THE OXFORD HANDBOOK OF

ITALIAN POLITICS

THE OXFORD HANDBOOK OF

ITALIAN

POLITICS

Edited by

ERIK JONES

and

GIANFRANCO PASQUINO

OXFORD

UNIVERSITY PRESS

OXFORD
UNIVERSITY PRESS

Great Clarendon Street, Oxford, OX2 6DP,
United Kingdom

Oxford University Press is a department of the University of Oxford.
It furthers the University's objective of excellence in research, scholarship,
and education by publishing worldwide. Oxford is a registered trade mark of
Oxford University Press in the UK and in certain other countries

© Oxford University Press 2015

The moral rights of the authors have been asserted

First Edition published in 2015

Impression: 2

Published in the United States of America by Oxford University Press
198 Madison Avenue, New York, NY 10016, United States of America

British Library Cataloguing in Publication Data

Data available

Library of Congress Control Number: 2015947358

ISBN 978-0-19-966974-5

Printed and bounded by
CPI Group (UK) Ltd, Croydon, CR0 4YY

Preface

When we set out to assemble an *Oxford Handbook of Italian Politics* in the early spring of 2011, we had no idea how much and how quickly Italy would change. Silvio Berlusconi was then prime minister with a nearly unassailable parliamentary majority. The center-left was divided. And while much of Europe was in the throes of an economic crisis, the impact on Italy was not yet apparent. There were ongoing debates about whether Italy had transitioned from a "second" to a "third" republic and there was renewed focus on the foibles of the Italian political class. But Italy was hardly in the throes of a political revolution; the more things changed the easier it was to see how they remained the same.

We sketched our ideas for the volume to highlight the core features of Italian politics. We commissioned authors who could write authoritatively about the country's evolution, primarily since the end of World War II but in some cases since Unification. We established a supportive working relationship with the provincial government of Bologna in order to organize seminars with politicians around some of the many themes in draft form. And we set our authors to work with little inkling of what the future had in store.

The result is a collection that speaks to the enduring characteristics of Italian political life rather than focusing on recent political developments. This is consistent with the aims of the Oxford Handbook series; it is also complementary to a collaborative project we have with the Istituto Cattaneo in Bologna to produce the annual volume *Politica in Italia* in the Italian edition or *Italian Politics* in the English version. Readers looking to catch up on what is happening in real time are encouraged to look at that contemporary survey of events. The goal of this handbook is to provide a comprehensive overview of Italian political history, institutions, traditions, actors, and concepts.

There are 54 chapters organized in nine sections. We start with the conceptual vocabulary that defines key aspects of Italian political life. This is where we commissioned chapters to focus on elites, the Risorgimento, *trasformismo, partitocrazia*, and the dualism between north and south. These concepts are not necessarily unique to Italy. Other countries also have elites, they have gone through a period of nation-building, they have politicians who change party affiliations, and they have political parties that try to run the show. Other countries also have important geographic cleavages. What they do not have is the distinctive mix of these elements or the reinforcing influence they represent.

This conceptual vocabulary provides the context for understanding Italy's political institutions. This is the second section of the volume. Starting with the Constitution of the Republic, we asked authors to explain the organization of executive, legislative, electoral, and bureaucratic power. The emphasis in these chapters is more descriptive than interpretative. They provide the frame within which Italian political life has evolved.

The third section explores Italy's political traditions from Christian Democracy through populism. The goal with these chapters is to show how each of these traditions has contributed to Italian political development. That set of parallel narratives comes together in the fourth section, where we look at the major periods in post-World War II Italian history. This periodization extends up to the present pattern of bi-polar alternation between center-right and center-left—setting the stage for what is likely to come after.

Such analysis should not ignore the individuals who have shaped Italian politics. However, a fair rendering of Italy's rich political tapestry of personalities would require a volume unto itself. What we offer is a study in contrasts. We have paired historical figures from similar or overlapping periods in order to elicit both their unique characteristics and some of the texture of their interaction. Most of these figures have played prominent parliamentary roles; we included a chapter on Gianni Agnelli and Enrico Mattei because not all major political figures are elected.

This point about politics outside the electoral process extends across the next three sections of our collection. We have clustered chapters on religion, economics, and society. The chapters on religion focus primarily on the Catholic Church but also consider Italy's growing religious differentiation and its enduring liberal or lay tradition. The chapters on economics draw attention to Italian families, firms, labor markets, and welfare state. They also highlight important roles played by specific institutions or groups, such as the Bank of Italy and the cooperative movement. The chapters on Italian society broaden the analysis to bring in different forms of mass media, to highlight public ethics, gender, immigration, and social movements—and to explore some of Italy's more violent forms of political expression through terrorism and organized crime.

The remaining chapters draw attention to Italy's relationship with the outside world using the concentric circles of the Atlantic Alliance, Europe, and the Mediterranean. These external relationships are present through much of the rest of the volume as well. It goes without saying that Italian politics has been heavily influenced by forces from abroad. It is also worth noting, however, that Italy exerts influence. In that sense, Italian politics is important not only for its own sake but also for what Italy has to offer to the rest of the world.

This collection would never have been possible without the professionalism, hard work, and commitment of our many contributors. As editors, we owe them more than the usual debt of gratitude. The Province of Bologna was a vital source of support and inspiration. They not only gave us a wealth of insights in the two seminars we held on their premises, but the resources they provided also made it possible for us to commission translations for eight of the chapters and so to facilitate participation from a number of vital contributors. Our thanks go to Valeria Calderoni for translating Chapter 26, and to Giulia Baldisseri and Valeria Elena Benko who together translated Chapters 9, 20, 27, 28, 31, 32, and 35. The project as a whole was overseen by Kathryn Knowles and managed by Dea Di Furia. Thanks go to them and to the direction of SAIS Europe for making this possible. A number of very talented students also contributed to our efforts. Of these, two deserve particular mention: Luigi Scazzieri prepared many of the abstracts and keywords and Chiara Monti formatted the text for publication.

The talented production staff at Oxford University Press also deserve mention. Our commissioning editor, Dominic Byatt, has encouraged us throughout this project. His colleagues at OUP have shown unfailing patience with a production schedule that often overran our initial estimates. They also provided tremendous support. If the text of this volume reads fluently, Elizabeth Stone deserves the lion's share of the credit. Any errors are ours alone.

A final word of thanks go to my co-editor Gianfranco Pasquino and my SAIS colleague Mark Gilbert. Oxford Handbooks are somewhat daunting publications both because of the scale of the exercise and because of the range of knowledge required. As such, they are best tackled as collaborative ventures. It is a great privilege to work at a place like SAIS Europe where we have such a wealth of talent.

Erik Jones
Oxford, UK
May 2015

Contents

PART I CORE CONCEPTS

PART II POLITICAL INSTITUTIONS

PART III POLITICAL TRADITIONS

PART IV POLITICAL PERIODS

PART V MAJOR FIGURES

PART VI RELIGION AND POLITICS

PART VII ECONOMIC INSTITUTIONS, ASSOCIATIONS, AND INTERESTS

PART VIII POLITICS, CULTURE, AND SOCIETY

PART IX EXTERNAL RELATIONS

List of Figures

List of Tables

List of Common Acronyms

AC	Azione Cattolica
ACI	Alleanza Cooperativa Italiana
AGCI	Alleanza Generale delle Cooperative Italiane
AGCOM	Autorità per le Garanzie nelle Comunicazioni
AGIP	Azienda Generale Italiana Petroli
AN	Alleanza Nazionale
ANAS	Azienda Nazionale Autonoma delle Strade
ANCC	Associazione Nazionale Cooperative Consumatori
ANCD	Associazione Nazionale Cooperative fra Dettaglianti
ANM	Associazione Nazionale Magistrati
ASPI	Assicurazione Sociale per l'Impiego
ATM	Azienda Trasporti Milanesi
BNL	Banca Nazionale del Lavoro
BR	Brigate Rosse
CAF	Craxi-Andreotti-Forlani
CCC	Consorzio Cooperative Costruzioni
CCD	Centro Cristiano Democratico
CdM	Consiglio dei Ministri
CEE	Central and Eastern Europe
CEI	Conferenza Episcopale Italiana
CGIL	Confederazione Generale Italiana del Lavoro
CIA	Central Intelligence Agency
CIG	Casse Integrazione Guadagni
CISL	Confederazione Italiana Sindacati Lavoratori
CL	Communione e Liberazione
CLN	Comitato di Liberazione Nazionale
CNEL	Consiglio Nazionale Economia e Lavoro
CNS	Consorzio Nazionale Servizi

Comintern	Communist International
CPI	Corruption Perception Index
CpM	Cassa per il Mezzogiorno
DC	Democrazia Cristiana
DIA	Direzione Investigativa Antimafia
DRIA	Disintegration, Reconstruction, Integration and Alienation
DS	Democratici di Sinistra
EC	European Community
ECB	European Central Bank
ECPI	Excess Perceived Corruption Index
EDC	European Defence Community
EEC	European Economic Community
EMS	European Monetary System
EMU	Economic and Monetary Union
ENEL	Ente Nazionale per l'Energia Elettrica
ENEP	Effective Number of Electoral Parties
ENI	Ente Nazionale Idrocarburi
ENPG	Effective Number of Parliamentary Groups
ENPP	Effective Number of Parliamentary Parties
ERM	Exchange Rate Mechanism
ESCB	European System of Central Banks
ESRB	European Systemic Risk Board
EUR	Esposizione Universale Roma
FCC	Formazioni Comuniste Combattenti
FGCI	Federazione Giovanile Comunista Italiana
FI	Forza Italia
FIAT	Fabbrica Italiana Automobili Torino
FIOM	Federazione Impiegati Operai Metallurgici
FLI	Futuro e Libertà per l'Italia
FRG	Federal Republic of Germany
FSB	Financial Stability Board
FSF	Financial Stability Forum
FUCI	Federazione Universitaria Cattolica Italiana
G-7	Group of Seven Leading Industrial Nations

GDP	Gross Domestic Product
GJM	Global Justice Movement
GRECO	Group of States against Corruption
GSF	Genoa Social Forum
HDI	Human Development Index
IAA	Independent Administrative Agency
IDV	Italia dei Valori
IMI	Istituto Mobiliare Italiano
INA	Istituto Nazionale Assicurazioni
INAIL	Istituto Nazionale per l'Assicurazione contro gli Infortuni sul Lavoro
IOTA	Identity, Opposition, Totality, Alternative
IPAB	Istituti Pubblici di Assistenza e Beneficenza
IRES	Imposta sul Reddito delle Società
IRI	Istituto per la Ricostruzione Industriale
ISTAT	Istituto Nazionale di Statistica
IT	Information Technology
LN	Lega Nord
M5S	Movimento 5 Stelle
MP	Member of Parliament
MSI	Movimento Sociale Italiano
NAR	Nuclei Armati Rivoluzionari
NATO	North Atlantic Treaty Organization
NCD	Nuovo Centrodestra
NEET	Not in Education, Employment or Training
NGO	Non-Governmental Organization
NHS	National Health Service
NIMBY	Not In My Backyard
OECD	Organisation for Economic Co-operation and Development
OLIR	Osservatorio delle Libertà ed Istituzioni Religiose
ON	Centro Studi Ordine Nuovo
OPEC	Organization of Petroleum Exporting Countries
P2	Propaganda Due
PCI	Partito Comunista Italiano
PES	Public Employment Services

PD	Partito Democratico
PdAz	Partito d'Azione
PdCI	Partito dei Comunisti Italiani
PdL	Il Popolo della Libertà
PDS	Partito Democratico della Sinistra
PL	Prima Linea
PLI	Partito Liberale Italiano
PLO	Palestine Liberation Organization
PNF	Partito Nazionale Fascista
PPI	Partito Popolare Italiano
PR	Partito Radicale
PRC	Partito della Rifondazione Comunista—see also RC
PRI	Partito Repubblicano Italiano
PSDI	Partito Socialista Democratico Italiano
PSI	Partito Socialista Italiano
PSIUP	Partito Socialista Italiano di Unità Proletaria
RAI	Radiotelevisione Italiana
RC	Partito della Rifondazione Comunista—see also PRC
RSA	Rappresentanze Sindacali Aziendali
RSI	Repubblica Sociale Italiana
RSU	Rappresentanza Sindacale Unitaria
SEL	Sinistra Ecologia Libertà
SISMI	Servizio per le Informazioni e la Sicurezza Militare
SME	Small or Medium-sized Enterprise
SVIMEZ	Associazione per lo Sviluppo dell'Industria nel Mezzogiorno
TEU	Treaty on European Union
TFR	Trattamento di Fine Rapporto
TV	Television
UB	Unemployment Benefits
UDC	Unione di Centro
UDEUR	Unione Democratici per l'Europa
UFM	Union for the Mediterranean
UIL	Unione Italiana del Lavoro
UNIFIL	United Nations Interim Force in Lebanon

UQ   Fronte dell'Uomo Qualunque
USSR   Union of Soviet Socialist Republics
WGI   World Governance Index
WSF   World Social Forum
WTO   World Trade Organization

LIST OF CONTRIBUTORS

Paolo Acanfora is a Lecturer of History and Institutions of the European Union at the International University of Languages and Media in Milan.

Aldo Agosti is Honorary Professor of Contemporary History at the University of Turin.

Roberto Aliboni is a Scientific Counsellor in the Istituto Affari Internazionali-IAI in Rome and former Director and Vice President of the same institute.

Giuliano Amato is a Judge in the Italian Constitutional Court.

Gianfranco Baldini is Associate Professor of Political Science at the University of Bologna.

Paolo Bellucci is Professor of Political Science at the University of Siena.

Emanuele Bernardi is a Researcher in Contemporary and Economic History at the Università "La Sapienza" in Rome.

Giuseppe Berta is Professor in Contemporary History at the Università Bocconi in Milan.

Anna Cento Bull is Professor of Italian History and Politics at the University of Bath.

Martin J. Bull is Professor of Politics at the University of Salford.

Mauro Calise is Professor of Political Science, University of Naples Federico II.

Donatella Campus is Associate Professor of Political Science at the University of Bologna.

Carlo Carboni is Professor of Economic Sociology at the Università Politecnica delle Marche.

Anthony L. Cardoza is Professor of History at Loyola University Chicago.

Valerio Castronovo is President of the Istituto di Studi Storici "Gaetano Salvemini" in Turin.

Roberto Cipriani is Professor of Sociology at the University Roma Tre.

Nicolò Conti is Associate Professor of Political Science at the Unitelma Sapienza University of Rome.

Maurizio Cotta is Professor of Political Science at the University of Siena.

John A. Davis is Professor of Modern Italian History at the University of Connecticut and a fellow of the Institute for Advanced Studies in Paris.

Mario Del Pero is Professor of International History at the Institut d'études politiques in Paris.

Donatella Della Porta is Professor of Sociology at the European University Institute.

Vincent Della Sala teaches political science at the University of Trento and is Adjunct Professor of European Studies at SAIS Europe.

Mark Donovan is Senior Lecturer in the Department of Politics and International Relations at Cardiff University.

Ilaria Favretto is Professor of Contemporary European History at Kingston University, London.

Maurizio Ferrera is Professor of Political Science at the University of Milan.

Mark Gilbert is Professor of History and International Studies at SAIS Europe.

Carlo Guarnieri is Professor of Political Science at the University of Bologna.

Stephen Gundle is Professor of Film and Television Studies at the University of Warwick.

Stephen Hellman is Professor of Political Science at York University, Toronto.

David Hine is Associate Professor of Politics at Oxford University.

Jonathan Hopkin is Associate Professor of Comparative Politics at the London School of Economics.

Piero Ignazi is Professor of Comparative Politics at the University of Bologna.

Matteo Jessoula is Associate Professor of Political Science at the University of Milan.

Erik Jones is Professor of European Studies and International Political Economy at SAIS Europe and Senior Research Fellow at Nuffield College, Oxford.

Paolo Mancini is Professor of Sociology of Communication at the University of Perugia.

Alberto Melloni is Director of the Foundation for Religious Studies (fscire.it) and Professor of History of Christianity at the University of Modena/Reggio.

Carol Mershon is Professor of Politics at the University of Virginia.

James L. Newell is Professor of Politics at the University of Salford.

Giovanni Orsina is Professor of History at Luiss-Guido Carli University in Rome.

Letizia Paoli is Professor of Criminology at the University of Leuven.

Gianfranco Pasquino is Professor Emeritus in Political Science at the University of Bologna and James Anderson Senior Adjunct Professor at SAIS Europe.

Gianluca Passarelli is Associate Professor of Political Science at the Università "La Sapienza" in Rome.

Simona Piattoni is Professor of Political Science at the University of Trento.

Paolo Pombeni is Emeritus Professor of the History of European Political Systems at the University of Bologna and is Director of the Italian-German Historical Institute in Trento.

Lucia Quaglia is Professor of Political Science at the University of York.

Marta Regalia is a Researcher attached to the University of Bologna.

Marino Regini is Emeritus Professor of Economic Sociology at the University of Milan.

Martin Rhodes is Professor and Co-Director of the Colorado European Union Center of Excellence at the Josef Korbel School of International Studies at the University of Denver.

Verónica Roldán is Professor of Sociology of Values at the University Roma Tre.

Chiara Saraceno is an Honorary Fellow at the Collegio Carlo Alberto in Moncalieri/ Torino.

Giuseppe Sciortino is Professor of Sociology at the University of Trento.

Massimo Teodori was Professor of the History and Institutions of the United States at the University of Perugia.

Nadia Urbinati is Kyriakos Tsakopoulos Professor of Political Theory at Columbia University.

Marco Valbruzzi is a PhD Researcher in the Department of Political and Social Sciences of the European University Institute.

Antonio Varsori is Professor of History of International Relations at the University of Padua.

Salvatore Vassallo is Professor of Political Science at the University of Bologna.

Patrik Vesan is Assistant Professor of Political Science at the University of Aosta Valley.

Vera Zamagni is Professor of Economic History at the University of Bologna.

PART I

CORE CONCEPTS

CHAPTER 1

··

LA CLASSE DIRIGENTE

··

JAMES L. NEWELL

THE term *classe dirigente* is not easy to translate. *Bourgeoisie* or "capitalist class"—
Marxian terms referring to ownership of the means of production—do not fully
capture the sense: a *dirigente* is one who leads, and leadership takes place in other
spheres besides the economy. Not exclusive to the economy, leadership is not exclusive to politics either. For this reason, *classe dirigente* is not synonymous with *classe
politica*, which consists of those occupying positions in the institutions of government
at national and sub-national levels. Nor does the term *elite* constitute an adequate
translation: elites are those who excel in some respect, whether in material possessions or abilities, and they may or may not lead, depending on the quality of the role
models they furnish for those who have fewer of the possessions or abilities in question. Nevertheless, the term inevitably brings to mind the work of the elite theorists
Vilfredo Pareto and Gaetano Mosca.

For Pareto, since people are unequally endowed, political change is inevitably
the work of elites, ordinary people in most circumstances acting as little more than
bystanders. Regime change, through revolution or otherwise, then, is a matter of the
circulation of elites and Marx was wrong in thinking that revolution could be used as
a tool to end their domination. For Mosca, whatever the principles according to which
people were theoretically governed, in practice all but the most primitive societies
were ruled by small minorities. For both thinkers, as for members of the school of elite
theorists they founded, the essential point is that power relationships in contemporary
society are more or less independent of its formal political arrangements, democratic
or otherwise. Given these reflections, "ruling class" seems to offer the best translation.
It is the class which, thanks to its extraordinary endowments and therefore its status,
leads and manages a society either by the influence it has over the actions of the political class or by the influence it has over popular attitudes and behavior, or by both
types of influence.

A Contentious Term

It is entirely fitting that Mosca and Pareto were Italians writing at the time of Huttington's[1] first wave of democratization; for in stark contrast to countries such as Britain and the United States, Italy at the time had a state that found it difficult to use principles of democracy to establish a firm foundation of legitimacy for itself.[2] In Britain, nascent democracy, beginning with Magna Carta in 1215, was about the breakdown of feudalism; about placing limits on royal power; about empowering groups other than those with connections to the court. The purpose of government was to facilitate the unfettered pursuit of the action of free individuals in civil society—requiring divided government and constitutional government. From such a perspective, with the addition of universal suffrage, there can be no "ruling class" as such: the people as a whole rule through institutions explicitly designed to *prevent* such rule in fact being exercised by any one part, much less rule that is *arbitrary*. To acknowledge that *alongside* the institutions of political democracy there exists a "ruling class" is to agree to the proposition that the power that can be wielded by some relative to others undermines the empowerment the latter are supposed to enjoy through political institutions to the point of throwing a question mark over the extent to which the polity can in any meaningful sense be regarded as "democratic" at all. It is no wonder then, that in English-speaking countries, the notion of a "ruling class" has never been popular.

Italy represents a very different case. There, the term "ruling class" is used much more widely and in a much more relaxed way. In the south, the breakdown of feudal jurisdiction and the abolition of feudal land tenures have to await the French Revolution and Napoleon's conquest of Italy after 1796. In 1815, the peninsula is divided into eight separate states. "Most [are] under the direct or indirect control of Austria, and those that [are] not [are] ruled by conservative, absolutist kings."[3] Unification, when it comes, is essentially the work of a restricted Piedmontese elite unable to win the allegiance of vast swathes of the population or to place the authority of the state on any kind of firm foundations, this for reasons that are political (the opposition of the Church and a restricted franchise), economic (elites' rapacity, and grinding poverty), social (widespread illiteracy), and geographical (communications difficulties over a largely mountainous and rugged terrain). In some parts of the country, the state's writ does not run at all and people look for alternative means of underwriting contracts. In Sicily, the Mafia supplies, as a private good, the protection and dispute settlement that would otherwise be supplied, publicly, by the state.

Decline in the state's capacity and lack of public confidence in it become mutually reinforcing in a vicious circle. By 1913, while the per capita level of industrialization for the United Kingdom is 115 (UK in 1900 = 100), for Italy it is 26.[4] A weak manufacturing base combined with a weak state mean, not surprisingly, that the distinctively bourgeois values of law and order and due process find relatively infertile terrain. With the complicity of economic and political elites in the rise of Fascism, a refusal to acknowledge the existence of a ruling class or something approximating it seems unsustainable. Consequently, Italians, and people like the British or Americans, find themselves at opposite ends of a spectrum: while the latter refuse to accept the idea that they have a ruling class at all, the former not only accept that they have one, they wish it were stronger and more effective.

THE EMPIRICAL SIGNIFICANCE
OF THE *CLASSE DIRIGENTE*

Aside from what is *perceived* to be the case, it is worthwhile asking whether suggestions of the existence of a "ruling class" in fact make sense empirically. The term "class" implies, first, the internal homogeneity, in some respect, of its members and, second, some qualitative, not merely quantitative, distinction that sets its members apart from those who are not members. Third, if it is to be more than merely the concept of an observer, a class must have some kind of existence in the minds of its putative members: it must, to use Marxian terminology, not only be a *Klasse an sich* but also a *Klasse für sich*.

With regard to the first of these criteria, social scientists usually think of common location in the social structure as being what counts, the relevant indicator being occupation. The second criterion, meanwhile, points to the drawback associated with many attempts to operationalize the class concept: as occupations are typically grouped according to some continuous variable such as status, the placement of class boundaries is essentially arbitrary "and the utility of the resulting class schema correspondingly diminished: if using such a schema we find that there is a relationship between class position and vote, for example, essentially all we learn is that hierarchy is related to voting; we get little insight into what it might be *about* such classes that they influence voting patterns".[5] Third, since classes, unlike feudal estates, do not constitute legally defined sets of rights and obligations, it cannot be assumed that there will be any necessary connections between social structural position on the one hand and social consciousness and action on the other. Classes, unlike feudal estates, reflect power disparities that are the outcome of free exchanges between legally equal contracting parties. Consequently, they have no necessary bearing on people's self understandings or behavior; much less is there any guarantee that they will fulfill any of Michael Mann's IOTA (identity, opposition, totality, alternative) conditions.[6]

On what grounds, then, is it possible to point to the existence—in Italy or any other case—of a *classe dirigente* that goes any way to meeting the three criteria? Clearly, at the apex of various fields—law, politics, business, scientific research, culture and entertainment, religion—there exist people whose occupations enable them to exercise an unusual degree of influence over the life of society: that much is obvious. But what makes it legitimate to regard Mario Monti as belonging to a class together with the Agnelli family and Luca Cordero de Montezemolo, and all three as belonging to a class together with Ferruccio de Bortoli, Eugenio Scalfari, Rita Levi-Montalcini, or the Pope?

First, they all restrict access to rewards and privileges by exclusionary forms of social closure, the two main devices of which are "first, those surrounding the institutions of property; and, second, academic or professional qualifications and credentials."[7] However, this is a characteristic they share with a not insignificant proportion of the population, most of whom are not members of the *classe dirigente*. What sets the latter apart, within the broader category, is that the status they have by virtue of the sheer quantities of property or certified competence at their command—the impact they single-handedly can have on public policy thanks to their property or their positions—gives them a *public reputation*, actual or potential. They talk to and are talked about in the media and are therefore known to the public. This in turn means that they have a resource which those who are not known to the public do not have. The prestige, recognized competence, the respect that is accorded them: these are by definition forms of authority and therefore power resources enabling them to access the media and politicians in a way that those who are not publicly known cannot. When they speak, other important people and the public sit up and listen.[8]

Their public reputation gives members of the *classe dirigente* a second common characteristic, the need to employ assistants and gatekeepers of various kinds: rarely can they be contacted directly—a reflection of the fact that their reputations are also their vulnerability. They are scandal prone. As used-car dealers know, reputations are very difficult to acquire but very easy to lose. As celebrities, actual or potential, members of the *classe dirigente* are of special interest to investigative journalists; as celebrities they are, like it or not, used by the public as role models. Transgressions—which, if committed by ordinary people would not be of the slightest interest outside their immediate circles—may damage celebrities' reputations and therefore their power if they become public; so they require staff to assist them in the continuous effort of reputation maintenance and to shield them from prying eyes.

Finally, as members of the *classe dirigente*, they each perform, in various ways and to various degrees, a role for society as a whole that is not dissimilar to the role the President of the Republic performs for the Italian polity. The President's supreme function is to mediate and regulate the interaction of political actors with the aim of ensuring that politics is carried on without threatening national integration. This means that the President's role is not simply juridical or ceremonial but also political in character; and it is precisely to facilitate the exercise of the supreme function that the Italian Constitution is rather unspecific about the President's powers: these are like an accordion, available to play to its full extent when the weakness of other actors (notably the parties) so requires, otherwise kept relatively "closed" by these other actors' strength.[9] Correspondingly, members of the *classe dirigente* are expected, by the public, to conduct themselves in ways that are conducive to the maintenance of order even when they are advocating changes; as individuals with very large stakes in the existing social order it is in their interests so to do.[10] The substance of the conduct that is required of them is not necessarily prescribed in detail anywhere; like that of the President it will vary greatly depending on that of other significant actors. The decision of Monti—a leading academic—to accept the responsibilities of prime minister; the decision of Montezemolo—an industrialist—to set up a political movement and then to participate in the 2013 general election, are both clear examples of this.

Trade union leaders occupy an interesting position in relation to the definition just developed. On the one hand, they head organizations whose purposes lead them to challenge the distribution of power and resources sanctioned by the exclusionary activities of the ruling class. On the other hand, thanks to their capacity to deploy scarce resources of their own (skills of speech-making and handling meetings if nothing else) they occupy positions of power and influence which they can only retain to the extent that they are able to ensure the continuity of stable and cordial bargaining relationships with employers. And in order to ensure that, they must ensure that the organizations they lead exert at least as much power *over* their members as they exert power *for* them.[11] They must, in C. Wright Mills's famous phrase, act as "mangers of discontent."[12]

THE COMPOSITION
OF THE *CLASSE DIRIGENTE*

Given the above-discussed criteria, the *classe dirigente* can be defined in operational terms as consisting of all those who make it into *Who's Who in Italy*, the current edition of which includes about 8,000 entries.[13] This means that the class comprises about 0.02 percent of the adult resident population; that is, about 1 in 5,000 is a member.[14] In November 2012, the private research institute Eurispes undertook an analysis of *Who's Who* data relating to 1992 and 2012, making possible a description of the socio-demographic characteristics of the *classe dirigente* and how they have changed over the past 20 years.[15] The main findings were the following:

- The class consists predominantly of older males: the proportion of females has doubled in the last 20 years but still only 15 percent are female. Meanwhile, 4 out of 5 (79.5 percent) are over 50, and 39.3 percent over 65. Some 20 years ago the proportion of those over 50 had been 3 out of 4, the proportion over 65, 25.2 percent. Carboni and Pavolini analyzing *Who's Who* data for the period from 1990 to 2004 note that the process of aging has been particularly marked among business people and those employed in cultural occupations and the professions.[16] They therefore argue that aging has reflected not only the aging of the population in general but two specific processes. On the one hand, Italian capitalism, which flourished in the 1960s and 1970s, was built above all on family firms dominated by life-time owner-managers. The more recent transition to a post-industrial economy, and global competition, has limited the availability of new opportunities and therefore the proportion of new generations of entrepreneurs to be found in the *classe dirigente*. On the other hand, recent years have seen severe cut backs in the availability of places in the universities, hospitals, research centers, and so on responsible for producing cultural products, as well as severe restrictions on access to the professions.

- The marked regional disparities apparent in other areas of political, economic, and social life in Italy are also reflected in the composition of the *classe dirigente*. As one would expect, a large majority of members of the class are resident either in Rome (47.2 percent) or in Milan (21.0 percent), which are the political and economic capitals, respectively, but also the main artistic and cultural centers. Of the 95.4 percent born in Italy, only 16.7 percent were born in the south, thus appearing to confirm the disadvantages faced by those originating in this part of the world in gaining access to positions of power. And when they do gain such access they go elsewhere: of those born in the south some 90 percent are resident in Lazio or in the main industrial regions of the centre and the north.

- At least in terms of formal qualifications, members of the *classe dirigente* are better educated now than they were 20 years ago, with 83.3 percent having a university degree as compared with 66.1 percent in 1992. While this presumably reflects the general growth of the better-educated in each generational cohort since the war, it is likely, at least in part, also to reflect the significant shift that has taken place in the distribution of members of the class among sectors of activity: as one would expect, the proportion of degree holders is larger among those working in the fields of culture and the professions than it is among businesspeople, and while the latter have declined as a proportion of the class, there has been an equally significant growth in the former.[17]

- The occupations accounting for the largest proportions of the *classe dirigente* are politicians (21.7 percent), university professors (18.5 percent), and company directors (14.7 percent) followed by sportspeople, actors, artists and entertainers (14.0 percent), and by journalists (5.3 percent). Lawyers, doctors, military, and judicial personnel together account for only 4.4 percent. The obvious overrepresentation of some occupations (notably politicians and journalists) as compared with others reflects the tendency towards a high public profile of its members as a function of its role in maintaining social integration.

Taken together, the changes in the characteristics of the *classe dirigente* arguably reflect important shifts in the performance of this integration role since the 1990s in the direction of more explicit efforts to manufacture consent. As is well known, key institutions like political parties have suffered drastic declines in public confidence, with falling memberships and falling turnouts at elections, while recent years have also seen, in part as cause in part as consequence, a growing mediatization of politics. These twin processes may in part explain the growth in the proportion of politicians making up the *classe dirigente*; the growing relative significance of journalists, writers, and university professors relative to company directors and entrepreneurs, and the growing numbers with degrees in the arts and humanities as compared with technical and scientific disciplines.[18] The increase in significance of politicians probably reflects an expansion of institutional networks designed to increase public confidence by responding to decentralizing pressures such as those of the Northern League. As public confidence has declined so has there been a growing need for communications experts and experts in the processing and interpreting of information. Mediatization has meant a growing tendency for political communication to depend on and be shaped by the media and therefore a growth in the power of the latter vis-à-vis other institutions. Arguably, therefore, the power and profile of those whose job it is to select and interpret information (writers, journalists, and academics) through the media has grown correspondingly.

The Performance
of the *Classe Dirigente*

By definition, the function of a *classe dirigente* is to lead. "To lead" means to "enlist the aid and support of others in the achievement of a common task" and obviously a leader is unlikely to be successful in this if s/he does not enjoy the trust and confidence of those whose support s/he is seeking to enlist.[19] Clearly, Italians do not have much confidence in their leaders, or in some of them, because, as is well known, survey data regularly show that they don't have much confidence in the key institutions these leaders are responsible for running (see Table 1.1). Politicians are spectacularly unsuccessful in inspiring confidence, while entrepreneurs and others responsible for managing the economic life of the country fare only marginally better. Far more successful are those with responsibility for institutions that are either close to citizens (voluntary associations), have direct responsibility for protecting them (the forces of law and order), or have succeeded in capturing the public imagination (the Corpo Forestale in the area of environmental protection and the army with its contributions to international peace missions).

Why is the *classe dirigente* less than completely successful in inspiring public confidence in the institutions it runs? Why, in short, is it *weak*? One reason is that it does not have, or significant numbers of its members, do not have—or take insufficient steps to be seen to have—the necessary degree of probity: they behave as "amoral individualists."[20] Transparency International's corruption perceptions index—measuring "perceptions of the extent of corruption in the public sector from the perceptions of business people and country experts"—shows this clearly: Italy regularly emerges among the bottom handful of EU member states and sometimes even behind such Third World countries as Ghana, Rwanda, or Puerto Rico. Corruption, real or perceived, is disastrous from the point of view of maintaining public confidence, as it blatantly contradicts those principles of legality, due process, and formal equality on which the power and authority of the *classe dirigente* as a whole depends.[21] It is a form of free riding that threatens the class collectively.

Table 1.1 Confidence of Italian Citizens in Institutions, 2013 (percent)

Institution	Confidence*
Corpo Forestale	77.1
Carabinieri	76.3
Voluntary organizations	75.4
Police	75.0
Armed forces	71.3
Guardia di Finanza	71.0
Consumers' associations	63.8
Schools	48.2
Secret services	45.3
President of the Republic	44.7
Judiciary	42.0
Church	36.6
Entrepreneurs' associations	29.8
Trade unions	19.5
Public administration	17.6
Government	15.9
Parliament	9.0
Political parties	7.3

* Percentages of respondents declaring "some" or "a great deal" of confidence in the institution in question.

Source: "La fiducia dei citadini nelle istituzioni: Rapporto Italia 2013", Eurispes <http://www.eurispes.eu/content/la-fiducia-dei-cittadini-nelle-istituzioni-rapporto-it alia-2013>.

The point can be made by means of another comparison with Britain whose *classe dirigente* understands the importance of probity very well and is for this reason absolutely ruthless with any of its members who (are perceived to) step out of line: not for them the tolerance of tax evasion, the *ad personam* legislation, and the amnesties that make such regular appearances on the Italian political stage. One is bound to ask, then, why it is that, in the land that gave us Machiavelli and a host of other original and astute political thinkers, the *classe dirigente* has been so apparently inept at keeping its members in line.

Anything approaching a "complete" answer would have to appeal to social patterns with roots stretching back deep into the past, and to many other issues besides.[22] Here we focus on the way in which the class organized its internal affairs having emerged from the ruins of Fascism. The power vacuum created by this event meant that the only authority available for Italians to turn to was the Church or the Resistance movement, which was dominated by the political parties. Central, therefore, to the reconstruction of social organizations and interest groups, the parties were able—as "the principal channels of access to the bureaucracy and the principal transmission belts in the allocation of resources from centre to periphery"—to penetrate the interstices of civil society and the state.[23] In short, in the aftermath of Fascism, the *classe dirigente* came to be dominated by one of its parts—the politicians—and it was through their organizations—the parties—that the class mainly organized its affairs. The politicians, however—thanks to the Cold War and the "polarized pluralist" character of the party system—were obliged to rely heavily on patronage to mobilize popular consent; and they were unable to offer to the business representatives among the members of the class, the coherent policy-making they needed in order to make sound, long-term investment decisions.[24] Thus it was that—needing politicians' patronage for a range of routine business matters, from town-planning decisions to those concerning the award of public-works contracts, and keen to overcome inefficiencies—entrepreneurs sought to establish stable relation-ships with politicians whereby, in exchange for financial support at a time when the cost of politics was rising, they would obtain more of the certainty needed for finance and investment to be managed and planned rationally.[25]

What emerged, therefore, was a whole series of improper relations between economic and political power, including concomitants like the P2 Masonic lodge, giving rise to:

> veritable clans whose purpose was nothing other than mutual assistance in the man-agement and enhancement of the power of their members. Thus … Andreotti had a clan, comprising the chemicals industrialist, Nino Rovelli, the building contractors of the Caltagirone family, parts of the Catholic banking sector and numerous pol-iticians … while Berlusconi (who would hardly have been able to make his fortune without political support) belonged to Craxi's clan.[26]

For a short while after the great *Tangentopoli* corruption scandal, with its bipolar-izing effects on the party system, it seemed that there might be a clean-up. But the emergent centre-right was dominated by Berlusconi, who has managed to undermine still further the capacity of the *classe dirigente* to inspire confidence in the country's institutions—this by managing power as a court system: "The principal characteristic of a court system is its ability to spread or reinforce servile attitudes and habits: adulation, simulation, cynicism, disdain for free spirits, venality and corruption."[27]

A second reason for the weakness of the *classe dirigente*, therefore, has to do with its lack of the cohesion without which leadership is difficult if not impossible. As con-servative political thinkers have taught, cohesion requires that interaction between the components of a social body reflect the interaction between the parts of a living body, each of whose organs contributes to the survival of the body as a whole by performing a unique function in harmonious interaction with each of the others. Three instances of disharmony have been particularly important in recent years, first, the inability of the politicians on either side of the left–right divide to accord each other legitimacy as potential governing actors. For those on the centre-left, this has been impossible given Berlusconi's conflict of interests. The *classe dirigente*, in capitalist liberal democracies, is the body of commanders within the larger dominant class formed around practices of social closure based on principles of legality and due process. These principles, through the rules of property and credentials, guarantee unequal access to resources, while legit-imizing that inequality in the eyes of the population as a whole. So, to accord Berlusconi legitimacy is to undermine the bases on which the *classe dirigente* maintains itself in the first place.

Second, Berlusconi's power, and the way he has chosen to manage that power, has provided the basis for often bitter conflicts between the political and judicial branches of the state—which the *classe dirigente* has been unable to resolve because they cut right through the class itself: on the one side stand Berlusconi and his courtesans; on the other, "the austerity, ethical rectitude and idea of service to the state embodied in the figure of Francesco Saverio Borrelli, the chief prosecuting magistrate of Milan."[28]

Third, those members of the *classe dirigente* who are meant to keep the membership as a whole in line by playing the role of the fourth estate—those with media responsibilities—have been unable to do so effectively because they have lacked the authority that comes with independence: traditionally, Italian newspapers have found it difficult to make a profit, and hence have either been party newspapers or papers owned by other companies (e.g., FIAT) wanting to use them as tools to further their interests, or else by others wanting to use them to pursue some specific political ambition. "[T]he public service broadcaster RAI has, since its inception, been subject to political interference of varying intensity," while the main commercial broadcasting group, Mediaset, is of course owned by Silvio Berlusconi.[29] Hired to pursue a political line, journalists have helped to create that line: it is as if, as an organ of the body, they had been taken over by another organ. To be sure, they *do* criticize; but being perceived as being closely associated with one or the other of the political line-ups, they lack the authority that would enable them to set the political agenda and oblige politicians to respond.[30]

Finally, effective leadership requires a vision shared by leaders and led: in this case, a shared idea, however vague, of what the ideal Italy looks like, of what it means to be Italian. Yet the circumstances surrounding Unification were such as to obstruct the emergence of a national integrative ideology. Fascism's attempt to plug the gap was discredited beyond appeal with the outcome of World War II. While the anti-fascist ideals that inspired the 1948 Constitution provided some social glue, the latter was the work of the Communists and Christian Democrats: neither considered themselves heirs of the liberal tradition of the Risorgimento, and both had communities of reference that lay outside, and were in some respects opposed to, the national community. Moreover, the ideals automatically excluded those who, in the aftermath of 1943 had chosen to fight against the Resistance. Their capacity to promote a sense of nation was therefore limited. Lacking self-esteem as Italians, citizens had difficulty in developing feelings of allegiance to their national institutions, their leaders difficulty in creating them.

Conclusion

The problems of Italy are problems of its ruling class, which currently finds itself between the devil of a growing economic crisis and the deep-blue sea of growing citizen dissatisfaction.[31] It is not well placed to handle the dilemma because—thanks precisely to amoral individualism, a lack of cohesion, and the absence of a clear vision—it is unable to exercise hegemony: to impose on citizens norms and values that they view as inevitable and take for granted so that they behave in ways functional to the maintenance and development of a social and political order with which all might be content. And because it cannot exercise hegemony, so the ruling class finds it difficult to lead and manage—in a never-ending vicious circle. Within and outside the class are individuals and groups driven by an ethic of social responsibility. In the absence of a class able effectively to lead, it is on the clash between these groups and the amoral individualists that the future of Italian society will depend.

Notes

1. Samuel P. Huntington, *The Third Wave: Democratization in the Late 20th Century* (London: University of Oklahoma Press, 1991).
2. Ibid.
3. John Gooch, *The Unification of Italy* (London: Routledge, 1986), 1.
4. P. Bairoch, "International Industrialization Levels from 1750 to 1980," pp. 3–35 in Patrick O'Brien (ed.), *Industrialisation: Critical Perspectives on the World Economy* (London: Routledge, 1998), 12.
5. James L. Newell, "Labourism, Ideology and the British Middle Class," PhD thesis (Florence: European University Institute, 1991), 38.
6. Michael Mann, *Consciousness and Action among the Western Working Class* (London: Macmillan, 1973). In this book, Mann sets out four conditions that have to be fulfilled if classes are to exist as compartmentalized social collectives cemented by a shared sense of group consciousness, first, a shared "identity" must exist between the group's members. Second, this identity must include a perception of "opposition" to other group interests. Third, these components must combine in a "totality" that defines the group members' social situation and society in general. Fourth, an "alternative" to the existing power relations must be conceived.
7. Frank Parkin, *Marxism and Class Theory: A Bourgeois Critique* (London: Tavistock, 1979), 48.
8. I am not suggesting that being known to the public is necessary in order to qualify for membership of the *classe dirigente*. Obviously, there are many members of the class, past and present, who have been and are, incredibly powerful (e.g., the head of the Italian army), but whom few have ever heard of (e.g., Enrico Cuccia). What I am saying is that these people's power gives them a capacity for publicity should they choose to seek it, a capacity that others do not have. The test, therefore, of whether one is a member of the *classe dirigente* as opposed to the broader category of those whose property rights and credentials give them privileged access to resources is that one can make pronouncements that cause others to pay attention. It is this *capacity* for publicity that distinguishes the *classe dirigente*, whose job, after all, is precisely to *lead*.
9. Gianfranco Pasquino, "Italian Presidents and their Accordion: Pre-1992 and Post-1994," *Parliamentary Affairs*, 65 no. 4 (October 2012), 847.
10. Honors and awards, with their imposing titles and therefore the additional status they confer—"Commendatore dell'Ordine al merito della Repubblica Italiana," "Cavaliere

del lavoro," "Grande Ufficiale dell'Ordine al merito della Repubblica Italiana" and so on—further enhance the size of this stake and it is not indulging in conspiracy theories to suggest that they are often used to keep potentially troublesome public figures in line. The British are experts at this, the Italians much less so largely because of the explicitly anti-fascist and egalitarian principles that inspired the drafting of the 1948 Constitution and underpinned the post-war settlement bringing the abolition of former aristocratic titles and thus a degree of diffidence toward honors generally.

11. Richard Hyman, *Industrial Relations: A Marxist Introduction* (London: Macmillan, 1975), ch. 3

12. C. Wright Mills, *The New Men of Power: America's Labor Leaders* (New York: Harcourt Brace, 1948), 9.

13. The reference here is to the online edition published by WHO'S WHO Sutter's international red series available at <http://www.whoswho.eu>. "The *Who's Who* database includes only those occupying positions at the top of Italian institutions, organizations, associations, firms and societies with an international profile." "The selection of people to include is made by an international committee of *Who's Who* experts which remains anonymous so as not to be subject to any kind of influence," "Nota metodologica alla ricerca," pp. 149–151 in Carlo Carboni (ed.), *Élite e classi dirigenti in Italia* (Rome and Bari: Laterza, 2007), 150.

14. Bearing in mind that the adult resident population on January 1, 2011 was 50,396,628, the latest date for which Istat figures are available: <http://dati.istat.it/Index.aspx?DataSetCode =DCIS_POPORESBIL1&Lang=>

15. See "Il profilo del potere in Italia" (available at <http://www.whoswho.eu/doc/ita_news-paper_embed/4665_ita_newspaper_embed.pdf>) from which the figures cited in the following paragraphs have been taken unless stated otherwise.

16. Carlo Carboni and Emmanuele Pavolini, "Una radiografia delle élite: chi sono e che caratteristiche hanno," pp. 3–52 in Carlo Carboni (ed.), *Élite e classi dirigenti in Italia* (Rome and Bari: Laterza, 2007), 20–26.

17. Carboni and Pavolini (ibid.) suggest that businesspeople declined from 47 to 18 percent between 1990 and 2004, while those working in cultural and professional occupations rose from 27.5 to 42.0 percent over the same period.

18. According to Carboni and Pavolini (ibid., p. 11), politicians grew from 14.4 to 26.3 percent between 1990 and 2004; in 2004 only a quarter had degrees in economics or science subjects as compared to one third in 1990 (ibid., p.27); entrepreneurs and managers in private industry declined significantly while university professors, journalists, and writers remained steady or increased (ibid., table 1.1).

19. Martin M. Chemers, *An Integrative Theory of Leadership* (Mahwah, NJ: Lawrence Erlbaum Associates, 1997).

20. Carlo Carboni, "Epilogo. Potere, élite e classe dirigente: un breve repertorio sociologico," pp. 125–147 in Carlo Carboni (ed.), *Élite e classi dirigenti in Italia*, Rome and Bari: Laterza), 141.

21. (<http://cpi.transparency.org/cpi2012/in_detail/>.)

22. Robert Putnam, *Making Democracy Work: Civic Traditions in Modern Italy* (Princeton, NJ: Princeton University Press, 1993).

23. James L. Newell, *Parties and Democracy in Italy* (Aldershot: Ashgate, 2000), 47.

24. For party systems, see Giovanni Sartori, *Parties and Party Systems: A Framework for Analysis* (Cambridge: Cambridge University Press, 1976). These matters are explored in some depth in the chapters by Valbruzzi and Calise in this volume.

25. Martin Rhodes, "Financing Party Politics in Italy: A Case of System Corruption," pp. 54–80 in Martin Bull and Martin Rhodes (eds.), *Crisis and Transition in Italian Politics* (London: Frank Cass, 1997), 65–66; Mauro Magatti, *Corruzione politica e società italiana* (Bologna: Il Mulino, 1996), 71–74.

26. Newell, *Parties and Democracy in Italy*, 107–108.

27. Maurizio Viroli, *The Liberty of Servants: Berlusconi's Italy* (Princeton, NJ: Princeton Universiy Press, 2012), xii.

28. Paul Ginsborg, "Explaining Italy's Crisis," pp. 19–39 in Stephen Gundle and Simon Parker (eds.), *The New Italian Republic: From the Fall of the Berlin Wall to Berlusconi* (London and New York: Routledge, 1996), 29.

29. Chris Hanretty, "The Media between Market and Politics," pp. 85–98 in Andrea Mammone and Giuseppe A. Veltri (eds.), *Italy Today: The Sick Man of Europe* (Abingdon, Oxford, and New York: Routledge, 2010), 85–86.

30. Martin J. Bull and James L. Newell, "Negatività in nome del liberalismo: Ritratti dell'Italia nell' *Economost*," *Comunicazione Politica*, no. 1 (2011), 33–34.

31. Carboni, "Epilogo," 147.

CHAPTER 2

....

THE RISORGIMENTO

....

ANTHONY L. CARDOZA

As the acrimonious debates engendered by the 150th anniversary of national unification in 2011 clearly attest, the Risorgimento remains very much at the center of contemporary Italian political life. Indeed, since the end of the Cold War, the collapse of Italy's First Republic in the 1990s, the Northern League's challenge to national unity, the frustrated hopes for progressive reform, and a surge in non-European immigration have given the subject a new lease on life as a principal source of Italian national identity. The term, Risorgimento, which translates as "revival" or "resurrection," covers three distinct but interrelated projects. Traditionally, it has referred to a movement and sequence of events that culminated in national unification and independence between 1859 and 1861. As such, the Risorgimento represented the decisive moment in the emergence of Italy as a nation-state with defined geographical boundaries and a common institutional structure. At the same time, other scholars have applied the term to a broader process of social, economic, and political modernization after 1815, a time that ostensibly witnessed the gradual decline of traditional rural society, the rise of modern urban life, a shift from an agricultural to an industrial economy, and the creation of a new parliamentary political system. In this respect, the long-term goal of the Risorgimento was to forge a new modern Italy firmly ensconced in the first ranks of the most advanced nations of Europe. The lion's share of scholarship and popular media attention in the past 15 years, however, has focused on the role of the Risorgimento as an ideological and cultural movement that created and disseminated the idea of Italy as an "imagined national community." The nineteenth-century protagonists of this movement included novelists, painters, and composers, as well as nationalist propagandists like Giuseppe Mazzini, who provided the images, metaphors, and narratives of a new patriotic discourse that has shaped the ways political leaders, intellectuals, and the media have understood, interpreted, and acted upon Italian developments over the past century and a half.[1]

The perfect storm of events that resulted in the political unification of the Italian peninsula between 1859 and 1861 was largely the unanticipated product of conventional and guerrilla warfare, diplomacy, and popular revolution carried out by a diverse cast of mutually hostile forces against seemingly overwhelming odds. Italian nationalists faced daunting obstacles in the nineteenth century. From the outset, they had to over-come a millennial history of political, geographic, economic, and linguistic fragmenta-tion on the peninsula. To make matters worse, Roman Catholicism, a powerful source of national identity in Poland and Ireland, played a decidedly anti-national role in the Italian setting, where the Pope was not only a spiritual leader, but also a temporal power, a status deemed essential to papal authority and independence. At the same time, nationalists faced a hostile coalition of the great powers of Europe, dominated by the Habsburg Empire, which controlled much of northern Italy directly, while its other family members ruled over many of the smaller states on the peninsula. Finally, Italian patriots were themselves bitterly divided between moderate liberal monarchists and more radical democratic republicans. Mazzini, the leading figure in the radical camp, played a crucial role in publicizing the national cause, promoting the martial exploits of Giuseppe Garibaldi, and in influencing public opinion abroad. Still, his attempts at direct action via revolutionary conspiracies, violent insurrections, and military expedi-tions all ended in failure.

A key turning point in the unification process came in the early 1850s, when Count Camillo Benso di Cavour became prime minister of the Kingdom of Sardinia, Italy's only indigenous dynasty, the most liberal progressive state on the peninsula, and the home of a proud monarchy and military nobility. An ardent proponent of free trade, sec-ularism, and constitutional government, and an opponent of revolution and republican-ism at home, Cavour was also a gifted statesman with an extraordinary talent for seizing opportunities. He was initially a reluctant nationalist, whose goals were limited to dis-lodging Austria from Italy and extending the boundaries of the Savoyard monarchy to the northern part of the peninsula. Such reservations did not keep Cavour from exploit-ing patriotic sentiments by enlisting the support of the Nationalist Society to promote Piedmontese leadership of the independence movement in northern and central Italy. The collapse of the conservative bloc of great powers in the wake of the Crimean War, Austria's relative isolation on the Italian peninsula after 1856, and the imperial ambitions of the French emperor, Napoleon III, created new diplomatic opportunities that Cavour skillfully exploited. In the spring of 1859, he negotiated the Treaty of Plombières with the French ruler, who promised military support against Austria in exchange for the Piedmontese territories of Nice and Savoy. The ensuing war ended prematurely when Napoleon III withdrew in July before Piedmont could seize Venice and the surrounding Veneto region. Nevertheless, Cavour and the House of Savoy's military–political cam-paign had achieved most of its principal objectives by the beginning of 1860, while keep-ing the democratic and republican forces at bay. Their state now included Lombardy, Emilia, and Tuscany, the most modernized and prosperous regions on the peninsula.

Piedmont's success in the north and center, however, had unintended and undesired consequences for Cavour in the south, where the withdrawal of the Austrian Empire destabilized the Bourbon dynasty in Naples and allowed the political initiative to shift to the democratic nationalists. Revolts in Sicily in the spring of 1860 inspired Garibaldi to lead an expedition of "one thousand red shirts" to the island, and then cross to the mainland in August to overthrow the Bourbon dynasty in Naples. The prospect of a democratic republic in the south and a Garibaldian advance on papal Rome forced Cavour and King Victor Emanuel II to accept a much larger unified Italian nation in the name of the monarchy, in order to avoid hostile intervention on the peninsula by both the Habsburgs and Napoleon III and the possible loss of the territorial gains of the previous year. After assuring the French ruler that the status quo in Rome and the Vatican would remain unchanged, the monarch led his army into the rest of the papal territories and then south to the town of Teano, where Garibaldi handed over his conquests to the new "King of Italy." Plebiscites in the fall of 1860 resulted in the annexation of these territories and the formal proclamation of the Kingdom of Italy on March 17, 1861.[2]

While the unification of most of the peninsula was an extraordinary achievement, all the protagonists saw the resulting product as a decidedly mixed blessing. Cavour and the moderate liberals now ruled over a new national territory, but not the one that they had envisioned or necessarily wanted. Conversely, the democratic nationalists got most of the territorial edifice they had hoped for, but found themselves largely excluded from the new nation-state. At the same time, the forced merger of the north and south left a legacy of resentment, distrust, and popular unrest that would prove to be remarkably enduring. Nor did the emergence of a unified nation-state automatically resolve long-standing problems on the peninsula. The governments of the new state not only had to defend its independence abroad and resolve immediate financial challenges, but were also confronted with the enormous tasks of overcoming entrenched local and regional loyalties and rivalries, forging a new connection between the Italian state and society, and stabilizing their relations with the Catholic Church. Significantly, many of these tasks have continued to absorb the attention and shape the policies of the various regimes that have governed the country in the ensuing century and a half.

The Risorgimento's second project of economic and social modernization has also proven to be an arduous undertaking. From the outset, the ostensibly more advanced societies and economies of France, Great Britain, and Germany provided the yardsticks by which the country's "modernity" was measured and judged. As a nation-state based on a parliamentary system after 1861, Italy did enter the political vanguard of Western Europe, while recent scholarship has shown that its infrastructural investments in transportation, communications, and education contributed to gradual but steady economic growth in the half century after unification. Nonetheless, the country's overreliance on the old textile industry limited long-term sustainable expansion, and its economy continued to lag behind its northern and western European neighbors.[3] The combination of two world wars, a global depression, and Fascism in the first half of the twentieth century further delayed growth and the transformation of the economy. As a consequence, Italy remained a predominantly poor, rural society into the early 1950s. Only in the second half of the twentieth century, with the postwar "economic miracle" and the ensuing transformations, did the country join the ranks of the major European economies and become an affluent, "postindustrial," urban, mass consumer society. Even then, the persistence of the north–south divide and the absence of broader political and institutional reform led scholars, by the 1990s, to refer to Italy as an example of "modernization without growth."[4]

The Risorgimento's third project—the construction and inculcation of a collective national identity—received relatively limited attention in the academic community and the media during the decades of the economic miracle, a period when the excesses of Fascism had discredited the ideals of nationalism, and the opposing transnational ideologies and institutions of Marxism and Catholicism dominated Italian political and institutional life. After 1990, the end of the Cold War and the ensuing resurgence of old regional loyalties and tensions at home and across the European continent coincided with a sea change in the scholarly world to postmodern cultural approaches. As a result, there has been a surge in the past decade and a half of new research on the Risorgimento as a source of Italy's supposedly fragile sense of national identity. In the process, this work has re-envisioned the Risorgimento less as a concrete political movement or series of events and more as a set of discursive themes, symbols, metaphors, and images articulated by patriotic artists, writers, and propagandists to give meaning to and promote the idea of the "nation" and "Italian people" both on the peninsula and abroad.

The nineteenth-century architects of the idea of the Italian nation attempted to blend a pre-existing secular and religious culture of "Italian-ness" with the rhetoric of the French Revolution and the language of Romanticism. The result included a romantic nostalgia for past glory, a condemnation of present decadence, and a vision of future greatness for Italy's national community. Patriotic intellectuals and creative artists highlighted the glories of Ancient Roman civilization and the achievements of the Renaissance, when the peninsula stood proudly at the forefront of European economic and cultural life. According to their historical narrative, however, the centuries after 1500 saw Italy and its people fall into decline, decay, and corruption in the wake of military defeats, foreign domination, clerical rule, and domestic divisions. Thus, Italy lapsed into a long slumber, and was still mired in conditions of civil, individual, and collective degradation and fragmentation at the beginning of the nineteenth century. Significantly, the Risorgimento's condemnation of national decline and squalor involved not only institutional life, but also the character traits of the Italian people, who were depicted as excessively subservient, lazy, undisciplined, and effeminate shadows of their glorious ancestors. In this context of decadence and failure, nationalists envisioned unification and independence both as a means of reviving and resurrecting the greatness of Italy's past and as a force for the moral regeneration of its people. Italian national identity and national character became, in this fashion, inseparably intertwined in the vision and rhetoric of the Risorgimento, which offered an explanation for Italian degeneration as well as the remedies for its regeneration.[5]

As Lucy Riall has recently noted, historians initially refocused on the Risorgimento as a cultural phenomenon in the first half of the nineteenth century in order to understand how it shaped the consciousness and sensibilities of a growing segment of the educated classes, and thereby transformed them into active protagonists willing to fight and die for the nationalist cause.[6] Alberto Banti, for instance, identified a set of canonical novels, poems, theatrical works, paintings, and melodramas that, he argued, reached a growing audience by tapping into powerful emotions tied to kinship, honor, and sacrifice, which were adaptable to an ethno-cultural community rooted in bonds of blood, land, memories, and self-consciousness.[7] In a similar vein, Christopher Duggan has shown how Mazzini redeployed the language and practices of Roman Catholicism on behalf of the national cause by emphasizing the themes of God, faith, doctrinal purity, and martyrdom in his writings and propaganda.[8] Banti and Paul Ginsborg have claimed that this "deep culture" of the Risorgimento had successfully given birth to a "mass movement" by the early 1860s, mobilizing tens of thousands of Italians, who enjoyed the support and sympathy of additional hundreds of thousand others.[9] Such claims need to be viewed with some caution, since a majority of Italy's middle classes and peasants still remained hostile or indifferent to the national cause both before and after 1861.

A subsequent body of scholarship has examined the ways in which the romantic ideals and rhetoric of the Risorgimento have continued to influence the terms and language of public debate and political conflict on the Italian peninsula in the century and a half after national unification. From the outset, the Risorgimento served as a partisan tool in recurring battles among competing political projects over the definition of what constituted a successful and modern nation and society. Such conflicts were already embedded in the contrasting hopes and expectations of the original participants in a movement that included republicans and monarchists, centralizers and federalists, democrats and liberals. Not surprisingly, these groups attached sharply different meanings to the terms nation, Italian people, rebirth, and regeneration, which they passed on to successive generations. The struggles of the Liberal state against the harsh social, economic, and political realities of the peninsula in the second half of the nineteenth century further exacerbated these divisions. The romantic image constructed by patriotic intellectuals of the Italian nation as a holistic, cohesive, and organic ethno-cultural community stood in stark contrast to concrete experiences of persistent divisions and fragmentation after 1861. The perceived gap between the heroic "poetry" of the Risorgimento and the mundane "prose" of the successive Liberal era's accomplishments nourished, in turn, a sense of disappointment and failure within the ranks of the intelligentsia and the educated classes in general, that took the form of repeated criticism of and disdain for the Italian nation-state.[10]

Dissatisfaction with the Liberal regime's perceived shortcomings and inadequacies led, on the one hand, some of its ideological opponents to attack the Risorgimento, per se, as a failed, flawed, or misguided project that had given birth to an illegitimate nation-state. Militant Catholics, for instance, argued that the parliamentary monarchy's secularist roots alienated it from the "authentic nation" or real Italy, whose true identity and greatness lay in its essentially Catholic character and its central role in a larger European Christian civilization.[11] On the other end of the ideological spectrum, Marxists challenged Liberal Italy's "grand narrative" of national triumph with a "counter-narrative" of the Risorgimento as a passive or failed revolution. For Antonio Gramsci, the moderate liberals' national-building project rested upon a fatal compromise between the modern capitalist bourgeoisie of the north and the semi-feudal landed elites of the south, a compromise that precluded any genuine economic, social, and political reform in the half century after unification. On the contrary, Gramsci argued, the unification process created an enduring gulf between the Italian state and

civil society that found expression in persistent parliamentary paralysis, political instability, social conflict, and distorted industrial development on the peninsula. In this
fashion, the Marxist critique of the Liberal state linked the ostensible problems of the
Risorgimento to a broader interpretation of the trajectory of modern Italian history,
which led inexorably from unification to the post-World War I crisis and triumph of
Fascism in the 1920s and 1930s. This interpretation of Risorgimento as a failed "passive
revolution" did not go unchallenged after World War II. Rosario Romeo, in particular,
argued that the Marxists' French Revolutionary model could not have worked under the
conditions prevailing on the Italian peninsula. Here, the Risorgimento liberals' focus
on the urban capitalist economy of the north and the unification of the national market,
Romeo argued, represented the best possible path to development for the entire country.[12] Nonetheless, Gramsci's interpretation proved to have a long shelf life, dominating
scholarly debates and discussion in Italy until the 1970s, when the work of the "new"
social historians demonstrated the inadequacy of class-based analysis for explaining either popular revolts or the relationship between the socioeconomic interests and
political views of the bourgeois elites.[13]

On the other hand, new right-wing nationalist forces enthusiastically embraced their
own version of the Risorgimento and its rhetoric in order to advance their own authoritarian and expansionist agendas in the late nineteenth and the first half of the twentieth century. Above all, they seized on its romantic vision of Italy's glorious future as a
virile, resurgent, and powerful new state, which they used to highlight the shortcomings of the liberal monarchy and to challenge its legitimacy as the political embodiment
of the nation. In their propaganda, parliamentary transformism, the emerging threat
of socialism, and the "Southern Question" all served as proof that the aspirations of
the Risorgimento had been betrayed.[14] Nationalist ideologues devoted special attention to the supposed inability of the Liberal state to achieve the essential moral regeneration of the Italian people, whom, in their narrative, remained mired in their old
vices and character flaws. At the same time, they employed the themes and models of
Risorgimento discourses to articulate and legitimize their own authoritarian projects,
which, they claimed, would strengthen the central state and solidify the national community. Through repression of subversion at home, in tandem with war and imperial
expansion abroad, they promised to eliminate internal divisions, redeem past national
humiliations, remake Italians into a heroic and virile people, and reassert Italy's prestige
abroad. The extraordinary nature of Italian unification in 1861 encouraged nationalists
in their endeavors, since it seemed to have rewarded foreign policies of adventurism and
risk-taking. Disasters like the Battle of Adowa in 1896, which temporarily ended Italian
imperial ambitions in Ethiopia, did little to temper nationalists' enthusiasm for war and
expansionism as the best means for achieving Risorgimento goals of moral, cultural,
and political redemption. On the contrary, nationalists became passionate supporters of
the Libyan War in 1911 and Italian intervention in World War I.

In the explosive climate of revolutionary unrest and inflamed nationalistic passions after World War I, both Fascists and anti-fascist forces selectively made use of
Risorgimento aspirations and ideals to bolster their own legitimacy and to discredit

their adversaries. Mussolini's propaganda apparatus boasted that his regime was carrying to completion the project of the Risorgimento and thus represented the fullest embodiment of the historically ordained Italian nation. In particular, the Fascists exploited the belief in Italy's pre-destined superiority and greatness, and the corresponding need for the spiritual and physical regeneration of the Italians to achieve that destiny. The regime's propaganda played on the country's past record of military and foreign policy defeats to disparage the Liberal parliamentary state and to mobilize popular support for its own project of remaking Italians into a more disciplined, "virile," and militaristic people, capable of achieving "glory and power" abroad and establishing the country as a great power on the world stage. In pursuit of these goals, the Fascist educational and cultural initiatives emphasized the historical continuities that linked the dictatorship to Imperial Rome and the Risorgimento. They highlighted the supposed affinities between Garibaldi's "red shirts" and Mussolini's "blackshirts" to present the Fascists as the natural heirs of these heroic, nineteenth-century freedom fighters. At the same time, the regime glorified physical strength and violence as part of a larger project of remaking Italians into new "fascist men." Unlike their liberal, individualistic, effeminate, peace-loving ancestors, they were depicted as hypermasculine warriors who formed a disciplined, unified force, obedient to the Duce and determined to establish Italy's rights as a great power in the Mediterranean and in Europe. The aspirations of the Risorgimento thus offered a framework for Mussolini's increasingly aggressive imperialist policies in the mid-1930s. Accordingly, the invasion of Ethiopia was presented to the Italian public as the first step in gaining revenge for past humiliations and in achieving the long-promised greatness of their nation in the Mediterranean.

At the same time, the Risorgimento provided a set of the rhetorical tools for Mussolini's political adversaries. While the Marxist left viewed the Fascist dictatorship as the end product of a fatally flawed passive revolution in the nineteenth century, liberal anti-fascists like Piero Gobetti advanced their own counter-narrative of Fascism as the betrayal of Risorgimento hopes and ideals. Far from being the engine of national rebirth, Mussolini's regime embodied, in their view, all the "old illnesses of immature Italy" that the national movement of the nineteenth century had sought to overcome. For his part, the Duce himself personified the worst "defects" of the "Italian soul and character" inherited from the past, with his "superficiality, effrontery, rhetorical emptiness, lack of political education, and boastfulness." Gobetti envisioned, as an alternative to the Fascist dictatorship, a "Risorgimento without Heroes" grounded in the modern, pragmatic, and industrious values of his native region of Piedmont.[15]

In the wake of the collapse of the original Fascist regime in World War II, each side in the ensuing civil war continued to employ the patriotic ideals of the Risorgimento to mobilize its supporters and legitimize its own political cause. Propagandists for Mussolini's Republic of Salò, for instance, constantly linked his government to the honor of the *patria* and invoked the names of the heroes of the Risorgimento against the traitors of the "fatherland," who had surrendered to the allies. For their part, the Resistance forces attacked Fascism for having "obliterated the nation," and portrayed their actions as a "war of liberation" in defense of the "honor of Italy," the "ideal of the

Fatherland," and the "independence of the nation." Through their "blood and sacrifices," the partisan brigades claimed to be united in a common cause of national regeneration or, in the words of Vittorio Foa, "the need to reconstruct an identity for ourselves in the face of fascism."[16]

In the decades after 1945, the Risorgimento and its nineteenth-century vision of the nation appeared to be an historical anachronism without relevance to the new Italy emerging from the war. The catastrophic legacy of Fascism, which had culminated in military defeat, economic chaos, and civil war, had discredited its nationalistic ideals and its accompanying patriotic rhetoric and celebration. In an era of the Cold War ideological blocs and the supranationalism of the emerging European community, the two dominant and sharply polarized parties of the first Italian Republic, Christian Democracy and the Italian Communist Party, both rested upon ostensibly universal values and institutions that, as Duggan has argued, precluded them from appealing "to the 'nation' as an overarching pole of reference."[17] The diminished status of the Risorgimento was strikingly evident in the positions of the two parties on the one hundredth anniversary of Italian unification in 1961. Echoing the rhetoric of their nineteenth-century predecessors, the Christian Democrats argued that the true nation was the community of Catholic believers and dismissed the events of 1859–61 as a failed "hasty and almost improvised diplomatic–military solution of the Italian problem."[18] While the Communists contested this view of Italian development, they also attacked the commemorations of a movement that had led to war and Fascist dictatorship. In the absence of an ideological foundation grounded in patriotic ideals and emotions, both blocs relied instead their own political subcultures and institutional communities to galvanize their supporters and consolidate their power bases in the Italian Republic. As more recent commentators have observed, post-1945 Republican Italy thereby perpetuated some of the historical shortcomings that had alarmed and mobilized the protagonists of the Risorgimento a century earlier: a lack of shared national values, a cohesive vision of the nation, and a sense of moral unity.

The economic miracle and the ensuing consumer revolution of the 1960s further complicated the situation. On the one hand, some political pundits worried that new patterns of mass private consumption reinforced the problems of excessive individualism and materialism that had concerned nineteenth-century patriotic intellectuals. On the other hand, the same material and cultural changes tended to erode traditional local customs and identities that had long impeded the development of a common national identity. The growing urbanization and secularism of the Italian people undermined, in particular, the old religious base of the Christian Democrats and forced them to rely on state largesse to preserve their virtual monopoly of power. Increasingly, short-term party and factional political interests, rather than a larger vision of the welfare of the nation, dictated government policies, setting the stage for the crisis of the First Republic at the beginning of the 1990s.

The Risorgimento and the theme of national identity have returned with a vengeance to the arena of public debate and discussion since 1990. The end of the Cold War and its transnational ideological blocs, combined with a public debt crisis triggered by Italy's efforts to qualify for membership in the Eurozone, aroused popular discontent and undermined the raison d'etre of the old parties. In the void left by the collapse of the Christian Democratic regime, new political forces once again redeployed the question of Italian national identity as a device to mobilize their bases and discredit their foes. No movement more closely reflected this shift than the Northern League, which denounced the Risorgimento's unification of the peninsula in 1861 as a disastrous mistake, since it yoked together two separate and mutually incompatible national communities: the north and the south. In place of the existing Italian state, the League has advanced solutions that ranged from the independence of the northern regions to the introduction of a decentralized federal system. Although there was little popular support for the idea of secession, even in its own ranks, the Northern League did succeed in stoking widespread anxieties and worries about the supposed fragility of the unitary state and the dangers of national disintegration, at least judging by the tidal wave of new publications devoted to these topics over the past 15 years. At the same time, the erosion of older religious and class-based identities has led to what Silvana Patriarca has described as a "neo-patriotic … renationalization of the political landscape" in Italy.[19] The parties of the center-right, especially Berlusconi's Forza Italia and National Alliance, reappropriated national symbols and appealed actively to Italian patriotism in their electoral propaganda, attacking the parties of the left for their ostensible lack of commitment to the nation.

The 150th anniversary of Italian unification in March 2011 dramatically illustrates how the preoccupations of the Risorgimento patriots still can shape the agenda of contemporary Italian politics. As one might expect, the state commemorated the anniversary with various public ceremonies, sporting events, and other activities intended to display collective national solidarity and pride. At the same time, however, the anniversary also became yet another occasion for bitter public debates and disagreements about the nation's identity and the relative achievements, failures, and betrayals of the Risorgimento and its historical legacy. In response to this "destructive quarrelsomeness" and the "sowers of division," the President of Italian Republic, Giorgio Napolitano, used a series of public speeches at celebrations of the anniversary to launch a vigorous defense of the Risorgimento. For Napolitano, the "greatness" of the unification movement in Italy lay "precisely in the richness and multiplicity of its inspirations and its components" as well as in its "identification of the idea of the nation with the idea of liberty." Accordingly, he argued that the anniversary represented an opportunity to reawaken "a unified national consciousness" in the Italian people, in a difficult moment "laden with uncertainties and challenges for our country."[20] While these polemics attracted a great deal of media attention, both on the peninsula and abroad, it is difficult to disagree with Lucy Riall's observation that the nation "is only a metaphor which displaces discussion of more intractable problems" and Risorgimento's failings "an allegory for … the present-day erosion of democratic institutions."[21]

NOTES

1. See Lucy Riall, *Risorgimento: The History of Italy from Napoleon to Nation-State* (New York: Palgrave Macmillan, 2009), 37–39.

2. Anthony L. Cardoza, "Cavour and Piedmont," in John A. Davis, ed., *Italy in the Nineteenth Century* (Oxford: Oxford University Press, 2000), 108–131.

3. Nick Carter, *Modern Italy in Historical Perspective*, (London: Bloomsbury Academic, 2010), 48–52.

4. John A. Davis, "Remapping Italy's Path to the Twentieth Century," *Journal of Modern History* 66, no. 2 (June 1994), 293.

5. See Silvana Patriarca, *Italian Vices: Nation and Character from the Risorgimento to the Republic* (Cambridge: Cambridge University Press, 2010).

6. Riall, *Risorgimento*, 122–124.

7. Alberto Banti, *La Nazione del Risorgimento. Parentela, santita' e onore alle origini dell'Italia unita'* (Turin: Einaudi, 2000).

8. Christopher Duggan, *The Force of Destiny: A History of Italy since 1796* (London: Allen Lane, 2007), 125–129.

9. Alberto Banti and Paul Ginsborg, eds., *Storia d'Italia. Annali 22, Il Risorgimento* (Turin: Einaudi, 2007), xxiii–xxiv. For an approach that highlights conflicts within the unification movement, see Mario Isnenghi and Eva Cecchinato, eds., *Fare l'Italia: unita' e disunita' nel Risorgimento* (Turin: UTET, 2008).

10. Banti, *La Nazione del Risorgimento*, 199–205.

11. Oliver Logan, "Italian Identity: Catholic Responses to Secularist Definitions, c1910–48," *Modern Italy* 2, no.1 (January 1997) 52–71.

12. Rosario Romeo, *Risorgimento e capitalism* (Rome-Bari: Laterza, 1959).

13. Riall, *Risorgimento*, 74–77.

14. On the concept of transformism, see Marco Valbruzzi's contribution "Trasformismo," Chapter 3 in this volume.

15. Patriarca, *Italian Vices*, 172–174.

16. Duggan, *The Force of Destiny*, 535–537.

17. Duggan, *The Force of Destiny*, 543.

18. Duggan, *The Force of Destiny*, 561.

19. Patriarca, *Italian Vices,* 237.

20. Giorgio Napolitano, *Una e indivisibile. Riflessioni sui 150 anni della nostra Italia* (Milan: Rizzoli, 2011), 9, 46, 68. On the role of the presidents of the Italian Republic, see Gianfrano Pasquino's chapter in this volume (Chapter 7).

21. Lucy Riall, "Sum of all Defects," *Times Literary Supplement*, August 19 and 26, 2011, 11.

CHAPTER 3

....

TRASFORMISMO

....

MARCO VALBRUZZI

"*Trasformismo*, an ugly word for an uglier thing." This is how, at the end of the nineteenth century, one of Italy's most famous poets, Giosuè Carducci, described and stigmatized what many historians consider to be the Italian vice par excellence: *trasformismo*. As a rule, it is preferable to be skeptical of words that we cannot easily translate into other languages, especially into English. Political concepts, such as the one this chapter deals with, should be able to "travel" across different countries and different time periods. Unfortunately, this is not the case with *trasformismo*, which has recently and aptly been added to the list of *les intraduisibles*, that is, those words that cannot be divorced from the deep-rooted tradition of a given country. Moreover, *trasformismo* has quickly become one of the most enduring features of the Italian national identity; a political phenomenology that, as Galli Della Loggia pointed out,[1] cannot be separated from "Italian social life."

What we know for certain is that *trasformismo* is a complex concept that encompasses a vast array of often contradictory definitions. In particular, during its long historical trajectory, different scholars have emphasized different aspects of the concept, while neglecting one or more of its defining features. For instance, many historians have focused on the relationship between *trasformismo* and the process of Italian unification. From this perspective, *trasformismo* has been treated almost as a synonym of "centrism" or, to parody Abraham Lincoln, a government of the center, by the center, for the center. To be more precise, *trasformismo* has been seen as a peculiar system of government, the Italian way to democratization and modernization. Conversely, other scholars, especially political scientists, have preferred to make their focus the individual behavior of those who "transform" their opinions and decisions in order to reach a particular opportunistic goal. In this case, transformism has come to be known as little more than a form of "party switching," that is, the changing of party affiliation by individual politicians. Accordingly, those politicians who practice the ancient art of *trasformismo* have been labelled "switchers" or, more figuratively, "turncoats" (*voltagabbana*). Finally, there are scholars, especially sociologists and anthropologists, who have approached the concept of transformism from a cultural perspective. For many among them, *trasformismo* is neither the product of a difficult historical conjuncture nor the behavior of a single opportunist politician. Briefly put, *trasformismo* should be interpreted as a prototypical Italian trait: a distinctive national vice (for its critics) or the best example of Italy's quintessential ability to survive (for its apologists).

Nevertheless, despite its profound ambiguities and contradictions, *trasformismo* has become the *fil rouge* that links the heroic days of the Risorgimento to the far less heroic age of governmental instability during the republican phase that began in Italy after World War II. Looking for a single, or the most apt, interpretation of transformism would be wrong in itself and, above all, a mission that is unlikely to be accomplished. Instead, it is more constructive to chart its long and fortunate historical trajectory—from its birth at the dawn of the Italian nation to the aftermath of the party system breakdown in the 1990s. This is the aim of the following sections.

THE LONG HISTORY OF A SUCCESSFUL WORD

Trasformismo is a concept with many definitions and, as a consequence, many referents. With no *consensus scholarum* in the scientific literature as to what the term actually means, transformism has, thus far, been treated as an umbrella concept under which we find many different ideas. To some extent, the flexibility and universality of the concept has represented, until today, its good fortune. Because of its long history and the lack of clear borders vis-à-vis other confining concepts such as "centrism," "consociativism," "clientelism," "opportunism," and so on, and, above all, because it has always been at the center of a strong debate between, on the one hand, its realistic defenders and, on the other, its moralistic detractors, *trasformismo* is a magic box with ever-changing content.

If we observe the historical trajectory of the word carefully, it is interesting to note that, when it first appeared, it had no negative connotations. Quite the contrary: in a letter written in 1874, by the senator Carlo Alfieri to the deputy Francesco De Sanctis, Alfieri claimed that the "traditions of the past," namely the exhausted division between left and right, ought to be substituted by the "sane doctrine of the *parliamentary trasformismo*." Hence, at the beginning of its story, *trasformismo* was something good and sound—a practice that the parties should consider carefully. If the letter written by Alfieri signals the etymological birth of the term, its formal entry in the public debate occurred two years later in a speech by the Italian Prime Minister Agostino Depretis. On October 11, 1876, Depretis declared that his ultimate goal was to "facilitate that fruitful transformation of parties, that unification of the Liberal elements of the Chamber, which would constitute the solid majority so long invoked [. . .]. Good ideas, the really good practices: I will take them from anywhere, even from my opponents." That famous speech, delivered to his constituents in his hometown, Stradella, by one of the most important leaders of the left, marks the ideological debut of *trasformismo* in Italian history. At the same time, it implicitly recognizes that a political era, namely the period characterized by the (not so neat) contrast between the "historic right" and "historic left," was coming to an end. More specifically, the ideological formation of the *transformist practice*—that had solved the Roman question in 1870, and balanced the budget—was the unavoidable consequence of the "break-up of the great political parties, and their change of colour, or rather, the varied hues which their representatives assumed from time to time, and the disappearance of any particular significance from the old names, which were not replaced by others with a more definite meaning."[2]

The positive atmosphere surrounding the practice of government theorized and implemented by Depretis quickly disappeared when *trasformismo* moved from the world of ideas to the world of empirical and real phenomena. At this point, it is worth recalling that the *political* birth of *trasformismo* dates back to 1883, with the formation of Depretis's fifth cabinet. At that time, a sizeable group of former rightists, inspired and led by one of the leaders of the fragmented "historic right," the Bolognese Marco Minghetti, entered and reinforced the incumbent governing majority formed by Depretis, who, only one year earlier, in a remarkable speech to his Piedmontese constituency, stated that: "If anyone wishes to *transform* himself and become progressive by accepting my very modest program, how can I refuse him?" This seemingly disinterested invitation from the head of government was enthusiastically accepted by Minghetti who strongly believed in the virtues of the "center virile parties," that is, the *conjonction des centres*—the moderate liberals and the moderate conservatives—against the threat posed by the extremist or anti-system parties. Incidentally, it is worth noting that, for Croce:

> [A]fter 1885, "transformism" was so much an accomplished fact that it was no longer talked about, and the word itself went out of use. Nevertheless, when the name recurred it always suggested something equivocal and unworthy, a sign of Italian weakness, and the echo of this impression is to be found in historical literature. Historians are usually professors or other simple-minded people, who are bewildered by successive changes of ministry, by the perpetual failure to realize their coveted hope of a "stable government" and above all by the mutability of human affairs. The secret desire of their hearts is that things should remain as they are, and they do not consider that, if they did so, there would be no history to write, or at least none of the kind which they are accustomed to write.[3]

Nevertheless, and perhaps against Croce's wishes, the word "*trasformismo*" did not disappear from the public debate. On the contrary, it became an ideal target for any kind of critic, both from the left and the right.

Despite, or perhaps thanks to, its highly negative connotations, *trasformismo* remained a constant element in the history of Italy. Its success was certified, once for all, by the fact that, curiously, when Crispi become President of the Council in 1887, he agreed to form his majority and govern the country in a very "transformist" way. The telling case of Crispi, formerly a fierce opponent of the misdeeds of transformism, illustrates perfectly the secret and irresistible charm of this parliamentary technique, which had the power to change and *transform* the minds of even those who had previously criticized it. The absolute flexibility of *trasformismo* to adapt to the different phases of Italian history is proved once again by its capacity to face the emergence, at the end of the nineteenth century, of the first mass-based political parties: the Italian Socialist Party and, later on, the Catholic Popular Party. As Antonio Gramsci correctly pointed out, the advent of these new models of political organization led to a different kind of transformism which, after the tragic Fascist "parenthesis," would accompany the history of the country until the complete collapse of its party system in the early 1990s. More specifically, the "molecular transformism" working under the strict control of Depretis and Crispi, whereby "individual political figures were incorporated one by one into the conservative-moderate 'political class,'" was substituted by the "transformism of whole groups," especially extremists "who crossed over the moderate camp."[4] This second kind of *trasformismo* made its first appearance during the disputable "Giolittian era" and later, after World War II, it would become the defining feature of the party system that existed in Italy almost until the end of the twentieth century.

Needless to say, there are many (substantiated) reasons as to why *trasformismo* was unable to shake off its negative associations, in particular its strong connection with the idea of political *immobilismo* and corruption. What is more, this complex set of meanings and interpretations found its main exegete in the Sicilian writer Giuseppe Tomasi di Lampedusa who, in his unique masterpiece *Il Gattopardo*, perfectly described the intrinsic logic of any "transformist" arrangement: "If we want things to stay as they are, things will have to change." With the (posthumous) publication of *Il Gattopardo* in 1958, *trasformismo* found its perfect icon and manifesto.

THE DIFFERENT TYPES AND PHASES OF *TRASFORMISMO*

Cavour's *Connubio*

For many scholars *trasformismo* has an eminent forefather and a noted precedent: Camillo Benso, count of Cavour, the leader of the process of Italian unification and the undisputed leader of that political coalition of competent and distinguished politicians that we know as the "Destra Storica." The noted, and much debated, precedent dates back to 1852, when Cavour decided to reach an agreement—which has passed into the annals of history as *il Connubio* (literally: the "marriage" or "union")—with the leader of the radical (and relatively leftist) wing of the Parliament, Umberto Rattazzi, in order to isolate both the extreme monarchic right and the Mazzinian left. Observed from this viewpoint, the agreement between Cavour and Rattazzi, with the subsequent formation of a workable and sizeable centrist majority, was neither an isolated incident in the history of Italy nor simply an antecedent of that peculiar mode of government (re)launched, 30 years later, by Depretis and Minghetti. As Luigi Musella has recently highlighted, Cavour was the first Italian politician "to put into practice a *transformist* politics which remained a constant in the political history of the country."[5] Thus, the count of Cavour has been considered as the actual putative father of *trasformismo* or, worse still, the first ever *trasformista*.[6] However, other scholars and historians, approaching the same phenomenon from different perspectives, have reached different, if not opposite, conclusions. For instance, Luciano Cafagna, having recognized that "'trasformismo' was actually born—as it has been frequently and correctly suggested—with Cavour's *connubio* in 1852,"[7] stresses the progressive and dynamic orientation of Cavourian politics and its governing majority. If the *transformist* practices carried out decades later by Depretis, Crispi, and Giolitti had a defensive, tactical, and purely spontaneous nature, the mode of government developed by Cavour was absolutely strategic, progressive, and programmatic.

Depretis's (Liberal or Historic) Transformism

Only three months after the declaration of the Kingdom of Italy, Cavour unexpectedly passed away. His death meant not only the tragic disappearance of the most important and ingenious figure of the Italian Risorgimento, but also the gradual disintegration of his political party. Moreover, after the challenging rebalancing of the budget and the tormented conquest of Rome, the "historic right" had implemented its historic platform. Consequently, the "legitimate" right was, at that time, both lacking an uncontested leader and a clear mission. This situation opened the way to the "parliamentary revolution" that, in 1876, brought Agostino Depretis and the "historic left" into power. However, as Maurizio Cotta has noted, the governmental alternation occurred in Parliament (not at election time) in 1876, and "far from constituting an unexpected 'revolution', can be seen as the culmination of a gradual convergence among the two elite camps that took place in the parliamentary arena during the preceding ten years."[8]

It was during this period that "historic *trasformismo*" made inroads in the history of Italy and became a concrete political reality. More precisely, it was the October 1882 general election, with the electoral deal struck by Depretis and Minghetti, which marked the formal inauguration of what was then called (without any negative connotation) transformism. It is worth highlighting that 1882 was the year that saw, following a long and complicated process,[9] the electoral reform that extended the vote to literate males over the age of 21—even those who did not pay any direct taxes. As Salvemini noted, the "Italian Risorgimento between 1859 and 1870 was the work of an oligarchy of upper and middle classes [where the] right to vote was granted only to males over twenty-five who paid a minimum of eight dollars in direct taxation and knew how to read and write."[10] Consequently, until 1882, the enfranchised citizens numbered 620,000, that is, 2 percent of the overall population. After the reform headed by Depretis, the electorate rose from 2.2 percent (in 1880) to 6.9 percent of the Italian population

The extension of the vote, both for the left and the right, was approved with the common purpose of reducing the distance between the so-called (originally by the

Catholics) *paese legale* ("legal country") and *paese reale* ("real country"); that is, the liberal elites, on one hand, and the popular masses, on the other. However, and, in some cases, even against the hopes of the governing elite, the electoral reform of 1882 made the electoral bases of the two loose parties in power more unstable and "unmanageable" and, at the same time, electorally strengthened the extreme forces. In sum, *trasformismo* as a parliamentary technique was "not improvised, nor particularly original",[11] and was devised by the liberal elite in order to deal with, on the one hand, the increasing fragmentation of the parliamentary arena, and, on the other, the growing and converging threat posed by the extreme left (radicals, republicans, and, later, socialists) and the extreme right.

In 1882–83 the Italian political system was still undergoing that "molecular" phase of transformism which entailed individual co-optation of single parliamentarians within the so-called "area of legitimacy." This kind of parliamentary arrangement came into being as the result of many steps and phases. The first step took place during the pre-electoral period, thanks to the meticulous operation of the prefects at the local level. In this respect, suffice to say that by (ab)using the local power of the prefects, the ruling elite was able to mold its parliamentary majority well in advance. The second step toward the formation of the "transformist coalition" occurred at the electoral level and took the form of "semi coordinated electoral stand-downs,"[12] namely pre-electoral agreements between politicians of the "liberal-conservative" camp. Finally, although this process proceeded as a never-ending vicious circle from the local level up to the central level, the third step required the formation, at the center of the party system, of a sort of "coalition of the willing" made up of all those parliamentarians willing or, in many cases, eager to trade their vote and consensus to the government in exchange for pork barrel favors. It is no coincidence that this was the precise point at which *trasformismo* meets and espouses (for mutual convenience) *clientelismo* (clientelism).

Crispi's (Conservative) Transformism

The death of Agostino Depretis in 1887 marked both the end of the so-called "historic trasformismo" and the arrival of the "dictatorship of an old wolf, following the regime of an old fox."[13] The "old wolf" was Francesco Crispi, who became prime minister after the uncontested political supremacy of the "old fox" Depretis. What the new President of Council inherited from his direct predecessor was, in part, his mobile and flexible parliamentary majority and, above all, his ability to reach flexible compromises between different groups and individuals. Many scholars have identified only small differences of degree between "Depretis's transformism" and "Crispi's transformism." By contrast, other scholars have emphasized differences in kind between what they call the "liberal transformism" inaugurated by Depretis and the "conservative transformism" of Crispi (and, later, of di Rudinì).[14] More precisely, with the approval of the protectionist trade policy of 1887, Crispi created the conditions for a strict alliance between traditional landowners (especially from the south) and new entrepreneurial groups in the north.

The creation of this new "historic bloc" (to use Gramsci's terms), masterminded by the prime minister himself, allowed the formation of that "'permanent' alliance of interests and values" which formed the basis of the "new" conservative transformism.[15]

Despite the aforementioned differences, "liberal" and "conservative" *trasformismo* shared the same defensive, or exclusive, approaches. In order to avoid and reduce the convergent threats of the extreme parties, both Depretis and Crispi created centrist governing majorities with the support of available legislators from the liberal pro-system camp. The birth of the Italian Socialist Party (PSI) in 1892 and, more than twenty years later, the formation of the Catholic Italian Popular Party (PPI), engendered new and unprecedented challenges for the ruling liberal class. The age of the mass-based political parties was making its gradual—albeit belated, but undoubtedly triumphant in the long run—entrance into the Italian political system. It was the challenge launched by this new kind of party that drove *trasformismo*: the necessity to deal with new and stronger political actors required an overhaul of the old and weakened transformist practices. In this sense, Giovanni Giolitti can be considered the "updater" of the old practices to meet the new demands of a changing society on the road toward industrialization and political modernization. Unsurprisingly, during the so-called "Giolittian Era" many scholars have seen the emergence of what they aptly label "*neotrasformismo*."[16] While in the past the practice of *trasformismo* took place within the borders of the centrist, liberal, and "legitimate" coalition, Giolitti's new inclusive project tended to absorb and co-opt into the governing majority those parties and forces outside or, more precisely, *against* the system. Briefly put, Giolittian *neotrasformismo* completely changed the logic of competition between the ins (liberal ruling class) and the outs (anti-system parties from the extreme left and right): the new defensive strategy masterminded by Giolitti required on "opening," first, to the extreme left and later to the extreme right.

That said, another relevant difference between the old and the new version of *trasformismo* involves the nature of those political actors that needed (more or less reluctantly) to be "transformed." At its inception, transformism had a "molecular" nature: single legislators were co-opted from time to time in the flexible parliamentary majorities. Conversely, at the beginning of the twentieth century, in particular as a consequence of the emergence of the new mass parties, (neo)*trasformismo* became a collective action, that is, a strategy to absorb distinct groups within the centrist majority. Incidentally, the new strategy designed by Giolitti, albeit original and meticulous, was not as successful as its creator had hoped. In spite of the ambitions of "the statesman of Dronero," his project was unable to either reduce the distance between the rulers and the ruled or to govern effectively and consistently. The so-called "*giolittismo* was a sort of centrism tilted toward the center-left in the first phase and a sort of center-right centrism in the second phase, with the war in Libya and the Gentiloni Pact. The historic expressions of this oscillatory centrist defense were a peculiar method of 'trasformismo.' "[17] Securing the parliamentary support of the radicals and, with much more difficulty, the socialists, Giolitti tried (without success) to absorb the emerging "social question" within his amorphous political majority.

Fascist Interlude and Republican Transformism

Thus, the failure of the "transformist system" paved the way for the Fascist regime, whose inception, incidentally, was based on a "great and successful transformist operation,"[18] namely, the creation of a "big list" (*listone*) of all the truly "national" (approved) candidates. In so doing, *trasformismo* signed its own death warrant: Mussolini transformed the "gloomy" Parliament into a "bivouac for his platoons," and transformism, at least as a purely parliamentary phenomenon, disappeared suddenly.

After the end of World War II and with the return to a democratic political regime, the Italian political system relied once again on the old practices of centrist majorities fabricated in Parliament after the elections and without any clear associations to the preferences of the voters. As in the past, the party system was "blocked" at the center: alternation in power was impossible and the oppositions were plural, bilateral, and, above all, anti-system. The presence of the so-called *conventio ad excludendum* against the Italian Communist Party, established because of its strong links with the Soviet Union, and the presence of an "excluded pole" harboring the not so different heirs of the Fascist regime, reduced the "area of legitimacy" to a few centrist political parties: the dominant Christian Democracy and their small laical or liberal satellites (the Republican Party, the Italian Liberal Party, and the Italian Democratic Socialist Party). It was under these conditions, where the center was "bound to govern" and the oppositions were obliged to stay out of power, that what we can label "republican transformism" made its first appearance in 1962: when the PSI left the benches of the opposition and joined those far more hospitable and rewarding benches of the centrist parliamentary majority and, one year later, those reserved for the cabinet. Unlike the old "liberal" transformism, based on "mobile majorities formed day-by-day through agreements with single parliamentarians or local interest groups,"[19] *trasformismo* of the "first Italian party system" (1946–93, the period in Italian history known as the "First Republic") was much more static or rigid. The leaders (of the factions) of the governing parties decided the coalition agreements and post-electoral alliances. However, the rigidity of the system did not reduce the frequency of cabinet turnover or the instability of the governments. If the Kingdom of Italy experienced 58 governments from 1861 to 1922, the Italian Republic did not fare much better, with 59 governments between 1948 and 2013 (with an average tenure of about 13 months for both periods). *Plus ça change, plus c'est la même chose*: another immortal motto of transformism.

The (new) "opening to the left" (*apertura a sinistra*) made in the early 1960s by several leaders of the Christian Democrats (DC) aimed to broaden the decreasing consensus in the Italian polity by enlarging the area of democratic legitimacy to the PSI. This strategic move, which can be seen as an episode of "inclusive transformism," opened the way to the period of the "center-left," a stable governmental coalition that lasted for more than a decade (1962–75) and followed the phase of "centrism" inaugurated in 1948 by the governments headed by the Christian Democrat Alcide De Gasperi. The second episode in the trajectory of the republican *trasformismo* occurred in the mid-1970s, when Enrico Berlinguer, leader of the PCI, and Aldo Moro, leader of the Christian Democrats, decided, in the midst of a profound economic crisis and the growth of terrorist movements, to build a "grand coalition" between those political forces "which group together and represent the great majority of the Italian people."[20] This agreement, which Berlinguer himself described as a "historic compromise," brought about a consociation between the DC and the PCI that lasted only from 1976 to 1979, during which time Giulio Andreotti led two monocolor governments supported by a large parliamentary majority. Likewise, the "opening to the left" and the period of "national solidarity" (the other label attached to the "historic compromise") entailed a form of "inclusive" transformism as the DC tried to absorb the anti-system menace by including the PCI into the area of the pro-system, that is liberal-democratic, parliamentary majority. This was, at least in the vague project of Aldo Moro, "an unprecedented and 'total' form of transformism" that,[21] however, ended in a "total" failure: the PCI did not become *ipso facto* a pro-system actor; the *convention ad excludendum* remained firmly in place; and, above all, the "governments of national solidarity" lasted little longer than *l'espace d'un matin.*

After the failure of the "historic compromise," *trasformismo* turned out to be a form of defensive or restrictive strategy exclusively regarding those five parties included in the area of democratic legitimacy. Indeed, the five-party coalition era (*pentapartito*), which lasted from 1980 to 1992, was an alliance containing all five main non-communist parties that, after several more or less centrist governments led mainly by Giovanni Spadolini, Bettino Craxi, and Giulio Andreotti, was destroyed by the 1992–94 anticorruption and anti-Mafia investigations.

The Second Italian Party System

The complete and unexpected collapse of the first Italian party system was hailed, perhaps overly optimistically, as the advent of a new political era that would eradicate the innate vices that have accompanied Italian politics since the Unification. The discovery of government alternation, a complete novelty for the Italian people, particularly if "dictated" by the electorate, was greeted as the death knell for any kind of *trasformismo.* However, as many scholars have emphasized, the "second Italian party system" ("Second Republic" in the journalistic jargon) was based on purely transformist foundations. Ernesto Galli della Loggia is right to highlight that both the PCI and DC faced (and to some extent overcame) the crisis of the party system thanks to transformist and only cosmetic changes. On the one hand, the PCI suddenly "chang[ed] its name in a day" and its party leaders "denied ever having been Communists." On the other hand, the DC changed its name to Partito Popolare Italiano, "whose current leaders were nearly all, in the past, ministers or important representatives of the DC's nomenclature but preferred now to forget this." And so, Della Loggia asked rhetorically: "Is not trasformismo this manipulation of memory?"[22] Indeed it was. And these were the foundations upon which the so-called Second Republic was built.

However, unlike in previous decades, the kind of transformism that has occurred since 1994 was, in a way, far more similar to the original practice inaugurated by Depretis. Indeed, as Figure 3.1 shows clearly, since the inception of the second party system (1994–2013), party switching, that is, the changing of party affiliation of a single legislator, became a significant and frequent phenomenon. From a historical perspective, after a phase of "group transformism" dominated by the mass parties, and since 1994, Italy has experienced a return to the form of molecular transformism that characterized the Liberal state, albeit in a more bipolar context.

Although not explicitly supported by large bureaucratic organizations, these forms of individual party switching have had profound consequences in the history of Italy. Two examples may suffice to illustrate this point. The first example dates back to 1998, when the former President of the Republic, Francesco Cossiga, in the vanguard of the few parliamentarians that he described as *straccioni di Valmy* ("beggars from Valmy") caused the defeat of the Prodi government and, at the same time, the formation of the new D'Alema government. The second and more recent example is related to the crisis created by the decision of Gianfranco Fini, one of the main representatives of the (Berlusconi's) People of Freedom, to leave the government led by Silvio Berlusconi in 2010. While the parliamentary group Futuro e Libertà (Future and Freedom)—created by Fini and his loyal supporters after the 2008 general elections—passed in the opposition camp, Berlusconi received the support and, more importantly, the vote of confidence, of single parliamentarians (self-defined as I Responsabili, "The Responsible Ones") coming from parties elected outside the center-right, pre-electoral, coalition. In light of these two examples, it is clear that the 1992 breakdown of the party system has not cancelled the practice of *trasformismo*. It has merely *transformed* it, which is not a paradox, but yet further proof of its chameleon-like ability to adapt to different political habits and environments.

To summarize, all the historical episodes of Italian *trasformismo* can be categorized into two distinct dimensions. The first separates cases of "molecular transformism" from those of "group transformism." While the former identifies examples of legislators who, as individual parliamentarians, cross the floor and/or change party

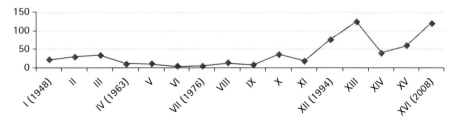

FIGURE 3.1 Absolute Numbers of Party Switching in the Chamber of Deputies, by Parliamentary Term

Source: Author's own elaboration. Data from: CIRCaP Archive on Parliamentary Elites in Italy (<http://www.circap.org/data-on-political-elites.html>) and Italian Chamber of Deputies (<http://storia.camera.it/deputati#nav>).

Table 3.1 A Typology of *Trasformismo* in Italy

	Molecular transformism	Group transformism
Exclusive transformism	"Liberal transformism" (1876–87) "Conservative transformism" (1887–1900)	*Pentapartito* (1980–92)
Inclusive transformism	Second Party System (1994–2013)	Giolittian era (1901–14) Center-left (1962–75) Historic compromise (1976–79)

affiliation, the latter concerns those cases in which entire groups of politicians are co-opted within a given parliamentary majority. Instead, the second dimension distinguishes between cases of "inclusive transformism," whereby parties in government sought to increase the existing majority through the assimilation of other parties excluded from the customary coalitions, and cases of "exclusive transformism" by which different centrist majorities are formed through different combinations of the existing pro-system parties. The four cells created by crossing these two dimensions (see Table 3.1) allow us to chart all the episodes (to date) of Italian *trasformismo*. As the table shows, transformism—whilst not an innate moral characteristic of Italian politicians—can undoubtedly be considered a "constant" of the Italian polity.

INTERPRETATIONS
AND VIEWS OF *TRASFORMISMO*

"An Italy without Italians. A unification without unity. A nation excommunicated. A centralism without centre. A political system that works with difficulty."[23] These were, and in many cases still are, the problems that the ruling elite had to tackle after the creation of the Kingdom of Italy. The Liberal state was, in Gramsci's terms, the result of a "passive revolution"; a process carried out by the elite without any meaningful participation of the popular masses. In line with this perspective, *trasformismo* has been considered, especially in the Marxist historiography literature, as the parliamentary expression of the ruling class's hegemony. More accurately, the creation of amorphous centrist majorities was the strategic device that the "political class" adopted in order to exclude permanently the popular masses represented in Parliament by the extreme political parties (republicans, radicals, socialists, and Catholics). As a purely conservative strategy employed (in turn) by the leaders of the Destra Storica and Sinistra Storica, many historians, in Italy as well as in other countries, have wholly condemned the transformist system.

Strictly attached to this negative view of *trasformismo*, there is a moralist stream of literature that has specifically emphasized the extreme corruption and manipulation of the whole electoral process.[24] Gaetano Salvemini, famous historian and southern socialist, can be considered the preeminent representative of this strand of literature. The main target of his vehement critiques against *"il Ministro della malavita"*—this is the, perhaps unwarranted, nickname Salvemini gave to Prime Minister Giolitti—was the corrupted "management" and gerrymandering of the general elections, thanks to a problematic control of the public bureaucracy at both the central and local level. This vicious triangular relationship between government, single parliamentarians, and public administration was used by the prime minister to build his "personal" majority, and by the politicians to favor the re-election and satisfy the requests of his restricted constituency.

In marked contrast to the (neo)Marxist and moralist accounts of *trasformismo*, the Idealist literature, in particular, Benedetto Croce and Rosario Romeo, has preferred to interpret it as the best strategy employed by the liberal ruling elite in order to face the threat of the "red ones," on the extreme left, and the "black ones," on the extreme right. Briefly put, the creation of floating and amorphous centrist majorities was a sort of automatic self-preservation device by the governing political class which has the responsibility to govern an "Italy without Italians" and, what is more, a nation directly "excommunicated" by the Church with its formal prohibition (*non expedit*) for Catholics to vote and participate in public affairs. In such a difficult context, *trasformismo* represented not only a life-support system for the liberal elite (and, *sensu lato*, for the entire country), but also an effective political arrangement that "provided a remarkable level of stability, while Italy was making huge progress in sectors like economic development, of the North but also of the South, civic growth, education, healthcare and so on and so forth."[25] In sum, for the Idealist, historiography transformism was neither the epiphenomenon of the ruling class's hegemony nor the easy target of preachy politicians or scholars. Essentially, it was the best option in the worst situation.

At the midpoint between Marxists and Idealists, we find the interpretation of those we can describe as "Realists." For them, *trasformismo* was not the "best option" but the "only option" in the worst situation. This point has been finely illustrated by Giovanni Sartori: "transformism was an 'equilibrium' between two opposite disequilibria."[26] In a context characterized by the existence of strong anti-system parties, the only feasible solution was the creation of a large centrist majority, which encompassed all the pro-system actors. It was, as Giulio Bollati described it, "a defensive reflex"; that is to say, a system of government based on the center of the party system, which excluded any alternative government.[27] In this sense, *trasformismo* implied the impossibility of any kind of alternation in power because the hypothetical "alternatives" were illegitimate and anti-system. In this way, transformism has quickly become an apt synonym for "centripetalism" or "centrism." Ultimately, transformism conceived as the product of a troubled process of national unification is anything but the "Italian version—neither particularly corrupted nor specifically virtuous—of a model of government, and of a political system" that prevailed elsewhere in Europe during the nineteenth century.[28]

CONCLUDING REMARKS

At the end of this historical and conceptual journey, one question remains: Is *trasformismo* an Italian specialty? Put another way, is its worldwide success deserved or just a by-product of an eye-catching label? In order to effectively address these questions, it is worth noting that, historically, transformism masquerading as "centrism" "has been anything but peculiar to Italy."[29] As many scholars have pointed out,[30] the tendency among centrist parties to converge in "the middle" of the party system was a common trend throughout Europe in the late nineteenth century, and transformism *qua* centrism was not an invention that we can say was made in Italy.

The same argument holds true with regard to that specific facet of *trasformismo* that political scientists call "party switching," or "party hopping." As Heller and Mershon argue: "even where switching is rare, it is not utterly absent and its occurrence varies over time."[31] The Italian party system is far from the only example in which switchers and turncoats have existed and proliferated. Indeed, the term "*transfuguismo*" was coined in Spain, during the years of the Restauración, precisely to describe any change in party affiliation on the part of a single parliamentarian. No different from what happened to the word "*trasformismo*," "*transfuguismo*" also became a negatively charged word—characterizing, in Spain and elsewhere (but particularly in Latin America), any blameworthy and opportunistic behavior exhibited by politicians. In short, there is nothing new about the Italian transformism.

Finally, there are those works that have put an emphasis on the cultural side of *trasformismo*. In such a context, several scholars have seen it as an extreme example of political corruption, the "Italian version of the patronage system" or a tricky form of electoral malpractice.[32] However, it is worth noting that neither clientelism and patronage, on the one hand, nor political and electoral corruption, on the other, are phenomena strictly confined to Italy. Hence, even in this field Italians have not discovered anything new: they have simply pushed already existing trends to extreme limits.

But then, in conclusion, is *trasformismo* a useful category for analyzing modern Italian history? In the light of the discussion in this chapter, the answer should be a straightforward "no": transformism as "centrism" or "clientelism" or "*transfuguismo*" is a concept that is common, diffused, and well-known beyond Italy. As we have seen in this chapter, *trasformismo* is a complex category that encompasses many different entities. It is not only a *system of government* based on the inclusion of the "centers" and the parallel exclusion or transformation of the "extremes," but also a *mode of governance* that implies the more or less covert cooperation of several public authorities at different levels. In other words, it involves the tendency of mainstream parties to converge to the center, excluding the extreme forces, as well as the ability of the politicians to change their opinions and affiliations in order to protect/promote particularistic interests, controlling the bureaucratic apparatus. *Trasformismo* contains all this, and much more. It is its special mixture of events and episodes, deeds and misdeeds, feelings and strategies, tendencies and constants, that makes it absolutely singular and unquestionably Italian. I have no doubt that the true "autobiography of the nation" can and must be read among the folds of the enduring transformist trajectory.

NOTES

1. Ernesto Galli della Loggia, *L'identità italiana* (Bologna: Il Mulino, 1998), 98.
2. Benedetto Croce, *A History of Italy: 1871–1915* (Oxford: Oxford University Press, 1963), 13.
3. Ibid., 20.
4. Antonio Gramsci, *Prison Notebooks, III* (New York: Columbia University Press, 2011), 257.
5. Luigi Musella, *Il trasformismo* (Bologna: Il Mulino, 2003), 9.
6. See, e.g., Giorgio Candeloro, *Storia dell'Italia moderna,* Vol. IV (Milan: Feltrinelli, 1967) and Fabio Vander, *La democrazia in Italia. Ideologia e storia del trasformismo* (Genoa: Marietti, 2004).
7. Luciano Cafagna, *Cavour* (Bologna: Il Mulino, 1999), 231–232.
8. Maurizio Cotta, "Elite Unification and Democratic Consolidation in Italy: A Historical Overview," in John Highley and Richard Gunther (eds), *Elites and Democratic Consolidation in Latin America and Southern Europe* (Cambridge: Cambridge University Press, 1992), 150.
9. See: Sandro Rogari, *Alle origini del trasformismo. Partiti e sistema politico nell'Italia liberale* (Rome and Bari: Laterza, 1998).
10. Gaetano Salvemini, "Introductory Essay," in William A. Salomone, *Italian Democracy in the Making: The Political Scene in the Giolittian Era, 1900–1914* (Philadelphia: University of Pennsylvania Press, 1945), vii.
11. Alfio Mastropaolo, "Notabili, clientelismo, trasformismo," in Luciano Violante (ed.), *Storia d'Italia. Annali 17. Il Parlamento* (Turin: Einaudi, 2001), 810.
12. See: Mark Donovan and James L. Newell, "Centrism in Italian Politics," *Modern Italy* 13, no. 4 (2008), 381–397.
13. Pietro Vigo, *Annali d'Italia,* vol. 5: *1887–1890* (Milan: Treves, 1947), 103.
14. See, for instance, Musella, *Trasformismo,* 2003.
15. Martin Clark, *Modern Italy: 1871 to the Present* (Essex: Pearson, 2008), 116.
16. See, e.g., Rogari, *Alle origini del trasformismo*; Giovanni Sabbatucci, *Il trasformismo come sistema* (Rome and Bari: Laterza, 2003); Massimo L. Salvadori, "Trasformismo," in Angelo d'Orsi (ed.), *Gli* ismi *della politica* (Rome: Viella, 2010), 467–474.
17. Luciano Cafagna, "Legittimazione e delegittimazione nella storia politica italiana," in Loreto Di Nucci and Ernesto Galli della Loggia (eds), *Due Nazioni. Legittimazione e delegittimazione nella storia dell'Italia contemporanea* (Bologna: Il Mulino, 2003), 17–40.
18. Sabbatucci, *Il trasformismo come sistema,* 66.
19. Ibid., 78.
20. Enrico Berlinguer, *La questione comunista. 1969–1975* (Rome: Editori Riuniti), 1975.
21. Giampiero Carocci, *Il trasformismo dall'Unità ad oggi* (Milan: Edizioni Unicopli), 21.
22. Ernesto Galli della Loggia, "L'Italia trasformista," *Il Corriere della Sera,* March 17, 1999, 1.
23. Cafagna, *Cavour,* 220.
24. See, e.g., Carlo Tullio-Altan, *Populismo e trasformismo. Saggio sulle ideologie politiche italiane* (Milan: Feltrinelli, 1989).
25. Mastropaolo, "Notabili, clientelismo, trasformismo," 814.

26. Giovanni Sartori, *Mala tempora* (Rome and Bari: Laterza, 2004), 502.

27. Giulio Bollati, *L'Italiano: Il carattere nazionale come storia e come invenzione* (Torino: Einaudi, 2011), xxvii.

28. Sabbatucci, *Il trasformismo come sistema*, 32.

29. Donovan and Newell, "Centrism in Italian Politics," 381–397.

30. See, e.g., Paolo Pombeni, *La trasformazione politica nell'Europa liberale. 1870–1890* (Bologna: Il Mulino, 1994).

31. William Heller and Carol Mershon, *Political Parties and Legislative Party Switching* (New York: Palgrave Macmillan, 2009), 10.

32. Simona Piattoni, "Le clientélisme revisité. Politique clientéliste et développement éeconomique dans l'Italie de l'après-guerre," *Pôle Sud*, 19 (November 2003), 161.

CHAPTER 4

PARTITOCRACY

Parties and their Critics in Italian Political Life

MAURIZIO COTTA

THE word *partitocrazia* appeared in the Italian vocabulary after World War II, most likely coined by Roberto Lucifero, a right-wing and monarchical journalist,[1] and received a more scientific interpretation by Giuseppe Maranini, a prestigious constitutional lawyer of the University of Florence.[2] The word was used in a broad sense to express a critique of the role of organized parties and to uphold the role and independence of individual parliamentarians against collective party discipline. We can see this expression as part of a long-term tradition of criticism toward parties and their role and influence within the Italian political system.

The acceptance of parties as a normal, or even as a necessary, component of modern representative democracy has not been easy in Italy and many other Continental countries. Against this acceptance has long been the simple and deep-rooted idea that political divisions are not compatible with the common good. An established history, especially in the "republican" tradition, of condemning "factions" as the major enemies of good governance, has contributed to the perception of parties, and the partisan spirit in which they originated, as sources of conflict and thus a serious danger to the orderly running of the polity. This negative view has been reinforced, in some Continental countries more than others, by the emerging "sacralization" of the state. The Hegelian view that the modern state,[3] as a unified and coherent system of authority, represented the pinnacle of civilization and morality, was difficult to reconcile with parties competing to win a place at the helm of the state and implement their "particularistic" views of government. Only a more pragmatic and pluralistic political culture could accept that the common good was not a monolithic and predefined entity, but rather the result of a dynamic process of approximation which could indeed be enhanced by competition among differing views,[4] and that the state (as an authority and administrative system) should be viewed as an instrument, rather than the absolute good of political life. In such a framework, far from being a negative factor, parties would positively contribute to a real-life (fully functional) democracy.[5]

A critical view of parties can also be traced to a rather different origin. From an individualistic liberal conception of politics with the independent amateur politician as its ideal, the party as a collective and disciplined organization had to be seen as a threat. The individual parliamentarian subjected to the orders of an external party bureaucracy was reduced to a pure executor deprived of any autonomous role, while the role of the parliament itself was diminished to that of a voting machine. In this way, parties were seen as a danger to "true" parliamentarism.

And, finally, these negative views about parties of a theoretical and normative type could easily be reinforced by the practical evaluation of their very real flaws.

To conclude from the existence of a strong critical tradition that parties have always been strong in Italian politics would, however, be wrong. Rather, the truth is probably the opposite. For long periods and from many different points of view Italian parties have in fact been weak and unable to implement a true party government.[6] In a wide historical view, the periods characterized by strong party control over political life are significant but far from dominant. A synthetic historical excursus could probably identify the following phases with regard to the role of parties in Italian politics: (1) a prolonged phase of notable parliamentary parties; (2) the delayed ascendance (and rapid failure) of mass organized parties before Fascism; (3) the authoritarian single-party monopoly of the fascist period; (4) the "golden age" of mass parties after World War II; and (5) the decline of mass parties and the challenge of leader-dominated parties after 1994. In the following discussion I will briefly outline the state of affairs for the first three periods and then devote more attention to the last two.

ITALY AS A LATECOMER IN THE DEVELOPMENT OF ORGANIZED MASS PARTIES

The not so linear "parliamentarization" process of Italian politics found its early origins in the "predecessor state," the Kingdom of Sardinia, under the constitution gracefully conceded (*octroyé*) by King Charles Albert in 1848 (the so-called Statuto Albertino, which, in 1861, became the first constitution of a unified Italy). Although the distinguished politician and political writer Marco Minghetti wrote that "parliamentary government meant party government,"[7] parties hardly emerged as a strong political actor in that context. For quite a long time they consisted of fairly loose parliamentary aggregations of notables, and their presence at the electoral level remained extremely weak and scarcely visible. In spite of this, from the outset parties were a frequent target of criticism. On the one hand, they were criticized from a more philosophical perspective, for example by political thinkers such as Rosmini (1839)[8] and Gioberti (1850)[9] for their particularistic views. On the other hand, more practically oriented observers accused them of having a clientelistic role and excessive influence over the public bureaucracy and judiciary.[10] Paradoxically, these early parties could simultaneously be criticized for being weak in exercising some of the typical functions of parties in a developed party government system, as well as for their excessive intrusions in areas of public administration. Their ability to develop clearly distinguishable and alternative political platforms was limited, as was their capacity to produce cohesive majorities in parliament and to sustain the government in office. In addition, their ability to control the selection of the prime minister and some of the ministers (against the influence of the king) was far from fully established. At the same time, politicians (especially those in government) did not refrain from using their influence in an expanding state bureaucracy to position their clients. It could be said here that the inability to fulfil the higher political functions of parties was, to some extent, compensated by their clientelistic instruments of influence.

The rise of organized parties with a formal membership structure was a relatively late phenomenon. It was the Socialist Party and, somewhat later, the Christian Democratic People's Party of Luigi Sturzo that initiated the era of a more modern type of party. In the face of this new challenge, even the "liberals," who had so far dominated political life without being an organized party, decided in 1922 to establish a true party—in fact not so long before political parties were banned by the incoming Fascist regime. The new style of political action brought by the organized mass parties, and, in particular, the influence of their external membership structure and leadership over the parliamentary component, once again stimulated criticism toward parties from the right side of the ideological spectrum. As this party model was particularly associated with the rise of the socialists, conservative opinion was understandably negative. Very soon, however, the new Christian Democratic Partito Popolare, guided from outside the Parliament by its leader, a priest (Luigi Sturzo), also received strong criticism from the liberal side due to the preeminent role of the external membership structure.

With regard to the development of strong party organizations Italy was in fact a latecomer in Europe, and the process could not reach a stable level as it was soon interrupted by the authoritarian experience of Fascism. Compared to other contemporary experiences, the Italian Socialist Party was not able to develop a very strong membership structure before the advent of Fascism; the rate of members to voters was among the lowest in Europe.[11] The strong internal divisions that marred the life of the party and produced repeated schisms further increased this organizational weakness. As for the Partito Popolare, its organization was, to a significant extent, dependent on religious organizations, and its short life between 1919 and 1925 did not allow it a full organizational deployment. It can be said, then, that, before the advent of Fascism, the build-up of a fully developed system of modern mass parties was less than midway. Old parties of notables found themselves in an uneasy coexistence with the new organizations, making a true party government far from an accomplished feat.

THE FASCIST EXPERIENCE

In 1925, within a couple of years of its takeover, the Fascist regime outlawed and destroyed all pre-existing party formations; at the same time, however, it initiated a new phase of party influence in Italian political life. For the first time, albeit in a non-competitive framework, a dense and ubiquitous party organization came to cover the entire country and mass membership acquired an unprecedented high. The Partito Nazionale Fascista (PNF) was, until Mussolini's rise to power in 1922, a rather small organization in terms of membership (members in 1920 only numbered 27,430, though rapidly rose to more than 100,000 by May 1921);[12] more important, however, was its significant paramilitary branch, which was a crucial instrument for the political takeover.

The role of the PNF went through a progressive transformation as Mussolini's regime consolidated. With Mussolini, strongly placed at the regime's helm, using the government and the bureaucratic apparatus (in particular that of the Ministry of Interiors), at this point unchallenged by parliament and opposition, as the main instruments of power, any strong dualism between party and state was to be a source of embarrassment rather than a resource. In this way, the paramilitary branch of the party, often with strong local roots, was to be disciplined. By 1925, with the banning of all the other parties, the PNF reached a monopolistic status yet was clearly and increasingly placed in a subordinate position vis-à-vis the highly personalized rule of the dictator. Any autonomous initiative of the party and its top ranks was not tolerated. The party was to be the instrument for the consolidation of the regime's control over Italian society, but not the driver of the process. It was not in the party that the leadership role of Mussolini was to be decided; on the contrary, it was the Duce who decided the role of the party.[13] Only at the end of the regime, in July 1943, when military defeat had dramatically exposed the failure of the dictator, could the party become the arena for deciding to put an end to the political career of Mussolini (and, at the same time, decreeing the end of the party itself).

After a first phase, during which access to the party remained relatively restricted and members were supposed to be "true" fascists, membership of the party and its auxiliary organization covering all sectors and milieus of society expanded enormously to the point where the majority of the population was, in some form, organized into the machine. Being a party member became almost mandatory for obtaining a post in public administration and, more generally, for not being relegated to the status of second-class citizen in the country. From around 600,000 members of the party in 1926,[14] when Farinacci was forced to resign as party secretary after his attempts to exert a relative autonomy over Mussolini, the numbers more than quadrupled (to approx. 2.6 million) in 1939; if we add all the ancillary associations of the party, nearly half of the Italian population (20 million out of 43.7) came to be enrolled in this gigantic machine before World War II. Particularly important was the network of youth organizations.[15] The party and its organizations not only oversaw the political regimentation of the population, but also distributed a vast array of "welfare" benefits (from health care and holidays to sports and cultural activities) for a large strata of the population that had been thus far denied access to these. From this viewpoint, it could be said that Fascism brought about the first true period of partitocratic penetration in Italian society. At the same time, this gigantic machine had become deeply bureaucratized and in a way even depoliticized: the highest political direction was not produced from the party, but from the personal dictator.

THE COMPETITIVE BUILD-UP OF PARTY ORGANIZATIONS AFTER WORLD WAR II AND THEIR INSTITUTIONALIZATION

The war defeat, the collapse of Mussolini's regime, and the reconstruction of a democratic state in the new international context that followed these events opened the way for a period of undeniable party ascendancy. Two large parties, the Christian Democracy (DC) and the Communist Party (PCI), became the major players of the new political regime and, together with a few smaller ones (Socialist Party, Social Democratic Party, Republican Party, Liberal Party), they inaugurated a period of more than forty years of relatively stable electoral alignments, government arrangements, and a broad political penetration into Italian society. This was a period that, from many points of view, can be defined as partitocracy,[16] or, to use a different terminology, as having a fairly strong system of party government.[17]

The fall of Mussolini's dictatorship left the new regime with an inheritance that should not be underestimated. The huge heritage of PNF buildings and structures was, to a large extent, incorporated into the new democratic state, but some were appropriated by the reborn parties. A large number of intermediary cadres were "recycled" by the democratic parties. More important, perhaps, was the fact that people had become accustomed to the idea that a political party should play a role that went beyond the purely political debate of ideas, and instead extend to more mundane aspects of day-to-day life, essentially working as a subsidiary to the state.[18]

Beside the inheritance from the Fascist period, a number of other concomitant factors likely contributed to the strong role acquired by organized mass parties in the new democratic regime. The almost complete disappearance of the pre-fascist liberal political class, and the collapse of the state in the wake of military defeat, gave the reborn mass parties (Communists, Christian Democrats, and Socialists) an opportunity to gain a central role in shaping the new democratic regime while the state machine was being rebuilt. The harsh competition between the Christian Democratic Party and the Communist Party, which erupted soon after the new regime was inaugurated, added a strong incentive for the main actors of this dramatic game to strengthen their organizational bases.

In the competitive game of organizational build-up, the Communist Party was originally in the lead and the DC could only counteract, mainly using the support of the Catholic Church's organizations. With time, albeit without lessening the strong ties with religious organizations, the DC also developed a much more articulated organization of its own.

The Communist Party was rapidly able to achieve what the Italian Socialists had failed to obtain: a cohesive and locally ramified membership organization. Within two years after the end of World War II, the party had reached more than 2 million members, around 10,000 local sections, and 50,000 cells in workplaces.[19] A large proportion of communist voters were, in fact, mobilized in the party organization.[20] No other party could display such a strong organizational machine at that time. The DC, which, at the electoral level, already had the largest following in 1946 and was about to win a landslide in 1948, had, in 1947, less than half the members of the PCI and a much less structured network of local units.

At the organizational level, the great strategic electoral battles of 1948 and 1953, which established the period's political winners and losers and defined the long-term political equilibrium of the country, were not decided by the membership organizations of the parties alone. It was quite clear that the DC could count upon the decisive support of another crucial actor in the Italian system, the Catholic Church with the powerful lay organizations of the Azione Cattolica.[21] On the other side, the PCI was supported by the leftist trade union CGIL.

The stabilization of the political system on two main fronts, a permanent party of government, the DC, with its smaller allies, and a permanent party of opposition, the PCI, gave Italian politics the semblance of "trench warfare," with parties engaged in a constant struggle to strengthen and defend their political and social bases. The opposition party, deprived of central government resources (but not those of local government) counted not only upon its membership organization, but also upon a broad set of ancillary associations in the fields of culture, sport, and leisure to consolidate its following. This type of social penetration was not, however, equally successful across all regions of Italy. In the so-called "red regions" of central Italy (Emilia-Romagna, Tuscany, and Umbria) this produced a strong "subcultural" entrenchment, and the party became the center of a dense and integrated network of influence. In other regions (the "white regions"), however, the opposition party could not compete with the entrenchment of the DC and had to count on a less structured relationship with voters.[22] In spite of some difficult moments, such as the shock produced by the Russian intervention in Hungary in 1956, or the challenges coming from the students and social movements and the birth of "red" terrorism in the late 1960s and 1970s, the party was able to organize itself for a long-term strategy of survival in opposition.

The DC, having firmly established its control of the central government (and much of local government), was keen to develop its own organizational apparatus in a way that would make it more independent from the lay organizations of the Catholic Church, without rejecting the electoral support that could be derived from them. Under the leadership of Fanfani in the 1950s, a great effort was made to establish a stronger membership organization with a diffuse local presence. In spite of this, the local units of the DC never acquired the importance and activism of communist units. With the increasing fragmentation of the party into organized factions (*correnti*), the membership organization became the arena for an intense internal competition of power at the local and national levels. This led to an inflation of membership numbers, and quite often cast doubt on the quality of the membership: a significant number of cards would simply be paid for by local caciques.

Owing to its permanent government position, the DC party could extensively exploit other important resources. Patronage applied to the central and peripheral state administration, and even more to the large parallel bureaucracies that had developed over the years, became an extremely important instrument in the hands of the party leadership. Schools, the post, the railroads, and the police offered opportunities to exert clientelistic influence in the recruitment, career advancements, and geographical mobility of employees and high-level officers. The large public sector of the economy, especially in the industrial and financial subfields—in part a legacy of the economic crises of the 1920s and the fascist period, but also a product of the more recent policy choices of postwar governments and their attempts to foster industrial development in less favored areas of the county and so safeguard employment—created particularly favorable opportunities for party intervention. In fact, some of the party's internal factions developed very close relations with state industries.

With the decline of ideological tensions and under pressure to make the system work, the competitive and conflictual entrenchment of the two main Italian parties gradually mellowed, and, from the 1970s onwards, was increasingly balanced by instances of more cooperative behavior. Examples of this behavior were the reforms of parliamentary regulations (1971), allowing the opposition a greater role in the agenda setting of the representative assembly, then the external support granted by the PCI to the Andreotti governments in 1976–79, the assignment of some leading parliamentary positions to the opposition, and also some areas of influence granted on state television. If we further consider the introduction of a system of state financing of parties in 1974, it is reasonable to say that some elements of the cartel party model were emerging.[23]

In spite of these transformations and a decline in the original ideological conflict that had defined the competition among parties, the Italian political system remained frozen throughout the 1980s with regard to the original allocation of governing and opposition roles. In this view, the Italian party system seemed unchangeable. The inertia of political dynamics and the lack of any significant alternation of executive power were to exact an increasingly high price from both governing and opposition parties. The main parties increasingly lost contact with society, and their ability to mobilize popular support declined significantly.[24] This was well attested, for instance, in the plunging numbers of affiliates of the PCI (according to the Istituto Cattaneo, the party lost about one third of its members between 1977 and 1990).[25] The increasing volatility of the vote from 1979 to 1992, before reaching an unprecedented peak in 1994,[26] as well as the unexpected success of new parties (the Northern League in particular), were other signs of the crisis of the old order. An even more dramatic indicator of this crisis was the combined electoral weight of the two largest parties (DC and PCI) which, between 1976 and 1992, declined from 73.1 percent to 45.8 percent.

With the arrival of the 1990s, it became clear that, while the old partitocratic mold appeared to persist unchanged, in reality its ability to control Italian society was rapidly disappearing and the stage was being prepared for a political earthquake.[27] Evaporating electoral and organizational control meant it was increasingly difficult for parties to obtain the traditional allegiance of the media, the judiciary, and organized economic groups.

THE COLLAPSE OF THE OLD PARTY SYSTEM, THE DECLINE OF THE ORGANIZED PARTY: LEADEROCRACY AFTER PARTITOCRACY?

The party system that had dominated Italian politics for nearly forty years came to an abrupt end at the beginning of the 1990s. A combination of factors contributed to the sudden and unexpected collapse of all "governing parties"—Christian Democracy Party, Socialist Party, Social Democratic Party, Republican Party, Liberal Party—which had been at the helm of the executive without alternation of power since 1947. The inquiries of Milanese prosecutors, soon followed in other parts of Italy, unveiled to the public the diffuse practices of illegal financing of parties and the large recourse to corruption in procurements and tenders, discrediting the leadership of the governing parties. The fact that all attempts to renew their leadership failed to save the parties from political bankruptcy suggests that corruption was but one aspect of a deeper crisis, which, above all, had a political component. The system of parties, frozen into shape by the harsh ideological confrontation of Cold War years, had not benefited from the stimuli of open competition and alternation in government. The security of their position in government, assured by the ideological (self-)exclusion of those in opposition, had made the governing parties increasingly unable to face the new problems of the country and to innovate in policymaking. Particularistic distribution of benefits and clientelism had become their main instruments of action. The collapse of the Soviet Union and the end of the Cold War in 1991 deprived them of their ideological superiority, while the dramatic rise in costs of a huge public debt curtailed resources for sustaining the spending policies of the past.[28] In this context, mainstream parties had become significantly more vulnerable to external challenges. The breakdown of the governing parties, coupled with the difficulty of the main traditional opposition party, the PCI (now renamed PDS), to redefine its identity after the sunset of world communism, created a wide opening for political innovation. Some of this opening seemed bound to be occupied by a new territorially based party (the Northern League) that, for the first time in a non-peripheral

area of Italy, introduced a brand new political discourse challenging the central government. Yet, given the intrinsic geographical limitations of that appeal, there was still a
very large part of the electorate that was in want of representation. The appearance and
immediate electoral success in 1994 of a new leader, Silvio Berlusconi, and of his party
(Forza Italia) initiated a new phase in Italian politics. Berlusconi's success certified, on
the one hand, the end of the old parties, while, on the other hand, it offered a new model
of efficient political organization with which the other political actors had to come to
terms sooner or later.

Between 1994 and 2011, the dynamics of the political system were defined by asym-
metric competition between the new model party, the "personal party" of Berlusconi,[29]
and the post-communist PDS/DS/PD trying to adapt the surviving elements of a more
traditional model of party organization to the new political context. Forza Italia profited
from the extraordinary resources of its leader (not only financial and the media, but
also Berlusconi's personal electoral appeal and intuitive strategizing in the formation
of coalitions); at the same time, it was entirely dependent on the leader. This symbiosis
was the source of the party's success, but also of some of its problems. The party had to
follow the personal strategies of the leader (for instance, in matters of judicial policy)
even when they were not necessarily productive in terms of consensus; at some points,
the party became embroiled in the private problems of its leader. As can happen with
personalistic leaderships, the entourage of the leader is often selected more for its loyalty
that for its merits. It is therefore difficult for such a party to nurture a political class of
a high standing. These limits especially started to weigh down on local politics, where
decisions were made directly from the center of the party, often leading to suboptimal
results. Increasingly, these limits became relevant at the national level as well.

Difficulties and problems were, however, for some time much greater on the other
side of the political spectrum. The only party that had survived from the collapse of the
so-called "First Republic," the successor party of the PCI, found itself faced with the
dilemma of preserving its old organizational machine and, at the same time, adapting
to the deeply changed political landscape post-1994. A particular challenge for the party
was to adapt to a bipolar and leader-centered arena of competition. The party, which had
lived for so many decades guarding a well-identifiable left position, now had to fight for
center voters in order to have any chance of winning against a strong competitor that
had conquered a broad space spanning the center and right. To face this challenge, the
party was compelled to redefine its identity, open its ranks to politicians coming from
very different origins (mainly former Christian Democrats), and incorporate other parties under a broader ideological umbrella. After the electoral failure of 1994, it also had
to accept an external leader, Prodi (a Christian Democrat by background), for the electoral battle and leadership of government. In a way, the main left party also had to recognize, not without strong internal doubts, the preeminent importance of leadership in the
new competitive framework. Yet while Forza Italia, and later its successor, the PdL, were
intrinsically adapted to accepting the domineering role of the leader, things were very
different for a party which, in its long tradition, had not refused the role of leaders (from
Togliatti to Enrico Berlinguer), but had only accepted those grown into this role from

inside the party apparatus and strongly identifying with it. It has probably to do with this that, twice, the electorally winning leadership of Prodi was weakened from within the party, and, in the end, rejected. At the same time attempts to relaunch the party with leaders (such as D'Alema, Veltroni and Bersani) coming from the traditional ranks of the organization, repeatedly failed or at best obtained a Pyrrhic victory (as with Bersani in 2013). In an attempt to give greater authority to its leaders, the party started to experiment with primaries to select the candidate for governmental leadership, and to organize popular elections (open to all sympathizers), also commonly called "primaries," for the party secretary. This instrument was at first largely controlled by the party apparatus and used to confirm the existing leaders, but, more recently, it has opened the way for a significant transformation in the relationship between party organization and leader. Through this instrument, a new young leader, Matteo Renzi, coming from an absolutely peripheral position in the party apparatus, has managed, with the help of his own personal electoral machine, to win, first locally in 2008 (becoming the mayor of Florence) and then nationally in 2013, against the worn-out representatives of the party establishment, and so rapidly reach the premiership. The innovative aspect of this occurrence is what we might call a sort of "semi-hostile takeover" of the party from an individual political entrepreneur. The success of this takeover against a largely hostile party apparatus also suggests the possibility of a deep transformation for the main party of the left. Despite differences, the PD might also take on some of the features of its main opponent, the Berlusconi party. The leader, with his personal entourage, becomes the real engine of the party, while the party organization becomes something between an obstacle to be neutralized and an instrument to be used when needed—but not the political core of the party. The central element becomes the ability of the leader to win political battles and to command the loyalty of his followers.

The picture of the new Italian world of parties would not be complete without mentioning the third actor that has moved even more innovatively in the direction of a leader-centered model, the Five Star Movement. The movement, launched between 2007 and 2009 by the popular television comedian and blogger Grillo, features a strong anti-political message and, after some victories in municipal elections, obtained an unexpected success in the 2013 elections and inaugurated a very special organizational style. The leader of the movement, not elected in parliament, has guided the parliamentarians from the outside with a very strong hand and by means of internet communication.[30]

At this stage, then, the three main Italian parties are all strongly guided by a leader (albeit each with a peculiar style) who is, in a sense, above the party, either because he has created the party (Berlusconi and Grillo), or because he has won the party against the apparatus (Renzi). The long cycle of partitocracy, inaugurated after World War II, seems to have ended in what we might call the phase of "leaderocracy." In this type of party, a leader with a strong personal control over resources and a sophisticated ability to communicate directly with the voters through the media prevails over the burdensome permanent organization of the party. The leader and his loyal entourage now increasingly control some of the peculiar functions of the party apparatus, such as programmatic elaboration, patronage, and the recruitment of middle-level elites.

It is still too early to say how stable and lasting this new phase will be. For the time being, three points deserve to be highlighted. The first is that no significant alternative model of party organization seems available in Italy today. The second is that the new model features some crucial advantages (a greater programmatic flexibility, better adaptation to the new world of media, more immediate rapport with individualistic voters, etc.), but also some relevant problems. Of the latter, the foremost are linked to the personal characteristics of the leader. As the example of PdL/Forza Italia has shown since 2011, the decline of the strategic capacities of the leader, his private problems, and his aging may become a serious disadvantage for the party. At the same time, the obvious solution of substituting the leader may be very difficult to implement because the party as such has lost any autonomous capacity to generate alternative leaders. The third point worth mentioning concerns the compatibility between this new model and a parliamentary form of government. A form of government such as a parliamentary one based on indirect legitimation of the executive and a need to have a collective discipline in the assembly may not be easily compatible with the new type of leader-centered party. Almost inevitably, a push in the direction of presidential or semi-presidential forms of government will most likely gain momentum. The recent electoral reform initiated by Renzi indicates that even without a constitutional reform an electoral system with a bonus for the largest party (and runoff among the two strongest competitors) may be used to produce de facto the direct investiture of the leader.

NOTES

1. R. Lucifero, *Introduzione alla libertà* Rome, OET Edizioni del secolo, 1944.
2. G. Maranini, *Governo parlamentare e partitocrazia: lezione inaugurale dell'anno accademico '49–'50*, Florence, Editrice Universitaria, 1950.
3. G. W. F. Hegel, *Grundlinien der Philosophie des Rechts*, Berlin, In der Nikolaischen Buchhandlung, 1821.
4. For a discussion of the difficult cultural process through which this idea was attained in the seventeenth century see S. Cotta, *La nascita dell'idea di partito nel secolo XVIII*, in S. Cotta, *I limiti della politica*, Bologna, Il Mulino, 2002, pp. 21–63.
5. G. Sartori, *Democratic Theory*, Detroit, Wayne State University, 1962.
6. R. Katz, "Party Government: A Rationalistic Conception," in F. G. Castles and R. Wildenmann (eds.), *Visions and Realities of Party Government*, Berlin, de Gruyter, 1986, pp. 31–71.
7. M. Minghetti, *I partiti politici e la loro ingerenza nella giustizia e nell'amministrazione*, Bologna, Zanichelli, 1881, pp. 59–81.
8. A. Rosmini, *Filosofia della politica*, Milan, Pogliani, 1839.
9. V. Gioberti, *Del rinnovamento civile d'Italia*, Turin, Bocca, 1850.
10. Minghetti, *I partiti politici*.

11. S. Bartolini, *The Political Mobilization of the European Left: 1860–1890*. Cambridge, Cambridge University Press, 2000, pp. 240–277; S. Cannarsa, *Il socialismo e i XXV congressi del Partito Socialista Italiano*, Florence, Società Editrice Avanti, 1950.

12. L. Di Nucci, *Lo Stato-partito del fascismo*, Bologna, Il Mulino, 2009, p. 46; E. Gentile, *Storia del partito fascista*, Bari, Laterza, 1989.

13. A. Aquarone, *L'organizzazione dello stato totalitario*, Turin, Einaudi, 1965.

14. L. Di Nucci, *Lo Stato-partito del fascismo*, Bologna, Il Mulino, 2009, p. 274.

15. Ibid., p. 488.

16. M. Vinciguerra, *I partiti italiani: dallo statuto albertino alla partitocrazia*, Calderini, Bologna, 1968.

17. G. Pasquino, 'Party Government in Italy: Achievements and Prospects', in R. S. Katz (ed.), *Party Governments: European and American Perspectives*, Berlin, de Gruyter, 1987, pp. 202–242.

18. L. Cafagna, *La grande slavina. L'Italia verso la crisi della democrazia*, Venice, Marsilio, 1993.

19. G. Poggi, ed., *L'organizzazione partitica del PCI e della DC*, Bologna, Il Mulino, 1968.

20. Bartolini, *The Political Mobilization of the European Left*.

21. A. Manoukian, ed., *La presenza sociale del PCI e della DC*, Bologna, Il Mulino 1968.

22. A. Parisi and G. Pasquino, "Changes in Italian Electoral Behavior: The Relationships between Parties and Voters," in S. Tarrow and P. Lange (eds.), *Italy in Transition: Conflict and Consensus*, London, Frank Cass, 1980, pp. 6–30.

23. R. Katz and P. Mair, "Changing Models of Party Organisations and Party Democracy, the Emergence of the Cartel Party," in *Party Politics*, 1, 1995, pp. 5–28. N. Conti, M. Cotta, and F. Tronconi, "Le parti-cartel en Italie. Un tableau contrasté," in Y. Aucante and A. Dézé (eds.), *Les systèmes de partis dans les démocraties occidentales. Le modèle du parti-cartel en question*, Paris, SciencesPo Les Presses, 2008, pp. 195–218.

24. G. Pasquino, *Crisi dei partiti e governabilità*, Bologna, Il Mulino, 1980.

25. Corresponding figures for the DC (with a peak in 1990) seem to contradict this assertion, but most probably they should be interpreted as suggesting the increasingly strong competition among factions which produced a boom of affiliations, rather than a genuine surge of participation.

26. R. D'Alimonte and S. Bartolini, "Plurality Competition and Party Realignment in Italy: The 1994 Parliamentary Elections," *European Journal of Political Research* 29, 1996, pp. 105–142.

27. L. Bardi and L. Morlino, "Italy: Tracing the Roots of the Great Transformation," in R. S. Katz and P. Mair (eds.), *How Parties Organize: Change and Adaptation in Party Organisations in Western Democracies*. London, Sage, 1994, pp. 242–277.

28. M. Cotta, "La crisi del governo di partito all'italiana," in M. Cotta and P. Isernia (eds.), *Il gigante dai piedi di argilla*, Bologna, Il Mulino, 1996, pp. 11–52.

29. M. Calise, *Il partito personale*, Bari, Laterza, 2010.

30. P. Corbetta and G. Gualmini (eds.), *Il partito di Grillo*, Bologna, Il Mulino, 2013.

CHAPTER 5

A TALE OF TWO ITALYS? THE "SOUTHERN QUESTION" PAST AND PRESENT

JOHN A. DAVIS

A 2010 report from the Organisation for Economic Co-operation and Development (OECD) noted that Italy suffers from the widest geographical dualism of all the European Union states, and, while he was still Governor of the Bank of Italy, Mario Draghi described Italy's south as the "most extensive and most densely populated backward territory in the European Union."[1] There are many examples of regional economic imbalances in other Western European states, but none have proved to be as long lasting as the gap between Italy's north and south.

At the time of Unification, the economic differences were less apparent than they would become later. But, above all, it was the mass emigration from the impoverished south in the 1890s that made the "Southern Question" a national rather than a regional issue, and led to the first measures of public intervention early in the new century. Since then, the economic disparities between north and south have tested the technical ingenuity of successive generations of Italian policymakers and public figures, as well as national and international economists and social scientists.

In the meantime the south, like the rest of Italy and Europe, has changed beyond recognition, especially in the last half-century. In the 1950s, southern Italy was the theater for the biggest regional development project in postwar Europe, and today the world of rural poverty and despair evocatively described in postwar Italy's first international bestseller, Carlo Levi's *Christ Stopped at Eboli* (1945) no longer exists. On the contrary, levels of consumption and living standards in the south are at the higher end of European Union norms. But the differences remain and, in terms of output and productivity, the south still lags far behind the rest of Italy, rates of unemployment are higher, capital investment is low, while public services and infrastructures are poor. Indeed, since Italy's Unification there have been only two brief moments of economic convergence between the north and the south: the first in the decade before World War I and the second in the 1950s and 1960s. Hence, despite more than half a century of government intervention, and internal and external (most recently European Union) funding, the economic disparities persist.

These disparities are its surest measure, but Italy's "Southern Question" has always been about much more than economics. The perception of the south as a problem was first framed in the aftermath of Unification and from the start raised issues about historical and cultural differences and doubts about whether the north and the south had been, could be, or should be unified. Since the "Southern Question" inevitably touches directly on essential questions of national unity, it has never been simply a regional issue. Indeed, the south has played a critical role in shaping the evolution of modern Italian politics and at every major turning point in Italy's history since Unification resolving the "Southern Question" has been invoked as the key to building a new and better Italy. Giuseppe Mazzini may, or may not, have predicted, that "Italy's destiny will depend on what happens in the south," but that slogan was frequently invoked after the fall of Fascism and is heard no less often today. For the critics of Italian unity, by contrast, the persistence of the "Southern Question" remains the clearest proof that political Unification has benefited neither of the "two Italies". As the economic disparities between the north and the nouth have widened in recent decades, it is not surprising that the "Southern Question" has become a focus for deeper contemporary Italian discontents.

ORIGINS: FROM UNIFICATION TO WORLD WAR I

Without the collapse of the former Bourbon Kingdom of the Two Sicilies in 1860, a unified Italian state would never have been created. But if Italy was made in the south, northern and southern liberals were agreed that the collapse of the Bourbon monarchy was an inevitable consequence of centuries of misgovernment, corruption, ignorance, and backwardness. Such views were reinforced by the brief but violent rural protests that swept through the mainland south after Unification, the seriousness of which the new government tried to conceal by attributing them to the work of brigands and common criminals. But the restoration of order in the mainland south required more troops and cost more lives (those of the brigands) than all of Italy's wars of national independence. By 1864 order had been restored on the mainland, but two years later, during Italy's Third War of Independence against Austria, an armed revolt took place in Palermo.[2]

Liberals saw these disturbances as a consequence of the social backwardness of the south and as part of a reactionary conspiracy against the progressive and secular values of the new state, orchestrated by its principal enemies the Roman Curia and supporters of the former Bourbon rulers. For the latter, the unrest instead revealed that Unification had been imposed by force on an unwilling south. The lines along which the place of the south in the new state would be contested were set, and they continue to haunt the memories of the Risorgimento and Italian Unification to the present day.

After Unification, the south was associated with poverty, primitive lifestyles, endemic corruption, banditry, and arcane criminal subcultures like the Neapolitan "*camorra*" and its more recent Sicilian counterpart the "*mafia.*" In an age of Darwinian positivism, southerners were placed well below their northern neighbors on the evolutionary ladder. Such stereotypes helped perpetuate the belief that there were still two quite different Italies, even though many of the staunchest champions of the new state were southerners, most notably Francesco Crispi, the Sicilian who became Italy's first southern prime minister and the Neapolitan philosopher and historian Benedetto Croce.[3]

The "Southern Question" was never static, however, and the closing decade of the century saw important shifts in perceptions. At the time of Unification, the economic differences between the north and south had not been immediately apparent: poverty was, after all, the condition of most Italians at the time. But forty years later, the rapid industrialization of many parts of the north made more visible the desperate structural weaknesses of the southern economies, giving rise to the first great debates on how best to promote economic development and the first attempts to map the true economic conditions of the south.

It was the ensuing massive exodus of impoverished rural southerners, however, that made the "Southern Question" a matter of pressing national concern. Between 1896 and 1915, some 11 million Italians would emigrate, the majority from the southern mainland and Sicily. Most headed for the cities of America's Atlantic seaboard where they hoped to accumulate some savings before returning home. Although many, perhaps most, did return, the scale of the emigration caused alarm. The newly founded nationalist movement warned vociferously that the exodus of Italy's fittest and finest sons posed a vital threat to the nation, and showed that Italy must acquire colonies for its surplus population. Others called for action to remedy the causes, and the Apulian socialist Gaetano Salvemini took the lead in blaming the poverty of the rural south on the power and avarice of the reactionary southern landowners. As the key component of a reactionary conservative political alliance, Salvemini claimed that after Unification the southern landowners had been the main opponents of democracy not only in the south, but in Italy as a whole. Those conclusions were widely support on the political left, making the poverty of the south first and foremost a political question that could be resolved only by realizing the democratic objectives promised but never delivered in the Risorgimento.

In 1904, Giovanni Giolitti's government introduced the first measures of direct public intervention in the south. Although initially limited to modernizing the port of Naples and promoting land reclamation projects in the province of Basilicata, under the direction of Francesco Saverio Nitti the project's objectives became much broader. Convinced that agriculture alone could not bring growth to the south, Nitti believed that new technologies, especially hydroelectric energy, had made industrialization in the south possible. His proposals met with strong opposition, but they also won the support of significant northern industrial and banking concerns and, by 1915, much had been achieved. In 1910, the south's first steel plant had been commissioned at Bagnoli, on the coast between Naples and Pozzuoli, and quickly attracted other industries. Hydroelectric energy projects were being developed along the Volturno river, work on the Apulian aqueduct had begun, and the first express rail connection between Naples and Rome was opened.[4]

For the first time since Unification, the economies of the two Italies briefly converged. But even though a new industrial sector had by 1914 been created in the immediate vicinity of Naples, convergence owed more to emigration than to Nitti's initiatives. In fact the principal beneficiary of southern emigration was the north, because the remittances that the southern emigrants sent back to their families helped balance Italy's foreign exchange account and hence kept interest rates low during a critical phase of industrial expansion.[5] In the south there were also signs of change, especially where emigration had reduced the surplus rural labor force and enabled the laborers and peasants to start organizing unions to negotiate better wages. But this revealed other obstacles to change and the responses of the landowners were ferocious. In Apulia, they deployed armed and mounted militias to smash the unions and terrorize the laborers, and Salvemini would claim that these militias were forerunners of the post-war fascist squads in northern Italy. Similarly, in Sicily the remarkable expansion of independent peasant cooperative farms, whose backers included the cofounder of the Christian Democrat movement, Don Luigi Sturzo, met with open hostility from the landowners. In 1911 a Parliamentary Commission concluded that the conditions of the rural poor in the south had changed little.

FASCISM AND THE "SOUTHERN QUESTION"

Italy's entry into World War I in 1915 brought any prospects for economic development in the south to an end. Emigration ceased, southern laborers were conscripted, and the massive expansion of Italy's industrial production during the war was concentrated overwhelmingly in the north. Once the war was over, in the south, as in the north, industrial workers were laid off and the violent prewar agrarian conflicts reopened. Apulia was again the epicenter, and well before Mussolini's March on Rome (October 1922), the landowners had rallied to the fascist counter-revolution and taken the offensive against the labor unions and the socialists..

To write the history of the "Southern Question" in the interwar years in the fascists' own terms would be a story of unending victories. The regime declared victory over the mafia and, by the mid-1930s, a supporter could claim that "it is no longer legitimate to speak of a 'Southern Question.'"[6] But although the regime's intervention in the south thereafter was stronger on rhetoric than practical results, land reclamation and irrigation projects (including the Apulian aqueduct) did progress, as did attempts to improve agricultural productivity as part of the fascist bid for national economic self-sufficiency ("autarchy") that was designed to reduce Italy's dependence on food imports. But even before 1929 and the collapse of world trade, economic and social conditions in the southern regions were deteriorating. The expansion of small peasant properties that began during the War came a halt in the 1920s, while the fascist government's policies favored the big estates and the landowners. The situation was exacerbated by new restrictions on Italian immigration imposed by the United States in 1922. As a consequence, between 1930 and 1950 (when the next wave of emigration began) the rural population in the south grew from 35 million to 37 million by 1950. Underemployment and unemployment rose, living standards and consumption fell.

To make matters worse, the fascist bid to increase the productivity of agriculture (the "Battle for Wheat") proved counter-productive and by overtaxing arid and infertile soils caused yields to fall. In the 1930s the imposition of production quotas by the regime also began to alienate the landowners and when, in 1940, the government requisitioned the Sicilian lemon harvest to pay for imports of Nazi war materials the landowners effectively went on strike and refused to harvest the crop.[7] By the time of the fall of Mussolini's regime, conditions in the rural south were as bad as they had been before the great pre-World War I emigration.

The "Southern Question" and Italy's Postwar Reconstruction

Mussolini's war made things even worse. When Italy declared war on Britain and France in June 1940 the southern cities were defenseless against Allied bombing, while the Allied landings in Sicily and on the mainland (at Salerno) on July and September 1943 turned the south into a major a theater of war, followed by military occupation. Damage to buildings, industrial plants, communications, and infrastructures was extensive, as were civilian casualties. Throughout the occupation there were severe shortages of essential food supplies, clothing, fuel, and work, resulting in epidemic diseases, malnutrition, and even starvation. Only the black market thrived.[8]

Following the fall of Mussolini and Italy's surrender to the Allies on 8 September 1944, King Victor Emanuel III abandoned Rome and moved the government to the Adriatic port of Bari. This meant that until the liberation of Milan in April 1945, Italy remained divided, but the "Southern Question" re-emerged dramatically without waiting for the war to end. The collapse of Mussolini's regime had reignited pre-fascist rural conflicts which were now exacerbated by population increases and mass rural unemployment. These discontents focused above all on the need for land to work or farm, resulting in collective occupations of uncultivated estates and repeated violent clashes between the laborers and the police and security forces. In Sicily the landowners recruited mafia and other criminal groups to combat the rural laborers and peasants and the rising tensions and death tolls caused many to fear that the south was on the brink of civil war.

In an attempt to restore order, the Communist Minister for Agriculture, Fausto Gullo, in October 1944, decreed the compulsory division of uncultivated absentee estates in the Sila region of Calabria and the establishment of peasant cooperative farms. But this only caused the land occupations to spread and, it was against this background Manlio Rossi-Doria, a reformist socialist and prominent agrarian economist warned that, without a solution to the "Southern Question," Italy would remain "a weakened and incomplete Nation without the means to nurture a truly modern and civil democracy."

Many shared Rossi-Doria's concerns and his belief that the south was the key to Italy's post-fascist future. But when it came to what should be done there was little agreement. Liberals acknowledged the need for some form of state intervention, providing it was minimal. Those on the left agreed that the south was the key to the success of Italy's "second Risorgimento," but were divided when it came to choosing whether the re-establishment of democracy required reformist or revolutionary measures.[9]

THE POSTWAR SOUTHERN DEVELOPMENT PROJECT

After the war, the unrest in the south showed no sign of diminishing, while the outbreak of civil war in Greece and the onset of the Cold War raised new fears of about the situation in southern Italy and possible Communist infiltration. But there were other alarming signs of political disaffection, and in the plebiscite of 1946 the south voted heavily against the abolition of the monarchy, while support for the Uomo Qualunque anti-party movement grew. In western Sicily a new separatist movement was calling for regional autonomy, although this served primarily as a cover for a campaign of violence against the peasants, the unions and the democratic left that culminated in the notorious May Day massacre of unarmed peasants and their families perpetrated by the bandit Salvatore Giuliano and his gang at Portella della Ginestra in 1947.[10]

The confused and tense political situation following the expulsion of the Communist Party (PCI) from the government in May 1947, the massive electoral victory of De Gasperi's Christian Democrats (DC) in April 1948, and shortly afterwards the attempt to assassinate the Communist leader, Palmiro Togliatti, complicated the formulation of new initiatives for the south. An ambitious land reform proposed by the Minister for Agriculture, Antonio Segni, proved too radical, and it was not until 1950 that De Gasperi's government finally introduced a package of measures designed to accelerate the break-up of the larger uncultivated estates and create small peasant farms.[11]

At the same time, support from the World Bank made possible the creation, in August 1950, of a special fund. The Cassa per il Mezzogiorno ("Southern Development Fund": CpM) that was designed to support a much broader and more focused development program. This project had been formulated by group of technical experts who, although not fascists, had formerly held senior positions under the regime, especially in the Institute for Industrial Recovery (IRI) that had been founded in 1931. The experts included, among many others, Pasquale Saraceno, a senior official in IRI, a socialist economist Rodolfo Morandi who, in 1944, had been President of the Committee for National Liberation in Upper Italy, and Donato Menichella, who, in 1945, was appointed Governor of the Bank of Italy. Menichella had also served in IRI and was a close friend of the future Christian Democrat Prime Minister, Alcide De Gasperi.

Morandi was the key strategist and in 1946 he had founded the Association for the Industrial Development of Southern Italy (SVIMEZ), to prepare and implement new development programs. Morandi and his associates admired Nitti's pre-1915 projects and, like him, were convinced that industry was essential for generating sustained economic development in the south. The group's influence was greatly enhanced by its international contacts, especially in the United States, whose government became even more closely involved in postwar economic and political reconstruction when Italy was included in the provision of the European Recovery Program (ERP), or the Marshall Plan in June 1948. Both Saraceno and Morandi were already in close contact with Paul Rosenstein-Rosen at the World Bank and with Paul Hoffman at the international Economic Cooperation Administration, with whose support the CpM was set up.[12]

THE PROGRAM OF "SPECIAL INTERVENTION" (*INTERVENTO STRAORDINARIO*)

ERP funds went to revive Italy's northern industries, but they also made southern Italy the setting for the biggest regional development project in postwar Europe. The program was based on the principle of "special intervention," since the funds made available were in addition to normal state and local government budgets and the CpM operated outside standard ministerial boundaries. For that reason the project met with strong opposition from both free trade liberals and the Communists (PCI), while Saraceno was concerned that the CpM did not have adequate political autonomy.

The achievements of the first decades were, nonetheless, far from negligible, although this owed much to new waves of mass emigration from the south. While many headed for destinations outside Italy in Europe, the US, Australia, New Zealand, and South Africa, others now moved to the expanding industrial cities of the north. Here their lives were rarely easy, and the southern immigrants were often greeted with hostility similar to that awaiting Commonwealth immigrants in postwar Britain and non-EU immigrants in Italy today. But despite the anti-immigrant sentiments, the new internal migration was indicative of how deeply Italian society and its economy were being transformed in the postwar decades.

Despite the priority that Saraceno and Morandi had placed on industrial development, it was not until the end of the first decade that new chemical, engineering, and steel industries were established in Taranto, Brindisi, Pomigliano d'Arco, and Milazzo (Sicily). Nonetheless, mass emigration, infrastructural investment, and the agrarian reforms were beginning to transform the rural south during the decade of Italy's so-called "economic miracle". As rural unemployment shrank and industrial and tertiary employment expanded, the economies of the two Italies converged again for only the second time since the start of the century.[13]

A Strategy in Doubt?

The convergence would prove to be short-lived, however, and even before the oil crisis of the early 1970s the southern development project was coming under critical scrutiny. The economist Vera Lutz voiced the wider concerns of opponents of state intervention when she claimed that emigration and wage differentials alone were all that was needed to solve the key problems of overpopulation, underemployment, and underinvestment in the south.[14] As Lutz's intervention indicates, by now the southern Italian development project was drawing the attention of economists, sociologists, anthropologists, and technical experts from all over the world, especially from the United States, and offered an international platform for testing the strategic viabilities of state intervention as opposed to market forces and free enterprise.

The south could never be just a laboratory for rival economic development theories, however, not least because of its importance in Italy's political geography. After the establishment of the Republic, the south offered Italy's leading political parties major opportunities to expand their existing electoral support. In this, none had been more successful than the Christian Democrat Party (DC), whose dominant national position was assured by its electoral successes in the south. With the parties of the left drawing their support predominantly from northern and central Italy, those of the center and the right relied on votes from the south.

This meant that the two Italies were now very closely united again, but in ways that, for many, evoked parallels with the south's political role after Unification. It was against that background that the ideas of the former Communist leader and intellectual, Antonio Gramsci, began to attract wide attention. In his posthumously published *Prison Notebooks*, Gramsci, like Salvemini, argued that the reactionary southern landowners had been responsible for wrecking the democratic aspirations of the Risorgimento and thereafter had been the principal obstacle to the development of Italian democracy. Those conclusions led others to focus on the political role played by the new class of political intermediaries and brokers that had grown up in the shadows of the political ascendancy of the Christian Democrats and their allies.

Widely seen as the political successors of the old landowner class, the new political elites were now the principal target of growing public anger over the inadequacy of public services in the principal southern cities and with corruption in local government. That outrage was vividly captured in Francesco Rosi's 1963 movie on building speculation and housing shortages in postwar Naples (*Le Mani sulla Città, Hand on the City*). Giuseppe Tomasi di Lampedusa's cynical portrayal of the Risorgimento in his best-selling novel *The Leopard* (1958), popularized in Luchino Visconti's epic film version (1964), similarly reflected popular disillusionment with the postwar promises of renewal in the south.

Although the north was the principal theater for the protest movements with which the 1960s ended, there were significant episodes of popular unrest in many parts of the south as well. But while the government grappled in the next decade with the economic crisis and terrorism in the north, the development program in the south was losing direction. A worse moment could hardly have been chosen for a strategic shift from supporting small and medium-size enterprises to promoting large-scale projects. The shiny modern steel plants at Taranto and Gioia Tauro were completed at time of global overproduction and would never be put to use. Ridiculed by the press as "cathedrals in the desert," they quickly came to embody the flaws of the "top-down" planning mentality of the "special intervention" program. Many suspected, too, that their real aim was not to benefit the south but to support crisis-hit northern industrial concerns, just as many saw the new FIAT automobile factories at Cassano, Temoli, and Melfi as a way of escaping the constraints imposed by the powerful northern labor unions.

Criticism of the prevailing strategies was reinforced by new studies, many by distinguished foreign scholars, which documented the scale of political corruption in the south and the misuse of public funds.[15] These studies also revealed that over the previous decades the "Southern Question" had changed profoundly, and that no longer concerned the rural areas but above all the massively congested southern cities and decaying metropolitan areas. The situation changed rapidly for the worse following the earthquakes of December 1980 that caused heavy loss of life and massive structural damage across an area from Irpinia to the city of Naples. Emergency funds were quickly made available for housing the victims and rebuilding, but there was soon evidence of systematic misuse of the relief funds and materials and of massive corruption involving local political figures and organized crime. A key role was played by the recently reorganized Neapolitan *camorra* and its leader Raffaele Cutolo, but in the same decade criminal organizations were expanding in many other parts of the south (notably the Calabrian 'Ndrangheta and the Apulian Sacra Corona Unita). The most open challenge to the authority of the state came from Sicily, however, where, in May 1982, General Carlo Alberto Dalla Chiesa, the police chief who had defeated the Red Brigades and had been sent to Palermo to investigate mafia activities, was assassinated, with his wife, in the center of the city.

After the 'decade of bullets' and terrorism the north was by now experiencing a new consumption-led boom while, in central Italy, a "Third Italy" had emerged from the spectacular rise of family-based enterprises operating on world markets. Behind the façade of economic expansion, however Italy's public expenditure was running dangerously high, in part because lavish welfare and income support transfers were being used to sustain southern living standards and consumption. As Pasquale Saraceno bitterly noted, the south was enjoying the appearances but not the realities of growth, a judgment that could have been applied to Italy as a whole.[16]

NEW APPROACHES

By the late 1980s, crime and the south's dependence on state funds had become favored targets of the newly formed Northern Leagues, while a sense that the state was no longer an effective presence in the south was part of the broader crisis that overwhelmed the First Republic in the early 1990s.[17] In fact, the most open challenge to the state came not before but during the crisis, with the assassinations in 1992 of the leading the anti-Mafia magistrates, Giovanni Falcone and Paolo Borsellino. Yet, despite the enormity of the crime, many saw, in the public horror provoked by the assassinations, signs that the south was ready for a new political departure.[18] Such an interpretation was reinforced by the exposure of the scale of political corruption that implicated a remarkable cross-section of Italy's political parties, national and local politicians, and public administrators. Since Milan was the original focus of the investigations that precipitated the crisis, it appeared that political corruption in the south was less a special case than one more variant of a norm that was Italian. That meant, too, that many saw in the proposed reshaping of the Italian Republic and its political system the critical opportunities for finally resolving the "Southern Question," and for adopting new strategies for growth.

These developments coincided with the conclusion of the post-war program of 'special intervention' in the south. In 1984 the CpM had been wound up and by that time the policies with which it was associated were seen not as a remedy, but as a cause of economic stagnation in the south. There was little sympathy in Italy for the neoliberal policies popularized by Ronald Reagan and Margaret Thatcher, but opposition to state intervention and regulations was gaining momentum as was illustrated by the debates that followed the publication of Robert D. Putnam study *Making Democracy Work* in 1993. Putnam argued that economic growth and political democracy in the north were the results of traditions of "civic culture" that stretched back to the Middle Ages, whereas the lack of economic growth in the south was in turn the legacy of a history of feudalism and foreign occupation that had stifled the growth of independent civic virtues.[19]

The debates on Putnam's thesis served to give broader publicity to the critical role of "human and social capital" in the development of modern democratic, free enterprise economies which had acquired special relevance in Italy because of the dramatic expansion of small and medium sized family run enterprises in central Italy in the previous decade. Putnam's conclusions gave authoritative endorsement to the notion that the "Third Italy" offered a specifically Italian model for development. This had important implications for the south and the economic sociologist, Carlo Trigilia, was among those who argued that the example of the "Third Italy" demonstrated the need to pursue development strategies in the south that would create human capital and networks capable of mobilizing local resources. In contrast to the top-down strategies of the past, the emphasis should be on local initiatives that could build on the diversity of economic conditions. The task of the state was to remove the regulations and layers of intermediaries and brokers created by previous policies, to improve education, training, public health, welfare, and public services, and combat organized crime.[20]

Support for new approaches grew and the journal *Meridiana* offered an influential platform for promoting the case for de-regulation and greater autonomy to release the human resources and capital of the south. But others, including SVIMEZ, continued to warn that the lack of strategic industries and the deficiencies of public services, communications, together with high transaction and credit costs in the south could not be remedied without further direct intervention.[21]

THE SOUTHERN QUESTION TODAY

Twenty years on, the high hopes that the crisis of the First Republic would result in a thorough reorganization of Italian politics, that the south would acquire greater political autonomy and experience new growth have not been realized.[22] In economic terms, the north–south divergence has increased notably since 1992, and in 2013 the annual SVIMEZ report warned that the performance of the southern economies over the previous 12 months was the worst in the last 50 years. Industrial development fell by 2 percent in a single year, as did GDP per capita, investment, family incomes and consumption, production, and exports. One family in four is estimated to be on, or below, the poverty line, while the total number of jobs has fallen to 6 million: a figure last seen in 1978. Over the last 20 years, 2.7 million individuals have emigrated from the south, and, in recent years, 64.5 percent of the emigrants have been high school and university graduates. With 35 percent of the Italian population and unemployment rates four times higher than in the north and center, the economy of southern regions faces the dual challenge of dwindling investment and a major exodus of human capital. The report concluded bleakly that the south risks becoming "an industrial desert."[23]

The situation is by no means uniform, but even the most successful regions in the south (Apulia, Basilicata) have not matched growth rates in the least dynamic regions in the north and center. Many of the difficulties reflect the flat performance of the Italian economy as a whole, and the broader impact of globalization and deindustrialization. But the south has in addition suffered disproportionately from cuts in government spending, while a succession of short-lived governments has inhibited coherent policy implementation. The situation has often been exacerbated by the presence of the Northern League in government coalitions, as witness the notorious decision of Silvio Berlusconi's government in 1994 to allow 56 percent of the Italian regions, including some of the wealthiest parts of northern Italy, to receive EU funds designated for "distressed economic areas".

After Italy joined the Euro, in 1998 Romano Prodi and Carlo Azeglio Ciampi launched what was to be a "new Spring for the South": the first serious attempt to reconfigure development policies for the south since the start of the crisis at the beginning of the decade. But after the fall of the Prodi government there was little follow-up, while new federalist initiatives and the devolution of powers to regional governments placed new emphasis on local initiatives. Indeed, after the end of the "special intervention," the south exists not as a whole but only as the sum of its parts.[24]

Regional differences have increased, but in many parts of the south the situation has continued to deteriorate in ways that Roberto Saviano's fictional documentary *Gomorrah* and the images of burning refuse on the streets of Naples have brought to international attention.[25] The presence of organized crime is more localized than these images might suggest, but it remains a major threat, and the economist Paolo Barucci has warned that the widespread phenomenon of "unlawful forms of intermediation" challenges both the authority and the legitimacy of the state and means that the " markets no longer function." Agreeing that, in many parts of the south, organized crime "is the market," Piero Vigna, a former legal adviser to the Parliamentary Anti-Mafia Commission, has underlined its increasingly global and technologically sophisticated features.[26]

Organized crime deters foreign investment and jeopardizes the only major source of external funding, as in the well-publicized case of the withdrawal EU funding for the Salerno to Reggio Calabria motorway in 2013, because of suspected mafia contamination of the contracts. Leandra D'Antone has argued that the motorway encapsulates the essential features of the recent history of the "Southern Question." Work began on what was to be the principal transport link between Naples and the deep south in the 1960s, but today key stretches of the motorway are still unfinished construction sites as a consequence of the constant interpenetration of organized crime and political corruption.[27] Yet this intricate interplay of local and national interests suggests that, despite repeated claims that there are two Italies, the "Southern Question" remains primarily an Italian question. Or, as the Sicilian writer Leonardo Sciascia put it in one of his novels: "In Sicily, all roads lead to Rome."

The formation of Enrico Letta's government in 2013 raised hopes that Prodi's 1998 "Southern Spring" would be revived. Carlo Trigilia served in that government as Minster for Regional Development and Cohesion, and emphasized the importance of policy implementation, closer cooperation with the relevant EU agencies, and concerted action to reduce the power of "political capitalism" and organized crime in the south.[28] But institutional and cultural change are, obviously, long-term processes, while, like its predecessors, Letta's government proved short-lived. The lack of political stability that has characterized Italian politics for the last two decades undermines effective policy implementation and for as long as what Gianfranco Pasquino terms a "never-ending transition" continues it is not easy to see how solutions to the political dimensions of the "Southern Question" can be found.[29]

Far from diminishing, the distorting stereotypes of the "two Italies" that are constructs of a century and half of debate on the "Southern Question" have recently found a new lease of life. The "Southern Question" offers a contentious public forum where the cost-benefits of Unification are constantly debated, and a mirror in which Italian identities, unities, and disunities are reflected. The old images of an idle, unproductive, and crime-ridden south that acts as a dead weight that holds back the development of a more dynamic and entrepreneurial north have been reactivated in the polemical language of the Northern Leagues. In response, southerners claim that they are the true victims of Unification, and of policies and politics that have consistently promoted the interests of the north at the expense of the south.[30]

Adding to a climate of reciprocal vilification, "revisionist" rewritings of the past have contributed to the rise of new separatist movements in both the north and the south whose strong populist undertones continue to attract enthusiastic media attention. These movements reflect resentments at the persisting disparities between north and south, but they are also a manifestation of the broader "anti-politics" and "anti-party" movements that have gained momentum in many different parts of Europe, and especially in Italy in recent decades. Despite their apparently contradictory objectives, the Northern Leagues' nostalgia for a mythical independent northern Padania or the newfound attraction of a mythologized pre-Unification Bourbon south reflect discontents provoked by impact of economic globalization that have much in common with the anti-politics and anti-party sentiments of Silvio Berlusconi and Beppe Grillo's Five Star Movement.[31] These new developments can only further complicate the politics of the "Southern Question" which remain as contentious today as at any previous time in the history of modern Italy.

Notes

1. Cited in Francesco Barbagallo, *La Questione Italiana. Il Nord ed il Sud dal 1860 a oggi* (Rome and Bari: Laterza Editori, 2013); Piero Bevilacqua, *Breve Storia dell'Italia Meridionale dall'Ottocento a oggi* (Donzelli: Rome, 2005); and Guido Pescosolido "Questione Meridionale," in *Enciclopedia del Novecento* (III Supplemento) (Rome: Treccani, 2004). The best English-language surveys are in Paul Ginsborg, *A History of Contemporary Italy: Society and Politics 1945–1980* (London: Allen Lane, 1990); Vera Zamagni, *The Economic History of Italy 1860–1990* (Oxford: Oxford University Press, 1993); and the essays in Gianno Toniolo (ed.), *The Oxford Handbook of the Italian Economy since Unification* (New York and Oxford: Oxford University Press, 2013).
2. Paolo Macry, *Unità a Mezzogiorno. Come l'Italia ha messo assieme i pezzi* (Bologna: Il Mulino, 2012).
3. See John Dickie, *Darkest Italy: The Nation and the Stereotypes of the Mezzogiorno 1860–1900* (Houndsmill and London: Palgrave Macmillan 1999) and Antonino De Francesco, *La palla al piede. Una storia del pregiudizio antimeridionale* (Milan: Feltinelli Editori, 2012).
4. Barbagallo, *La Questione Italiana*; Luigi De Rosa *La Provincia Subordinata. Saggio sulla questione meridionale* (Rome and Bari: Editori Laterza 2004).
5. Zamagni, *The Economic History of Italy*.
6. Raffaele Ciassca cited in Emmanuele Felice, *Perché il Sud è rimasto addietro?* (Bologna: Il Mulino, 2013), p. 109.
7. Salvatore Lupo, *Il Giardino degli Aranci. Il mondo degli agrumi nella storia del Mezzogiorno* (Milan: Feltrinelli, 1990).

8. See David W. Ellwood, *Italy 1943–1945: The Politics of Liberation* (London and New York: Longman, 1985).

9. See Barbagallo, *La Questione Italiana*, and Simone Misiano, *Manlio Ross-Doria. Un Riformatore del Novecento* (Soveria Mannelli: Rubbettino Editore, 2010).

10. See Salvatore Lupo, "The Mafia," in Patrick McCarthy (ed.), *Italy since 1945* (Oxford: Oxford University Press, 2000), 153–166, and Lupo *History of the Mafia* (New York: Columbia University Press, 2011).

11. Barbagallo, *La Questione Italiana*, 134.

12. See especially Michele Alacevich, 'Postwar Development in the Italian Mezzogiorno: Analyses and Policies," *Journal of Modern Italian Studies* 18/1 (2013), 90–112.

13. Toniolo, *The Oxford Handbook of the Italian Economy since Unification*; De Rosa, *La Provincia Subordinata*.

14. Vera Lutz, *Italy: A Study in Economic Development* (Oxford: Oxford University Press, 1962).

15. Sidney G. Tarrow, *Peasant Communism in Southern Italy* (New Haven: Yale University Press, 1967); Percy A. Allum, *Politics and Society in Post-War Naples* (Cambridge: Cambridge University Press, 1973); Judith Chubb, *Poverty, Power and Politics in Southern Italy: A Tale of Two Cities* (Cambridge: Cambridge University Press, 1982).

16. Barbagallo, *La Questione Italiana*, pp. 185–186.

17. For an analysis of the crisis see Patrick McCarthy, *The Crisis of the Italian State: From the Origins of the Cold War to the Fall of Berlusconi* (New York: St. Martins Press, 1995) and Gianfranco Pasquino "Political Development," in McCarthy (ed.), *Italy since 1945*, 69–93.

18. Jane and Peter Schneider, *Reversible Destiny: Mafia, Anti-Mafia, and the Struggle for Palermo* (Berkeley and Los Angeles: University of California Press, 2003).

19. Robert D. Putnam with Robert Leonardi and Raffaella Nardini, *Making Democracy Work: Civic Traditions in Modern Italy* (Princeton: Princeton University Press, 1993). See also Filippo Sabetti, *The Search for Good Governance: Understanding the Paradoxes of Italian Democracy* (Toronto: McGill-Queens University Press, 2000); Michele Salvati, "Politiche di sviluppo. Una riflessione critica," in Marta Pertrusewicz, Jane Schneider, and Peter Schneider (eds.), *Il Sud. Conoscere, capire, cambiare* (Bologna: Il Mulino, 2009), 257–273; and Dario Gaggio, "Do Social Historians Need Social Capital," *Social History* 29 (2004), 499–513.

20. Carlo Trigilia, *Sviluppo senza autonomia. Effetti perversi delle politiche nel Mezzogiorno* (Milan: Feltrinelli, 1992); and Arnaldo Bagnasco's earlier *Tre Italie. La problematica territorial dello sviluppo italiano* (Bologna: Il Mulino, 1977).

21. See Vera Negri Zamagani and Mario Sanfilippo, *Nuovo meridionalismo e intervento straordinario. La SVIMEZ dal 1946 al 1950* (Bologna: Il Mulino, 1988); Salvatore Cafiero, *Questione meridionale e unità nazionale:1861–1995* (Rome: NIS, 1996), Salvatore Cafiero, *Storia dell'intervento straordinario nel Mezzogiorno (1950–1993)* (Manduria: Lacaita, 2000); Nino Novacco (ed.), *Per il Mezzogiorno e per l'Italia. Un sogno ed un impegno che dura da 60 anni* (Bologna: Il Mulino, 2007).

22. See Gianfranco Pasquino, "Political Development," in McCarthy (ed.), *Italy since 1945*, 69–93, and Felice, *Perché il Sud è rimasto addietro?*

23. SVIMEZ (Associazione per lo Sviluppo dell'Industria nel Mezzogiorno) *Rapporto 2013 sull'economia del Mezzogiorno* (Bologna: Il Mulino, 2013) (http://www.svimez.info).

24. Christopher Roux, "Italy's Path to Federalism: Origins and Paradoxes," *Journal of Modern Italian Studies* 13/3 (2008), 325–338; Alfonsina Iona, Leone Davide, and Giuseppe Sobbrio,

"'O Convergence where art thou?' Regional Growth and Industrialization in Italy," *Journal of Modern Italian Studies* 18/3 (2008) 366–387; Emmanuele Felice, "Regional Development: Reviewing the Italian Mosaic," *Journal of Modern Italian Studies* (Special Issue on "150 Years of the Italian Economy," ed. Vera Zamagni and Paolo Malanima) 15/1 (2010), 64–80.

25. Roberto Saviano, *Gomorrah* (New York: Straus & Farrar, 2007). See also Felia Allum and Percy Allum, "Revisiting Naples: Clientelism and Organized Crime," in *Journal of Modern Italian Studies* 13/3 (2008), 340–365.

26. Cited in Barbagallo, *La Questione Italiana*, 201.

27. Leandra D'Antone, *Senza pedaggio. Storia dell'autostrada Salerno-Reggio Calabria* (Rome: Donzelli, 2008).

28. Carlo Trigilia, *Non c'è Nord senza Sud. Perché la crescita dell'Italia si decide nel Mezzogiorno* (Bologna: Il Mulino, 2012).

29. Gianfranco Pasquino, "Post-Electoral Politics in Italy: Institutional Problems and Political Perspectives," *Journal of Modern Italian Studies* 18/4 (2013), 484.

30. See, for example, Giovanni De Luna, *La Repubblica del dolore. La memoria di un'Italia divisa* (Milan: Feltrinelli Editori, 2011), and Guido Crainz, *Autobiografia di una Reppublica* (Rome: Donzelli, 2009).

31. See Guido Crainz "Italy's political system since 1989," *Journal of Modern Italian Studies* 20/2 (2015), 176–188, and Chapter 18 in this volume.

PART II

POLITICAL
INSTITUTIONS

CHAPTER 6

···

THE CONSTITUTION

···

GIULIANO AMATO

MOST of the patriots who fought for Italian Unification in the nineteenth century expected the new Italy to have a Constitution, approved by an elected Constitutional Assembly. Constitutions were at the origin of the Risorgimento, from the self-proclaimed republics of the late eighteenth century to those of the revolts in 1848–49.[1] How could a unified Italy be denied her own Constitution?

Unfortunately, Italy was denied it: initially, the paramount purposes of the Kingdom of Sardinia—the driving force of the unification process—prevailed. The kingdom already had a constitution, called a "Statuto": in 1848 the king had unilaterally granted it to his citizens. The legal force of the Statuto was extended to the Kingdom of Italy, thereby underlying the continuity between the two states. Not only that: the King of Sardinia—who was Vittorio Emanuele the Second when Italian Unification was accomplished—became the first King of Italy but remained "the Second."[2] This proved even more difficult to digest for those who had dreamt of a Constitutional Assembly as the new foundation for a new state.

It took more than eighty years for this dream to come true. World War II, the fall of the fascist regime (which, formally, had not touched the Statuto, though it had subverted the constitutional architecture based on that document), and the role of the anti-fascist movement were sufficient reasons for the principle of continuity to be set aside. Initially, the king, Vittorio Emanuele III, had envisaged a post-fascist return to his Statuto and, for this reason, had proposed nothing more than the election of a new Chamber of Deputies. However, both the Allied Powers and the anti-fascist parties united in the National Liberation Committee supported a future democratic decision on the institutions to be given to postwar Italy.[3] Eventually, this position was finalized in the legislative act that remained as the "Transitional Constitution" of that time, namely legislative decree n. 151, June 25, 1944. Article 1 of the Transitional Constitution stated: "After the liberation of the national territory, the institutions will be chosen by the people, who by universal, direct and secret vote will elect a Constitutional Assembly in order to approve the new Constitution of the State."

The political choice enshrined in this article is clear. The Constitutional Assembly was supposed, firstly, to decide if Italy should preserve the monarchy or become a republic; secondly, it was to adopt the ensuing constitutional rules. But in the following months this choice was modified. On the assumption that the Constitutional Assembly would more likely have a republican majority while the citizens were still divided, the Allied Powers (who feared a leftist bias in any possible republic) and the political parties (mostly the Christian Democrats) who had followers on both sides, succeeded in transferring the fundamental choice between a monarchy or republic to a popular referendum. Legislative decree n. 98, March 16, 1946, stated that, on June 2, 1946, the citizens would vote for the referendum and also elect the Constitutional Assembly. And so it was. The Republic won by roughly 2 million votes (out of 22 million voters) and the Constitutional Assembly was elected to give Italy a republican constitution. For the first time in Italian history, women too cast their votes at a national election.[4]

The 556 members elected to the Assembly were not unprepared for their job. Not only had an ad hoc ministry previously been set up to prepare studies and investigations on behalf of the future assembly,[5] but the parties, or at least some of them, had produced ideas and drafted proposals on the organization to be given to the new state.[6] Furthermore, the Assembly membership was highly qualified and included both key political figures and prestigious scholars.[7] Therefore, the cultural background of the Assembly was not in doubt. Doubts did exist, however, about whether the Assembly would succeed in reaching reliable and solid agreements. The distance was wide between those parties that wanted to reinstall Italy among the Western liberal democracies and those whose final aim was the construction of a socialist republic, following the Soviet example. Bridging such a distance seemed even more unlikely when the Cold War broke out in 1947 and the leftist parties were thrown out of the Cabinet, then led by the Christian Democrat Alcide De Gasperi.

Despite all this, the Assembly succeeded in writing a Constitution which its members believed in profoundly. Naturally, members maintained different expectations for the future, but the miracle was that all the players agreed both upon the rules of the game and upon the substantive principles defining the boundaries of the playground. It is for this reason that the Constitution has gradually become a sort of cult object for Italians, who see it as the best fruit of a golden age, drafted when political parties were ready to overcome their conflicts for the sake of a common national interest.

Beyond the rhetoric, the miracle has several (more prosaic) explanations. First of all, the parties were quite uncertain as to future developments. At the time, who the winner would be really was an open question; consequently, it was advisable for all of them to set a common and well-balanced ground. Secondly, academic representatives, so transversally present in the Assembly, played a role in facilitating agreements that were shared by its scholars, if only in technical terms. Last but not least, the cultural threads upon which the Constitution was built were due mostly to a small group of leading Catholic figures (Giuseppe Dossetti, Giorgio La Pira, Amintore Fanfani, Giuseppe Lazzati, Aldo Moro), who had drawn them from the Catholic social doctrine.[8] By offering a common platform based on this doctrine, the Christian Democrats made it much more acceptable for the socialists and the communists than any traditional pro-market vision would have been. As we will see, it is this key that allows us to understand several passages of the Italian Constitution and the levels of consent it garnered.

The general orientation of the Assembly was not only against the fascist regime, its organization, and its contempt for individual and collective freedoms, but was also very critical toward the previous liberal architecture, which had been narrowly elitist and had never accepted that, between the state and individuals, there exist legitimate collective interests and groups, whose role must be recognized. Fascism had gone too far in such recognition, for whatever collective interest its principles might legitimately admit was directly absorbed into the public sphere and therefore became a public entity. It had been the wrong answer for the society of the twentieth century, but twentieth-century society was irreversibly the society that needed to be coped with.

Articles 1, 2, and 3 of the Constitution are very eloquent in explaining the vision adopted by its founding fathers. By defining Italy as a democracy based on labor, they denied legitimacy to the recognition of any higher status not based on personal qualities or on the quality of one's work. By asserting the rights of each person, both as an individual and as a member of the social group and community he/she belongs to, the founding fathers also asserted the legitimacy and the liberties of such groups and communities. By including an equal protection clause that was not limited to prohibiting discriminations, but also required the Republic to remove the social and economic impediments to the full development of each citizen's personality, they abandoned the abstract notions both of "citizen" and of "equal treatment under the law" of the nineteenth century's legal systems.

Moving from this incipit, the Constitution follows an architecture that differs considerably from that of previous ones. One of its architects, Aldo Moro, defined this architecture in terms of "increasing sociality." In his mind, after a series of fundamental principles, the rights and freedoms of the individual had to be stated; then, the rights, freedoms, and responsibilities connected to the first communities an individual comes into contact with (namely family and school); then, rights, freedoms, and responsibilities in economic, social, and political contexts; and, finally, the organization of the state. This outline proved a fair prediction of what the Constitution would indeed look like.[9]

Fundamental principles go from article 1 to article 12 and touch upon several crucial issues: from the need for a decentralized governance within the framework of an "indivisible" national unity to the protection of linguistic minorities; from the principle of agreements with religious confessions as the necessary basis for their statutory regulations (which, in the case of the Catholic Church, is upgraded to the level of "Concordatarian" and therefore bilateral regulation) to the protection of the natural, historical, and artistic heritage of the country; from the respect due to generally recognized norms of international law and that due to the right of asylum to the rejection of war as a means of aggression and as a means to solve international conflicts.

Much should be said about the impact of each of these principles on Italian life over the last sixty years. It cannot be done here. However, at least a mention is needed of some of the developments upon which the impact has been particularly remarkable, namely:

(a) the role of the "indivisibility" of the Republic in the rejection of recent, regional legislative acts trying to reach far beyond the boundaries of regional autonomy; (b) the success of the agreements with religious confessions, which have proved a very satisfactory means to enhance the opportunities for believers to practice their creeds; (c) the increasing importance given to the protection of Italy's natural, historic, and artistic heritage, despite initial opinions that it was "extravagant" for a Constitution to insert such an item among its fundamental principles;[10] (d) the political use made of the Constitution by pacifist movements in rejecting war: the relevant text has been read as an absolute prohibition of any use of military resources—peacemaking and peacekeeping included— and not, as was intended, as the prohibition of unilateral aggression.[11]

Individual freedoms, traditionally called "civil liberties," are guaranteed under Title I ("Civil relations") of Part I ("Rights and duties of the citizens"). What is new in the articles running from 13 to 28, which makes them substantially different from the similar list of clauses in the previous Statuto? First of all, the items included go beyond the freedoms taken into account in any nineteenth-century Constitution, where there is no mention of freedom of association. Indeed, at the time, even the most generous interpretations considered freedom of association to be an implied derivative of individual freedom. But, even more than this, the constitutional guarantee is different and much stronger. In the nineteenth century, the long fight against the arbitrary powers of the king—which peaked in the Great Revolutions—eventually succeeded in granting the exclusive power to introduce new limitations to individual freedoms to the law (which meant the representative parliaments). This development embodied the kind of guarantee that was deemed essential. It was the seal of victory in that fight.

However, faced with the totalitarian political forces that took over in Italy—and not only there—in the first decades of the twentieth century, this guarantee did not provide an adequate shield and was easily bypassed. By law of the Parliament, and therefore without formally violating the Statuto, civil liberties were either denied or put in the hands of the Executive or of special tribunals. After the tragedies stemming from this experience, the new Constitution innovated and strengthened the shield. The Italian Constitution not only proclaims that individual freedoms can be limited exclusively by law (or on the basis of a law), but it also establishes—freedom by freedom—which limits can be introduced and which authority (judicial or administrative) is empowered to do so. Therefore, for example, since freedom of movement can be limited only for sanitary and security reasons, a statute limiting the movements of prostitutes for moral reasons was upheld by the Constitutional Court as long as such reasons were so compelling as to affect security.[12] In Italian legal language, such a special constitutional protection is defined as "enhanced statutory reserve," while the traditional protection is called simply "statutory reserve."

The Constitution is even more innovative in its Title II, devoted to what it calls "ethical-social" relations. The family, health, and education are dealt with here. Precedents can be found in other twentieth-century constitutions—first of all in the Weimar Constitution—but certainly the values and principles contained in the Italian document far surpass the constitutional culture of the nineteenth century. The traditional horizon of civil liberties as they were perceived in the nineteenth century is widened and now also includes social rights, viewed and defined, in some cases, with a Catholic bias. Take the case of the family. Both in the Weimar Constitution (article 119) and in the Italian one (article 29), the solemn recognition and protection of the family are granted based on marriage. However, in the Italian one, there is something more: namely, the family based on marriage is defined as a "natural society." Here the Catholic influence is transparent; today this is still an obstacle to the full recognition of equal rights of other existing forms of family (the so-called de facto families).

In other cases, however, the old liberal democracy's secular principles prevailed over the Catholic influence. So it was for the schools. According to article 33, the Republic has the task of establishing state schools for all levels of education. Private schools are free to operate, but must create no burdens on the state. However, public funding to private, and mostly Catholic, schools was introduced later. Indeed, in the 1960s, a Cabinet supported by a center-left coalition lost its parliamentary majority for this reason.[13] This would no longer happen: in the name of free choice, which families and students are entitled to enjoy, limited funding is widely accepted.

Beyond the diverging views on this specific matter, the clause upon which the founding fathers unanimously agreed is in article 34. According to this article, those who are "talented and deserving" are entitled to reach the highest levels of education. The Republic is charged with making this right "effective" by distributing grants, and by supporting families and providing other benefits, to be conferred by competition. In recent years, the harshness of financial readjustment has severely affected the implementation of this crucial clause.

Health is the third important item under this title. The memory of the Nazi experience played a decisive role in shaping the article devoted to health in Italy. The second paragraph of article 32 affirms that only by specific legislative provisions can a sanitary treatment be mandatory, and not even the law may violate the limits due to the respect of human dignity. The treatment of mental disease was profoundly and positively affected by this clause, while the general transformation of health assistance has been based on the first paragraph of the same article, which defines health as a fundamental right of the individual and an interest of the national community, to be protected by the Republic. Herein lie the origins of the Italian National Health System, one of the best in the world. Moreover, the Constitutional Court has found in this article the legal basis to grant everybody—illegal immigrants included—the right to be protected as regards "essential" sanitary needs.[14]

Title III, formally devoted to "Economic relations," deals with the most settled social rights, with the limitations that may be imposed on property rights and, more generally, with the role of the state in the economy. The rights to a fair salary, to a fair pension, and also to strike were much less disputed than the rest. While the divergence between the Christian Democrats and the Communist left was wide here, the Catholic social doctrine succeeded in defining a common platform. The final agreement was reached on defining property both as "public and private" (ten years later the Treaty of Rome did the same in launching the European Economic Community), on admitting that private property has to be "guaranteed"—though also limited in view of its "social function" and of the need to be accessible to all (article 42)—and finally on the complex construction of article 41 on the general theme of the state and the market.

Here, the free marketeers and the supporters of the state economy were at odds on several issues. The admissibility of public planning was one such issue. Eventually, a final text was approved in which the market is not mentioned at all (nor is it mentioned in any other article of the Constitution), but the freedom to private economic initiative is formally guaranteed, thereby going far beyond the old constitutions, in which property (and not economic initiative) was recognized. At the same time, public planning was excluded, though the last paragraph of the articles states that public programs may be established by law, in order to address and coordinate public and private economic activities toward social ends.[15]

It has to be admitted that the future of a free market economy based on such a platform was, at the time, quite fragile. Article 41 was not a real and solid compromise; it was more an open option. It was used to confirm that Italy was part of the Western world, but it was also used to demonstrate that a socialist transformation of the Italian economy was feasible, without violating the Constitution.[16] As events have unfolded since then, the second option has proved purely hypothetical. Little by little—due also to Italy's increasingly deep roots in the European common market—the initial leftist purpose of an exit from capitalism faded away. When the Communists themselves became part of the parliamentary majority in the late 1970s, they did not even think of an overall and coercive public planning of the economy; they were satisfied rather with programming and coordinating, which implies a much lighter public role. In thirty years, upon the subtle wording of article 41, a thick and robust divide had been built.

The last "relations" considered by the Constitution are the political ones, in Title IV. The core of this Title is in article 48, on the right to vote, and in article 49, on political parties. Article 48 is quite predictable in proclaiming the right to a vote that must be equal, secret, and free. The first paragraph is also to be expected, where it confers the right to vote on all citizens—men and women—who have reached their full legal age. However, the text, in truth, is the conclusion of a long and difficult history. In the first parliamentary elections of the newly formed Kingdom of Italy (eighty years before) only a restricted elite of wealthy males had enjoyed the right to vote. After World War I, the right was extended to all men. Italy had a new beginning with gender equality in voting when in was admitted for the referendum and for the election of the Constitutional Assembly and subsequently enshrined in the Constitution.

The plain formulation of article 49 conceals the controversy at the time over the role of political parties in Italy as compared to that in similar democracies. Article 49 recognizes the right of all citizens to freely associate in political parties, "to concur with democratic method to the determination of national policies." After the fascist experience and to prevent any totalitarian adventure of whatever nature, several requests were tabled to make it clear that democracy should, first of all, be an internal method for the parties of the new Italy. But the requests were rejected, and not only by the Communists, who feared being singled out for such a reason. Eventually, they all agreed on a "democratic method," to be referred to the external action of the parties. None of them wanted to be subject to state controls: these were deemed inadmissible by all. The difference is striking between this article and article 21 of the German Grundgesetz, which speaks openly of "internal" democracy and provides for a declaration of unconstitutionality of any party whose aims and behavior might subvert the free and democratic legal system of the country.[17]

The past histories of Italy and Germany were similar, but the two countries arrived at their postwar constitutions in very different conditions. Germany was still in the hands of the Allied Powers and the Grundgesetz was deliberated and approved by a parliamentary assembly composed of representatives of the Laender (not directly elected by the German citizens) under the supervision of the Western Powers. Italy, due to its "Resistenza," its transitional arrangements and the recent democratic elections, had political parties with a strong popular legitimacy, who considered themselves the new holders of sovereignty. This attitude affected not only article 49, but also the very organization of the government.

In Part II, all the aspects of such organization are dealt with. Three crucial innovations were introduced: strongly promoted by the Christian Democrats, these innovations were opposed or only tepidly accepted by the Communist left and by the pre-fascist liberals. The first one, in Title V, is the regional organization of the state, which goes back to an unaccomplished dream of the Italian Risorgimento. At the time, the paramount reasons of unification prevailed and led to centralization and a uniform administrative ruling of the entire country. Eighty years later, the Catholic vision of a multilayer democracy that bestows governmental responsibilities upon its "intermediate" communities prevailed. The overall design provides not only for municipalities and provinces, with their own autonomous spheres, but most of all for regions, who share the legislative power that was once an exclusive prerogative of the national Parliament. The model here was the Spanish Constitution of 1931. It should be noted that Title V was not applied for more than twenty years. Finally in power, after winning the political elections of 1948, the Christian Democrats were not at all happy to share that power with the Communists, who held the majority in some regions. The Communists became supporters of the regions, and, in 1970, an agreement was finally reached to implement this part of the Constitution.

The second innovation (in Title VI) is "constitutional rigidity": the Constitution can be amended only by special procedures and not by ordinary legislation. Furthermore, a Constitutional Court is entitled to judicial review of any such legislation. The Austrian Constitution of 1920 had been the front-runner in abandoning the principle of parliamentary supremacy inherited from the French Revolution. Germany and Italy needed to live through the tragedy of their totalitarian regimes to follow suit. Only France remained firm, until, in 2008, by constitutional reform, France too joined the mainstream of the twentieth century.

The third innovation (in Title IV) is a strongly independent judiciary. Italy had been part of that continental tradition by which an originally exclusive power—that of the Crown—had limited itself by admitting other public powers, to be exercised "in the name of the king." In the new Constitution, the judiciary is on the same footing as the other powers of the state; it is not a derivative of any of them. Therefore, the division of powers is duly accomplished, even though it is still resented and wrongly criticized by those who consider it essential for a democracy to recognize a paramount role for those institutions that derive their legitimacy from a popular and political vote.

The system of government, which runs from Title I to Title III of Part II, is much less innovative than one might expect after reading the heavy criticism levied by several members of the Constitutional Assembly about the weakness and the shortcomings of "parliamentarism," which had paved the way to fascism. The proposal of a presidential form of government was opposed by those who, after having lived under a fascist regime, were fearful of any kind of monocracy. It was also pointed out that an elected president had failed to protect the Weimar Republic from the Nazi takeover. The so-called "rationalization" of the parliamentary form of government seemed to be much more agreeable: vote of confidence to the prime minister only and not to individual ministers, plus vote of no confidence to be accompanied by the majoritarian election of a successor (as in the German Grundgesetz). In the end, a resolution was almost unanimously approved, outlining just such a solution.[18] Afterwards, however, almost nothing was done along these lines, and the only "rationalization" that was actually adopted is the one concerning the timing of the request for a motion of confidence. For the rest, the prime minister (still named President of the Council) remained a *primus inter pares* and the traditional political powers of the Parliament remained untouched.

Two reasons explain the Assembly's conservative attitude. The first is the already mentioned uncertainty over the future political winner. Neither the Christian Democrats nor the left were ready to make the future executive stronger, thereby running the risk of giving such enhanced strength to their respective political enemy. The second reason is the position of the parties; they believed that the job of making the executive strong lay with them—not with any institutional device: "Giving the Executive the strength it needs has to depend on our political will, nothing else is needed." And so it was.[19]

After coming into force, on January 1, 1948, the Constitution remained undisputed for years. Political conflicts delayed the implementation of some of its innovations and this aroused passions, mostly on the left ("the betrayed Constitution"). However, Title V on the regions was actually implemented in 1970, and the Constitutional Court—from its inception in 1956 and against the initial views of the highest ordinary court (Corte di Cassazione)—clearly stated the immediate justiciability of the constitutional clauses on civil liberties.

The lack of institutional stabilizers of the executive was not an issue. On the one side, the parties were still sufficiently strong to support the Executive's policies in Parliament with their "political will." On the other side, the role of the Parliament in the decision-making process gave the opposition a voice—and frequently more than a voice—in its deliberations and decisions. The impact was truly remarkable. Over the common platform of such procedural democracy, the substantive principles of democracy also gained ground. When the Communist Party abandoned its original aims and became an "ordinary" party—to the point of joining the Christian Democrats in a parliamentary majority in the 1970s—credit was given to the Constitution itself. Its farsighted flexibility had powerfully bridged the cleavage upon which the Republic had initially been built.[20]

It could have been a happy ending, but it was not. Other developments were occurring, in relation to which those very constitutional features that had played the role of an asset started to appear as a liability. The effective adoption of a multilayered system of government, with regions, provinces, municipalities, and other local institutions in charge of specific missions, made the system itself complex and cumbersome. All too frequently, too many participants had a say in a single procedure, while none of them was empowered to make a final decision. At the same time, political parties were losing both their role and their legitimacy. In order to reach their electors, it had been crucial for the parties to act as channels of participatory democracy. Now, mass media had intervened, and active citizens were forced to become spectators, with the leaders more and more on the front stage. At the same time, a high rate of corruption was discovered in political life and the power exercised by those parties lost its legitimacy.

Constitutional reform aimed at "giving back" to the citizens the power to make fundamental decisions about who should run the country. That the executive lacked strength became a popular issue. The debate on this reform has accompanied the last thirty years of Italian life, and the fact that the issue is still open is, in part, responsible for the piling up of distortions and of partial transformations of existing mechanisms that has intervened, rendering the current picture far from satisfactory.

Not by amending the Constitution, but by modifying the electoral law and passing from proportional to majority rule, has the condition of the executive been changed. Over the last few years, Cabinets have enjoyed more solid parliamentary majorities and, by relying on them, they have made an expanded use of law decrees and votes of confidence, thereby transforming the Parliament into a ratifying institution. Not even in the Fifth French Republic could Parliament approve a financial bill of more than 800 paragraphs with just one vote (a vote of confidence). But such a strong executive has no reach over the powers of the regions, extended by a constitutional reform approved in 2001, which has intensified conflict between them and the central state.

In 2005, the center-right supported a wider reform, amending several clauses of the Constitution and enhancing the role of the prime minister, also vis-à-vis the President of the Republic. The reform passed in Parliament, but was rejected in a popular referendum in 2006.

Nine years later, in the spring of 2015, one of the main missions of the Cabinet in office is to promote constitutional reform. What is the conclusion at the moment? Italians love their Constitution, they praise it as "the most beautiful in the world," in the words of their most popular actor, Roberto Benigni.[21] In truth, they love Part I of it, where their rights and liberties are protected; they consider it untouchable, yet they are very unsatisfied with politics and with national and local political institutions. Some Italians, mostly on the right, also complain about the judiciary, accusing that branch of government of political bias and unfairness.

A new reform is now under way, that reduces the legislative sphere of the Regions and streamlines the Parliament, by transforming the Senate into a less powerful chamber of only 100 members, elected by the regional councils. The most beautiful Constitution of the world might soon enjoy the embellishments it badly needs.

Notes

1. Christopher Duggan, *The Force of Destiny: A History of Italy since 1796*, London, Allen Lane-Penguin Books, 2007; Lucy Riall, *Risorgimento: The History of Italy from Napoleon to Nation State*, New York, Palgrave Macmillan, 2009.
2. Giselle S. Godkin, *Life of Victor Emmanuel II*, New York, Macmillan, 1880; Denis Mack Smith, *Victor Emanuel, Cavour and the Risorgimento*, Oxford: Oxford University Press, 1971.
3. Enzo Cheli, *Costituzione e sviluppo delle istituzioni in Italia*, Bologna, Il Mulino, 1978.
4. Women had the right to vote by Legislative Decree January 31, 1945. Therefore, their very first elections were the local ones on March 10, 1946.
5. The founding act of the Ministry was Legislative Decree July 31, 1945, n.435. Its main mission was to collect "domestic and foreign" documents on constitutions. Actually several committees worked in it. Among them, the Committee on the Reorganization of the State, chaired by Professor Ugo Forti, and the Committee on the Economy, chaired by Professor Giovanni De Maria.
6. Roberto Ruffilli (ed.), *Cultura politica e partiti nell'età della Costituente*, Bologna, Il Mulino, 1979.
7. There were political figures such as Lelio Basso, Epicarmo Corbino, Alcide De Gasperi, Ugo La Malfa, Luigi Longo, Emilio Lussu, Pietro Nenni, Sandro Pertini, Meuccio Ruini, Palmiro Togliatti, Leo Valiani, and intellectuals and scholars such as Luigi Einaudi, Concetto Marchesi, Costantino Mortati, Tommaso Perassi, Ignazio Silone, and Egidio Tosato. Also prominent figures of the pre-fascist Italy were members of the Assembly: Benedetto Croce, Saverio Nitti, and Vittorio Emanuele Orlando.
8. Roberto Ruffilli (ed.), *Cultura politica e partiti nell'età della Costituente*, vol. 1: *L'area liberal democratica. Il mondo cattolico. La Democrazia Cristiana*, Bologna, Il Mulino, 1979.
9. Leopoldo Elia, *Costituzione, partiti, istituzioni*, Bologna, Il Mulino, 2009.
10. Gastone Baschieri, Luigi Bianchi d'Espinosa, and Carlo Giannattasio, *La Costituzione italiana. Commento analitico*, Florence, Noccioli, 1949.
11. Mario Dogliani, *Il valore costituzionale della pace e il divieto della guerra*, in www.studiperlapace.it, 2002, argues that art. 11 should be interpreted as a prohibition of any use of military means except for the case of defense from aggression.
12. Decision December 28, 1962, in <www.cortecostituzionale.it>.
13. In June 1964 the Moro Cabinet resigned after the Socialists voted in Parliament against the budget. In that budget 149 million lire had been allocated on behalf of private schools.
14. Decision July 7, 2010, n.269, in <www.cortecostituzionale.it>.
15. A Communist amendment, according to which a "plan" would subordinate productive activities to state direction was rejected and an amendment was approved which referred to " coordinating programs" in the sense—the author explained—given to them by the liberal economist Friedrich Hayek. See Luigi Gianniti, "Note sul dibattito alla Costituente sulla 'Costituzione economica,'" in *Diritto Pubblico*, 2000, p. 918.

16. Carlo Lavagna, *Costituzione e socialismo*, Bologna, Il Mulino, 1977.

17. Gianfranco Pasquino, *Commentario della Costituzione, Artt.48–52*, Bologna, Zanichelli, 1992.

18. The resolution is usually quoted under the name of Tomaso Perassi, who wrote and tabled it on September 4, 1946.

19. Frederic Spotts and Theodor Wieser, *Italy: A Difficult Democracy*, Cambridge: Cambridge University Press, 1986. The weakness of the state as the main historical problem of Italy is at the core of Sabino Cassese's analysis in *L'Italia. Una società senza Stato*, Bologna, Il Mulino, 2011.

20. Joseph La Palombara, *Democracy Italian Style*, New Haven, Yale University Press, 1987. According to Giuseppe Palma, *Surviving without Governing: The Italian Parties in Parliament*, Berkeley, University of California Press, 1977, this broadened consensus had a price, namely an increasing reduction of the decision-making capacity. While Giovanni Sartori, *Parties and Party Systems: A Framework for Analysis*, Cambridge, Cambridge University Press, 1976, was not at all convinced of the intervened depolarization of the Italian system.

21. Roberto Benigni had more than 12 million viewers when he explained the fundamental principles of the Constitution in a TV show, "La più bella del mondo," on December 17, 2012.

CHAPTER 7

···

THE PRESIDENTS
OF THE REPUBLIC

···

GIANFRANCO PASQUINO

SINCE 1948, Italy has seen 12 Presidents of the Republic: Luigi Einaudi (1948–55, Partito Liberale Italiano [PLI]); Giovanni Gronchi (1955–62, Democrazia Cristiana [DC]); Antonio Segni (1962–64, DC); Giuseppe Saragat (1964–71, Partito Socialista Democratico Italiano [PSDI]); Giovanni Leone (1971–78, DC); Sandro Pertini (1978–85, Partito Socialista Italiano [PSI]); Francesco Cossiga (1985–92, DC); Oscar Luigi Scalfaro (1992–99, DC); Carlo Azeglio Ciampi (1999–2006, no party affiliation); Giorgio Napolitano (2006–15, former Communist, at the time of his election no party affiliation, though member of the Democratic Party/Olive Tree Senate parliamentary group; re-elected in 2013); and Sergio Mattarella (2015–, former Christian Democrat and former member of the Democratic Party, at the time of his election no party affiliation). The president is the head of the Italian state. He is elected by a body made up of the members of the House of Deputies (630) and the Senate (315 plus all senators for life) joined by 58 representatives of Italy's 20 regional councils. The total is approximately 1010. The candidate to the presidency must obtain three fourths of the votes in the first three ballots. Starting with the fourth ballot, an absolute majority is required. In a parliament in which strict voting discipline has always been quite rare, even more so when the vote is secret, both thresholds are rather high. No surprise that, in several cases, for instance, Leone (23), Saragat (21), Scalfaro (16), Pertini (16), a long sequence of voting has been necessary. There have also been two exceptional cases, Francesco Cossiga (1985) and Carlo Azeglio Ciampi (1999), when the largest parties reached an agreement before the vote and, as a consequence, the president was elected by a sizable majority on the first ballot. On April 22, 2013, Giorgio Napolitano won an unprecedented re-election on the sixth ballot, obtaining more votes (738) than he had received seven years before (543). In Italy, there is no Vice-President. In emergency situations, the Speaker of the Senate temporarily exercises the functions and the powers of the president.

The president is in office for seven years. In the Italian Constitution there is no term limit for the President of the Republic. However, before the fateful and dramatic re-election of Napolitano, no president had ever been re-elected, despite indications on the part of some of them (for instance, Saragat and Pertini) to be available and more than willing to serve a second term. All former presidents automatically become senators for life. Though often considered, wrongly, a largely ceremonial office, endowed with limited institutional and political powers, the presidency of the Italian Republic has been coveted by many politicians as the crowning of their political life. There is no previous, open, public, and transparent debate on the merits and the qualities of the candidates before the actual voting begins, and there are no official candidates, that is, no political personality has ever declared his intention to "run for" the presidency. Usually, even several months before the election, a certain number of names are tossed around by political supporters, pundits, and commentators. While the pool of personalities owning the necessary credentials—paramount among which is a long political career—is quite limited, it has always been extremely difficult to predict the winner. Overall, in almost all the cases, the front-runners have not succeeded in being elected.

THE ELECTIONS OF THE PRESIDENTS

The narratives referring to the way the 12 Italian presidents have been elected reveal a lot of information about Italian politics as a whole. This is usefully presented and synthesized in Table 7.1.

While no pattern is clearly detectable, and each and every election and president tells a specific story, there is an important common element. All elections have been highly politicized. They have revolved not just around the selection of the best candidate

Table 7.1 Presidents of the Italian Republic, 1948–2013

Year	No. of ballots	President elected	Age	Votes	Electoral college	% of votes	Party of the President
1948	4	Einaudi	74	518	900	57,6	Liberal Party
1955	4	Gronchi	68	658	843	78,1	Christian Democracy
1962	9	Segni	71	443	855	51,8	Christian Democracy
1964	21	Saragat	66	646	963	67,1	Social Democratic Party
1971	23	Leone	63	518	1008	51,4	Christian Democracy
1978	16	Pertini	82	832	1011	82,3	Italian Socialist Party
1985	1	Cossiga	57	752	1011	74,4	Christian Democracy
1992	16	Scalfaro	74	672	1015	66,2	Christian Democracy
1999	1	Ciampi	79	707	1010	70	Independent
2006	4	Napolitano I	81	543	1009	53,8	former PCI/ Olive Tree
2013	6	Napolitano II	88	738	1007	73,3	no party affiliation
2015	4	Mattarella	74	665	1010	*60.2*	Former Democratic Party

Source: author's calculation based on the information available at: <www.quirinale.it>.

for that office, but of the candidate who could strengthen or weaken a specific strategy pursued by some parties, their leaders, and even the actual and potential governing coalitions. The 2013 election is a testimony that all the protagonists were deeply engaged in a complex and dangerous political game that only the re-election of the incumbent Napolitano could, albeit temporarily, regulate.

An election in which there are no official candidates must be organized around some informal, though practical and applicable, rules. Indeed, up to 1992 there existed a precise, though unwritten, but abided by, agreement among the governing parties (DC, PSI, PSDI, PRI, PLI). For the election of the President of the Republic the rule of alternation would be applied, that is, a non-Christian Democratic President had to be followed by a Christian Democratic one. No other specific criterion, for instance, the taking into account of the regional origins of the candidates (three of them have come from Piedmont, two each from Campania, Tuscany, and Sardinia, one from Liguria), was ever spelt out. However, informally there was a widespread belief that the personality who could aim at the presidency had to be somewhat distant from active politics and above it—*au dessus de la mêlée*—and someone who had not behaved in a highly partisan and controversial manner. This explains why five out of the twelve elected presidents have served as Speakers of the House (four) and the Senate (one). In fact, the office of Speaker was (all too) often considered a stepping stone toward the presidency, and all incumbent Speakers felt they were potential candidates. Finally, in a way, all governing majorities attempted to choose a President of the Republic who would strengthen their coalition and help them to pursue their political goals, while both the Communists and the Neo-Fascists always attempted to weaken those majorities by "interfering" in the electoral process and, possibly, becoming determining. Since all Italian governing majorities have been subject to internal tensions and conflicts, they have rarely succeeded in electing their first choice; partially due to the fact that there was rarely just one agreed-upon and impeccable "first" choice. Some fractions of the usually composite governmental majorities often found themselves willing and/ or obliged to look for the votes of the Communists, and, in one blatant case (Leone's election in 1971), even of the Neo-Fascists. Hence, most of the candidates, as well as their party leaders, had to take into serious account, if not the preferences, certainly the sheer numerical strength (and party discipline) of Communist parliamentarians. All this said, partisan affiliation, together with the rule of alternation, remained the dominant criterion throughout 44 years and 7 presidential elections until 1992, when the party system collapsed.

The first President of the Italian Republic was a non-Christian Democrat, the prominent liberal leader Luigi Einaudi, former Governor of the Bank of Italy and former Minister of Finance. Piedmontese, Einaudi was the wise choice of the powerful Christian Democratic leader Alcide De Gasperi, at the time prime minister, for two reasons. First, De Gasperi did not want his own party to occupy all top institutional offices. Second, he considered it advisable to distribute some of the most coveted positions to his coalition partners in order to keep together and to strengthen the governing coalition. A sober, austere, competent professor of economics, Einaudi (1948–55) performed his institutional task with a British-style restraint, never openly interfering with the activities of the government and parliament. He has made available his interpretation of the presidential office in the book *Lo scrittoio del Presidente* (1955, *The President's Desk*). Clearly understating his role and influence, Einaudi decided to offer a personal evaluation of the impact of his "presidential" opinions and views, publishing *Le prediche inutili* (1959, *Useless Preachings*).

Implementing the above-mentioned unwritten rules, after Einaudi, it was the turn of a Christian Democrat. The then secretary of the DC indicated Cesare Merzagora, then Speaker of the Senate (1953–67), not a member of the party, but very close to it. However, the centrist coalition proved unable to master the necessary majority of votes because quite a number of, especially left-leaning, Christian Democratic members of parliament were unwilling to support Merzagora. The DC internal divisions allowed the Socialists and the Communists to get into the game. A left-wing Christian Democrat, who had already served in parliament before the advent of Fascism, the Tuscan Giovanni Gronchi, Speaker of the House of Deputies since 1948, was elected on the fourth ballot, receiving also the votes of the PSI and the PCI. Gronchi played a very active political role, especially in foreign policy, showing a more cooperative attitude toward the Soviet Union. He also tried to have his way in promoting and supporting a government led by Christian Democrat Fernando Tambroni, who also received the "unacceptable" votes of the Neo-Fascists. Opposed by several mass demonstrations and rejected by his fellow Christian Democrats, Tambroni was obliged to resign. Gronchi's Presidency ended in disgrace. Following the completion of his term (1955–62), the Christian Democrats reminded their governmental partners that Gronchi had not been their official candidate and that they could not be considered fully responsible for his objectionable and controversial behavior. Therefore, they claimed it was still up to them to indicate the name of the next President.

In order to counterbalance the burgeoning center-left coalition (DC, PSI, PSDI, PRI) in which the Socialists replaced the right-wing liberals, the secretary of the DC proposed a prominent representative of the conservative wing of the party: the Sardinian Antonio Segni. Several times minister, twice prime minister, Segni served for a very short time. Elected in 1962, he became incapacitated in July 1964 in the midst of an obscure phase of the Republic, after what seemed to have been a military coup in the making, and was persuaded to resign in December 1964. The turn had arrived for another non-Christian Democrat. The choice fell on the Piedmontese Giuseppe Saragat, the man who had split the Socialist Party in 1947 and created the Social Democratic Party. Several times deputy prime minister and minister, lastly of Foreign Affairs, at the time of his complicated election that required an unprecedented number of ballots (21) Saragat was still the secretary of the PSDI. Indeed, he never ceased in his attempts to shape Italian politics. From the presidency, he first facilitated the merger between his Social Democrats and Pietro Nenni's Socialists (1966). Then (1969), he encouraged a split of the Unified Socialist Party (PSU) when he realized that, better organized and politically more capable, the Socialists were set to control the new party. Saragat (1964–71) has also been criticized for not having understood that the terrorist challenge that began in 1969 was the product of several Neo-Fascist groups which enjoyed the connivance of some sectors of the Italian state.

The most prominent candidate the Christian Democrats could put up in 1971 was definitely Aldo Moro. However, Ugo La Malfa, the secretary of the Republican Party, formulated a strong veto, alleging that Moro would open the path to a greater (and unacceptable) role in Italian politics for the Communist Party. When the secretary of the DC, Amintore Fanfani, already an unofficial candidate himself in 1964, realized that not even this time could he successfully aim at the presidency, the Christian Democrats began supporting the former Speaker of the House of Deputies (1955–63) and twice prime minister of short-lived governments, Giovanni Leone. On Christmas Eve, on the 23rd ballot, Leone barely obtained the absolute majority of votes, and then only because the Neo-Fascist parliamentarians were influenced into supporting him in exchange for an early dissolution of parliament. Amidst an obscure occurrence of violent terrorist activities, new elections offered the Neo-Fascists the best opportunity to reach their highest percentage of votes ever. Leone (December 1971–June 1978) was the second Italian President not to complete his term. Notwithstanding the precise nature of the events that led to Leone's (never a popular president) resignation, what really counts are the manifest and latent interpretations that were given for his dramatic decision.

Several commentators have stressed that Leone's position had become untenable following three extremely serious events. First, there was the discovery of Moro's corpse on May 8 that, among other elements, revealed the inability of the entire political class to confront the Red Brigades. Second, there was the outcome of a popular referendum to repeal the highly controversial law on state financing of political parties. Only thinly won by those who wanted to retain the law, the outcome was, in any case, considered a signal of major citizens' dissatisfaction with all Italian political parties and their politics. Third, and probably decisive, there appeared the likelihood of the involvement of Leone's lawyers and associates in a law firm, in what proved to be one of the major political–economic scandals of the time, and not only in Europe: the Lockheed Company having bribed several top officeholders to sell their new expensive aircraft. Under the pressure of public opinion and of fellow Christian Democrats, Leone yielded and tendered his resignation.

Not only had the turn of a non-Christian Democrat arrived, but the Socialist secretary Bettino Craxi badly wanted to assert his recently acquired political power by promoting someone from the ranks of the PSI and representing the Socialists at large and their political culture to the office of President of the Republic. In principle, most of the Christian Democrats and the Communists believed that the Socialist request was legitimate, but neither party was willing to accept any candidate perceived as politically too close and too loyal to the Socialist secretary. As a consequence, his preferred candidates were shunned and the choice fell on Sandro Pertini. Anti-fascist, prestigious leader of the Resistance movement, Speaker of the House of Deputies from 1968 to 1976, and, though a member of the Socialist Party, a political maverick all his life, Pertini, most certainly not a Craxi supporter, was elected on the 16th ballot at the age of 82. Fully and visibly enjoying his new office, flamboyant and outspoken, Pertini (1978–85) became a very popular president and played a very incisive political role. Often speaking on behalf of the Italian citizens, he appointed the first non-Christian Democratic prime minister, the Republican Giovanni Spadolini (1980–82). Later, defying the reservations of the DC, he also appointed Bettino Craxi to the office of prime minister (1983–87).

Though the ageing Pertini never hid his aspiration to be re-elected, in 1985 it was again the turn of a Christian Democrat candidate. The secretary of the party, Ciriaco De Mita, wisely decided to find a way to avoid yet another long series of ballots. Therefore, he held a round of informal negotiations with the leaders of all the parties, to the exclusion of the Neo-Fascists, and got his candidate, Francesco Cossiga, elected on the first ballot. At the time of his election, Cossiga was the Speaker of the Senate (1983–85). A prominent Christian Democratic politician from Sardinia, he had occupied several ministerial offices. He had been twice prime minister, several times minister, and, above all, Minister of Internal Affairs at the time of Moro's kidnapping (March–May 1978) by the Red Brigades. Cossiga took full responsibility for his failure and his collaborators' in discovering Moro's prison and apprehending the members of the Red Brigades. As a consequence, in a rare act of personal and political consistency, he resigned. For several years, Cossiga's presidential term was characterized by his political silence and aloofness from day-to-day events. At the beginning of the 1990s, Cossiga suddenly started a long sequence of scathing declarations criticizing the political class and deriding some of its most prominent members (whose indignant reactions only indicated that they had no sense of humor at all). His actions were called *picconate* (axe blows), since they were aimed at demolishing Italian politics as it had been practiced until then. When Cossiga sent a message to parliament asking for significant constitutional reforms made necessary in the wake of the collapse of communism, he was accused of undermining the political system and even of subverting the Constitution that he was supposed to protect and promote. An ill-advised request for impeachment came from the former Communists recently regrouped in the Party of the Democratic Left. There was no parliamentary debate on Cossiga's impeachment (later quickly shelved in the new parliament), because the president decided to resign (April 25, 1992) only a few months before the end of his term (July 1992). It was a slap in the face of a flabbergasted political class, immediately after the April 1992 general elections that had revealed the decline of all traditional parties and the beginning of a major political and institutional crisis.

With hindsight, one can state that the abrupt end of President Cossiga's term fundamentally (and appropriately) coincided with the end of the first long phase (1948–92) of the Italian Republic. Cossiga's bitter resignation added one factor to those events—that were, namely, the fall of the Berlin Wall, the Clean Hands investigation, and a wave of anti-partyocracy referendums—that had already been undermining the life of the traditional parties and their arrogant and exaggerated exercise of political power. As for the presidency, none of the parties was in the position to revive the old rule of alternation and impose its implementation. What made the election of Cossiga's successor extremely difficult and acrimonious was the attempt by both the Socialists and the majority of the Christian Democrats to blatantly exploit that opportunity for purely short-term partisan advantage(s). The political game was strictly interwoven with the institutional game, because the first act of the newly elected President of the Republic had, necessarily, to be the appointment of the prime minister. The gridlock/stalemate appeared unbreakable/impenetrable. The secretary of the Christian Democrats, Arnaldo Forlani, could not muster enough votes for himself, mostly because all the friends of the powerful outgoing Prime Minister Giulio Andreotti were fighting for their life—this being, for reasons of age, Andreotti's last chance to be elected. To put it bluntly, it was the Mafia that broke the stalemate. The assassination on May 22, 1992, of the judge Giovanni Falcone, his wife, and their bodyguards on the way from the airport to the city of Palermo, provoked an intense and widespread emotional and political anti-Mafia backlash, the first target being Andreotti himself, whose party faction in Sicily was considered contiguous with too many Mafia "friends" and activities. Spurred on by this dramatic event, on the 16th ballot parliament elected the 74-year-old Piedmontese Oscar Luigi Scalfaro to the Presidency of the Italian Republic.

While a Member of Parliament since 1946, and having several times been a minister in different departments, notably the Department of Domestic Affairs, Scalfaro was not an especially distinguished conservative Christian Democrat. A few weeks before the presidential election, he had been elected to the office of Speaker of the House of Deputies because he was considered a staunch defender of the powers and the prerogatives of parliament. Once in office, the vicissitudes and the vagaries of Italian politics obliged President Scalfaro to behave in a rather unpredictable and unprecedented way, emphasizing and asserting the powers of the presidency. Twice, in 1994 and in 1998, he rejected the requests both by Berlusconi and by Prodi for an early dissolution of parliament. Twice, in 1995 and in 1998, he encouraged, facilitated, and gave his support to governments enjoying the confidence of majorities born in parliament thanks to the migration of dozens of parliamentarians (yet another instance of Italian *trasformismo*, though nonetheless legitimate according to the Italian Constitution). On the whole, Scalfaro successfully attempted to give stability to a political system in turmoil.

His succession was quite smooth. In May 1999, Carlo Azeglio Ciampi's election on the first ballot was masterminded by Walter Veltroni, then secretary of the Left Democrats, who was capable of winning even Berlusconi's support for Ciampi, principally in order to stop the growing popular support expressed for the candidacy of an outstanding female politician, Emma Bonino, one of the leaders of the tiny, but not uninfluential, Radical Party. Never a Member of Parliament, Ciampi was a former Governor of the Bank of Italy, prime minister from April 1993 to April 1994, and Minister of the Treasury from 1996 to 1998. His term coincided with two governments led by Berlusconi, from April 2001 to April 2006. In a way, President Ciampi was obliged to act as an institutional countervailing power to the political behavior and the governmental initiatives by Berlusconi in three major areas: the judiciary, the mass media, and the conflict of interests. Also, because of a timely intervention by the Constitutional Court, Berlusconi did not get what he wanted in his attempt to tame the judiciary. His bill on the reorganization of the mass media was sent back to Parliament by President Ciampi, who accompanied it with a message stressing the need for a regulation capable of guaranteeing pluralism and impartiality of all sources of information. The law passed by Berlusconi's government on the conflict of interests fundamentally recognized its existence, but did nothing to enforce the necessary changes. Notwithstanding Ciampi's lack of personal political power, because he had no specific party support, his presidential vicissitude suggested that a strong parliamentary majority could get its way unless he was willing to run the risk of an institutional clash. Ciampi was not. His moral suasion did not fare effectively against Berlusconi's obstinacy and restlessness with all rules and procedures.

In May 2006, there existed many ambitious personalities within the center-left coalition that had barely won the legislative elections. When it became clear that none of those personalities would have received the votes of the center-right, the leaders of the center-left parties reached an agreement on the name of an impeccable candidate. Senator for life Giorgio Napolitano obtained the necessary absolute majority of votes (543 out of 990) on the fourth ballot without any convergence by the center-right. A distinguished reformist Communist politician, Napolitano had been Member of Parliament since 1953, Speaker of the House of Deputies from 1992 to 1994, Minister of Domestic Affairs from 1996 to 1998, member of the European Parliament and Chairman of the Committee on Institutional Affairs from 1999 to 2004. Appointed senator for life in 2005, at the age of 82, he became the oldest of the Italian presidents.

Napolitano's presidency deployed itself in extremely difficult times, economically and politically. A staunch believer in the centrality of Parliament in the Italian democratic Republic, the president was nevertheless gradually obliged to play a very active and incisive institutional and political role. First, in 2007 he rescued Prodi's weak government, torn by insurmountable internal contradictions. Then, between 2008 and 2011, he followed, step by step, the deterioration of the governing capabilities by Berlusconi and his changing parliamentary majority. Finally, in November 2011, he was instrumental in creating a situation that gave birth to yet another non-partisan government led by the Professor of Economics Mario Monti, for ten years European Commissioner for the Internal Market, whom he had just appointed senator for life. Throughout his intense and passionate presidency, Napolitano pressed the case for an indispensable reform of the electoral law. Taking advantage of the celebrations for the 150th anniversary of the Unification of Italy, Napolitano constantly preached the values of civic duty and political commitment, and the importance that Italy be a loyal and active member of the European Union. From many points of view, Napolitano's interpretation and fulfillment of his presidential role became not too dissimilar from that of the presidents in semi-presidential regimes. His exemplary presidency has set a high standard for his successors.

Unexpectedly, it was Napolitano himself who was asked to remain in office for another term. He had solemnly and clearly declared that a second mandate was inappropriate for two reasons: one institutional, the second personal. Institutionally, Napolitano felt that the already long seven-year term should not be replicated and he stressed that in the past no president had been re-elected. Personally, he considered himself too old for a second term that he would complete at the age of 95. In any case, he felt it would be inappropriate to accept a proposal to be re-elected in the expectation of his retirement. Two sets of political circumstances obliged him to change his mind. One, was the fact that no viable political majority existed in the Parliament elected on February 24–25, 2013, so much so that the president was unable to appoint a prime minister. The sizable parliamentary representation of a technically anti-system political movement called Five Stars made any agreement on the name of the next president fundamentally impossible. Following the dramatic defeat of two candidates chosen by the Democratic Party, the largest parliamentary group, the leaders of three parties processed sadly to the Quirinale, the presidential headquarters or mansion. Humbly they had to beg Napolitano to accept re-election. This he did, delivering a strong accusatory speech against the behavior of those politicians. In few days, Napolitano masterminded the formation of a government including the center-left, the center-right, and the center, yet one instance of a "government of the president," that is, strongly backed by him and more than willing to accept his suggestions.

In his acceptance speech, Napolitano chastised all parties and clearly stated his willingness to serve only for a time. He would go as soon as the political circumstances allowed him to do so. Hence on January 15, 2015, when he felt that the new government was solidly in office and that the reform process was effectively launched, Napolitano resigned. The election of his successor was largely masterminded by Matteo Renzi, the leader of the largest parliamentary party, the Democratic Party. The sitting Constitutional justice 74-year-old Sergio Matteralla, several times Minister (Education and Defense), had had a distinguished political career. Napolitano held him in high consideration. His personality and stature explain why he could be easily elected on the fourth ballot, on January 31, 2015.

Unfortunately, contrary to other cases—for instance, the admittedly much more important office of President of the USA—neither historians nor political scientists have ranked the Italian presidents with reference to their capabilities and performance. This task is made highly complicated, first, by the existence of two quite different phases in the history of the Italian Republic (1948–92; 1994–2013) and, second, by the lack of even a general agreement on the qualities of the president, on his political and institutional duties, and on the powers the officeholder has and can in practice wield. This is the topic of the next section.

THE ROLE OF THE PRESIDENT
AND PRESIDENTIAL POWERS

There was not much of a debate in the Constituent Assembly elected in 1946 concerning the role and the powers of the President of the Italian Republic. Once the king had been ousted by a popular referendum (June 2), it became necessary to design the figure of a president capable of exercising some of the "royal" prerogatives and powers, thus preventing any possible authoritarian degeneration. Curiously, no satisfactory example could come from the other European countries. After excluding the Southern European authoritarian regimes and the Eastern European Communist regimes, all remaining European democracies, but one, were parliamentary *monarchies* that could by no means be taken into consideration. The exception was France, whose Fourth Republic Constitution, much to General De Gaulle's political disappointment and institutional fury, designed a weak president destined to be an easy prey for the political parties. In the Italian Constituent Assembly only one alternative proposal was formulated: a strong president, directly elected by all the voters, to be accompanied and checked by a network of powerful local governments, the communes being the real backbone of the Italian state. Though introduced by Piero Calamandrei, illustrious Professor of Constitutional Law, one of the leaders of the small Action Party, his proposal never took off and was quickly put aside. Thus, the model for the Italian President was and remained essentially the one that was written into the Constitution of the Fourth French Republic. Several decades after the approval of the Italian Constitution, a distinguished scholar of the presidency, Livio Paladin (later President of the Constitutional Court) wrote that, though elastic and flexible, the role and the powers of the President of the Italian Republic were ill-defined and ambiguous.[1] A short enumeration of the tasks and the powers of the Italian President seems to suggest that his overall role is by no means simply ceremonial.

Most certainly, the Italian President is not a constitutional king in disguise. He is the official head of the state and is asked to represent the national unity. He presides over the Supreme Military Council and the Higher Council of the Judiciary. In practice, he has never been tested in his "military" role, and he has always taken the side of the judiciary in any confrontation with Parliament, the government, or the prime minister. Italian presidents enjoy the privilege of appointing as life senators personalities who have honored the country in their artistic, social, cultural, and entrepreneurial activities. The Constitution indicates that there should be only five life senators appointed by the presidents, not that each and every president can appoint five of them. Unfortunately, beginning with President Cossiga, who appointed long-time politician Giulio Andreotti senator for life, subsequent presidents, excluding Napolitano, have, in contrast with the letter and the spirit of the Constitution, appointed former prominent politicians senators for life.

The president's political and institutional activities revolve around four quite significant powers. First, he has the power of authorizing the presentation to Parliament of all bills drafted and submitted by the government and the ministers. Second, he has the power to enact the laws, but also of returning to Parliament all the bills he may consider unsatisfactorily drafted or containing elements that may potentially conflict with the constitutional principles and articles. However, it is unclear whether he can still return any bill re-examined and reapproved by Parliament after only cosmetic changes. In any case, no president has so far asked Parliament to reconsider a bill more than once. Third, the President of the Republic appoints the prime minister and, on his request, the ministers. Fourth, the president of the Republic can, "after having heard from the Speakers of both Houses, dissolve Parliament." Finally, though belonging to the category neither of prerogatives nor of powers, the president has the possibility of sending to both Houses formal messages in which he offers his guidelines for legislation and his evaluation of necessary policies. These messages must be discussed by both Houses. So far, most of these have been formally discussed, but, at best, they have only influenced the lawmaking process quite marginally.[2]

Especially in the past twenty years or so, most of the discussion concerning the powers of the president has been focused on the formation of the government and on the dissolution of Parliament (or the president's opposition to an early dissolution). From a purely descriptive point of view, one must keep in mind the fact that all Italian presidents up to 1992 simply forfeited their power to appoint the prime minister and, on his proposal, the ministers. In fact, the presidents were simply ratifying the choices made by party leaders. Only rarely were they asked by party leaders to choose the prime minister most acceptable to the DC's minor allies from among a small roster of names, usually all Christian Democrats. The only exception to this widely accepted procedure was made when, against the preferences of the Christian Democrats, President Gronchi appointed Fernando Tambroni, whose short-lived government lasted only 116 days; he was obliged to resign following major street protests and demonstrations. Most of the few known rejections by the presidents of the names of potential ministers have been the consequence of informal communications and negotiations. However, two cases stand out. President Pertini rejected the appointment of a Christian Democrat, asserting his lack of competence and integrity for the office. President Scalfaro refused to appoint Cesare Previti, Berlusconi's personal lawyer, to the office of Minister of Justice, but he could not reject Previti's appointment to the office of Minister of Defense, despite his total lack of experience and knowledge in the field.

From 1994 on, following the reform of the electoral law imposed by a popular referendum, the Italian party system had to be organized around two competing coalitions. Defined as "bipolarism," this unusual coalitional arrangement meant that coalitions had to be formed before the vote, that the voters were offered a clear choice, and that it could become immediately clear who had won the elections. The leader of the winning coalition found himself in the position of convincingly claiming the office of prime minister. Indeed, none of the three presidents of the Republic of the 1994–2012 period ever questioned the political and constitutional legitimacy of this outcome. However, serious political and constitutional problems arose when victorious prime ministers lost their parliamentary majority. This was the case with Berlusconi in 1994 and Prodi in 1998. President Scalfaro's interpretation and implementation of the Constitution strictly followed article 94: "The government must have the confidence of both houses." Therefore, he both rejected Berlusconi's and Prodi's request for an immediate dissolution of Parliament following their loss of parliamentary confidence, and actively allowed the formation of another government. In a way, the same interpretation was provided by President Napolitano when the 2008 Berlusconi's parliamentary majority proved to be no longer operational/functional. In November 2011, Napolitano explored whether another parliamentary majority existed that would be willing and capable to support a non-partisan government made of professors, *grands commis*, and technocrats, and led by Mario Monti.

In all these quite important cases, the Italian presidents have been shown to wield significant powers to implement the Constitution. Once they received from both Speakers the indispensable information that there was a majority of parliamentarians willing to support a new government promising to function with effectiveness, the presidents could legitimately reject all requests for an early dissolution of Parliament. On the whole, though with some differences deriving from the political circumstances and their personalities, Scalfaro, Ciampi, and Napolitano have consistently fulfilled the image and the substance of an active and incisive role for their office. The best way to evaluate the role of the President of the Italian Republic is contained in a metaphor formulated by Giuliano Amato, Professor of Constitutional Law, twice prime minister, and several times minister. According to Amato, the battery of the presidential powers is like an *accordion*. When the parties are strong they may, and most often will, prevent the president from "opening" the accordion and playing it to its full extension. This was largely the situation between 1948 and 1992. All the players knew and accepted the rules of the game. Only rarely did the presidents challenge the power of the parties and their leaders, usually with negative results. When, for a variety of reasons, the parties are weak, that is, in the post-1992 situation, then not only do the presidents enjoy the opportunity to put to work their institutional powers, they must do so because their actions are indispensable in making the system work.

How then, can the overall role of the President of the Italian Republic be defined? No doubt, from time to time, he has been asked to play the role of referee in a complex game involving the government, parliament, and the judiciary. Though it would be highly inappropriate for him to counterbalance the government by siding with the parliamentary opposition, in some exceptional circumstances he may still try to convey to the government, parliament, and public opinion his interpretation of the preferences of the citizens. This he can do more effectively if he defines his role, above all, as that of the guardian of the Constitution, perhaps of the living *voice* of the Constitution, and attempts to exercise his moral suasion. In all likelihood, it has been Napolitano who has best interpreted and implemented his role as the voice of the Constitution. Throughout his Presidency, on many an occasion, he has truly preached the values of the Constitution, the importance of national unity, the learning and practicing of civic duties.

THE FUTURE OF THE PRESIDENCY

As long as Italian democracy was, at the high cost of becoming a suffocating *partyocracy*, tightly controlled and guided by the political parties, there was little or no discussion at all about the role of the presidency. The parties chose the President of the Republic to play a largely ceremonial role and to rubberstamp all the decisions taken and the policies formulated by the parties. Few, though not minor, attempts actively to intervene in political matters have characterized in different ways the presidencies of Gronchi, Segni,

Saragat, Leone, and perhaps Pertini. On the whole, however, the "ceremonial" inter-pretation established clear limits to the presidential practice. When the parties became weaker and the postwar party system collapsed, the presidents discovered not only that their constitutional powers were significant, but also that they had to utilize them for the sake of the preservation and functioning of the political system and Italian democracy. The last two years of Cossiga's presidency (1990–92) were a sort of watershed. Two ques-tions have been raised since. First, if the Italian President is indeed so powerful, should it not become necessary to devise and apply precise checks on his behavior? Second, if the President's role is no longer confined to a limited number of tasks to be fulfilled in a trad-itional parliamentary democracy, should not a clear and visible conscious transition to a different model of government, for instance, French-type semi-presidentialism, that entails the direct popular election of the president, endowed with executive powers, be entertained, formulated, and implemented?

The political and institutional trajectory of the Italian president(s) of the Republic is, at the same time, a consequence of the many problems existing in the relationships between the government and parliament, and a factor in their always temporary solu-tion. The role and powers of the president will have to be redefined, together with the model of government the Italians choose and will be able to shape.

NOTES

1. L. Paladin, "Presidente della Repubblica," in *Enciclopedia del Diritto*, vol. 35 (Milan: Giuffré, 1988), 165–242.
2. The chapters in M. Luciani and M. Volpi (eds.), *Il Presidente della Repubblica*, (Bologna: Il Mulino, 1997) closely analyze all the presidential powers.

CHAPTER 8

GOVERNMENT AND PRIME MINISTER

MAURO CALISE

THE Italian government is commonly seen as the Cinderella among European nations. When compared to other democracies, the Italian Consiglio dei Ministri (Council of Ministers, CdM) is singled out for its lack of cohesion as well as effective steering capacity. Elements which can only be enhanced by the weakness—both institutional and political—of its president, or prime minister.[1] Does this conventional picture still hold true? As we shall see in this chapter, the Italian republican government has gone through three distinct phases. The first one has characterized the golden age of *partitocrazia*, spanning from 1946 to 1976. Cabinet duration was among the shortest of all European democracies, and crises to form a new government—often with pretty much the same ministers—often lasted several months. However, cabinet instability was, to a large extent, compensated by the fact that most succeeding governments were composed by the same political coalition, with the same major party—the Christian Democrats— always nominating the prime minister from its own ranks. This also resulted in the extraordinary continuity of the ministerial elite, with a high degree of role institutionalization. The party era of Italian governments can thus be properly described by the noted formula of a "stable instability."

The second phase covers roughly 15 years, from the end of the 1970s to 1992, when the *Tangentopoli* crisis suddenly brought the partitocratic regime to an end. This is the "age of reform," as it was characterized by a silent revolution in the governmental structure, leading to a considerable increase in its normative and organizational powers. These changes were brought about by a series of cumulative efforts developed by a top-ranking group of *commis-d'Etat*, who could mainly rely on the political backing of the lay parties—the Socialists and the Republicans—which had, by the early eighties, at last gained access to Palazzo Chigi.

The third period covers the last twenty years, the so-called Second Republic. For lack of a better epigraph, I shall title it "The Winter of Discontent." In the dismal recollection of Giuliano Amato—one of the key personalities of the "Age of Reform"—the

Italian First Republic collapsed just when it seemed that a more efficient executive had at last been set in place, if not in motion. The demise of the old ruling parties suddenly deprived the governmental machinery of an experienced ruling class. On the other side, it seemed at first to pave the way for a larger and much more outspoken movement for governmental change, a movement based on repeated and extensive referendum campaigns to spearhead widespread innovation in the political system. The core of the referendum manifesto was to introduce a new electoral law, which would rapidly align Italy to the Westminster model, based on the alternance between two parties winning the election on a clear popular mandate. History, as it often the case, took a different path.

An incoherent bipolarism took the place of the bipartitism dream. And the Berlusconi *ventennio* gave to executive dominance a very different flavor—and results—from those that the referendum movement had hoped for. The Cavaliere showed little interest into institutional reforms, and only tried to further enlarge the absolute command he enjoyed within his personal party. Thus, he became a prisoner of his own strength, until the inevitable political—and physical—decay.

In the middle of one more transition, now from the Second to the Third Republic, the Italian government seems to have lost the "*spinta propulsiva*" it had eventually gained by the end of the First Republic. In retrospect, it may sound like a bitter irony that the partitocratic regime would collapse, only to give way to a much more risky and unstable party rule, based on personal entrepreneurship rather than on oligarchic cohesion. The road to the Westminster model of party government still appears a long and winding one.

A Stable Instability

The best insight into the original framing of the Italian Council of Ministers is the definition of its president as a *primus inter pares*. That is, from the very beginning, the Italian cabinet was organized on the basis of the explicit refusal of a leadership role of its chief executive. There are two main explanations for this choice. One concerns the fascist legacy of a strong anti-monocratic bias. All through the Constituent Assembly debates, the presidentialist option—which was heralded by influential jurists such as Piero Calamandrei—was rejected on the grounds that it could open the way to the resurgence of an authoritarian regime. Such an argument would easily spill over into the more general statement that a strong executive was not only dangerous, but unnecessary. The guarantee for governmental stability and efficiency should not rely on the constitutional framework, but on a clear political mandate. One which could only be provided by the political parties' support. In fact, the second explanation for the government's institutional fragility leads to the dominant role of mass parties as the main pillar of the overall political system.[2] This was a shared conviction between the two larger parties, the Christian Democrats and the Communists.

The weakening of the government as a separate institution and the centrality of parties had, as a direct consequence, strengthened the role of parliament, leading to an all-parliamentarian regime which would be defined as "*parlamentarismo integrale*."[3] Its main characteristic consisted in the frequent co-optation of the opposition party in the legislative process. If the banning of the PCI from Palazzo Chigi—for geopolitical reasons—had led many observers to speak of a *conventio ad excludendum*, one could argue that, in most policy arenas, there, in turn, existed a *conventio ad includendum* which would make Italy the prototype of a "consociational democracy," in sharp contrast with the radical ideological struggles which, in many occasions, pitted one party fiercely against the other.[4]

Consociational democracy was a major trait of the First Republic and influenced several areas of its political system. With respect to the executive sphere, the lack of an alternance in government further contributed to cabinet instability. Since the cabinet would not fear being ousted by an alternative political majority, its worst enemies resided within the very parties composing the ruling alliance. One should then not be surprised that, during the first three decades of existence, the average length of a cabinet, in Italy, would be less than a year. Yet, in spite of continuous crises, which should have resulted in a disorderly and unpredictable decision-making environment, the Italian governments showed one remarkable stabilizing feature in the composition and recruitment of its ministerial elite. One of the most important contributions of the Christian Democrats to the democratic foundations of the republican regime was through the very close connection established between the party electoral roots in the periphery and its governing leadership at the top.[5]

There are three features which stand out as the cornerstones of the governmental elite. The first one was territorial representation. There was a constant and clear-cut relationship between the size of a region—measured by the number of its voters—and the number of ministerial posts allocated to representatives from that region. And—not surprisingly—an even stronger relationship existed between the votes to the DC and the regional distribution of government seats.[6] The overall picture was one with a very close correspondence between consent for the dominant party in the periphery and the composition of the top decision-making body. To better appreciate the role of such a balanced distribution one needs only look at the lack of any territorial equilibrium in the governments of the Second Republic, which have been characterized by a fierce antagonism among the various sections of the country.

The second cornerstone of the First Republic's ministerial elite was the weight of preference votes in determining career progression, from junior ministers to the most influential cabinet posts. Up until 1991, Italy had a proportional electoral system. Seats at the Chamber of Deputies were assigned on the basis of the percentage of votes each party had gained in each electoral district. Within the party list, candidates were elected according to the number of preference votes each one had been able to collect. Once we turn to the preference counting for all undersecretaries and ministers over a 30-year time span, we can observe three distinctive traits. The first one is that, in a great majority of cases, access to an undersecretary post was reserved to MPs scoring the highest preference votes' percentage. An even stricter rule was applied for the promotion from undersecretary to a ministerial position, where scoring among the top preference percentages became a prerequisite. Last not least, no less than 100,000 preference votes were necessary in order to be nominated to core ministries, such as Interior, Defense, or Foreign Affairs. It should be noted that the ministries with the highest preference score do not belong to the traditional clientelistic sectors—such as Public Works, Education, or Mail and Communication—but are concentrated at the very heart of the state apparatus.[7]

With territorial distribution and preference accumulation, a third factor distinguished the career pathways of the ministerial elite: its institutionalization. We can measure this through a number of indicators. The first one concerned membership of the parliament. Cases of outsiders were extremely rare. The ministerial career was clearly reserved for those who had previously passed through the electoral test, and spent several years in getting acquainted with committee and assembly routines and procedures. Second, the percentage of ministers which had previously held a position as undersecretaries grew from 16.2 in the first legislature to 73.2 in the fifth. A number which became even higher when referred to the inner circle of the superelite, the 152 politicians who scored at least 5 presences, that is, higher than the average of 4 for the overall group of 452 ministerial appointments.

This leads us to the third institutionalization indicator, the lengthy permanence of a restricted number of people in the higher echelons of government. The superelite, while making up a third of the whole group, concentrated in its hands two thirds of the governmental positions, as minister and/or undersecretary. This trend became strongest for the core oligarchy of 27 people, who numbered at least 12 appointments. The continuity and institutionalization of the governmental elite became an important countervailing factor for the frequent cabinet crises;[8] a phenomenon which closely resembles what had been observed in the French case.[9]

Territorial distribution and preferences accumulation as a mark of a strong connection between center and periphery, along with the "stable instability" of the governmental leadership tightly held in the expert hands of a core group of superelite: this is the picture of the Italian party oligarchy as it stood after the first three decades of the Republic. A picture which may seem to figure as a tribute to a self-confident and ever-lasting partitocratic regime. Yet, as it is often the case with historical trends, the peak in the strength of the governing elite was only a prelude to its quick demise.

If we look at the same picture just ten years after, the main pillars of ministerial pathways and stability had collapsed. The weight of the superelite was rapidly cut by over a half, clearly a sign of the passing of age of a generation which had not found as stable a substitute. This was also coincident with a higher rate of turnover in the composition of each cabinet and, even more important, a sharp decrease in the percentage of ministers who had been previously also been appointed as undersecretary. This was a clear sign that many of the new entries didn't pass through the traditional career pathways and, in many cases, directly accessed the ministerial post from outside the party milieu. These elements of discontinuity were emphasized by the sheer drop in the average number of preference votes per minister, which went down by over a third from its peak at 100,000 in the sixth legislature.[10]

According to our main indicators, the Italian governing elite had already shown, by the mid-eighties, evident signs of an internal disruption. Well ahead of the dramatic collapse in the wake of *Tangentopoli*'s scandals, we can see that the traditional hold on the decision-making process was changing hands and, to a large extent, shape. This change appears to be coincident with—as well as caused by—the weakening of the party machines as the stronghold of the political system. In analyzing the transition from the First to the Second Republic, there has been a general consensus that the crisis of the governing parties was mainly due to the spread of corruption within political ranks. It is interesting to note that this phenomenon may have been facilitated by the turnover we have observed in the governing class. While the change in the ruling class would become most evident after the prosecution, between 1992 and 1994, of about a half of the Italian MPs,[11] it appears that the final breakdown followed a decade-long erosion of established party linkages.

It would take two decades to fully measure the depth of the political void opened up by the demise of the party-based governing class. At first, it seemed that the end of the partitocratic regime would give birth to a stronger as well as a more stable executive, thanks to two major institutional changes. The most visible one was the new electoral law, a quasi-majoritarian system which replaced the proportional one which had been in existence since the founding of the Republic. With the "Mattarellum," Italy would at last move into the club of the alternance democracies, where a clear winner would result directly from the ballot, one which could be defeated, and dismissed, in the following election. The second change was, perhaps, even more important. All through the eighties, Italy had witnessed a silent revolution of its top executive.[12] The Council of Ministers had begun to strip a relevant part of the legislative process away from parliament. At the same time, Palazzo Chigi witnessed a thorough reorganization of its administrative powers, with most of the new and more efficient functions falling under the direct control of the prime minister. The merging of both processes—a new electoral law and a reformed executive—seemed to be at last moving Italy toward the promised land of a stronger government.

THE AGE OF REFORM

The early phases of the transformation of the Italian executive were outlined in a seminal study by Sabino Cassese,[13] who was the first to question the general assumption that, in Italy, "there existed no government." The drive for change gained momentum all through the eighties, as a combination of two main trends. The first trend concerned the shift of legislative power from parliament to the Council of Ministers. The second trend consisted of the strengthening of the Executive Office on organizational grounds. In both cases, a pivotal role was played by the tenacious efforts of a think tank which included several of the most prominent Italian jurists, some of whom were also politically active: Andrea Manzella became General Secretary of the Presidency of the Council of Ministers; Sabino Cassese and Franco Bassanini served as Ministers for the Public Function; while Giuliano Amato became prime minister in 1992 and 2000.

The expansion of cabinet legislation occurred through two main channels, the emergency bills and delegated legislation. On strict constitutional grounds, *emergency bills* can be enacted on the condition of exceptional urgency. They then need to gain parliament's approval within the next 60 days. However, by the late seventies, it became an ordinary practice to emanate emergency decrees without any evident reason of urgency, and to reiterate them, shortly before their expiry date, up to six or seven times.[14] This often made approval or rejection by the parliament useless, the more so if the bill was related to some kind of expenditure which had, in meantime, already been deployed. In spite of continuous criticism on the media and in constitutional debates, emergency bills have since become one of the main sources of all Italian legislation.

As for *delegated legislation*, its increase mainly derived from the parliament's adoption of EU regulations, through broad guideline laws calling for later enactment of more specific bills by the government. This was also the channel through which a growing number of major reforms were handled, including those of the pension system and the overall reorganization of the ministries, or, more recently, with the new provisions for tax regulation, the reform of the radio and television broadcasting system, or the new dispositions regarding fiscal federalism. Along with the rise of its direct legislative power, the Council of Ministers also improved its indirect normative role through a better control of the legislative agenda in the parliament, both on the floor and in the committees, thus promoting its own bills more effectively.

The expansion of the government's normative power could only be possible thanks to a thorough reorganization of its administrative capacities.[15] The reform process, dating from the early 1980s, took a more coherent turn with the August 1988 law 400 eventually providing the legislative framework for a brand new executive office, one that Italy had been badly in need of since its unification.[16]

Along with further improvements enacted, ten years after, by the Prodi and D'Alema cabinets, there emerged three main innovation trends. The first one was the creation of a strong administrative machinery, with a general secretariat which served as the coordination unit for all presidential branches of activity. The secretary general oversees over a wide range of offices supporting the premier's institutional leadership, from those directly interacting with the premier to what is perhaps the most important innovation: the offices in charge of personnel and budget management where Palazzo Chigi was at last granted full autonomy, as had long been the case with other constitutional bodies as the House, the Senate, and the Presidency of the Republic. The premier became thus able to "freely build and dismantle its own offices (. . .) with internal decrees which are not subject to the preliminary legitimacy control by the *Corte dei conti*."[17]

The secretary general also became the first and foremost representative of a fiduciary relationship between the premier and the top executives within Palazzo Chigi, thus inaugurating a law abiding spoils-system based on the temporary recruitment of highly specialized professionals. A notable example is offered by the Department of Economic

Affairs, once a marginal place for handling union relations and now transformed into a think tank providing guidelines and proposals for internal and international purposes. The Department for Juridical and Legal Affairs (DAGL) also plays a strategic role and has become the brain trust and operational branch for the massive amount of normative Acts, which, mainly through delegated legislation, represent the rise of government influence in the lawmaking process.

Along with the rapid increase of Palazzo Chigi's vertical control over policymaking, a no less relevant expansion concerned the outreach of the Executive Office into a number of key internal and international domains through interinstitutional networking. A major role is played by the Ministry for Parliamentary Relationships, who could count on a specific department within the Presidency of the Council in his task of dealing with both the floor and the committees in order to streamline legislative activities according to the government's agenda. A second interinstitutional front is represented by the relationships with local authorities, both at the regional and the municipal level, through the Stato-Regioni and Stato-Città conferences, where the government rapidly became the key player in the complex game of redistribution of institutional power. As a consequence of a series of devolutionary reforms, regional and municipal administrations were being allocated a set of relevant functions stripped from the ministries. Through its pivotal intermediary role, the Executive office became the recipient of the ultimate decision-making power.

The third area of interinstitutional intervention by the Executive Office concerns its relationships with the European Union; it aims to keep in close touch with and, if necessary, lobby the offices in Brussels where the main guidelines and budgetary provisions of EU legislation are drafted.

THE WINTER OF DISCONTENT

At the onset of the Second Republic, there seemed to be several favorable conditions for the consolidation of a stronger executive, both at the institutional and the political level. A number of legislative reforms, culminating in law 400 of August 1988, had paved the way for a more autonomous and more efficient prime ministerial office. One which could more effectively steer a growing number of normative prerogatives that the government had been stripping from parliament, a trend which would be reinforced in the following decade. At the same time, the collapse of the old-style partitocracy and the adoption of a new and quasi-majoritarian electoral law seemed to create the perfect political environment for the emergence of a two-party system, inspired by the Westminster model that had been the constant benchmark for the reform movement and its referendum campaigns.[18] Why is it so that events took such a different turn, leading to a permanent condition of political instability.

There are several factors which contributed to derailing the Italian progress toward a stronger and more stable executive. The first, and perhaps foremost, was the failure of the new electoral law to provide the bipartisan outcome envisioned by its proposers. According to the most orthodox Westminster supporters, so disappointing an outcome was mainly due to the fact that the law kept smaller parties alive through the provision that one fourth of parliamentary seats be allocated on a proportional basis. This thus led to one of the main obstacles to a full-fledged working of a majoritarian electoral system, as pointed out in Giovanni Sartori's seminal criticism to Maurice Duverger: the survival of radical, non-coalitional parties.[19] This thesis was to be fully confirmed by the role of Rifondazione Comunista on the left and Lega Nord on the right in undermining the cohesion of their respective coalitions.

Secondly, the survival of the radical parties' determinant role in coalition building was also instrumental in fostering an ideological opposition to any further strengthening of the chief executive. The North League relentlessly pushed toward a devolution of the state machinery, thus opposing any form of reinforcement of political and institutional control at the top. On the opposite side, the radical left fiercely contrasted any form of constitutional reform which could revive the presidentialist option that had been banned at the very onset of the Italian Republic. This stance received a very favorable reception in the wider center-left establishment. Both former communist and Christian Democratic politicians were themselves only too eager to use Berlusconi's strong personality and authoritarian leadership style as a pretext to dismiss any major change to the prime ministerial office. With the partial—and unfulfilled—exception of the Ulivo's 1996 original manifesto, the strengthening of the Italian executive through a completion of the 1980s reforms was never on the center-left agenda.

Strangely enough, it also never became a distinct and firmly sought after objective of Silvio Berlusconi. In retrospect, the lack of a clear-cut presidentialist design looms large as the main limit of the Cavaliere's political career. Perhaps the main reason for Berlusconi's passive record as an institutional reformer lies in his absolute control over his party. By inventing and rapidly building a prototype personal party,[20] which transferred to a political organization the same kind of full-fledged command he had enjoyed as an entrepreneur over his own companies, Berlusconi remained intimately convinced that institutional settings and procedures, even in a presidentialist mold, would be a filter, if not an obstacle, for his need for unconstrained decision-making power. His only major wide-ranging organizational reform—after the invention of Forza Italia—consisted in his attempt to enlarge the scope of his original party, transforming Forza Italia into the Popolo della Libertà in an attempt to annex and incorporate his former allies. But the attempt to shape a superpersonal party in order to stabilize the center-right coalition rapidly failed, leading to the eventual collapse of the Second Republic.

On strictly institutional grounds, it may appear a paradox that Italy's stable instability, which characterized the First Republic, would lead the way to the unstable stability that has been the crucible of the Second. When measured in terms of cabinet duration there is a wide difference between the two periods, with Berlusconi's *ventennio* scoring an unprecedented executive continuity. The average length moves sharply higher, from 315 days in the First Republic to 678 days in the Second. The more so if one considers that the longest cabinet in the First Republic, Craxi I, was a clear exception with its three years of duration, while there are three cases in the Second Republic which score a similar or better result, with the first Prodi government lasting 874 days, the second Berlusconi setting the 1412 all-time record, almost matched by his fourth cabinet, with 1287.[21] Yet a closer look behind these number shows that mere duration is not, by itself, an indicator of improved government stability.

One first consideration concerns the fact that government duration is hampered by an extremely high rate of alternation. During the First Republic, a short cabinet duration was compensated by the extraordinary continuity of the same party as the main ruling actor for almost half a century, an even more decisive factor when measured through the tenure of the ministerial elite we have analyzed earlier in this chapter. To the contrary, the much longer cabinet duration in the Second Republic seems to be mainly caused by the risk that a cabinet crisis could quickly lead to an alternation in government by the opposing coalition.[22] In fact, among all European nations, Italy scores by far the maximum alternation risk, thus showing that a decisive cause for cabinet duration may have been fear that the ruling coalition be ousted from power. This fear would not, however, restrain governmental partners from fierce intercoalitional feuds. Besides daily chronicles detailing each coalition party, as well as their leaders, as being continuously engaged in battling and discrediting one another, one needs only to recall that, in several cases, a cabinet was terminated by a no-confidence vote from within its own ranks, the so-called *ribaltone* or *ribaltino*.

Along with political intra-coalition divisiveness, another major indicator of cabinet instability during the Second Republic is offered by the composition and recruitment of its ministerial elite. Several characteristics accounting for the cohesiveness of the First Republic's "superelite" seem to have been weakened, if not altogether eliminated. The "classic unwritten rule of the need for a junior ministerial apprenticeship is no longer at work," thus paving the way for a growing number of "expert ministers—technicians or 'semi-technicians' (politicians with a strong policy profile)"[23] to directly enter the ministerial ranks. This eventually led to a "remarkable, though not dramatic, reduction of the typical parliamentary origin of government ministers in Italy."[24] In light of such widespread political and ministerial fragmentation, it comes as no surprise that even the longest lasting cabinets were "characterized by an unusual number of reshuffles and internal changes."[25]

If then evaluated on the more substantive grounds of governmental cohesiveness, the Italian executive seems rather to have been marching the Leninist way, one step forward and two backwards. The result was an eventual collapse of the so-called bipolarity, in the wake of the February 2013 elections, and the unprecedented formation of a facade coalition between two fiercely antagonistic parties.

PARTIES AGAINST PRESIDENTS

The substitution of the traditional party oligarchies with more personalized actors and roles is a process which has impacted upon all Western democracies, both at the political and institutional levels, as is shown through the analytical framework of "presidentialization."[26] Yet the impact has been gradual, and parties have, in most countries, learned to coexist with—and be mutually helpful to—stronger leaders. To the contrary, the Italian case showed an outright clash between presidents and parties.[27]

On the right, the rise of Silvio Berlusconi marked a sharp discontinuity from the oligarchic decision-making system run by the Christian Democrats. A highly successful entrepreneur, both by biography and self-representation, the Cavaliere tried to impose his managerial style to the executive bureaucratic maze, only to rapidly discover that running one's own company was a quite different job than steering the governmental apparatus. While the founder of Forza Italia certainly was, for a long time, in the most favorable position to complete the process of institutional reform of the Italian executive through a fully-fledged prime ministerial dominance, he ended up becoming the captive of his own parliamentary majority. He ended his political career as a "divided premier,"[28] and, eventually, as a divided leader within the party he had once ruled as his personal property.

In the center-left camp, the dismantling of the two mass parties which had dominated the political system failed to produce the "new model army" that many reformers had envisioned. As we have seen in the first section of this chapter, the main contribution of the mass parties, both in the government and the opposition, was to establish a solid connection between center and periphery. This happened through grounding ministerial careers firmly in the territorial roots of electoral consensus and regional representation, and by intermingling the political class command line with the state bureaucratic apparatus. This fusion would cost the Italian party-based governmental system the unfriendly tag of "*partitocrazia*." But—with all its costs and limitations—this also provided the young Republic and recently constituted nation with a viable mechanism to hold the country together.

By eventually joining forces in the founding of the Democratic Party, neither the former Christian Democrats nor the post-Communist political class proved able to reinvent their legacy. The PD, by refusing to adapt itself to the new environment of personalized leadership, both at the institutional and the party level, continued to cherish the restoration of the "good ol' system," based on oligarchic party rule. Such a conservative approach eventually resulted in two major setbacks. On one side, the ostracism of a strong leader as the main catalyst of electoral consensus brought about the disastrous defeat of the February 2013 national elections. On the other side, it soon became clear that the defense of collective leadership was little more than a desperate attempt to hide the far less illustrious reality of extreme internal factionalism. As of the spring 2013, Wikipedia listed 19 *correnti* (the Italian euphemism for faction), and the party organization had become the battleground of fiercely competing micro-notables;[29] thus leaving hardly any doubt that the main surviving legacy of the First Republic's party environment was the persistence of clientelistic networks.

All through the 1980s, the main avenue toward a stronger and more stable executive seemed to have been paved by a number of reforms concerning the reorganization of the executive office, aiming at establishing a model of prime ministerial dominance influenced by the German or British systems. The failure to consolidate this trend during the Second Republic, due to the joint outcome of Berlusconi's incapacity and the center-left's hostility, left the Italian political system in an unprecedented state of disarray. The deterioration of both major parties and the rise of Grillo's protest movement turned fragile Italian bipolarism into a tripolar system, which doesn't allow for any stable cabinet formation. Unless the route to reform is quickly resumed by forceful leadership, in the struggle between presidents and parties—whoever wins the next battle—Italy will have lost the war.

Notes

1. Note that the formal Italian title for the Cabinet is the Council of Minsters ("Consiglio dei Ministri"), while the title of the prime minister is actually the President of the Council of Ministers. In order to avoid confusion with the President of the Republic (the formal head of state in Italy), and to ease comparison with other parliamentary regimes, this chapter will refer to the President of the Council as prime minister or premier, and the Council of Ministers as the government or Cabinet.
2. Pietro Scoppola, *La repubblica dei partiti: evoluzione e crisi di un sistema politico 1945–1996* (Bologna: Il Mulino, 1997).
3. Gianfranco Miglio, "Le contraddizioni interne del sistema parlamentare-integrale," *Rivista Italiana di Scienza Politica* 14 (1984), 209–232.
4. Arendt Lijphart, *Patterns of Democracy: Government Forms and Performance in Thirty-Six Countries* (New Haven: Yale University Press, 1999); Alessandro Pizzorno, "Le difficoltà del consociativismo," in *Le radici della politica assoluta* (Milan: Feltrinelli, 1993), 285–313.
5. Mauro Calise and Renato Mannheimer, *Governanti in Italia: un trentennio repubblicano 1946–1976* (Bologna: Il Mulino, 1982).
6. Ibid., 45–68.
7. Ibid., 69–107.
8. Ibid., 109–142.
9. Mattei Dogan, "How to Become a Cabinet Minister in France: Career Pathways, 1870–1978," *Comparative Politics* 12 (1979), 1–25.
10. Mauro Calise and Renato Mannheimer, "Come cambiano i governanti di partito," *Rivista Italiana di Scienza Politica* 16 (1986), 461–484.
11. Luca Ricolfi, *L'ultimo Parlamento: sulla fine della prima Repubblica* (Rome: Carocci, 1993), 117.
12. Mauro Calise, "Il governo," in Francesco Barbagallo, *Storia dell'Italia repubblicana* (Turin: Einaudi, 1997), 347–397.
13. Sabino Cassese, "Is There a Government in Italy? Politics and Administration at the Top," in Richard Rose and Ezra N. Suleiman, *Presidents and Prime Ministers* (Washington: American Enterprise Institute for Public Policy, 1980), 171–199.
14. Vincent Della Sala and Amie Kreppel, "Dancing without a Lead: Legislative Decrees in Italy," in John M. Carey and Matthew Soberg Shugart, *Executive Decree Authority* (Cambridge: Cambridge University Press, 1998), 175–196.
15. Annarita Criscitiello, *Il cuore dei governi: le politiche di riforma degli esecutivi in prospettiva comparata* (Naples: Edizioni scientifiche italiane, 2004).

16. Alessandro Pajno and Luisa Torchia, eds., *La riforma del governo. Commento ai decreti legislativi n. 300 e n. 303 del 1999 sulla riorganizzazione della Presidenza del consiglio e dei ministeri* (Bologna: Il Mulino, 2000).

17. Francesco Battini, "La presidenza del consiglio: il modello organizzativo," in Pajno and Torchia, eds., *La riforma del governo*, 107–121.

18. Gianfranco Pasquino, *Restituire lo scettro al principe. Proposte di riforme istituzionali* (Rome and Bari: Laterza, 1985).

19. Giovanni Sartori, "The Influence of Electoral Systems: Faulty Laws or Faulty Methods?," in Bernard Grofman and Arendt Lijphart, eds., *Electoral Laws and their Political Consequences* (New York: Agathon Press, 1986), 43–68.

20. Mauro Calise, *Il partito personale. I due corpi del leader* (Rome and Bari: Laterza, 2010 [2000]); and Mauro Calise, "The personal party: an analytical framework", in *Italian Political Science review / Rivista Italiana di Scienza Politica*, 3 (2015).

21. Andrea Pritoni, "La durata in carica dei governi italiani tra Prima e Seconda Repubblica," *Rivista italiana di scienza politica* 2 (2012), 221–246, 228.

22. Ibid., 242.

23. Luca Verzichelli, "The Difficult Road Towards a More Effective Process of Ministerial Selection," in Keith Dowding and Patrick Dumont, *The Selection of Ministers in Europe: Hiring and Firing* (London: Taylor & Francis, 2009), 79–100, 86.

24. Ibid.

25. Ibid.

26. Thomas Poguntke and Paul Webb, eds., *The Presidentialization of Politics: A Comparative Study of Modern Democracies* (Oxford: Oxford University Press, 2005).

27. Mauro Calise, *La Terza Repubblica* (Rome and Bari: Laterza, 2006).

28. Fortunato Musella, *Il premier diviso. Italia tra presidenzialismo e parlamentarismo* (Milan: Bocconi, 2012).

29. Mauro Calise, *Fuorigioco. La sinistra contro i suoi leader* (Rome and Bari: Laterza, 2013), 83–91.

CHAPTER 9

....

PARLIAMENT

....

SALVATORE VASSALLO

DURING the so-called First Republic (1945–1992), parliament was considered an institution central to Italian political life. Having peaked in the 1960s and 1970s, its prominence started to decline during the 1980s (section 1). During the Second Republic, parliament registered a further loss of power. Its right to bestow or deny a government the vote of confidence was curtailed on one hand by the dynamics of political bipolarity, and on the other—when elections failed to determine a clear majority—by the activism of the Presidents of the Republic (section 2). Legislative powers had been progressively handed down to government, particularly due to the changes that were made to Chamber of Deputies and Senate regulations (section 3) in order to cater for the pressing need of urgent "financial measures" (sections 4 and 5). According to the manuals and regulations, parliament should also monitor and guide governmental activity, but the proceedings through which this "directing and controlling" function should be fulfilled often become idle political role play (section 6).

Since the early 2000s, parliament has also been the subject of a heavy handed denigration campaign and subject to widespread blame, due to its huge maintenance costs, the excessive number of its members, lack of transparency, and the reputedly exorbitant indemnities paid out to individual MPs. Moreover, the 2005 electoral law effectively denies voters any control over the appointment of MPs, leaving control entirely in the hands of party heads or current leaders.[1] This makes it seemingly impossible for parliament to fulfill that pedagogical role within society to which Walter Bagehot attributed great importance in his mid-1800s overview of British parliament (section 7).

Furthermore, it is broadly recognized that the Italian Parliament might regain a more dignified reputation and greater strength in its dealings with government if the unjustifiable duplicity of structures and purpose that exists between the twin chambers—which are at present endowed with identical powers—were abolished: a reform which all political parties have pleaded for, not without remarkable hypocrisies, yet repeatedly failed to implement (section 8). The proposals advanced by Renzi's Government, that took office at the beginning of 2014, have swiftly accelerated this 20-year long debate, and may lead to further changes to the role of parliament within the political system (section 8).

Lost Centrality

The central standing of parliament in the First Republic had very different purposes with respect to those referred to when it is—or was—said, that "parliament matters" in reference to the "Westminster model."[2]

First, the Italian parliament was central because it was the arena in which negotiations were staged, and compromises found, between parties that were indispensable to the life of the unstable governments that succeeded one another in the immediate aftermath of World War II until 1994. Coalition agreements were stipulated among the political forces allied, at any given point, with the the party that found itself in relative majority—the Christian Democrats (DC)—and the main currents within it. Such coalition agreements were not reached through lengthy debates that determined detailed government platforms, as was and still is the case, for example, in Belgium and Holland; hence the coalition's strength and the government's stability were tried daily, monthly, in parliamentary halls and commissions.[3]

Second, parliament acted as a springboard for securing government positions. The chances of becoming minister or undersecretary were linked, albeit not directly, to the number of preferences with which any one MP was elected to the Chamber of Deputies.[4] The Senate's electoral system was proportional, with uninominal colleges, and so devoid of competition regarding preferences. In both cases though, reputations built in—or during the struggle to enter—parliament were the cards to play in order to access the roles of minister or undersecretary.

Third, parliament was also the place in which governing parties had to find common ground with the main opposition party. The communists, despite being consistently excluded from government alliances due to their numbers and discipline within parliament, were able to contrast the majority's stances both in the commission and during parliamentary debates.[5] They were also able to mobilize large numbers of militants and a vast array of collateral organizations that represented important social interests, and which therefore somehow had to be included in the game of pacts. Accordingly, until 1974, 75 percent of laws were directly sanctioned within the commissions, and during the first four governmental terms of office the communist parliamentary group voted in favor of 74 percent of laws passed. The percentage of commission-approved laws decreased in later legislatures, and plummeted to 20 percent in 1994.[6]

This particular kind of pact-building was induced by parliamentary regulations which gave the government no guarantees regarding the timetable for the approval of its bills while they endowed the opposition with a de facto power of veto.

Until 1971, the parliament's work schedule was drafted daily. With the regulations implemented in that year, a tame form of planning was introduced, which still had to be approved unanimously by the group leader's conference, thus making Partito Comunista Italiano (PCI) consensus essential. No time limits were envisaged for either the discussion of legislative texts or the presentation and debate of amendments. It followed that even minuscule groups, if they were as fierce as the Radials happened to be, could obstruct the debate on a single project for weeks on end. The regulations also allowed for an essentially generalized use of the secret ballot, which in turn facilitated the incursions of the so called "snipers": members of the parliamentary majority who failed to comply with party guidelines regarding a vote, either because they were representatives of particular interests or because they wished to send a specific message to the prime minister, the party secretariat, or to a minister.

Parliament also legislated on matters of detail and on internal public administration proceedings. Through impromptu yet very frequent laws—the so-called little laws—funds were allocated to single categories, groups, institutions, or local communities, and it was precisely on this ground that the individual activism of MPs was greater, and the exchanges between the majority and the opposition continuous. The centrality of parliament had thus become, during the First Republic, a professional ideology of sorts, one of the most typically Italian implications of "consensual democracy," and the other side of government inefficiency and instability.

GRANTING AND DENYING PARLIAMENTARY CONFIDENCE

If in the course of the First Republic parliament had acquired a certain centrality, it rapidly lost its bearings during the Second Republic. Bipolar dynamics, despite the many individual side bargains that were made during legislatures, limited the feasibility, effectiveness, and scope of parliamentary agreements aimed at reshaping the structure of those government coalitions the elections originated.[7] In effect, none of Second Republic's legislatures was able to reach the end of the five-year parliamentary mandate and avoid political crises.

Only in the case of the XVI legislature (2001–2006) did the crisis not entail a change of prime minister—Silvio Berlusconi—and in the combination of parties forming the parliamentary majority. During the XV legislature (2006–2008) the crisis of the second Prodi Government required anticipated general elections, precisely due to the impossibility of building a new parliamentary majority. Conversely, ten years earlier—during the XIII legislature (1996–2001)—when Romano Prodi's first government was denied confidence following the defection of the Communist Refoundation Party (PRC) in October 1998, the leader of the Democratic Party of the Left (PDS), Massimo D'Alema, was successful in his bid to be elected prime minister, thanks to the aid of a group of centre-right MPs mobilized by former President of the Republic Francesco Cossiga. However, D'Alema resigned 18 months later, in the aftermath of the centre-left's crushing defeat in the regional elections, handing the reins of government over to Giuliano Amato until the end of the legislature.

In the XVI legislature (2008–2013) a rift broke out between Silvio Berlusconi, then prime minister for the fourth time, and former National Alliance (AN) leader Gianfranco Fini, then President of the Chamber of Deputies. Following this a new parliamentary group emerged, "Future and Freedom for Italy" (FLI), composed of those centre-right MPs that had quit the governing majority. Then too, "parliamentary maneuvers" were limited to Berlusconi's search for single opposition party MPs that may have been be inclined to switch sides in order to support his government, using as leverage the dread of an anticipated general election, the promise of government posts, and other incentives. On this occasion, the term "*scilipotismo*" was coined to describe this extreme, bizarre, and politically shady form of "transformism."[8] The expression was derived from the case of Domenico Scilipoti, an Italy of Values (IDV) MP—a starkly anti-Berlusconi party founded by ex-magistrate Antonio Di Pietro—that in December 2010, after having entered the new "People and Land" parliamentary group, together with two other IDV, two Democratic Party, and six Union of the Center (UDC) MPs, had given the government his vote of confidence.

The bipolar set-up had thus left little room for transparent negotiation among parties for the modification, within parliament, of the composition of the majority coalition. Therefore, faced with a looming early end to the legislature, the role of coalition-maker fell directly into the hands of the Presidents of the Republic. In 1995 it was Oscar Luigi Scalfaro who encouraged the establishment of Lamberto Dini's Caretaker Government. Likewise, Giorgio Napolitano fostered, halfway through the XVI legislature, and after the crisis that befell Silvio Berlusconi's fourth government, the installation of Mario Monti's "technical government" (2011–2013) with the support of the PdL parliamentary group, the centrist groups and the PD. Napolitano himself, at the start of the XVII legislature, when faced with the deadlock produced by the electoral results, went as far as naming the establishment of a so-called large coalition government involving the same parties that had supported the Monti Government, as a precondition for his acceptance of a second term as President of the Republic.

Parliamentary Regulations and Management of the Parliamentary Agenda

The centrality of parliament, characteristic of the First Republic, had become embedded into the regulations and practices of the legislative process. But, with the advent of the Second Republic, some of the rules changed, and some were used creatively in order to bypass the parliamentary assembly.

Already in the early 1980s, after the crises of the governments presided over by Giulio Andreotti between 1976 and 1979 with the support of the Communist Party, a debate had begun regarding an overhaul of regulations geared at strengthening the governments' position in parliament. Yet it was only in 1988 that a series of alterations were actually approved both in the Chamber of Deputies and in the Senate.

In 1988 the Senate saw the drastic reduction of the use of the secret ballot, and it was envisaged that its working schedule be drawn up taking into account not only the parliamentary groups' or single MP's suggestions but also the priorities indicated by the executive. In order to ensure that government policy is implemented in a timely manner, the work program was designed to include the specific date in which voting on every bill was to take place. However, the approval of the agenda remains, to this day, in the hands of the parties constituting the governing majority. The schedule requires the approval of the "conference of parliamentary group leaders," in which each group has a weight proportional to its size in the parliamentary assembly. Alternatively, it may be approved by the assembly itself. Generally, the agenda is approved unanimously, though, as a measure of last resort it may also be sanctioned by absolute majority by either the conference or the assembly.

Within the Chamber of Deputies, the changes in the rules were initially less effective. Only in 1990 was government was endowed with the right to provide non-binding indications regarding the agenda. Since then, the shortfalls in granting the government a more active role in leading the legislative initiative were balanced by the greater influence granted to the President of the parliamentary assembly. Indeed, in the Chamber, when the conference of parliamentary groups leaders fails to reach unanimity in approving the working agenda, it falls within the President's duties to dictate a viable solution, taking into account both the government's indications and the preferences of minority groups. Furthermore, in 1990 the review of the Chamber's regulations did not limit the room of maneuver available to obstructionism. It was also because of this that the reforms launched in the 1990s would be rather more deep-seated in the Chamber of Deputies than in the Senate. The greatest changes were introduced, significantly, in 1997, as the works of the Bicameral Commission were carried out, and it appeared as though the centre-left and centre-right might reach an agreement on an overall review of the design of institutions, in keeping with a majoritarian democratic model.

Ever since then, the President of the Chamber has become the ultimate warrantor ensuring compliance with governmental agenda. It is due to this that it is, at present, hard to imagine a scenario in which the majority coalition might decide—as it happened in the 1970s and 1980s—to arrange for the election of an exponent of the opposition to the role of President of the Chamber. Within the Senate, the President of that Chamber is a less relevant figure, because should the conference of parliamentary groups leaders fail to vote unanimously, it falls to the assembly to make a decision, following a brief debate. Thus today, the opposition has very few tools it can use in preventing the government from continuing to pursue its agenda if the majority party leaders and the presidents of the two chambers are loyal to the prime minister.

RULING BY DECREE

In the course of the last 20 years, governments have progressively incremented their level of control over the legislative process thanks to an ever increasing use of decrees in the two forms the Italian Constitution envisages.

According to the Constitution, "law decrees" (*decreti-legge*) may be issued in instances of "necessity and urgency," without prior parliamentary authorization. They effectively hold the same validity as laws, but need to be "converted to law" by parliament in order to maintain that validity; parliament can emend them, as it adopts them. Article 77 of the Constitution states that the adoption of the decree must occur within 60 days from the date on which the decree was published.

Conversely, "legislative decrees" (*decreti legislativi*) are issued by the government on the basis of a previous parliamentary mandate and immediately become law, and do not require parliamentary ratification. In compliance with Article 76 of the Constitution, parliament, in order to assign the government a mandate to issue legislative decrees, must pass a law in which the subject, the "principles and directive criteria," and the deadline before which the decree is to be issued are specified.

Since the start of the 1980s, Italian governments have often resorted to their right to issue "law decrees" for presumed and often non-existent reasons of "necessity and urgency." In practice, government has used law decrees because it has not been in a position to ensure its bills are approved, by parliament in a timely fashion and without an impractical number of changes. However, there remained the need to return to parliament for the "conversion to law" of the decree. Whenever the approval of the conversion turned out to be impossible within the Constitutional timeline—60 days from issue—the government would repeatedly "reiterate" the decree, issuing it again as the 60 days expired, in order to save it from obsolescence.

Thus, by the mid-1990s there was a vast number of accumulated "reiterated, non-converted decrees," until, in 1996, the Constitutional Court outlawed the reiteration of decrees that had not been converted within 60 days from their date of issue. That sentence compelled Prodi's Government, in office at that time, to undertake to dispose of all previously issued decrees. Yet this did not deter subsequent governments from using decrees as a speedy substitute for ordinary law-making processes.

Nevertheless, the main innovation introduced in the 1990s—and maintained in the years that followed—concerning the relationship between government and parliament was undoubtedly the inauguration of the mandate to issue decrees, namely the possibility for parliament to approve a law mandating the right of government to legislate through decree.[9]

During the First Republic, this facility had not been widely taken advantage of. Governments began to make use of it in the latter half of the 1980s, in order to recoup the great delay Italy had accumulated in complying with EU guidelines regarding the creation of the common market, that were based on the Single European Act. Giuliano Amato's Government, pressured by the early 1990s dire currency and financial crisis, used it instead to intervene on important sectors of public policy. Toward the end of 1992, and contextually with the financial law for 1993, parliament approved four mandates of ample scope for the rationalization and reorganization of the civil service, healthcare and pension schemes, and local government finances.

Following this example, later governments, despite not finding themselves in contexts as extraordinary as that in which the Amato Government operated, continued to have recourse to the mandated decree.

In order to complete this sketch, it must be mentioned that beside law and legislative decrees, Second Republic governments learned to make more extensive use of "regulations," that is to say of those sets of norms issued by government that carry the status of law.[10] From 1997 onward, thanks to an initiative of Romano Prodi's first government, various realms that had previously been regulated by parliament-approved "little laws"—such as the internal organization of ministries—switched to being disciplined by regulations directly issued by the executive. Moreover, since that time, every year the government is expected to present parliament with a "bill for simplification" in which an array of fields are listed, on which the government itself will be authorized to intervene through legislative decrees or "simplifying regulations."

In order to portray, albeit imprecisely, the measure in which the legislative agency of government has diminished, let us consider that during the X legislature (1987–1992) over a total of 1,428 approved legislative acts, 75 percent were laws, 9 percent were legislative decrees, and 15 percent law decrees. Between the XIII (1996–2001) and XVI (2008–2013) legislatures, the percentage of laws within the total of all normative acts hovered around the 50 percent mark, the quota of law decrees remained almost unchanged, and the number of legislative decrees doubled, while about 10 percent of normative production was represented by law-abating regulations.

MAXI-AMENDMENTS AND CONFIDENCE VOTES

It must be added that the most relevant reforms are now often a part of the annual budget, actualized through the "financial measures bill," the "stability law," and the "collateral law drafts." These provisions can be submitted by government alone and are examined though a special procedure that limits the right of intervention of individual MPs. Thus, excluding annual special laws—such as those linked to the budget, decrees, and the ratifications of international agreements—not much is left. There were 407 "other laws" approved during the XII legislature (1996–2001), an average of little less than seven per month. The average decreased to about four laws passed per month during the XIV legislature (2001–2006), and less than two per month in the XVI legislature (2008–2012).

Nevertheless, even when government could count on a relatively wide majority, such as that of the XIII and XVI legislatures, it continued to be faced with many difficulties when attempting to pass bills, often because those submitted to parliamentary scrutiny proved to be technically incomplete. Hence two further tools were used to put pressure on parliament—or rather, the majority's own parliamentary groups: the vote of confidence and the so-called maxi-amendments.

According to Chamber of Deputies and Senate regulations, when a confidence vote is linked to an article or single amendment, the text submitted by government must be accorded priority in the process of parliamentary scrutiny. If it is approved, all alternative texts and amendments are considered annulled. This is due to the fact that the government, by superimposing the vote of confidence, places its own continuity on the line, and even dissenting parliamentary groups are induced to cast a favorable vote. Once the vote of confidence is placed alongside a bill, each group or individual MP can report to its electoral base that all attempts were made to safeguard one interest or another—perhaps even though blatantly incompatible with national financial interests—but that, in the end, breaking down the wall erected by government proved impossible.

"Maxi-amendments" are usually submitted by the government as the scrutiny of a bill draws to a close. They are amendments that entirely substitute the text undergoing examination, and perhaps integrate norms that were not included in the original project.

As can be easily inferred, the combination of these two techniques—the submission of a maxi-amendment alongside the superimposition of a confidence vote—effectively impedes debate and eliminates all margins for negotiation between government and the majority's parliamentary groups. This strategy has also been repeatedly used for the conversion of decrees to law, and for ensuring the approval of financial budgets since 2003 by centre-right and centre-left governments alike, but above all by "technical" governments.

Functions of Direction and Control

The parliament, as well as legislating, should monitor and direct government activities: it should supervise—through parliamentary questions and points of order—and provide political direction—with motions, resolutions, and orders of business. These manifold forms of parliamentary initiative, however, often degenerate into political role play that proves to be far from incisive either in communication with the public or as a way of achieving tangible results.

In Italian parliamentary jargon, "orders of business" are those acts that supply the government with "instructions" regarding the way in which it should implement legislative measures. They are displayed and voted upon immediately after the close article-by-article scrutiny of the proposed bill has been completed and just prior to moving on the final poll. They are oftentimes used as a way of taking or dispensing compensation for the failed approval of amendments that might have effectively changed the law but did not get through or were recalled, upon the request of the speaker or government—perhaps because there was not the financial means to implement them. Thus, a defeated amendment that aimed at increasing contributions to schools, the police, or the care of the disabled—which may not be reinserted in the order of business in the same form—turns into an exhortation of sorts, on which the government representatives can easily agree, without the annoyance of financial considerations. So much so that, according to an expression commonly used among MPs, "no one can be denied an order of business."

The "motions" are general orientation acts that address specific issues or sectors of public policy, ranging from the overcrowded conditions in jails to decisions on foreign affairs. Approval of such motions rarely influences public policy. When they are not merely rhetorical they serve to furnish proof of sufficient consensus among parliamentary groups around decisions that government made or is about to make, perhaps with the help of parliamentary groups located outside the governing majority, that compensate for the dissent present within that majority.

Parliamentary questions and points of order are intended to be instrumental in pursuing those ministries that are erring or struggling, politically or bureaucratically, and oblige the government to clarify, correct or, at the very least, take a stand on the issue at hand. But the substantial number of questions and points of order, the lack of filters leading to a great number of individual presenters, and the fact that the government is, in practice, not obliged to consider them, greatly diminishes their effectiveness. The only exceptions are the "urgent questions" and the "points of order requiring immediate response"—two kinds of acts through which the parliament monitors the governmental activity—with which the government must deal within a very short time span, according to a regulation introduced to the Chamber of Deputies in 1997. In both instances, the requests have to be supported with a sufficient number of signatures and are counted as part of an allowed quota: no one MP can subscribe to more than one urgent parliamentary question per month, and any question requires 30 signatures before it can be submitted.

Essentially, the "points of order requiring immediate response" are a *question time* of sorts, intended to emulate the lively and direct confrontation that occurs between the prime minister and the main opposition leader at Westminster. Yet Italian prime ministers have rarely agreed to take part in such a debate, and this type of "point of order" procedure has become little more than a monotonous read-aloud of a previously known text, composed of predictable questions to which a secondary member of government will provide answers—often simply reading a bureaucratic note prepared by the offices of his ministry of reference.[11]

The oversaturation of parliamentary initiative, coupled with a redundant bicameral system, has led to the undermining of parliament's role as controller, due to the scarce visibility afforded to these initiatives. The members of government and ministry leaders that supply the answers can easily hide behind ultimately elusive responses.

SOCIAL REPRESENTATION
AND PEDAGOGICAL FUNCTION

During the First Republic, MPs elected with the main parties usually acted as an interface with local constituencies, albeit not always with virtuous motives and noble means. The competition for preference votes meant that that all MPs and parliamentary candidates had to build and nurture the support of their electoral base, as well as their financial resources. In the case of the PCI this further meant obtaining the backing of the party as a whole, in the Democrazia Cristiana (DC) and Partito Socialista Italiano (PSI) it translated into affiliation with a current or faction, and, particularly in the south, building support often entailed the creation of webs of nepotism.[12] The work within the parliamentary commissions, focusing on laws and "little laws," or reiterated contacts with the ministries, thus made it possible for parliamentarians to reward their supporters, ensuring the goodwill of interest groups gravitating around the party current of choice, signaling involvement in the constituency—streaming toward it, perhaps, some public infrastructure funds—and helping electors/clients with employment procedures, relocation, careers, and social security issues.

Single member constituencies, introduced in 1993, could perhaps foster, in time, the building of a new kind of link between those elected and their electoral base. But that learning curve was brusquely interrupted in 2005, when an electoral law was approved based on long, "blocked" lists to be presented in constituencies as large as whole regions or clusters of provinces. The link between MPs and constituencies thus became much feebler, because, in order to be elected or confirmed in office, the decisive ties were now those built with the individuals responsible for the drafting of candidate lists, rather than with the electors.

Partly due to this new electoral system, parliament and MPs have become widely discredited. A campaign regarding the privileges of the "political caste," originating from the publication of a successful book following a 2007 journalistic inquiry, has stigmatized the excessive costs of parliament, parliamentary groups, and indemnities.[13] Therefore, after a decade of economic decline, during which gross domestic product (GDP) registered an annual growth of 0.25 percent and public expenditure for parliament and party financing steadily increased, citizen trust in the parliamentary machine entirely disappeared.

According to data periodically gathered by Eurobarometer, in the years between 2003 and 2007, the percentage of Italians that confirmed their trust in parliament oscillated between 31 and 39 percent, a trend in keeping with that registered in other European countries during that same time span. In the years that followed, a generalized decline in the trust afforded to national parliaments was noted. Within European countries, the percentage of citizens that "tended to trust them" reached 25 percent in 2003. Yet in Italy that same decline has been much steeper. The level of trust toward Italian parliament, measured by that indicator, totaled 10 percent in 2013. Rather than fulfilling a "pedagogical" role in society, as Bagehot had hoped, parliament became the object of widespread blame.

Reforms toward a New Parliamentary Credibility

Effectively, the existence of twin chambers, composed of representatives elected according to the same party affiliations in both chambers, and endowed with exactly the same powers—with the consequent duplication of every parliamentary structure, and with a high number of MPs—was never convincing. When the 1947 constituents decided to maintain the Senate, formerly appointed by the king, they debated the ways in which its composition might be differentiated from that of the Chamber of Deputies. Many Christian Democrat members of the Constituent Assembly were in favor of a Senate that mirrored social categories shaped according to a corporate model. Conversely, some of the Republican exponents had a propensity for a "Chamber of Regions." Socialists and Communists were staunch supporters of a single-chamber system, as they felt that there could not be two distinct expressions of "the people's will." After the "corporate" solution had been rejected, an attempt was made to justify the maintenance of the Senate, envisaging that, unlike the Chamber of Deputies, its members would be chosen with the regions in mind—thus alluding to the Chamber of Regions concept—and that the legal age for both electors and members would be raised with respect to that required for the Chamber of Deputies—thus hinting at the Senate's higher degree of wisdom. Yet the composition of the two chambers has always been similar. The procedure requiring any law to be approved twice does not seem to have led to great improvements in their quality, while the complexity of the ordinary legislative process has, time and again, undoubtedly become a tool in the hands of the guardians of the status quo, or an alibi for governments to legitimize their efforts to bypass parliament.

Thus, for many years the need to overcome the bicameral system, by differentiating the composition and powers of the chambers, has been invoked. All the hypotheses made by the main political parties have, however, been based upon the assumption that the existence of two distinct, full-time parliamentary bodies, endowed with identical status and indemnities, should be preserved—due to the presumed unwillingness on the part of those MPs directly concerned with the unpalatable prospective of nullifying their chance of re-election to approve the reform otherwise. As a result, the proposed suggestions have been of a kind bound to render the legislative process and the interactions between government and parliament more complex, rather than offering any simplification.

The 1997 Bicameral Commission, for instance, adopted the so called Senate of Guarantees hypothesis, one that envisaged a Senate with an equivalent power to that of the Chamber of Deputies in matters of electoral and constitutional laws, on the regulation of authorities, on information and telecommunications, civil and political rights, penal law, judicial system, and local government. But the Senators, in their roles as full-time MPs, would be elected through proportional representation. The Senate would thus have become a "veto player," wielding even more power over governments.[14]

The "federalist" constitutional reform approved by the centre-right in 2005—and subsequently rejected by the 2006 referendum—revoked the Senate's power to grant or deny governments a vote of confidence. It established that Senators would be elected through proportional representation in conjunction with the regional councils, making the dissolution of the Senate impossible. But then, in order to maintain the "equal status" of Senate and Chamber of Deputies members, it accorded the Senate equal powers on social and healthcare policy, fiscal federalism, and constitutional review. Furthermore, the Senate would have the last word on laws concerning the numerous matters that fall under the jurisdiction of both national and local government.[15]

All proposals subsequently advanced by the leading political parties have always adhered to the same lines. Matteo Renzi's Government, in office since 2014, has suggested instead that the Senate be transformed into a body composed of regional institution representatives, with limited responsibilities and a veto power the Chamber of Deputies may surmount, along lines similar to the Austrian and German Bundesrat. At the same time, in the context of negotiations with the centre-right opposition forces, it proposed amendments to the electoral laws aimed at reducing the size of constituencies, and thus the length of candidate lists, as well as guaranteeing the appointment of the majority of seats to the party with the most votes. If these reforms were to be finally approved, the functions and procedures of parliament could alter significantly. An architecture less baroque in style might prove to gain in authoritativeness.

NOTES

1. Marta Regalia, Chapter 11, this volume.
2. Maurizio Cotta, "The 'centrality' of Parliament in a protracted democratic consolidation: the Italian case," in Ulrike Liebert and Maurizio Cotta (eds), *Parliament and Democratic Consolidation in Southern Europe: Greece, Italy, Portugal, Spain and Turkey* (London and New York: Pinter, 1990), 55–91.
3. Luca Verzichelli and Maurizio Cotta, "Italy: from 'Constrained' Coalitions to Alternating Governments," in W. G. Müller and K. Strom (eds), *Coalition Governments in Western Europe* (Oxford: Oxford University Press, 2000), 456–460.
4. Mauro Calise and Renato Mannheimer, *Governanti in Italia: un trentennio repubblicano, 1946-1976* (Bologna: Il Mulino, 1982).
5. Giuseppe Di Palma, *Surviving Without Governing: The Italian Parties in Parliament* (Berkeley: University of California Press, 1977).
6. Chiara De Micheli and Luca Verzichelli, *Il Parlamento* (Bologna: Il Mulino, 2004), 199.
7. Carol Mershon, Chapter 12, this volume.
8. Marco Valbruzzi, Chapter 3, this volume.
9. Salvatore Vassallo, "Le leggi del Governo: come gli esecutivi della transizione hanno superato i veti incrociati," in Giliberto Capano and Marco Giuliani (eds), *Parlamento e processo legislativo in Italia: continuità e mutamento* (Bologna: Il Mulino, 2001), 85–126.
10. Nicola Lupo, *Dalla legge al regolamento: Lo sviluppo della potestà normativa del governo nella disciplina delle pubbliche amministrazioni* (Bologna: Il Mulino, 2003).
11. Luigi Gianniti and Nicola Lupo, *Corso di diritto parlamentare* (Bologna: Il Mulino, 2008), 161.
12. Luigi Graziano, *Clientelismo e sistema politico. Il caso dell'Italia* (Milan: Franco Angeli, 1984); Gianfranco Pasquino, *Votare un solo candidato. Le conseguenze politiche della preferenza unica* (Bologna: Il Mulino, 1993).
13. Gian Antonio Stella and Sergio Rizzo, *La Casta. Così i politici italiani sono diventati intoccabili* (Milan: Rizzoli, 2007).

14. Salvatore Vassallo, "The Third Bicamerale," in Luciano Bardi and Martin Rhodes (eds.), *Italian Politics. Mapping the Future* (Boulder, CO: Westview Press, 1998), 111–131.

15. Salvatore Vassallo, "The Constitutional Reforms of the Center-Right," in Carlo Guarnieri and James Newell (eds), *Italian Politics. Quo vadis?* (Oxford and New York: Berghahn Books, 2005), 117–135.

CHAPTER 10

···

THE COURTS

···

CARLO GUARNIERI

DURING the second part of the twentieth century the institutional setting of the Italian judiciary was massively reformed. Judicial prerogatives have been strengthened and courts have come to play an increasingly significant role in Italian politics. This development has been followed by a growing politicization of the judicial corps—with the emergence of several ideologically different groups—and by a persistent conflict with the political environment. However, the expansion of judicial power is likely to remain a permanent trait of Italian democracy.

JUDICIAL ORGANIZATION AND CHANGE
···

At least until the middle of the twentieth century, the Italian judiciary was organized according to the model prevailing in civil law countries.[1] Judges were civil servants, with only some additional guarantees: they were—and still are—recruited through a national public competition, the judiciary being a unitary organization. Law graduates sat the national examination immediately after completing their studies, and still tend to do so. Once in the corps, the graduates became part of a hierarchical organization, controlled by high-ranking judges, with the Ministry of Justice at the top. In addition, following the French Napoleonic tradition, judges and prosecutors belonged—and still do—to the same corps: both were—and are—defined as "magistrates." During their professional life, they can switch from one function to another.

Also in Italy, as in most Continental European countries, the judicial function was largely defined in passive, executory terms: the judge was considered to be the "mouth of the law," faithfully applying the will of the legislator.[2] The Court of Cassation—the traditional apex of the judicial pyramid—exerted its control on inferior courts, formally through its review powers, informally through its influence over promotions and—in extreme cases—discipline. Therefore, even without considering the fascist period—when civil and political rights were severely restricted—traditionally courts played a subordinate role in the Italian political system. On the other hand, their minor role assured a relative insulation from political pressure. Italian magistrates could pursue their career without significant political interferences. Only the top of the judicial hierarchy was appointed by the government, although, even in such cases, professional qualifications mattered.

The Constitution of 1948 introduced significant changes to this set-up. Among its most relevant innovations were a constitutional review of legislation and a strong increase in judicial independence. Constitutional review was assigned to a specialized court (Corte costituzionale), separated from the ordinary judiciary, and organized more or less according to the teaching of Hans Kelsen, allowing access to separation of powers questions and, more importantly, to *any* court having doubts on the constitutionality of a statute it had to apply in a concrete case. Judicial independence had to be guaranteed by entrusting all decisions regarding the status of judges and prosecutors to a body—the Higher Council of the Judiciary—composed of magistrates elected by their colleagues (two thirds), and lawyers elected by parliament and therefore having a political imprinting.

After the experience of the fascist regime, the need for assuring better protection of political and civil rights was deeply felt. The major political parties in the Constituent Assembly—Christian Democrats, Socialists, and Communists—did not trust each other much and, in any case, not one alone could muster a majority to pass the Constitution. With the development of the Cold War and the Stalinization of Eastern Europe, Christian Democrats—and the other small centrist parties—were fearful of a possible communist-dominated executive. Also the left became increasingly worried about being isolated in opposition and maybe subjected to legal restrictions. Moreover, the uncertainty about which party would govern in the future was high. Therefore, the Constitution provided an impressive array of guarantees against possible executive and legislative abuses, and can be considered a good example of "new constitutionalism."[3] Constitutional review and the strengthening of judicial independence were designed as a way to check the political branches by political actors uncertain about their future power and divided by a low level of trust.[4]

An additional confirmation of this fact is provided by what happened after the first parliamentary elections, in 1948, which had seen the Christian Democrats triumph. While the parties of the left began to reconsider their traditional mistrust of courts and to advocate a strengthening of judicial power, Christian Democrats' enthusiasm for judicial checks cooled down. Giving up the traditional instruments of executive influence on the judiciary seemed a gratuitous gift to the Communist opposition. Moreover, the Court of Cassation had quickly aligned itself with the new political order. For instance, after 1948, its former president—Antonio Azara—accepted a Christian Democratic seat in the Senate and also filled the Justice portfolio for a while.

Only after the 1953 elections, when Christian Democrats' power was circumscribed, did the implementation of the Constitution resume, leading to the institution of the Constitutional Court, in 1956, and of the Higher Council of the Judiciary, in 1959. The new Constitutional Court began to vigorously "clean up" the legal system—getting rid of the remains of fascist legislation—an action substantially tolerated, if not welcomed, by most political parties.[5] The only significant opposition came from the Court of Cassation. In the 1960s, the two courts entered into a collision on the final power of interpreting statutes. The real issue was that the Court of Cassation—more ideologically conservative in any case—was jealous of the fact that the Constitutional Court, by performing its institutional function of reviewing the constitutionality of the laws, had to decide their meaning and therefore impinged on the Cassation's traditional prerogative of determining the "exact" interpretation of the law. In the end, with the support of most academics, a sort of alliance between lower-ranking judges and the Constitutional Court was able to report a victory in the battle, thanks also to the increasing independence of lower courts judges.

The composition of the Higher Council of the Judiciary was another subject of conflict. The initial decision—in 1959—that the judicial component be made to represent, above all, the higher-ranking magistrates, was strongly contested by the rest of the judiciary. The conflict led to the leadership of the main judicial association (the ANM: Associazione nazionale magistrati) being conquered by the "innovators": that is, by those advocating a reform—actually the dismantling—of the traditional hierarchical setting. Thus, between the mid-1960s and the mid-1970s the power of the judicial hierarchy was destroyed—promotions were entrusted to the Council, which was now elected according to the principle "one magistrate, one vote"[6] —with the result that the independence of judges and prosecutors was strengthened in both dimensions: external, from political power, and internal, from higher ranks. In practice, promotions have become automatic, with the result that judicial salaries are related only to career seniority, while specific positions are allocated through a variable consideration of seniority and party and judicial unions' politics.

In fact, since the end of the 1950s, magistrates began to organize themselves in various, ideologically different groups. The ANM has divided itself into organized factions (*correnti*), each with a stable organizational structure and a more or less defined political ideology. Thus, "leftist" factions—the Movimento per la Giustizia (Movement for Justice) and the more radical Magistratura Democratica (Democratic Magistrates)—have criticized the traditional "mouth of the law" definition of the judicial role, underlining instead the duty of the judge to implement "constitutional values" and especially the equality principle (art. 3 of the Constitution). As well, Magistratura Democratica has openly proclaimed the need for the judge to side with "progressive" political forces. On the other hand, a moderate group like Unità per la Costituzione (Unity for the Constitution) has always advocated more self-restraint vis-à-vis the political branches, focusing its activity on union-like matters such as career and salary, while a conservative group like Magistratura Indipendente (Independent Judiciary) has emphasized the need for judges to safeguard their impartiality by avoiding any involvement with politics. All these groups played a crucial role in the reform process by putting pressure on the political parties, a fact made easier by each faction developing relationships with the more ideologically proximate parties. Moreover, since the 1970s, they have monopolized the judicial component of the Council, deeply affecting its decision-making process and especially appointments to more important positions. Since support by one of the judicial factions represented in the Council plays a significant role in the process, this fact helps explain the need for magistrates—or at least for those willing to rise in the field—to affiliate themselves with such factions and, thus, the strong influence exerted by the *correnti* inside the judicial corps.

THE JUDICIALIZATION OF POLITICS IN THE FIRST REPUBLIC

Thanks to all these changes, since at least the 1970s, Italian courts began to accumulate power. The institution of the Higher Council and its "democratization" increased judicial guarantees of independence to the highest level in Continental Europe.[7] As we have seen in the section "Judicial Organization and Change," the Constitutional Court contributed to the decline of the traditional influence of the Court of Cassation. Moreover, the practice of judicial review became diffused among ordinary courts. Now, ordinary courts had to make a first appraisal of the constitutionality of a statute in order to decide whether or not to send a case to the Constitutional Court, therefore accustoming themselves to critically evaluating the legislation, a practice foreign to the traditional "mouth of the law" approach to legal interpretation. The Constitutional Court invited ordinary judges to interpret existing statutes in such a way to make them compatible with the Constitution, in this way justifying judicial lawmaking.[8] The result—thanks also to the role played by the *correnti*—was a decline of the traditional stereotype of the judge as "mouth of the law," an increase in judicial creativity, and the development, inside the judicial corps, of new, more activist conceptions of the judicial—and also prosecutorial—role.

Changes in the structure of public prosecution were even more significant. First of all, especially after the institution of the Higher Council in 1959, the powers of the Minister of Justice over prosecution were progressively reduced. The Constitution had already recognized the principle of mandatory prosecution (art. 112): it increasingly came to be interpreted as sparing prosecutors from any kind of supervision from outside the judicial system, with the result that their actual degree of discretion was expanded. Also, the powers of the higher ranks were gradually reduced, with the consequence that the approximately 150 prosecution offices in first-instance courts began to act in a substantially autonomous way.

Moreover, the long season of political violence in the 1970s, and, later, the still unfinished struggle against organized crime, had important effects on the judicial system. Traditional systems of coordination, based on the hierarchy of offices, proved themselves to be slow, cumbersome, and ineffective, and were also weakened by the increasing autonomy of lower-ranking judges and prosecutors. Thus, new, direct, face-to-face relationships developed between prosecutors and instructing judges of different offices.[9]

These developments enhanced the role of the Higher Council—with its powers over the career and discipline of magistrates—which increasingly played a coordinating role.

Another important change was the growing influence of the judiciary on police forces from the mid-1970s. Traditionally, prosecutors and instructing judges did not interfere with police investigations. Often they just waited for the police to provide them with the evidence for pursuing a prosecution in court. However, some initial police failings in the fight against terrorism and organized crime pushed the judiciary to take a more proactive stance: for example, by directly leading investigations in these areas.[10] In this way, the magistrates were able to improve their investigative skills and to exert a growing influence on police forces. The reform of the code of criminal procedure in 1989 ratified this situation, by abolishing the instructing judge and by entrusting the investigation to the prosecutor. Prosecutors—many of whom had been instructing judges before 1989—were able to employ their powers and skills, as well as their good relationships with police forces, to broaden the range of their investigations and, as we will see in the section "The Crisis of 1992 and Clean Hands," to strongly pursue cases of political corruption.

All these developments were supported by the consensual trend that has characterized Italian politics since the end of the 1950s. The decision to systematically dismantle the old judicial arrangement has to be understood in light of the fact that the political environment was receptive to judicial demands. Once the traditional alliance between the executive and the senior judiciary was weakened, new and increasingly important relationships developed between political parties and representatives of magistrates' associations. The parties permanently in opposition (such as the Communists) or those slowly moving from opposition to government (such as the Socialists in the 1960s) were obviously interested in developing contacts with a strategic body like the judiciary, and in strengthening the judiciary's independence from an executive branch they did not expect to fully control. The party traditionally in government, the Christian Democrats, was confronted with new and powerful rivals. But competition among the various factions within the Christian Democrats meant that the judiciary found allies even within the governing party. The new relationships between the judiciary and Italian political parties, together with the growth of Socialist and Communist influence on parliamentary decision-making, resulted in the reforms that satisfied magistrates' demands: the dismantling of the traditional career path and the increasing role of the Higher Council, where judicial groups began to play a crucial role, especially after the introduction—in 1975—of proportional representation in Council elections.[11]

THE CRISIS OF 1992 AND CLEAN HANDS

For a while, judicial power, although growing, was kept somewhat in check by the strength of the political parties. The Christian Democrats, although divided in several factions, were always the largest party and therefore remained firmly in power. In the

Higher Council, party members were sometimes able to profit from the competition between different judicial groups in order to exert some influence. In turn, parliament often declined to waive immunity from prosecution for its members, and conflicts of jurisdiction obstructed the development of complex investigations. But the political crisis of the early 1990s gave courts a significant chance to assert the power already accumulated. The fall of the Berlin Wall, with the resultant breakdown of socialist regimes in Central and East Europe and Russia, had a major influence on Italian politics. To cut a long story short, the failure of the communist experiment fueled internal conflict and damaged the electoral appeal of Italian communists, even if, in the past, they had tried to dissociate themselves from the Soviet Union. The result was a split in the party—between the social democratic PDS and the more radical RC—and a strong decline of electoral support at the 1992 parliamentary elections. The dissolving of the "red threat" had a corresponding effect on the main anti-communist party, the Christian Democrats. For the first time in the postwar period, the party plunged under 30 percent in the polls. In the meantime, European constraints made more difficult to pursue the policy of deficit spending that had supported the clientelistic policies of governing parties: the governments had therefore to cut expenses and to raise taxes, with the result they further increased popular dissatisfaction. This state of public opinion made itself known: support for the centrist governing coalition (the *pentapartito*) fell to under 50 percent of votes and the coalition only received a thin majority of seats in parliament.

The political landscape was ready for the so-called "Clean Hands" to erupt. The weakening of the governing parties radically undermined the traditional ways in which they were able to contain judicial power. In a few months, the investigations undertaken by prosecutors in Milan—and later also in other cities—hit prominent politicians of the governing coalition, as well as managers of state and private companies, with charges of corruption and other related crimes. The Amato government, formed in July 1992 after a three-month crisis, survived less than one year, but saw several of its ministers forced to resign, after being put under investigation. Meanwhile, the "anti-corruption pool" of Milan acquired an enormous popularity. Judicial investigations continued to develop. Although there are no complete data on final convictions, it seems that more than 5000 people were in some way involved: among them 4 prime ministers, various ministers, and about 200 Members of Parliament. The changed political environment of the early 1990s allowed judicial investigations to develop all their capabilities and to invest the political system with a maximum of impact. Prosecutors were able to exploit the resources accumulated in the past in the fight against terrorism and organized crime. Their more proactive stance, and their influence with the police, allowed the development of investigations "in search" for crimes, in contrast to the traditional attitude of acting only after a prosecutor had been formally notified of a crime.[12] Often the accused were induced to collaborate, by giving evidence in exchange for more lenient treatment (especially avoiding pretrial detention).

Another important element supporting the development of judicial investigations was the role played by the media. Between 1992 and 1994 especially, the media were overwhelmingly supportive of the investigations, often anticipating their results and, in any case, siding with the judiciary and against the political class. Only after 1994, did part of the media—especially those under the direct or indirect influence of the new leader of the right, Berlusconi—begin to take a more critical stance, leading to division of sorts between those for and those against the tycoon. As a consequence, the impact of the "judicial-mediatic circus,"[13] at the beginning extremely strong, lessened. Today, it can still be felt among left-wing electors, but much less among those of the right.

However, at least for a while, the overwhelmingly favorable attitude of the media supported the strong impact of judicial investigations on public opinion and on the political system. The charges upon which most investigations were based—illegal financing and bribery—were represented by the media as the principal causes of waste of public money and maladministration. In this way, high fiscal pressure was also related to political corruption. So, the popularity of "Clean Hands" was due also to the fact that it was discovering a network of illegalities at the very moment the ordinary citizen had to pay more taxes in order to balance the state budget, whose deficit could be understood as being, at least in part, the consequence of corruption.

The Judicialization of Politics
in the Second Republic

Clean Hands has had a long-lasting impact on Italian politics, ratifying the power of criminal justice. Since then, many prosecutors have become public figures, often starring in the media. Several of them have entered the electoral arena, as Antonio Di Pietro, a protagonist of Clean Hands and later the leader of a small but not insignificant political party (Italia dei Valori), or Antonio Ingroia, an anti-Mafia prosecutor of Palermo, who, in 2013, failed to enter parliament as the leader of a leftist party. Recently, two former prosecutors have been elected mayors of important cities such as Naples and Bari.

The political impact of public prosecution was also magnified by changes in the institutional setting. In the fall of 1993, a constitutional amendment radically reduced the range of parliamentarians' immunity from judicial investigations. In the past, by denying the lifting of parliamentary immunity political parties had been able to keep judicial investigations under control. Since 1993, investigations, as well as judicial proceedings, have been able to develop without the need of previous authorization—only pretrial arrests must be authorized—a fact that makes the prosecution of political figures easier.

The high degree of involvement of courts in the political process has entailed different reactions from the political class. Following the election of March 1994—under a new semi-majoritarian electoral law—a new center-right coalition, led by Silvio Berlusconi, came into government. Just before the elections, Milan prosecutors had become interested in Berlusconi. Later, in November, when attending a United Nations conference on the fight against crime in Naples, he was publicly notified he was under investigation—a fact that contributed to the fall of his first cabinet. Since the middle of the 1990s, the

Milan investigations have focused on Berlusconi: a sort of continuous duel that is still ongoing. It goes without saying that the center-right has been critical of these developments. For example, as we will see later in this section, after 2001, when again in power, the center-right coalition tried, in different ways, to reduce judicial power. Sympathy for courts remains widespread in the center-left, although we must distinguish between the so-called *giustizialisti*—passionate supporters of judicial power—and the much more tepid attitude of the rest, worried that judicialization could also hit their parties (as, to some extent, it did).

On the other hand, the evolution of the party system was not without consequences for judicial power. Between 1996 and 2011, Italy has been governed by two coalitions—center-left and center-right—as a direct result of the elections. In 2001, for the first time in Italian electoral history, an incumbent—the left—was replaced by the opposition—the right—a fact which was repeated in 2006, although in a more fragmented contest, and in 2008, when the right was been returned to power with a strong parliamentary majority. However, the immediate consequence of the decrease of political fragmentation has been an increase in the conflict between courts and politics.

A first example is provided by the application in 1989 of the new code of criminal procedure. As we have seen in the section "The Judicialization of Politics in the First Republic," the code abolished the instructing judge and shifted the task of preparing the case to the public prosecutor. However, although the code had foreseen many limitations to the powers of prosecutor, understood to be only one of the parties in the case, in the early 1990s, in the context of the dramatic assassination of two prominent anti-Mafia magistrates (Falcone and Borsellino) and under pressure from the judiciary, a series of Constitutional Court decisions brought about a strong reinforcement of prosecutorial prerogatives.[14] The Court restored to the prosecutor many of the traditional powers of the old instructing judge, making it easier for the prosecution's dossier to be taken into consideration as evidence at the trial, even though it contained proofs obtained *inaudita altera parte* and therefore in violation of the adversary principle. A long confrontation followed between the Parliament, trying to strengthen the individual rights of the defendant, and also under pressure from the criminal bar, and the Constitutional Court, with its emphasis on the primacy of the search of truth at trial. In 1999, an amendment was voted in order to insert into the Constitution the principle of the accusatorial trial: the first and most explicit case of overruling the Court in Italian constitutional history. The amendment was voted by a wide majority composed of the right and large part of the left—irritated by the Constitutional Court's persistently negative attitude toward its legislation—with only a small group of *giustizialisti* against.

After 2001, with the right in power, the conflict between courts and politics rose to new heights. Berlusconi, already the target of several investigations, began a systematic policy of circumscribing the guarantees of independence of judges and prosecutors and reducing the significance of judicial investigations. An example of the first was, in 2005, a reform aiming at somewhat restoring the old hierarchical structure. The reform was passed, but it was not fully implemented: after the election of 2006, the new left majority quickly intervened by watering down much of its content. As for the second, the list is long. We can mention the reform, in 2002, of the crime of "false accounting" introducing a sort of tolerance area in which the difference between what is reported in the official financial statement of a company and the reality, as ascertained by the court, is no longer to be considered a crime. The new law had the main effect of dismantling some of the cases against Berlusconi. Later, the right concentrated its effort in trying to provide a sort of legal "shield" for the prime minister: in 2003 and 2008 two statutes—the so-called Lodo Schifani and Lodo Alfano—were enacted, suspending all criminal investigations against the President of the Republic, the prime minister, and the presidents of both Chambers of Parliament; however, both were subsequently declared unconstitutional by the Constitutional Court.

Although we should not overemphasize the majoritarian turn of the 1996–2008 period—since the elections of 2013 suggest that the decline of political fragmentation has been only temporary—it is clear that stronger political majorities have had the consequence of increasing the level of conflict between the judiciary and the political branches. Notwithstanding the cases against him, which even produced some convictions, Berlusconi did not resign, claiming to be the victim of a persecution by politically inspired—that is, leftist—magistrates. Even after the fall of his cabinet in 2011—a consequence of the economic and financial crisis—and his expulsion from Parliament in 2013—a consequence of a conviction becoming final—he has been able to survive politically somewhat and to remain one of the main protagonists of the Italian political scene.

COURTS AND POLITICS IN ITALY: A COMPLEX RELATIONSHIP

As we have seen in the section "The Judicialization of Politics in the Second Republic," the role of courts has been one of the main issues of recent Italian politics. Although criminal justice has been the focus of the conflict, judicial decisions in other areas have also triggered critical reactions on the part of the political system. We have already considered the role of the Constitutional Court in the reform of the criminal process. Other significant interventions by the Court have been those dealing with popular referendums. The Italian Constitution allows popular referendums in order to repeal legislation. However, their admissibility has to be checked by the Constitutional Court. Since the middle of the 1970s, many referendums have been proposed for all sorts of political issues: from divorce to abortion, from hunting to the abolition of state financing of political parties. In an effort to reform the much criticized political institutions, referendums were also proposed in order to change national and local electoral laws. The decisions of the Court in the matter have deeply oscillated, often without the support of clear principles. The complexity of the arguments developed by the Court has had the actual effect of increasing its margin of discretion, a fact strongly criticized by, for instance, civil rights groups.[15] Without any doubt, the most significant intervention of the Constitutional Court in Italian politics has been, at the end of 2013, the declaration of unconstitutionality of the national electoral law, the much criticized Porcellum (pig's law).

Significant decisions in non-criminal cases have also been laid down by other courts. For instance, in 2008, in absence of clear legislation, the Court of Cassation ruled that a father was authorized to terminate the feeding of his daughter, in a coma for 18 years. The decision triggered a deep conflict at the social and political level. It was strongly criticized, not only by the Catholic Church, but also by the right-wing parties. The conflict escalated when Prime Minister Berlusconi attempted to issue a decree in order to void the decision by the Court. The attempt was stopped by the President of the Republic, but the issue pitted the right against the left; the latter, in this case, siding with the courts.

Summing up, the relationships between the courts and political institutions in Italy have been characterized by a high degree of conflict. Of course, constitutional democracies, being based on some form of separation of powers, are always characterized by some institutional tensions, which will involve the judiciary. However, since the 1980s, the conflict between the courts and the institutions in Italy—that is, government and parliament—has been a permanent trait of the political landscape. The temperature of the conflict has obviously risen sky-high during "Clean Hands" investigations and since then it has not subsided. The tension between Berlusconi and his supporters, on one hand, and large sections of the judiciary, on the other, has been consistently high.

The conflict between courts and politics has been explained in different ways. According to a popular view, based also on several international assessments, the Italian political class shows a high degree of corruption—at least in comparison with that in other democratic countries—justifying the high rate of judicial investigations.[16] The conflict should therefore be understood as between courts trying to enforce standards of governmental integrity and a large part of the political class unable or unwilling to abide by these. A more theoretical interpretation maintains that judicialization is related to long-term changes in democratic political systems.[17] The traditional "programmatic" politics—in which parties compete with different policy programs—has given way to a kind of "moralistic" politics, in which the personal attributes of candidates play a major part. In this new situation, the check on candidates' moral qualities—the so-called *controllo di virtù* (virtue check)—cannot be performed by the opposition any longer, as it, at least in Italy, has been involved in a web of transactions with the governing parties. At this point, also thanks to the support of the media, the chance is there for courts to play a significant part in the process. In other words, courts could perform as a sort of mechanism of political accountability in a new situation in which traditional forms do not function any longer in a satisfactory way.

Although these interpretations contain, without doubt, several elements of truth, the strong political impact of—especially criminal—courts should also be taken into account. As we have seen in the section "The Judicialization of Politics in the First Republic", at least since the 1970s, Italian prosecutors have enjoyed a remarkable degree of independence—likely the highest among consolidated democracies—and significant powers, thanks also to their influence with the police. In addition, since 1993, the

traditional immunity of parliamentarians from criminal suits has been severely circumscribed, and today prosecutors can freely investigate, indict, bring to trial, and possibly
convict any Member of Parliament. All these elements make more likely for an Italian
politician to be investigated and also be subject to some form of criminal proceeding.[18]

On the whole, the case of Italy can be interpreted as another case of judicialization of
politics, a trend already evident in a large number of democratic political systems.[19] The
expansion of judicial power has been supported by the institutional setting designed
by the Constitution, and brought about by a divided Constituent Assembly and, later,
by a growing state of political fragmentation. In the 1990s, with the traditional party
system in disarray, the judiciary was able to further expand its prerogatives. Moreover,
the experience of the last 20 years has shown that the strong position acquired by the
judiciary in the 1990s is unlikely to be reversed. Although most magistrates are coming
to realize the need of an overall reform of their careers and their activities, and the issue
will remain highly salient in the next few years, judicialization is likely to remain a permanent trait of Italian politics.

The fragmentation thesis, put forward especially by Tom Ginsburg,[20] finds in Italy
an additional confirmation. The strong consensualism of Italian political institutions,
together with a fragmented party system, makes any attempt at curbing judicial power
extremely difficult. Therefore, unlike what was supposed in the past,[21] civil law countries
can exhibit a strong judicial power, although some of its traits tend to be different from
other classical cases of judicialization, such as in the United States.

Notes

1. John H. Merryman and Rogelio Perdomo, *The Civil Law Tradition* (Stanford: Stanford
   University Press, 2007).
2. Carlo Guarnieri and Patrizia Pederzoli, *The Power of Judges* (Oxford: Oxford University
   Press, 2002).
3. Alec Stone Sweet, *Governing with Judges: Constitutional Politics in Europe* (Oxford: Oxford
   University Press, 2000).
4. See Chapters 6 and 8, this volume.
5. Patrizia Pederzoli, *La corte costituzionale* (Bologna: Il Mulino, 2008) and Gustavo
   Zagrebelsky and Valeria Marcenò, *Giustizia costituzionale* (Bologna: Il Mulino, 2012).
6. After the last reform, in 2002, the body is composed of sixteen magistrates elected directly
   by all magistrates with a proportional electoral law—therefore, faithfully representing the
   landscape of judicial factions (the *correnti*) and of eight lawyers or law professors elected
   by parliament with a 60 percent majority. The President of the Republic and the president
   and the prosecutor general at the Court of Cassation are *ex officio* members of the Council.
7. John Bell, *Judiciaries within Europe* (Cambridge: Cambridge University Press, 2006) and
   Guarnieri and Pederzoli, *The Power of Judges*.
8. Pederzoli, *La corte costituzionale*.
9. Until 1989, Italian criminal justice was organized along the traditional French-style
   semi-inquisitorial model, in which the investigation of significant cases was entrusted to
   an instructing judge.

10. Giuseppe Di Federico, *Ordinamento giudiziario: uffici giudiziari, CSM e governo della magistratura* (Padua: Cedam, 2012).

11. Daniela Piana and Antoine Vauchez, *Il Consiglio Superiore della Magistratura* (Bologna: Il Mulino, 2012).

12. Luciano Violante, *Magistrati* (Turin: Einaudi, 2009).

13. Daniel Soulez-Larivière, *Du cirque médiatico-judiciaire et des moyens d'en sortir* (Paris: Seuil, 1993).

14. Pederzoli, *La corte costituzionale.*

15. Pederzoli, *La corte costituzionale*, 221–235.

16. Alberto Vannucci, "The Controversial Legacy of '*Mani Pulite*': A Critical Analysis of Italian Corruption and Anti-Corruption Policies," *Bulletin of Italian Politics* 2, no. 1 (2009), 233–264.

17. Alessandro Pizzorno, *Il potere dei giudici* (Bari: Laterza, 1998).

18. Carlo Guarnieri, "Courts Enforcing Political Accountability: The Role of Criminal Justice in Italy," in Diana Kapiszewski et al., *Consequential Courts* (Cambridge: Cambridge University Press, 2013), 163–180.

19. C. Neal Tate and Torbjorn Vallinder, eds., *The Global Expansion of Judicial Power* (New York: New York University Press, 1995).

20. Tom Ginsburg, *Judicial Review in New Democracies* (Cambridge: Cambridge University Press, 2003).

21. Merryman and Perdomo, *The Civil Law Tradition.*

CHAPTER 11

ELECTORAL SYSTEMS

MARTA REGALIA

SINCE 1861, Italy has gone through six electoral systems. While there were even more reforms, and while those reforms were sometimes more than minor adjustments, Italy experienced, substantially, a two-round system and a proportional system during the liberal era; a proportional system with a sizable majority premium at the beginning of the fascist regime; and, during the republican era, a list proportional system with preferences, a mixed-member majoritarian system, and, finally, a closed list proportional system with a majority premium.[1] As it will become clear by reading this chapter, the permanent feature of each of these conspicuous reforms was the predominant interest of the actors involved: notables and/or parties. The Italian electoral history was driven by their concerns in terms of seats.

LIBERAL STATE

In 1861 the Italian state inherited its electoral system from the Kingdom of Piedmont. All adult literate citizens, at least 25 years old, paying an annual census of forty *lire*, or, regardless of the revenues, with a profession that could warrant sufficient intellectual ability (like professors, public officials, judges, etc.) were entitled to vote. Those conditions, taken together, granted the right to vote to about 2 percent of the entire Italian population.[2] Deputies were elected by a two-round system in single-member constituencies (508, as the number of deputies) with a closed second round. In fact, if no candidate in the first round won the absolute majority—provided that at least one third of the electorate went to the polls—a second round, run-off contest had to be held between the two best placed candidates. This system, which produced truly majoritarian results, seemed appropriate to a political elite made of notables, which drew their forces locally and whose task was to protect the interests of their constituencies.

The reform of the electoral system, including the enlargement of suffrage, became a priority when, in 1876, the so-called Sinistra Storica (historic left) came to power. At this point, a parliamentary struggle between conservatives and progressives took place on the contrasting values of census and capacity. The historic left, in fact, after passing the legge Coppino on compulsory elementary education, promoted an electoral reform to grant the vote to all literate citizens over 21 years of age, regardless of census. The Destra Storica (historic right), aware that the enlargement would have benefited the urban, (potentially) progressive electorate, imposed a correction: regardless of capacity, the right to vote was extended to all adult citizens paying a census of about twenty *lire*. Consequently, 7 percent of the population was enfranchised.[3] Apart from suffrage enlargement, the historic left tried to break the strong link between the deputies and their electoral constituencies, ensured by the majoritarian system, which, in its opinion, was responsible for the existence of electoral clienteles and the absence of party competition. Thus, a peculiar form of two-round system based on lists in multimember constituencies was introduced. According to this system, 508 deputies were elected in 135 districts. Each constituency could elect from two to five deputies, depending on its population. Voters had the possibility of casting a number of votes equal to the number of deputies to be elected (only, in case of five seats' constituencies, voters had four votes). Candidates obtaining the highest number of votes won the seats, provided that they received at least a number of votes equal or superior to one eighth of the eligible citizens. If one or more seats remained unassigned—a very rare event—a run-off election was held the following week, between the candidates with the most votes.[4] Since political parties were not organized and well established, this system encouraged agreements over "official" lists among candidates of different leanings, thus supporting the politics of *trasformismo* (see Chapter 3, this volume) initiated by Prime Minister Depretis.

Once it became clear that the two-round multimember system had not reached the expected gains in terms of party competition, in 1891 the Kingdom of Italy reverted to single-member constituencies,[5] and, a year later, to a majority run-off system, which required candidates, to be elected in the first round, to gain the absolute majority of votes, provided that this amounted at least to one sixth of the electorate. However, the harshest struggle between the nineteenth and the twentieth centuries was fought over universal male suffrage—the debate over allowing women to vote was postponed. In an attempt to overstep the left, but without calling into question the liberal principle of the right to vote as derived from capacity and not from a subjective, individual entitlement, Giolitti fostered a revolutionary enlargement. In 1912, the right to vote was extended to all adult citizens over 30 years of age, regardless of literacy, and to all citizens between 21 and 30 years who were literate or who had served the army. This brought the enfranchised to about 23 percent of the population.[6] This reform also introduced a parliamentary indemnity, earlier formally excluded.

After a last passionate debate inside and outside Parliament, in 1918 Italy introduced universal male suffrage (all adult citizens over 21) and, in 1919, the single-member constituency was abandoned in favor of a proportional representation in 54 multimember districts with the d'Hondt formula. This change toward a proportional system represented an attempt to maintain some representation in a deeply changed political and social scene for the political forces who had governed the country since Unification—and who were in a minority due to universal suffrage—with the new socialist and Catholic mass parties collecting the majority of the electorate after World War I. The only attempt to preserve the liberal system of personal representation and to weaken the parties' role was made through electoral technicalities that allowed the citizens to vote for a list and to express a number of preferences for that list, or, alternatively, to add the names of candidates from other lists (*panachage*) to the list they had chosen.[7] The Parliament coming out after the first application of the 1919 reform was deeply divided into rival fronts, representing the socialist and Catholic subcultures, and thus causing immobility, confusion, and indecision: a stalemate exploited by Mussolini immediately thereafter.

UNDER FASCISM

One of the first acts of the fascists, once in the government, was the reform of the electoral system. Taking advantage of the parliamentary divisions between those in favor of a proportional law and those in favor of a plurality system, in November 1923, Mussolini sponsored the so-called legge Acerbo, which introduced a multimember proportional system with a majority premium. The most voted list at the national level, provided it had obtained at least 25 percent of the valid votes, would receive a majority premium of two thirds of the 535 parliamentary seats. The remaining 179 seats were to be divided among other lists, in each of the 16 constituencies, following the Hare formula.[8] Each voter could indicate two or three preferences,[9] but, since each list was made of a maximum number of candidates equal to two thirds of seats, the preferences expressed for the winning party—the fascist one—were meaningless, emphasizing the predominant role of the Fascist Party in the selection of the deputies.

Less than two years later, in 1925, the fascist regime showed again its willingness to manipulate the political system through the electoral system, when a new reform, a plurality system in single-member constituencies, was approved. However, this reform was not implemented because, in 1928, the fascist regime approved its third electoral reform. Within a more general subversion of the principles of liberal democracy, the fascists imposed a new, plebiscitary representation model, reducing the number of enfranchised citizens and the number of deputies. That system envisaged a single national constituency with the power of validating or rejecting a list of 400 candidates selected by the Gran Consiglio del Fascismo. Finally, in 1939, what remained of the representative system was wiped out: the Camera dei Deputati ceased to be elected and was totally replaced by the Camera dei Fasci e delle Corporazioni, composed of members selected by the fascist regime.

During the Republic

After World War II, the suffrage, extended to women, became universal. The Constituent Assembly was elected, on June 2, 1946, with a proportional system in 31 multimember constituencies. The choice of a proportional system was passionately debated among the political class. The pre-fascist liberal elite (see Chapter 19, this volume) accused the proportional system of the demolition of liberal democracy, while party elites who went underground during Fascism saw, in proportional representation, an instrument to return to the parties the power to govern the country. In the end, party politics prevailed, and the result was a very fragmented political spectrum, partly unable, partly unwilling, to include the electoral system in the Constitution (see Chapter 6, this volume).

Two years later, on April 18, 1948, the first post-World War II elections to the Camera dei Deputati (the lower Chamber) and to the Senato della Repubblica (the Senate, elected for the first time) were held. The Chamber was elected with the same rules used to elect the Constituent Assembly. With minor modifications, that electoral system remained in place till 1992. All citizens, male and female, over 21 years of age could vote, (18 after the 1975 reform) and those over 25 years could be elected. The number of deputies hinged on the size of the population (one per 80,000 inhabitants) and was fixed at 630 only in 1963.[10] The electoral law foresaw a party-list proportional system (using the strengthened Imperiali quota) with preferential voting in 31 multimember constituencies,[11] and remainders allocated in a single national district among parties that had won at least a constituency seat. Each voter could vote for a party and express a number of preferences depending on the district magnitude: 3 in up to 15 members' constituencies, 4 otherwise. Following the June 1991 referendum, in 1992 voters could express just one preference. This system did not, however, prevent the political fragmentation endemic to the Italian party system (see Chapter 12, this volume). On the contrary, it was specifically conceived, along with the hyperconsensual constitutional architecture, in order to safeguard an idea of party democracy that found its natural expression in the list proportional representation.

In 1953, with the so-called legge truffa (swindle law), the DC (and its centrist allies) tried to deeply modify the existing proportional system, giving a majority premium of 65 percent of seats to the party (or the coalition of parties) that had obtained the absolute majority of votes. The goal of the Christian Democrats (see Chapter 14, this volume) was to slow down the electoral growth of left and right extremist parties: actually, reform backers perceived the law as a way to strengthen democracy against anti-systemic forces by way of reinforcing the government thanks to a premium of up to 15 percent of seats.[12] However, since no group succeeded in reaching that percentage, the majority premium was not attributed and seats were allocated according to a proportional system very similar to the previous one.[13] In 1954, the legge truffa was repealed and the proportional system was restored. In 1956, however, that system was slightly modified: seats were allocated with the Imperiali quota and remainders were distributed in a single national constituency, but without national lists, among parties that gained at least one constituency seat and 300,000 votes. This electoral system remained in place until 1992.

As mentioned, for the first time in 1948 the Senate was elected. All citizens at least 25 years old were allowed to vote, while, to be elected, the candidates had to be 40 years old. The electoral system selected for the upper Chamber foresaw a peculiar plurality system that, indeed, was a proportional one: each of the twenty Italian regions was divided into a number of single-member constituencies proportional to the number of inhabitants. Voters had to express one vote for one candidate and the candidate reaching at least 65 percent of the valid votes was declared elected. If no candidate reached this (extremely high) threshold, as occurred most of the time, the unassigned seats were allocated, according to the d'Hondt formula, in a single regional constituency to groups of connected candidates. This electoral system produced a very close translation of votes into seats and, fostering fragmentation, ensured the survival of smaller parties. Actually, parties with less than 1 percent of votes could gain parliamentary representation.

While the system for the Senate tended to slightly favor bigger parties, the two systems did not produce very dissimilar effects on the competition *among* parties. What really differed were the dynamics of competition *inside* parties: preferential votes for the lower Chamber boosted the competition among candidates of the same party, especially when parties were divided, as the DC, into *correnti* (factions), which found in the preference vote the instrument for assessing their strength. Preferences were used especially by DC voters and, even more, in the south of the country. Only about one third of the possible preferences were expressed, although, in 1992, when voters could mark just one preference, slightly less than 50 percent of the electorate used the preferential vote.[14] According to Cazzola,[15] preferential voting was tied to economic underdevelopment and clientelism, and was more frequent the weaker the party organization and the stronger intraparty competition. In fact, the strict party discipline of PCI (see Chapter 15, this volume) hindered individual electoral campaigns, since the Communist Party was able to control its electorate and to direct its preferences. On the contrary, DC candidates spent most of their time and resources in campaigning for preferences.[16] DC and PCI were, in fact, the archetype of, respectively, *partito di centro* (high internal fragmentation and strict control of public resources for clientele) and *partito di opposizione* (high party discipline and weak control of public resources).[17] This resulted also in the high substitution rate of DC deputies through electoral defeat, an experience very rare among PCI candidates. Preferences were also the basis of what Parisi and Pasquino called *voto di scambio* (vote of exchange),[18] that is, the routine to use preferences, by voters, as a barter good and, by candidates, as an asset to purchase. Nevertheless, it was very rare that preferential votes overturned party-list order.[19] An important and often neglected consequence of preferential voting was its capacity to influence the formation of government coalitions. The Christian Democrats were, in fact, the essential element of whichever coalition, but the relative electoral strength of their factions contributed to establishing which other parties could be included in the government. This meant that the changes in the governmental coalitions (see Chapter 8, this volume) were due also—but not only—to the weight of the different factions (produced by preference votes) inside the DC.[20]

As mentioned, the June 1991 referendum reduced the number of preferences from three/four to one, to be expressed by writing on the ballot the name of the candidate. Beyond contributing to the lessening of electoral fraud, the effects of the reform were mainly three.[21] First, well-recognized national leaders were forced to do their best when campaigning inside their district, in order to grab the preferences required to be elected; second, candidates were made less dependent on their national faction leaders: competing against each other for the same preferences, national leaders were no longer in the position to distribute preferences among their followers who, therefore, being less dependent on their leader for re-election, became more autonomous also during the legislature; third, losing the power of their network, national leaders were defeated, inside some provinces, by local candidates deeply rooted in their electoral districts, causing what Ceccanti called "leadership provincialization."[22]

Concluding, the Italian proportional electoral law tended to emphasize both party system fragmentation and the lack of internal party cohesion. In fact, it was a highly proportional law without strong constraining clauses: the only threshold was to obtain at least 300,000 votes nationally and to win a seat in one constituency, which meant having a concentrated electorate of about 62,000–65,000 votes.[23]

The system put in place in 1948, though with some minor adjustment, was the longest lasting electoral system in the Italian history since Unification. On April 18, 1993, a referendum modified the electoral law for the Senate, overturning the proportional principle in favor of the plurality one. Referendum advocates claimed that a majoritarian electoral law would, on the one hand, strengthen the relationship between voters and candidates through the single-member constituency, and, on the other hand, simplify the political framework through the creation of two well-defined coalitions. Solid parliamentary majorities, stable governments, accountability, and alternation in government would all follow.[24] The expected result was a bipolar competition (see Chapter 25, this volume).

In 1993, following the scandals of *Tangentopoli* (see Chapter 24, this volume), and just some months after the referendum, a new electoral law was enacted, setting up a mixed-member majoritarian system, called Mattarellum by Giovanni Sartori, after the name of its rapporteur deputy Sergio Mattarella. As far as the lower Chamber was concerned, in each of the 26 constituencies,[25] three fourths of seats were attributed in single-member constituencies by a plurality system, while the remaining one fourth was attributed through a list proportional system using the Hare quota and the largest remainder method with a threshold of 4 percent at national level. Each voter had two ballots: one for the plurality and one for the proportional part. Moreover, that system had a technicality, called *scorporo parziale*, meant to prevent the overrepresentation of parties that had already gained one or more seats in single-member constituencies. When computing the amount of votes that each list collected in the proportional part, a number of votes equal to the second-placed candidate in the single-member constituency plus one was subtracted to the list connected with the winning candidate in the single-member constituency.[26]

As far as the upper Chamber was concerned, the new electoral system allocated three fourths of the seats, in each region, with the plurality system, while one fourth was attributed with the proportional d'Hondt formula on regional constituencies among connected candidates not elected in single-member districts (proportionally to the number of votes obtained in each constituency) and therefore with the so-called *scorporo totale* (i.e. the winning candidates' votes were not computed). Each voter had just one vote to cast for their preferred candidate in the single-member constituency.

The 1993 electoral reform produced contrasting results. The party system format continued to be highly fragmented. According to Giovanni Sartori,[27] in fact, the proportional system in force till 1992 produced only five/six relevant parties,[28] while the Mattarellum tripled them. And this was due not to the proportional mechanism, but to the plurality one, which allowed small parties significant blackmail power. Therefore, if we consider the reduction of the number of parties as one of the primary goals of the 1993 electoral reform, then the Mattarellum failed miserably. On the other hand, the undeniable merit of this mixed-member majoritarian system was to have launched a phase, still lasting, of bipolar competition and alternation in government. In fact, in 2001, Italy experienced its first true alternation in government since 1876. However, it is not easy to establish if the Mattarellum did work in creating a bipolar system of competition because, as Sartori highlighted,[29] bipolarism is the "natural" dynamic of Western European party systems, even the ones with a proportional electoral system. Actually, Sartori underlined the fact that no plurality system in single-member constituencies can reduce the number of parties if parties are weak, even less so if plurality is accompanied by a proportional correction.

Nevertheless, the Mattarellum did favor the formation of pre-electoral coalitions, which, in turn, supported the affirmation of a bipolar dynamic of competition, since coalitions presented themselves to the electorate as two alternative choices for the government of the country. Undoubtedly, the new party system was more competitive and most parties were driven toward aggregation (even if not uniformly over the entire national territory). Unquestionably, voters became more decisive in determining government formation. Since two coalitions were competing, voters could foresee who would become prime minister in case of the electoral victory of either coalition. Voters and parties, therefore, learned the electoral benefits of pre-electoral coalitions and the party system started to progressively structure itself as bipolar, but still fragmented.[30] Paradoxically, in fact, the plurality mechanism provided incentives to the fragmentation inside each of the two main coalitions. Actually, smaller parties used to negotiate their support in some constituencies in exchange for stand-down agreements in their favor in other constituencies. Therefore, while at the district level the plurality logic did work, at the national level it did not produce the desired reduction of political fragmentation. Especially as far as the lower Chamber is concerned, the two votes for the plurality and the proportional parts, the division of safe constituencies among allies, the *scorporo* mechanism, and the side payments for smaller parties, hindered the development of a logic of majoritarian competition to such an extent that they represented an element of "proportionalization" of the plurality system.[31] This "proportionalization" produced another effect: it hampered the development of strong linkages among candidates and their constituency. In fact, the heterogeneity of coalitions brought about a series of complex negotiations regarding the single-member constituencies which could be managed only by central party leaders, leaving voters aside. Often, in fact, the same candidate was moved, from one election to another, from one constituency to another, preventing his/her territorial rooting and the development of a direct relationship between voters and candidates.[32] Moreover, the Mattarellum was not immune from another problem: the risk of institutional stalemate. In fact, the small differences in the electoral systems for the two Chambers (number of votes, proportional formula, thresholds, *scorporo*) were able to produce very narrow or even opposite majorities in the two branches of Parliament[33] (see Chapter 9, this volume).

Another, but not the last, electoral reform was enacted in 2005. Fostered by the center-right parliamentary majority, the new law was also a response to some of the partisan problems of the previous electoral system. Single-member districts, in fact, were more favorable to the center-left, whose electorate was more loyal and did not betray its coalition even if the uninominal candidate was not well accepted. On the contrary, center-right candidates used to receive fewer votes than the sum of votes of the lists supporting the same candidates in the proportional part.[34] Thus, the House of Freedom and the Northern League sponsored a proportional electoral reform which eliminated the(ir) problems with single-member districts.

According to this law, seats are allocated on the basis of a party-list proportional system (without preferences) and a majority premium. In the 26 electoral constituencies,[35] to which seats are attributed in proportion to the population,[36] parties can run alone or in coalitions. Seats are allocated, first nationally, with a list proportional system using the Hare quota and the largest remainder method to parties or coalitions that have overcome one of the following thresholds: for coalitions, 10 percent of valid votes, provided that at least one list obtained 2 percent nationally; for single lists or for lists being part of coalitions under the 10 percent threshold, 4 percent of valid votes. The most voted coalition or list is awarded a majority premium amounting to 340 seats out of 630.

Soon after, Parliament also modified the upper Chamber electoral law. The Senate continues to be elected on a regional basis. In each region, seats are attributed proportionally to the population and then allocated according to a party-list proportional system without preferences using the Hare quota and the largest remainder method. Parties can run alone or in coalition and the majority premium is attributed at the regional level to political organizations that have overcome one of the following thresholds: for coalitions, 20 percent of valid votes, provided that at least one list obtained 3 percent regionally; for single lists or for lists being part of coalitions under the 20 percent threshold, 8 percent of valid votes. The most voted coalition or list is awarded a majority premium of 55 percent of the seats in that specific region.

The 2005 reform was scathingly criticized on three fronts. First, providing a majority premium on two different bases (national for the Chamber, regional for the Senate) could cause a dangerous phenomenon: two different majorities in the two parliamentary branches, thus political and institutional stalemate. Second, the law required that parties or coalitions make explicit their political program and the name of their leader, thus apparently conflicting with the constitutional powers of the President of the Republic. Third, the long and closed lists of candidates provide party leaders with the power to select, in their "smoke-filled rooms," the entire parliamentary class.

This system—known as Sartori Porcellum since its principal creator, the former minister Roberto Calderoli, defined his own law as a *porcata* (a dirty trick)—made it less dangerous, at least for parties able to overcome the mentioned thresholds, to run alone outside coalitions.[37] Actually, "fragmented bipolarism" had its peak in the 2006 elections. However, voters and parties learned very quickly the rules of the game imposed by the new electoral law, and, in 2008, a form of "limited bipolarism" was established. In fact, the 2005 electoral reform retained the incentives to form pre-electoral coalitions, simplifying bargaining processes and strategic coordination among parties: no more wrangling on single-member constituencies, but broad coalition agreements.[38] The competitive dynamic did not change, but the party system format saw the appearance of two big parties (PD and PDL), both from the supply side (party strategies) and from the voters' reactions side (in fact, voters mainly focused on those two alternatives). This caused a reduction in party fragmentation at the electoral, the parliamentary, and the governmental level.[39] Therefore, despite criticism, the new electoral law produced *decisive* (a winning coalition with a political leader legitimated to become prime minister) and *competitive* (alternation in government) elections by "manufacturing" a sizable parliamentary majority. The new law made even clearer the decisive power of voters on the choice of government. In fact, parties and coalitions must file an electoral program and their leader's name. In this way, elections are a zero sum game in which what is at stake is the majority premium which allows the winning coalition to govern. Nonetheless, in the 2013 elections, something extraordinary and unpredictable happened: a new party, the MoVimento 5 Stelle, led by a comedian, Beppe Grillo, became the most voted-for party in Italy. Due to the different bases for the allocation of the majority premium in the lower and upper Chambers, the center-left winning coalition was not able to form a government on its own. Suddenly, therefore, elections ceased to be *decisive*, and a *Große Koalition* made its way, with the M5S putting in place a *conventio ad (self-)excludendum* which has marked (and will mark) contemporary Italian political history.

It is not an easy task to draw some conclusions on the Porcellum. I dare to define it "an electoral law without decisive effects" since, in three consecutive elections, it produced three very dissimilar electoral, parliamentary, and governmental consequences. In fact, in 2006, the bipolarism reached its maximum level of fragmentation, no party running outside coalitions was able to gain parliamentary representation and a high level of government instability followed. In 2008, two more cohesive coalitions competed, a centrist party (UDC) overcame the threshold and the Berlusconi government was the second longest-lived government in Italian republican history. In 2013, finally, the number of electoral parties rose again, three coalitions and one party entered the Parliament, giving birth to an oversized government coalition.

Conclusions

At the beginning of December 2013, the Constitutional Court (see Chapter 10, this volume) passed a judgment on Porcellum declaring it unconstitutional for two main reasons: because it did not foresee a minimum threshold in order to attain the majority premium and because of long and closed lists of candidates. The immediate effect of the sentence was to speed up the electoral reform. The proposal came from Prime Minister Matteo Renzi after an agreement with Silvio Berlusconi, whose party, however, did not vote the final approval of the so-called Italicum. The new electoral law foresees a majority-assuring semi-open list proportional representation system. Seats are allocated, first at the national level, with the Hare formula and the largest remainders method among the lists that have overcome the 3 percent threshold nationally. Then, they are assigned to the 100 districts (with a magnitude range from 3 to 9 seats). The allocation, however, is not fully proportional, since it assigns a majority bonus to the party (coalitions are not allowed) that obtains at least 40 percent of the votes. If no party goes beyond that threshold, the two most voted parties compete in a second, run-off election. The winning one will receive 340 seats (out of 630). The remaining seats are allocated proportionally among the other parties. Lists of candidates are semi-open: the first candidate in each list is blocked (and will be the first to be elected, if his party wins a seat in that district). All the other candidates are elected on the basis of preferential voting. Multiple candidacies are allowed, only for list leaders, in up to 10 districts. Lists must present gender alternation and voters can express two preferences, but only if in favor of candidates of different gender, otherwise only the first preference will be considered valid. The law will apply only to the Chamber of Deputies starting from July 2016, since the parallel constitutional reform will transform the Senate in an assembly not elected by the citizens but representative of Italian regions. Italicum supporters underline mainly three points: voters can choose not only their representative, but also, substantially, the Prime Minister; the majority bonus favors governability without distorting too much representation; it fosters the presence of women in Parliament. Those who criticize the Italicum highlight that: governability will not be assured, since it depends not just on the electoral system, but on other, most important elements of the political system; that the law gives the majority of seats to a single party that might represent a tiny minority of the electorate; that the 3 percent threshold is too low to prevent party fragmentation; and, finally, that multiple candidacies in up to 10 districts will significantly distort the relationship between voters and candidates.

The electoral law remains an object of intense and acrimonious debate. Most of the proposals are marred by intense and irreconcilable partisanship. When and where voters have little power, as is the case in Italy because of the 2005 electoral law, parties, *trasformismo*, and lobbies prevail. Bad electoral laws are one important reason why the Italian political system cannot be decently governed and why the quality of Italian democracy is not satisfactory.

NOTES

1. These pages deal with electoral systems for parliamentary elections. Though interesting, no mention will be made of systems for the election of local councils, provinces, and regions, which include strong majoritarian and personalizing elements.
2. Giorgio Galli, Vittorio Capecchi, Vittoria Cioni Polacchini, and Giordano Sivini, *Il comportamento elettorale in Italia: un'indagine ecologica sulle elezioni in Italia tra il 1946 e il 1963* (Bologna: Il Mulino, 1968), 23.
3. Ibid.
4. The number of candidates admitted to the run-off was double that of the unassigned seats; e.g. if two seats remained unassigned, four candidates took part in the run-off.
5. The problem of malapportionment was not solved, and elections continued to be held in constituencies whose boundaries had been drawn according to the 1882 population census.
6. Galli et al., *Il comportamento elettorale in Italia*, 23.
7. One preference in up to 5 member constituencies, two preferences in 6 to 10 member constituencies, three preferences in 11 to 15 member constituencies, and four preferences in more than 15 member constituencies.
8. If no list gained at least 25 percent of the votes, seats would have been distributed proportionally with the Hare formula.
9. Two preferences in less than twenty member constituencies, three otherwise.
10. Also the number of senators was fixed at 315 in 1963.
11. Thirty-two since 1958, when Trieste was added.
12. Maria Serena Piretti, *La legge truffa. Il fallimento dell'ingegneria politica* (Bologna: Il Mulino, 2003). Gaetano Quagliariello, "Cinquanta anni dopo la riforma elettorale del 1953," in Stefano Ceccanti and Salvatore Vassallo, *Come chiudere la transizione. Cambiamento, apprendimento e adattamento nel sistema politico italiano* (Bologna: Il Mulino, 2004), 71–88.
13. The only difference was represented by the remainders distribution, since national lists were suppressed.
14. Stefano Ceccanti, "Nessuna falcidia: i giovani, le donne e l'elettore razionale," in Gianfranco Pasquino, *Votare un solo candidato. Le conseguenze politiche della preferenza unica* (Bologna: Il Mulino, 1993), 31–79.
15. Franco Cazzola, "Partiti, correnti e voto di preferenza," *Rivista Italiana di Scienza Politica* 2, no. 3 (1972), 569–588.
16. Richard S. Katz and Luciano Bardi, "Voto di preferenza e ricambio del personale parlamentare in Italia (1963–1976)," *Rivista Italiana di Scienza Politica* 9, no. 1 (1979), 71–95.
17. Renato D'Amico, "Voto di preferenza, movimento dell'elettorato e modelli di partito: l'andamento delle preferenze nelle elezioni politiche italiane del quindicennio 1968-1983," *Quaderni dell'osservatorio elettorale* 18 (1987), 91–147.
18. Arturo Parisi and Gianfranco Pasquino, "Relazioni partiti-elettori e tipi di voto," in Arturo Parisi and Gianfranco Pasquino, *Continuità e mutamento elettorale in Italia. Le elezioni del 20 giugno 1976 e il sistema politico italiano* (Bologna: Il Mulino, 1977), 215–249.

19. Gianfranco Pasquino, "Le radici del frazionismo e il voto di preferenza," *Rivista Italiana di Scienza Politica* 2, no. 2 (1972), 353–368.

20. Katz and Bardi, "Voto di preferenza e ricambio del personale parlamentare in Italia," 71–95.

21. Gianfranco Pasquino, ed., *Votare un solo candidato. Le conseguenze politiche della preferenza unica* (Bologna: Il Mulino, 1993).

22. Ceccanti, "Nessuna falcidia."

23. Gianfranco Pasquino, "Tricks and Treats: The 2005 Italian Electoral Law and Its Consequences," *South European Society and Politics* 12, no. 1 (2007), 79–93.

24. Alessandro Chiaramonte and Roberto D'Alimonte, "Dieci anni di (quasi) maggioritario: una riforma (quasi) riuscita," in Ceccanti and Vassallo, *Come Chiudere la transizione*, 105–123. On the debate see Richard S. Katz, "Reforming the Italian Electoral Law, 1993," in Matthew Soberg Shugart and Martin P. Wattenberg, *Mixed-Member Electoral Systems: The Best of Both Worlds?* (Oxford: Oxford University Press, 2003), 96–122.

25. Plus one single-member constituency: Valle d'Aosta.

26. If the elected candidate was linked with more than one list, the subtraction was made *pro quota*, i.e. proportionally to the number of votes that each list connected to the winning candidate obtained.

27. Giovanni Sartori, "Il sistema elettorale resta cattivo," *Rivista Italiana di Scienza Politica* 31, no. 3 (2001), 471–480.

28. As defined by Sartori himself in his 1976 book: Giovanni Sartori, *Parties and Party Systems: A Framework for Analysis* (Cambridge: Cambridge University Press, 1976).

29. Ibid.

30. Chiaramonte and D'Alimonte, "Dieci anni di (quasi) maggioritario."

31. Roberto D'Alimonte and Alessandro Chiaramonte, "Il nuovo sistema elettorale italiano: le opportunità e le scelte," in Stefano Bartolini and Roberto D'Alimonte, *Maggioritario ma non troppo. Le elezioni politiche del 1994* (Bologna: Il Mulino, 1995), 37–81.

32. Chiaramonte and D'Alimonte, "Dieci anni di (quasi) maggioritario."

33. Ibid.

34. Paolo Feltrin and Davide Fabrizio, "Proporzionale con premio di maggioranza: un sistema elettorale (inconsapevolmente) efficace," in Paolo Feltrin, Paolo Natale, and Luca Ricolfi, *Nel segreto dell'urna. Un'analisi delle elezioni politiche del 2006* (Turin: Utet, 2007), 323–338.

35. Plus one single-member constituency: Valle d'Aosta.

36. Since the 2006 elections, moreover, 12 deputies and 6 senators are attributed to foreign constituencies.

37. Alessandro Chiaramonte and Aldo Di Virgilio, "Da una riforma elettorale all'altra: partiti, coalizioni e processi di apprendimento," *Rivista Italiana di Scienza Politica* 36, no. 3 (2006), 363–391.

38. Aldo Di Virgilio, "La riforma elettorale della Casa delle libertà alla prova del voto," *Polis* 21, no. 1 (2007), 119–146.

39. Alessandro Chiaramonte, "Dal bipolarismo frammentato al bipolarismo limitato? Evoluzione del sistema partitico italiano," in Roberto D'Alimonte and Alessandro Chiaramonte, *Proporzionale se vi pare. Le elezioni politiche del 2008* (Bologna: Il Mulino, 2010), 203–228.

CHAPTER 12

PARTY SYSTEMS IN POST-WORLD WAR II ITALY

CAROL MERSHON

PARTIES and party systems are foundational to democratic politics. This conventional wisdom has particular resonance in post-World War II Italy. Parties have so thoroughly permeated Italian political life that the term *partitocrazia* has gained wide currency (cf. Chapter 4, this volume). Parties have had such a central place that the changes in the Italian party system dating from the early 1990s have led many observers to refer to a "Second Republic," even though the 1948 Constitution is still in effect.[1]

Given the context, this chapter addresses four major questions. How has the Italian party system evolved since the end of World War II? What explains systemic changes over time? How much do continuities with the past leave an imprint on the contemporary system? The recent record of flux invites a fourth: how might party system dynamics be analyzed with a new lens?

To preview, the Italian party system has evinced change so profound that it is essential to identify multiple systems after World War II. The chapter's first section focuses on two party systems as established in elections. Although societal factors help account for systemic shifts, the second section emphasizes strategic and institutional explanations. The third section weighs the impact of the past on the contemporary party system, and the fourth considers inter-electoral party system change. The conclusion highlights the fact that the study of postwar Italian party systems enhances understanding of party systems writ large.

DISTINCT PARTY SYSTEMS IN POSTWAR ITALY

In accord with the scholarly consensus, I define a political party as a team of politicians competing or intending to compete for popular support so as to hold elective office, and a party system as a patterned set of interactions among parties.[2] Many political scientists echo Sartori in maintaining that the number and policy positions of parties suffice to characterize a party system.[3] Mainwaring adds institutionalization as another property separating party systems.[4] Some scholars analyze the configuration of the number, sizes, and positions of parties in order to discern the presence or absence of a core party and thus distinguish party systems.[5] Mair designates the structure of interparty competition for control of the executive as the sole criterion demarcating party systems.[6]

Even though scholars disagree on how to differentiate party systems, all criteria in widespread use point to one party system in Italy from the first postwar elections of 1946 until the early 1990s. Some criteria signal another systemic rupture in the early 2010s.

For now, I focus on the first two party systems created in postwar Italian elections. From 1946 to the early 1990s, five attributes can be observed: a relatively high number of parties and relatively great distances among parties; relatively high system institutionalization; the Christian Democrats' continuous occupation of the core; and closed competition for the executive. From the early 1990s to at least 2010, shifts appear on all five fronts. Amid continuing party system fragmentation, two large pre-electoral alliances emerged, integrating the now-moderate heirs of once extremist parties. The level of system institutionalization arguably declined. Starting in 1992, elections yielded an empty core. In 1994, closed competition for the executive ended. In 1996, open competition began.

Consider the number of parties and distances among them. Giovanni Sartori homes in on these two traits to classify Italy as a case of polarized pluralism.[7] To Sartori, relatively high fragmentation and polarization link to other traits, including the presence of one or several centrist parties (for Italy, the DC), anti-system parties, irresponsible oppositions, and centrifugal competition. Although this seminal contribution has sparked debate, it underscores the fact that the DC and its circle of governing allies implemented an agreement to exclude the Communists and neo-Fascist MSI from the executive.[8] The end of the Cold War in 1989 triggered the multistep transformation of the PCI—and next the transformation of the MSI.[9] In 1994, the reformed PDS anchored one pre-electoral cartel, and the AN joined its main opponent. Center-left and center-right alliances have competed in the electoral arena since 1994.

The postwar Italian party system was born institutionalized, so to speak, given the parties' role in directing the anti-Fascist Resistance, building mass organizations, and mobilizing mass support.[10] Granted, partisans fought the Resistance only in the center and north. And the first few national postwar elections registered somewhat high electoral volatility, an index measuring one aspect of party system institutionalization.[11] Yet, compared to other new democracies, Italy had an institutionalized party system in the early postwar years that would rapidly institutionalize further. Even so, the electoral volatility recorded in the 1992 parliamentary elections—which rose further in 1994—might have ended the entrenchment of high institutionalization.[12] Other scholars, however, perceive relatively high party system institutionalization in Italy from the mid-1990s to the early 2010s.[13]

The DC qualified as a core party from 1946 up to, but not including, the 1992 elections.[14] For that span, that is, the DC was the essential member of all policy-feasible majority coalitions, given the seat shares and policy positions of all parties in the Italian policy space. This analysis, grounded in spatial theories of voting, imparts precise meaning to party dominance of a party system: a party inhabiting the core need not command a seat majority on its own; its power derives from its ability to make all majorities. A core party, if present, should govern. The DC as a core party fulfilled that expectation.[15] According to this school, Italian electoral outcomes in and since 1992 have produced an empty core.[16]

Given the DC's uninterrupted control of government, the Italian party system exhibited a closed structure of party competition for the executive until 1994.[17] In the mid-1990s, questions surrounding the first Berlusconi cabinet suggested "uncertainty"[18] in the structure of competition. With alternation in government starting in 1996 and continuing since then, competition over the Italian executive has opened up.

Thus, although scholars use different criteria to distinguish party systems, all criteria mark the passage from one Italian party system to another in the early 1990s. The precise dates of the transformation may vary slightly, but the consensus stands. Table 12.1

Table 12.1 Italian Election Results, Chamber Seats and Vote Shares, Selected Parties and Selected Parliamentary Elections 1946–1992

Party	1946	1963	1976	1987	1992
DC	207 (35.2%)	260 (38.3%)	262 (38.7%)	234 (34.3%)	206 (29.7%)
PCI	104 (18.9)	166 (25.3)	228 (34.4)	177 (26.6)	–
PSI	115 (20.7)	87 (13.8)	57 (9.6)	94 (14.3)	92 (13.6)
PSDI	–	33 (6.1)	15 (3.4)	17 (3.0)	16 (2.7)
PRI	23 (4.4)	6 (1.4)	14 (3.1)	21 (3.7)	27 (4.4)
PLI	–	39 (7.0)	5 (1.3)	11 (2.1)	17 (2.9)
MSI	–	27 (5.1)	35 (6.1)	36 (5.9)	34 (5.4)
LL/LN	–	–	–	1 (0.5)	55 (8.7)
PDS	–	–	–	–	107 (16.1)
RC	–	–	–	–	35 (5.6)

Key to party acronyms:

DC Christian Democracy
LL Lombard League (LN, Northern League 1992)
MSI Italian Social Movement (MSI)
PCI Italian Communist Party (PCI heir)
PDS Democratic Party of the Left
PLI Italian Liberal Party
PRI Italian Republican Party
PSDI Italian Social Democratic Party (name changes disregarded)
PSI Italian Socialist Party
RC Communist Refoundation (PCI heir)

Note: The table lists only those parties that are among the largest in at least one election reported and/or that recur in the executive. For each party, number of seats appears first and share of votes appears in parentheses. For 1946, results are for the unicameral Constituent Assembly.[19]

profiles the first Italian party system by illustrating the ingredients of successive governing coalition formulae centered in the DC,[20] as well as such important shifts as the apex of PCI strength in 1976 and the DC's losses in 1992.

Together, Tables 12.1 and 12.2 contrast the first two postwar Italian party systems. Whereas Table 12.1 spotlights the recurrence of key players in the electoral arena between 1946 and 1992, Table 12.2 conveys the redefinition of contestants from 1992 to 2013. Ironically, perhaps the most striking quality of Table 12.2 is its understatement: for simplicity, most rows report first on a baseline 1992 party and then on its principal heir(s). Only the Northern League—which debuted in 1992 and whose predecessor entered Parliament in 1987, as seen in Table 12.1—has run in all parliamentary elections between 1992 and 2013.

By several, but not all, criteria, the 2013 elections ushered in a third Italian party system. Party system fragmentation has increased, and new policy disputes have arisen.

Table 12.2 Italian Election Results, Chamber Seats and Vote Shares, Selected Parties and All Parliamentary Elections 1992–2013

Party	1992	1994	1996	2001	2006	2008	2013
PDS / DS / PD	107 (16.1%)	109 (20.4%)	150 (21.1%)	135 (16.6%)	220 (30.4%)	217 (33.1%)	297 (25.5%)
RC / SA / SEL	35 (5.6)	39 (6.1)	35 (8.6)	11 (5.0)	41 (5.7)	2 (3.1)	37 (3.2)
FI / PDL	–	99 (21.0)	123 (20.6)	189 (29.4)	140 (23.6)	276 (37.2)	98 (15.6)
MSI / AN / PDL / FDI	34 (5.4)	109 (13.5)	93 (15.7)	99 (12.0)	71 (12.0)		9 (2.0)
LN	55 (8.7)	117 (8.4)	59 (10.1)	30 (3.94)	26 (4.5)	60 (8.3)	18 (4.1)
M5S	–	–	–	–	–	–	109 (25.1)

Key to party acronyms (with relevant elections):

AN National Alliance ('94, '96, '01, '06) ('08)
DS Left Democrats ('96, '01, '06; ran with Daisy as Ulivo in '06)
FDI Brothers of Italy ('13)
FI Forza Italia ('94, '96, '01, '06)
LN Northern League (all elections 1992 to 2013)
M5S Five Stars Movement ('13)
MSI Italian Social Movement ('92)
PD Democratic Party ('08, '13)
PDL People of Freedom ('08, '13)
PDS Democratic Party of the Left ('92)
RC Communist Refoundation ('92, '94. '96, '01, '06)
SA Rainbow Left ('08)
SEL Left, Ecology, Freedom ('13)

Note: The table lists only those parties that are among the largest in a few elections, save for one class of exceptions: it omits parties belonging to the variegated DC diaspora (Chapter 14, this volume). For each party, the number of seats appears first and the share of votes appears in parentheses. For 1994–2001 elections, vote shares from proportional representation (PR) ballot appear.

The vertical waved lines indicate the 1993 and 2005 electoral reforms. The table largely disregards pre-electoral alliances.[21]

System institutionalization has declined, as flagged by extraordinary electoral volatility. The 2013 election, like all others since 1992, created an empty core.[22] Open party competition for government has continued.

The two postwar Italian party systems are distinct. Recent developments point to the possibility of a third party system. The discussion leads naturally to explaining systemic change.

EXPLANATIONS FOR SYSTEMIC CHANGE

Postwar Italian society has witnessed far-reaching change, with manifold political repercussions, as multiple chapters in this volume attest. Broad societal trends have altered the Italian party system from the bottom up, as voter attitudes and voter-party linkages have evolved. In the early postwar decades, the Italian electorate was firmly aligned behind parties and party organizations. By the 1970s, however, a process of electoral dealignment and realignment was underway, due to secularization and urbanization, along with generational replacement and increased educational attainment among voters.[23] Survey research in the 1980s indicated that the subcultural "vote of belonging," motivated by fidelity to either the DC or the PCI, was eroding; voters who cast a potentially mobile "vote of opinion," based on parties' policy promises and performance, had become more numerous.[24] The end of the Cold War in 1989, the PCI's moves along its post-Cold War road to reform, and the rapidly spreading corruption scandal that erupted in early 1992 all increased voters' willingness to back new and refashioned party options. Voters' orientations thus helped produce the electoral earthquake of 1992 and the seismic shift of greater magnitude of 1994.

Yet voters' orientations do not suffice to explain party system change. Voters choose from the options available at election time: starting in 1994, as noted, party leaders have forged pre-electoral alliances; voters have used the cartels as heuristics in making vote decisions,[25] and have been able to do so, given their ability to rapidly learn about the workings of new electoral laws.[26] Electoral institutions influence voters' choices. Politicians' strategic choices, as conditioned by institutions and, at times, redesigning institutions, modify party systems from the top down.

Electoral institutions underlie both enduring fragmentation in the Italian party system and turning points in its evolution. The highly proportional version of open-list proportional representation in effect from 1946 to 1993 for Chamber elections established very low barriers to entry; the electoral rules for the Senate, while not quite as permissive, also awarded seats to miniscule parties.[27] The 1975 advent of elections to regional councils across Italy and the 1976 lowering of the age requirement for voting in Chamber elections helped strengthen the PCI in the mid-1970s. Under Italy's highly proportional variant of proportional representation, in 1992 the DC's vote losses accompanied a rise in overall party system fragmentation, as Table 12.1 suggests.

The revolving door of parties displayed in Table 12.2 reflects in part the impact of two electoral reforms. In 1993, Members of Parliament (MPs) approved mixed-member electoral laws for the Chamber and Senate, deliberately aiming to assure representation to small parties.[28] These rules, inaugurated in 1994, engendered that intended effect. Other outcomes ensued. In particular, old parties crumbled and new parties arose. The DC, engulfed by corruption, split apart in early 1994; its immediate heirs hoped for survival under the new rules. Media magnate Berlusconi founded Forza Italia shortly before the 1994 elections. In late 2005, the center-right government, headed by Berlusconi, enacted bonus-adjusted closed-list proportional representation, given perceived disadvantages for the center-right under the mixed-member rules.[29] It might seem that the 2005 reform would enhance governability. Yet the different bases for allocating the seat bonus across the two houses—nationwide for the lower house, regionally for the upper—have ended up threatening governments: a pre-electoral coalition's comfortable majority in the Chamber has accompanied a razor-thin Senate majority (the case of the center-left in 2006), a dwindling Senate majority (the center-right over the 2008–13 legislature), and even a Senate minority (the center-left in 2013).[30]

Both sets of rules have given politicians incentives to compete in multiparty alliances in the electoral arena. The leaders of relatively large parties have spearheaded the construction of pre-electoral cartels on the center-left and center-right. Under the mixed-member laws, cartel leaders bargained single-member district candidacies among member parties so as to allot districts in proportion to anticipated party strength.[31] With the first use of bonus-adjusted PR in 2006, the quest for the majority prize produced the most fragmented and heterogeneous pre-electoral coalitions up to that point.[32]

Politicians can update strategies without any change in institutions. In the run-up to the 2008 Italian parliamentary elections, Left Democrat leader Veltroni created the Democratic Party by effecting a merger of the DS, the Daisy, and smaller parties. This move prompted adaptation on the center-right: the FI and AN, with minor parties, founded the People of Freedom; the fusion officially fell after the 2008 election but the announcement beforehand included the member parties' commitment to form a single PDL parliamentary group.[33] The systemic attribute of "fragmented bipolarism," wherein two pre-electoral cartels coexisted with and even facilitated the survival of many parties from 1994 to 2006, thus gave way, in 2008, to "limited pluralism."[34]

Politicians' strategic behavior extends beyond the response to and reform of political institutions. Politicians also seek to manipulate the chief issues defining the space of party competition.[35] To illustrate, during the Cold War, the DC's emphasis on anti-communism perpetuated the party's appeal to its faithful electorate and reinforced its exclusion of the PCI from government. In the second Italian party system, Berlusconi tried to revive anti-communism, and the Northern League brought center-periphery relations and anti-establishment populism into national debate.[36] In the early 2010s, the Five Star Movement (M5S) has broadcast a new brand of anti-establishment sentiment, based on citizen rejection of austerity measures imposed by the European Union.

Societal, institutional, and strategic influences have thus reshaped party systems in postwar Italy. In that light, we now evaluate continuity and change in the contemporary party system.

The Contemporary Italian Party System

The 2013 parliamentary election may have upended the Italian party system—again. Table 12.2 confirms that the PD, the second largest party in 2008, dropped to a quarter of the national vote in 2013. The largest party in 2008, the PDL, sank to a sixth. The pre-electoral alliance led by outgoing premier Monti barely passed the 10 percent barrier for Chamber representation. The anti-party M5S scored an electoral victory without parallel in Western Europe for a party in its national debut.[37] Under these conditions, in 2013 the center-left pre-electoral cartel won the premium of 54 percent of Chamber seats with only 29.6 percent of the vote.

Figures 12.1 and 12.2 assess the magnitude of party system change in 2013 by tracking several indexes of electoral outcomes for every national contest since 1946. Figure 12.1

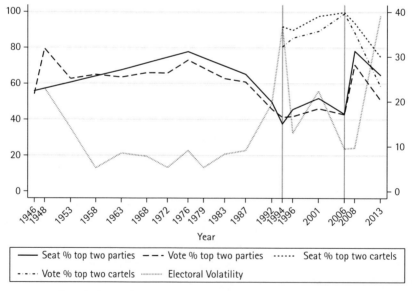

FIGURE 12.1 Results of Electoral Competition among Italian Parties, All National Legislative Elections, Lower House, 1946–2013: Two Largest Parties, Two Largest Pre-Electoral Alliances, and Electoral Volatility

Note: Figures 12.1 and 12.2 report 1946 results for the unicameral Constituent Assembly. The 1948 vote datum reflects the result for the combined Popular Front alliance of the PCI and PSI (along with the first-place DC). The vertical lines mark the first elections in which the electoral reforms of 1993 and 2005 were implemented.[38]

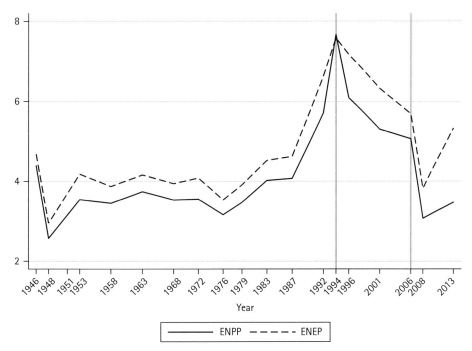

FIGURE 12.2 Results of Electoral Competition among Italian Parties, All National Legislative Elections, Lower House, 1946–2013: Effective Numbers of Parliamentary Parties and Electoral Parties

reports the combined vote and seat shares of the two largest parties, which fell to their postwar nadir in 1994 and dipped in 2006 after a rise; recall that both dates coincide with the first use of new electoral rules. After elite strategic innovation boosted the combined vote and seat shares of the two largest parties in 2008, those shares tumbled in 2013, as noted. Consider next the performance of the center-left and center-right pre-electoral cartels since 1994, whose combined vote and seat shares expanded through 2006, ebbed in 2008 (yet remained near 90 percent), and plummeted in 2013 to the unprecedented levels of 59 percent and 75 percent, respectively. The 2013 plunge in the cartels' combined seats occurred even with the bonus applied. Electoral volatility spiked in 2013 to the highest value ever seen in postwar Italy—and one of the highest observed in an established democracy.

Affording another view, Figure 12.2 charts party system fragmentation by focusing on two frequently adopted indexes, the effective number of parliamentary parties (ENPP) and the effective number of electoral parties (ENEP). The first measure weights the raw number of parties by the share of seats each party wins at election time, and the second weights the raw number of parties by their vote shares. Both reached a maximum in 1994, when the first electoral reform took effect, and declined after that—until a reversal in 2013. The widened gap in 2013 between the lines for the two indexes represents increased disproportionality in the distribution of votes and seats, the greatest ever in postwar Italy.[39]

The spectacular entry of the Five Stars Movement into the national electoral arena in 2013 posed a post-electoral conundrum, because the M5S refused to assume a role in the executive. Lengthy negotiations preceded the inauguration of the Letta cabinet (of the PD, PDL, Civic Choice, Centrist Union, and Radicals), whose complement of undersecretaries extended further to two micro-parties. For the first time in the Italian Republic, parties constructed an executive grand coalition.[40] The coalition not only encompassed but also split the center-left and center-right pre-electoral alliances: the SEL and the Brothers of Italy, of the center-left and center-right cartels respectively, joined the M5S in opposing the Letta government at its investiture, while the League abstained.

The systemic break of the early 2010s might seem complete. Yet signs of persistence appear. I start with the Five Star Movement, whose sudden, disruptive addition to the party system biases the appraisal *against* continuity.

Despite its clamorous novelty, the M5S exhibits at least seven links with the past. First, survey data disclose that the M5S drew an interclass electorate in 2013, thus evoking an enduring trait of the DC.[41] Second, surveys conducted just before the 2013 election reveal that M5S voters stood apart from others in relying on the Internet as a principal source of news.[42] Yet patterns of media usage have long helped segment the Italian electorate. In the first postwar party system, voters belonging to the Catholic and Communist subcultures read different newspapers and watched different RAI-TV channels. Since the early 1990s, center-right voters have provided a loyal audience for Berlusconi's media empire, largely shunned by center-left voters.[43] Third, the M5S advertises its extra-parliamentary origins in part through its name. Previous extra-parliamentary movements, including the League, have shaken the Italian party system by earning parliamentary representation. Fourth, although the M5S rode a wave of success in subnational elections from 2010 to 2012, such contests have repeatedly remolded the Italian party system; witness, for example, the regional gains of the PCI in 1975 and the League in 1990. Fifth, the M5S has reiterated the theme of participatory democracy characteristic of Greens in Italy and across Europe since the 1980s. Sixth, again, the anti-establishment message sent by the M5S finds an echo in the League's fierce criticism of the political class in the early 1990s. Last, the M5S has introduced opposition to the EU into the set of issues structuring party competition. Yet international issues have done much to drive postwar Italian party competition. The Cold War underpinned the confrontation between the DC and PCI. When the Cold War ended, the first postwar Italian party system yielded to the second.

Now, more broadly, I revisit the criteria for distinguishing party systems. Relative to party systems in other advanced democracies, the Italian system has long manifested fragmentation. This trait shows both continuity and change, with the 2013 election reaffirming heterogeneous, many-party pre-electoral alliances—and boosting the strength of formations outside the two major cartels. Relative to others, the Italian party system long displayed strong parties styled by others (or self-styled) as anti-system. That attribute waned in the early 1990s, despite the center-right's attempts to resuscitate anti-communism. It may have returned, given the stance of the Five Star Movement; but signs of M5S weakness after the 2013 elections suggest caution in drawing conclusions about renewed polarization.[44] Electoral volatility, treated by many analysts as a key indicator of party system institutionalization, climbed to an astonishing peak in 2013. Yet, after the 1994 peak, volatility settled to a degree up to 2013, so that whether a variant of that pattern will reassert itself is unclear. Recall two elements of continuity dating from the 1990s. Starting in 1992, no parliamentary election has produced a core party. Since 1996, parties have engaged in open competition for government.

Thus, it is likely, but not certain, that a third postwar Italian party system has emerged. Its features are still taking shape. Indeed, party leaders have attached top priority to electoral and constitutional reforms. New electoral institutions, if approved, will offer new incentives and constraints to parties and voters. Parties will also learn under new rules, revising the strategies that write the menu of options for voters as party competition recurs in the electoral arena.

ON INTER-ELECTORAL PARTY SYSTEM CHANGE

The discussion so far rests on the premise that parties and party systems are creatures of elections. But party systems are not only products of the electoral arena; their constituent parties are neither unitary nor fixed actors from one parliamentary election to the next. Individual legislators make choices of affiliation that can redefine the strength of legislative parties during a parliamentary term, without recourse to the voters' verdict. MPs' decisions made outside the electoral arena shape voters' options at the next election.[45]

To open a window on inter-electoral party system change in postwar Italy, Table 12.3 tracks MP choices on party membership in the lower house for the five legislatures serving between 1994 and 2013. Specifically, for each legislature, Table 12.3 compares the effective number of parliamentary parties in the election launching the term, reported in Table 12.2, with three other measures: the effective number of parliamentary groups (ENPG), weighting the raw number of parliamentary groups by their seat shares, at the inception and end of the term; total MP switches during the term; and within-term seat volatility, a summary score of the membership gains and losses of each parliamentary group, computed here for the term's start and end.[46] In all legislatures, the ENPG at the term's start differs from the ENPP at election time, reflecting legislators' responses to parliamentary rules. In all legislatures, the ENPG rose from the outset to the close of the term, although the movement was most contained from 1996 to 2001. Nonetheless, as seen on the second row, during that term the near-stasis in the ENPG masks what other indicators reveal as substantial inter-electoral party system change: a total of 295 MP switches occurred and seat volatility exceeded 20 percent. Whereas electoral volatility of more than 15 or 20 percent, in an established democracy, is routinely viewed as high, party seat shares overall can exhibit this much

Table 12.3 Inter-Electoral Party System Change in the Italian Chamber
of Deputies, 1994–2013

Legislature	ENPP at election	ENPG		Total MP switches	Seat volatility within term
		Start term	End term		
XII: 1994–1996	7.67	6.15	6.50	208	13.6
XIII: 1996–2001	6.09	6.14	6.18	295	21.1
XIV: 2001–2006	5.30	5.35	5.63	44	4.15
XV: 2006–2008	5.06	5.22	6.04	65	6.99
XVI: 2008–2013	3.07	3.09	4.28	180*	16.2

*The total of MP switches is reported up to November 8, 2011, whereas the legislature ended its activities in January 2013. Some deputies switched party more than once.[47]

or even more variation in the interval between elections, as a result of incumbents' choices—changes—of party affiliation.

One way to drive home the import of inter-electoral party system change is to look at how MP switches determined the fate of two executives during the two legislatures evincing the greatest within-term seat volatility since 1994: Prodi I, in the 13th legislature (1996–2001); and Berlusconi IV, in the 16th (2008–2013). Prodi I collapsed in October 1998, the first government in the Italian Republic to fall due to defeat on a motion of confidence. The Communist Refoundation Party split into two on the confidence vote, with its hardliner heir depriving the executive of a Chamber majority. The Democratic Union for the Republic, formed of mobile MPs in early 1998, during the term, also denied support to Prodi. The UDR, its successor party, and the moderate heir to the once-unified RC, entered all cabinets after Prodi's during the 13th legislature.

Berlusconi IV began the 16th legislature with ample majorities in both houses. While the government's contingent shrank in the Senate slightly over the term, it suffered a greater decline in the Chamber. In July 2010, Fini and his followers defected from the PDL to create Future and Freedom as a parliamentary group. Fini broke with the government in mid-November 2010, although a few MPs re-entered the ruling majority by mid-December; additional MP switches in January 2011, founding the Responsible Initiative parliamentary group, bolstered Berlusconi further. Yet by November 2011, ongoing shifts in the partisan balance of power left the government without a Chamber majority. Berlusconi resigned, and the non-party Monti cabinet was quickly installed.[48]

CONCLUSION

The investigation of Italian party systems offers general insights into parties, party systems, and democratic political life. In studying Italy, we gain appreciation for the ways that distinct criteria for demarcating party systems can identify (roughly) the same boundaries between successive systems, even while the systemic features emphasized differ. Whereas that lesson applies to the first and second Italian party systems as established in elections, another appears for the (probable) third: it is difficult to discern the contours of a new party system when institutional reform is well-nigh inevitable.

The Italian case makes it clear that explanations for party system change must take multiple factors into account. Not only voters' choices, as shaped by societal trends, but also parties' choices, as structured by institutional opportunities and constraints, have contributed to the evolution of the Italian party system. In particular, electoral institutions mold party systems and yet are themselves malleable in the hands of party politicians.

In contemporary Italy, the anti-party Five Star Movement has entered the political fray and public approval ratings for parties have descended to abysmal lows.[49] All the same, parties in Italy, as in other democracies, organize the teams and terms of elite competition, and thus frame and defend alternative choices to voters. Parties organize the work of the legislature, and thus translate citizen preferences into policy decisions. Agreements among parties enable the installation and functioning of executives, even when a crisis non-party cabinet takes the reins. Parties and the party system continue to occupy an essential place in contemporary Italy, as in other democracies.

When we adopt a new lens for analyzing party systems and look at incumbents' changes of partisanship in Parliament, we discover that elections set up but do not settle party systems once and for all.[50] Legislators' choices of affiliation can alter the partisan balance of power and even undo executives between elections. The interaction of voters' and parties' choices, as conditioned by institutions, establishes party systems within the electoral arena. Elected representatives, whose choices are also structured by institutions, can remake party systems outside the electoral arena. Through this lens, a party system in a democracy is a delicate balance, a result of the ongoing choices of multiple players within the political elite, which are periodically checked via the elemental democratic practice of elections.

NOTES

1. Acknowledgements. I thank the editors and Olga Shvetsova for helpful comments, and Elaina Faust for research assistance.
2. E.g., Anthony Downs. 1957. *An Economic Theory of Democracy*. New York: Harper & Row; Peter Mair. 1997. *Party System Change: Approaches and Interpretations*. Oxford: Oxford University Press.
3. Giovanni Sartori. 1976. *Parties and Party Systems*. New York: Cambridge University Press.
4. Scott Mainwaring. 1999. *Rethinking Party Systems in the Third Wave of Democratization: The Case of Brazil*. Stanford: Stanford University of Press.
5. E.g., Norman Schofield and Itai Sened. 2006. *Multiparty Democracy: Elections and Legislative Politics*. Cambridge: Cambridge University Press.
6. Mair, *Party System Change*.

7. Sartori, *Parties and Party Systems*.

8. For cross-national treatment, Kaare Strøm, Ian Budge, and Michael J. Laver. 1994. "Constraints on Cabinet Formation in Parliamentary Democracies." *American Journal of Political Science* 38 (2): 303–335.

9. Chapters 15 and 17, respectively, this volume.

10. Cf. Gianfranco Pasquino. 1986. "The Demise of the First Fascist Regime and Italy's Transition to Democracy: 1943–1948." In *Transitions from Authoritarian Rule: Southern Europe*, ed. Guillermo O'Donnell, Philippe C. Schmitter, and Laurence Whitehead. Baltimore, MD: The Johns Hopkins University Press, 45–70.

11. Electoral volatility, a score of the aggregate shift in party vote shares between two successive elections, captures predictability in party competition. The other three aspects of party system institutionalization are societal anchoring of, popular support for, and solidity of parties (e.g. Mainwaring, *Rethinking Party Systems in the Third Wave of Democratization*).

12. E.g., Ibid., 25.

13. E.g., Luigi Ceccarini, Ilvo Diamanti, and Marc Lazar. 2012. "Fine di un ciclo. La destrutturazione del sistema partitico italiano." *Politica in Italia. I fatti e le interpretazioni dell'anno*, ed. Anna Bosco and Duncan McDonnell. Bologna: Il Mulino, 63–82.

14. The core is a policy position that, given the number, sizes, and positions of all actors in a system, is invulnerable to defeat; a core party occupies such a position.

15. E.g., Carol Mershon. 2002. *The Costs of Coalition*. Stanford: Stanford University Press.

16. E.g., Schofield and Sened, *Multiparty Democracy*.

17. Mair, *Party System Change*.

18. Ibid., 216.

19. Italy, Ministero dell'Interno. "Archivio storico delle elezioni."

20. Mershon, *The Costs of Coalition*.

21. Sources: Roberto D'Alimonte and Lorenzo De Sio. 2010. "Il voto. Perché ha rivinto il centrodestra." In *Proporzionale se vi pare*, ed. D'Alimonte and Chiaramonte, 76; Lorenzo De Sio. 2007. "Al di là delle apparenze. Il risultato delle elezioni." In *Proporzionale ma non solo. Le elezioni politiche del 2006*, ed. Roberto D'Alimonte and Alessandro Chiaramonte. Bologna: Il Mulino, 262; Lorenzo De Sio, Matteo Cataldo, and Federico De Lucia, eds. 2013. *Le elezioni politiche 2013*. Rome: Centro Italiano Studi Elettorali, 190–191; Italy, Ministero dell'Interno, "Archivio storico delle elezioni"; Italy, Ministero dell'Interno. "Elezioni 2013"; Maria Chiara Pacini. 2002. "Appendice." In *Maggioritario finalmente? La transizione elettorale 1994–2001*, ed. Roberto D'Alimonte and Stefano Bartolini. Bologna: Il Mulino.

22. Party seat shares and likely party policy positions strongly suggest the absence of a core party in the 2013 elections, even though the measures typically used to locate parties in policy space (as in, e.g., Schofield and Sened, *Multiparty Democracy*) are not yet available.

23. E.g., Samuel H. Barnes, 2004. "Secular Trends and Partisan Realignment in Italy." In *Electoral Change in Advanced Industrial Democracies,* ed. Russell J. Dalton, Scott C. Flanagan, and Paul Allen Beck. Princeton: Princeton University Press, 205–230.

24. E.g., Mannheimer, Renato, and Giacomo Sani. 1987. *Il mercato elettorale. Identikit dell'elettore italiano*. Bologna: Il Mulino; Arturo Parisi and Gianfranco Pasquino. 1977. "Relazioni partiti-elettori e tipi di voto." In *Continuità e mutamento elettorale in Italia*, ed. Arturo Parisi. Bologna: Il Mulino, 215–249; cf. Gary W. Cox, 1997. *Making Votes Count: Strategic Coordination in the World's Electoral Systems*. Cambridge: Cambridge University Press. Parisi and Pasquino also discuss the "vote of exchange," anchored in individualized relationships between voters and candidates.

25. Delia Baldassarri. 2012. *The Simple Art of Voting: The Cognitive Shortcuts of Italian Voters*. Oxford: Oxford University Press.

26. E.g., Francesco Zucchini. 1997. "La decisione di voto. I tempi, l'oggetto, i modi." In *A domanda risponde*, ed. Piergiorgio Corbetta and Arturo M. L. Parisi. Bologna: Il Mulino, 91–137.

27. E.g., Chapter 11, this volume.

28. Steven Warner and Diego Gambetta. 1994. *La retorica della riforma. Fine del sistema proporzionale in Italia*. Turin: Einaudi.

29. E.g., Gianfranco Pasquino. 2007. "Tricks and Treats: The 2005 Electoral Law and Its Consequences." *South European Society and Politics* 12 (1): 79–93.

30. Under Italy's symmetric bicameralism, any executive must win a vote of investiture in both houses, and either house can deny confidence later in the life of a government.

31. E.g., Aldo Di Virgilio. 1997. "Le alleanze elettorali. Identità partitiche e logiche coalizionali." In *Maggioritario per caso. Le elezioni politiche del 1996*, ed. Roberto D'Alimonte and Stefano Bartolini. Bologna: Il Mulino, 71–136.

32. Aldo Di Virgilio. 2010. "Cambiare strategia a regole invariate. La rivoluzione dell'offerta." In *Proporzionale se vi pare. Le elezioni politiche del 2008*, ed. Roberto D'Alimonte and Alessandro Chiaramonte. Bologna: Il Mulino, 33–73.

33. Ibid.

34. Alessandro Chiaramonte. 2010. "Dal bipolarismo frammentato al bipolarismo limitato? Evoluzione del sistema partitico italiano." In *Proporzionale se vi pare.* ed. D'Alimonte and Chiaramonte, 226, 227; cf. Chapter 25, this volume.

35. Cf. William H. Riker. 1986. *The Art of Political Manipulation*. New Haven: Yale University Press.

36. Cf. Chapter 18, this volume.

37. Alessandro Chiaramonte and Vincenzo Emanuele. 2013. "Volatile e tripolare. Il nuovo sistema partitico italiano." In *Le elezioni politiche 2013*, ed. Lorenzo De Sio, Matteo Cataldo, and Federico De Lucia. Rome: Centro Italiano Studi Elettorali, 95. This comparison leaves aside founding elections of a democratic regime.

38. Sources: Italy, Camera dei deputati. 2013. "Legislature precedenti"; Giannetti Di Virgilio and Pinto. 2012. "Patterns of Party Switching in the Italian Chamber of Deputies 2008–2011," 32; Mershon and Shvetsova, *Party System Change in Legislatures Worldwide*, 60.

39. Michael Gallagher. 2013. Election Indices Dataset. <http://www.tcd.ie/Political_Science/ staff/michael_gallagher/ElSystems/Docts/ElectionIndices.pdf>.

40. To clarify, the Monti non-party cabinet relied on a legislative interparty grand coalition. Letta included left, right, and center parties in the executive.

41. Ilvo Diamanti. 2013. "Destra e sinistra perdono il proprio popolo. M5S come la vecchia Dc: interclassista." (Originally published, *La Repubblica*, March 11.) <http://www.demos. it/a00832.php>.

42. Lorenzo De Sio. 2013. "Una 'frattura mediale' nel voto del 25 febbraio?" In *Le elezioni politiche 2013*, ed. Lorenzo De Sio, Matteo Cataldo, and Federico De Lucia. Rome: Centro Italiano Studi Elettorali, 101–104.

43. ITANES 2001; Baldassarri, *The Simple Art of Voting*.

44. E.g., Renato Mannheimer. 2013b. "Sale la disaffezione. E si aggiungono i delusi dal Movimento." *Corriere della Sera*, May 28. <http://archiviostorico.corriere.it/2013/maggio/28/Sale_disaffezione_aggiungono_delusi_dal_co_0_20130528_4f0ec41c-c75c-11e2-8 a1b-37b6707e1336.shtml>.

45. Carol Mershon and Olga Shvetsova. 2013. *Party System Change in Legislatures Worldwide: Moving Outside the Electoral Arena*. Cambridge: Cambridge University Press. Cf. William B. Heller and Carol Mershon. 2009. "Integrating Theoretical and Empirical Models of Party Switching." In *Political Parties and Legislative Party Switching*, ed. William B. Heller and Carol Mershon. New York: Palgrave Macmillan, 29–51.

46. Within-term seat volatility can also be tracked continuously, e.g., at monthly intervals, over one or more legislative terms.

47. As of December 2013, two parliamentary groups in the 17th legislature, the PDL and Civic Choice, have seen splits. Letta has survived in office, but his government is not intact: the re-established FI exited in late November.

48. E.g., Ilvo Diamanti. 2012. "Rapporto gli italiani e lo Stato 2012." <http://www.demos.it/rapporto.php>.

49. Mershon and Shvetsova, *Party System Change in Legislatures Worldwide*. Carol Mershon and Olga Shvetsova. 2014. "Change in Parliamentary Party Systems and Policy Outcomes: Hunting the Core." *Journal of Theoretical Politics* 26 (2): 331–351; Carol Mershon and Olga Shvetsova, 2013. "The Micro-Foundations of Party System Stability in Legislatures." *Journal of Politics* 75 (4): 865–878.

50. Sources: Chiaramonte and Emanuele, "Volatile e tripolare," 99; Gallagher, "Election Indices Dataset"; Italy, Ministero dell'Interno. 2015. "Archivio storico delle elezioni." <http://elezionistorico.interno.it/>; Italy, Ministero dell'Interno. 2013b. "Elezioni 2013." <http://elezioni.interno.it/camera/scrutini/20130224/C000000000.htm>.

CHAPTER 13

....

BUREAUCRACY

....

SIMONA PIATTONI

WITH few exceptions, in most of Europe, state building has historically preceded nation building. Italy is arguably one of these exceptions. Despite the trite dictum "Having made Italy, we must now make Italians," presumably proffered by Massimo d'Azeglio in the wake of Italian Unification, it can be argued that Italians have been characterized by a common vernacular and a common culture long before they ever acquired a state. Whatever the sequence between these two fundamental processes (see Chapter 2, this volume), it is probably beyond dispute that the Italian state reveals peculiar weaknesses that also characterize social relations. For example, the well-known phenomenon of *familismo* (Banfield 1958),[1] which characterizes interactions in the private sphere, can be found in the public sphere too, as *parentela* and *clientela* (La Palombara 1964).[2] These phenomena hardly elevate the state above society and rather make it the prey of particular interests. By analyzing the Italian bureaucracy, we gain a heightened feel for the checkered history of the Italian state and its still unsettled and contested nature.

As in most other nations, national historiography in Italy has developed its own particular brand of "exceptionalism." Italy's exceptionalism is premised on the idea of an unfulfilled political, social, and economic project, and on the consequent need for Italians to continuously reform and reinvent their politics, society, economy, and state. Italian official and scholarly rhetoric is replete with concepts that hint at unfulfilled promises that should finally be kept in a yet-to-come future. The theme of "rebirth" continuously runs through Italian history and rhetoric. The Risorgimento is as much at the core of this exceptionalism as the "unaccomplished economic unification" (*riunificazione economica*) of the peninsula.[3] The many electoral reforms enacted in the postwar period stand in stark contrast to the enduring fragmentation of the Italian party system. The repeated attempts at institutional reform clash against the resilience of some of the distinguishing traits of the Italian state, particularly its centralized and unitary character. These tensions and contradictions are revealed with particular clarity by an analysis of Italian bureaucracy.

A mix of continuous attempts at reform and surprising continuity has characterized this quintessential state institution. And yet—summoning up another often-used dictum, "*Eppur si muove!*"—Italian bureaucracy has undergone a period of real change. During the 1990s and 2000s, the Italian bureaucracy has begun a significant process of change which, however, has once more not been fully carried through. In this chapter, I will examine both change and continuity, taking into account four main aspects. First, the increasing *differentiation* of the Italian administration due to an attempt to keep up with changes in the national and global economy. Second, the increasing *devolution* of powers to lower levels of government and to independent administrative agencies in an effort to offload some of the administrative burdens from the central state and to respond to the increasing demand of self-government from the periphery. Third, changes in Italy's modes of *governance* to take into account a surging demand of participation from civil society organizations and the need to secure the involvement of multiple levels of government, including the European Union (EU). Fourth, the growing "*Europeanization*" of the public administration, increasingly called to translate into practice decisions made at European Union level according to EU procedures. These have engendered many changes along four dimensions: structures, functions, personnel, and procedures.[4] This chapter highlights these changes in the Italian bureaucracy, focusing mostly on the structures and functions performed by it and only hinting at the transformations of its personnel and procedures.

Particularly during the postwar period, the Italian bureaucracy has responded mainly to the challenges and opportunities coming from the European and global context, and to pressures stemming from Italian economic development as interpreted and filtered through the political system (see Chapter 36, this volume). Admittedly, the bureaucracy—despite the Weberian imagery of a machinery impersonally carrying out tasks and functions decided by the political level—is also part and parcel of the political system itself, particularly in a country like Italy in which state and society were never completely disentangled from one another. By examining the social background, career paths, and partisan affiliations of state bureaucrats, the concluding section of this chapter will critically assess the plausibility of two contradictory theses that have characterized the scholarly debate on the Italian bureaucracy: on the one hand, the thesis of the existence of "family bonds" between the Italian bureaucracy and important sectors of the Italian political society,[5] and, on the other, the thesis of the negotiated detachment between bureaucracy and political power.[6] In-between these two extremes, lies a whole series of contradictory phenomena that are difficult to discern and leave Italian scholars and citizens equally perplexed.

ITALIAN BUREAUCRACY FROM UNIFICATION TO THE PRESENT

I will here offer a brief overview of the transformation of the Italian bureaucracy since Unification, using a by-now conventional periodization and focusing on structures and

functions. Stress will be placed on the relative independence of the timing of bureaucratic reforms vis-à-vis other important historical and political events (World Wars,
Republican Constitution, electoral reforms) and on the noticeable capacity of the
administrative class to stall reform as well as on the interest of the political class to keep
the bureaucracy as a tame reservoir of votes and support. Despite the many attempts at
reforming the Italian state, the evolution of the Italian bureaucracy reflects the inevitable economic and social changes more than self-conscious political strategies, since
these have aimed at keeping the bureaucracy as a pliable tool in the hands of the parties
currently in power, rather than reforming it in order to equip the Italian economy and
society with a state that could sustain the country's social and economic growth.

More than we realize, then, the Italian bureaucracy has been impacted by pressures
coming from the economic and institutional context, particularly the European Union
and the global context, rather than by self-conscious attempts at reforming it. Politics
acts as a filter and, more often than not, as a delaying factor in the adaptation of bureaucratic structures, functions, procedures, and personnel to these pressures. The *reinven-
tion* of the Italian state and bureaucracy has thus proceeded haltingly and piecemeal,
through repeated cycles of reform which have increased their internal organizational
diversity and fragmentation without fundamentally altering their original traits. Still,
the contours of a new state can be gleaned even underneath this confused evidence.
Whether these efforts will allow Italy to (as it were) "catch up with history" or, rather,
land it in a yet-to-come future, is to be seen.

FROM UNIFICATION TO WORLD WAR II

The Italian administration was modeled on the Piedmontese administration, in its turn
very similar to the French one (although possibly more militarily oriented).[7] The Italian
state was created as a centralized unitary state organized along two main administrative tiers: the central and the municipal level.[8] Municipal governments were originally
headed by a mayor appointed by the monarch, but this later became an elective post.
The center interacted with the periphery through provincial offices, which were a direct
expression of central government, and, in particular, through prefects appointed by the
Minister of the Interior and responding directly to him. Italian prefects, although modeled on the French prototype, were less powerful and mostly had a "police" function, testimony to the limited trust (if not outright distrust) that characterized center–periphery
relations in Italy after Unification (hence the dictum recalled in the opening paragraph,
which certainly originally indicated the scarce sense of national identity among the
rather different populations unified through military conquest and plebiscites).

The central state was organized along a limited number of ministries, which reflected
the minimalist conception of the state characteristic of the liberal period (1861–1919).
The Savoy monarchy had reformed its state (the Kingdom of Sardinia) in 1853, central-
izing all decisions in the hands of a few ministers, who answered directly to the prime

minister and the king. Ministries were hierarchically organized: below the minister stood a secretary general, who acted as *trait d'union* between the political level (the minister) and career officials (the bureaucratic apparatus) entrusted with implementing the laws. In 1888, the Crispi reform abolished the position of secretary general and replaced it with that of state undersecretary (*sottosegretario di stato*), a member of Parliament—hence a political figure—who had the task of supervising the operation of the ministerial offices. As the number of tasks managed by the central state increased, the number of ministries also increased: for example, the Treasury was instituted in 1877 and the Ministry for Post and Telecommunications in 1889.[9]

The post-World War I period witnessed the increasing differentiation of the Italian economy and the expanded role of the state in it. Consequently, two new organizational forms were introduced in the public administration: the *azienda autonoma* and the public company. The former was used particularly at the municipal level (hence it was also called *azienda municipalizzata*) to allow the municipal administration to perform functions of public utility (water management and distribution, electric power production and distribution, garbage collection, etc.). At the central level, the national railways (Ferrovie dello Stato) also initially belonged to this category. The latter were publicly owned companies operating under private company law entrusted with economic activities, which also, however, served a public goal (e.g. investing in underdeveloped areas, extending loans to low-income households, maintaining minor roads, etc.). Early examples of this type are companies operating in the fields of insurance (INA), road construction and maintenance (ANAS), official statistics (ISTAT), and the mixed public–private petrol company (AGIP).[10] The difference between the two types can be appreciated considering the source of their revenues: use-related fees (for *aziende autonome*), sale of products and services (for public companies).

During the fascist period, public companies further multiplied, not just to sustain and promote more effectively an expanding economy, but also to tie entire functional sectors of the Italian economy more closely with the state according to the fascist corporatist ideology. The national institute for credit to enterprises (IMI), the institute for industrial reconversion (IRI) and the national institute for insurance on work-related accidents (INAIL) were created between 1931 and 1933, but the trend also continued after World War II with INA-Casa (a section of INA promoting the construction of low-income housing), the Fund for the South (Cassa per il Mezzogiorno), the national company for fossil fuels (ENI), and the national company for electric power (ENEL) were created between 1949 and 1963. The unintended consequence of this expansion of the "para-state" has been to create a distance between the ministerial bureaucracy and the rest of the public administration in charge of these companies. This not only signaled a distrust of the state toward its own bureaucracy, but also reinforced the original traits of the latter (i.e. sole attention to the formal implementation of the law rather than to its effectiveness).

The post-World War II period saw an even more rapid increase in the number of ministries, driven in part by the further expanding tasks of the state, but in part also by the need of the fractious Christian Democracy-led governments to satisfy the many inner factions present within the DC and the coalition parties, each eager to control a certain number of ministerial and undersecretarial positions from which to dispense jobs (in the public administration) and, when possible, public largesse (funds, projects, permits, etc.) in exchange for votes. The Italian bureaucracy was thus part and parcel of that system of patronage and clientelism that characterized the postwar Italian political system.[11] As a consequence, several ministries (for Transportation, Merchant Marine, Budget, Public Companies, Health, Tourism and Entertainment, etc.) were created after the war, leading to further confusion and pulverization of competences. This situation led, in the seventies, to the first attempt to rein in this multiplication of ministerial structures, while, at the same time, new mixed public–private bodies were entrusted with the management of ailing industries.

THE SEVENTIES: THE FORGOTTEN CRITICAL JUNCTURE

Many things changed at the end of the sixties, sowing the seeds for a momentous transformation of the Italian economy and society in the decades to come. Much of what we experience today is the long-term consequence of decisions made at the turn of that decade, and of the reforms that were introduced in the eighties and nineties as a response to them.

On the economic front, a model of development—based on mass production of material-intensive products produced through energy-intensive processes—came to an end. As a consequence of the end of the Bretton Woods system of fixed exchange rates and the momentous increases in the price of oil, Italian industry was forced to reconvert and restructure and to begin the long search for a new development model. In particular, the development model driven by public companies investing in the south in unprofitable circumstances—the so-called undue burdens (*oneri impropri*) placed on public companies was abandoned.[12] The discovery in the eighties of the surprising vitality of Third Italy's small and medium-sized enterprises (SMEs) temporarily bridged the gap to the new industrial era,[13] but the bridge was too short and left Italian industrial transformation suspended in mid-air. Macroeconomic intervention should have also changed, switching from the subsidization of large publicly owned industries (as a means to developing the lagging south) to what should have been a far-sighted strategy aimed at retraining the workforce, promoting new skills, and sustaining private entrepreneurship, but this vision was never consistently pursued and Italian firms were left to fend for themselves. Italian SMEs valiantly managed to temporarily fill the gap, but the Italian public administration never made the transition to a different type of industrial and labor policy.

Socially, these years saw equally dramatic changes. While ailing industries were nationalized and workers either parked in compensatory schemes or absorbed in the traditional tertiary sector, welfare expenditures began to grow and outpace the tax-ing capacity (or will) of the Italian state. The root causes of the current national debt grew. The contemporaneous (sometimes violent) mobilization of society—demanding greater economic, civil, and political rights—induced the governments of the day to buy consensus through social expenditures. The public administration had difficulties keeping up with these changes. The only innovative response was a certain amount of administrative and political devolution, which finally enacted the 1948 constitutional provision establishing ordinary regions to which major competences were entrusted (health, development, agriculture, and tourism).[14] New administrative and politi-cal positions were created at the regional level and, after the reform of the provincial tier from a purely administrative to a political level of government (law 122/1951, law 142/1990), also at the provincial level, which partly absorbed the redundant workforce. The structure, status, and career paths of bureaucratic personnel were also reformed (law 312/1980, legislative decree 748/982, law 93/1983). The transformation of bureau-cratic employment from a public to a private regime was perfected in the 1990s with a series of legislative decrees (29/1993 and 80/1998), later systematized in the early 2000s.

THE EIGHTIES: THE PRESSURE OF EUROPEANIZATION

In the eighties, as the economy pulled itself slowly out of recession and successive gov-ernments tried to put a stop to double-digit inflation, Italian bureaucracy started to feel the pressure coming from the "Europeanization" of a number of policy areas, from regional development to the monetary and exchange rate, from environment to gender equality. Europeanization refers to a process whereby policy goals, standard operating procedures, and even cognitive frameworks increasingly reflect decisions and practices adopted at European Union level.[15] While reflecting no national state tradition in par-ticular, hence posing problems to all member states' bureaucracies, Europeanization has represented a particularly fierce challenge for the Italian bureaucracy.[16] In the new context of floating currencies and increasing economic interdependency—in 1983 Italy joined the Exchange Rate Mechanism or "snake" with a larger band of oscillations than the other European Community (EC) countries—these constraints became increasingly more stringent. Escape from budgetary constraints, traditionally obtained by printing money and devaluing the lira, could no longer be sustained and the famous "divorce" between Italian governments and the Bank of Italy in 1981 ushered in a period of tighter fiscal policy.[17]

The eighties closed with the end of the Cold War and the demise of communist regimes in Eastern Europe, while the nineties opened with German reunification and the decision, taken in Maastricht, to move toward an Economic and Monetary Union and a single currency by 2004. The space of maneuver for the management of social and economic conflicts began to shrink: the Italian bureaucracy should have been reformed to facilitate such momentous structural transformations but, once again, reform was hesitant, piecemeal, and incomplete. The first partial reforms were implemented toward the end of the 1980s. Law August 8, 1988, n. 400, regulated governmental activity and the structure of the Presidency of the Council of Ministers, which foreshadowed a more general reform of the ministries (later carried out by law 300/1999, but then partially reversed by law 317/2001). Law June 8, 1990, n. 142, regulated local governments (provinces, communes, metropolitan areas, etc.) as well as the relationship between these and the regions. Law 241/1990 regulated bureaucratic procedures, making them simpler and more transparent and allowing citizens to be more easily informed, as each dossier was entrusted to a particular functionary who was "responsible" for it. A new era of decentralization, privatization, and "destatization" was thus ushered in, leading to a veritable spate of reforms during the late nineties.

Once more, this organizational development grew out of the awareness that the "typical" ministerial structure was ill-equipped to perform the new functions expected of the state. In the seventies and eighties, together with a growing disillusionment with Keynesian macroeconomic intervention, a new theory of the state and its role in the economy emerged: rather than intervening directly in the economy, creating demand or offering supply of goods and services, it was now believed that the state should supervise and regulate the production and consumption of goods and services carried out by private entities. Regulation, though, is no menial task: it requires expert knowledge of a number of technically challenging fields. Since the central bureaucracy had been traditionally selected on the basis of its legal competence, it was unable to monitor production, management, and distribution of technically specific services from telecommunications to food safety, from stock exchange supervision to financial transactions regulation. For this reason, a growing number of independent administrative agencies (IAAs) have been created since the seventies in a growing number of fields.[18]

THE NINETIES: INSTITUTIONAL REFORMS, AT LAST

As we have seen, the accumulated effect of these changes had not just been quantitative, but also qualitative: the original hierarchical model—based on a single chain of command from the minister to the undersecretary to the divisions—had, in some instances, been modified to accommodate the needs of ministries presiding over rather different tasks. The goal of preserving a common and uniform organizational design progressively gave way to increasing differentiation across ministries and to the need to create a fairly complex structure servicing the prime minister's office.

Meanwhile, the country had been shaken by the Mani Pulite earthquake caused by corruption and malfeasance investigations that swept away the main postwar parties, which, in turn, led to significant electoral reforms both at the center and at the periphery. This brought to power new political formations and allowed for the formation of the first "technocratic governments" with a clear reformist mandate. At the same time, as a consequence of the alternation in power between center-right and center-left governments, a more spasmodic period of reforms was inaugurated. Rather than aiming at a radical institutional reform that would simultaneously change the form of state, the form of government, and the public administration—reforms that had escaped the reach of Italian legislators for decades (Commissione Bozzi 1983–85, Commissione De Mita-Iotti 1993–94, Commissione D'Alema 1997)—Franco Bassanini, Minister of the Public Administration during several center-left governments between 1996 and 2001,[19] managed to pass and implement four laws which had a profound impact on precisely the form of state.[20] Under the second Berlusconi government (June 2001–April 2005), the fifth chapter of part two of the Italian Constitution was reformed by constitutional law October 18, 2001, n. 3 (the reform had been confirmed by a constitutional referendum held on October 7, 2001). The upshot of these reforms has been to transform, in part, the Italian state from a clearly unitary to a quasi-federal state, and to more forcefully diffuse both political power and administrative responsibility to multiple governmental tiers. While responding to growing and historically overdue demands for greater regional and local autonomy, the reform has proven to be a source of increased public expenditures and an opportunity for ever-expanding patronage and corruption.

The new context of alternation in power among opposed coalitions—which broke with the postwar tradition of DC-centered governments—meant that the tendency to make the ministerial bureaucracies even more pliable to the will of current powerholders was strengthened. To this end, a number of high-level positions were placed at the disposal of the various ministers (a sort of *spoils system*), thus skipping the usual recruitment procedure based on *concorsi* (open public competitions), which supposedly selected bureaucrats on the basis of their certifications and selection tests—a procedure which, while in practice amply circumvented, had remained formally in place.[21] In the nineties, moreover, this official system was supplemented by a different type of competition, based on a *concorso*, which gave access to year-long training, after which the successful candidates could access directly the highest rungs of the administration: the level of manager (the so-called *corso-concorso*). This was meant to inject younger and more skilled elements into an ageing and generally unqualified workforce.

These were the years during which the structure of the public administration was changed and its numbers were reduced,[22] but also during which the qualification of the bureaucratic personnel was not substantially altered. And, despite the favorable economic conjuncture in the second half of the eighties, nothing was done to downsize the deficit and reduce the public debt either. While social mobilization, so typical of the seventies, had started to subside, the public administration, both at the central and at the regional level, seemed unable to produce credible development plans to jump-start the economy again or even to use effectively the structural funds that were coming from European cohesion policy. At the end of the decade, the simultaneous pressures from worsened budgetary circumstances and tighter external constraints finally drove home the need to embrace a new administrative paradigm, that is, to offload some public activities through privatization, and to rely even more on the supervisory activity of the independent administrative agencies: a sort of Italian version of new public management, implemented through the introduction of new contractual instruments in public administrations.

The upshot of this organizational innovation has been the yet greater multiplication of organizational types, while the results in terms of the actual independence of these agencies from political power have been, at best, mixed.[23] Some of these agencies (first and foremost the agency for telecommunications, AGCOM) are only nominally independent: both their leaders and the commissioners are politically elected (with specific guarantees for parliamentary minorities) with their independence theoretically protected by incompatibility rules, the non-renewability of the appointment, the required approval of the President of the Republic, and by quarantine rules. These guarantees notwithstanding, the standing of these commissioners is more akin to that of the highest institutional political posts (Presidents of the House of Deputies and the Senate), hence subjected to political pork-barreling, than to that of independent magistrates. The real independence of these agencies is therefore questionable. The quasi-political appointment of the personnel of these agencies is one of the manifestations of the changes which have taken place in the Italian political system since the nineties and which eventually also reverberated onto the Italian bureaucracy.

While these changes responded in part to the need to upgrade and widen the set of skills present in the Italian bureaucracy, they also lent themselves to patronage practices, reinforcing the political character of the public administration. Political appointments—that is, appointments of top-level administrative managers openly leaning toward specific political formations—have become common practice, particularly in the still large population of semi-public companies that govern many sensitive services. All in all, these two evils have not cancelled each other out: while the basis of the central administration is still made of employees who have entered at the bottom of the pyramid with low skills and purely legal qualifications, the upper echelons are now populated by more qualified individuals who, however, often got their job thanks to political connections. The sum of these two evils does not endow Italy with a qualified, autonomous, and competent bureaucracy, but rather with an oddly qualified, dependent, and often still incompetent administration.

CONCLUSION: THE ILLUSIONARY REFORMS OF THE ITALIAN BUREAUCRACY

Changes in the public administration, therefore, continuously occurred since Unification, but did not manage to amend the traditional weaknesses of the Italian bureaucracy or to equip it with that *esprit de corps* and sense of mission which is the immaterial manifestation of a solid national state.[24] The paradox of constant reforms that keep missing the mark has been interpreted in different ways.

According to a first interpretation,[25] the political and bureaucratic classes had arrived early on at a "mutual accommodation," according to which the political class would use the bureaucracy as a reservoir of jobs and votes, but would not attempt to modernize it, and the bureaucratic class would accept this subordinate role in exchange for its protected status. Low-paid but secure jobs and promotion by seniority rather than through quality assessment were the terms of the deal. This would explain why, particularly since the second postwar period, the bureaucracy was increasingly "southernized" and colonized by distinct political formations, societal groups, and functional interests (what have been labeled as *parentela* and *clientela*).[26] The political class thus relinquished all attempts to reform and modernize the bureaucracy, and rather resorted to creating "parallel bureaucracies" (*enti pubblici, aziende municipalizzate, imprese pubbliche, autorità amministrative indipendenti*) to carry out the new tasks that became progressively necessary (from the nationalization of utilities and public services to the promotion of particular industries, from the delivery of welfare services to the regulation of economic and social activities). This strategy created growing fragmentation and inefficiency, and ultimately failed to equip Italy with a modern and professional bureaucracy capable of carrying out those complex governance functions made necessary by global transformations and European integration.

A second interpretation rather emphasizes the resilience of the original Continental (French and German) state tradition.[27] Part and parcel of this tradition was the idea that legislative activity must be carried out by Parliament and entrusted to government for its execution through a machine-like bureaucracy. This original imprint had been strengthened by the planning frenzy that gripped governments, in both France and Italy, during the postwar period. In the late eighties and nineties, the Anglo-Saxon less *étatist* and more liberal approach to policymaking had only superficially been grafted onto this template, which had revealed its limits in the globalized and turbulent context of the twentieth-century *fin de siècle*. This transition had been incomplete, though, with the centralized institutional template checking the full unfolding of the new administrative culture. The preservation of this division of labor between legislation and execution is a "myth" which has become particularly out of tune with reality, at least since the state ceased to be a "minimal state" and began to provide welfare services. It has been the delusionary attempt to minutely regulate the economy and the society which has led to an overproduction of extremely detailed laws that are difficult to interpret and implement, and which prompts calls for successive rounds of legislation (and adjudication) in endless, self-reinforcing circles. Not until a new "paradigm" is adopted and the division of labor between the political and the administrative classes is sought on different grounds—that is, until the political system concentrates on overseeing change, while the administrative system presides over "ordinary administration," but both legislate in their spheres of competence—will there be any real progress in terms of efficiency and effectiveness.

Finally, a third, highly unconventional and distinctive interpretation,[28] suggests that the postwar reforms have only revealed a design that was implicit in the very conception of the Italian republican constitution: that of a state *jointly constituted by autonomous spheres of authority and self-governing units at multiple territorial and social levels*, whose interrelations are regulated by the principles of subsidiarity. According to this view, this original design had been somehow disguised under a constitutional language that only apparently referred to unitary concepts, but which had never really inspired the constitutional legislators. Much like Michelangelo described the work of the sculptor as that of freeing the already formed statue from a layer of marble that concealed its form, the work of the legislator should be that of freeing the Italian bureaucracy of cumbersome legal concretions that have been placed onto it and allow the new Italian state to reveal its true form.

NOTES

1. Edward Banfield, *The Moral Basis of a Backward Society* (New York: The Free Press, 1958).
2. Joseph La Palombara, *Interest Groups and Italian Politics* (Princeton, NJ: Princeton University Press, 1964).
3. Luigi Einaudi, *Il buongoverno: saggi di economia e politica (1897–1954)*, ed. Ernesto Rossi (Bari: Laterza, 2004 [1955]).
4. Giliberto Capano and Elisabetta Gualmini, *La pubblica amministrazione in Italia* (Bologna: Il Mulino, 2006).
5. La Palombara, *Interest Groups and Italian Politics*.
6. Sabino Cassese, *Il sistema amministrativo italiano* (Bologna: Il Mulino, 1983).
7. Thomas Ertman, *Birth of the Leviathan: Building States and Regimes in Medieval and Early Modern Europe* (Cambridge: Cambridge University Press, 1997).
8. In reality there were four administrative levels below the central state—*provincia, circondario, mandamento*, and *comune*—but the provincial and the communal levels were clearly the most important ones.
9. Capano and Gualmini, *La pubblica amministrazione in Italia*, 29.
10. Ibid., 34.
11. Simona Piattoni, *Il clientelismo. L'Italia in prospettiva comparata* (Rome: Carocci, 2005).
12. Italian economic historiography has never quite agreed whether investment in the south by public companies substantially failed because the original idea was flawed—how can a company operating in a competitive market succeed if it has to produce in underinfrastructured areas hiring unskilled labor?—or because bad investment decisions were made, or, again, because public companies were run more according to a logic aimed at buying votes than at making profits. Probably the answer lies in a mix of all three.
13. The term Third Italy indicates the regions of the northeast and center of the peninsula which were characterized by an economic model (based on small and medium-sized enterprises) distinct from that of the First Italy (the northwest of large private enterprises) and of the Second Italy (of large public companies investing in the south). See Arnaldo Bagnasco and Rossella Pini, *Sviluppo economico e trasformazioni sociopolitiche dei sistemi territoriali a economia diffusa. Economia e struttura sociale*, Quaderni della Fondazione Giangiacomo Feltrinelli, N. 14, 1981; Arnaldo Bagnasco, *La costruzione sociale del mercato*

(Bologna: Il Mulino, 1988); Carlo Trigilia, *Sviluppo economico e trasformazioni sociopolitiche dei sistemi territoriali a economia diffusa. Le subculture politiche territoriali*, Quaderni della Fondazione Giangiacomo Feltrinelli, N. 16, 1981; Carlo Trigilia, *Grandi partiti, piccole imprese* (Bologna: Il Mulino, 1986).

14. Robert Putnam, Robert Leonardi, and Raffaella Nanetti, *La pianta e le radici. Il radicamento dell'istituto regionale nel sistema politico italiano* (Bologna: Il Mulino, 1985).

15. For a by-now classical definition, see Caludio M. Radaelli, "The Europeanization of Public Policy," in Kevin Featherstone and Claudio M. Radaelli (eds.), *The Politics of Europeanization* (Oxford: Oxford University Press, 2003), 27–56.

16. Martin Bull and Joerg Baudner, "Europeanization of Italian Policy for the Mezzogiorno," *Journal of European Public Policy* 11, n. 6 (2004), 1058–1076; Paolo Graziano, *Europeizzazione e politiche pubbliche italiane. Coesione e lavoro a confronto* (Bologna: Il Mulino, 2004); Sergio Fabbrini and Simona Piattoni (eds.), *Italy in the EU: Redefining National Interest in a Compound Polity* (Lanham, MD: Rowman & Littlefield, 2008).

17. Carlo Azeglio Ciampi, *L'autonomia della politica monetaria. Il divorzio Tesoro-Banca d'Italia trent'anni dopo* (Bologna: Il Mulino, collana pubblicazioni AREL, 2011).

18. For detailed overviews, see Sabino Cassese and Claudio Franchini, *I garanti delle regole* (Bologna: Il Mulino, 1996); Giorgio Giraudi and Maria Stella Righettini, *Le autorità amministrative indipendenti* (Bari and Rome: Laterza, 2001).

19. More precisely, Franco Bassanini was Minister for Public Administration and Regional Affairs during the first Prodi government (May 1996–October 1998), then undersecretary of the prime minister during the first D'Alema government (October 1998–December 1999), and again Minister for Public Administration during the second D'Alema government (December 1999–April 2000) and the second Amato government (April 2000–June 2001).

20. These are the so-called Bassanini laws: law 15 March 1997, n. 59; law 15 May 1997, n. 127 (Bassanini bis); law 16 June 1998, n. 191 (Bassanini ter); and law 8 March 1999, n. 50 (Bassanini quater).

21. Miriam Golden and Lucio Picci, "Pork Barrel Politics in Postwar Italy, 1953–1992," *American Journal of Political Science* 52, n. 2 (2008), 268–289.

22. Capano and Gualmini, *La pubblica amministrazione in Italia*, 48–51.

23. Ibid., ch. 3.

24. Shefter would argue that in Italy a "constituency for bureaucratic autonomy" never gained sufficient force. Martin Shefter, *Political Parties and the State* (Princeton: Princeton University Press, 1994), 28.

25. Cassese, *Il sistema amministrativo italiano*.

26. La Palombara, *Interest Groups and Italian Politics*.

27. Bruno Dente, *In un diverso stato. Come rifare la pubblica amministrazione italiana* (Bologna: Il Mulino, 1995).

28. Franco Bassanini, "Vent'anni di riforme del sistema amministrativo italiano," ASTRID Working Papers (n.d.), http://www.astrid-online.it/Riforma-de1/Studi-e-ri/BASSANINI_Vent-anni-di-riforma-PA_20_02_10.pdf>; Franco Bassanini, "La forma dello stato della Repubblica italiana dopo la riforma costituzionale del 2001," ASTRID Working Papers (n.d.), http://www.astrid-online.it/Dossier--r/Studi--ric/Bassanini_Forma-Stato_Titolo-V_04_2010.pdf>.

PART III

POLITICAL TRADITIONS

CHAPTER 14

CHRISTIAN DEMOCRACY

The *Italian Party*

GIANFRANCO BALDINI

FOR almost half a century, since party leader Alcide De Gasperi was first named prime minister in December 1945, until the party was dissolved in January 1994, the DC (Democrazia Cristiana) was the veritable *partito italiano*. The DC was unmovable from power. The Cold War cleavage meant that its main adversary, the Partito Comunista Italiano (PCI), the strongest communist party in Western Europe, could not provide a viable alternative. All Italian republican governments were led by the DC for 35 years (1946–81). And even when the party temporarily gave up the premiership to long-time allies in the 1980s, it still kept the largest share of seats in every government until 1993. How could a party, founded just a few years before Italy became a Republic, keep such a permanent hold on power? The DC was the plurality party in all general elections from 1946 to 1992, with an impressive average vote of 38.7 percent until 1987, and still 29.7 in 1992. This was due to three main factors: the solid anti-communist barrier it provided, the capacity to represent Italian Catholicism, and, most of all, its nature as a party of mediation, both between the deeply divided internal factions, the other parties, and society at large. Hence, the DC was not just an Italian party, but *the* Italian party, until it collapsed under the combined (exogenous) pressures of the fall of communism, the EU financial constraints on public spending, but especially the judicial investigations into corruption.

While other contributions in this Handbook explore the party's hegemonic period (M. Gilbert) as personified by Alcide De Gasperi (see also Chapters 26 and 32, this volume) this chapter examines how the party became a state-centered party, while progressively losing touch with both society and the Church. Organizational and systemic elements are therefore the main focus of this chapter, which is divided into four sections. Before looking at the organization (and how the party came about), I analyze the systemic causes and consequences of the record-long party rule. Then, looking at the shifting dynamics between state, Church and society, and especially at the occupation of state resources, I argue that the DC symbolized, in a unique way, the many contradictions of Italian politics, some of which predated its birth, while others remain as peculiar DC heritages.

The Party of Government, with No Alternatives

The DC had many faces. Seen from abroad, the party was identified with the ambivalent perceptions that Italy commanded: a nation able to recover and prosper through a veritable economic miracle in the early 1960s, but also plagued by low social capital, endemic corruption, and, last but not least, the enduring success of many criminal organizations. In many ways, Giulio Andreotti—seven times prime minister and in Parliament from 1946 until his death in 2013 (as life senator since 1991)—personified the continuity as much as the ambiguities of DC's power.

When the DC collapsed in 1994, several small parties fought to preserve its heritage, to no avail, despite some efforts by Forza Italia.[1] In 2000, Marco Follini—later to become leader of currently the main center heir party to the DC, the UDC (Union of Center)—wrote a book that,[2] in many ways, captures the multifaceted nature of the DC. For this reason, I shall use parts of it, as related to my arguments. Follini correctly put it like this: the DC was, at the same time, "the party of society, the party of the State, and the Party of the Church."[3] After having been a catch-all party *ante litteram*, the DC used state resources probably like no other party in Western Europe. State occupation began in the 1950s, and developed thoroughly in the following two decades. Unclear—and, most of all, unaccountable—control of state resources meant that there was never a genuine competition between parties on policy alternatives: either macro policies as those related to international affairs, or micro policies based on patronage and distribution of selective incentives dominated electoral competition during the so-called First Republic.[4]

DC's predominance, and the PCI's anti-systemic nature—as captured by Giovanni Sartori's polarized pluralism model[5]—made government turnover less a consequence of electoral results than of the DC's internal factional struggle, as channeled also by preference voting in a very proportional electoral system.[6] According to Sartori, the DC was germane in differentiating polarized pluralism, Italian style, from other comparable cases belonging to the same category (the French Fourth Republic 1946–58, but also the German Weimar Republic 1919–33). Among other systemic factors, this was related to the fact that the center, as a political space in Italy, was occupied by a strong Catholic party, able to fill this central location on its own (rather than as part of a coalition). Slightly different, and more concentrated on the PCI's ideological profile as a key factor for explaining the "imperfect bipartitism" pattern, Giorgio Galli's analysis had a more limited theoretical leverage.[7] In terms of electoral behavior, the key model was elaborated at the end of the 1970s. The progressive occupation of the state by the DC was captured by the growth of the vote of exchange at the expense of both the vote of belonging (as expressed especially in the so-called subcultures: northeast for the DC and center, or Red Zone, for the PCI) and of the vote of opinion, linked to alternative judgment on welfare, fiscal, or other policies.[8]

These patterns were embedded on long-term political dynamics and cultural roots. The DC was never a truly conservative party, at least if we mean by that a party which also aims to preserve the country's cultural traditions and institutions. While De Gasperi was a key protagonist in the crucial phase of democratization (1943–48), his party was split on institutional solutions. The Constituent Assembly had to work in a context of deep polarization, reflected in the nature of the 1948 Constitution, which included a panoply of liberal mechanisms aimed at constraining the executive in favor of parliament (in itself structured as bicameral and redundant), in order to exorcise the resurgence of Fascism. But the roots of division went even deeper.

Italy as a state was born out of many conflicts, and Catholic opposition to the state was one of the strongest elements for its problematic consolidation. In Liberal Italy there had been no alternation either: *trasformismo* was the main pattern of government turnover. Italy as a Republic was born with low legitimacy, and out of excluding dynamics, rather than with the aim of a "common destiny" shared by all political parties and areas. The choice over the form of the state revealed big (and persistent) geographical divisions: in the 1946 referendum, behind an overall 54.3 percent for the Republic, as many as 85 percent of the voters supported change in the northern Trento Province, as contrasted with as few as 23.5 percent in southern Campania.[9]

Then, after the Constitution was born as an anti-fascist pact (which made the neo-fascist MSI an anti-system party), the political system would be marked by the 48 percent support the DC obtained in the 1948 election (see Chapter 26, this volume). The second—and indeed most relevant exclusion of a political actor (the PCI, which would increase its votes for the following 30 years)—gave the DC a key responsibility in governing the country. This lends plausibility to the legend which quotes De Gasperi as asking: "What are we going to do with all these votes?"

The first decision De Gasperi took was to govern in coalition, despite not being forced to do so by parliamentary arithmetic. And the polarized climate also affected the second key decision, that is, to look for a majoritarian mechanism to stabilize centrism in 1953.[10] This was not successful and the-then so-called swindle law (legge truffa) brought De Gasperi's leadership to an end. So the party did much with those votes, but also missed key opportunities to modernize the country.[11] When the PSI entered into government in the 1960s, the patterns of DC's predominance were set. Government instability would be triggered by factional rivalries. More generally, the DC would lack both strong leadership and concertative capacities to govern the economy while keeping an eye not just on consensus, but also on financial stability and economic modernization. Political culture also played a role: the predominance of Catholicism and Marxism made the search for reformist solutions very difficult.

MANY PART(IE)S IN ONE: A PARTY OF FACTIONS

The DC was, first of all, a party built on internal mediation, between the different factions, which made it resemble a rather loose assembly of different parties.[12] The DC's factionalization was inscribed in its genetic phase, which resulted from the concomitant efforts of several organizations. The birth of a Catholic party had proved very problematic in two previous cases. The Vatican had played a critical role in limiting the success of both Romolo Murri's Opera dei Congressi (founded in the 1870s) and of the short-lived Italian Popular Party (PPI, 1919–26) led by Luigi Sturzo.[13] De Gasperi had been PPI's last party secretary, and he had learned important lessons from both these experiences.[14] The DC was founded on the remnants of the PPI in 1942, still under fascist ruling. Along with the leaders of the former party (Popolari), all main leaders came from different organizations (mainly university students), directly mobilized by the Church.[15] These components—bound together by Catholic inspiration—can be perceived as an external "source of legitimation" for the party.[16] Coupled with a geographical organization based on diffusion (rather than penetration led by a single center, often supplanted by the Catholic organizations, both in voters' mobilization and for the party's local activities[17]) this meant that the party was weakly institutionalized.

The dominant coalition—that is, the actors who controlled the party's most vital zones of uncertainty, including financing, recruitment, competency, and so on[18]—was dispersed, and no single actor would clearly dominate over the others for a substantial period of time.[19] While De Gasperi's role was very important in setting up the party, his leadership never went beyond the status of "situational charisma";[20] a pattern in which the leader, while symbolizing the party in the eyes of members and voters, is more constrained in the way in which he leads the party than in "pure" charisma. De Gasperi's role as mediator between the different factions, which had emerged already in the first party congresses (despite being them formally forbidden by the party's statute), was already apparent in the widespread opposition to his double role as party leader and premier (which he only kept for a few months).[21]

Hostility to the merging of party and government leadership, as emerged during De Gasperi's tenure, was to mark the party forever: only two leaders, Amintore Fanfani (1958–59) and Ciriaco De Mita (1988–89) shortly managed to escape it. It was not incidental that these two leaders have been the most committed to organizational reforms, which have had, respectively, the aim of building a more independent organization (shedding the influence of Catholic organizations), and overcoming the power of factions, by granting more powers to regional party bodies (especially via a stratagem to detonate factional power to the advantage of the party leader). It is no coincidence that both efforts, thirty years after each other, ultimately backfired. In the first case, the big centrist *dorotei* faction was built (1959), and duly dominated party politics for over a decade; in the second, the end of the record-long De Mita's party leadership (1982–89) led to the victory of "neo-doroteism."[22]

Factional rule was institutionalized in the early 1960s, with the adoption of proportional rules in the election of party organs. Each faction had its own organization, stronger than the overall party structure: when the party organization is described as "federal" this meant that internal groups could establish their own relations with the external environment, often acting independently from the rest of the party. Although both the *ideological* and the *power-oriented* criteria can be found in the origins of the main factions,[23] the former were soon replaced by the fight for power and resources, on a pattern consistent with a progressive shift from cooperative, to competitive and finally degenerative factionalism.[24] At the height of internal divisions, in 1982, there were as many as 12 different factions.

Factional leaders could either be famous politicians or second- or third-rank ministers. During De Gasperi's tenure as prime minister (1945–53), the so-called second generation of DC leaders emerged: Fanfani, Aldo Moro, and Andreotti. All in all, these leaders were *presidenti del consiglio* for over 18 years. Andreotti was never party secretary, but had a role in all Italian governments from 1946 to 1992, when his name also entered the list of candidates for the presidency of the Republic. While De Gasperi gave an identity to the DC and a leadership to Italy, Fanfani, Moro, and Andreotti later represented the different souls of a party which would not tolerate the emergence of a too powerful leader: "Fanfani's organizational skills, Andreotti's administrative capacities or the depth of Moro's thought could have been the basis for a more consistent DC profile (but …) ended up as threats to the party's more safe, anonymous and impersonal habits of coexistence."[25]

A frequent postulate on DC's ideology is that while the party elite often claimed it looked to the left, its electorate was mainly rightist. As a matter of fact, the DC always kept an interclassist approach, and to the right of the liberals there was no viable potential ally: when the MSI was the only party supporting Fernando Tambroni's government in summer 1960, people took it to the street, some demonstrators were killed, and the government fell. Despite the Church's many reservations—it was only with Second Vatican Council (1962–65) that the Church fully recognized the principle of liberal democracy—the opening to the left came to be tolerated: first with the PSI in the 1960s (in governments led first by Fanfani, then by Moro), then with the PCI's external support to the National Solidarity governments in the second half of the 1970s (with Andreotti at Palazzo Chigi, 1976–79). More generally, given the impossibility of alternation, in Italy, left and right acquired a peculiar meaning: with parties not competing on substantive programmatic issues, patterns associated with micro policies through the use of patronage and clientelistic relations became more and more important. While this was consistent with a long tradition of patron–client relations in Italy, dating to the Liberal age, when many local notables, mainly in the underdeveloped and traditionalist south, distributed favors in exchange for votes, factional divisions exasperated this process.

The short-lived ideological nature of factional divisions also applies to Italian foreign policy, a key concern for the United States (US) in the first decade of DC's rule.[26] While never really questioning the Western alliance, leaders such as Giuseppe Dossetti and Giorgio La Pira were hostile to NATO membership, and President of the Republic Giovanni Gronchi arguably cultivated "micro-Gaullist" aspirations at the turn of the 1960s (when Enrico Mattei's Middle East policy was also controversial).[27] Later, while the DC kept a rock-solid hold on the Interior Ministry, the party was keener on letting allies take up the Foreign Affairs and especially the Defense ministries.[28] This was part of a difficult trading balance with the emergence of a kind of convention that saw, for many years, the cohabitation of pro-Israeli and a pro-Palestine politicians balancing Italian Mediterranean policy in the Ministry of Foreign Affairs and the Ministry of Defense, or vice versa.[29]

THE SHIFTING BALANCE BETWEEN CHURCH, STATE, AND SOCIETY

DC's power was built on mediation. The party had to struggle in the search for an adequate balance between the three different corners of its identity—Church, state and society. Although the role of the Church decreased after 1948, it never disappeared. During most of the electoral campaigns, the Vatican continued to express the desirability of the permanence of the Catholics under the DC flag, and Catholic political unity (*unità dei cattolici*) remained a major issue throughout the 1980s, and arguably even after.

However, Fanfani understood that the party needed an organization to limit both the influence of external supporters (not just the Church, but also the US and Confindustria) and to tame the PCI's penetration of society via its mass-party dimension. In 1954–55 the first campaign for membership recruitment was organized, and in the 1958 general elections the party profited from new activists' participation, which boosted them to as many as 1.4 million members, thus recovering from the 1953 result. Fanfani's efforts were fruitful to an extent in strengthening the organization (local branches and activists' festivals were organized, later to become Feste dell'Amicizia; never, however, reaching the scale of PCI's Feste dell'Unità). However, a true emancipation from flanking organizations was never achieved, and these efforts (both for party organization and in building a veritable state party) also had a clear side effect. The geography of party support had already started to change in the 1958 election—a process that would speed up in the following decade: the northeast was overtaken by the south as the region where the DC electorate was most concentrated. A similar pattern of *meridionalizzazione* also affected party membership.[30] These trends were due to the steady increase in clientelistic relations as main sources of electoral support: the party was focusing more and more on exchange votes, and the absence of any proper check on membership registers meant that a veritable rank-and-file of *anime morte* (dead souls) became possible.

DC's societal links continued to be mediated by Catholic organizations, despite a growing secularization, which accelerated during the second half of the 1960s.[31] With hindsight, one can argue that 1974 provided some key tests about the changing challenges the DC had to face in order to preserve its pivotal position. The (lost) referendum on divorce, in itself triggered by the Church and supported by Fanfani, showed the party had lost touch with a modernizing society. The second element was the insurgence of violence, with the Piazza della Loggia bombing (in Brescia) by extreme right terrorist groups, on a scale soon to be overtaken by the rise of Brigate Rosse, which killed Moro in 1978. The third event was the approval of the law on political parties' public financing, which provided no effective means to avoid bribes or tackle the institutionalized system of corruption which the DC, and many other parties—with different degrees and dynamics—had by then set up. On the contrary, the law, "by establishing strict and cumbersome regulations and procedures, (. . .) also made it very difficult to provide for *legal* contributions."[32]

Indeed, it is only with hindsight that one can underline these events as really signifi-cant in the history of the party. All in all, the 1970s were most of all marked by violence and social conflict, a fact that made the PCI's parliamentary support of the National Solidarity executives more digestible to the latter party's electorate.

More generally, it would be wrong to assume that the party became part of the state while leaving behind its function of broker between society and the state itself. The DC's "colonization of the State," was achieved through the expansion of the public sector. State colonization was pursued via different means, including state agencies to promote underdeveloped areas (Cassa per il Mezzogiorno, 1950), the creation of a Ministry for State Holdings (1956) and the set-up, or indeed the strengthening, of state-holding com-panies. In this respect, with the center-left governments (1963–68), DC's strategies came to be shared by PSI, and other minor partners.

Research on the political economy underlines a key element of the DC's state-centered status, not often caught by scholars focusing solely on the party. Much like political dynamics, such as the lack of alternation, so the state–entrepreneur dynamics predated the DC's existence. Also in this regard, then, one can argue that the DC could strengthen state assets with regard to key long-term dynamics, such as early public intervention in the Italian economy, the familial model of Italian capitalism, and the fact that "banks performed the functions that should have been fulfilled by the financial markets."[33] Following Salvati,[34] one can argue that industrial policies, as devised by the DC and allies since the 1960s, contributed to hampering the process of economic growth and therefore the possibility of designing strategies more aligned with other European coun-tries. In other words, Italian state capitalism, as led by the DC and its allies since the 1960s, worsened—rather than resolving—Italy's known structural problems: the under-development of the south; the fragility of big industry, concentrated in one part of the country and largely public; the weakness of government in industrial relations, all con-tributed to Italian decline. This made the search for a European anchorage all the more urgent: the Maastricht Treaty was signed by Andreotti during his last spell (the seventh!) as Presidente del Consiglio. How state occupation was managed is a story often told, which nonetheless deserves some space, for at least two reasons: the way in which DC's pervasiveness came to be shared by long-time coalition partners (and, in some ways, also by the PCI, hence the pervasiveness of *partitocrazia*); and the fact that partisan embeddedness in the economy was so strong that it still marks Italy today, 20 years after DC's disappearance.

Though selecting indicators is by no means easy, and many aspects are still poorly researched, one can start from ministerial spoils. Ministers for State Holdings were DC members for 80 percent of the governments, until the ministry's dissolution in 1992. The DC also kept a rock-solid hold on the agricultural sector, securing 97 percent of the ministries in this field, which was strategic both for the Mezzogiorno, and for providing electoral support and membership recruitment.[35] More precisely, the clientelistic use of the institutions was in the hands of the local leaders of the factions (the *capicorrente*), who controlled the organization of the party through artificial expansion of its member-ship. Relations with the territory and linkage with the constituencies was held through the distribution of financial benefits, easily managed via the firm control of the DC on all the main institutes regulating the flux of economic aids to the south.

Research on cities like Naples and Catania showed that clientelism,[36] as traditionally managed by notables, had been replaced in the Mezzogiorno by party clientelism led by *capicorrente*. But clientelism would not just shape local politics and the way in which the party collected the votes. Rather, it would also become a key element of the Italian welfare system: a clientelistic system based on an hypertrophic pension system,[37] and on benefits for the public sector that would soon hamper public finance stability: by 1990 public debt reached 100 percent of GDP and fiscal revenues almost reached "Scandinavian levels" at around 40 percent of GDP, while quality of services remained, on average, low and geographically very differentiated. These pattern were made possible by multiple shared interests among coalition partners, but they could often also count on non-belligerency from opposition parties. In the 1970s, consociationalism "Italian style" was built on the PCI's accommodating behavior in Parliament, as well as on its partial share of some spoils.

Following Leonardi and Wertman,[38] one can also focus on three crucial sectors: the control over the public broadcasting sector (RAI); the direction of the state-holding companies; and the direction of the main Italian banks. In a nutshell, while the DC had governed public broadcasting since the beginning, in the 1980s the "political direction" of the three public channels was divided among the three main parties: RAI 1 to DC, RAI 2 to PSI, and RAI 3 to PCI.[39] In the same period, the DC lost some of its control on state-holding companies. In 1992 privatizations began for IRI, Istituto per la Ricostruzione Industriale (Institute for Industrial Reconstruction), which was the largest institute, controlling over two-thirds of state holdings; ENI, which controlled over 400 firms in the energy sector; ENEL Ente Nazionale Energia Elettrica (National Energy Trust), the State Trust which controls the sector of energy; and INA (Istituto Nazionale Assicurazioni), the biggest Italian insurance institute. However, even after the reform—which reset all the executive boards, but distributed the seats among the governmental parties—the DC was still firmly holding the key positions in all the firms.[40] Finally, the party had also to give up some positions in the banking sector: while, in 1976, as many as 90 percent of the presidents belonged to the DC area, in 1992 the party still controlled 70 percent of the main Italian banks.[41]

CONCLUSION: A PARTY ON TRIAL

In 1992, the Mani Pulite inquiries and the poor result in the general election marked the first signs of the DC's crisis, which precipitated the following year. The new (and last) leadership of Mino Martinazzoli (October 1992–January 1994), clearly an outsider in the party's dominant coalition, could not do much: despite important innovations and a radical renewal of party membership, reforms proved too late to be effective. The last chapter of Follini's book refers to a party on trial. The DC was a master of media-tion, but the crisis long predates its disappearance. The stickiness and immobility of the DC's system by the 1980s—the incapacity to recognize how much society had changed in the previous two decades—were symbolized by the permanence as party leader of Arnaldo Forlani (a long-time *doroteo*) until after the 1992 elections. Asked by a jour-nalist about the ineffectiveness of his reply during an interview, he famously rebuked "Did I say nothing? Well, I could keep on like this for hours." And yet, especially for many Italians who have not experienced DC's rule, Forlani's most famous image comes from another "interview," this time in a Milan tribunal. In one of the symbolic images of *Tangentopoli*, Forlani stood, hesitatingly and vaguely answering, almost mumbling in front of prosecutor Antonio Di Pietro, who was questioning him about the DC's involvement in illicit party financing. Despite all its shortcomings, the party deserved a better end.

For over 40 years, the DC was the cornerstone of the First Republic, a dysfunctional political system. It was the political party that most dominated the public sphere by exploiting the weakness of the state to its own benefit. This colonization of state insti-tutions had particularly negative consequences in the south, where distrust vis-à-vis the state was traditionally higher, and where clienteles were built upon state-depend-ent beneficiaries, such as public officials, and state-subsidized businesses to such an extent that borders between local control of the "exchange vote" and highly successful criminal organizations such as the Sicilian Mafia, Campania's *camorra* and Calabria's 'Ndrangheta became more and more blurred. Lack of alternation meant also that par-ties did not compete on substantive programmatic issues. This, combined with the fac-tionalized control over government composition—and therefore the substantial lack of direct accountability to the voter—meant that the DC institutionalized a system of using public resources without restraint, thus fuelling public debt. Indeed, while preference voting gave the appearance of creating more direct popular influence on the political process, it actually became the main mechanism through which party factions could prosper and cultivate their slice of the cake.

While the 1974 referendum on divorce had shown the extent to which the party was misinterpreting Italian modernization, those of 1991 on single preference voting and especially the 1993 referendum on electoral reform, marked significant institutional challenges to a giant with feet of clay. Almost twenty years after Pier Paolo Pasolini had evoked the need to put the DC on trial, a party born underground had to change its name and identity without having ever been in opposition. This process would leave a mark of low legitimacy both to various DC inheritors and to the party system in gen-eral. A giant first became a dwarf and then its remnants spread to the right, center, and left.[42] Most voters went to the right (Forza Italia and Northern League especially), while the leaders less involved in investigations turned left. And it is no coincidence that it is on the left that two recurrent DC organizational and institutional dilemmas here analyzed—factional divisions and the "double leadership" question—are today so much affecting the life and destiny of the Partito Democratico.

Notes

1. C. Paolucci, "From Democrazia Cristiana to Forza Italia and the Popolo della Libertà: Partisan Change in Italy," *Modern Italy*, 13, n. 4, 2008, pp. 465–480.
2. M. Follini, *La DC*. Bologna: Il Mulino, 2000.
3. Ibid, p. 8.
4. M. Cotta and L. Verzichelli, *Political Institutions in Italy*. Oxford: Oxford University Press, 2007.
5. G. Sartori, *Parties and Party Systems: A Framework for Analysis*. Cambridge: Cambridge University Press, 1976.
6. G. Pasquino (ed.), *Votare un solo candidato*, Bologna, Il Mulino, 1993.
7. G. Galli, *Il bipartitismo imperfetto. Comunisti e democristiani in Italia*. Bologna: Il Mulino, 1966.
8. A.M.L. Parisi and G. Pasquino, "Changes in Italian Electoral Behavior: The Relationships between Parties and Voters," *West European Politics*, 1, n. 2/3, 1979, pp. 6–30.
9. In these two areas the DC vote, respectively, was record-high in the simultaneous vote for the Constituent Assembly, and well above average since the early 1960s. These data are just an example of the political dimension of the very resilient north–south cleavage.
10. G. Baldini, "The Different Trajectories of Italian Electoral Reforms," *West European Politics*, 34, n. 3, 2011, pp. 644–663.
11. M. Salvati, *Tre pezzi facili sull'Italia*. Bologna: Il Mulino, 2011.
12. A. Zuckerman, *The Politics of Faction: Christian Democratic Rule in Italy*. New Haven: Yale University Press, 1979.
13. C. Warner, "Christian Democracy in Italy: An Alternative Path to Religious Party Moderation," *Party Politics*, 18, 2, 2013, pp. 256–276.
14. P. Allum, " 'From two into one': The Faces of the Italian Christian Democracy," *Party Politics*, 3, n. 1, 1997, pp. 23–50.
15. On DC's initial years see G. Galli, *Storia della DC*. Milan: Kaos, 2007; G. Baget Bozzo, *Il Partito Cristiano al Potere*, 2 vols. Florence: Vallecchi, 1977; A. Giovagnoli, *Il Partito Italiano. La Democrazia Cristiana dal 1942 al 1994*. Bari: Laterza, 1996.
16. A. Panebianco, *Political Parties: Organization and Power*. Cambridge: Cambridge University Press, 1988; originally published as *Modelli di Partito*. Bologna: Il Mulino, 1982.
17. G. Poggi (ed.), *L'Organizzazione Partitica del Pci e della DC*. Bologna: Il Mulino, 1968.
18. Panebianco, *Political Parties*, pp. 33–36.
19. R. Leonardi and D. Wertman, *Italian Christian Democracy: The Politics of Dominance*. New York: Macmillan, 1989, pp. 21–46.
20. Panebianco, *Political Parties*.
21. Factional power was so embedded that, even after the 1992 general elections, when the DC, for the first time, scored below 30 percent, and the Clean Hands investigations started to hit hard, the traditional dynamics could be preserved. This meant that Giuliano Amato (PSI) only received the list with the names of the DC's (potential) ministers from DC's party secretary a few hours before his visit to the President of the Republic, to be sworn in as prime minister. G. Amato, *Un governo nella transizione. La mia esperienza di Presidente del Consiglio*, in "Quaderni costituzionali," 14, 3, 1994, p. 362.
22. M. Caciagli, "The 18th Congress: From De Mita to Forlani and the Victory of 'Neodoroteism'," in F. Sabetti and R. Catanzaro (eds.), *Italian Politics: A Review*. Boulder, CO, Westview Press, 1991, pp. 8–22.

23. D. Hine, "Factionalism in West European Parties: A Framework for Analysis," *West European Politics* 5, 1, 1982, pp. 36–53.

24. F. Boucek, "Rethinking Factionalism: Typologies, Intra-Party Dynamics and Three Faces of Factionalism," *Party Politics*, 15, 4, 2009, pp. 455–485.

25. Follini, *La DC*. p. 114.

26. M. Del Pero, *L'alleato scomodo. Gli Usa e la DC negli anni del centrismo (1948–55)*. Rome: Carocci, 2001.

27. Mattei was the first chairman of ENI, Ente Nazionale Idrocarburi (National Hydrocarbons Trust).

28. Leonardi and Wertman, *Italian Christian Democracy*, p. 229.

29. L. Caracciolo, "L'Italia alla ricerca di sé stessa," in G. Sabbatucci and V. Vidotto (eds.), *Storia d'Italia*, vol. 6: *L'Italia contemporanea. Dal 1963 a oggi*, Rome and Bari: Laterza, 1999, pp. 541–604.

30. F. Anderlini, "La DC: Iscritti e Modello di Partito," *Polis*, 3, 1989, pp. 277–304.

31. P. Ignazi and S. Wellhofer, "Votes and Votive Candles: Modernization, Secularization, Vatican II, and the Decline of Religious Voting in Italy 1953–1992," *Comparative Political Studies*, 46, n. 1, 2013, pp. 31–62.

32. L. Bardi and L. Morlino, "Italy: Tracing the Roots of the Great Transformation," in Richard S. Katz and Peter Mair (eds.), *How Parties Organize*. London: Sage, 1994, pp. 242–277, p. 258.

33. R. Cafferata, "The Enduring Presence of Groups and Public Enterprises in the Italian Economy," *Journal of Management & Governance*, 14, 2010, pp. 199–220, p. 200.

34. Salvati, *Tre pezzi facili sull'Italia*.

35. S. Tarrow, *Peasant Communism in Southern Italy*. New Haven: Yale University Press, 1967; L. Graziano, *Clientelismo e Sistema Politico: Il caso dell'Italia*. Milan: Franco Angeli, 1980.

36. P. Allum, *Politics and Society in Postwar Naples*. Cambridge: Cambridge University Press, 1973; M. Caciagli, *Democrazia Cristiana e potere nel Mezzogiorno*. Rimini and Florence: Guaraldi, 1977.

37. J. Lynch, "Italy: A Catholic or Clientelist Welfare State?," in K Van Kersbergen and P. Manow (eds.), *Religion, Class Coalitions and Welfare States*. Cambridge: Cambridge University Press, 2009, pp. 91–118.

38. Leonardi and Wertman, *Italian Christian Democracy*, pp. 236–241.

39. The DC kept a strong hold on the key position of the directorship of the RAI. Ettore Bernabei was promoted by Fanfani as director general from a similar position in the DC's party newspaper *Il Popolo* in the early 1960s; in the 1980s, this position was given to De Mita's close friend, Biagio Agnes.

40. G. Baldini, "The Failed Renewal: The DC from 1982 to 1994," in P.Ignazi and C. Ysmal (eds.), *The Organization of Political Parties in Southern Europe*. Praeger: Boulder, 1998, pp. 110–133.

41. *Il Corriere della Sera*, September 15, 1976; *Il Mondo*, August 24–31, 1992.

42. C. Baccetti, *Postdemocristiani*. Bologna: Il Mulino, 2007.

CHAPTER 15

....

COMMUNISTS

....

PAOLO BELLUCCI

THE Italian Communist Party (Partito Comunista Italiano—PCI) has attracted sustained scholarly attention since the reinstallation of democracy in Italy after the end of World War II. Such attention has not only come from historians. Sociologists and political scientists have also analyzed in depth the structure and organization of the party, its electoral and social base, its political class, the relations with unions and secondary organizations, and its international alignment. Such a great interest was not only due to the obvious scientific relevance of one of the major actors and pillars of the Italian party system, and of Italian democracy. It was the apparent contradiction between Italy's position in the Western camp of the international divide during the Cold War years and the presence of the strongest Communist Party in democratic Europe that made the PCI the object of a lively political and historical concern.

The main foci were the democratic credentials of a Communist Party in a Western polity, either as a Leninist party aimed at overthrowing capitalism to install a socialist regime, or as a slowly evolving social democratic party fighting to achieve its goals through electoral democracy. An extensive historical literature has analyzed the trajectory of the PCI: from the leading Communist involvement in the Resistance during Italy's liberation from Nazi Fascism in 1943–45 and the early Togliatti' s refusal of a Socialist national revolution, to the endorsement of the Soviet invasion of Hungary in 1956; from the PCI's criticism of the Warsaw Pact's military repression of the "Prague Spring" in 1968, to the full acceptance of NATO's military alliance in the mid-70s; from the Historic Compromise in 1976 with the PCI supporting a Christian Democratic Party minority government, to support for the European Common Market, to the open criticism of the Soviet regime in 1981, and to, finally, the demise of the old party and the transformation into the Partito Democratico della Sinistra in 1991, after the fall of the Berlin Wall and the implosion of the Soviet Union.[1]

With hindsight, this looks very much like a story of a slow moving away of the party from the tenets and practice of international Marxism under the pressure of outside events, while holding for a long time to the myth of a socialist change of Italian society as a mobilization tool for electoral purposes. This was especially so in the 1950s and 1960s, when the Italian foreign policy and the West–East confrontation offered the party "high politics" issues to engage voters, while it tried domestically to accommodate and attenuate radical economic demands by unions.[2] The socialist myth—associated to criticism of Italy's overall pro-US foreign policy—allowed the party to postpone indefinitely the final class struggle, in order to allow itself to survive and grow electorally. This reading by no means wants to suggest a distinction between grand strategies and daily tactics, or the downgrading of political ideologies to electoral campaign manipulation. Both party elites and rank-and-file militants—and voters—had, for a long time, a positive image of socialism. They pressed for a radical socioeconomic change of Italy. With time, they also came to uphold to a radical pluralistic vision of democracy—stressing equality, but also the virtues of negotiation, compromise, and consensus. A kind of "constitutional radicalism," as suggested by a scholar of Italian communism who, writing on the verge of the Historic Compromise, and arguing against those who feared the PCI would assume a government role ("the PCI leadership … would be directed at socioeconomic change rather than political-constitutional change"), reported the closing line of an interview with a Communist politician, who described the party as: *"Siamo dei curiosi comunisti!—*We're peculiar Communists!"[3]

This chapter does not aim at providing a story of the Italian Communist Party, nor of Communist ideology. Rather, it purports to review social science empirical research on the development and transformation of the Italian "peculiar Communists." To do so, it looks at the PCI as a cleavage party,[4] analyzing, in turn, its social base, the value orientations of voters and militants, and the organizational structure. The focus will be on some selected features of the electorate and of the three faces of the party:[5] the party on the ground (rank-and-file militants); the party in central office (the party elite and structures); and the party in public office (the Communist representatives in Parliament).

THE COMMUNIST ELECTORATE: THE SLOW EROSION OF A CLEAVAGE ENCAPSULATION

In the first election of the Italian Republic in 1946, to elect the Constituent Assembly, which was to write the Italian Constitution, the PCI polled 18.9 percent of the vote.[6] It was a result below expectations, given the prestige acquired by the party during the Resistance, and lower than the vote share of the Socialists, at 20.7 percent. When the two parties joined forces in the Democratic Front to contest the vote against the Christian Democratic Party (Democrazia Cristiana—DC) in the highly polarized 1948 elections, they polled 31 percent, once again below expectations, and one fifth short of the combined result of the parties two years earlier. Nevertheless, it was clear that the Socialist and Communist political orientations were an important part of Italian political culture. In fact, a constitutive element of a new polity which saw the reappearance of the mass parties—including the party of the Catholics—which 29 years earlier, in the 1919 Parliament, already had the majority of seats.

The juxtaposition between the Democratic Front and the Christian Democratic Party in 1948 was based on an overlap of internal and international political spheres. Each coalition sided with one of the two antagonist international blocs in Europe: the DC supported the West and Christian values, market economy, and multiparty democracy; the United Front supported social equality and justice, democracy, national pride, and neutrality between the blocs, although it also openly sided with the Soviet Union.[7] The inception of the new Italian polity was, therefore, characterized by a strong polarization on the tenets of the political regime whose legacy lasted almost fifty years, and implied a systematic exclusion of the largest opposition party from government. On the other hand, and of particular importance, the ideological polarization on the meta-polity was not matched by a similar divide along meso and micro politics, especially economic and social policies. Content analyses of party manifestoes showed clearly that "Overall ... there has been remarkably little difference between the Christian Democrats and the Communists during the post-war era."[8] The two parties remained distant on foreign policy, but their policy appeals on welfare and the market economy were rather similar.[9] This was mirrored in the consensual lawmaking in Parliament, where the Communist opposition approved 70 percent of government and DC proposals between 1948 and 1972,[10] and afterwards. Why this happened has to do with the mass, catch-all nature of the two parties, which had important consequences for the PCI's electoral strategy.

After the disappointing 1948 results, the United Front split, with the Socialist half reducing, over time, its electoral consensus on its path to join the DC in government in the early 60s, while the PCI progressively gained electoral support. The latter polled an average of 22.6 percent in the two elections of the 1950s, and 26.1 percent in those during the 1960s, to increase to an average of 30.6 percent in the 1970s, when, in 1976, it reached the largest ever share of the vote: 34.4 percent, just 4.3 percentage points below the DC vote. PCI's consensus ebbed in the 1980s, polling in the last elections waged with the traditional name a share (26.6 percent, in 1987) similar to that of twenty years earlier, at the peak of the workers' unrest in the Autunno Caldo.

Between 1953 and 1987, DC and PCI together received the vote, on average, of 65.4 percent of Italians (with the zenith reached in 1976, 73.1 percent). [11] Such bipolarization of electoral consensus assigned the two parties a prominent role in the Italian party system: the former as the constitutive hinge of every government and the latter as the uninterrupted leader of the opposition, in a regime which was to be described as an "imperfect bipolarism," given the absence of alternation in government by the PCI.[12] Both were mass-based organizations, able to translate early involvement in the Resistance into wide political participation through the parties, the unions, and the flanking organizations they contributed to establishing, which together constituted a dense web of social networks capable of upholding partisanship.[13]

What, then, were the sources of the PCI's wide popular support? The first systematic study of Italian political behavior—conducted by the Istituto Carlo Cattaneo on aggregate socioeconomic and electoral data[14]—revealed, with some surprise, that the economic class conflict explained relatively little of the PCI's vote. There was, in other words, just a modest correlation between social stratification and political choice. The PCI vote was not uniquely concentrated in the working class, neither was it much stronger in the industrial areas of the country. The research showed a geography of voting closely resembling that of the pre-Fascism elections, with the PCI's strongholds in central Italy—later dubbed the Red Belt—and in the urban areas of the northwest. The Cattaneo study found the roots of electoral support to be in the party's cultural and organizational structure rather than in social class, that is, in the subcultural attachment of voters to the party, later framed by Parisi and Pasquino as a "vote of belonging" (*voto di appartenenza*).[15] This was a form of partisanship based on cultural values, a location in the social structure, and a membership (or feeling of closeness/trust) in secondary organizations on a territorial base. Voting for the PCI was, then, the result of a social and political cleavage, a social embeddedness—or closure—in a political enclave (the Communist–Socialist). As such, it was to be for a long time a rather stable vote, but with a growing interclass appeal.

This was the result of an explicit party strategy. As Sani recalled, quoting Secretary Togliatti, since the 1940s the leadership had openly rejected a view of the party as a "restricted association of propagandists for the general ideas of communism," calling for a popular party based on the working class as well as on other social strata, accommodating the multilayered cleavages of Italian society, based on occupation, religion, and the economic northern–southern divide.[16] While, in the 1950s, the working class was certainly overrepresented in the PCI vote—the party eliciting the support of around 40 percent of the working class, although a significant 30 percent of them voted for the DC—since the early 1960s the party had also attracted sectors of the service class and the petty bourgeois, acquiring an interclass representation which it has kept ever since.[17] Yet class itself did not explain vote choice in absence of the intermediation channel provided by organizational ties with leftist associations.

Those involved in Italian social–economic modernization and political secularization backed the electoral expansion of the PCI in the 1970s; however, this undermined the strength of the Communist subculture. The available evidence shows, over time, an increasing cultural heterogeneity in the Communist voters, who lost most of their distinctiveness with respect to the general public. In a key area for the PCI's self-image—international alignment—voters were even able to affect the party position, as the growing appeal of the European project and a positive image of the United States among PCI voters led the party, in 1975, to attenuate its anti-Americanism and openly support NATO and the European Community.[18] Esteem for the socialist regimes had, in fact, fallen dramatically: while, in 1957, a Doxa survey showed 60 percent of Communist voters expressing positive feelings toward Soviet Union, by 1968 this had dropped to 30 percent, further halving in 1985.[19] Other indicators of the Communist subculture followed a similar trend: identification with the working class, membership and trust in unions declined; the gap in religious attendance decreased; closeness to the party shrunk; ties with secondary organizations were mostly severed. By the mid-1980s, 40 percent of the PCI's electoral consensus came from voters "external" to the political

subculture, and the party's electoral base was, overall, representative of the general electorate. In the last election the party contested, in 1987, only one third of its votes came
from people politically engaged and identified with the party.[20] The majority of voters
were mild sympathizers and/or voters who chose the party on policy grounds. The PCI
had fully become a catch-all party. It was, of course, a radical left-wing party, whose voters demanded social equality, social rights, and redistribution. But the Socialist myth
had been badly tarnished, and the allegiance to liberal electoral democracy had been
increasing over a long period. Yet the PCI's electoral appeal in the 1980s showed a steady
decline, which paved the way to radical, albeit tardive, change.[21]

THE PARTY ON THE GROUND: SOLID
TO THE END

The ebbs and flows of PCI's electoral consensus were accompanied by a reduction in
party membership: from 2 million members in 1946 (with a ratio of members to votes of
47.5) to 1.8 million in 1958 (a ratio of 20.8), to 1.6 million in 1972 (a ratio members/vote
of 17.4) and 1.5 million in 1987 (a ratio of 14.7).[22] While the reduction of the ratios mem-
bers/votes meant that the party was slowly expanding its reach beyond subcultural borders, the decline of membership—which was, of course, also common to other parties,
reflecting the social and economic modernization Italy experienced over time and the
ensuing political secularization—was revealing a deep transformation of the social relations between the party and the environment, and of the nature of the political engagement of the rank and file.

The 1960s' Istituto Cattaneo's research program on the penetration of both PCI
and DC in Italian society,[23] on the roots and involvement of their militants,[24] and on
the parties' organizational structures[25]—together with the previously quoted research
on electoral behavior—offer a remarkable understanding of the Communist Party in
the early phase of the Republic, based on in-depth inquiries still exemplary for their
breadth and methodological richness (relying on qualitative and quantitative analyses
of local communities, secondary organizations, life stories and interviews with militants, party documents, survey data). The overall image of the PCI which came out from
these studies was one of a party—observed between 1946 and 1965—quite distant from
the Leninist model, and described as a political organization "in-between a modern
mass-based party with an inter-class social base and a vanguard party ... although of
this latter model it has kept only some behavioural traits while, concerning its goals, the
constant appeal to an ideological organizational structure and a revolutionary 'rhetoric'
is to a large extent only verbal."[26] Social science research thus documented early on the
distance between an anti-system image of the PCI—shared by its critics but also by most
of the party elite—and the reality of a cleavage mass party, showing its contradictions
slowly emerging. The party's early strategy was then to organize a hierarchical party,

to keep alive a revolutionary sentiment adhering to the myth of the Soviet society, and to organize an efficient economic structure and be represented in local communities. At the same time, the PCI prevented the "revolutionary spirit" it aroused from bursting, postponing indefinitely the advent of a classless society.[27] In a first phase (1945–50) militants perceived the democratic and legal approach of the party as a tactic, with few doubts regarding the PCI's real revolutionary goal. In a second phase (1951–56), when the party's organizational strength was at its apex, a thick web of local branches and secondary organizations allowed militants to experience a communitarian life and to develop a subcultural allegiance which was to be the backbone of its electoral strength. The Socialist myth was, however, tarnished by de-Stalinization in the USSR and the invasion of Hungary, which affected the cohesiveness of the party's leadership and of the militants. This was reflected in an organizational crisis (the third phase of the party, between 1956 and 1963), with declining membership and the beginning of political secularization among militants.[28] The social turmoil of the late 1960s, the USSR occupation of Prague, and, later, the advent of dictatorship in Chile, pushed the PCI in the 1970s to open to the Western Alliance and to further distance the party from the Soviet Union—although the link was severed only later, in 1981—and to elaborate, first, a "third way" to democratic socialism (the so-called "Eurocommunism") and then to propose, in 1980, a "democratic alternative," which tried, although with little success, to cope with the crisis of the Marxist culture.[29]

The tight structure of the party implied that these changes came mainly from the top, with rank and file following suit, although resistance to change emerged noticeably. The early Cattaneo's studies clearly detected continuity and change among party members. They described the PCI's militants in the 1950s as embedded in a deep and close web of party and secondary associations' activities, with political involvements rooted in the family and socially transmitted. Cleavage encapsulation was high and integration within the party intense: only 38 percent of PCI militants attended church when young and only 22 percent believed in God (respectively 81 percent and 100 percent among DC's rank and file); 44 percent reported having chosen a spouse on ideological affinity (only 16 percent did so among Christian Democrats); 39 percent reported only having friends among party members or sympathizers (27 percent among DCs); 88 percent of the party members read the official party newspaper daily (only 2 percent did the same among DC militants); 96 percent of members engaged intensively in proselytism and canvassing (44 percent among DC militants). The party as a "church" meant, therefore, that militants' loyalty to the party and its leaders was an overriding concern, and explained their adaptation to the changing party's strategies.

At the same time, different generations exhibited varying attitudes, in particular on the nature of social change and on democracy. Among the 1945–50 generation of activists, 88 percent thought taking power through elections was just a tactic, an opinion which dropped to 50 percent among the 1956–63 cohort of party members. Likewise, the Soviet Union appeared a positive model of society for 50 percent of the earlier generation, but only 28 percent of the younger one shared the same opinion.[30]

Research carried out 15 years later—again by researchers at the Istituto Cattaneo and by CESPE,[31] a PCI-related think tank (the first research on its militants approved by the party, traditionally weary of social sciences, on the occasion of the 15th Congress of the PCI in 1979), allows us to trace the further evolution of the PCI party base after the experience of the Historical Compromise and the formal abandonment of Marxism–Leninism as the official party ideology. The CESPE study portrays a party still "cleavage encapsulated," with a continuity in identity and integration which surprised the authors.[32] The profile of the party member, and of the party's functionaries, revealed a strong socialization within the Communist subculture. The strongest influence was still exerted by the family, and only among the younger generation—those entering the party after 1977—does the subcultural milieu decline.[33] Even among young militants, friend networks were still composed significantly of PCI members/sympathizers (44 percent among 1977–79 joiners vs 60 percent for earlier generations); daily readership of the party press had spread (69 percent); and the traditional identity motivation for joining the party had intensified (65 percent agreed with the statement: "It's the party of the working class" and 58 percent with, "It's the most democratic and anti-fascist party").[34] Also, the social composition of the party base reflected a traditional cleavage structure, with the largest share of delegates—40 percent—being industrial and agricultural workers.

The overall image of the PCI on the ground which emerges from the CESPE study was one of a strong allegiance of the base to the party's organizational structure. However, the study did not deal with the ideology and strategy of the PCI, which was the object of the Cattaneo research, showing that a solid party structure did not necessarily imply full acceptance by the rank and file of elites' strategic changes. Barbagli and Corbetta's 1979 study, on the opinion and attitudes of PCI's militants facing both a drastic revision of the party's antagonistic relationship with the Christian Democrats and its traditional closeness with the Soviet Union's Communism, uncovered still a great esteem for Socialist regimes, in stark contrast with the prevailing opinion within the party's electorate. Younger militants held a more critical view of socialism, lamenting the violation of civil and political rights, with 9 percent maintaining that USSR was as imperialist as the USA. But, even among them, the opinion that socialist regimes allowed substantial social rights—welfare in particular—meant a prevailing view of democracy interpreted as "social justice," rather than as pluralism and protection of individual rights. Moreover, the study showed how the party base appeared rather skeptical of the Historic Compromise, while there was a potential consensus for an alternative strategy centered on a left coalition competing with government parties, which, in 1980, was suddenly and unexpectedly announced by Secretary Berlinguer.

A subsequent study, carried out by Piero Ignazi, on the delegates attending the PCI's 19th Congress in 1990, just before the transformation into the Democratic Party of the Left (Partito Democratico della Sinistra—PDS) the following year, sheds light on the attitudes of the party base during the final phase. The intent of the last secretary, Occhetto—who, in the 1989 Congress, failed to have approved a drastic change in the ideology and organization of the party, on a platform of pluralist democracy, market economy, ecology, and feminism—was, after the fall of the Berlin Wall, to dismiss the old name and to give birth to a new party which would explicitly and finally sever any link with the Communist tradition. Initially widely supported, he found that, before and during the Congress, several criticisms were voiced, and organized fractions emerged for the first time.[35] Occhetto's proposal was eventually voted by 65.8 percent of the delegates. It was based on the rejection of any Italian road toward socialism and of the tight hierarchical structure of the party organization, openly legitimizing dissent and decentralizing the party structure.[36] The old party was, therefore, doomed, and a new party—PDS—was launched in the following year's last PCI Congress; at the price, however, of a bitter breakup with unrefounded Communists, who went ahead with a new party, Rifondazione Comunista, with the support of one third of the delegates.

Such disagreement was well reflected in the delegates' attitudes.[37] The political culture they express shows, in fact, a mix of continuity and change. A first instance of the latter comes from the sociodemographic composition of the delegates. It reveals—even discounting among them a certain degree of unrepresentativeness of the rank-and-file base—a strong departure from the past, given the marginalization of the working class—just 6 percent of the delegates—and a massive presence of the service class, concentrated in the public administration, with a significant presence of professional politicians (44 percent). The Communist Party had, then, lost its traditional social outlook. Also, the ideological one had changed: 70 percent of delegates looked now at Marxism as only one among many different ideological sources of action, although 50 percent agreed on Marx's thought as being up to date. Six in 10 delegates gave a negative evaluation of the Communist regimes ("Between the 1940s and 1989 there has been a brutal dictatorship in Eastern countries"). However, attitudes toward the market economy describe only a slight acceptance of capitalist institutions: two thirds agreed that "a fair society cannot do without a market," but four out of five delegates also repute capitalism as an economic system that exploits people. Likewise, foreign policy attitudes revealed a traditional view, hinged on anti-imperialism (98 percent thought Third World poverty was due to Western exploitation) and anti-Americanism (93 percent agreed that the US is imperialist). On the other hand, a liberal-procedural (based on pluralism and rights) rather than a substantial (based on social justice) vision of democracy had greatly expanded (51 percent), as well as a pragmatic view of the party itself: 60 percent thought that the party should compromise and try to expand electorally, rather than being always loyal to its ideological principle.

Overall, the study showed that the party had begun a great transformation, departing sensibly from the Communist tradition, but documented also the legacy of the past political culture. However, breaking down the attitudes according to the political leaning of the delegates (radical left, left, moderate left) provides a more homogeneous distribution of attitudes within each group, with the largest differentiation being observed between the radical left and the others. Among the latter, appreciation of the market and criticism of socialist regimes were most intense; the least shared view was of the traditional relevance of the working class (the *classe gardèe*) for party strategies. Conversely, the opposite is observed for the delegates of the radical left. From this perspective, the split the PCI experienced in the process of changing name and identity mirrored a significant attitude polarization. On the other hand, the distinction between professional politicians and simple party delegates shows that the harbingers of the change were to be found among the former, who were more malleable and with more material incentives than the rank and file (more loyal to symbolic-indentitarian incentives) in pushing forward the transformation of the party.[38]

The Party in Central and Public Office: Co-optation and (Lack of) Dissent

As we have seen, the party on the ground, at least in two occasions documented by social research, has proved able to disagree with the strategic changes enacted by the PCI elite. Such research cannot, however, overlook the main characteristics of the structure of the PCI, exposed clearly in the 1968 Cattaneo study, which remained stable for the next twenty years: it was a large, complex, territorially and functionally articulated hierarchical organization—whose recruitment in the top decision-making elite was by co-optation—supported centrally and locally by a professional staff with the goal of permanently mobilizing joiners and voters. Mobilization was also possible thanks to the organized links that the party had with secondary organizations it promoted or controlled (mainly unions and cooperatives) through overlapping membership both at the rank-and-file and at the executive levels.[39] Even if the principle of collegiality would formally operate at all levels: "the working of the organization shows the prevalence of executive roles over assemblies, and the concentration of the power in restricted groups when not in a few individuals."[40]

Although such description would more or less fit many parties in the Europe of the 1950s and 1960s—in keeping with the classical literature on parties by the elitist school—both a strong organization and the practice of "democratic centralism," that is, the ban over organized dissent in party fractions,[41] epitomized the Italian Communist Party. The puzzle over the nature of the PCI originated, then, in the contradiction between its claim to be a variation of Communist parties and, at the same time, having a large bureaucratic structure similar to many European social democratic movements.

Baccetti's analysis aptly describes the unsolved problem of the PCI: between 1973 and 1978—in the period of the maximum electoral expansion of the party—professional staff (excluding clerical jobs) increased from 1850 to 2350, to reach a high of 2560 staff in 1988. However, the intake of new generations of party professionals did not affect the classical organizational model of co-optation: both at the center as well at the periphery, party functionaries were selected by executive offices. Since becoming a professional in the party structure meant assuming a political role, such a procedure did reverse the virtuous sequence of holding a political role only after a successful leadership experience. Working for the party apparatus was thus the key to leadership roles in the party.[42]

Co-optation operated at all levels, including the top positions in the national Central Committee and party's Executive Office, where change was very slow. Between 1951 and 1989 incumbents filled, on average, 75 percent of the available seats in the Central Committee. Only in the 1956 Congress—after the Hungary repression—and in the 1989 one—with Occhetto as new secretary—did the percentage of new entrants hover at around 50. The rate of change was even smaller in the more elitist Executive Office (Direzione Nazionale): in the same period, on average, 82 percent of incumbents were reconfirmed.[43]

Also, the parliamentary political class was fully dependent on the party, whose selection showed a distinct pattern, quite diverse from that of other Italian mass parties. Whereas, for Socialist and Christian Democratic MPs the Parliament was the locus of their political career—as shown by high rates of incumbency and intraparty electoral fights—Communist MPs found in the party–rather than Parliament—the center of their political activity, showing a significant smaller parliamentary seniority. The selection and career were within the extra-parliamentary organization, and political turnover was not the result of an electoral defeat—as for the others—but, rather, the outcome of the decision (jointly with, or imposed by, the party) of an MP not to seek re-election and return to party activity.[44] The parliamentary class of the PCI represented, then, a model of unitary-centralized and extra-parliamentary political class, while other parties' MPs adhered to an opposite pluralistic-decentralized-parliamentary model.[45]

The dismantlement of such a structure was thus a very slow process, started for sure within the party, but only accelerated by the 1987 electoral defeat and by the later end of West–East confrontation. The 1979 15th PCI Congress approved a liberal conception of representation of party delegates—abolishing any mandate constraint—and the 1986 17th Congress affirmed the legitimacy of dissent in executive offices, overcoming the long-standing tradition of "democratic centralism." Finally, the 1989 18th Congress allowed the presentation of alternative lists of candidates for the party's executive assembly,[46] laying the ground for the party's transformation the following year.

CONCLUDING REMARKS

The birth of the PDS in January 1991 has not put an end to the distress of the Italian Left. On the contrary, it started a long transition toward a new party of the Left which is, to some extent, still ongoing. The new party had to face a turbulent political environment with the collapse of the entire party system of the First Republic, new electoral institutions, and a bipolarization of the political space. It did not perform well and, after PDS, another party—Democratici di Sinistra, DS—was launched in 2000,[47] followed by the Democratic Party (Partito Democratico—PD) in 2007, with the goal—paradoxically—to unite the main political subcultures—the Socialist–Communist and the Catholic—which had fiercely fought each other for forty long years. Maybe the Democratic Party is the actual mooring of the Italian Communist Party.

NOTES

1. See, among others, Paolo Spriano, *Storia del Partito comunista italiano* (Turin, Einaudi, 1976); Paul Ginsborg, *Storia d'Italia dal dopoguerra a oggi. Società e politica 1943–1988* (Turin, Einaudi, 1989); Aldo Agosti, *Storia del Partito comunista italiano 1921–1991* (Bari, Laterza, 1999); Roberto Gualtieri (ed.), *Il PCI nell'Italia repubblicana 1943–1991* (Rome, Carocci, 2001); Victor Zaslavsky, *Lo stalinismo e la sinistra italiana: dal mito dell'Urss alla fine del comunismo: 1945–1991* (Milan, Mondadori, 2004); Vittoria Albertina, *Storia del PCI 1921–1991* (Rome, Carocci, 2006); Silvio Pons. *La rivoluzione globale: storia del comunismo internazionale, 1917–1991* (Turin, Einaudi, 2012).

2. Alessandro Pizzorno, *I soggetti del pluralismo. Classi Partiti Sindacati* (Bologna, Il Mulino, 1980), 99–154.

3. Robert D. Putnam, "The Italian Communist Politician," in Donald L. M. Blackmer and Sidney Tarrow, eds., *Communism in Italy and France* (Princeton, Princeton University Press, 1976), 173–217; 217.

4. Stefano Bartolini, *The Political Mobilisation of the European Left, 1860–1980.* (Cambridge, Cambridge University Press, 2000).

5. Richard Katz and Peter Mair, eds., *How Parties Organise* (London, Sage, 1994).

6. Piergiorgio Corbetta and Maria Serena Piretti, *Atlante storico-elettorale d'Italia. 1861–2008.* Istituto Carlo Cattaneo (Bologna, Zanichelli, 2009).

7. Maurizio Cotta and Luca Verzichelli, *Political Institutions in Italy* (Oxford, Oxford University Press, 2007), 22–23.

8. Alfio Mastropaolo and Martin Slater, "Italy 1946–1979: Party Platforms and Electoral Programmes under the Republic," in Ian Budge, David Robertson, and Derek Hearl, eds., *Ideology, Strategy and Party Change: Spatial Analyses of Post-War Election Programmes in 19 Democracies* (Cambridge, Cambridge University Press, 1987), 345–368; 368.

9. Ian Budge, Hans Dieter Klingemann, Andrea Volkens, Judith Bara, and Eric Tanenbaum, *Mapping Political Preferences: Estimates for Parties, Electors and Governments, 1945–1998,* 239 (Oxford, Oxford University Press, 2001).

10. Giuseppe Di Palma, *Surviving without Governing: The Italian Parties in Parliament* (Berkeley, University of California Press, 1977).

11. Piergiorgio Corbetta, Arturo M.L. Parisi, and Hans M.A. Schadee, *Elezioni in Italia. Struttura e tipologia delle consultazioni politiche* (Bologna, Il Mulino, 1988).

12. Gorgio Galli, *Il bipartitismo imperfetto* (Bologna, Il Mulino, 1966).

13. James Newell, *Italy: Governance in a Normal Country* (Cambridge, Cambridge University Press, 2010).

14. Giorgio Galli, ed., *Il comportamento elettorale in Italia.* Istituto di studi e ricerche Carlo Cattaneo (Bologna, Il Mulino, 1968).

15. Arturo M. Parisi and Gianfranco Pasquino, "Relazioni partiti-elettori e tipi di voto," in Arturo M. Parisi and Gianfranco Pasquino, eds., *Continuità e mutamento elettorale in Italia* (Bologna, Il Mulino, 1987), 215–249]

16. Giacomo Sani, "Mass-Level Response to Party Strategy: The Italian Electorate and the Communist Party," in Donald L. M. Blackmer and Sidney Tarrow, eds., *Communism in Italy and France* (Princeton, Princeton University Press, 1976), 456–503; 462.

17. Maurizio Pisati, *Voto di classe. Posizione sociale e preferenze politiche in Italia* (Bologna, Il Mulino, 2010).

18. Robert D. Putnam, "Italian Foreign Policy: The Emergent Consensus," in Howard R. Penniman, ed., *Italy at the Polls: The Parliamentary Elections of 1976* (Washington, DC, American Enterprise Institute for Public Policy Research, 1977), 287–326; Pierangelo Isernia, "Present at Creation: Italian Mass Support for European Integration in the Formative Years," *European Journal of Political Research* 47 (2008), 383–410.

19. Pierpaolo Luzzato Fegiz, *Il volto sconosciuto dell'Italia* (Milan, Giuffrè, 1966); Giovanna Guidorossi, *Gli italiani e la politica. Valori, opinioni, atteggiamenti dal dopoguerra ad oggi* (Milan, Franco Angeli, 1984); Renato Mannheimer and Giacomo Sani, *Il mercato elettorale. Identikit dell'elettore italiano* (Bologna, Il Mulino, 1987).

20. Paolo Bellucci, "All'origine delle identità politiche," in A.M.L. Parisi and H.M.A. Schadee, eds., *Sulla soglia del cambiamento. Elettori e partiti alla fine della prima Repubblica* (Bologna, Il Mulino, 1995), 185–226; Paolo Bellucci and Paolo Segatti eds., *Votare in Italia. Dall'appartenenza alla scelta* (Bologna, Il Mulino, 2010).

21. Giorgio Galli, ed., *Il comportamento elettorale in Italia*. Istituto di studi e ricerche Carlo Cattaneo, (Bologna, Il Mulino, 1968), 21.

22. Leonardo Morlino, "Le tre fasi dei partiti italiani," in Leonardo Morlino and Mario Tarchi, eds., *Partiti e caso italiano* (Bologna, Il Mulino, 2006), 105–144.

23. Agopik Manoukian, ed., *La presenza sociale del PCI e della DC* (Bologna, Il Mulino, 1968).

24. Francesco Alberoni, ed., *L'attivista di partito* (Bologna Il Mulino, 1967).

25. Gianfranco Poggi, ed., *L'organizzazione partitica del PCI e della DC* (Bologna, Il Mulino, 1968).

26. Ibid., 186.

27. Alberoni, *L'attivista di partito*, 24.

28. Ibid., 30–35.

29. Piero Ignazi, *Dal PCI al PDS* (Bologna, Il Mulino, 1992), 36.

30. Alberoni, *L'attivista di partito*, 369–374.

31. Marzio Barbagli and Piergiorgio Corbetta, "Una tattica e due strategie. Inchiesta sulla base del PCI," in Marzio Barbagli, Piergiorgio Corbetta, and Salvatore Sechi, *Dentro il PCI* (Bologna, Il Mulino, 1979), 9–59; Aris Accornero, Renato Mannheimer, and Chiara Sebastiani, eds., *L'identità comunista. I militanti, la struttura, la cultura del Pci* (Rome, Editori Riuniti, 1983).

32. Ignazi, *Dal PCI al PDS*, 45.

33. Chiara Sebastiani, "I funzionari," in Accornero, Mannheimer, and Sebastiani, eds., *L'identità comunista*, 103.

34. Nino Magna, "Dirigenza e base," in Accornero, Mannheimer, and Sebastiani, eds., *L'identità comunista*, 220–221.

35. Carlo Baccetti, *Il Pds* (Bologna, Il Mulino, 1997), 29.

36. Ibid., 53–69.

37. Ignazi, *Dal PCI al PDS*, 137–164.

38. Ibid., 164.

39. Poggi, *L'organizzazione partitica del PCI e della DC*, 178–179.

40. Ibid., 179.

41. Salvatore Sechi, "L'austero fascino del centralismo democratico," in Barbagli, Corbetta, and Sechi, *Dentro il PCI*, 61–111.

42. Baccetti, *Il Pds*, 173.

43. Ignazi, *Dal PCI al PDS*, 113–114.

44. Maurizio Cotta and Luca Verzichelli, "La classe politica italiana: cronaca di una morte annunciata," in Maurizio Cotta and Pierangelo Isernia (eds.), *Il gigante dai piedi d'argilla. La crisi del regime partitocratico in Italia* (Bologna, Il Mulino, 1996), 373–408, 391.

45. Maurizio Cotta, *Classe politica e parlamento in Italia* (Bologna, Il Mulino, 1979), 363.

46. Ignazi, *Dal PCI al PDS*, 88–96.

47. Paolo Bellucci, Marco Maraffi, and Paolo Segatti, *PCI, PDS, DS. La trasformazione dell'identità politica della sinistra di governo* (Rome, Donzelli, 2000).

CHAPTER 16

SOCIALISTS, REPUBLICANS, AND RADICALS

NICOLÒ CONTI

THE Italian Socialist Party (PSI), the Italian Social Democratic Party (PSDI), the Italian Republican Party (PRI), and the Radical Party (PR), in different ways, all played a significant role in the Italian political system of the First Republic. The former three were mainstream parties many times in government, while the latter was a more unconventional party, known especially for having politicized post-materialist issues within a system otherwise locked in more traditional cleavage representation. These four parties are considered together in this chapter because of their commonalities. First, they all shared a secular ideology, on this ground being alternatives to the Christian Democrats symbolized the permanence of a state/Church cleavage in Italian society. Second—with the only exception of the PR—these parties have been in government most of the time during the First Republic as they were favorite partners of the Christian Democrats in coalition building. Given the fragmented nature of the Italian party system where a single party did not ever reach a majority in the Parliament and the DC was always the party winning a plurality of votes, coalitions incontestably favored those parties that were closest to the centrist DC. Indeed, these four parties all leaned toward left of center: the PSI more to the left, particularly until the 1960s, when it started a process of realignment that, by the 1980s, led the socialists to more centrist positions; the PSDI and the PRI were closer to center; the PR had a more maverick position, with a mix of libertarian radicalism and economic liberalism. Their ideological moderation and pragmatic behavior made the PSI, PSDI, and PRI particularly able to coalesce with the Christian Democrats. Exactly for this reason, in the First Republic these parties became strongly associated with government. On the contrary, the PR demarcated itself as an anti-system party, severely blaming the government for incompetence, corruption, and proximity with the Church.

Beyond their broad ideological similarities, the origins and belief systems of these four parties present, however, important differences. As it will be discussed in greater detail in the following sections, the PSI, PSDI, and PRI have older foundations, and their roots can be traced back to the nineteenth century, while the PR only became established in the 1960s. In the First Republic, they have all become commonly known as the "lay parties," because they supported principles of secularism, balancing the confessional stance of the dominant DC. However, beyond this cleavage, the PSI and PSDI also politicized conflict between employers and workers, taking, in this context, a position in defense of labor, while the PRI and PR held a more ambivalent stance, mixing elements of socialism and liberalism (see Chapter 19, this volume).[1] Otherwise, the PR was the party more directly associated with politicization of post-materialist issues, particularly those related to the defense of civil rights. On those issues, the radicals exerted a sort of issue-ownership within the Italian political system, as, although the other lay parties nominally shared same point of view as the PR (for example, on issues of divorce and abortion), they did not take as much initiative to politicize those issues, probably in order to maintain their alliance with the DC. Finally, in terms of world vision, during the Cold War years these parties proved to be broadly anti-Marxist and pro-Atlanticist; however, the PSI moved from a Marxist to a pro-West vision, starting from the 1960s and more unequivocally from the mid-1970s,[2] while the PR was mainly a pacifist movement. In the end, although these parties have become associated with defense of secularism, their strategies and behavior, as well as their preferences on socioeconomic issues and foreign policy, were more diversified. However, with the only exception of the PR, their mutual ideological distance progressively reduced over time and, with few exceptions, issues of government formation and termination among these parties and with the DC often depended on allocation of portfolios more than serious policy disputes.[3]

The organizational features of these parties varied remarkably. The PSI was more linked to a class-based mass-party model, with a permanent organization and extensive territorial ramifications. The PSDI started as a splinter group of the PSI and, although originally inspired by the same organizational model, together with the PRI never managed to achieve a truly nation-wide mass organization, so the two developed more as elite parties. On the contrary, the PR became established at a time of general decline of the mass-party model,[4] with the specific goal of mobilizing those groups (young people, minority right activists, libertarians, pacifists) who did not identify with the traditional parties: its internal organization was similar to a social movement.

The electoral size of these parties was also different. The PSI was always the strongest one, with a share of votes in the lower Chamber varying between 10 and 14 percent in the period between 1953 and 1992, while, in the same period, the PSDI share of votes was between 2 and 7 percent, that of the PRI between 2 and 5 percent, and that of the PR between 1 and 3 percent (see Table 16.1). The combined effect of ideology and electoral weight induced the Christian Democrats to build coalitions with the PSI–PRI (each took part in 18 cabinets out of a total number of 50 during the First Republic) and PSDI (29 cabinets),[5] but not with the PR. When in government, the PSI, PSDI, and PRI often enjoyed a disproportionate blackmail power compared to their size, and could negotiate some of the better government spoils with the DC, since they were necessary to secure a minimum winning coalition (see Chapter 23, this volume). When the system imploded in the early 1990s, largely because of the unpopularity of the government as a consequence of its widespread practices of bribery and corruption (see Chapter 24, this volume), participation in power meant that the PSI, PSDI, and PRI were also identified with political misconduct, thus leading to their eventual demise. Although the PR was never in government, and therefore was not involved in the same corruption scandals, it did not capitalize on the other parties' crisis and never developed as a real party organization with a vote-seeking strategy, but continued to confine itself to its social movement character. In the Second Republic, these four parties have systematically reached an average share of votes of only few decimals in the general elections. It is thanks to their pre-electoral agreements with larger parties that, even after 1994, they have occasionally managed to appoint a very limited number of MPs.

THE SOCIALISTS

The Italian Workers' Party was founded in 1892 with an unambiguous Marxist platform. In 1893 it incorporated other smaller radical forces and changed its name to the Socialist Party of the Italian Workers. Finally, it was renamed the Italian Socialist Party after having been banned by the Italian government in 1894 because it was considered a threat to the state. It continued to exist uninterruptedly for a century until, after being involved in corruption scandals, it lost most of its votes and was finally dissolved in 1994. Since then, many former PSI members have joined other parties of both left (mainly the Left Democrats and the Democratic Party) and right (mainly Forza Italia and the People of Freedom). A small group of former socialists founded a new party that, over the years, was given different names before finally being renamed Italian Socialist Party in 2009 and becoming part of the larger center-left coalition.

During its history, the PSI was often characterized by internal tensions among pragmatists and radicals, Atlanticists and believers in the Soviet Union and its way to socialism, supporters of a domestic alliance with the Christian Democrats or, alternatively, with the Communists. These divisions explain why, during its long existence, the party went through various internal divisions and splits, as well as different patterns of party competition. To name a few, after the breakout of several party factions of both revolutionary unionists and moderate pragmatists, in the 1920s, a former member who had just been expelled by the party, Benito Mussolini, founded the Fascist National Party. In the same period, a group of socialists split from the PSI to create the Italian Communist Party (PCI) and joined the Communist International. Only between the two world wars, after the banning of all opposition parties and the murder of some prominent socialist leaders by the fascist regime, did the exiled socialists find their unity again and cohesively take an active role in the liberation movement against Mussolini's dictatorship and the Nazi occupation. The party was also very active in the aftermath of World War II in constitution building and in the democratization of the country (the socialist Giuseppe Saragat was President of the Constitutional Assembly in 1946–47). At the time, the PSI was still the second largest party of the country after the DC.

However, the internal conflicts between radicals and moderates became salient again after the new democratic constitution was introduced and the government of national unity that took the country out of the war process was dissolved. The system's polarization immediately became apparent (see Chapter 12, this volume) and the socialists were compelled to decide whether to align with the Christian Democrats or with the communists in the view of the first democratic elections of 1948. The pro-Moscow orientation of the socialists was majoritarian at the time, rather than unanimous.[6] In the end, the second option prevailed within the party but it proved electorally unsuccessful.[7] It also caused a new split of moderate members, who considered the party too much aligned with the communists in the domestic arena and with the Soviet Union in the international scene. This splinter group created a new party (ultimately renamed in 1952 as the Italian Social Democratic Party, PSDI), which included some prominent socialist figures (such as Saragat) who had played a crucial role after the fall of the fascist regime. Although this splinter party was never as strong as the PSI electorally, thanks to its early moderate stance it was considered able to participate in government by the DC well before the PSI, so, after the end of the governments of national unity in 1947, the PSDI replaced the PSI in the cabinet (with Saragat as deputy prime minister). This new division among socialists marked a definite electoral rebalancing within the left in favor of the more cohesive and disciplined PCI, which became the largest party of the left. Since that time, the PSI has been compelled to be a third force within the Italian party system, behind the Christian Democrats and the communists. The party was an anomaly in the Western European context, where socialist parties tended, instead, to be more sizeable. It should be noted that the PSDI proved a real competitor for the left, for example, with its 7 percent of votes, it certainly contributed to the disappointing electoral result of the PSI–PCI alliance in 1948. Its influence on the third largest workers' union (UIL) also gave the PSDI a significant social basis, contributing to the overall fragmentation of the Italian left.

As a consequence of its internal ideological diversity, and even after the split of PSDI, the broad position of the PSI was always a matter of power balance among its internal factions. Until the 1950s, under the leadership of Nenni, the leftists prevailed and the party aligned with the communists. After the late 1950s, particularly after the invasion of Hungary by the Soviet Union and the electoral defeats at home when it was in alliance with the communists, it was again Nenni who led the PSI toward more moderate stances, and acceptance of Atlanticism, the Common Market, and capitalism. After the mid-1960s, this realignment allowed the party to join a coalition government with the Christian Democrats, an alliance that would last a whole decade—until the DC opted for a grand coalition with the PCI. The PSDI also contributed to bringing the DC and the PSI closer, and finally reunited with the PSI in 1966 under the banner of the Unified Socialist Party (Partito Socialista Unificato). During this period, Saragat confirmed his influential role and was elected President of the Republic in 1964 (proving a more convincing candidate for this role than Nenni, who finally withdrew his candidacy). However, the unification of the socialists lasted only two years, then the PSI and PSDI spilt again after the unsatisfactory electoral result of 1968. This division was also evidence of the eternal divisions within the socialist camp: many members of the PSI believed that the incumbent government should represent a transitional solution until the time was right for a PSI–PCI alliance that could be majoritarian in the country; the former PSDI members, of course, did not agree with this line.

At the same time, the PCI was experiencing its greatest electoral success (with more than triple the votes of the PSI and just slightly behind the DC), becoming the largest communist party in a Western democracy. In 1976, the PSI party secretary, Francesco De Martino, withdrew support for government and declared his intention to build a leftist alternative to DC-led cabinets, together with the communists. However, his strategy did not prove electorally successful for the PSI; when Bettino Craxi was appointed new party secretary in the same year, a convinced ideological shift was introduced, with total rejection of Marxism and a consequent embracement of liberalism (although mitigated by some elements of social market economy), by the PSI. This shift could be compared to the ideological realignment of the Social Democratic Party (SPD) of Germany, decided almost twenty years before, in 1959, in the famous party convention in Bad Godesberg. Similarly to the SPD, the PSI sought to move beyond its working-class base to the full spectrum of potential voters, with an appeal to the middle class and to professionals. Nenni died in 1980, other old members were marginalized within the party, and the PSI central office was drastically renewed: at that point the new political course of the party went unchallenged. Craxi held leadership and ruled the PSI until 1993, just before its dissolution in 1994. The internal hegemony of Craxi, and his capacity to successfully bargain with the DC and secure high gains for his party, made the PSI, for the first time, a rather personalistic organization and a real competitor to the DC.[8] As a consequence, the party proved more cohesive than in the past, but lost the internal checks and balances that could better guarantee not only intraparty pluralism, but also sound finance management. Instead, the concentration of power in the hands of the party leader and the opaque internal controls favored corruption and financial mismanagement within the PSI, at a scale that ultimately led to colossal scandals and drove the party to collapse in the early 1990s. A similar destiny was shared by the PSDI, which, although never reaching the same weight as the PSI, was almost always in government and equally involved in the corruption scandals that led, in the end, to its demise.

From the electoral point of view, the PSI was rather stable as a third force during the First Republic and went through vote losses only in 1948, when it contested the elections in alliance with the Communists, and, again, in the 1970s, when it aligned with the PCI, which was at maximum strength (see Table 16.1). Thus, evidence shows that the PSI was electorally stronger when it was in alliance with the Christian Democrats but weaker when it aligned with the PCI (see also Chapter 23, this volume). As well, the success of the PCI developed at a time of decline of the PSI (1970s), while the socialists grew when the communists declined (1980s). So, it is evident that there was competition within the left camp, and we can interpret an alliance with the Christian Democrats and the isolation of the communists by the PSI as a strategy to challenge their main competitor, one that found in Craxi one of the main advocates. Some criticized this strategy as it created the conditions for non-alternation in government and for immovability of the

Table 16.1 Electoral Results of the PSI, PRI, and PR in the General Elections. Proportional Vote in the House of Deputies (percent)

	1946*	1948	1953	1958	1963	1968	1972	1976	1979	1983	1987	1992	1994±	1996±	2001±	2006	2008	2013
PSI (renamed SDI in 2001–2008)	20.7	32 In joint list with PCI	12.6	14.2	13.8	14.4 Joint PSI–PSDI list	9.6	9.6	9.8	11.4	14.2	13.6	2.1	0.4	0.9	2.6** In joint list with PR	1	***
PSDI		7.1 In joint list with other PSI splinters	4.5	4.6	6.1		5.1	3.4	3.8	4.1	3	2.7	≈	≈	≈	≈	≈	≈
PRI	4.4	2.5	1.6	1.4	1.4	2	2.9	3	3	5.1	3.7	4.4	≈	≈	≈	≈	≈	0
PR (renamed Bonino-Pannella List in 1992–2013)				1.4		0	1.1	3.5	3.5	2.2	2.6	1.2	3.5	1.9	2.2	2.6 In joint list with SDI	≈	0.2

* Election of the Constitutional Assembly

** A group of socialists contested the elections separately in a joint list named "Christian Democracy–New PSI" that obtained 0.7 percent of votes

*** The PSI gained 4 seats in the House of Deputies in a joint list with the PD (25.4 percent), but it gained only 0.2 percent of votes and no seats in the Senate with its own list

± Proportional seats under a mixed plurality-proportional electoral system

≈ The party did not present its own list, but some of its candidates contested the elections under other party lists

Source: Italian Ministry of Interior.

government mandate of the DC, something that favored, in the end, a blocked government and led to the consequent spillover of corruption.[9] The PSDI was instead a minor electoral force, albeit one able to contain the expansion of the PSI and to maximize gains despite its limited electoral weight, thanks to ideological positioning exactly in-between the DC and the PSI.

The PSI was third in terms of membership as well. As Figure 16.1 shows, on average, the main left competitor, the PCI, tripled the membership rate of the socialists. This pattern developed well before the PCI was actually able to translate its membership domination within the left camp into electoral domination as well. The DC started instead to diverge from the PSI later in the 1950s, but over a decade reached membership rates similar to those of PCI. Divisions among the socialists did not help their overall capacity to affiliate members and establish a party in the ground as large as those of DC and PCI. It should also be noted that the PSI and PSDI competed with each other on this ground: the electoral threat of the latter and its capacity to affiliate members (also thanks to its affiliate union, UIL) should not be underestimated.[10] In the end, from the point of view of electoral capacity and organizational ramification through membership, the PSI was always squeezed by the concurrent competition of the PCI to its left and the PSDI and DC to its right. Its efforts to maintain a mass-based organization were particularly challenged by the limited size of Italian party membership (even though this was quite sizeable by comparative standards),[11] combined with the congested presence of parties seeking a mass organization status.

In spite of its rank as a third force, however, the institutional record of the PSI was one of a force actually in government most of the time (since the 1960s). For example, the PSI held prime ministership twice, with Craxi in 1983–87 and Giuliano Amato in 1992–93. Both times, this happened after electoral losses of the main coalition partner DC, while, on the same occasions, the PSI proved more electorally stable. This situation also arose due to internal factional conflicts within the DC that prevented the Christian Democrats from expressing a unitary candidate for prime minister who would be backed by a majority of the party.[12] In both junctures, a cohesive PSI guided by Craxi was able to take advantage of the weakness of the DC and take the lead in a cabinet that, particularly under his leadership in 1983–87, proved unusually stable by Italian standards.[13] The Socialist Party family also held the Italian presidency, with Saragat of the PSDI in office in 1964–71 and Sandro Pertini of the PSI in 1978–85,[14] thus proving its crucial role in national institutions. The election of the latter, particularly, was an enormous success for the socialists. Not only was Pertini elected with 832 out of 995 votes by the parliament, thus proving the respect of other parties for this founding father of Italian democracy and the credibility of a PSI candidate for this role, but he also opened the way for the first executives led by non-Christian Democrat chiefs: he appointed Craxi as *formateur* in 1979 (but this time he could not find a majority of parties to form a government), then the republican Spadolini in 1981, then again Craxi in 1983. Hence, the election of Pertini as President of the Republic created the conditions for real competition among government parties, and the overall influence of the PSI on the government grew as a consequence.

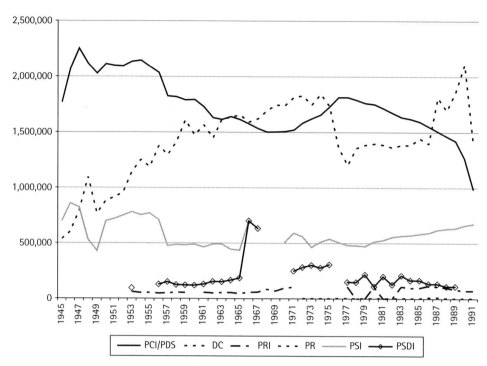

FIGURE 16.1 Membership in PSI, PSDI, PRI, and PR, in Comparison with the Two Largest Parties, DC and PCI

Source: Istituto Cattaneo.

The socialists played a fundamental role at the local level too. Since the 1970s, Italy had started a process of decentralization, with important developments in terms of delegation of powers from the state to the local layers of government (regions, provinces, municipalities). As a consequence, local institutions have been substantially empowered and their role in the management of important policies, such as health and the environment, has increased. These new government tiers opened opportunities for the PCI to take government responsibility in those territories where it was majoritarian, as it became possible to have different government compositions at the local and at the national level. In this context, given the polarization between DC and PCI, almost everywhere the PSI proved a pivotal party. Indeed, the overall number of local single-party governments was very limited, so similar to what happened at the national level, even at the local level the two larger parties were compelled to build coalitions with smaller parties. The PSI—more than the PSDI, which was unequivocally attached to the DC and anti-communist from its inception—was able to build coalitions with either DC or PCI. In the end, once the process of regionalism and decentralization allowed the creation of a new relevant level of government, the institutional record of the PSI has become one of a party in government most of the time, at the national level, and also at the local level. The advantage of pivotality was such that, in many cases, even a major change in coalition making at the local level did not hamper the role of the PSI, as it easily jumped from a coalition with DC to one with PCI, and vice versa. On these occasions, the PSI was often able to bargain very advantageous conditions in exchange for its participation in coalitions. To give an example, the socialist Carlo Tognoli was mayor of a city as important as Milan uninterruptedly from 1976 to 1986 under both center-left (DC–PSI) and leftist (PCI–PSI) coalitions.

Since 1993, the socialists have declined enormously and have almost disappeared from the political scene, with the exception of some individual figures (such as Giuliano Amato), who have joined other parties. After being involved in large-scale cases of bribery, the socialist leader Craxi fled from justice in 1994 and settled in Tunisia, where he died in 2000. The former party secretary of PSDI, Pietro Longo, was arrested for the same reasons in 1992, and the incumbent secretary, Antonio Cariglia, was similarly prosecuted. A very insidious system of illegal financing of these parties was uncovered, leading to public indignation and to the parties' demise. After the crisis of the PSI and PSDI, their members became very divided due to the new bipolar party system of the Second Republic. By that point, the parties' ideological shift had been so ample that the idea that they belonged to the left of the political spectrum was not so evident anymore; in particular, this sense of belonging would not be shared by the new party elite recruited under Craxi. Many socialists associated the Italian left (particularly the former Italian Communist Party, just renamed the Party of Left Democrats, PDS) with the mobilization of citizens and the judiciary against corruption and the government parties; this, of course, increased their antagonism with the left, as they considered it responsible for its own collapse. As a result, a socialist diaspora started from 1994, with many former members of PSI and PSDI dividing among the opposite camps of left and right, while the reconstructed Italian Socialist Party only occasionally managed to appoint some of its representatives to public office thanks to pre-electoral agreements with the new parties.

The Republicans

Among the Italian parties, the one with the oldest historical roots is the PRI. Its origins date back to the Italian Risorgimento, particularly to the first illegal organizations (such as the Giovane Italia led by Giuseppe Mazzini) that, since the 1830s, fought for the unification of the country. However, the republicans had serious problems with the actual form of state building in Italy, as this was carried out as an incorporation of new territories by the conservative Piedmontese monarchy, while the republicans were leftist and fiercely anti-monarchist. Thus, after a period of rejection of the national institutions of the new Kingdom of Italy, the republicans started to take part in the elections only from the 1880s when, together with the socialists, they started to occupy the extreme left of the political spectrum. However, their ideology was not Marxist, but left liberal, and over the years their stance became even more distinctive from the rest of the Italian left, as the republicans quickly became anti-communist and Atlanticists.[15] However, it was only after the end of the Kingdom of Italy and the advent of the Italian Republic in 1946 that the republicans stopped being considered extremists and started instead being included in the political mainstream as a privileged partner of the Christian Democrats. Since then, they have occupied a tiny space in the political spectrum to the right of the PCI and PSI and to the left of the DC.

From the electoral point of view, the PRI was always a small force within the Italian party system (see Table 16.1). With few exceptions, the party electoral stronghold was always very limited in scope and confined to the central regions of the country. Although some of the party members were prominent figures with high personal recognition and key posts in government (such as the Minister of Foreign Affairs, Carlo Sforza, in the crucial years after World War II, the Budget Minister, Ugo La Malfa, during the social reforms of the 1960s, or Prime Minister Giovanni Spadolini in 1981–82[16]), the PRI never succeeded in increasing its electoral base, and remained, instead, squeezed between those of the larger, more ideological, and better organized parties (DC, PCI, and PSI). Indeed, in the First Republic, the vote share of the PRI in the lower Chamber varied between 1 and 5 percent. However, even its small share of votes was, on many occasions, necessary for a larger party to secure a majority in Parliament; thus, the PRI's blackmail potential and coalition behavior was not so different from that of the other lay parties.

The recurrent presence of the republicans in the most relevant institutions of the country was indeed linked to their stable relationship with the Christian Democrats, something that allowed the PRI to be in government almost uninterruptedly between 1946 and 1953, 1962 and 1972, and 1979 and 1991. In the remaining years, the PRI was either in government intermittently, or gave its external support to DC-led cabinets (such as in 1953–62). Thanks to their broad government practice, the republicans became part of an experienced elite, even though poor in extra-parliamentary structures and organization in the ground, as is also proved by the very limited membership of the PRI (see Figure 16.1). However, the main party leaders could well be included in the founding fathers of the Italian democratic state, and their contribution in terms of values and ideas to the major decisions of the Italian government has been significant. For example, La Malfa was appointed minister in the transitional governments of national unity immediately after World War II, and again several times in the following decades, including as deputy prime minister (1974–76). As Minister of Foreign Trade (1951–53) he played a crucial role in liberalizing international exchange after the closure imposed by fascism. He also took an active role in promoting, within the Italian government, the ideals of European market integration in the years that led to the Treaty of Rome in 1957.[17] He was one of the advocates of a progressive opening of the government arena to the Italian left, first to the PSI in 1960s and later to the PCI in the 1970s. His personal influence was also central in major economic decisions concerning, for example, nationalized industry and Italian membership in the European monetary system. After he died, his successor to the leadership of the Republican Party, Spadolini, played an important institutional role, particularly as the first non-Christian Democrat prime minister since World War II. It is evident that, despite its reduced electoral weight, the

PRI has shared with the DC (and has even been in the forefront of) some of the most crucial steps in the making of the Italian democracy.

Even if at a lower scale than the DC and PSI, the PRI was also involved in corruption scandals in 1992–93 and, consequently, almost disappeared from the political scene. In 1994, after the outbreak of new parties and of bipolar politics in Italy, the republicans, like the socialists, spread between the new left and right parties. However, some of the original members continued to exist as PRI, but the party never managed to appoint more than three MPs in the Parliament and this was possible only thanks to pre-electoral alliances with the center-left (in 1996) or the center-right coalition (from 2001 on).

THE RADICALS

The PR was founded in 1956, for the most part by a splinter group of the Italian Liberal Party and some non-aligned leftists. Its original mission consisted of promotion of secularism and fight against government corruption and its proximity with the Church. But, over the years, the most moderate affiliates of liberal origins left the party after disagreement with its political extremism, fierce anticlericalism, and alignment with the left. This group of critics included most of the party founders, thus, since the 1960s, the PR was handled by a new generation of political activists with little political experience or past party affiliations (see Chapter 19, this volume). In this respect, it was a unique case in the Italian context, as the other parties tended to have much older origins. It was precisely in the 1970s that the PR acquired its very nature of a new-left post-materialist movement, mainly interested in politicizing new issues, such as those related to divorce, abortion, euthanasia, civil rights, equal opportunities, pacifism, and defense of the environment. By petitioning for popular referenda on these issues, the PR found an innovative way to politicize subjects that would otherwise have remained marginal in the impermeable Italian party system.

Radicals were, overall, rather isolated within the domestic system due to their lack of coalition potential: a consequence of both their political radicalism and very limited electoral size. Moreover, the only credible interlocutors for this purpose had left the party during its early days, thus exposing the party's actual character of radical antagonist. Hence, lacking any power of influence within the representative institutions, the PR successfully managed to bring its favorite issues onto the agenda by petitioning directly with citizens in order to call referenda,[18] and so to circumvent Parliament (where radicals would not be able to coalesce and build a majority around their position). This strategy was also perfectly consistent with their search for an innovative image and in order to demarcate themselves from the traditional parties, which had, in Parliament and in bargaining among the respective central offices, their own favorite arenas for issue conflict and management. Politicization through referendum was also a way for the radicals to have a maverick impact on the party system, as some of the issues they raised were transverse to the other parties and party alliances. As a matter of fact, on the occasion of referenda, the lay parties often abandoned (and defeated) the DC to side with the radicals. Among the main referenda proposed or contested by the radicals, one could mention those in favor of divorce, abortion, assisted pregnancy, legalization of light drugs, or against nuclear power and the state financing of parties.

Ultimately, the party worked mostly as a referendum committee. Still, even in presence of very limited central and public office structures,[19] or territorial ramification and membership (see Figure 16.1), its success in mobilizing citizens in referendum campaigns was impressive. This was mainly due to innovative communication strategies through shock initiatives,[20] but also to the party capacity to mobilize underrepresented groups (feminists, pacifists, greens) over specific goals, also thanks to formal merger with some non-partisan groups of civil society (such as the gay movement or the pro-abortion movement in the early 1970s) that was unusual in the Italian political scene.

At the end of the 1980s, the PR merged in the Transnational Radical Party and ceased to exist as an independent national organization. Like the socialists and the republicans, from 1994 its members joined larger parties of both left and right, while a small group of independent radicals contested the elections under the Bonino-Pannella List (after the name of the two main historical leaders of the PR); however, they could only appoint few members in the Italian Parliament and only when they established a pre-electoral alliance with one of the two major coalitions.

Final Remarks

Even though they played a significant role in the First Republic—in terms of overall government life (socialists and republicans) or issue politicization and agenda making (radicals)—the parties that were analyzed in this chapter have almost disappeared from the political scene of the Second Republic. No relevant (in terms of electoral size or coalition potential) organization recalling those parties exists in this new political system, and even the capacity of groups such as the radicals to force their favorite issues into the political agenda through referenda and more unconventional initiatives has gradually vanished. Although some organizations of very limited scope stemming from those parties exist nowadays, it seems more appropriate to refer to the original organizations as historical parties that have marked, in different ways and with varying intensity, some of the main steps in the political life of the First Republic, but failed to survive the political turmoil and party system change that has led to the Second Republic.

Notes

1. Often this ambivalence was a reflection of intraparty divisions. For example, the liberal component of the PRI split in the early 1960s when the party opened to a government

alliance with the socialists, and to principles of state interventionism and social market economy.

2. The geopolitical division was a major reason for the split of the PSDI from the PSI in 1947.

3. Gianfranco Pasquino (1995), "Il pentapartito," in G. Pasquino (ed.), *La politica italiana. Dizionario critico, 1945–1995* (Bari: Laterza).

4. Otto Kirchheimer (1966), "The transformation of the Western European party systems," in Weiner Myron and Joseph LaPalombara (eds.) *Political Parties and Political Development* (Princeton: Princeton University Press).

5. The overall number of cabinets of the First Republic was very high and this was also due to a large number of (normally single-party) cabinets lasting only few months, whose main goal was to pass specific legislation, such as the annual budgetary law.

6. The socialist leader Nenni, who was the party secretary in 1931–45 and 1949–63, was, at that time, one of the main advocates of the pro-Moscow line and a fierce opponent to the Atlantic Pact. Ten years later, he became one of the main proponents of the ideological realignment of the PSI that also included acceptance of Atlanticism and denunciation of the undemocratic nature of the Soviet Union, particularly after repression of the Hungarian revolution of 1956.

7. The combined vote for PSI and PCI declined from 39.6 percent in the elections of the Constitutional Assembly of 1946, to 32 percent in the general elections of 1948.

8. Wolfgang Merkel (1987), *Prima e dopo Craxi: le trasformazioni del PSI* (Padua: Liviana).

9. Giorgio Galli (2007), *Storia del socialismo italiano: da Turati al dopo Craxi* (Milan: Dalai).

10. For the first twenty years after its birth, between 1953 and 1972 (with the exclusion of 1968 when it unified with the PSI), the PSDI had an average share of votes of 5 percent in the House of Deputies and a peak of 6.1 percent in 1963. In the same period, its membership rate was, on average, just over 226,000, but it reached a peak of over 300,000 members in 1973–75. A decline in the votes and membership of PSDI started in the second half of the 1970s.

11. Richard S. Katz and Peter Mair (eds.) (1994), *How Parties Organize: Change and Adaptation in Party Organizations in Western Democracies* (London: Sage).

12. Although it was a highly factional party whose internal consensus was difficult to reach, the DC still managed to appoint the prime minister of 45 cabinets out of the total 50 of the First Republic.

13. The Craxi I–II cabinets lasted between August 1983 and April 1987 with only one reshuffle in August 1986 and a record as second-longest cabinet of the First Republic after De Gasperi's (1946–53). Amato's cabinet was shorter (June 1992–April 1993) and its end was determined by the disappearance of all its supporting parties consequent to corruption scandals; still, its action was very important, for example, his cabinet passed the largest budgetary law in Italian history.

14. He was also Speaker of the House of Deputies in 1968–76.

15. Giovanni Spadolini (1980), *I repubblicani dopo l'unità* (Florence: Felice Le Monnier).

16. He was also Speaker of the Senate in 1987–94.

17. Lorenzo Mechi (2003), *L' Europa di Ugo La Malfa. La via italiana alla modernizzazione (1942–1979)* (Milan: Franco Angeli).

18. According to the Italian Constitution, in order to call a referendum to repeal a law it is necessary to collect 500,000 signatures.

19. The main exception is represented by the radio channel Radio Radicale, always a major organizational asset of the party, which has received official recognition, along with public financing by the state, for quality journalism and information.
20. One could mention the extreme hunger strikes, or the self-accusation of the practice of abortion in clandestine hospitals and illegal drug consumption by radical leaders such as Marco Pannella and Emma Bonino.

CHAPTER 17

....

FASCISTS AND
POST-FASCISTS

....

PIERO IGNAZI

NEO-FASCISM in Italy presents unique features compared with other European countries. In the postwar period, Italy displayed the largest, most enduring, and established neo-fascist party, and the most numerous and violent radical right groups devoted not only to aggressive initiatives but to terrorist actions too, provoking an incomparable number of causalities compared to similar movements in other countries.

On the "partisan side" of neo-fascism, only in Italy did an openly declared neo-fascist party, the Movimento Sociale Italiano (MSI) (Italian Social Movement), emerge officially and legally almost immediately after the end of World War II; only in Italy was it able to compete in local elections in 1947 and get parliamentary representation after the first parliamentary election in 1948; only in Italy did it maintain parliamentary representation among all postwar legislatures, occupying the fourth position in the party system following the 1958 general election; only in Italy did it enter local government, including in large cities such as Naples, Catania, and Bari, in the 1950s (even though in the 1960s it was dismissed from local government almost everywhere); only in Italy did it play a partial role in democratic politics, contributing to the instalment of some governments in the late 1950s and the election of a President of the Republic in 1971. And, finally, only in Italy did neo-fascism evolve outside the realm of fascism, moving toward the moderate conservative camp and finally dissolving in it, rather than radicalizing along the extreme right agenda prevailing in Europe since the late 1980s.

On the "non-partisan" side of neo-fascism, the radical right groups acquired particular relevance in Italian politics from the late 1960s until the early 1980s. Well beyond their membership and their resources, which are difficult to ascertain (Italy did not avail itself of an agency for the "protection of the Constitution" as in Germany), they could play a role thanks to the relationships with, and the protection assured by, some component of the state apparatuses (security forces, Army, secret services), and by the MSI too in certain periods. These groups purportedly undertook numerous violent street actions and terrorist acts up to the apex of the Bologna railway station bombing in 1980, which caused 85 deaths. The extension over time and the number of people involved—both as perpetrators and victims—make the radical right wing of Italian neo-fascism a unique phenomenon in comparative terms.

This uniqueness is linked to the role of fascism in Italian history. Fascism is an Italian invention. Albeit its intellectual premises could be found in the *fin de siècle* French anti-liberal and anti-democratic elaboration, it was politically accomplished in Italy. In this country it created a regime which lasted for more than two decades, ending with a traumatic two-year (1943–45) civil war between pro-German fascists and pro-Allied anti-fascists. In sum, in Italy, fascism had such relevance that it passed on an unavoidable, heavy heritage to postwar politics.

The Neo-Fascist Nostalgic and Radical Period: 1946–95

The First Years: Rebirth and Positive Reception

The neo-fascist party Movimento Sociale Italiano (MSI) (Italian Social Movement) was founded at the end of 1946 by a group of young fascist war veterans, who had fought under Mussolini' s Repubblica Sociale Italiana (RSI) (Italian Social Republic), in 1943–45. Actually, this group was backed, under the radar, by more experienced former members of the fascist regime apparatus, who could not yet operate openly. As sketched out in the very minimal first party manifesto (the "Ten Points" program), the foremost concern was national conciliation and pacification in order to gain full—or at least adequate—political viability. However, while veiled and disguised, all the symbolic and cultural references of the new party suggested a close linkage to fascism.

This genetic imprint raised the problem of the party's legitimacy in the democratic *anti-fascist* regime, and, at the same time, of the anti-fascist regime's legitimacy for the MSI followers. This inner contradiction was solved quite soon, as the party opted for legal conduct and participation in the elections. In fact, in October 1947, the MSI entered its first electoral contest for Rome's city council. This was a critical choice because the far from negligible result (4 percent of the votes) enabled the MSI to present itself as the key reference for the nostalgic milieu, which was looking for a political representative. Moreover, as the party increasingly exhibited a legalistic attitude, it enlarged the gulf between the variegated world of right extremism, which, on the contrary, went on maintaining its radical stance against the new democratic system, even supporting violent actions. The MSI publicly distanced itself from these extremist groups, displaying loyalty to the democratic rules, because only in doing so could a neo-fascist party survive in an "anti-fascist" regime (which the party, at any rate, did not accept as such, given its anti-system identity). However, a covert relationship with the radical right groups remained active for a long time, even if the latter recurrently denounced the party's accommodation with the "anti-fascist regime" and thus the "betrayal" of the fascist ideals.

The MSI contested the first parliamentary elections held in 1948 and, with 2.2 percent of the votes, obtained six MPs. The electoral results demonstrated the existence of a deep north–south cleavage: 69.6 percent of the MSI votes were cast in the regions south of Rome and all the MPs were elected in southern constituencies. This skewed geographical distribution of votes had a direct impact on the party's politics. In fact, the party itself was politically and ideologically split into two diverging factions that followed the geographical divide. The "northern" faction, more militant and radical, claimed to be the heir of the socialistic and anti-bourgeois republican fascism of the 1943–45 period, while the "southern" faction followed the clerical and conservative-authoritarian fascist tendency of the 1922–43 years. This differentiation, which recalls, Renzo De Felice's famous distinction between the "fascist-movement" (revolutionary, anti-capitalist, nonconformist, utopian, etc.) and the "fascist-regime" (authoritarian, pro-clergy, corporatist, traditionalist, etc.) marked the MSI political ideological debate for a long time.

The MSI leadership of the first years identified itself with the northern "movement" tendency: according to the first "Ten Points" program, the party, beyond advocating a national reconciliation after the civil war, called for an anti-capitalist and anti-bourgeois policy reminiscent of the so-called "Verona Chart" adopted by the RSI in 1944. However, the geographical distribution of votes in the 1948 elections had shown that the MSI had its electoral reservoir in the south and that the old guard of the fascist notables still had a say. As a consequence, the young, northern, and more militant leadership group, led by Giorgio Almirante, was unable run the party any longer: in January 1950, Almirante was replaced by Alfredo De Marsanich, a former member of government in the fascist regime, and a perfect representative of the party's southern faction.

Whereas the party's radical faction expressed hard-line opposition to the democratic system, the moderate faction was inclined to exploit any circumstance whatsoever in order to be accepted as a "normal" political partner by the government parties and thus *to fit in with the system*. De Marsanich's leadership emphasized the MSI's role as a *national force* for the defense of the Christian, Western world against Communism and, consequently, promoted an electoral alliance with the monarchist party. The party leadership called for the acceptance of NATO—which the MSI had opposed in Parliament a few years earlier—and an alliance (aborted at the eleventh hour) with the DC for the 1952 Rome city council election.

This policy of accommodation was amply rewarded by the electorate: in the local elections throughout the south in 1952 the MSI–Monarchist alliance was granted 11.8 percent of votes. This means that, in only a few years, the MSI had moved from a semi-legal and marginal organization to a sizeable force (at least in the south of Italy), governing, together with the monarchists and other minor conservative groups, important cities such as Naples, Bari, and Catania. Correspondingly, the party organization boomed—notwithstanding a quite selective and controlled recruitment process—attracting tens of thousands of members and installing branches all over the country, above all in the center-south. The party could thus consolidate its organization along the mass party model.

The MSI's accommodating strategy did not go unchallenged inside the party. Despite the electoral successes (in the 1953 general election the party scored 5.8 percent of the votes, almost tripling its votes and quadrupling its seats), the radical faction remained very active and tried repeatedly to overthrow the party leadership. The showdown occurred in the 1956 Congress, where the radical faction, led by former secretary Almirante, lost by seven votes only. This defeat provoked a split within the party: the radical component finally quit the party (but Almirante remained in the party) and founded the movement Ordine Nuovo (New Order) under the leadership of Pino Rauti. This movement would prove to be the most important right extremist group in the following decades. Under the leadership of Rauti, and inspired by the works and the personality of Julius Evola, an original, anti-modern, and somewhat esoteric intellectual whose works have been a source of inspiration for over a generation of both neo-fascists and right extremists, Ordine Nuovo moved toward a radical opposition to the democratic system. In particular, Ordine Nuovo looked for sponsorship in the Army and the secret service, in order to stop the "communist infiltration" and its incoming, inevitable conquest of the power.

The MSI, freed of the most turbulent faction, elected as secretary the most effective leader of the moderate component, Arturo Michelini, former vice-secretary of Rome's Fascist Party in the 1930s. The new leadership pursued, with more emphasis and appeal, the strategy of accommodation and "insertion into the system" by attempting to establish fair relationships with the DC. Actually, until 1960, the party achieved unprecedented political successes. At first, *together* with monarchists and liberals, the MSI supported two DC minority governments in 1957 and in 1959. Then, it backed a DC minority government in 1960. This government could secure investiture *only thanks to the MSI votes*. The political impact of the latter agreement was enormous: for the first time in postwar democratic Italy, a government had received the vote of confidence thanks *exclusively* to neo-fascist support. The MSI was on the verge of finally being accepted as a legitimate governing partner by the Christian Democracy Party.

The sixth MSI Congress planned for July 1960 in Genoa was intended to celebrate the accomplishment of Michelini's strategy. However, the growing role of the MSI had created deep concern among the leftist parties. In Genoa, on the eve of the MSI Congress, a militant anti-fascist reaction broke out, and then spread to other Italian cities over the next fortnight. The wave of protest, culminating in violent clashes with the police and the death of some leftist demonstrators, led to the government banning the Congress from taking place. A few days later the government itself resigned. As a result of both events, the MSI was again sent to the wall. Its zenith had been reached, and the decline had begun.

Isolation, Recovery, and Back Again to Marginalization

The collapse of Michelini's strategy had two main effects. On the one hand, it enfeebled the party organization and revitalized the inner factionalism. On the other, it marginalized the party and fostered the development of new extreme right groups which contested the "wet" MSI policy and claimed a hard-line confrontation with the left, employing whatever means necessary. Beside Ordino Nuovo, a less intellectual group, which was more prone to street action, emerged in those years: Avanguadia Nazionale (National Vanguard). Ordine Nuovo and Avanguardia Nazionale have been, for a long time, the most active and militant movements. However, in the late 1960s they were flanked by a blooming of right-wing radical groups which, while sometime flashy and only locally based, sprang up all over the country. All this implies that the MSI was on the verge of losing its hegemony on the extreme right milieu.

The party crisis reached its peak in 1968, when it plummeted to 4.5 percent of the vote in the general elections, while its youth organization, which was the party's backbone, was deeply shaken by the student movement, since some young neo-fascists were fascinated by that wind of protest and abandoned the party. The exit from the crisis came with the change of leadership due to Michelini's death in 1969. A profound *organizational, strategic, and ideological* renewal was initiated by the new party secretary, the once "radical" Giorgio Almirante, who came back with a vengeance. The new leader gave new impetus to the party, innovating the organization, the strategy, and the discourse.

At the *organizational* level, the party was reformed through a higher centralization of the decision-making process, a stricter control over (but, at the same time, a higher support for) local party cadres, and a restructured youth organization. The membership increased dramatically and the party militant gained more room and attention in the political scene.

The party *strategy* aimed at diluting the neo-fascist connotation by setting up a novel party structure, called the "Destra Nazionale" (National Right), which could attract conservative political groups and independent opinion leaders thanks to a softening of the neo-fascist nostalgia. This strategy enabled the MSI to attract new forces: the Monarchist Party merged with the MSI, and some DC and PLI (Italian Liberal Party) politicians as well as some of the Army's high-ranking officers joined the party. However, such a strategy was inherently contradicted by a concomitant appeal for a tough confrontation in the streets with the "Reds," an appeal intended to mobilize the party *and* recapture the extreme right movements outside the party. In fact, Ordine Nuovo (with the exception of a fringe) and its leader, Pino Rauti, rejoined the MSI. The attempt at merging a respectable, "clean," and updated image with a militant and tough one, in order to both increase the party's coalition potential and defend the "silent majority" troubled by the social unrest of that period, proved an impossible task.

The third major change, closely related to the strategic one, was related to *ideological renewal*. Almirante repeatedly asserted his acceptance of the democratic system, but these declarations remained superficial and specious since no revision of the fascist identity was carried out. The ideological renewal was limited to a reframing of the image and symbols (less black shirts and Roman salutes), rather than a redefinition of the founding principles.

Up to the mid-1970s, Almirante succeeded in the recapture of dominance over the extreme right field, and in the conquest of the DC's more moderate conservative constituency. The MSI reached its peak in organizational terms with more than 400,000 members, articulated in 102 provincial federations and 4,335 local branches, and gained its highest-ever electoral score (8.7 percent of the votes in 1972). However, beyond its insufficient ideological renovation and its unrestrained radical militantism, the party's strategy was endangered by the DC's counter-initiatives to marginalize the MSI, denouncing its responsibility for the spread of violence in that period. In fact, the party did not neatly distance itself from the spread of violence activated by right extremist groups. The party leadership had meant to control and manage these fringes, but these movements intended to combat the "communist danger" not only by confronting the leftist organizations in street clashes (that the MSI leadership would have accepted and even favored), but with murderous terrorist actions. The bombing at the Banca dell'Agricoltura in December 1969 in Milan (which resulted in 16 casualties) was only the first episode in long stream of "black" terrorist attacks which plagued the country in the following decade.

Consequently, the MSI lost the support of a large share of the moderate electorate, and it fell back to 6.1 percent of the votes (-2.6 percent) in the 1976 parliamentary elections. This defeat opened the way to a critical review of Almirante's leadership and policies. A new party faction, led by the MSI speaker in the Chamber of Deputies, called for an effective enforcement of the "Destra Nazionale" strategy and the development of a better relationship with the DC. This faction failed to dismiss Almirante and thus left the party on the eve of the ninth National Congress (1977), founding the ephemeral National Democracy (Democrazia Nazionale) Party, which disappeared three years later after its fiasco of a performance in the 1979 parliamentary elections (0.6 percent of the votes).

The exit of the more moderate and accommodating faction altered the party's discourse and strategy (but without any leap backward). The key player in this phase was the former leader of Ordine Nuovo, Pino Rauti, who had re-entered the party in 1969. At the head of new internal party faction, he promoted a fresh cultural–ideological approach, reminiscent either of some "fascist-movement" suggestions or of new elaborations mainly offered by the French Nouvelle Droite, a cultural movement born in France, which aimed to modernize right-wing thought—even advocating overcoming the left–right cleavage. In a nutshell, the Nouvelle Droite rejects many core elements of the present ideologies. It rejects fascism and nationalism, but also liberalism for its supposed reduction of every relationship to commodity; the Westernization of the world, and the American political–cultural hegemony that entails the levelling of every difference and the annihilation of "natural communities"; the liberal democratic means of political participation; egalitarianism, which is the inevitable by-product of the conjugation of liberal individualism and mass society, whereas the differences should be appreciated and exalted; and utilitarianism as the key to any relationship. The faction led by Rauti accepted many of these ideas and, as a consequence, it introduced a major cleavage in the political–ideological party's culture: in fact, now the real enemy was capitalism rather than communism, as capitalist dominance in Western societies had dispossessed people of a real, authentic, communitarian life, enhancing standardization, consumerism, and alienation. This change of paradigm, while not accepted by the majority of the party, attracted an unprecedented number of students and young people. The youth summer camps organized at the turn of the 1970s by Rauti's faction, expressed the new mood of the younger generation: the open, casual, and relaxed atmosphere of those camps, not by chance called Hobbit camps—as a nod to fascination for a world of fantasy rather than of war—had nothing in common with the gloomy and militaristic atmosphere of previous similar initiatives. Above all, these young activists expressed a clear desire to stop the harsh and violent confrontation with the "Reds" and to get out of the neo-fascist "ghetto," the encapsulated and closed world where the anti-fascists had encased the neo-fascists and the latter had actually accepted living in. In sum, *this new party component expressed the need to take part in Italian society.*

In this period, the MSI was highly isolated, mainly because of its (more or less conscious) complicity with street violence and terrorist groups. The number of extremist groups, of terrorist actions, and of casualties reached unprecedented levels and outnumbered Red terrorism in terms of causalities in the 1970s and early 1980s. In particular, after the student unrest of 1977, a new wave of terrorist groups emerged (among them, Nuclei Armati Rivoluzionari, Terza Posizione, and Costruiamo l'Azione), loosely organized but very deadly. Only by the mid-1980s, after a further bombing in a train (Christmas 1984) near Bologna, the protection and complicities such groups availed themselves of in the past (either from the MSI or the state apparatus) were finally over. The desire to close down the "lead year" of violence was finally shared by both extreme rightist and leftist militants.

Also, the MSI had moved, at the end of the 1970s, to an unequivocal refusal of violence. That move was consequent to a new strategy inspired by Rauti's ideas. According to such strategy, the anti-Communist appeal was to be replaced by a call for an anti-system, anti-DC opposition, and the silent majority constituency by a young, underprivileged, and anti-establishment one. Following this new approach, the party self-defined itself as the collector of the "protest" against the all-party "partitocracy," which was considered "the" responsible for Italy's agony.

All these changes, however, did not lead to the abandonment of MSI's traditional ideological identity: the party *glued* the new image of a peaceful "protest party" to its traditional neo-fascist references such as political and economic corporatism, and authoritarian and nationalistic preferences. This resilience was, somewhat paradoxically, favored by a different reception of fascism, which started circulating in the early 1980s: in a nutshell, fascism was seen in a more historical perspective rather than in political–ideological terms, as had occurred in the past. In this way, fascism was losing its demonizing flavor. This did not entail any, even latent, recognition or acceptance of that regime: it just damped down the ostracism toward the (small) constituency of neo-fascists represented by the MSI.

The Two-Steps Entry into the Political System: From Failure and Inability to Sudden Success and Legitimacy

The deradicalization of the political conflict, with the demise of the violence and the "historicization" of fascism, made the MSI less stigmatized than in the past. A few examples demonstrate this change of political climate: in 1983 the socialist prime minister, Bettino Craxi, declared, during the parliamentary confidence debate, that he would treat all parliamentary groups in the same vein without any discrimination; MSI leaders were invited, for the first time, to public meetings together with other anti-fascist party leaders; and the MSI secretary, Almirante, was admitted to the PCI headquarters, in June 1984, at the funeral of the PCI secretary, Enrico Berlinguer.

These modifications of the external environment did not impact on the party ideology and strategy. Instead of abandoning its cultural and ideological identity, the party leadership maintained its ties with fascism. Therefore, in the mid-1980s, the MSI continued to oscillate between verbal radicalism and the desire to be overtly accommodated within the system. Even Almirante's resignation, due to poor health, at the 15th National Congress (1987) and the new leadership of the 35-year-old Almirante dauphin, Gianfranco Fini, did not solve the conundrum. In fact, the new secretary maintained the traditional line, stressing the fascist identity and proclaiming the party's extraneousness to the "partitocracy." As a consequence, the party remained politically isolated. The party's inevitable stalemate moved the old guard to withdraw its support to Fini, who was replaced, in the 16th Congress (January 1990), by Pino Rauti.

Rauti was to replace the MSI's traditional authoritarian, conservative, *petit bourgeois* political culture with a "leftward," anti-capitalist, and anti-Western one—without contesting, incidentally, its loyalty to fascism. Actually, the most novel element introduced by Rauti, even before his appointment as secretary, namely the emphasis on, *and the right to*, "distinctiveness," provided the ideological–cultural tool for the rejection of xenophobic or racist attitudes. Given the rise of the immigrant question in Italy in the late 1980s to early 1990s, that position—and Rauti's more general quite eccentric political vision—did not (and could not) please the traditional MSI electorate. At the 1990 regional election the party got the lowest score ever: 3.9 percent of the votes. Instead of leading a mass movement against the capitalist regime and the establishment, the party was becoming more and more isolated, and verging on irrelevance. When Rauti was confronted by a further devastating defeat at the local election in Sicily, where the party vote dropped from 9.2 percent to 4.8 percent, he was forced to resign. In July 1991, Fini, who had led the internal opposition, regained the secretaryship.

Notwithstanding the recovery of its traditional electorate after the bewildering setback suffered during Rauti's secretaryship (in the general election of 1992 the MSI scored 5.3 percent of the vote, a result similar to the previous ones), the MSI future became quite gloomy because of a new electoral law, which substituted proportional representation for plurality. Actually, in a plurality system, a small and geographically dispersed party runs the risk of being devoid of parliamentary representation if it does not ally with any other party. In order to find a way out of this cul de sac, the MSI promoted a new umbrella organization "Alleanza Nazionale" (National Alliance) in order to draw in some independents unlikely to join the party directly. When this project was launched in the summer of 1993, no one paid any attention, because it did not offer anything new compared to the traditional issues of the party (presidentialism, plebiscitarianism, moral conservatism, etc.) and it was seen as one of the many attempts already experienced in the past—like Almirante's 1970s "Destra Nazionale"—to gain wider support.

In conclusion, when the MSI had almost achieved full legitimacy, its incapacity to promote an ideological renewal, along the same path experienced by the PCI a few years earlier, could sanction once again, the party's marginality—or, even worse, its irrelevance.

The MSI's fate radically changed in December of 1993 with the local elections in some of the largest Italian cities (Rome, Naples, Genoa, Venice, and others), to be held with the new, two-ballot electoral system for the election of the mayor. When these elections were called, the activities of the magistrates against political corruption, the "Clean Hands" investigations initiated the year before, had reached their peak. All governmental parties were hurt by the investigations and all party leaders had resigned: the DC and, even more so, the PSI, were in total disarray. Consequently, the DC was not even able to present plausible candidates in the main cities where the electoral contest for the mayorship was to be held with the new, double ballot electoral system. On the contrary, the MSI put its best assets into the two most important cities: the party leader, Gianfranco Fini, stood in Rome, and Alessandra Mussolini, the Duce's granddaughter, in Naples. Unexpectedly, both MSI candidates surpassed the other moderate conservative candidates presented by the DC and former governing parties in the first ballot, and thus both contested the second ballot against the leftist candidates. At the end, Fini and Mussolini lost, but scored in the second ballot an impressive 46.9 percent and 44.4 percent of the votes, respectively. Moreover, for the first time since the 1950s, the party gained the mayorship in 19 medium-size cities (over 15,000 inhabitants) and in 4 provinces (all in the center-south of the country).

This unaccountable and resounding success greatly increased the MSI's "coalition potential." However, on the eve of the general elections of March 1994, none of the traditional parties had yet expressed any interest. The DC in particular, led by a leftist faction, was totally unavailable for any partnership with the MSI. What was needed, then, was a new political actor, immune from the "mold" which characterized all of the established parties, that is, *anti-fascism*.

The entry of Berlusconi's Forza Italia (Go Italy) provided that tool. First, the declaration in favor of Fini in his contest for the Rome mayorship, and second, the offer of a coalition with the MSI in the south in the 1994 legislative elections, both constituted a watershed compared to the traditional attitude of the political establishment regarding the MSI. This overture was immediately exploited by Fini, who paid formal homage to the principles of democracy and market economy, and implemented the Alleanza Nazionale (National Alliance) umbrella organization, contesting the incoming election under that name and restyling the party symbol. This image lifting proved very successful: in the 1994 general elections the party scored an unprecedented 13.5 percent of the votes (+8.1 percent) and elected 109 MPs (17.3 percent) in the lower Chamber. Such an impressive breakthrough could be explained by two sets of factors.

The first set concerns the *long-term* changes in Italian society, in particular the above-mentioned deradicalization of the political conflict and "historicization" of fascism. Therefore, the MSI was progressively perceived as an acceptable political actor, despite its proclaimed loyalty to fascism. The second set of factors comprises *short-term* elements, ranging from the collapse of the DC to the party's non-involvement in the investigations on political corruption, from the legitimacy offered by Berlusconi to the excellent performance of Fini in the media, where he appeared cool, quiet, reasonable, and apparently accountable.

The MSI Transformation into AN and the Exit from Neo-Fascism: 1995–2007

The combination of these long-term and short-term factors, *rather than a new party message*, enabled the MSI to remove its marginalization, electorally and politically. On one hand, the party collected votes from all of the old governing parties in the 1994 elections: 29.3 percent of its voters were former DC voters, 16.8 percent former PSI voters, and 13.2 percent came from the other three minor governing parties. On the other hand, the party—as partner of the winning right-wing coalition—the Polo per le Libertà (Freedom Pole)—entered the Berlusconi I government in May 1994. *For the first time in postwar Europe an extreme right party, while still imbued with fascist nostalgia, had become members of a cabinet.*

During the short-lived Berlusconi government (May–December 1994) the MSI tried to de-emphasize its ideological leaning in order to be fully legitimized. However, throughout all of 1994, party officials, and Fini himself, alternated between official declarations of acceptance of the "democratic method" and the refusal to overtly disown their fascist mold. Fini continued to offer a rather positive interpretation of fascism, declaring that it had been a fair regime up until 1938 (when the racial laws were enacted), because "in certain periods freedom is not an essential value" (*La Stampa*, June 4, 1994). Moreover, the party manifesto still paid homage to the fascist and anti-democratic political culture without enduring any criticism. In fact, when the MSI launched the AN project, it rejected approaching a different ideological space, stating that "Alleanza Nazionale does not imply a liberal-democratic *regression*" (*Il Secolo d'Italia*, July 29, 1993; our italics).

Given these premises, the Congress which celebrated the transformation of the MSI into the AN in January 1995 produced no more than a change of name. The long-awaited debate on the roots of the party was concentrated into a single, albeit highly relevant, sentence, whereby the Congress recognized that anti-fascism was "an historically necessary moment to regain the freedom that fascism had denied." This important declaration was, however, tempered by the solid loyalty to the fascist tradition emerging from the participants at the 1995 Congress: an overwhelming majority (62 percent) agreed with the item which stated that "notwithstanding some questionable choices, fascism was a good regime"; and another 7 percent considered fascism to be "the best regime ever conceived." *Almost none* (0.2 percent) criticized it as a "brutal dictatorship" and only 18 percent conceded that it was "an authoritarian regime." The remaining 13 percent avoided a condemnation of fascism stating that it was "the inevitable answer to the communist threat." This amazingly positive evaluation of fascism was reinforced by the data on the preference for a list of political thinkers (from fascists to liberals). Of all the listed names, those who scored the highest were the representatives of the fascist and right radical tradition, starting from Gentile (91 percent), followed by Mussolini (82 percent) and Evola (71 percent). Only the exit from AN of Pino Rauti and the foundation of the tiny and die-hard Movimento Sociale–Fiamma Tricolore (Social Movement–Tricolor Flame), due to the refusal of the supposed AN acquiescence to capitalist and liberal democratic references, gave some credibility to the new party.

Therefore, one can state that the cultural ideological references of the new party were still embedded in the fascist and anti-democratic tradition. *However, whilst true, this is only part of the picture*. A rather different profile from the traditional nostalgic and neo-fascist image exists in reality, and *it even emerged well before the process of transformation into the AN*. The data collected by two similar surveys carried out earlier, at the 15th (1987) and the 16th (1990) MSI Congresses on a set of items ranging from clericalism to nationalism, from racism to militarism, from traditionalism to authoritarianism, demonstrated that the MSI middle-level elites exhibited attitudes quite divergent from the authoritarian and nostalgic party's official politics and manifest ideology. In fact, on a series of issues related to civil rights (drug addiction, homosexuality, police questioning, death penalty, conscientious objection, gender relationships, and, to a certain extent, even immigrants' rights) the MSI cadres displayed a somewhat tolerant and flexible view. The level of acceptance of liberal positions on these issues was remarkable.

However, *notwithstanding these more open attitudes, the party's official ideology did not move from the standardized reminiscence of the fascist and anti-democratic tradition.* Paradoxically, where the party leadership had modified some elements of the anti-democratic ideology, as in the case of xenophobia and racism, it did not convince its party cadres. In fact, the 1995 Congress final document unequivocally condemned any form of racism and anti-Semitism, but the middle-level elite remained quite skeptical on those issues: fear of foreigners as a danger to national identity was supported by 59 percent of the participants, and 47 percent wanted to reduce the "Jewish power in international finance."

In conclusion, *well before the transformation into AN,* the party cadres demonstrated a surprising openness to salient civil rights questions, typical of the post-modern society. However, these stances were contradicted by both a leaning toward racism and anti-Semitism (which the leadership had tried to modify), and a solid loyalty to the original identity provided by fascism (which had not been questioned until the—rather timid—revision in 1995 with the passing to AN). These contradictions were still present after the party's breakthrough in 1994.

The party leadership activated a more substantial change when it realized that, even at the heights of its success, it could not make a real breakthrough. At the general elections of 1996, in fact, AN had reached the highest score ever: 15.7 percent of the votes (+2.2 percent). That resounding success, however, contained the seed of a crisis because the party had not succeed in conquering the leadership within the right-wing coalition, which remained in the hands of Berlusconi's Forza Italia: AN was handicapped by the still widespread perception of its extreme location in the political spectrum (point 8.2 on 0–10 left–right scale) and its feeble accountability as a truly non-nostalgic party.

Precisely to redefine or reframe its image and identity, the party promoted an "ideological conference," held in Verona in early 1998. More so than the innovative manifesto issued at that party conference, the series of declarations by Fini himself on very sensitive issues created a turning point. The most dramatic statement referred to his distancing from the 1943–45 RSI epic: Fini declared that he would have not flanked the last Mussolini regime because it was "on the wrong side" in the fight for democracy. This quite explicit statement hit one of the more solid party taboos, and it was not by chance the AN cadres appeared very skeptical, as only one out of four agreed with this. In addition, Fini maintained a very clear stand against any racist, xenophobic, or anti-Semitic positions, leaving the monopoly of these issues to Rauti's MS–FT and even Bossi's Northern League.

Actually, the new party manifesto and Fini's statements did not find adequate support from the party's middle-level elite. The survey carried out at the same 1998 conference highlights the persistence of a widespread compliance vis-à-vis the fascist regime. *The large majority (61 percent) still agreed with the idea that fascism was, overall, a good regime.* Even the newcomers (those who joined the party after 1994) shared this view by 55.1 percent. The same ideological viscosity emerged in the most reputed thinkers: once more, Gentile, Mussolini, and Evola came first—while the gap with the liberal thinkers, especially Croce and Tocqueville, shrank. The contradiction was still there: *while, on authoritarian issues, the party cadres show an evolution toward conservative-democratic positions, they still remain quite prone to nostalgia and, to a certain extent, to xenophobia.*

Even if Fini's innovative statements on AN ideological references did not receive attention in the party's ranks, he kept moving out of neo-fascism. In contrast to the superficial modifications adopted through the marketing-style operation of the MSI passage to the AN, the party leader, backed by the faction of the renovators gathered around the journal *Charta Minuta*, introduced groundbreaking political–ideological changes, partly accepted, party refused, by the rank and file. The party manifestos at the beginning of the 2000s exhibit a significant, while still patchy and faltering, step out of the reach of both neo-fascism and right-wing extremism. AN perceives itself—and is perceived by the other Italian parties—as a mainstream right-wing party, fully legitimate as a governmental partner and even more moderate than the Lega Nord. A key example supports this assumption: in the fall of 2003 Fini proposed extending the right to vote to legal immigrants in local elections, a blasphemy for whichever right extremist party all over Europe. But what is more relevant is the agreement in the party rank and file as well as in the party members *interviewed in 2001*, well before Fini's statement. The gulf between the party leadership and the followers appeared largely closed.

A further and final passage which stated the exit from neo-fascism was expressed, during Fini's visit to Israel, at the Yad Vashem in 2003. On that occasion Fini pronounced a radical condemnation of fascism, defining it as "*un male assoluto*" (an absolute evil). This statement provoked a furor by some die-hard members; they left the party and founded more radical, but much smaller and almost irrelevant parties (Alessandra Mussolini's Alternativa Sociale (Social Alternative) and Francesco Storace's La Destra (The Right)). But many surveys assessed that the statement was accepted by the largest part of the electorate and the rank and file. Neo-fascist nostalgia was no longer part of AN identity.

This new profile was acknowledged by the "others," either at home and abroad. In particular, Fini's role as Italian member in the EU convention for the Treaty of Lisbon and later as Minister of Foreign Affairs in the period 2004–06 provided him with recognition in the international milieu as a responsible, moderate conservative figure. One example is the introduction he wrote for the Italian translation of the book by the UMP leader and France's President Nicolas Sarkozy.

In conclusion, the long march out of neo-fascism, effectively initiated by Fini leadership in the late 1990s, was accomplished in the mid-2000s. The final act was represented by the fusion of AN with Forza Italia and the common foundation of a new party, the Popolo della Libertà (People's Freedom) in 2009. Neo-fascism nowadays survives in tiny chapels and extremist parties as Forza Nuova (New Force) or the less militant La Destra, or in youth movements such as Casa Pound (Pound House). But the story of the neo-fascist *party* as such has expired ideologically and organizationally.

CHAPTER 18

···

POPULISM AND THE
LEGA NORD

···

GIANLUCA PASSARELLI

A populist party that has been at the core of the Italian political system for at least the last 15 years, the Lega Nord (Northern League, LN) was formed in the wake of the political and economic crisis that overwhelmed Italy in the late 1980s and at the beginning of the 1990s. The Lega Nord was formed in 1989, while its main branch—the Lega Lombarda—was established in 1984. In fact, the explosion of political crisis subsequent to the party's birth is unsurprising, as the LN was one of the causes of the downfall of the political system. The LN's big electoral success of the 1990s (especially in 1992), and the incipient Christian Democracy's (DC) political and electoral weakening were among the most relevant factors of the Italian political system's crash. The crumbling of the political system that had dominated Italy since 1948 afforded the LN many advantages and opportunities. Moreover, the LN was the political actor that benefited most from this systemic collapse, as this party, formed by Umberto Bossi, served to politically highlight the weaknesses and contradictions of that system. The ways in which the LN achieved its political and electoral success were typical of populist movements. The *leghisti* appealed to the people with (northern) civic virtues against the corruption of "*loro*" (them), and the ineffectiveness of the political and financial leadership, which had led the country to collapse. In particular, the Lega's anti-southern rhetoric was stressed, since southern people were described by the party as lazy, idle, and favoring ineffective local governments. Moreover, the LN stressed its anti-immigrant position, and, above all, its condemnation of *Roma ladrona* (thieving Rome). By stressing its anti-government rhetoric, anti-national issue positions, and its will to separate from Italy, elements of a populist framework were clear, with political and institutional distrust, anti-system attitudes, racism, and attacks on the political elite. In this chapter we present and describe LN's populist features within the general framework of Italian populist history and characteristics.

POPULISM AND ITS DEFINITIONS

In the literature on populism there are no shared definitions, although there is a more or less broad consensus on some aspects. The "structural" features of populism include: a strong leadership, a challenging of the law, an appeal to the people, an "us *v.* them" dichotomy, a common-sense apologia, and an emphasis on the community.[1] Moreover, it is also possible to talk of the "ideology" of populism, which is clearly different from these parties' organizational features. Indeed, there can be right-wing populism as well as left-wing libertarian and anti-establishment parties.[2] Populism is "an ubiquitous phenomenon in modern politics," and it shows a chameleonic nature.[3] Attacks against war, banks, and political and financial elites are often a common battlefield for both left and right populisms.

However, right-wing populist movements have, for the most part, stressed issues related to "safety," such as opposition against immigration since the 1990s, and the dangers of a multicultural society, especially defined in terms of the socioreligious clash arising from the Islamic movements in Europe after the events in New York on 9/11. Instead, leftist populist movements and parties are essentially against representative democracy. Those "new" populists have called for a much more deliberative and participatory democracy, stressing the need to overcome the differences between the delegates and *normal* people, who are only allowed to vote for the Parliament but are then excluded from the decisional arena.[4] Despite having a distinctive "essence," widespread populism seems to show a "weak ideology,"[5] emphasizing the clear contrast between "them" and "us." Indeed, the struggle between the politicians, who represent all the vices in the people's eyes, and the *normal* people, who defend all the virtues, is at the core of populist propaganda. Populism's most important trait is related to its appealing to the people and its empathy with the *true* needs of the people, strongly emphasized by populist leadership. The latter often consider populism as democratic and legitimate precisely because of this popular support. Thus, it has been underlined that, in some ways, there is an intimate connection between democracy and populism.[6] After all, a "government of the people, by the people, for the people," the well-known sentence pronounced by President Abraham Lincoln in his 1863 Gettysburg Address, could easily be accepted by democrats and populists alike. Indeed, both "have been competing for the people for centuries."[7]

POPULISM AND POPULISTS IN ITALY
DURING THE FIRST AND SECOND REPUBLICS

The history of Italian democratic politics is strongly related to the presence of movements and parties that can be defined as populist. It is possible to affirm that, to some extent, Italy (along with France) has been the cradle of populism in Europe. During the election of the Constituent Assembly in 1946, and again during the first democratic election in 1948, the presence of the so-called Uomo Qualunque (Common Man) electoral list achieved interesting results. The list was created by Guglielmo Giannini, a journalist who founded a weekly newspaper that inspired the political activities of the namesake political movement. The list won 5.3 percent of votes in the 1946 elections and 3.8 percent of the votes in the 1948 elections. The Uomo Qualunque was formed *before* the end of World War II, and, since 1944, Giannini had been strongly attacking the outgoing fascist elite and the new politicians of the democratic parties unified in the so-called CLN (Committee of National Liberation). The birth of Uomo Qualunque was triggered by the humiliation Italy was subjected to during and after World War II. In particular, *Qualunquismo* used mainly humor to address the people's dissatisfaction with Italy's dramatic socioeconomic conditions. Further, it tried to gain the trust of those people scared of being purged due to their adhesion to Fascism. The main issues Uomo Qualunque was able capitalize on were related to the supposed exploitation of normal people oppressed by politicians, banks, bureaucrats, and so on. The international context helped Giannini to emphasize the oppression of Italy caught between the USA and the USSR. Nevertheless, Giannini's political incertitude and Italy's new economic growth reduced any room for the Uomo Qualunque, whose relevant history ended before 1950 (see Chapter 20, this volume).

The second wave of populist, or better yet, anti-establishment movements in Italy came in the late 1960s.[8] The Italian 1968 started thanks to the impetus provided by the civil rights protests in the USA and the so-called May 1968 in France. In the latter case, there were important protests, including the first wildcat general strikes ever, which commenced with a series of student occupation protests (especially at the University of Paris), and continued with millions of workers striking for two weeks. Its impact was such that it almost caused the collapse of President Charles de Gaulle's government. In staging wildcat strikes, the movement clashed with the trade unions and the French Communist Party, so that the students were largely against the "official" politics and parties.

Similarly, the rise of the so-called extra-parliamentary movements in Italy was, for the most part, based on student and worker activism, which peaked in 1968–69 (the *hot autumn*, with numerous strikes). Those movements called for a new model of economic development, and for peace and disarmament, and spoke out against the Vietnam War. The social issues promoted were based on a new regulation of hierarchical relationships between generations, and on a new, important role for young people. It must be stressed that such movements were different from new right populist parties because they represented the demands for peace, ecology, nuclear disarmament, and women's rights. Nevertheless, these two sides of Italian populism shared a negative experience with established parties, and their strong criticism of government.[9]

From the political point of view, the trigger was the fight within the Italian Communist Party (PCI) in 1969 between a faction of dissidents (especially concerning the relationship with the USSR) and the party's leadership. The *Manifesto* was founded as a monthly review (and then as a newspaper) in 1969 by a collective of left-wing journalists engaged in the wave of critical thought and activity on the PCI. In the following general election, a *Manifesto* list of candidates ran for office, earning about 1 percent of the votes,[10] and a myriad of extra-parliamentary groups put forth anti-establishment claims. Moreover, different groups (not always linked to the social movements born as a generational protest), both from the extreme left and the extreme right, then turned to violence during the so-called *years of lead*, a period of political and social turmoil. From a social point of view, those movements appealed to a defined class, to use Mény and Surel's typology.

After the long period of *Black and Red* terrorism, a new political actor in the late 1980s burst onto the Italian political scene, directly addressing its political and electoral message against the old parties to the "people." That party was *the* Lega Nord. Of course, there is no direct linkage between the movements of the 1960s and 1970s and the "new" populism of the Second Republic, after 1992. For example, the Radical Party, founded by Marco Pannella, is a libertarian party formed in the 1970s that we cannot consider as a populist party due to the fact that it recognizes the legitimacy of the centrality of law,[11] despite the fact that radicals also fight to change many policies and laws. Instead, populist parties and movements do not recognize the role of law, which they publicly contest and which they try to delegitimize.

The electoral dealignment process, the weakening of ideological influence, the increase in the personalization of politics, and, to some extent, the "weakening" of political parties, made room on the political and electoral stage for "new" populist parties. Indeed, the most significant Italian populist parties were formed in the so-called Second Republic. In 1994, the Italian tycoon Silvio Berlusconi formed Forza Italia (FI—Go, Italy!) and, soon after, he won the general elections and became prime minister. Up to 2009, Forza Italia regularly called out to the people both to legitimize its electoral strength and to strengthen its leadership's political and governmental choices. Berlusconi, on many occasions, explicitly referred to the people as the *only* political actor allowed to judge his actions, and stated that, in order to solve Italy's problems, he would "take care of everything." Similarly, in the electoral arena Forza Italia's leader has always stressed his link with the people, using an appeal to them to earn more votes. In fact, his slogans, such as "president worker" to identify himself with the aims and expectations of the working class, are legendary. Moreover, during campaign events, Berlusconi clearly expressed populist claims.

In addition, the 2013 general elections saw the latest, though arguably certainly not the last,[12] wave of a populist party. The Movimento 5 Stelle (Five Star Movement, M5S), after a few years of political activity and participation in local and regional elections, earned more than one quarter of the votes (25.6 percent).[13] The issues proposed and stressed by the M5S are, to some extent, related to the intergenerational value changes that emerged in the 1970s, and which revealed a switch to a new set of "post-materialist" values that emphasized autonomy and self-expression.[14] Other aspects clearly reflect the populist claims of the normal people subjugated by the elite, the banks, and the politicians/government. M5S's great political and electoral success resulted from the increasing corruption of many politicians, the inequality between ordinary people and the ruling class, and the economic crisis. International events, in particular the role of the European Central Bank, gave the M5S the opportunity to try to overcome traditional cleavages (*left and right do not exist anymore*) and to address issues that appealed to a vast segment of voters. The leader appealed to the people, repudiated party power and union representation, and focused on the concept of community. Moreover, following the line of opposition between "old" and "new" politics, the M5S strongly emphasized the dichotomy of young versus old also in terms of the generation gap including lesser social protections for younger people than "privileged" older people. The M5S received the most votes of any national party in the 2013 elections both in electoral terms (the nationalization of its geographical implantation),[15] and in socioprofessional representation.[16]

L'Uomo Qualunque, the LN, Forza Italia, Italia dei Valori (a party founded by Antonio Di Pietro, a public prosecutor who opposed corruption),[17] M5S, and other small political forces contributed to the Italian electoral and political development by proposing a populist political platform. Populist parties are persistent in Italian politics, even if populism has mostly been like an underground river. There have been, in fact, both periods when populist parties have flourished and phases during which both the electoral and political effects of populist movements have been irrelevant. After having defined what populism is and what it is not, and after introducing the main movements and populist parties of the Italian political system since 1946, it is now time to present the case of the Lega Nord. The LN represents a very peculiar case of a populist party in both the Italian and comparative perspective, due to its "relevancy" and organizational features.

The Northern League: Populism, Regionalism, and Extreme Right

The early 1990s were marked by the Mani Pulite (Clean Hands) and *Tangentopoli* (Bribe City) corruption investigations in Milan, and the Communist Party's (PCI) change of name, organization, and ideology after 1989's international events. The referendum of 1991 that reduced the number of preference votes voters were allowed to cast in parliamentary elections also significantly changed the political landscape, paving the way for the LN. Even though Bossi announced, like the Socialist Party's (PSI) leader Bettino Craxi, that he would be at the seaside rather than vote, with the LN playing no part in the campaign, the result opened a window of opportunity for the party. The limitation in the number of preference votes voters could cast had strongly affected intraparty dynamics, shaping the balance of power between different leaders and influencing the process of candidates' selection. Thus, the two main parties, the DC and the PSI, were strongly negatively influenced by the electoral reform, which weakened their "sick" bodies, so paving the way for new populist parties, such as the LN.

Former DC voters were now free to vote for other parties since the historical enemy that had justified the long tradition of the so-called "*voto di appartenenza*" had disappeared.[18] In this context, a new political movement took shape that was the product of an attempt to unify ethno-regionalist and autonomist movements based on solid and historically rooted tradition.[19] However, this path was not very effective, as Bossi himself recognized the negligible electoral results of using ethno-politics as a cleavage issue in the Lega Lombarda's experience.[20] Bossi, whose charisma had given him a strong relationship with the party's members and voters, was the uncontested leader—his position was uncontested as he regularly and brutally excluded any attempt at challenge or dissent. The new party was strongly critical of the DC, and of the *pentapartito* (five-party government) coalition to which the DC belonged, in its failure to address the issues that were near and dear to the north's heart, and its failure to secure modern solutions for the most developed Italian regions, giving force to the LN's anti-system attitudes.[21] In particular, the party rudely expressed its anti-immigrant positions, and its anti-southern policies and political program. The party brought to the political agenda the "Northern Question,"[22] the so-called northern malaise,[23] by reversing the long-standing focus on the problem of the southern regions. During the 1992 general elections, the LN was, for the first time, seen by a broader public at a national level, and it won 8.7 percent of the votes.

The Lega was the topic of widespread discussion from 1987 onwards when it elected two MPs (Bossi as senator and a deputy). Moreover, in local elections the party reached remarkable electoral results, especially in the election of the mayor in small and medium-sized cities of the Lombardy. Similarly, at the European election of 1989, the list created by the Lega and its allies obtained about 6 percent in the northeast district and more than 10 percent in some provinces, such as Bergamo. Its breakthrough came in the regional elections in 1990, when it obtained 18.9 percent in Lombardy, becoming the second party after the DC. This was partly in response to institutions that favored the minor political parties, namely, the electoral systems characterized by low disproportionality. It must be remembered, too, that the LN rapidly adopted organizational models and policies since its "three faces" were highly centralized and controlled by a charismatic leadership. Though the LN has, so far, never formed an electoral alliance with the center-left, it has demonstrated a multifaceted attitude both when it was in power—as an anti-system party—and when in the opposition—through an "anti-state populism."[24] At this outset, the LN was considered a "flash party," an opportunity for voters who were against the existing parties and a "split vote" that occasionally expressed itself inside the solid framework of the Italian political system.

With the changing of political alliances, the LN's electoral performance—after its entrance into government in 1994 (8.4 percent)—was uneven. The Lega's highest national performance was in 1996 at 10.1 percent, when it invented the Padania (a project to create a macro region including all the Italian northern regions) and ran on its own, taking over 30 percent of the votes in some provinces of the Veneto and upper Lombardy. It again showed a strong resurgence immediately after the 2008 general elections. From a handful of small towns and militant groups, the LN won over 8.3 percent of the votes in the 2008 general elections, 10.1 percent in the 2009 European elections, and 13.3 percent in the 2010 regional elections.[25] This electoral strengthening of LN party vote was not totally unexpected,[26] and some important socioeconomic elements combined to weaken the political and governmental system that has rightly been described as a "giant with feet of clay."[27]

Each electoral phase in LN's history is well connected with its U-turns in terms of policies strictly related to change of strategy. Between the 1980s and 1992 the LN built up its organization and electoral roots by especially strengthening its identity opposing southern people, old parties, and immigrants. After participation in the national government in 1994, Bossi decided to give up the coalition with Berlusconi and started to emphasize the idea of separation from Italy, the so-called Padania, especially in 1996 when the LN ran alone and after 1998 when Italy accepted to join the European single currency. Between 1996 and 2000 the LN was politically and electorally isolated, and this phase coincided with its deepest anti-national rhetoric, embracing criticism of the European Union's policies and globalization. For the 2000 regional elections, Bossi, as charismatic leader and party founder, imposed, even on the party's recalcitrant faction, a new alliance with Berlusconi and the center-right. Thenceforth, the party embraced the defense of Western values and, after the 9/11 events, the LN started a very aggressive attack on Muslims, foreign trade, and immigrants. All those policies were kept together by Bossi's ability and rhetoric. Still during its third participation in government (2008–11), the LN stressed the need for security. The latter was also related to *welfare chauvinism*, the defense of the Italian welfare state against newcomers such as immigrants, as the party played on public fears during the years of the incipient economic crisis.

The exit from the government in 2011 and the dramatic change in the leadership after the Bossi family's involvement in public funds scandals, produced an electoral disaster for the LN (the party fell to about 4 percent). After the 2013 elections, the party newly radicalized its policies, especially those targeting immigrants, the theme of unemployment, and the fear of economic crisis. The conflict with Cécile Kyenge—the Minister of Integration—who originates from Congo, was a dramatic yet easy move to try to regain the political stage. More than twenty years on, the LN is now the oldest of the newly formed Italian political parties. It has been a member of three Italian governments, and it governs three regions (Lombardy, Piedmont, and Veneto), as well as a significant number of provinces and cities in many parts of northern Italy.

Even though the LN is a "new" party, it has differentiated itself from the "new" left and "new" right post-materialist parties.[28] The LN's voters, by rapidly manifesting a radical anti-establishment position,[29] as well as discriminatory attitudes toward southern Italians, were not placed at the right end of the left–right continuum; they self-located at the middle of the political spectrum, consistent with the LN's view of itself as being a "super partes" party with regard to the "old" parties, with "neither a left nor right" position typical of many populist parties. The LN's racist attitude and extreme political trend were evident from the party's propaganda and posters. Images represent immigrants, dangers from a multicultural society, and a Rome dedicated to stealing resources from northern regions.

With these foci, can the LN (still) be seen as a populist party? Its expansion has been made possible not only because of its localist claims, but for three other deeply rooted and interrelated reasons: (1) the diminishing importance of subcultures and traditional affiliations; (2) the decrease in the significance of the left–right dimension; and (3) the contempt for traditional parties and elites.[30] These three factors are the most relevant variables in explaining the rise of the "new" parties in Italy between the 1980s and 1990s. The unfreezing of the political system structured around the cleavages emerging at the beginning of the twentieth century, the fall of the Berlin Wall, and so on, provided the LN with a very advantageous window of opportunity.[31] All these factors are important when assessing the LN: in particular, they offered a new political–electoral entrepreneur the chance to emphasize, in *latu sensu*, some of the anti-establishment policies, which were then positively received by voters.

According to the Mény and Surel's categories,[32] we can see that the LN appealed to the people on all three platforms, which are not mutually exclusive. The LN's populist traits are clearly identifiable in the first stage as "sovereign people": the attacks against "*Roma ladrona*" and the elites. Further, we can see the populist trait related to the *economic* meaning of populism in the party's appeal to those categories penalized by economic and financial globalization (small entrepreneurs, the middle class, and so on). Finally, the LN has constantly addressed a community (Lombardy, the northern regions, Padania) to stress the feeling of belonging, and consequently has excluded non-members of that community.

The LN's history is linked in an inextricable way to populism. We can say that populism represents a sort of ontological trait of the Northern League since its birth; its populist features have never been doubted, nor has it overcome or abandoned them. However, it is possible to detect different phases in the LN's life and to stress different levels of populism in each.

Territory was the LN's founding and fundamental issue and its political framework. The party, especially at the beginning, used the protection of the northern territories to develop its electoral campaigns and regionalism project.[33] Nevertheless, sample surveys conducted in the 1980s showed that the level of regional identification in Lombardy was not significantly higher than in other regions.[34] To a greater degree than the League of Lombardy, the largest branch of the future LN party, the Łiga Veneta had specific ethnic demographics, such as population, dialect, and customs, which were typical of other ethno-regionalist parties.[35] Nevertheless, ethno-regionalism proved to be no more than an "awkward attempt" to explain the LN's formation,[36] and a set of largely fictitious specificities.[37] Thus, the "center-periphery" cleavage theory only offers one possible interpretative key for the development of the LN.

In any case, territory was a constant issue in the LN's political message. The antagonist frame between the *hard-working* north and the *lazy* south was systematically at the core of the party's slogans. The *leghisti* hurled abuse at southern people and especially against Rome (*Roma ladrona*). The attack on the capital did not have only a geographical meaning; indeed, it was used by the party as a symbol to oppose a broader range of messages typical of its populist trait: anti-establishment, anti-immigrant, anti-politician, and so on. Those attitudes were confirmed and amplified by the party's manifestos, which periodically updated the LN programs and political views. In these documents it is possible to detect the search for a regional identity, the fight to introduce federalism, the welfare chauvinism and the related opposition to extra-European immigration, the defense of the "traditional" family, the centrality of Christian values (especially after 9/11 events), and the growing intolerance to European Union rules.

In this latter context it is very interesting to observe the party's U-turn, which coincided with Italy's entrance into the euro in 1998.With the emergence of new political actors on both the right and left wings, the relevance of territorial subcultures waned. Nevertheless, the presence of the localistic parties in the mid-1980s and the LN's electoral breakthrough in 1992 dramatically indicated that, if anything, the political subcultures were changing but had not vanished. In fact, the LN not only symbolically evoked the role of territory in its political mission; its electoral background had also been geographically well defined since the beginning. Moreover, the party also tried to reinvent a local and cultural "tradition" of the northern regions and of Padania.[38] Nevertheless, from the territorial point of view, the party's implantation had been clear since the beginning. As Diamanti suggested in his first studies,[39] the presence of the LN has become stronger in the territories where the previous DC implantation was more evident, such as in Veneto and Lombardy.[40] From a different perspective, other scholars found that the League was first successful in Veneto in peripheral areas,[41] only to later – although rapidly enough –colonize the heartlands of the DC.[42]

At the beginning, the LN used the territory, and especially the Lombardy, one of the richest Italian regions, to defend the northern people's interest. In particular, the LN focused on the supposed northern regions' exploitation by the south's ineffectiveness, and Rome's inability to govern. Soon after their first role in government (1994), and after having discarded the "regionalist" option, the LN focused more on the defense of a new territorial entity, the so-called Padania,[43] in an attempt to invent an identity and to exit from the isolation in which the party had been relegated. Once again, territory was used against both Roma Polo and Roma Ulivo—the names of the two main coalitions against which the party was opposed—to stress their similarities. Thus, the LN's populist trait was based on the rejection of all traditional political options and offers. The project of building a new nation/state—Padania—was then abandoned at the beginning of 2000, when the party rejoined the center-right coalition and became a member of the 2001–06 government led by Berlusconi. The LN shifted its position by opting for a less divisive and less "revolutionary" institutional proposal: so-called devolution. The LN has always argued for separation from Rome. First the *leghisti* called it federalism, then Padania, then devolution, now "*Prima il nord*" and the creation of a macro-region (the union of the three northern big regions: Lombardy, Piedmont, and Veneto). It is this demand, stated through populism propaganda, which is the core of LN's identity. Populism is its style. When the *leghisti* are in government they become more moderate, when they are out they are more radical, though they are often both at the same time. Finally, during the last 2013 general elections, as mentioned, the party supported the project of creating a macro-region territorial aggregate which should unify Piedmont, Veneto, and Lombardy. The new slogan, *Prima il Nord!* (The North first!), coined by Roberto Maroni, the new secretary, then substituted by Matteo Salvini, a younger and more radical one, clearly represents the attempt to overcome the period of Bossi's leadership, which mostly (but not exclusively) focused on a northern region identity (the so-called Padania became a sort of obsession[44]) and on the related project of independence. Maroni's program, instead, is mostly founded on a view that stresses the crucial role of northern regions in the Italian economic system, and (over)represents the stakeholders and the citizens of those areas. Nevertheless, Maroni himself spectacularly emphasized populist themes, such as the anti-elite message, both against the political class in general and against the LN leadership's ongoing involvement in judicial affairs. Indeed, Maroni, elected in 2012, has publicly called for the use of brooms to make a clean sweep inside and outside the party.

Along with this partially innovative campaign, Maroni's strategy, in some ways, replicates the old cliché of the LN's racism and defense of subnational identity,[45] and it also served to test the political waters and therefore to reframe the electoral message. Territorial cleavage has been a subject used essentially in order to emphasize the populist approach of the party rather than pursue a political goal; and geographical differentiation, to a great extent, has masked an agenda of discrimination and opposition to *them*, meaning politicians and the people's enemies. This interpretive key was determined by voter attitudes toward a set of crucial issues, and debates on the party's organization, especially anti-party and anti-politics attitudes, shifted as voters followed the party's changes.[46] In the last twenty years, the LN partially changed its public policies with reference to the issues most often emphasized by extreme right parties, notably immigration,[47] the European Union, religion, and civil rights. LN's voters and sympathizers have moved from a "moderate" position on the left–right continuum toward a more rightist positioning,[48] especially in more recent years. In particular, a diachronic comparison of the party's electorate attitudes on certain crucial issues, as well as a change in how the LN places itself on the left–right spectrum, confirm the radicalization of the party.[49] Thus, the party has clearly emphasized populist attitudes toward a set of themes typical of populist movements of the extreme right in Europe.[50]

The party's leadership, clearly a charismatic one, has often been the most evident organizational face in presenting the LN's political project, in particular, Bossi's speaking out on populist themes, for the most part through the use of rough language and crude manners. The party general secretary's speeches have become famous precisely because of his provocative oratory. By using truly politically incorrect language, the leader has introduced issues into political discourse which have often been long unaddressed by historical parties. Bossi strongly attacked the *partitocrazia* (the long-established parties, especially those in power since Italy became a democracy), and also criticized the political equivalence of parties in the government and the PCI, the most relevant force of the opposition. The LN cried out against the oligarchy, the ineffective management of public debt, and the muddled bureaucratic process, which negatively affects the small northern industries. Bossi focused on the corruption of incumbent governmental parties, and, at the same time, underlined the stability of politicians, neither of which changed after many years both in government and in the Parliament. In this sense the LN was able to intercept and promote the long-lasting "dissatisfied society."[51] The leadership has not only given a clear anti-elite message by drawing attention to the *us* v. *them* dichotomy; it has also centralized power in Bossi's hands—delegating to one single man all the power and all virtues is typical of populist movements.

The LN's leader played the role of victim so as to bring to light old parties' intolerance against the innovative force of this newcomer, thereby strengthening the LN's cohesion and stressing the fight between "friends and enemies." Moreover, Bossi has also very skillfully weakened, or better yet, destroyed every form of opposition to his leadership: he adopted a form of action typical of populist leaders, that is, the dismissal of any dissident. The centralization of power leadership highlights the uselessness of representative democratic processes in which an assembly takes decisions. In contrast, the LN's leader pointed out the need to avoid exhausting bargaining processes typical of the ineffective and vacillatory political elite responsible for Italy's (and, indeed, the northern regions') socioeconomic troubles. That personal leadership thus had the explicit aim of also challenging the democratic rule of state.

The LN has been a populist party since its formation (except, perhaps, for the short period at the very beginning when the leadership stressed more the party's "ethno-regionalist" features).[52] Populism is the quintessence of the LN, its ontological trait and its uncompromising feature. A non-populist LN would be a completely different political entity and, distanced from populist elements, would represent the end of the party as we know it. Since its inception, the party has maintained its populist characteristics even though, in some phases, it has changed the intensity of populist claims in a chameleonic way. These changes, however, have been essentially tactical shifts and not radical variations from its historical core, which the party has never abandoned. The issues that the LN has sponsored, and the ways in which the leadership has dealt with them, have the typical traits of populist attitudes. The ideology on which the party bases its actions is clearly oriented toward a compelling challenge of the incumbent elite and the defense of ordinary people against the oligarchy and politicians. Finally, the leadership has deliberately shown highly centralized power in order to normalize dissent and to strengthen the adversarial model of politics against all kinds of communitarian enemies against which the charismatic leader is called to defend *his* people.

CONCLUSION

The Italian Lega Nord has clearly shown a marked populist trait during almost all of its thirty years of life. Even though the party's leadership has stressed the territorial claim in particular, the main element defining the LN's activity and style is its strongly rooted populism. This party was born at the crossroads of the resurgence of localism and neo-regionalist parties and the rise of new parties of the so-called "counter-silent revolution" on the right of the new political continuum.[53] However, if the call to a territorial identity, which has had strong and unquestionably crucial relevance, has undergone many tactical shifts, the general traits of the party's populism have never disappeared. Moreover, the changes to its "territorial" issue have allowed the party to avoid falling into the trap of becoming a single-issue movement based on the Northern region; [54] in fact the latter is another element, which also characterizes regionalism—a fanaticism for its heartland.[55] General elements of LN's populism have been detectable since the party's origins. After all, building and defending an idealized community is one of the typical traits of populist movements, which try to defend their members from all kinds of external dangers that could contaminate the community's integrity and homogeneity.

The extraordinary political and institutional crisis that befell Italy in the late 1980s and early 1990s offered the party an exceptional opportunity. A lethal—for the political system—blend of both international events and national changes provided a new political entrepreneur with the unique opportunity to enter the Italian political arena. The Lega Nord, thanks to the ability and lack of scruples of its leadership, significantly impacted the solemn and formal ways of the political oligarchy. Adopting a campaign that emphasized populist themes, such as immigration, anti-state feeling, and anti-political traits, the party was able to quickly gain a foothold on the political stage. It skillfully mixed an emphasis on the defense of territorial identity with a permanent spotlight on populist issues. Focusing on a well-defined territorial area, which represents its main electoral strength, the LN has been capable of broadening its political appeal thanks to its populist themes.

Since the 2013 general elections, the party founded by Bossi has been facing many challenges brought forth by the dramatic and profound changes that took place after 2008. Thenceforth, the LN's electoral trend has been extraordinarily positive, and the party has expanded its influence, even in "southern" regions, where it was historically less established. However, after the regional elections of 2010 (the LN won 13 percent of votes), the party was faced with a big problem related to its leadership: the party organization, and, in particular, the national leadership, underwent serious changes, a process that is still taking place. Between 2010 and 2012, the struggle between the party's various factions culminated with the substitution of the leader and founder, Bossi. In the 2013 elections the party's vote collapsed and it now cannot even win local elections in areas of historical electoral settlement. This dramatic change has happened in particular due to the legal proceedings that involved the Bossi family, specifically Bossi's son, and the party's treasurer. They were under investigation in relation to the personal use of public party's funds. The political and the legal proceedings that involved the so-called "magic circle" (*il cerchio magico*), that is, the political and personal inner circle of Bossi's leadership, have dealt a fatal blow to the party's organization.[56] In particular, those circumstances allowed the above-mentioned transition in the party in central office from Bossi and his main allies to Maroni.

Moreover, the party change has been visible not only in issues and policies but also in politics, and especially in the political dimension on the "left–right" continuum. LN's voters, as well as activists and politicians, have become radicalized in recent years, shifting from an intermediate "centrist" position to the extreme right. Data from both national and European mass surveys provide additional support of this shift from "left to right" and the accompanying changes in criteria (i.e. immigration, democracy, civil rights, European integration, and politics), indicating that LN voters have evolved into a body that fits well the new extreme-right family. Of course, there was an ultra-right party faction from the beginning but it was not hegemonic as it has recently become. The LN made a pretty obvious shift to the right in the late 1990s when FI stole its moderate electorate. But there has always been a "Lega of government" and a Lega movement and tensions between the two. Thus, considering the LN as a "new" extreme right party implies a contradiction of the thesis according to which "populist parties are by nature neither durable nor sustainable parties of government."[57] The LN is a populist party that still governs three main northern Italian regions. Thus, the LN is a sort of outlier case among right-wing populist parties, who usually have success (only) in opposition.[58]

The LN continues to be a relevant party in the Italian political system. Its populist traits matter and they are, in some ways, in harmony with the "populist" side, and to some extent, nature of Italian politics. Thus, continuing to study the Northern League is a very good way to continue to shed light on developments in contemporary Italian politics and populism.

Notes

1. See: Margaret Canovan, *Populism*, New York, Harcourt Brace Jovanovich (1981); Paul A. Taggart, "New Populist Parties in Western Europe," *West European Politics*, 18, n. 1 (1995), 34–51; Pierre-Andrè Taguieff, "La rhétorique du National populisme," *Mots*, 2, n. 9 (1984), 113–119.

2. Thomas Poguntke, "New Politics and Party Systems: The Emergence of a New Type of Party?," *West European Politics*, 10, n. 1 (1987), 76–88. Herbert Kitschelt, "Left-Libertarian Parties: Explaining Innovation in Competitive Party Systems," *World Politics*, 40, n. 2 (1988), 194–234. Ferdinand Müller-Rommel, "The New Challengers: Greens and Right-Wing Populist Parties in Western Europe," *European Review*, 6, n. 2 (1998), 191–202. Andreas Schedler, "Anti-Political-Establishment Parties," *Party Politics*, 2, n. 3 (1996), 291–312.

3. Paul A. Taggart, *Populism*, Philadelphia, PA, Open University Press (2000), 115.

4. Müller-Rommel, "The New Challengers," 193.

5. Peter Wiles, "A Syndrome, Not a Doctrine: Some Elementary Theses on Populism," in Ghita Ionescu and Ernest Gellner (eds.), *Populism: Its Meaning and National Characteristics*, London, Macmillan (1969), 163–179; 167.

6. Canovan, *Populism*; Yves Mény and Yves Surel (eds.), *Democracy and the Populist challenge*, London, Palgrave (2002).

7. G. Hermet, *Les populismes dans le monde*, Paris, Fayard (2001), 15.

8. They significantly differed from other populist movements because they were only occasionally electorally engaged (Alfio Mastropaolo, *La mucca pazza della democrazia. Nuove destre, populismo, antipolitica*, Turin, Bollati Boringhieri (2005).

9. Müller-Rommel, "The New Challengers."

10. A total of 224,313 votes (0.7 percent).

11. For a different interpretation see: Marco Tarchi, *L'Italia populista. Dal qualunquismo ai girotondi*, Bologna, Il Mulino (2003), 109 ff.

12. In particular, the two anti-Berlusconi movements, the so-called Girotondi, which were set up by Italian artists and intellectuals in 2002 to defend Italian justice from Berlusconi's attempts to delegitimize the judiciary and to favor the approval of self-interest laws, and *Il popolo viola* (People in purple).

13. The M5S obtained 44,935 more votes than the second biggest party, the Democratic Party. Nevertheless, if we also consider the "foreign district," which includes Italian voters abroad, the Democratic Party surpasses the M5S by 148,116 votes.

14. Gianluca Passarelli, Filippo Tronconi, and Dario Tuorto, "Dentro il movimento. Organizzazione, attivisti e programmi," in Piergiorgio Corbetta and Elisabetta Gualmini (eds.), *Il partito di Grillo*, Bologna, Il Mulino (2013), 123–167.

15. Piergiorgio Corbetta and Gianluca Passarelli, "Fisionomia elettorale delle regioni italiane," in Mariuccia Salvati and Loredana Sciolla (eds.), *L'Italia e le sue regioni (1945–2011)*, Rome, Treccani (forthcoming).

16. Luigi Ceccarini and Fabio Bordignon, "Five Stars and a Cricket: Beppe Grillo Shakes Italian Politics," *South European Society and Politics*, 18 (2013), 427–49.

17. Tarchi, *L'Italia populista*, 183 ff.

18. Arturo Parisi and Gianfranco Pasquino, "Changes in Italian Electoral Behaviour: The Relationships between Parties and Voters," *West European Politics*, 2, n. 3 (1979), 6–30.

19. Ilvo Diamanti, *La Lega. Geografia, storia e sociologia di un nuovo soggetto politico*, Rome, Donzelli (1993).

20. The two most important ethno-regionalist parties were the Łiga veneta and the Union Valdôtaine.

21. Luciano Bardi, "Anti-Party Sentiment and Party System Change in Italy," *European Journal of Political Research*, 29, n. 3 (1996), 345–363.

22. Margarita Gómez-Reino Cachafeiro, *Ethnicity and Nationalism in Italian Politics: Inventing the Padania: Lega Nord and the Northern Question*, Aldershot, Ashgate (2002).

23. Ilvo Diamanti, *Il male del Nord: Lega, localismo, secessione*, Rome, Donzelli (1996).

24. Herbert Kitschelt and Anthony McGann, *The Radical Right in Western Europe: A Comparative Analysis*, Ann Arbor, MI, University of Michigan Press (1995).

25. Michael Shin and Gianluca Passarelli, "Northern League in National, European and Regional Elections: A Spatial Analysis," *Polis*, 26, n. 3 (2012), 355–369.

26. Gianluca Passarelli and Dario Tuorto, *Lega & Padania. Storie e luoghi delle camicie verdi*, Bologna, Il Mulino (2012a).

27. Maurizio Cotta and Pierangelo Isernia, *Il gigante dai piedi di argilla. Il governo di partito e la sua crisi nell'Italia degli anni novanta*, Bologna, Il Mulino (1996).

28. Ronald Inglehart, *The Silent Revolution: Changing Values and Political Styles among Western Publics*, Princeton, NJ, Princeton University Press (1977). Piero Ignazi, "The Silent Counter-Revolution: Hypotheses on the Emergence of Extreme Right-Wing Parties in Europe," *European Journal of Political Research*, 22, n. 1 (1992), 3–34.

29. Schedler, "Anti-Political-Establishment Parties." Müller-Rommel, "The New Challengers."

30. Renato Mannheimer (ed.), *La Lega Lombarda*, Milan, Feltrinelli (1991), 18 ff.

31. Roberto Cartocci, *Fra Lega e Chiesa: l'Italia in cerca di integrazione*, Bologna, Il Mulino (1994).

32. Yves Mény and Yves Surel, *Par le peuple, pour le peuple*, Paris, Fayard (2000).

33. John Agnew, "The Rhetoric of Regionalism: The Northern League in Italian Politics, 1983–94," *Transactions, Institute of British Geographers (TIBG)*, New Series, 20, n. 2 (1995), 156–172.

34. Ibid., 49–50.
35. Lieven De Winter and Huri Türsan (eds.), *Regionalist Parties in Europe*, London, Routledge (1998). Giorgia Bulli and Filippo Tronconi, "Regionalism, Right-Wing Extremism, Populism: The Elusive Nature of the Lega Nord," in Andrea Mammone, Emmanuel Godin, and Brian Jenkins (eds.), *Mapping the Far Right in Contemporary Europe: Local, National, Comparative, Transnational*, London, Routledge (2012), 78–92.
36. Gianfranco Pasquino, "Meno partiti più Lega," *Polis*, 5, n. 1 (1991), 555–564.
37. Anna Cento Bull and Mark Gilbert, *The Lega Nord and the Northern Question in Italian Politics*, London, Palgrave (2001), 57.
38. E. Hobsbawm and T. Ranger, *The Invention of Tradition*, Cambridge, Cambridge University Press (1983); M. Huysseune, "Landscapes as a Symbol of Nationhood: The Alps in the Rhetoric of the Lega Nord," in *Nations and Nationalism*, 16, n. 2 (2010), 354–373.
39. Diamanti, *La Lega*.
40. Anna Cento Bull "The Politics of Industrial Districts in Lombardy: Replacing Christian Democracy with the Northern League," *The Italianist*, 13, n. 1 (1993), 209–229.
41. Michael Shin and Agnew, John A., *Berlusconi's Italy: Mapping Contemporary Italian Politics*, Philadelphia, PA, Temple University Press (2008).
42. Gianluca Passarelli and Dario Tuorto, "The Lega Nord Goes South: The Electoral Advance in Emilia-Romagna: A New Territorial Model?," *Political Geography*, 31, n. 7 (2012b), 419–428.
43. Roberto Biorcio, *La Padania promessa*, Milan, Il Saggiatore (1997). D. McDonnell, "A Weekend in Padania: Regionalist Populism and the Lega Nord," in *Politics*, 26, n. 2 (2006), 126–132.
44. Taggart, *Populism*.
45. The official video of the 2013 electoral campaign clearly sounds like a subliminal attack on southern people (in the north people wake up first, etc.), and on immigrants (in northern regions the public health-care service takes care of everybody [. . .] even immigrants).
46. Thomas Pogunkte and Susan Scarrow, "The politics of Anti-Party Sentiment: Introduction," *European Journal of Political Research*, 29, n. 3 (1996), 257–262.
47. Anna Cento Bull "Addressing Contradictory Needs: The Lega Nord and Italian Immigration Policy," *Patterns of Prejudice*, 44, n. 5 (2010), 411–431.
48. Piero Ignazi, *Extreme Right Parties in Western Europe*, Oxford, Oxford University Press (2003).
49. Gianluca Passarelli, "Extreme Right Parties in Western Europe: The Case of the Italian Northern League," *Journal of Modern Italian Studies*, 18, n. 1 (2013), 53–71.
50. Ignazi, *Extreme Right Parties in Western Europe*. Cas Mudde, *Populist Radical Right Parties in Europe*, Cambridge, Cambridge University Press (2007).
51. Leonardo Morlino and Marco Tarchi, "The Dissatisfied Society: The Roots of Political Change in Italy," *European Journal of Political Research*, 30, n. 1 (1996), 41–63.
52. Hans-Georg Betz, *Radical Right-Wing Populism in Western Europe*, New York, St. Martin's Press (1994). Tarchi, *L'Italia populista*.
53. Ignazi, "The Silent Counter-Revolution."
54. Mannheimer (ed.), *La Lega Lombarda*, 32.
55. See Tarchi's writings on identity populism: "Italy: A Country of Many Populisms," in D. Albertazzi and D. McDonnell (eds.), *Twenty-First Century Populism: The Spectre of Western European Democracy*, Houndmills, Palgrave Macmillan, 82–100.

56. Gianluca Passarelli and Dario Tuorto, "Attivisti di partito in Italia. Il caso della Lega Nord: un partito anomalo?," *Polis*, 36, n. 2 (2012), 255–284.

57. Mény and Surel (eds.), *Democracy and the Populist Challenge*, 18.

58. Passarelli, "Extreme Right Parties in Western Europe."

CHAPTER 19

··

LIBERALISM AND LIBERALS

··

GIOVANNI ORSINA

POST-1945, Italian political liberalism is a complicated creature. From the downfall of fascism until the early 1990s there was a small liberal party. However, liberalism cannot be reduced to the Italian Liberal Party (Partito Liberale Italiano; PLI): other parties must be considered—Partito d'azione, republicans and radicals at least—and liberal political culture more generally. The elusive nature of liberalism and the seldom innocent debates on its definition and boundaries do not help. Finally, postwar Italian liberalism cannot be understood other than in a long-term perspective: the Risorgimento and pre-fascist Italy being inextricably intertwined with the national liberal tradition. This chapter will try to provide a map of the territory—a map that the reader should not expect to be overly detailed, given the amount of territory it aims to chart. The first section will sketch the essential features of Italian political liberalism from the Risorgimento to the downfall of fascism. The second to the fourth sections will confront the years 1943 to 1992 in a chronological order. The epilogue will briefly deal with the last decade of the twentieth century and the beginning of the twenty-first.

LIBERTY, NATION, AND MODERNITY

The origins of Italian liberalism cannot be understood other than in their connection with the two major challenges that Italians had to face in the nineteenth century: creating a nation-state and pushing a backward country onto the path of civilization that Western European countries were treading. The interaction between the distinct but not disconnected concepts of liberty, nation, and modernity contributed to making the Risorgimento political landscape particularly bumpy. The lessons of 1848–49 were essential in convincing the liberals that a liberal solution for the Italian question could not be reached by liberal means: interstate relationships in the pre-unitary peninsula, the weight of the Habsburg Empire, and the Roman question made detaching liberty and modernity from national independence impossible. And national independence was a matter of political and military might. Whatever their abstract values and preferences, in sum, Risorgimento liberals had to tread the narrow path that history was offering them: accepting the leadership of the Savoy monarchy and bearing with warfare, diplomacy, and political power.[1]

Even after Unification, mainstream Italian liberalism remained deeply embedded in the political and institutional contingencies of the Risorgimento that had become the founding blocs of the new state: the monarchy, the nation, state/Church separation, and the Statuto—the Piedmontese-turned-Italian Constitution. Moreover, once they began building the new state, the liberals realized that even in an independent and unified country the virtuous spiral of liberty and modernity was not easily set in motion and did not roll on half as fast as they had wished and expected. Both this awareness, that was heavily influenced by the "Southern Question", and the features acquired during the Risorgimento, gave Italian political liberalism a particularly statist and interventionist character: it postulated that the governing elite and the state were more advanced than the country and had the right and duty to make it ready for liberty—forcibly, if necessary.[2] This opened up the space for a small, but robust and vocal, group of intellectuals who recognized Carlo Cattaneo as their forerunner and upheld a different brand of liberalism: more confident in civil society and the market, a great deal less statist and more democratic, advocating federalism and free trade.[3] Matters were further complicated by the cultural and political evolution of the late nineteenth century. Whereas in the middle decades of the century, liberty, the nation, and modernity were considered inextricable, after 1870 that was no longer the case, and many who defined themselves liberals were, in fact, ready to give priority to the nation and/or modernity. The social question and the growth of socialism on the one hand, and the evolution of political Catholicism on the other, opened up further cleavages inside the liberal camp.[4]

Liberal Italy can be considered, to a certain extent, a success story—not just from the point of view of economic growth and modernization, but also from that of liberty: freedoms, rights, and political participation increased notably between 1870 and 1915.[5] Yet the liberal regime remained fragile. Distrustful as it was of a country that it considered backward and thought its duty to civilize, the liberal elite identified itself with the state and occupied it, trying to de-ideologize the political struggle so as to fend off the Catholic and socialist challenges and to reabsorb those forces in a subordinate position. This significantly weakened the ability of the institutions to gain legitimacy.[6] With World War I, liberalism and liberal parties entered a deep and prolonged crisis in all European countries. In Italy, the impossibility of detaching the institutions from the ruling elite and its ideology transformed the political collapse into an institutional one. And fascism entered the political arena.[7]

Fascism had various effects on the liberal tradition. In the first place, it contributed to showing that liberalism had been defeated and left behind by history. Second, fascism wrestled many of the symbolic and institutional items with which liberalism had been enmeshed, such as the nation and the state, away from it. After 1945, this would make it difficult for liberals to reconnect with their tradition. Finally, fascism prompted a number of efforts aimed at salvaging liberalism from its defeat. Here we can consider only four such instances, and very briefly. Luigi Einaudi kept alive the intellectual strand originating with Cattaneo that had always been politically marginal in the pre-fascist period. In his interpretation, fascism was the ripest fruit of the centralism, dirigisme, and corporatism that that tradition had always fought. Piero Gobetti, reconnecting with a long-standing radical tradition and building on Einaudi's teaching, believed that the moral deficiencies of the Italians could be healed only by enacting the revolution that Italy had never had, and identified liberalism as the ideology of such a revolution. Carlo Rosselli sought a synthesis between liberalism and democratic socialism. Benedetto Croce, with his *Storia d'Italia dal 1871 al 1915* (1928) vindicated liberal Italy as a period of stability and progress; and with his *Storia d'Europa nel secolo decimonono* (1931) postulated the historical contingency of the spiritual crisis of liberalism and the eternal and imperishable value of liberty.[8]

THE ORIGINS OF THE REPUBLIC

Post-1945 liberalisms stand at the crossroads between the tradition hitherto described and the political contingencies of their times.[9] There was a significant liberal element in the armed resistance against Nazi Germany and the Repubblica Sociale Italiana. It is difficult to pin it down because its liberalism was seldom declared—it labelled itself independent and gave its allegiance to the fatherland or the monarchy. Recent studies have drawn attention to this component of the Resistenza, however, demonstrating that its patriotism and independence were often part of a more general allegiance to the pre-fascist liberal tradition. Relevant figures of the pre-fascist elite such as Vittorio Emanuele Orlando, Francesco Saverio Nitti, Meuccio Ruini, Benedetto Croce, Ivanoe Bonomi, and the Partito Liberale, who began reforming in 1942, also played an important role in the birth of the Italian Republic. The PLI was one of the six parties of the National Liberation Committee (CLN) that, alongside the monarchy and the Allies, managed the early phase of the post-fascist period.

Traditionally fragmented by a web of cross-cutting cleavages, Italian liberalism had been unified by its being embedded in Risorgimento culture and institutions—state, nation, and monarchy. Fascism, however, had remolded and appropriated that culture and those institutions. To what extent was it expedient, or even possible, to retrieve the loose end of the historical thread that had been cut in 1922–25? PLI liberals found it very difficult to reach an agreement on how this question should be answered. In the CLN they took a cautious position, opposing any attempt to enact a political and institutional revolution. The future of Italy, they argued, should be decided by the Italians: the parties and the CLN should not predetermine any solution, but create the conditions for the voters to decide freely. The hope for a national palingenesis that would break the country free of its past, however, was far from absent in the ranks of the PLI. Liberal features, moreover, were also visible in the Partito d'Azione (PdAz), the expression par excellence of postwar palingenetic expectations. The PdAz was a heterogeneous entity, and much of it lay outside the liberal camp. Yet a strongly social and equalitarian liberalism inspired by Carlo Rosselli, and a revolutionary liberalism inspired by Piero Gobetti, were part of its ideology.[10]

If the Partito d'Azione represented the liberal tradition to the left of the PLI, others were embodying that tradition on the party's right: some of the great personalities of the pre-fascist period; a number of monarchist parties rooted in southern Italy; and the Uomo Qualunque (Common Man) movement. The weekly *L'Uomo qualunque* was founded by playwright Guglielmo Giannini at the end of 1944. It met with great success, and in the fall of 1945 it evolved into a political movement. Giannini argued that the only relevant social division was that between professional politicians and "the crowd"—defined as a sum of individuals not a cultural or ethnic community. He refused all ideologies as mystification, and thought that public institutions should merely administer a virtuous and progressive society and not endeavor to change it. In many ways the mirror image of *azionismo, qualunquismo* was by no means a liberal phenomenon altogether. Yet it did not lie entirely outside the liberal camp, and it has correctly been defined as "a plebeian form of liberalism in populist clothing."[11]

Disagreements within, and contrasting pressures from without, made the story of the PLI from 1945 to 1948 rife with secessions. On June 2, 1946, the elections for the Constituent Assembly gave the liberals less than 7 percent, showing that they could never dream of regaining their pre-fascist hegemonic position. The Partito d'Azione polled less than 1.5 percent and dissolved the following year, not without leaving a long-lasting intellectual legacy. With more than 5 percent, the Uomo Qualunque demonstrated that many, above all in the south, were unhappy with anti-fascist parties. In 1946 and 1947 the liberals took part in the compromise leading to a Constitution that was open in several directions, many of them scarcely liberal, but which was clear enough in its defense of individual rights. The warnings of the elderly Vittorio Emanuele Orlando, the most influential pre-fascist scholar of constitutional law, that the checks and balances were insufficient, went unheeded.[12]

Between mid-1946 and mid-1947 the liberals were very critical of Alcide De Gasperi's governments with the socialists and communists. In May 1947, the Marxist parties were excluded from the governing majority and De Gasperi gave birth to its fourth cabinet, where the liberals occupied prominent positions: Luigi Einaudi was deputy premier and key economic minister, Giuseppe Grassi was Minister of Justice. From that moment on, liberal economists took control of postwar reconstruction, implementing a policy of monetary stability that provided the basis for the subsequent economic miracle. Yet the PLI still did not know how to position itself, since the Christian Democracy (Democrazia Cristiana; DC) had occupied the political center which the liberals used to hold before fascism. In the PLI Congress of December 1947, with a clear move to the right aimed at exploiting anti-communism, Roberto Lucifero led the party into an electoral alliance with the Uomo Qualunque. A relevant component of the PLI elite then seceded—many of them would create the Independent Liberal Movement (MLI) in June 1948.[13] The move to the right was not rewarded by the voters, either: by then the DC had monopolized the role of bulwark against Moscow, and, in April 1948, the liberal–qualunquisti alliance polled less than 4 percent for the Chamber of Deputies and 5.4 percent for the Senate.

FROM *CENTRISMO* TO *CENTRO SINISTRA*

Although, in parliament, the DC had the absolute majority, after the 1948 elections De Gasperi opted for a coalition government: in the Cold War, the Catholics having an uneasy relationship with the nation-state, he thought a wider alliance necessary. The liberals kept their role in steering the economic reconstruction process, and provided the government with both a symbolic link to the Risorgimento and a more practical relationship to the bureaucracy and entrepreneurs. Luigi Einaudi was elected first President of the Republic. The clear hegemonic position of the DC and the absence of any alternatives to the four-party "centrist" alliance of the DC with the PLI, the republicans, and the social democrats made the first legislature (1948–53) a relatively less quarrelsome period for the liberals. In 1951 many of the 1947–48 seceders who had given birth to the MLI re-entered the PLI.

In a similar way to the liberal tradition, the Italian republican tradition has been extremely complicated—suffice it to point out the very different thought and personality of its two most prominent "spiritual fathers," Mazzini and Cattaneo. A relevant part of that tradition, the elements connected to Cattaneo, much more than those related to Mazzini, cannot be excluded from the liberal ideological camp. In September 1946, Ugo La Malfa, who had quit the Partito d'Azione in February, entered the Partito Repubblicano Italiano (PRI), where he would gain importance over time. In 1951–53, as Minister of Foreign Trade, he played a crucial role in the liberalization of Italian exchanges. In more general terms, La Malfa can be considered the most important political exponent of the progressive and interventionist brand of liberalism that emerged out of the 1930s. Eager to modernize Italy according to Western models, and, in principle, anti-communist, liberals of this shade were also convinced that, to accelerate the modernization process, the country had to be radically transformed by a strong state backed by a firm political will. In time, La Malfa and many others who shared his opinions would conclude that such a revolution needed the votes of the socialists first (mid-1950s), and later on (after the end of the 1960s) of the communists.[14]

De Gasperi's failure in the 1953 elections and his death in 1954 saw a new generation, epitomized by Amintore Fanfani, at the head of the DC: people who had not grown up in the liberal Europe of the *belle epoque* but in the much less liberal interwar period. Faced with this new situation, the grand entrepreneurs, who, after the war, had entrusted the defense of their interests chiefly to the DC, began wondering whether they should change their strategy. Strengthening the traditionally pro-market PLI was an option that they pursued by promoting, in agreement with the party's secretary general Bruno Villabruna, the election of Giovanni Malagodi to parliament. Malagodi, a cultivated, cosmopolitan, and polyglot man with an impeccable liberal pedigree, had long worked as a banker and, after 1947, as a consultant to the Italian government in international economic organizations. Born in 1904, although he had become an adult while fascism was seizing power and had played a role in the restructuring of the Italian economy after 1929, he believed, with Croce, that the crisis of liberalism was not due to any internal flaws but to a failure of self-confidence. As a consequence, his recipe for Italy was an unwavering allegiance to the West, to liberal democracy, and—with a degree of flexibility, in this latter case—to market economy. In 1954, just one year after having become a deputy, Malagodi was elected secretary general of the PLI. While the favor of the entrepreneurs certainly helped him, it must also be stressed that his clarity of mind and ability were uncommon, and came together with an organizational talent that the PLI had never seen before.[15]

In the years 1953–62 the Italian political system was tormented by the agony of the centrist alliance and the painful birth of the new center-left majority with the socialists. There was a continuous strategic and tactical tension between those who wanted to revive the centrist formula, those who wanted to move to the left, including the socialists into the governing majority, and those who were ready to move to the right, including the monarchists and the neo-fascists. All governing parties, notably the DC, were cross-cut by those cleavages.[16] Malagodi was not a right-wing liberal, as he demonstrated in his long militancy in the Liberal International, over which he presided twice (1958–66; 1982–89). Yet his close ties with the entrepreneurs, anti-communist intransigence, refusal to consider the socialist option, and unprejudiced attitude with regard to the monarchists (never to the neo-fascists) placed his PLI firmly to the right of the Italian political arena. The reaction of the liberal left was prompt, leading, in 1955–56, to a new secession and the birth of the "first" Partito Radicale. The new party led a short unhappy life, but was surrounded by a very lively intellectual milieu, animated by influential magazines such as Mario Pannunzio's *Il Mondo* (1949), Arrigo Benedetti's *L'Espresso* (1955), and Francesco Compagna's *Nord e Sud* (1954). In the late 1950s and early 1960s, the gulf between the PLI and progressive liberal culture widened, as Malagodi strenuously fought against the birth of a new governing majority with the socialists, while the liberal left became ever more convinced that getting the PSI onboard was Italy's only hope for finally breaking up any resistance to modernity.[17]

In 1962–64, as the center-left majority was born and consolidated, Malagodi encountered his defeat. In the 1963 elections, the PLI benefited from being the only democratic alternative to the new alliance, and polled its best-ever 7 percent. Yet in the following years the liberal opposition remained sterile, and the possibility of the party having an impact—as in 1972–73, when it briefly returned back into power—was very much subordinated to external circumstances, notably the byzantine circumvolutions of the DC. As a result, the PLI continuously lost votes, until in 1976 it came very close to disappearing from parliament. Yet the birth of the center-left did not bring any luck to the progressive liberal culture that had advocated it, either. As Malagodi had correctly prophesied, the new alliance turned out to be a power deal between non-liberal forces such as the DC and the PSI, strengthening the grip of political parties on the state and of the state on social and economic dynamics. Progressive liberal culture, which had expected a lot from the governments with the socialists, was terribly disillusioned. The decision to close down *Il Mondo* in 1966 can be considered the epitome of this crisis—the editor Mario Pannunzio himself interpreted it as such. In 1969, Ugo La Malfa, a strenuous advocate and protagonist of the center-left, declared the alliance a failure. Progressive liberals had either to place their hopes in a second opening to the left, this time to the communists, or to give way to their elitist tendency to behave as strangers in fatherland, declaring the country hopelessly flawed for its refusal to listen to them.[18]

LIBERALS AND PARTYOCRACY

The contingencies mentioned, as well as the Zeitgeist, made the second half of the 1960s and the 1970s an unfavorable moment for political liberalisms of all shades. Some liberal instances could then be found in the marginal groups and cultures that were unhappy with the hegemony acquired by political parties. The birth of the center-left alliance was paralleled by a double consolidation: that of the crucial position occupied by parties in the political system—notably their supremacy over, and colonization of, both state and society ("partyocracy")—and that of a rather radical brand of antifascism as the Republic's cultural backbone. This mechanism delegitimized all critiques to parties and any attempt to reform the Constitution as fascist or akin to fascism. Yet while, in many cases, attacks to partyocracy were, in fact, based on scarcely (or not at all) democratic premises, in other cases they stemmed from genuinely liberal concerns: that the hollowing out of public institutions by parties was nullifying the separation and balance of powers, and that the rights which Italians were given in theory as citizens, in practice were subordinate to their being party members. According to this interpretation, the accusation that critiques to partyocracy were akin to fascism should be overturned: it was partyocracy that was importing quasi-fascist features into the Republic. These arguments had been refined since the mid-1940s in liberal milieus such as that of *Il Mondo* and by liberal personalities—or liberal Catholic, as in the notable case of Luigi Sturzo. In the 1960s and 1970s, the intellectual and political battle against partyocracy was continued by the Professor of Constitutional Law, Giuseppe Maranini, the hero of the Spanish Civil War and former PRI leader, Randolfo Pacciardi, the Resistenza hero and PLI member, Edgardo Sogno, the journalist and former leading member of the PLI, Panfilo Gentile.[19]

By the end of the 1960s, a number of indicators started showing that the ability of the party system to represent Italian society was waning. This gradually widened the space for initiatives either independent of, or even contrary to, traditional parties. The "second" Partito Radicale had started taking shape in the 1960s, building on the leftovers of the first PR, and had gained momentum thanks to the social movements of the late 1960s, developing the libertarian tendencies of those movements under Marco Pannella's charismatic leadership. It is doubtful whether the PR can be entirely encompassed within the liberal ideological camp. Most certainly, however, it cannot be excluded from it altogether. In the 1970s, the radicals waged a vehement battle in favor of divorce and abortion, notably in the 1974 and 1981 referendums, and picked up the campaign against the partyocracy, using the referendum to bypass parties and give the voters a direct voice.[20] The inability of the PLI to represent the right-wing liberal sections of public opinion, the repeated political failures of progressive liberalism, and the parties' loss of representative power, furthermore, led to the foundation of two newspapers that explicitly aimed at fulfilling a political function: Indro Montanelli's right-wing *Il Giornale* (Milan, 1974), and Eugenio Scalfari's left-wing *La Repubblica* (Rome, 1976). Once again, neither newspaper can be considered entirely liberal, but both deserve to be mentioned in a history of Italian liberalism.[21]

In the second half of the 1970s, prompted also by the near-extinction of the party in the 1976 elections, Malagodi relinquished his control over the PLI, handing it over to a younger generation led by Valerio Zanone (general secretary, 1976–85), and, later on, Renato Altissimo (1986–93). This implied a left-wing turn and a change of strategy: whereas Malagodi had dialogued mainly with the DC, the new leadership believed its main interlocutor to be the PSI. The liberals' new course, however, as well as the fact that they got back into government in the 1980s in the new five-party majority (*pentapartito*), must also be understood as a reaction to the changing political environment: the PSI itself, under Bettino Craxi's leadership, was then undergoing a momentous transformation, as was the entire political system after Aldo Moro's assassination and the failure of the "national solidarity" formula.[22]

The Anglo-Saxon pro-market turn of the 1980s did not have a great practical impact in Italy. In that decade, the country piled up an enormous public debt. Italian political cultures, of course, were not unaware of neoliberalism and were ready to meet the challenge it presented, but with the exception of single intellectuals and the right-wing of the PLI nobody embraced it fully or even predominantly. Yet the Zeitgeist of the 1980s had a significant impact on Italian culture at large: individualism, consumerism, entrepreneurship became watchwords in the peninsula too. Much of this was represented and amplified by commercial television, which had grown in the 1970s, exploiting the loopholes of an illiberal legislation: the most important of which were gathered in a network by real estate developer Silvio Berlusconi.[23]

In the 1980s, the parties' inability to govern such a vital and inordinate society became more evident, and this triggered a debate on political and constitutional change that was lively and theoretically rich, yet unable to bear any practical fruit. The first parliamentary commission on institutional reforms was created in 1983 and presided over by former Constituent Assembly member and longtime liberal deputy Aldo Bozzi. The counterposition between societal virtues and political vices became a commonplace of public debate.[24] It was an ambiguous counterposition, though. It could be used by right-wing, anti-statist, pro-market liberals arguing that the state should be rolled back (e.g. Montanelli's *Il Giornale*), as well as by left-wing, "stranger-in-fatherland," ethical reformist liberals convinced that the "good ones" should take control of both society and politics and finally even up the level of moral modernity of the country with that of its material modernity (e.g. Scalfari's *La Repubblica*).

This chapter does not deal with liberal culture except insofar as it had a direct political impact. Since 1945, however, the historical and theoretical debate on liberalism has been quite lively in Italy. So many people contributed that it is impossible to mention them here. Yet any chapter on Italian liberalism in the second half of the twentieth century cannot but name at least four intellectuals. Norberto Bobbio (1909–2004) was the most important advocate of a progressive brand of liberalism ready to incorporate much of the socialist tradition. Bruno Leoni (1913–1967) developed an original strongly individualistic version of liberalism related to that of the Austrian School. Rosario Romeo (1924–1987) gave a crucial contribution to the understanding of the Risorgimento and of Italian history more generally, stressing the positive role that the state had played and should continue playing in the moral and material growth of the country. Building on an exceptional knowledge of European political thought as well as on Croce's inheritance, Nicola Matteucci (1926–2006) espoused an anti-utilitarian, ethical brand of liberalism attentive to historical challenges and the legacy of tradition.[25]

Epilogue: Liberalisms in Berlusconi's Age

After 1989, "liberalism" and "liberal," which in the 1960s and 1970s had been generally considered outmoded if not reactionary words, enjoyed a new lease of life. Many, if not all, endeavored to appropriate them. In order to fully understand this ideological event, however, we must consider it against the very peculiar historical background of the early 1990s: the myth of civil society; the debate on institutional reform; the parties' increasing loss of representative ability and the critiques to partyocracy; the rise of the League in northern Italy; the unbearable situation of the public finances; the judicial earthquake that destroyed all governing parties, PLI and PRI included; Berlusconi's entry into politics.[26]

Mani Pulite—"Clean Hands," the tidal wave of prosecutions for illegal financing of parties and political corruption—was greeted favorably by the vast majority of both left- and right-wing liberal opinion. Surely this was the case for both *Il Giornale* and *La Repubblica*.[27] This favor however—not unlike the counterposition between societal virtues and political vices in the 1980s—had diverse ideological sources. To the eyes of conservative liberals, Mani Pulite demonstrated the failure of a bloated public sector and vindicated long-standing critiques of partyocracy, creating a unique chance for both reducing the size of the state and giving it back the powers that parties had usurped. Progressive liberals considered the magistrates a quasi-revolutionary instrument capable of making the Italians ready for liberty by throwing the ballast of Italian history overboard: corruption, privileges, and clientelism, as well as social egoism and widespread illegality. The two interpretations converged in the "destructive" phase of Mani Pulite but diverged when it became clear that the post-communist Partito Democratico della

Sinistra would survive the judicial tempest and was about to hegemonize the new political phase. And even more when Berlusconi disrupted that expectation of hegemony.

As an ideology, Berlusconism was an "emulsion" of right-wing liberalism and populism[28]. Confidence in the positive character of Italian society and its capability for progressive self-organization was its kernel. Three further arguments ensued: the state is a problem, not a solution, and should be rolled back and restructured so that it becomes a friendly aid to citizens rather than a paternalist oppressor; political and ideological strife is legitimate, but Italy has historically been soaked in an excess of it (hyperpolitics), while it should be kept within reasonable limits (hypo-politics); professional politicians have failed and ought to be substituted by a new elite issued from society—especially from the entrepreneurial class—and epitomized by Berlusconi himself. The liberal elements in Berlusconi's rhetoric and his liberal way of appropriating the adjective "liberal" attracted right-wing liberal public opinion and gave new prominence to the word liberalism among right-wing voters in general. Some of Berlusconi's early ideologues—such as Giuliano Urbani and Antonio Martino—were pro-market liberals who had been active in the PLI. Many PLI voters and politicians went with Berlusconi, and even Pannella's radicals have never been prejudicially hostile to him.

Many other liberals, however, above all progressive ones, have been antagonized if not horrified by the non-liberal components of Berlusconism: both ideological, such as its populist emphasis on leadership and efficiency and its impatience with institutional checks and balances, and practical, such as Berlusconi's media empire and wealth, generating multiple conflicts of interests.[29] The "cold civil war" between Berlusconians and anti-Berlusconians that has raged since 1994, therefore, has cleaved the liberal camp once again. This is hardly surprising: Berlusconi has exacerbated the division that we have seen throughout these pages between a conservative brand of liberalism, diffident of the state and ready to accept Italian society as it is, and a progressive "liberationist" brand, convinced that only public institutions can civilize the country and make it fit for liberty. While the liberals were busy fighting this civil war, the post-1989 liberal high tide has ebbed away. The Zeitgeist began to change in the second half of the 1990s. After the turn of the century, 9/11 first, and then the recession, accelerated and consolidated this transformation—to which the mismatch between the ideological fortune enjoyed by liberalism and the little political fruit it bore also contributed. At least as far as economic liberalism is concerned, opinion polls make it clear that, during the first decade of the twenty-first century, voters have increasingly become less market oriented. Accordingly, the free-market component of Berlusconism has been progressively toned down, while its socially conservative elements have become more prominent.[30]

Notes

1. References here could be innumerable. Two evergreen classics are: Guido De Ruggiero, *The History of European Liberalism* (Boston: Beacon Press, 1927), first part, ch. 4, "Italian Liberalism"; Rosario Romeo, *Cavour e il suo tempo* (Bari: Laterza, 1969–84). For a general

introduction see Antonino De Francesco, "Ideologie e movimenti politici," in Giovanni Sabbatucci and Vittorio Vidotto, eds., *Storia d'Italia*, vol. I: *Le premesse dell'Unità dalla fine del Settecento al 1861* (Rome and Bari: Laterza, 1995), 229–336. Recent scholarship is discussed in Domenico M. Bruni, ed., *Libertà e modernizzazione. La cultura politica del liberalismo risorgimentale* (Milan: Guerini, 2012).

2. Cf. Alberto Aquarone, *Alla ricerca dell'Italia liberale* (Naples: Guida, 1972); Raffaele Romanelli, *Il comando impossibile. Stato e società nell'Italia liberale* (Bologna: Il Mulino, 1988).

3. On Cattaneo see Norberto Bobbio's classic *Una filosofia militante. Studi su Carlo Cattaneo* (Turin: Einaudi, 1971). On this alternative liberal tradition see Antonio Cardini, *Stato liberale e protezionismo in Italia, 1890–1900* (Bologna: Il Mulino, 1981); Luca Tedesco, *L'alternativa liberista in Italia. Crisi di fine secolo, antiprotezionismo e finanza democratica nei liberali radicali* (Soveria Mannelli: Rubbettino, 2002).

4. Cf. Fulvio Cammarano, *Storia dell'Italia liberale* (Rome and Bari: Laterza, 2011).

5. See, for instance, Raffaele Romanelli, ed., *Storia dello Stato italiano dall'Unità a oggi* (Rome: Donzelli, 1995). For a classic account of the "growth" of liberal Italy, as rich and skillful as it is ideologically oriented, see Gioacchino Volpe, *Italia moderna* (Florence: Sansoni, 1958).

6. Cammarano, *Storia dell'Italia liberale*.

7. Fabio Grassi Orsini and Gaetano Quagliariello, eds., *Il partito politico dalla grande guerra al fascismo. Crisi della rappresentanza e riforma dello Stato nell'età dei sistemi politici di massa, 1918–1925* (Bologna: Il Mulino, 1996); Roberto Vivarelli, *Storia delle origini del fascismo* (Bologna: Il Mulino, 2012).

8. Even an essential bibliography on these four people would require a chapter of its own. Brief introductions to their thinking, written from the point of view of liberalism, and references, can be found in *Dizionario del liberalismo italiano*, vol. II (Soveria Mannelli: Rubbettino, 2014): Luigi Compagna, "Benedetto Croce," 364–370; Francesco Forte and Paolo Silvestri, "Luigi Einaudi," 437–445; Alberto Giordano, "Piero Gobetti," 570–573; Zeffiro Ciuffoletti, "Carlo e Nello Rosselli," 959–961.

9. Liberals and liberalisms of the 1943–48 period have been researched extensively in the last decade. This paragraph is based on: "I liberali e la repubblica," special issue of *Ventunesimo Secolo* 4, no. 8 (October 2005); Fabio Grassi Orsini and Gerardo Nicolosi, eds., *I liberali italiani dall'antifascismo alla repubblica*, vol. I (Soveria Mannelli, Rubbettino, 2008); Giampietro Berti, Eugenio Capozzi, and Piero Craveri, eds., *I liberali italiani dall'antifascismo alla repubblica*, vol. II (Soveria Mannelli, Rubbettino, 2010); Gerardo Nicolosi, *Risorgimento liberale: il giornale del nuovo liberalismo, 1943–1948* (Soveria Mannelli: Rubbettino 2012). For a recent analysis of the origins of the Republic, taking the liberals into due account, see also Giancarlo Monina, ed., *1945–1946. Le origini della Repubblica* (Soveria Mannelli, Rubbettino, 2007).

10. Giovanni De Luna, *Storia del Partito d'Azione* (Turin: UTET, 2006); Luca Polese, "Azione (Partito d')," in *Dizionario del liberalismo italiano*, vol. I, 95–98. See also Dino Cofrancesco, "Azionismo," ibid., 99–108, that emphasizes the distance between *azionismo* and the liberal tradition.

11. Dino Cofrancesco, "L'Uomo qualunque. Analisi di un movimento politico," *Nuova Storia Contemporanea* 16, no. 3 (May–June 2012), 5–38. See also: Guglielmo Giannini, *La Folla. Seimila anni di lotta contro la tirannide* (Soveria Mannelli: Rubbettino, 2002); Sandro Setta, *L'Uomo qualunque, 1944–1948* (Rome and Bari: Laterza, 2005); Dino Cofrancesco,

"Qualunquismo," in *Dizionario del liberalismo italiano*, vol. I, 842–849; Giovanni Orsina, "Guglielmo Giannini," in *Dizionario del liberalismo italiano*, vol. II, 541–545.

12. Fabio Grassi Orsini, "Orlando, profilo dell'uomo politico e dello statista: la fortuna e la virtù," in Vittorio Emanuele Orlando, *Discorsi parlamentari* (Bologna: Il Mulino, 2002), 13–120.

13. Cf. Christian Blasberg, *Die Liberale Linke und das Schicksal der Dritten Kraft im italienischen Zentrismus, 1947–1951* (Frankfurt am Main: Peter Lang, 2008).

14. On the PRI see Chapter 16, this volume. On Ugo La Malfa, see Paolo Soddu, *Ugo La Malfa. Il riformista moderno* (Rome: Carocci, 2009).

15. Giovanni Orsina, *L'alternativa liberale. Malagodi e l'opposizione al centro sinistra* (Venice: Marsilio, 2010).

16. The best, although non-neutral, reconstruction of this web from a DC perspective is still Gianni Baget Bozzo, *Il partito cristiano e l'apertura a sinistra: la DC di Fanfani e di Moro, 1954–1962* (Florence: Vallecchi, 1977).

17. For the radical secession see Chapter 16, this volume; Gerardo Nicolosi, "Partito radicale (anni della Repubblica)," in *Dizionario del liberalismo italiano*, vol. I, 770–775. On the intellectual milieu, see Antonio Cardini, *Tempi di ferro. Il Mondo e l'Italia del dopoguerra* (Bologna: Il Mulino, 1992); Roberto Pertici, "Riviste," in *Dizionario del liberalismo italiano*, vol. I, 906–915.

18. On Malagodi's defeat and prophecies see Orsina, *L'alternativa liberale*. For the crisis of liberal culture, Roberto Pertici, "La crisi della cultura liberale in Italia nel primo ventennio repubblicano," *Ventunesimo Secolo* 4, no. 8 (October 2005), 121–157. For La Malfa's assessment of the *centro sinistra* cf. Paul J. Cook, *Ugo La Malfa* (Bologna: Il Mulino, 1999), 229–230.

19. For an overview see Eugenio Capozzi, *Partitocrazia. Il regime italiano e i suoi critici* (Naples: Guida, 2009). Cf. also: idem, *Il sogno di una costituzione. Giuseppe Maranini e l'Italia del Novecento* (Bologna: Il Mulino, 2008); Alberto Giordano, *Contro il regime. Panfilo Gentile e l'opposizione liberale alla partitocrazia* (Soveria Mannelli: Rubbettino, 2010).

20. Chapter 16, this volume; Gerardo Nicolosi, "Il secondo Partito radicale: idea di partito e organizzazione," in Gerardo Nicolosi, ed., *I partiti politici nell'Italia repubblicana* (Soveria Mannelli: Rubbettino 2006), 331–364; Gerardo Nicolosi, "Partito radicale (anni della Repubblica)."

21. Cf. Paolo Murialdi, *Storia del giornalismo italiano* (Bologna: Il Mulino, 1999), 252ff.; Andrea Ungari, "Indro Montanelli," in *Dizionario del liberalismo italiano*, vol. II, 770–773.

22. Giovanni Orsina, "Il 'luogo politico' del Partito liberale nell'Italia repubblicana," in Giovanni Orsina, ed., *Il partito liberale nell'Italia repubblicana* (Soveria Mannelli: Rubbettino, 2004), 11–59; Franco Chiarenza, "Partito liberale italiano. La fine," in *Dizionario del liberalismo italiano*, vol. I, 761–765. See also Chapter 23, this volume.

23. Cf. Marco Gervasoni, *Storia degli anni Ottanta. Quando eravamo moderni* (Venice: Marsilio, 2010).

24. Cf. Alfio Mastropaolo, "A Democracy Bereft of Parties: Antipolitical Uses of Civil Society in Italy," in Bruno Jobert and Beate Kohler-Koch, eds., *Changing Images of Civil Society: From Protest to Governance* (London and New York: Routledge, 2008), 32–46.

25. For an introduction to these four liberal intellectuals and for an essential bibliography we cannot but refer once again to the entries in the *Dizionario del liberalismo italiano*, vol. II: Roberto Giannetti, "Norberto Bobbio," 146–151; Antonio Masala, "Bruno Leoni," 652–655; Giovanni Giorgini, "Nicola Matteucci," 732–735; Guido Pescosolido, "Rosario Romeo," 950–954.

26. Cf. Simona Colarizi and Marco Gervasoni, *La tela di Penelope. Storia della seconda Repubblica, 1989–2011* (Rome and Bari: Laterza, 2012).

27. Marco Damilano, *Eutanasia di un potere. Storia politica d'Italia da Tangentopoli alla Seconda Repubblica* (Rome and Bari: Laterza, 2012).

28. Giovanni Orsina, *Berlusconism and Italy: A Historical Interpretation* (Basingstoke and New York: Palgrave Macmillan, 2014).

29. See, for instance, Vittorio Bufacchi and Simon Burgess, *Italy since 1989: Events and Interpretations* (Basingstoke and New York: Palgrave Macmillan, 2001).

30. Orsina, *Berlusconism and Italy*, ch. 5.

PART IV

POLITICAL PERIODS

CHAPTER 20

CHRISTIAN DEMOCRACY IN POWER, 1946–63

PAOLO POMBENI

THE years between 1946 and 1963 represent, in many ways, the "heroic" phase of the Christian Democratic Party (Democrazia Cristiana; DC), as well as the foundational era of Italian democracy. It was in this period that the DC took on three fundamental roles. First, with its leader De Gasperi, it inspired and directed political stabilization immediately after the war, through its decision to launch—in a stern but not jacobinic fashion—the new democratic regime. Second, it fostered—albeit via one of its minority currents, the so-called little professors led by Giuseppe Dossetti—the construction of a constitutional ideology that could harmonize the disquietudes of European political thought from the 1920s to the Resistance. Third, following the founding years 1945–48, it took on the issues concerning the management of the country's modernization, combining, again, a moderate defense of social and cultural traditions while accepting the changes induced by significant economic development.

These developments did not proceed in linear fashion but were fraught with social and ideological conflict, first and foremost the difficult confrontation with the traditional Catholic culture that the ecclesiastical hierarchies struggled to abandon; and during this time the DC had to grapple with a multi-party democratic system that proved hard to control. Today's historians should not underestimate results such as the Communist Party's permanence within the democratic system, against all proposed special laws that envisaged its expulsion; or the creation of a broad alliance encompassing all those forces open to the adventure of modernization, including the socialist party; or the choice of a broadly Keynesian governance of economic development.

Recalling those years' events means appraising both the hurdles faced by, and the creative abilities of, a generation of leaders confronted with a complex task. This peculiar leadership was by no means a given, for, as we shall see, at the end of this "heroic" phase a fresh story would commence: the DC and the Italian political system as a whole would quiver in the face of opposition to the achievements of the reforms proposed on the founding years and ultimately fall back on a cautious administration of the power system in accordance with the way in which it had consolidated. Thus our story starts with a crucial choice.

De Gasperi's first real political masterpiece was the decision to refer the choice regarding the state's institutional form, republican or monarchic, to a popular referendum. In 1945, following a crisis among the member parties of a coalition linked to the National Liberation Committee, De Gasperi took on a position of high rank. In a sense his appointment had been a compromise, since the advancement of a leftist candidate proved impossible and all wished to avoid the return to government of the old pre-fascist liberal leaders. Very few realized they had put power into the hands of a man endowed with great political capabilities, who would be present throughout the process of reconstruction.

De Gasperi was no longer a young man.[1] Born in 1881 in a village of the Trentino region, then under Habsburg rule, he had made his debut as one of the founders of the Trentino-Alto Adige Catholic Party and as an MP in Vienna's parliament from 1911 to 1918. Then, after Trentino-Alto Adige was annexed to the Italian state, he became part of Don Luigi Sturzo's Italian Popular Party, and was present in parliament as an MP from 1921 to 1924. At that time he had to confront the fascists who, once securely in power in 1924, had him arrested, tried, and briefly jailed in order to force him into virtual exile, away from public life. He then worked, not without certain difficulties, in the Vatican Library, until in 1943 the fall of Fascism led him to join the committee of anti-fascist parties (Comitato di Liberazione Nazionale; CLN), due to his having been the last secretary of the Italian Popular Party (Partito Popolare Italiano; PPI). The PPI, along with others, had participated in the anti-Mussolini protests after the assassination of socialist MP Giacomo Matteotti at the hands of fascist Blackshirts.

De Gasperi's choice to rely on the people's vote in order to find an answer to the institutional question came as a surprise. According to the agreements made during the Resistance, this choice was to be left to the future constituent assembly, in keeping with the tradition of the American and French Revolutions, and the more recent Weimar Republic. The people were considered to be unreliable, mainly due to the belief that, especially in the south, a legitimist sentiment prevailed. Hence, the prime minister's choice, one nearly forced on the government with the support of the occupying allies, was interpreted by many as an implicit endorsement of the monarchy. This interpretation was shared by the man who would become the leader of the leftist current within the DC, young university professor Giuseppe Dossetti—born in 1913—who resigned from his role of party vice-secretary in protest.[2]

In fact, with this decision De Gasperi was offering a foretaste of his future political course of action: managing what he expected to be a complex task of reconstruction while avoiding ungovernable rifts within the nation. He was familiar with the German experience, and he understood what had eroded and caused the crisis of the Weimar Republic: the delegitimation of the republican system as it emerged from World War I, a system which appeared to be imposed from without by the radicalism of the new authorities in power.[3]

If the choice regarding the institutional system had been left to the constituent assembly's vote, a never-ending quarrel might have ensued: regardless of the outcome, the defeated camp would not fail to accuse the other of having betrayed the people's true will. Both republicans and monarchists had influential sponsors, the first among the left-wing parties and in almost all the Resistance's intelligentsia, the latter in the imposing bureaucracy and within national and Vatican ecclesiastic circles. The people's direct say would have rendered it impossible for any and all to suggest that a decision had been made against its will.

De Gasperi's decision proved appropriate. Despite the small margin yielded by the vote held on June 2, 1946—12,718,641 for the republic and 10,718,512 for the monarchy—and the attempts to suggest that the results had been manipulated by the authorities, Italy has known no relevant phenomenon of monarchic legitimism since.[4]

One of the factors that allowed a smooth change of institutional regime was the caution used by all in managing the transition. Many controversies arose around the fact that fascists had not been purged, and above all regarding the failed prosecution of those crimes committed by fascists during both the 20-year-long regime and the months between September 1943 and April 1945. In fact, the law granting a general amnesty passed on June 22, 1946 bore the signature of the minister of justice and communist party leader Palmiro Togliatti.[5] There was a trailing off of feuds, and undoubtedly there were murderers who did not pay for their crimes, but overall this decision averted the risk of violent organized clashes, and, more importantly, it limited the ability of many forces that identified with fascism to reorganize. Despite the fact that on December 26, 1946 a group of ex-fascists, among whom were Giorgio Almirante, Pino Romualdi, and Arturo Michelini, had founded an extreme right party—the Movimento Sociale Italiano (MSI)—that party remained for a long time a marginal backward-looking force, characterized by the ambiguity of proudly recalling its origins but, at the same time, of denying the will to re-establish the fascist regime—as Augusto De Marsanich famously put it, "don't deny, don't restore."[6]

The art of stabilizing the political system was further perfected by De Gasperi with a policy that was very tolerant of the state's public bureaucracy. For obvious reasons this was, largely a product of the dynamics of fascism's colonization of the public sphere. To say that the Italian bureaucracy at that time was composed solely of fascists would be incorrect. Italy had a long tradition of functionaries and clerks trained to obey, whatever the color of the political elite. Hence De Gasperi felt that, once allowed to maintain their positions, they would not obstruct the new policy makers' will. On this issue he was partly mistaken: if, on the one hand, the bureaucrats did not revolt against their benefactors, on the other they represented a conservative force that lacked openness, and they certainly did not aid in the necessary modernization of public infrastructure, failing to actively support the new policies.[7]

The constitutional issue remained, nonetheless, the government's principal concern.[8] With few exceptions it was thought that it was necessary to review the Constitution, which was formally fixed at its 1848 Albertine Statute form, yet had been relevantly manipulated during Fascism. Thus, a Constituent Assembly was elected, on that same June 2, 1946 to tackle this issue.

This was a complex stage. The elections constituted the first test of the political parties' ability to gather popular support. Those defined as the three great people's parties were revealed to be dominant: first place went to the DC with 35.2 percent of the vote; in second place the socialist party—then the Partito Socialista Italiano di Unità Proletaria (PSIUP) and later the Partito Socialista Italiano (PSI)—with 20.6 percent; and the communist party (PCI) came in as a close third with 18.9 percent. All other parties were much smaller in size: the two parties that laid claim to the pre-fascist liberal legacy, the National Democratic Union (Unione Democratica Nazionale; UDN), and the National Bloc of Freedom, totaled respectively 6.7 and 2.7 percent of the vote. Mazzini and Garibaldi's old republican party (PRI) gathered 4.3 percent of consensus. There were two new developments. First, the self-defined Fronte dell'Uomo Qualunque ("Common Man's Front"), which achieved an astounding 5.2 percent result. Recently funded by playwright Guglielmo Giannini, it polemicized against the parties' excessive power that oppressed the average citizen—an expression of middle-class clerkship's widespread fear that the new politicians might deprive them of their livelihoods. Its success would prove ephemeral, as the party effectively disappeared at the following elections, merging in part with the DC and in part with extreme right parties.

The second development was the unforeseen and catastrophic failure of the Partitio d'Azione ("Action Party"). Rooted in left-wing liberalism, successful among intellectuals, boasting participation in the Resistance, and having seen its own Ferruccio Parri fulfill the role of prime minister between June and December 1945, it claimed to represent, in a somewhat jacobinic fashion, the spirit of a new Italy and to be the natural judge of, and guide into, the new era. It won a meager 1.4 percent of the vote and never recovered from that defeat.[9]

In order to provide visibility for the rejuvenated representative democracy, the Constituent Assembly had been imagined as a large parliament composed of 556 MPs, a number disproportionate to the tasks at hand. Its objectives were but three: to cast a vote of confidence in favor of the government, approve the peace treaty, and draft the new constitution. It did not have to deal with ordinary law, which was to be passed by governments via decrees, without the need for further ratification.

This gave rise to frustration during the assembly's activities. The vote of confidence was initially a matter of course: in the first phases, the parties opted for a large coalition in which all three major parties—DC, PSIUP, and PCI—took part, having gathered between them 75 percent of the consensus. Alcide De Gasperi was confirmed as head of government. The peace treaty, signed in Paris on February 10, 1947, was ratified by the assembly, though not without difficulties. It was rather harsh, while Italian public opinion had believed that Mussolini's fall in July 1943, and above all the work of the Resistance, had earned Italy a measure of leniency. In a heated debate, a former exponent of liberal pre-fascist governments, Vittorio Emanuele Orlando, went as far as accusing De Gasperi, wholly without reason, of "servile greed" toward those who had won the war.[10]

The drafting of the Constitution was effectively delegated to a special 75-member commission presided over by Meuccio Ruini. It was here that the intellectual process of constructing the legal code of the new republic took place. The document was made of two parts. The first dealt with its major principles and the constitutional design. Here a group of young DC members headed by Giuseppe Dossetti took the lead.[11] Their ambition was to compose a charter that affirmed the new conception of man and society that had taken hold in the 1930s and 1940s' intellectual debate, an adventure in which exponents of Catholic political thought, such as Maritain and Mounier, also partook. They found support in communist leader Palmiro Togliatti who, having been immersed in the struggles of the European "popular fronts," partly shared that sensibility.[12] Because, in retrospect, this agreement appeared to be suspicious, a legend emerged about a compromise between the DC and the communists, the so-called half Russian, half Latin constitution. In truth this was simply a formalization of the *zeitgeist*.

The second half, dealing with the organization of state power, was dominated by the debate among jurists in the aftermath of the shock caused by the great dictatorships. This discussion, in which one of the dominant figures was jurist and Christian Democrat MP Costantino Mortati, saw a staunchly civil libertarian division of power prevail, in an attempt to prevent that which all feared, namely the possibility of an adversary exploiting an electoral victory and concentrating all power in its own hands. The constitutional arrangement which weakened the power of every component of the decision-making process (parliament, government, judiciary, etc.) but gave to each one a sort of veto thus hindered the decision-making process.

The new Constitution was approved in December, and came into effect on January 1, 1948. In the meantime the political context had changed. The alliance between the three great people's parties was strained by disagreement on foreign relation issues—the US was not favorable to the idea of the PCI being in power, and the USSR found it hard to stomach the alliance of communists with bourgeois parties—but also because of internal turmoil. The socialist party fractured in January 1947 following the birth of a social-democratic party that openly argued against the PCI, while the communists found it hard to forego their traditional revolutionary party roots; the slogan that defined them as a "party of struggle and government" could scarcely resolve its inherent ideological inconsistencies. At the same time, it became apparent to De Gasperi that in order to be assured of US backing and to avoid tensions on the conservative front—to which the Vatican did not deny a certain support—it had become necessary to bring the governing coalition to an end.[13]

This duly occurred in May 1947, formally in order to launch a shared government of the DC with "technicians," the most relevant of whom was Luigi Einaudi, a prominent economist and the Governor of the Bank of Italy. Shortly after that event, a vote was expected to take place, which would establish the real nature of the political equilibrium.

In fact, however, the elections were delayed by a few months, taking place on April 18, 1948. The electoral campaign had been rather bitter. The communists, in an attempt to gain the majority of the consensus, had resumed the old "Popular Front" formula. This involved an alliance among the left-wing parties and "bourgeois" progressives, which had been developed in 1930s Europe, and constructed as the most effective anti-fascist tool. The problem was that it consisted simply of an alliance between the PCI and PSI, and as such was limited to the traditional left. The DC then chose to portray itself as the anti-communist bulwark and guarantor of a stability that carefully merged a measure of social progress with the preservation of the traditional values that characterized Italian society. In undertaking this task, the DC could, for the first time, count on structured Catholic Church support, because Pius XII, increasingly preoccupied with the challenge posed by Eastern communism, supported this new image and engaged with it personally.[14]

The result of this duel was unambiguous: the DC totaled 48.5 percent of the vote, obtaining 305 MPs over 574 in the Chamber of Deputies and 131 Senators out of 237. The Popular Front did not fare well: with 31 percent of the vote, it failed to increase the sum total the PCI and PSI had gathered in 1946, and communist MPs now outnumbered the socialists. It also became clear that the political system was destined to be multi-party: Giuseppe Saragat's social-democrats scored 7.1 percent of the vote, with the republicans at 2.5 percent and the liberals at 3.8 percent. And then there were the extreme rights, which, all things considered, met with reasonable success: the monarchist came in at 2.8 percent, and the MSI at 2 percent.

This presented a first political problem. Theoretically, the DC could have attempted to govern on its own: this was the course of action suggested by the party's own leftist current, headed by Dossetti, that saw alliances as a shackle restraining any party that wished to be reformist. De Gasperi chose instead to involve center parties—the social-democrats, the republicans, and the liberals—in the government. His logic, which he would share years later in a letter to the Pope, was as follows: while the DC could count on strong public support, prominent national economic forces, high-ranking bureaucrats, and the press were loyal to the so-called lay sphere, which resented being ousted from power. Thus, in order to prevent such a situation it was necessary to include them in government, capitalizing on their awareness that the DC was the only force that could forestall a communist victory.

De Gasperi was indeed shaping the Italian political system, basing it on what, many years later, political analyst Giorgio Galli would call "an imperfect two-party system."[15] The system was based on competition between the center, occupied by the DC—which kept the moderate right-wing parties at bay and excluded the extreme right—and the left, in the form of the communist party. The latter, due to reasons linked to international equilibria—namely its affiliation with the USSR—could not become associated with power, in a mechanism that jurist Leopoldo Elia defined a *conventio ad excludendum*, an informal but binding agreement that a Communist Party could not become a governing force in a system included in the Western Alliance's sphere.[16]

This political setup earned the name of "centrism." As long as De Gasperi managed to hold on to power, the lay parties remained marginal. Nevertheless, in validation of their role, in 1948 the presidency of the Republic was assigned to Luigi Einaudi—not De Gasperi's choice, who favored the republican Sforza. De Gasperi worked both to consolidate Italian presence within the "Atlantic" alliance—Italy joined NATO in 1949—and to pass, thanks to the agreement with Dossetti's internal leftist current, a series of reforms between 1950 and 1951.[17]

The embitterment caused by the Cold War, however, disrupted this fragile equilibrium, not solely due to Dossetti's exit from the party in October 1951—in a bid to focus on the reform of the Church—but rather because of the escalation of both Catholic and the lay right's demands in the wake of ever stauncher anti-communist sentiment. In order to free himself from this blackmail of sorts, which put him in a difficult position with regard to what remained of the internal leftist current, De Gasperi resorted to the passing of a majoritarian electoral law, tailored around the centrist coalition. The law envisaged assigning 65 percent of seats to any coalition totaling 50 percent plus one of votes. It was a law clearly made-to-measure for the centrist coalition, the only one in a position to manage such a result: the left were at least 15 percent short, and the extreme right was decidedly out of the game with its meager 5 percent. Due to this, the left in opposition branded the law as a scam.[18]

On July 7, 1953 elections were held under the new electoral law, but the outcome did not live up to expectations. The DC lost consensus, plummeting to 40.1 percent, while none of its allies was able to bring to the table the percentages needed to meet the quorum (PSDI 4.5 percent, PRI 1.6 percent, PLI 3 percent). Instead, support both for the extreme right—with the monarchist and MSI reaching 6.9 and 5.9 percent respectively—and extreme left—PCI 22.6 percent, PSI 12.7 percent—increased.

That result effectively marked De Gasperi's political demise—he passed away a short time after, on August 19, 1954—but it also inaugurated what was to become a long transitional phase in Italian politics.

On paper, DC-led centrism continued to shape government, but the formula had lost its shine. After De Gasperi's death, the party was left in the hands of a pre-fascist Catholic old guard that coexisted alongside a new generation, reared by Dossetti's leftist current, a generation that had not followed its leader when he chose to abandon politics.[19]

Amintore Fanfani, the new appointed leader, was an economic history professor who had sided with Dosssetti. He was endowed with a feisty temperament and sharp intelligence, but was little loved by a party torn apart by internal currents. Nevertheless, he was successful in his bid to become DC secretary, and was elected at the Napoli congress held in 1954. He immediately started working toward enfranchising the party from ecclesiastical support, as well as endeavoring to characterize it as a force able to lead a moderate modernization of the country's social and economic structures.[20]

This meant breaking free from the mindsets of the Cold War, which, after Stalin's death in 1953, seemed to have entered into a new phase. Thus, things started to shift. PSI leader Pietro Nenni spoke, at his party's congress in the spring of 1955, of the need of finding some common ground with the Catholics, in the knowledge that the DC was itself open to this possibility. The so-called opening to the left was underway.[21]

On April 29, 1955 Giovanni Gronchi, President of the Chamber of Deputies for the DC, was elected to the presidency of the Republic, with the support of the left, and against the northern economic and financial milieu's candidate Cesare Merzagora. From the start Gronchi favored a measure of political openness, tearing down a few anti-communist fences by launching some authorities that were envisaged by the Constitution but had remained dormant, such as the Constitutional Court.

The PCI attempted to take advantage of this new scenario, but was preempted by international events. The Hungarian uprising, and its brutal repression at the hands of the USSR in October 1956, were the opposite of what was needed to consolidate the image of a communism that was open and willing to engage in debate. Furthermore, the events allowed the PSI, with its libertarian tradition, to condemn Soviet policy, thus eroding the perception of the party as being dominated by Togliatti's political practices.

The issue of an opening to the left of the governmental coalition became more pressing, mainly because it had become paramount to grapple with the modernization that was taking place in Italian society. The overcoming of post-war difficulties and the positive turn in international finances were triggering what would later be defined as the economic miracle. This state of affairs also induced corresponding changes in lifestyles: increased urbanization, the assertion of a culture ever more dependent on the models conveyed by the media—particularly television, which was then becoming a mass phenomenon—and the consequent rise of demands for wage increases.[22]

This context called for a more dynamic management of Italian politics than that allowed by a coalition in which the combined weights of liberal and Catholic conservatism reduced the scope for effective interventions and compelled the government to negotiate, often rather openly, with the extreme right parties.

The situation was very tense, also due to the crisis within the high ranks of the Catholic Church. Pius XII was nearing the end of his life, and conservative forces headed by Cardinal Ottaviani and Genoa's Bishop Giuseppe Siri dominated the Vatican.[23] These forces often accused the DC of an irresponsible openness to the "Marxists," who were officially condemned by Church doctrine, although, in reality, it was a question of the fear felt by a conservative culture in the face of great social changes—the ecclesiastical leaders at that time were apprehensive of ubiquitous "lay threats."

It was against this background that the DC's most strenuous political phase began. The party's secretary, Amintore Fanfani, chose to use a strong arm, taking on the burden of reform and, for the elections held on May 25, 1958, he presented a program rich in economic and social interventions. The elections marked a shift in electoral consensus: the DC earned a significant 42.4 percent, but the PSI also registered an increase at 14.2 percent. Surprisingly, the communists remained stable at 22.7 percent, and were little affected by the crisis which followed the Hungarian incident, which saw many prominent intellectuals leave the party. There were other small adjustments, yet none was truly significant.

The time seemed to be ripe for a reformist experiment, partly due to the passing of Pope Pius XII and the advent of his successor Angelo Roncalli—elected to the papal throne on October 28, 1958, with the name of Giovanni XXIII—that fueled hopes of greater openness on the part of the Vatican. In reality, this would take a few more years.

Fanfani gave rise to fears within the party due to his unwillingness to delegate and the amount of power he had acquired: he was party secretary, prime minister, and minister of foreign affairs. Within the DC, factionalism flourished, and it was a fracture within

Fanfani's own current that caused his downfall. In the Party Congress held from March 14 to 18, 1959, Fanfani was forced by an agreement between a group of notable exponents of his current, and some other group's members, to resign from his post of secretary. Because the men had convened in the convent of Santa Dorotea, they would be known from then on, as the dorothean current.[24]

Forty-two-year-old Aldo Moro was called upon to substitute Fanfani, and he was expected to manage the party with a degree of caution. Moro, previously a member of Giuseppe Dossetti's current, revealed himself to be executing a precise plan, envisaging a measure of openness to the left. He would realize it step by step, always careful not to fall prey to the traps set by his many adversaries, both Catholic and lay, opposing his policy.

Moro got a cautious all clear to open to the left at the DC congress held in Florence from 24 to 27 October, 1959, yet he was faced with the complex circumstances the government was in. Leading the executive was the moderate conservative Antonio Segni, and when he had to leave the post the situation became so problematic that it seemed inevitable to launch a transitional government headed by a less prominent politician, Fernando Tambroni. In order for him to take office, the DC had to accept, not without internal turmoil, the favorable votes of the extreme right party MSI. Tambroni was under the impression that this would be a chance for personal success, and he inaugurated a policy of intervention. Having been minister of the interior, he believed he could count on a power derived from the knowledge and acquaintances he had acquired through the political services of the police and its apparatus.

Vatican conservatism had been unleashed in the attempt to block any and all hypothesis of openness to the left.[25] On May 17 the Holy See's official publication, the *Roman Observer*, published an article significantly titled "certainties" (*Punti Fermi*), which reiterated that Catholics could not form alliances with Marxists—and thus with the PSI—while some bishops and Jesuit contributors to the periodical *Civiltà Cattolica* attacked Moro himself, weakening his position within the party and with his electoral base.

The breakthrough came following an unforeseen crisis. The MSI had planned for its 1960 congress to be held in Genoa, a city that was a symbol of anti-fascist Resistance. The lefts took advantage of this, and organized a protest against neo-fascism. It became clear that the memory of the Resistance was still vivid in the people's consciousness. Tambroni wished to appear able to stand his ground, perhaps in a bid to gain credibility in the eyes of the US, and promoted a climate that precipitated violent clashes between the police and protestors. There were two casualties, and the country seemed to be on the verge of a generalized conflict.[26]

It was at that moment that political rationality prevailed. Moro led the DC to forsake Tambroni, who ingloriously resigned on July 19. The socialists, facing internal problems of their own—with the leftist side of the party criticizing the agreement with the DC, viewed as a bourgeois, conservative party—were persuaded by leader Nenni that the only progress possible for Italian democracy would come through the alliance with the Catholic party. Togliatti himself was initially partial to the turn, in which he hoped the

PCI would eventually be able to take part. Even the Vatican was experiencing a change of wind: Mons. Angelo Dell'Acqua was taking over the post of secretary of state. A friend of Moro's and Fanfani's, he had the chance to convince the Pope that the policy brought forward by Ottaviani and his associates would lead only to bitter conflict in Italian politics, a conflict that might at length threaten the hegemony of the Catholic party.[27]

Moro was thus able to take a small step forward, and a single-sided government formed, headed by Fanfani, on July 26, 1960. It became known as the government of democratic convergence, in order to stress the wide unity of perspectives fostered by the crisis experienced during Tambroni's experiment. In the meantime, PSI "autonomists" registered a victory, albeit relative, during the party's 1961 Milan congress. This group opposed the theory stating that the absence of working-class unity—that is to say the lack of unity with the communist party—meant a loss of legitimacy for the PSI. This was of course an indispensable step both in securing benevolent neutrality from the US—where John F. Kennedy had recently become president—and to escape ecclesiastical vetoes regarding the agreement with the communists.[28]

During the DC congress convened in Naples toward the end of January 1962, Moro won further support for his policies, which by now were seen favorably by the finest Catholic intellectuals, thus compelling even the right-most section of the party to fall into line. To the latter faction, the secretary—re-elected with a consensus of 92 percent—gave a guarantee that the presidency of the Republic would be assigned to moderate conservative Antonio Segni, one of the current's main participants, as was confirmed on May 6, 1962.

Meanwhile, on February 22, 1962, Fanfani became his own successor as prime minister, but this time with a government coalition formed by the PSDI and the PRI, relying on the external support of the PSI. It was the launch of the first center-left coalition, which the liberals, having moved to the opposition benches, constructed as the advent of political disaster. Their secretary, Malagodi, felt defeated in his attempt to erect what he defined as, with an hyperbole best suited to a more deserving cause, "a fortification to hold off barbarians."[29]

It was this government which began and partly accomplished the economic reforms that would characterize the center-left's short-lived creative phase: the nationalization of the electric grid, the launch of a commission for economic planning, new taxation on shares and real estate revenue, a pension reform, and a reform of the educational system that restructured compulsive schooling to age 14, concentrating it into a single three-year cycle that followed the five years of primary school—before it had been divided into two separate paths, middle school for those intending to progress to higher education, and a professional school for children to be precociously incorporated into the workforce.

As could be expected, the reformist dash met with strong opposition, in which authentically conservative interests, and more trivial fears of the upheavals that supposedly were to be caused by such innovations, converged. This climate reverberated on the political elections held on April, 28. The DC lost consensus and its electoral results fell to 38.3 percent, the PSI also failed to benefit from its openness, and saw its votes decreasing slightly to 13.8 percent, while the PRI that with its leader, Ugo La Malfa, had been supportive of the turn, stopped at 1.4 percent.

Only the PSDI, a party with a strong history of nepotism, made the best of its position in government, and managed a result of 6.1 percent. The two forces most vehemently opposed to the new run were the ones who reaped the greater benefits: the PLI jumped to 7 percent, a result that would be reshaped in the following consultation, and the PCI reached a conspicuous 25.3 percent.

These results were not as catastrophic as they were portrayed to be by many interested commentators, yet they did force the DC to tone down its propositions. Moro aimed at a government that would now include the PSI, albeit with a moderate program able to calm conservative apprehensions present both in his party and in the electoral base. Nenni found it difficult to accept his role as auxiliary in a project which lost sight of the turn that was supposedly to be achieved with the entrance of the socialists into the mythical government control room.

The first reaction was to opt for another transitional government entrusted to MP Giovanni Leone, while waiting for the PSI to unravel the threads of internal conflict during the 25th Congress held from 25 to he 29 October, 1963. Nenni won by a small margin with 57 percent of the vote, but leftist socialist opposition remained firm. Nevertheless, this victory set the wheels of negotiation in motion once again, and on December 5, 1963, the first "organic" center-left government was launched, with Moro and Nenni as prime minister and vice-president of the council of ministers respectively.[30]

It appeared to be the crowning achievement of a political strategy that had developed in little less than a century, yet it proved to be a classic case of Indian summer. The conservative forces were all but defeated. The PCI, after its initial openness, would return to steadfast opposition, compelled partly by the resistance it faced due to Italy's international positioning, and by the persistence of old Catholic prejudices, despite the changes induced by Vatican II.

The first Moro government lasted only a few months, from December 4, 1963, to June, 26 1964. The spring and summer of 1964 witnessed a crisis of notable proportions, with obscure instances of pressures applied by high bureaucracy and by the military. In reality this marked the inception of a new historical phase: the DC would long endure as the hegemonic party, but it would, from now on, put to one side its tradition of innovation and awareness of modernity's challenges that had hitherto been important components of its political culture.

NOTES

1. De Gasperi's biography has been extensively researched: on the early years see: Paolo Pombeni, *Il primo De Gasperi. La formazione di un leader* politico (Bologna: Il Mulino, 2007); an ample biography can be found in *Alcide De Gasperi*, 3 vols. (Soveria Mannelli: Rubettino, 2009); introductive essays are in: Alcide De Gasperi, *Scritti e Discorsi Politici*, 4 vols. (Bologna: Il Mulino, 2006–09). A more compact biography is: Piero

Craveri, *De Gasperi* (Bologna: Il Mulino, 2006); A comprehensive analysis in English can be read in: Paolo Pombeni (ed.), "De Gasperi's scritti e discorsi politici," *Modern Italy* 14, 4 (2009).

2. On Giuseppe Dossetti's political biography, see: Luigi Giorgi, *Una vicenda politica. Giuseppe Dossetti, 1945-1956* (Milan: Scriptorium, 2003); Paolo Pombeni, *Giuseppe Dossetti. L'avventura politica di un riformatore cristiano* (Bologna: Il Mulino 2013); Fernando Bruno, *Dossetti, un innovatore nella democrazia cristiana del dopoguerra* (Turin: Bollati Boringhieri, 2014).

3. Paolo Pombeni, "De Gasperi Costituente," *Quaderni Degasperiani per la storia dell'Italia contemporanea* 1 (2009), 55–123.

4. It must be noted that 1,148,136 ballots were unmarked or spoiled.

5. Hans Woller, *I conti col fascismo* (Bologna: Il Mulino, 1997); Cecilia Nubola, "I provvedimenti di clemenza nei confronti dei 'collaborazionisti' nell'Italia del secondo dopoguerra," in Paolo Pombeni and Heinz-Gerhard Haupt (eds.), *La transizione come problema storiografico* (Bologna: Il Mulino, 2013), 319–344.

6. Giuseppe Parlato, *Fascisti senza Mussolini: le origini del neofascismo in Italia, 1943-1948* (Bologna: Il Mulino, 2006)

7. Guido Melis, *Storia dell'amministrazione italiana* (Bologna: Il Mulino, 1996), 383–500.

8. Paolo Pombeni, *La Costituente. Un problema storico-politico* (Bologna: Il Mulino, 1995).

9. On the first phase of the Republic and of the party system see: Giancarlo Monina (ed.), *1945-1946. Le origini della Repubblica* (Soveria Mannelli: Rubbettino, 2007); Giovanni De Luna, *Storia del Partito d'Azione 1942-1947* (Rome: Editori Riuniti, 1997); Giovanni Sale, *Dalla monarchia alla repubblica. Santa Sede, cattolici italiani e referendum (1943-1946)* (Milan: Jaca Book, 2003).

10. Sara Lorenzini, *L'Italia e il trattato di pace del 1947* (Bologna: Il Mulino, 2007).

11. Enrico Galavotti, *Il professorino. Giuseppe Dossetti fra crisi del fascismo e costruzione della democrazia, 1940-1948* (Bologna: Il Mulino 2013)

12. Aldo Agosti, *Togliatti. Un uomo di frontiera* (Turin: Utet, 2003); Roberto Gualtieri, Carlo Spagnolo, Ermanno Taviani (eds.), *Togliatti nel suo tempo* (Rome: Carocci, 2007).

13. Pietro Di Loreto, *Togliatti e la "doppiezza". Il PCI tra democrazia e insurrezione, 1944-1949* (Bologna: Il Mulino 1991); Elena Aga Rossi and Victor Zaslavsky, *Togliatti e Stalin. Il PCI e la politica estera staliniana negli archivi di Mosca* (Bologna: Il Mulino, 2007); Giovanni Sale, *De Gasperi gli Usa e il Vaticano agli inizi della guerra fredda* (Milan: Jaca Book, 2005); Roberto Gualtieri, *L'Italia dal 1943 al 1992. DC e PCI nella storia della repubblica* (Rome: Carocci, 2006); Gustavo Corni and Paolo Pombeni, "La politica come esperienza della storia," in Eckart Conze, Gustavo Corni, Paolo Pombeni (eds.), *Alcide De Gasperi: un percorso europeo* (Bologna: Il Mulino, 2005); Salvatore Lupo, *Partito e antipartito. Una storia politica della prima Repubblica, 1946-1978* (Rome: Donzelli, 2004); Michele Donno, *Socialisti democratici. Giuseppe Saragat e il Psli, 1945-1952* (Soveria Mannelli: Rubbettino, 2009).

14. Paolo Pombeni, "I partiti e la politica dal 1948 al 1963," in Giovanni Sabbatucci and Vittorio Vidotto (eds.), *Storia d'Italia*, vol. 5: *La Repubblica* (Rome and Bari: Laterza, 1997), 127–251.

15. Giorgio Galli, *Il bipartitismo imperfetto. Comunisti e democristiani in Italia* (Bologna: Il Mulino, 1966).

16. Agostino Giovagnoli, *Il partito italiano. La Democrazia cristiana dal 1942 al 1994* (Rome and Bari: Laterza, 1996)

17. Guido Formigoni, *La Democrazia cristiana e l'alleanza occidentale, 1943-1953* (Bologna: Il Mulino, 1996); Mario Del Pero, *L'alleato scomodo. Gli Usa e la Dc negli anni del centrismo, 1948--1955* (Rome: Carocci, 2001); Paolo Acanfora, *Miti e ideologie nella politica estera democristiana. Nazione, Europa e comunità atlantica, 1943-1954* (Bologna: Il Mulino, 2014); Giovanni Tassani, "Il vicesegretario intransigente. Giuseppe Dossetti e la Dc: 1950-1951, dinamica di un distacco" *Nuova Storia Contemporanea* 11, 5 (2007), 55–86.

18. Maria Serena Piretti, *La legge truffa. Il fallimento dell'ingegneria politica* (Bologna: Il Mulino 2003)

19. Pietro Di Loreto, *La difficile transizione. Dalla fine del centrismo al centro-sinistra, 1953-1961* (Bologna: Il Mulino, 1993).

20. Francesco Malgeri, *La stagione del centrismo. Politica e società nell'Italia del secondo dopoguerra, 1945-1946* (Soveria Mannelli: Rubettino, 2002), and "Gli anni di transizione da Fanfani a Moro," in Francesco Malgeri (ed.), *Storia della Democrazia Cristiana*, vol. 3 (Rome: Cinque Lune, 1988), 5–265. Gianni Baget Bozzo, *Il partito cristiano e l'apertura a sinistra. La DC di Fanfani e Moro, 1954-1962* (Florence: Vallecchi, 1977).

21. Gianluca Scroccu, *Il partito al bivio. Il PSI dall'opposizione al governo, 1953-1963* (Rome: Carocci, 2011).

22. Guido Crainz, *Storia del miracolo italiano. Culture, identità, trasformazioni fra anni Cinquanta e Sessanta* (Rome: Donzelli, 1996).

23. Nicla Buonasorte, *Siri. Tradizione e Novecento* (Bologna: Il Mulino, 2006); Paolo Pombeni, "Aldo Moro e l'apertura a sinistra," in Renato Moro and Daniele Mezzana (eds.), *Una vita, un paese. Aldo Moro e l'Italia del 900,* (Soveria Mannelli: Rubettino, 2014), 67–96.

24. Vera Capperucci, *Il partito dei cattolici. Dall'Italia degasperiana alle correnti democristiane* (Soveria Mannelli: Rubbettino, 2010).

25. Michele Marchi, "Politica e religione dal centrismo al centro-sinistra. Luigi Gedda, i Comitati Civici, l'Azione Cattolica e la Santa Sede," *Mondo Contemporaneo* 1, 2013, 43–89; Michele Marchi, "La DC, la Chiesa e il centro-sinistra. Fanfani, Moro e "l'asse vaticano" "1959-1962," *Contemporanea* 2, 2008, 41–90.

26. Guido Formigoni and Andrea Guiso (eds.), "Tambroni e la crisi del 1960," *Ricerche di Storia Politica* 4 (2001), 361–386.

27. Enrico Galavotti, "Dell'Acqua sostituto e la politica italiana (1953-1967)," in Alberto Melloni (ed.), *Angelo Dell'Acqua. Prete, Diplomatico e Cardinale al cuore della politica vaticana, 1903-1972* (Bologna: Il Mulino, 2004), 119–160.

28. Leopoldo Nuti, *Gli Stati Uniti e l'apertura a sinistra. Importanza e limiti della presenza americana in Italia* (Rome-Bari: Laterza, 1999); Umberto Gentiloni Silveri, *L'italia e la nuova frontiera. Stati Uniti e centro-sinistra, 1958-1965* (Bologna: Il Mulino, 1988).

29. Giovanni Orsina, *L'alternativa liberale. Malagodi e l'opposizione al centro-sinistra* (Venice: Marsilio, 2010)

30. Mimmo Franzinelli and Alessandro Giacone, *Il riformismo alla prova. Il primo governo Moro nei documenti e nelle parole dei protagonisti, Ottobre 1963-Agosto 1964* (Milan: Feltrinelli, 2012)

CHAPTER 21

THE "OPENING TO THE LEFT"

ILARIA FAVRETTO

THE "opening to the left" was a key moment of transition in the Italian political system, as the Italian Socialists returned to power after over 15 years of opposition. Faced with the political and electoral crisis of the centrist formula, discussed in Chapter 20, some Christian Democrats (Democrazia Cristiana; DC) began to look at an alliance with Pietro Nenni's PSI as the way forward. The center-left formula would, they argued, provide Italian governments with a stable majority. Equally important, in the wake of the economic miracle, the inclusion of the Partito Socialista Italiano (PSI) in a coalition government was meant to secure a smooth and peaceful transition to modernity, as had previously been the case with the "Lib–Lab" alliance promoted by Giovanni Giolitti in pre-Fascist Liberal Italy.

THE "OPENING TO THE RIGHT" OPTION AND THE FAILURE OF THE TAMBRONI EXPERIMENT

The 1953–58 legislature was marked by great instability. By the mid-1950s it was obvious to many that the centrist formula had exhausted its possibilities. However, agreement ended there, as there was no consensus on the way forward: whether coalition governments should increase their majority by opening to the left, to Nenni's Socialists, or to the right, to parties such as the Monarchists and the neo-Fascists (MSI).

The opening to the right was viewed sympathetically by the Christian Democrats' right-wing factions, the Vatican, and the US Italian embassy.[1] Both Monarchists and neo-Fascists had increased their vote considerably at the 1953 elections, polling 6.9 percent and 5.8 percent respectively. Their vote shrank slightly in 1958,[2] but was still deemed sufficiently large to allow the DC to lead a stable center-right coalition government, also including the Liberals.

Numerically, this option made sense, and gained support particularly after the sorry ending of the 1958 government of Amintore Fanfani. This had been formed straight after the 1958 election and given an ambitious reformist agenda by its DC leader. However, after a few months it was deprived of a majority by the DC's internal defectors,[3] which ruled out—at least temporarily—any further flirtation with the Italian Socialists.

Nevertheless, numbers in politics are often not enough. The opening to the right was, in fact, tried out in March 1960 by the Christian Democrat Fernando Tambroni, but to no avail. After the fall of the Fanfani government, and following a short-lived administration led by Antonio Segni, Tambroni decided to challenge the anti-Fascist consensus and accepted the MSI's support for his newly formed government. This met with widespread opposition, not just within the Left but also across the political spectrum (including from sections of the DC). When, a few months after this government's formation, the MSI provocatively decided to organize their party congress in Genoa, an anti-Fascist stronghold due to the leading role played by this city in the Resistance, open protest broke out. The MSI Congress was eventually cancelled. However, the summer of 1960 was marred by escalating violence and tensions between anti-Fascist demonstrators and police. In July Tambroni was forced to resign by his own party.[4]

The brief Tambroni experiment delivered a fatal blow to the opening to the right option. Memories of Fascism were still very strong, making cooperation with the MSI taboo. In the same fashion that anti-communism ruled out the PCI's participation in government, anti-Fascism stood throughout the postwar period as an obstacle to the neo-Fascist vote being used to support faltering coalition governments. The events of the summer of 1960, therefore, revived the "opening to the left" debate, which increasingly came to be regarded as the only way out of the centrist coalition impasse.

THE ITALIAN SOCIALISTS' AUTONOMIST COURSE

The Socialists' inclusion in a coalition government would have been unthinkable in the late 1940s. After the end of Alcide De Gasperi's national coalition government in May 1947, Nenni's party followed the PCI in their Cold War-driven radicalization; throughout the reconstruction years and up to the mid-1950s, they pursued a policy of alignment with Palmiro Togliatti's Communists.[5]

Two beliefs were crucial to the PSI leadership's full adherence to Stalinism and alliance with the Communists. First, they regarded the DC and center parties as a new Fascist threat, which only a common front with the PCI could counter. The memory of the role that the disunity of working-class parties had played in the triumph of Fascism in the 1920s was still vivid.[6] Second, socialist cadres were strongly convinced of the imminence of a third world war. Key party figures who favored "autonomy" from the Communist Party, such as Riccardo Lombardi, advocated a position of neutrality. This contrasted with the PSI leadership's opinion that socialist parties throughout the world should close ranks and openly side with the country of "really existing socialism," the USSR, against the "party of war," the USA.[7]

Nenni's decision to stick to the policy of alignment with the Communists had caused the breakaway of the reformist group of Giuseppe Saragat in 1947. Equally important, it had signaled the definitive estrangement of Nenni's party from the reformist mainstream of European socialism, confirmed in 1949 by its expulsion from the Socialist International. However, the death of Stalin in 1953, and the "*disgelo*" (thaw) that de-Stalinization brought about in the international sphere, opened a new phase in the party's history. War no longer seemed so imminent.[8] Moreover, following the Soviet crushing of the Hungarian revolt in 1956 and the Khrushchev revelations in the same year, the image of the USSR as the country of "really existing Socialism" was badly tarnished.[9] The Socialists embarked upon a process of dealignment from the Communists, which was accelerated by the electoral and political crisis of the centrist formula, and the new opportunities that this presented for Nenni's party.

From 1956, Nenni's socialists, led by the autonomist faction that won the majority at the 1957 party congress, abandoned the "united front" strategy, questioned their previous assumptions and substantially revised their earlier fellow-traveler agenda. Parliamentary democracy was now accepted.[10] Italy's economic miracle and exceptional growth rates challenged the PSI's earlier belief in the inevitability of the crisis of capitalism. Capitalism was working, and had been gaining increasing stability. Most importantly, in line with other European countries, Italy had seen, in the previous few years, a considerable expansion of state intervention in the economy. The preconditions for exercising increased control of the economy had been established.

The PSI's rediscovery of a peaceful and democratic road to socialism was marred by contradictions and ambiguities. The long-term goal of socialism was not dropped; in the 1950s and 1960s most European socialist parties, whilst moving toward the center, nevertheless retained a long-term commitment to socialism, however this was defined. Nenni's change of direction in 1956 was, in fact, to bring the Socialists into line with all other Western European socialist parties, and to open the road to reunification with Saragat's Social Democrats (eventually achieved in 1966). It was also to lead to reacceptance of the PSI within the ranks of the Socialist International.

THE HISTORIOGRAPHICAL DEBATE
ON THE "OPENING TO THE LEFT"

Some scholars have recently taken issue with the dominant historiographical interpretations of post-1945 Italy which, they argue, have been far too sympathetic to left-wing parties and have intentionally ignored and downplayed alternative solutions to the opening to the left. They suggest that institutional reform, such as that carried out in Charles De Gaulle's France, could well have provided centrist coalitions with stable majorities and so made the Socialists' inclusion in a coalition government unnecessary.[11]

This view seems to forget that this approach was attempted in 1953 with no success. Faced with setbacks in the local elections of 1951 and 1952, centrist coalition parties, led by the Christian Democrats, passed an electoral law in March 1953 that assigned two thirds of the seats in Parliament to any coalition of parties securing more than 50 percent of the votes.[12] This was instantly compared with the Acerbo electoral law, passed in 1924 by Benito Mussolini, which had opened the way to his government's progress toward authoritarianism. Memories of Fascism, combined with Italy's political polarization, made this law—dubbed by its opponents a "swindle law" (legge truffa)—unacceptable, not just to opposition parties, but also to some within the centrist coalition. Prominent figures left both the Social Democrats (PSDI) and the Republican Party (PRI) to form Unità Popolare, which campaigned vigorously against the new electoral law prior to the 1953 election.[13] The centrist electoral alliance eventually failed to reach 50 percent of the vote; in the wake of the electorate's rebuttal, the law was repealed in July 1953.[14]

One should also note that, by the late 1950s, support for the opening to the left did not only come from political and electoral calculations. Advocates of the dialogue with Nenni's Socialists, such as the Republicans or left-wing Christian Democrats, believed that including the Socialists in a coalition government would also be crucial for Italy's modernization and sustained economic growth.[15]

In the wake of the economic miracle came a series of major problems, which demanded an immediate political response in terms of enacting reforms. First, from the late 1950s, wages and salaries began to rise. The increased bargaining power and strength of the trade unions, resulting from full employment, now made a strong case for an incomes policy. Second, the spurt in growth experienced by northern industries further widened the historical gap between north and south.[16] Italy's economic structure also suffered from profound sectorial imbalances. In contrast to extremely dynamic and advanced industries like those in the "industrial triangle," other sectors, such as agriculture and retailing, persisted in their backwardness and low productivity rates. Finally there was the disparity between private prosperity and low social investment, which J. K. Galbraith famously described as the "public squalor" issue.[17] State intervention was grossly inadequate in the most essential social services. While there was a growth in demand for consumer products typical of high income levels, such as luxury properties, cars, and household appliances, spending on other, far more essential, consumer products, which would have guaranteed minimum standards of living, remained under the per capita level of most developed countries in Western Europe.[18]

The unregulated framework within which Italy's economy had been expanding posed a real threat to further growth if not immediately reformed. In this context, state intervention, planning, and reform made significant inroads on the national political agenda. This was a common pattern in Western Europe and, as De Gaulle's policies in France clearly show, conservative and moderate parties could be as committed to planning and state intervention as center-left and left-wing parties. However, both the Italian Liberals and Christian Democracy's center-right factions fiercely opposed state intervention. The opening to the Socialists, and the strengthening of state interventionists within the Cabinet, was, to many, the only way by which the wealth and resources unleashed by the economic miracle could be more equitably redistributed and, more importantly, sustained in the years to come.

Republicans acted as staunch supporters of the center-left formula, particularly after the victory of Ugo La Malfa's left-wing faction at the PRI Congress in March 1960, and played a crucial role in laying the intellectual foundations of the center-left experiment. La Malfa also played an important part in fostering and facilitating the *rapprochement* between political and ideological strands—social liberalism, social reformism, and social Catholicism—that had been divided by the Cold War.[19] By the mid-1950s, planning and state intervention had, in fact, also made significant inroads in political debate within the Christian Democrats.

Christian Democracy and the Center-Left Solution

Following the victory at the 1954 DC Congress of the center-left-leaning faction Iniziativa Democratica and the election of their leader Fanfani as party secretary, the attitude of the DC toward the state underwent a substantial change. In December of that year, the Christian Democrat Finance Minister, Ezio Vanoni, announced his landmark plan, in which he introduced the guiding principle of state-managed direction of the economy. Two years later, in 1956, the Ministry of State Shareholding (Ministero delle Partecipazioni Statali) was created to oversee and coordinate the two existing giant public enterprises, the Ente Nazionale Idrocarburi (ENI) and the Istituto per la Ricostruzione Industriale (IRI), as well as the rest of the vast but rather dispersed and disconnected public sector.[20]

Fanfani's election also emboldened those sections of his party who, since 1953, had looked sympathetically on the opening to the left. The Socialists' inclusion in a coalition government, the DC's Left argued, would secure greater stability for governments, would isolate and possibly weaken the Communist Party, and, last but not least, would be crucial in carrying out a long overdue program of socioeconomic reforms.[21]

Throughout the 1950s, the opening to the left debate was extremely divisive within the Christian Democrats. The idea of an alliance with Nenni's party met with fierce resistance from the DC's center-right factions and even within Fanfani's Iniziativa Democratica itself. The latter was an extremely heterogeneous group both politically and ideologically: it included former members of Cronache Sociali, Giuseppe Dossetti's left-wing faction which had dissolved in 1949, as well as moderate Christian Democrats such as Mariano Rumor, Antonio Segni, Aldo Moro, and Emilio Colombo, who all regarded the center-left project with suspicion.[22] Moderates believed that Nenni's inclusion in a coalition government would pose a threat to Italy's commitment to NATO, as well as to traditional Catholic values.

After the 1958 election and the formation of the Fanfani government, resentment of the DC leader's domineering style (in 1958 he was prime minister, Minister for Foreign Affairs, and party leader), as well as unease about his attempt to press ahead with a shift to the left to which the party had not agreed, turned into open dissent. Fanfani's government was left short of a stable majority, and he had to resign.[23]

The election of Aldo Moro as party secretary at the 1959 DC Congress, and the rise of the newly created moderate Dorotei faction in the party's hierarchy, temporarily put the center-left project in abeyance. Moro did not, in principle, oppose the inclusion of the Socialists in a coalition government, because he appreciated that this would politically isolate the Communists and possibly weaken them electorally. However, he also knew that this was a move that could not be forced upon the party, but should be achieved by means of a strategy to gradually build consensus. He embarked on the latter, and at the eighth DC Congress, held in Naples in January 1962, the opening to the left was eventually given the go-ahead by 80 percent of party members.[24]

Moro's skillful leadership, as well as his moderate credentials, played an important role in winning over center-left skeptics. However, one should also note that, by 1962, the Vatican had also given the go-ahead to the opening to the left experiment, something that did not go unnoticed in the Christian Democrat headquarters.

THE VATICAN'S BLESSING

The death of Pius XII and the election of John XXIII in 1958 acted as a watershed. The former, an exceptionally "political" Pope,[25] who had excommunicated the Communists in 1949 and, throughout his papacy, expected the Christian Democrats to operate as the secular arm of the Church, had made no secret of Vatican opposition to the opening to the left. In 1957 the Church threw cold water on the consensus that the center-left formula had been gaining in the Catholic world and within some sections of the DC, when the ban on the cooperation of Catholics with Marxist-inspired political parties was reiterated.[26]

However, the pontificate of John XXIII signaled a new era in state–Church relations and the beginning of a process of the Church's disengagement from Italian politics. As the Pope put it to Fanfani during a private conversation in April 1961, "the 'two banks of the Tiber' [the Vatican and Montecitorio, the seat of secular power] [are] united in their respect for shared values, but aware that their areas of competence and objectives are very different."[27] Two years later, the encyclical *Pacem in Terris* (1963) was to state formally the Church's neutrality in politics and to advocate the return to a more spiritual role for religious organizations. Decolonization was then in full swing, and for the

Church to retain some influence in the newly created independent states it was crucial that it placed itself above the US–USSR divide.[28]

The loosening of the Church's grip on Italian politics was not a smooth process and, as scholars have emphasized, enemies of the center-left formula continued to abound within the Italian episcopate.[29] However, from 1961 onwards, the Vatican took a number of symbolic steps that suggested that the veto on the opening to the left had been lifted, or at least softened. In particular, in May 1961, the Pope published the encyclical *Mater Magistra*, which stated the Church's condemnation of the worst abuses and wastes of capitalism and the need for some form of regulation. This provided center-left advocates in the Catholic world with moral legitimacy and support. A few months later, Pasquale Saraceno, a leading economist who spent most of his intellectual life searching for a Catholic "third way," was invited to give a speech at the DC conference of September 1961 in San Pellegrino on the state's right to intervene in guiding the economy.[30] Left to itself, he argued, the market had exacerbated rather than resolved the geographical and sectorial imbalances of the Italian economy. The state had to intervene by means of economic planning in order to ensure balanced development.

THE UNITED STATES AND THE CENTER-LEFT

The hostility of the American embassy to the opening to the left strengthened the hand of center-left opponents throughout the 1950s and, at the very least, suggested some caution to center-left advocates within Christian Democracy. Recent research has shown how the US attitude toward the opening to the left was not as unwavering as it has long been depicted. We now know that, from 1953, units such as the Office of Intelligence Research in Washington looked at the center-left as a possible option to resolve the centrist impasse.[31] Interestingly, in the mid-1950s the British embassy in Rome also began to look at the opening to the left as the most effective and possibly only way of containing the Communists; for this reason the British ambassador cooperated closely with the British Labour Party, and indirectly with the Socialist International, with a view to facilitating and accelerating Nenni's break from the Communists and the PSI's reunification with Saragat's PSDI.[32] However, Clare Boothe Luce, the US ambassador in Rome, was vehemently anti-communist and had no time for Washington speculations about the Socialists' trustworthiness: throughout her stay at the embassy (May 1953 to December 1956) she kept her door firmly closed to center-left supporters of any kind.[33]

By 1962, though, the US attitude toward the center-left had changed considerably. The election of Kennedy and the return of the Democrats to the White House in January 1961, resulted in a more open attitude toward Nenni's Socialists. The center-left formula was consistent with Kennedy's "New Frontier" philosophy and was now regarded as the best way forward for Italian politics,[34] both because it would result in governmental stability and because the newly formed center-left government was expected to implement a wide-ranging and ambitious program of social reforms and modernization, thereby reversing the Communists' electoral growth.

Hesitation and suspicion did not, however, completely evaporate. The State Department's Italian desk and a number of officials at the Rome embassy remained highly skeptical of the opening to the left solution. The biggest fear was that a center-left government might result in the loosening of Italy's commitment to the Western bloc. However, Nenni had, by then, formally accepted Italian membership of both NATO and the European Community.[35] Moreover, De Gaulle's anti-Americanism and neutralist leanings, which had in fact met some sympathy in certain factions of the DC,[36] had clearly shown that moderate and conservative parties could pose a similar and possibly more insidious threat to US foreign policy than their center-left counterparts.

THE BIRTH OF THE CENTER-LEFT

By 1962, the center-left formula had the informal blessing of the US and the Vatican, and the formal support of the DC. In March 1962, Fanfani formed a government that included Christian Democrats, the PSDI, and the PRI, while the PSI abstained from voting against this.

This was a sort of hybrid center-left as the Socialists were not yet included in the coalition government. However, the first ten months of the Fanfani government are widely regarded in the literature as the most vibrant, and possibly the only, dynamic phase of the whole center-left experience. Two key (and highly controversial) reforms were carried out in areas that had long dominated Italian political debate: the nationalization of the electricity industry and the establishment of a single compulsory school system for children aged 11 to 14 (the *scuola media unica*).[37] Ugo La Malfa was appointed budget minister; the "Nota aggiuntiva" (additional note) that he presented to accompany his "General Report on the Economic Situation of the Country in 1961"[38] is generally considered to be one of the key documents that laid the theoretical and empirical foundations for economic planning in 1960s Italy, together with the Giolitti Plan (1965) and the Pieraccini Plan (1966–70). The main objectives remained virtually unchanged in all of them: the achievement of full employment, the elimination of both sectorial imbalances between industry and agriculture and regional differences, and a better balance between private and public consumption.

The Christian Democrats' U-turn over the issues of regional government and urban planning reform, to which we shall return in the following section, 'The 1963–68 center-left governments', further alienated left-wing factions within the Socialists from the center-left formula, and triggered tensions within the autonomist faction itself. However, Nenni's autonomist group succeeded once again in winning a majority, albeit slight, at the October 1963 party congress.[39] Two months later, in December 1963, the first center-left government including Socialists in the Cabinet was at last formed by the DC leader Aldo Moro. The program put forward in January 1964 during Moro's presentation of the new Cabinet to parliament included a wide and ambitious range of measures: planning, agrarian reform, municipal reform, educational reform, fiscal reform, and a package of anti-monopoly laws. Not without reason, it was dubbed by the Liberal leader Giovanni Malagodi "short observations on the universe."[40]

THE 1963–68 CENTER-LEFT GOVERNMENTS

For all the expectations that the opening to the left had raised—if only because of the length of its gestation period—the 1963–68 center-left legislature proved a source of major disappointment. This is reflected in the way the literature labels these years as characterized by "missed political opportunity,"[41] "missed reforms,"[42] "directionless progress,"[43] and "reformism without reforms."[44]

The center-left governments have, in fact, a more mixed record than these assessments suggest. By the end of the legislature some important pieces of social legislation had been passed, notably the reform of mental institutions in July 1967, and, in 1968, the establishment of state nursery schools and pensions reform.[45] However, there is no doubt that these governments failed to deliver on most of the defining items of their promised agenda, and in particular on planning reform, which was left unimplemented. In the space that remains I will summarize the factors that contributed to undermining the center-left experiment at the very time of its inception (1962–64).

Scholars of post-1945 Italy have, in general, not been lenient toward the Christian Democrats, and, when it comes to the 1960s, most explanations of the center-left governments' sorry record emphasize the role played by the DC and its "*riformismo senza riforme*" (reformism without reforms) attitude. The Christian Democrats, it has been argued, eventually came to support the opening to the left merely out of political calculation, hoping that the Socialists' inclusion in a coalition would secure greater governmental stability, halt communist electoral growth, break the PSI–PCI alliance, and, by so doing, defuse the threat of an alternative left-wing government. With the exception of left-wing factions within the DC, such as La Base, the large majority of the party was firmly anchored to the political center ground and wary of the risks that the opening to the left posed to their popular support.

The local elections held in June 1962, three months after the formation of the Fanfani government, provided a salutary warning for the Christian Democrats: the alliance with the Socialists led to a loss of almost 2 percent, mainly to parties to the right of the DC such as the Liberals. Gains were not, however, made among the moderate left-wing electorate, which tended to favor the PSDI: Saragat's party grew by almost 2 percent. The April 1963 national elections dealt a further blow to Christian Democracy, whose vote declined from 42.3 percent (1958) to 38.3 percent. Again, this worked to the advantage of Malagodi's Liberals, who in 1963 doubled their vote by polling 7 percent; this was the best result that they ever achieved in the post-1945 period.[46]

The message was clear. If the DC's electoral base was to be preserved, no further concessions should be made to the PSI and to the reformists' agenda. And so it was. During the 1962 Fanfani government, the party had already disowned and rejected the urban planning reform put forward in Parliament by the left-wing Christian Democrat Minister of Public Works Fiorentino Sullo in July of that year. In subsequent years the moderate Dorotei faction, which kept firm control over the party leadership throughout the center-left period, would do their best to halt or water down any piece of legislation regarded as too threatening to the DC's traditional electorate.[47]

This brings us to another factor often highlighted in the literature to explain the center-left government's mixed record, namely the exceptional strength within the Italian economic structure of the "backward" sectors, and the fierce resistance they offered to reform.[48] Center-left policies were to be of great advantage to the advanced industrial sector. Large companies such as Fiat and Pirelli depended heavily on exports and looked to the center-left agenda and to planning and investment in public housing, public transport, and improved welfare as effective ways of containing the cost of labor (and, indirectly, production costs). Moreover, they hoped that Socialist participation in a coalition government would facilitate better relationships with the unions at a time of growing industrial unrest and, possibly, the implementation of an incomes policy. Lastly, they believed that investment in research and education would provide highly technological industries with skilled and properly trained manpower.

However, center-left reforms had little to offer, and in fact posed a threat, to sectors of Italian society such as small businesses, shopkeepers, and rural smallholders. Due to the patchy development of Italian capitalism, these were all still of a significant size and were electorally very influential.[49] The attitude of Confindustria, the Italian Employers Federation, is revealing in this regard. Dominated by small-scale entrepreneurs, throughout the 1950s Confindustria opposed the center-left option, and, when this became a reality, they adopted a rather confrontational attitude. The formation in 1962 of the Fanfani government triggered an unprecedented flight of capital.[50] Moreover, during the 1962–63 period, the Bank of Italy exerted increasing pressure on the Christian Democrats to contain reformism by deflationary measures.

By early 1963, the economy had deteriorated considerably. The increasingly large balance of payments deficit and growing inflation, both partly the outcome of wage increases that resulted from the labor demands of 1962, became matters of concern and alarm. Proposals to implement deflationary measures were increasingly discussed within Italian economic and political elites. In the autumn of 1963, the Leone government, a short-lived (June–December 1963) DC-only administration, which was quickly formed in April 1963 to fill the political vacuum created by the election and ongoing negotiations between the DC and the PSI, passed an exceptionally harsh austerity budget. As the memoirs of the then head of the Bank of Italy, Guido Carli, reveal, deflationary measures were then designed to tackle Italy's balance of payments crisis, but also, if not mostly, to "rebalance power relations in favor of the entrepreneurial world and away from the possibility that the Socialists, especially the super-interventionists such as Antonio Giolitti, joined the government."[51]

The deflationary measures introduced in 1963 delivered a fatal blow to the center-left's reforms and provided the context in which, a few months after the formation of the December 1963 center-left government, Aldo Moro coined the notorious formula of the "*politica dei due tempi*" (two-stage policy).[52] In his opinion, the government should prioritize anti-inflationary measures and leave long-term reforms for a time when economic recovery had been achieved. The center-left formula survived, but it was to become an increasingly empty vessel.

Another factor that may explain the center-left's mixed record is that the DC's coalition allies, including the Socialists, played far too subordinate a role in the coalition to be able to challenge the Christian Democrats' "minimalist" notion of reforms. When Nenni's party entered the Moro government in December 1963, its electoral weight was 13.8 percent in contrast to the DC's 38.3 percent.[53] Furthermore, Nenni's party was by then deeply divided. The Fanfani government of 1962 had put considerable strain on the autonomist faction. Although Lombardi voted in favor of Nenni's line at the PSI's 1963 Congress, he refused to join him in the December 1963 Moro government.[54] Nenni's troubles did not end there. In January 1964, one month later, the party's left-wing factions, having opposed coalition membership at the October 1963 Congress, decided to break away and form the PSIUP.[55] This, of course, further weakened the Socialists' bargaining power within the coalition.

The influence exerted by political parties in a coalition government is not always directly related to their electoral strength. However, Nenni's room for maneuver was fairly limited. By 1964, fears had grown that Italian democracy might not survive the political mayhem that the Socialists' decision to abandon their center-left strategy would have created. In June 1964, the Socialists, Social Democrats, and Republicans opposed a Christian Democrat-sponsored bill on state funding for private education, and the Moro government resigned. When Moro started negotiations to form a second administration, the agenda Socialists were asked to agree was far more moderate than that of his first government. In particular, urban planning reform and the creation of regions had been dropped. Weeks passed with no agreement, until, in July 1964, a new government finally emerged. As Nenni famously wrote in his memoirs, in the background of negotiations Socialists could hear a distinct "*rumor di sciabole*" (rattle of sabers). [56] He referred to the machinations exposed in 1967 in a series of articles in the left-wing weekly *Espresso*, and known as the Piano Solo: in the summer of 1964, led by General Giovanni De Lorenzo, the *carabinieri* (military police) were preparing to step into the political vacuum and support a new Tambroni-like center-right government, or possibly a coup.[57] The "authoritarian threat," which the Socialists believed would engulf Italian democracy if they rejected the DC's requests, prevented the PSI from wielding the kind of power that is typical of relatively small parties in sustaining a coalition government, and that the party would come to have in the 1980s.[58]

Most of the reforms promoted by center-left supporters were designed to modernize the economy and secure balanced growth and better allocation of resources in the future. However, in the context of the exceptional polarization that marked the Italian political landscape, hostile media successfully portrayed these reforms as a prelude to Socialism. Nenni's party did, of course, play its part, as the Socialists cloaked their proposed reforms with profuse radical rhetoric; scholars have described this as their "*ideologismo dimostrativo*" (ostentatious radicalism).[59] The very same reforms that the Republicans and Christian Democrats described as "corrective" were presented by the Socialists as "structural," that is, as reforms that would not just correct the imbalances of Italy's economy, but change the very nature of Italian capitalism.[60] The revolutionary tones used by the PSI provided opponents of the center-left coalition with powerful ammunition and played a crucial role in undermining its legitimacy with the wider public.

In the eyes of some historians, the PSI position amounted to weak reformist culture, a historical anomaly in relation to other European socialist parties due to the prominence, right from the party's foundation, of radical maximalist tendencies within their ideological baggage.[61] Such an interpretation carries some elements of truth. However, one should not forget the electoral competition from the PCI. Up to 1962, the attitude of Togliatti's party toward the opening to the left was one of "wait and see." However, particularly after the 1963 deflationary measures and the DC's U-turn on policies such as urban planning reform, the Communists became more confrontational and adopted increasingly hostile tones toward the center-left governments.[62] This put the PSI in a rather unfortunate electoral position: over the decade it was not to win any votes to its right, while it lost considerable support from the electorate to the left. Those to gain were the PCI, whose support grew from 22.7 percent in the 1959 election to 25.3 percent in 1963, 26.9 percent in 1968, and 27.2 percent in 1972,[63] and the PSIUP, which scored 4.5 percent in 1968, although in 1972 this fell to 1.9 percent, to the advantage of the PCI and minor radical groups such as Il Manifesto.[64] After the 1972 elections, the Socialists' leader Francesco De Martino famously stated that the PSI would stop shaking the tree only for the PCI to pick up the fruit.

For all the radical rhetoric utilized by the Socialists in the years when they were promoting the center-left agenda, and the scaremongering warnings of center-left opponents, the center-left years in fact amount to a period of extremely mild reformism. Scholars of post-1945 Italian history have pointed to the ineffectiveness of center-left governments in addressing the sectorial and territorial imbalances exacerbated by the economic miracle, and to their failure to implement long-overdue reforms in the areas of public housing, health, and education, as key factors that explain the radicalization of Italian society and polarization of Italian politics in later years.[65] The end of the 1963–68 legislature coincided with widespread mobilization both among students and factory workers: the scale of protest would be exceptional compared to most European countries, both in scale and duration. This will be the focus of the next chapter.

Notes

1. Leopoldo Nuti, *Gli Stati Uniti e l'apertura a sinistra. Importanza e limiti della presenza americana in Italia* (Rome and Bari: Laterza, 1999).

2. Martin Clark, *Modern Italy 1871–1995* (London: Longman, 1997 (1st edn. 1984)), 328.

3. Yannis Voulgaris, *L'Italia del centro-sinistra, 1960–1968* (Rome: Carocci, 1998), 90.

4. Paul Ginsborg, *A History of Contemporary Italy* (Harmondsworth: Penguin, 1990), 347–348.

5. Paolo Mattera, *Il partito inquieto. Organizzazione, passioni e politica dei socialisti italiani dalla Resistenza al miracolo economico* (Rome: Carocci, 2004), chs 4, 5, and 6.

6. Maurizio Degl'Innocenti, *Storia del PSI dal dopoguerra ad oggi* (Rome and Bari: Laterza, 1993), 34.

7. Giovanni Scirocco, *"Politique d'abord." Il PSI, la Guerra fredda e la politica internazionale (1948–1957)* (Milan: Unicopli, 2010), 136.

8. Ibid., 137.

9. Pietro Nenni, "Luci e ombre del congresso di Mosca," *Mondo Operaio*, 9 (March 1956), 146–154.

10. Ilaria Favretto, *Alle radici della svolta autonomista. PSI e Labour Party, due vicende parallele* (Rome: Carocci, 2003); and Albertina Vittoria, "Organizzazione e istituti della cultura," in *Storia dell'Italia repubblicana*, vol. 2 (tomo 1): *La trasformazione dell'Italia: sviluppo e squilibri* (Turin: Einaudi, 1995), 637–703.

11. Giovanni Orsina, "Il sistema politico: lineamenti di un'interpretazione revisionistica," in Pier Luigi Ballini, Sandro Guerrieri, and Antonio Varsori (eds.), *Le istituzioni repubblicane dal centrismo al centro-sinistra (1953–1968)* (Rome: Carocci, 2006), 309–333.

12. Domenico Rosati, *Biografia del centro-sinistra (1945–1995)* (Palermo: Sellerio, 1996), 53.

13. Francesco Barbagallo, *L'Italia repubblicana. Dallo sviluppo alle riforme mancate (1945–2008)* (Rome: Carocci, 2009), 48.

14. Maria Serena Piretti, *La legge truffa. Il fallimento dell'ingegneria politica* (Bologna: Il Mulino, 2003).

15. Franco De Felice, "Nazione e sviluppo: un nodo non sciolto," in *Storia dell'Italia repubblicana*, vol. 2 (tomo 1), 783–882, 783ff.

16. Giorgio Fuà and Paolo Sylos Labini, *Idee per la programmazione economica* (Rome and Bari: Laterza, 1963), 22–25.

17. John K. Galbraith, *The Affluent Society* (London: Hamish Hamilton, 1958—Italian transl.: *Economia e benessere*, ed. di Comunità, Milan, 1959).

18. Carmela D'Apice, *L'arcipelago dei consumi. Consumi e redditi delle famiglie italiane dal dopoguerra a oggi* (Bari: De Donato, 1981), 39–40.

19. Vittoria, "Organizzazione e istituti della cultura," 638–648.

20. Francesco Malgeri, *La stagione del centrismo. Politica e società nell'Italia del secondo dopoguerra (1945-1960)* (Soveria Mannelli: Rubbettino, 2002), 277–281.

21. Agostino Giovagnoli, *Il partito italiano. La Democrazia cristiana dal 1942 al 1994* (Rome and Bari: Laterza, 1996); Voulgaris, *L'Italia del centro-sinistra, 1960–1968*, 23–24.

22. Francesco Malgeri, "Cambiamenti sociali e mutamenti politici: il partito di maggioranza," in Ballini, Guerrieri, and Varsori (eds.), *Le istituzioni repubblicane dal centrismo al centro-sinistra (1953–1968)*, 334–350, 335.

23. Nicola Tranfaglia, "La modernità squilibrata. Dalla crisi del centrismo al 'compromesso storico,'" in *Storia dell'Italia repubblicana*, vol. 2 (tomo 1), 7–111, 30–31.

24. Voulgaris, *L'Italia del centro-sinistra, 1960–1968*, 13.

25. Malgeri, *La stagione del centrismo*, 322.

26. Michele Marchi, "La DC, la Chiesa e il centro-sinistra: Fanfani e l'asse vaticano," 1959–1962," *Mondo contemporaneo*, no. 2 (2008), 41–90, 45.

27. Ibid., 39.

28. Ibid., 41–90.

29. Guido Verucci, "La Chiesa postconciliare," in *Storia dell'Italia repubblicana*, vol. 2 (tomo 1), 303.

30. Pasquale Saraceno, *"Lo Stato e l'economia," relazione al I° Convegno Nazionale di Studio della Democrazia Cristiana, San Pellegrino, 13–16 settembre 1961* (Rome: Edizioni Cinque Lune, 1963). The speech is also included in Pasquale Saraceno, *L'Italia verso la piena occupazione* (Milan: Feltrinelli, 1963).

31. Mario Del Pero, "Gli Stati Uniti e il dilemma italiano," in Ballini, Guerrieri, and Varsori (eds.), *Le istituzioni repubblicane dal centrismo al centro-sinistra (1953-1968)*, 212–226, 213.

32. Ilaria Favretto, "La nascita del centro-sinistra e la Gran Bretagna. Partito socialista, laburisti, Foreign Office," *Italia Contemporanea*, no. 202 (1996), 5–43.

33. Nuti, *Gli Stati Uniti e l'apertura a sinistra*.

34.. Ibid.

35. Pietro Nenni, "Where the Italian Socialists Stand," *Foreign Affairs*, no. 2 (November 1962). On this see also Giovanni Scirocco, "Il PSI dall'antiatlantismo alla riscoperta dell'Europa (1948–1957)," in Piero Craveri and Gaetano Quagliariello (eds.), *Atlantismo ed Europeismo* (Soveria Mannelli: Rubbettino, 2003), 135–204.

36. Massimo de Leonardis, "L'Atlantismo dell'Italia tra guerra fredda, interessi nazionali e politica interna," in *Storia dell'Italia repubblicana*, vol. 2 (tomo 1), 253–271, 259–261.

37. Giuseppe Ricuperati, "La politica scolastica," in *Storia dell'Italia repubblicana*, vol. 2 (tomo 1), 707–778.

38. Ugo La Malfa, *Verso la politica di piano* (Naples: Edizioni Scientifiche Italiane, 1962).

39. Gianluca Scroccu, *Il partito al bivio. Il PSI dall'opposizione al governo (1953–1963)* (Rome: Carocci, 2011), 331–338.

40. Giuseppe Tamburrano, *Storia e cronaca del centro-sinistra* (Milan: Rizzoli, 1984), 276.

41. Ginsborg, *A History of Contemporary Italy*, 283.

42. De Felice, "Nazione e sviluppo: un nodo non sciolto," 859. See also Massimiliano Amato and Marcello Ravveduto, *Riformismo mancato. Società, consumi e politica nell'Italia del miracolo* (Rome: Castelvecchi Editore, 2014).

43. Cecilia Dau Novelli, *Politica e nuove identità nell'Italia del "miracolo"* (Rome: Studium, 1999), 18.

44. Guido Crainz, *Storia del miracolo italiano. Culture, identità, trasformazioni fra anni cinquanta e sessanta* (Rome: Donzelli, 2005 (1st edn. 1996)), part VI: "Il riformismo perduto." For similar interpretations see also Guido Crainz, *Il paese mancato. Dal miracolo economico agli anni ottanta* (Rome: Donzelli, 2005 (1st edn. 2003)); Barbagallo, *L'Italia repubblicana*, 79, 87–88; Tranfaglia, "La modernità squilibrata," 75.

45. Degl'Innocenti, *Storia del PSI dal dopoguerra ad oggi*, 382–383.

46. Tranfaglia, "La modernità squilibrata," 62.

47. Voulgaris, *L'Italia del centro-sinistra, 1960–1968*, 200.

48. Barbagallo, *L'Italia repubblicana. Dallo sviluppo alle riforme mancate (1945–2008)*, 88.

49. Tamburrano, *Storia e cronaca del centro-sinistra*, 355.

50. Voulgaris, *L'Italia del centro-sinistra, 1960–1968*, 137.

51. Guido Carli, *Cinquant'anni di vita italiana* (Rome and Bari: Laterza, 1993).

52. De Felice, "Nazione e sviluppo: un nodo non sciolto," 835.

53. Tamburrano, *Storia e cronaca del centro-sinistra*, 233.

54. Andrea Ricciardi, "Riccardo Lombardi e l'apertura a sinistra, 1956–1964," in Andrea Ricciardi and Giovanni Scirocco (eds.), *Per una società diversamente ricca. Scritti in onore di Riccardo Lombardi* (Rome: Edizioni di Storia e Letteratura Roma, 2004), 63–112.

55. Aldo Agosti, *Il partito provvisorio. Storia del Psiup nel lungo Sessantotto italiano* (Rome and Bari: Laterza, 2013); on the PSIUP see also Anna Celadin, *Mondo Nuovo e le origini del PSIUP. La vicenda socialista dal 1963 al 1967* (Rome: Ediesse, 2006).

56. Ricciardi, "Riccardo Lombardi e l'apertura a sinistra, 1956–1964," 98.

57. Mimmo Franzinelli, *Il Piano Solo. I servizi segreti, il centro-sinistra e il "golpe" del 1964* (Milan: Mondadori, 2010).

58. Marco Gervasoni and Simona Colarizi, *La cruna dell'ago. Craxi, il partito socialista e la crisi della Repubblica* (Rome and Bari: Laterza, 2006).

59. Giuseppe Vacca, "Introduzione. Per la storia del centro-sinistra," in Voulgaris, *L'Italia del centro-sinistra, 1960–1968*, p. xviii.

60. Antonio Giolitti, *Riforme e Rivoluzione* (Turin: Einaudi, 1957); Simona Colarizi (ed.), *Riccardo Lombardi. Scritti politici 1945–1963. Dalla Resistenza al centro-sinistra* (Venice: Marsilio, 1978).

61. See, for instance, Marco Gervasoni (ed.), *Riformismo socialista e Italia repubblicana* (Milan: MBPublishing, 2005), 7–18, 7 and 14; Luciano Cafagna, *Una strana disfatta* (Venice: Marsilio, 1996), 100; and Giovanni Sabbatucci, *Il riformismo impossibile. Storia del socialismo italiano* (Rome and Bari: Laterza, 1991).

62. Ermanno Taviani, "Le riforme del centro-sinistra," in Ballini, Guerrieri, and Varsori (eds.), *Le istituzioni repubblicane dal centrismo al centro-sinistra (1953–1968)*, 360–386, 379.

63. Giorgio Galli, *Storia del socialismo italiano* (Rome and Bari: Laterza, 1980), 132, 160.

64. Ibid., 160.

65. Crainz, *Il paese mancato*.

CHAPTER 22

···

THE *COMPROMESSO STORICO*

···

STEPHEN HELLMAN

THE historic compromise (*compromesso storico*) was, strictly speaking, simply the strategy of the Italian Communist Party (PCI) through most of the 1970s. This strategy failed. Yet it deserves attention because of its influence on Italian politics between the end of the center-left and the beginning of the *pentapartito*.

This was a period of monumental upheavals that saw Italy's economic, social, and political equilibria dramatically altered. Labor militancy rose dramatically through the 1960s, and was reaching outside the workplace (e.g. housing, transport, pensions) by the end of the decade. A student movement disrupted high schools as well as Italy's rapidly expanding universities. Militancy spilled out of schools and workplaces, into the streets (squatters' and tenants' movements) but also into professional organizations (magistrates, the military, prisons).[1] By the end of the 1960s, a right-wing backlash increased polarization, and fears for the stability of democratic institutions. The 1969 bombing of a bank in Milan killed 17 people and signaled the start of a decade-long overt assault on Italian democracy that became known as "the strategy of tension."[2] As the massive mobilizations began to wane in the early 1970s, violence between left-and right-wing groups increased dramatically, and the neo-fascist Italian Social Movement (MSI) made unprecedented electoral gains in the south.

The already-tense political equilibrium of the 1960s broke down, producing a stalemate and early elections in 1972 that resolved nothing, and seemingly strengthened the hand of the far right and the most conservative elements in the government. And these events were all well underway *before* the first "oil shock" of 1973—following the destabilization of global exchange rates two years earlier—threw economies into a crisis that would last until the end of the decade.

The *compromesso* was first spelled out in its entirety in 1973, though its outlines were clear a year earlier.[3] The PCI came closest to implementing the *compromesso* between 1976 and 1979, when it became part of the governing majority, but it never got farther than providing external support to Christian Democratic (DC) governments. These (two) governments lasted from mid-1976 until the very beginning of 1979, when the frustrated PCI finally withdrew its support, forcing new elections. It abandoned the *compromesso* not long afterward. Three phases characterize events between 1972/73 and 1980.

THE BIRTH OF THE HISTORIC COMPROMISE

The breakthroughs of the mid-1970s—the referendum upholding divorce and the 1975 local, and 1976 general, elections—followed the upheavals of a few years earlier. But this complex period emitted confusing signals. The trade unions, divided along political lines since 1950, appeared to be uniting, which would increase their already-formidable bargaining (and disruptive) leverage. And various new movements seemed to herald unstoppable social change. Yet this period also witnessed a powerful anti-left, anti-worker reaction by parts of the middle strata, and mass discontent in the south, ably manipulated by the MSI. The "strategy of tension," aimed at destabilizing the country and provoking a coup, appeared to have support in some parts of the military and security apparatuses.

Then, the 1972 general elections, following the most sustained popular mobilization in postwar history, offered no comfort at all to the left. The Italian Socialist Party (PSI), coming off its second split in less than a decade, slipped to 10 percent. The far left was so fragmented that a million votes produced not a single seat. The PCI barely held its own. The biggest winner was the MSI, reaching an historic high (nearly 9 percent). When the battered Socialists refused to rejoin the DC in a re-edition of the center-left, the old centrist formula was resuscitated.

Enrico Berlinguer had assumed leadership of the PCI in 1972, and had struck a cautious tone from the very start.[4] These elections confirmed his wariness. Then, in September 1973, Chile's elected Socialist government was violently overthrown. Berlinguer immediately produced three articles in the PCI weekly entitled "Reflections on Italy after the Events in Chile," in which he laid out the *compromesso storico*.[5] He had been making the broad points for over a year, but now he articulated the strategy systematically. Being democratically elected had not saved the Unidad Popular government from being smashed by a reactionary coup, Berlinguer stated: even an absolute majority could not guarantee success for a program of serious reforms. Italy, he asserted, could avoid worsening an already serious crisis only if the country's three great "democratic and popular" forces—Communists, Socialists, and Catholics—worked together. This would require long-term collaboration, demanding significant compromises on the part of all actors, and the PCI was willing to play its part.

Global events then provided further dramatic punctuation: the October 1973 OPEC oil embargo quadrupled petroleum prices. Inflation soared, and struggling economies saw a simultaneous drop in investments and productivity, contributing to the phenomenon of "stagflation." In these generally dismal conditions, Italy stood out: its inflation rate moved into double digits, where it would remain for the rest of the decade.[6] Because of the crisis, the PCI leadership, and much of the rank and file, quickly accepted the new strategy, even though the compromises Berlinguer called for implied the need for restraint on the part of many of the party's constituents, starting with the working class.

To be sure, Berlinguer was not simply promising to bring the unions to heel as the price for admitting the PCI into the government. He made clear that, in exchange for restraint, which would be necessary to dampen runaway inflation, investments and policies would be required that favored the least well-off strata, above all in the south, while extensive institutional reforms would be required to guarantee democratic stability. Still, this was a departure from the PCI's (and the unions') previous attitudes. And there is no question that to have the Communist Party acknowledge that austerity and rigor were required to confront such serious challenges exerted an appeal well beyond the PCI's usual bases of support.

The strategy raised questions from the beginning. How far had the PCI moved away from the USSR? How committed was it to liberal democratic norms? The mid-seventies were the heyday of what became known as "Eurocommunism," named for the apparent increasingly Western orientation of the Communist Parties of Western Europe. The PCI was the largest by far of these parties (in membership and in its share of the vote) and, for that reason alone, attracted the most attention.[7] When it surged to over a third of the vote, the focus on Italian Communism grew even more. Indeed, by 1976, Berlinguer went so far as to say that he felt safer under NATO's umbrella than he would under a destabilized international system. This was a dramatic departure from pro-Soviet orthodoxy and reflected the party leadership's commitment to increasing the PCI's legitimacy, and democratic *bona fides*.

But in 1973 and 1974, even sympathetic observers could wonder whether the PCI was "crying crisis" as a way to obtain at least a share of political power without having to undertake a dramatic makeover. Moreover, proposing to save Italian democracy by relying on the established mass parties suggested a vision of a country unaltered over recent decades.[8] The parties were indeed well rooted, and exerted significant control through their numerous flanking organizations—but had nothing changed since 1945? What did the *compromesso* therefore suggest about the PCI's understanding of Christian Democracy? The DC was not simply a den of thieves or mere patronage dispensers. But would this complex political organization be willing to reform the very system of power it had spent three decades constructing? The *compromesso* was not proposing radical changes, but it did demand reformed management of society and the economy. Yet many of the DC's factions depended, for their survival and competitive edge, on the exact opposite of the discipline and much more efficient management of resources that such reforms implied.

Thanks to the electoral advances of 1975–76, the Communists could avoid having to question their assumptions. These gains came after the PCI's moderate strategy was put forward, and party leaders took that as evidence of growing public support for the *compromesso*. Moreover, the PCI seriously misinterpreted those new votes.[9] Rather than grasp that most new supporters were *opinion* voters, persuaded by the party's proposals in a given moment, these new electors were viewed as the same as the PCI's traditional supporters. The latter's loyalty could be assumed through thick and thin, as votes "belonging" to the party (*voti di appartenenza*). This mistaken conviction, which I heard often in the mid-1970s, was built on past experience as well as wishful thinking. It would cost the PCI dearly.

Although Berlinguer referred to *three* "great historic forces," his real target was the DC. The PSI was viewed as having dissipated its once-great heritage in the 1960s, between subordination to the DC and two crippling schisms. Its pivotal position between the PCI and DC gave it considerable leverage, but the Socialists also repeatedly found that their location could be extremely perilous.[10] By the early 1970s, when the PCI was taking the PSI for granted, it often barely hid its dismissive—or contemptuous—attitude. Bettino Craxi, who became PSI secretary in 1976, never forgot this.[11] Yet while personal resentment may have played a role in the parties' interaction, it is important to understand that the Socialists were in an impossible position. If the *compromesso storico* were ever realized, the PSI would be crushed between Italy's "two Churches." And if the strategy indeed signaled a speed-up in the PCI's democratic evolution, what would become of the PSI, less than half the Communists' size?

The Socialists carried out several ideological and strategic flip-flops in the course of the 1970s.[12] Some were sincere, and some were cynical maneuvers aimed at embarrassing the Communists. Some indicated that the PSI actually understood—as the PCI and DC did not—that Italy had changed in ways that rendered many old assumptions obsolete. But all grew out of the PSI's desperate need to carve out an autonomous identity for itself.

POLITICAL TURMOIL AND STALEMATE

By the mid-1970s, right-wing threats subsided and the winds of change blew more strongly. The 1974 referendum to abolish divorce witnessed a dramatic 41–59 percent failure for the DC. This was a watershed in Italian history, for what it revealed about the diminished role of the Church in Italian society and, more broadly, as a harbinger of changes anticipated since the 1960s. Yet even as the PCI celebrated this victory, its cautious reading of events continued. For instance, immediately after the referendum, Berlinguer warned his party to expect a conservative counteroffensive.[13]

Local elections in 1975 then saw the Communist vote draw within 2 percent of the DC, which led to speculation whether they would "overtake" the DC in the 1976 general elections. The PCI did reach its historic high (34.4 percent) in 1976, but the DC recuperated almost all the previous year's losses—by draining votes from its smaller allies and the MSI. The Socialists slipped below 10 percent, producing a dramatic shakeup that brought Craxi and a group of younger leaders to the helm.

The result was a parliamentary standoff: a center-left coalition remained numerically possible, but after their bitter experience between 1964 and 1972, the Socialists had sworn never again to join a government that excluded the PCI. The PSI's call in this period for a "left alternative" sounds quite radical, but it was ambiguous by design. Left-wing

Socialists very much hoped for a unified left alliance, like the one being constructed in France between Communists and Socialists at the time. But many Socialists wished for no such alliance, and deeply distrusted the PCI, or simply feared that their party would inevitably lose if it embraced the much larger, better-organized Communists. Their interpretation of the "left alternative" was conditional: if the PCI *eventually* changed, they then could support an alliance. Neither position mattered to the PCI. Simply put, "the left" did not figure in the *compromesso*, which consciously obscured the likely polarization that invoking left and right would create. Only the unity of *all* "democratic and popular" forces could guarantee democracy's survival and the implementation of much-needed reforms.[14]

Three years after the *compromesso storico* was first enunciated, the stage was set for something new, but not exactly what Berlinguer had hoped for: national solidarity.

NATIONAL SOLIDARITY (1976–79)

The divorce referendum was only the most dramatic sign of increasing secularization. For the DC, secularization also meant the decline of Catholic flanking organizations, particularly student and working-class organizations, historic training grounds of party leaders. The DC was divided over how to proceed, but all contending factions—and they were numerous—agreed that the unity of the party, and its centrality in the system it had shaped for 30 years, was absolutely essential. Reform-minded Catholics who believed that a true reform of the DC would require ridding the party of its most corrupt and compromised elements were either outside the DC or represented a small and relatively isolated internal fringe.[15]

Aldo Moro was no exception, despite espousing an "encounter" with the Communists. He had a clear sense of the need to collaborate with the PCI. But it is hard to argue with Paul Ginsborg's assessment that Moro's vision was framed "in the honoured tradition of Italian *trasformismo*," that countenanced no serious challenge to the DC's state system, and envisioned the PCI ending up very much as the Socialists had under the center-left. Without calling it *trasformismo*, Scoppola makes the same point.[16] Of course, many Christian Democrats opposed Moro's long-range plan, cautious as it might have been.[17] This helps explain why Giulio Andreotti—a wily veteran from the party's right wing—was tapped to lead the national solidarity governments.

These were, technically, single-party (*monocolore*) Christian Democratic cabinets. The first was known by the curious but accurate term, *non-sfiducia*, or "no non-confidence," since it counted on the abstention of the parties of the "constitutional arc" within Parliament, explicitly including the PCI. Frustrated with DC stalling tactics, and under increasing pressure from the unions to obtain meaningful results, the PCI finally insisted on a more direct governing role, forcing the first cabinet's resignation in late 1977. In the period between governments, the American ambassador reiterated US opposition to any further concessions to the Communists. This surprised those who thought that the Democratic Carter administration might have a "softer" attitude toward the PCI than its predecessor. But faced with domestic pressure and a complicated foreign scene, Carter did not bend. Andreotti, supremely confident of his ability to handle the PCI without outside pressure, looked back on this episode as "useless and interfering."[18] His second government was, in fact, identical to the first. It received a confidence vote from the constitutional arc of parties—on the day Aldo Moro was kidnapped. That was the closest the PCI came to being formally included in a government after 1947.

A Mixed Legacy I: Legislative and Social Reform

The legislative record of the governments of national solidarity is quite respectable by the standards of the governments that preceded and followed them. If we include some legislation passed in 1975, clearly in response to mass mobilization, the accomplishments grow—for better and for worse. But these governments did not meet the expectations raised when they were formed. This posed no problems for the DC, but it frustrated and ultimately damaged the PCI.

There are several clear successes. A dramatic example is the abortion law, passed in 1978 following considerable mobilization by the women's movement. It passed after years of obstructionism and stalling; only the DC and the MSI voted no. At the time of its passage, it was one of the most liberal abortion laws in Western Europe, permitting women over the age of 18 to request termination of a first-trimester pregnancy for various reasons, including economic, social, or psychological hardship. A dramatic reform of family law was passed in 1975: while technically not instituted by a national solidarity government, it was unquestionably the product of the same mobilization that disrupted the old equilibria. It took eight years to overcome DC foot-dragging, but, in the wake of the divorce referendum, the heavily sexist and authoritarian 1942 (Fascist) Civil Code was finally rewritten.[19]

National solidarity governments produced modest institutional improvements by streamlining and opening up seemingly mundane, but actually quite important, parliamentary procedures.[20] Another area where these governments made an important difference—directly traceable to unrelenting pressure from the Communists and Socialists—concerned the regions. Despite being recognized in the constitution, regional government was only implemented in 1970, when foot-dragging by the DC and the central bureaucracy was finally overcome. Both had been loath to give local left-wing strongholds additional tools. In 1977, Rome finally devolved more powers to the regions, including a measure of financial autonomy. Urban planning, housing policy, and control over health policy figured among these powers; the latter became especially relevant when a national health system was implemented in 1978.

These were long-overdue reforms, but, overall, the record was mixed. Efforts to reform housing and urban planning met fierce resistance from entrenched bureaucratic interests as well as from builders and land speculators. And while health-care reform started on an encouraging note, the vices of the political system soon distorted a promising idea as local health-care units increasingly fell victim to appointments based on political affiliation rather than professional competence.

On the labor relations front, save for the 1970 Statuto dei Lavoratori (Workers' Charter) most significant achievements took place outside of Parliament, but very much in response to earlier social mobilization and the presence of the left in the governments of national solidarity. Starting in 1975, there were signs of improved labor–capital relations.[21] Parts of organized labor remained quite militant (and helped force the PCI's hand in demanding greater progress in late 1977). But, in the course of the solidarity governments, the major union confederations expressed a willingness to moderate wage demands and make other concessions in exchange for measures to improve employment, especially in the south. The unions' new policy was articulated in a meeting in Rome. Held in a convention center that is part of the massive EUR complex (Esposizione Universale Roma, originally built by Mussolini to host the never-held 1942 World's Fair), this policy was instantly dubbed the "EUR line."[22] This line was not dictated by the PCI, but the influence is obvious.

While this partial truce had a moderate economic impact, it was negligible in terms of the deeper problems of employment and investment. The main proponent of the EUR line later admitted that union leaders might have felt the line was necessary, but it never won the support of most activists.[23] When it became clear that more ambitious improvements were not forthcoming, the line fell into disfavor even among some supporters. In any event, by the end of the 1970s, the labor movement had been seriously weakened by the economic crisis, so that industrialists who had been more accommodating in the middle of the decade sensed the turning tide and became much more aggressive.

A Mixed Legacy II: *Strategia della Tensione* and *Anni di Piombo*

The "strategy of tension" and the "years of lead" overlap almost entirely with the period we are examining.[24] For our purposes, two points are crucial. The first is that there was considerable "background" violence, starting in the late 1960s, among demonstrators and in clashes between political groups; this was not terrorism, but, nonetheless, frequently caused serious injuries and occasionally deaths. The most spectacular bombings, kidnappings, and murders carried out by clandestine organizations understandably stand out decades after the events, but it is important to realize how much "low-intensity" violence, in addition to blatant acts of terrorism, conditioned the politics of the period. A few statistics tell a dramatic tale: Donatella della Porta reported that more than 4,300 events could be classified as politically violent in the 1970s. Another 2,712 events were explicitly claimed by terrorist groups, with a total death toll of 351.[25] These numbers help explain the deep scars, both figurative and literal, left on the Italian body politic. The second point is that the most dramatic events came from the extreme right from the late 1960s until the mid-seventies. After that, the headlines generally went to the violent operations of left-wing organizations, of which the Red Brigades are the most well-known. But both "Black" and "Red" terrorism existed throughout the entire period: the single most devastating "Black" attack (the bombing of Bologna's train station that took 85 lives) took place in 1980.

Political responses to violence and terrorism followed predictable patterns. Following its centrist vocation, the DC positioned itself as the essential bulwark against both left and right extremism. In the early 1970s it often suggested that "Red" terrorists and Communists had much in common. It did not always distinguish disruptive demonstrations and strikes from genuinely violent or extremist episodes. Desperate for legitimation, the PCI initially would not even acknowledge that there was such a thing as "Red" terrorism, and constantly affirmed its allegiance to "the democratic Republic, born in the Resistance." Its law-and-order posture occasionally became quite heavy-handed during the period of national solidarity. Once it recognized that "Red" terrorism did indeed exist, the PCI followed a policy of creating "scorched earth" around it. As the DC had done earlier, Communists frequently lumped together acts that were slightly transgressive with truly violent and subversive activities, and were frequently quite insulting when referring to rebellious youth. This stance created serious problems for the party among young people—and among many intellectuals. The Socialists vacillated between the major parties' firmness and the flexible, civil-libertarian position of the Radicals and far left. The hardest line of all, not surprisingly, was that of the MSI, which, among other things, called for the reinstitution of the death penalty and revealed an often tenuous commitment to democratic norms.

REFERENDA AND THE MORO AFFAIR

Two cases illustrate some aspects of this multilayered phenomenon. In 1975, amidst the local election campaign, the DC pushed through a law on public order. Known as the Legge Reale after then Justice Minister, Eugenio Reale, it reacted quite repressively to increasingly confrontational public demonstrations. Numerous provisions facilitated both preventive detention and holding suspects without charges. The law also allowed the use of deadly force when it was deemed that this would prevent a range of serious, but not always easily ascertained, criminal acts. The PSI had softened its position on public order, but, back in the government and contesting an election, it voted for the Legge Reale. The Communists, in the opposition, voted against, but without making a big issue out of it.[26]

Three years later, under a national solidarity government, the Reale Law was subjected to an abrogative referendum, sponsored by the Radicals, but joined by a heterogeneous array of forces. Radicals and a cluster of small far-left formations found themselves making common cause with the (conservative) Liberal Party (PLI) and the MSI. The other parties, accounting for 90 percent of the electorate, all favored upholding the law.

Aldo Moro was already in the hands of the Red Brigades when the referendum campaign was set in motion; his body was recovered a month before the vote. With this in mind, the outcome was striking: 43.6 percent of voters—with a turnout of just over 81 percent—favored abolishing the law. This was a Pyrrhic victory for the constitutional arc of parties. It revealed a high level of tolerance for protest during the most dramatic episode in postwar history—despite some parties' inclinations to lump together legitimate protest and illegitimate actions. Another fairly obvious interpretation would be that the vote suggested strong reservations about providing the authorities with too much power and discretion. Over 1,400 people were eventually charged with participation in "Red" terrorist organizations, and 6,000 were charged with far more nebulous crimes, such as "subversive association."[27] These prosecutions clearly affected the political climate.

Given what we now know about the subsequent gulf that has come to exist between the public and the parties, it is tempting to read backward from the present and see this vote as an early sign of voters' growing alienation from the parties. But powerful evidence calls this interpretation into question. For there were *two* referenda held that day, and the second was a vote to abolish the 1974 law that provided for parties' public funding. A reaction to scandals, that law was meant to eliminate the undue influence of powerful economic interests on the parties.

Here again the Radicals set the referendum in motion. Only one party of any size—the Socialists—joined the abolition campaign. But here, in contrast to the Legge Reale, a very strong majority (76.5 percent) voted to uphold the law. This could thus be seen as a sort of moral victory for the abolitionists. But this vote can hardly be read as an implied denunciation of the parties. (Within 15 years, in the midst of *Tangentopoli*,[28] a whopping 90 percent would vote against public funding; *that* is a resounding vote of non-confidence!)

Aldo Moro's 55-day ordeal at the hands of the Red Brigades, ending with his murder, was, first and foremost, a trauma for the country and government. It created heart-wrenching dramas in Moro's own party, as the DC refused to negotiate with the *brigatisti*, who promised to spare Moro's life if some convicted terrorists were freed. Opponents of negotiations said that any such steps would represent de facto recognition of the terrorists, and would likely encourage further kidnappings, or worse. True to its form throughout the period of national solidarity, the PCI was the most unyielding proponent of firmness in the face of the terrorist threat, but the DC was not far behind.

Craxi and the Socialists espoused a softer line favoring negotiations. Here as well, different pressures pointed in the same direction for the PSI. It could present itself as more humanitarian than either of the larger parties, which it happened to believe to be true. More cynical observers could also point to the Socialists putting themselves in a win–win situation: if negotiations led to Moro's release, they would rightly be able to claim credit for being first to espouse this position. Should the worst come to pass, no one would be able to blame them for the outcome. The most visible other protagonist of a "soft" line was Pope Paul VI, who publicly called for Moro's release. Most far left groups also favored negotiations, usually taking pains to criticize the Red Brigades.

The Moro affair left many questions unanswered, but for all the remaining uncertainty, Italian democracy unquestionably emerged stronger in the aftermath of the *anni di piombo*. Yet there were too many occasions where civil liberties appeared to take a back seat to prosecutorial zeal and the law-and-order excesses of the government—and a PCI that was occasionally more royalist than the king. Most disturbing of all is the finding that the sweepingly repressive emergency legislation employed by the government when violent incidents were at their peak actually aggravated the problem by facilitating recruitment to these organizations.[29] Considering the extent of the phenomenon, Italy's response was actually quite constrained.

The End of National Solidarity—and the Historic Compromise

In 1979, the PCI's patience finally ran out: unless it gained entry into the government, it would return to the opposition. This ultimatum brought down the government and forced new elections. The DC quickly moved to reassure its own right wing while calming Socialist fears: with the goal of quickly bringing them back into a stable alliance, it renounced further collaboration with the PCI.[30] Craxi executed a rapid *volte-face* in the 1979 general election campaign. A year earlier, his party had solemnly affirmed its call for a "left alternative." But now the PSI was in effect running against the PCI, stressing "governability" to ensure safe passage out of the crisis, while promising not to repeat the subordination to the DC suffered by the Socialists in the original center-left.[31]

Falling to 30 percent in 1979, the PCI dropped the *compromesso* with none of the drama that accompanied its adoption. Rather, the expression "democratic alternative" began appearing a few months after the election. The fact that Berlinguer never used the phrase "left alternative" was perhaps a reflection of his continued commitment to try to woo Catholics, who might be leery of the term "left." Or the phrase might have been a parting shot at the Socialists, since they (however insincerely) had constantly used "left alternative." Not that it mattered: the PCI's turnaround was never paid serious attention by Craxi and the PSI, continuing the waltz without partners that marked Communist–Socialist interaction throughout the 1970s.

With the door closed definitively on the PCI, the DC and PSI initiated the final phase of the First Republic, the *pentapartito*. Far from a return to a slightly expanded version of the old center-left, the *pentapartito* actually represented a qualitative change. As Gianfranco Pasquino has persuasively argued, no longer having to worry about any challenge to their permanence in office, the DC and PSI also left behind any need to reform themselves.[32] They launched an unceasing (and ever-more-corrupt) struggle over spoils, just as the material resources to be distributed were shrinking. The resulting degeneration eventually led to the implosion of the party system. But that takes us beyond the topic under examination here.

More directly relevant is the question: Did events have to unfold as they did? There is no such thing as historical inevitability, but the short answer is almost certainly yes—given the history and strategic evolution of the PCI and PSI by the early 1970s. Had the Communists not adopted the historic compromise, and tried to woo the very vulnerable Socialists, an Italian variant of the French Union of the Left might have been plausible. The French Socialists, Communists, and Radicals were separated by far greater differences than the PCI and PSI. But the French institutional environment (especially the electoral system) was far more favorable to the construction of alliances than was the Italian.[33] And, above all, Berlinguer's commitment to the *compromesso* was unshakable.

Once Craxi was in charge, the Socialists were going to oppose whatever the PCI did. The PSI desperately needed to rebrand itself, to use current parlance, and, "alternative" rhetoric aside, this did not mean strengthening its left-wing identity. On the contrary, following the general trend among all Socialist Parties of southern Europe at the time, it chose to emphasize "modernization." This meant reducing links to organized labor and moving toward a "lighter," more middle-class, media-savvy organization that emphasized leaders' personalities.[34]

None of the parties—starting with the DC—considered dramatic changes to their own way of being in the 1970s. The PCI changed the most, but then it had the greatest distance to cover. Once back in the opposition, it took a harder line on domestic issues as it scrambled to recover credibility and support from the working class. This was a step back from its previous moderation, but it was a more stylistic than substantive change. In 1981, following the imposition of martial law in Poland, Berlinguer declared that the "propulsive thrust" that began with the Russian Revolution was exhausted. Most observers considered this to be the clear break with the Soviets that had long been demanded of the PCI. But by then, it didn't matter: the *pentapartito* was in full flight, and the Communists would remain isolated until the First Republic collapsed.

Conclusions

Aside from explaining what the *compromesso storico* was, this chapter has emphasized the fact that it bracketed the period when the political equilibrium of the First Republic was challenged, but not changed. And when the key actors did not change, or did not change sufficiently, the party system entered its terminal stage.

The period was also important because it saw the beginning of trends that would profoundly impact Italian politics. The 1978 referendum on the public financing of parties demonstrated that, while the parties might have slipped in public esteem by the late 1970s, they continued to enjoy broad public support—or at least acceptance. Referenda would eventually be overused and indeed abused, with as many as 7 (1997 and 2000) or even 12 (1995) often unrelated items put to a vote at the same time. Not surprisingly, voters' attention, and hence their participation, tended to wane, resulting in many referenda that failed because fewer than half of all voters turned out, as the law requires. But from the 1970s into the 1990s, and to a lesser degree more recently, the selective use of the abrogative referendum has occasionally had a powerful impact on Italian politics.

A negative phenomenon that first appeared in the late 1970s was the decline in voter turnout in general elections. On the surface, the concern at the time appears almost risible: turnout fell from 93.4 percent in 1976 to 90.6 percent in 1979. Yet the rate had been so astonishingly consistent at around 93 percent for nearly thirty years that the drop attracted attention almost immediately, particularly when it became clear that this was not a temporary aberration, but a clear trend.[35] Since 1979, the decline has been interrupted, modestly, in only one election (2006).

But for all the disappointments, and troubling symptoms, that flowed from the national solidarity experience, it is worth recalling that Italian democracy was consolidated and strengthened by the PCI's firm commitment to the democratic rules of the game, and to the defense of Italy's institutions, which were genuinely under constant stress and, often, direct attack. It is one of the many ironies of the period that the Italian Communists, denied a full seat at the governing table because of doubts about their democratic *bona fides*, helped ensure that the table remained solid nonetheless. And that, even taking into account the party's occasional overzealousness, is no small achievement.

Notes

1. For more on social movements, see Chapter 49, this volume. For a broader sociohistorical perspective on this period: Paul Ginsborg, *A History of Contemporary Italy: Society and Politics, 1943–1988* (London: Penguin Books, 1990), ch. 9 and pp. 366–370.
2. See Chapter 50, this volume.
3. For a detailed discussion, Stephen Hellman, *Italian Communism in Transition: The Rise and Fall of the Historic Compromise in Turin, 1975–1980* (New York: Oxford University Press, 1988), 21–27.
4. "Relazione di Enrico Berlinguer," in PCI, *XIII Congresso del PCI: Atti e risoluzioni.* (Rome: Editori Riuniti, 1972), 54–59.
5. Enrico Berlinguer, "Riflessioni sull'Italia dopo I fatti del Cile," in Gustavo Tomsic, ed., *Berlinguer. Governo di unità democratica e compromesso storico. Discorsi 1969–1976* (Rome: Sarmi, 1976), 85–105.
6. For the inflation rates 1972–74, CISL, *CISL 1984* (Rome: Edizioni Lavoro, 1984), 28 and 32.
7. To provide an idea of the attention attracted by Eurocommunism, consider the fact that a bibliography published in 1987 is 188 pages long: Olga A. Narkiewicz, *Eurocommunism, 1968–1986: A Select Bibliography* (London and New York: Mansell Publishers, 1987).

8. Marcello Flores and Nicola Gallerano, *Sul PCI. Un'interpretazione storica* (Bologna: Il Mulino, 1992), 241–249.

9. Arturo Parisi and Gianfranco Pasquino, "Relazioni partiti-elettori e tipi di voto," in idem, eds., *Continuità e mutamento elettorale in Italia* (Bologna: Il Mulino, 1977), 215–249.

10. Wolfgang Merkel, *Prima e dopo Craxi. Le trasformazioni del PSI* (Padua: Liviana Editrice, 1987), 7–25.

11. Ginsborg, *A History of Contemporary Italy*, 377.

12. See the relevant sections of Chapter 16, this volume.

13. In the Central Committee meeting of June 1974. Enrico Berlinguer in Antonio Tatò, ed., *La "questione comunista" 1969–1975* (Rome: Editori Riuniti, 1975), vol. 2, 758–759.

14. Berlinguer, "Riflessioni sull'Italia dopo I fatti del Cile," 99–101.

15. Pietro Scoppola, *La democrazia dei cristiani. Il cattolicesimo politico nell'Italia unita. Intervista a cura di Giuseppe Tognon* (3rd edn, Bari: Laterza 2006), 135.

16. Scoppola, *La democrazia dei cristiani*, 46 and 142; Ginsborg, *A History of Contemporary Italy*, 338.

17. See Chapter 28, this volume, for more details.

18. Quoted in Roberto Fornasier, "The DC and the PCI in the Seventies: A Complex Relationship Supervised by the United States," *Bulletin of Italian Politics* 4, no. 2 (2012), 222.

19. For a contemporary discussion, see Valerio Pocar and Paola Ronfani, "Family Law in Italy: Legislative Innovations and Social Change," *Law and Society Review* 12, no. 4 (Summer, 1978), 607–644.

20. Robert Leonardi, Rafaella Nanetti, and Gianfranco Pasquino, "Institutionalization of Parliament and Parliamentarization of Parties in Italy," *Legislative Studies Quarterly* 3, no. 1 (February 1978), 161–186.

21. Piero Ignazi, *Il potere dei partiti. La politica in Italia dagli anni Sessanta a oggi* (Bari: Laterza 2002), 68.

22. For relevant documents and discussion, Stefano Bevacqua and Giuseppe Turani, eds., *La svolta del '78* (Milan: Feltrinelli, 1978).

23. Giampaolo Pansa, ed., *Luciano Lama. Intervista sul mio partito* (Bari: Laterza 1987), 73–77.

24. Readers are again referred to Chapters 49 and 50, this volume.

25. Donatella della Porta, "Institutional Responses to Terrorism: The Italian Case," *Terrorism and Political Violence* 4, no. 4 (1992), 151.

26. Romano Canosa, *La polizia in Italia dal 1945 a oggi* (Bologna: Il Mulino, 1976), 320–352.

27. Della Porta, "Institutional Responses to Terrorism," 151.

28. See Chapter 24 by Martin Rhodes, this volume, on *Tangentopoli*.

29. Della Porta, "Institutional Responses to Terrorism."

30. Pietro Scoppola, *La repubblica dei partiti. Evoluzione e crisi di un sistema politico 1945–1996* (Bologna: Il Mulino, 1997), 424.

31. Merkel, *Prima e dopo Craxi*, ch. 5.

32. Gianfranco Pasquino, *Il sistema politico italiano. Autorità, istituzioni, società.* (Bologna: Bononia University Press, 2002), 38–44.

33. W. Rand Smith, *Enemy Brothers: Socialists and Communists in France, Italy, and Spain* (Lanham, MD: Rowman & Littlefield, 2012).

34. For a thorough overview of these trends, see Gerassimos Moschonas, *In the Name of Social Democracy: The Great Transformation 1945 to the Present* (London: Verso, 2002).

35. Piergiorgio Corbetta, Arturo M. L. Parisi, and Hans M. A. Schadee, *Elezioni in Italia. Struttura e tipologia delle consultazioni politiche* (Bologna: Il Mulino, 1988), 285–302.

CHAPTER 23

THE *PENTAPARTITO*

MARTIN J. BULL

THE *pentapartito* was the five-party governing coalition which, aside from two brief interruptions, held office between June 1981 and April 1991. The parties making up the coalition were: Christian Democracy (DC), the Italian Socialist Party (PSI), the Italian Republican Party (PRI), the Italian Social Democratic Party (PSDI), and the Italian Liberal Party (PLI). There were seven *pentapartito* governments in total during this decade, spanning three legislatures (the eighth, ninth, and tenth), interspersed by two non-*pentapartito* governments in the period, both headed by Fanfani (see Table 23.1).

The statistics in Table 23.1 paint a picture of government instability and difficulty in forming governments. The average life of a government during the whole period was less than a year and, for the *pentapartito* governments, 429 days. Furthermore, during the entire period, more than twelve months—and, during the *pentapartito* governments, 204 days—were spent in the absence of any government. The statistics also highlight one government in this period whose duration improves the average significantly: that of Craxi I, which proved to be (until that time) the longest-lasting government of the Republic.[1] At the time, therefore, the *pentapartito* was seen as combining two contrasting images: on the one hand, instability, party and faction fighting; and, on the other hand, *craxismo*, the rise of the PSI and greater stability.

Yet, seen in a historical perspective, and especially since the implosion of the party system between 1992 and 1994, the *pentapartito* has taken on a very different image: that of laying the foundations for the collapse of the "First Republic" through the excess of its politicians and parties, who took the malfunctioning of the political system to heights not seen before. In this image, the *pentapartito* marked the high point of the first republican "empire," and therefore the beginning of its decline and fall. Indeed, following the final collapse of the *pentapartito* formula in 1991, the two governments which followed (Andreotti VII and Amato) were four-party coalitions (*pentapartito* less the PRI), the first running for just over a year until the 1992 "earthquake" elections, and the second running for less than a year before its collapse and replacement by a technical government (Ciampi), this marking the definitive end to the old parties as the basis for party government in Italy. In the same period, most of the politicians associated with

Table 23.1 *Pentapartito* Governments 1981–91

Prime Minister	Start Date	End Date	Duration: days	Interval/Crisis
Spadolini I	June 28, 1981	Aug 7, 1982	405	16
Spadolini II	Aug 23, 1982	Nov 13, 1982	82	18
Fanfani V*	Dec 1, 1982	April 29, 1983	149	97
Craxi I	Aug 4, 1983	June 27, 1986	1058	34
Craxi II	Aug 1, 1986	March 3, 1987	214	45
Fanfani VI*	April 17, 1987	April 28, 1987	11	91
Goria	April 28, 1987	March 11, 1988	227	13
De Mita	April 13, 1988	May 19, 1989	401	64
Andreotti VI	July 22, 1989	March 29, 1991	615	14
Total overall			3162 (av: 351)	392
Total *pentapart*			3002 (av: 429)	204

* Non-*pentapartito* governments: Fanfani V did not include the PRI; Fanfani VI was a minority DC government with some independents

the *pentapartito* era had their reputations tarnished by revelations of systemic corruption. By the end of the Amato government (April 1993), nearly half of the ministers had had to resign because they had been served with formal notices of judicial investigation, and, by the 1994 national elections, all of the *pentapartito* party leaders had either been removed or were undergoing trial, save Craxi, who had escaped to Tunisia to avoid imprisonment.[2]

This defining image of the *pentapartito* (the "years of mud"[3]), while not lacking in accuracy, is perhaps too simplistic a portrayal of the experience, based as it was on a complex and changing power play between its principal partners. This chapter, therefore, having outlined the broader political and economic context to the *pentapartito*, analyses the changing nature of the relations between the parties at the heart of the *pentapartito* formula before then examining the rise and fall of the experiment.

THE POLITICAL AND ECONOMIC CONTEXT

The birth of the *pentapartito* in 1981 is best seen in the context of the collapse of the "Historic Compromise" (between the DC and the Italian Communist Party, PCI) in 1979, and the struggle to find an alternative configuration.[4] There followed four weak, unstable, and short-lived governments (Andreotti V, Cossiga I and II, Forlani), the first three based on three-party support (DC–PRI–PSDI; DC–PSDI–PLI; DC–PSI–PRI) and the last on four parties (DC–PSDI–PRI–PSI). These governments experienced high social tensions, including the massive strike at FIAT in 1980 and terrorism. The fall of the Forlani government, which paved the way to a more durable political alliance, was due to the exposure of the "secret masonic" lodge P2. Forlani resigned over the time it had taken for the government to publish the list of P2 members, which included a significant proportion of the establishment and, notably, members of the DC. It was the biggest scandal of the Italian Republic.

At the same time, however, the economy was undergoing unprecedented change and this provided the context for the success of the *pentapartito* in staying in office (see Table 23.2). The severe economic recession of the early 1980s quickly gave way to a period of renewed economic growth that lasted almost until the end of the decade, with consistent growth in GDP above 2.5 percent combined with declining inflation. This was part of a recovery on a world scale, but there were also national factors at work. A restructuring of Italian industry was underway, incorporating electronic and automated techniques, as well as a number of industrial mergers and takeovers. This was accompanied by an acceleration of the trend of decentralization of production through the performance of small and medium-sized enterprises (SMEs), which, in the 1980s, became the mainstay of employment in the industrial sector and made famous the "made in Italy" mark.

Organized labor was no longer in a position to resist these changes. A 33-day strike in 1980 over FIAT's restructuring plans split the workforce and was ended by a demonstration of 40,000 workers in support of FIAT's terms: other large companies followed FIAT's lead. In 1983, an agreement was signed between the government, trade unions, and industry, which reduced labor market rigidities, placed a limit on wage increases, and reduced the coverage of the wage-indexation system (*scala mobile*). The following year, the Craxi government passed a decree further reducing its coverage, a measure which split the trade union movement. A referendum to nullify the decree failed,

Table 23.2 Economic Performance during the *Pentapartito* Years

Year	Growth (GDP)	Inflation	Public deficit*	Public debt*	Unemployment
1981	0.6	19.3	11.4	59.8	8.4
1982	0.2	16.3	11.3	64.9	9.1
1983	1.0	15.0	10.6	70.0	9.9
1984	2.7	10.6	11.6	75.2	10.0
1985	2.6	8.6	12.6	82.4	10.3
1986	2.9	6.1	11.6	86.5	11.1
1987	3.1	4.6	11.0	90.6	12.0
1988	4.1	5.0	10.7	92.7	12.0
1989	2.9	6.6	9.9	95.7	12.0
1990	2.1	6.1	11.0	97.8	11.0
1991	1.2	6.4	10.0	100.6	10.9

*As percentage of GDP

Source: Extracted from Martin J. Bull and James L. Newell, *Italian Politics: Adjustment under Duress* (London: Polity, 2005), 29 (Table 2.3) and 33 (Table 2.4).

54.3 percent of voters voting against the proposal, thus marking the "end of an era" for trade union power, which had begun with the "Hot Fall" in the late 1960s.[5]

These changes explain why the *pentapartito*—despite its axis being no different to the "center-left" of the 1960s (DC–PSI)—was not simply a reversion to an old formula; and nor did the difference lie simply in the inclusion of a fifth party (the center-right PLI). The *pentapartito* was in power during a veritable transformation of the economy and of organized labor, presenting significant opportunities for the government in office. However, the period was also marked a significant shift in the political relations between the parties, underpinned by changes in their electoral fortunes (see Table 23.3), which undermined government stability and effectiveness.

The Principal Characteristics
of the *Pentapartito*

The *pentapartito* was characterized by four features relating to the changing fortunes of the parties and relations between them: decline of the DC; crisis of the PCI; rise of third parties (and especially the PSI); and an inherently conflictual relationship between the governing parties.

First, the *pentapartito* marked an extended decline in the monopoly of the DC, symbolized both in the DC's defeat in its 1981 referendum campaign against the abortion law of 1978 and in the party's loss of the prime minister's office for the first time since the war: the first four *pentapartito* governments were led by non-DC prime ministers.[6] Indeed, the very genesis of the *pentapartito* was premised on the removal of the DC from this office and an understanding that any of the five coalition parties might provide the prime minister. This owed much to President Sandro Pertini, the first ever Socialist President of the Republic (elected in 1978) who, in 1981, recognizing the manner in which the exposure of the P2 membership list had discredited the DC, chose the PRI leader, Giovanni Spadolini, to form the first non-DC-led government since the war. The two Spadolini governments of the early 1980s, furthermore, paved the way for two socialist-led governments under Craxi, 1983–86.

The DC's difficulties reflected its failure to reform itself over the previous decade. Furthermore, the PSI threatened to steal its image as the principal bulwark against communism and make inroads into its state patronage resources. This situation set in motion a new quest for Christian Democratic renewal under leader Ciriaco De Mita, elected in May 1982. De Mita's solution was to carry through party reform involving strong leadership, a reduction in factionalism, and the development of an image as a "modern conservative party capable of sound economic management and attractive to the growing numbers of managers and technocrats."[7] It was ironic that this reform, to be effective, would have to undermine the sort of power base of the southern notables spearheading the reform in the first place. In any case, this strategy was not shared across the party, and De Mita—despite being, in 1988, only the second DC politician (after Fanfani 1958–59) to become both party leader and prime minister at the same time—was consistently opposed, and his reform program failed to reverse the party's decline. In the five elections between 1963 and 1983, the DC's vote had been largely stable (between a low of 41.3 percent in 1963 and a high of 42.2 percent in 1968 and 1972). In 1983, however, its vote declined steeply to 35.7 percent (its worst performance since the war) and recovered only marginally in 1987 to 37.1 percent. It further suffered the ignobility of being, in the 1984 European elections, "surpassed" by the PCI as the party with the largest vote (although this was partly explained by a large communist sympathy vote following the premature death of its leader, Enrico Berlinguer). Other features of the DC continued unarrested: the increasing "southernization" of its vote and membership, its ageing leadership, its internal party factionalism, its enrolment of membership for purely internal struggles, its clientelistic activities, and its apparent involvement in the murky underworld (P2, organized crime).

Second, the decline of the DC was paralleled by a crisis in the other main party, the opposition PCI. In the period until the mid-1970s, the PCI's vote in national elections had consistently increased to a high point of 36 percent in 1976. The PCI, therefore, was consistently regarded as a powerful political player whose presence could not be disregarded when it came to formulating governing coalitions. Indeed, between 1976 and 1979 the party allowed the survival of DC minority governments through a policy of "not no-confidence" (dubbed the "Historic Compromise"). However, the electoral defeat of 1979, where the PCI's votes declined to 32 percent, the subsequent collapse of the formula and the PCI's retreat into opposition, combined with leader Berlinguer's definitive break (*lo strappo*) with the Soviet Union after the *coup d'état* in Poland in 1981 and a failure of the party to respond to the modernization of the economy taking place (demonstrated in its response to the strike at FIAT and the referendum on wage indexation) left the PCI in disarray. Its political alternatives were exhausted, its identity in crisis, its policies out of date, its leadership weak (under Alessandro Natta who replaced Berlinguer), and its internal factionalism growing.

This changed the dynamic amongst the parties in the *pentapartito* because the PCI could safely be regarded as bordering on political irrelevance, a position advanced primarily by PSI leader Craxi, whose renewed anti-communist rhetoric differed markedly from the traditional anti-communism of the DC: "while the Christian Democrats had always taken into account what they thought would be the reactions of the Communist Party to their decisions, Craxi deliberately tried to show the Communists' irrelevance."[8] This meant neither consulting the PCI nor anticipating its positions in deciding one's own.

The third feature of the *pentapartito* was the rise of other parties relevant to the coalition, and especially the Socialists.[9] The "center" parties (PRI, PSDI, PLI) saw their combined vote rise from 7.1 percent in the 1979s elections to 10.8 percent in 1983 and then back to 7.7 percent in 1987, a rise largely accounted for by the PRI, evidently profiting from Spadolini's role as prime minister in 1981–82. While the PSDI and PLI, which had seen declines in their votes since the 1960s, saw marginal—and temporary—recoveries

Table 23.3 Elections to Chamber of Deputies during *Pentapartito* Years
(percentage vote)

	1979 *Pentapartito* from June 1981	1983 *Pentapartito*	1987 *Pentapartito*	1992 *Pentapartito* until March 1991
DC	41.6	35.7	37.1	32.7
PCI	32.0	31.4	28.1	
PDS				17.0
RC				5.6
PSI	9.8	11.6	14.9	14.6
PSDI	3.2	3.7	2.7	2.5
PRI	2.5	4.6	3.3	4.3
PLI	1.4	2.5	1.7	2.7
MSI	4.8	6.7	5.6	5.4
Radicals	2.8	1.7	2.1	1.1
DP	1.0*	1.1	1.3	
Greens			2.1	2.5
Lega Nord			0.2	8.9
Rete				1.9
Others	0.9	1.0	0.9	0.8
Total	100.0	100.0	100.0	100.0

* PdUP in 1979

Key: DC: Christian Democracy; PCI: Italian Communist Party; PDS: Democratic Party of the Left; RC: Communist Refoundation; PSI: Italian Socialist Party; PSDI: Italian Social Democratic Party; PRI: Italian Republican Party; PLI: Italian Liberal Party; MSI: Italian Social Movement; DP: Proletarian Democracy; PdUP: Democratic Party of Proletarian Unity; Lega Nord: Northern League; Rete: Network.

Source: Extracted from Table 3.1, Bull and Newell, *Italian Politics*, 46.

in the 1980s (the PLI's move toward the center-left under leader Valerio Zanone made possible the creation of the *pentapartito*), the PRI's vote nearly doubled from a very low base of 2.5 percent in 1979 to a high point of 4.6 percent in 1983 before dropping back to 3.3 percent in 1987. However, the center parties—while reflecting the increasing electoral volatility of Italian voters—were only ever going to be "satellites" to the DC, occasionally being granted some of the better spoils of government. Craxi, on the other hand, had entirely bigger goals in mind, part of which involved using the electoral effect of holding the prime ministership. (It was primarily Craxi's initiatives that brought the second Spadolini government to an end.)

Craxi, having become leader of the PSI in 1976, had spent the first few years repositioning and changing the party. Surrounded by a core group of younger members, he set about removing symbolic aspects of the party which he felt compromised its image and ability to reposition itself: out went Marxist ideology (replaced with Western social democracy) and the hammer and sickle (replaced by the red rose—symbol of the 1974 Portuguese revolution). At the same time, however, he changed the internal organization of the party, in the process quashing factionalism and removing any opposition to his leadership. The party was then repositioned as a "third party" aimed at securing votes from both the left and right and therefore redefining the center (left) as a fulcrum of opposition to the bipolarism between the PCI and DC.[10] This repositioning involved, on the one hand, fierce competition with a declining DC for a greater share of the spoils of office, including, ultimately, the prime ministership, and, on the other hand, vitriolic opposition to the PCI, with the PSI under Craxi effectively reintroducing the *conventio ad excludendum* (the agreement amongst the parties to exclude the PCI from office) which former DC leader Aldo Moro had done so much to overcome. The overall goal was to increase the power and influence of the PSI within the political system. There can be little doubt that this strategy had some electoral success, the PSI's vote increasing from 9.8 percent in 1979 to 11.6 percent in 1983 and then peaking at 14.9 percent in 1987. Yet it was nothing like the rise in vote that was expected (after two Socialist-led governments) or needed if the PSI were to replace the PCI as the second main party.

The fourth feature was the highly conflictual nature of the *pentapartito*, which was a product of two factors. The first was the high number (five) and wide range (from center-right to center-left) of parties making up the coalition, which reinforced the long-standing Italian practice of government formation being dependent almost entirely on the basis of sharing out ministries, agencies, and boards (with policy rarely, if ever, being a consideration).[11] It also meant that governments were inherently fragile, since the exit of any of the five parties would bring down the whole edifice (even if the government still had a majority), and government reshuffles were, consequently, protracted exercises. The second was the relationship between the two core parties, the DC and PSI, which—at least during the central years of the *pentapartito*—was highly competitive, "devoid of mutual trust, parity or programmatic accord, and riven by suspicion and by an eternal jockeying for position," largely as a consequence of the dominance of two leaders (Craxi and De Mita) and their "modernization" strategies.[12]

The composition and main features of the *pentapartito* as a coalition help explain the performance of the *pentapartito* governments in this period, which is best viewed in two broad phases: first, the two Craxi governments, which were regarded as the golden age of the *pentapartito* experiment; and, second, the so-called "CAF" (Craxi–Andreotti–Forlani) years, which witnessed the decline and end of the experiment.

Pentapartito in Ascension: The Craxi Years

In many political histories of Italy, the Spadolini governments appear almost as an *antipasto* and the Goria government as a *digestivo* to the *pentapartito*'s main course—the two Craxi governments. Although not an entirely fair reflection on the *pentapartito* experience and achievements, there is, nonetheless, little dispute that Craxi in government symbolized the *pentapartito* experience: Craxi engineered the election that brought him to power (by withdrawing support from the Spadolini government) in order to exploit the DC's crisis; De Mita ran an election campaign predicated on the modernization of the DC which secured the party's worst ever defeat; and the two Craxi governments that followed spanned almost the entire ninth legislature and were an essential part of the PSI's strategic goal both to dominate and change the functioning of the political system.

Moreover, despite the eventual failure of both goals, the very attempt certainly shook the foundations of the Italian political system, especially its consociational aspects. If the prevailing characteristic of the postwar Italian political system was a "politics of bargained pluralism"—in which decisions were taken after a long process of consultation with all relevant actors—then Craxi's goal was to break with this and introduce a more decisive form of politics based on strong government (or increased governability) and, where necessary, confrontation to achieve one's goals ("*decisionismo*").[13] If nothing else, there can be little doubt that Craxi brought a new style to Italian politics, and it was one that matched the era of the 1980s, symbolized in Thatcherism and Reaganomics: aggressive individualism, neoliberalism, a "get rich quick" mentality, and the emergence of a "new bourgeoisie" with these values at their heart.

In terms of actual substance, however, the record was more mixed. Certainly, Craxi's approach was markedly different to his predecessors, using his power and influence to affect change or force debate on issues, from which there were clear outcomes, for example: the signing of the new Concordat with the Vatican in 1984; the reduction of the coverage of the wage-indexation system (*scala mobile*) and the successful stand Craxi took against the PCI and the referendum which threatened to overturn it; the tightening up of legislation on the tax returns of shopkeepers; and the much more forceful presence of Italy in foreign affairs, symbolized by the Sigonella affair, where Craxi stood up to the United States on the grounds of national sovereignty and the Americans eventually backed down.[14]

On other issues he promoted, however, his record was either unsuccessful or controversial. His launching in 1976 of the "great reform" (root-and-branch institutional reform) was apparently aimed at forging a modern progressive constitutional framework to match the changes in the style of politics his party was introducing. Yet the main emphasis of the Socialists' ill-defined preferences, when the Bozzi Commission on institutional reform was set up in 1983, was an increase in powers of the office of prime minister. In reality, Craxi sought to use institutional reform to break the bipolarism of the DC–PCI and secure a larger role for the PSI, and so his reformism was heavily circumscribed by partisan considerations—where these failed to be met by proposed reforms he was a conservative, insofar as he viewed the existing consociational system as offering the PSI sufficient space to achieve its goals. This failure to separate systemic from partisan interests was common across the parties, and the Bozzi Commission ended in failure in 1985. An analogous approach was adopted with regard to the issue of commercial television, as Craxi, in 1984, carried through a decree law to allow his long-term friend, Silvio Berlusconi, to continue building up his private monopoly of television stations, a monopoly that was subsequently confirmed by legislation passed five years later (the Mammì Law).

Beyond these examples, there was little or no attempt to tackle what were regarded as major areas in need of reform (public administration, the welfare state, local government, education, dealing with EU legislation, and so on). This failure was perhaps all the more damning in view of the economic boom that Italy was undergoing during the decade, in common with other Western democracies. This brought sustained economic growth combined with dramatic falls in inflation, allowing Craxi to bask in the glow of economic success—indeed, at the time, some observers dubbed it as a "second economic miracle" (after the first in the 1950s). Yet other economic indicators painted a more ominous, if not sinister, picture (see Table 23.2). The rate of unemployment grew during the decade, peaking at 12 percent between 1987 and 1989. No action was taken to bring down the rate of the public deficit, and, as a consequence, the public debt as a percentage of GDP rose, during the Craxi years alone, from 70 percent to 90.6 percent and, during the *pentapartito* as a whole, from 59.8 percent to 100.6 percent. In short, despite a significant rise in taxation in the same period, there was profligacy in public spending, the seriousness of which would have consequences even 20 years later. Finally, although not known at the time, it became apparent that Craxi and the PSI—as part of their strategic goal of dominance—were the chief protagonists of illicit and corrupt activities which would lead to the dénouement of the existing parties and party system.[15]

PENTAPARTITO IN DECLINE ... AND FALL: THE "CAF" YEARS

Whatever one's judgment on the Craxi years, it could be argued that they generated significant expectations in terms of reform and, in terms of style, they brought something new to Italian politics. In the period following the 1987 elections, both the promise of reform and the new style began to disappear. The results of the elections confirmed the growing dilemma at the heart of the party system: that there was declining support for and evident dissatisfaction with the existing parties, but no real alternatives to what could be offered in terms of governing coalitions, and it was notable (from hindsight) that these elections saw the first electoral share of the vote (albeit only 0.2 percent) going to what was then a largely unknown party called the Northern League.

The decline and crisis of the PCI continued and allowed the *pentapartito* to strengthen its hold on the system, but the failure of the PSI to increase its vote substantially (it went up by only 3.3 percent), combined with a marginal recovery of the DC's vote (but still below its level of support in the 1970s), increased the level of competition between the parties. More importantly, the degree of factionalism inside the DC increased, as De Mita, in 1988, managed to become, at the same time, both party leader and prime minister—a feat not achieved since Fanfani in 1958–59. If this reinforced his hold over the DC (and increased tensions with the PSI) in the short term it also signaled the beginning of the end of the De Mita period: in wielding too much influence he ensured that the other factions would oust him. The birth of a new centrist faction, Azione Poplare (dubbed the "neo-Dorotei" after the faction which had dominated the DC in the post-war period), which brought together leading figures in the party, was principally aimed at removing De Mita: he was stripped of the party leadership in February 1989 (when the party split and Forlani was elected) and the prime ministership a few months later (when Forlani struck a deal with Craxi to replace De Mita with Andreotti—a position he held for the final two *pentapartito* governments), a process which ended what would be the party's last attempt at reform before its organizational collapse in the early 1990s.

The ousting of De Mita by the so-called "CAF (Craxi–Andreotti–Forlani) axis" saw a fundamental shift in the nature of the *pentapartito* coalition. If, under De Mita, the DC had been seeking to compete with the PSI at every turn—which had been the main cause of instability—Andreotti and Forlani, by contrast, were exponents of the art of accommodating the PSI's needs and therefore reducing the tensions between the two parties. This took the form of a secret power-sharing agreement between the DC and PSI, allegedly forged in a camper van by Forlani and Craxi behind the scenes at the PSI's Congress, based on Andreotti becoming prime minister and a longer-term division of the spoils of government. This undoubtedly signaled a shift to the right and the effective abandonment of any program of reform: the new programmatic alliance became based on little more than a systematic and corrupt sharing out of the country's resources to retain power, made possible by Italy having the largest public sector of any of the advanced Western democracies.[16]

This emphasis on accommodation and power sharing for the long term introduced a stronger element of stability into the coalition, perhaps best exemplified in the handling of the Mammì Law, which effectively sanctioned Berlusconi's commercial television monopoly. When faced with an unwelcome amendment to the bill (from the left) the government made it subject to a vote of confidence (meaning it had to be accepted or rejected in its entirety). When, on being passed, five DC ministers resigned in protest, Andreotti replaced them within 24 hours and the government survived intact. This demonstrated both the strength of the CAF axis and the interests at stake in this legislation. The stability also gave planned, pending, or EU-dictated legislation space to come onto the statute books, as well as individual ministers (e.g. Giuliano Amato and Guido Carli) the space to take forward initiatives. As a consequence, the two years of the final *pentapartito* government saw the passage of legislation in various areas, for example: the La Pergola Law (1989), which reformed the manner in which Italy handled EU legislation; Italy's entry into the narrow band of the European Monetary System and the abolition of restrictions on the free flow of capital (1990); the Amato Law (1990), which allowed banks to become joint stock corporations; an anti-trust law (1990); an inside-trading law (1990); a reform of local government and public administration (both 1990); the Martelli Law on immigration; an equal opportunities law (1991); laws on land protection (1989) and national parks (1991); and the already cited Mammì Law on media regulation.

However, whether these reforms justify Ginsborg's description of the tenth legislature (1987–92) as "a period of considerable reforming zeal" is questionable—and even if accurate, it could be said that it was too little too late.[17] The reforms should not hide the general stagnation of the coalition and the demise that was occurring in this period. There were no moves undertaken to reduce public expenditure or get the public deficit under control, and the level of public debt in 1991 exceeded 100 percent of GDP for the first time. Furthermore, economic growth in 1991 fell to its lowest level for seven years. The opportunities in the 1980s to carry through structural reforms (to the public sector, pensions, and the welfare state) were all but gone. More importantly, changes were occurring during the period of the tenth legislature of a deeper political and social nature, which would sweep away not just the *pentapartito* variant of Italian governing coalitions but—starting with the 1992 elections—virtually all of the parties and coalitions that had governed Italy since the war.

The long-term high levels of popular dissatisfaction with Italian democracy were becoming increasingly visible in the 1980s, reflected not only in an increase in protest voting and spoilt ballots, but also in the rise (in the north) of the Northern League, founded in 1984, and (in the south) of the Network (Rete), founded in 1990. By the early 1990s, these changes were translated into a serious protest against the DC regime.[18] This was largely because the main factor that had held them in check until then (the "Communist question") effectively disappeared after 1989 when PCI leader Achille Occhetto began a process of transformation of the party into the non-communist Democratic Party of the Left (PDS). Voters no longer felt obliged to "hold their noses and vote Christian Democrat," and public prosecutors no longer felt constrained in investigating the corruption of the governing parties, since there was no longer, in such actions, the risk of favoring a "communist advance." In this situation, a "referendum movement," founded by a dissident Christian Democrat, Mario Segni, used the referendum to force change on an unwilling political establishment, notably through the abolition (in June 1991) of preference voting (long held to be at the core of the DC's system). At the same time, the negotiations over the Maastricht Treaty (eventually signed in February 1992) revealed the tough convergence criteria that would have to be met for Italy to enter European Monetary Union in the first wave, meaning severe economic adjustments (public expenditure cuts and tax rises) would have to be made, which could only undermine the power bases of the DC and its allies.

The *pentapartito*'s contextual role in this dénouement is apparent from its failures during the Craxi years, yet it made a more direct contribution too, in the sense that it was precisely the lack of response by the CAF axis in the late 1980s to the fast-changing political and social environment that hastened the meltdown of the old party system. On the one hand, the PSI underestimated the likely impact on the party system of the PCI's crisis, assuming that there could only be gains from it: Craxi in particular adopted a series of short-term tactical moves to justify continued rejection of any rapprochement with the emerging PDS. On the other hand, the DC underestimated the impact that these changes would have on its privileged relationship with the Catholic world. And neither party seemed cognizant of the significance, for their methods of governing and respective power bases, of the moves toward European Monetary Union. In short, at a point in time when pressures on the political class to reform itself and the system became the most intense in nearly half a century, the *pentapartito* appeared set on a reactionary course, complacently reinforcing its stranglehold on the system.

The glaring nature of this paradox was brought home by the behavior of the Italian President, former Christian Democrat Francesco Cossiga who, in 1990, changed from being rather conventional in outlook into an outspoken President who engaged in a wholesale crusade against the Italian body politic, declaring that he was taking a "pick axe" to the political system to drive its politicians and parties toward reform. This campaign by the supposed guardian of the Constitution brought into sharp relief the shortcomings of the political system as well as the inability of the existing political class to carry through reform.

Seen in this context, there was a certain inevitability about the meltdown and transformation of the party system, which occurred between 1992 and 1994. By that point in time, however, the *pentapartito* was long gone. Indeed, it could be said that, like the end of the world in T. S. Eliot's "Hollow Men," the *pentapartito* ended "not with a bang but a whimper." In March 1991, the Andreotti VI government collapsed due to the PRI withdrawing its support over its failure to be given the Ministry of Communications, and it was replaced by a non-*pentapartito* formula: a four-party Andreotti VII government, subsequently described by Giorgio Galli as amongst "the most inert in Republican history."[19] One year later the party system itself went out with a "bang" on the back of the 1992 election results—yet the role of the *pentapartito* in this dénouement would never be forgotten.

Notes

1. It was subsequently beaten by Berlusconi's second government, which ran for nearly four years between 2001 and 2005.
2. Gianfranco Pasquino, "Political Development," in Patrick McCarthy, ed., *Italy since 1945* (Oxford: Oxford University Press), 83.
3. "Mud-raking" following the *anni di piombo* ("years of lead"—bullets) of the 1970s (Indro Montanelli and Mario Cervi, *L'Italia degli anni di fango, 1978–1993* (Milan: Rizzoli, 2012)).
4. On the Historic Compromise see Chapter 22, this volume.
5. Peter Lange, "End of an Era: The Referendum on the *Scala Mobile*," in Raffaella Nanetti and Robert Leonardi, eds., *Italian Politics: A Review*, vol. 1 (London: Pinter, 1986).
6. On the DC's difficulties see Chapter 14, this volume.
7. Philip Daniels, "The End of the Craxi Era? The Italian Parliamentary Elections of June 1987," *Parliamentary Affairs*, 41, no. 2 (April 1988), 269.
8. Pasquino, "Political Development," 77–78.
9. See Chapter 16, this volume.
10. Paolo Farneti, *Il sistema dei partiti in Italia 1946–1979* (Bologna: Il Mulino, 1983), 218.
11. Gianfranco Pasquino, "Il pentapartito," in Gianfranco Pasquino, ed., *La politica italiana. Dizionario critico, 1945–1995* (Bari: Laterza, 1995).
12. Paul Ginsborg, *Italy and its Discontents 1980–2001* (London: Penguin, 2003), 142.

13. David Hine, *Governing Italy: The Politics of Bargained Pluralism* (Oxford: Clarendon Press, 1993).
14. Montanelli and Cervi, *L'Italia degli anni di fango*, ch. 8.
15. On the exposure of corruption and its impact see Chapter 24, this volume.
16. Gianfranco Pasquino, "Le coalizioni di pentapartito (1980–91): quale governo dei partiti?," in Mario Caciagli, Franco Cazzola, Leonardo Morlino, and Stefano Passigli, eds., *L'Italia fra crisi e transizione* (Bari: Laterza, 1994).
17. Ginsborg, *Italy and its Discontents*, ch. 5.
18. Leonardo Morlino and Marco Tarchi, "The Dissatisfied Society: The Roots of Political Change in Italy," *European Journal of Political Research*, 30 (July 1996), 41–63.
19. Quoted in Enzo Santarelli, *Storia critica della Repubblica* (Milan: Feltrinelli, 1997), 300.

CHAPTER 24

TANGENTOPOLI—MORE THAN 20 YEARS ON

MARTIN RHODES

In 1992–94, a sudden and unanticipated explosion of corruption investigations and prosecutions in Italy (nicknamed *Mani Pulite*, or Clean Hands) produced a series of seismic shocks that radically transformed Italy's political landscape. Within two years, the political class was decapitated, the parties that had dominated the country either collapsed and disappeared or broke into smaller successor organizations, and the electoral and party financing systems were radically reformed via popular referendum.

In early 1994, the prosecuting magistrates of the Milan "pool"[1]—the so-called *troika anti-tangenti* (anti-bribe troika) of Antonio De Pietro, Gherardo Colombo, and Piercamillo Davigo, coordinated by Gerardo d'Ambrosio, and led by chief prosecutor (*procuratore capo*) Francesco Saverio Borrelli—seemed triumphant, and what remained of Italy's caste of established politicians were cowering before judicial onslaughts, hostile public opinion, and the emergence of newly powerful political actors. Yet, in retrospect, the "revolution of the judges" had already peaked and the "counterrevolution of the politicians" was about to begin.

Although focusing on the events of the period, the following discussion also seeks to answer a number of questions about why *Tangentopoli* happened when it did, what it signified, and—in the conclusion—what its legacy has been. Although the early 1990s was clearly a moment of social, political, and economic disarray, creating an unprecedented opportunity for challengers to the postwar political status quo, without an extremely aggressive prosecuting magistracy with a talent for courting public opinion and relatively untrammeled powers in launching investigations and imprisoning suspects, the humble origins of *Tangentopoli* would not have assumed national dimensions - or dragged ever higher ranks of politicians across all political parties into the morass. But those same strengths also made the magistrates highly vulnerable to political counterattack and—eventually—to a decline in popular support.[2]

PHASE 1: MARIO CHIESA
AND CORRUPTION IN MILAN

The first phase of corruption revelations and prosecutions were entirely local, and began with the arrest on February 17, 1992, of Mario Chiesa, president of the Pio Albergo Trivulzio retirement home in Milan, and leading member of the Milanese Socialist Party (PSI). Magistrate Antonio Di Pietro had been led to Chiesa by the owner of a small cleaning firm, Luca Magni, who, tired of being asked to pay bribes, or *tangenti*, to secure contracts, had taken his complaints to the police. Supposed to pay a bribe of 14 million lire (approximately 7,000 euros[3]) on a contract worth 140 million lire, Magni was wired for his meeting with Chiesa and instructed to take only 7 million lire with him, the aim being to provoke Chiesa into demanding the rest, thereby revealing his guilt.

Chiesa spent five weeks behind bars before agreeing to talk on March 23, by which time it was clear that his party had abandoned him. But the reaction to his arrest was immediate. Bobo Craxi, secretary of the Milan PSI, and son of Socialist Party leader Bettino Craxi, attributed the arrest to political motives and the "beginning of the electoral campaign." His father called Chiesa "*un mariuolo*" (a rogue) who had cast a shadow over the reputation of an honest party. Rather than seeing this as an isolated case, the Lega Nord, which would see its vote leap from 0.5 percent to over 8 percent in the April elections, quickly linked Chiesa's early revelations to its slogan "*Roma ladrona*" ("thieving Rome")—a much more accurate characterization, as it turned out, than Craxi's.

For what Chiesa began to reveal was a complex web of corruption involving all of Italy's major political parties, with Craxi's PSI the pivotal player. Chiesa portrayed a system of bribes as taxes on public contracts, some of which ended up in personal bank accounts, in Italy and abroad, but much of it fed into a *mercato occulto* (hidden market) of funds for electoral and factional party competition. The PSI had become, to use Gianfranco Pasquino's description from the mid-1980s, a party of "political entrepreneurs and gamblers,"[4] and Chiesa an example par excellence of the "business politician"[5]—an intermediary (nicknamed "Mr. 10 percent") highly skilled at extortion on behalf of his party.

Despite the gathering clouds, the PSI and the other small centrist governing parties—the Republican PRI, Social Democratic PSDI, and the Liberal PLI—all emerged relatively unscathed from the April 1992 elections. The PSI's larger coalition partner, Christian Democracy (DC), lost 28 seats in the Chamber and 18 in the Senate, but the biggest loser by far was the former Italian Communist Party's Social Democratic successor, the Democratic Party of the Left (PDS), losing 70 seats in the Chamber and 37 in the Senate. Yet, only a year later, both the DC and PSI would be on life support, and the country's voters on the verge of switching off the machine.

Events during those 12 months were cataclysmic. By May 1992, more senior members of the PSI had been caught up in the anti-corruption net, including Carlo Tognoli (a former PSI mayor of Milan and outgoing Minister of Tourism in the Andreotti government) and Paolo Pillitteri (another former PSI mayor of Milan and brother-in-law of Bettino Craxi). That month, investigations into bribes connected to the Milan Metro system began to touch politicians from the DC and eventually the former communist PDS, with the arrests of Maurizio Prada, the DC president of the Milanese municipal transport company (ATM), and Sergio Radaelli, its former PSI vice president.

The Milan Metro affair revealed a cross-party cartel to collect and distribute *tangenti*, mirrored by collusion amongst private sector firms in sharing out contracts. A phenomenon discovered by multiple inquiries, the costs of such networks of corruption to the tax payer and their impact on the efficiency and quality of public works was (and is) extraordinary.[6] In Milan, all companies that worked on the third line of the Milan Metro had to pay bribes equivalent to 4 percent of the contract obtained. According to the prosecutors, 1 percent each went to the DC and the PCI/PDS, while the PSI garnered 2 percent.[7] Between 1980 and 1991, some 30 billion lire was allegedly channeled into the party system via the ATM.[8]

Before proceeding, it is worth considering the dynamics underpinning the events of early 1992 and what exactly was being uncovered. The critical actor was the Milan pool of magistrates. Equipped with the twin tools of "mandatory criminal initiative" (whereby a prosecutor must open a file on an individual when the suspicion of a crime arises, notifying the suspect with an *avviso di garanzia*, or notice of investigation) and *carcere preventivo* or *cautelare* (imprisonment, prior to the proving of guilt, if there is a danger of tampering with evidence or flight from justice), the prosecuting magistrates were able to extend their investigations quickly across the local political–administrative system.[9] In the next phase they were to follow their leads from the lowest to the highest levels of the political party hierarchy.

PHASE 2: "*MANI PULITE*" EXTENDS TO NATIONAL-LEVEL POLITICS

What the magistrates were revealing was a form of systemic corruption that was far from new. Only two decades earlier, the 1970s' "oil scandal" exposed illegal price fixing in the oil derivatives market and a large system of bribes involving the oil producers' association, Unione Petrolifera, ENEL (the state electricity company), and the parties of Italy's governing coalitions—the DC, PSI, Social Democrats (PSDI), Republicans (PRI), and Liberals (PLI).

This kind of arrangement was already routine. As Ciriaco De Mita, then Minister for Industry and future DC leader and prime minister put it: "ENEL finances parties but this is among the, shall we say, 'sub-institutional obligations' of ENEL."[10] The political crisis triggered by the scandal was resolved with no convictions, for a more timid magistracy and rather supine press at the time allowed the parties to collude in burying the scandal. And although a new law on party financing (195/2 May 1974) was introduced (parties would get public subventions if winning more than 2 percent of votes, payments from public sector companies were outlawed, and parties were required to publish annual accounts), absent standardized accounting practices and an effective monitoring system—and regardless of a further strengthening of the rules by new legislation in the early 1980s—the system was easily manipulated.[11] Parliamentary immunity from prosecution was maintained, and illicit party funding continued as before.

In the late 1980s, it was conservatively estimated that, from 1970 to 1987, Italian parties received some 60 billion lire (in 1986 lire) in illegal funding.[12] But investigations in the early 1990s were to reveal a massive escalation in those sums and an enormous expansion in political corruption.

May 1992 saw those investigations reach the summit of the party system when the first of 74 *avvisi di garanzia* (a record during *Tangentopoli*) was delivered to Severino Citaristi, a senator and national treasurer of the Christian Democrats (DC). Citaristi, like many others, freely admitted to the illicit financing of political parties but not to corruption. A similar refrain was repeated in speeches by Bettino Craxi, most notably on July 3, 1992, when Craxi stated that yes, there had been extensive illegal party financing, and that all parties had been involved, and that if these were criminal acts then the entire political system was a criminal one; but that no, this did not justify overturning the system, or delegitimizing the whole political class, or creating a climate in which a careful policy of dealing with the problem might be prevented.

At that point, Craxi, like other leading politicians, was still trying to keep a lid on the revelations. He had aspired to lead the new government formed after the April elections, but was bypassed, due to his connections with the scandals in Milan, by the new President of the Republic, Oscar Luigi Scalfaro, in favor of Giuliano Amato. Amato (Craxi's *éminence grise*) remained unsullied by the corruption allegations hurting the PSI. But any hope that normality would soon be restored was dashed on July 14, when an *avviso di garanzia* was delivered to Craxi's faithful lieutenant Gianni De Michelis, deputy leader of the PSI and Minister of Foreign Affairs (1989–92), alleging the negotiation of bribes linked to highway construction in the Veneto and illegal party financing. In August, Craxi launched the first of a series of attacks on the Milan magistrates, stating, in the PSI paper *Avanti*, that "Con il tempo e attraverso una migliore conoscenza dei fatti di cui qualcuno dovrebbe finalmente occuparsi, potrebbe persino risultare che il dott. Di Pietro è tutt'altro che l'eroe di cui si sente parlare" ("That with time and a better knowledge of the facts that someone should attend to, it may well result that Di Pietro is far from being the hero he is acclaimed to be").[13]

On September 2, Sergio Moroni, Socialist deputy for Bergamo-Brescia and member of the PSI executive, shot himself after receiving two *avvisi di garanzia* alleging corruption relating to public works on the Ferrovie Nord (Northern Railways) and a hospital in Lecco. Moroni's was the first of a series of high-profile deaths linked to *Tangentopoli*. He had sent a suicide note to President Scalfaro stating that a great veil of hypocrisy had shrouded the financing of political parties, but that he had never profited from bribes, was always motivated by political idealism, and that there was no justice to be found in a newspaper and televisual "pogrom" of the political class.[14] Craxi and his *dauphin*, Claudio Martelli, both attacked the magistrates, Craxi blaming them for creating "*un clima infame*" ("a vile atmosphere").[15]

PHASE 3: COMPETITION FOR PUBLIC OPINION AND THE DECAPITATION OF THE PARTIES

The reporting of *avvisi di garanzia* in the media had indeed begun to create a climate in which there was a successful "criminalization of corruption,"[16] but also a growing assumption that a notification of investigation was the same as a guilty verdict. At this stage, some opinion polls gave 80 percent of support to the prosecuting magistrates. But this was also the point at which outright competition between politicians and the Milan pool for public support began, with the words "*il rogo*" (the stake, as in "burning at") and "*caccia alle streghe*" (witch hunt) gaining growing currency. And as the number of "*cadaveri eccellenti*" ("illustrious corpses") grew with further suicides, so public and press opinion slowly began to shift.

Craxi received his first of many *avvisi di garanzia* alleging illegal party financing and corruption on December 15, 1992, and resigned as party leader on February 11. Martelli—who hoped to succeed him—was removed from the scene himself that same week when, due to fallout from a new scandal ("Conto Protezione"), he was forced to relinquish the justice portfolio in the Amato government and his position in the PSI. Former trade unionist Giorgio Benvenuto replaced Craxi at the head of the party instead. This new scandal emerged from the confessions of Silvano Larini, an entrepreneur and PSI *faccendiere* (middleman or fixer), who had revealed a Swiss bank account (Ubs 633369) used (among other things) by Bettino Craxi for foreign financial operations on behalf of his party. Larini alleged that funds had also been destined for the personal use of Craxi and Martelli.

The other small centrist parties were also decapitated in early 1993. On February 25, Giorgio La Malfa, leader of the Republican Party (PRI)—presented as the "*partito degli onesti*" ("party of the honest") in the April elections—resigned after receiving an *avviso* linking him to the Enimont affair (see section 4 below). On March 15, the same fate—in connection with the same scandal—befell Liberal Party (PLI) leader Renato Altissimo. Primo Greganti—a national functionary of the PCI/PDS—was arrested on related charges. Social Democrat Party (PSDI) leader, Carlo Vizzini, was also linked to the Enimont affair, but resigned in March 1993 when he discovered that his party was bankrupt (a case of illegal party financing that failed to finance the party).

Most seriously, on March 31, Socialist Senator Franco Reviglio was forced to resign as Finance Minister in the Amato government after being linked to the emerging ENI affair. ENI turned out to be a case par excellence of the complex web of relationships, established via *lotizzazzione*—the distribution of administrative positions according to party and party faction membership and influence—between politicians and public sector bosses. Regardless of the outlawing of such practices by Law 195/1974, ENI (and other public sector companies) had continued to finance political parties. Reviglio had been chairman of ENI (Italy's national hydrocarbons company, and a Socialist Party fiefdom after 1979) between 1983 and 1989. His Craxi-appointed successor at ENI, Gabriele Cagliari, was also arrested on similar charges.

The Amato government's response to the escalating scandals was twofold, as it attempted both to defuse the crisis and protect *la casta*[17]—the political class—from further prosecution. Those two aims proved to be quite incompatible. If the government imagined that hostile public opinion could be mollified by Amato's request in March that ministers receiving an *avviso di garanzia* surrender their portfolios, it was inflamed by a simultaneous attempt—by Justice Minister, Giovanni Conso—to limit the political impact of the scandals. Legislative provisions included the repayment of bribes and a ban on holding public office in cases of corruption for five years, but also—in a decree law of March 5, 1993—the decriminalization of illegal political financing with retroactive effect, covering those already under investigation.

Referred to as the "*decreto colpo di spugna*" ("wipe the slate clean decree") it provoked an immediate denunciation in the media by the leader of the Milan pool, Francesco Saverio Borrelli.[18] Considered by some a misuse of judicial power in seeking to influence the legislative process,[19] the tactic was nevertheless very successful—the subsequent outcry led President Scalfaro to reject the decree law—and provided proof of the magistrates' ability to mobilize public opinion.

The fate of the Amato government, and its attempts to contain *Tangentopoli*, was effectively sealed by voters' revolt when, in two national referendums (of a total eight) on April 18–19, they backed a majoritarian electoral system for the Italian Senate (82 percent in favor with a 77 percent turnout) and—critically for the future of anti-corruption policy—the abolition of the public financing of political parties (90.3 percent in favor) both for campaigns and organizations. If the magistrates were adept in getting the public behind them, so too was the reform movement led by former DC politician Mario Segni, which, allied with Marco Pannella's Radical Party, put the referendums on the political agenda and secured sufficient support for them at the polls.

Stepping back from these events, it is worth emphasizing that, although elaborated in the heat of an intense and volatile political moment, the 1993 referendum on party financing, and the new legislation (Law 515/December 1993) it spawned, departed substantially from the 1974 law, both in eliminating public subsidies to parties and reimbursing the campaign expenditure of candidates instead, while also introducing a new regulatory structure (with both national and regional agencies) for monitoring and sanctioning party funding. In the 1994 elections, large fines were levied on all parties for exceeding spending limits and failing to reveal the sources of their funds. This was unsurprising given the nature of funding revealed by *Mani Pulite*. Still less surprising was the way in which parties fought back against these regulations and subverted them once the judicial inquiries began to subside, and public support for them faded.

But for the moment, the judges and political reformers seemed triumphant. The referendums were seen as vote of no confidence by Amato and his team which resigned on April 21 to be replaced by a "technical administration" under Carlo Azeglio Ciampi. But the Chamber of Deputies appeared unrepentant when on April 29, it denied authorization for the magistrates to proceed against Craxi, provoking calls for the dissolution of the Chamber by opposition parties and street protests across the country—including one outside Craxi's hotel in Rome later that day: he was showered with coins and bank notes when he emerged amid chants of "Bettino, vuoi pure queste, Bettino, vuoi pure queste" ("Bettino, do you want these as well"), to the tune of *Guantanamera*.[20]

PHASE 4: ENIMONT, "ILLUSTRIOUS CORPSES," AND THE CUSANI TRIAL

Far from containing the turmoil, the inauguration of the Ciampi government on April 28, 1993 opened a new season of *Tangentopoli* with some of its most dramatic events and revelations. Information had begun to appear from what would be the largest scandal of the period, involving ENI and ENEL (the state electricity company) and Enimont, a planned joint venture between ENI and private-sector chemical giant Montedison, owned by industrialist Raul Gardini's Ferruzzi group. Once again, Craxi's PSI took the role of principal protagonist.

Gabriele Cagliari, chairman of ENI and Craxi appointee after 1989, had been arrested on March 9. Cagliari admitted paying four billion lire to a representative of the PSI to secure a contract on a power station being built by ENEL, and revealed some 50 billion in illegal funding through ENI and its subsidiaries to the Socialists and Christian Democrats. Former ENI finance director, Florio Fiorini, alleged that 1.2 billion lire per annum had been channeled to the DC, PSI, Liberals and Social Democrats during the 1970s and 40 million each month to the DC and PSI in the 1980s. Cagliari was also caught up in the "Montedison-Enimont" affair.

Cagliari spent 133 days in Milan's San Vittore prison under *carcerazione preventive*, before committing suicide on July 20. Raul Gardini, colourful industrialist, *bon vivant* and the main architect of the Enimont deal, had agreed to meet Antonio Di Pietro to explain his role in the affair on July 23. But shaken by the death of Cagliari, and aware that his industrial empire was about to crumble, Gardini took his own life with a pistol early that day. These two deaths sent a shock wave through Italy, provoking second thoughts by many who had celebrated the members of the Milan pool as heroes, and leading supporters in the national press to reflect somberly on the appropriateness of their judicial tactics.

Eugenio Scalfari, a journalist who had campaigned against corruption since the 1950s, and distinguished founder, and at the time, editor of *La Repubblica*, had cautioned the Milan magistrates a week or so before Cagliari's suicide, advising them to be careful in their use of *carcerazione preventive*—to consign suspects to trial as quickly as possible and avoid expressions of triumphalism. The danger, he wrote, with some prescience, was that this strategy could "boomerang back" on the judges.[21] With Cagliari's death, Scalfari wrote that if *carcere preventivo* was used injudiciously and prolonged "saremmo allora in presenza di uno stravolgimento che minerebbe dalle fondamenta il corretto esercizio della giurisdizione penale" ("this would represent a misuse and distortion that would undermine the correct implementation of criminal law").[22] As it turned out, it was precisely this issue that would give credibility to an increasing number of attacks on the magistrates.

But the most spectacular event of the era had yet to come. The trial of Sergio Cusani—a key financial intermediary between Raul Gardini and the entire spectrum of Italian political parties who was arrested on the day of Gardini's death—began on October 28 and was transmitted live on television, attracting in its most popular moments a peak audience of 4 million (some 16 percent of viewers). Variously analyzed as a "ritual of degradation," "a collective purification ceremony" or even "public pornography,"[23] the Cusani trial certainly entwined moral and legal elements in novel prime time fashion. As Cusani himself remarked if "la tangente Enimont è stata definita la madre di tutte le tangenti … il processo è diventato il padre di tutti i processi" ("if the Enimont bribe was the mother of all bribes … the trial was the father of all trials").[24]

Testimony from Giuseppe Garofano, a former Montedison chairman, and two other former Ferruzzi group executives, revealed that huge kickbacks were given to leading politicians in return for the purchase at an inflated price of Montedison's 40 percent stake in Enimont. Cusani revealed details of his role in disbursing the *maxi-tangente* (of some 150 billion lire—77.5 million euros) deriving from the Enimont deal. Craxi and DC leader Arnaldo Forlani were alleged to have received the lion's share (75 and 35 billion lire respectively), with smaller sums allegedly going to Claudio Martelli and a host of other politicians, mainly from the small centrist parties which, in addition to sharing power with the DC and PSI, had also shared in the profits from collusive, cross-party corruption.

With all of the qualities of a court room drama series, Di Pietro, the rough-edged prosecutor, engaged in a four-month long duel with Cusani's lawyer Giuliano Spazzali, and confronted a long cast of witness/suspects, including Craxi, the combative defendant, who sought, though not convincingly, to justify his actions ("everybody did it"), and Arnaldo Forlani his hapless DC counterpart ("I don't remember"; "it wasn't me"). Leading representatives from almost all of Italy's political parties were paraded through the court. More than a dozen of these were eventually convicted of illegal party financing—including some, like Umberto Bossi and Alessandro Patellei from the Lega Nord, who had been cheering the prosecution from the gallery, only to find themselves in the dock. The entire political system was truly on trial—and in full public view.

Some have attempted to separate analytically political from administrative corruption, or to link corruption in Italy solely to its system of proportional representation and preference voting (abolished by referendum in 1991), rather than to a more diffuse form of bad governance.[25] But it was clear from the revelations from the Cusani and other trials that corruption had multiple causes, and was manifest in many spheres, generating a series of vicious circles contributing to the "parallel growth of corruption, inefficiency, clientelism and (under certain conditions) the political protection of organized crime."[26] It was unlikely that new rules—or even the arrival of new parties in power—could undermine this level of systemic corruption or convince politicians to accept a change of regime. And so it turned out to be with the arrival of Berlusconi on the Italian political scene from early 1994.

PHASE 5: BERLUSCONI AND THE RESIGNATION OF DI PIETRO

The Cusani trial was not the end of *Tangentopoli*, but it was certainly its zenith. Two further major scandals were unearthed in the months that followed. On 20 September 1993 came the arrest in Switzerland of Duilio Poggiolini, after several months on the run. Director-general of the *Servizio farmaceutico nazionale* of the Ministry of Health, Poggiolini confessed to receiving bribes (what he called "contributions") from pharmaceutical companies between 1974 and 1992. Police discovered a treasure trove of banknotes, Krugerrand, and jewels worth hundreds of billions of lire in his house.

Francesco De Lorenzo—Liberal Party member and Health Minister from 1989 to 1992—was also caught up in the wider National Health Service scandal and eventually sentenced for having taken 8 billion lire in *tangenti* from the pharmaceutical industry. Then, in April 1994, 80 members of Italy's financial police (Guardia di Finanza—popularly known as "Le Fiamme Gialle," or "Yellow Flames") and hundreds of industrialists were accused of corruption and bribes linked to tax evasion—an investigation nicknamed "Fiamme Sporche," or "Dirty Flames." By June, those inquiries had extended to Silvio Berlusconi's holding company Fininvest—creating a new and formidable enemy of the anti-corruption campaign.

Italy's local elections in November 1993 saw the DC and what was left of the country's other traditional parties massacred—primarily by the former communists, the Lega Nord and neo-fascists—a result expected to be repeated in forthcoming national elections. But the emergence of entrepreneur Silvio Berlusconi and his new political party *Forza Italia* in January 1994 changed everything. The election of a government led by Berlusconi at the end of March not only consigned the traditional governing parties to history—to be replaced by Forza Italia, the right-wing Alleanza Nazionale (succeeding the post-fascist Movimento Sociale Italiano, or MSI) and Umberto Bossi's Lega Nord—but also opened a new (and final) phase of *Tangentopoli*.

Prior to the election of Berlusconi, there had been many attacks on the magistrates, both open and public and covert (including death threats from the mysterious "Falange armata"—a shady organization reputed to be connected to right-wing terrorism). But those attacks would now increase, placing greater pressure on Di Pietro and his colleagues. They would also impact their hitherto very high levels of public backing as the "politicization of anti-corruption" began to polarize society between center-left support for the judicial system and center-right opposition to it.[27]

The "Fiamme Sporche" investigations may also have impacted public support for the "judge's revolution," for as Francesco Saverio Borrelli would later comment, once the corruption inquiries moved to lower levels, affecting small and medium-business owners—ordinary citizens—"people began to say that's enough: you've liberated us from the old political class that sucked our blood, now you can leave us in peace."[28]

The removal of Bettino Craxi from the Italian scene (Craxi fled to Tunisia to avoid arrest in mid-May, where he would remain until his death in early 2000) did not bring the political fight he had initiated to an end. Already under investigation himself, Berlusconi quickly took up the gauntlet. As Massimo D'Alema, then leader of the PDS, acutely remarked in early September, "Far from disappearing from Italian political life, Berlusconi represents the highest form of Craxismo."[29] Thus, while the previous parliament had voted to abolish parliamentary immunity from investigation at the end of October 1993, the new government tried to revisit the rejected Conso decree in what became known as the "*decreto salva-ladri*" ("save the thieves" decree) presented by new Justice Minister Alfredo Biondi. The Biondi decree, issued on July 13, made the illicit financing of political parties a non-custodial offence.

On July 16 the new decree allowed a number of high profile prisoners to be released—including Francesco Di Lorenzo, whose corruption charges connected to the National Health Service had especially enraged public opinion. In response, the magistrates went on the offensive once again in the media, and the so-called "popolo dei fax" (the concerned general public) sent faxes and telegrams to newspapers and television stations protesting the Biondi decree. Alleanza Nazionale and the Lega Nord threatened to withdraw their support from the government, while Berlusconi threatened to resign, in turn, if the decree was not retained. But on July 19, the Commission of Constitutional Affairs of the Chamber of Deputies blocked the Biondi decree and the government was forced to withdraw it.

The fight was now fully on between Berlusconi and his allies and the magistrates. The late summer and autumn of 1994 saw a series of attacks on the latter as their inquiries began to close in on Berlusconi, his family and his business interests—the opening salvos, as it turned out, in a war that was to continue for the next two decades. On July 29 his brother Paolo was placed under house arrest on charges of bribing the *Guardia di Finanza*. In September, Giuliano Ferrara, the Minister for Relations with Parliament (and one of many political transplants from the PSI to Forza Italia) denounced the Milan magistrates for attacking the constitution. Meanwhile, Sergio Cusani accused them of defamation, and one of the high ranking financial police charged under "Fiamme Sporche" attacked them for manipulating the legal process.

In early October, Fininvest manager Giulio Tradati was arrested and more charges brought against Paolo Berlusconi. Tradati would reveal the existence of Swiss bank accounts employed for financing illegal corporate activities in Italy and an off-shore company, All Iberian, and allegedly used to channel very large bribes from Berlusconi to Craxi.[30] Ten days later, Justice Minister Biondi sent a team of inspectors to investigate the operations of the Milan magistrates, but to his annoyance nothing untoward was revealed. Inquiries into the activities of Massimo Berruti, a lawyer and *forzista*, led the Milan magistrates to allege tampering with evidence relating to Fininvest corruption on Berlusconi's behalf: on 21 November they sent an *avviso di garanzia* to Berlusconi himself while he was hosting, somewhat ironically, a UN conference in Naples on international organized crime.

Two days later, an attempt to destroy the reputation of Antonio Di Pietro, with murky origins, was launched by businessman Giancarlo Gorrini. Gorrini denounced Di Pietro for having received from him an interest free loan of 100 million lire, a Mercedes and repayment of debts incurred from betting on horses. The next day, November 24, Alfredo Biondi launched another inquiry—this time covert—into the work of the Milan magistrates. In the background, it was alleged by those involved in the inquiry that Defense Minister Cesare Previti, a close confidante of Berlusconi (who President Scalfaro had rejected as Justice Minister due to his past shady dealings) had said that Di Pietro was to be destroyed and that Gorrini had been paid to do so.[31]

Faced with the prospect of further attacks, and fearing that his constant political and media attention was threatening the integrity of the judicial investigations, Antonio Di Pietro resigned from the Milan pool on December 6, 2004—effectively bringing *Mani Pulite* to a close. His resignation letter stated that "The only thing I can hope for is that without me there will be a 'depersonalization' of the '*Mani Pulite*' inquiries and a calming of the passions that I have involuntarily excited."[32]

The first Berlusconi government was forced to resign itself only two weeks later on December 22 when Umberto Bossi's Lega Nord withdrew its support, to be replaced by yet another "technical" administration led by former Treasury Minister Lamberto Dini. But, regardless, the "passions excited" by Di Pietro and the other members of the Milan pool continued to redound on them over the next few years in the form of multiple attacks on their record and reputation. It was only 14 months later that Gorrini's accusations against Di Pietro were dismissed by a court in Brescia, and those accused of plotting against Di Pietro—notably Paolo Berlusconi and Cesare Previti—themselves charged with pressuring him to resign to distract judicial attention from Silvio Berlusconi and Fininvest.[33]

Throughout 1995 and 1996, further accusations were levelled at the magistrates and rumors circulated in the press to undermine their credibility, including the oft-repeated attack from Berlusconi against "*le toghe rosse*" (red togas)—referring to the robes of magistrates, and their alleged left-wing leanings (even though most members of the Milan pool were on the center-right). In early May 1995, another Minister of Justice, Filippo Mancuso, launched an investigation into the Milan magistrates for misusing *custodio cautelare*—provoking a vote of no confidence in Mancuso by many parties supporting the Dini government.

Predictably, Di Pietro continued to attract much attention after he entered politics as Minister for Public Works in the government of Romano Prodi that took office in April 1996—a position he held for only six months before resigning on November 14 after being notified of further charges related to his role in *Mani Pulite*. As stated in his resignation letter to Prodi, he was driven from government by the same pressures that forced his departure from the magistracy: "I've had enough of those who seek to use my person to delegitimize the *Mani Pulite* inquiries on the one hand and the government and its institutions on the other."[34]

CONCLUSIONS

The events and revelations of 1992–94 tell us much about the Italian political and judicial systems, both then and since, regarding the timing of *Tangentopoli*, its significance and its longer term consequences.

As for why *Tangentopoli* happened when it did, regularly rehearsed macro arguments point to the end of the Cold War, the subsequent erosion of the cross-party consensus (and US veto) on keeping the Italian Communist Party out of power, and the expansion of political and administrative corruption to systemic dimensions, with ever-escalating costs for those caught up in the market for bribes. The coincidence of *Tangentopoli* with the economic crisis of the early to mid-1990s and an intensification of the war between the Italian state and the mafia also undoubtedly contributed to a context of political tumult and disorder,[35] in which the space for an unprecedented prosecution of corruption was expanded. But the real significance of these factors is hard to ascertain, compared to the one critical element—the extraordinary power of the Italian prosecuting magistrates (and the equally extraordinary determination of Antonio Di Pietro)—without which *Tangentopoli* simply could not have occurred.

With respect to *Tangentopoli*'s significance, there are various interpretations: was this an explosion of pent-up anger and frustration on the part of Italians, after decades of stagnation in a blocked "consociational" political status quo, or was it simply a moment of diffuse dissatisfaction exploited by new political challengers to that order, rather than a de-legitimization and rejection of the entire system? The fact that public opinion support for anti-corruption weakened considerably once Berlusconi and his allies politicized the judicial inquiries (although some 92 percent of Italians polled in 1996 saw corruption as very or quite important, that figure collapsed to just 5.5 percent in 2001[36]) undermines the notion that public opinion was either a constant or an independent force.

Moreover, neither public opinion nor press scrutiny have prevented what Antonio Di Pietro has called the "metastasizing of the cancer discovered by *Mani Pulite* to the entire system" over the last 20 years.[37] Much more convincing are analyses that point to the importance of a novel and mutually reinforcing interaction in the period between the magistrates and the press—both much stronger and more independent than in the past—in fueling popular outrage and the role, in turn, of new political actors intent on exploiting the opportunity to undermine the status quo.[38]

The decline in public support for anti-corruption after 1994 was not simply due to Berlusconi's politicization of the issue. It was also linked to a mutual delegitimization of judicial activity and political power in the ever bitter clashes between the two.[39] The politicians behaved abysmally, and were guilty of both actively attacking and undermining the magistrates and failing, under any of the governments of the period, to tackle corruption seriously: not a single law or decree was passed in 1992–94 (nor much besides in the years thereafter) to support the investigations or clamp down on corruption.[40] But the magistrates also overplayed their hand in their use of *carcerazione preventive*, thereby losing powerful supporters in the media, and opening themselves unnecessarily to credible critiques from their opponents.[41] The politicization of the Italian magistracy itself, and its organization along ideological lines, may not have characterized the Milan pool as such. But anti-judicial rhetoric, and some hard evidence, regarding political bias in judicial investigations,[42] clearly hurt *Mani Pulite* at the time, and Italy's broader anti-corruption struggle since, by giving some credence to dubious political attacks on magistrates' impartiality, notably by Berlusconi but also many others.

Finally, although outside the scope of this chapter, the lack of a more incisive, longer-term impact by *Mani Pulite* on corruption and illicit party financing tells us much about the embeddedness of corruption in Italy's institutions, political class and political culture. In the years after *Tangentopoli*, successive Italian parliaments have introduced more restrictions on the prosecution of political corruption - including *ad personam* laws to protect politicians involved in criminal proceedings, a perpetuation of absurdly short statutes of limitation, and the decriminalization of certain corruption offences - than they have policies to support it. The spirit and letter of the 1993 referendum on party financing were completely abused by legislators as they sought over the following years to expand and exploit public funding and to protect its use from external scrutiny. In the words of one analyst "Italian political parties formed a cartel to protect their collective financial security."[43] *Plus ça change*.

In 2012, after a new series of party finance scandals, and amidst another economic crisis and voters' revolt—with strong similarities to 1992–94—a new party finance law was passed (Law 96/2012) which sought to place greater controls and surveillance on the misuse of funds.[44] The difference this time was that external pressures on Italy—from the Council of Europe, the European Commission and the Organisation for Economic Co-operation and Development—cast a new and harsh light on the self-serving behavior of Italy's political class.

NOTES

1. The word" "pool" used in relation to the Italian magistracy, refers to a tight and closed group of magistrates who share amongst themselves all the information relating to an investigation but also keep that information secret. Originally adopted by anti-Mafia

judges in the early 1980s, the aim was to allow the group to continue working if one of the magistrates was murdered.

2. This analysis relies on multiple sources, including the Italian press and secondary accounts. Among the latter, the most useful were Gianni Barbacetto, Peter Gomez, and Marco Travaglio, *Mani pulite: La vera storia* (Milan: Chiaralettere, 2012), (a monumental and indispensable piece of investigative journalism) and the shorter but nonetheless useful and highly readable account by Paolo Posteraro, *I peggiori anni della nosta vita—Da Craxi alla caduta di Berlusconi,* (Rome: Newton Compton Editori, 2010).

3. There are 1,936.27 lire to the euro.

4. Gianfranco Pasquino, "Modernity and Reform: The PSI between Political Entrepreneurs and Gamblers," *West European Politics* 9, 1986: 118–141.

5. Donatella Della Porta (1996), "Actors in Corruption: Business Politicians in Italy," *International Social Science Journal*, 48, 149: 349–364.

6. Donatella Della Porta and Alberto Vannucci, "Corruption and Anti-Corruption: The Political Defeat of 'Clean Hands' in Italy," *West European Politics*, 30, 4, 2007: 830–853

7. Martin Rhodes, "Financing Party Politics in Italy: A Case of Systemic Corruption," *West European Politics*, 20, 1, 1997: 55–80.

8. Donatella Della Porta and Alberto Vannucci, *Corrupt Exchanges: Actors, Resources, and Mechanisms of Political Corruption*, De Gruyter 1999, p. 33.

9. Carlo Guarnieri, "The Judiciary in the Italian Political Crisis," *West European Politics*, 20, 1, 1997: 157–175 and David Nelken, "The Judges and Political Corruption in Italy," *Journal of Law and Society*, 23, 1, 1996: 95–112.

10. Cited in A. M. Chiesi, "I meccanismi di allocazione nello scambio corrotto," *Stato e Mercato*, 43, 1995, p. 147.

11. See Rhodes, "Financing Party Politics in Italy," 58–65; E. Auci, "Verita e problem dei bilanci dei partiti," *Il Mulino* 253, 1978, 65–73; and F. Cazzola, *Della corruzione: Fisiologia e patalogia di un sistema politico*, (Bologna: Il Mulino, 1988).

12. Cazzola, *Della Corruzione*, note 6, pp. 138–139.

13. *La Repubblica*, August 23,1992.

14. "L'ultima lettera di Sergio Moroni," <http://www.ossimoro.it/massacro.htm>.

15. Sebastiano Messina, "L'Accusa di Craxi: 'Clima Infame'," *La Repubblica*, September 4, 1992.

16. S. Sberna and Alberto Vanucci, "It's the Politics, Stupid': The Politicization of Anti-Corruption in Italy," *Crime, Law and Social Change*, 60, 5, 2013: 565–593.

17. See *La casta: Così i politici italiani sono diventati intoccabili,* by Sergio Rizzo and Gian Antonio Stella, Rizzoli 2007.

18. Franco Coppola, "E da Conso mano tesa a Borrelli," *La Repubblica*, February 27, 1993.

19. E.g. Posteraro, *I peggiori anni della nosta vita*, pp. 51–52.

20. This extraordinary scene can be viewed at <https://www.youtube.com/watch?v =2lOrwLu8sjA>.

21. Eugenio Scalfari, "Modesti suggerimenti a Di Pietro," *La Repubblica*, July 11, 1993.

22. Eugenio Scalfari, "Un morto sulla coscienza del paese," *La Repubblica*, July 21, 1993.

23. See, respectively, Pier Paolo Giglioli, Sandra Cavicchioli and Giolo Fele, *Rituali di degradazione: Anatomia del processo Cusani*, Bologna: il Mulino, 1997; Roberta Sassatelli, "Justice, Television and Delegitimation: On the Cultural Codification of the Italian Political Crisis," *Modern Italy*, 3, 1, 1998, pp. 108–115; and Ruth Miller, *The Erotics of Corruption: Law, Scandal, and Political Perversion*, SUNY Press 2009, pp. 22–24.

24. Cited in Piero Colaprico, 'Al processo Cusani un gran finale da 'guerre stellari', *La Repubblica*, April 18, 1994.

25. E.g., M. A. Golden and E. C. C. Chang, "Competitive Corruption: Factional Conflict and Political Malfeasance in Postwar Italian Christian Democracy," *World Politics*, 53, 4, 2001: 588–622.

26. D. Della Porta and A. Vannucci, "The 'Perverse Effects' of Political Corruption," *Political Studies*, 45, 3, 1997: 516–538, at p. 537.

27. Sberna and Vanucci, "It's the Politics, Stupid."

28. "Quando, con l'indagine sulla Guardia di finanza, si andò oltre, apparve chiaro che il problema della corruzione in Italia investiva gli alti livelli proprio in quanto partiva dal basso. Ho l'impressione che la gente abbia cominciato a dire: adesso basta, avete fatto il vostro lavoro, ci avete liberato dalla piovra della vecchia classe politica che ci succhiava il sangue, ma adesso lasciateci campare in pace," cited in Giorgio Dell'Arti, "Cinquantamila Giorni," *Corriere della Sera*, November 5, 2013, http://cinquantamila.corriere.it/storyTellerThread.php?threadId=BORRELLI+Francesco+Saverio>.

29. "Lo dice Craxi, che è una figura tutt' altro che scomparsa dalla vita politica italiana. Il berlusconismo potrebbe essere definite … la fase suprema del craxismo" in Alessandra Longo, 'E contro la destra ecco i 'Democratici', *La Repubblica*, September 3, 1994.

30. Luca Fazzo, "Tangenti, errori e misteri nel grande affare All Iberian," *La Repubblica*, 15 June 1998.

31. Cinzia Sasso, "E Previti ci disse: Di Pietro va distrutto," *La Repubblica*, January 18, 1996.

32. "L'unica cosa che riesco ad immaginare (e che è nelle mie possibilità) è quella di "spersonalizzare" l'inchiesta "Mani pulite," nella speranza che, senza di me, le passioni, che la mia persona può aver involontariamente acceso intorno alla normale dialettica processuale, si plachino," "Lettera di Di Pietro al procuratore capo Borrelli, 6 dicembre 1994," *Corriere della Sera*, "Cinquantamila Giorni," <http://cinquantamila.corriere.it/storyTellerArticolo.php?storyId=4e678c06e7798>.

33. They, in turn, were absolved by the Brescia court in late January 1997 for lack of evidence—although Previti was to be charged and convicted for corruption in the late 1990s.

34. "Basta, soprattutto, con chi vuole usare la mia persona per delegittimare per un verso l'inchiesta Mani pulite e per l'altro il Governo e le Istituzioni," 'Lettera di dimissioni di Antonio Di Pietro', November 14, 1996, *Corriere della Sera*, Cinquantamila Giorni, <http://cinquantamila.corriere.it/storyTellerArticolo.php?storyId=4e67948bb36c5>.

35. Leading anti-mafia judges Giovanni Falcone and Paolo Borsellino were murdered by the mafia on May 23 and July 19, 1992 respectively, and in May–July 1993 a mafia bombing campaign hit Florence, Milan and Rome killing a dozen people.

36. Alberto Vannucci, "The Controversial Legacy of 'Mani Pulite': A Critical Analysis of Italian Corruption and Anti-Corruption Policies," *Bulletin of Italian Politics*, 1, 2: 235.

37. "Mani Pulite, le lacrime di Di Pietro e la contestazione di Stefania Craxi," *Corriere della Sera*, February 17, 2012.

38. See Véronique Pujas and Martin Rhodes, "Party Finance and Political Scandal in Italy, Spain and France," *West European Politics*, 22, 3, 1999: 41–63 and J.-L. Briquet, "A Crisis of Legitimacy in Italy: The Scandals Facing the First Republic (1992-1994)," *International Social Science Journal*, 60, 196, 2009: 297–309.

39. S. Belligni, "Magistrati e politici nella crisis italiana. Democrazia dei guardiani e neopopulismo," Political Theory Series Working Paper, No. 11, 2000, Department of Public Policy and Public Choice, University of Eastern Piedmont.

40. Della Porta and Vanucci, "Corruption and Anti-Corruption," p. 839.

41. See M. Maor, "Feeling the Heat? Anticorruption Mechanisms in Comparative Perspective," *Governance*, 17, 1, 2004: 1–28 on the risks to anti-corruption campaigns in combining legal with moral appeals to the public and over-reaching in their use of strong judicial tactics.

42. A. Ceron and M. Mainenti, "Toga Party: The Political Basis of Judicial Investigations against MPs in Italy (1983-2013)," EPSA 2013 Annual General Conference Paper No. 234. <http://ssrn.com/abstract=2224735>.

43. R. Pelizzo, "From Principal to Practice: Constitutional Principles and the Transformation of Party Finance in Germany and Italy," *Comparative European Politics*, 2, 2, 2004, p. 138.

44. See Daniela Piccio, "A Self-Interested Legislator? Party Regulation in Italy," *South European Society and Politics*, 19, 1, 2014: 135–152 and European Commission, *Italy: Annex to the EU Anti-Corruption Report*, Brussels, 3.2.2014 COM (2014) 38 Final—Annex 12.

CHAPTER 25

....

BIPOLARITY (AND AFTER)

....

JONATHAN HOPKIN

THE period after the 1994 elections marked a clear break with the party politics of Italy's postwar "First Republic." Italy's party system in the postwar period was famously described by Giovanni Sartori as an exemplar of "polarized pluralism"[1]—a fragmented multi-party system with extremist "anti-system" parties on either flank and a governing coalition in the center, making alternation in power impossible. From 1994 on, Italian elections took on a bipolar dynamic, with two broad electoral coalitions competing to take control of the government, and a number of reasonably clean alternations in power, with almost total turnover of government personnel. Two factors conspired to bring about these dramatic changes in the party system and the relationship between government and parliament: the *Tangentopoli* scandals (described in Chapter 24, this volume) which wiped out much of the existing political elite and the major parties of government, and the change to the electoral system, with the highly proportional electoral law of the postwar period replaced by a largely majoritarian one in 1993, after a popular referendum (see Chapter 11, this volume).

This chapter charts the emergence and evolution of a broadly bipolar or majoritarian pattern of party competition and explains how, without any formal change to Italy's constitutional arrangements, the changes in the party system brought about a dramatic transformation in how Italy is governed. The chapter looks at the collapse of the center and the emergence of both new parties and new electoral coalitions on the center-left and the center-right. It shows the ways in which the new party system approximated the classic two-party model associated with majoritarian electoral systems and the important differences due to the continued high levels of fragmentation within the center-left and center-right electoral blocs. It also shows how the changing pattern of partisan competition affected the relations between prime ministers and their governments, and between governments and the parliament. It concludes by assessing the consequences of the Eurozone crisis after 2008 for Italy's incipient electoral bipolarity.

From Consensus to Competition?
The 1994 Elections and the Birth
of the Second Republic

The transformation of the Italian party system in 1994 was more than simply a "critical election," changing the balance of power between parties or the dynamics of coalition formation. Between 1992 and 1994 the incumbent parliamentary elite—which had enjoyed a high degree of continuity in the postwar period, with some leading politicians at the heart of power since the war—was swept away, along with the main political parties. Parliamentary turnover reached 70 percent for the Chamber of Deputies,[2] and the party labels under which the new legislators were elected were for the most part completely different from those in the previous election just two years earlier. Not only was there a wholesale renewal of the political elite; the political parties that structured the voters' choices in 1994 were, with few exceptions, either entirely new organizations or existing parties that had radically changed their ideological and electoral identities (electoral volatility as measured by the Pedersen index was 36 percent). Moreover, the new electoral law changed the relationship between parties, forcing them to compete in entirely new ways. All this amounted to a sea-change in Italian politics.[3]

The politics of what came to be named the "First Republic" (1948–92) was dominated by the Christian Democrats (Democrazia Cristiana; DC), which was not only the largest party in electoral terms, but also occupied the pivotal, central space in the party system, making it an indispensable component of any governing coalition (see Chapter 12, this volume). As a result, the DC led all government coalitions in Italy from 1948 to 1992, particularly since its most powerful rival, the Italian Communist Party (Partito Comunista Italiano; PCI), was in practice excluded from the process of government formation by a combination of domestic and international vetoes. This arrangement was described by Galli as an "imperfect two-party system" (*bipartitismo imperfetto*), with an essentially bipolar dynamic of electoral competition, but without the possibility of the government changing hands.[4] Indeed, despite the large and growing number of parties achieving parliamentary representation in postwar Italy, the combined vote share of the DC and PCI did not fall below 60 percent until 1992.[5] But the DC's gradually declining vote share meant that, over time, governing coalitions increasingly included a broader range of parties. This centrist coalition was the only feasible government due to the large share of votes won by the anti-system parties identified by Sartori. For most of the period after 1962, the DC relied on the support of the Socialists (Partito Socialista Italiano; PSI), and through the 1980s, they were joined by three microparties—the Liberals, Republicans, and Social Democrats—in a five-party coalition known as the *pentapartito* (see Chapter 23, this volume).

The *Tangentopoli* crisis hit the centrist governing parties hardest, whilst the adoption of an electoral law based on single-member constituencies exposed these parties

Table 25.1 Index of Bipolarism (Combined Vote Share of Two Largest Parties, Chamber of Deputies)

Year	DC	PCI	Total
1950s	41.2	22.7	63.9
1960s	38.7	26.1	64.8
1970s	38.6	30.6	69.2
1980s	33.7	31.6	65.3
	DC	PDS	
1992	29.7	16.1	45.8
	FI	PDS/DS	
1994	21.0	20.4	41.4
1996	20.6	21.1	41.7
2001	29.4	16.6	46.0
	FI	Olive-Tree	
2006	23.7	31.3	55.0
	PDL	PD	
2008	37.4	33.2	70.6
	M5S	PD	
2013	25.5	25.4	50.9

Source: Bufacchi and Burgess, *Italy Since 1989*, p.173; adapted and updated by author. For 1994-2001, the table reports vote shares in the proportional section of the ballot.

to the winner-take-all dynamics of first past the post-electoral competition.[6] The prospect of fighting elections under majoritarian rules with almost all of their leaders fighting corruption charges brought the implosion of the political forces of the *pentapartito*, opening up a void in the center and center-right of the political spectrum. Threatened by the possible victory of the left in these conditions, media magnate Silvio Berlusconi mobilized his own public image and his corporate resources to reorganize the fragmented center-right into a single electoral coalition, drawing on the emergent Northern League and the extreme-right National Alliance. In response, the post-communist left (the Democratic Party of the Left— Partito Democratico della Sinistra; PDS) built an electoral alliance with its radical left rivals the Communist Refoundation Party (Partito della Rifondazione Comunista; PRC), and other center-left forces. The *bipartitismo imperfetto* of the First Republic began to transform into a genuinely bipolar competition between left and right, albeit maintaining a high degree of fragmentation.[7]

Squeezed uncomfortably between these two was the Italian Popular Party (Partito Popolare Italiano; PPI), the successor party to the DC, which was formally dissolved in January 1994. Under the PR electoral law of the First Republic the DC had been "condemned to govern,"[8] since no feasible parliamentary majority could be constructed without it. Under the new electoral system, the PPI was now in the position of having to face both ways before the electorate, with powerful threats to both its left and right. The well-known effects of single-member constituencies, whereby voters tend to cast tactical votes in favor of one of the two strongest candidates,[9] polarized electoral support around the electoral alliances on either flank of the PPI. The predictable consequence was that despite polling a respectable, if much reduced, vote share, the PPI won few seats, and the Christian Democratic presence in the new parliament was limited to a small centrist rump, although a number of more conservative DC refugees won election in Berlusconi's coalition (under the label CCD— Centro Cristiano Democratico or Christian Democratic Center). After the 1994 elections, the Italian Parliament revolved around two large electoral alliances, each aiming to win majority support and form governments led by identifiable prime ministerial candidates. The next section describes the development over time of these two electoral blocs.

MAJORITARIAN POLITICS IN ITALY: FROM POLARIZED PLURALISM TO A TWO-PARTY SYSTEM?

The shift to bipolarity is closely related to the momentous changes in Eastern Europe in the late 1980s that led to the collapse of the Soviet bloc and the end of communist regimes in Europe. Geography, and the political and electoral strength of the PCI, had placed Italy in the frontline of the Cold War, but the PCI had increasingly distanced itself from the Soviet Union in the 1970s and 1980s, developing the concept of Eurocommunism and seeking to challenge the effective veto on communists participating in government. This culminated in PCI leader Achille Occhetto's proposing the formal abandonment of the party's communist identity at the end of 1989, as the communist regimes in the East were collapsing. The new party, formally launched at the Rimini Congress of 1991, was named the Partito Democratico della Sinistra (Democratic Party of the Left; the PDS was subsequently relaunched as the Democratici di Sinistra [Left Democrats; DS] in 1998), and adhered to the tradition of European social democracy, joining the Socialist International and the Party of European Socialists in the European Parliament. The aim was to move beyond the PCI's exclusion from the inner core of the party system and become a governing party, perhaps in alliance with the Socialists.[10] The collapse of the centrist coalition in 1992-94, and the quasi-majoritarian electoral reform which the PDS supported, appeared to present the reformed party with an unmissable opportunity to capitalize on its new identity.

The 1994 election illustrated the limitations of this strategy. Occhetto's shift to the center had met with opposition on the left of the PCI, a sector of which departed to form the Party of the Communist Refoundation (PRC).[11] In order to maximize the chances of a left victory, Occhetto formed a broad-based alliance, the Progressives, which included PRC on the left as well as some smaller socialist and liberal groups to the right of the PDS. The retention of a hammer and sickle (albeit in miniature) in the PDS symbol and the deal with PRC allowed Berlusconi to depict the Progressive Alliance as a coalition of communists, nullifying Occhetto's attempts to move beyond the communist past and appeal to a broader electorate. The PDS's weak showing in the election, winning just over 20 percent of the proportional vote, compared with 6 percent for PRC, cautioned against abandoning the broad left strategy. But an electoral alliance spanning from the communist left to the center (represented by Democratic Alliance, some of whose leaders subsequently joined Berlusconi on the right) created problems of credibility and internal coherence. The evolution of the center-left after 1994 can be seen as a series of attempts to resolve this dilemma.

The fall of the Berlusconi government in late 1994 revealed that the center-right, although electorally more successful, faced similar problems. Berlusconi's dramatic entry onto the political scene at the head of a completely new party, Forza Italia,[12] entirely reconfigured the center-right political space. Forza Italia was the big winner of the 1994 poll but could only ensure victory by building a broad electoral alliance—the Pole of Freedoms in the North with the populist Northern League, which advocated the separation of the North from the rest of Italy[13], and the Pole of Good Government in the South with National Alliance,[14] the successor party to the post-fascist Italian Social Movement, a strongly nationalist party with deep roots in the South. A common interest in averting a communist victory and the temptations of political power were not enough to overcome the obvious divisions between the Northern League and its coalition partners, and the League split with Berlusconi, returning the fold only at the 2001 elections.

The Northern League's estrangement from Berlusconi meant that the center-right was divided at the 1996 elections, with the predictable consequence that the center-right parties were penalized by the workings of the new electoral system. Despite their overall vote share of over 50 percent in the constituency votes, the divided center-right won fewer seats than the center-left Olive Tree coalition led by Romano Prodi, who was able to form a government with majority support in the Chamber of Deputies and a narrow but unstable majority in the Senate. The center-right's defeat, despite a strong showing (both National Alliance and the Northern League made significant gains) demonstrated that there were very clear incentives for the two main electoral blocs to field joint candidates for the constituency votes. The Olive Tree was the left's response to these incentives, with the PDS forming the core of a broad alliance that included former Socialists and Christian Democrats, and which relied upon the external support of Communist Refoundation to achieve a governing majority. This support was withdrawn after little more than two years, forcing Prodi's resignation and effectively terminating the Olive Tree experience. The precarious life of the center-left government demonstrated that shared electoral interests did not automatically translate into workable governing coalitions.

The initial experience of the new electoral law seemed to call into question "Duverger's Law," the political science theory whereby single-member districts produce two-party systems.[15] In 1994, the combined vote share of the two largest parties was just 41.4 percent, even lower than in 1992, when the Christian Democrats' electoral collapse brought an end to the postwar party system. In 1996 it barely budged at 41.7 percent (see Table 25.1). However, the lessons learned in the 1990s were taken on board and the party system became increasingly polarized around the two strongest parties, Forza Italia and the Left Democrats. This growing polarization had more to do with elite decisions to cooperate to maximize parliamentary representation than any increased affect for these two parties on the part of the electorate. Italian voters continued to disperse their votes amongst a bewildering number of parties: the effective number of electoral parties (ENEP), a standard measure of party system fragmentation, was on average much higher after the electoral reform of 1993 (5.99) than in the golden age of Italian polarized pluralism (3.83) (see Table 25.2). But the quasi-majoritarian electoral system reduced the fragmentation of the party system within the parliamentary institutions, by distorting the allocation of seats in favor of the larger parties, as is indicated by the much higher scores on Gallagher's Index of Disproportionality after 1992 (Table 25.2).

By 2001, the center-right had settled into a stable, if uneasy alliance. After the Northern League's flirtation with populism in the second half of the 1990s, advocating separation from the Italian state, it reached an accommodation with Berlusconi in time for the 2001 elections.[16] As a result the center-right, this time under the label House of Liberties, won comfortably against a center-left alliance under yet another leader, this

Table 25.2 Effective Number of Electoral and Parliamentary Parties in Italy (ENEP and ENPP*)

Year	ENEP	ENPP	Index of Disproportionality**
1950s	4.03	3.50	2.21
1960s	4.05	3.64	2.62
1970s	3.84	3.39	2.90
1980s	4.57	4.05	2.55
1992	6.63	5.71	2.51
1994	7.58	7.67	7.81
1996	7.17	6.09	6.91
2001	6.32	5.30	10.22
2006	5.69	5.06	3.61
2008	3.82	3.07	5.73
2013	5.33	3.47	17.34

Source: Gallagher, Michael, 2014. Election indices dataset at <http://www.tcd.ie/Political_Science/staff/michael_gallagher/ElSystems/index.php>, accessed June 23, 2014.

* The effective number of parties is calculated used the Laakso and Taagepera formula (Markku Laakso and Rein Taagepera, "'Effective' Number of Parties: a Measure with Application to West Europe," *Comparative Political Studies* 12:1 (1979), pp. 3–27). "Electoral" refers to the number of parties according to the distribution of votes, "parliamentary" the number according to the distribution of seats in the Parliament (Chamber of Deputies)

** Least Squares Index, using Michael Gallagher's formula (Michael Gallagher, "Proportionality, disproportionality and electoral systems," *Electoral Studies* 10:1 (1991) 33–51). This indicates the difference between the share of votes and share of seats allocated to each party; a higher number indicates a greater disparity between the two.

time the centrist Mayor of Rome Francesco Rutelli. Although Berlusconi's second government proved more durable than any other in the history of the Republic, lasting all
the way through to the end of the legislature, it was once again marked by intra-coalition
wrangling, this time with Fini's National Alliance and the Christian Democrats of the
UDC challenging Berlusconi's governing strategy and his closeness to the Northern
League. The House of Liberties remained intact, but lost the 2006 election to a reconstituted center-left coalition, again under Romano Prodi, returning from his spell as
European Commission President.

The center-left's victory in 2006 was excruciatingly narrow, and achieved only
by building an electoral coalition—the Union—spanning from the communist left
(itself divided into two parties, Communist Refoundation and the Party of Italian
Communists [PdCI]) all the way to the Christian Democratic Unione Democratici per
l'Europa (UDEUR) of Clemente Mastella, many of whose components had previously
stood under the center-right banner in the mid-1990s.[17] Moreover, the new electoral law
adopted for these elections—which became known as the "Porcellum" (pigsty) after a
candid comment by one of its authors, the Northern League's Calderoli[18]—was based on
proportional representation, but with a nationwide majority premium for the Chamber
of Deputies, and a regional premium for the Senate, making a center-left majority in
both chambers highly unlikely. The new system formally abandoned single-member
districts but maintained the bipolar dynamic of the party system by forcing parties
into broad pre-electoral coalitions in order to compete for the majority bonuses (see
Chapter 11, this volume). But the arrangements for the Senate, biased in favor of the
center-right, who dominated the most populous regions, made clean government alternation more difficult. Not surprisingly, the center-left opposed the reform.

The consequences for alternation quickly became evident as Mastella and a small
number of other senators defected from Prodi's governing majority in early 2008, forcing a new election which Berlusconi won.[19] But the bipolarity of the party system was
if anything reinforced by the new law, which introduced closed proportional lists and
higher thresholds. This handed much greater power to the leaders of the larger parties
and weakened the bargaining position of the smaller parties, which had retained a pivotal position in the post-1993 period thanks to the allocation of 25 percent of seats in the
chamber through proportional representation with minimal thresholds. The 2006–08
legislature saw a dramatic reconfiguration of the party system, as most of the center-left
parties merged into a single party organization, the Democratic Party (Partito
Democratico; PD), in early 2007, whilst Berlusconi responded by moving to merge Forza
Italia, the National Alliance and several center-right microparties into a single structure,
the People of Freedom (Il Popolo della Libertà; PdL), which formally became a political party in early 2009. Although the Northern League, the post-communist left and
Antonio di Pietro's Italy of Values (Italia dei Valori; IDV) retained their independence,
the party system thus became more coherently bipolar, structured around competition
for government office between the PD and PdL. These two parties won just over 70 percent of the vote between them, the highest share for the largest two parties since 1976,
when the Christian Democrats and communists forged their "historic compromise."

Government and Opposition: From Peripheral Turnover to Alternation

The emergence of bipolar electoral competition, and the electoral alliances' practice (later institutionalized in the Calderoli electoral reform) of adopting prime ministerial candidates to lead their electoral campaigns, had an immediate impact on the process of government formation and the relations between parties in the Italian Parliament. Under the PR arrangements of the "First Republic," parties fought elections as entirely independent entities, and the process of identifying possible governing majorities took place—at least visibly—after the votes had been counted and parliamentary seats allocated to the different party lists. Prime ministers emerged out of weeks, sometimes months of complex negotiations between party leaders, and were often not formal party leaders themselves, making them dependent on power games within their parliamentary support base. Governments rarely lasted anywhere near to the full parliamentary term, falling at a rate of one every year or so, to be replaced by very similar governments, with only "peripheral turnover" in ministerial portfolios.[20]

The post-1994 party system produced a very different dynamic. The logic of the majoritarian electoral law, reflected in the arguments presented by its proponents, was to banish the backroom post-election dealings which had dominated postwar politics and appeared to undermine voters' ability to choose governments and hold them to account.[21] In 1994, the first election under the new electoral law, the political parties took their cue from the momentum behind majoritarianism and fought the election under the leadership of prime ministerial candidates (Occhetto on the left, Berlusconi on the right), even adopting the American presidential practice of televised debates between coalitional leaders.[22] This transformed the process of government formation, as the legitimacy derived from a kind of electoral mandate for the winning coalitional leader forced the hand of the president and the parliamentary elites in the designation of a prime ministerial candidate, and enhanced his authority within the Cabinet.[23]

But as far as government stability is concerned, this bipolar presidential pattern took time to bed down. Despite the decisive victory of Berlusconi's coalition in the 1994 elections, and the relatively swift investiture of its leader as prime minister, the new government fell after less than a year. Berlusconi's heterogeneous electoral alliance found itself commanding a parliamentary majority after the election, but was defined more by its opposition to the post-communist left than any coherent political program. As a result, Berlusconi's first government collapsed after only eight months, with the Northern League withdrawing its support. Berlusconi's coalition split further when his choice as Treasury Minister Lamberto Dini formed a technocratic government with parliamentary support from the center-left, the Christian Democratic PPI and National Alliance. The bipolar electoral competition instituted in 1994 therefore failed at first to generate a pattern of government formation based around the competing electoral coalitions, with

Dini's caretaker administration occupying the center of the party system, replicating the pattern of the First Republic.

The 1996 election did produce a more stable governing majority, with Prodi lasting some 887 days as prime minister, second only to Bettino Craxi in the history of the Republic. However the extension of the Olive Tree alliance all the way to the communist left led to the collapse of the governing majority when part of Communist Refoundation withdrew its support.[24] There was still almost half a legislature left to run at the time of Prodi's resignation, and Prodi was succeeded by the Left Democrat leader D'Alema, with a slightly modified parliamentary majority, which lacked the PRC defectors but gained a group of Christian Democrats led by former President of the Republic Cossiga. D'Alema's first government lasted just over a year before requiring a major reshuffle, and his second ended a few months later, his resignation following the center-left's defeat in the regional elections held in spring 2000. Giuliano Amato, the last prime minister of the First Republic, took over for the final year of the legislature.

These experiences demonstrate that Italian bipolarism in the years after 1994 retained many of the features of the "First Republic," with unstable parliamentary majorities, weak prime ministers and high government turnover. Although the electoral system brought about a transformation of the party system, the Italian constitution (with the exception of a reform of the status of regional governments in 2001) remained unchanged. Italian prime ministers lacked the kind of constitutional resources that strengthened the position of government leaders in other parliamentary democracies, such as the constructive vote of censure in Germany or the Royal Prerogative in the United Kingdom.[25] Even a powerful political leader such as Berlusconi, with key electoral resources such as money, media power and personal popularity, remained vulnerable to "blackmail" by minor coalition partners, or even individual deputies.[26] Prodi delivered a parliamentary majority for the center-left, but was weakened in internal coalition politics by his lack of his own party organization. In short, majoritarianism was incomplete, and the aspirations of electoral reformers remained mostly unfulfilled.

The 2001 elections marked a shift toward a more "presidentialist" arrangement with Berlusconi's coalition, once again including the Northern League, winning a comfortable majority in both the Chamber and the Senate, and entrenching Berlusconi firmly in the prime minister's office. This time the government remained in office for the full five years of the legislature, and the parliamentary majority remained sufficiently cohesive to pass a major electoral reform shortly before the 2006 elections, replacing the single-member districts with a closed list proportional system with a majority bonus and formal candidacies for the prime minister's office.[27] The Prodi government that succeeded Berlusconi lasted less than two years, before being brought down once again by a small group of defectors (this time on the center-right), but in 2008 Berlusconi once again won a majority in both houses and governed until the global financial crisis whose consequences for Italy's solvency ushered in yet another period of technocratic government.

As in the case of voter behavior and party alliances, the experience of government formation suggests a gradual learning process as the political elites adapted to the new institutional and political environment emerging out of the 1993 electoral reform and the collapse of the First Republic party system. Just as the electoral alliances became more cohesive (particularly on the center-right) and ultimately transformed for the most part into unitary parties, so government stability increased, again particularly on the center-right. Berlusconi's second government lasted 1,412 days, comfortably beating Bettino Craxi's record and indeed any other Italian government since Unification (excepting Mussolini's dictatorship). After a ministerial reshuffle, a third Berlusconi government saw out the legislature. Although Prodi's second spell as prime minister ended rather more abruptly, Berlusconi's fourth government lasted 1,287 days, but ended in circumstances that suggested a further shift in the Italian party system and patterns of government formation. The consequences of the 2008 financial crisis and the resultant run on Italian government debt in 2011 brought the fourth Berlusconi government down and with it, the consolidation of bipolarity and government alternation.

Crisis and Change: Back to Polarized Pluralism?

The transformation of the Italian party system in the early 1990s had a variety of causes, but one key catalyst was the financial crisis of the Italian state that became increasingly acute in 1992, shortly after the "earthquake elections" that saw the Northern League challenge the Christian Democrats across the prosperous north of Italy. The unstable governments of the 1970s and 1980s had contributed to the growth in government deficits and the accumulation of a large stock of public debt, as the political parties extracted spending commitments in exchange for parliamentary support, but paid little attention to the revenue flows required to cover them. This fiscal crisis was accompanied by a foreign exchange crisis, as in the late summer of 1992, the pressure on the Italian lira became unsustainable and Italy, along with the UK, crashed out of the European Exchange Rate Mechanism. The end of the First Republic was in part the result of the exhaustion of a political model based on fiscal expansion to pay for the political parties' increasingly demanding constituents.[28]

The political reforms of the early 1990s and the replacement of a discredited political elite could therefore be seen in part as a response to economic failure and the need for both political and economic reforms in the light of the European Union's push toward monetary union. The initial experiences, particularly under the Dini and Prodi governments, suggested that the new party system could be an effective mechanism for pushing through the reforms required by Europe. The pensions reform of 1995, and bargains with unions to reduce wage inflation, alongside administrative and deregulatory reforms and fiscal reform, all pointed toward a more policy-focused style of governing in the Second Republic. The result was Italy's qualification for the first wave of European Monetary Union, despite its public debt remaining well above the threshold established in the Maastricht Treaty. If Europe had proved an effective spur for reform, the Italian political system appeared to have delivered its own side of the bargain.[29]

Where the theory of bipolar electoral competition falls short is that the center-left government that piloted this process received no electoral reward, being roundly defeated in the 2001 election (although its own internal wranglings certainly played an important role in this defeat). The Berlusconi governments that dominated Italy's first decade in the euro were less inclined to adhere to European strictures, and when the global financial crisis of the late 2000s struck, Berlusconi's administration was unable to avoid a crisis of confidence in Italian government debt issues which led to his government falling, under heavy pressure from the European Central Bank and other EU bodies, to be replaced by yet another caretaker administration under Mario Monti.[30] Berlusconi agreed to provide parliamentary backing for the Monti government, which received the votes of all the major parties save the League in its investiture, although the center-right adopted an increasingly oppositional stance as the legislature reached its end. In sum, despite the trend toward an increasingly bipolar politics since 1993, the European debt crisis overturned the elected government and replaced it with a technocratic administration supported by practically the full spectrum of Italian parties.

The 2013 election further disrupted the bipolar pattern. Mario Monti, despite his initial commitment to remain above the electoral fray, decided shortly before the election to create his own list, a broadly centrist party called Scelta civica (Civic Choice), in a bid to retain his office. But rather than Monti, who polled a disappointing 8.3 percent of the vote, it was a completely new party, the Five Stars Movement (M5S) that broke the bipolar system,[31] winning a spectacular 25 percent of the vote, more than either the PD or the PdL. The M5S's success split parliament three ways, with the largest coalition, the PD's "Common Good" alliance, short of a majority in the Senate, and the center-right coalition just a few votes behind. The result was an awkward compromise between bipolarism and technocracy, with the PD's Enrico Letta forming a broad-based government relying on the votes of the center-right, which itself began to split between Alfano, who favored cooperation with the PD, and Berlusconi, who adopted an aggressive approach toward the new government.

In many respects the 2013 election marked a return to the fragmented and unstable politics of the mid-1990s, with no stable majority available and an increasingly unpredictable electorate. Perhaps the most striking feature of the M5S's remarkable success is that it mobilized opposition to the bipolar party system itself. Formed by comedian Beppe Grillo in 2009, M5S has an inchoate political identity, but its main focus is on the corruption and collusion between the two main parties of the bipolar era, the PdL and PD (which Grillo satirically calls the "PD without the 'L'"). Grillo's appeal relies on a perception that, rather than competing for power, the PD and PdL are in fact involved in a joint enterprise to exploit the Italian electorate through corrupt dealings and generous state financing of political campaigns. Although the M5S targets both the main parties, in many respects it has supplanted Berlusconi as the repository of "anti-politics" feeling in Italy, as is suggested by the PDL's much greater losses in the 2013 election.[32] But its position up to the time of writing has been to shun any kind of contact with the other parties, making the formation of a broad left–right coalition inevitable, and relacing the bipolar dynamic that had been slowly institutionalizing since the mid-1990s with a "tripolar" one.[33]

Conclusions: From Fragmentation to Bipolarity, and Back Again?

The transformation of Italian politics after 1994 provides a range of insights for social and political scientists, and is all the more interesting a case for the fact that almost no one predicted any major departures from the postwar pattern of Christian Democrat-dominated coalition governments, held together by a combination of antipathy toward the communist left and corrupt, pork-barrel politics. Similarly, no-one predicted the spectacular emergence of the Five Stars Movement in the 2010s, which shook a two-party system which had appeared to be stabilizing after a long gestation.

The Italian experience therefore provides some valuable insights into the effects of electoral systems and electoral reforms, and the limitations of institutional engineering. The change from a proportional to a mostly majoritarian electoral law in 1993 set the stage for a revolution in Italy's party politics, with most of the political parties either disappearing altogether or changing their names before the 1994 poll. However, this transformation did not bring about a stable two-party pattern of electoral competition, and high levels of fragmentation of the party system remained, coexisting with a broadly bipolar presidential-style battle between electoral alliances led by candidates for government leadership. Then, when the 2005 electoral reform appeared to have stabilized a two-party system by raising the effective electoral threshold and forcing small parties to align with their more powerful rivals, the euro debt crisis came along to discredit the main parties and create the opportunity first for a return to technocracy imposed by Europe, then, in response to the populist backlash, for a broad-based government coalition backed by both the PD and PdL. It is difficult to draw anything other than tentative conclusions given the pace of change in contemporary Italian politics, but the history of the "Second Republic" does seem to underline the limits of electoral reform as a tool for enhancing political accountability and government stability.

Notes

1. Giovanni Sartori, *Parties and Party Systems: A Framework for Analysis* (Cambridge: Cambridge University Press, 1976).
2. Luca Verzichelli, "The Parliamentary Elite in Transition," *European Journal of Political Research* 34:1 (1998): 121–150.
3. For an excellent overview of the changes, see Leonardo Morlino, "Crisis of Parties and Change of Party System in Italy," *Party Politics* 2: 1 (1996): 5–30.

4. Giorgio Galli, *Bipartitismo imperfetto. Comunisti e democristiani in Italia* (Bologna: Il Mulino, 1966).

5. Vittorio Bufacchi and Simon Burgess, *Italy Since 1989. Events and Interpretations* (Basingstoke: Palgrave Macmillan, 1998), p. 173.

6. Sartori, *Parties and Party Systems.*

7. Leading one scholar to describe the new party system as "fragmented bipolarism"; Roberto D'Alimonte, "Italy: A Case of Fragmented Bipolarism," in Michael Gallagher and Paul Mitchell (eds.), *The Politics of Electoral Systems* (Oxford: Oxford University Press, 2005), pp. 253–277.

8. Mario Caciagli, "Doomed to govern? Christian Democracy in the Italian Political System," in Mario Caciagli *et al.* (eds.), *Christian Democracy in Europe* (Barcelona: Institut de Ciències Polítiques i Socials, 1992).

9. Maurice Duverger, *Political Parties: Their Organization and Activity in the Modern State* (London: Methuen, 1964); Gary Cox, *Making Votes Count* (New York: Cambridge University Press, 1997).

10. Anna Bosco, "Four Actors in Search of a Role: The Southern European Communist Parties," in Nikiforos Diamandouros and Richard Gunther (eds.), *Parties, Politics and Democracy in the New Southern Europe* (Baltimore, MD: The Johns Hopkins University Press, 2001), pp. 329–387.

11. See Simone Bertolino, *Rifondazione comunista. Storia e organizzazione* (Bologna: Il Mulino, 2004).

12. Jonathan Hopkin and Caterina Paolucci, "The Business Firm Model of Party Organization: Cases from Italy and Spain," *European Journal of Political Research* 35:3 (1999): 307–339.

13. On the Northern League, see Renato Mannheimer (ed.), *La Lega Lombarda* (Milan: Feltrinelli, 1991); Ilvo Diamanti, *Il male del Nord. Lega, localismo, secessione* (Rome: Donzelli, 1996); and in English, Anna Cento Bull, and Mark Gilbert, *The Lega Nord and the Northern Question in Italian Politics* (Basingstoke: Palgrave Macmillan, 2001).

14. See Piero Ignazi, *Postfascisti? Dal Movimento sociale italiano ad Alleanza Nazionale* (Bologna: Il Mulino, 1994). In English, Carlo Ruzza and Oliver Schmidtke, "Towards a Modern Right: Alleanza Nazionale and the 'Italian Revolution,'" in Stephen Gundle and Simon Parker (eds.), *The New Italian Republic. From the Fall of the Berlin Wall to Berlusconi* (London: Routledge, 1996), pp. 147–158.

15. Duverger, *Political Parties.*

16. See Agazio Loiero, *Il patto di ferro. Berlusconi, Bossi e la devolution contro il Sud con i voti del Sud* (Rome: Donzelli, 2003).

17. See Jonathan Hopkin, "From Federation to Union, From Parties to Primaries: The Search for Unity on the Center-Left," in Grant Amyot and Luca Verzichelli (eds.), *The End of the Berlusconi Era?* (Oxford: Berghahn Books, 2006), pp. 67–84.

18. "Calderoli: La legge elettorale? L'ho scritta io, ma e' una porcata," *La Repubblica*, 15 March 2006. http://www.repubblica.it/2006/c/sezioni/politica/versoelezioni38/caldporcata/caldporcata.html>.

19. It was alleged that payments were made to bribe the defectors into voting down the Prodi government: "Respinto il rito immediato a Silvio Berlusconi," *La Repubblica*, 19 March 2013. http://napoli.repubblica.it/cronaca/2013/03/19/news/la_difesa_respinto_il_rito_immediato_per_silvio_berlusconi-54880091/?ref=search>.

20. See Maurizio Cotta and Luca Verzichelli, *Political Institutions in Italy* (Oxford: Oxford University Press, 2007), Chapter 4. The best illustration of "peripheral turnover" is the career of Giulio Andreotti, who held uninterrupted government office for 45 years between 1947 and 1992, a period in which there were 46 different governments.

21. Maurizio Cotta and Luca Verzichelli, "Italy: From 'Constrained' Coalitions to Alternative Governments?," in Wolfgang Müller and Kaare Strøm (eds.), *Coalition Governments in Western Europe* (Oxford: Oxford University Press, 2000), pp. 433–497.

22. Gianfranco Pasquino, "The New Campaign Politics in Southern Europe," in Nikiforos Diamandouros and Richard Gunther (eds.), *Parties, Politics and Democracy in the New Southern Europe* (Baltimore, MD: The Johns Hopkins University Press, 2001), pp. 183–223.

23. Donatella Campus and Gianfranco Pasquino, "Leadership in Italy. The Changing Role of Leaders in Elections and in Government," *Journal of Contemporary European Studies* 14:1 (2006): 25–40.

24. To underline the fissiparous nature of the Italian left, the defectors from Communist Refoundation, led by Armando Cossutta, went on to form a rival party, the Party of Italian Communists (PdCI).

25. Giovanni Sartori, *Comparative Constitutional Engineering* (Basingstoke: Palgrave Macmillan, 1994).

26. To use Giovanni Sartori's term; "European Political Parties: The Case of Polarized Pluralism," in Joseph LaPalombra and Myron Weiner (eds.), *Political Parties and Political Development* (Princeton, NJ: Princeton University Press, 1966), pp. 137–176.

27. Alan Renwick, Chris Hanretty and David Hine, "Partisan self-interest and electoral reform: The new Italian electoral law of 2005," *Electoral Studies* 28: 3 (2006): 437–447.

28. Stefano Guzzini, "The Long Night of the Italian First Republic. Years of Clientelistic Implosion in Italy," *Review of International Political Economy* 2:1 (1995): 27–61.

29. Maurizio Ferrera and Elisabetta Gualmini, *Salvati dall'Europa? Welfare e lavoro in Italia fra gli anni '70 e gli anni '90* (Bologna: Il Mulino, 1999).

30. Jonathan Hopkin, "A Slow Fuse: Italy and the EU Debt Crisis," *International Spectator* 47:4 (2012): 35–48.

31. On the Five Stars Movement, see Piergiorgio Corbetta and Elisabetta Gualmini (eds), *Il partito di Grillo* (Bologna: Il Mulino, 2013).

32. Stefano Fella and Carlo Ruzza, "Populism and the Fall of the Center-Right in Italy," *Journal of Contemporary European Studies* 21:1 (2013): 38–52.

33. Alessandro Chiaramonte and Vincenzo Emanuele, "Volatile and Tripolar: The New Italian Party System," Lorenzo De Sio ,Vincenzo Emanuele, Nicola Maggini and Aldo Paparo (eds.), *The Italian General Elections of 2013: A Dangerous Stalemate?* (Rome: CISE, 2013), pp. 63–68.

PART V

MAJOR FIGURES

CHAPTER 26

ALCIDE DE GASPERI
AND PALMIRO TOGLIATTI

ALDO AGOSTI

It has been said that "the ultimate stabilization of Italian democracy [was accomplished] through the central role of the DC and the PCI."[1] A whole discussion could be opened around the adjective "ultimate"; however, the profound crisis upsetting the Italian political system is more likely a variation—although one made particularly complex by endogenous peculiarities—of a generic disease that is threatening democracy today,[2] rather than a manifestation of its alleged inborn defects. Moreover, the historical era of Italian democracy, effectively summarized by Pietro Scoppola as the "Republic of the parties,"[3] gave undeniable evidence of its remarkable longevity, whatever the pattern of its long decline. The viewpoint quoted at the start of this paragraph might thus be shared by others, although it leaves in the background the other forces and political cultures that played an important role in shaping the constitution of the Italian Republic. The history of the First Republic (let us call it so) did actually revolve around two main actors, the Christian Democratic Party (DC) and the Communist Party (PCI). As the tendency is to label a more or less long-lasting historical era with the name of the main personality that marked it ("De Gaulle's France," "Adenauer's Germany") it is not surprising to see the frequent recurrence of the coupled name De Gasperi–Togliatti as the symbol of an entire era of Italian political history that goes from the return of the Communist leader in March 1944 to the death of the Christian Democratic leader in August 1954.

The "couple," in truth, almost immediately took shape, right after the liberation of Rome: one need only look at the electoral propaganda or browse through the satirical press of the first postwar years to see how the images and caricatures of the two figures surpass in number and frequency of appearance those of any other politician, showing a widespread, stabilized perception of their role among the mass public.[4] But the combination of the two has an intrinsic force which can withstand even the historian's examination. This point was highlighted by Ernesto Ragionieri who, while distancing himself from a "scenographic comparison" of the two figures, wrote in 1975 that the one and the other knew they could play an important role in Italian politics "for having served, although in different roles of a different importance, in two great universalistic institutions, the Church and the Communist International. Both aware of the conditioning, as well as the force, that the respective political parties derived from the connections with such formations, they probably discerned, at least to a certain point, the opportunity to acquire a broader margin of autonomy of action through their provisional agreement."[5]

The starting points were undeniably far from one another and from the solution they were aiming for. However, they did have something in common, something quite peculiar for two founding fathers of a republican democracy: in their respective worlds, democracy represented a conceptual framework for the reconstruction of society and of the state that was in drastic conflict with some fundamental principles and significant experiences of both the Catholic and the Communist movements. Neither of them, it was observed, "came to democracy through the royal path of long, gradual development," and the democracy of the years 1944–45 was an arena to which both rushed "rather unexpectedly and without too much experience in mediation:"[6] this is an element that cannot be overlooked if one wishes to understand the meaning and importance of the outlook embraced by Togliatti on one side and De Gasperi on the other at the time of the foundation of the new Italian state. Apart from this, until 1944 their biographical backgrounds were very different from each another.

Togliatti's cultural and political training took place at the same time as the incubation, birth, and first maturity of Italian fascism, and this left an even deeper mark on his life than the October revolution.[7] Fascism was the negative point of reference in respect to which Togliatti came to embrace militant political engagement as a life rule; it was the defeat inflicted by fascism on the Italian working-class movement that, while forcing him to an 18-year exile, tied him indissolubly to a project of world revolution where defeat could be read as a lost battle in a war destined to be victorious. Togliatti saw himself and his party as part of a vast project aimed at humanity's redemption, with Soviet Russia as its guide and driving force, provided the fight against fascism with an abiding conceptual anchor. It was his commitment to this leading idea along with his tactical skills and uncommon political flair, that enabled him to accept and share the most tragic aspects of Stalinism, paying a high price for it but without ever being completely crushed by it. In 1944, his return to Italy as a leading actor on the political scene offered him new room for initiative. The awareness of the decisive weight of the international scenario, which he acquired in the Comintern years, never abandoned him, remaining in many respects the compass of his political action. From this moment on, however, the central goal of his project became to think up a new role for a Communist party operating in the environment of a western political democracy, and, more concretely, to integrate the PCI into the republican democratic system. With regard to this objective, that overlaps with the USSR's *Realpolitik* stance—the latter being fully aware that Italy remained outside its sphere of influence—Togliatti observed with concern the northern Resistance's most radical trends, including those of a section of his own party.

De Gasperi, 12 years his senior, had relatively extensive experience as Member of Parliament representing Trentino in the Austrian Parliament, soon gaining a deep knowledge of the mechanisms and strategies of the political machine.[8] Already from his first public appearances he internalized a political method "resulting from a cautious rejection of the forms of radicalism typical of over structured theory-building,"[9] and he stuck to this in the years of his engagement in the People's Party (PPI), culminating in his appointment as Secretary between 1924 and 1926. His stance towards Fascism was initially prudent and cautious, as he regarded it as a stabilizing factor, despite its excesses; in fact, as president of the parliamentary group of the PPI, he was not, unlike Sturzo, a priori contrary to a governmental collaboration with Mussolini after the march on Rome. His opposition, however, became sharper and more determined, to the point of being arrested and held in jail for more than a year between 1927 and 1928. De Gasperi was thus an anti-fascist as well, and he remained anti-fascist during the years of the Fascist regime, although in a more private way and in the perspective of a Catholic reformation of society, envisaging coexistence as well as compromise with the dictatorship as long as it didn't hurt the interests and projects of the Church.[10] However, as the end of the war got closer and its outcome clearer, the idea of a state emerging from his writings suggested "a clear return to a full adoption of the democratic parliamentary notion based on political freedom and administrative decentralization:"[11] something very different from the aims of a pure and simple Catholic restoration that prevailed in many sectors of the clerical hierarchy. In the perspective of transition from dictatorship to democracy, however, the Resistance was and remained for him essentially a phenomenon endured from necessity and whose possible outcomes were always dreaded, a phenonmenon to be observed largely to be able to control it and empty it of its inherent dangers. In this, he was closer to Togliatti than the PCI later tended to portray him.

How well and in what way did Togliatti and De Gasperi know each other in 1944–1945 when they first were asked to collaborate in the governments led by Bonomi, Parri, and De Gasperi himself? How well did each of them know the party led by the other? Togliatti, in his early journalistic pieces, had shown a precocious interest in the PPI, and in that respect he had proven his sharpness and freshness of judgment. In the 1930s, however, his attention for what was left of the Catholic opposition to the regime was very limited, crushed under the weight of the Conciliation, in which he had seen the consolidation of a new power block where "the Church had covered much of the distance that separated it from the other forces of the capitalist world."[12] It appears that Togliatti did not talk about the Catholics in the "Course on the adversaries" he held for the Italian students of the Comintern school in Moscow in 1935:[13] if he did, the records of that lesson were not preserved. In the following years, corresponding to the season of the Popular Front, his mentions of Catholicism were sporadic and noncommittal. When, after the downfall of Fascism, the PCI leader turned to look to the various forces of the Italian political line-up with greater attention, his initial evaluation of Christian Democracy was cautious and ambivalent: on the one side he considered it important, as he attributed to it a base of supporters "mainly among farmers and catholic organizations" and a programmatic goal "aiming for the republic and the reconstruction of the country based on democracy;" on the other he foresaw that the "catholic reactionary circles" would exercise their influence on it.[14] After his return to Italy, Togliatti appeared more and more convinced that the DC would play a key role in the reconstruction of the political system. He believed that only the fundamental union of the three main "mass parties" (the Socialist, Communist, and Christian Democratic parties), as an expression of the most well-established political cultures of the Italian society, could allow for a democratic transformation of the country and warrant full legitimization of the PCI within it. In this perspective, he attributed to the DC, as a party of "the catholic farmer masses" who "suffered fascism and hate fascism as much as we do,"[15] an objectively progressive role that could be able to influence the most conservative manifestations of the bourgeois and liberal hegemony. This outlook shows the limit of identifying the DC with its alleged rural social base (underestimating instead the Catholic consensus among the urban middle class) and overestimating the room for maneuver granted to it from the Church: which, on the other hand, kept sending contradictory signals.[16]

Since the liberation of Rome, this idea of making the Christian Democracy one of the pillars of the restoration of an Italian state that is rejuvenated and open to significant social changes seemed to be a recurring thought for Togliatti. The unity pact with the Socialist Party (agreed in 1943) was considered an important achievement itself, but it was also seen as the cornerstone of an alliance among the three mass parties that "should provide for the struggle of the huge Communist masses and the huge Catholic masses for a program of economic, political, and social renewal."[17] The result achieved through the restoration of a uniform union confederation, the CGIL (ratified with the Rome pact of June 9, 1944) had to be extended to the political field: on September 9, in a letter to De Gasperi, Togliatti suggested the creation of a "bloc of forces of the people that should guarantee the triumph and stability of a democratic, progressive regime that matches the aspirations of the workers of our nation;"[18] moreover, after the crisis of the Bonomi government and the decision to continue to take part in it despite the withdrawal of the other left-wing parties, the PSIUP and the PdA, Togliatti, in a letter to Longo of December 1944, listed "the absence of a specific bond, sanctioned by a political pact, among the three main mass parties"[19] as one of the reasons that slowed down the resolution of that crisis. In February 1945, with the administrative elections in sight after the liberation of the north, he a "shared socialist and Communist list with the support of the DC" as "the best possible solution."[20]

As for De Gasperi, in his time as leader of the People's Party he obviously followed the tribulation of Italian socialism with great attention, but his comments on Communists are infrequent and rather disdainful, such as that he made following the Congress in Livorno;[21] however, in the articles devoted to the international scenario that the wrote for the magazine *Ilustrazione Vaticana* in the second half of the 1930s, he gave proof of remarkable sensitivity by showing, as noted by Pietro Scoppola, "that he does not judge a historical institution like communism solely by the principles it invokes."[22] It is surely not irrelevant that, in evaluating the change in orientation of international communism after 1934, he acknowledged at least "some semblance of truth" in the idea that it had been "the Communists who went one step closer to democracy, and not the democrats who got closer to Bolshevik socialism."[23]

However, these "flares," as Piergiorgio Zunino defines them, were destined to be replaced by "the deep, unshakeable, historical opposition of Catholicism to

Communism" that, in the summer of 1941,[24] would bring De Gasperi to the point of rejoicing for the news—later revealed as unfounded—of the German conquest of Moscow.[25] Earlier, his attention for Italian communism remained limited, if not completely absent—and it was not in any way stirred by the effects of the PCF's "outstretched hand policy towards the Christian workers" on the PCI after its launch at the time of the creation of the popular front. The changes in the political scenario brought about by the fall of Mussolini and the creation of the committees of national liberation caused De Gasperi to be extremely skeptical about the role of the PCI in those committees, to the point of making him question the validity of their participation.[26] Not even the appeasing statements by the Italian Communists on the theme of religious freedom induced him to let his guard down, as he considered them specious: soon, however, he was persuaded that "breaking up with them would be inappropriate, and keeping a close eye on their work is the best practice."[27] Togliatti's return to Italy strengthened De Gasperi's belief: he hoped that the presence of Togliatti in the country could "in any case help to avoid the negative experiments and the mistakes of Russian communism,"[28] and publicly gave him credit for expressing himself in favor of respect for religious faith, trusting that "the whole party will concretely take their own conclusions."

In the months that followed, the relationship between the two men became stronger. In September 1944 Togliatti sent his greetings to the National Council of Christian Democracy and reiterated his call for cooperation. De Gasperi responded by agreeing "on the need to cooperate at this time with all democratic and anti-fascist Italian forces, and about possible future collaborations," but signaled the violent interruption of several DC rallies carried out by Communist militants, and addressed Togliatti directly with a heartfelt appeal: "You will acquire for yourself great merit in the country if you can dispel [fears and distrust] with facts and create a climate that is a pledge of a climate of freedom for the future."[29] However, in the last months of 1944, De Gasperi's trust in the possibility of a fruitful collaboration with the Communists was cracked by growing doubts: he wrote to Sturzo on November 12, 1944 that the tactic of the PCI pursuing a future collaboration with Catholics is "the most effective feature of Italian politics,"[30] but he actually saw in it the expression of a "tactic" above all: "I have the impression"—he revealed to the founder of the PPI—"that they hope to win a de facto dictatorship through democratic forms." However, he added a significant comment: "Much of the country is anti-Communist, but it is not on the basis of anti-communism that we can rally our forces, otherwise we run the risk of getting confused with reactionary currents."[31] It is clear that on top of De Gasperi's personal, rooted hostility to communism came the predicament in which he was forced to move, under the growing pressure of the Vatican who considered the collaboration with the PCI, and in general with left-wing parties, in an increasingly negative light; and it is equally clear that becoming the point of reference for a coalition of clerical and openly reactionary interests did not suit him.

During the second Bonomi government and then again after the liberation of the north, relations between the PCI and the DC suffered no further deterioration. The presence of De Gasperi and Togliatti in the executive helped to stabilize understanding. The PCI did not support the candidacy of the leader from Trentino as prime minister after the resignation of Bonomi, but neither did the party peremptorily oppose it, and its support for the government of actionist Ferruccio Parri was rather lukewarm. Only in the summer of 1945 did relations between the two parties deteriorate, and even the personal relationship between the two leaders, although based on fairness and outward show of confidence, tended to cool down. In July, Togliatti wrote De Gasperi to complain about "the campaign of slander and personal vilification devoid of any foundations that is conducted by Christian Democracy propagandists against the men of my party," and called for De Gasperi's personal "authoritative intervention to put an end to this tide of nonsense and rubbish, which does not serve any other purpose than to create, with the poison of irritating and stupid slander, that atmosphere of mutual intolerance which in turn produces clashes and conflicts."[32] In general, his judgment on the DC became much more critical, to the point that in July he wrote that "the direction of De Gasperi raises concerns about a development not à la Don Sturzo, but à la Salazar or Dollfuss, i.e. towards totalitarianism of the distinctive clerical kind."[33]

However, when the Parri government fell in November 1945 on the initiative of the Liberals—without the Communist Party striving to support it or keep it alive—the designation of De Gasperi as prime minister was judged by the PCI leader as "proof that democracy begins to have relatively solid bases in Italy, that are not easily shaken."

He observed in an interview with the party newspaper that De Gasperi "is the leader of a party with a mass base. This fact alone makes him more acceptable to us than those so-called 'independent' politicians who do not account for their actions if not to their four friends and their own vanity. Moreover, after the election, when we and the Socialists will find ourselves without any doubt at the head of the strongest electoral alignment, the political agreement with the Christian Democrats will become the axis of governmental stability in a republican regime. We have been working with this prospect in mind since the liberation of Rome."[34]

The collaboration between the two men during the first De Gasperi government unfolded without too much friction, and Togliatti signed one of his key measures, the amnesty for common and military crimes committed during the war.[35] However, already during the campaign for the elections of the Constituent Assembly and of the institutional referendum of June 2, 1946, the Catholic columnists' direct attack against the Communist leader rose higher in pitch. Togliatti again expressed his regret in a personal letter to De Gasperi, but the latter replied with a certain harshness, thus alluding to the insurmountable limits which he saw in their collaboration: "Even if we were to completely agree on everything—the republic, the land reform, the industrial reform—we [Christian Democrats] would always carry the duty of promoting and defending the postulates of the spirit and of Christian civilization, as the foundation and guarantee of morality which alone can preserve the State from decadence and corruption. [. . .] Everyone is born with their own features and, even if evolutions are always possible and indeed desirable, it is not legitimate to confuse tactical reasons with beliefs."[36] And he concluded: "And so, dear Togliatti, the matter is neither about you nor me, but rather about an antithesis that is beyond our own selves."

Actually, this antithesis took on more and more decisive features as early as 1946, especially after Togliatti left the government to give priority to his leadership role of the party. In this regard, we must immediately underline the sharp difference in their perceptions of the role of party and government. For De Gasperi, the party represented "a limited organism,"[37] inevitably dependent on the government and parliament; and it was the government—as an expression of the parliamentary majority—that had to act as engine of institutional dynamics. He never lost this belief in the complete subordination of the party to the institutions of government and the congenital inability to think of the party as an instrument of the political synthesis of the Catholic world, and it was a conviction that led to increasing friction with a part of the DC, in particular that of *Cronache Sociali*.[38] By contrast, for Togliatti the role of the party was crucial: among his most original contributions to the reconstitution of a democratic political system in Italy was his rethinking of the party in such as way as to strengthen the strategy of seizure of power without a direct revolutionary break. For him it was important that "the only real corrective action with respect to bourgeois democracy is the action of a mass party that, based on the renewed strength and renewed prestige of the working class as the fundamental core of anti-fascist struggle, gets to become [. . .] the compact nucleus of a society and of a state in the making within society and the state of the bourgeoisie, using all their contradictions and divisions."[39]

The contrast, however, became more acute, especially in regard to the government's economic policy (the PCI wanted to put the brakes on the government's excessive liberalism[40]) and foreign policy, considered by Togliatti to be contradictory and excessively weak before the demands of the Anglo-Saxon powers. The alliance in government became more and more contrived for both parties and for their leaders, but while Togliatti did not have the ability or the strength to dictate conditions and was therefore willing to prolong it, De Gasperi was able to exploit the objective convergence between the desire of the DC to get rid of uncomfortable allies and the needs of American foreign policy, more and more inclined towards the exclusion of the Communists from government.[41] He knew, however, that it would have been unwise to take responsibility for signing the peace treaty with the Left parties in opposition: he then began to test the water, catching the occasion offered by the resignation of the socialist ministers after the January 1947 split, and formally opened the crisis.[42] The reaction of the PCI was ambivalent: on the one hand Togliatti spoke of "a decision if not imposed, at least persistently suggested abroad," that is by American conservative political circles, thus trying to remain faithful to the representation of the DC as a party that basically expressed the people's interests, and blaming the crisis on the context of international power relations. On the other hand, when the crisis ended with the formation of a DC-PSI-PCI government in which the weight of the left was reduced, he underlined the "anti-Communist inspiration that guided the uncertain and, in the end, unrealistic behavior of the party of relative majority."[43]

However, the path was by then mapped out: in the face of increasing inflation, pressures from the economic power were also increasing in favor of a deflationary policy which was inevitably at odds with the social interests represented by the left. Under pressure from the Church, at the very least encouraged by Washington, further alarmed by the defeat in the local elections in Sicily, De Gasperi made his decision: he suggested in a radio message on April 27, which was taken up in the Council of Ministers on the 30th, that it was no longer possible to govern without the support "of the natural organs of economic life, i.e. the financial institutions and the categories of the industrialists, employers, and workers."[44]

Throughout this phase, and probably until the elections of April 1948, Togliatti's conduct may appear to have been less clear and coherent as a whole than that of De Gasperi. The much-discussed decision he made that March, during the Constituent Assembly—disputed even by a small minority of his party—to approve the Article 7 of the future Constitution, which entrusted the regulation of relations between the Italian State and the Church to the Concordat of 1929, had the desired effect of preventing the imminent ideological confrontation of the Cold War from assuming the character of a war of religion (a perspective that was actually averted by the evolution of Italian society itself more than by the responsible attitude of the PCI); but, while it did not extend the permanence of the PCI in the government for more than a few months, it opened a wound that would not easily heal in the relations with the secular forces of the left and with the socialist party itself. Equally awkward was the conduct of the PCI when the crisis deteriorated in May. In an article titled "Ma come sono cretini!" ("They are such jerks!") published on May 20, Togliatti answered with an ostentatiously over-the-top tone to the insinuations of former US Secretary of State Sumner Welles, according to which the PCI was ready for civil war because it received funding from Moscow. This was perhaps an extreme attempt to force De Gasperi and the DC to choose between appearing to the public as consenting victims of the "atrocious insult to the whole nation," that is American interference, or going back to their cooperation with the left.[45] In fact, on May 26, the two leaders had a long conversation, of which we can read a brief report in the notes taken by De Gasperi: Togliatti was willing to "dismiss the incident" with a statement of clarification, and also ready to provide "economic guarantees" (basically to waive any proposal of socialization) but he warned: "we do not tolerate exclusions, otherwise it would mean admitting to be outside of the nation." The solution of the crisis, however, was well underway through the formation of a government of Christian Democrats alone, qualified by the presence of Einaudi at the Treasury. Even at this point, while De Gasperi already seemed fully aware of the irreversible nature of the breach with the PCI (as opposed to the one with PSI, which still considered it reparable), Togliatti seemed not to have yet archived the policy he followed with such determination in the previous years, and appeared not to consider the season of collaboration with DC to be over. This apparently uncertain and contradictory behavior left room for criticism from an increasingly restless party, but, in reality, it can be explained in light of the overall attitude of the PCI in the Constituent Assembly. The immediate ratification of the peace treaty in July (to which the Communists were midly opposed, offering merely lukewarm support to the motion by Orlando that sought to postpone it) probably was believed by Togliatti to be a necessary condition to prevent the increasingly clear dissent that separated the PCI from the DC in the field of foreign policy from affecting the final phase of the works of the Constituent process.[46] And in this, his convergence with De Gasperi—beyond the increasingly heated political skirmish—was out of the question: neither the one nor the other considered it appropriate to let the tension rise beyond measure on foreign policy issues while the definition of the constitutional framework was still at stake.

The scale of the commitment to the work of the Constituent Assembly, as the Communist secretary didn't fail to point out while evaluating his opponent's work after his death, was not the same for the two leaders: Gasperi remained relatively aloof,[47] leaving to the so-called *professorini* (Dossetti, La Pira, Moro) the task of designing the founding principles of the constitutional pact; Togliatti was instead personally engaged, with a determination that can only be explained with the high importance he attached to the task of finding "common ground [. . .] solid enough to establish a new state on top of it, beyond [the] political agreements determined by individual political parties that make up [. . .] a parliamentary majority." From this point of view, the Constitution represented for Togliatti a kind of insurance that gave legitimacy to the PCI and which was endorsed by the meeting of "two great currents," two "solidarisms," the one "human and social" typical of the workers' parties, the other Catholic in its origin and inspiration.[48] The method—which he fundamentally shared with the Christian Democrat and Socialist constituents—of reaching an agreement on the basis of the common elements in the concrete proposals, confining the ideological principles to the background—would allow for this result to be achieved in the end.

However, when elections were held for the first parliament of the Italian Republic on April 18, 1948, the international situation had become even more tense, resulting in a further deterioration of the already lukewarm relationship between De Gasperi and Togliatti. The tones of the campaign were extremely harsh. The United States intervened with all its political and economic weight, and the Catholic Church took the field by force as it mobilized its peripheral organizations in support of the DC, in an atmosphere of an out-and-out crusade against communism. In the February editorial of the monthly party magazine, Togliatti accused De Gasperi of not having "opened his mouth [. . .] if not to utter words that mean not only discord, but true provocation and incitement to civil war," of having spoken of "the supreme struggle, to fight and win now or never, facing death, and so on." and commented: "things that are said when it comes, precisely, to war, and not to a free and democratic expression of popular will."[49] However, in the final stages of the election campaign, the leader of the PCI was, in turn, drawn to fraught expressions that were unusual for him,[50] and in fact he didn't rule out the prospect of civil war either, as suggested in a meeting with the Soviet ambassador Kostylev on March 23.[51] That possibility, contemplated but feared by both, seemed to become alarmingly real after the attack of July 14, 1948 on Togliatti. In the days that followed, the tones of the debate in parliament were dramatically harsh, and the cold and ritual character of the condemnation from De Gasperi was striking, in that it sharply contrasted with the much greater emphasis he put on denouncing the alleged plan of insurrection by the PCI and the danger it posed to democracy.[52] But at that decisive moment each of the two opposing sides took a step back from the edge of abyss: the Communists held back, preventing that revolt from becoming an insurrection, and soon after that they also dropped their demands for the government's resignation. The latter, in turn—and in this the equilibrium of the statesman from Trentino was crucial—did not yield to the temptation to ban the PCI. The war of movement in the hottest months from February to July slowly turned into war of position. Opposing allegiances, although deep-rooted and destined to last, did not erase all sense of common citizenship and compliance with a set of rules, albeit reluctantly shared. Democracy, despite everything, survived.

However, from then on, and in the following five years, the political horizons of Togliatti and De Gasperi became increasingly distant and incompatible. On the international level, the formation of the Cominform removed any margin of autonomy from the socialist bloc that the PCI had tried to keep open until 1947, and Togliatti remained crushed by it until the death of Stalin. On the other hand, De Gasperi's atlanticist choice—though opposed by a minority of his own party—became the central pivot of his conception of a politically united Europe, that would have been able to finally overcome the wounds that made it sink in two wars, but that was so firmly and prejudicially anti-Communist as to hinder any prospects of detente. On the domestic level, the stabilization of the "democratic perspective of moderate colors [. . .] that was safeguarded and guaranteed by the continuity of the more established national realities: the Church, the major economic interests, the most significant hinges of the judicial and bureaucratic structures, the aspirations spread among the different social strata of the stability and security of individuals and family groups" took place,[53] with the consequence that "the consolidation within the DC of a moderate and conservative opinion who saw in the 'national party' announced by De Gasperi only the function of anti-Communist bulwark opened a new political issue, for his leadership and for the role of the party in the future political system."[54]

On the other hand the "secular" motion—which had been held firm unequivocally, albeit with some fluctuations, by the statesman from Trentino until the elections of April 18—appeared to grow dim. As has been rightly observed, "no less strong than the propensity of the Vatican to penetrate into the fibers of the Italian civil society and the state [is] in De Gasperi the tendency to seek its intervention to block the expansion of the left," so much so that between him and Pius XII an "undoubted welding of perspectives, a meeting halfway" was achieved.[55] This offered the PCI the opportunity for effective action, especially on the cultural level, against a clerical extremism that bordered on obscurantism: and Togliatti seemed particularly comfortable on this ground.[56]

The distances that were dug between the DC and the PCI therefore became deeper, and 30 years would have to pass before they could at least be partially filled. However, the connective tissue that was formed toward the end of the war had not completely frayed: at least secretly, a mechanism of mutual legitimation—which was also mutually conditioning—was still at work.[57] On the one hand, the distressing but effective balance between international obligations and the internal role of the PCI that Togliatti had managed to achieve—while also keeping under control the pressure for radicalization arising within his party—and the ability of the "new party" to ensure, along with the organization of the social protest, an effective education to citizenship, achieved the result of constraining the policies of centrist governments, even in a difficult time like that of the first phase of the Cold War. The rapid growth of peasant struggles in the south and the ability of the PCI and the CGIL to maintain their own action on the democratic and popular ground, by elaborating concrete objectives of reform and by building social alliances and synergies of different political cultures around them, left an important mark in the history of the country. However, this may have happened partly because of De Gasperi's ability in containing, especially after the outbreak of the Korean War, the strong domestic and international pressures to a militarization of the fight against communism and a transformation of the development model so strong as to shrink the reformist thrust of 1950 "in a sort of Atlantic dirigisme of neo-corporatist sort,"[58] bound to result in a center-right majority. If Togliatti managed to keep the action of the Communist Party on the democratic grounds this was thus not only due to his personal determination (in tune with Stalin's prudence), but also to De Gasperi's action. As prime minister, the statesman from Trentino was committed to underground confrontation with the US government and with the internal components that were pushing for a shift to the right. But he always avoided provoking an irreversible break in the constitutional pact and proved capable, despite everything, of responding to social pressures and policy proposals from the left and the unions by following a path—surely incomplete but real—of reform and development

Of course, particularly acute moments of tension periodically recurred: on the delicate ground of relations with the Church, the slender thread of De Gasperi's relationship with the left opposition almost broke when the Vatican decided in 1949 to excommunicate the Communists and their allies. But, in reality, this measure did not please the Christian Democrat leader, for whom the battle for party's political autonomy remained a key challenge, though never flaunted in a noticeable way. Indeed, what complicated and ended up unbalancing his relationship with the Vatican was the fact that, once the most acute phase of the contrast with the left between 1948 and 1951 was over, the forces of the ecclesiastical apparatus were deprived of an external object against which they could discharge, so that "it is De Gasperi himself who finds himself under the fire of extremism inspired by the Vatican."[59] The discord that used to characterize—although not openly—the relations between his leadership and the Church hierarchy, was then rekindled: an underlying tension that during the so-called operation Sturzo—when, on the occasion of the administrative elections in Rome, the Vatican wanted to impose an alliance with the forces of the extreme right on the DC—emerged so strongly that a rift was barely avoided.[60]

De Gasperi was still guided by a conception of state that, superior to the parties, was to be based on a balance between the guarantee of freedom for its citizens and the assertion of its authority. Indeed, as has been observed, "in the moment when it leaves out the left wing parties and thus a large proportion of its members, this 'strong state, but still inspired by freedom' is generally inclined to tip the scales in favor of force rather than freedom, and ends up producing a continuous administrative practice that De Gasperi wanted to sum up in the formula of 'shielded democracy'."[61] On the legislative side, the Christian Democrat leader, in order to give strength to this project, attempted to launch an operation that eventually backfired on him, by passing a new electoral law based on the first-past-the-post system that was branded as "swindle law" through a successful propagandist expression destined to last in time, and that provided for the party or group of allied parties who scored 50 percent plus one vote to receive 65 percent of the seats in the Chamber of Deputies. On this ground the clash with the Communist Party, and with Togliatti on a personal level, took on harsh and exaggerated tones: the stakes were high, due to the fact that, if the centrist coalition that De Gasperi had in mind to involve in its projects was to conquer two-thirds of the seats, not only would the leftist opposition have been even more marginalized, but the parliamentary majority would have been dangerously close to the threshold needed to amend the Constitution. Therefore, the opposition of the PCI was very tough. A debate on the subject was carried on for more than a month in the chamber, at times with dramatic tones; De Gasperi was left "to deal with this emergency showing a certain anxiety that was unusual for him, even if the determination was unchanged,"[62] while Togliatti distinguished himself as one of the protagonists in the battle carried on by the opposition. On December 8, the Communist leader presented and explained to the chamber a ruling of unconstitutionality, and ominously evoked the possible consequences of a breach in the covenant which the Constitution had enshrined among different forces and interests: "when you destroy the constitutional order, the social revolution, that in presence of a democratic order is considered only as an act of force, is also valid as law."[63] However, when the battle was reproduced in the Senate and Secchia proposed to leave the sessions as an act of boycott aimed at the President of the Senate, Meuccio Ruini, Togliatti objected that this would have meant civil war: "we are in the parliamentary regime [. . .] refusing to enter parliament would mean bringing the fight to another level."[64]

As is known, the "swindle law," although approved by parliament, did not pass at the elections of June 7, 1953 for a few tens of thousands votes. That moment constituted the beginning of a new tormented season of Italian politics where Togliatti would still be in the limelight, unlike De Gasperi, who died a little more than a year later. But, on closer inspection, the very pillars of De Gasperi's centrism were already fractured in the early 1950s. The problem of relations with the Church hierarchy was unsolved; De Gasperi's hegemony was less and less solid within the party, which witnessed the rise of strong currents of opposition to his policies; there was a widespread attitude of total closure toward the left and a reluctance to grasp the changes in international politics that it recorded; and lastly, the party's conception of the state had failed to result in a real and widespread cultural hegemony: "De Gasperi's policy was stuck at April 18th, but the country, albeit with many difficulties, was no longer the same."[65]

When the news of the death of his great antagonist—to whom he directed harsh comments only a few months before[66]—reached him on August 19, 1954, Togliatti displayed coldness and detachment by letting his party know that he would not be attending the funeral, "not only because, he wrote, I stand against any form of *embrassons-nous* in the presence of the corpse, and indeed it is repugnant to me as a vulgarity and hypocrisy," but also because he could not forget that De Gasperi "fought against us with no holds barred, rejecting any sense of humanity."[67] This sentence still expressed all the tension and hatred that built up over the years during which the confrontations and the social, political, and cultural clashes that set the leftists against the DC and its allies took on the character of a true "cold civil war."[68] However, the homage to the opponent he dictated to "*L'Unità*" was not only loaded with respect, but also a political message that stopped to consider "the common aspects, what was lived in community of purpose, albeit temporarily."[69]

A year later, Togliatti drew a more thoughtful evaluation of De Gasperi's work. Of course it cannot be defined as "fair-minded," as fair-minded could not have been, with inverted roles, an overall assessment by De Gasperi of the role of Togliatti in Italian history; and overall it resulted in a harsh final judgment, which nowadays appears to be ungenerous. But the Communist leader, who was at times capable of the sharp analysis of a great historian, was able almost unwittingly to trace parameters that identified "the touchstone of the ability of the politician:"

> To what extent do his ideal guidelines and his personal insight enable him to understand the course of events, to decipher, among the confusion of the individual events, what is essential and what is especially new, and in which, therefore, the germ of the future is contained? And to what extent is he able to derive from his principles a course of action that makes him master of the events, so that they take and retain the mark that he wanted to give them? The real research is between intentions and reality, on the one hand, and between the intentions and actualization on the other.[70]

He who wishes to analyze the work of both of the two major players in the reconstruction of postwar Italy to obtain a "fair-minded" judgment should try to conform to these criteria even today, although we are now far from the passions of that time. And if one also keeps in mind the "main task of the biography" indicated by Goethe—"to represent the individual in dealing with his time, to show how everything is against him, everything favors him, how he drew a vision the world and humanity from it and how, in turn, he reflects it,"[71] one will likely come to the conclusion that both De Gasperi and Togliatti were great politicians.

NOTES

1. R. Gualtieri, "Palmiro Togliatti e la costruzione della Repubblica," in R. Gualtieri, C. Spagnolo, and E. Taviani, eds, *Togliatti nel suo tempo* (Rome: Carocci, 2007), 336.
2. See, to pick only a few significant works in Italian, A. Mastropaolo, *La mucca pazza della democrazia. Nuove destre, populismo, antipolitica* (Turin: Bollati Boringhieri, 2005); A.Burgio, *Senza democrazia. Per un'analisi della crisi* (Rome: Derive e approdi, 2009); M. L.Salvadori, *Democrazie senza democrazia* (Rome and Bari: Laterza, 2009).
3. P. Scoppola, *La repubblica dei partiti. Evoluzione e crisi di un sistema politico 1945–1996* (Bologna: Il Mulino, 1997).
4. See M. T. Di Marco, "Metterci e rimetterci la faccia. Una lettura fisiognomica dei manifesti elettorali italiani," in *Zapruder. Storie in movimento*, Sept–Oct 2008, 7, 61–76.

5. E.Ragionieri, "La storia politica e sociale," in *Storia d'Italia*, vol. 4, *Dall'unità ad oggi* (Turin: Einaudi, 1976), 2419, 2416.

6. P. G. Zunino, "Comunisti e cattolici di fronte alla democrazia tra la crisi del fascismo e la Repubblica," in A. Agosti, ed., *Togliatti e la fondazione dello Stato democratico* (Milan: Angeli, 1986), 158.

7. Here I draw on the observations made in A. Agosti, *Togliatti. Un uomo di frontiera* (Turin: UTET Libreria, 2003), 557–558 (English transl. *Palmiro Togliatti. A Biography* (London: I.B.Tauris, 2008), 293–294.

8. On the formation of De Gasperi, see P. Pombeni, *Il primo De Gasperi: la formazione di un leader politico* (Bologna: Il Mulino, 2007. The most recent comprehensive biography of De Gasperi is the one by P. Craveri, *De Gasperi* (Bologna: Il Mulino, 2006). A critical edition of the entire corpus of his work has been published in several volumes: A. De Gasperi, *Scritti e discorsi politici*, 4 vols., ed. E. Tonezzer, M. Bigaran, M. Cau, S. Lorenzini, V. Capperucci, and B. Taverni, general ed., P. Pombeni (Bologna: Il Mulino, 2005–09). Each of the four volumes includes substantial historical essays that offer an overview of the situation.

9. M. Cau, "Alcide De Gasperi. Un personalità direttiva alla guida della ricostruzione," *Acta Concordium*, April 2012, 12.

10. It has been sharply observed—and this remark also applies to De Gasperi—that "the appearance of a consensus on the requirements of political democracy continued to be accompanied by the ancient fear that democracy would contain within it important factors of secularization and fragmentation of the social body." F. Traniello, " Il mondo cattolico nella seconda guerra mondiale' , in his *Città dell'uomo. Cattolici, partito e Stato nella storia d'Italia* (Bologna: Il Mulino, 1998), 267.

11. P. G. Zunino, *Saggio introduttivo* a *Scritti politici di Alcide De Gasperi* (Milan: Feltrinelli, 1979), 56.

12. P. Togliatti, *Fine della questione romana*, in *Opere*, ed. E. Ragionieri, vol. 2 (Rome: Editori Riuniti, 1972), 658; P. G. Zunino, *La questione cattolica e la sinistra italiana*, 300.

13. Better known as *Lectures on fascism*, a first version of them can be found in P. Togliatti, *Opere*, vol. 3, ed. E. Ragionieri (Rome: Editori Riuniti, 1979). Subsequent research has allowed us to identify two other lectures, both dedicated to social democracy: see the new edition edited by F. M. Biscione, *Corso sugli avversari. Le lezioni sul fascismo* (Turin: Einaudi, 2010).

14. P. Togliatti, *L'Italia e la guerra contro la Germania hitleriana*, in *Opere*, ed. Ragionieri, vol. 3, 381.

15. P. Togliatti, *La politica di unità nazionale dei comunisti, in Opere*, ed. Gruppi, vol. 5 (Rome: Editori Riuniti, 1984), 18.

16. In January 1945, Monsignor Montini, substitute of the Vatican Secretariat of State, reassured Eugenio Reale (then Secretary for Foreign Affairs in the government of Bonomi and close associate of Togliatti) that "the Vatican has never proclaimed the incompatibility between Catholic faith and membership in a party of the left, so that a Catholic may very well be a member of the socialist or Communist Party," and even proposed him to arrange talks "between his Holiness and the leader of your party, which now has such a great influence in Italy" (the report of Reale's talk with Montini is now published in P. Togliatti, *La guerra di posizione in Italia. Epistolario 1944-1964* ed. G.Fiocco and M.L.Righi, (Turin: Einaudi 2014), 38-40). This proposal seemed to have no appeal, and from the report of Reale emerged a reluctance of the Communist Party to follow up on it, but the episode reveals a climate still far from that of the Cold War.

17. P. Togliatti, *Per la libertà d'Italia, per la creazione di un vero regime democratico*, in *Opere*, ed. Gruppi, vol. 5, 73.

18. Togliatti, *La guerra di posizione in Italia*, 27.

19. L. Longo, *I centri dirigenti del PCI nella resistenza* (Rome: Editori Riuniti, 1973), 455.

20. Report of Comrade Togliatti held on February 5, 1945 at the Congress of Tuscany, in P. Secchia, *Il Partito comunista italiano e la guerra di liberazione. Ricordi, documenti inediti, testimonianze*, (Milan: Feltrinelli, 1973), 857.

21. "The new Communist Party will try by all legal and illegal means [. . .] to snatch organizations from socialism, getting them drunk, if not with the Asian narcotic, with the practical means that Lenin won't spare to some of his Italian minions." See Zunino, *Scritti politici di Alcide De Gasperi*, 136.

22. P. Scoppola, *La proposta politica di De Gasperi* (Bologna: Il Mulino, 1977), 255.

23. *Scritti politici di Alcide De Gasperi*, 235.

24. Zunino, *Saggio introduttivo*, 51.

25. G. Andreotti, *De Gasperi e il suo tempo* (Milan: Mondadori, 1964), 186.

26. G. Spataro, *I democratici cristiani dalla dittatura alla Repubblica* (Milan: Mondadori, 1972), 205–206.

27. De Gasperi's Memorandum for the Vatican, cited in Scoppola, *La proposta politica*, 266.

28. A. De Gasperi, *Scritti e discorsi politici*, cited in R. Moro, "Togliatti nel giudizio del mondo cattolico", in R. Gualtieri, C. Spagnolo, and E. Taviani, eds, *Togliatti nel suo tempo. Togliatti nel suo tempo* (Rome: Carocci, 2007), 343.

29. Both Togliatti's and De Gasperi's letters are in P. Togliatti, *La guerra di posizione in Italia*, 27–29. According to Scoppola, *La proposta politica*, 271, De Gasperi "appears in the letter to be fully convinced of the sincerity of the effort of the Communist leader and determined to concede him a loan agreement, so to speak" (p. 272).

30. Cited in Sturzo, *Scritti inediti*, vol. 3, *1940–1946*, ed. F. Malgeri (Rome: Cinque Lune, 1976), 334.

31. Sturzo, *Scritti inediti*, 336.

32. Letter from Togliatti to De Gasperi from July 10, 1945, cited in Moro, *Togliatti nel giudizio del mondo cattolico*, 346–347.

33. "Il malcontento di De Gasperi," *L'Unità*, July 8, 1946.

34. *L'Unità*, December 11, 1945.

35. The measure, highly controversial, was issued June 22, 1946, and is widely analyzed by M. Franzinelli, *L'amnistia Togliatti. 22 giugno 1946. Colpo di spugna sui crimini fascisti* (Milan: Mondadori, 2006). It is quoting to quote the comment Nenni wrote in his diary: "De Gasperi's tendency: leaving out all the fascists. Togliatti's tendency: dumping as few of them as possible." P. Nenni, *Tempo di guerra fredda, Diari 1943–1956* (Milan: Sugarco, 1981), 231.

36. Togliatti, *La guerra di posizione in Italia*, 68–71. Togliatti emphasizes the sentence and sarcastically writes, "Man is like a horse, on which either God or Satan ride since his birth."

37. *Scritti e discorsi politici*, vol. 3, 1, 660

38. Cau, *Alcide De Gasperi: una "personalità direttiva,"* 17.

39. G. Quazza, *Resistenza e storia d'Italia* (Milan: Feltrinelli, 1976), 188.

40. Togliatti, *Nuovo corso*, in *Opere*, ed. Gruppi, vol. 5, 232–235.

41. See S. Galante, *La fine di un compromesso storico. PCI e DC nella crisi del 1947* (Milan: Franco Angeli, 1980), 30–61.

42. On the way De Gasperi handles the crisis of January–February 1947, see F. Malgeri, *Dal fascismo alla democrazia*, in A.Canavero et al., ed., *Alcide De Gasperi* (Soveria Mannelli: Rubbettino, 2009), 282–295.

43. See Agosti, *Togliatti*, 334.

44. See G. Formigoni, "Alcide De Gasperi 1943-1948. Il politico vincente alla guida della transizione, " in De Gasperi, *Scritti e discorsi politici*, vol. 4, 125. In a subsequent speech to the Constituent Assembly (Parliamentary Speeches, Chamber of Deputies, Rome 1985, vol. 1, 150) he would then speak of a "fourth party," in addition to the three who were part of the government coalition in April, "belonging to all strata of society, but especially to the middle class." Taking a cue from an annotation by Emilio Sereni, who had been part of the government DCI -PCI- PSI, a great part of historiography will later interpret the definition of "fourth party" as a mere expression of the dominant economic and financial interests of big capital, erecting it to a "dogma of historiography." P. Craveri, who retraced in a philologically exemplary manner the use of the term by De Gasperi in parliamentary and government debates admits however to its "purely liberal" meaning and does not deny the will of the Prime Minister to dramatize the situation "to get rid of the participation of the left." (De Gasperi, *Scritti e discorsi politici*, 289–290.)

45. On the crisis of May 1947, the most accurate reconstructions, even from different points of view, are those of di Scoppola, *La proposta politica*, 306–318, and A. Gambino, *Storia del dopoguerra. Dalla Liberazione al potere DC* (Rome and Bari: Laterza, 1988), 391–394, making use in particular of the Francesco Bartolotta fund, from which Togliatti's quotations are taken. See also G. Amendola, *La rottura della coalizione tripartita*, in *Gli anni della Repubblica* (Rome: Editori Riuniti, 1976), 66–87.

46. See R. Martinelli, *Storia del Partito comunista italiano. Il "Partito nuovo" dalla Liberazione al 18 aprile* (Turin: Einaudi, 1996), 300–301; G. Procacci, "Togliatti e la politica estera italiana," *Ricerche storiche*, 1986, 14, n. 2.

47. See, despite the valorization of the cultural background of liberal Catholicism that was its source of inspiration, P. Pombeni, "De Gasperi Costituente," in *Quaderni Degasperiani per la storia dell'Italia contemporanea*, 2009, n. 1.

48.. *Discorsi parlamentari*, 1, 62–63.

49. *Rinascita*, February 1948.

50. As in the famous speech of Piazza San Giovanni in Rome, in which he promises to De Gasperi, after the victory of the Front, of "affixing to him" his own shoes, properly nailed "on a body part that I will not name." On the election campaign of 1948, see Gambino, *Storia del dopoguerra*, 480–517.

51. E. Aga-Rossi and V. Zaslavskij, *Togliatti e Stalin. Il PCI e la politica estera staliniana negli archivi di Mosca* (Bologna: Il Mulino, 1997), 233–234.

52. See De Gasperi, *Scritti e discorsi parlamentari*, vol. 4, section 1, 330–368.

53. F. Barbagallo, "La formazione dell'Italia democratica," in *Storia dell'Italia repubblicana*, vol. 1: *La costruzione della democrazia* (Turin: Einaudi, 1994), 100.

54. Formigoni, *Alcide De Gasperi*, 146.

55. Zunino, *Saggio introduttivo*, 75.

56. In 1949 he personally edits, opening it with a brilliant introduction, the translation of Voltaire's *Treatise on Tolerance* (Milan: Universale Economica).

57. Gualtieri, *PalmiroTogliatti*, 333–336.

58. Gualtieri, *PalmiroTogliatti*, 335.

59. Zunino, *Saggio introduttivo*, 55.

60. Craveri, *De Gasperi*, 542–551.

61. Zunino, *Saggio introduttivo*, 86.

62. Craveri, *De Gasperi*, 598.

63. *Discorsi parlamentari*, morning session of December 8, 1952, vol. 2, 733.

64. *Archivio Pietro Secchia 1945-1973*, introduction and editing by E. Collotti, in *Annali della Fondazione Giangiacomo Feltrinelli*, XIX (Milan: Feltrinelli, 1979), 428.

65. Zunino, *Saggio introduttivo*, p 88.

66. Even in the aftermath of the Christian Democrat Congress of Naples he had labeled his "Sanfedist fanaticism," attributing him the goal of a "paternalistic authoritarian regime": "L'imbroglio di Napoli," *L'Unità*, 4 luglio 1954.

67. Letter to Edoardo D'Onofrio, August 20, 1954, in P. Spriano, *Le passioni di un decennio (1946-1956)* (Milan: Garzanti, 1986), 68.

68. A. Lepre, *Storia della prima Repubblica. L'Italia dal 1943 al 1998* (Bologna : Il Mulino, 1999), 119–165.

69. "La dichiarazione di Togliatti," *L'Unità*, 20 Aug. 1954.

70. "Per un giudizio equanime sull'opera di Alcide De Gasperi" (1955), in *Momenti di storia d'Italia* (Rome: Editori Riuniti, 1963), 225–226.

71. J. W. Goethe, *Poesia e verità*, in *Opere*, vol. 5, Italian translation ed, L. Mazzucchetti (Florence: Sansoni, 1963), 573.

CHAPTER 27

....

GIANNI AGNELLI
AND ENRICO MATTEI

....

VALERIO CASTRONOVO

GIANNI Agnelli, born in 1921, was 15 years younger than Enrico Mattei. They came from very different social backgrounds. The Agnelli family belonged to Turin's bourgeoisie and headed a large industrial venture; Mattei was the son of a non-commissioned police officer and had made his living as an industrial worker in a small village of the Marche region until the founding of his small business, dealing in chemical products, halfway through the 1930s. Despite these differences, they had come to share the same experience during the German occupation and after the armistice of September 8, 1943, albeit on different fronts: Agnelli in the south as liaison officer for the Italian "Legnano" division, fighting beside the Allies, and Mattei in the north as a commander to the Catholic anti-Fascist insurgents (*Partigiani*).[1]

Mattei was nominated by the government for the post of Special Commissioner in Northern Italy for the Italian Oil Agency (Agip)—founded in 1926 under the Fascist regime—soon after the Liberation from Nazi-fascism (*Liberazione*). He contributed to salvaging it from closure by putting his trust in the promising results of research, conducted in 1944, that had been hidden from the German occupant. The Minister for Foreign Trade, Ezio Vanoni, strongly endorsed his effort. Edison, leading firm in private electrical industry, counted on the disinvestment of Agip, and had managed to beat Montecatini industries in the race—after Montecatini found itself in trouble due to the death of Guido Donegani, the man who had been responsible for its good fortunes, in mid-April 1947. Once Edison too was out of the picture, some large foreign firms came forward, while the Communist Party, in an effort to avert privatization, had called for Agip's nationalization. The latter solution, in Mattei's view, meant jumping from the frying pan into the fire, because it would let the company fall into the hands of a state bureaucracy he considered to be muddled and incompetent.

Mattei's antagonists also insinuated that his success was due to an arrangement with De Gasperi, given that the prime minister had entrusted him with the task of deconstructing the left parties' political monopoly of the Italian Resistance Movement

(*Resistenza*). That is to say that Mattei used the mission that had been entrusted to him as leverage to request the salvage of Agip. In fact, Mattei's action on behalf of De Gasperi, geared at claiming the "white" *Partigiani*'s role in the struggle that lead to the *Liberazione*, was something that he, as former commander of those forces, had always strongly upheld, as can be inferred from his public speeches.[2] After all, his aversion to the political formations of Marxist ideology was well known; and it was motivated by the knowledge that numerous extreme left militants were convinced that the battle they had fought during the *Resistenza* was not yet over, despite Togliatti's clear rejection of this view, based on his awareness of what the Yalta treaty meant.

Mattei was elected MP with the Christian Democrats (DC) in 1948, for the Milan-Pavia constituency. This role, coupled with his being vice-president of Agip, gave him the opportunity to act within parliament together with Vanoni, Minister for Finance in De Gasperi's fifth government, and thus in charge of the department responsible for the management of 60 percent of Agip's capital.

Agnelli had, in the meantime, become vice-president and main shareholder of Riv—FIAT's ball-bearings factory—representing his family in the role of chief beneficiary to his grandfather's inheritance; Senator Giovanni Agnelli had, in fact, died in 1954.

Mattei and Agnelli's paths crossed again after Agip manifested the intent to extend its mining activities in northern Italy, enacting a struggle with Anglo-American companies, at a time when FIAT was attempting to conquer the internal market, in competition with Ford and General Motors. Furthermore, FIAT's managers, headed by a capable and shrewd Vittorio Valletta, thought well of Mattei's policy, because the natural gas Agip had found was contributing sensibly to Italian economy by partly alleviating fuel shortages.[3] Agip's head had sensed that gas was to be an important energy source form the start, while Anglo-American companies had underestimated it, considering its distribution costs to be too onerous. Agip's president Marcello Boldrini and Mattei devised a four-year plan, aimed at constructing a vast web of gas pipelines able to guarantee stable, long-distance procurements at affordable prices. When the plan was launched, at a cost of 52 billion lire—15 billion of which were to be sourced via foreign loans and the remainder through company profit—the Anglo-American companies remained convinced that Agip would lose its money.

Meanwhile, the income generated by gas had not only assured Agip's survival but was also confirming the validity of Vanoni's hypothesis: that it represented a steady source of funds for the state, and thus was worthy of being supported in order to increase its profit margins.[4]

Dealings between Agip and FIAT intensified after the launch, in February 1953, of the National Authority for Hydrocarbon (ENI), which had obtained exclusive mining rights in the Val Padana region. This resulted, on the one hand, in accusations that a monopoly was being created, and, on the other, in bitter political condemnation from the liberals, fueled, amongst others, by Claire Boothe Luce. Wife to Henry Luce, the owner of America's largest newspaper chain, Claire Boothe Luce had been a US representative in Rome since 1953. On this occasion Agnelli and FIAT's managing director Valletta had attempted to mitigate the ambassador's intransigent stance, who was ill disposed toward

FIAT's representative because the CGIL, a leftist trade union, had managed to maintain a prominent place in internal labor commissions elected in that company's plants.[5]

On the American side, the "Seven Sisters" had not heeded FIAT's request to include ENI in the Abadan consortium for the exploitation of Iranian oilfields—FIAT had then been a partner of Texaco in the management of Petrolcatex within Italy. And so it was that ENI, after having opened its own production site on the Sinai in Nasser's Egypt, to the dismay London and Paris, came to stipulate an agreement with Iran in March 1957. As well as the customary 50 percent royalties, it envisaged the founding of a company by the two signatories, and the equal sharing of profits generated by oil extraction. This agreement, signed by Mattei together with the Shah of Persia Reza Palhavi brought other Arab oil producing countries to ask companies that had until then benefitted from conspicuous incomes linked to their standing for analogous terms. Once again, under these circumstances, FIAT tried to get across to its American counterparts that it would be wiser to try to come to some sort of understanding with Mattei, instead of persisting in underestimating both his tenacity and his lack of scruples.[6]

At that time Agnelli was still being portrayed by the press as a distracted, pleasure-seeking billionaire. A very different view was held by Mediobanca's president Enrico Cuccia: "I liked him straight away, because everything seemed to be too small for him, Turin, Italy ... And he was not scared of making enemies."[7]

After all, David Rockefeller had opened the doors of the international business community for Agnelli. "We clicked on a human, social and political level as well as on business matters," the American magnate would later recall. He had already wanted Agnelli to become a member of Bilderberg, the club he had created for European, American, and Canadian eminencies of the economic and political worlds to negotiate privately those issues that took on particular relevance in the West.[8]

Meanwhile, Agnelli established another important friendship, that with John Kennedy. The two met in London shortly after the war, when Kennedy, already a Democrat congressman, was in Great Britain to pursue his studies in economics. They met again in America: "He is a bit of a snob, a fully fledged Bostonian, London School of Economics, Harvard, solid knowledge in economics, very fit, he sails and he rides. Progressive ideas, typical of an American liberal, very open to the colored minorities. He is friends with actors and actresses, but intellectual through and through. And rich, very rich." So ran Agnelli's take on Kennedy, after the latter became a senator in 1952. Agnelli continued to be impressed by his "exceptional vitality," coupled with "his view of politics as a service he owed." Yet he was not oblivious to certain peculiar traits of the character: "his love of women, his restlessness and curiosity." These were traits akin to Agnelli's own: a style attractive and nonchalant, the elegant countenance and articulated speech, the openness to all new things and, last but not least, a certain *art de vivre*, a bent to enjoy the pleasures of life, with little heed of conventions.[9]

FIAT had inaugurated mass motorization in Italy in 1955, through purchase plans that allowed consumers to spread the cost of their economy cars over a considerable time span. And ENI, with its service stations along the *Autostrada del Sole* selling fuel at discounted prices had become, alongside Finsider—IRI's holding in the integrated steel mills public sector—the other main agent in the achievement of the "economic miracle."

In the meantime, Mattei had been playing a significant role in fostering the growth of the more progressive currents within the Christian Democrats as well as in supporting the election of Giovanni Gronchi as President of the Republic in the May 1955 election. Thus he felt that, at the end of the 1950s, the time was ripe to bring home another of his daring bets, in which, as always, he poured a good dose of audacity coupled with the coolness of the expert gambler. Mattei wished to reach a multi-year agreement regarding a large supply of crude oil for Eni from the USSR, a supply even greater than that already imported since 1958. To that end, secret negotiations had been undertaken—secret enough for the Italian ambassador Luca Pietromacchi to have been kept in the dark about their details—by the manager of foreign business for Eni, Giuseppe Ratti. The latter had been introduced to Moscow's diplomatic circles by Piero Savoretti, a veteran of FIAT's dealings with Russia, who had known Mattei when he was involved in the resistance movement (or *Partigiani*).[10]

Meanwhile, FIAT was bringing to a close the transactions with Eni regarding the transfer of all its oil-related enterprises—from Petrolcaltex to Sarpam—to the state authority for oil, keeping only a small shareholding interest in Aquila.[11]

Mattei's initiative in the USSR had received support from Turin and had reaped success during Gronchi's official visit to the Kremlin, planned between February 6 and February 10, 1960, after Krushev had authorized Minister for Foreign Commerce Nicolaj Patolicev to stipulate an agreement with ENI. After all, oil production in the Volga river basin and in the Ural Mountains had surpassed planned government needs, and the Kremlin had judged it convenient to place a larger quota of the surplus on the Western market, in exchange for specific materials that were needed. In return, ENI pledged to deliver 50,000 tons of synthetic rubber, various industrial systems to be built by its factory in Nuovo Pignone, 240,000 tons of Finsider-produced large steel pipes and other materials. Essentially the agreement would open the doors of the Soviet market to the products of some of Italy's largest companies, both private and public.

The contract between ENI and the Soviet government provoked quite a storm in the United States. The *New York Times* went as far as defining, on November 11, Mattei's decision to sell pumps and pipes to the USSR as "an attack to the security of the free world," deeming these supplies as strategically relevant. And all because, according to the Department of State, they would be used by the Kremlin for the construction of a vast web of oil pipelines traveling from Siberia through to South-Eastern Europe. This infrastructure would thus facilitate the procurement of oil by the armored divisions of the Red Army, based between Poland and Eastern Germany, in the event of a Soviet invasion in the heart of Europe. Furthermore, Washington feared that, with the acquisition of equipment and technical know-how, Russia would strengthen its economic structures, in a way detrimental to the West in the context of "competitive coexistence" that was being put in place between the East and the West.[12]

In response to the vehement attacks against him for having introduced a "Trojan horse" in NATO's defense apparatus, Mattei expressed his views in a long interview given to the American journalist Ernestine Adams on December 28, 1960. First and foremost, he pointed out how not only Britain but also the German Federal Republic, through groups such as Krupp and Mannesmann, had been long in the business of selling the USSR goods that were much more relevant to a potential use in war than the pipes and micro-compressors ENI was providing. He also underlined that it was in the collective interest of the West to foster, through business, the consolidation amongst Kremlin officials of a political will oriented to the relaxation of the relations between the blocs.[13]

In practice, it was Prime Minister Amintore Fanfani who defused the tension caused by the agreement with the USSR by persuading Western diplomacies that the deal was a legitimate way of pursuing national interests while favoring the "thawing" of relations between the West and the East—without in any way jeopardizing Italy's utmost loyalty to the Atlantic Pact.

In addition, the fact that, a few months later, the Democrat John Kennedy was elected to take office at the White House further helped to blunt the sharper edges of criticism to the agreement. So much so that, in March 1961, Averell Harriman, "itinerant ambassador" to the newly appointed American president, sought to meet Mattei in Rome, in order to personally ascertain who this man was who had earned great support in the Third World and so much opposition from the United States. ENI's president reassured him that the Italian people were and wished to "remain beside" America, but also wished to be treated as "friends, allies, and as such as peers not only in theory or in what concerned military alliances, but also on an economic level."[14] And this was what, in fact, the "Seven Sisters" had always ruled out, because of their "stubborn clinging to their conspicuous profits." With the result, he added, that "Africa is now filled with Russians, Poles, Czechs, Chinese" and that "if the governments and great industries of the West will fail to understand all this, Africa will turn its head elsewhere. And so will Asia and Latin America."[15]

Nonetheless, Mattei's dealings with the Third World had also raised serious concerns for Western Diplomacy—"in the war Italy had lost its colonies. Some think that it was a misfortune: it was, in fact, a great advantage," he commented on August 10, 1961, to the Frenchman Gilles Martinet. Moreover, there were suspicions that Agip, through some of its functionaries in Tunis, was providing support in more than one way to the Algerian movement for national liberation in its fight for independence from France. This is what was, in fact, happening behind the scenes.

Therefore, in many European capitals, opinions went as far as conjecturing that Mattei's intent might be that of directing Italian foreign policy towards neutralism: even more so after the coming into office, in 1962 Rome, of a centre-left government that was externally backed by the Socialist party.

Agnelli's familiarity with Kennedy led him to believe the American president to be moved by a strong desire for political change; he also deemed the time to be ripe for a change in Italian political structures, given the Socialist's repudiation of the pact of commonality of action they held with the Communist party after witnessing Russian repression in Budapest.[16] After all, it was known in Turin that Reinhardt, the American ambassador in Rome, had been authorized on April 22 by the Secretary of State Dean Rusk to launch negotiations with Rome regarding a decrease in ENI's purchases of Russian oil, in exchange for the willingness of a few American companies—Esso or Mobil—to guarantee an adequate supply of crude on favorable terms.[17]

Thus Agnelli and Valletta, during a meeting held with Kennedy on May 15, 1962 at the White House, had discussed the issue of commercial dealings with the USSR, in order to mitigate the State Department's worries that these economic associations might weaken Italy's loyalty to the Atlantic Alliance.[18] At stake were FIAT's project concerning the construction of a plant in Russia, as well as ENI's contract with Moscow.[19] The two thus hoped that the US president's staff would facilitate a solution to the controversies amongst American oil companies and ENI. When Valletta was asked, in a subsequent interview with John McCone, head of the CIA, what his opinions were regarding the new centre-left government in Italy, he stated that it was a "product of the new era," and went on to mention his hopes for a "better tolerance and understanding" of Mattei.[20]

And so it was that, after various diplomatic efforts and a meeting held on May 22 at the US embassy in Rome, attended by the Under Secretary of State George Ball and Mattei, ENI's president formed the opinion that the US were finally willing to offer him official, tangible, and undoubtable recognition. He thus transmitted to the Department of State a memorandum in which—after mentioning his having been honored in May 1945 at the hands of General Clarke, commander of US forces in Italy at the time, of the Bronze Star for his "military actions and loyalty" during the *Resistenza*—he requested an audience with Kennedy as well as a *Honoris Causa* degree to be awarded to him by the University of Stanford. His stay in the US would also be the occasion in which to stipulate a particularly important agreement between ENI and Esso.[21]

Affairs had thus come close to a "truce" with Standard Oil and to Mattei's official visit to the US when he tragically lost his life on October 27 of that year: his private plane, during a flight from Catania to Milan, crashed a few minutes before landing. The cause of the tragedy has remained unknown to this day, be it linked to malicious intent or otherwise.

A few days later, during a meeting, FIAT's board of directors commemorated Mattei with an address by Valletta, who stated that "the late Enrico Mattei was a man whose actions were the object of many a debate, yet he was undoubtedly a brilliant mind, instrumental to the growth of ENI, a company he brought onto the international stage, achieving great successes both in Italy and abroad ..." The feats accomplished by ENI's main man, he specified, were "perhaps aimed primarily at the valorization of Italian resources and prestige, rather than at short-term financial gain." In fact, the commitment to elevate Italy's international status was one FIAT's management had always claimed as its own. And the solidarity FIAT repeatedly showed in supporting Mattei's action was due to this affinity of intent.[22]

Four years later, on May 4, 1966, Agnelli, in his role as FIAT's president, sealed an agreement with the Soviet government that planned for the construction of a large car manufacturing plant in the Russian city of Togliattigrad. This important arrangement, which caused great stir in the Western world, showed how ENI and FIAT had been pursuing parallel industrial policies which converged in the intent to reinforce their autonomy and enlarge their groups' sphere of interest. Their strategy served to strengthen Italy's role on the international arena, as the country joined the circle of industrially advanced countries.

Agnelli would continue, in subsequent years and as a staunch supporter of the European project, to back European economic and political integration in his public speeches, and to voice his hope for a bolstering of US–Italian relations in the context of transatlantic economic cooperation. In this respect he made use both of his links with influential America circles—particularly Rockefeller's and those of the Franco-Anglo-American bank Lazard—and of his personal friendships with some Washington politicians, especially Henry Kissinger, whom he met in Rome in 1970, during Nixon's visit to Italy.[23]

Furthermore, until his death in January 2003, Agnelli had no difficulty in securing the attentiveness of American presidents, even in spite of his obtaining, in 1976, the participation of Muhammad al Gaddafi bankers in the recapitalization of FIAT, a move that gave rise to strong negative reactions from the US Department of State. Even Republican presidents, though aware of Agnelli's Democratic leanings, would not deny him their consideration.[24]

Agnelli was seen as a "shadow foreign minister" for Italy, a representative par excellence of the Italian industrial establishment, as well as a financial crutch of sorts for the peninsula. Through him, Washington could informally communicate political orientations and opinions to Rome.

Specifically, in 1976, Agnelli had been instrumental in reassuring the Department of State that the entrance of the Italian Communist party (PCI) in the governmental majority would not have any repercussions on Italian foreign policy. According to him, the Communists had been requested to back a government of national reconciliation solely in order to implement an "emergency program" that would curb inflation, improve the balance of payments, and reduce public deficit. Agnelli knew only too well how much Washington's prejudicial hostility to the Italian Communists—often reiterated by US ambassador in Rome Graham Martin—still weighed. Nevertheless, after Democrat Jimmy Carter's victory in November in the race to the White House, Italy felt that the new president would soften US attitudes in this respect. The Trilateral Commission, of which Agnelli was a prominent partner, had endorsed the ascent of the former Governor of Georgia, who would otherwise have been largely unknown, confident that he would implement a change with respect to Ford's presidency, which had proved both dull and lacking in force. And Trilateral Commission director Zbigniew Brzezinski had been nominated National Security Advisor for the Carter administration.

In a conference held on February 24, 1977, in New York, invited by the Foreign Policy Association, Agnelli had tackled the issue of the PCI's role, mainly because he was of the opinion that the issue would be relevant in deciding on the allocation of international loans that Italy desperately needed. He pointed out how he thought that it would be unadvisable to dictate overly harsh conditions to go hand in hand with the granting of such loans to a country like Italy, both because of its strategic position as frontier

state between the West and the Communist East and Middle East, and because an externally imposed "austerity" would further exacerbate social tensions, in a climate made
incandescent by the terrorist offensive carried out by the "Red Brigades" against state
representatives and exponents of the great industries. He then went on to examine the
fundamental political question that, in his view, continued to hinder a satisfactory resolution to the negotiations with the International Monetary Fund, of which the US held
the keys. He did not hide the fact that many unanswered questions still lingered concerning the ideological evolution of the PCI and its links with Moscow. As far as he was
concerned, the Italian Communists had not yet made significant advances, but they had
"changed enough" to "sway new sectors of the electorate." Nevertheless, it was necessary
to give PCI leaders time to tangibly show that their party had in fact become a "responsible party," thus effectively putting Enrico Berlinguer and his comrades to the test, in
order to assess how far they would abide by the laws of the market economy, and the
truthfulness of their declarations regarding Italy's indisputable loyalty to the Atlantic
Alliance.[25]

This address, on Agnelli's part, amounted to a cautiously appreciative act of openness
towards the PCI, corroborated by the fact that he had been outspoken about his hope
that US visas would be granted to some exponents of the party, enabling them to enter
the country. After all, he considered that Carter had chosen to appoint an astute man
such as Richard Gardner as US ambassador in Rome in order to realistically assess the
way in which the US might help Italy to overcome the economic crises it was engulfed by.

In practice, if Mattei's ENI had been defined as a "state within the state" because
of the strong links Mattei had with the DC's "chiefs of staff" and the nonchalance he
displayed in his dealings with the government in pursuing the economic goals of his
company—albeit with no view to personal gains—the same had been said of Agnelli's
FIAT, to the extent that Agnelli was referred to as a "king of republican Italy:" the
economic strength of this flagship enterprise of Italian capitalism being so strong as
to cause the heirs of FIAT's founder to appear to public opinion as a royal family of
sorts.

Naturally, it is undoubtable that Agnelli played a protagonist's role in Italian public life
pervasively and for a considerable span of time, not least due to his constantly being in
the limelight through the reports of relevant organs of the press—but not because he felt
invested of prerogatives such as to induce him to act as if FIAT was in fact a "state within
the state." He recognized without hesitation or pretense the priority held by political
power with respect to economic power. His identity could perhaps be described as that
of a liberal with a lay background culture, and a strong sense of state.

After all, one of the basic rules Agnelli always abided by was a scrupulous respect for
institutions. And regarding his role as "permanent ambassador" for Italy, with no mandate but with recognizable and recognized authoritativeness, he saw this role as a task
to be accomplished, albeit without ever losing sight of FIAT's interests. He felt he had
an obligation to the forwarding of his country's cause, no matter what government took
office, and at the same time he felt this was a way in which to live the events of his historical era to the full and to take active part in them.

Mattei, too, saw himself as a servant to his country's cause. As a man of the *Resistenza* he had been amongst the protagonists of the armed fight against the Salò regime and the German occupier, calling for the rebirth of Italy after dictatorship and war. And thus, after the liberation he had believed that the main task facing those who had fought was to lay the foundations of a new democratic order, as well as a robust development process that would enable Italians, once again, to be masters of their own their destiny. Since then, a tireless dedication to the defense of Italian interests and a strong civic passion had constituted the dominant notes of Mattei's action, both in public and economic life and on the international arena. The motivation behind such a resolute and steadfast commitment—as he gave proof of in the process of achieving what was dear to him—would otherwise be difficult to understand. This shows how deeply the ideals and resolutions of national redemption he matured during the *Resistenza*, together with his political upbringing, had shaped his personality, his world view, and his actions.

In essence, Mattei and Agnelli contributed, each in their own way and measure, to influence Italian foreign policy. The first by wisely promoting a series of fruitful dealings with Third World Countries, which would be further consolidated in later years by ENI management. The second by concurring to reinforce the relationship between Italy and the US, and through his participation in the process of integration among the European Community, something that would remain a consistent *fil rouge* in Italian diplomacy.

NOTES

1. Valerio Castronovo, *Fiat 1899–1999. Un secolo di storia italiana* (Milan: Rizzoli, 1999), 696.
2. Translator's note: The term "White" refers to the Catholic groups within the anti-fascist insurgent movement. Enrico Mattei, *Scritti e discorsi 1945-1962*, edited by P. Mieli (Milan: Rizzoli, 2012), 56–207.
3. Castronovo, *Fiat 1895–1999*, 850–858.
4. Castronovo, "Enrico Mattei ed Eni: l'Italia riparte dall'energia," in Mattei, *Scritti e discorsi*, 26–28.
5. Castronovo, *Fiat 1899–1999*, 888–890.
6. Castronovo, *Fiat 1899–1999*, 971–975.
7. Castronovo, *Fiat 1899–1999*, 1148.
8. Valerio Castronovo, "Introduction," in Gianni Agnelli, *Una certa idea dell'Europa e dell'America* (Turin: Einaudi, 2004), p. xiii.
9. Castronovo, "Introduction," in Agnelli, *Una certa idea*, pp. xiv–xvi.
10. Castronovo, "Enrico Mattei ed Eni," 44–45.
11. Castronovo, *Fiat 1899–1999*, 1090.
12. On this and on other opinions Mattei expressed in his role as ENI's President, see E. Mattei, *Scritti e discorsi*, 376 ff.
13. Castronovo, "Enrico Mattei ed Eni," 46.
14. Castronovo, "Enrico Mattei ed Eni," 46.
15. Castronovo, "Enrico Mattei ed Eni," 46.
16. Castronovo, "Introduction," in Agnelli, *Una certa idea* p. xvi.
17. Castronovo, "Enrico Mattei ed Eni," 50.

18. Castronovo, *Fiat 1899–1999*, 1063–1064.
19. Castronovo, *Fiat 1899–1999*, 1058–1059.
20. Castronovo, *Fiat 1899–1999*, 1072.
21. Castronovo, *Fiat 1899–1999*, 1072.
22. Castronovo, *Fiat 1899–1999*, 1089.
23. Castronovo, "Introduction," in Agnelli, *Una certa idea* p. xxxii.
24. Castronovo, "Introduction," pp. xxxix–xl.
25. For all the above, and the ensuing opinions of Agnelli, see Castronovo, "Introduction," in Agnelli, *Una certa idea* xl ff and the various speeches by Agnelli reproduced in the rest of the volume, 82ff.

CHAPTER 28

....

ALDO MORO AND ENRICO
BERLINGUER

....

EMANUELE BERNARDI

ALDO Moro and Enrico Berlinguer, two of the most well-known exponents of the leading parties—Christian Democracy DC and the Italian Communist Party (PCI)—that
were involved in the making of Italian history during the second half of the 1900s, had
very different biographical trajectories. Moro (1916–1978), was a Catholic. He completed
his education in the Italian Catholic Federation of University Students (FUCI) and, after
the war, became involved with Dossetti's leftist current within the DC. As a young man,
he was assigned government roles—he was Undersecretary of State for Foreign Affairs
between 1948 and 1950—and was eventually appointed as prime minister.

Berlinguer (1922–1984) came from a lay family. His political career started with his
post as secretary of the Italian Communist Youth Federation (FGCI), which he held
from 1949 to 1956, but did not take on any official roles during the short-lived communist participation in the post-war cabinets that ran from 1944 through to 1947. He
became PCI secretary from 1972 until his death.

Toward the end of the 1970s, these two figures rose to an ever-increasing importance
within their parties, and contributed to the creation of a climate which historians have
defined in various ways: "strategy of attention" on Moro's part with regard to the PCI,
debate politics, crisis of the *convention ad excludendum,* and so forth. Some scholars have argued that the contact between these two political forces had been "inevitable," after more than two decades from 1947 in which the PCI had remained outside
of government. The PCI sat in the opposition benches both during De Gasperi's centrist governments, formed in alliance with the minor parties (Liberals, Republicans and
Social Democrats; respectively the PLI, PRI, PSLI), and during the center-left coalition
governments that pivoted on the agreement between the DC and the Italian Socialist
Party (PSI). The entirety of Italy's post-war history would unravel along these two
political axes.[1]

The political encounter that was consumed all but straight forwardly between the
DC and the PCI during the 1970s was something other than an inevitable answer to the

political inadequacies of De Gasperi's centrism or those of the center-left governments. These governments' limits would render necessary the enlargement of the area comprising those entities considered to be politically "legitimate," as well as a newly found openness towards the left.

But it was ultimately the changes in Italian and international socio-economic circumstances that were to modify the conditions of political action. Among the most relevant occurrences on the international arena were the oil crisis and the end of the Bretton Woods system, together with an unprecedented commercial dynamism on the part of the United States.[2] On the national front, Italy faced the increasing electoral weakness of the DC and the growth of the PCI, contradictions intrinsic to its development strategy, the secularization of society in the presence of a Church that had been renovated by Vatican II, and the increasing relevance of the PCI's national profile following the Prague revolt and URRS military repression.

During this period, two diverse sensibilities—two outlooks on the peninsula's fate—met halfway. Starting out from two different mind-sets, Moro and Berlinguer arrived at a shared reading of some of the fundamental characteristics of Italian historical development in the international context. Among them, the obligations Italy had incurred on an international level, and the threats to national sovereignty they posed; the value of the Resistance movement and of the Constituent Assembly's work for the rebirth of the Italian Republic; the importance of the struggles of workers and peasants during the 1950s; the imbalances in economic development—especially with regard to the issue of north–south dualism and the inadequacies of the process of national unification—as well as Italy's role and pacifist "developmentalist" projection in the Third World. Moro and Berlinguer were also united in their heightened perception of the ethical and moral dimension of politics, and in a universalistic vision that brought them to consider questions not solely concerned with national contingencies but also with mankind's future on earth. Their political encounter, in other words, was also, and perhaps above all, a cultural one.[3]

Berlinguer followed, for the most part, the lines elaborated by Palmiro Togliatti. Despite operating during the most complex phase in the relation between the PCI and the USSR, Togliatti had recognized the Catholic Church and the Vatican to be an important reference point for the Italian masses which the PCI wanted and needed to represent, while striving to adhere to national specificities.[4] With respect to Togliatti's policy, Berlinguer widened the concept of debate with the DC, with which the PCI declared itself ready to collaborate in government—the so-called "historical compromise." More precisely, Berlinguer spelled out the communist project in relation to Italy's economic development agenda—the country could not afford to overlook the south and the new relationship between agriculture and industry, city and countryside—and reformulated the PCI's international position in relation to other communist parties and the USSR itself. The Italian Communist Party was critical of Soviet collectivistic experience, openly recognizing its limits and costs, and proceeded to sketch a new independent stance in contrast with the past—"Eurocommunism"—albeit it being still unable to modify the norms and the logics of the Cold War.

It was a set of analyses, propositions, and political initiatives that used Aldo Moro and the leftist current of the Christian Democrats as political referents. Already in the late 1960s, and more so after the historical compromise theorized in 1973 in an issue of *Rinascita*, in the view of Berlinguer and the PCI Italian democracy could be strengthened—and prevent a drift to the right—solely through the *rapprochement* and convergence of the left-wing masses with the Catholic masses, to overcome the divisions that had been created in the name of anti-communism.

In more general terms, in order to achieve radical and pervasive changes in Italian politics, it appeared necessary to trigger political processes capable of involving large sections of the DC and its electorate. To this end, a "confidential debate" was initiated between Moro and Berlinguer that dealt with varied themes, ranging from the law on divorce to the referendum, from the political perspective of the PCI and the DC to the election of the President of the Republic, internal and foreign policy, as well as the political parties' relationships with unions and other worker and farm laborer organizations.[5]

Moro identified weaknesses in Italy's structure and development patterns that previous political formulas, and the economic policies that accompanied them, had been unable to address, despite—and partly because of—the significant growth that had taken off with the "economic miracle" of the late 1950s. Italian society was still backward and divided, and within it youth protest exploded; Italy bore the weight of a subordination to the American ally that conditioned it heavily both politically and economically. Furthermore, the country was still searching for a social and economic unification of north and south, and its policies were unduly influenced by commercial interests, conveyed above all by Confindustria, the Italian employers' federation, and Confagricoltura, the federation of Italian farmers. Regulating the imbalances and contradictions that the first three decades of DC-led governments had generated, with the terrorist emergency in their wake, was for Moro the goal of an administration that must preserve the party's identity, unity and centrality, consolidate Italy's social structure, and revitalize the country.[6]

Although never fully accepting the communist proposal for a "historical compromise," Moro believed that this modernization could not be achieved without the active integration in the country's political fabric of those sections of society that stood to the left, in a way compatible with the international equilibria inherited from previous historical phases. It meant also balancing the "old" anticommunism with a revival of the antifascism. Rumors alleging Moro's enrollment in the PCI in the 1940s are perhaps unreliable: but they do confirm the deep differences of opinion that existed within the DC, and they also signaled a preoccupation with social issues shared by the left. Equally relevant is Berlinguer's belief that Moro was an ideal candidate for the Presidency of the Republic, due to his ability to interpret national interests and his balanced outlook.[7]

The proposal to pursue a working agreement with the PCI resulted from a conviction that past political formulas no longer corresponded to the electoral tendencies that had emerged in elections such as those of 1976—when the PCI gained 7.2 percent of the consensus to reach 34.3 percent overall, while the DC had stabilized at 38.7 percent. Nor were past political formula sufficient to meet the challenges posed by international relations, which were becoming increasingly complex on the trade and monetary fronts, and were subject to dramatic and sudden changes, bringing to the fore new queries concerning the limits and purposes of economic growth. Thus, there was a shared awareness of this critical phase in the capitalist system. And Italian politicians had to look for innovative approaches, on the economic, social, humanitarian, ethical, and moral fronts.

With Berlinguer's 1977 speech on austerity, the Communist Party Secretary attempted to identify the constitutive elements of an alternative economic policy, capable of rectifying the accumulated imbalances and which aimed not solely to achieve economic growth but rather to build a healthier relationship between the population and natural resources, in the name of quality, public services, and the reduction of individual consumption. A manifesto and appeal of sorts, the address was strongly criticized by the right and by the left; yet it won the sympathies of those minor but relevant Catholic currents that were sensitive to all reflections concerning the relationship between man and environment, and were not entirely persuaded by the market-led and production-oriented message that had been advanced by the "economic miracle."

Consistent political difficulties needed to be overcome in order to shape those hypotheses of convergence. Already at the start of the 1960s, the openness shown towards the socialists and the formation of the center-left governments had incurred opposition from the Vatican, DC leaders, and the American administration. This foreshadowed the strength of the forces that would coalesce around the anti-communist, moderate option.[8]

After a long incubation in 1976, the debate between the DC and the PCI appeared to yield its first political outcomes. On August 6, the Andreotti government obtained a vote of confidence thanks both to the favorable vote of DC parliamentary groups and South-Tyrol MPs, and to the abstention of the PCI, PSI, PSDI, PRI, PLI and the "Left-wing Independents." In abstaining for the vote, the PCI allowed the formation of a government it would be watching closely.

Moro, once elected President to the DC National Council, wrote in an article published by *Il Giorno* on December 10, that the PCI's electoral advance and the endurance of the DC signaled the advent of a polarization that must be taken into account. The debate with the PCI became central, as well as the issue of "the relationship that must be built with it." Moro believed that from the experience of such a government "interesting things" could emerge, despite the situation not having any "obliged solutions." In that context, the government "of abstentions" was the best that could be achieved, while, he went on, "thinking that going beyond it might be possible is to ignore internal and international factors."[9]

Despite a backdrop of major political, economic, and security adversities, the debate between the PCI and the DC, which mirrored a broader debate between laymen, Catholics, and Paul VI's Church, continued. On October 12, 1977, the press published a letter written by Berlinguer to Ivrea's bishop Mons. Luigi Bettazzi. After having reiterated the PCI's Marxist inspiration, the Secretary of the Communist Party declared that the old ideological dogmatism had been left behind and that Marxism should now be "seen and used in an informed way, as a teaching, not as a dogmatically immutable text." He went on to declare the PCI to be "fully and rigorously" lay in political terms, and "willing to build, and allow Italy to experience, a lay democratic party: a party that as such would not be theist, atheist or anti-atheists." For the first time a left-wing force was theorizing the concept of laity.

A few days later, through allowing his letter to be published in *Rinascita*—under the significant title "Communists and Catholics: clear principles and bases for understanding"—in light of the goals of the historic compromise Berlinguer stated that he "wished to build a society that, without being Christian in the sense of being attached to a radical ideological stance, would organize itself in such a way as to be ever more open and welcoming to Christian values."[10]

Catholic reactions to Berlinguer's initiative rapidly followed. According to the *Osservatore Romano*, Berlinguer's letter commanded a "particularly careful reading, in keeping with its indisputably great relevance." The Vatican's publication observed that atheism and the materialistic conceptualization of the world were not the only aspects of communism to be incompatible or "difficult to conciliate" with Christianity, if only due to the restrictions of freedom imposed in the name of justice in Soviet-controlled countries, where totalitarian regimes had discriminated fiercely against Catholics. The publication, however, viewed positively the potential emancipation of a party such as the PCI—a mass party "so strong and ebullient"—from its Marxist-Leninist ideological framework, and a move toward democratic, secular, leanings. No one, the journalist went on to say, wanted to "discourage" a "sincere willingness," yet it was important to remember that the Church's teachings regarding the incompatibility of Christianity and Communism were still valid.[11] According to the diary of communist leader Luciano Barca, "despite the implicit misgivings, these comments were interpreted, and not solely by us, as a cautious support on the part of Paul VI for Moro's inception of a far reaching political operation."[12] Faced with a situation that was felt to be eluding PCI control—youth protests, terrorism, rising inflation—Berlinguer decided to press ahead and quicken the pace of the race toward direct governmental responsibilities. After one of Moro's speeches in Benevento, which showed signs of a cautious openness towards the PCI, on January 5, 1978, the two men met.[13]

The PCI viewed Andreotti's "government of abstentions" as having become unsatisfactory: participation in government was the *conditio sine qua non* in dealing with the emergencies Italy was facing, for the implementation of reforms and for mending the rift that had originated in 1947, thus allowing for the reinstatement of a natural alternation. Barca provided a long but very interesting description of the encounter in his diary:

> [Moro] is on his last bid to persuade Enrico [Berlinguer] to postpone the reshuffling of the majority for a few months. But Enrico is very firm on this point. It is not only a question of reassuring the country with regards to the threat of eversion, of guiding it out of the rising trend inflation, nor is it simply a matter of proceeding with reforms that can no longer be delayed, such as those on justice and public administration. All of that is indeed necessary. But it is also necessary, through mending the rift of

1947 and legitimizing each other by a shared involvement in "a transition govern-ment"—in which "the PCI must vouch for the DC with the working classes, and the DC must validate the PCI in the eyes of the moderates and international allies"—to create the premises of a deliverance from a phase of stalled democracy (Moro clearly signals assent) in which a lack of political alternation has jumbled roles and worn out institutions.[14]

Support grew around the idea of new relations between DC and PCI; but even with the favorable stance of Republican La Malfa, and of the Christian Democrat leader Fanfani it was the DC that was not ready, and likewise the opposition of the American adminis-tration was all but overcome.[15] Furthermore, would the entry of the Communist Party into government not risk denying political representation to those troubled youth movements that seemed to feed an increasingly worrying trend of extra-parliamentary street violence? The meeting ended with Moro's promise to follow in the path that had been undertaken, in order to create the political spaces, both national and interna-tional, that were still insufficient to allow a political alliance with the PCI. Accordingly, he intended to contact the U.S. State Department; but only a few days after that meet-ing, the Department published a note criticizing the position DC leaders had taken with regard to the PCI, thus confirming the American administration's traditional stance.[16] On February 16, during the last of Berlinguer and Moro's meetings, just before Moro's abduction, the DC's leader continued to strongly highlight these difficulties. Moro, while recognizing the impossibility of an organic alliance with the PCI in the short term, reiterated his commitment to modifying and making more flexible the DC's positions, with the long-term objective of accomplishing Italian democracy.[17]

In light of a shared analysis of Italy's situation, and despite the cautious words spo-ken in public, at the basis of Moro and Berlinguer's relationship lay an important and substantial, though inchoate, reciprocal legitimation—alongside the acknowledgment that different cultural traditions and values could perhaps contribute to the process of changing Italy. On Moro and the DC's side, there was a recognition of the peculiarity of the PCI when compared with the international communist movement, and of its mod-eration and respect for republican institutions, in spite of its enduring financial links to Moscow. On the part of Berlinguer's PCI, accepting the concept of pluralism, there was a refusal to endorse simplistic judgments that portrayed the DC as a reactionary anti-Communist Party, suggesting instead that it was a complex party, popular and with multiple visions, which the PCI had to keep safe from conservative influences.

Moro's abduction on March 16, 1978, and his subsequent murder on May 9 at the hands of the Red Brigades, brought the strategy of historical compromise to a close and significantly conditioned Italian political structures. Antonio Tatò, a close collaborator of Berlinguer's, offered the following description of the possible outcomes of that initia-tive on PCI policy:

> The Red Brigades's strategy is to drag things out in the hope that the blackmailing of
> Moro, and the threat of his alleged "revelations," would enable them to cause alarm

and divisions within the DC and the government, a rift between us and the DC, between us and the PSI, between us and the so-called "leftist dissent," a crisis in the new majority, a crisis in the latter's relationship with the government; in other words it is, once again, a design to destabilize, crumble, subvert not only the new political framework, but also the national order and democratic institutions.[18]

The policy of steadfastness and the refusal to legitimize and negotiate with the Red Brigades was taken on and shared by the whole of the PCI's Directorate. In the Chamber of Deputies, on May 16, declaring his willingness to support an emergency government, Berlinguer spoke of a "threat to the Republic," and invited everyone to "take part in the actions necessary to thwart the maneuvers and provocations aimed at subverting our democracy."[19] On March 17, *L'Unità* published an article titled "Extraordinary democratic upsurge. The Italian people come together to defend the Republic." The entire country became involved. "A republican tragedy," a telling description ran.[20]

They were months of frantic legislative activity which facilitated communications between leading exponents of the DC and the PCI that had previously remained distant.[21] But the adhesion to Andreotti's government of national solidarity soon provoked a difficult debate within the PCI on the possible outcomes that this exceptional state of affairs might provoke. It was Giorgio Amendola, in a long letter to Enrico Berlinguer on June 1, 1978, who pointed out the limits of a political formula that, instead of having been imagined as a coalition of distinct forces able to deal with the emergency and legitimize the PCI, was blurring the boundaries that separated the DC and the PCI, undermining the characterization of the latter as an "alternative" to the former. This flawed inception, added to the lack of international prospects and to an inadequate culture of government, exposed the party to the pressures both of extremism and corporatism. It also determined a subordination to the DC within the governments of national solidarity which wore out the PCI, as the administrative elections held on May 14 and 15 proved.[22]

Tatò offered a different reading, in agreement with Franco Rodano: the historical compromise first, and the government of national unity later, were the tools with which the communists sought to shift the DC's political positioning, in keeping with a process that was at once "conservative and revolutionary," within the framework of rekindled relations with the USSR. Thus the PCI's main foe was not the DC, but Bettino Craxi's PSI; and the PCI should have supported the election of a Christian Democrat to the presidency of the Republic.[23]

These distinct readings were unable to provide the PCI with the political perspective necessary to steer in new directions both its relationship with the Soviet Union and with the other political parties. This policy atoned for quixotic attitudes in the face of the limited legitimation the PCI could rely on in the international political arena. This was partly due to American opposition to the party's involvement in government, and partly to the weakness of the communist ideal itself, engaged as it was in the never-ending search to reconcile justice, social equality, and freedom—and at the same time to create a model of modernity different from that represented by American consumerism.[24]

On the internal and electoral fronts, Moro's death marked the defeat of the Communist Party, in a way that made its decline irreversible. On the international front, during his October trip to Moscow, Berlinguer could not avoid taking note of the crisis of Soviet Socialism, a fact that did not, however, result in the legitimation of the PCI's Eurocommunist project and its participation in government. In an exceptional time in Italian politics, the historical compromise and Eurocommunism could not avoid the impact of the boundaries imposed by the Cold War, and the PCI could not disown its deep ideological roots. Nevertheless, these years left the marks on Italian society of intense political and social debate.[25]

NOTES

1. Roberto Gualtieri, *L'Italia dal 1943 al 1992. DC e PCI nella storia della Repubblica* (Rome: Carocci, 2006).

2. See Robert Gilpin, "I mutamenti economici degli anni settanta e le loro conseguenze," in Agostino Giovagnoli and Silvio Pons (eds.), *L'Italia repubblicana nella crisi degli anni settanta. Tra guerra fredda e distensione* (Soveria Mannelli: Rubbettino, 2003), 159–172.

3. See Francesco Barbagallo, *Enrico Berlinguer* (Rome: Carocci, 2006); Agostino Giovagnoli, "Berlinguer, la DC e il mondo cattolico," in Francesco Barbagallo and Albertina Vittoria (eds.), *Enrico Berlinguer, la politica italiana e la crisi mondiale* (Rome: Carocci, 2007), 77–104. On Moro and Berlinguer's global political visions, see also Giovanni Mario Ceci, *Moro e il Pci. La strategia dell'attenzione e il dibattito politico italiano (1967–1969)* (Rome: Carocci: 2013), 132.

4. And so it was that an area of contact with the Vatican developed in the immediate aftermath of the war, both within and without the PCI, that served the purpose of overcoming Cold War bipolar logic. The responsible attitude that was adopted in the vote regarding the constitutional article on the Lateran Pacts, as well as following the decision made by the Holy Office to excommunicate communists in 1949, marked the initial stages of an adversarial debate with the Vatican, that was both publicly portrayed in the national press and carried out in the secrecy of bilateral dealings that Berlinguer's PC inevitably inherited. On a philosophical and cultural level, the Yalta memorial and the Bergamo speech of 1963 embodied the highest example of Togliatti's reflection, which attempted to couple the originality of Italian socialism with the allegiance to the international communist movement, economic development and awareness of world unity. Also see Carlo Spagnolo, *Sul memoriale di Yalta. Togliatti e la crisi del movimento comunista internazionale* (Rome: Carocci, 2007).

5. Also see the numerous references in Luciano Barca, *Cronache dall'interno dei vertici del PCI. Con Berlinguer*, vol. 2 (Soveria Mannelli: Rubbettino, 2005), 517–518 and seq.; On the impact of the relationship between the National Alliance of Farmers and the Coldiretti, see Emanuele Bernardi, Fabrizio Nunnari, Luigi Scoppola Iacopini, *Storia della Confederazione Italiana Agricoltori. Rappresentanza, politiche e unità contadina dal secondo dopoguerra ad oggi* (Bologna: Il Mulino, 2013), 75–77.

6. See Agostino Giovagnoli, "Aldo Moro e la democrazia italiana," in Gabriele De Rosa and Giancarlo Monina (eds.), *L'Italia repubblicana nella crisi degli anni settanta. Sistema politico e istituzioni* (Soveria Mannelli: Rubbettino, 2003), 53–57; Renato Moro and Daniele

Mezzana (eds.), *Una vita, un paese: Aldo Moro e l'Italia del Novecento* (Soveria Mannelli: Rubbettino, 2015); Alfonso Alfonsi (ed.), *Aldo Moro nella dimensione internazionale. Dalla memoria alla storia* (Milan: Franco Angeli, 2013); Francesco Perfetti, Andrea Ungari, Davide Caviglia, Daniele De Luca (eds.), *Aldo Moro nell'Italia contemporanea* (Florence: Le Lettere, 2011).

7. Giovagnoli, "Aldo Moro e la democrazia italiana."
8. On the center-left see, among others: Luciano Radi, *Tambroni 30 anni dopo. Il luglio 1960 e la nascita del centro-sinistra* (Bologna: Il Mulino, 1990); Giuseppe Tamburrano, *Storia e cronaca del centro-sinistra* (Milan: Rizzoli, 1990); Pietro Di Loreto, *La difficile transizione dal centrismo al centro-sinistra. 1953–1960* (Bologna: Il Mulino, 1993); Yannis Voulgaris, *L'Italia del centro-sinistra 1960–1968* (Rome: Carocci, 1998). Also see Gianni Baget Bozzo, *Il partito cristiano e l'apertura a sinistra. La DC di Fanfani e di Moro (1954–1962)* (Florence: Vallecchi, 1977), and Francesco Malgeri (ed.), *Storia della Democrazia Cristiana*, vol. 3, *Verso il centro-sinistra. 1954–1962*, and vol. 4, *Dal centro-sinistra agli anni di piombo. 1962–1978* (Rome: Cinque Lune, 1989). On the international context, see Umberto Gentiloni Silveri, *Sistema politico e contesto internazionale nell'Italia repubblicana* (Rome: Carocci, 2008), 65 et seq.
9. Moro, "Riflessione," *Il Giorno* (December 10, 1976).
10. "Comunisti e cattolici: chiarezza di principi e base di un'intesa," *Rinascita* (October 14, 1977).
11. "A long and difficult labour of clarification concerning doctrine, and of reassurance with respect to procedures, is, however, still lacking: a labour so fraught with difficulties that it appears impossible to many—Catholics and non-Catholics—due to a radical opposition and incompatibility of ideological axioms," "Partito comunista e cattolici in Italia," *L'Osservatore romano* (October 18, 1977).
12. Barca, *Cronache dall'interno dei vertici del PCI. Con Berlinguer*, 699.
13. Moro pointed out that in the preceding thirty years there had never been a lack of debate with the PCI, albeit within the governmental framework of majority and opposition. "Now," he stated, "the situation is no longer one of institutional opposition" and to this new context "two circumstances are inherent: the programmatic agreement and the permanent differentiation (. . .) between the Christian Democrats and the Communist Party, that confirm themselves as representatives of two ideological alternatives. In this phase, according to Moro, a clash between these two parties would damage the country greatly. Because of this, he highlighted, "we have chosen the path of programmatic agreement." Tackling Italian democracy and plurality within the changes brought about by international factors, induced, according to the leader of the Christian Democrats, an indisputable evolution of the PCI. This evolution, he observed, aimed at the construction of a "socialist society that declares itself democratic (. . .) But let me add that the characteristics of this socialist democracy (. . .) are still hazy (. . .), they are intuitions, moods, aspirations (. . .). Thus we would like to understand the end goal of this new experiment, resulting from the mediation with proletarian internationalism and path to socialism, independent path to socialism (. . .), and perhaps this drives us to gaze too far into the horizon (. . .) they are a distant tomorrow." In Aldo Moro, *L'intelligenza e gli avvenimenti, 1959–1978* (Milan: Garzanti, 1979), 364 ff.
14. Barca, *Cronache dall'interno dei vertici del PCI. Con Berlinguer*, vol. 2, 709.
15. After a long phase of hostility with regard to the hypothesis of a greater, potentially programmatic, openness towards the PCI, Fanfani eventually planned, with Moro and

Berlinguer, the manner in which to manage that difficult transition; See the entry in Fanfani's diary on December 15, 1977, in "Diario 1977," *Archivio A. Fanfani, Senato della Repubblica*, Rome.

16. On the note, and on the United States' resistance to DC's positions, see Umberto Gentiloni Silveri, *L'Italia sospesa. La crisi degli anni Settanta vista da Washington* (Turin: Einaudi, 2009).

17. See: Luciano Barca, "Gli incontri segreti con Moro," in *Enrico Berlinguer* (Rome: l'Unità, 1985), 104 and seq.

18. Antonio Tatò, *Caro Berlinguer. Note e appunti riservati di Antonio Tatò a Enrico Berlinguer 1969–1984* (Turin: Einaudi, 2003), 66.

19. Barbagallo, *Enrico Berlinguer*, 323.

20. Agostino Giovagnoli, *Il caso Moro: una tragedia repubblicana* (Bologna: Il Mulino, 2005).

21. Giovagnoli, *Berlinguer, la DC e il mondo cattolico*, 97; Gualtieri, *L'Italia dal 1943 al 1992. DC e PCI nella storia della Repubblica*, 191.

22. In these elections, in which four million citizens voted, the PCI lost those votes it had previously won: the DC registered a great success; the PSI confirmed the results it had registered on the previous administrative elections and had a four percent rise in comparison with the previous political elections. On Amendola's letter see Roberto Gualtieri, "Il PCI tra solidarietà nazionale e 'alternativa democratica' nelle lettere e nelle note di Antonio Tatò a Enrico Berlinguer," in Gabriele De Rosa and Giancarlo Monina (eds.), *L'Italia repubblicana nella crisi degli anni settanta. Sistema politico e istituzioni* (Soveria Mannelli: Rubbettino, 2003), 279–280; on the political situation, see Barbagallo, *Enrico Berlinguer*, 326–327.

23. Gualtieri, "Il PCI tra solidarietà nazionale e 'alternativa democratica' nelle lettere e nelle note di Antonio Tatò a Enrico Berlinguer," 283–285.

24. On the concept of modernity for the PCI, see Silvio Pons, *La rivoluzione globale. Storia del comunismo internazionale (1917–1991)* (Turin: Einaudi, 2012); on the relations between the United States and Europe, see Federico Romero, *Storia della guerra fredda. L'ultimo conflitto per l'Europa* (Turin: Einaudi, 2010), and David Ellwood, *Una sfida per la modernità. Europa e America nel lungo Novecento* (Rome: Carocci, 2012).

25. See: Silvio Pons, *Berlinguer e la fine del comunismo* (Turin: Einaudi, 2006), 158–161; Andrea Guiso, "Moro e Berlinguer. Crisi dei partiti e crisi del comunismo nell'Italia degli anni Settanta," in Francesco Perfetti e Andrea Ungari (eds.) *Aldo Moro nella politica italiana* (Florence: Le Lettere, 2010), 139–177; for a critical perpective on the effects of the historical compromise, see Guido Crainz, *Il paese mancato. Dal miracolo economico agli anni ottanta* (Rome: Donzelli, 2005), 444 ff.

CHAPTER 29

BETTINO CRAXI
AND GIULIO ANDREOTTI

ANTONIO VARSORI

IT may not be immediately apparent why, in the same chapter, we are examining two personalities as different as Giulio Andreotti and Bettino Craxi. They belonged to different generations and they were leaders of political parties that, although often allied, often tried to undermine each other's position among Italian voters. Andreotti was portrayed as a cautious, secretive, sometimes devious politician, a devoted conservative Catholic with traditional and close ties with the Papal Curia. He was regarded as a cynical politician ready to accept any compromise in order to preserve his power. Though suspected of being involved in several scandals he was considered personally honest. His cynicism, as well as his witty jokes, appealed to large sectors of Italy's moderate public opinion; last but not least he was a conservative-minded politician with whom the Italian Communists thought it was possible to cooperate, a supporter of Italy's traditional Western choice, who could meet Yasser Arafat at a time when in the United States the Palestinian leader was labeled as a terrorist.

On the other side, Craxi had been regarded as a strong-willed and outspoken politician since the beginning of his political career. He became a leader who was able to exert iron control over his party; he was respected and feared, but he was seldom loved; his positions and projects were often the object of heated debate. During the 1980s he built a close alliance with the Christian Democracy, but he had stormy relations with leading representatives of the Christian Democrat party. Although he was part of the wider family of the European Left, he was hated by most Italian Communists, who regarded him as one of their worst foes, a sort of cunning "scoundrel" with no moral principles. As a consequence of his aspiration for transforming the Socialist Party (PSI) into the most important actor of the Italian left through undermining the strong influence exerted by the Communist Party (PCI) he became the target of serious criticism by left-wing intellectuals, "liberal" opinion-makers, and the most influential sectors of the progressive press.

In spite of those stark differences Andreotti and Craxi had several elements in common: they were perhaps the most significant representatives of the so-called First

Republic; they were both aware of the importance of power in everyday politics and in long-term political strategies. They played a leading role in Italy's political life during the 1980s; moreover they both exerted a strong influence on the nation's international role in a period in which Italy appeared to recover a central position in various international contexts—the Atlantic Alliance, the European integration, and the Mediterranean and Middle East. Last but not least, with *Tangentopoli*, both Craxi and Andreotti became the main targets of the various inquiries related to the "Clean Hands" investigations and for a long time they were—and they still are—regarded by some sectors of Italian public opinion as guilty of all the contradictions and evils of the country's political system (corruption, inefficiency, economic bankruptcy, etc.), while for another sector of the Italian public, they are perceived as almost forgotten heroes, the easiest scapegoats of a plot organized by an unholy alliance formed by left-wing public prosecutors, "liberal" newspapers, radical television anchor-men, and unscrupulous businessmen. In any case their fate was the symbol of both the achievements and the failure of the First Republic.

The Steady Progress of a Christian Democrat Leader

Giulio Andreotti was born in Rome on January 14, 1919 from a lower middle-class family. His father was an elementary teacher who died in 1921 as a consequence of wounds suffered during World War I.[1] The Andreotti family professed strong Catholic beliefs and Giulio was influenced by both his Catholic education and his Roman roots, to which he always felt closely tied. He was a brilliant student and attended one of the best Roman high schools, then he enrolled at the University of Rome and in 1941 graduated in Law. During his years as a university student he joined the Federation of Catholic University Students (FUCI), of which he became one of the leading representatives and where he made the acquaintance of another future Christian Democrat leader, Aldo Moro. From this early period he began to develop close ties with the Papal Curia and several authors (including his biographer, Massimo Franco) claim that Pope Pius XII held him in high esteem. After Rome's liberation from the Nazi occupation in June 1944, in spite of his young age, Andreotti was already perceived as one of the most trusted advisers of Alcide De Gasperi and a promising young member of the new Catholic party, Democrazia Cristiana (Christian Democracy; DC). In 1947 he held office for the first time as a very young under-secretary to the Presidency of the Council, and in that role he confirmed his close relationship with De Gasperi and dealt with various issues from film censorship to sport. Throughout his life Andreotti always maintained a deep interest in the Italian film industry and he enjoyed playing himself in a film with Alberto Sordi. Although in 1953 De Gasperi lost the leadership of the DC, so paving the way to a new generation of Catholic personalities such as Amintore Fanfani and Giovanni Gronchi, who at that time belonged to the left wing of the DC, Andreotti's political career experienced a steady progress. During the 1950s and the 1960s the Catholic party began to be characterized by the presence of powerful, well-organized factions (the so-called *correnti*). Andreotti was not the leader of a nation-wide faction, but he built up a strong electoral support in the more conservative areas of the Lazio region and he had followers in other regions, such as in Sicily, where some *andreottiani* had contacts with the Mafia. Although he was not among the promoters of the "turn to the left" and of the dialogue between the Christian Democracy and the Nenni Socialist Party, during the second half of the 1950s he was in office as Finance Minister and Treasury Minister. With the imminent center-left experiment, in 1959 he was appointed Defense Minister and he maintained this post until 1966, when he moved to the Ministry for Industry and Trade. As Defense Minister Andreotti began to develop close contacts with the Washington authorities and his office was characterized by several official visits to the US. Until the early 1970s, however, Andreotti was regarded as a mid-level Christian Democrat figure, but he was not considered an outstanding leader; between 1968 and 1972 he experienced a partial political eclipse and he had no ministerial responsibilities.

The late 1960s were shaped by the origins of the crisis in Italy which lasted for more than a decade: fading confidence in the political system was aggravated by economic problems and growing social turmoil, which paved the way to serious issues such as a violent terrorist threat from both extreme right and extreme left origins.[2] During the early 1970s Italy was ruled by weak and short-lived governmental coalitions, usually based on uneasy agreements between the Christian Democrats and the Socialists, whose position was threatened by the growing electoral and social influence exerted by the Italian Communist Party. Both the Socialists and the left-wing of the Christian Democracy began to look to the PCI as a useful partner, although everybody knew that the Communists' involvement in government would face the strong opposition of the US Nixon administration, which between 1970 and 1972, through Ambassador Graham Martin's covert activities, tried to influence Italy's internal situation.[3] Moreover as a reaction to the increasing influence exerted by the Left some sectors of the Italian voters began to look to the extreme right, which was represented by the neo-Fascist Movimento Sociale Italiano (MSI). In 1972 the Italian President of the Republic, Giovanni Leone, called a national election whose outcome was uncertain. But the moderate and conservative sectors of the DC rejected the idea of a renewed alliance with the Socialists; in this context Andreotti became the representative of the turn to the right by the Catholic Party; for the first time he became prime minister and he led a center coalition government, which was composed of Christian Democrats, Social Democrats, and Liberals. Andreotti's first government was short-lived, but it was characterized by the attempt at putting back the watch of Italy's political scenario to the 1950s.[4] However, Andreotti was unable to cope with both Italy's social turmoil and economic difficulties; as far as the international context was concerned, if the prime minister was regarded favorably by the US administration,[5] Italy's position in the European scenario was undermined by the nation's economic and financial problems; Italy joined the European Community's early attempt at creating an embryo monetary system, the so-called "snake," but, as a consequence of the lira's weakness, the Treasury Minister, the Liberal Giovanni

Malagodi, decided that the Italian currency had to leave the "snake" and to depreciate. This choice marked one of the lowest points in Italy's role in the European Community and Italy was labeled as "Europe's Cinderella."[6] The revival of a center coalition government was doomed to failure and in summer 1973 Andreotti was compelled to resign, so paving the way to a series of further weak governments led by Aldo Moro, who appeared to be interested in starting a dialogue with the PCI. In spite of that, Andreotti became a member of those cabinets, though he was in charge of the lesser Ministry for Budget and Economic Planning. His involvement in the Moro governments of the mid-1970s was the symbol both of his role as the guarantor of certain moderate sections of the Christian Democracy and of his clever maneuvering among the various factions of the Catholic Party. In 1976, owing to the growing difficulties in the relationship between the Socialists, who advocated an alliance with the PCI, and the more cautious Christian Democrats, parliament was dissolved and the President of the Republic called a national election. It was felt that the PCI could achieve an outstanding victory in the elections and outdo the DC. Such a possibility was regarded with deep concern by the major Western powers, which were hostile to such a development, since in their opinion, the involvement of the PCI in an Italian governmental coalition would threaten the cohesion of both the Atlantic Alliance and the European Economic Community.[7] The Italian internal situation was perceived by Western leaders as a part of a wider crisis in Southern Europe, from Cyprus to Greece, from Portugal to Spain to Italy. The outcome of the elections confirmed the central role of the Christian Democracy which scored about 38 percent of the votes, but also the growing influence of the PCI with close to 34 percent. Yet there was still evidence of social turmoil, owing to the power exerted by the unions, an increasing terrorist threat, and renewed serious financial difficulties. On the occasion of the G-7 held in Puerto Rico in summer 1976, on the morrow of the Italian elections, the representatives of the US, the UK, France, and the Federal Republic of Germany decided that the West would give Italy the much needed financial help on the condition that the PCI would not join the future Italian Government.[8] The task to form a new government fell on Giulio Andreotti, who was regarded as the only Christian Democrat leader who could work out a compromise solution. Andreotti was indeed able to form a cabinet which could rely on the Communists' abstention and he reached an agreement with the unions, which was welcomed by the Western powers as an early attempt at launching a policy of economic austerity. As a consequence Italy got the financial loans which were vital to relieve the country's economic plight. So Andreotti confirmed his political skill as well as his good relationship with the US authorities. In 1977, during an official visit to Washington, Andreotti met President Carter and assured him that he would never accept the Communists in the government and that the DC unanimously rejected such a perspective. Andreotti added that his government was the best solution for Western interests: the PCI supported it but was not a part of it, so it would lose consensus among its voters. In spite of a worsening internal situation and of the crisis of his government, in early 1978 Andreotti was confirmed as prime minister and he was called to face one of the most dramatic periods in post-war Italian history as a consequence of the kidnapping and subsequently the murder of Aldo Moro by the Red Brigades. Andreotti, with the support of the majority of the DC, as well as of the other political parties, with the exception of the Socialists, was in favor of a "hard line" approach to the terrorist group, rejecting any compromise. As a consequence of such an attitude he was charged with cynicism, if not personal interest, in sacrificing Moro's life, but those allegations neglect the most obvious reason for Andreotti's position: the defense of state prerogatives. Andreotti had always been closely tied to state structures owing to his long-term ministerial experiences; moreover, he regarded himself more as a statesman than a party man, an attitude that may be interpreted as a legacy of De Gasperi's ideals.[9] Andreotti's concept of a statesman's duties was further confirmed in late 1978 when he played a key role in Italy's European policy. In 1978 the West German Chancellor Schmidt and the French President Girscard d'Estaing launched a project which would lead to the creation of the European Monetary System (EMS). The Italian authorities immediately joined the project, as they hoped to achieve important concessions from their European partners, although Italian public opinion at the time was focused on the serious internal situation and paid scant interest to the European issues, even though these would involve a radical change in Italy's economic policy. Only on the eve of the final decision on the creation of the EMS did awareness of the economic consequences of the nation's involvement in the European project come to the fore. Strong opposition began to surface from various quarters—the PCI in particular feared the social implications of a policy of austerity—and although the Communists had a positive opinion of the EMS, they thought that Italy should not immediately join. It was primarily Andreotti who decided in favor of Italy's immediate involvement in the European project, although he was aware that such a choice would threaten the cohesion of the shaky governmental coalition. Italy's adhesion to the EMS was perhaps the first example of what would be later labeled as the "external constraint" (*vincolo esterno*): that is, a European obligation would help a weak political leadership to impose on the Italian people the sacrifices they would not otherwise accept.[10] In March 1979 Andreotti resigned and the end of his government appeared to represent the end of a phase in the political history of the First Republic. Andreotti experienced a new political eclipse and, although he maintained an important role in Christian Democracy he was unable to return to office until 1983. Such an eclipse was partly due to suspicions about his involvement in political and financial scandals, such as the P2 and the Sindona affairs, as well as to the contrasts with the emerging figure of the new secretary of the Italian Socialist Party, Bettino Craxi.[11]

THE SOCIALIST RISING STAR

Bettino Craxi was born on February 24, 1934 in Milan into a middle class family. Although his father, a convinced anti-fascist, was of Sicilian origins, Bettino Craxi always felt tied to Milan, where he started his political career. Craxi joined the PSI in the early 1950s and he became a supporter of Nenni, as well as of the elderly leader's decision to start the dialogue with the Christian Democrats which would lead to the center-left experience. In 1968 Craxi was elected to parliament and in a few years he was able to impose himself as one of the most influential leaders of the PSI.[12] The 1970s were characterized by a steady decline of the Socialists' fortunes; the tendency to play the role of supporter of the PCI's involvement in governmental responsibilities was a fateful mistake, especially since from 1973, owing to Berlinguer's decision to forge a "historical compromise" with the Christian Democracy, the position of the PSI was regarded by most Italian voters as largely uninfluential. The outcome of this misguided strategy led to the utter defeat of the PSI at the 1976 elections when the Socialists scored less than 10 percent of the votes. On the morrow of the electoral setback Craxi was elected Party Secretary. It is of some significance that the appointment of a strong-willed representative of a younger generation aroused interest in foreign socialist circles, especially the German SPD, which in this period was led by Helmut Schmidt: the West German Social Democrats perceived Craxi as the new leader who could detach the PSI from its political and psychological subservience to the PCI.[13] By contrast, the Communist leaders almost immediately regarded Craxi as a political buccaneer and a man with no moral principles.[14] Craxi's task to strengthen a chaotic and demoralized party, negatively influenced by warring factions, was not easy. The Moro affair offered him an early opportunity to bring the PSI to the attention of the public opinion as, in stark contrast with the positions developed by the Christian Democrats and the Communists, the Socialist leader favored the idea that saving Aldo Moro's life was more important than the defense of the state's prerogatives, so he did not rule out the possibility of negotiation with the Red Brigades. Craxi's position was fiercely criticized by numerous sectors of Italy's political world; both Andreotti and the Communist leader Berlinguer openly disagreed with him; yet this meant that he appeared as the defender of humanitarian ideals, tied to the non-Marxist socialist tradition. Although the "hard line" prevailed and it was usually thought that Moro's sacrifice was a vital choice in order to counter the Red Brigades, the Italian Socialists entered a new stage in their political trajectory.[15] Moreover, between the late 1970s and the early 1980s Craxi benefitted from the election to the Presidency of the Republic of the Socialist Alessandro Pertini, who always enjoyed a strong popular consensus. After a fierce internal struggle Craxi was able to impose himself on the left-wing faction of his party and to achieve a firm leadership of the PSI thanks largely to Italian Socialist traditions prior to the creation of the Italian Communist Party, that is the party's libertarian, non-Marxist, humanitarian roots. He also began to be perceived by numerous sectors of the public opinion as a young leader with clear-cut ideas and with an ambitious program of important reforms which aimed at radical institutional and political changes. Such positions appeared to be coherent with the new political and social atmosphere which was to characterize the whole Western world in the 1980s. As far as Italy was concerned, the nation was emerging from the "years of lead" and it was heading toward a period of social transformation, economic modernization, and political change, while in the international context, owing to the "new cold war," the PCI went back into isolation and Italy would strengthen its traditional bonds with the Western system, both the Atlantic Alliance and the European Community. Such a change appeared to be epitomized by the appointment in 1981—for the first time since

1945—of a non-Christian Democrat, the Republican Giovanni Spadolini, as prime minister. If a Republican could become prime minister why not a Socialist? In 1983 the elections showed positive results for the Socialist Party (about 11 percent of the votes) while the DC suffered a partial setback (about 32 percent). Owing to an agreement between the Socialists and the Christian Democrats, Craxi was appointed prime minister: he would lead the country for about four years in two different cabinets (August 1983–August 1986 and August 1986–April 1987).[16]

ITALY'S ROARING EIGHTIES: FOREIGN AND DOMESTIC ISSUES

It would be difficult to understand Craxi's political fortunes and Andreotti's renewed political achievements without taking into consideration the social atmosphere which characterized Italy in the mid-1980s. The country appeared to experience an optimistic mood, as a consequence of several factors: a general improvement of the economic situation, which was due both to a transformation in Italy's industrial and financial system and to favorable international trends (e.g. a sharp decrease in oil prices); the defeat of the terrorist menace owing to a more efficient action by the judiciary and the police forces; the spreading of "positive" values and "modern" ways of life which were the consequence of the "neo-liberal" revolution from the Regan-era United States and from Thatcher's Britain. Political and institutional reforms, as well as social and economic modernization appeared to be at close hand; that at least was the widespread perception, not only in Italian public opinion but also in the attitude of most Western political elites and international media which would build up a positive image of Italy in those years.[17] The Craxi cabinets could boast achievements in internal policy: a governmental stability which had never been experienced in the previous history of the Republic, a change in the relationship between the unions and the political power, mainly as a consequence of Craxi's decision to reform the mechanism which closely tied the increase in salaries to the rate of inflation. The signature of a new Concordat between the Italian state and the Holy See was less a foreign policy issue than a personal achievement on the part of the Socialist Prime Minister, and it marked a new, more modern relationship between Italian society and the Catholic world.[18] But, in spite of several statements about the need for significant institutional change, the Socialist leader was unable to achieve the constitutional reforms which could modernize the Italian political system—and, incidentally, to increase the powers of the prime minister; on the contrary, in order to strengthen his leadership on the PSI and to challenge the powerful hold of the Christian Democracy and the Communist Party, Craxi thought he was almost compelled to resort to negative and illicit systems which favored widespread corruption and strengthened the negative ties between the political parties and the economic and financial world, especially in a country such as Italy which was characterized by powerful state-controlled industrial and financial sectors.[19] In terms of economic policy, the Craxi governments were able to stem inflation, which fell from about 22 percent in the early 1980s to about 4 to 5 percent at the end of the decade, but the state deficit increased and it was almost impossible to cope with all the factors that presented serious obstacles to a steady economic growth: the inefficiency of the civil service, widespread corruption, the failed modernization of local authority structures, parliament's slow and clumsy decision-making process, which favored increasing state spending. So, in spite of a modern façade and some areas of efficiency, the Italian economic system suffered from inherent weaknesses and was, more than other Western European nations, sensitive to international economic trends that almost concealed the country's internal contradictions until the late 1980s.[20]

The most significant successes achieved by the Craxi governments, however, were those related to the international scenario.[21] In this context Craxi appointed as Foreign Minister Giulio Andreotti, who, in spite of the previous uneasy relations with the Socialist leader owing to the Moro case and his apparently good relations with the PCI, was able to develop an effective, sometimes successful, foreign policy, whose main aims Craxi fully shared. As far as the relationship with the US and the Atlantic context, Craxi and Andreotti confirmed Italy's loyalty to the Atlantic Alliance, especially to the decision to deploy the so-called euro-missiles on Italian territory. Such a decision was fiercely contested by a powerful pacifist movement, which involved not only the PCI and the radical left but also some influential sectors of Catholic opinion. During the mid-1980s this movement organized nation-wide demonstratoins, which made a strong impact on Italian public opinion. However, the steady and uncompromising attitude shown by the Italian government won the favor and the support of the Reagan administrations, which regarded Italy as a steady and reliable ally, whose position was of paramount importance to defend the cohesion of the Western European partners, especially the Federal German Republic, on the euro-missiles issue.[22] In practice such expression of Atlantic loyalty gave Craxi and Andreotti more room for maneuver in other areas of the relationship with the US. The most obvious and well-known episode is the Sigonella affair, when the Italian government was able to resist Washington's attempt at capturing the Palestinians who were responsible for the hijacking of the *Achille Lauro* without Rome's consent and against the rules of Italian jurisdiction. Craxi's popularity in Italian public opinion reached its climax at this time.[23] Yet this was also a period when the Italian authorities were often critical of US foreign policy, especially as far as Central America and the Middle East were concerned. The Craxi governments openly stated their disagreement with the warmongering attitude showed by the Reagan administration towards the radical Libyan regime led by Colonel Gaddafi. Moreover, Craxi and Andreotti pursued a consistent dialogue with Yasser Arafat and the Palestinian Liberation Organization (PLO), as in their opinion the Western world could not forget the Palestinian plight and the Western powers had to put pressure on the PLO in order to convince its leader to abandon terrorist activities and to open a dialogue with the US, as only an Israeli-Palestinian compromise could solve the crisis in the Middle East. Although some sectors of Italian public opinion were often critical of Craxi's and Andreotti's Middle Eastern policy, which was regarded as too pro-Arab, neither the Prime Minister nor the Foreign Minister forgot that among their aims was the peaceful solution of a crisis that was threatening Italy's and Western interests in the Mediterranean. Moreover, the Andreotti papers demonstrate that the Christian Democrat statesman, with Craxi's support, always took into consideration the position of the US. In the conversations he had with the American authorities Andreotti always pointed out that it was Italy's intention to transform the PLO into a political actor and to lead Arafat to regard the US administration not as an enemy but as the partner which could favor the solution of the conflict between Israel and the Palestinians.[24] Last but not least, the Italian authorities often argued that the continuation of the Israeli-Arab conflict would strengthen the Soviet position in the Mediterranean and the Middle East, a dangerous factor for Western interests in the context of the "second cold war."

As far as European integration was concerned, at least one Italian historian has pointed out the vital role that both Craxi and Andreotti played in June 1985 at the European Council held in Milan.[25] The two Italian leaders decided to call a majority vote on the convening of the inter-governmental conference which would lead to the signature of the Single European Act, a turning point in the integration process. With the support of Helmut Kohl and François Mitterrand the decision was taken, in spite of Margaret Thatcher's fierce opposition. The outcome of the Milan European Council was a major achievement and revealed the strong commitment to the integration process which characterized the activities of the Craxi governments, especially of the Italian Foreign Ministry under the leadership of Giulio Andreotti, who was able to create an image of himself as one of the most clever and successful foreign ministers of the Italian Republic; in this connection one could also point out Italy's support for Spain's and Portugal's candidature to the EEC, Rome's commitment to the political initiatives developed by Altiero Spinelli in the European Parliament, the recognition of the country's European role by Italy's partners through the regular bilateral meetings with Mitterrand and Kohl.[26] Italy's role in the Western European context appeared to be further confirmed at the numerous G-7 conferences held during the 1980s. But the climax in Italy's recovery of its international role was achieved in 1987 when Craxi boasted that the country's GDP had overcome that of the UK.

Yet most of Italy's international successes during the Craxi era had slippery foundations and were the consequence of contingent favorable situations. With the coming to power in 1985 of Gorbachev and the new growing dialogue between the US and the Soviet Union—which would lead to the so-called "zero option" agreement on the euromissiles issue—the interest of the US administration in Italy's position in the Atlantic Alliance began to wane. Furthermore, although the Italian Government had been the promoter of an inter-governmental conference, its commitment to the federalist option and to the strengthening of the European Parliament's powers was in stark contrast with the more cautious approach favored by both West Germany and France, as well as by the European Commission led by Jacques Delors. The Italian authorities were very critical of the Single European Act, but they were unable to understand the relevance of such a treaty, which would give the Commission the powers to launch new important initiatives such as the structural funds and the creation of a real common market with free mobility for goods, labor, and capital, a project which would be at the origins of the Economic and Monetary Union (EMU). Moreover, Italian decision-makers were unable to realize that in order to pursue an effective and fruitful European policy it was not enough to rely on a clever foreign minister and efficient diplomats (i.e. on traditional "high politics") but the whole country had to show its efficiency, from parliament to the regions, from the civil service to the economic actors. So by the late 1980s there was a growing gap between the Italian Government's European commitment and the poor performance by the Italian state and local authorities, with a growing number of procedures for infractions to the EC directives. In Brussels, therefore, Italy was regarded with increasing concern and less and less confidence.[27]

This slow decline in Italy's international role was also the consequence of the emerging difficulties in the "five party" coalition (*pentapartito*), especially in the relationship between Craxi and certain Christian Democrat leaders, such as Ciriaco De Mita, who aimed to re-impose the central role of the Christian Democracy in the political scenario. The general elections held in spring 1987 gave no definite response. Craxi had pinned his ambitions on these elections as he hoped for a Socialist electoral success. Although the outcome for the PSI was not shameful (about 14 percent in the Chamber and 11 percent in the Senate), the party was unable to claim an important role as the party of the left as the Communists scored about 27 percent of the votes, and the Christian Democracy confirmed their central role with about 34 percent of the votes. Craxi had aimed at imitating Mitterrand who had been able to create a new Socialist Party and to make it the leader of the French left to the detriment of the French Communists. But the Italian Communists' roots in Italian society were definitely stronger, as was their cultural grip on influential sectors of Italian society, while moderate voters still preferred to support the Christian Democracy. Moreover, Craxi's unconventional political methods and the involvement of Socialist leaders in financial scandals led elements in the media and public opinion to develop a negative image of the Socialist leadership, believing that its primary goals were to secure power and personal advantage. Between 1987 and 1989 Italy experienced three different governments (Fanfani, Goria, and De Mita) which were evidence of the uncertainties in the "five party" coalition. Although Craxi was still regarded as one of the most influential leaders and he exerted a strong hold on the PSI, his capacity to shape Italian policy and to develop a long-term political vision sharply decreased. On the contrary, Andreotti maintained his office as foreign minister and he appeared a sort of point of reference in a growing chaotic political debate.

CONCLUSIONS: ANDREOTTI, CRAXI, AND THE CRISIS AND COLLAPSE OF THE FIRST REPUBLIC

In summer 1989 Giulio Andreotti formed a new government (his sixth cabinet); the Christian Democrat leader maintained his office until spring 1992, although in 1991 he was compelled to work out a governmental reshuffle. When the government was created in 1989 Andreotti's appointment was perceived as the outcome of a renewed agreement among the five coalition parties, based on an undeclared alliance which tied Craxi to the DC Secretary, Arnaldo Forlani. Such an accord seemed destined to favor the continuation of the political formula which had characterized the previous decade. Moreover, the future perspectives for the center-left coalition seemed to be fairly positive as the most important opponent, the PCI, was going to face a dramatic crisis due to the impending fall of Communism in East-Central Europe which sealed the fate of the Communist parties in both parts of the crumbling European "iron curtain." In 1989 Italy's economic situation was still positive, at least that was the perception held by most economic and financial actors in Italy and abroad. As far as Italy's international position, Italy's new Foreign Minister, the Socialist Gianni De Michelis, was a brilliant and ambitious politician who pointed out Italy's aspiration to renew its influence in Central Europe, owing to the new situation which the crisis of the Communist regimes was creating.

Yet the position of Andreotti's government rapidly worsened and in less than three years the so-called First Republic suffered ignominious collapse under the burden of numerous scandals and judicial inquiries that wiped out a whole political class. Although the immediate reasons for the crisis appeared to be of a domestic character, such a collapse had its roots in an essentially foreign context, especially in the end of the international system based on the Cold War and the ensuing acceleration of the integration process that would lead to the Maastricht Treaty.[28] As far as the domestic situation was concerned the Andreotti governments, in spite of the strenuous efforts of some ministers, such as Treasury Minister Guido Carli and the President of the Council himself, were unable to deal with issues which had a strong impact on the public opinion: the spreading of the corruption closely tied to the party system, the growing challenge posed by criminal organizations such as the Mafia, which would reach its apex in 1992 with the murders of Giovanni Falcone and Paolo Borsellino, the sudden worsening of the economic situation, especially from 1991. Those phenomena were not new to the history of the Italian Republic, but the end of the Cold War was creating a political vacuum among Italian moderate voters, and many felt free to express their growing dissatisfaction toward the traditional party system. Although this system had appeared almost totally discredited in the 1970s, the terrorist threat and the "second cold war" had renewed the bond between the moderate electorate and its political parties, compelling them to vote "against" what they perceived as an impending Communist danger (at first "red" terrorism, later on the USSR). By the mid-1980s Craxi's attempt at modernizing the country had renewed hopes of a more modern and efficient political class, but such hopes had been rapidly frustrated due to the widespread belief that Craxi's policies had developed into mere exploitation of political influence in the interests of a corrupt party system. Such a perception may have been exaggerated but the end of the Cold War led some influential pressure groups, especially from key financial and economic quarters and the media, to develop and spread harsh criticism of the ruling political class, which would have been almost unconceivable a few years earlier. So politicians such as Craxi and Andreotti became the targets of violent attacks by both the media and leading opinion-makers. Such an attitude was barely evident in 1989 or in 1990, but it began to surface rapidly in 1991 and it reached its climax from 1992 with the beginning of the "Clean Hands" inquiry.[29]

The dramatic changes in the international system and Italy's unsuccessful attempts to cope with such developments fueled the crisis of the nation's party system. At first the Andreotti government had to face the consequences of the fall of the Berlin Wall, including the prospect of rapid German reunification. Andreotti was not enthusiastic about the creation of a reunified German state. Like Mitterrand and Margaret Thatcher, Andreotti had had direct experience of World War II and of Nazi Germany; moreover, as a statesman he had been critical of the partition of Europe into Eastern and Western blocs, but he also believed that the Cold War had guaranteed global stability, which in turn had led to the longest period of peace in Europe. In spite of that, Andreotti, always a realist politician, in a few months reconciled himself with the prospect of German reunification, although he hoped to contain the new German power through the safeguard of the Atlantic Alliance, that is the close bond between Europe and the US, and the deepening of the European integration, both in the political and the economic fields. In spite of the fact that Kohl's Germany favored both options, it became evident after 1990 that Germany had a different and far more influential role in the European balance and that especially Italy's position would be progressively reduced, as would be demonstrated by the negotiations leading to the Maastricht Treaty.[30]

The Gulf War, another byproduct of the end of the Cold War, was a further blow to Italy's international credibility. Once again domestic problems and international factors were closely interlocked. Although at first the Andreotti government had firmly condemned Iraq's aggression against its Kuwaiti neighbor, the Italian Government was compelled to develop a low profile attitude, mainly as a consequence of a strong pacifist movement, which was not led by the PCI but by Catholic groups and which appeared to enjoy the support of both the Pope and the Holy See. Divisions and contrasts surfaced in the Christian Democracy and Andreotti seemed to lose the traditional link with the Papal Curia and Catholic opinion. Yet Italy could not give up its close alliance with the US and the Italian Government felt itself compelled to take part in the military initiatives—both "Desert Shield" and "Desert Storm"—with poor military results. Last but not least, Andreotti hoped that the Soviet Union could play a useful role of mediator, an attitude which would lead nowhere and would lead in Washington to suspicions about Italy's reliability. The US military victory in the Gulf War and the weakening Soviet role in this part of the world were at the origins of a temporary change in the Middle East balance which appeared to leave the US as the only super-power. Moreover, Arafat's ill-guided support of Saddam Hussein's claims weakened the PLO's position and in 1991 it was compelled to comply with Washington's wishes. Italy, which by 1989, had been able to play a role of mediator between Washington and the PLO in the aftermath of the Gulf War, became a minor actor in the opinion of Washington's decision-makers: one of the most interesting, if controversial, achievements of Craxi's and Andreotti's foreign policy disappeared in a few months.[31]

The fall of Communism in Yugoslavia and Albania transformed itself into a nightmare for the Italian authorities. Between 1990 and 1992 De Michelis and the Farnesina, fearing the potential dramatic consequences of the Yugoslav Federation's implosion, made every effort to save some form of Yugoslav unity. Rome's initiatives seemed to be in part successful, but in early 1992 Italy's cautious "Balkan" policy was completely frustrated by the German decision to recognize Croatia's and Slovenia's independence. Moreover, the Italian government was confronted by the Vatican's open support for the two Catholic republics. Once again the traditional bond between the Holy See and the Italian Catholic leadership had been broken and the Yugoslav issue was a further factor dividing the Christian Democracy.[32] To compound its problems, Italy was suddenly confronted with flows of illegal immigrants from Albania, which confirmed in both national and international opinion the weakness of the Italian state.[33]

The Maastricht Treaty, and EMU in particular, was the last and more severe blow to the Andreotti governments and to the First Republic. Although in 1990 Italy was still able to exert some influence in the negotiations that paved the way to the two intergovernmental conferences, since 1991 the domestic crisis and the increasing economic difficulties led Italy's partners, especially Germany, to doubt Rome's capability to face the challenges posed by the creation of EMU, especially in light of its growing state deficit. Carli and an emerging technocratic Europeanist elite that had its stronghold in the Bank of Italy played a leading role in the EMU negotiations. Carli tried to defend Italy's position but he was compelled to accept the so-called five Maastricht criteria, which were the guarantee that if Italy would not comply with the economic dictates of Brussels and Germany it would be left out of the future European currency.[34] On their part the Europeanist technocrats hoped once again that an external European constraint would compel a weak political class to pursue sound and coherent economic policies, not only to limit state spending but also to promote a series of privatizations which would put an end to state and party political control of key areas of Italy's industrial and financial systems. Andreotti and certain leading Christian Democrats realized the vital importance of the issue at stake and that the Maastricht Treaty was a sort of time bomb for the future of the Italian political class; but it is very likely that Andreotti hoped to have more time at his disposal in order to comply with the "suggestions" from the European Community, the IMF, and some European partners.[35] It is significant that Craxi was almost unable to express a coherent attitude on the main foreign policy issues and appeared to focus his attention on short-term domestic problems. In the meantime there were signals of an impending institutional and political crisis, such as the conflict between President Cossiga and the party system, the increasing disagreements in the five-party coalition on the issue of the role played by private television networks, the electorate's rejection of Craxi's negative interpretation of the referendum on the electoral system. All these episodes revealed the growing gap between public opinion and the party system, especially the two parties which had ruled the country for decades and were the symbols of the First Republic. But this alarm bell was ignored by Craxi and Andreotti, who, although aware that something was changing, perhaps hoped that it would be possible to cope with such a challenge. But in 1992 the two time bombs detonated: the end of the Cold War gave Italian voters room for maneuver which had been almost unconceivable during previous decades, and the difficulties tied to the implementation of the economic clauses of the Maastricht Treaty led to a serious economic crisis, which, coupled with judicial inquiries and a renewed threat by organized criminality, led to the collapse of the First Republic and also the end of the political career of its two most influential representatives: although in different ways and with different "styles," both Craxi and Andreotti shared the same political fate.[36]

NOTES

1. For a biography of Giulio Andreotti see Massimo Franco, *Andreotti. La vita di un uomo politico, la storia di un'epoca* (Milan: Mondadori, 2010); see also N. Barone and Ennio Di Nolfo (eds.), *Giulio Andreotti: l'uomo, il cattolico, lo statista* (Soveria Mannelli: Rubbettino, 2010). Andreotti left a rich archive, which is kept by the Luigi Sturzo Institute in Rome. See <http://www.sturzo.it>.

2. On the Italian crisis of the 1970s see AA.VV, *L'Italia repubblicana nella crisi degli anni Settanta*, 4 vols. (Soveria Mannelli: Rubbettino, 2003).

3. On the US attitude towards Italy during the 1970s see Umberto Gentiloni Silveri, *L'Italia sospesa. La crisi degli anni Settanta vista da Washington* (Turin: Einaudi, 2009).

4. On the First Andreotti Government see the evaluations in Piero Craveri, *La Repubblica dal 1958 al 1992* (Milan: TEA, 1996), pp. 489–498.

5. See the documents in Historical Archives Luigi Sturzo Institute (hereafter ASILS), Giulio Andreotti Archives (hereafter AGA), USA, box 618.

6. Antonio Varsori, *La Cenerentola d'Europa? L'Italia e l'integrazione europea dal 1947 a oggi* (Soveria Mannelli: Rubbettino, 2010), pp. 248–249, 258–260.

7. On this period see especially Silvio Pons, *Berlinguer e la fine del comunismo* (Turin: Einaudi, 2006).

8. Antonio Varsori, "Puerto Rico 1976: le potenze occidentali e il problema comunista in Italia," *Ventunesimo Secolo*, 16 (June 2008) pp. 89–121.

9. On Andreotti and the Moro affair see in general Agostino Giovagnoli, *Il caso Moro: una tragedia repubblicana* (Bologna: Il Mulino, 2005).

10. Varsori, *La Cenerentola*, pp. 314–330.

11. Franco, *Andreotti, passim.*

12. On Craxi see the biography by Massimo Pini, *Craxi. Una vita, un'era politica* (Milan: Mondadori, 2007). Craxi left a personal archive which is kept at the Bettino Craxi Foundation in Rome. For further information see <http://www.fondazionecraxi.org>.

13. Giovanni Bernardini, "Stability and Socialist Autonomy: The SPD, the PSI and the Italian Political Crisis of the 1970s," *Journal of European Integration History*, 15/1 (2009), pp. 95–102.

14. See for example the negative evaluations in Antonio Tatò, *Caro Berlinguer. Note e appunti riservati di Antonio Tatò a Enrico Berlinguer* (Turin: Einaudi, 2003) pp. 74–83. The remarks by Tatò on Craxi were written in July 1978. On the relationship between the PSI and the PCI see also Gennaro Avcquaviva and Marco Gervasoni (eds.), *Socialisti e comunisti negli anni di Craxi* (Venice: Marslio, 2011).

15. On Craxi and the Moro affair see Gennaro Acquaviva and Luigi Covatta (eds.), *Moro-Craxi: fermezza e trattativa trent'anni dopo* (Venice: Marsilio, 2009).

16. On the process which led to the appointment of the Craxi government see Craveri, *La Repubblica*, pp. 959–1038.

17. On the 1980s see Marco Gervasoni, *Storia d'Italia negli anni Ottanta. Quando eravamo moderni* (Venice: Marsilio, 2011).

18. Gennaro Acquaviva (ed.), *La grande riforma del Concordato* (Venice: Marsilio, 2006).

19. On the obstacles which Craxi had to face in his attempts at modernising the country see Simona Colarizi and Marco Gervasoni, *La cruna dell'ago. Craxi, il Partito Socialista e la crisi della Repubblica* (Rome and Bari: Laterza, 2005); see also Daniele Caviglia and Silvio Labbate (eds.), *Al governo del cambiamento. L'Italia di Craxi tra rinnovamento e obiettivi mancati* (Soveria Mannelli: Rubbettino, 2014). See also Gennaro Acquaviva and Luigi Covatta (eds.), *La "grande riforma" di Craxi* (Venice: Marsilio, 2010).

20. See Gennaro Acquaviva (ed.), *La politica economica italiana negli anni Ottanta* (Venice: Marsilio, 2010).

21. For an assessment of general character see Ennio Di Nolfo (ed.), *La politica estera italiana negli anni Ottanta* (Venice: Marsilio, 2007).

22. On the euro-missiles issue see Leopoldo Nuti, *La sfida nucleare. La politica estera italiana e le armi atomiche 1945–1991* (Bologna: Il Mulino, 2007).

23. On the Sigonella episode see Di Nolfo (ed.), *La politica estera italiana*, pp. 99–148.

24. See ASILS, AGA, "USA—viaggi G. Andreotti," box 631, letter R. Petrignani (Italian Embassy Washington) to G. Andreotti, secret, 16 August 1984.

25. For example, Giuseppe Mammarella, "Il Consiglio Europeo di Milano del giugno 1985," in Ennio Di Nolfo (ed.), *La politica estera italiama degli anni Ottanta* (Manduria: Lacaita, 2003), pp. 205–231.

26. See Antonio Varsori, "The Relaunching of Europe in the mid-1980s," in Kiran Klaus Patel and Kenneth Weisbrode (eds.), *European integration and the Atlantic Community in the 1980s* (New York: Cambridge University Press, 2013), pp. 226–242.

27. Varsori, *La Cenerentola*, pp. 353–359.

28. For a general interpretation see Antonio Varsori, *L'Italia e la fine della guerra fredda. La politica estera dei governi Andreotti (1989–1992)* (Bologna: Il Mulino, 2013).

29. See the interesting evaluations in Gennaro Acquaviva and Luigi Covatta (eds.), *Il crollo. Il PSI nella crisi della prima repubblica* (Venice: Marsilio, 2012).

30. Varsori, *L'Italia e la fine*, pp. 19–46.

31. *Ivi*, pp. 47–120.

32. *Ivi*, pp. 121–188.

33. Antonio Varsori, "Italy and the End of Communism in Albania 1989–1991," *Cold War History*, 112/4 (November 2012), pp. 615–636; see also Luca Micheletta, *Diplomazia e democrazia. Il contributo dell'Italia alla transizione dell'Albania verso la libertà* (Soveria Mannelli: Rubbettino, 2013).

34. On Carli's position see Piero Craveri (ed.), *Guido Carli senatore e ministro del Tesoro 1983–1992* (Milan: Bollati Boringhieri, 2009).

35. Antonio Varsori, "The Andreotti Governments and the Maastricht Treaty: Between European Hopes and Domestic Constraints," *Journal of European Integration History*, 19/1 (2013), pp. 23–44.

36. It is well know that Craxi was condemned but he always refused to be judged and he took refuge in Tunisia, where he died in 2000—for his supporters as an "exiled" leader, for his

enemies as a "criminal" who had left the country in order to avoid "just punishment". As far as Andreotti was concerned, he faced long and difficult trials, from which he emerged acquitted. In spite of continuing suspicions about his relations with the Mafia, he maintained his role of Senator and died in 2013 at the age of 94 as a sort of living survivor of the First Republic. See Massimo Pini, *Craxi*, pp. 645 ff. and Franco, *Andreotti*, pp. 245 ff.

CHAPTER 30

SILVIO BERLUSCONI AND ROMANO PRODI

MARK DONOVAN AND MARK GILBERT

THE two dominant politicians of the "Second Republic," that is, the period that has elapsed since the collapse of the "First Republic" in 1992–93, have been Silvio Berlusconi and Romano Prodi. Berlusconi reinvented the Italian right after the downfall of Christian Democracy (DC) and the Socialist Party (PSI) in the corruption scandals known as *Tangentopoli*. Calling upon his lengthy and successful experience as an entrepreneur, Berlusconi created a new political brand, Forza Italia, from scratch and dexterously made it the principal point of reference in the party system, in alliance with the populist Northern League (LN) and the former fascists and nationalist conservatives gathered in the National Alliance (AN).

Romano Prodi achieved something similar on the center-left. After the end of the First Republic, no coalition of the left was strong enough to take power, even when allied to the misnamed Popular Party (PPI), which was the largest surviving remnant of the DC. Middle-class hostility to the Communist Party (PCI) remained strong, even though it had renamed itself the Democratic Party of the Left (PDS) and jettisoned Marxist ideology. Prodi, an academic economist from Bologna who had also served as the chief executive of a major state-owned holding company, argued that the center-left needed to enthuse its communist, Catholic, socialist and liberal elements with a common project. He put himself forward as leader of the so-called Ulivo (Olive Tree) coalition in the 1996 elections and was able to mobilize much enthusiastic support from progressive Catholics and the young, although the professional politicians within his coalition never accepted his sudden elevation to leadership and subsequently twice made him pay for his presumption. The Ulivo concept did, however, give the center-left a banner to rally around until, in 2008, the Democrat Party was created.

In Italy's "Second Republic," in short, a heterogeneous coalition of right-wing parties led by a charismatic and glib billionaire entrepreneur has faced an even more variegated coalition of centrist and left-wing parties. Only when the center-left coalition was led by Prodi, who is anything but charismatic (or glib), but who possesses an authentic common touch and a tough streak stiffened in the Hobbesian world of Italian university politics, has the center-left managed to defeat Berlusconi's right-wing alliance. Italy is a right-wing country—in places, a very right-wing country. Only the reassuring *professore* has succeeded in making the center-left palatable. Even he, however, never succeeded in persuading his own coalition—let alone the Italians as a whole—of the need for long-term, painful, structural reforms to ready the economy for membership of the Eurozone (although he did persuade both his coalition and the Italians of the need for short-term sacrifices to get into the Eurozone in the first place).

Outsiders and Insiders

Silvio Berlusconi was born on September 29, 1936 and educated at a Catholic school and at Milan University. His father was a banker who retired as managing director of the Banca Rasini, a small but important Milanese bank. In his youth, he made the friendship of the men who would become his key business partners and political backers: Fedele Confalonieri, his principal associate in the construction industry and subsequently the head of Berlusconi's media company, Mediaset, and Marcello Dell'Utri, a Sicilian who became Berlusconi's right-hand man in the early 1970s and was the driving force behind the creation of Forza Italia in the 1990s.

Undeniably able, Dell'Utri was a man with dangerous connections. According to several court sentences, in 1974 Dell'Utri brokered a protection deal on Berlusconi's behalf (his son, Piersilvio, had been threatened with kidnap) with a prominent Sicilian crime family whereby Berlusconi hired a mafia soldier called Vittorio Mangano as a "groom" for the stables at Arcore, Berlusconi's then recently acquired country house in the hinterland of Milan. Berlusconi has consistently denied that he knew that Mangano was anything other than a stableman. Mangano nevertheless became a key member of the Porta Nuova crime family. He was convicted in 1995 on extortion and drug trafficking charges, and in 2000 for murder, although he died before his appeal was heard. In March 2013, Dell'Utri, who has been under investigation or on trial for "association with the mafia" since 1994, was condemned by the Court of Appeal to seven years' imprisonment for having had links with mafia clans until 1992. The case continues, but Dell'Utri's links with the mafia, at any rate in the 1970s, are now proven beyond reasonable doubt.

By the time Berlusconi hired Mangano as a groom, he was emerging as a prominent businessman. Between 1972 and 1979, he constructed the Milano 2 residential complex in Segrate, a town in the outskirts of the city. Milano 2 was widely praised for its futuristic architecture and Berlusconi was made *Cavaliere del Lavoro* by President Giovanni Leone in 1977. *Il Cavaliere*, often shortened to *Il Cav*, has been his nickname for obsequious journalists ever since. From construction, Berlusconi moved into other fields—advertising, magazine and book publishing, and an insurance company were all incorporated into the portfolio of his family-controlled holding company, Fininvest.

Above all, he began a career as a television tycoon. Telemilano, founded in 1978, was a cable TV company that broadcast initially to the residents of Milano 2, and before long all over Lombardy. In 1980, Berlusconi broke the monopoly of the state broadcaster, RAI, by launching Canale 5, the first privately owned national television channel. Canale 5 was followed by Italia 1 and Rete 4 in 1982 and 1984, and by TV channels in Spain and France. Millions bored with the RAI's pedestrian fare switched to Berlusconi's high-energy mix of quiz shows, tacky comedies, Hollywood blockbusters, and lengthy commercial breaks. Berlusconi's broadcasting ambitions were resolutely opposed by the RAI, which sent the police to shut Canale 5 down. In a hagiography written by Berlusconi's supporters, the fight to break the state TV monopoly is depicted as "a battle for freedom, a battle against statism and the unjust coercion that the state presumed to exert over its citizens."[1]

One cannot understand the Berlusconi phenomenon unless one grasps that the Milanese entrepreneur regarded himself as an outsider; as somebody whose media outlets were bringing pluralism and democracy to a political and economic system that was in the hands of traditional, conservative elites. Berlusconi was treated as an upstart by the *salotti buoni* of Rome and Milan. At the same time, Berlusconi undeniably owed his success to being an insider. Without the friendship of the PSI leader, Bettino Craxi, who was best man when Berlusconi married the actress Veronica Lario in 1990, the Milanese tycoon could never have won his battle against the RAI. Craxi became Berlusconi's political patron and forced through an *ad personam* law in October 1984 legalizing private television (the so-called *decreto Berlusconi*). Berlusconi was politically savvy long before he became an entrepreneur in politics.

Berlusconi cemented his image by saving the AC Milan soccer club from bankruptcy in 1986. By January 1994, when he publicly "took to the field" in politics, AC Milan had won both the Italian league and the European Cup three times and the Intercontinental Cup twice. Many experts consider it to be the greatest club team of all time. In soccer-mad Italy, such success was a passport to politics, although it is doubtful that Berlusconi would ever have taken the stage if the "judicial *coup d'état*" of the early 1990s had not swept away his friends in high places. His position as AC Milan's chairman, and as an entrepreneur who had "never asked for state aid, never laid anybody off, never sent anybody into early retirement,"[2] gave him an aura of achievement which middle-class Italians, shaken by the collapse of the political system and alarmed by the threat of the former communists taking power, could only respond to favorably.

On January 26, 1994, in a meticulously choreographed broadcast on his TV networks, Berlusconi shrewdly promised national renewal, an end to corruption, an end to class hatred and greater opportunities for all. He contrasted his businessman's pragmatism with the ideological dogmatism of a left that "does not believe in the market, does not believe in private initiative, does not believe in profits, does not believe in the individual."[3] A brilliant piece of marketing, the broadcast immediately made Forza Italia—a party whose candidates had been selected and groomed, more or less in secret, by Publitalia 80, the advertising agency for Berlusconi's three television networks—a political force to be reckoned with. Whatever else Berlusconi may be, even his critics have acknowledged that he is "the world's greatest salesman."[4]

Romano Prodi is in many ways the polar opposite of Berlusconi, although he, too, was a political insider who was able, at a critical moment, to portray himself as an outsider. Prodi's career until the mid-1990s was as impressive in its own way as Berlusconi's. Born near Bologna in 1939, Prodi's first career was as a university professor. He became full professor of Economics and Industrial Policy when he was in his early thirties. For six months in 1978–79, Prodi was minister for industry in the second government of "national solidarity" headed by Giulio Andreotti.

Prodi was politically close to Ciriaco De Mita, the leader of the DC from May 1982 until February 1989, and during De Mita's ascendancy he became the chairman of the Istituto per la Ricostruzione Industriale (IRI), a giant holding company created in the 1930s that was one of the largest industrial conglomerates in Europe. Major banks, manufacturers and utilities were all part of IRI's portfolio, but the firm as a whole was making huge losses. Prodi undertook the politically sensitive task of rationalizing the company, notably by presiding over the sale of Alfa Romeo to FIAT. Prodi would have preferred to sell the carmaker to Ford, to create greater competition in the Italian domestic market, but FIAT's political connections were too strong.

Prodi's first clash with Berlusconi came as a result of his rationalization of IRI. Berlusconi, at Craxi's behest, intervened together with several other entrepreneurs in 1984 to block the privatization of a food services conglomerate to a businessman, Carlo De Benedetti, who was politically averse to the PSI leader but who was willing to pay Prodi's price for the company. The deal fell through, thanks to Berlusconi's intervention. When De Benedetti took IRI to court for failing to honor its contractual obligations to him, he lost. It was later established by the Milan Court of Appeal that Cesare Previti, Berlusconi's lawyer, had forwarded $434,404 paid to him by one of Fininvest's many subsidiaries to a shell company whose beneficiary was Renato Squillante, one of the judges that presided over De Benedetti's case. Although Berlusconi was explicitly exonerated of all wrongdoing, the case was emblematic of the poisonous combination of corruption, politics, and business interests that existed in 1980s Italy. [5]

Prodi's entry into politics was not made with the same éclat as Berlusconi's. The launching of the Ulivo in 1995 aroused genuine interest among the general public but, unlike Berlusconi, the professor's electoral added value was never great enough for him to be able to claim the undisputed leadership of the center-left. Before and during the campaign that led to the general elections of April 1996, Prodi was obliged to negotiate constantly with the leader of the PDS, Massimo D'Alema, and with the heads of the numerous minor parties that clustered, like bushes, around the Olive Tree.[6] Prodi was consequently never able to project an image of strong leadership. Berlusconi, by contrast, portrayed himself as a man of destiny.

THE PERSONALIZATION OF POLITICS?

It is widely argued that elections in the Second Republic became referendums on Berlusconi: for him, or against him. Indeed, the party system seemed to rotate about him. Elections became personalized and presidential, about determining who would become prime minister, with the left reluctantly, and rather ineptly, following developments which the conservative leader championed. The 2005 electoral reform reinforced the tendency towards personalization by requiring parties to identify who their prime ministerial candidate was. In the 2006 elections, coalitions backing either Prodi or Berlusconi won 98.9 percent of the vote. Italy was not going to become, as many feared, a system hegemonized by the media magnate. Prodi's presence at any rate guaranteed "bi-leaderism." Another major development in the 2006 campaign seemed to confirm the significance of the personalization and presidentialization thesis. For the first time, an Italian election campaign saw a head-to-head TV debate. These confrontations (there were two) between Prodi and Berlusconi seemed to epitomize Italian politics becoming candidate- rather than party–centered. Scholars suggested that by 2006 Italy had become "a prototype of personalization among established parliamentary democracies."[7]

This development was by no means universally welcomed. "Skyrocketing" personalization of politics was a development that some regarded as a liability for democracy itself;[8] the Second Republic seemed to have created a plebiscitary form of democracy hostile in principle to government accountability.[9] Yet voters did hold governments to account. In the Second Republic, the rascals, as the quaint term has it, were repeatedly thrown out. No government was re-elected. Thus Berlusconi lost the 1996 and 2006 elections, to say nothing of the wider, 2013 debacle, whilst the only challenger to beat Berlusconi, Prodi, found it impossible to maintain his leadership within the center-left (and the center-left found it impossible to win back-to-back elections).

Unsurprisingly, therefore, not everyone agrees that Italian politics have become personalized, even if nobody disputes that Berlusconi has thrown a long shadow over the party system. Until 2013, at least, electoral behavior is argued to have remained rooted in traditional voting patterns, understood in left–right terms,[10] not in a vote for high-profile candidates. Ex-PCI voters switched their support to its successor parties and, eventually, the Democratic Party (PD) and other left parties, and accordingly supported Prodi when he was the left's prime ministerial candidate. Equally, former government supporters turned to the center-right—and Berlusconi. In this perspective, individual leaders such as Prodi and Berlusconi still mattered, but more for their successes and failures in party and alliance building. What determined election outcomes, given the relative stability of the electorate, or "demand side," were developments on the "supply side": the appearance of new political formations, like the Ulivo and Forza Italia, and the alliances made, or unmade.

It is certainly true that the ability to build alliances is what has characterized the political activity of both men—though neither has been so gifted at managing the coalitions they constructed. Berlusconi's 1994 triumph resulted from his creation of Forza Italia and his stitching together of separate alliances with the National Alliance and the Northern League which, once they were part of the same parliamentary majority, briefly reconciled their many differences to form a government coalition. Berlusconi's defeat in 1996, by contrast, resulted in good part from the defection of the League and the success of Prodi's Ulivo, an alliance which, improbably, brought together the principal successor parties to the DC and PCI (the PPI and PDS), the great rivals of the First Republic. The League's return to alliance with Berlusconi in 2000 then enabled further victory for the right in 2001, reigniting fears of a permanent conservative majority.

In 2006, however, Prodi gained a second victory over Berlusconi thanks to his artful assembling of all the parties of the left into a single alliance. It was the first time the notoriously fissile Italian left had been united in the Republic's history. Prodi's battle to unify—or, at any rate, to amalgamate—the left began whilst he was President of the European Commission (1999–2004) and was aided by the 2005 electoral reform and the fear that if Berlusconi were re-elected, his power would become entrenched, giving rise to another dominant party regime like the DC's. In 2006, Prodi's pan-left alliance, the Union, narrowly prevailed at the polls. Its majority in the Senate was tiny, however, and two years later Prodi was forced to resign. The early 2008 elections were then dominated by two, new, would-be catch-all parties, the Democratic Party and Berlusconi's People of Freedom (PdL), which was a merger of Forza Italia with the National Alliance, in coalition with the Northern League and the far right. Berlusconi won again, largely because the PD spurned key allies. The PdL was more promiscuous—certainly the right word in Berlusconi's case—in its choice of partners.

The electoral stability thesis not only acknowledges the importance of alliance formation. It also recognizes two forms of electoral volatility. First, the polarized or gladiatorial nature of electoral combat initiated by Berlusconi's resurrection of anti-communism in 1994 and reciprocated in the visceral anti-Berlusconism of much of the left, meant that those voters most disillusioned by the government they had voted for at the previous election tended to abstain at the subsequent one, rather than switching to the opposition. Ulivo voters disenchanted in 2001 by the center-left's performance in power did not regard Berlusconi as a wholesome alternative; center-right voters annoyed by the failure of Berlusconi's governments to reduce taxes still shrank from voting for the former communists. So-called differential abstention thus punished primarily the incumbent parties, yet did so without boosting the opposition. Second, though, there was a small but growing proportion of opinion voters who did switch "cross block," left to right or vice versa, to the opposition—which duly came to power.[11] For both these types of voters, voting had become more instrumental and less expressive, more about retrospectively punishing inadequate government performance and less about confirming the voter's own identity. Elections, then, have primarily been about voters' values and their evaluations of what governments have done and not done. Contrary to popular belief then, they have not been a "referendum" for or against Berlusconi.[12]

The outcome of the 2013 election confirmed the significance of punitive, retrospective voting. It also highlighted one consequence of Berlusconi's charismatic leadership style. Since the 2011 economic crisis had brought down the Berlusconi IV government, Italy had been governed by a technocratic administration backed by left and right. Now, in 2013, the right lost a half of its 2008 vote, the left almost a quarter, both being punished for the austerity politics that the government of Mario Monti had implemented, whilst the right was further punished for not having prevented the crisis in the first place. A further, part explanation for the truly extraordinary success of Grillo's Five Star Movement in the 2013 election campaign lies in the way Berlusconi consistently prevented Forza Italia (and then the PdL) from institutionalizing itself, that is, consolidating as an organizational structure potentially independent of him. When Berlusconi stepped down as leader, abdicating any political role for nearly 18 months, the party fell apart, making it easier for Grillo's campaign to strike into the hearts of conservative voters who, hitherto, had been largely immune to it. Let us turn now, though, to the question of government performance.

PERFORMANCE IN GOVERNMENT

Romano Prodi was prime minister for two and a half years (1996–98), and two years (2006–08); Silvio Berlusconi for eight months (1994–95), all but five years (2001–06), and three and a half years (2008–11). In sum, Berlusconi was prime minister almost twice as long as Prodi and for most of the decade 2001–10. Interestingly, that decade saw a significant increase in reported levels of satisfaction with Italy's political system. This was remarkable because these had been well below the European average for some decades, which partly explains why the First Republic collapsed.[13] Although dissatisfaction with "actually existing democracy" initially remained high in the Second Republic, a fluctuating trend of growing satisfaction can be identified. This peaked in the period 2004–10 when it averaged 44 percent, significantly surpassing the previous "high" of 1984–91, which averaged just 28 percent (Gesis, 2010).[14] Satisfaction then fell sharply in 2012, arguably because the realities of Italy's economic situation had become clear following the 2011 economic and political crisis which had seen Monti replace Berlusconi as prime minister.[15]

Two politico-institutional reasons can be suggested for the trend of increasing satisfaction to 2010. The first is that it reflects the consistent support shown by Italians for the new bipolar structuration of politics. The years from 2001 are largely those, let it be remembered, in which Berlusconi and Prodi incarnated right and left alternating in government and which saw the TV duels of 2006. Other factors matter, of course, such as relatively low unemployment, but they are not the focus here. The second politico-institutional factor relates more specifically to Berlusconi. Arguably, the dominance of center-right government from 2001 reconciled part of the conservative right, which had long been hostile to the First Republic, with Italy's political institutions. Berlusconi thus identified the left as the continuation of the hated partyocracy whilst Forza Italia and the Northern League were emanations of civil society, and particularly of the business world. Berlusconi's moral message, moreover, that Italy was fundamentally sound, even including its propensity for bending, and even flouting, the rules, was highly welcome.[16]

Whilst Berlusconi's political message and his victories over the left were applauded, his more specific government performance evoked more mixed reactions and, overall, saw a repeated cycle of high expectations and a classic "honeymoon period" followed by declining support and electoral defeat (a pattern mirrored on the left). A major reason for disillusion was his failure to cut taxes and more generally his failure to carry out the depth and range of structural reforms needed to boost economic growth. In fact, in the decade to 2010 the overall tax burden in Italy increased from 41.5 to 42.5 percent whereas the average EU17 tax rate fell from 40.9 to 39.0 percent.[17] Economic growth equally has proved elusive, with the entire period of the Second Republic coinciding with near economic stagnation. Berlusconi's governments were, nevertheless, rather active. A notable feature was the simplification of several areas of law through their codification, for example regarding consumer protection, data protection, and a new highway code. These measures were in line with a strategy seeking to rationalize Italy's "legal jungle," creating a more modern and more effectively regulated polity. In fact the regulatory type of policymaking had been neglected in the First Republic in favor of distributive, often clientelist-inspired legislation. Some important structural reforms were also implemented, most notably of pensions and the labor market, whilst a number of major social reforms were also carried out, not least of the school and university education systems. A major reform of the judicial system enacted in 2005 was substantially modified by the subsequent Prodi government of 2006–08.

Potentially the most significant reform of the 2001–06 Berlusconi governments was their overhaul of the constitution. Promoted above all by the Northern League which sought radical devolution to the regions, the process became a political football within the coalition, with the National Alliance and Christian Democrats seeking to maintain the supremacy of "the national interest" and to guarantee the ultimate authority of the center. In the event the legislation was overturned by referendum following the right's defeat in the 2006 election. Significantly, the provinces that showed most popular support for the proposals roughly corresponded with the League's putative "*Padania*".

The Achilles heel of the Berlusconi governments, at least in terms of its impact on liberal public opinion, not least internationally, was the range of legislation that appeared primarily to serve the interests of Silvio Berlusconi and his allies in the legal, business, and political worlds. The 2004 Gasparri law regulating radio and television broadcasting was widely accused of enabling Berlusconi's media business to fend off the challenge of competition—an opinion seemingly shared by the European Court of Justice which, in 2008, ruled that the Gasparri law breached European law in several respects. There were also successive attempts by parliamentarians close to Berlusconi to secure immunity from prosecution for the prime minister (and other senior officers of state), at least whilst they held office. Thus the Schifani bill, which was declared unconstitutional in 2004, and the Alfano bill, 2008, judged unconstitutional in 2009. Some of these bills brought a degree of conflict with presidents of the republic who more than once exercised their right to return them to parliament for further consideration.

Finally, Berlusconi's performance in the international sphere should not be neglected. Here he was perceived by his supporters at least as rather effective in furthering Italy's national interest. His governments were seen as maintaining Italy's traditional alignment with the US in a more robust fashion than the left, and as favoring this relationship over the one with Europe, which the left, by contrast, tended to prefer. Italy was not, nevertheless, among the coalition of the willing that invaded Iraq in 2003, given strong public opposition and constitutional constraints on the use of force to resolve international disputes. Berlusconi was also seen as redressing the balance of Italy's foreign policy in the Middle East which, in the First Republic and then with the left in the Second Republic had been rather pro-Palestinian. Foreign policy was, moreover, another area where the personalization of politics seemed prominent, with Berlusconi adopting a form of personal diplomacy with such notorious leaders as Vladimir Putin and Colonel Gaddafi.

Prodi's two periods in office were, as we have seen, both relatively short. His major government achievement was certainly that of enabling Italy to enter the Eurozone, which it did on January 1, 1999. Italy was thus one of the 11 member states, of 15 at the time, to enter the Eurozone in the first wave. The most striking domestic measure taken in relation to this was the imposition of a one-off "Euro-tax" paid in instalments through 1997. Supposed to be repaid in full, in 1999 about half the sum raised was returned. The measure brought the public deficit to under three percent of GDP, thus enabling Italy to meet one of the three key criteria for entry to the Eurozone, and was of great symbolic significance. First, it was probably the last time that an Italian government could mobilize support for a project of deepening European integration. Second, it appeared to confirm that the new, majoritarian system of party government could furnish the country with governments able to govern, that is, to take strong measures rooted in consent based on winning a competitive election. This was particularly significant after the false start of the brief Berlusconi I government, and subsequent technocratic government of Lamberto Dini. It was for this reason, too, that the fall of the Prodi government in 1998 was so significant, for the three subsequent center-left governments (1998–2001) were the products not of elections but maneuvring by party elites. Indeed, the second D'Alema government (1999–2000) included a new, short-lived party comprising MPs elected under Berlusconi's flag who had, thus, transformed themselves from opposition status into government supporters—the sin of transformism conventionally seen as having repeatedly disfigured Italy's parliamentary history since the late nineteenth century. Italy's participation in the new monetary system from 1999 was also significant because it deflated the Northern League's secessionist mobilization which nominally sought for a putative "Padania" to become part of core Europe, which Italy was thought to be incapable of joining.

The impression of effective government was reinforced by the 1997 Bassanini reforms. Named after the Minister for Public Administration and Regional Affairs, these sought to reform Italy's public administration, including local government, perhaps one of the most difficult tasks for any national government. Specifically, the reforms sought to simplify and modernize public administration processes and to strengthen devolution to the local authorities. The fact that Bassanini did not keep his post in subsequent governments contributed to undermining the effectiveness of the reforms, however.

In 2006, Prodi sought to launch his second government in rather heroic style, championing a liberalization package promoted by the Minister for Economic Development, Pier Luigi Bersani. Intended to remove professional and trade barriers hindering more

market-based and competitive practices, many professions actually escaped deregulation through vigorous lobby action. Some success was achieved in creating a degree of
independence for pharmacists from medical prescriptions and in the reregulation of
taxi firms. The government was notable for the internal divisions generated by the left's
unsuccessful attempt to improve the rights of cohabiting couples which were successfully opposed by conservative Catholics, not least because the proposed legislation did
not discriminate between hetero- and homosexual couples. In international affairs, the
government disappointed many on the left. First, it reversed its initial opposition to the
US increasing the size of its air base in the province of Vicenza, a decision that was particularly controversial given the base's strategic role in supporting operations in Iraq and
Afghanistan. Second, the government did not give clear backing to the judicial investigation and prosecution of the several intelligence officers, including the head and deputy head of the Military Intelligence and Security Service, SISMI, for their involvement
in one of the best documented cases of "extraordinary rendition," or CIA kidnapping, of
the imam known as Abu Omar in 2003.

In sum, both Prodi and Berlusconi have some significant governmental and political
accomplishments to their name. It is, then, exaggerated to suggest that under their leadership governments "survived without governing," a judgment passed on the Christian
Democrats in the First Republic. Nevertheless, neither was re-elected on merit, and
both saw their personal levels of support decline whilst in office. Increased support
for the political system before 2011 was, indeed, for the system rather than for government performance. It was probably also based on the delusion that Italy was "OK,"
as Berlusconi insisted, when it was not. The major failing of both leaders, in short, is
what they did not do. Italy is regarded by many commentators today as bordering on
being a "failed state," not, of course, in the sense of utter lawlessness, but as having a
party political elite incapable of delivering the structural reforms the country needs
as a major industrial power and key member of the Eurozone. Yet every Italian prime
minister seeking major structural reform faces massive resistance, which is why there is
some scant hope that Matteo Renzi's populist mobilisation of support for decisive government action might be sufficient to overcome the many barriers to institutional and
socio-economic reforms.

ITALIAN ANOMALIES

It is impossible to assess Silvio Berlusconi's career purely in terms of the legislation his
government passed, or the reforms he introduced. In 2001, *The Economist* printed a
notorious front-page accusation that Berlusconi was "unfit" to hold office less because
it doubted his abilities as chief executive (although it did doubt them) than because of
his ethical problems.[18] No Western statesman in the past 20 years, even US President Bill
Clinton, has been so plagued by legal issues as Silvio Berlusconi. Italian politics has been

dominated since 1994 by the numerous judicial investigations into Berlusconi's finances, political dealings, and allegedly aberrant sex life.

Prodi, by contrast, has emerged as an elder statesman in world affairs since he lost office for the second time, in 2008. A regular contributor to the Op-Ed pages of national and international newspapers on global policy issues, Prodi has also become an advisor to the United Nations on peacekeeping in Africa and the president of an international foundation sponsoring "Cooperation among Peoples." Prodi enjoys good personal relations with many leaders in the developing nations of the world, especially China, and has become a figure of genuine international standing. Paradoxically, however, Prodi's relations with the other leaders of the Italian left have remained tense. In May 2013, Prodi was the natural candidate of the center-left for the presidency of the republic, an office which is elected by a secret ballot of the two chambers of parliament together with representatives from the regions. In a striking act of political spite, more than 100 center-left parliamentarians took the opportunity provided by the secret ballot to sink his candidacy.

There is no space here to list all the crimes of which Berlusconi has been accused. He has been involved in nearly 20 criminal trials. In some he was acquitted; in several others he was found guilty by one or more grades of the justice system but the statute of limitations ran out before he could be sentenced definitively; in two, both of which regarded the falsification of company accounts, his governments passed a law decriminalizing the act of which he was accused. In July 2013, however, he was definitively sentenced to four years' imprisonment for fraud and embezzlement. Berlusconi was never in fact placed behind iron bars. He served less than one year of the sentence, which was in any case transmuted into social work. He nevertheless had to surrender his passport and was debarred from holding public office for six years. He was also obliged to resign his knighthood. Berlusconi has also been accused of paying €3 million to Senator Sergio De Gregorio to persuade him to cross the floor in parliament in 2006. De Gregorio plea-bargained a 20-month sentence and, in July 2015, Berlusconi was sentenced to three-years' imprisonment for corruption. The statute of limitations was effective from later that year, however.

In addition to these financial and political scandals, Berlusconi's private life has become a public issue. Berlusconi's wife, Veronica Lario, filed for divorce in 2009 and publicly denounced "virgins offering themselves up to the dragon" to explain her decision. The year 2011 in Italian politics was dominated by the so-called "Ruby affair." As stories surfaced of sex parties at his country residence at Arcore, near Milan, Berlusconi was accused by prosecutors of having paid for sex with a 17-year-old girl nicknamed "Ruby the Heartstealer" and of having abused his authority to cover up his relationship with the young woman. It is not in dispute that Karima El Mahroug (Ruby's real name) frequented Berlusconi's country residence, was in regular telephone contact with the then premier and, along with a score of other young ladies who testified at the trial, was given handsome presents in cash and jewels. In June 2013 Berlusconi was condemned to seven years' imprisonment by a Milan court, but the sentence was subsequently quashed upon appeal in 2015. The scandals surrounding Berlusconi took a serious toll on his reputation and, by the autumn of 2011, contributed to making his position as premier untenable. The Milanese businessman no longer possessed the necessary credibility with his peers in other European capitals. In November 2011, Berlusconi was, in effect, sacked by President Giorgio Napolitano and replaced by Mario Monti, a former European Commissioner. Berlusconi's removal from power was not accepted by the Italian right. Some of Berlusconi's closest followers—notably Angelino Alfano, an able Sicilian lawyer who was widely regarded as Berlusconi's *delfino*, or heir apparent—have since broken with the Milanese businessman politically, but even they loudly proclaim their conviction that Berlusconi is an innocent victim of a gigantic judicial conspiracy by left-wing prosecutors. Berlusconi's most fanatical devotees—middle-aged women politicians collectively known as "the Amazons"—deride the institutions of the Italian state with a vehemence that has no parallel in any other European country. Barely 10 percent of the shrinking share of the electorate that intends to vote now supports Forza Italia, but this hard core of perhaps three million people identifies with Berlusconi viscerally. He is a symbol of that part of the Italian middle class that detests regulation, taxes, socialism, and intellectuals.

Berlusconi's legacy for Italian politics has been to make his own person and conduct the principal subject of contention for the political class. Instead of governing the country, and resolving its problems, Italy's politicians have spent most of the last 20 years dealing with Berlusconi and his problems with the law. Romano Prodi, by contrast, fell victim to the endless intrigues that have characterized the internal politics of the center-left since the end of the First Republic. This is the real personalization of Italian politics: politics as an internecine, costly, unprincipled battle for or against individual leaders. The Italian electorate will not tolerate such conduct much longer. The Second Republic seems ever more likely to end in the same way as its predecessor.

NOTES

1. Silvio Berlusconi, *Una Storia Italiana* (Milan: Mondadori, 2001), 57–58.
2. Berlusconi, *Una Storia Italiana*, 46.
3. Berlusconi, *Una Storia Italiana*, 77.
4. Alexander Stille, "The World's Greatest Salesman," *New York Times Magazine*, March 17, 1996, 26–28.
5. Squillante was subsequently sentenced to eight years' imprisonment (reduced to four on appeal); Previti to five years. The Court of Cassation—Italy's final court of appeal—ruled on November 30, 2006 that the case should anyway have been heard in Rome, not Milan, and ordered a retrial. This decision had the effect of ensuring that the statute of limitations ran out before the new trial could conclude, and both Previti and Squillante were released. Previti was found guilty of other serious charges, however, and forced to resign as an MP in 2007.
6. Mark Gilbert, "The Oak Tree and the Olive Tree," in M. Caciagli and D. Kertzer (eds.), *Italian Politics: The Stalled Transition* (Boulder, CO: Westview Press, 1996), 101–117.
7. D. Garzia and F. Viotti, "Party Identification, Leader Effects and Vote Choice in Italy, 1990–2008," *World Political Science Review*, 8, 1:2 (2012), 1–23.

8. P. Ignazi. "The Three Ages of Party Politics in Postwar Italy," in K. Lawson (ed.), *Political Parties and Democracy* (Oxford: Praeger, 2010), 47–69.

9. D. Piana and F. Raniolo , "Conclusioni. Quale democrazia in Italia," in L. Morlino et al., *La qualità della democrazia in Italia* (Bologna: Il Mulino, 2013), 293–316, at 298.

10. A. Di Virgilio, "Nuovo sistema elettorale e strategie di competizione: quanto è cambiata l'offerta politica?," in R. D'Alimonte and A. Chiaromonte (eds.), *Proporzionale ma non solo. Le elezioni politiche del 2006* (Bologna: Il Mulino, 2007), 191–241; A. Chiaromonte, "Dal bipolarismo frammentato al bipolarismo limitato? Evoluzione del sistema partitico italiano," in R. D'Alimonte and A. Chiaromonte (eds.), *Proporzionale se vi pare. Le elezioni del 2008* (Bologna: Il Mulino, 2010), 203–228.

11. P. Bellucci, "Government accountability and voting choice in Italy, 1990–2008," *Electoral Studies*, 31 (2012), 492.

12. P. Bellucci and P. Segatti, *Votare in Italia: 1968–2008. Dall'appartenenza all scelta* (Bologna: Il Mulino, 2010), 400–401.

13. L. Morlino and M. Tarchi (2006), "La società insoddisfatta e i suoi nemici. I partiti nella crisi italiana," in L. Morlino and M. Tarchi (eds.), *Partiti e caso italiano* (Bologna: Il Mulino, 2006), 207–243.

14. Gesis(2010):<http://www.gesis.org/en/eurobarometer/topics-trends/eb-trends-trend-files/list-of-trends/democracy-satisf/> (accessed September 10, 2013).

15. Eurobarometer, Standard Eurobarometer, 78, December 2012, T74.

16. G. Orsina, *Il berlusconismo nella storia d'Italia* (Venice, Marsilio, 2013).

17. Eurostat, News release 68/2013, 29 April 2013. Taxation trends in the European Union. http://ec.europa.eu/eurostat/documents/2995521/5171906/2-29042013-CP-EN.PDF/bf853a7e-2ba1-4d00-b21e-78264f16b671?version=1.0>.

18. "Why Silvio Berlusconi is Unfit to Lead Italy," *The Economist,* April 28, 2001, 1.

PART VI

....

RELIGION
AND POLITICS

....

CHAPTER 31

···

THE ITALIAN CATHOLIC HIERARCHY

···

ALBERTO MELLONI

DEALING with the issue of Catholic hierarchy in relation to Italian politics requires some preliminary clarifications in regard to terminology. Canon law states that clerics are part of the hierarchy, defining them as those Catholics who have been ordained, have received episcopal consecration—or, after the 1970s, permanent diaconate—and thus have been confirmed *in sacris*. But journalistic Italian prose, and parliamentary language in its tow, commonly use the term "hierarchy" when referring to the episcopate. The reference here is not to the College of Bishops as a whole but to a specific entity endowed with the responsibility to represent the episcopate by its leaders. From Italian Unification to the Second Vatican Council, the Pope governed himself. From the Second Vatican Council onward, the Pope governed through the Italian Episcopal Conference, which is the only episcopal conference in the world that does not elect its own president but instead has one nominated by the Pope. Lastly, in a State that has become less and less attached to the practice of Catholicism, but that is still profoundly influenced by a mentality that belongs to that Christian denomination, the popular perception is that, whatever the ecclesiological doctrine may say, the only "hierarchy" to look at, is the Pope's own. All others—from bishops to parish priests—must simply follow: they can be validated by "the" hierarchy, nothing more. The Pope's authority towers above all others and is the only authority discussed in terms of emotional engagement—"love for the Pope"—while other ranks lack this sentimental connection. The only problem this scenario poses is that the Pope does not govern alone, nor does he govern with the aid of his bishops alone; rather, he governs through the decision-making apparatus that is the Roman Curia (*Curia Romana*). Restructured at the end of 1500, in the twentieth century this body underwent further "reforms," in law and in practice, which allowed its members to exercise a power that was in principle impossible to delegate, like that of the Pontiff himself. In fact, this power ended up being delegated and was used to political ends and within the country's political debate, especially after the end of World War II.

The Two Problems: the Spaniards and the Pope

Italy's exit from World War II was unparalleled on the European stage. Italians "invented" Fascism, but they also believed that Fascism was the cause of Italy's defeat. Italy saw democratic forces prevail in a bloody civil war, but within these forces militants and leaders that did not entirely belong to the persecuted anti-fascists played a decisive role. The country invested its best minds in the process of liberation, but a predominant role was also played by the Marxist parties that were waiting not for the reinstatement of a bourgeois state but for socialist transformation of society.

Above all, the nation that was born from a war with the Papal States, a culture-shaping conflict that found in Roman Catholicism a strong ideological and cultural binding agent. The mentality of Italian Unification (the Risorgimento) used to regard the legacy of Spanish power and the papacy as the two entities that had hindered the nation-building process, making it unachievable until both had been defeated. In contrast, popular and educated sensibilities of the post World War II Italy no longer had any interest in Spanish domination and blamed the dramatic differences between north and south on the conservative policies of the liberal regime and on fascist miscalculations; and, above all else, saw not only in Catholicism but in the papacy itself—and in particular that of Pope Pius XII—an essential element for ensuring national endurance.

Consul Dei

During the nineteenth century Italian history had witnessed the liberal aspirations of Catholicism and at the end of the century saw the birth of an organized Catholic movement. In the next century this popular participation was used in a conservative sense until World War II. In 1919 a Sicilian priest Don Luigi Sturzo founded a Catholic party, albeit too late to hinder the slide into Fascism—and had then been condemned to exile in order to please the Duce. Mussolini's regime had been able to take full advantage of ecclesiastical support. However, all this had in the end been outdone by the sincerity with which small Catholic minorities had taken part in the Resistance, as well as by Pope Pius XII's decision to remain in Rome after September 8, 1943, the date of the armistice between the Allies and the Kingdom of Italy. When the structure of the state shattered, the Pope became a stabilizing force, at once *consul Dei* and *defensor civitatis*. Although devoid of temporal power, he presented himself as the holder of a sovereignty to which Italy was not unresponsive.

The shy and empirical openness to "healthy" democracy was showed by Pope Pacelli in his radio broadcast at Christmas 1944: he said that its goal is the "execution of God's order," rather than the exercise of a "pure and simple absolutism". It was not only a green light for the Catholic parties' involvement in the birth of this new form of State, but also a final renunciation of hopes to restore a confessional regime *sic and simpliciter.* The latter possibility had its supporters in Italy, so much so that some prelates, particularly Palermo's Archbishop Ernesto Ruffini, and the Secretary of the *Sant'Uffizio* Alfredo Ottaviani, were not afraid to declare their support publicly.

THE HOLY SEE AND THE EPISCOPATE

Turning this openness into a politically relevant element in a liberated Italy inevitably shed light on a contradiction, and sometimes a source of conflict, that remained unresolved for the following seven decades.

In the opinion of the Holy See, the Pope, as Primate of Italy, has a legitimate political role—although the political nuances of that role underwent many modifications over the years. In fact, the layered structure of the Roman Curia includes two congregations, which later became sections of the Secretary of State Bureau, each led by a "Substitute," one for International Relations—overlapping slightly with the domain of the Sacred Congregation for the Propagation of the Faith (*Propaganda Fide*) and of the Congregation for the Oriental Churches—and one for Italy. In Pacelli's Curia, in which the Pope left the post of Secretary of State vacant from 1945 until his death in 1958, it fell to the Substitute to engage with Italian politics. This second Substitute happened to be Giovanni Battista Montini, the son of an Italian People's Party Member of Parliament (MP), a reader of Jacques Maritain, and the educator of a generation of democratic Catholics. His nomination signaled a pledge, on the Pontiff's part, to the birth of democracy and to its subsequent Christian Democratic character, but this proved to be a difficult terrain. Indeed, toward the end of 1953, a conspiracy whose supporters included Cardinal Pizzardo banished Montini from Rome, by arranging that the Pope appoint him Archbishop of Milan. This Northern city—the economic capital of the reconstruction—had never been a peripheral or minor seat. Blessed Andrea Ferrari had worked there, future Pope Achille Ratti had stood at that pulpit, and after him personalities such as Carlo Maria Martini and Angelo Scola would make Milan a true counterbalance to Rome's power. But in 1953 sending the Substitute to Milan meant physically distancing him from the power structures and from the Papal Court, rendering his contribution to the processes that generated "Vatican" policies irrelevant. Furthermore, convincing Pacelli not to ordain any further cardinals, thus depriving Archbishop Montini of the cardinal's hat, was to serve as a guarantee against this feared prelate with "democratic tendencies" entering the conclave, or walking out of it in papal robes, as was indeed to happen in 1963.

Montini had to deal with the Italian bishops; this problem concerned different political sides but remained intact through to the end of Benedict XVI's papacy. The episcopate, at the time, was even devoid of an episcopal conference, due to Italian bishops having the Pope as a natural president and as the Primate of Italy, and feeling that a nation born from the Risorgimento should not possess such a body. Furthermore, the

Italian episcopate held its own view of politics, in fact it held many, bonded by a strong anti-communist commitment, which would often represent the sole principle guiding the bishops. Additionally, the more charismatic bishops brought with them diverse political leanings: from the very spiritual figures of Milan's Cardinal Ildefonso Schuster and Florence's Elia Dalla Costa, to the bishops of the great southern cities who, in turn, had a strong reactionary streak. The political weight of each tendency was lesser or greater depending on its accord with papal directives, or, more precisely, with the directives that the Pope, as he received people and information, believed he should impart. Because of this, Cardinal Giuseppe Siri, the young, proactive and fiercely reactionary Archbishop of Genoa, played an important role in the first phase of republican history. He distrusted Montini's democratic faith, and he was famed as Pacelli's heir apparent—if not quite his designated successor. Although he proved unable to gather consensus in any of the four conclaves he took part in, he managed to inspire a conservative current that, with and after him, would reap important public positions.

Montini's democratic vision, however, encountered opposition not solely outside the Holy See. Even within it, resistance was manifest, in particular around another issue destined to have weight in the first seven decades of post-fascist Italy: the decision regarding the form and nature of the political parties. In fact, the other Substitute, Domenico Tardini, was persuaded that in liberated Italy there should be numerous parties for and of Catholics: so much so that even the birth of the "Catholic Left" would find some support and endorsement among ecclesiastics. For, ideology aside—which would be first deprecated and then condemned—this multiparty setup seemed to be the Holy See's best tool for influencing Italian politics. This current of thought lost, and Montini's position on the "political unity" of Catholics would prevail from 1943 to 1993 through the Christian Democratic party (DC). The party did not deliver on the front of votes—Catholic electors were spread across the political spectrum—but did build, via a sort of *unitas ficta,* a screen that would enable the DC to reap the support of the clergy and the faithful, quite independently from ecclesiastical moods and pressures—or at least much more so than the parties of the so-called Second Republic.

THE CONSTITUTION

The first and most relevant trial for this set of impulses was the drafting of the Italian Constitution. The DC's institutional agnosticism in the referendum on the choice between a monarchy and a republic is that of the Church—indeed, Pope Pius XII wrote in 1944 that democracy could be compatible with both institutional forms. Hence, at first, Alcide De Gasperi's choice was to reserve governmental action for himself, and his decision to entrust the Constitution to a young professor trained at Milan's Cattolica, Giuseppe Dossetti, did not cause alarm. Much like his University colleagues—Giuseppe Lazzati, Amintore Fanfani, but also Giorgio Lapira and Aldo Moro—Dossetti represented the paradoxical results of Padre Agostino Gemelli's academic institution. The

Università Cattolica del Sacro Cuore strived to educate the future ruling class of a confessional, post-fascist state, while aiming at academic excellence, and thus found itself educating the leadership of a democratic Italy that would last, Romano Prodi's government included, until the start of the twenty-first century. The democratic elements that Dossetti and his followers would bring to the Constitution were worthy of note, especially given the circumstances in which they operated.

The steadfast fathers of *La Civiltà Cattolica*, the Jesuit periodical that expresses the off-the-record thinking of the Secretary of State Bureau, had in fact prepared three constitutional drafts in order to "guide" Catholic constituent: one bluntly confessional aspired to the Spanish "ideal" of "Nacionalcatolicismo", one moderately confessional, and a minimal one in which the Lateran Pacts (*Patti Lateranensi*) signed in 1929 between Fascist Regime and the Holy See, were at least protected. Faced with this move, Dossetti, Montini, and Angelo Dell'Acqua chose to ensure a channel of communication and contact remained open. During a series of weekly meetings, DC constituents were able to persuade both the few ecclesiastics who already agreed, and those who mistrusted the choice, that Italy's problem was that of obtaining not a formal democracy but a substantial one. This move was compensated by adding a mention of the Lateran Pacts to the Constitution, as the Holy See desired, and not of the formula of the "existing pacts" (or "Pacts") as De Gasperi had wished. However, the Pacts were incorporated into the constitution in Article 7, along with Article 8 on religious freedom and the right of other churches and religions to sign "Intese" with the state. A "cocktail" that allowed the Constitutional Court of Italy to declare in 1989 that the Constitution of the Republic enshrines a "supreme principle of *laicità*"—despite the fact that neither this term nor *laicité*, the key term of French early twentieth-century politics for the separation between church and state, were ever mentioned.

For Dossetti, the problem with regard to the Constitution was not that of challenging the Church or yielding to the Pope's will—two things he would indeed do in 1948 and 1956 when pressured to run in two separate elections—but rather that of preventing the birth of a democracy with the Catholic masses opposing it, as had happened during the Risorgimento. He considered that the absence of Catholic popular support as well as that of the masses of workers was the reason for the weakness shown by the Liberal regime when confronted with Fascism.

THE VICEROY

The wish to turn the Constitution into a rallying point for bishops and for the faithful imbued with clerical Fascism, in order to persuade them to coalesce around a democratic republic and a pluralist society, can be said to have been fulfilled. At the elections of April 18, 1948, the attempt made by a clerical organization known as the Roman party, headed by Monsignor Roberto Ronca, to push the DC toward authoritarianism, failed. Instead, the first republican Chamber of Deputies arose out of a clash between the

Socialists and Communists on one side, and the DC on the other. Cardinal Giuseppe Siri's effort to turn the Commission of Cardinals, an assembly of those Cardinals presiding over ecclesiastical regions, into a lever pushing for a move to the right in DC's political line also failed. Undeterred, Siri, acting as viceroy to Pius XII especially after his death, would not give up his claim to a central role in political dealings.

However, the ecclesiastical authorities, both at the episcopal and at the Vatican levels, still kept an ongoing negotiation table open with the DC, deciding on candidatures for to vast array of political roles and even on the composition of the government. Nevertheless, this influence did not impact the DC's political line: after De Gasperi's death, the party dismissed its centrist formula and postulated an "opening to the left" in order to engage with the Socialist Party in government, and it did so despite all the resistance, both quiet and violent, of the ecclesiastical authorities. What was influenced, however, was not the outcome of this political process, but its speed: this stalling, caused by conservative and reactionary forces, constituted another persistent factor in Italian history, one destined to extend beyond the twentieth century.

The 1950s were the years of the DC's structural "collateralism," but they were also years in which indications of discontent with that political line emerged from the trade unions and from politics. There was no lack of dramatic incidents, such as the trial of Prato's Bishop Monsignor Pietro Fiordelli, convicted for having slandered a young couple who chose to wed in the town hall, by labeling them "public concubines". The anticommunist paradigm and the allegiance to the Pope, however, screened and absorbed these incidents, as well as the first cases of dishonesty in ecclesiastical finances—as in the Monsignor Edward P. Cippico case. After all, the bishops yearned only for guidance. They were often called to the provincial meetings convened by the region's cardinal; the cardinal would in turn be summoned by the Substitute who would draft the meeting's order of the day, without this dynamic being perceived as frustrating, but rather as a show of solidarity with the Pope's directives. The episcopate, in fact, built a relationship with political power only after Pope Pius's death, on October 10, 1958.

Pope Pius XII passed away just before signing the condemnation of Jaques Maritain, an act that would have overturned the political equilibria of the Church. He left a Church in which his former Substitute, Montini, devoid of a cardinal's hat, could not aim for the papacy. It was a Church facing a political context in which, after the 1949 excommunication of those who adhered and endorsed "atheist Communism," the pastoral and political problems faced by the rapidly developing nation were increasingly worrisome.

A WIDER TEVERE

The Pope elected on October 28, 1958, Venetian Patriarch Angelo Giuseppe Roncalli, who took the name of John XXIII, was certainly not favorable to the center-left, nor to the strategy that called for the involvement of the Socialists in government. Misinterpreting a welcome of his to the congressmen of the Socialist Party (PSI), which in fact constituted a reductive interpretation on his part of the excommunication of 1949, it was believed that the new Pope was sympathetic to Aldo Moro and Amintore Fanfani's political strategy, and that his inclination was the cause of the de facto permission provided by the Holy See. Pope John, however, did not endorse this openness, and he distrusted Pietro Nenni's PSI: he was convinced that an overly narrow Tiber (which is the river that runs between the Vatican and Rome) would prove detrimental to the Church, and that allowing the DC some leeway was a deserved gesture of magnanimity.

In previous years the Pope had refused De Gasperi an audience, because he considered him guilty of having hindered the so-called "Sturzo Operation". Through a civic list headed by the elderly priest and filled with neo-fascist and reactionary personalities, the operation was an attempt at blocking access to the Roman municipality. Conversely, with Pope John, Amintore Fanfani, who emerged as new leader of the DC after De Gasperi, found a political hearing. Fanfani was well capable to give weight to, in an admittedly complex situation. Sure enough, the Pope could not count on unconditional compliance with his directives: the "Roman party" and parts of the Curia linked to Cardinal Alfredo Ottaviani did not hesitate, for example, to publish in the Holy See's daily newspaper, on May 18, 1960, an article on the *Punti Fermi*, that the Pope had forbidden should go to print: and that sounded like an excommunication of the center-left in the making.

However, Pope John's policy of "distance" was associated with two consequences of the Second Vatican Council that had great institutional relevance to the Holy See's attitude to Italian politics. On the one hand, before the Council, Roncalli gave the Secretary of State a leading position within the Vatican's system of government, and appointed as its head a diplomat of similar convictions, Cardinal Amleto Giovanni Cicognani. These regulations, devised by Paul VI in 1968, subordinated "La Suprema," the *Sant'Uffizio* Congregation, to the Second Lodge of the Apostolic Palace, and in fact completed the transformation of the Pontifical government into a system that included an effective prime minister—although the fact that it was not so by law would become a source of lasting conflict. Furthermore, given that all Churches would come to the Council with a plenary episcopal conference, Italy too formed its own, the "Conferenza Episcopale Italiana" (CEI)). This conference, with Siri as its first president, and then with the Venetian Patriarch Giovanni Urbani, became a secondary force in the Council's works, but a very relevant one in post-Conciliar times.

THE REFORMING PRINCE

The times following the Second Vatican Council—starting on October 11, 1962, after three years of preparation, and ending on December 8, 1965—were marked by Montini's rise to the pontiff's seat. Having been created cardinal by John XXIII, Milan's Archbishop prevailed over the Curia's opposition, and became Pope on June 18, 1963, taking the name Paul VI. He was a "Christian Democrat" Pope, as Jan Grootaers would define him: an irreverent definition, though not devoid of meaning. For Montini did not only come from a family active in the Italian People's Party (PPI), but he was also a sort of "founder" of that DC which, throughout his papacy, would see its prestige but not its power fade, during the complex years spanning from the youth revolts of 1968 to Aldo Moro's assassination in 1978.

In the last sessions of Vatican II, and in the beginning of the post-Conciliar phase, Montini experienced first hand the weakness of the Italian Church: an episcopate that, with the exception of Bologna's Cardinal Giacomo Lercaro, held no authority in any of the great debates—liturgy, collegiality, and ecumenism. It was a Church that, after having offered the DC the best of its managerial class, found itself deprived of the intellectual tools with which to comprehend the Church shaped by the Council and the 1960s world. The outcome of the brief trajectory of the "organic center-left," which in 1969 was already struggling on a political level, was not accidental. At a stage when, as Moro declared at DC's national congress in February 1969, "new times are coming," Catholic militants identified the DC's political culture as the enemy. They started organizing so-called dissent groups that absorbed forms of politicization of left-wing faith, the most relevant example being the "Christians for Socialism"; grass-roots communities that showed solidarity with parties of the extreme left, one of the most famous amongst them being the "Comunità di San Paolo"; and intellectual circles that provided the Communist Party with a group of parliamentary candidates, known as "left-wind independents," amongst them, Mario Gozzini, Raniero La Valle, and Boris Ulianich.

For Paul VI, the challenge represented by the left was in conflict with his plan for the post-conciliar phase in Italy and in the world. Instead of acting as a "reformist prince" regulating the tempo of a renewal he believed in—although he feared it could proceed too fast—Pope Montini found himself having to contain a political process which shifted the focal point to the left. This undermined the formula of "political unity amongst Catholics," and broke that balance which, in his youth, he had imagined as the weapon to brandish against the possibility of Italy acquiring its own Bavarian-style Catholic conservative party, much in the same way as he had prevented Dossetti's group from conceptualizing a Catholic labor party.

All the above combined to mobilize the Italian episcopate as it was acquiring a new form through harsh internal conflict, which had started with the removal from his seat of Bologna Archbishop, Giacomo Lercaro, in January-February of 1968. Lercaro, with the aid of his pro-vicar Giuseppe Dossetti, ordained as a priest in 1959, had decided to dedicate the sermon on the first World Peace Day to the condemnation of the US intense bombing of North Vietnam. His sermon effectively superimposed the Church's position onto that of the PCI, unwittingly interfering with the attempts at mediation between the Americans and the Vietcong that the Pontiff had been pursuing. The removal, unprecedented save for the actions of a few inquisitors in 1500, was a symptom of an ecclesiastical authority acting on ecclesiastical dynamics for reasons directly linked to the political context.

Montinians

A new generations of bishops, ordained by Pope Paul VI in the last ten years of his papacy before his death in 1978, operated according to the same principles. These "followers of Montini," presided over by Bologna's Cardinal Antonio Poma—who succeeded Lercaro and was aware or more of the plot against him—are the ones with whom the Pope proceeded to renovate the episcopal conference, endowing it with a fresh profile and new responsibilities.

Italian society was changing. Pressure was mounting for a review of the 1929 Gasparri–Mussolini concordat, and divorce became regulated through a law—passed by a referendum held on May 11 and 12, 1974, that Fanfani and the Pope expected to be abrogated. The Church found itself a component of this new society and tried to enter a political debate in which many observant Catholics voted PCI or PSI, declaring they were"contributing to" a mission pursued by previous generations of DC affiliates or PPI militants.

Paul VI organized this Montinian episcopacy in a new episcopal conference, whose de facto leader was the Secretary General Enrico Bartoletti. A very spiritual man, endowed with great political tact, Bartoletti promptly realized the consequences of the referendum on divorce. The referendum had been won by the anti-abrogation parties not against Catholic vote but with the aid of that vote and with that of those Catholics such as Giuseppe Alberigo and Pietro Scoppola, who believed that defending the theological principle of the indissolubility of marriage through civil law was wrong. Bartoletti, who died before being able to launch the process of making an "Italian Church," convened in 1976 a major ecclesiastical *convegno* halfway between a holy synod and a parliament, on "evangelization and the promotion of humankind," aimed at bringing to the fore the political urgencies that were polarizing the Church and were accompanying the difficult path of the DC in the years between the oil crisis and Moro's assassination.

In the very same years, Moro was theorizing the third phase of Italian politics. In this phase, as the Socialists had already done, Moro thought that the PCI should have been involved in government alongside the DC, with a view to creating a system of alternation typical of mature democracies. Meanwhile, the Pope and bishops were grappling with internal conflicts on matters of theology as well as on the moral and political realms. Open channels of communication were scarce: Ivrea's Bishop Monsignor Luigi Bettazzi—author in 1976 of a famous "letter to Enrico Berlinguer"—gained the consensus of the left; while other ecclesiastical sectors, such as Cardinal Fiorenzo Angelini's, delegate to the Catholic Hospitals on behalf of the Holy See and well acquainted with the vast Roman system of sanitary care—were supporting Giulio Andreotti's conservative current within the DC.

Support given to the PCI and other left-wing formations by lone or organized Catholics shuffled the cards in the Italian political game. An extreme example is that of the Genoese priest Gianni Badget Bozzo, a former collaborator of Dossetti and later one of Siri's right-hand men, who ran for election with Craxi's PSI in 1985 and would, at the close of the century, become a theological advisor to Silvio Berlusconi. This politically generated tension gave rise to internal struggles and was dealt with through tools of canonical repression (the formula of "self-exclusion from the ecclesiastical community" was used several times). In some cases a suspension "*a divinis*" occurred, as in the case of St. Paul's Outside the Walls's Abbot Giovanni Franzoni, who was deprived of his ministry because of his electoral support for the PCI.

Few prelates, like Cardinal Michele Pellegrino, Archbishop of Turin, voiced their discomfort when confronted by the tendency to overlap doctrinal faithfulness and political obedience. In many cases, such as that of Napoli's Cardinal Ursi, the dioceses attempted to mediate between a political system characterized by a slow turnover and a rapidly changing society. Others, like Palermo's Cardinal Salvatore Pappalardo, began the slow shifting of the Church from general indifference to the issue of "legality" in a society imbued with Mafia undercurrents to belligerent stances; a change that a few years later would make the Sicilian capital a protagonist in the anti-mafia "spring," with exponents of the Catholic faith in the front lines. But the ultimate reference point is the Pope: for or against him; only he could decide what was politically intolerable.

The change in moral paradigms that occurred after widespread disobedience to the 1968 encyclical "Humanae vitae" continued with support for certain behaviors and practices that would eventually lead to approval of the abortion law in May 1978. But, mostly, it was the idea that a full understanding of Vatican II would come about too slowly, and the perception of a "Council betrayed," that were the lifeblood of many fragmented ecclesiastical experiences, diverting militants away from the large structure that was Azione Cattolica (AC). Despite the AC's "religious choice," endorsed by its then president Vittorio Bachelet in the aftermath of Vatican II, the AC lost ground to other entities, many of which felt that the party-trade union-AC circuit supplying a large part of the country's leading class, was an embodiment of privilege and collateralism.

The experience of the new "movements" that were rising out of the fumes created by the magma of aggregation and subsequent disaggregation was very different. These new movements sought legitimization, often political, from the ecclesiastical authorities. If some amongst them—the Focolare Movement, the Neocatechumenals, Rinnovamento dello Spirito—had no political agenda, and were content with ecclesiastical acknowledgment, others, such as the Community of Sant'Egidio (Comunità di Sant'Egidio), that entered parliament and the government in 2011–2013, had a very political future.

A peculiar movement, Communion and Liberation (Comunione e Liberazone, CL), chose very early on, in 1973, to cultivate its own political brand, and to cast it within the DC—particularly before Carlo Maria Martini became Archbishop of Milan in 1981. The vacancy left by a Catholic conservatism that, as imagined by the conservative president of the Catholic Action Luigi Gedda and Cardinal Giuseppe Siri, should have been a direct expression of the Pope and episcopate, was occupied, at first on a local and subsequently with increasing political ambitions, by this generation of Don Luigi Giussani's disciples. First through their own Popular Movement (Movimento Popolare), and later through events such as the Rimini Meeting and the Compagnia delle Opere, they stepped forward as a new right-wing oriented militia, within a Church in which the *gauchiste* trend appeared to be prevailing, if not in numbers, because of its strong voice.

POLISH MISTRUST

Aldo Moro's tragic death in May 1978 brought this phase—and in a way the Italian papacy—to an end. The president of the DC was kidnapped by the Brigate Rosse—a terrorist group that counted few but significant members who came from, or were close to, Catholic entities. When both the DC and the Church failed to find a way to free him, Moro was killed, after a 55-day imprisonment. The strenuous effort of Agostino Casaroli, modern Catholic history's most experienced negotiator, collapsed "thanks" to Giulio Andreotti, prime minister. The letters and memoirs that Moro wrote during his time as a captive were an excruciating analysis of the powerlessness of a Catholicism that, through its politicians and ecclesiastics, had held power for 30 years and still sank when faced with PCI firmness; for the Communist Party, in fact, it was impossible to engage in any form of negotiation, due to its ideological proximity with the terrorist who theorized the armed struggle.

Paul VI, who was a longtime personal friend of Moro, was unable to find his own definite position in the Moro affair, and died a few months after that devastating experience, on August 6, 1978. The unexpected and sudden death of John Paul I, caused by a heart attack, makes that year the end of the line for Italian popes—at least for more than one third of a century. The election of a Polish pope in 1978, John Paul II, seemed at first a mere interjection, but would ultimately mark the end of a papacy "*naturaliter*" Italian, which would never come back as an unquestioned rule as it was for centuries. The Polish papacy would carry decisive weight in the relationship between politics and the ecclesiastical authorities. As he took on the role of Bishop of Rome, Karol Wojtyła came to live, for the first time in his life, in a Western parliamentary democracy—and also in a country whose spiritual leader was not "the prince of politics." Furthermore, Wojtyła, and those who had endorsed his election, viewed the Italian context as one which had lost its energy and its nerve under the guidance of Paul VI, as wells as its inflexibility, solidity, and certainties.

"Don't be afraid," the motto addressed to believers and non-believers at the start of his papacy, implied laying a claim to a faith that publicly declared its strength: not an ideologically conservative strength—John Paul II would later openly criticize e.g. the Iraq/Afghanistan wars pursued by George W. Bush—but one committed to fighting an individualistic culture with a strong voice, and without turning its nose up at a close relationship with the world's conservative parties.

The problem facing Wojtyła was twofold. In Italy, a conservative party of the ideological orientation that Wojtyła would come to appreciate, for instance, in Ronald Reagan, did not exist. Instead there existed a Montinian CEI, of which he soon rid himself. The Pope called an ecclesiastical meeting in Loreto in 1985, during which he dispatched not only the leaders of the episcopal conference but also the cultural and political mode of action that had assumed dialogue and mediation as its main tools. Papal trust in Anastasio Ballestrero's CEI (the Archbishop of Turin was the President at that time) was being eroded, and for the first time the organization witnessed the rise of an episcopate out of, or close to, the ranks of CL—the Archbishop of Bologna Giacomo Biffi, for instance. As a result, the CEI was unable to express leadership of the episcopacy. But Wojtyła nominated his vicar in Rome, Ugo Poletti, for the presidency of the CEI as if he were the legal ward to a generation of bishops—that of Alberto Ablondi, Andrea Mariano Magrassi, Gilberto Baroni and Antonio Bello—that could no longer count on the Pope's explicit support. In 1991 John Paul II substituted Poletti due to his age, but did not free the CEI from compulsory administration: he nominated Camillo Ruini—a theologian well acquainted with the internal struggles of the DC—who would, for his part, enact Wojtyła's strategy, as president of the bishops and Cardinal Vicar of Rome (*Vicario dell'Urbe*).

This strategy benefited from the great turning point reached with the 1984 concordat between Agostino Casaroli and Bettino Craxi, a turn whose implications were not fully understood by all. On one hand, the new Villa Madama agreement made the changes necessary for the 1929 concordat to be in accordance with constitutional principles as well as with conciliar viewpoints, albeit without renouncing the privilege-granting nature of the chosen tool. On the other, it brought about a great change because the beneficiary of the economic rewards that concordate granted was no longer the clergy, as per the previous instrument which was a small state stipend called "congrua," but the CEI. Furthermore, the size of these rewards would no longer be regulated through a head-count system, allowing, as for the German taxation made on behalf of the Churches and called *Kirchensteuer*, to allocate funds to a Church within certain limits, but through a weighted system. More precisely, the concordat established that a quota of the eight per thousand from the income tax levy (*IRPEF*)—the size of which was to be determined by the number of signatures collected—would be assigned to the national Catholic Church. In the space of a few years this scheme would turn the CEI, in terms of net profit, into one of the main national "companies."

The Ruini Years

Camillo Ruini came to lead the CEI as the crisis of the CEI's political parties came to a head. He progressively did away with the formula of "Catholic political unity," and he recognized that, as Tardini had felt, post-DC fragmentation could enlarge the CEI's scope of action. But, above all, he was able to utilize the economic leverage of the eight per thousand not only for necessary deeds of restoration, charity, and clerical sustenance—an Italian priest earns the same salary as a specialized factory worker while being free from rent and family obligations—but also for the development of a media strategy. Through an old newspaper, called "*Avvenire*", now fundamentally overhauled by Ruini's political right hand and director Dino Boffo, a television channel eventually entrusted to that same journalist, as well as conventions and cultural events, this media operation increased the force and weight of a CEI that was strongly identified with its president rather than with its secretary general. Indeed, the latter was relegated to tasks that were subordinate to the president, both during Dionigi Tattemanzi's mandate, later Archbishop of Genoa and Milan, and during the mandate of Giuseppe Betori, who would later become Archbishop of Florence.

Ruini found a great antagonist in Carlo Maria Martini. A biblical philologist that became Archbishop of Milan, Martini promoted and removed his predecessor's assistants—particularly Giacomo Biffi and Giovanni Saldarini—thus strengthening the faction he did not belong to. By doing so, he put himself forward as a reference point for an entirely new way of imagining politics and the Church's role, but he never became an opponent of the CEI and of Ruini's policy.

On Silvio Berlusconi's first electoral victory in 1994, and subsequently during the crisis faced by the Prodi government in 1998, Ruini made a choice, accepting that the hierarchy's support—which greatly differed from Catholic support *tout court* and was significantly smaller—was shifting to the right. Not because of a particular political affinity, nor due to naiveté in respect of Berlusconi and his party, but rather in virtue of the view that those forces would guarantee better public visibility for the Church, and particularly so on the "non-negotiable" issues that offered Italian right-wing politicians the chance to qualify as *defensor fidei*—despite behaving, both individually and in the cultural sphere, in a way all but fitting to the precepts of the Holy Roman Church.

In this political plan, Ruini's strategy had two objectives, which were secured successfully and in a timely fashion. The first was to weaken Romano Prodi's position which, precisely because of his being an exemplary Catholic, constituted a disruptive element in his designs. The second was reducing communication both within the episcopal conference and across the ecclesiastical world. The unconditional support provided by John Paul II made these objectives attainable. The fragile alliances that brought Prodi to government allowed the Church to ensure his downfall without investing too many energies, playing against the Catholic economist now his allies, now the electoral system, as well as the abstentions from the 2005 referendum against a restrictive law on medically assisted procreation—which did not make the quorum it needed to ensure validity and therefore preserved a law which was later dismantled by the Constitutional Court.

On the other hand, the cultural weakness of Italian Catholicism, apparent since liberation and particularly after Vatican II, ensured that for nearly all bishops, all movements, and for much of the laity, it was more convenient to rely on the trust that existed between Ruini and the Pope rather than to voice opinions or dissatisfaction, and to be content with taking over those voids in spiritual discourse that would make Carlo Maria Martini famous.

Ruini failed on only one issue, the constitution. Indeed, when Berlusconi's first government put forward suggestions for constitutional reform, the CEI remained indifferent. By contrast, Dossetti, now a monk, made a comeback onto the political arena in an attempt to dispute the drafted constitutional changes. His move, which would be victorious well after his death, speaks volumes for the fact that the more anti-communism remains the only political content of Catholic culture, even after the demise of the PCI, the more the value of the constitution is weakened. And this offers an implicit ecclesiastical blessing for those who wanted to rewrite the constitution written after the liberation.

TARCISO BERTONE AND THE CHAOS

Ruinism seemed to have survived both Wojtyła's long agony and the 2005 conclave that elected Joseph Ratzinger as his successor. Ruini, excluded from the agreements that led to the rise of Pope Benedict XVI, found himself having to manage Romano Prodi's second yet ephemeral victory, followed by the return of Berlusconi's government. However, the old antagonism between the bishops and the Secretary of State Bureau resurfaced as Benedict XVI appointed the new Secretary in 2006. After the experienced diplomat Angelo Sodano, the German Pope chose Tarciso Bertone, a confidant of his; given that the CEI's president is not elected but nominated by the Pope, this designation of the cardinal of Genoa, Angelo Bagnasco, was the only way to favor turnover.

The renewal of the Presidency of CEI occurred after a serious infringement— Ruini denied a patient who had refused treatment the religious funeral his family had demanded—and after a political battle unanimously directed by all the bishops against civil partnerships, which are accepted by most episcopates as a compromise instrumental in avoiding the word "marriage" being used to refer to same-sex unions. Opposition to civil partnerships, proposed by the Prodi government under the acronym DICO (Rights and Duties for Stably Cohabiting People), wore out Prodi's frail parliamentary majority, while giving the Secretary of State the chance to choose a new president for the CEI, and to spell out the terms that were to condition his action.

As a consequence in 2007 Bertone accelerated change and he favored Angelo Bagnasco's ascent to the CEI's leadership over Angelo Scola, despite the fact that the latter could boast a much greater intellectual proximity to Benedict XVI. In a letter to the new president, Bertone established that the Secretary of State Bureau would overlook relations with the Italian government, while the CEI was to dedicate its efforts to solving social and pastoral problems.

The turn did not influence political equilibria: Bertone maintained relations with the Italian right as they had been before, and Bagnasco attempted to find his place in this dialogue with the priorities of Berlusconi's ideology, not solely because of a firm belief in it, but also due to the pressure Ruini's policies continued to exert on an episcopate in which every movement could rely on its chapter.

Judiciary documents on a crime and police misconduct obliged *Avvenire*'s director Dino Boffo to resign. A letter to the Pope's secretary, in which he accused the editor of *L'Osservatore Romano* and the Secretary of State, was stolen together with other official papers that discredited other prelates, particularly Angelo Scola. The latter, being transferred in the meantime from Venice to Milan by Pope Ratzinger, was described, in a letter from CL's leader, as an archbishop able to end the conflicts his predecessor Tettamanzi had created with the Lega Nord and with CL—the entities in control of the decision-making processes of the Lombardia region.

This stream of leaks—or Vatileaks, as they would be known in journalistic jargon—was clearly linked to Italian political conflicts and could not but appear as the outcome of an overly closeknit relationship between the Italian Church and the Italian right; it also implied drastic and demanding choices. These conclusions did not fail to influence Benedict XVI's sensational decision to renounce the papacy, a decision made public on February 11, 2013 and that became effective on February 28 of that same year.

GOODBYE MARIO MONTI

All this occurred during a serious political crisis that started with a sharp rise of the credit spread on Italian sovereign debt, and with the emergence of incidents that made Berlusconi a target for blackmail. Once his government fell, the President of the Republic entrusted Mario Monti—a Catholic economist and former European commissioner—with the task of forming a new government.

Finding himself in the confronted with a scandal caused by the theft of papal documents, and enmeshed in the conflicts between the CEI and the Secretary of State Bureau, Monti developed a direct relationship with Benedict XVI, one that was to prove more useful to the Pope than to the professor, elevated to the dignity of life-long Senator by President Giorgio Napolitano, while he appointed him as prime minister. Thanks to Monti, Ratzinger abandoned his euro-skeptic positions that had some bearing in creating the crisis, and took reconciliatory steps, especially toward German Chancellor Angela Merkel, which had some effect in sedating the trend of the sovereign debt index.

Before the birth of the Monti government, the CEI had undertaken an operation—culminating in the Todi convention—aimed at regrouping certain components and movements in order to give Catholics a presence in the public domain. Some of the Todi conference's main actors—the Community of Sant'Egidio's founder Andrea Riccardi, and Corrado Passera, a former CEO of state and private companies, who moved on to banking—would later became prominent figures in the Monti government. Others, such as the leaders of CL and of the Italian Confederation of Trade Unions (CISL), struggled to free themselves from the ties with Berlusconi's government and to prepare their comeback in other political formations or paths.

The line-up that ensued from the Todi conference—and that, however, failed to absorb all Italian Catholics—continued to point to those "non-negotiable" principles and values as a discerning element. But at the end of 2012, with the general political elections scheduled for February 2013 looming, the group became divided. Mario Monti, with strong encouragement not only from the Vatican but also from the Pope himself, founded his own party, Civic Choice (Scelta Civica), toward which the CEI, and above all the old guard of Ruini's acolytes, tuned a cold shoulder.

Because of this, the most relevant Catholic persons did not join Monti's party; only their representatives did so. The electoral failure of that ambitious project, aimed at holding the balance in a system unused to bipolarism, coincided with Ratzinger's resignation and then with the election of the first non-European Pope, Francis.

With Pope Bergoglio the political positioning of Catholic hierarchies started to shift rapidly. His pastoral style obliged the bishops to redefine their political profiles, the appointment of Pietro Parolin as the Secretary of State aimed at reducing contact with the Italian right, and the economic crisis, headed toward a profound social crisis, modified priorities.

However, in all, it is not difficult to see that, once the political juncture has regained some stability, the positions held by the many institutional and cultural components of Italian Catholicism—and the center of Roman Catholicism—will continue to be an essential element in any analysis of Italian politics.

BIBLIOGRAPHY

Alberigo, Giuseppe, *Il cristianesimo in Italia* (Milan: Mondadori, 1992).

Cristiani d'Italia. Chiese, stato, società, 1861-2011, ed. A. Melloni and l'Alto Patronato del Presidente della Repubblica, Istituto della Enciclopedia Italiana, Rome, 2011, vol. 2. pp. lx and 1872.

Jemolo, Arturo Carlo, *Chiesa e Stato in Italia negli ultimi cent'anni* (Turin, Einaudi, 1973).

Martina, Giacomo, *La chiesa in Italia negli ultimi trent'anni* (Rome: Studium, 1977).

Melloni, Alberto, "Some Historical Consideration on the Vatileaks: Eating in the Capital," *Journal of Modern Italian Studies* 17(2012)/1.

Melloni, Alberto, *Tutto e niente. I nodi della storia dei cristiani d'Italia, 1861-2011* (Roma-Bari: Laterza, 2013).

Pollard, John, *Money and the Rise of the Modern Papacy: Financing the Vatican, 1850-1950* (Cambridge, Cambridge University Press, 2005).

Pollard, John, *Catholicism in Modern Italy: Religion, Politics and Society, 1861-2005* (London: Routledge, 2007).

Riccardi, Andrea, *Il potere del papa. Da Pio XII a Giovanni Paolo II* (Roma-Bari: Laterza, 1993).

CHAPTER 32

....

THE CATHOLIC RIGHT

....

PAOLO ACANFORA

RATHER than speaking of one Catholic right in post-World War II Italy, it would be more appropriate to speak of many Catholic right-wing movements, of diverse projects and of different experiments in political culture. To this end, it is necessary to take into consideration three different entities: a right that could be defined as ecclesiastical, whose aim is to influence Italian politics by exerting direct pressure on the Christian Democracy Party (DC), and by swaying the Catholic electorate; a Christian democratic right, internal to the sole Catholic party; and a politically engaged Catholic right, active in various organizations other than the DC.

Diverse ideas and political projects coexist within each of these entities, evolving through time, and not always surfacing to become visible. The ecclesiastical world, for instance, has its own specificity, originating from different takes on issues such as the relationship between politics and religion, as well as that between members of the Church and laymen. Such issues have sometimes caused very deep divisions, within the Church but also amongst Catholic organizations. Furthermore, while on some occasions the existing contact points between these entities have managed to find a specific political definition for themselves, they have failed to do so in other instances. This state of affairs naturally calls for a specific periodization of the issue.

Another aspect that must be considered is the specificity of the Christian Democratic Party. The party was formed, between the end of 1942 and the beginning of 1943, with the intent of building Catholic political unity. The path to unity proved to be all but free from strife. Within the Vatican, the option of the plural participation of Catholics, and of their deployment in different political formations, had not been discarded. It was through Alcide De Gasperi's activities, and thanks to the presence of Giovan Battista Montini in the Vatican, that the church was eventually pushed to support the unitary solution.[1]

This outcome brought the DC to present itself as a pluralist party, within which different political cultures, held together by a common Catholic inspiration, coexisted. Such pluralism, throughout the years, crystallized the currents running through the party, each representing an independent dimension, so much so that it was hinted that the DC was a federative party.[2] This peculiarity makes it difficult to position the DC in a political framework based on dichotomies such as right/left and progressive/conservative. The ideological and political definition of a "centrist" party, on which numerous efforts of further elaboration have been focused, could not avoid importing those same dichotomies into the party.

Nevertheless, despite this perspective, the complexity of internal dynamics is such as to hinder the description of one political entity. Furthermore, on a historiographical level, an exhaustive mapping of the DC's internal factions is still lacking, in spite of the numerous works on single groups.[3] Amongst these, there is a specific deficiency in regard to the right wing of the party.[4]

Thus, this chapter aims to analyze the main aspects of the Catholic right, appraising its relevance in the policy of a party such as the DC, which had a pivotal role within the Italian political system. The analysis has been framed by using the beginning of the center-left era as the *ad quem* limit in time. This choice is essentially due to the consideration that, with the first government lead by Aldo Moro in December 1963, a chapter in republican history drew to a close and another begun in which the role of the Catholic right changed considerably. The new setup, despite undergoing various and at times dramatic phases, would last until the radical upheavals of the 1990s, marking the end of the feasibility of opening and enlarging the Italian political lineup towards the right. The widening of the circle of those involved in government happened structurally toward the left and, despite the right-wing Catholic movements continuing to play a significant role within the Italian political system, the fundamental options that had characterized their political course and physiognomy up to that point became, in many ways, unavailable. The end of the centrist government formula, and the launch of the center-left that ensued, imposed new strategies and different political elaborations.

THE INSTITUTIONAL QUESTION
AND NATIONAL RECONCILIATION

The first fundamental fact to be considered is the importance and the complexity of the relationship between Italian Catholicism and the fascist experience. Clearly, in considering the issue of the Catholic right in the immediate aftermath of World War II, it is impossible to ignore assessments of Catholic participation in Fascist political and cultural life. Historiography has dealt extensively with the issue, reaching numerous and contrasting formulations, yet it is beyond doubt that the Catholic world claimed and played an active role within the fascist political and cultural debate, representing one of its souls—whose foundations were mainly based in the criticism of Gentile[5]—and being able to build a peculiar Catholic nationalism.[6] The relationship with a totalitarian regime, whose aim was to carry out an anthropological revolution and construct a new man on the basis of values that were not Catholic but that belonged to the fascist political religion, proved complex. But this complexity did not hinder the development of profound affinities, especially in regard to a shared hostility to modern liberal democracy.

In this sense, full acceptance of the democratic regime, as per Pope Pius XII's radio message on December 24, 1944, proved to be all but quick and simple in the ecclesiastical world. Even support for the newly founded DC was to know hesitations and conditionings that impaired and reduced the scope of Catholics' autonomous action in the political arena, even if the autonomy of lay authorities represented a crucial value within a liberal democratic regime.[7]

And it was precisely in the context of the relationship between religious action and political action, between Church authority and the autonomy of laymen engaged in politics, that the most acute controversies amongst the DC and Church hierarchies took place. The ecclesiastical right was particularly active in this sense. It applied pressure, including through the action of important sectors of Catholic lay associations, in order to push for a greater subordination of the party to the wishes and orientations of the Vatican; and it did so in the name of the indisputable right of the Church to dictate policy not only in religious matters but also in the political arena.

The clearest evidence of the existence of an ecclesiastical right bent on conditioning DC policy and prepared to go as far as constructing a second Catholic party—of the conservative sort—was the so called "Roman party," a "poly-centric" entity that in general terms represented "the current opinions of the middle class within the Roman Curia (Curia Romana)."[8] This group, gathered around the movement known as Civiltà Italica led by Monsignor Roberto Ronca and inspired, amongst others, by Monsignor Alfredo Ottaviani, criticized De Gasperi's majority within the DC chiefly for the quality of its anti-communist effort.

De Gasperi had wanted to make the DC the "party of the nation," not because of its implicit vocation to govern, which translated into pure pragmatism, but because of its being an entity able to channel all the diverse expressions of society.[9] It was to be an inter-class party, which portrayed itself as the authentic heir of the political traditions inherited from the Italian unification process (Risorgimento), and as the best representative of the nation's spirit. Through an articulate elaboration of the myth of the nation, DC leaders legitimized themselves as the country's new guiding force, the only force able to bring the process of Risorgimento to a close. This procedure was articulated in two fundamental concepts. First and foremost was the recovery of the "neo-guelph" paradigm, according to which Italy is a Catholic nation and thus cannot be led by an atheistic and materialistic hierarchy, antagonistic to the religious soul of the Italian people. The second broad concept was an interpretation of Risorgimento in which three fundamental elements can be traced: 1) the marginalization of the contrasts between the Church and the political forces that had achieved Italian unification; 2) overemphasis of the Catholic world's role in the unification process; 3) the individuation of a common Christian origin for all the cultures that had been the at the basis of Risorgimento.[10] Because of this interpretation, which allowed the party to place itself in perfect continuity with national history, the DC, by introducing the Catholic masses into the state, completed, after the fascist interlude, what the Risorgimento had initiated. It thus enacted the "second Risorgimento," a social Risorgimento that followed the political one and was not accomplished on April 25, 1945, a date that signified the end of war and the liberation from Nazi-fascism in national liturgy. Nor was it accomplished on June 2, 1946, with the birth of the Republic, but on April 18, 1948, when the DC had very successfully prevailed, in the first general election, over the popular social communist front.[11]

As well as these three dates, there was another important moment that marked Italian history in the aftermath of World War II: the fracture in the tripartite government, composed of the DC and the socialist and communist parties, in May 1947. This event, which occurred just a few weeks prior to the launch of the Marshall Plan, had sanctioned the definitive wreckage of the antifascist front.

The right-wing faction within the DC that had emerged with Stefano Jacini's *Centro di studi politici* and through the magazines *Parola nuova* and *Realtà politica*, had publicly been pushing for this solution since the end of 1946.[12] For the conservative half of the party anti-communism represented a crucial and essential element. This was not, of course, particular to the more right-wing faction in the Christian Democrats. Anti-communism was an ideological trait shared by the whole of the Catholic party. Nevertheless, the different ways in which it was interpreted caused significant divergences. De Gasperi's centrist group sternly supported an anti-totalitarian democracy that viewed both communism and fascism as totalitarian, and both were interpreted as expressions of forces foreign to the interests and spirit of the nation—fascism because it was linked to an anti-historical nationalistic conception that denied the universalistic vocation of Italian tradition, and communism for being subordinate to Soviet expansionism and shackled to an ideology in conflict with the religious spirit of the nation.

Furthermore, De Gasperi's group declared itself not entirely averse to reforming Italian society and institutions geared at consolidating democracy. The alliance with socialist and communist forces was undoubtedly a tactical one, but it also stemmed from the need to build a new state, capable of answering the masses' call for integration—masses which had been marginalized in liberal Italy and mobilized on the ideological basis of the fascist totalitarian regime.

On this subject the Christian Democratic right was bewildered. Coupled with radical anti-communism, which called for a union of the DC with those parties on the right of the political spectrum, was a rejection of social and institutional progressivism, of which the republican question was a clear expression.

It was a delicate question, and one which divided the party. The internal struggle had brought to the toppling of republican majority groups by others of monarchical tendencies. This was the case, for instance, of the party's Roman committee. The decision, significantly, was legitimized as a consequence of the intensifying fight against communism.[13] Even among the young Christian Democrats, Giulio Andreotti had obtained consensus ensuring that the national congress declared inadmissible the participation of party members to "political groups outside the party," such as the youth republican committees, thus adopting a "clear stance against those young DC members belonging to the leftist current."[14]

During the party's national congress in April 1946, the DC, while not providing its electorate with directives regarding the referendum of June 2, 1946, expressed its support for the republican option with a clear majority of 68.8 percent. However, the monarchical minority was not only a substantial one at 23.7 percent—compared with 7.5 percent abstention—but it was also aware of representing the views of a great part of the Catholic electorate. Important figures such as Stefano Reggio d'Aci, Gaspare Buffa, Vincenzo Rivera, Angelo Maria Nasalli Rocca, Stefano Jacini, Carlo Petrone, and Cesare degli Occhi represented, albeit with different sensibilities, a current bent on making itself heard in order to sway party policy.

The government's alliances with the socialist and communist parties, combined with the republican victory, increased tension within the party and the ecclesiastical world.[15] Former PPI (Partito Popolare Italiano) member Degli Occhi, for instance, had left the DC in order to join the national monarchic party, a path Rivera would follow in 1963. Drives towards a rupture in the party, and the consequent formation of a new Catholic party on the right of the DC, were perceived as an important threat. The question was not confined to internal debate. In August 1946 the Ministry of the Interior commented on the relevance of Reggio d'Aci's action, which had brought the questions of the collaboration with socialists and communists—as well as that of unity within the Italian General Confederation of Labor (CGIL)—to the fore. The "threat of a rupture, arisen as early as the last national congress, when it became necessary to decide on a stance regarding the institutional question," continued to appear real, and was essentially postponed until the following national congress.[16]

In general terms, it is necessary to avoid overstating the role played by these components, both within the DC and in ecclesiastical hierarchies. For the right-wing current of the party was made up of diverse personalities—amongst whom the intellectual Stefano Jacini stood out—and, more importantly, during De Gasperi's era it was essentially assimilated into the majoritarian group that had taken on a markedly centrist physiognomy. Even the ecclesiastical right that in those years was composed of two fundamental factions—that of Monsignor Ronca and Civiltà Italica and that of the Jesuits of Civiltà Cattolica[17]—appeared not to have a fixed reference point within the party, least of all one that could be used to maneuver it. After all, the aim was to push the party to unite around a conservative stance, rather than to foster competition amongst inner groups. Nevertheless, we must not overlook the weight certain positions held within the ecclesiastical world or how pervasive criticism of De Gasperi's line really was—among his critics was Pope Pius XII himself. His policy was judged to be too soft on communism and not responsive enough to the Vatican's wishes; this pressure weighed down the party's ruling class and caused numerous problems.

In fact, various attempts were made to mobilize those sectors of Italian right-wing politics that openly asserted their affinity with Catholicism, such as the monarchists and neo-fascists. The aim of such mobilization was that of building a common conservative front that would include the DC and various right-wing movements, particularly during the 1940s and the 1950s.

The relationship between the DC and the right-wing parties was complex. Criticism of the DC's claim to be the sole representative of Catholic identity was a constant in Italian right-wing debate. As early as 1944 the democratic monarchical party (Partito Democratico Italiano) had made "the first, open objection to the DC's right to declare itself the only Catholic party."[18] Yet the most threatening challenge for the DC came from the Common Man's Front (Fronte dell'Uomo Qualunque), a movement lead by Guglielmo Giannini, which since its first congress defined itself as "the authentic exponent of the values associated with Catholic religion."[19] The movement attracted wide support in the southern regions, based on the rejection of the ideological party that portrayed itself as the "party-nation"[20]—that is a new allegiance which substituted the sense of national belonging—and criticized the DC's inability to effectively lead the struggle against communism and protect Catholic interests. The electoral success obtained by this new organization, and its ability to intercept the support of a significant number of southern Catholics, represented a serious threat to the DC leadership. And even within the openly neofascist front, which crystallized in the Movimento Sociale Italiano (MSI), there was a Catholic presence that wished to turn the MSI into "the second, truly Catholic party, as an alternative to the DC."[21]

Clearly, threats came from all directions. The DC's reaction was essentially twofold. On the one hand, it proceeded on a purely pragmatic level, taking advantage of the various opposing forces in order to "sustain its own centrist majorities, though never accepting, as with the liberals, their official participation in national government, and opting instead for alliances on a local scale."[22] On the other hand, it continued to stress its absolute and indisputable centrality within the Italian political system, as well as the importance of party unity, not only for the party's survival, but—more poignantly—for that of the entire nation. As the only organization able to represent and protect the nation's spirit and traditions, and to pursue authentic democratic and anti-totalitarian policies, the DC gave itself a "redeeming mission": to preserve the party's central role and unity became equivalent to saving the country.[23]

Thus, for all right-wing movements one problem arose, that of juggling their claim to Catholic identity with a critical attitude toward the DC. Such an attitude had to be contained enough to ensure that the building of a united front would not be compromised, to avoid losing ecclesiastical support. This issue became a crucial one, and one that weakened each group's position.

In order to rally the Catholic electorate that had been attracted by the Common Man's Front, or by monarchical and neofascist stances, De Gasperi's majority had given prominence to its policy of national reconciliation. Post-fascist Italy, after the totalitarian experience that had led it to identify national belonging with a specific ideological affiliation—defining those who were anti-fascist as also anti-nation[24]—had to become, once again, everyone's homeland. Necessary provisions were, on the one hand the abandonment of all nostalgic stances, and on the other the recognition of the obsolescence of the fascist/anti-fascist divide. This meant that anti-fascism, and consequently the Italian resistance movement (*Resistenza*)—to which great historical significance was attached—had to be viewed as an "incidental political phenomenon," one limited in time and from which a new, finally reconciled Italy must rise, as De Gasperi wrote in 1944.[25]

All political forces had to be involved in the effort to overcome the nation/anti-nation dialectic. The only possible exception was perhaps the Communist Party, not only because it had to adhere to the directives of a foreign power, but also because its ideology was distant from national tradition.[26] As Jacini maintained, with the exception of Carlo Pisacane, Marxism had had no hand in the process of unification.[27]

National reconciliation was further advocated by other actors, external to the party, such as the magazines *Candido, Il Brancaleone*, and *Il merlo giallo*. They aimed to rally those sectors of the Catholic world that were receptive to "nationalist and radically anti-communist political right-wing" issues.[28] Former opinion-makers of the regime continued to express their views along these lines, holding the DC as the last bastion to resist the totalitarian and materialistic values of communism. This line of argument engaged them in a pacifying effort, one able to transcend the purges and bring the nation back on the road to unity, against the only really anti-national actors, the communists.[29]

Even in the ecclesiastical world, these tendencies emerged at an early stage. In a letter to Giulio Rondinò, vice prime minister and member of the DC, Monsignor Roberto Ronca invited the DC to protect the southern bourgeoisie from communist purging of ex-fascists, thus respecting "that profound need for justice that is an innate quality of the Italian soul."[30] The right-wing Christian Democrats wished to voice these issues. Reggio d'Aci, in an argument with his fellow party members, spurred them to get over the "misconstruction of specifying justice in fascist or anti-fascist terms."[31] This would bring the woeful chapter of civil war to a close "through the prevailing of the law rather than the prevailing of a single faction."[32] Purges, wherever they may take place, were to be seen in light of the protection of the bourgeois and middle classes, the overcoming of the fascist/anti-fascist divide, and the rallying of all those individuals that might be instrumental in the construction of a conservative anti-communist front.

THE AFTERMATH OF APRIL 18, 1948

The elections held on April 18, 1948 were undoubtedly an important milestone in Italian republican history. The influence of Catholic associations proved to be particularly effective and efficient. A vigorous mobilization, based on capillary groundwork, was formed in order to combat socialist and communist propaganda nationwide. Central to the process that led to victory were the Catholic Action's (AC) Civil Committees, led by Luigi Gedda.[33]

It would be inappropriate, however, to think of the AC as a monolithic block. Within it, diverse opinions coexisted, and many opposed the idea of creating Civil Committees that would create propaganda to unite all Catholics, even those who did not identify with the DC. However, Gedda's recommendation that the Committees should form was fully endorsed by the ecclesiastical hierarchy and by Pope Pius XII.

Viewed as a response to the core claims and interests of the Catholic right, Gedda's strategy can be considered according to the following classification. The Committees acted upon needs that large sections of Catholics felt very strongly about: 1) the construction of a broad anti-communist front channeled into a conservative bloc; 2) the defense of interests, principles, and values belonging to "Christian civilization," understood as Catholic civilization; 3) the Church's claims to the right of dictating, through its ministry, fundamental guidelines, both in theory and practice, for those Catholics that engaged in political activity. The last point was especially sensitive, as it undermined the principle of autonomy for lay Catholics with respect to their concrete actions in the world, and in particular the autonomy of DC leaders in determining policy. Gedda's strategy thus led a large section of the party to unite in voicing their uneasiness over the Church's interference with and blurring the boundaries of the religious and the political worlds, which in their minds were to be kept strictly separate.

The electoral struggle substantially contributed to the creation of a context in which religion and politics were entwined. The decision to adhere to a Christian civilization was construed as an "integral political" choice catering to the needs of the masses which, after World War II, had lost all reference points.[34] The crucial importance of the April 18 election resides in its having been perceived as a political showdown between two diverging ideals of man, state, society, and historical processes. A few days before the vote the party's newspaper read: "it is not a question of voting for or against a ministry, for or against a political program. It is about solving multiple political, moral, social and economic problems that concern all we hold dear: family, faith, Country, freedom, the self and our future."[35] On the day of the ballot, the newspaper summarized the ultimate significance of the election: "today Italians will defend their reasons for being with their vote."[36]

In this context the Civil Committees 'contribution was decisive, not only in practical terms—though securing the votes of the elderly and the ill—but also in terms of a theoretical and propagandist elaboration based on the paradigm of the battle for civilization. The DC's were ill at ease with the political presence of the Committees, as we have seen. In the hours following the victory, the party's leaders rushed to point out that, despite their fruitful collaboration, the responsibilities assigned to the two entities (the DC and civic committees) were to remain strictly separate,[37] and that measures were to be taken both to avoid overlap[38] and to protect the party from being demoted.[39] The leaders feared a loss of independence, and it was not solely a procedural concern: a large section of the DC feared that Gedda's explicitly right-wing policy might cause the party to drift in that direction.

The goal for most of the DC was to take hold of the Catholic electorate without compromising the party's centrist policy line. In order to achieve this, it was necessary to use, albeit with due caution, certain specific tools. Amongst them was the newspaper *Brancaleone*, edited by Attilio Crepas. Aside from its contribution for the election campaign—not unlike that made by *Il Merlo Giallo* and *Candido*, which through cofounder Giovanni Mosca took to insistently campaign in favor of the party—both the newspaper and its editor unrelentingly engaged in pro-DC propaganda. Crepas had contacts with various levels of the DC hierarchy. With Secretary Guido Gonnella he was even able to discuss the creation of new secret bodies, such as the "psychological office," an entity that was to develop an anti-communist strategy of propaganda for the DC, making use of innovative techniques.[40]

Nevertheless, there was much resistance from prominent party members to publicly expose themselves on this terrain. During a party general meeting in July 1949, De Gasperi sympathizer Paolo Emilio Taviani intervened, warning that whilst valuing the role of this part-DC subsidized newspaper, "contacts with Crepas [must remain] indirect, in order not to assume responsibility for the paper." Furthermore, he added, MPs should not collaborate with the publication in any obvious way.[41] A similar contribution came from the movement of Italian Catholic Vanguards.[42] The movement aimed to "unreservedly support" the DC, and to "begin an open battle with the MSI, from which the arbitrary monopoly of Italian honor must be taken away," as it represented its only claim to young people's consensus.[43] Crepas and the *Brancaleone* team also initiated the birth of Alleanza Tricolore, born in Rome in 1952. The movement, self-defined as a "third force, strongly loyal and supportive of the DC," had the declared goal of supporting "the plan for national pacification headed by De Gasperi," winning back "to democracy ex-fascists and wide sections of Italian youth, which were being seduced by MSI propaganda."[44]

These leanings, despite placing the DC in direct competition with neofascism on the one hand, favored the identification of common values and ideals on the other. The situation was a rather complex one. The right-most component of the party, which had interpreted the election result as an endorsement of its conservative positions, and was requesting the "effects" of DC reformism on "middle class masses" to be carefully scrutinized,[45] had clustered around a heterogeneous group called La Vespa. This heterogeneous group had no easily identifiable political and cultural common origin, yet it did add another element to the traditional positions of the right-wing currents inside the party. Until then, this current had presented as its fundamental traits a prevalently monarchical outlook, an economic and social conservatism—as per Jacini, Rivera and Carmine de Martino's agrarian right—a sensitivity to ecclesiastical demands, and the marking of national pacification as a stepping stone towards the creation of an anti-communist, conservative political force. La Vespa members now forcefully posed the problem of the autonomy of parliamentary groups from party authorities. In a secret meeting of the group, MP Rivera had prepared a document to this effect, in which he claimed total independence for MPs, whose only tie to the party should be that of "mutual respect and consideration."[46] This issue was of paramount importance, as it informed the very notions of political party and of its relationship with the government and institutions.

These positions joined, personal inclinations aside, with the endeavors of Catholic groups located outside of the DC and sectors of Gedda's AC that aimed at reinforcing the DC's conservative profile and at putting pressure on De Gasperi's policies. The most visible manifestation of this pressure was undoubtedly the so called Sturzo operation, made ready for the administrative elections of 1952.[47] In the face of a decrease in votes cast for centrist parties, and the increase of those in favor of the left, those elections became crucial. Electoral results in Rome were, obviously, particularly relevant. In order to prevent the city of Rome from having a left-wing administration, Gedda, as newly appointed president of the AC, worked on an initiative that would have deep repercussions on the DC. The idea, endorsed by large sectors of the Vatican, was to put together a unified electoral list comprising the DC and right-wing parties, including the neo-fascists, led by the personality of Luigi Sturzo. This implied an array of consequences, amongst which the undermining of both the party's centrist configuration, and its Vatican support base. De Gasperi and Gonella, then party secretary, defined this hypothesis as a "grave catastrophe,"[48] and worked to convince ecclesiastical hierarchies of the peril it represented for the Italian political system. Even the AC leadership expressed aversion and doubts.

Despite the episode ending in the withdrawal of the proposition, fears of the possible coming into being of a second Catholic party on the right of the DC remained ingrained in party consciousness.

The Enduring Issue of Dialogue with the Socialists

The aforementioned hypothesis did not fade with the end of the Sturzo operation. Gedda, notably, persisted in challenging the DC, which in his view lacked in political vision, and showed commitment only to day-to-day matters. The Civil Committees continued to be his preferred tool. Despite having to face strong dissent, Gedda's political line remained unchanged. His enemies included De Gasperi's "democratic liberalism," leftist tendencies, and particularly the so called lapirism (*lapirismo*), accused of fashioning, on a psychological level, a softened political climate that anticipated collaboration with the socialists.[49]

After De Gasperi's death, the nomination of Amintore Fanfani as DC secretary, and the electoral results of 1953 which had not yielded a stable majority, the right current within the party once again proposed a partnership with conservative forces. On the occasion of the fifth party general meeting, Andreotti stated that "the fight against communism must be the priority, if not the sole objective of the Christian Democrats, and in order to win no strategic alliances must be excluded."[50] And the only possible leeway was, in this sense, to the right.

Even Giuseppe Togni, reinforcing some of Scelba's government leanings, underlined the issue insistently. New and more poignant definitions needed to be found for anti-communism. The state and its structures needed to be "purged" from the "grave detrimental menace posed by clerks and officials that were communist or sympathized with communism."[51] This was the path to ensure an efficient defense of democratic institutions. In a speech given in Rome, repeating the words of a critical intervention of his which he had delivered a few days prior in the lower house of parliament, Togni spurred the DC to "make a comeback" calling "all true Italians" to Italy's rescue. Thus the nation/anti-nation dialectic was being brought back: "Italy's foreign policy will never be a prestigious policy, recognized by all other countries, whilst Italy continues to harbor millions of people who are the subjects of a foreign power, who do not recognize Rome's law, but plot instead against Rome and the Italian people." Communists, anti-Italian by definition, were seen as "rapacious soldiers of fortune, descending from the northern mists to plunder the most sacred endowments of state and religion."[52]

The adhesion to western organizations managed by De Gasperi became,[53] as time unfolded, another element to be used to promote the conservative outlook, and not only in predictably anti-communist terms, but also in order to arrest any possible collaboration with the socialists. The anti-Atlantic positions of the socialists made that party entirely unreliable as regards international cooperation. The slow evolution of the PSI and Italy's unstable democracy imposed, in the mind of parts of the DC, a necessary but not easily attainable dialogue with the left. This issue is the one Aldo Moro would find himself grappling with in 1959, as his term as party secretary unfolded.

Fanfani spent the years from 1954 to 1959 shifting between mildly initiating and shrinking away from dialogue, whilst attempting to keep the party united and disciplined through a very authoritarian mode of leadership. This approach to power would eventually lead to a shift in the party's internal policies, fostering the rise of a heterogeneous front critical of Fanfani.

If the Vatican was gradually abandoning plans for a second Catholic party, despite Gedda's activism and initiatives such as Vanni Teodorani's clerical-fascist *Rivista Romana*, fractures within the party, political instability and demands for a more forceful opposition to communism contributed to create the threat of a secession.[54] A threat that became more menacing every time the issue of dialogue with the lefts arose. In the new internal structure of the party, those on the right, still struggling to create a definite profile for themselves, would side with the centrists in order to fight against suggestions of dialogue with the socialists.

Within the party, ecclesiastical vetoes clearly had great relevance. Opposition to the socialists was not solely about parliamentary dynamics, or the simple distrust of a party that had—unlike its European counterparts—engaged in Communist-like policies. It was about fundamentals, about different conceptions of life. In an article published in his current's magazine, Andreotti warned the DC not to make dangerous choices: "our responsibility would be grave, if we were to hold as democratic those people and groups that we have always considered natural enemies of our conception of life, both on a political and economic level, and as regards spiritual and religious values."[55] The impossibility of collaborating with the socialists sprung from different outlooks on life as well as from incompatibility in moral, religious, and political grounds; refusing to allow dialogue with them meant averting the danger of "the Tevere's waters" turning red.[56]

These stances were reintroduced from multiple sides through the evocation of De Gasperi's memory. It was in the name of De Gasperi's centrism that people such as Gonella and Scelba, as well as a young Oscar Luigi Scalfaro, opposed dialogue with the socialists, in the same way as Andreotti was doing from the pages of *Concretezza*. And it was a rereading of De Gasperi's experience that directed the course of Catholic philosopher Augusto del Noce's personal intellectual journey.

Some of these figures would eventually enter, often in a non-systemic, chaotic fashion, into Catholic political experiences that could be broadly defined as pertaining to the right of the political spectrum. A meaningful example of this is the fortnightly publication *L'Ordine Civile*, edited by Gianni Baget-Bozzo, with Gedda's support, between 1959 and 1960. The publication had amongst its collaborators various fascist supporters, in addition to Del Noce himself, and functioned as tool to express criticism of Fanfani and of the dialogue with the socialists, advocating instead for a strong state, on the lines of De Gaulle's France.[57]

Eventually, Moro's political talent in his term as secretary would allow the party to overcome opposition to interactions with the left. Moro found the path to ideological reconciliation of the party's heterogeneous currents, skilfully including the Catholic world in the process,[58] a world that had been changing its perspective on modernity through the Second Vatican Council. Unable to continue opposing such interactions after 1963, the right-wing current internal to the DC would fight for the chance to influence the construction of the center-left, thus preparing the battles that were to follow in subsequent years.

The possibility of a second Catholic party emerging was gradually fading. Persisting with the idea seemed obsolete and harmful even to Vatican conservative circles.[59] Amid the contradictions that existed amongst right-wing parties, the ecclesiastical will not to undermine the Catholic front, and the complex position of Christian Democrats' internal right-wing current—which aimed at representing even those conservatives that lay outside Catholic culture—the hypothesis of creating a second Catholic party weakened, despite still exercising a certain influence on party policy.

Notes

1. Agostino Giovagnoli, *La cultura democristiana* (Rome and Bari: Laterza, 1991), 157–186. On the topic, see also Chapter 31, this volume.
2. *L'organizzazione partitica del Pci e della DC*, ed. Gianfranco Poggi (Bologna: Il Mulino, 1968), 298–299; Gianni Baget-Bozzo, *Il partito cristiano e l'apertura a sinistra* (Florence: Vallecchi, 1977), 215. See also Chapter 14, this volume.
3. A description of the origin of the factions can be found in Vera Capperucci, *Il partito dei cattolici: dall'Italia degasperiana alle correnti dei cattolici* (Soveria Mannelli: Rubbettino, 2010). A shorter assessment, covering a longer time frame but rather partisan in its judgements can be read in Attilio Tempestini, "Le correnti democristiane: struttura e ideologia dal 1943 al 1980," in *Il Ponte*, no. 5 (1982), 457–475.
4. A first contribution is in Capperucci, "La destra democristiana," in *Storia delle destre nell'Italia repubblicana*, ed. Giovanni Orsina (Soveria Mannelli: Rubbettino, 2014), 41–84.
5. On Gentile see Alessandra Tarquini, *Il Gentile dei fascisti. Gentiliani e antigentiliani nel regime fascista* (Bologna: Il Mulino, 2009), 107–163.

6. Francesco Traniello, *Religione cattolica e stato nazionale. Dal risorgimento al secondo dopoguerra* (Bologna: Il Mulino, 2007), 221–264.

7. Emilio Gentile, *Contro Cesare. Cristianesimo e totalitarismi nell'epoca dei fascismi* (Milan: Feltrinelli, 2010), 81–230.

8. Andrea Riccardi, *Il partito romano nel secondo dopoguerra (1945–1954)* (Brescia: Morcelliana, 1983), 45.

9. On DC's vocation to govern, see Carlo Masala, "Born for government: the Democrazia Cristiana in Italy," in *Christian Democracy in Europe since 1945*, vol. 2, ed. Michael Gehler and Wolfram Kaiser (London and New York: Routledge, 2004), 101–117; Mark Donovan, "Democrazia Cristiana: Party of Government," in *Christian Democracy in Europe. A Comparative Perspective,* ed. David Hanley (London and New York: Pinter, 1994), 71–86.

10. Paolo Acanfora, "La Democrazia cristiana e il mito della nazione: le interpretazioni del Risorgimento," *Ricerche di storia politica*, no. 12 (2009), 177–196.

11. Acanfora, "Myths and the political use of religion in Christian Democratic Culture," *Journal of Modern Italian Studies*, no. 12 (2007), 307–338.

12. Giovanni Tassani, "Cattolici e destre. Dalle destre marginali o inespresse di ieri al centro-destra di governo di oggi" in *La nazione cattolica. Chiesa e società in Italia dal 1958 a oggi*, edited by Marco Impagliazzo (Milan: Guerini e Associati, 2004), 407.

13. Archivio Centrale dello Stato (hereafter: ACS), Ministero dell'Interno (hereafter: MI), Gabinetto Partiti Politici (hereafter: GPP), b. 57, fold. 165/P/93, document dated 23/4/1945.

14. ACS, MI, GPP, b. 57, fasc. 165/P/94-1, document dated March 5, 1945.

15. Luigi Gedda, for example, adamantly maintained that "the institutional question had divided those who supported the DC"; Augusto D'Angelo, "Il disegno politico di Luigi Gedda," *Giornale di storia contemporanea*, no. 2 (2010), 26.

16. ACS, MI, GPP, b. 57, fasc. 165/P/94-1, Direzione generale pubblica sicurezza (hereafter: DGPS), sec. I, document dated August 24, 1946.

17. Roberto Sani, *Da De Gasperi a Fanfani: la Civiltà cattolica e il mondo cattolico italiano nel secondo dopoguerra, 1945–1962* (Brescia: Morcelliana, 1986).

18. Sandro Setta, "La DC e i partiti di destra" in *Storia del movimento cattolico*, vol. 6, edited by Francesco Malgeri (Rome: Il Poligono, 1981), 192.

19. Ibid., 199.

20. Gentile, *La grande Italia. Ascesa e declino del mito della nazione nel ventesimo secolo* (Milan: Mondadori, 1997), 348–353.

21. Setta, "La DC e i partiti di destra," 212.

22. Ibid., 209.

23. Acanfora, "Myhts and the political use of religion in Christian democratic party," 318–319.

24. Gentile, "La nazione del fascismo. Alle origini del declino dello stato nazionale," in *Nazione e nazionalità in Italia*, edited by Giovanni Spadolini (Rome and Bari: Laterza, 1994), 65–124.

25. Alcide De Gasperi, "Il programma della Democrazia cristiana" (February 1944) in *Atti e documenti della Democrazia cristiana, 1943–1967*, vol. 1, edited by Andrea Damilano (Rome: Cinque Lune, 1968), 49.

26. Luigi Sturzo, "Travaglio intimo degli italiani" in *Il Popolo*, February 8, 1951.

27. Speech by Stefano Jacini to the Senate, July 29, 1949, published in Jacini, *Consiglio d'Europa e patto atlantico* (Rome: Tipografia del Senato, 1949), 30.

28. Tassani, "Cattolici e destre," 408.

29. Pierluigi Allotti, *Giornalisti di regime. La stampa italiana tra fascismo e antifascismo (1922–1948)* (Rome: Carocci, 2012), 191–221.

30. Archivio Storico dell'Istituto Luigi Sturzo, (hereafter: ASILS) Fondo Giulio Rodinò, fold. 51.1, letter by R. Ronca to G. Rodinò, dated between December 12, 1944 and June 19, 1945.

31. Stefano Reggio d'Aci, "Il colpo di spugna e la fiducia nella giustizia" in *Il Popolo*, July 9, 1944.

32. Reggio d'Aci, "La legge contro i delitti fascisti" in *Il Popolo*, June 23, 1944.

33. Mario Casella, *18 aprile 1948. La mobilitazione delle organizzazioni cattoliche* (Galatina: Congedo editore, 1992).

34. G. L. Mosse, *La cultura dell'Europa occidentale nell'Ottocento e nel Novecento* (Milan: Mondadori, 1987), 482–483.

35. "Cento ragioni" in *Il Popolo*, April 15, 1948.

36. L.A. Mondini, "Dovere di italiani" in *Il Popolo*, April 18, 1948.

37. ASILS, Democrazia cristiana, consigli nazionali (hereafter: cn), box 3, fold. 8, speech by Attilio Piccioni, May 4, 1948.

38. ASILS, DC, cn, box 4, fold. 9, speech by Mario Cingolani, July 26, 1948.

39. ASILS, DC, cn, box 4, fold. 11, speech by Umberto Merlin, December 21, 1948.

40. ASILS, DC, Segreteria politica (hereafter: SP), AS/5-Gonella/UC-corrispondenza, box. 13, fold. 1, marked "riservatissima personale" to the Secretary of the Spes Giorgio Tupini by Attilio Crepas, September 28, 1950.

41. ASILS, DC, Direzione nazionale, box. 4, fold. 44, speech by Paolo Emilio Taviani, July 16, 1949.

42. The Movement, born in 1919, was rebuilt on November 20, 1945, and from June 28, 1947 adopted the acronym MACI, and the motto "Christ or Death".

43. ASILS, SP, AS/5-Gonella/UC-corrispondenza, box. 13, fold. 1, note from the central secretary of MACI to Giorgio Tupini, May 13, 1950.

44. ACS, MI, GPP, b. 107, fold. 1408, confidential letter, April 9, 1952.

45. ASILS, DC, cn, box 4, fold. 11, speech by Stefano Jacini, December 21, 1948.

46. ACS, MI, DGPS, AA.GG. e RR. (General Confidential Affairs), 1950, b. 25, memo dated December 21, 1950.

47.. D'Angelo, *De Gasperi le destre e l'operazione Sturzo* (Rome: Studium, 2002).

48. Ibid., 79.

49. Michele Marchi, "Politica e religione dal centrismo al centrosinistra. Luigi Gedda, i Comitati civici, l'Azione cattolica e la Santa Sede" in *Mondo contemporaneo*, no. 1 (2013), 43–89.

50. ASILS, Congressi nazionali, box 5, fold. 6, sub-folder. 1, speech by Giulio Andreotti at the Fifth National Congress, June 29, 1954.

51. ACS, MI, DGPS, AAGG e RR, 1954, b. 26, conference by Giuseppe Togni, province of Livorno, October 11, 1954.

52. ACS, MI, DGPS, AAGG e RR, 1954, b. 27, speech by Giuseppe Togni, Rome, October 31, 1954.

53. Guido Formigoni, *La Democrazia cristiana e l'alleanza occidentale* (Bologna: Il Mulino, 1996) and Acanfora, *Miti e ideologia nella politica estera DC. Nazione, Europa e comunità atlantica (1943–1954)* (Bologna: Il Mulino, 2013).

54. Giovanni Tassani, *La cultura politica della destra cattolica* (Rome: Coines, 1976), 68.

55. Andreotti, "Appunti per Trento" in *Concretezza*, October 1, 1956.

56. Andreotti, "Il Tevere rosso" in *Concretezza*, November 15, 1956.

57. Giovanni Tassani, *Il Belpaese dei cattolici* (Siena: Cantagalli, 2010), 207–212. On the topic, also see Eugenio Capuozzi, "Nuova destra cattolica e riformismo istituzionale: l'eredità della terza generazione democristiana" in *Ventunesimo Secolo*, no. 30 (2013), 119–129.

58. D'Angelo, *Moro i vescovi e l'apertura a sinistra* (Rome: Studium, 2005).

59. See, for example, the observations Cardinal Siri made on Gedda; D'Angelo, "Il disegno politico di Luigi Gedda," 39.

....

CHAPTER 33

RELIGIOUS DIFFERENTIATION AND NEW RELIGIONS IN ITALY

....

ROBERTO CIPRIANI AND VERÓNICA ROLDÁN

COMPARED with a past when Italy was dominated by the Catholic Church, which influenced practically every area of community life (steering preference in favor of certain political parties and orienting social and ethical choices), the situation at the time of writing in 2015 appears less homogeneous, more subject to variation at both national and local levels.[1] Dedicated centers have been set up to study and observe developing phenomena as well as the dynamics relative to legislation. For example, the Osservatorio delle Libertà ed Istituzioni Religiose (OLIR, Observatory of Religious Freedom and Institutions) is collecting data on law and religions in collaboration with the Ufficio Studi e Rapporti Istituzionali (the Institutional Studies and Relations Office), an agency for religious denominational affairs and the institutional relations of the prime minister's office. In Milan, the Centro Ambrosiano di Dialogo con le Religioni (the Ambrosian Center for Dialogue with Religions) provides a wealth of documentation regarding the agreements between the Italian state and the religious denominations, as per Article 8 of the Constitution of the Italian Republic.

According to Article 47 of Law no. 222 of May 20, 1985, the following religious organizations may receive eight per thousand (8 euros for every 1,000 euros paid) of Private Income Tax returns: the Roman Catholic Church, the Waldensian Church, the Italian Union of 7th-Day Adventist Churches, the Assemblies of God in Italy, the Union of Italian Jewish Communities, the Evangelical Lutheran Church in Italy, the Christian Evangelical Baptist Union of Italy, the Holy Orthodox Archdiocese of Italy and Exarchate of Southern Europe, the Apostolic Church in Italy, the Italian Hindu Union, the Italian Buddhist Union. Furthermore, Italian taxpayers may deduct from private income sums of up to 1,032.91 euros in favor of the above-mentioned congregations (as well as of the Church of Jesus Christ of Latter-Day Saints).

Under Law no. 400 of August 23, 1988, Article 2, paras i) and l), assigned to the Cabinet of Ministers the task of deliberating on matters concerning relations between the state and the Catholic Church as well as issues indicated in the aforementioned Article 8 of the Italian Constitution: "All religious denominations enjoy equal freedom before the law. Religious denominations other than Roman Catholicism have the right to organize according to their own statutes, as long as they do not enter into conflict with the Italian legal system. Their relations with the State are regulated by law according to agreements stipulated with their respective representatives."

According to Article 14, Decree no. 300 of July 30 1999, the Home Office is charged, among other things with "safeguarding civil rights, including those of religious denominations."

Furthermore, a General Secretariat is called upon—according to Decree no. 303, Article 12, para 10 of July 30, 1999—to "assist the Prime Minister in the performance of his/her institutional duties regarding relations with the religious denominations, subject to the powers of the Home Office as per Article 14 par. 2 let. *d* of law no. 300/1999."

Over the years, various committees have been set up to handle questions regarding both the Concordat (relations between the Italian state and the Roman Catholic Church, following the Concordat of 1929 and the Agreement of 1984) and agreements with other denominations, according to constitutional principles and the laws relating to freedom of conscience, religion, and belief.

Furthermore, the Italian state has been granted the right to distinguish between "authentic" and "non-authentic" religion, and recognize the rights thus ensuing. From this stems a further fundamental socio-political issue, that relating to religious freedom,[2] as well as to the freedom to change religions and the legal recognition of marriages, including mixed unions between subjects belonging to different religious affiliations.

In other words, it is an issue of equality among citizens whatever their religion or non-religion may be. The year 1984 saw the beginning of a series of agreements with other religions; on September 13, 1991 parliament rejected a bill regarding religious freedom, a bill which had been approved by the Cabinet led by the then Prime Minister Giulio Andreotti, and later endorsed by the Commission for Constitutional Affairs. The aim was to replace legislation on "recognized cults" that was passed in fascist times, and to remodel the fragmentary nature of government regulations on religious affairs in order to create impartial, pluralist state legislation that expressed openness toward all cultures, religions, traditions, and innovation.

But perhaps the most complex question that remains to be addressed today is the relationship between culture and religion and between politics and religion. If a religious practice is recognized, its associated cultural features must also be accepted—for example, the veil worn by Islamic women, the exhibition of the Christian cross in public places, the inclusion or not of religion or religions as subjects in school curricula,[3] religious dietary customs, the areas reserved to the different denominations in cemeteries, the more or less patent public display of symbols of faith and so on.

THE NEW ITALIAN REALITY

Since 2007 there has been a manifest increase in Italy in the number of Orthodox believers, in particular people from Romania and Bulgaria, who will probably be joined by other Christians of the Catholic religion because Croatia has joined the European Union as its twenty-eighth member. The figure of 2.6 percent for religions other than Roman Catholicism, recorded in a survey dating 1995,[4] is likely to increase.

Meanwhile, in 2007, Franco Garelli calculated the numbers of non-Catholics in Italy at around 5 percent,[5] pointing to the increase in Muslim (over the past 40 years) and Orthodox Christian (over the past ten years) immigrants in Italy as a major contributory cause. As Garelli observes, Islam and the Orthodox Church (or rather the Orthodox Churches on the whole, regardless of nationality) are competing, as far as numbers are concerned, for second place in Italy after the Roman Catholic Church.

The percentage of non-religious seems to be increasing, although by only a bare 0.3 compared with 1995, rising from 8.8 percent to 9.1 percent. To these we may add the minority of those who believe without belonging to a church and those who belong without believing.

If Muslims and Orthodox Christians represent the most recent addition to the contemporary Italian religious scenario, one should not fail to mention the increase of other denominations and practices, some of which (Hindus and Buddhists) have been present in the country for five decades now, while others have taken root more recently.

However, the most recent development is the massive influx of Orthodox Christians, above all Romanians (841,000, though some believe the figure to be 968,576 or even 1,110,000), Ukrainians (168,000), Moldavians (122,000), Macedonians (49,000) and Albanians (42,000), and an almost analogous number of Bulgarians (51,000). The The Statistical Dossier on Immigration informs us that, in 2011,[6] 5,011,307 foreigners resided in Italy, of whom 2,702,074 were Christians (1,482,648 Orthodox Christians, 960,359 Catholics, 222,960 Protestants, 36,107 other Christian denominations), 1,650,902 Muslims, 131,254 Hindus, 97,362 Buddhists, 7,300 Jews, and 69,215 the members of other oriental religions, while those practicing other traditional religions numbered 50,498. The non-religious (atheists, agnostics, the indifferent) totaled 215,135, while 87,567 claimed being of another persuasion.

In percentages, the greatest increase has occurred among the Christians in the broad sense, with numbers rising from 44.6 percent in 1991 to 49.8 percent in 2009 (one should emphasize the increment to 28.9 percent of the Orthodox Christians) while all the other religions remained at much the same level as in the past.

Proof of the increase in Italy of Orthodox Christians is the fact that, in 2011, there were as many as 35 Orthodox churches in Rome alone. In Italy there are 355 Orthodox parishes, 166 of which refer to the Romanian Patriarch, a further 84 to the

Patriarch of Constantinople, and 44 to that of Moscow.[7] This is a relatively recent development.

On the other hand, the numbers of those who practice the Islamic religion seem to have stood still or increased only marginally, along with religions other than Christian. There are about one and a half million Muslims in Italy at the time of writing. This leads one to surmise that, in the near future, issues regarding relations between religion and politics, religion and the Italian state will see the Islamic religion and the Orthodox Churches at the forefront and lead to juridical discussions, linked also to differences between subjects from EU member states and people from other nations.

As such statistics are not easy to draw up, due to the fact that religious affiliation is not usually included in the data found in official archives, documents and sources in this country, we must resort to the figures provided by immigrants' mother countries to weigh their distribution in the country they have chosen to reside in; in other words, we attribute to immigrants the same percentiles as those likely to have applied had they chosen to remain in their home countries. These calculations are, therefore, only approximate estimates.

The data available for the many other religiously oriented subjects residing in Italy, whether Sikhs, Jehovah's Witnesses, Mormons, Shintoists, and so on, are so fragmentary that they are difficult piece together.

However, the following points are clear:

1) the majority of those who emigrate to Italy are members of a Christian church and account for about half of all the immigrant population;

2) of the Christian immigrants, members of the Orthodox Church account for the lion's share, even compared with Catholics, while Protestants appear to be the minority;

3) Muslims comprise the second most numerous religious group in terms of numbers and communities in Italy;

4) Hindus and Buddhists account for only a very small percentage (around 3 percent);

5) figures for both Jews and other religions are even smaller than figures for Hindus and Buddhists;

6) non-believers amount to about 12 percent;

7) the Orthodox presence has increased also thanks to flows from Greece, Egypt, Ethiopia, and Eritrea;

8) Muslims (especially Moroccans) are concentrated mainly in regions such as Puglia, Sicilia, Trentino Alto Adige, Valle d'Aosta, Romagna, Marche, Lombardy, and Lazio;

9) the numbers of Hindus and Buddhists in Italy are almost identical, though the former are slightly more numerous;

10) the Italian Sikh population (30,000 people only) is a special case. They live above all in northern Italy, especially in the Po valley, where they look after livestock;

11) Philippinos and Bangladeshis account for numerical increase since the 1970s, the former in the Catholic and Protestant, the latter in the Muslim population;
12) most Indian immigrants in Italy are Hindus;
13) most of those from Sri Lanka are Buddhists;
14) among Africans there is a prevalence of traditional religions (animism, but also blends of historical religions and ancestral practice).

OTHER RELIGIONS AMONG
ITALIAN CITIZENS

If one pays particular attention to Italy's "autochthonous" population, it emerges that those who embrace creeds other than Roman Catholicism are a small minority. And yet the "new" denominations are quite numerous, as is a widespread perception of growing religious pluralism, which may be seen as indicative of a kind of modernity inclined to appreciate freedom of individual inquiry and a broad range of religious choices.

According to the results of a pluriannual survey carried out by Turin's Centro Studi sulle Nuove Religioni (New Religions Study Center), led by Massimo Introvigne, today, about 2.5 percent of the national Italian population claims professing a faith other than Roman Catholicism and being a member of one of the creeds we find within the multifarious range of historical and recently installed religions. The data published in the latest edition of the *Enciclopedia delle religioni in Italia* (The Encyclopaedia of Religions in Italy) revealed that 836 religions are practiced in this country (compared with 616 in 2001 and 647 in 2006),[8] but that the number of those who belong to these congregations, be they "historical" creeds or "new religious movements", is limited.

Scholars and experts of religious matters hold that the actual congregations of many of these denominations, however relevant they may be from a cultural and typological point of view, are infinitesimal, so that, rather than "an invasion of other religions," one might speak of an "invasion of denominations." In any case, in Italy, that sector of the population (2.5 percent of the whole) which claims a religious identity different from Roman Catholicism accounts for 1,417,000 out of a total population of 60,820,764.[9] Italian religious diversity is illustrated in Table 33.1.

This degree of religious diversity among Italians brings with it certain consequences in relation to relations between the state and civil society, which, as far as the explicitly religious scenario is concerned, entails interaction between the state and non-Catholic denominations; and this in turn has a direct impact on the question of religious freedom, which, in last three decades has led to political, juridical, sociological, philosophical, and historical consideration of the need to adapt the Italian legal system to the country's present-day religious situation.

Table 33.1 Italian religious minorities (2012 estimate)

	Total	%
Jews	36,000	2.5%
"Fringe" and dissident Roman Catholics	25,000	1.8%
Orthodox Christians	110,000	7.8%
Protestants	435,000	30.7%
Jehovah's Witnesses (and analogous)	415,000	29.3%
Mormons (and analogous)	25,000	1.8%
Other Christian creeds	5,000	0.4%
Muslims	115,000	8.1%
Baha'i and other religions of Islamic inspiration	4,000	0.3%
Hindus and neo-Hindus	26,000	1.8%
Buddhists	135,000	9.5%
Osho and derivative groups	4,000	0.3%
Sikh, Radha Swami and derivative groups	6,000	0.4%
Other oriental groups	2,000	0.1%
New Japanese religions	3,000	0.2%
Exoteric and "ancient wisdom" groups	15,000	1.1%
Human potential groups	30,000	2.1%
Organized New Age and Next Age groups	20,000	1.4%
Others	6,000	0.4%
Total	**1,417,000**	100.0%

Source: Massimo Introvigne and Pierluigi Zoccatelli (eds), Enciclopedia delle religioni in Italia (Leumann: Elledici, 2013), 8.

RELATIONS BETWEEN THE STATE AND RELIGIOUS CONFESSIONS IN ITALY (1848–2013)

The following is a brief historical account of how the theme of relationships between the state and religious denominations was addressed on several occasions with a view to producing norms compatible with the country's multifaceted jurisprudential, historical, and political make-up.

From a historical point of view, February 17, 1848 is a seminal date; it was the date when King Carlo Alberto granted religious freedom, by promulgating the *Lettere patenti* (Patent Letters), permitting the Waldesian Protestants "to enjoy all the (same) civil and political rights as Our subjects."[10] At the same time, with the enforcement of the *Statuto Albertino* (Albertine Statute) of 1848, which remained a fundamental law of the Kingdom of Italy until 1948, the Roman Catholic and Apostolic Church was proclaimed the "only religion of the state." Other creeds were permitted, on the other hand, to be "tolerated compatibly with the law." This concession initially related to the Waldesian Church, then the Jewish community, and was eventually extended to embrace all the other evangelical religions practiced in the country.

In 1848, Count Camillo Benso di Cavour, destined to become the protagonist of Piedmontese politics until the foundation of the Kingdom of Italy in 1861, the year of his death—according to Michele Madonna (2011) statements in a historical study of religious freedom in Italy—stated being "greatly disappointed at the lack of recognition of full Constitutional 'freedom of worship,' a principle which, in his opinion, should not be introduced indirectly into the constitution of a highly civilized people, but be proclaimed as 'one of the fundamental premises of the social covenant.'" The future statesman expressed, however, the hope that Article 1 might simply take the form of a "tribute to the Catholic religion." Upon closer examination, this hope reflected reality. A clear provision favoring a denomination does not prevent the simultaneous development of legislation designed to guarantee the equality of citizens regardless of religious affiliation. A few weeks prior to the adoption of the constitution, in February 1848, the sovereign issued letters patent to "emancipate" the Waldensians, while at the end of March of the same year, Jews were accorded civil rights, and in April gained access to military office.

But above all, the Sineo Law (June 19, 1848) established in its single article, that "religious difference does not pose an obstacle to the enjoyment of civil and political rights or to eligibility for civil and military offices." It is a broad statement of the equality of all citizens, whatever their denomination, a formula open to other religions, new compared to those previously "emancipated."[11]

In March 1871, the Italian House of Deputies voted the "Mancini" Order of the Day, which established equality in the eyes of the state of all religions as far as personal freedom of creed was concerned. This separatist state of affairs continued until the Patti Lateranensi (Lateran Pacts) of 1929, a Concordat between the Roman Catholic Church and the Fascist state. Article 1 of this agreement stated that "the Roman Catholic Christian and Apostolic faith was the official religion of the state" while the Kingdom of Italy "admitted" the other denominations.

Although, at first sight, this represented a statutory improvement for all the non-Catholic creeds, which, rather than being "tolerated" were now "admitted" according to Law no. 1159 of 1929. In practice, however, many of the restrictions laid down by regulations regarding public order and the "admitted creeds" remained. The congregations that were not as yet recognized—for example, the Pentecostal churches, the Salvation Army, and Jehovah's Witnesses—were heavily discriminated against and, at times, even arrested and banished.

Article 2 of the same law (no. 1159/1929) also proclaimed that "institutions other than the state religion might be considered charitable organizations" and accorded juridical status. This gave some denominations the possibility of becoming legal entities.[12]

In 1948, the Republican Constitution recognized "equal freedom" of practice and the right for religions to be founded and draw up their own statutes. In Article 7, the Constitution accepted the Lateran Pacts of 1929 *in toto* without amending them, but

Article 8 pointed out that "all religious confessions are equally free in the eyes of the law." The third clause of this article established that relations between the state and the non-Catholic creeds were to be regulated by *Settlements*, that is, by bilateral agreements.

The previous laws (no. 810/1929, and no. 1159/1929) regarding the "admitted creeds" remained in force, and were only partially abrogated by the Constitutional Court at the beginning of the 1960s in keeping with the new attitudes expressed by the Roman Catholic Church from the Second Vatican Council.

Articles 3, 19, 20, and 21 of the Constitution also recognized the equality of citizens regardless of creed, the equal freedom of all religions, and the right for people to practice their various faiths. Citizens, foreigners, and the stateless were allowed to propagate and practice their relative faiths, on the sole condition that their rites did not breach Italian laws of common decency.

Yet the third clause of Article 8 of the Constitution, that regarding the Settlements, was not applied immediately and had to await the mid 1970's before transactions regarding the first Settlement with the Waldesian Church were begun and endorsed by the then Prime Minister Bettino Craxi (Italian Socialist Party) on February 21, 1984, a week after ratification of a new Concordat with the Roman Catholic Church, which abolished some of the norms incompatible with religious freedom.

On November 22, 1988 Settlements were made between the Italian Republic and the Adventist Church and Assemblies of God. This first set of Settlements concluded with those established with the Union of Italian Jewish Communities, on February 8, 1989,[13] with the Christian Evangelical Baptist Union of Italy, on April 12, 1995, and with the Evangelical Lutheran Church in Italy, on November 29, 1995.

From the 1980s, however slowly, changes were introduced to safeguard religious freedom in Italy, within the context of a religiously and culturally pluralist and essentially secular state. Sentence no. 203 of April 11, 1989 revoked the "compulsory" teaching of the Roman Catholic religion in Italian state schools. In a series of sentences (no. 440 of October 18, 1995, no. 329 of November 14, 1997, no. 508 of November 13, 2000, no. 327 of July 9, 2002, no. 168 of April 18, 2005), the Constitutional Tribunal, referring to the principle of secularity, declared the privileged position regarding matters of penal law enjoyed by the Roman Catholic Church to be illegitimate. The entire issue was reformed in 2006 when all religions were placed on an equal footing, even in terms of town planning, namely church buildings (an Abruzzi regional law of 1988 and a Lombard regional law of 1992); previously the concession of benefits was subject to the stipulation of a Settlement with the state.[14]

Today, for the congregations that have stipulated Settlements with the state, particular laws apply and are subject to implementation by the Minister of the Interior. July 30 and December 31, 2012, during Mario Monti's Government (technical government), parliament approved the last five Settlements. In 2013, therefore, the following Settlements were approved by law:

- The Waldesian Church (Law no. 449, August 11, 1984; Law no. 409, October 5, 1993; Law no. 68, June 18, 2009);

- The Italian Union of Seventh-day Adventist Christian Churches (Law no. 516, November 22, 1988; Law no. 637, December 20, 1996; Law no. 67, June 8, 2009);
- The Assemblies of God in Italy (Law no. 517, November 22, 1988);
- The Union of Italian Jewish Communities (Law, no. 101, March 8, 1989; Law no. 638, December 20, 1996);
- The Christian Evangelical Baptist Union of Italy (UCEBI) (Law no. 116, April 12, 1995; Law no. 34 of April 4, 2012);
- The Evangelical Lutheran Church in Italy (CELI) (Law no. 520, November 29, 1995);
- The Holy Orthodox Archdiocese of Italy and Exarchate of Southern Europe (Law no. 126, July 30, 2012);
- The Church of Jesus Christ of Latter-day Saints (Law no. 127, July 30, 2012);
- The Apostolic Church in Italy (Law no. 128, July 30, 2012);
- The Italian Buddhist Union (Law no. 245, Dec. 31, 2012);
- The Italian Hindu Union Sanatana Dharma Samgha (Law no. 246, December 31, 2012)[15].

A Settlement with the Christian Congregation of Jehovah Witnesses was signed on April 4, 2007.

A New Bill Concerning Religious Freedom

Between the end of the 1980s and the early 1990s, a need was felt for a general law governing religious freedom. This was because at that time many new denominations extraneous to the country's age-old Judaic-Christian tradition—such as Islam (practiced by many immigrants[16]), Buddhism, Baha'i, as well as a number of atypical Christian creeds like the Jehovah's Witnesses and the Mormons—had become an integral part of the Italian religious scenario.

In 1989, the then head of government, Ciriaco De Mita (Christian Democrat), declared that a new law regulating freedom of religion, capable of surpassing the old 1929 laws of "admitted creeds" was needed. This proposal was taken up again by Giulio Andreotti's (1989–1992, Christian Democrat) government, but the bill did not even make it to the parliament.

During Giuliano Amato's (1992–1993, Italian Socialist Party) government further Settlements were signed with the Baptist and Lutheran churches and ratified during Silvio Berlusconi's (Forza Italia) and Lamberto Dini's (1994–1995, technical government) terms of office.

The bill concerning religious freedom was introduced again during the 13th Legislature headed by a left-center Ulivo government (in office from May 9, 1996 to May 29, 2001) led, in turn, by Romano Prodi, Massimo D'Alema, and Giuliano Amato. In this instance, Domenico Maselli, a Christian Socialist, Evangelical pastor and historian of Christianity, was appointed rapporteur, but the bill did not make it to the final vote. In view of changes within the religious ambit in Italy, Maselli sought to promote a general law which did not exclude but, rather, facilitated the stipulation of Settlements between the state and non-Catholic creeds, whose members were also non-Italians. It is important to point out that the state can legally stipulate Settlements only with Italian citizens who represent religions practiced in the country.

An *erga omnes* law proposed securing individual rights and the legal obligations governing cohabitation, while the system of Settlements had the task of guaranteeing the particular needs of single religions. Among the changes recommended was to make the Department for Religious Creeds autommomous (it was originally part of the Ministry of Justice, later of the Minister of the Interior), or else that the Prefects and not the Police be put in charge of religious matters. The overarching idea was that relations between the state and religion should not appear to be a matter of "public order."

The Prodi government re-opened Settlement negotiations, almost completing agreements with the Jehovah's Witnesses and Buddhists; but, on the eve of ratification, matters entered a stalemate, and had to wait five more years in the case of the Buddhists, while the Settlement with the Jehovah's Witnesses has not been concluded to date.

In 2001, when Valdo Spini (Democratic Left) reintroduced a new bill regarding freedom of religion, Silvio Berlusconi, the head of government, declared being in favor and Mario Bondi was appointed rapporteur. But, due to the opposition of Umberto Bossi's Northern League, the bill was rejected once again.

A further attempt was made in the parliament during the following legislature, and the bill was championed by Valdo Spini and Marco Boato (Green Party) with Roberto Zaccaria (Democratic Party) as rapporteur, while Lucio Malan (Forza Italia) presented a similar bill in the Senate. But after several hearings by the Commission for Constitutional Affairs, in which representatives of all the religious confessions took part, and following lengthy discussions, the bill was postponed once more.

The various proposals, despite a few differences, tend to be homogeneous: their first part is dedicated to individual and collective freedom of religion, the second refers to the legal position of religious denominations and the third deals with procedures accruing to the stipulation of a Settlement.

It is clear from the above that a general law on religious freedom in Italy has not been forthcoming to date, despite support for such a law from various political movements (both center-right and center-left, with the exception of Northern League), and the favor expressed by the various religious organizations, and notwithstanding the objections raised by the Catholic Church and other denominations regarding the general configuration of the proposed bills.

At the time of writing, the parliamentary journey of the religious freedom issue has ground to a halt, but the following commissions of the Prime Minister's office have been set up to address issues concerning ecclesiastical affairs and religious freedom:[17]

- The Inter-ministerial Commission for Settlements with the religious denominations;
- The Religious Freedom Advisory Committee;
- The Government Commission for the implementation of the provisions as per the Agreement between the Holy See and Italy, signed on February 18, 1984 and ratified by Law no. 121 of March 25, 1985;
- The Government Commission for the solution of the difficulties encountered when interpreting the rules and regulations of the Concordat;
- The Government Commission for the revision of the personal income tax deductions and shares with a view to carrying out changes;
- The Commission for the recovery of the bibliographic heritage of Rome's Jewish community, pillaged in 1943;
- The Committee for the co-ordination of Shoah memorial ceremonies.

CONCLUSIONS

Italian Law foresees different kinds of relational modes between the state and religious denominations. The first mode concerns the Roman Catholic Church, which stipulated a Concordat with the state in 1929 and ratified it in 1984. This is an "international agreement" between two sovereign states, Italy and the Vatican. It envisages not only religious freedom but concessions regarding other matters such as the inclusion of the Catholic religion as a subject in Italian state-school curricula, the display of Roman Catholic symbols in public places, the salaried presence of Catholic chaplains in the army and in prisons, the reservation of transmission time for religious programmes on the state radio and television networks.

Another mode is that regarding relations between the state and non-Catholic religions and their representatives, regulated by Settlements. This does not have the same juridical and constitutional status as the Concordat reserved only to the Roman Catholic Church, whose exclusive historical and cultural role the Fathers of the Constitution wished to acknowledge.

Settlements are stipulated with those religious denominations which are structured, organized, hierarchical, and whose leaders have the authority to represent the faithful and interact with the state on their behalf: for example, the Waldesian Synod and the chairman of the Italian Jewish Communities. A Settlement is a bilateral agreement between the state and the authorities of the religious confession in question. This is why a Settlement with the Islamic faith is difficult to put into practice given the absence of a hierarchical structure capable of representing the various Islamic realities present in Italy.

Then there are the "admitted creeds," declared such by Law no. 1159 passed by the Mussolini Government in 1929 and still in force, concerning the majority of the many non-Catholic religions practiced in this country. This law foresees two levels of recognition, one for confessions with juridical status, another for those devoid of it. The latter can only obtain official recognition of their ministers for the celebration of civil marriages and ministry in hospitals and prisons.

Finally, there are also religious communities that have no form of legal or administrative recognition, at times due to their own choice, at others because of bureaucratic difficulties.

Concluding, we can say that the Italian scenario, characterized historically by a culturally and religiously homogeneous tradition, is today quite variegated.[18] Although the diversities are limited, their social significance is far greater than their statistical value. Of considerable interest is the prevailing perception that society in Italy is now multi-ethnic and multidenominational. Of comparable importance is the fact that the immigrant population in Italy now numbers 4,859,000, equal to 8.0 percent of the whole population (higher than the EU average which stands at 6.6 percent). These immigrants, thanks to their cultural and religious practices, have brought the national figures for non-Catholic practice up from 2.5 percent to 7,[19] and have thus made a considerable contribution towards change in the composition of Italian society, which, to those who live here, spells pluralism, multiculturalism, and multi-denominationalism. In this context, politics and the law are called on to address this new social complexity born of an increasingly varied religious reality.

Notes

1. Francesco Margiotta Broglio, *Religione, diritto e cultura politica nell'Italia del Novecento* (Bologna: Il Mulino, 2011).
2. Alessandro Ferrari, *La libertà religiosa in Italia. Un percorso incompiuto* (Rome: Carocci, 2012).
3. *IRInews: Insegnare le Religioni in Italia*, quarterly review edited by Mariachiara Giorda, Current documents, opinions on the teaching of religion and religious studies in Italy (IRInews2010@gmail.com).
4. Vincenzo Cesareo, Roberto Cipriani, Franco Garelli, Clemente Lanzetti, and Giancarlo Rovati, *La religiosità in Italia* (Milan: Arnoldo Mondadori Editore, 1995), 330.
5. Franco Garelli, *Religione all'italiana* (Bologna: Il Mulino, 2011); see also Franco Garelli, "Flexible Catholicism, Religion and the Church: The Italian Case," *Religions*, no. 4 (2013), 1–13.
6. Dossier Statistico Immigrazione 2012 (Rome: Idos, 2012).
7. Giuseppe Giordan, "La costellazione delle chiese ortodosse in Italia," in Enzo Pace (ed.), *Le religioni nell'Italia che cambia. Mappe e bussole* (Rome: Carocci, 2013).
8. Massimo Introvigne, Pierluigi Zoccatelli, Nelly Ippolito Macrina, and Verónica Roldán, *Enciclopedia delle Religioni in Italia* (Leumann: Elledici, 2001); Massimo Introvigne and Pierluigi Zoccatelli, (eds.), *Le religioni in Italia*, (Leumann: Elledici, 2006).
9. Demographic data, issued in 2012 by the National Statistics Agency.
10. Paolo Naso, *Protestanti, evangelici, Testimoni e Santi*, in Enzo Pace, *Le religioni nell'Italia che cambia. Mappe e bussole* (Rome: Carocci, 2013), 99.

11. Michele Madonna, *Breve storia della libertà religiosa in Italia. Aspetti giuridici e problemi pratici* (2011), <http://www.treccani.it/enciclopedia/breve-storia-della-liberta-religiosa-in-italia-aspetti-giuridici-e-problemi-pratici_(Cristiani_d'Italia)/>.

12. Today, recognition of the legal status of institutions (organizations, associations, or foundations) of this kind of confession is conceded after careful and detailed investigation by the office responsible for these affairs and is granted by decree of the President of the Republic at the proposal of the Home Office, in consultation wtih the Board of State and the Council of Ministers.

13. Enzo Pace, *Le religioni nell'Italia che cambia. Mappe e bussole* (Rome: Carocci, 2013), 133.

14. Michele Madonna, *Breve storia della libertà religiosa in Italia. Aspetti giuridici e problemi pratici* (2011), cit.

15. See the website of the Italian Minister of the Interior: <http://www.interno.gov.it/mininterno/export/sites/default/it/temi/religioni/sottotema002.html.>.

16. Stefano Allievi, *Islam italiano. Viaggio nella seconda religione del paese* (Turin: Einaudi, 2003).

17. < http://www.governo.it/Presidenza/USRI/confessioni/commissioni.html>.

18. Enzo Pace, *Vecchi e nuovi dei. La geografia religiosa dell'Italia che cambia* (Milan: Edizioni Paoline, 2011).

19. Introvigne and Zoccatelli, *Enciclopedia delle religioni in Italia*.

CHAPTER 34

....

THE LAITY

....

MASSIMO TEODORI

THE term lay is used to refer to a political current running through Italian history in the nineteenth and twentieth centuries, and has its origin in the Italian Unification (Risorgimento), when Italian unity and the nation state came into being in antithesis to the Church and Catholic movements. Contributing to the unification process, and to the construction of the national spirit, were two main lay political currents, the Right and the Left. The Liberal Right, also known as the Historical Right, had its roots in the Kingdom of Sardinia, and in its capital, Turin. The current's main exponent was the Kingdom's Prime Minister, Camillo Benso Conte di Cavour, who had taken office in November 1852. In February 1861 he became prime minister of the newly created Kingdom of Italy, and remained in that role until his death on June 6 of that same year. Cavour was responsible, alongside other representatives of the liberal current, for the main lay innovations that marked the unification process. In the Kingdom of Sardinia that meant the emancipation of Jews and Waldensians—who were granted equality, in terms of civil rights, regardless of their religious beliefs—and the nationalization of the educational system previously controlled by the Jesuits, who were excluded from public life and whose property was seized. In 1850 the Siccardi Laws abolished the ecclesiastical courts, the legal institution of clerical immunity, and the right of asylum in the Church's premises. It also revoked tax reductions for the clergy, disbanded contemplative religious orders, and confiscated their possessions. It liquidated seized Church properties, and it forbade religious bodies to add to their wealth without the monarch's authorization. In 1861, in the wake of the Kingdom's foundation, Cavour used the expression "a free Church in a free nation," that would inspire the many nineteenth-century lay and liberal currents, to articulate the principle of Church–State separation. As Italian territorial unity advanced, Turin parliament's lay legislation was extended first to northern, then to central and southern Italy, until the conquest of Rome on September 20, 1870. From 1861 to 1976, the governments lead by the Historical Right and presided over by liberals such as Bettino Ricasoli, Marco Minghetti, Alfonso La Marmora, and Giovanni Lanza, undertook a secularization of the new state through legislation and administrative regulations such as the suppression of state contributions to the Church, the introduction of civil marriage, and the elimination of ecclesiastical bodies. In 1871, after the military conquest of Rome snatched the city from papal rule, the Law of Guarantees (*Legge delle Guarentigie*) was passed: it safeguarded papal freedom with regard to ecclesiastical issues, the immunity of ecclesiastical residences, the independence of the clergy from state control, the abolition of the bishops' compulsory oath of allegiance to the king, and an endowment for the upkeep of the Holy See.

The other lay current during the Risorgimento was the Left, in its varied "democratic" and "republican" denominations. Its most prominent ideologue was Carlo Cattaneo, a father of radical liberalism and lay federalism from Lombardy, committed to constructing Italian unity through a federal pact between territories, without annexing them to the Kingdom of Savoy, which had been extending its jurisdiction to the rest of Italy in the years from 1848 to 1870. Cattaneo's republican federalism was inspired by European scientific Enlightenment, and aimed at a cultural transformation of society to be pursued through the liberating practices of self-government, decentralization, and adversarial democracy. If Cattaneo was the intellectual godfather of anticlerical secularism, Giuseppe Garibaldi represented its most popular embodiment, gathering the support of the patriotic multitudes that contested religious influence and ecclesiastical power. In 1860, the expedition of the Thousand (*La spedizione dei Mille*), led by Garibaldi, won Sicily and the south to the rule of the Italian state. Famous to his death in 1882 for his military courage, Garibaldi was the legendary champion of radical and republican, lay, masonic, and anticlerical movements that, in 1879, gave birth to the League for Democracy (Lega della Democrazia). The league's agenda was devised by prominent intellectuals and politicians such as Aurelio Saffi, former triumvir of the 1849 Roman Republic, Garibaldi follower Agostino Bertani, Matteo Renato Imbriani, Felice Cavallotti, a Radical Party leader, Giovanni Bovio, republican jurist, and poet Giosué Carducci. It envisaged the revision of the monarchic statute, the suppression of the Law of Guarantees, the introduction of universal suffrage, state ownership of all ecclesiastical property, fiscal reform, the reclamation of all peninsular territories, and the conversion of the army into a people's militias.

A United Italy

After 1876 Italian administration changed hands, as the Left overtook the Right in the race to form government. Cavour's lay and liberal stances, that had been a marker of the national unitary movement's institutional development while the Historical Right was in office, continued to influence Left-lead and transformist governments until the end of the 1800s. Cavour's Free Church in a Free State policy, though interpreted in varied ways, prevailed over jurisdictionalist tendencies—which were also lay and sometimes anticlerical—that supported state rights to meddle in Church affairs. In unified Italy, those intransigent democrats that had radical leanings joined the republicans at first, and later the socialists, to form the Extreme Left. This group would, in the last years

of the nineteenth century, be instrumental in defending united Italy's secular profile in alternative to moderate liberalism, as well as in spurring the political and social
reorganization of the clergy. During the 50 years of unity between 1861 and 1918, the
Freemasonry constituted a lay network gathering not only the anticlerical Left, the radicals, the republicans, and some socialists, but also many moderate and liberal constitu-
tionalists. It represented the middle class' means to gain supremacy over Italian politics,
and to try to elaborate a "civic religion" of sorts, based upon secularism and on its universalistic values—scientific progress, free exchange between cultures, and tolerance
for all religions, ideologies, and customs—and explicitly presented an alternative to the
only other unifying cultural force for the Italian people: Catholic tradition. The theory
which holds Freemasonry to be the ruling classes' trestle in liberal Italy is witnessed by
the presence, in its lodges, of the fathers of the Risorgimento—Garibaldi and Cattaneo,
Cavour and, though more marginally, Giuseppe Mazzini—of almost all end-of-century
statesmen, such as prime ministers Agostino Depretis, Benedetto Cairoli, Francesco
Crispi, Antonio di Rudinì, Giuseppe Zanardelli, Alessandro Fortis, Sidney Sonnino;
of a consistent number of prominent intellectuals—Bertrando Spaventa, Francesco De
Sanctis, Giosué Carducci, Arturo Labriola; and of about 60 percent of the Chamber of
Deputies' MPs in the 1890s. Around Freemasonry there existed a myriad of lay groups
such as radical reactionary and positivist societies, associations for the freedom of
thought and religious freedom, for cremation, for lay schools, as well as other leagues
like the student organization Corda Fratres.

At the beginning of the 1900s two liberal reformers, Giuseppe Zanardelli and
Giovanni Giolitti, became prime ministers, and started leading national institutions
toward modernization. Zanardelli enacted a new markedly secular and liberal penal
code. It envisaged the repression of the clergy, the abolition of the death penalty, and the
introduction of a limited right to strike. He could not, however, pass a law on divorce,
which came within a framework of new regulations regarding the family. Giolitti, at the
cusp of the nation's liberal and secular modernization, opened the doors to Catholic
entrance into political life, a prospect sanctioned by the Gentiloni pact in 1913. From
the first time since 1870, Catholics were allowed to vote in political elections, overruling the Pope's 1874 "*non expedit*" ban that forbade Italian Catholics to participate in
the Kingdom of Italy's political activities. The introduction of universal male suffrage
in 1912, and of a proportional voting system based on party lists in 1919, made it possible for Catholics and Socialists to enter parliament, and marked a decisive loss of
political weight on the part of the liberal ruling class, both conservative and reformist, that had for centuries been society's pillar of strength in matters of social and state
secularism. Before the political rupture caused by Fascism in 1922, a number of politicians and intellectuals emerged that would leave their mark in the lay world. Ernesto
Nathan, of Jewish descent, a radical and member of the Grand Orient of Italy, of which
he was Grand Master at the end of the 1800s and again in 1917, became Mayor of Rome
for the liberal-republican-socialist bloc, remaining in office from 1907 to 1913. He radically modernized the capital and stimulated construction work and other provisions
that would benefit the poorer classes. Francesco Saverio Nitti, a scholar of economic

and southern issues, prime minister between 1920 and 1921, represented the secular, liberal, and radical tendency that favored state intervention in economic matters. Giovanni Amendola, an MP leading the liberal-democratic current from a liberal prospective, fought for the improvement of individual rights and the ascent of the masses into power, as well as leading the struggle against Fascism known as the Aventine secession. Francesco Ruffini—a jurist and Minister for Education in the Giolitti government—personified continuity with the lay spirit of the Risorgimento, and, in his role of theorist of the right to freedom, he reclaimed the trend that advocated the separation of Church and State which had been upheld by Cavour. And, lastly, philosopher of freedom Benedetto Croce defended lay culture and the secular state from the historical falsifications undertaken by Catholic writers. Croce also led a small group of senators—Luigi Albertini, Francesco Ruffini, Emanuele Paternò di Sessa, Tito Sinibaldi, and Alberto Bergamini—that, in 1929, voted against the Concordat between the Church and the fascist regime, and delivered the famous "Paris is not worth a Mass" speech.

THE POSTWAR PERIOD

After the fall of Fascism, postwar Italy presented a party system very different from that which had been operating before the regime. Fascism had caused, directly or indirectly, the death of three main lay party leaders: liberal-progressive Giovanni Amendola, socialist reformer Giacomo Matteotti, and liberal socialist Carlo Rosselli. The National Liberation Committee (CLN), in which those antifascist parties responsible for the Resistenza and for the first post-regime governments had gathered, comprised the Christian Democracy (DC) and the Italian Communist Party (PCI), as well as four lay forces: the moderate Italian Liberal Party (PLI), the liberal-democratic Labour Democratic Party (PdL), the Italian Socialist Party (PSI), and the new Action Party of liberal-socialist tendency. The balance of power that, before the regime, had been in favor of those who supported secularism, had changed in the post-fascist era, and was now leaning toward the Catholics and the communists. The elections held on June 2, 1946, for the formation of the Constituent Assembly, and for the constitutional referendum which founded the Republic, yielded the following results: Christian Democracy 35.2 percent, Italian Socialist Party of Proletarian Unity 20.7 percent, Italian Communist Party 18.9 percent, National Democratic Union (PLI and PdL) 6.8 percent, Common Man's Front (UQ, populist Right) 5.3 percent, Italian Republican Party (PRI) 4.4 percent, National Bloc of Freedom (monarchical Right) 2.8 percent, Action Party together with Sardinian Action Party 1 percent. The secular forces, spread across various parties within the political spectrum, were a minority that lost further ground in the general political elections on April 18, 1948. They were strongly influenced by Cold War polarization on the international arena, which in Italy translated into a direct contrast between the Christian Democrats, with 48.5 percent of the vote, and the Popular Democratic Front—formed by the PCI and the Socialists—with 31 percent of the vote. The lay parties, also known as "minor" parties, counted on little popular support: Giuseppe Saragat's Socialist Unity—an anticommunist Italian Socialist Party of Proletarian Unity's break-away group—gathered 7.1 percent of the vote, the liberals and other right-wing moderate groups converging into the National Bloc totaled 3.8 percent, and the Republican Party 2.5 percent. The Action Party disappeared, despite its key role during the Resistenza and in the first antifascist governments between 1944 and 1945, with Prime Minister Ferruccio Parri.

In March 1947 the lay forces were defeated, within the Constituent Assembly, on the vote regarding the addition of the Lateran Pacts—Treaty and Concordat—stipulated by Church and State in 1929, as the seventh article of the republican Constitution. It read: "the State and the Catholic Church are, each in its own order, independent and sovereign. Their interactions are governed by the Lateran Pacts." DC, UQ and PCI members voted in favor of the Concordat, whereas the Socialists, Republicans, Actionists, and the majority of liberals and PdL affiliates opposed it. On the occasion of this key event for the definition of Church–State relations, the political forces identifiable as lay and non-secular clashed, and the PCI's intentions to mediate with the Catholics and withdraw from lay battle grounds became manifest. The secular parties split when faced with the Church–State Concordat: on one side were those who opposed it, had liberal and socialist leanings, and who believed religious peace to be founded on constitutional freedom; on the other the PCI, upholder of the idea of a power pact between the government political rationale and the Church's doctrinal authority. From 1948 and throughout the 1950s, Italy was governed by DC-led coalitions that were loyal to the Western anti-Soviet bloc. These coalitions included the "minor" lay parties, Giuseppe Saragat's Socialist Democratic Party, Bruno Villabruna and Giovanni Malagodi's Liberal Party, and Randolfo Pacciardi and Ugo La Malfa's Republican Party. Their role, with regard to secularism, was to counterbalance the pressures of clerical and fundamentalist forces that were acting upon the DC during Pius IX's papacy, as well as those exerted by Catholic organizations linked to the Civic Committees founded by Luigi Gedda, an admirer of Franco's authoritarian regime in Spain.

In the 20 years that followed World War II, the laity—as well as the PLI, PRI, and PSDI that were involved in government with the DC, and a faction of the PSI, with ties to the PCI—found a means of expression in the creation of a myriad of associations and periodicals dealing with political and cultural issues; in 1955 they were joined by the newly founded Radical Party. The Italian Association for Demographic Education, created by Luigi De Marchi, was committed to introducing birth control to Italy, the use of which, at the time, was forbidden by the penal code; the Association for Religious Freedom In Italy defended the rights of religious minorities in the face of the Concordat's illiberal regulations; the Association for the Defense and Development of Public Schools fought in favor of public schools and against state funding for private schools; the Italian Association for Cultural Freedom, set up by Ignazio Silone and Nicola Chiaromonte, was part of the international Western network of the Congress For Cultural Freedom; and the Italian Goliardic Union brought together lay students in order to participate in the universities' political debate and contrast Catholic, communist and neofascist students. In addition, a number of periodicals specializing in political culture made up society's secular fabric, as an alternative to Catholic and communist organizations. *Tempo Presente* was the expressive tool for freedom and culture that worked alongside Silone and Chiaromonte's organization, and in conjunction with similar international publications such as the *Prevues* for France and *Encounter* for Great Britain. Bologna's *Il Mulino* was based on secular stances, and aimed to facilitate exchanges among young people with liberal, social democrat, and liberal Catholic tendencies. Francesco Compagna and Vittorio De Caprariis' *Nord e Sud*, in Naples, continued the democratic and lay tradition of meridionalism that had an eminent predecessor in Gaetano Salvemini. Adriano Olivetti's *Community*, expressing the orientation of the movement which bore that same name, was centered on social humanism and had its headquarters in Ivrea's typewriter factory.

The weekly publication *Il Mondo*, founded in 1949, was the secular world's main voice during the 20 years that followed the war; and its editor, Mario Pannunzio, was one of the leading lay intellectuals of the 1900s. Liberal philosopher Benedetto Croce and the radical democratic historian Gaetano Salvemini were the periodical's tutelary deities, and the publication could boast of collaborations with some of the most prominent cultural and political personalities of its time. The weekly magazine's mission, in the years of its circulation between 1949 and 1966, was the creation of a "third secular force" that would counterbalance the DC and PCI. With that same aim the Radical Party was founded in 1955, into which leading figures from the liberal Left—Mario Pannunzio, Nicolo Carandini—and from the social democracy, such as Leopoldo Piccardi, merged to form a unified electoral bloc with the Republican Party in 1958, albeit with little success. *Il Mondo* also sponsored the "Convegni Del Mondo" conference series between 1955 and 1962. The conferences dealt with the momentous question of Italy's modernization—with regards to schools, public administration, finance, justice, State–Church interactions and economic monopolies—and were meant to aid, as a Fabian Society of sorts, in drafting the political program of a reformist government.

THE SECULAR STRUGGLES

The last issue of the lay weekly publication *Il Mondo*, voice of the lay "third force," was published in 1966. In those same years the monthly *Tempo Presente*, another anti-totalitarian voice of democratic anti-fascism and anti-communism, was closing down. As the 1960s unfolded, new phenomena arose on the international scene: the process of détente between the US and the USSR, the end of European colonialism and the start of Western neocolonialism, Vatican II, the student protests on both sides of the Atlantic, and a new kind of society, based on affluence and consumerism. In 1963 Italy, the first Centre-Left led government formed, through the alliance of the Christian Democrats, the Autonomous Socialist Party, the PCI, and the minor lay parties PSDI and PRI. The governmental front of those parties characterized by secular tendencies also experienced a change, as it became stronger through the Socialist's Party contribution, while the liberals lined up to form the opposition. The Radical Party, in turn, changed its political profile from that of a party representing an enlightened urban middle class to that of a small and mainly young extra-parliamentary formation that, under Marco Pannella's guidance, emphasized lay and libertarian ideals in an anticlerical, antimilitarist, and anti-totalitarian sense.

In this context, some very relevant secular battles developed both within society and in the institutions, battles that would lead to new European-style laws—such as those on divorce and abortion—that had never been introduced in Italy due to the opposition of the Catholic Church. Between 1969 and 1970 divorce legislation—supported by the people, and based on a draft by MPs Loris Fortuna and Antonio Baulini of socialist and liberal affiliations respectively—was approved with the PCI, PSIUP, PSI, PSDI, PRI, and PLI voting in favor, and the DC, the National Monarchical Party, and the neofascist Italian Social Movement (MSI), voting against. It was the first time in the Republic's history that a secular parliamentary front, which included a reluctant Communist Party, and was urged by the Radical Party-inspired Italian League for Divorce, prevailed over the alliance of the Catholic center with the monarchical Right and the MSI. The secular parliamentary victory was ratified by the referendum on divorce held on May 12, 1974, which rejected with 59.3 percent of the popular vote the abrogation of divorce, requested by clerical formations collateral to the Christian Democrats. The action of the lay parties, together with the secularization of Italian society, prevailed over Cristian Democrat opposition and the inadequate lay commitment of the PCI, which prioritized its relationship with the ecclesiastical hierarchy over interpreting Italian society's widespread sensibilities. After divorce was legalized in April 1975, new legislation regarding the family was approved, despite the opposing vote of the MSI and liberal abstention, establishing the juridical equality of spouses. In May 1978, a law legalizing abortion was passed and countersigned by some Christian Democrat statesmen, riding the wave of secular and feminist movements that had been making their weight felt in society. A few years later, in 1984, during the mandate of socialist prime minister Bettino Craxi, the Concordat signed by the state and the Holy See was reviewed, and some of its obsolete sections—such as that which defined the "Catholic religion as the only Italian state religion," and that which provided for the retention of the Church's economic privileges, were abolished. The balance of power between secular and non-secular parties remained in favor of the latter formations, as the general political elections held in 1979 showed: the Christian Democrats totaled a percentage of 38.3 of the vote, followed by the PCI with 30.4 percent, the Italian Socialist Party at 9.8 percent, MSI 5.3 percent, Radical Party 3.5 percent, Italian Republican Party 3 percent, Italian Liberal Party 1.9 percent, and lastly the Party for Proletarian Unity at 1.4 percent. The success of civil rights battles in the 1970s was largely due to the efforts of the Radicals, who were present in parliament since 1976 and were able to introduce the awareness that it was indeed possible to pursue lay goals within that institution, despite the resistance of Catholic and communist forces alike. Through the Radical Party's efforts, during the years between 1960 and 1980, secularism became no longer simply the Risorgimento's legacy to a liberal and pre-fascist Italy, but a dynamic tendency able to transform the country in a way that was consistent with the shared perceptions of the Italian people.

THE SO-CALLED SECOND REPUBLIC

During the so-called Second Republic, born after the crisis brought about by the *Tangentopoli* (Bribesville) inquiry which ran between 1992 and 1994, and implicated all the political parties that had governed Italy for the previous 50 years, the lay forces disappeared from the political and parliamentary scenes. Political exponents and relevant cultural personalities with a history in the socialist, lay-democratic, and liberal formations joined either the Centre-Right headed by Silvio Berlusconi—Forza Italia, Freedom Party (Partito della Libertà), The People of Freedom (Popolo della Libertà)—the post-communist Center-Left—DS, PDS, Democratic Party (PD)—or the post-DC parties—Segni Pact (Patto Segni), The Populars (Popolari), The Daisy (Margherita). The Radicals later dispelled and regrouped into the Pannella List (Lista Pannella), which became increasingly marginal, while segments of other lay formations such as the Socialists, Republicans and Liberals, were running for election—with a majoritarian electoral system since 1994—autonomously or in alliances with the Left or Right, with little success.

At first, in the view of the lay, the dissolution of the political unity of Catholics—DC—appeared to be a sign of progress toward European democratic models, based on turnover between the Center-Left and Center-Right, which were both inspired by non-religious principles. Despite this, the subsequent evolution of politics showed a tendency opposed to the secularization of politics prevailing. Indeed Catholic influence—strongly swayed by the Italian Episcopal Conference—deeply penetrated not only Berlusconi's Right, which was ready to take on a power pact with the Vatican, but also the main post-communist left-wing force, that showed great openness toward the Catholic political and religious world and its legislative demands on ethical issues. The front headed by Berlusconi, despite stressing its links to the old centrist parties'—form the DC to the PSI—liberal legacy, showed a generic clerical and traditionalist leaning that, in legislation concerning ethical matters and freedom of scientific research, placed Italy in the rear-guard when compared with other Western countries. Similarly, the reformist Left, which had merged into the Democratic Party (PD) in 2008, failed to show a greater degree of independence from the Vatican. Fears of losing touch with the Catholic world induced the Democratic Party, heir to the communist tradition and the Christian Democrat Left, to embrace an attitude of reticence and cautiousness when confronted with issues inherent to secularism. Another contributing factor to the decline of lay political forces was the inactive presence of former Socialists, Social-Democrats, Republicans, Liberals, and Radicals in the great formations of the Left and Right. These political and intellectual lay personalities in the Left and Right alike did nothing to oppose illiberal civil right laws.

During the "Second Republic"'s 20 years, parliament approved fundamentalist laws concerning ethical questions—such as birth, death, gender and sexual issues, abortion, stem cells, scientific research, biotechnology—which were inspired by the Church, a body that lay a claim to the monopoly of public ethics in Italy, in the belief that religious moral precepts should transfer into national law. In February 2004, law 40 on assisted reproductive technology was passed which forbade the donation of sperm or female gametes, the creation of more than three embryos all of which must be implanted, and conferred juridical personality to embryos. In 2005, the Italian Episcopal Conference, presided over by Cardinal Camillo Ruini, caused the legislative "abrogative" referendum on law 40 to fail via its public request that citizens abstain from the vote. At the same time, the Church put pressure on parliament not to discuss legislation drafts regarding the rights of "*de facto* spouses," drafts comparable to those held by the majority of other European countries. In 2007 a campaign was launched with the support of many Centre-Left and Centre-Right MPs to limit the right to abortion sanctioned by law 194—a law that had been approved by the lay majority in 1978—and to increase the number of conscientious objectors among doctors and nurses employed in public healthcare who refuse to carry out abortions. In 2009, thanks only to a Constitutional Court sentence which opposed the parliamentary majority, doctors were allowed to cease the force feeding of Eluana Englaro, who had been a prisoner of her lifeless body for the 17 years she spent in an irreversible coma. Immediately after the incident parliament passed a law concerning the "living will" which essentially prevents the individual from freely making arrangements regarding his or her own death. The last but certainly not least example of the anti-secular offensive that developed during the "Second Republic" has to be the confirmation, in favor of the Vatican and Episcopal Conference, of the fiscal privileges on the Church's real estate properties that were introduced by the new Concordat of 1984.

From a lay perspective, during the "Second Republic" the worst laws that Italy has ever known were passed, marking a clear regression in comparison with the previous political phase. If during the 1970s new civil rights were introduced, in keeping with a society that was becoming increasingly secularized, as the new century unfolded the parliament proceeded to approve legislation on ethical matters that was in stark contrast with the shared sensibilities of the Italian people. Why did this regressive tendency arise? Because both the Centre-Left and Centre-Right fronts that made up the new political and electoral systems embraced and made dominant within their formations clerical petitions, despite their being of scarce relevance in the country. The residual secular groups of liberal and socialist inspiration within the Centre-Left and the Centre-Right have become marginal, and have largely accepted the obsequious mood pervading their respective parties when dealings with the Vatican are concerned. Reinforcing this regressive tendency was the disappearance of lay forces from Italian parliament that, although minoritarian, had triggered the civil rights campaigns of the "First Republic," eventually also engaging the Communist Party.

PART VII

....

ECONOMIC INSTITUTIONS, ASSOCIATIONS, AND INTERESTS

....

CHAPTER 35

TRENDS AND TENSIONS WITHIN THE ITALIAN FAMILY

CHIARA SARACENO

WHEN one speaks of the Italian family, stereotypes are likely to come to mind: "strong families" that protect their members but do not allow them much autonomy, while creating the so-called amoral familism syndrome; a family where wives are subjugated but mothers are strong; and so forth. As all stereotypes, they both reveal and distort the truth.

Since the late 1960s, patterns of family formation and organization have undergone profound transformations in Italy. These changes, in turn, have led to important modifications of family law, with the introduction of (no fault) divorce in 1970, the legalization of contraception and abortion in 1977, and in 1975 a new family law granting equality between spouses and turning parent–child obligations upside down. In those same years, important changes also took place in social welfare arrangements (extension of maternity leaves, expansion of childcare services, individualization of the taxation system).[1]

Changes in behavior and cultural patterns continued in the following years and are still taking place, without, however, being met by comparable changes in civil law and in welfare state arrangements. These are still largely based on a presumption of extended family solidarities,[2] a sharp gender division of labor and a long economic dependency of children well beyond the legal age of 18. In the meantime, family and sexuality themes have become increasingly divisive issues in public discourse, as well as objects of explicit political negotiations with the Catholic Church.

This chapter first gives an overview of the main trends in patterns of family formation and organization, focusing mainly on the 1990s onwards. Then it moves on to discuss how these trends are (or are not) met by legal regulations and social policies.

AN OVERVIEW OF THE MAIN TRENDS
IN PATTERNS OF FAMILY FORMATION

Increasing Delay in the Formation of New Families

In contrast to their European contemporaries, the majority of Italian youth enter marriage without having previously lived outside the parental home, alone or with a partner. This phenomenon is not new, particularly for males. On the contrary, it is a long-standing feature of Italian society, due to a combination of patrilocality in patterns of family formation and of late entrance in economic activity.[3] Yet this feature has persisted throughout changes both in patterns of family formation, and in the economy and the labor market. The age for exiting the parental household has even increased in recent decades. In 2009–10, 40.9 percent of all 25–34 years old were still living as children in their parents' household, compared with 33.1 percent in 1992–93.[4] The percentage is higher in the Center-North than in the South. The cause of this increasingly late exit from the parental household cannot be simplistically found in the persistence, and even strengthening, of so called *mammismo*, that is, in an emotional inability, coupled with practical opportunism, to be free of one's mother's care and services. The young meet increasing difficulties in finding a job and having a proper wage, compounded by an overall lack of social protection and by a housing market where renting is both difficult, given the low offer, and expensive. A study has shown that the opportunities for the younger cohorts of 25–34-year-olds have substantially worsened compared with those of their parents (fathers) with regard to age of entrance in the labor market, level of wages, job security, notwithstanding the fact that this generation is on average better educated than their parents' generation. [5] It is true that the majority of the young and their parents still feel that a child does not need to exit the parental household until he/she is ready to (unless forced by exceptional circumstances such as emigration, severe family conflicts, severe deviant behavior). Yet, a growing minority would like to become autonomous but finds it increasingly difficult to do so.[6]

This delay in achieving autonomy, this dependence on parental support, together with the specific difficulties encountered by young mothers in balancing paid work with childcare, accounts for the Italian low fertility rate. Already below 1.5 children per woman in the mid-1980s, the fertility rate dipped to 1.19 in 1996, slowly increased to 1.46 in 2010 (mostly because of the contribution of migrant women), to decrease again to 1.39 in 2013.[7] A too exclusive dependency on family solidarity, in a society and welfare state that support neither the autonomy of the young nor mothers' employment, produces a kind of reproductive anorexia and slows down the transition from the status of children to that of parents.

Delay in family formation has been accompanied by a lowering of age for entry into sexual relations, particularly for women. Unlike their mothers, most women today no longer expect to be married to have sex. The average age at first intercourse for women is now about 17, only about one year later than for men, whose "beginning age" has remained stable at around 16.[8]

Weakening of Marriage as the Basis of Family Formation

Marriage in Italy is still the event that marks (and allows) entrance into cohabitation as a couple and into parenthood for the majority. There are, however, signals of rapid change among the younger cohorts. Over 33 percent of first marriages, on average, are now preceded by cohabitation of at least one year, compared with 2 percent in the cohorts who married in the 1970s, 7.7 percent of those who married in the 1980s, and 13.7 percent of those who married in the 1990s. The phenomenon is more widespread in the Center-North than in the South. Furthermore, the number of unmarried cohabitant couples who have children is also increasing: from 8 percent of all unmarried cohabitant couples in 1996 to about 20 percent in 2009.[9] This largely explains the increase in births outside marriage despite the general context of low fertility, from 8 percent of all births in the early 1990s; to 25,9 percent in 2013 (although these were mostly within a cohabitation). In some of the Center-North regions, where cohabitation is more widespread, almost 30 percent of all births occur outside marriage.[10] Finally, the characteristics of those who choose to cohabit without (or before) marrying have also changed. Until the mid-1990s, cohabitation without marriage was mainly restricted to couples where at least one partner was widowed or separated/divorced and did not want to marry (for economic or inheritance reasons) or could not marry (because of the waiting time imposed by the divorce law). These conditions still apply but now the young also consider the option of cohabitation without marriage at their first partnership. The number of unmarried cohabitant couples where neither partner comes from a previous marriage increased more than eight times between 1993–1994 and 2010–2011.[11]

Marriage as an institution is also being weakened, as in other countries, by an increasing marital instability, notwithstanding all the procedural and economic obstacles that make ending a marriage a more complex process in Italy than in most countries. A divorce, save for few and extreme exceptions, must always be preceded by a legal separation and by a waiting period. Until April 2015, when a new law was approved, there was a waiting period of at least three years. With the new law this has reduced to six to twelve months, depending on whether the procedure is consensual or contentious. While in 1980 there were only 7.7 marital separations for every 100 marriages, in 1995 the corresponding number had already doubled to 15.8, almost redoubling again by 2011, at 31.1 per cent.[12] The figures for divorces are lower, since not all separations are transformed into divorces, but they follow the same trend, with a slight reduction of the gap between separation and divorce rates. There were 7.97 divorces for every 100 marriages in 1995. This figure more than doubled in 2011, to 18.19 per 100.

As in the case of unmarried cohabitation, there are wide regional differences in marriage instability, with the Center-North having rates similar to those of continental Europe and the South very low rates, albeit increasing faster than elsewhere. These differences may be partly imputed to different family cultures and gender norms, partly to the higher incidence of low income families and to a lower women's employment rate in the South, which render marital separation too costly.

The weakening of marriage as the founding institution of the family for the heterosexual population is counterbalanced by an increasing demand for legal acknowledgment—up to marriage, adoption and other forms of filiation—by homosexuals. A recent national survey found that, although politicians are still reluctant to grant such an acknowledgment, the majority of the Italian population is in favor of granting legal status to homosexual couples, even if not through access to marriage.[13] There is less support for adoption by homosexuals, but same-sex couples are having children, however. Within the present legal framework, these children by law have only one (the biological) parent.

A Gender Contract under Tension

At the core of many of the changes within the family are changes in women's expectations and behavior, which put the traditional gender contract under stress.

Women are the willing or constrained protagonists of the fertility decline. They are also, to some degree, the main protagonists of marital instability, in that when they find their marriage to be no longer acceptable they are more ready than men to put an end to it, if they can afford it, that is, if they have a job and a wage. Although in Italy women's labor force participation is still lower than the EU average, with an activity rate of 51.1 percent, it constantly, if slowly, increased between the early 1990s and the 2007 economic crisis. Furthermore, women mostly work full time. The majority of mothers of preschool children is now in the labor market. Women's employment in Italy, however, irrespective of motherhood, is heavily dependent both on education and on the region of residence. Activity and employment rates are much higher among the better educated and those living in the Center-North regions than in the South, where most of women's inactivity is concentrated. The educational and territorial differences are greater than those found in most EU countries. They also affect the degree to which becoming a mother represents a risk, from the point of view of labor market participation: the better educated, who have better jobs and can count on a comparatively higher personal and family income, are better able to remain in the labor market than the lower educated women in low income households. Marriage and children still are a cause of exiting the labor force. In the 2010s, women's employment rate in the 35–44 age bracket is 83 percent among the unmarried and childless, 75.4 percent among those who are married and childless, 56.9 percent among the married with children (40.5 percent if they have three or more children).Overall, between 20 percent and 30 percent of women still interrupt their labor market participation for considerable lengths of time due to family responsibilities, mostly because of the birth of a child.[14] The persistent and increasing precariousness in the labor market is causing a new type of inequality among women with regard to motherhood: in the 25–34 age group, 34 per cent of women with an indefinite work contract already have a child, compared with 23.8 per cent of those with fixed term contract.

Achieving an acceptable work–family balance is difficult for Italian women, not only because of the prevalence of full-time work and of a weak development of women's and family friendly policies (something we will turn to later), but also because of a persistent gender asymmetry in unpaid family work. The division of unpaid family work in Italian couples is among the most unbalanced in the developed countries, even when both partners are in paid work.[15] There has been some change, however, particularly among the younger cohorts and among husbands of working women and fathers of very young children. In particular, employed women have reduced the time devoted to housework (not to the care of children) and young fathers have increased the time for their children. Among dual worker young couples with small children, time use seems to have changed by comparison with older generations: more time is spent caring for children and doing things together, less time in performing housework. Children may benefit from more father's time. Fatherhood is the dimension of maleness that appears to be the most changed, particularly among better educated men. Men, however, even when they share part of the unpaid work, tend to be selective, choosing the most pleasurable activities and leaving the less pleasurable and more routine ones to women.

The increasing precariousness of jobs,[16] particularly among the young, might not only constrain family formation and fertility; it might also slow down the more egalitarian trends in the gender division of labor. Uncertainty and vulnerability, in fact, might induce both women and men, but particularly the latter, to avoid negotiations in the workplace around time use for family or personal reasons.

Kinship Ageing and Family Solidarity under Stress

Close kinship is important in Italy and, to a larger degree than in most developed countries, the locus of many forms of emotional and practical support.[17] One of the main forms of support is intergenerational cohabitation. Through cohabitation, parents support adult children who are unemployed, or earn too little or too irregularly to be able to live on their own, or have divorced and cannot afford to pay for their own accommodation. (Re)cohabitation may be also the solution to the caring needs of a frail elderly parent.

There are, however, other important ways in which close kin operates as a resource and a buffer. Most young couples have access to their own housing through their parents' financial support.[18] In Italy, to a much larger degree than in most EU countries, working mothers rely substantially on the support of grandmothers, both as an alternative to paid services and as a stopgap, an emergency resource.[19] Frail elderly parents are mostly taken care of, on a regular basis, by their children, mainly daughters, even when they live on their own.

This solidarity has proven largely efficacious. Its very necessity—for lack of alternatives— however, has indirectly strengthened the intergenerational reproduction of social inequality. As the data of the first National Report on Equitable and Sustainable Wellbeing indicate,[20] such solidarity worked as a crucial buffer in the first years of the financial and employment crisis that started in 2007. Yet, as the crisis continues and youth unemployment rates skyrocket while middle-aged parents experience reduced incomes because of reduced working hours or loss of job, the capacity of family solidarity to keep family members from falling into poverty and experiencing deprivation has dramatically weakened. Since 2010, the number of individuals and households experiencing poverty and deprivation has increased because many families have exhausted their financial reserves while the crisis continues.

Family solidarity is also under tension for reasons other than the financial crisis, however. The Italian family, from the point of view of close kinship, has become increasingly a clear example of the so-called beanpole family typical of aging societies, due to the dual impact of a rapid fertility decline and increasing life expectancy. This has opened up the possibility to develop three generational relationships for long life spans. It has also made available a relatively numerous generation of "young old" (55–70-year-olds) that is on average in good health, often already retired (in the case of women often never entered into the labor market), often with relatively good pensions. This generation is on the forefront of the demands for financial support and care coming from the younger and the older ones. Kinship ageing, however, has also created caring demands and unbalances within kinship networks (fewer adult children for more frail elderly parents). Between 1983 and 2003, for instance, help provided to the old by family members diminished, in favor of help provided to young households where the mother is in employment.[21]

Faced with the scarcity of non-health care services for the frail old, families have developed a kind of self-made welfare, exploiting the new (for Italy) immigration phenomenon by hiring migrant cheap (and often irregular) mostly female labor: the so called *badanti*. Recourse to migrant care labor is present in other countries too. Within the EU, however, only two other Mediterranean countries—Spain and Portugal, which share with Italy many features of family culture and arrangements and of an unbalanced welfare state—present this phenomenon with an analogous consistency and intensity.[22]

Migrant, Foreign, and Mixed Families

Since the mid-1990s, migrants have contributed to change the panorama of family arrangements not only as paid family workers, often living within Italian households, caring for the frail elderly and small children, but also through their own households and families. This is indirectly testified by the fact that a large number of regular migrants now enter Italy for reasons of family reunification (see Chapter 48, this volume). This contribution is visible demographically, in that migrant women have a higher (although declining) average fertility rate than Italian women. In 2012, the average number of children per woman was respectively 1.29 and 2.37 for Italian and foreign women. The presence of foreign families enriches and complicates the variety of family cultures and life styles that meet in childcare services and schools.

Migration, together with the growing international mobility of the Italian population, has also caused an increase in the number of marriages where one of the spouses is a foreigner. The number of mixed marriages reached a peak in 2008, when in 15 percent of all marriages celebrated that year at least one spouse, generally the wife, was a foreigner, declining slightly and then stabilizing in the following years.[23]

LEGAL NORMS AND SOCIAL POLICIES IN THE FACE OF FAMILY CHANGE

Laws concerning the family have adapted late, slowly, and only partially to changes in patterns of family formation, family cultures, gender and intergenerational relations, and the demography of kinship networks. They continue to reflect a rigid and univocal definition of family, while stressing the role of financial obligations well beyond household boundaries. This definition of the family and its obligations, in turn, remains the implicit and explicit assumption of most social policies.

Laws: Very Slow Moving

 Article 29 of the Italian democratic Constitution stipulates gender equality in marriage and Article 30 stipulates equality between children born inside and outside marriage. Yet in the first 25 years of democracy after World War II, family relationships were still regulated by the Fascist civil code. In civil law, husbands and wives were still treated differently; children born outside marriage were still defined as illegitimate and had very few rights. Furthermore, both contraception and abortion were illegal. Divorce did not exist.

Most legal innovations in the area of family law were introduced in the 1970s, largely because of a very vocal and active women's movement, but also because of the changed political climate. The alliance between the Socialist and the Communist parties broke down, opening the way, after decades of Center-Right governments, to the first Center-Left one, more open to revision in family law. At the same time, the social movements of the time, while criticizing the Left and specifically the Communist Party for its "conservatism," put pressure on this same party to support their demands in Parliament. In 1970, no fault divorce was introduced, in the form of a two-step process with a long waiting time (five years) between the two steps. In 1971, contraception was legalized; in 1978, abortion was legally allowed under certain conditions. In 1975, a new family law was approved, giving legal implementation to the constitutional principle of gender equality within the couple and acknowledging a change in the balance of interests to be protected between parents and children, with the latter being defined as subjects of rights, rather than duties. Children born outside marriage were no longer defined as "illegitimate," but as "natural," and their entitlement to be acknowledged by their parents was strengthened. The 1975 reform, however, did not innovate with regard to the range of "obliged kin" and of the duration of the obligations involved. In accordance with the vision of a family based on extended solidarity, article 433 of the Italian civil code stipulates a wide range of "obliged kin" figures—that is, of relatives who are legally obliged to provide financial support in case of need: parents toward children (without age limitation), children toward parents, grandparents toward grandchildren, siblings reciprocally, children-in-law toward parents-in-law, aunts and uncles toward nieces and nephews.

Their limitations notwithstanding, these legal reforms opened up a conflict with the Catholic Church, culminating in two popular referenda called by the Christian Democrats and various Catholic organizations to repeal, first, the divorce law, and then the abortion law. Both referenda were lost by those wanting to repeal the laws, indicating the degree of cultural change that had taken place in these matters at the social level and the weakening influence of the Catholic Church in private life styles. It was the first, but also the last time the Catholic Church was defeated on this terrain and that a law was passed notwithstanding opposition from the Catholic hierarchy.

Following this period of legal reforms, the following decades saw little innovation in civil law in matters concerning the family, notwithstanding changes in behaviors and demography. In 1987, the compulsory waiting time required between legal separation and entitlement to apply for divorce was reduced from five to three years. Later bills intended to further reduce this waiting time, at least for couples without children, were defeated in Parliament by a bipartisan (Catholic) majority, or didn't even enter the Parliamentary agenda. Only in April 2015 did Parliament succeed in approving a law that reduces the waiting time. Italian divorce, however, remains a two-step process, requiring two court pronunciations and a waiting time. Before the 2015 reform, the main, legal change in the regulation of separation and divorce, concerned child custody. In 2006, following developments already in place in other countries and the mobilization of non-custodial fathers associations, shared custody became the standard legal form of custody and calculation of child support became more standardized.

The protection of children's rights and wellbeing were also the motivations behind the adoption and of foster parenthood reforms of 1983 and 2001. As late as December 2012, any residual difference in the rights and legal kinship of natural and legitimate children were eliminated, thus finally fulfilling the mandate of Article 30 of the Italian Constitution.

On the reproductive rights front, the law allowing abortion is periodically attacked and is increasingly difficult to implement. Through the mechanism of conscientious objection, largely induced by the professional marginalization and overburdening of the few gynaecologists who perform abortions in public hospitals, long waiting lists mean that it is difficult for women to have an abortion within the allowed period. The legalization of the RU486 pill that does not require that the woman performing an abortion be hospitalized, was long opposed by the Center-Right governments at the national and regional level. On the opposite side, support through Law no. 40/2004 on assisted reproduction for those who wish to have a child but cannot introduced a number of restrictions and infringements of personal freedom (for instance, only a maximum of three embryo may be allowed to develop and all three of them have to be simultaneously implanted). This law has been progressively dismantled by national and European courts' decisions. After these decisions, access to reproductive technologies, including recourse to third party donors, was open to all married or cohabitant heterosexual couples who are either infertile or bearers of serious genetic diseases. Same-sex couples and singles cannot access these techniques in Italy. Similarly, adoption remains limited to married couples.

Article 433 concerning "obliged kin"—one of the most extended in developed countries—remains in place. It has consequences for the definition of individual social rights with regard, in particular, to social assistance. Entitlement to social assistance is, in fact, residual and secondary to entitlement to family solidarity. Furthermore, social assistance measures are scarce. In particular, there is no nationally legislated minimum income provision for the poor (except for the elderly and the disabled).

Finally, Italy is one of the few European countries where unmarried heterosexual, but more so same-sex couples, have no acknowledgment in law, although recent court decisions have acknowledged their right to be treated "as a family," thus putting pressure on Parliament to legislate on the matter.

Social Policies

From an EU comparative perspective, public family policies in Italy have traditionally been and still are minimal, whether one considers income transfers or the provision of care services.[24]However, the increase in women's labor force participation, together with concerns for the low fertility rate, have solicited debate and also policy proposals. Yet moving from debates and proposals to decisions has proven difficult, for different reasons. In the first place, investing in this sector would have required a reorientation of social expenditure in a period of increasing budget constraints (see also Chapter 38, this volume). Strengthening individual rights to social security, particularly for the young, and increasing the offer of care services in order to improve work–family balance for women, conflicts with more established entitlements and interests at a time in which these are already perceived as under attack, therefore mobilizing traditional interest groups. Trade unions were not against a development of care services, or the introduction of a universal and decent unemployment indemnity, or a universal child allowance. But they first defended the interests of pensioners against any reform. As suggested by Bonoli,[25] the "timing" was not favorable. The so-called new social risks had a weak constituency. Social expenditure was in fact rebalanced (recalibrated), but through cutting (with the successive pension reforms), rather than through a different distribution across sectors. An example of this is the sharp increase in the pension age of women stipulated in November 2011, without any compensation through an increase of care services for children and the frail elderly, or an increase in compensation during parental leave.

The main policy innovation since the 1970s was reform of maternity and parental leave with law 53/2000. Under the dual pressure of the women's movement and European directives, this law introduced the status of "working father," giving working fathers individual entitlement to parental leave, improving the previous 1979 law that allowed fathers to take parental leave only if the mother renounced it. Parental leave follows the period of five months maternity leave to which only mothers are entitled and is compensated with at least 80% of pay. Parental couples (or single mothers) are entitled to ten months of additional leave up to when the child turns 8. They may share this period, but no parent may take more than six months. If the father takes at least three months, he can earn an extra month. Parental leave, however, is poorly compensated in comparison with maternal leave (30 percent of the parent's wage and only for the first six of the total ten months available for the couple) and is open only to dependent workers. In a context where many young men and women have temporary work contracts, often in the form of self-employment, many new parents are either not entitled to or cannot afford to take parental leave. And many young women incur the serious risk of losing their job or not having their contract renewed when they become pregnant and take the maternity leave they are legally entitled to.

Investments have been made for childcare services, particularly for the under three, since coverage for three- to six-year-old children was already among the highest in Europe in the 1970s. Notwithstanding an important financial investment by the second Prodi government in 2007, however, Italy did not achieve the target of at least 30 percent coverage for the under three-year-olds by 2010. Only one region, Emilia Romagna, reached that threshold. Wide differences persist between regions, with all the Southern ones, except Sardinia, being below 10 percent.[26]Furthermore, the sharp reduction of funding for the social services generally and for education since the onset of the financial crisis has made it difficult for local governments to maintain and develop their childcare services, while forcing a reduction in full-time classes at elementary school. The so-called child investment strategy, strongly sponsored by the EU and the Organisation for Economic Co-operation and Development, has not been fully implemented in Italy, where, on the contrary, there is increasing risk that the country's tradition of childcare services with a strong educational focus will be weakened in order to reduce costs.[27]

Particularly lacking have been developments in the area of care for the frail old. The only provision is an allowance paid to all those who have a very high (70 percent) level of inability. Yet even this provision does not grant that the individual receives proper care, assuming that a family member provides essential care. The availability of this allowance largely explains the explosion of the *badanti* phenomenon, since the allowance can be used to pay for some hours of care provided by cheap labor. Migrant laws, in turn, have further strengthened this phenomenon, as migrant carers have been systematically "privileged" in the periodical "regularization" waves. This has been an easy way to address the care needs of the frail elderly without touching the social budget. Only some municipalities have developed some kind of monitoring and support in the offer and demand market of this kind of work.[28]

The general framework of social policies, therefore, has remained premised on the implicit and often explicit assumption that the family should remain the main provider, directly and indirectly, with regard to both income support and care, even beyond the household boundaries.

Concluding Remarks

While remaining "strong," out of choice or necessity, Italian families have much changed since the post-war years and are still changing— demographically, in patterns of behavior, and in regard to gender and intergenerational relations—in some case strengthening traditional features (e.g., late exit from the parental household and kinship interdependency), in others marking a clear break. Legal and policy developments, however, have lagged behind these changes. Since the mid-1990s, trends in civil law and in welfare arrangements concerning family and work–family policies have significantly diverged from those adopted in most EU and Western countries.[29] This gap between behavioral and institutional changes is a cause of inequality. In particular, the strengthening of family interdependencies, while limiting individual autonomy, supports the intergenerational reproduction of social inequality. The late and inadequate development of social care services strengthens inequality not only between social classes but also between men and women. The resistance to change family law and to acknowledge new forms of families infringes the civil rights of many.

The influence of the Catholic Church and the weak secularity (*laicità*) of the Italian state and of Italian political culture have a central place in explaining the resistance to adapt civil law to the changing meanings and expectations concerning family relationships. But there are also other reasons, in particular linked to the role assigned to family solidarity in the Italian welfare state. Heavy and extended family obligations are coupled with a system of family-linked income transfers that partly supports dependencies: survivor pensions, tax deductions for dependent spouses and (even adult) children and other financially dependent family members. Extending these kinds of family-related transfers to "non-standard" families is costly and would necessitate a change in institutionalized expectations concerning the family, as would developing social policies that rely less on traditional assumptions concerning family solidarity and the gender division of labor.

Such assumptions, however, are proving increasingly untenable. As the economic crisis has shown, families do act as buffers, compensating individual losses and pooling resources. Yet, not all families have adequate resources to perform this role. And in the long run, those with modest economic means become vulnerable to poverty. Italy is one of the EU countries where the long fiscal crisis has not only increased the number of jobless households, but where the phenomenon of in work poverty is increased most, because of an imbalance between available income and number of family members who depend on it.[30] Traditional assumptions are also untenable for demographic reasons, since kinship aging has changed the balance between potential family caregivers and receivers, at a time when this balance was already under pressure because of women's increasing labor force participation.

Notes

1. Chiara Saraceno, *Mutamenti della famiglia e politiche sociali in Italia* (Bologna: Il Mulino, 2008).
2. Manuela Naldini, *The Family in the Mediterranean Welfare States* (London: Frank Cass, 2003).
3. Marzio Barbagli, Maria Castiglioni, and Giampiero Dalla Zuanna, *Fare famiglia in Italia* (Bologna: Il Mulino, 2003).
4. ISTAT Indagini Multiscopo. *Famiglia e soggetti sociali* (Rome: ISTAT, various years).
5. Antonio Schizzerotto, Ugo Trivellato, and Nicola Sartor (eds.), *Generazioni disuguali* (Bologna: Il Mulino, 2011).
6. ISTAT, *Le difficoltà nella transizione dei giovani allo stato adulto e le criticità nei percorsi di vita femminili* (Rome: ISTAT, December 28, 2009).
7. ISTAT, Natalità e fecondità della popolazione residente, *Report* (November 27, 2014).
8. Barbagli et al., *Fare famiglia in Italia*; Marzio Barbagli, Giampiero Dalla Zuanna, and Franco Garelli, *La sessualità degli italiani* (Bologna: Il Mulino, 2010).
9. ISTAT, Come cambiano le forme familiari, *Report* (September 15, 2011).
10. ISTAT Natalità e fecondità della popolazione residente, *Report* (November 27, 2014).
11. ISTAT, Come cambiano le forme familiari, *Report* (September 15, 2011).
12. ISTAT, Separazioni e divorzi in Italia. 1995–2011, *Report* (May 27, 2013); see also Marzio Barbagli and Chiara Saraceno, *Separarsi in Italia* (Bologna: Il Mulino, 1998).
13. ISTAT, La popolazione omosessuale nella società italiana, *Report* (May 17, 2012).
14. ISTAT, La conciliazione tra lavoro e famiglia, *Report* (December 28, 2011); Alessandro Rosina and Chiara Saraceno, "Interferenze a simmetriche. Uno studio sulla discontinuità lavorativa femminile," in *Economia & Lavoro*, 42, 2 (2008), 149–167; Manuela Naldini and Chiara Saraceno, *Conciliare famiglia e lavoro* (Bologna: Il Mulino, 2011); Linda Laura Sabbadini, *Il lavoro femminile in tempo di crisi, relazione presentata agli stati generali del lavoro delle donne in Italia* (Rome: Cnel, II Commissione, February 2, 2012), http://www.slideshare.net/slideistat/ll-sabbadini-il-lavoro-femminile-in-tempo-di-crisi.
15. EUROSTAT, *Reconciliation between Work, Private and Family Life in the European Union* (Eurostat Statistical Books, Luxembourg: 2009); ISTAT (2010) *Rapporto annuale 2010*. Rome: ISTAT.
16. See Chapter 37, this volume.
17. Matthijs Kalmijn and Chiara Saraceno, "A comparative perspective on intergenerational support," *European Societies*, 10, 3 (2008), 479–508; Martin Kohli, and Marco Albertini, "The family as a source of support for adult children's own family projects. European varieties," in Chiara Saraceno (ed.), *Families, Ageing and Social Policy: Intergenerational Solidarity in European Welfare States* (Cheltenham: Edward Elgar, 2008), 38–58.

18. Teresio Poggi, "The intergenerational transmission of home ownership and the repro-duction of the familialistic welfare regime", in Saraceno (ed.), *Families, Ageing and Social Policy*, 59–87.

19. Wolfgang Keck and Chiara Saraceno, "Grandchildhood in Germany and Italy: an explor-ation," in Arnlaug Leira and Chiara Saraceno (eds.), *Childhood: Changing Contexts* (Bingley: Emerald, 2008), 135–166.

20. ISTAT/CNEL, *Benessere equo e sostenibile in Italia* (Rome: ISTAT, 2013).

21. ISTAT, *Rapporto annuale 2010*.

22. Francesca Bettio, Alessandra Simonazzi, and Paola Villa, "Change in care regimes and female migration: the 'care drain' in the Mediterranean," *Journal of European Social Policy*, 16 (3, 2010), 271–285; Raimondo Catanzaro and Asher Colombo, *Badanti & Co. Il lavoro domestico straniero in Italia* (Bologna: Il Mulino, 2009); Manuela Naldini and Chiara Saraceno, "Social and family policies in Italy: not totally frozen but far from structural reforms," *Social Policy & Administration*, 42, 7 (2008), 733–748.

23. Anna Laura Zanatta, *Le nuove famiglie* (Bologna: Il Mulino, 2003); ISTAT, Il matrimonio in Italia, *Report* (November 28, 2012).

24. OECD, *Growing Unequal?* (Paris: OECD, 2008); OECD, *Doing Better for Families* (Paris: OECD, 2011).

25. Giuliano Bonoli, "Time matters: post-industrialization, new social risks and welfare state adaptation in advanced industrial democracies," *Comparative Political Studies*, 40 (5, 2007), 495–520. See also Trudie Knijn and Chiara Saraceno, "Changes in the regulation of responsibilities towards childcare needs in Italy and the Netherlands: different timing, increasingly different approaches," *Journal of European Social Policy*, 20, 5 (2010), 444–455.

26. Presidenza del consiglio dei ministri, *Rapporto di monitoraggio del piano di sviluppo dei servizi socio-educativi per la prima infanzia al 31 dicembre 2010*. (Rome: Dipartimento per le politiche della famiglia, 2011).

27. E.g. Peter Moss, "Early child education and care," in Sheila Kamerman, Shelley Phipps, and Asher Ben-Arieh (eds.), *From Child Welfare to Child Well-Being* (Heidelberg, London, and New York: Springer, 2009), 371–384.

28. Naldini and Saraceno, *Social and Family Policies*.

29. Margitta Mätzke and Ilona Ostner, "Introduction: change and continuity in recent family policies," *Journal of European Social Policy*, Special issue, 20, 5 (2010), 387–98.

30. Chiara Saraceno, *Il lavoro non basta. La povertà in Europa negli anni della crisi* (Milano: Feltrinelli, 2015).

CHAPTER 36

···

INDUSTRY AND THE FIRM

···

GIUSEPPE BERTA

THIS chapter analyzes the relationship between Italian industry and the Italian political system which evolved from the end of World War II to mid-2013, and specifically focuses upon the way in which the evolution of industry has been conditioned by Italy's political and institutional structure, which was itself influenced, in turn, by Italian industry. Thus, the key focus is on the political and social repercussions of Italian industrial development, which occurred within the framework of an institutional system which strongly affected the configuration of the industrial sector. The periods examined thus correspond to the major periods of development in contemporary Italy.

INDUSTRIAL DEVELOPMENT IN THE ITALIAN REPUBLIC

···

The period of fascism (1922–43) was decisive in configuring the mixed economic system that sustained the development of Italian industry during its most vigorous period of expansion in the 1950s and 1960s. An economic system in which private (free enterprise) and public (state) interests flourished had already emerged under the period of fascism. Industry was the ground on which this "relationship game" between the various subjects was acted out, with a constant flow of exchanges between the two poles of government and industry. From this point of view, the aftermath of World War II is both a continuity of the industrial framework of the 1930s and a logical development that increased this complementarity or reciprocity: the steel industry is a case in point, with the integrative role of Finsider with regard to the growth of private industry for the manufacture of durable consumer goods in the 1950s and 1960s.[1] The case of the national infrastructure can also be considered as emblematic, especially the motorway network, which was also created by IRI,[2] in order to promote the motor car industry and private car ownership.

The newly formed Italian Republic had inherited from the past the principle that industry not only constituted a means which was vital for the growth of wealth, but was also the main force capable of promoting the modernization of the country. The speed of social change was seen as being largely dependent on the capacity for industrial transformation. Furthermore, industry became a decisive link to the international economy, thus reflecting the results of the development policies introduced thanks to the Atlantic Alliance and the hegemony of the United States. The Marshall Plan, with its expansive vision of the economic process, designed to create a mechanism of global interdependence, with regard to the transfer of technology, expertise, competences, and organization, was decisive here. It was a modernization plan founded upon a political–institutional hegemony, which served to reinforce its potential as an agent of the country's wealth and modernity.

From the mid-1950s onwards, it became clear that industry basically corresponded to the process of modernization in Italy. For this reason, the state was ready to back private industry as far as possible. At the same time state industries were supported and strengthened thanks to the ever increasing expansion of the system of state (public) participation, the pole of state industry whose governance increased until it had to be managed with the introduction of a separate ministry (Ministero delle Partecipazioni Statali).

The Italy of the "economic miracle" was a country of strong complementarities: the large numbers of small businesses and enterprises had great weight in the economy, as has always been the case in the economic history of post-unification Italy. Notwithstanding, the hub of this productive system was based within the nucleus of the major industries, both state and private, and spearheaded the industrial transformation. Thus, the major enterprises (big businesses) formed the solid economic base of the nation, and, as such, were supported and protected by the state, from the very moment at which the modernity of the country became dependent, for the most part, on the major national enterprises. This privileged position paved the way for the adoption of incentives offering promotion and protection, which big businesses, first and foremost Fiat, had already enjoyed for a long time. These incentives were, in fact, a determining factor in the plan to modernize the nation thoroughly, especially when greater territorial integration was sought by extending the industrial system throughout Italy, with the creation of production plants in Southern Italy. In an undertaking to enable the South to become richer and more modern, incentives were offered to enterprises willing to invest in the South of Italy, the so-called *Mezzogiorno*. This witnessed the creation of the steel-making plant Italsider in Taranto (1962–70), an important turning point, followed by the creation of the car production plant for Alfa Romeo in Pomigliano d'Arco (1966–67), and that of Fiat in Termini Imerese (1970).

In this way, the state entrusted the dynamic economic equilibrium of the nation to Italian big business, which thus became part of the material constitution of the republic. This gave rise to a marriage of convenience between the system of government and Italian big business, with both partners convinced of the usefulness of the alliance, and which took place within a specific design for a mixed economy which was the outcome of Italian history. Not surprisingly, in periods of crisis such as the 1970s, this structure was heavily relied upon, with a steep increase of state aid to industry. The latter formed part of the political and institutional profile of the Republic, since its civil mission was established in the wake of the relationship between politics, state institutions, and the economy. This undoubtedly gave the world of Italian big business its political character, and not just those elements which were part of the archipelago of state participation, conditioned not only by the power coming from the state, but also by the power of the private sector, both of which shared a common final interest.

In this respect the trajectory of Fiat is emblematic: the biggest Italian industrial enterprise also profited from its links with politics and with state institutions. Until the end of the twentieth century it considered itself a part of these, even when it expressed critical views of political tendencies or policies. Its position always remained within the mechanisms of the elite within government. What is more, if we trace the profiles of the most important Italian entrepreneurs in the second half of the twentieth century, we can easily observe their particular political characters or tendencies.

Figures as different as Enrico Mattei, Vittorio Valletta, and Adriano Olivetti all express, albeit in different ways, clear political inclinations or tendencies. For example, Enrico Mattei, the founder of ENI in 1953,[3] would never have become one of the major economic actors of his time without the help of the political sphere or system. Mattei was a successful entrepreneur and self-made man who established himself in Milan in the 1930s. However, the core of his entrepreneurial action manifested itself first during his period at Agip, and then as the director of ENI, which was set up thanks to his political commitment in the rank and file of the Democrazia Cristiana (Christian Democrats). Mattei was thus able to use a political and institutional framework to support his efforts to create a major company in the field of energy sources, the first and foremost being petrol. Mattei personified the "interweaving" between politics and the economy at the highest levels. In the same way, the way in which he maneuvered reflected the very strong political legitimation of Italian big business, which was one of the mainsprings of the state holding system.

In contrast, Vittorio Valletta represented the big business development model pursued by the Americans. It was Valletta who was responsible for building up Fiat and bringing its economic power to a peak, working within the political and economic constraints of the Cold War, and reflecting both the limits and the opportunities posed by the Atlantic Alliance. He saw Fiat as an autonomous power, but one which was in constant dialogue and harmonious agreement with the state authorities. Valletta never hesitated to make himself heard when it came to new political line-ups, as in June 1962, when, in an interview for the newspaper *Il Messaggero*, he granted his own imprimatur or endorsement to the nascent center-left government, with the Partito Socialista Italiana (PSI) adhering to the majority in Parliament. Thus, even though it may seem that Fiat was not directly involved in politics, it was nevertheless active behind the scenes with regard to government alliances and coalitions, and offered its participation and perspectives to the political system during periods of political change.

The action of Adriano Olivetti (the head of a company set up by his father in 1908, which produced office machinery) differed from that of the other two entrepreneurs cited above. Disillusioned by the compromises that the major political parties imposed, he attempted to reach the public sphere by a direct route, through a cultural and political movement bearing his personal stamp, the Movimento Comunità or Community Movement, a federal-type political movement based upon territory. He led this with little success in the parliamentary elections of 1958 (he was the only member of the movement to be elected); but notwithstanding this, it still conditioned, by sheer force of example, the choices and behavior of successive governments, while simultaneously maintaining a critical distance from government circles. The insistence on the issue of urban planning undoubtedly helped enrich the political and administrative culture of the first center-left government.

But politics was not absent, not even from the horizon of the widespread entrepreneurship which, during the "economic miracle," provided the energy "from below" (as opposed to "from above," in big business and in the circles of the elite), which represented a vital economic base rooted in their own territorial contexts. The period of post-war reconstruction, and, immediately afterwards, the "economic miracle," appeared to be more shaped or determined by private and individual initiatives. But the latter could easily have become part of an economic system that offered a precise exchange of interdependency. It was in this way that the big businesses found their "reference points" in the world of credit, generally in the major national banks (Banca Commerciale Italiana, Credito Italiano, Banca Nazionale di Lavoro), while the small enterprises were mainly sustained by local circuits of country banks. This was how a system of economic organizations that guaranteed opportunity and margins of development for economic operators at different levels came into being. And this mechanism, partly spontaneous, and partly encouraged and sustained "from above," endorsed a positive relationship between the economy, politics, and the institutions. As noted above, this scenario began to change in the early 1960s, when the period of the "economic miracle" came to an end, and the period of attempted reformism implemented by the framework of the center-left government began. It is now clear that this phase was short-lived, at least regarding the reform projects. Thus, Italy did not follow the virtuous path of the other nations which had "lost the war, but won the peace." The country which had been second only to Japan in terms of growth rates, and had equaled or even, for brief periods, actually surpassed those of Germany, proved unable to reach a long-lasting stable economic equilibrium. The frequent political crises and, with regard to industry, the long period of intense conflict with the trade unions in the factories from 1969 to 1980, did not allow Italy to obtain stability, despite the persistent dynamism of its entrepreneurial system. What it lacked, above all in the 1960s and 1970s, was a system of reciprocal consultation (*concertazione*) or team play among the major organized interests that would have allowed both a more stable economic performance and less troubled and unstable public life.

Giovanni Agnelli, the most important member of the family that controlled the property of Fiat, succeeded Valletta as the head of the group in 1966. It was he who tried to establish a dialogue with the intention of putting pressure on the political system, on the one hand, while establishing a common meeting ground with the main trade unions, on the other. As President of the Confindustria (the Federation of Italian Industry) from 1974 to 1976,[4] in a period of great political and economic uncertainty, Agnelli wanted to attempt to beat a new path, consisting of "an agreement between manufacturers" that would reduce trade union conflicts in the workplace, on the one hand, and encourage the public (state) apparatus to change, on the other. This gave birth to one of the most controversial accords in Italian labor history, the agreement of January 1975, which closely indexed salaries to inflation (*scala mobile*), which was rising rapidly in the wake of the petrol crisis of 1973.

This move was not a success because it accelerated the inflationary process without reducing the trade union conflicts "from below" in the workplace. It also signaled a separation between the world of big business, be it private or public (state), and what is now called the "peripheral economy," that is, the areas and districts of small enterprises, which succeeded, thanks to their dimensions and de-centralized geographical positions in comparison to the major hubs of the Italian industrial system, in developing models of production which were more flexible and better equipped to satisfy both evolving and niche markets.

From among the parties in government, Agnelli found an interlocutor in the small Partito repubblicano (Republican Party) in the shape of Ugo La Malfa, who became the most diligent political referent, or key person, for the world of big business. Bruno Visentini, several times minister of the Partito repubblicano and a crucial "hinge" figure between public (state) and private industry, first heading IRI and then Olivetti, was also in close contact with La Malfa. In the 1970s, when Italy was in the grip of many problems, he played a role of autonomy and mediation, in dialogue with the same environs of lay or secular democracy as the Mediobanca of Enrico Cuccia, a person with a profound knowledge of the joints in the economic system, and who was continually called upon to "navigate" or manage successfully between the public (state) and private sphere.

The natural philo-government vocation of the leading industrial groups was undoubtedly an element of continuity, at least until the end of the twentieth century. The "interweaving"—or, some would say, collusion—between the leading economic groups and the political class was considered a constitutive element of the Italian Republic. As long as industry, or at least substantial parts of it, went to the opposition, the country had to await a new phase, one which was completely different, that of widespread industrialization which had invested in areas previously considered marginal to Italian development. It was the aggregate enterprises in the new manufacturing areas of the Northeast which first manifested their approval of the protest that brought the Lega Nord (the Northern League) to the fore, a movement which, when it appeared on the political horizon, seemed to represent a form of "territorial syndicalism," intent on claiming investment in local infrastructure and a revision of the distribution of the tax burden. But this "third Italy" failed, in the last part of the twentieth century, in its endeavors to undermine the primacy or domination of the elite, in terms of representation. The Confindustria chose to ignore the protest, and, instead, continued to pursue a task of institutional mediation, confirmed by a policy of "concertazione" or reciprocal consultation among the trade unions and other social actors, which took hold, above all, in the last decade of the twentieth century.

An End-of-the-Century Crisis

Even for the industrial system, the years of political and economic crisis that have gone down in history with the name *Tangentopoli* (bribesville or kickback city), which exposed the "*intreccio*," or collusion, of extortion and bribery which took place between enterprises and political parties, represent a decisive distinction. The 1990s saw the fall or disappearance of some of the major Italian enterprises, both private and public (Olivetti, Montedison), more or less concomitantly with the crisis in the political system. This signaled the end of an era and a discontinuity in Italy's economic and social history. It resulted in the new era in which the recipes of liberalization, privatization, and the dismantling of the public (state) apparatus in favor of organized production were all established, in short the particular themes that took form between 1992 and 1993 and which were destined to return in the international prescriptions in order to relaunch or restore the productivity and competitiveness of the Italian economy.

At this point we should focus on the role played by Guido Carli (1914–93), a vital figure who was Ministro per il commercio con l'estero (Minister for Foreign Trade) in the second half of the 1950s, Governor of the Bank of Italy (Banca d'Italia) from 1960 to 1975, President of the Confindustria from 1976 to 1980 (proposed by Agnelli), and, finally, Ministro del tesoro (Treasury Minister) at the moment of the Treaty of Maastricht. Through his actions, Carli determined the crucial stages in the evolution of the Italian economy: in many ways, he can be placed among the authors or creators of the dominant model of the mixed economy. And yet, in the last part of his life, he used the agreements for the unification of Europe to introduce the principle of the "*vincolo esterno*" or external constraint. Carli was convinced that Italy and its entrepreneurial system would not change of its own free will or be able to rely on its own economic and entrepreneurial force, and that in order to restore growth and promote industry, Italy needed to be subjected to external conditioning. In other words, the country needed the discipline which only the European Union was capable of applying, with the aim of reforming economic behavior, which, left to itself, was pushing the country towards economic collapse. With the transition to a single European currency, Italy would be obliged to abandon its resistance, bureaucratic staticity, and internal protection, thereby freeing an economic capacity which would then have repercussions on the dynamics of its economic development. It is worth noting how, at the end of his life, Carli lost the convictions that had previously guided him. After he graduated he went to work for IRI upon the suggestion of Giovanni Battista Montini, the future Pope Paul VI. It was only later, at the end of the Second World War, that he embraced the doctrine of liberal economics. As Minister for Foreign Trade and then, above all, in Banca d'Italia, it was Carli who had piloted Italian capitalism with authority; although, in his last years, he developed a deep pessimism regarding the economic destiny of a country that could not be left to its own devices, and which risked economic and civil decadence. In his final years as Treasury Minister, Carli dedicated himself to changing an economy which, he maintained, was drugged by public spending, by interference from government and politics, and from the competitive devaluation of the lira, which was a technique used in times of difficulty to save industrial enterprises. Carli had always observed how Italy had grown when it was able to connect itself to the cycles of international growth; hence the necessity to place Italy at the heart of European integration, in order to uproot the "*lacci e lacciuoli*" or traps and snares to which Carli attributed Italy's declining economic performance.

Twenty years on, we can reach the conclusion that the hypothesis of the *vincolo esterno* has not worked. The system of Italian big business is, for the most part, in decline; the entrepreneurial capitalism of medium-sized enterprises is a significant and interesting reality, but circumscribed, and the concern regarding the soundness and the efficiency of the vast area of small and very small enterprises remains. In the last twenty years, economic development in Italy has gradually, but consistently, slowed down. From the end of the twentieth century onwards, a radical change in Italy's history has been conjectured, modifying the model of development based upon the mixed economy and the role of the state at its very roots. The bases of this model were progressively eroded, starting from the 1970s when the configuration of the Italian economy in its entirety began to show signs of slowing down. At this time, the big businesses found themselves in difficulty, while the "small is beautiful" motto was used to extol the dynamism of small enterprises in the emerging industrial districts. It was at this moment that the hierarchies of the past found themselves in difficulty and Italy began to lose its own autonomous vision of economic development, without being able to identify a new productive infrastructure able to sustain growth in Italy, now devoid of its historical points of reference.

As is well known, the *Tangentopoli* scandal laid bare the gigantic linkages between the economy and the world of Italian politics which had fuelled a "perverse interweaving," or as stated earlier a perverse "collusion," which had remained unexplained. The proposed solution was that of shock therapy, inspired by the rules and dictates of Anglo-Saxon liberalism. In the so-called Second Republic,[5] we can almost say that industry was no longer included in the institutional system, as it had been in the First Republic. It is true that powerful collective lobbies existed, but the prime minister (Presidente del Consiglio) and entrepreneur Silvio Berlusconi, the man who has governed Italy for most of the last 20 years, is neither a representative of industry nor from the world of manufacturing. Instead, he is a representative of an economic activity born out of the mechanism of state concessions, an experience that brings us back to a "collusive form of capitalism," to use William J. Baumol's expression, and which has the tendency to reproduce some of the constants in the economic history of Italy, albeit in new forms. It can be easily verified how the loss of political and social prominence that industry underwent from the end of the twentieth century onwards correlated with the decline of the presence of big business in Italian society.

The entrepreneurial system with state participation and the companies that were grouped together in IRI was progressively fragmented and broken up as the logical effect of the dissolution of the public (state) holding company in the year 2000. At the same time, the long story of Fiat, in the configuration it had had for an entire century (1899–1999) also came to an end, almost contemporaneously with the tumultuous period of *Tangentopoli*, during which Fiat existed in a state of siege, together with other major industries (Montedison, ENI, Ferruzzi). In a certain sense, Fiat had been a material part of the constitution of the country, like the major political parties that had embodied or represented it. Even state aid and the other advantages which it had obtained seemed to be justified by the role it played in the economic system of a country which wished to identify itself with its great automobile industry. The state had sustained Fiat because it was the very embodiment of the great Italian private company, which had contributed with its vehicles and its productive capacity to model contemporary Italy, giving it a modern face. This mutual self-respect continued until the late 1980s, when the happy period of growth came to an end. Not surprisingly, Fiat found itself lost in the uncertain political waters of the Second Republic, which was established without its involvement. The center-right invented by Silvio Berlusconi and the even more disorganized center-left political alternative were alien creatures to the top managers in Turin, the logic of both sides being seen to be out of touch with the times (as occurred in 2000 with the election of the president of the Confindustria, which, for the first time, went to a candidate, Antonio D'Amato, in explicit opposition to the wishes of the Fiat group).

The worsening of the Fiat crisis in 2002 revealed all too clearly the very deep gap between the company and the center-right government, which observed the problems at the Lingotto, home to Fiat's management in Turin, with skepticism. The long period of Gianni Agnelli's industrial leadership was almost over (he died in January 2003), and many openly expressed their doubts about the prospects of saving a group which was heavily indebted, with a shrinking market, and lacking a strong and accredited management. Furthermore, in the summer of 2004, with the group at its worst moment, the choice of Sergio Marchionne, a manager trained exclusively abroad, as CEO was symptomatic. He has always underlined his separation from political mechanisms, defining his leadership as a return to pure business, no longer seeking a privileged position vis-à-vis the government and its institutions. Not even the global crisis of 2008 changed this approach: if anything, Fiat, under Marchionne's direction, emphasized that it would neither accept nor request state aid. On the other hand, it was this premise which enabled him to have a free hand in his search for an international alliance, which was achieved with Chrysler in 2009. Here, the project of creating a global car producer, Fiat-Chrysler, was born, which should allow the ties with Italy to be drastically cut back, and will in turn mean the end of its historic identification with the Republic.

By renouncing the national system of incentives and advantages, and, it can be added, the system of collusion, Fiat took a direction which, succumbing to the urgency of globalization, takes it away from Italy. The solution for a major Italian big business is to project itself internationally in order to free itself of the constraints of the Italian system.

ITALIAN INDUSTRY
IN THE TWENTY-FIRST CENTURY

The first ten years of the euro witnessed a period of transformation for the Italian economy and, in particular, for Italian manufacturing. This was a period of serious re-adjustment of the structure of industry and of enterprise, which saw a transformation in its configuration.

With the arrival of the euro, Italy was emerging from a problematical phase, as stated previously. These were the years in which the prospects of the major enterprises which had led the postwar industrial development of Italy faded: Fiat lost ground in the car sector; companies such as Montedison and Olivetti went into decline and eventually disappeared; in the tire sector, Pirelli had to be scaled down after it failed to gain control of the German tire producer Continental. Meanwhile, the dismantling of the state-owned enterprises proceeded unabated. Some interpreted this sequence of events as a sign that Italian economic production had gone into a cycle of irreversible decline, referring to the disappearance of industrial Italy (Luciano Gallino). Thus, the recurrent theme of Italy's economic and entrepreneurial decline made itself increasingly felt. The prospect of a so-called competitive devaluation of the lira in order to encourage exports vanished with the advent of the single currency, the euro; widespread skepticism regarding the country's economic destiny and its industrial production prevailed.

Notwithstanding this, Italian industry and manufacturing continued to exist. In October 2005, *The Economist* highlighted a fact which was usually omitted: the figures showed that, among the developed nations, only two—Germany and Italy—held a quota of employment in industry that was higher than 20 percent of the total employment figures. All the others, led by the United States and including Japan, were clearly below this threshold. This was easy to understand with an economic power such as Germany, which has some of the most important companies in the world, leaders in their sectors. But what about Italy with its myriad of micro-companies?

In reality, part of the business world had taken the double challenge of the euro and globalization very seriously. The companies which emerged as the most dynamic were neither the historic firms that remained, nor the small firms found in the territorial districts, which, moreover, had long been acclaimed. Instead, they were companies of intermediate size, which could be identified by a growing presence on the international markets and by their remarkable rate of innovation, which were taking on labor while the others were reducing their workforces. The function of these new companies was identified by an official survey carried out by Mediobanca, which, processing the data from Unioncamere,[6] succeeded in deciphering the structure of this new level of enterprise, which seized the opportunities offered by globalization and was able to wedge itself into global niche markets. These "pocket multinationals" are the real actors on the economic scene, and have, given their export capacity and notwithstanding everything, proven to be the most brilliant sector of Italian industry, and have not retreated since the introduction of the single currency. The figures show us that Italian businesses have performed well, above all, in the export sectors of the engineering industry, capital goods, and intermediary goods.

The crisis which spread from the end of 2008 onwards hit them hard, causing greater downturns in the volume of production than those experienced by their main European partners, Germany in particular. In percentage terms, Italy has exported less and imported more. In this way, it has paid for the heterogeneity of a productive system which is less solid and more fragmented, as well as the price of the repercussions of its financial situation. Nevertheless, one part of industry, the part dedicated to exports, was able to respond to the crisis with a certain degree of efficiency, at least until 2012. This is a sign that Italy's productive system has its levers and strong points, with a clear division between those who operate in international markets (and have learned how to penetrate the new world economies), and those who remain firmly anchored in an internal market which is, to all extents and purposes, stagnant.

During Italy's 150 years as a unified country, the history of its industry has been characterized by a peculiar conformation which appears to be the outcome of the interaction between private economic interests and public (state) intervention. It is what culminated in the configuration of a particular model of the mixed economy, that established itself between the 1930s and 1960s. It directed the transformation of the country and allowed Italy to become one of the most developed nations. For more than 20 years, however, this model has undergone a process of deconstruction which has progressively accelerated, until today, when we find ourselves with an economy that lacks a carefully defined structure.

The recent metamorphosis of Italian industry previously mentioned is one of the clearest indicators of this process of deconstruction. From this moment onwards, we will be able to observe whether the industrial economy of Italy has the resources to adopt a new configuration, an alternative to the one "in force" in the past, and whether the institutions will be able to accompany it and help it evolve. In the present phase, it appears that a sort of neutrality is emerging with regard to the country's economic and productive system, and this does not hold much hope for Italy's ability to maintain and update its industrial profile. Today, we are faced with the need to redraw the map of the geography and functions of industrial Italy, by resorting to taxonomies that cannot follow the patterns adopted in recent decades. We can no longer resort to the image of the Italy of industrial districts; it is no longer enough to evoke the profile of the dynamic medium-sized enterprises which export in order to grasp the specific character of a manufacturing system whose features are in reality uncertain and confused.

The impression is that the distances between the various types of industrial organizations have been reduced. Think about new factories that are considered large: Pomigliano d'Arco, with a workforce of 2000 people, is now an outpost of Fiat-Chrysler, just as the plant in Settimo Torinese is an outpost for Pirelli, with an even smaller number of workers (around 1250). In fact, in the near future, the gap, also in terms of productive units, between the different-sized enterprises will be much smaller. We are moving towards organizational models whose dimensions are no longer a basic distinction or a limitation. We are heading in the direction of leaner and more integrated structures, but which require high levels of investment. A first overview suggests that a new Italian industrial model is taking shape around a cluster of nodes or linkage points for "intelligent manufacturing," in companies where production is combined with high-level research in the areas of services and assistance. This design goes beyond the previous dimensional and territorial demarcation lines, but is still in its initial stages.

This evolution is accompanied by what the research center Censis has described—not in the most positive of terms—as a process of *"deindustrializzazione competitiva"* or competitive de-industrialization,[7] indicating a repositioning or realignment of a notable part of industry in the service sector. In the past, the vast archipelago of the service sector was able to compensate for the rapid downsizing of industrial organization but at a price of replacing factory work with less-qualified employment. In recent years, the opportunities created by the manufacturing system's response to the crisis seem to have favored the growth of a universe of businesses active in the most advanced segments of service industries, in particular those linked to the industrial sector.

The existence of a reciprocal influence between the service sector and industry is clearly highlighted by the very similar performance of value added in both sectors. A virtuous circle of reciprocal supply between the hubs of the manufacturing industry and the most advanced components of the service industry (logistics, storage, IT services, research services, machine hire, and professional counseling activities or services) should now be seen as the key to interpreting these processes of transformation. However, this needs to be encouraged by specific supportive actions, which question the capacity of a number of actors in the economic and industrial system to act in concert, following co-operative models. This will probably be crucial in formulating a development strategy which can help to overcome the stagnation in which the Italian economic system currently finds itself.

The convergence of the disintegration processes which occurred, above all, in 2012 and 2013 in the business system and the crisis in the Italian political system seems to be particularly significant. In a certain sense, it is as though the condition of the one reflected that of the other, and vice versa. In fact, the impasse within politics and political parties has been accentuated by the fact that economic and industrial Italy seems to have lost a clear perception of itself. Nothing, or almost nothing, seems to remain of the model on which the grand epoch of development in the 1950s and 1960s was based. The productive system has lost its distinctive physiognomy and the interdependencies that united the various components have failed, as two examples indicate. The first is the decline in the Italian steel industry, symbolized by the uncertainty of the fate of the Ilva Group, whose biggest plant in Taranto is at risk owing to the enormous costs of implementing anti-pollution regulations, costs which are certainly higher than the owners, the Riva family, are prepared to pay. The second, and in this case positive, example is the merger of Fiat and Chrysler, which is leading to a complete restructuring of the productive capacity of its plants in Italy, enhancing in perspective the Italian car production from the recent low levels (approximately 400,000 vehicles a year, a figure much below the production figures of other major European countries).

The new profile of these industrial sectors corresponds to the end of a historic phase in which the major production supply chains were identified as the cornerstones of the Italian economy. Vertical supply chains, currently in rapid decline, have been replaced by smaller businesses that are able to develop horizontal ties. But the deconstruction of the old Italian industrial model has not been accompanied by the introduction of an alternative model of production. Above all, we cannot assess the extent to which a new production model will be able to replace the old one, without leading to a drastic downsizing of industry.

And yet Italy could exploit what has been identified as the "new industrial revolution" (Peter Marsh), based upon technological paradigms that are extremely flexible and adaptable in comparison with those of mass production. In a world economy characterized by the continual multiplication of niche markets, both in the developed and developing countries, with highly versatile production technology symbolized by the 3D printer, the Italian industrial experience may find new ways to make its mark. Italy is, after all, the country that has shown an extraordinary degree of versatility in its industrial districts and with pocket multinationals. But in order to face this technological and economic watershed requires not only the traditional operative flexibility, but also a profound knowledge of new technologies and an optimum specialization of human capital, capable of exploiting all the opportunities available. Given the present state of affairs, it is difficult to predict whether the Italian business system is prepared to embark on such a challenging metamorphosis, operating for the most part "from below," in a way which is both spontaneous and uncoordinated, as in the past. It is even more difficult to imagine that the Italian political sphere will be able to drag itself out of its inertial swamp to accompany and to sustain a change of this magnitude, thereby overcoming the country's long-running impotence regarding its economic troubles. However, the restoration of an essential degree of coherence and systemic integration would seem to be a *sine qua non* for Italy to break the chains of stagnation and stalemate that currently hold it prisoner.

NOTES

1. Finsider was part of the major public holding IRI (Institute for Industrial Reconstruction, Istituto per la Ricostruzione Industriale), set up in 1933.
2. Acronym of Institute for Industrial Reconstruction, was an Italian public institute, established in 1933 and wound up in 2002.
3. The Ente nazionale idrocarburi (ENI) is today a multinational corporation. It was created by the Italian government as a public entity in 1953, and was converted into a limited company in 1992.
4. Founded in 1910, Confindustria is the main organization representing Italian manufacturing and services companies.
5. The period 1994–2011 was characterized by a strong dichotomy between the center-right, led by Silvio Berlusconi, and the center-left coalitions.

6. Unioncamere—the Italian Union of Chambers of Commerce, Industry, Artisans and Agriculture—is the public body that unites and institutionally represents the Italian Chamber of Commerce system.

7. The Censis (Social Investment Study Centre), is a socio-economic research institute founded in 1964.

CHAPTER 37

LABOR MARKET POLICY AND POLITICS

PATRIK VESAN

LABOR market policy has always been a key issue in Italian political debates. Since the 1950s, struggles over public employment services, workers' rights, wage regulation, and labor market flexibility have caught the attention of mass media and the parliamentary scene. Nevertheless, the political salience of Italian labor issues can hardly be explained by the financial burden associated with this policy domain. This latter (expressed as a percentage of gross domestic product) has always been below the average of the main European countries (except for the UK).[1] Moreover, if we consider the internal distribution of Italian social policy spending, even now labor market policy appears to be relatively minor, lagging behind pension and health policy expenditures. Why then has labor market policy featured so prominently in Italian politics?

A first reason is that most of the struggles in this policy domain have centered on regulatory provisions (labor laws, collective agreements), whose political relevance lies in redistributive conflicts on the allocation of rights and duties more than in its direct implications for public finance. A second reason is that Italian trade unions and political parties have often considered labor policy as an "arena of power" in which they tried to (re)assert their identity and legitimacy in the eyes of voters. As a consequence, debates on labor market policies have often exhibited a symbolic and ideological nature, rather than a programmatic and technical character. A third reason deals with the micro-distributive logic of Italian labor market policies. Measures such as public works, unemployment benefits, or employment incentives have represented important resources which have often been diverted by political parties in order to gain consensus at a national or local level.

The focus on regulatory provisions (and, conversely, the scarce attention paid to job-oriented services), the ideological nature of debates, and the clientelistic logic of policymaking are thus three important features of Italian labor policies that explain their political salience despite low associated expenditures. As we will argue, these characteristics have proven resilient in the face of important reforms that have been adopted throughout the decades.

The aim of this chapter is to reconstruct the development of Italian labor policy. In the next section, we present the institutional model that emerged and consolidated during the so-called "Golden Age" (1945–75). The third section focuses on a brief description of reform cycles that have, since the 1980s, led to some significant changes in the configuration of Italian labor policies. The main reasons behind these changes are briefly presented in the fourth section, while the last section concludes with some considerations on the future reform agenda.

Italian Labor Policies in the Golden Age

The original Italian labor policy model, which was developed between the 1950s and the end of the 1970s, was clearly geared towards the promotion of labor stability and the centrality of full-time, open-ended contracts.[2] Temporary employment contracts were considered an exception and were limited to specific sectors or jobs. The principle of a "guaranteed labor market" also informed the Workers' Statute, an important law adopted in 1970, concerning the protection of the rights of individuals in the workplace. The bulk of this law was contained in Article 18, which defined strict sanctions for illegitimate individual dismissals of workers with open-ended contracts.[3]

The unemployment benefit (UB) system was also devised to protect existing employment. Such a system was (and still is) based on a single insurance tier that embraced two main schemes. The first scheme consisted of rights-based unemployment insurance, providing minimal flat-rate benefits for a maximum duration of 180 days.[4] The second scheme was the *Cassa integrazione guadagni* (CIG), which is still in use. The CIG provides an ad hoc short-time work allowance that offers relatively generous wage replacement benefits (i.e. 80 percent of the gross salary for the employment suspension duration). In theory, the CIG should cover only temporary lay-offs in order to retain a skilled workforce during economic crises and industrial restructuring processes. However, since the 1970s, the CIG has often been used as a functional substitute for traditional income maintenance schemes, arbitrarily extending its standard duration in order to postpone moving people into formal unemployment status,[5] or to provide a bridge towards early retirement.

By contrast, no universal unemployment assistance and minimum income programs were established. As a consequence, first-time jobseekers and the long-term unemployed remained uncovered by unemployment protection support,[6] as did many employees because of the high contributory requirements of unemployment insurance.

Regarding active labor market policy, investments in training and job assistance were rather limited during the Golden Age. A further characteristic of the original labor policy model was the public monopoly of job placement services (PES) established in 1950, which managed a rigid and highly ineffective procedural hiring system.

In conclusion, the original model of Italian labor policies was strongly centered on the protection of the standard (full-time) employment of male breadwinners. By contrast, no passive or active security measures were universally guaranteed for first-time jobseekers and the many long-term unemployed, mainly represented by young workers.

Indeed, one important reason that can explain such institutional arrangements can be found in the (presumption of) extended family solidarities.[7] As in other Mediterranean countries, the main priority was the protection of the breadwinner's job, since close kinship was considered crucial in providing a last resort safety net. Furthermore, irregular jobs represented another widespread source of income for those people, especially in the South, formally registered as unemployed.

Nevertheless, the peculiar model of the Italian labor market policy can also be understood by looking at political factors. During the Golden Age, both the Christian Democracy (DC) and the Italian Communist Party (PCI) were not interested in investing in the adoption of a universal UB system or in advancing labor market flexibility. Their top priority was instead the creation and protection of employment opportunities, especially for male (adult) population.[8] This peculiar model of the Italian Golden Age labor policy quite closely reflected the predominant features of the strongly polarized party system, which often inhibited any attempt at programmatic dialogue on comprehensive and far-reaching labor market reforms.[9] However, the ideological nature of party competition was usually accompanied by the achievement of marginal accommodations between the main political forces addressed, for example, to the selective extension of the CIG, the clientelistic distribution of temporary public works, and other tangible benefits to specific groups of voters. Indeed, this micro-level legislation offered some types of compensation for the general distortions and inefficiencies of the national labor policy model. Nevertheless, it also enhanced the fragmented, discretionary, and occupationally defined nature of the policy model.

Once put in place, the original configuration of the Italian labor policy showed a self-reinforcing logic which was fuelled by the prevailing particularistic mode of political competition. Moreover, the scarce capacity of the State administration contributed to seriously slowing down the adoption of path-breaking reforms. This situation lasted until the end of the 1970s, when some new developments breached the consolidated model of Italian labor policy.

The Long March to Reform

Since the 1980s, a number of important changes have come about with respect to Italian labor market policy. In this section, we briefly describe the main innovations that have been adopted over the last few decades. To this end, we can distinguish four major reform cycles.[10]

The first cycle started at the beginning of the 1980s, in reaction to the rapid deterioration of economic and labor market conditions that followed the second oil crisis. The high level of inflation (21 percent in 1980) and the slowing down of the economy were among the main concerns at that time. From 1980 to 1989, the unemployment rate rose from 7.6 percent to 12 percent, while the employment rate, which registered minor fluctuations around 54 percent, showed an increase of about 10 percent in the service sector.

In order to mitigate the social consequences of the industrial restructuring processes, Italian governments made extensive use of the CIG and pre-retirement schemes, and in 1991 a new scheme (the mobility allowance) was adopted to protect workers in firms with more than 15 employees in case of collective redundancies. Moreover, at the end of the 1980s, two further innovations were introduced: an unemployment insurance scheme with reduced contributory requirements for workers ineligible for the ordinary UB, while the meager flat rate unemployment benefit was replaced by a nominal replacement rate.

Other important reforms were the revision of the automatic mechanism of wage indexation (the so-called *scala mobile*) to combat rising inflation and the introduction of new employment contracts, such as part-time and temporary training contracts for young jobseekers (*contratto di formazione lavoro*), whilst regulations on fixed-term jobs and hiring procedures were gradually relaxed. Although these measures opened the way to the gradual liberalization of the Italian labor market policy, their implementation was limited and subjected to the control of trade unions through contractual agreements. Thus, the main characteristics of the original institutional model remained largely resilient, at least until the beginning of the following decade.

The second reform cycle, which unfolded during the 1990s, began in the middle of a deep economic and political crisis, and in reaction to a rising unemployment rate (which reached 30 percent in the mid-1990s among young people) and a falling employment rate. During this cycle, five important agreements were signed between the government and social partners: in 1992, with the Amato government; in 1993, with the Ciampi government; in 1995, with the Dini government; in 1996, with the Prodi government; and finally in 1998, with the D'Alema government. These pacts focused on a wide array of issues, ranging from income, fiscal, local development, and employment policies, to the regulation of collective bargaining. Although this repeated recourse to trilateral agreements did not lead to the institutionalization of "social concertation" as a major policymaking strategy,[11] these agreements facilitated—on the Italian road to the euro—the adoption of some innovative labor policy measures. In particular, in 1997, an important reform of the PES system was undertaken. This reform was based on three pillars: the legalization of temporary agency work, the abolishment of the public monopoly on job services, and the devolution of competences on active labor market policy to the regions and the provinces. Alongside the introduction of temporary agency work, further liberalization of the labor market was realized thanks to the promotion of part-time, apprenticeship, and semi-independent work (*lavoro parasubordinato*). By contrast, no path-breaking unemployment benefit reforms were adopted, and would not be until 2012. Only some incremental changes can be observed in relation to the net average replacement rate of the CIG and the ordinary UB, which started to markedly converge. This effect was caused by a combination of factors: the incremental upgrading of ordinary unemployment insurance (which reached 40 percent of the previous wage in 2000) and the decrease in CIG payouts that followed the introduction of a benefit ceiling indexed at 80 percent of wage rises. Nevertheless, disparity in levels of protection for different categories of workers persisted, owing to the longer duration of the CIG.

The third reform cycle began in 2001, with the appointment of the new center-right government led by Silvio Berlusconi. The policy measures adopted in this period were mainly targeted at increasing the employment rate through the liberalization of the labor market. In 2001, the adoption of the European directive on fixed-term work lowered the restrictions applicable to this type of employment contract. Law 30/2003, partially inspired by the work of Marco Biagi, a government consultant assassinated by the Red Brigades (Brigate rosse), legalized several forms of atypical work contracts. It is worth noting that these measures, similar to many of the reforms realized in other European countries during this period,[12] affected labor market regulation only "at the margin" since they did not concern standard employment relationships. A more comprehensive liberalization was not possible, owing to the strong opposition of trade unions (in particular the CGIL, the Italian General Confederation of Labor), which neutralized the efforts made by the Berlusconi government to diminish the level of employment protection for open-ended workers by revising Article 18 of the Workers' Statute.

The attempt to adopt a comprehensive reform of the unemployment benefit system also turned out to be a blind alley. Again, only incremental changes were introduced. In particular, to face the social impacts of the economic crisis that started in 2007, the main instruments have been the so-called "emergency social shock absorbers" (*ammortizzatori sociali in deroga*). These are ad hoc UBs managed by regional authorities and trade unions, which extend the traditional coverage (both in terms of duration and categories of workers) of the "standard" CIG schemes and mobility allowances.[13] Recourse to discretionary and temporary measures has thus been preferred to the promotion of a more radical reform that would create a universal nationwide UB system.

The last reform cycle coincides with the adoption of Law 92 promoted by the Monti government in 2012. Once again, most of the political attention and efforts were devoted to regulatory measures, especially the revision of Article 18 of the Workers' Statute. For the first time, Law 92 broke with the strict Italian protective approach of core workers, stating that in the case of illegitimate dismissals for economic and disciplinary reasons the reinstatement of the worker in the previous job position is no longer compulsory, and the judge can only force the employer to pay a lump sum compensation.[14] There were no strong empirical evidences in favour of the Article 18 reform: its relevance for the better functioning of the Italian economy and labor market is debated. Moreover, the strictness of the Italian labor market, measured by the OECD employment protection legislation index, had already been significantly lowered from the mid-1990s, thanks to the sharp liberalization of temporary contracts. Nevertheless, as we will argue, the Monti government wanted primarily to send a clear message to international political and economic actors in order to regain their confidence.

A further innovation of the Law 92/2012 was the partial reform of the UB system, which abrogated the mobility allowance (but only by 2017) and introduced a new unemployment benefit (*assicurazione sociale per l'impiego*, or ASPI) characterized by a higher replacement rate, longer duration, and extended coverage.[15] By contrast, CIG schemes were not substantially modified, owing to strong vetoes from social partners, while no significant innovations were adopted with reference to active labor market policy.

In conclusion, the original labor policy model has been transformed over the years, both with gradual changes and abrupt shifts. Compared to recent decades, the level of protection guaranteed by the Italian UB system is now more similar to that provided by other European countries. Further, national employment regulation appears less rigid—thanks both to the liberalization of atypical contracts and the Article 18 reform, which has partially reduced employers' uncertainties related to individual dismissal costs.

Despite the adoption of several important reforms in recent years, the old distortions of the Italian labor policy have not been completely erased. The Italian UB system continues to be centered on ad hoc measures (short-term work schemes), whereas first-time jobseekers and a substantial share of workers (in particular atypical workers) are not yet covered by any kind of universal income-maintenance schemes.[16]

As far as active labor market policies are concerned, we can point out contradictory trends. On the one hand, we can observe several signs of "normative recalibration," that is a gradual reorientation of discourses on labor policies towards a more proactive approach.[17] On the other hand, public spending on active labor market policies has decreased since 2004, after a promising rise from 1994 to 2003. Moreover, public employment services remain highly fragmented on a regional basis and weak because of the traditional lack of investment and the limited institutional capacity of the Italian public administration.

The sharp increase in temporary workers owing to the liberalization reforms have worsened the dual character of the Italian labor market, in which a relatively well-protected group of core workers coexists with temporary workers (mostly young people) who are often trapped in poor quality jobs characterized by low pay and limited access to social security and training opportunities. With the changes introduced during the Monti government, the era of reform "at the margin" was supplanted by interventions aimed at reducing labor market segmentation through targeting hitertho unaffected core workers. As a consequence, the increase in flexibility for open-ended employees has made boundaries between "insiderness" and "outsiderness" more blurred than they were before the beginning of the "great recession." Moreover, the reform carried out by the Monti government has only partially been accompanied by thoughtful changes in the income maintenance benefits system. The adaptation of the Italian labor market policies to post-industrial economic conditions therefore remains a task to be accomplished. This task appears particularly urgent since the recent economic crisis has worsened some of the main problematic features which have charaterized the Italian labor market for decades, such as the territorial divide between North and South Italy and the generational segmentation of the labor market.[18]

EXPLAINING THE REFORMS

The four reform cycles that we have briefly described have been the result of a constellation of factors that have contributed to a partial break in the self-reinforcing logic of the old institutional model. The pressure for such reforms originated with the emergence of new problems and social needs that have followed the transformation of the Italian economy and labor market since the late 1980s. The gradual deindustrialization process and the late tertiarization of the Italian economy, the rise in the unemployment rate accompanied by a slow growth (if not a decrease) in the employment rate, and changes in the organization of modes of production have, indeed, represented common pressures which have favored the adoption of labor market reforms. However, beyond these functional drivers, political science literature has pointed out at least three other groups of factors which have triggered Italian labor market policy change.

The first group of factors focuses on transformations of the Italian political system, especially with reference to relationships between political and corporate actors. After the fall of the Berlin Wall, the old party system collapsed and new political groups appeared on the national scene. This political earthquake has had two consequences for the content of national labor policy.

Firstly, at the beginning of the 1990s, traditional political competition was partially suspended. The political void accompanying the end of the old party system was temporarily filled by technocratic governments and social partners who collaborated in the face of the serious economic crisis that hit Italy in 1992–3. As we have said, this climate of "social concertation," partially insulated from the influence of the old party politics, was propitious for adopting social pacts favoring budgetary restraint, wage moderation, and labor market reforms aimed at increasing the employment rate and reducing the high level of youth unemployment.

Secondly, the 1993 electoral reform facilitated the alignment of political parties around two major poles.[19] Since that time, this (partial) bipolarization has led to the gradual consolidation of a centripetal party coalition dynamic, despite the emergence of new forms of radicalization and the persistence of a high level of polarization within the Italian party system. The emergence of this dynamic, in addition to the convergence of the main political forces' positions on socio-economic issues,[20] has eased the acceptance of some labor market reforms that in the past had always been hampered by the prevailing centrifugal direction of party competition. In particular, both center-right parties, such as Forza Italia and Lega Nord, and center-left parties, albeit with some differences, favored the liberalization of the Italian labor market in a way that was never taken into consideration by the DC or PCI. However, until 2012 this liberalization process was realized at the margin, thus without affecting core workers. This was particularly due to the pressures exerted by radical left forces (the leftist part of DS-PD, Rifondazione comunista, and especially the CGIL), which continued to hold significant veto power over the center-left coalition and over the entire Italian political system generally. The context changed in 2012, when a double political and economic crisis once more caused a partial suspension of party competition, allowing the new technocratic Monti government to introduce a law that decreased, for the first time since 1970, the level of employment protection for open-ended workers.

As far as income support measures for the unemployed are concerned, the adoption of a comprehensive reform has been prevented by mutual vetoes: from the political and trade union Left (Rifondazione comunista and CGIL), on the one hand, and from employer associations and the Lega Nord, on the other, which opposed a radical change of the status quo. At the same time, the Lega Nord, which in the 2000s exerted a strong influence upon the center-right governments, was firmly against the introduction of minimum-income schemes, since—it argued—these schemes would have mainly allocated resources in favor of southern regions.[21]

This situation did not radically change under the Monti cabinet; no substantial reform of the CIG system was approved. The only changes with regard to unemployment benefits resulted from the introduction of the new ASPI scheme and the abrogation of the mobility allowance. This latter measure, however, was postponed to 2017, leaving, de facto, the door open for further regulatory intervention.

The second group of explanatory factors, which has been pointed out by the literature on Italian labor policy reforms, refers to the presence of exogenous pressures, in particular originating from Italy's membership of the European Union (EU). Ferrera and Gualmini focus, for example, on the role of economic internationalization and European Economic Monetary Union (EMU).[22] Since the 1980s, partial labor market liberalization has been promoted in order to increase the cost competitiveness of Italian firms, compensating them for the difficulties caused by the entry of the lira into the European Monetary System (1979) and the liberalization of capital movement following the adoption of the Single European Act. A further and more significant pressure on Italian labor market policies originated with the Maastricht package on the EMU, which engaged Italy in a process of restoring sound public finances. The reference to external constraints (*vincolo esterno*), such as the financial crisis and the need for action in the name of Europe, have been used by successive Italian governments to bolster support for the adoption of reforms that have been framed as necessary, fair, and in some cases, also inevitable.[23] This is what happened in the 1990s when several social pacts, including some important employment policy measures, were adopted.[24]

The *vincolo esterno* dynamic also held true when the Monti government passed a comprehensive reform of labor market policy in 2012. In this case, the *vincolo esterno* was represented by the need to send clear signals to international financial markets and to comply with the requests advanced by EU institutions.[25] Nevertheless we can highlight some differences in the recourse to the *vincolo esterno* strategy. In the 1990s, the *vincolo esterno* argument served the government by helping to *convince* potential veto players (in particular trade unions) that they could not further procrastinate about suggested reforms. In this case, the trigger for reforms was represented by the need to face the economic and financial crisis combined with the idea of "joining the club" of the euro, which enjoyed wide support at that time. By contrast, in 2012 the political context was rather different, since it was characterized by the growing Euroskepticism of both citizens and elites,[26] and by the tight pressures coming from EU institutions, which allowed the government to *impose* its decisions in a top-down policy style.[27] In such a situation, which was marked by the severe sovereign debt crisis of 2011, the need of financial support from international institutions exerted an implicit but harsh pressure for reforms.[28]

The *vincolo esterno* thesis thus refers to the strategic use of external constraints as catalysts for domestic change. Yet this thesis can be interpreted more broadly, with reference to the role of ideas and the activation of learning and cognitive convergence processes.[29] This conceptualization of the *vincolo esterno* leads us to a last explanation of labor policy change in Italy—one which has remained rather underdeveloped in literature up to now.

Such an explanation focuses on norm internalization processes at an elite level. According to this perspective, the Italian labor market reforms can be explained by a shift in policy beliefs: from state interventionism and employment protection goals to competitiveness and employment growth goals. This shift started in the mid-1980s, and subsequently was fostered by different stimuli such as the dramatic economic emergencies that hit Italy at the beginning of the 1990s and again after 2008, the macroeconomic challenges associated with Italy's EMU accession, the burgeoning public debt and, later, the sovereign debt crisis, and finally the new reformist discourses carried out by the OECD and the European institutions. This ideational turn has been mainly guided by technocratic elites who have played the role of "normative entrepreneurs" in persuading political and union leaders of the need to adopt new policy recipes inspired by the idea of "flexicurity," in other words some sort of compromise between greater labor flexibility and security for workers.[30] Nevertheless, this policy learning process has remained largely incomplete, since it has only partially translated into concrete institutional outputs.[31] This can be explained by the existence of severe budget constraints and by the fact that the technocratic reform coalition was confronted with the presence of nested cross-class interests, which firmly defended the status quo.[32] Finally, another obstacle to learning has been the weak coordination capacities of Italian unions, employers, and public administration, which have prevented the consolidation of valuable employment services and the vocational training system. As a consequence, Italian flexicurity-inspired reforms have been mainly weighted towards the flexibility dimension, without seriously addressing the challenges posed by the deep dualism of the Italian labor market.

CONCLUSIONS

The evolution of labor market policy in Italy has been a story of a profound, albeit uncoordinated, transformation, proceeding from the emergence and consolidation of a peculiar institutional model during the Golden Age to the reform of many of its original characteristics throughout the 1990s and 2000s. Despite some important steps that have been taken in the direction of a more universal and coherent model of public intervention in the labor market, the actual system remains imbalanced, guaranteeing an adequate level of protection (and services) only to some categories of workers.[33] In order to address the main distortions of the Italian labor policy model, three issues are crucial.

Firstly, a comprehensive reform of the UB system is needed. This reform should be aimed at reducing the wide disparities of treatment among workers and assuring adequate universal protection to those categories of workers and jobseekers who are still not covered by any form of unemployment or social security scheme.[34]

Secondly, the normative recalibration towards active labor market policies, despite recurrent pledges, has not yet led to sound investments in employment services and training programs. This clearly clashes with the fact that these measures should represent the cornerstone of a modern labor market policy based on securing transitions to, during, and out of employment.[35]

Thirdly, even though the adoption of sweeping reforms remains a fundamental step, their implementation has been often overlooked. This represents a serious mistake, since the outcome of labor policy measures largely depends on their effective enforcement, which often relies on a complex network of public and private actors at different levels of government. This implies developing a stronger coordination capability as well as reducing the likelihood of an impasse deriving from the excessive fragmentation and dispersion of decisional power.

The modernization of the Italian labor market is therefore still hampered by the regulatory and particularistic bias of employment policies, which have remained largely underdeveloped and ill-suited for the emerging post-industrial character of the Italian economy. Overcoming these hurdles requires furthering the shift in Italian party system dynamics towards a (more) programmatic mode of political competition and reinforcing the capacity of public administration—two conditions that still need to be fulfilled.

Notes

1. After the outbreak of the sovereign crisis which hit Italy in 2011, Italian labor market policy expenditure increased more than that of other countries, such as Germany, owing to the high level of unemployment rate.
2. Patrik Vesan, "La politica del lavoro," in Maurizio Ferrera, ed., *Politiche sociali* (Bologna: Il Mulino, 2012), 123–84.
3. Article 18, which applies only to firms with more than 15 employees, established that a labor court could mandate an employer who had fired a worker without "just cause" or "justified reasons" to reinstate the worker in his/her former position and to pay the entire wage and social contributions lost since the day of dismissal.
4. In order to get access to the unemployment insurance employees should have at least two years of insurance seniority and one year of social contributions paid in the two years

before the onset of unemployment. These entitlement requirements are still valid for the ASPI, the unemployment benefit scheme introduced in 2013.

5. It is worth noting that people covered by CIG schemes are not formally considered to be unemployed.

6. The only exception was represented by some discretionary unemployment benefits that were provided to specific categories of workers.

7. See Chapter 35, this volume.

8. Elisabetta Gualmini, *La politica del lavoro* (Bologna: Il Mulino, 1998); Maurizio Ferrera, Valeria Fargion, Matteo Jessoula, *Alle radici del welfare all'italiana: origini e futuro di un modello sociale squilibrato* (Venice: Marsilio, 2012).

9. Julia Lynch, *Age in the Welfare State: The Origins of Social Spending on Pensioners, Workers, and Children* (Cambridge: Cambridge University Press, 2006); Georg Picot, *Politics of Segmentation: Party Competition and Social Protection in Europe* (London and New York: Routledge, 2012).

10. For similar, but not completely overlapping, reform cycles in health and pension policy, see Chapter 38, this volume.

11. Marino Regini, Sabrina Colombo, "Italy: The Rise and Decline of Social Pacts," in Sabina Avdagic, Martin Rhodes, and Jelle Visser, eds., *Social Pacts in Europe: Emergence, Evolution and Institutionalization* (Oxford: Oxford University Press, 2011), 118–46.

12. Johan Bo Davidsson, "An Analytical Overview of Labour Market Reforms across the EU: Making Sense of the Variation," *LABORatorio R. Revelli working papers*, no. 111 (June 2011), 1–29.

13. Stefano Sacchi, Federico Pancaldi, and Claudia Arisi, "The Economic Crisis as a Trigger of Convergence? Short-time Work in Italy, Germany and Austria," *Social Policy and Administration* 45, no. 4 (August 2011), 465–87.

14. The reinstatement of employees illegitimately dismissed remains compulsory when the court recognizes the manifest nonexistence of the motive. Despite the changes introduced by Law 92, the real impact of the Article 18 reform on liberalization of the Italian labor market will depend on the predominant judicial approach to the issue.

15. The ASPI provides a benefit for one year (18 months for workers aged 55 years and over), equal to at least 75 percent of previous average wage, decreasing after six months. This benefit has also been extended to apprentices, cooperative workers, and art workers.

16. Stefano Sacchi and Patrik Vesan "Employment Policy: Segmentation, Deregulation and Reforms in the Italian Labour Market," in Ugo Ascoli and Emmanuele Pavolini, eds., *The Italian Welfare State in a European Perspective* (Bristol: Policy Press, 2015), 71–100.

17. Stefano Sacchi and Patrik Vesan, "Interpreting Employment Policy Change in Italy since the 1990s: Nature and Dynamics," *Carlo Alberto notes*, no. 228 (December, 2011), 1–35; Maurizio Ferrera, Anton Hemerijck, "Recalibrating European Welfare Regimes," in Jonathan Zeitlin and David Trubeck, eds., *Governing Work and Welfare in a New Economy: European and American Experiments* (Oxford, Oxford University Press, 2003), 88–128.

18. Sacchi and Vesan "Employment policy," 71–100.

19. See Chapters 11 and 25, this volume.

20. Picot, *Politics of Segmentation: Party Competition and Social Protection in Europe*; Giuseppe Ieraci, "Governments, Policy Space and Party Positions in the Italian Parliament (1996–2001): An Inductive Approach to Parliamentary Debate and Votes of Investiture," *South European Society and Politics* 11, no. 2 (June, 2006), 261–85.

21. Stefano Sacchi, Francesca Bastagli, "Italy: Striving Uphill but Stopping Halfway," in Maurizio Ferrera, ed., *Welfare State Reform in Southern Europe: Fighting Poverty and Social Exclusion in Italy, Spain, Portugal and Greece* (London/New York: Routledge, 2005), 84–140.

22. Maurizio Ferrera, Elisabetta Gualmini, *Rescued by Europe? Italy's Social Policy Reforms from Maastricht to Berlusconi* (Amsterdam: Amsterdam University Press, 2004).

23. Kenneth Dyson and Kevin Featherstone, "Italy and EMU as a "Vincolo Esterno": Empowering the Technocrats, Transforming the State" *South European Society & Politics* 1, no. 2 (Autumn, 1996), 272–99. On the importance of the *vincolo esterno* see also Chapters 36 and 38, this volume.

24. Bob Hancké and Martin Rhodes, "EMU and Labour Market Institutions in Europe: The Rise and Fall of National Social Pacts," *Work and Occupations* 32, no. 2 (May 2005), 196–228.

25. In 2011, Trichet, who was at the time President of the European Central Bank (ECB), and his designated successor Draghi, sent a "confidential" letter pressing the Berlusconi government to adopt sweeping reforms. As for labor policy, the letter strongly supported the promotion of firm-level agreements, a review of hiring and firing regulation, and a review of the unemployment insurance system.

26. Paolo Graziano and Matteo Jessoula, "'Eppur si muove(va). . .'. The Italian Trajectory of Recent Welfare Reforms: From 'Rescued by Europe' to Euro-Skepticism," in Sophie Jacquot, Paolo Graziano, and Bruno Palier, eds., *The EU and the Domestic Politics of Welfare State Reforms. Europa, Europae* (London: Palgrave Macmillan, 2010), 148–74.

27. Stefano Sacchi, "Italy's Labour Policy and Policymaking in the Crisis: From Distributive Coalitions to the Shadow of Hierarchy," in Hideko Magara and Stefano Sacchi, eds., *The Politics of Structural Reforms. Social and Industrial Policy Change in Italy and Japan* (Cheltenham: Edward Elgar, 2013), 192–214.

28. Stefano Sacchi, "Conditionality by Other Means: EU Involvement in Italy's Structural Reforms in the Sovereign Debt Crisis," *Comparative Politics* 13, no. 1 (2015), 77–92.

29. Kevin Featherstone, "The Political Dynamics of External Empowerment: The Emergence of EMU and the Challenge to the European Social Model," in Andrew Martin and George Ross, *Euros and Europeans. Monetary Integration and the European social model* (Cambridge: Cambridge University Press, 2004), 226–47.

30. Patrik Vesan, "The Emergence and Transformation of the European Agenda on Flexicurity," *Working Paper of the Department of Economic and Political Sciences*, University of Aosta Valley, no. 4 (October 2012), 1–31.

31. Matteo Jessoula and Patrik Vesan, "Italy – Partial Adaptation of an Atypical Benefit System," in Jochen Clasen and Daniel Clegg, eds., *Regulating the Risk of Unemployment. National Adaptations to Post-industrial Labour Markets in Europe* (Oxford: Oxford University Press, 2011), 191–222.

32. Sacchi, "Italy's Labour Policy and Policymaking in the Crisis," 192–214.

33. An overall reform of labor market policies is being carried out at the time this volume goes to press. This reform envisages a further liberalization of the new open-ended contracts and some important changes in the unemployment benefit system aimed at increasing the coverage for job seekers. Moreover, if it is fully implemented, this reform will also forsee a transformation of the governance of active labor market policies and public employment services.

34. Sacchi and Vesan "Employment Policy," 71–100. For more details on the labor market reform carried out by the Renzi government at the beginnnig of 2015, see Patrik Vesan and Emmanuele Pavolini "The Italian labour market policy reforms and the Economic Crisis: Toward the End of the Italian Exceptionalism?," in Sotiria Theodoropoulou, ed., *Auterity stategies and welfare states in Europe* (Brussels: European Trade Union Press, forthcoming).

35. Günter Schmid and Bernard Gazier, *The Dynamics of Full Employment. Social Integration through Transitional Labour Markets* (Cheltenham: Edward Elgar, 2002).

CHAPTER 38

....

THE WELFARE STATE

Pensions and Health Care

....

MAURIZIO FERRERA AND MATTEO JESSOULA

THE chapter analyzes the developmental trajectory of the two main pillars of the Italian welfare state—that is, pensions and health care, accounting for roughly 90 percent of total social expenditure—by identifying four different phases: i) expansion in the 1950s–70s, ii) ambivalent and chaotic restructuring in the 1980s, iii) encompassing reforms in the 1990s and 2000s, iv) austerity driven retrenchment since the start of the financial and economic crisis in 2007.[1]

We argue that, parallel to improvements in social and living standards, social protection expansion in Italy brought about imbalances and distortions—the so-called "five original sins"—that have led to the emergence of a very peculiar, as well as relatively dysfunctional, institutional arrangement: the "welfare state Italian style."[2] Despite thorough reforms in the last two decades, these sins—or vices—of the Italian welfare state are still partly visible and in need of being addressed.

WELFARE STATE ITALIAN STYLE: ORIGINS AND EXPANSION

....

The institutional framework inherited by the new Republican regime born in 1948 divided social protection into three separate parts: social insurance (*previdenza*), health and sanitation (*sanità*), and social assistance (*assistenza*). Insurance coverage was limited to employees, thus excluding the self-employed; most benefits were related to previous contributions (pensions) or flat rate (unemployment benefits). The provision of health services relied heavily on the private sector, while hospitals (called IPAB, Institutes of Public Assistance and Charity), were subject to state supervision, but with large administrative and financial autonomy—many of them were actually under control of the Catholic Church. Finally, a plethora of public and semi-public agencies provided social assistance for the needy at national and local level, paralleled by private and church charities.

While reforms started to extend coverage and increase generosity of social protection schemes especially in the field of pensions, the institutional architecture witnessed only a few alterations during the 1950s.[3] Yet, at the turn of the decade, things started to change.

The 1957–63 "economic miracle" brought about greater national well-being, also producing a growing "fiscal dividend" in the public budget. In a new cultural and political climate, social problems and policies received increasing visibility and attention. The political alliance between the Christian Democrats and the Socialists was based on the premise of a new wave of reforms and was committed to a radical modernization of the country. The formation of the new government coalition in 1962 was followed by several articulated reports on social reforms:[4] the list of the reforms actually implemented remained quite limited, however, at least up to the mid-1960s. From 1968 onwards, the institutional profile of the Italian welfare state started to change rapidly, in the wake of new and heated social conflicts and under popular and union pressures. Hospital care was thoroughly revised in its administrative and financial status. The reform transformed hospitals in public institutions owned and transparently administered by the state, changed the health care financing system, and introduced new coordinating and planning institutions within the Ministry of Health Care. The pension reforms of 1968 and 1969 introduced an "earnings-related" formula, guaranteeing to employees a replacement rate of up to 80 percent after 40 years of career, which turned out to be very generous especially in light of the loose eligibility conditions for retirement: pensionable age was at 60/55 years for men/women, and the latter reform also introduced for employees the possibility of retiring after 35 years of insurance membership, regardless of age, with a replacement rate of 70 percent (so-called *pensioni di anzianità*, i.e. seniority pensions).

This reformist zeal continued and indeed deepened throughout the 1970s. Following constitutional provisions, regions and local authorities were (very) gradually transformed into the main loci of welfare policy, gradually suppressing the health insurance and assistance funds run from the center. Social assistance, health care, housing, and vocational training thus gradually became the competence (at least formally) of sub-national governments. New social and personal services were organized, new housing and transport programs launched, and some first active labor market policies inaugurated. Last but not least, in 1978 a sweeping reform led to the establishment of the National Health Service, the NHS (Servizio Sanitario Nazionale), replacing all pre-existing separate professional insurance funds.

In the second half of the 1970s the Italian welfare state thus emerged as a relatively distinct and coherent institutional configuration. Though largely centered on the Bismarckian social insurance principle typical of all Continental, conservative-corporatist welfare regimes,[5] in the field of health care this configuration included a "Beveridgean" element (the NHS), or at least a Beveridgean aspiration to universal and uniform coverage—an

Table 38.1 Social Policy Reforms, 1952–1978

Social Insurance

1952	Pension reform: improvement of pension formula and establishment of pension minima
1955–66	Family allowances reform
1957–66	Pension insurance extended to farmers, artisans and traders
1958–65	Increase of pension levels and pension minima
1968	Pension reform: introduction of earnings-related pensions. Unemployment insurance improved.
1969	Pension reform: introduction of social pensions, cost of living indexation
1974	Reform of invalidity pensions
1975	Wage indexation of pensions

Health Care

1968	Reform of administrative and financial regulations for hospitals
1974	Hospital care transferred to regions
1978	Establishment of the National Health Service

Social Assistance

1972	Jurisdiction over social assistance and services transferred to the regions
1977	Social assistance "categorical" funds abolished; jurisdiction transferred to local authorities

aspiration which was already present in the 1948 Constitution. The Bismarckian transfer schemes provided adequate benefits, most of which were earnings-related and fully indexed: pensions, in particular, were based on a highly generous earnings-related formula. The formerly dispersed health care services had been replaced by a relatively unitary—though highly decentralized—national and universal service, based on citizenship; education had also been reformed and greatly expanded, and housing broadly decentralized. A process of incisive secularization, moreover, had accompanied these transformations, greatly reducing the role of the Catholic Church in social policy and clearly disconnecting the notion of "welfare" from that of "Christian charity." In the field of social assistance, however, the family continued to play a crucial role as redistributive agency (see Chapter 35, this volume).

The institutional growth of the welfare state was paralleled by a rapid and substantial quantitative expansion. In the mid-1950s, total social expenditure (including income maintenance, health care, and social assistance) absorbed around 10 percent of GDP—a relatively low level by international standards. In 1970 this percentage had risen to 17.4 percent, reaching 22.6 percent in 1975—a level in line with that of France or Belgium and higher than that of Britain.[6]

All these dynamics gave a great and unquestionable contribution to the overall modernization of the country. Similarly, they contributed to raise living standards while reducing poverty and inequality (which were still widespread in the 1950s). They left, however, a number of unresolved structural questions. Moreover, they planted some new, dangerous seeds that led to the emergence of additional problems: the 1970s witnessed the appearance of an endogenous crisis, the most visible symptoms of which were concentrated in the sector of welfare state financing. Using summary formulas, we can say that the Golden Age of welfare expansion witnessed the appearance of five "original sins," which have been (and still largely are) the object of articulated debates and policy actions in the subsequent decades.

The Five "Original Sins"

The first two sins can be characterized as "distortions." The social insurance reforms listed in Table 38.1 originated, firstly, a *functional* distortion, clearly favoring certain risks/functions of social policy—most notably, old age—at the expenses of certain others—most notably, family benefits and services, total lack of employment/income, and the relief of poverty. In particular, the schemes aimed at catering for the needs of large and poor families remained underdeveloped and underfunded. At the beginning of the 1950s, pensions and family benefits absorbed a roughly equal share of GDP.[7] By 1980, pension expenditure was almost seven times higher than family benefits: the highest ratio in the EC except for Greece.[8] The staged process of expansionary measures culminating in the 1969 pension reform set the country on the road to becoming a sort of "pension state" rather than a modern, fully fledged welfare state responding to a variety of needs with a variety of instruments. Even the new social activism of the regions could do little to contrast the expansive momentum of public pension growth, which started to crowd out—financially and institutionally—most other types of benefits and services.

The second distortion is of a *distributive* nature. Centered as they are on occupational status, all Bismarckian systems give rise to some disparity of treatment across sectors and categories—as well as between employed (insiders) and non-employed (outsiders). The fragmented development of Italy's social insurance originated a true "labyrinth" of categorical privileges which has very few comparative counterparts.[9] The main cleavage (which was already clearly visible in the 1970s) opposed workers located in the core sectors of the (industrial) labor market to those located in the more peripheral sectors (semi-regular and unemployed).

The third original sin which characterized the start-up, "Keynesian" constellation has to do with the *financing* of public, and in particular social, expenditure. In 1950–64 Italy's public finances witnessed a phase of relatively balanced growth, in which the expansion of outlays was matched by a parallel expansion of revenues. The subsequent decade was marked, however, by a new pattern of unbalanced growth, in which outlays continued to rise while revenues stagnated around a figure of 30 percent of GDP. This "flat decade" on the revenue side created a "gap" in Italy's public finances, which made things much worse when the exogenous shocks hit in the mid-1970s.[10] In the Italian debate, this gap is often referred to as the "original hole," because it marked the beginning of the public debt spiral of the subsequent decades. We count it among the "sins" because it was caused by the choice that was made not to raise taxes and to delay the modernization of the tax apparatus.

The remaining two original sins had to do with *legality* and *efficiency*. Though articulated from a legislative and organizational viewpoint, the social policy configuration built between the 1950s and the 1970s was characterized by high institutional "softness." Especially in some sectors and areas, the degree of compliance with the rules disciplining the access to benefits and the payment of contributions remained very low, not only on the side of the various clienteles of social programs, but also on the side of public authorities. This syndrome assumed inordinate proportions in the sector of disability pensions, which became the privileged currency of an extended clientelistic market: between 1960 and 1980 the total number of disability pensions rose almost five times, and in 1974 (following an expansive reform) it came to surpass the total number of old age pensions—an unparalleled record in the Organisation for Economic Co-operation and Development (OECD) area.[11]

As to the efficiency of public services (in virtually all fields of public intervention), the 1970s fell short of all expectations of the Keynesian modernizers of the 1960s. The lack of a pragmatic culture, the partisan colonization of the administrative apparatus, the opportunistic use of public employment by the patronage system, the failure to design rational systems of incentives: these and other factors gave rise to an oversized bureaucracy with very low levels of performance.[12] Within the welfare state, the problem was particularly acute in the case of health care. The 1978 reform establishing the NHS introduced many perverse incentives from a financial and organizational point of view; as a matter of fact, the institutional design of the 1978 reform was largely responsible for the chaotic developments and growing financial strains witnessed by this sector throughout the 1980s.

The Chaotic Restructuring
of the 1980s

Despite their unremitting lip service to the exigencies of financial adjustment, the various Penta-party governments which held office during the decade did not accomplish much in terms of welfare modernization. Proposals for cost containment pension reforms were included in the agenda of the different cabinets and started to be discussed in Parliament.[13] The financial and organizational problems raised by the newly established NHS prompted in their turn an articulated debate on how to "reform the (1978) reform." Neither the pension reform nor the "reform of the health reform" made much progress until the early 1990s. However, the 1980s did witness some first cuts in both sectors: relatively peripheral and not very effective cuts in the case of pensions, more substantial ones in the case of health.

In the pension field, starting from 1983 a number of measures were taken that aimed at subordinating some entitlements to the actual income conditions of recipients and at controlling abuses. Income ceilings were established for maintaining the right to minimum pensions and to multiple benefits (e.g. old age and survivor pensions). The rules concerning invalidity pensions were in their turn completely revised in 1984, tightening medical criteria and introducing periodical reviews of the physical conditions of the beneficiaries. At the turn of the decade, however, a major expansionary reform extended the earnings-related formula for old age pensions to the self-employed without any adjustment on the revenue side, as the contributions remained at a very low level for these categories. This greatly aggravated both the financial and economic unsustainability and the intergenerational unfairness of the Italian pension system.[14]

Though important in symbolic terms, the steps in the direction of a greater "targeting" of Italy's social insurance were only modestly effective in financial terms. Not only were they programmatically limited to the margins, so to speak, of the system, but they also activated some counter-developments which largely neutralized their positive impact on costs (especially in the field of disability pensions).

Co-payments, or tickets, as they are known by the Italian public, were (and still are) without doubt the most visible and the most unpopular instrument of government action in the health care sector throughout the 1980s. As in the field of pensions, the turning point was 1983. Alarmed at the worrying increase in health care costs (especially for prescription drugs) in the previous two years, the government decided to change the co-payment from a modest fixed fee to a percentage, making consumers pay 15 percent of the drugs' cost. This percentage was raised on several occasions in later years, reaching 30 percent in 1989. The ticket was also extended from drugs to diagnostic tests and referrals (i.e., consultations with specialized physicians prescribed by family doctors). Though heavily criticized, the co-payment policy generally achieved its aims, which were primarily financial. Besides bringing revenues to state coffers, co-payments stabilized health care consumptions, especially as regards pharmaceuticals.

As noted for the pension sector, health care "targeting" through user charges produced a number of perverse counter-developments. To mitigate the social impact of such charges, a detailed legislation on exemptions was passed during the decade, combining different criteria (income, type of illness, family and work status, age, etc.). But Italian patients soon learned how to exploit the loopholes of this legislation: the number of exempted consumers reached the impressive figure of 25 percent in 1989, accounting for 75 percent of total pharmaceutical expenditure.

If on the expenditure side the 1980s were an ambiguous decade (continuing expansion, accompanied by various chaotic attempts at retrenchment), on the revenue side the dominant trend was much clearer: increases on all fronts. Through a rapid and intense increase in contributions and taxes, during the 1980s Italy fully completed its march to catch up with the revenue levels of her European partners, covering the distance created by the "flat decade" of 1965–75. But this remarkable tax adjustment did not suffice to cure the structural imbalance of national accounts.

THE REFORM CYCLE
OF THE 1990S AND 2000S

After a decade of chaotic attempts at retrenchment, the 1990s and 2000s witnessed the emergence of a more coherent policy of restructuring and modernization parallel to a softening of union opposition. Several legislative interventions were passed in the field of pensions (see Table 38.2), the first one dating back to 1992–3. While maintaining the overall architecture of the system—occupational schemes and earnings-related formulas combined with a social pension for poor elderly—the 1992 Amato reform introduced a number of retrenchment measures after decades of ameliorations. At first the reform faced opposition from the trade unions; however, the climate of financial emergency of summer–autumn 1992 and the partly negotiated style of Amato eased the reform process.[15] The impact of the Amato reform was not insignificant, both in terms of cost-containment (see Figure 38.1) and in terms of equity, especially thanks to the tightening of eligibility conditions for civil servants' "baby pensions" (i.e. their traditional entitlement to retire with only twenty years of contributions, at very early ages, was eliminated). In order to compensate for the reduced generosity of public pensions, the Amato government planned to develop supplementary pensions, based on prefunded schemes. Introduced in extremely adverse conditions—for both economic and financial reasons-supplementary funded pensions were established in Italy on a voluntary basis and the possibility to use the pre-existing severance pay (*Trattamento di fine rapporto*—TFR) to finance these schemes was also legislated.[16]

In the fall of 1994 the Berlusconi government, voted into office in the spring elections, disclosed a new reform plan which would have entailed substantial savings in the short run. This would have affected unions' core constituencies—that is, retirees (via changes in the indexation mechanism) and older workers through penalizations in case of retirement via seniority pensions—and, as a consequence, it provoked the reaction of workers' organizations, which launched massive protests and were ultimately able to block the reform process. Actually, in the wake of a general strike, the Northern League—which opposed measures on seniority pensions—precipitated a cabinet crisis. In December 1994 Berlusconi fell and was replaced by Lamberto Dini's technocratic cabinet. The trade unions agreed to negotiate into force with this government a new broad reform by the first semester of 1995. In May 1995 the new Dini government succeeded in striking the agreement with the trade unions, which was approved by Parliament in the following August.

The main novelty of the Dini reform has been the introduction—with a very long phasing in period—of a new contributions-related formula (the so-called notional defined contribution system, NDC) in place of the earnings-related formula in force since 1968. The pension is no longer related to pensionable earnings, but to the total amount of contributions paid in throughout the working career. The Dini reform introduced other important novelties, above all a new flexible retirement age for both men and women (between 57 and 65 years), and the gradual tightening of eligibility conditions for seniority pensions to be completed by 2008.

The new co-operative approach of the trade unions can be explained by at least four factors.[17] First of all, the trade unions had undergone an internal process of maturation: the reform-oriented components of the movement grew stronger, supplying an articulated platform of proposals to the national leadership. The second factor was the concerted style of policymaking introduced by Dini—who was "technically" supported in the Parliament by center-left parties—jointly with (third) the distributional profile of the reform and the significant number of concessions granted to the trade unions by the Dini cabinet. Union support was actually gained by substantially protecting older workers' and retirees' entitlements while (over-)burdening younger generations with adjustment costs and introducing the new NDC system, which would bring to a halt the favorable treatment granted to the self-employed by the 1990 reform. Finally, there were the very concrete spurs of the international markets. As a consequence of the political crisis and the ensuing loss of credibility of the Italian government, interest rates started to soar in the winter of 1995 and the lira witnessed an alarming fall against the Deutschmark. The unions thus "learnt" that refusing the reform was not equal to maintaining the status quo, but made things much worse. In other words, they understood by means of a "negative reinforcement" that the arguments of the governments and of the Bank of Italy in favor of pension reform were well grounded, and accepted their proposals.[18]

The fall of 1992 also marked an important turning point as regards health care: the "reform of the reform" was finally approved. This transformed local health units into "public enterprises," with ample organizational autonomy and responsibility, but also the obligation to operate with balanced budgets. The reform also brought changes in the financing regulations, making regions more responsible, and it introduced ("managed") competition between public and private providers of health care sevices.

Table 38.2 Main Pension and Health-care Reforms, 1992–2012

Pensions	
1992–93	Amato reform
1995	Dini reform
1997	Prodi reform
2004–05	Maroni–Tremonti reform
2006–07	Damiano reform
2008–09	Sacconi reforms I & II
2011	Fornero reform
Health Care	
1993	"Reform of the (1978) reform"
1999	Bindi reform

The 1992–5 reforms represented major breakthroughs with respect to the institutional legacies of the past. They were also, however, the result of social and political compromises in which the government had to make a number of concessions with regard to its original plans. The most evident of these regarded the phasing in of the NDC system to calculate pensions: the Dini reform exempted all workers with at least 18 years of insurance seniority by December 1995 from the application of the new method (i.e., the same cohorts that had already been less affected by the Amato reform three years earlier).

But meeting Economic Monetary Union deadlines kept the Italian authorities under acute budgetary pressures. Hence, the new center-left "Olive-Tree" coalition led by Romano Prodi and voted into office in the spring of 1996 relaunched the reformist effort and even widened its ambitions by making a comprehensive reform of the *stato sociale* one of its highest priorities. In January 1997 Mr. Prodi appointed a commission of experts to draft a broad plan for reform. The report submitted by this Commission (known as the Onofri Commission, after the name of its chairperson, a Bologna economist) became the object of a rather heated debate in the summer and fall of 1997. In the budget law for 1998 the Prodi government tried to adopt many of the Commission's recommendations. However, fierce opposition from the Refounded Communists (whose votes were crucial for reaching a majority in Parliament) and difficult negotiations with social partners forced the government to substantially scale down its ambitions.

In the field of health care, a third reform (after those of 1978 and 1992) was introduced in June 1999. This established new rules with respect to the financing competences of the center and the periphery, a new regulation of the relationships between hospital doctors and the NHS (making full-time employment and private activities outside the hospital incompatible for doctors), and a new regulatory framework for supplementary health insurance funds.

The 2000s were mostly a period of parametric adjustments to the new rules introduced in the previous decade. In 2004 the Berlusconi cabinet intervened again in the field of pensions, substantially tightening eligibility conditions for seniority pensions and reintroducing a fixed and differentiated pensionable age for men (65 years) and women (60 years). In 2005 the government also adopted a reform of supplementary pensions in order to boost their take-up, via the introduction of the so called "silent consent" formula (*silenzio assenso*) for the transfer of TFR to funded schemes. The 2004–05 Maroni reforms resulted from a laborious compromise forged with social partners and financial institutions.[19] The center left and the CGIL were very critical of the 2004 public pension reform, and when the Prodi-led *Unione* coalition returned to power in 2006 it substantially relaxed eligibility conditions for seniority pensions—recently introduced by the Maroni reform—while reducing the generosity of pensions for younger generations that were subject to the NDC system.

The Berlusconi government did not promote any structural reform in health care. This was determined, in part, by the new balance of powers between state and regions created by the 2001 constitutional reform. Since 2001, central government has found it very difficult to implement significant reforms without the consent and the involvement of the regions. This is true not only for reforms aimed at changing the organization and management of the health care system, but also for any policy aimed at pursuing relevant health targets and, in part, at containing health care costs. Central and regional governments have entered a phase of permanent political and technical confrontation. Various practices of institutionalized joint policymaking have been developing from 2000–1 onwards, leading to a series of *Accordi* (agreements) or *Patti* (pacts) signed in the State–Regions Conference and then converted into legislation by Parliament. The most important took place in 2005, when central government and the regions agreed on a multi-step mechanism of regional expenditure monitoring and recovery plans in case of excessive deficits. After 2005 joint policymaking was extended to non-financial issues, though with difficulties.

From the Economic to the Sovereign Debt Crisis and Austerity Measures

Pension reforms adopted in 1992–2007 were crucial not only for the introduction of the NDC system in the first place and the design of the new multi-pillar pension architecture, but also for the stepwise tightening of eligibility conditions for old age and especially seniority pensions. However, as previously mentioned, most reforms included long phasing-in periods and exemptions from the new rules; and until 2008 eligibility conditions for standard old age pensions still varied between males and females as well as across professional categories.

After the outbreak of the financial and economic shock in 2008–09 and the following sovereign debt crisis in 2010, recent measures—adopted in 2009–10 and especially those enacted since May 2011—have mainly been aimed at shortening the transition period to the new rules in order to reduce expenditure in the short to medium term. Interventions have mostly regarded eligibility conditions for both old age and seniority pensions—as well as the rules to calculate benefits. As in the early to mid-1990s, recent measures were included in major "austerity packages" propelled by exogenous factors.

The most important measures included in the two reforms designed in 2009 and 2010 by the Berlusconi cabinet (Sacconi reforms I and II) were the fast (2010–12) equalization of pensionable age for female public servants to the male age, as requested by a ruling of the European Court of Justice (ECJ),[20] and the automatic link of pensionable ages to changes in life expectancy—as suggested by the European Commission.

Building on the 2009/10 reforms and a further adjustment in July 2011, the Fornero reform—included in the so-called "Rescue Italy" decree by the technocratic Monti government (Law Decree 201/11 converted into Law 214/11)—introduced major changes mostly aimed at i) promoting regulatory harmonization between genders, among professional categories, and across generations; and ii) raising the retirement age in the short to medium term by tightening eligibility conditions. The Fornero reform gradually harmonized the standard pensionable age for women employed in the private sector with other categories and anticipated the first adjustment of pensionable age to changes in life expectancy. These measures will likely entail a substantial increase of the standard pensionable age, which is expected to reach 66 years and 7 months for all categories in 2018 and 67 years in 2019, one of the highest in Europe.[21] The reform also shortened the phasing in of the NDC system: since January 2012 the latter will be applied pro rata (i.e. for working years after 2011) also to previously exempted workers. Importantly, the Fornero reform has also de facto reintroduced a flexible retirement age between 63 (*pensione anticipata*) and 70, by phasing out seniority pensions.

Measures approved in 2011 will thus further contribute to a reduction in the burden of public pension expenditure in the next decades by adding to the reforms of the 1990s and later adjustments in 2004–10. Figure 38.1 clearly shows the impressive cumulative contribution by the various reforms to containment of pension costs in the next decades.

Compared with the previous periods of reforms, the peculiarity of the more recent phase 2009–11 stands out in many respects: i) the relevance as well as the nature of external pressures—i.e. *vincolo esterno*; ii) its interplay with national political dynamics and the role played by the various actors (especially the unions); and finally iii) the distributive impact of reforms along the temporal dimension. First and foremost, after

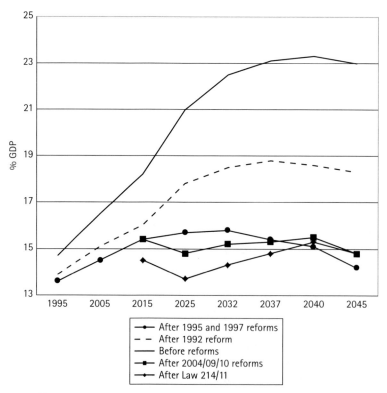

FIGURE 38.1 Public Pension Expenditure (percent GDP) after the Various Reforms

Source: Adapted from Ministero dell'Economia e delle Finanze, various years; Technical Annex—Law Decree 201/11.

the outbreak of the economic and especially the sovereign debt crises, the EU abruptly re-entered the domestic policy arena, and pension policies went through an intense series of reforms which were led by European pressures. External pressures grew stronger, and they were also of a different nature because traditional "hard and indirect" stimuli—those stemming from EU budgetary rules—were coupled with "hard and direct" constraints, as in the case of the 2008 ECJ ruling on the different pensionable age for male and female public sector employees. It was also striking that new institutional EU actors—in other words the European Central Bank (ECB)—became crucial in setting goals for domestic policy reform: in fact, the ECB did not simply call for austerity measures in the field of pensions, but indicated reforms in details—that is, making "more stringent the eligibility criteria for seniority pensions and rapidly aligning the retirement age of women in the private sector to that established for public employees, thereby achieving savings already in 2012."[22] The technocratic Monti government thus approved the latest pension reform in accordance with these recommendations which constitute an unprecedented intervention by supranational authorities in Italian pension policymaking.[23]

Clearly, this had implications for the ability of domestic actors to steer the policymaking process, especially regarding the veto power of the unions, and consequently on the distributive effects of reforms. Measures adopted in the 1990s provided key exemptions and very long phasing-in periods, but recent interventions have mainly been aimed at reducing expenditure not only in the long run but also in the very short term. This means that the interests of older workers (and pensioners) have been affected, as well as those of younger cohorts, thus provoking unions' disappointment and protest. From a slightly different perspective, it must be noted that reforms have essentially been pushed through by political actors (government, Parliament), by making claims to Brussels ahead of an increasingly Euroskeptical Italian population.

REFORMED BUT NOT YET VIRTUOUS

Have the five original sins of welfare Italian style been remedied? The reforms that have taken place since the 1990s have not fully eradicated the distributive and functional distortions of the Italian welfare state which have been described. They have, however, made significant steps in this direction; more importantly, they have planted promising institutional seeds for a dynamic of recalibration. On the one hand, the setting of more transparent and clear-cut boundaries between social insurance and social assistance has been working to strengthen the safety net of means-tested and need-based benefits and services which has been historically lacking (or very weak) in Italy—though much has still to be done to expand the traditionally underdeveloped sectors of the Italian welfare state. On the other hand, the new architecture of the pension system has been working to gradually downsize, or at least to contain, the further expansion of a sector which has been historically oversized. The stabilization of pension expenditure, the rationalization of NHS financing, and the increase in the tax take (now considered to be "excessive") have restored to quasi-health the state of public finances (at least in terms of deficits), thus responding to the third original sin.

Achievements have been less pronounced as regards efficiency and legality. There are still considerable gaps in terms of institutional capabilities and bureaucratic efficiency in the management of both pensions and health care. This latter sector is still fraught with corruption, clientelism, and extensive politicization, especially in the South.

"Vices" have thus been contrasted, some have been contained, some have reappeared under new guises. Meanwhile recent developments, above all labor market flexibility (see Chapter 37, this volume), represent new challenges to the institutional foundations of the Italian welfare state, and especially the pension system built in accordance with the typical employment patterns of the Fordist-industrial age.[24] For the Italian style welfare state, the time of "virtue" is yet to come.

NOTES

1. The chapter is the result of joint effort and reflection by the two authors; however, Sections 2, 3, 4, and 7 should be attributed to Maurizio Ferrera, Sections 1, 5, and 6 to Matteo Jessoula.

2. For a detailed analysis of the emergence of such a peculiar welfare state configuration, cf. Maurizio Ferrera, Valeria Fargion, and Matteo Jessoula, *Alle radici del welfare all'italiana. Origini e futuro di un modello sociale squilibrato* (Venice: Marsilio, 2012).

3. In this period, however, pension system coverage was significantly extended in order to include the main categories of self-employed, cf. Maurizio Ferrera and Matteo Jessoula, "Italy: A Narrow Gate for Path-shift," in Ellen Immergut, Karen Anderson, and Isabelle Schulze, eds, *Handbook of West European Pension Politics* (Oxford: Oxford University Press, 2007), 396–453; Ferrera, Fargion and Jessoula, *Alle radici del welfare all'italiana*.

4. CNEL, *Relazione preliminare sulla riforma della previdenza sociale* (Rome, Istituto Poligrafico dello Stato, 1963); Committee of Experts on Social Security, *Per un sistema di sicurezza sociale* (Bologna: Il Mulino, 1965).

5. Gøsta Esping-Andersen, *The Three Words of Welfare Capitalism* (Cambridge: Polity Press, 1990).

6. Peter Flora, *State, Economy, and Society in Western Europe 1815–1975: A Data Handbook in Two Volumes* (Frankfurt, New York, London, and Chicago: Campus/Macmillan Press/ St. James Press, 1983–87); Peter Flora, ed., *Growth to Limits. The Western European Welfare States since World War II* (Berlin: De Gruyter, 1986); Maurizio Ferrera, *Il Welfare State in Italia. Sviluppo e crisi in prospettiva comparata* (Bologna: Il Mulino, 1984).

7. Cf. Ferrera, Fargion, and Jessoula, *Alle radici del welfare all'italiana*.

8. European Commission, *Social Protection in Europe* (Luxembourg: Office for Official Publications of the European Community, 1993).

9. Maurizio Ferrera, "Il modello Sud-europeo di welfare state," *Rivista Italiana di Scienza Politica*, no. 1 (April 1996), 67–101.

10. Emilio Gerelli, Luigi Bernardi, and Alberto Majocchi, eds., *Il deficit pubblico: origini e problemi* (Milan: Angeli, 1984).

11. Ferrera, *Il Welfare State in Italia*.

12. Sabino Cassese, *L'amministrazione pubblica in Italia* (Bologna: Il Mulino, 1974).

13. Cf. Giuliano Cazzola, *Le nuove pensioni degli italiani* (Bologna: Il Mulino, 1995); Matteo Jessoula, *La politica pensionistica* (Bologna: Il Mulino, 2009).

14. cf. INPS, *Le pensioni domani* (Rome: Inps, 1993).

15. On the politics of pension reforms in 1992–2008, cf. Jessoula, *La politica pensionistica;* Ferrera and Jessoula, "Italy: A Narrow Gate for Path-shift."

16. On the development of supplementary funded pensions in Italy, cf. Matteo Jessoula, "Italy: from Bismarckian Pensions to Multi-pillarization Under Adverse Conditions," in Bernard Ebbinghaus, *Varieties of Pension Governance: Pension Privatization in Europe* (Oxford: Oxford University Press, 2011), 151–82.

17. For details see Lucio Baccaro, "Negotiating the Italian Pension Reform with the Unions: Lessons for Corporatist Theory," in *Industrial and Labor Relations Review*, 55 (3): 413–31; David Natali, *Vincitori e perdenti* (Bologna: Il Mulino, 2007) and Jessoula, *La politica pensionistica*.

18. On the interplay between the so called "vincolo esterno" and internal political dynamics, cf. Maurizio Ferrera and Elisabetta Gualmini, *Rescue by Europe? Social and Labour Market Reforms from Maastricht to Berlusconi* (Amsterdam: Amsterdam University Press, 2004).

19. Cf. Matteo Jessoula, "Italy: from Bismarckian Pensions to Multi-pillarization Under Adverse Conditions"; Matteo Jessoula, "Istituzioni, gruppi, interessi. La nuova politica pensionistica in Italia," *Rivista Italiana di Politiche Pubbliche*, no. 2 (August 2011), 211–41.

20. For details see Matteo Jessoula, "Recalibrating the Italian Welfare State: A Politics too Weak for a 'Necessary' Policy?," in Marco Giuliani and Erik Jones, *Italian Politics 2009* (Oxford: Berghahn Books, 2010).

21. A "safeguard clause" set the standard pensionable age at 67 in 2021.

22. Text of the joint letter sent, on August 5, 2011, to the Italian government by the then President of the European Central Bank Trichet and Mario Draghi (Governor of the Bank of Italy, now President of the ECB), urging actions aimed at reducing public expenditure in the short run.

23. Apart from relatively minor adjustments, Monti's successors (Enrico Letta and Matteo Renzi) have not changed the basic architecture of the 2011 pension reform.

24. For a comparative analysis of the interplay between labor market transformation and pension reforms, see Karl Hinrichs and Matteo Jessoula, eds, *Labour Market Flexibility and Pension Reforms. Flexible Today, Secure Tomorrow* (Basingstoke: Palgrave Macmillan, 2012).

CHAPTER 39

···

THE BANK OF ITALY

···

LUCIA QUAGLIA

THE Bank of Italy has always had a special place in the Italian system of governance because it has traditionally been one of the most efficient and least politicized institutions in Italy.[1] It has been a "strong" institution in a "weak" state, which explains its influence and independence over time. It is one of the three largest central banks in the Eurosystem, which it joined when the third stage of Economic and Monetary Union (EMU) began in 1999. This chapter discusses the Bank's independence from the political authorities prior to EMU; the Bank's policies in the 1980s and 1990s, and its attempts to reform the Italian economy; and the Bank's membership of the Eurosystem from 1999 onwards.

THE BUILDING UP OF THE BANK OF ITALY'S INDEPENDENCE PRIOR TO EMU

For most of the postwar period prior to the completion of EMU, most of the Bank of Italy's efforts were directed towards protecting and enhancing its independence from the political authorities. In the literature on central banks, the institutional independence of the central bank is generally regarded as very important.[2] A distinction is generally made between "political independence," which mainly concerns the government's influence on the procedures for the appointment (and the dismissal) of the Governor and other members of the Executive Board, and "economic independence," meaning that the central bank is not required to finance the public debt and deficit.

Until the changes introduced in the early 1990s in preparation for the final stage of EMU, in economists' rankings the Bank of Italy used to be awarded fairly high scores as far as political independence (especially personnel independence, more than decisional or institutional independence) was concerned, but scored rather low on economic independence.[3] The main legal provisions that underpin central bank personnel independence are the procedures for the appointment of the board, the length of tenure in office, and the incompatibility between political roles and positions within the bank.[4]

Prior to the reform introduced in 2005, the legislation very much limited the direct influence of the political authorities in the appointment process of the Governor and his/her deputies, who composed the Executive Board. The nomination of all four members of the Executive Board, hence also the Governor, were proposed by the Board of Directors (a body deeply integrated within the Bank) and had to be approved by a decree of the President of the Republic, acting on the proposal of the prime minister together with the Treasury minister, after discussion in the Council of Ministers. Furthermore, the practice of internal appointments to senior and top positions in the Bank generally prevailed, and therefore the Governor was generally chosen from among deputy governors, and deputy governors were normally chosen from among senior officials at the Bank. On the one hand, this tended to strengthen the autonomy of the central bank; on the other, critics argue that this made the Bank "self-referential."

The personnel independence of the Bank of Italy has at times been challenged, and the influence of the political authorities could not be completely excluded from the process of appointment. For example, in 1980 an outsider, Lamberto Dini, was appointed as Director-General, reportedly receiving the support of sectors of the Christian Democratic Party. In 1993 the junior Deputy Director, Antonio Fazio, reportedly supported by Catholic forces, was promoted to Governor, instead of the incumbent Director-General, Dini, who was not supported by the outgoing Governor or the senior Deputy Director-General, Tommaso Padoa-Schioppa, who lacked the support of the center-right coalition. The situation was similar in 1994, with the appointment of a new Director-General, rather than the promotion to this office of the senior Deputy Director-General, Padoa-Schioppa.

Until the 2005 reform, the Bank of Italy was one of the most centralized and hierarchical central banks in Europe. The Governor had wide powers and discretion within the Bank because all responsibilities in the field of monetary, exchange-rate, and supervisory policies were concentrated in his hands—there were no formal mechanisms for collegial decision-making procedures. Also, before 2005, all four members of the Executive Board were appointed *sine die*, that is, their mandates were open-ended and there was no age limit for these positions, which was exceptional among central banks. In practice, since the World War II, the longest period during which governors remained in office was a decade or more, as was also the case for other members of the Executive Board. This strengthened personnel independence from the political authorities.

In contrast to the relatively high political (especially personnel) independence, the economic independence (also referred to as instrument independence) of the Bank was very low before the institutional change introduced by the so-called divorce in 1981. With this divorce that took place between the Bank of Italy and the Treasury, the central bank was freed from the obligation to buy all the Treasury bills that remained unsold at auction.[5] The reform, initiated by the Treasury minister, Nino Andreatta, under the auspices of the Governor of the Bank of Italy, Carlo Azeglio Ciampi, was implemented by means of a formal exchange of letters between them, without any involvement of the parliament or the rest of the government. The economic independence of the Bank was completed only in 1993, when the overdraft account of the Treasury at the central bank was closed down to comply with the provisions on central bank independence outlined in the Treaty on European Union. The financial and organizational independence in terms of economic resources available to the central bank has always been remarkable.[6]

The independence of the Bank of Italy has been strengthened by the weaknesses of domestic political institutions—it has been a "strong" institution in a "weak state."[7] In the first republic, the Italian state was characterized by fragmented political institutions, whereby the executive had limited political capacity, which was further weakened by frequently changing coalition governments. This state of affairs explains some of the atypical functions performed by the central bank in the Italian political economy, discussed in the following section.

THE POLICIES PROMOTED BY THE BANK OF ITALY PRIOR TO EMU

For most of the post-war period, the Bank of Italy acted as an "economic counter-power to the government," trying to encourage the reform of the Italian economy. There was an inclination on the part of government, and politicians more generally, to let the Bank make difficult decisions, supposedly on technical rather than political grounds. This was part of a larger picture, where the tacit acknowledgment of the absence of strong political institutions fostered policymaking by technocrats, several of whom moved to important political positions in the 1990s. It was facilitated by the fact that until the early 1990s, the Bank of Italy had a near monopoly of expertise in Italy, a trend that continued in the 2000s, even though the Treasury augmented its technical capabilities from the 1990s onwards. Not only did the Bank of Italy have technical knowledge, but it was also very willing to use it to its best advantage.

In the 1980s and early 1990s two parallel financial market reforms—the processes of internal and external liberalization—took place under the aegis of the Bank of Italy and had a significant impact on the de facto economic independence of the Bank of Italy, previously discussed. Indeed, the Bank of Italy devoted much of its energies and its best minds to the introduction of these reforms, often deliberately presented as "technical" changes. As noted by the former Governor of the Bank of Italy and later Treasury Minister Guido Carli, "the political significance of these technical improvements was not understood" by the political class.[8]

The reforms introduced in the 1980s and 1990s were designed to make the Italian financial system more "market-oriented." First, they ended "internal protectionism" by promoting more efficient management of the public debt and competition in the banking system. At the same time, they reduced "external protectionism," mainly by introducing the freedom of capital movements and the freedom of establishment for banks.[9]

These reforms were motivated by the need for Italy to comply with the EU directives on banking and the free movement of capital. However, such external pressure was deliberately exploited in the national arena by the central bank, with some support from the Treasury. The goal of the market reforms implemented in the 1980s and early 1990s was to make monetary policy more independent of fiscal policy, by enabling the Treasury to place its bonds on the market without using the overdraft facility at the Bank of Italy.[10] Indeed, net subscription by the Bank of Italy of Treasury bills decreased over the 1980s and became negative in the 1990s.[11] Segmentation in the banking sector came to an end—the formal change took place with the implementation in 1992 of the Second Banking Directive issued in 1988, which introduced the all-purpose universal bank in Italy—and the banking system was privatized, modernized, and consolidated.

The Bank of Italy, especially during the governorship of Ciampi, used "external" economic policy constraints in the domestic environment to bring about domestic reforms.[12] A clear example was the exchange rate policy implemented by the Bank of Italy in the Exchange Rate Mechanism (ERM) (1978–92), which was an exchange-rate regime based on an adjustable peg.[13] Participation in the ERM, produced a major shift in Italian exchange-rate policy and monetary strategy. From the first half of the 1980s onwards, the realignments of the lira never fully compensated for the inflation differentials between Italy and the low-inflation countries within the ERM. Furthermore, from 1987 to 1992 no realignments took place, leading to an appreciation of the lira in real terms and reversing the exchange-rate policy of the 1970s.

The so-called "strong" exchange-rate policy (or "hard currency" option) implemented by the Bank consisted in deploying the exchange rate as an "external constraint" in the domestic arena, where it was used to fight inflation by disciplining the trade unions and promoting industrial restructuring.[14] It was also intended to force the political authorities to implement a restrictive fiscal policy.[15] In the period up to the early 1990s, the monetary and exchange-rate policies of the Bank were constrained more by the conduct of fiscal policy than by legal provisions concerning instrument independence, as explained above. The Bank performed a crucial role in macroeconomic policymaking, given that Italy was often forced to steer its economy by means of monetary policy alone, because fiscal policy was "paralyzed" by partitocracy.

More generally, the Bank of Italy has generally been a pro-European institution, especially during the governorship of Carlo Azeglio Ciampi (1980–93), who was prime minister in a caretaker government (1993) and Treasury Minister (1996–8) in the Prodi government. Ciampi was one of the main craftsmen of Italy's joining the third stage of EMU from the outset. Deputy Governor Tommaso Padoa-Schioppa (1979–97) was widely credited as being one of the founding fathers of the single currency, developing the idea of the "inconsistent quartet" in the so-called Padoa-Schioppa Report.[16] According to the report, which was named after the chairperson of the group that drafted it, the four elements on which European economic governance was being constructed—free trade, full capital mobility, managed exchange rates, and monetary policy autonomy—could not coexist without at least one collapsing. The notion of the "inconsistent quartet" was especially influential in the European Commission, also because Padoa-Schioppa had been seconded by the Bank of Italy to serve as Director General for Economic and Monetary Affairs at the Commission between 1975 and 1979 and was close to the President of the European Commission Jacques Delors. While at the Bank of Italy, Padoa-Schioppa was invited by Delors to serve as one of two secretaries to the Delors Committee (1988–9), which outlined the blueprint for EMU.[17]

The Bank has been at the forefront of the development of Italy's "economic culture." Its Research Department has been the research center par excellence in the economic field in Italy. The Bank has awarded scholarships for post-graduate education abroad, and many of these award holders later joined the Bank. The cutting-edge economic expertise deliberately developed by the Bank of Italy meant that the wider implications of certain "technical" decisions taken by the central bank were not always understood, a priori, by the government and the political class, which did not have direct access to technical knowledge. As explained later, in EMU the quality of economic knowledge and the caliber of experts to which central banks have access have become an important source of informal power in the Eurosystem, and the Bank of Italy is well positioned in this respect.

The Bank of Italy has been a breeding ground for talented civil servants and the financial elite. It has "exported" credibility, expertise, and personnel for the conduct of Italian economic policy to other parts of the Italian state apparatus, the private sector, and international organizations. Interestingly, the Bank has been the "exporting" institution, whereas central banks in other countries more usually "import" senior officials from outside (cf. the Bundesbank and the Banque de France).[18]

The Bank of Italy has represented a "credible interface" for Italy with the outside world. Since the postwar period it has interacted with foreign institutions (i.e. other monetary authorities and international organizations) and, more generally, has kept contacts with the outside world. After the upgrading of technical capabilities and human resources at the Ministry of the Treasury, which led to the "empowerment" of the Treasury (later reformed into the Ministry for the Economy), the function of external economic representation and credible interface between the domestic arena and the international environment has largely been taken over by this Ministry. Indeed, the relative strengthening of domestic political institutions in the second republic and the measures required to adapt to the single currency account for the (at times difficult) "normalization" of the functions performed by the central bank.

THE BANK OF ITALY IN EMU

In approaching the final stage of EMU, the Bank of Italy legally consolidated its independence, guaranteed by the Treaty of the European Union (TEU) and the statute of the Eurosystem. Since 1999, the monetary policy in the Euro Area is conducted by the European Central Bank (ECB) and the Eurosystem. The Bank of Italy participates in policy formulation and implementation as a member of the Eurosystem. Similarly, exchange-rate policy is conducted at Euro Area level. On the one hand, the Bank of Italy has lost the power to conduct these policies at the national level; on the other, this power is now shared with the ECB and other participating central banks at Euro Area level.

The Bank of Italy is one of the main central banks in the Eurosystem, within which it is rather influential not only because of the size of the country but also because of the macroeconomic expertise it can master. The number of research staff is the highest among European central banks, *ex equo* with the Bank of England.[19] Moreover, this is not a recent trend, as the Bank of Italy had one of the largest research departments in Europe throughout the period considered in the study (1990–2003), even though the Bank considerably expanded its research staff in the period 1996–2003. This was a deliberate strategy to strengthen the Bank's influence within the Eurosystem and in ECB decision-making. A study of the quantity, quality, and relevance of research in 36 central banks in developed countries since 1990 indicates that the number of journal articles published by staff of the Bank of Italy is one of the highest, with an upward trend since 1999.[20] Moreover, the Bank of Italy, the Bank of England, and the ECB are the sole non-American representatives among the top ten central banks in quality-adjusted output (i.e. publications in top-quality academic journals).

In the first five years or so in EMU, the Bank of Italy, under the governorship of Antonio Fazio, focused its efforts on promoting the consolidation of the Italian banking system. As part of the Bank's "grand design" for reshaping the banking system in Italy, Governor Fazio endeavored to protect the *italianita' delle banche* (essentially, Italian ownership of the banks operating in Italy). Consequently, Governor Fazio consistently opposed foreign shareholdings and never authorized a foreign takeover, in an attempt to prevent, or at least to slow down, foreign penetration of the Italian market.[21] The Bank's official explanation was that this strategy was designed to give the domestic banking system time to adjust and to become competitive internationally. Critics (the *Financial Times*, for example, was particularly vocal on this) argued that it was economic protectionism, coupled with *dirigiste* attitudes.

In 2005, two episodes threatened the credibility and reputation of the central bank, weakening its ability to resist changes, which were incorporated at the 11th hour in the Law on Savings. The cases made the headlines across Europe because they involved foreign banks and related to two proposed takeovers of Italian banks in 2004–5: one of Banca Nationale del Lavoro by a Spanish group, Banca Bilbao Vizcaya Argentaria; and the other of Banca Antoniana Popolare Veneta (Antonveneta) by ABN Amro. In both cases Governor Fazio intervened to block the foreign takeover bid, while endorsing counterbids launched by two Italian banks, Banca Popolare di Lodi and Unipol, respectively. Both foreign banks involved in the attempted takeovers complained to the European Commission, which had given its authorization on the grounds that the bids did not jeopardize competition in the banking sector. An antitrust enquiry launched by European Competition Commissioner Neelie Kroes was dropped on the grounds of lack of conclusive evidence. The European Internal Market Commissioner, Charlie McCreevy, also expressed his concern in a letter to Governor Fazio in 2005.[22]

Pressure from other EU member states, EU bodies, and financial markets, hence a mixture of Europeanization and globalization effects, coupled with sharp domestic criticisms, led to the resignation of Fazio in the fall of 2005, followed by a change of competition policy in the banking sector in Italy.[23] The reform, which was inserted into the Law on Savings, essentially left untouched the extensive supervisory powers of the central bank. However, banking competition policy was transferred to the Competition Authority, which had been established by law in 1990 and is separated from the central bank. Whereas the Bank of Italy would conduct its evaluation of mergers and acquisitions by taking into account "sound and prudent management issues," the Competition Authority based its assessment on the impact of mergers and acquisitions on competition.

It should also be noted that during the drafting of the Law on Savings, which amended central banking legislation, the Italian government requested the legal opinion of the ECB three times (May 2004, October 2005, and December 2005). In its opinion issued in October 2005, in the wake of the Fazio affair, the ECB suggested the introduction of the principle of collegiality for the Executive Board's decision-making on measures related to tasks of competence of the European System of Central Banks (ESCB) and the introduction of a fixed-term mandate, renewable once, for all members of the Executive Board. This suggestion was eventually incorporated into the relevant legislation in December 2005. The ECB also repeatedly highlighted the need for ensuring that the planned transfer of the Bank of Italy's share capital to the state was compatible with the provisions of the TEU concerning the avoidance of monetary financing and the need for sound fiscal policy.

Interestingly, in September 2005 the Italian government was keen to enlist the support of the ECB not only in the drafting of national legislation, as prescribed by the TEU, but also in its efforts to topple the Governor of the Bank of Italy. Since the Italian government lacked the legal power and the political will to dismiss the Governor, who was at the center of a major controversy after being accused of preventing foreign takeovers, an unsuccessful attempt was made by the Italian government to enlist the direct intervention of the ECB on this matter. The ECB, however, refrained from intervening, on the grounds that it was not part of its remit.[24]

It is telling that when the Treasury minister, Domenico Siniscalco, resigned in September 2005 following a serious disagreement with the Governor of the Bank of Italy, he wrote a letter to the President of the ECB, Jean-Claude Trichet, raising the issue of "independence of government from central banks."[25] The previous Treasury minister, Giulio Tremonti, had resigned in 2004 after falling out with the Governor of the Bank of Italy in an attempt to reduce his powers. Governor Fazio eventually resigned in December 2005, driven by heavy domestic political pressure from the government; indirect external pressure, mainly exerted through financial markets; and faltering support from within the Bank.

Following the Fazio affair, the governance structure of the Bank of Italy was reformed. The 2005 reform increased the influence of the government in the appointment procedures, in that the members of the Executive Board are appointed by a presidential decree, acting on the proposal of the prime minister, followed by a deliberation of the Council of Ministers, having consulted the Board of Directors. In other words, after the 2005 reform the Board is only consulted—its opinion is not legally binding. Since 2005 each member of the Executive Board has a six-year mandate, which can be renewed only once and can be repealed by the government. The decision-making process was also made more pluralistic, so that decisions with external implications for the Bank are no longer to be taken by the Governor alone, but are instead taken by the five members of the Executive Board, through a formal voting procedure. This procedure does not apply to decisions concerning the activities of the Eurosystem, where the Governor votes in his/her personal capacity, as is the case for the other member central banks.

Mario Draghi, former vice-president and managing director of Goldman Sachs (an international investment bank), based in London, and former Director General of the Italian Treasury in the 1990s, took over from Governor Fazio in 2006. From the outset, Draghi gave clear signals of change. With reference to banking supervision, he made it clear that his objective was to open up and modernize the Italian financial sector, in marked contrast to the approach taken by Fazio. More generally, Draghi faced the challenge of rehabilitating a tarnished institution. His success in doing so, shifting the Bank away from the defensive and protectionist approach associated with Fazio, was essential for his emergence as a credible candidate for the ECB presidency.

As Governor of the Bank of Italy, Draghi was not just *ex officio* member of the Governing Council of the ECB. He was also the chairperson of the Financial Stability Forum (FSF), later the Financial Stability Board (FSB). In this last role he played a leading part in international financial circles in coordinating proposals for international standards in financial market and banking reforms. This experience fitted well with the changing role definition of the ECB in the international financial crisis, as it began to emphasize its responsibility for promoting financial stability in the Euro Area, acting as secretariat for the new European Systemic Risk Board (ESRB). Draghi was appointed ECB President in 2011. In the summer of 2011, the outgoing ECB President Jean Claude Trichet and the Governor of the Bank of Italy and incoming president of the ECB, Mario Draghi, wrote a letter to the Italian government calling for urgent and radical structural reforms, including the liberalization of public services and professional activities.[26]

Conclusions

The Bank of Italy is a remarkable institution in the Italian system of governance for three main reasons. Italy has generally been portrayed as a "weak" state, in which the executive has limited political capacity. This, together with the weakness of successive coalition governments, plus the fact that political interests have fragmented voices in the Italian system, has increased the Bank of Italy's autonomy and influence in the policies in which it was involved. The Bank acquired and preserved a certain autonomy over time in a system typically "colonized" at all levels by the political parties.

A crucial specificity of the Italian central bank was the establishment of a particular kind of "credibility" that enabled it to extricate monetary issues from the influence, or for that matter, the interference of the political class, even before full independence was granted in approaching EMU. The Bank of Italy, in turn, seemed to be committed to fostering this view, in so far as its power rested on its perceived legitimacy based on performing technical tasks in an apolitical manner, which would have been lost if it had gained a reputation for acting in a partisan manner.

Second, the Bank was frequently forced to perform "atypical" functions, which should have been carried out by other parts of the state apparatus, but which the weak state, stalled by partitocracy, was unable to perform until the 1990s. These atypical functions mainly meant that the central bank was often a "technical" counter-power to the government, whereby the Bank was the main advocate of sound (stability-oriented) macroeconomic policies. The Bank of Italy has often been willing and able to use external constraints, such as the exchange rate, in the domestic environment.

Third, after joining EMU, there was a genuine difficulty in defining a new role for the Bank of Italy, partly because several special functions performed by it had been transferred to other parts of the state apparatus, and partly because it had lost many of its traditional functions, which had been transferred to the ECB. Some high-caliber officials (often the most outward-oriented ones) left the Bank to take up senior positions in international organizations, at the ECB, at the Treasury, and in private banks. Among the national central bank governors, Fazio was one of the most determined to safeguard the competences of national central banks within the Eurosystem.

In EMU, until the proposal for Banking Union put forward in 2012, financial stability and financial supervision remained mostly national competences, even though the mechanisms for institutional cooperation in the EU and the Euro Area were stepped up in the 2000s. The establishment of the Single Supervisory Mechanism will change the landscape of banking supervision in the Euro Area by transferring supervisory competences to the ECB. For domestic banks, national supervisors, including the Bank of Italy, will continue to perform supervisory tasks, but the final responsibility will rest with the ECB. One of the main open issues for the central bank is how to adapt to the Single Supervisory Mechanism.

Notes

1. Research for this chapter was conducted while I was visiting fellow at the European University Institute and Hanse Wissenschaftskolleg.
2. Alex Cukierman, *Central Bank Strategy, Credibility, and Independence: Theory and Evidence* (Cambridge, MA: MIT Press, 1992).
3. Vittorio Grilli, Donato Masciandaro, Guido Tabellini, Edmond Malinvaud, and Marco Pagano, "Political and Monetary Institutions and Public Financial Policies in the Industrial Countries," *Economic Policy*, 6, no. 13 (October 1991), 341–92.
4. Alberto Alesina and Lawrence Summers, "Central Bank Independence and Macroeconomic Performances," *Journal of Money, Credit and Banking*, 25, no. 2 (May 1993), 151–62.

5. Gerald Epstein and Juliet Schor, "The Divorce of the Banca d'Italia and the Italian Treasury: A Case of Central Bank Independence," in Peter Lange and Marino Regini (eds.), *State, Market and Social Regulation: New Perspectives on Italy* (Cambridge: Cambridge University Press, 1989), 147–164.

6. Reportedly, the Bank's officials are amongst the best paid civil servants in Italy. The Governor is one of the best paid governors in the world.

7. Lucia Quaglia, "Civil Servants, Economic Policies and Economic Ideas: Lessons from Italy," *Governance*, 18, no. 4 (October 2005), 545–66.

8. Giuseppe Berta, Chapter 36, this volume, and Guido Carli, *Cinquant' Anni di Vita Italiana* (Rome: Laterza, 1993).

9. Pierluigi Ciocca, *La Nuova Finanza in Italia* (Turin: Bollati Boringhieri, 2000).

10. Carli (1993) and Mario Sarcinelli, "Italian Monetary Policy in the '80s and '90s: The Revision of the Modus Operandi," *BNL Quarterly Review*, 195, no. 48 (April 1995), 397–422.

11. Franco Passacantando, "Building an Institutional Framework for Monetary Stability: The Case of Italy (1974–94)," *BNL Quarterly Review*, 196 (March 1996), 3–37.

12. Kenneth Dyson, Kevin Featherstone, and George Michalopoulos, "Strapped to the Mast: EC Central Bankers Between Global Financial Markets and Regional Integration," *Journal of European Public Policy*, 2, no. 3 (September 1995), 465–87.

13. James Walsh, *European Monetary Integration and Domestic Politics. Britain, France and Italy* (London: Lynne Rienner, 2000).

14. Jeffrey Frieden, "Making Commitments: France and Italy in the European Monetary System, 1979–85," in Barry Eichengreen and Jeffrey Frieden (eds.), *The Political Economy of European Monetary Unification* (Boulder, CO: Westview Press, 1994), 25–47.

15. Francesco Giavazzi, Luigi Spaventa, and Rainer Masera, "Italy: The Real Effects of Inflation and Disinflation," *Economic Policy*, 4, no.8 (April 1989), 133–71.

16. Tommaso Padoa-Schioppa, *Efficiency, Stability and Equity* (Oxford: Oxford University Press, 1987).

17. Committee for the Study of Economic and Monetary Union, *Report on Economic and Monetary Union in the European Community* (Delors Committee Report) (Brussels: CEC, 1989); and Kenneth Dyson and Lucia Quaglia, *European Economic Governance and Policies. Volume II: Commentary on Key Policy Documents* (Oxford: Oxford University Press, 2010).

18. John Goodman, *Monetary Sovereignty: The Politics of Central Banking in Western Europe* (Ithaca, NY: Cornell University Press, 1992).

19. Pierre St-Amant, Greg Tkacz, Annie Guérard-Langlois, and Louis Morel, "Quantity, Quality, and Relevance: Central Bank Research, 1990–2003', *Bank of Canada Working Paper 37* (Ottawa: Bank of Canada, 2005).

20. Ibid.

21. *Financial Times*, February 11, 2005; March 31, 2005.

22. *Financial Times*, February 18, 2005.

23. See Lucia Quaglia, *Central Banking Governance in the European Union: A Comparative Analysis* (London: Routledge, 2008).

24. Ibid.

25. *Financial Times*, September 22, 2005.

26. See Carlo Carboni, Chapter 41, this volume.

CHAPTER 40

....

TRADE UNIONS

....

MARINO REGINI

In comparative analyses Italian trade unions are often seen as a stereotypical example of the southern European model.[1] This model is characterized by low membership levels, organizational weakness, strong ideological divisions, and an adversarial logic of action. As a consequence of these features, trade unions enjoy limited recognition by employers and have a low degree of influence on economic and social policies.

Yet most of these features no longer apply to Italian trade unions or require qualifications that strongly limit the usefulness of such categorization. In fact, the ideal/typical southern European model largely corresponds to the picture of Italian trade unionism in the 1950s. But in the following decades trade unions have gone through different stages of development that have called into question the listed features one after the other, radically changing their initial configuration.

I will examine this evolution away from the original model, first in general terms, then looking at trade unions as organizations in the industrial relations system, and finally seeing them as actors in the political and institutional systems. However, one qualification is needed here to better understand the relative ease as well as the limits of this evolution.

Trade unions are less regulated in Italy than elsewhere in Europe. The 1948 Constitution defined Italy as "a democratic republic founded on labor" and declared (Articles 39 and 40) that employees have the rights to organize collectively and to strike. But subsequent governments failed to enact specific legislation giving detailed force to these principles, the most notable source of collective employment rights being the 1970 *Statuto dei lavoratori*. If unions enjoy few specific rights, they are subject to even fewer obligations. Their internal organizational arrangements and their objectives are not externally regulated. Until the 1990 law on disputes in essential public services, strike action was virtually unconstrained by law.

This low level of institutionalization, which has often coupled the Italian case with the British one as a polar model in comparative studies of European industrial relations, is a feature not just of trade unions but of all the major interest organizations in Italy.[2] Both unions and employers' associations are voluntary associations, and access to the arena of interest representation is relatively open. This has fostered the development of a pluralist and diversified system of representation.

Overall, the informality and voluntarism of the Italian industrial relations system has increased its ability to adapt to changing circumstances.[3] In fact, an informal system can be highly adaptive in phases of profound change, allowing arrangements adopted at the periphery of the system to be tailored to local conditions. It permits experimentation with innovations that would be difficult to introduce if they required institutional change. However, informality also has drawbacks, most notably the greater likelihood of unpredictable behavior by trade unions and other industrial relations actors, their tendency to adopt a short-term perspective, and their vulnerability to shifts in power relations.

STAGES OF DEVELOPMENT

Under the Pact of Rome concluded by the anti-fascist parties in 1944, free trade unionism was reconstituted as a unitary, class-oriented, centralized representative system. But the unitary nature of Confederazione generale italiana del lavoro (CGIL) proved fragile, as it was internally divided along ideological lines. In 1948–49, with the onset of the Cold War, the Christian democratic, reformist socialist, and republican factions withdrew, and soon afterwards formed two further confederations: Confederazione italiana sindacati dei lavoratori (CISL), connected to the Christian Democrats and Unione italiana del lavoro (UIL), linked to the small lay parties, the Republicans and Social Democrats, and to the reformist wing of the Socialists.

The split was to have enduring effects on relationships between unions and workers, which thereafter tended to be based on ideology and political alignment. CGIL, which remained the largest confederation, was linked to the Communist and the Socialist parties and was a class-oriented trade union, in that it aspired to organize all the country's workers—blue-collar and white-collar, employed and unemployed, unionized and non-unionized—rather than to provide different organizational channels for specific occupational groups or sectors, or for unionized workers. This was consistent with an economy characterized at the time by high unemployment, the continuing importance of agriculture, and the scant development of industry. Consequently, attention was long focused on general demands and issues, rather than on specific groups or on working conditions at the level of firms.

Union structure, particularly in CGIL, followed the dual horizontal and vertical pattern typical of southern European trade unionism; that is to say, interests were aggregated both geographically and by industry. Throughout the 1950s, horizontal structures and representative logic predominated—both at the national/confederal level and the decentralized level (chambers of labor)—in parallel with strategies of centralized and coordinated collective bargaining.

CISL, by contrast to CGIL, emphasized a "trade unionist" logic, an industry-based organizational structure, and a negotiation strategy oriented to more specific issues and which included company-level collective bargaining. However, against the background of labor's vulnerability in the market and of the weakening of the left in the political arena, employers sought simply to avoid dealing with the unions, although they showed a general but lukewarm preference for CISL and UIL on the shop floor. As a consequence, UIL and CISL developed in a manner substantially similar to CGIL. If anything, given their links with the government parties, they made greater direct or indirect use of party-political channels.

Prior to the split, membership of the unitary CGIL was high—an estimated 5,735,000 in 1947—reflecting the climate of social mobilization in which free trade unionism had been restored. However, for more than a decade and a half from 1950 union membership declined even while the "economic miracle" strengthened labor's market position. This was the result of union divisions and of the repression of union rank and file in the workplace during the 1950s. Within the overall decline, CGIL suffered a sharp drop in membership of more than two million, while CISL gained around half a million new members.

Only at the end of that decade did the economic boom and a partial thaw in the Cold War permit a degree of unity of action by the unions, together with some attempts to set up shop-floor organizations in the factories. However, this was too little to enable the unions to harness the growing discontent of broad sectors of the labor force; discontent which bred a period of severe conflict culminating in the "hot autumn" of 1969. In this year, the strike volume was three times higher than the already high level for the period 1959–67. However, strike statistics fail to convey the full impact of the general collective mobilization. Workers' struggles assumed much more radical and ideologically charged forms than those traditionally envisaged by the unions. Demands, driven by egalitarian aspirations and fiercely critical of the existing organization of work, were highly innovative.[4]

Collective mobilization added to the tensions in the relationship between workers and unions originating from changes in the composition of the labor force. The impact of Fordist production methods in large firms—the speeding up of work, fatigue, deskilling, and the loss of professional identity by workers—was neglected by unions dominated by skilled workers. At the same time, the cities of the booming northwest were flooded with a mass of mainly young and unskilled workers from the poorer regions, unused to urban life and factory discipline, or to the traditions of collective action and interest representation.

During the long phase of conflict which persisted until the late 1970s, the relationship between unions and their members was profoundly redefined. It now tended to center on the collective identity and solidarity created during the mobilization (rather than as before on political affiliations), giving rise to demands for direct democracy and control from below. In consequence, the ideological distance between the unions tended to narrow, and reunification seemed to be within reach. For the first time, unions were successful in establishing their workplace-based representations within firms, proposing a new system of shop-floor delegates and factory councils in recognition of the informal, direct forms of worker involvement and participation that had emerged during the period of collective mobilization.

The institutional/legal framework also changed. The enactment of the Workers' Statute in 1970 provided recognition and stability for union organization independent of shifts in the labor market position. A "federative pact" between CGIL, CISL, and UIL was signed in 1972, which ratified the highly popular factory councils. Social mobilization and the introduction of new organizational forms of representation encouraged increases in unionization throughout the 1970s. Membership peaked in 1978, when the overall rate reached 50.4 percent of the active labor force—a high level in a system of voluntary unionization and in an economy in which small and extremely small firms predominated.

However, the process of organizational consolidation was soon halted by the recession following the first oil crisis. The unions were compelled to recentralize their activity before a stable pattern of practices and rules could be defined at the decentralized level. This change—which gave rise to a bargaining strategy of restraint symbolized by the "Eur turning-point"—had the undesired effect of eroding support among workers and reopening ideological fault lines within the CGIL–CISL–UIL Federation.

Union membership began to decline gradually and employers were able to exploit episodes of worker protest and displays of intolerance by militants. The so-called "march of the forty thousand" Fiat middle managers and white-collar workers against the unions in 1980 is perhaps the best known of these episodes, but it was not the only one. Uncertainty in interpreting the attitudes of the rank and file exacerbated the already difficult relationship among the confederations, and in 1984 the Unitary Federation broke up over opposing views of wage restraint.

At the beginning of the 1990s, the strength of confederal trade unionism in Italy had diminished compared with ten years previously. One indicator was the fall in the membership of employed workers, from 7.1 million in 1980 to 5.9 million in 1990, representing a decrease in union density from 49.0 to 39.2 percent. Another symptom was the deteriorating relationship with the rank and file, manifested in the growth from 1987 of the *Cobas* (radical rank-and-file organizations) in the public sector,[5] and in the frequent outbreaks of dissent organized by factory councils in the private sector.

The 1990s was the decade of tripartite concertation, or "social pacts" between confederal unions, employers' associations, and the state.[6] The unions saw tripartite concertation as a means of cushioning the effects on workers of unemployment, industrial restructuring and the decentralization of production, and the rising cost of living, but especially of compensating for their declining market power by providing them with institutional functions and political recognition. For their part, employers accepted some form of union participation in economic policy because of their awareness of the remaining power of the unions to oppose a strategy of deregulation. Governments viewed the concertation of incomes policies in the first half of that decade, and of labor market and welfare policies afterwards, as a useful instrument for curbing inflation and for achieving socio-economic reforms in negotiated ways.

This focus on tripartite concertation did not, however, hinder union activity at company level. Quite to the contrary, the reform of the workplace representation system that was achieved in the period of social pacts revitalized the relationship with members and improved relations between unions. Overall, these processes strengthened confederal trade unionism and restored its public visibility and popularity.

The 2000s have been characterized by contrasting trends, which reflect the shifting balance of power of trade unions but also their search for new responses to the economic crisis and the difficulties of the political context. At the beginning of the decade the electoral victory of a center-right coalition, as well as the change in presidency of the largest employers' association, led to a more hostile environment for the trade unions. This resulted in a polarization between the CGIL, which tended to adopt a tough line of opposition, and the CISL and the UIL, which were more ready to compromise. In this situation, industrial conflict increased again after several years, and separate agreements were reached. The two high points of this renewed division among trade unions were the interconfederal agreement on collective bargaining reform, which in 2009 was strongly supported by the government but not signed by the CGIL; and the refusal by the metalworkers' trade union of CGIL (FIOM) to sign the agreements imposed by the Fiat management as a condition not to move production abroad.

On the other hand, attempts at unitary action between the trade unions have never been halted, until a unitary interconfederal agreement on union representation and collective bargaining was reached in June 2011. The deep economic and political crisis that characterizes the current decade seems indeed to have brought signs of a trend reversal in the previous union decline. The fall in union membership has stopped; the so-called "autonomous" trade unions which were a vehicle for the most radical demands have declined; unionization of new sectors of the labor force such as immigrant workers and employees with non-standard contracts has been launched with some success; and the system of workplace union representation established in 1993 has been institutionalized throughout the economy.

Trade Unions as Organizations in the Industrial Relations System

In all their stages of development, Italian trade unions have faced the typical organizational problems and dilemmas of interest associations that aim to represent their members' demands.

The first problem is of course to increase membership, with the double objective to enhance their "representativeness," that is the proportion of the active employees which is affiliated to a trade union (union density), and to increase their finances, since members usually pay dues. Trade union density in Italy is well above the EU27 average:[7] in 2011, 35.2 percent of employees were members of a trade union (retired employees excluded). Like in other advanced economies, the peak was reached in the late 1970s (50.4 percent in 1978) and it was followed by a sharp decline in the two next decades. However, while the 1980s showed a negative variation (–17.7 percent) and so did the 1990s (–11 percent), the trend has been reversed in the 2000s, when the rate of unionization increased again.[8]

A distinctive feature of Italian trade unionism is the very high rate of unionization of pensioners, which are not calculated in the union density rates but contribute to unions' finances substantially. About half of the 12.5 million total union members are in fact pensioners who belong to formally separate organizations affiliated to confederations. While active workers decreased by two million in the last 20 years, pensioners increased by four million. The growth of retired members partly reflects the general aging of the population, but is also due to a system of selective incentives offered by trade unions concerning administration of pensions and other welfare programs, and the organization of cultural and recreational activities for retired workers. This growth significantly affects unions' action, in that it keeps the attention of confederations focused on pensions and welfare and makes reforms in this field more difficult.[9]

A second problem is how to design a system of workplace representation, namely how to structure relations between the union organization and employees in the places where they work and need to meet their delegates. As with other aspects of trade unionism, workplace representation in Italy has long been characterized by the looseness of the rules governing its operation, a feature which, however, has facilitated adaptation and change. From the end of the war up until now, three main types can be identified.

The first was the *commissione interna* or internal commission, introduced after the fascist period by national agreement between employers' and workers' representatives. It was an elected body representing the workforce as a whole, hence, strictly speaking, it was not a union body. It had no bargaining powers and could not call strikes; its functions ranged from consultation with the employer to monitoring the implementation of collective agreements signed by external trade unions. Nevertheless, until the end of the 1960s internal commissions in many companies provided worker protection against management and sometimes undertook embryonic forms of bargaining on company issues. At the beginning of the 1970s, in the context of collective mobilization, the commissions were labeled "outdated," "bureaucratic," and "ineffective," and were abruptly replaced by other models of representation.

The second type of workplace representation was the *Rappresentanze sindacali aziendali* (RSA), envisaged by the Workers' Statute of 1970, which authorized workers from the "most representative" unions to establish workplace-based union representation. Accordingly, the RSA did replace the internal commissions. However, while the law granted them rights and entitled them to organizational resources, it did not regulate their constitution or operation. As a consequence, the RSA assumed a variety of forms.

The third type of workplace representation was the *Consiglio di fabbrica* or *Consiglio dei delegati* (factory council, council of delegates) which first appeared as an unexpected consequence of union initiatives to regain control over the spontaneous wave of worker mobilization. The factory councils then being set up were broad and heterogeneous groupings of both union members and non-members elected by the workforce as a whole. In 1972, the federative pact between CGIL, CISL, and UIL officially defined factory councils as workplace-based institutions of *worker and union* representation. Thus the two functions, of representing the workforce as a whole and of representing the external union, were embodied in a single institution, which was entitled to the resources provided for the RSA.

At the beginning of the 1980s, according to union figures, over 32,000 councils, consisting of 206,336 delegates, represented some five million workers. This means that around 50 percent of the labor force—excluding the public sector and agriculture, where representation took the form of unelected RSA appointed by the unions—was represented by councils. Their dual nature and loose regulation permitted the councils to give all workers a voice while enabling the unions to exert final control over their activity (not least because they could withdraw their recognition). The system performed a variety of functions, acting as a channel for information disclosure between management and unions, and as a permanent mechanism for workplace negotiation, joint consultation or decision-making.

However, the costs of the system should also be considered: the lack of clear boundaries between the respective powers of councils and unions; the uncertainty of roles and procedures; and the unpredictable behavior of the parties. A reform took place in 1993. With the tripartite accord signed in July, the social partners opted for a single organization in all workplaces which took the name of *Rappresentanze sindacali unitarie* (RSU, unitary union representation). The name was chosen to emphasize that this was a single institution recognized by the unions. The aim was to put an end to the organizational vagueness and terminological confusion of the previous 20 years.

Like the old councils, the RSU were bodies of both general and union representation. They continued to be elected by the whole workforce (not just union members), while unions had priority in nominating candidates. The novel feature, however, was that the reorganized bargaining system introduced by the July 1993 agreement also gave employers an interest in placing workplace representation on a more solid footing, so that they could count on a more reliable partner in decentralized bargaining. Accordingly, in December 1993, unions and employers' associations reached a national-level agreement on the RSU (followed in early 1994 by a similar agreement for the public sector), the first on such matters after nearly 30 years of substantially informal arrangements. As a consequence, a body of coherent—and above all formally defined—rules on the constitution and operation of workplace representative bodies took shape.

However, the tension between the voluntarism and (the lack of) institutionalization of Italian industrial relations has not been solved by this type of workplace representation. In the 2000s, it has become an object of dispute between the union confederations, especially between the CGIL, which calls for a law to set precise rules on the composition of RSU, and the CISL, which claims this is a matter of self-regulation. A unitary interconfederal agreement on trade union representativeness and collective bargaining was reached in 2011, but this agreement still requires further specifications before it can be implemented.[10] On the other hand, even in the new century the RSU has provided a relative stability to an industrial relations system often plagued by acute divisions and conflict at the central level.

TRADE UNIONS AS ACTORS IN THE
POLITICAL AND INSTITUTIONAL SYSTEMS

In the 1950s, the relationships between industrial relations actors and the political/institutional system were conditioned above all by the weakness of the trade unions. The three union confederations lacked the conventional power resources: a high level of membership; a monopoly of workers' representation; and (with the partial exception of CISL and UIL) recognition by the government and employers. This compelled the unions to depend heavily on the support of friendly political parties, which provided them with militants, funds, and legitimacy. At the beginning of the 1950s, for example, four of the eleven members of the CGIL governing council were senior officials from the Partito Comunista Italiano, and four of the nine members of the CISL governing council had leading roles in the Christian Democratic party; a decade later, the proportions were the same. However, such dependence on the parties tended to divide the unions and alienate them from their rank and file.[11]

Union weakness was compounded by the effects of the Cold War, which widened divisions and contributed to CGIL's political isolation. The unions' exclusion from economic policy choices also reflects the model of economic development pursued: exclusion may be seen as the guarantee offered by the government to industrialists in return for their relinquishing the traditional forms of state protection which conflicted with the decision to open up the Italian economy to international competition. The overall thrust of economic policy in those years was of non-interference in entrepreneurial decisions, making it difficult to envisage union involvement in economic policy goals of full employment and the growth of public consumption.

In the early 1960s, the center-left governments shifted from a strategy of union exclusion to one of limited union participation in experiments in incomes policy and labor market regulation, and even in economic planning. Having demonstrated a degree of united action and a moderate capacity for mobilization in negotiating a set of wage increases in 1962, the unions were now repeatedly consulted on a range of economic policy issues. Their dependence on political parties diminished with the easing of the Cold War and the new Christian Democrat strategy of "opening to the left," allowing greater attention to be paid to changes in the workplace and less to party-political allegiances.

Nevertheless, both the government's policy of union involvement and the unions' independence from the parties were frequently thwarted, and union influence on policy decisions was insubstantial. On the eve of the "hot autumn" of 1969, therefore, change was still embryonic.

In the early 1970s, at the height of mobilization, the unions launched a "struggle for social reforms" which constituted an attempt to undertake direct political action in competition with the political parties. This stemmed partly from factors common to other European countries, notably the confederations' desire to regain control over mobilization, and their need to forge alliances with other social groups. In other respects, however, the situation was anomalous in European terms. It reflected the unusual inability of the Italian party system to implement reforms even where a degree of consensus on goals existed; and the unions' determination to employ the mobilization tactics typical of the period to combat their exclusion (even under relatively "friendly" center-left governments) from social and economic policymaking.

Although implemented in a conflictual manner, the strategy of reforms marked a transition from exclusion to involvement in the formation of economic and social policy in the phase of political exchange of the second half of the 1970s and the first half of the 1980s. The "struggle for reforms" failed, however, to achieve significant results, both because the agreements reached with the government, for instance on housing policy, did not find their way into law, and because labor mobilization failed to engender major changes in voting patterns. This reduced the political weight of the unions vis-à-vis the political parties and the advantages accruing to the latter from supporting their demands.

From the mid-1970s, the unions' stance on economic and social policies changed; and there was an even more profound shift in the attitude of governments. These developments took place against a background of international recession and spiraling inflation. Until the appearance of Margaret Thatcher on the international scene, any solution to the most serious economic slump since World War II seemed impossible without active state intervention and the cooperation of the large interest organizations. In the period 1976–9, governments of "national solidarity," supported by a parliamentary majority including the Partito Comunista Italiano, attempted to handle the consequences of economic crisis through social pacts. The unions for their part were now prepared to engage in a wide-ranging process of political exchange involving wage restraint in return for full employment policies, controls on corporate restructuring, and social reform. Exchange rested, therefore, on the unions' undertaking not to exploit fully the market power of the strongest workers. The change in union approach was illustrated most vividly by the "Eur document" of 1978, in which CGIL set out publicly its new strategy of recognizing macro-economic constraints on its actions.

The Eur document was a turning point for Italian trade unions' participation in the economic and social policymaking. Tripartite concertation was successful in 1983 and, in spite of the division it produced among trade unions the following year, it remained very high on their agenda. The high point was reached in the 1990s, widely seen as the decade of "social pacts" between confederal unions, employers' associations, and the state.[12]

More generally, since the Eur document 11 major national pacts were agreed to, in addition to numerous territorial pacts: one in the late 1970s, two in the 1980s, five in the 1990s, and three in the 2000s. Italian social pacts were signed in periods characterized by quite different structural and institutional conditions, but we can highlight some general features. First, a sentiment of national economic emergency has characterized all social pacts. A second general feature has been the weakness of the governmental coalitions that looked to social pacts as an instrument for enhancing their legitimacy. A third feature has been the presence of moderately strong unions, capable of coordinating both industry-level and decentralized bargaining, but also permanently challenged by the risk (and often the reality) of internal divisions.

Italian trade unions are therefore important actors in the political and institutional systems. In the latter their role has been enhanced also by their relatively formalized and stable involvement in the implementation of public policies, as well as by the indirect intervention of public institutions in labor relations.

Trade unions have been active in public policy institutions in Italy ever since the period after World War II, when representatives of the major interest organizations were involved in the administration of social security bodies and welfare programs, from the pensions system to the Wages Guarantee Fund.[13] Their role then expanded through participation in the numerous tripartite committees that intervene in labor market management at the national and local level.[14] Added to these are the union representatives sitting on the administrative boards of ministries and public agencies, as well as on the hundreds of committees that regulate the employment relationship in the public sector.

Over time, these arrangements have generated a number of unforeseen effects. The results of the unions' institutional involvement have been generally disappointing, as regards their ability to influence the public administration's choices, and the efficiency and quality of public services. However, there have been a number of beneficial consequences for the industrial relations system. Institutional participation has created spaces for contact between the social partners even in periods when collective bargaining has faltered. A further effect has been the consolidation of the unwritten rule that implementation of major changes promoted by the public authorities requires some consent by the trade unions. This also means that the actual influence of the unions in Italy has always been somewhat greater than might appear from indicators such as membership levels or the results of collective bargaining. Institutional involvement has provided them with opportunities to obtain benefits and resources which they can then convert into selective incentives for their members.

CONCLUSIONS: THE DIFFICULT COEXISTENCE OF VOLUNTARISM AND INSTITUTIONALIZATION

As we have seen, trade unions are less regulated in Italy than elsewhere in Europe, and the Italian industrial relations system has often been described as having a low level of institutionalization, in the sense of lacking formalized and stable rules governing relations between the actors. However, I have shown that this captures only a part of the whole story. If we broaden our observation to include the ways in which services and public administration are regulated, especially as regards welfare and social security, the role of Italian trade unions stands out as being much more formalized. Thus one observes a pronounced voluntarism in relations between unions and employers (particularly in the private sector), coupled with the institutional involvement of trade unions in the implementation of social policies and in the regulation of public sector employment. This is a structural feature of the Italian system of industrial relations which has never been substantially altered, by either the 1970 Workers' Statute or the later legislation.

The fact that Italian trade unions are loosely regulated and operate in an arena of interest representation with few barriers to entry has favored the emergence of a system of pluralistic representation for both unions and employers' associations that is at once organizationally strong and unevenly representative. This fluidity has permitted the growth of institutions sufficiently flexible to adapt to change with relative success. As regards collective action, the general lack of legislative restrictions on strikes and the absence of compulsory arbitration in labor disputes encourages conflictual behavior even by small groups independent from, and sometimes hostile to, the major unions. Collective bargaining in Italy is also not subject to legal rules (as in Germany), nor is negotiation between the social partners compulsory (as in France). Consequently, the bargaining structure has moved back and forth between the center and the periphery according to circumstances and power relations, without well-established rules accepted by both sides.[15] This has given rise to overlaps in competences and in the issues addressed at different levels, and has hampered coordination by the union confederations.

However, this phenomenon is to some extent counterbalanced by the second fundamental aspect discussed above: namely, the relatively formalized and stable involvement of trade unions in the implementation of public policies. This second aspect has long been overlooked and its effects have gone largely unobserved. Actually, Italian trade unions have always been active in the administration of social security bodies and welfare programs, as well as in tripartite committees that intervene in labor market management. Trade unions are also often officially consulted by the public authorities on labor-related matters.

This dualism between voluntarism and informality, on the one hand, and involvement in public institutions, on the other, has its origins in the trade unions' economic and political weakness, which for many years allowed other industrial relations actors simply to ignore them. Informality could ensure flexibility at low cost and without excessive risks, while institutional involvement could to some extent counter the lack of a well-developed and formalized industrial relations system, and thereby help social cohesion. At a later stage, the informality and voluntarism of the Italian industrial relations system has increased its ability to adapt to changing circumstances, though this has been at the price of the often unpredictable behavior of actors; and their tendency to adopt a short-term perspective has been encouraged. When the need for predictability has increased, the advantages of informality have diminished, while the costs have increased.

The 1993 tripartite agreement can be seen in this light as the most determined attempt to overcome this dual character of trade union activity and of industrial relations in Italy. Trade unions and employers' associations have for the first time explicitly set out to impose a framework of formal regulation on the collective bargaining structure and on their own relationships. This commitment to a greater institutionalization of industrial relations showed a new awareness that informality has its drawbacks, most notably the unpredictability of actors' behavior and their vulnerability to shifts in power relations.

This awareness has not disappeared in the two decades that followed. On the contrary, in spite of ongoing internal divisions, trade unions have converged in relying on relatively institutionalized industrial relations as the only way to contain the growth of sub-standard positions in the labor market. Such considerations have since then tipped the balance in favor of regulation. While Italian trade unions are now holding to this position rather strongly, the uncertainties and internal divisions that have characterized their action in most recent years can to a large degree be related to this problem. Namely, is it possible for them, and to what extent, to recreate spaces for informal interaction at the periphery of the system (company level and local bargaining) in order to offset the potential inflexibility of institutionalized relations? Is it possible to substantially maintain the level of institutional protection traditionally enjoyed by core workers but at the same time to jointly manage the flexibilization that employers demand in the workplaces? The continuing relevance of trade unions in Italian industrial relations and political systems may largely depend on their ability to provide a unitary and convincing answer to these still unsolved questions.

Notes

1. Bernard Ebbinghaus, "Ever Larger unions: Organisational Restructuring and its Impact on Union Confederations," *Industrial Relations Journal*, 34, no. 5 (2003).
2. Gian Primo Cella, "Regulation in Italian Industrial Relations," in Peter Lange and Marino Regini (eds.), *State, Market and Social Regulation. New Perspectives on Italy,* (New York: Cambridge University Press, 1989).
3. Ida Regalia, Marino Regini, "Italy: The Dual Character of Industrial Relations," in Anthony Ferner and Richard Hyman (eds.), *Changing Industrial Relations in Europe* (Oxford: Blackwell, 1998).
4. Alessandro Pizzorno, Emilio Reyneri, Marino Regini, and Ida Regalia, *Lotte operaie e sindacato: il ciclo 1968–1972 in Italia* (Bologna: Il Mulino, 1978).
5. Lorenzo Bordogna, *Pluralismo senza mercato. Rappresentanza e conflitto nel settore pubblico* (Milano: Franco Angeli, 1994).
6. Marino Regini and Sabrina Colombo, "Italy: The Rise and Decline of Social Pacts," in S. Avdagic, M. Rhodes, and J. Visser (eds.), *Social Pacts in Europe: Emergence, Evolution and Institutionalization* (Oxford: Oxford University Press, 2011).

7. Jelle Visser, *Data base on institutional characteristics of trade unions, wage setting, state intervention and social pacts, 1960–2011 (ICTWSS)* (Amsterdam: AIAS, University of Amsterdam, 2013).

8. Mimmo Carrieri, *I sindacati* (Bologna: Il Mulino, 2012).

9. Ida Regalia, "Italian Trade Unions: Still Shifting between Consolidated Organizations and Social Movements?," *Management Review*, 23, no. 4 (2012).

10. Regalia, "Italian Trade Unions: Still Shifting between Consolidated Organizations and Social Movements?".

11. Alessandro Pizzorno, *I soggetti del pluralismo* (Bologna: Il Mulino, 1980).

12. Marino Regini, "Between Deregulation and Social Pacts. The Responses of European Economies to Globalization," *Politics and Society*, 28, no. 1 (2000). See also Lucio Baccaro, Mimmo Carrieri, and Cesare Damiano, "The Resurgence of the Italian Confederal Unions: Will it Last?" *European Journal of Industrial Relations*, 9, no. 1 (2003).

13. See Chapter 38, this volume.

14. See the Chapter 37, this volume.

15. Not even the 1993 tripartite accord has set the final word on it, as it has been variously interpreted by the different actors in the following decades.

CHAPTER 41

LIBERAL AND LICENSED PROFESSIONS

CARLO CARBONI

PROFESSIONALS are leading players in modern society,[1] and their power and importance have increased from the beginning of the "short century" to the present day. The professions that exploded with the new economy and financially driven capitalism from the mid-1990s rapidly became icons of the new modernity that drives ideas, solutions, and financial resources in real time, pushing ahead progress and knowledge in the fields of genetics, biomedicine, and technology. The numbers and roles of these professionals have continued to expand from the mid-1990s: as playmakers of the exchange between science and technology, between generative knowledge and economy, between codified knowledge and institutions. Consequently, they have conquered positions in all spheres, from economics to politics, culture, technology, health, training, communication and information, and the organization of civil society.

As a result, an emergent class composed of managers, executives, scientists, and technicians has taken root. These professionals in new and traditional fields are all highly educated and, above all, increasingly essential in institutional, social, and market networks. This new class has emerged as the repository for the application of cognitive, relational, methodological, and technological know-how. As such, it has fueled a new middle class that has rejected employment to profess its vocation, assuming a greater degree of autonomy, responsibility, and risk; a new professional middle class that is based not on property but on a codified knowledge that highlights the capabilities of modern individuals to transform resources by applying their knowledge and skills in respected activities.

The importance of the social role acquired by professionals is further underscored by the fact that a sizable number of them, in Old World countries, have entered not only the middle class but also other circles of the power elites, which are the most restricted and powerful (see Chapter 1, this volume). After all, the new global world requires increasing skills and professionalism in the key relational roles of exchange. These factors encourage the view of professionalism and its top ranks as a combination inclined to potential developmental guidance in times of relational capitalism, whose power structures are increasingly less guaranteed by asset inheritance, and—perhaps—are increasingly related to access and the relational skills that distinguish a networking elite.[2]

The economic crisis in the West, however, has revealed another side of the coin. The most disturbing themes tackled in this chapter include: (a) the role played by moral hazard among top professionals and management; (b) the privileged status behavior, extending to forms of crony-capitalist nepotism displayed by professionals and other elites; (c) the frequent interlocking of figures running large corporations and banking and financial institutions; and (d) the punishing and depriving effect of the recession on the incomes and employment of professionals.

Furthermore, since the mid-1980s, modernity has changed its tone and paradigm alongside the emergence of new expertise and new elites. When the market went into top gear, society experienced meltdown and the net elites assumed a significantly unconventional role to bring about a cultural change, as Christopher Lasch so aptly pointed out.[3]

Italian Particularism

Many of the trends defined by the expansion of the liberal professions in Western societies over a century or so can also be found in Italy, where the media have often criticized a growing number of corporate and political barriers that have been erected by the boards of professional associations to limit the numbers and boundaries of particular professions. In Italy, liberal and licensed professions constitute the only socioeconomic group that has managed to double in size since the mid-1990s, now counting over 2.4 million members including management. More precisely, between 1997 and 2009, the number of associated professionals rose by 35.9 percent, from 1.476 million to 2.006 million. In terms of members, the medical register is the largest, with approximately 400,000 physicians, surgeons, and dentists, followed by 380,000 nurses and 220,000 engineers.[4]

The number of women has also risen drastically, since the 1990s and approximately 70 percent of the growth of the professions is attributable to the large-scale arrival of women in their ranks. This phenomenon is not restricted to caring jobs that were once considered semi-professional (e.g. nurses, social workers). In fact, during the 2007–11 recession, the number of women "specialists in legal sciences" rose by 44.5 percent, engineers by 16 percent, and physicians by 14 percent.

The overall growth of the professions is attributable chiefly to the strengthening of the relational networks between knowledge and economy, and between science and its economic application. The new power of the professional elites arose within these networks, and their relational and reputational capital enabled them to exercise effective institutional and corporate lobbying pressure.

Most of the professions have undergone technological, social, and economic transformation in recent decades. Even the most traditional have experienced a change in partners, means, and relationships. E-working has opened up new functions and opportunities, and the experiences of young professionals show that their vocation is marked by a desire for self-fulfillment in their profession. In the second half of the twentieth century, standardization processes for professionals—from private practitioners to salaried employees in large firms—continued to expand, intensifying impersonality in the relationship with the customer and a service ethic that increasingly conceals business relations. The differentiation processes of economic and social activities introduced new professions and changed the order of things, relaunching a new professional cultural software as a free choice for individuals who had invested in training.

With the emergence of new professions, two association networks are taking shape within the Italian professional system. On the one hand, there are the regulated professions, with around 2 million registered members; on the other, non-regulated professional activities (at least another 2 million practitioners) undertaken by numerous associations that are linked across the country and coordinated at the national level. The drive for recognition and regulation of the "new professions" sector continues.

After the "practice of codified knowledge" (73 percent), the most widespread activity among the professions is the cultivation of interpersonal relations (69 percent), while the most important working activities are the processing and interpretation of information (58 percent) and creative thinking (56 percent). Their imprinting is relationality, information, skill. The professional elites (of economic, political, scientific, and mass media networks) constitute the majority of the Italian elites, accounting for 69 percent of Italy's driving forces and 81 percent of the country's leaders.[5] In the sphere of net elites, the members of the liberal and licensed professions have a significant impact on the total of elites: 5 percent of journalists, 4 percent of consultants and lawyers, 1.5 percent of architects, and 1 percent of physicians.[6] Moreover, the widespread penetration of the professions commences from local and regional elites, in which liberal and licensed professions are deeply rooted.[7]

The strength of the liberal and licensed professions is attested to primarily by interlocking, in which they often play a leading role on the boards of companies, banks, financial institutions, and in the political world. Recent research on the multiple positions held by board members of Italian companies in Fortune's Global 500 list showed the presence of professionals in ensuring transversal power and intermediation, with these multiple positions acting as common denominators driven by a ubiquity that has brought the exponential growth of conflicts of interest. Moreover, these ubiquitous figures vaunt important political backers.

The multiple positions originated in post-Unification with lawyers practicing their profession, as well as being university teachers and pursuing political careers (the latter seen as rich in positional advantages).[8] So the legal profession was the first to became a symbol of social mobility, which is a historical blindspot for Italy. Secondly, the high value set on this profession spotlights the historical undervaluation of the role of scientific and technical professions that, in turn, depend on the difficult relationship with a public bureaucracy. The state's apparatus demands skills linked to its bureaucratic logic, which is reluctant both to admit the primacy of professional competence and the role of experts.[9] Aside from the fascism that valorized architects and engineers, the role of experts in elite Italy has been reduced to the legal framework, with little appreciation of techno-scientific roles. Thirdly, the institutionalization of the Bar (1874) showed the state monopoly on higher education as well as on the liberal professions, since both these worlds are intrinsically tied together. Only by the twentieth century, after the divorce between the nobility and the professions, did the liberal professions take on the characteristics of unwaged, self-employed, and organized occupations, which are linked to high levels of education that certifies legal abstract knowledge. The transition to modern professions, which are more tied to market logic and the use of experts to resolve the complex issues faced by governments, has therefore been very slow in Italy, like the rest of continental Europe and in contrast to the Anglo-Saxon world.

The history of the country since Unification shows that Italian particularism lies not in figures or trends, but primarily in the strong bond between Italy's professional associations and its resilient political capitalism. More precisely, professional associations are a flexible and adaptable piece of the state. They were regulated by Act No. 897 (1938), which extended to other major professions a ban that already applied to lawyers (1933) and physicians (1933), whereby they could not practice their profession unless they were members of the appropriate professional association. Today, the 2,000 branches of professional associations turn over almost 200 billion euros (just under 15 percent of the GDP), not to mention a further 50 billion euros or so in the form of the total assets of the 16 independent social security funds they regulate and manage.[10] The strength of the associations lies in the fact that they actually represent a piece of the state—which has granted them regulatory, disciplinary, and ethical powers—in a tangle of interests and connections that traditionally break off from the spoils system to merge with the professionals who are board members of big banks and leading public and private companies. Professional associations have now acquired the power to veto decisions affecting them, a power recently reconfirmed, as will be explained in the closing paragraph. In turn, the professional groups are struggling to preserve their market positions in terms of both their profession and their pension schemes. They may be seeking a new professional welfare system and, above all, will have to solve the problem of access for young professionals, as the high numbers in some professions in Italy, such as lawyers (almost five times higher than in France) or architects (four times more than currently in Spain), constitute a real thorn in society's side.

Therefore, the professional book in Italy is open in the middle, and has long been awaiting a new page that shows routes around these obstacles and free deployment of this social and vocational potential based on merit that is encapsulated instead in state legislation. Free associations that make reputation and self-regulation their emblems could, in fact, trigger greater social mobility in a country that needs to shrug off the shackles and parasitical ballast that have been generated by privilege. Several professionals, interviewed in our recent surveys,[11] have pointed out that their activities are often stifled by pan-politicism and difficult relationships with the public sphere. Many of them did not hesitate to condemn dependence on politicians and the need to make more decisive inroads into proficiency, competition, and transparency; that is, pathways of merit in a competitive market of professions.

These opinions are at odds with the political-corporate filtering imposed by each professional association. Some commentators, observing the low pass rates in state professional examinations, have asked whether Italy is an unbearable gerontocracy, as young professionals now have the poor prospect of a sub-contracted job, or of becoming "gophers" in professional firms, taking insecure and often underpaid positions. Italian professionals consider themselves fulfilled (89 percent), but only just over 48 percent feel gratified in terms of remuneration. Moreover, professionals are more prone to stress (51.8 percent) than office (24.1 percent) and manual (37.8 percent) workers.

MIDDLE CLASS OR A NEW PROFESSIONAL BOURGEOISIE?

After politicians, businessmen, and trade-union leaders, professionals constitute the "fourth estate" in Italy, but public opinion considers them a top community in terms of privileges. Italians perceive professionals as belonging to a class that enjoys privileges as well as wealth generated by their position. Consequently, privilege is the resource that distinguishes professionals in the Italian social system. Their currency of power is constituted by skill and relationality, and as a result they are perceived as groups occupying the middle–upper strata of the social system. Indeed, not all young people can afford sufficient training to become professionals, even when they possess merit and vocation, owing to the frailty of the right to education in Italy.

The position of the class itself generates an exclusive status that uses professional registers and associations as a sort of system whose output is a neo-elite class, if not actual castes, as in the case of powerful groups such as lawyers, physicians, and architects. The institutionalization of professional associations in Italy has been structured as a corporate process, which began in the last quarter of the nineteenth century with notaries and lawyers. Each professional group has organized itself with its own role, association, individualized training system, and a self-disciplinary ethical system, while the qualifying system constitutes a mechanism of selective status control and corporate exclusion.

Moreover, the affiliation between social status and family is well known, and consequently the perpetuation of the class system often occurs through family ties and nepotism. Recent reports by Alma Laurea show that over 40 percent of architects are the children of architects, and similar percentages can be found for each of the major associations,[12] such as lawyers, engineers, and physicians, confirming that the Italy of professional associations also constitutes a familial brake on social mobility.

The status privileges of professionals can also be deduced from their ability to avoid or evade taxes, a national sport in Italy. The propensity of artisans, professionals, and traders not to issue till receipts, invoices, or receipts persists, and tax evasion is rapidly increasing among all professionals; respondents assigned the highest index of tax evasion to lawyers (42.7 percent of cases), followed by surveyors (40.2), psychologists and psychiatrists (40), architects (38.7), dieticians (38), medical specialists (34), dentists (34), veterinarians (25.3), accountants (23.5), and notaries (19.6).[13]

However, if we refer to young adult professionals (aged 30 to 40), their average incomes are very low: in architectural firms a young engineer is paid 250–500 euros a month, much less than a waiter in the restaurant trade. In Italy, the growth of the professional middle class was initially thwarted by economic decline and then seriously damaged by the recession. In the professions, especially among the young, a "penniless" middle class has emerged, referring to the status of relative deprivation suffered by this social pillar of democracy. In fact, compared with a decline of 5 percent in the real available income of Italian families in the period 2005–10, that of professionals registered with their independent social security funds fell by roughly twice that amount, reaching 20 percent in the legal profession.

The recession (2008–13) has also frozen employment dynamics that were very lively in the decades either side of the new millennium, during which the number of professionals registered with orders increased and the number of professional women doubled. Indeed, the early 1990s revealed that the number of new professionals with technical and technological vocations was also finally growing in social and economic importance in Italy, albeit with the familiar contradictions derived from the country's small and medium-sided enterprise (SME)-type manufacturing structure, and services marked by an endemic backwardness in terms of productivity and efficiency. We refer to the whole area of new professions associated particularly with business services, and consequently information technology and quality, design and communication, internationalization, and product marketing.[14] Moreover, with a cognitive patrimony of codified, generative, and creative knowledge, this area had appeared resistant to the recession until 2009, when financial troubles began to infect the real economy and hence also the service sector. Subsequently, falling employment and incomes began to affect almost the entire array of professionals. The only exceptions were the health professions that we could define as counter-cyclical, alongside the medical expenses of Italian families, which have continued to rise during these years of economic crisis.

In affecting professionals, the recession not only contributes to pulverizing the traditional social bond provided by the middle classes, but also deals a blow to the (albeit slow) modernization of national human resources, which seemed to have started with a significant expansion of brainpower in production and services. The collapse of professionalism is therefore very bad news for the national economy, which is generally detached from the technological frontier and must rely on innovation to act as a precious revolving door: new professionals could be an excellent lubricant for improving and renewing the economic motors around which most of the labor world revolves. The traditional social elevators, such as self-employment, professionalism, and also higher education, have been damaged. The fallout is being felt above all by young people, already under pressure from an unprecedented "intellectual" unemployment rate. Ten years after graduation the salaries of our young graduates have decreased by as much as 50 percent compared to the turn of the century.[15] Three decades ago a university education was seen as the key for being upwardly mobile in society. Vance Packard's analysis (*The Status Seekers* 1959) of new graduate elites had come to the same conclusion twenty years earlier, in the USA. These situations now pale into insignificance, with professionalism having a stronger but less advantageous role. Even the number of young people inclined to set up their own businesses has fallen in the recession, with fewer under-35s involved in entrepreneurial activities, especially in the center and north of the country, where they had played a leading role in economic development.

RECENT CHANGES: THE RECESSION REINFORCES PROFESSIONAL GERONTOCRACY

The typical ideal requirements for professions as established more than a century ago by Max Weber (autonomy, intellectual independence, competence, ethics, etc.) are disappearing under the impact of standardization of professional activities. The definition of professionalism is inexorably lost in the rivers of description that substantiate it (self-employed, employee, intern), as well as stratification (insecurity, lack of protection, aim of achievement) and differentiation (emerging professions, sector changes) classifications. Consequently, figures fluctuate, with the Consiglio Nazionale Economia e Lavoro (CNEL) claiming there are 3.5 million professionals in Italy, while the Istituto di ricerche economiche e sociali (IRES) says there are 5 million (2 million are members of registers and rolls; 3 million are unprotected). If we consider only self-employed professionals, the Istituto nazionale di statistica. (ISTAT) states there are about 1 million (plus 500,000 contract and jobbing workers), but the Istituto nazionale previdenza sociale (INPS) talks of about 900,000, and the Ministry of Finance indicates 1.3 million. The second aspect to consider is that the image of the "career professional," typical of the second half of the twentieth century, today looks drab and drained. The professionals who were the heirs to the nineteenth- and twentieth-century elite and "educated classes," from the second half of the twentieth century to the present, acquired an image as "well-to-do" and, in any case, seemed to be the main artery fueling the Italian middle classes. Indeed, the group of successful professionals (slightly more than one in ten) is an integral part of the "bourgeoisie" and contributes to creating one of the largest corporation elites.

However, this image is applicable to small numbers and is increasingly less a reflection of reality for independent professionals in this recession. In 2012, one in five professionals were at risk of insecurity and more than 40 percent appear to earn less than 15,000 euros a year: the data describe professional groups as suffering the most. The credit crunch, lengthy payment terms, increasingly erratic commissions due to the recession, all constitute the weaknesses, the soft underbelly of today's independent professions. About one freelance professional in two declares they are forced to work in this system, which erodes the enthusiasm and drive that underpins professional freelance culture. More recent sociological research suggests the independent professions overall seem to have lost their appeal and bargaining power in the job market. The difficulties encountered by professionals today show the reality of a declining section of the middle classes. In some cases, the social elevator is stuck, and in others it is plummeting relentlessly downwards. This loss of status contributes to the spreading of the unhealthy idea that a degree—which at least 90 percent of self-employed professionals have—has become a "piece of paper" of little use, especially to the young.

Our young professionals, even in scientific and technical areas, either resign themselves to ridiculously low "takings" or are forced to take the route of intellectual migration, which is a great risk because it deprives Italy of important skills. In the last century Italian emigrants were manual workers, labor power, while at the beginning of the twenty-first century they are increasingly becoming brain power. Annually this depressed country loses enough young emigrants to populate a city the size of Mantua. So why are we surprised when there are so many disappointed graduates and professionals among the protesters attending Beppe Grillo's M5S meet-ups?[16] Or that the most talented of our youth are resentful that their merits are never acknowledged? Never so much as in these hard times have connections and recommendations been the passports that allow youngsters to enter the professional world.

During the recession, bad news for young Italians arrives daily, sinking them further into social depression. High youth unemployment is not a novelty for Italy, having reached 40 percent in the late 1980s during a time of complete employment restructuring and deindustrialization. After reading the ISTAT statement that Italy holds the European record for NEETs (Not (engaged) in Education, Employment or Training) (one in five youths neither studies nor works), learning the rate of youth unemployment and the significant decrease in undergraduates after six years of the recession, we witness the implacable wave of frustration overwhelming our young professional brain power. This is shown by the two-digit fall in the number of those examined and certificated to access the liberal professions,[17] indicating a tendency to depress professional expectations in our young graduates. Not only in Italy, but throughout the former "Western World," those who have lost their jobs are mostly young people. In short, the mechanisms of exclusion fielded by the "elders" continue to prevail over the weak actions of usurpation implemented by youth. Teachers are scarce, and the young are offered meager access to professional elevators.

Gerontocracy is the order of the day among professional association executives and stops social elevators for the professions. Professional job opportunities are scarce, and when they occur they offer merely lengthy traineeships at little or no remuneration. In many cases, rather than learning to practice a profession, young people are used as "gophers" (as there are no teachers). However, it is shocking to learn that 60 percent of young Italians are against reforming, let alone abolishing, professional associations.[18] Perhaps rather than a rational preference for protection (which is actually negligible), mistaken for the possibility of a free market, we are seeing a universe of lost and confused youth that is easy prey for the recession and above all for historic corporatism.

The professional market in Italy was never a lush garden for vocation, even before the crisis. It has always been marked by closures and the corporate clientele of powerful professional associations, expression of a cultural software widespread in society, avid for protection and never completely won over by the idea of a competitive and transparent market. Thus a professional culture has developed that is often gridlocked and covertly immersed in the political and corporate filters of the individual professional associations. The result is that it has never been possible to apply the pragmatic reforms that distinguish an open society in the face of self-referencing corporations that open and close the hatches of access to professional markets at their own discretion, making them impervious to competitive stimuli.

Certifications are also declining because examinations often have unpredictable outcomes, depending on geographical areas and professions: it is no exaggeration to say that it is like throwing dice. The absurd aspect is that in recent years the drop in certified young people has not just affected traditional professions such as accountancy, penalized by long placements, but also engineering, the decline of which is only partially offset by the growth in IT specialists and civil engineers (for whom certification is obligatory). This is a signal that the country wastes efficiency, struggling to make rational use of its best and most modern human resources.[19] It is a sign that something more profound is happening. In the past, at the height of the industrial society, the most evident crises mainly affected manual workers. In the post-industrial society, social depression fallout involves precisely the finest figures in terms of cognitive and technological knowledge. It will be precisely the knowledge workers—on whom our country had begun to wager for a better twenty-first century—who will pay the price.

The risk is that during the recession, skepticism will take root in Italy with regard to investments in knowledge; that is, families will begin to believe the alarming notion that tertiary education is useless, that it does not increase a young person's chances of finding a professional, adequately remunerated, and qualified job. Most importantly, we are forfeiting the work culture of our youth, who feel they are being led astray by the promised arrival of an economy based on professional knowledge. Their defeatist and pessimistic weariness threatens to extinguish the vocational fire that the culture of *Beruf* requires. Italy had not sufficiently espoused the idea that its industrial manufacturing system requires tertiary and professional functions to manage processes of enhancement, and that to restore efficiency to "system Italy" there is a need to give a value to the professional knowledge of the younger generations.

Awaiting Reforms for Italian Particularism

The professional world continues to garner the trust of the Italians: about half of the population recognizes the merit of professionals, second only to entrepreneurs in this ranking compiled by both the Italians and their elites.[20] As a result, with the new century public opinion has become persuaded that a reform of professional associations was appropriate and overdue. Opening the floodgates to attract new forces of young brain power to the professional market should be the main purpose of such a reform project, so as to foster the emergence of talented youth that has been held back until now. Pierluigi Bersani's 2006 blanket deregulation (rates, advertising, and professional associations) at least appeared courageous, and that trace of reform was recovered timidly by Silvio Berlusconi (2008–11)[21] and with a little more decisiveness by Mario Monti's "technical" government (2011–13).

In the debate on the reform of the professions that has now lasted several decades, there are issues that have been explored directly, including the abolition of the legal value of the educational qualification—which about 80 percent of Italians see as a necessary measure in order to increase the role of merit—and also of professional associations, something that 55 percent of executives interviewed for the second LUISS Report (2008) feel to be appropriate. In the professions jungle there are many other issues to address, discuss, and resolve, from the mass of semi-professions to be upgraded, to the ethical issues associated with *Beruf*, new pension schemes to deal with numerical growth, and the remarkable overpopulation reached by several traditional professions. These are important groups that interface daily with citizens, business and family networks, producers, and consumers, establishing professional and relational connections that are important for the country. Consequently it seemed necessary to implement pragmatic, operational reform that would be able to dismantle the monopoly that each association enjoys and which the European Parliament and the Council pinpointed as negative with their Directive 2005/36/EC on the recognition of professional qualifications (September 7, 2005).

"A radical and credible overall reform strategy is required, including full liberalization of local public services and professional services." Thus wrote Jean-Claude Trichet in the famous letter from the European Central Bank (ECB) to the Italian government, dated August 5, 2011, actually the first of the ten heartfelt recommendations in which it suggested urgent injections of massive doses of competition within the liberal professions.

Under pressure from the EU and ECB, the governments of Silvio Berlusconi and Mario Monti tried to touch on a subject—liberal professions—that had remained impervious to any substantive modification for over 30 years. If, on the one hand, Trichet's decree stressed the freedom of access to professions, on the other it did not deal with the problem of the overpopulation of certain Italian liberal professions, in particular law, accountancy, engineering, architecture, and journalism.

Bersani, Berlusconi, and Monti's hesitant attempts clashed with a veritable jungle of veto powers from the Italy that counts, both in mind and "gut." However, it is no secret that in Italy—a breeding ground of privileges and protection—"real" liberalizations would be a real hornet's nest. At the first hint of a proposal for a thorough reform of professional associations (proposed by Mario Monti), the force of the associations mobilized, and by the time of implementation, what had been called a mini-reform of the professions had shrunk to a sort of mini-liberalization. The associations that should have been extensively reformed were given an affable opportunity for self-reform.

What happened? The professional lobbies took the field in defense of traditional mechanisms of consensus that bind state powers to a vast industrial and professional middle class: the head and the gut of the country. The policy of small steps on these issues that have been debated since 1983 (under Minister Darida) appears to be the only one practicable at this time of drained state coffers, and taking into account the corporative strength, the complexity, and the additional processes of differentiation and stratification that the professional sphere has encountered in recent years. However, the results appear to be minimal, because the state is struggling to reform a piece of itself—institutionalized corporations—and also because in 2011, for example, 44 percent of parliamentarians were members of a professional association.

In fact, far more than a few timid liberalizations or law reforms are needed, particularly to solve the glaring problems of the weak and the young in the professions: incentives, loans, venture capital; in other words, bold, challenging steps that cannot be sustained today owing to the poor state of the public finances. In these hard times the remedy for the liberal professions must come primarily from the social partners who organize them in cities and regions, where the creation of professional communities, of networks of codified and generative competence, could represent added value for local development and businesses. Universities could also play a role, strengthening their "third mission," that of placements for professions that offer training. The banks too should be able to "financialize" technological and generative professional knowledge. Most importantly, the solution lies in young people, if they are capable of interpreting positively the metamorphosis of professions, thereby creating new cultural and motivational software that is able to give value to their own innovative knowledge, applying criteria of excellence and competitiveness.

Economic decline, society at a standstill, the ruling classes shattered by sector and sectionalist corporatism, have devastated central powers and released a weak state and strong corporations. So far, Italy has stubbornly ignored pressures and calls (by the EU) to liberalize markets and professions completely, to dismantle protectionist clientele fabric. Here are a culture and forces that once formed the backbone of civil society that are long institutionalized, and thus are capable of applying a de facto obstruction to liberalization, caring nothing for evidence from Europe and the wider world that proves that liberalization and professional trade associations help a country to free itself. Greater competition would involve a downsizing of political capitalism in favor of a modern market democracy, and also the removal of a corporative society in favor of an open system.[22] Now, more than ever, the economy driven by technology and finance has definitely shifted the emphasis from labor power to brain power, the latter being the area preferred by the professions. This is why the diffusion of professional communities should be considered the circulatory system of the social capital and the technological change which shall characterize the next Italian development.

Notes

1. In Max Weber the professions are vehicles of modern rationality and, at the same time, *Beruf* (vocation) is the modern individual's free choice. Emile Durkheim saw the professions as a product of social differentiation, and underscored that corporate and professional associations could curb the growth of individualism and industrial rationality by adopting a shared code of professional ethics. Parsons, the third classical interpreter of modernity, emphasized that the professions are distinguished by possession and use of a system of scientific and theoretical knowledge that is tied to community values and principles. The three classical theorists thus agree both on the importance of morality and ethics, and on a high degree of competence as an ingredient of the professional mind set (see Luciano Gallino, "Sociologia delle Professioni," in Luciano Gallino, *Dizionario di Sociologia* (Turin: Utet, 1978) and Terence James Johnson, *Professions and Power* (London: Macmillan Press, 1972).
2. Jeremy Rifkin, *The Age of Access: The New Culture of Hypercapitalism, Where All of Life is a Paid-For Experience* (New York: Putnam Publishing Group, 2000); on net-elite concept, see Carlo Carboni, *La società cinica. Le classi dirigenti nell'epoca dell'antipolitica* (Rome and Bari: Laterza, 2008).
3. Christopher Lasch, *The Revolt of the Elites and the Betrayal of Democracy* (New York: W.W. Norton & Co, 1995).
4. CENSIS, *Rapporto sulla situazione del paese* (Milan: Franco Angeli, 2010).
5. Carlo Carboni "Net-elites e doppia identità del capitalismo relazionale," in Third Report, *Generare classe dirigente. Una mutazione del paese da accompagnare oltre la crisi* (Rome: Luiss University Press, 2009), 299–363.
6. Carlo Carboni, ed., *Élite e classi dirigenti in Italia* (Rome and Bari: Laterza, 2007), 122.
7. For example, with the regionalization of the national health system, many physicians served as regional health officers, as happened in Calabria: see Carlo Carboni, *L'implosione delle élite. Leader* contro *in Italia e in Europa* (Soveria: Rubbettino, 2015), 116.
8. Maria Malatesta, "Professioni e professionisti," in Maria Malatesta, ed., *Annali Storia d'Italia (no.10). I professionisti* (Turin: Einaudi, 1996), xvi-xvii.
9. Willem Tousijn stressed that within the Italian bureaucracy there is not a hierarchy based on professional competence ("Tra stato e mercato: le libere professioni in Italia in una prospettiva storico-evolutiva," in Willem Tousin, ed., *Le libere professioni in Italia* (Bologna: Il Mulino, 1987), 49–50.
10. Michele Ainis, *Privilegium. L'Italia divorata dalle lobby* (Milano: Rizzoli, 2012), 32.
11. See four Reports, *Generare classe dirigente* (Rome: Luiss University Press, 2007–10).
12. "Profile of Italian graduates," *IX–XV Reports 2008-2013 of the Alma Laurea*: http://www.almalaurea.it/>.
13. "Legalità ed evasione fiscale in Italia viste dai cittadini," *III Report of the Eures*, Rome 2012.
14. Gian Paolo Prandstraller, ed., *Le nuove professioni nel terziario* (Milan: Franco Angeli, 1994).

15. "Profile of Italian graduate," *XV Report of the Alma Laurea,* 2013: http://almalaurea.it/files/comunicati/2013/sintesi_rapporto_condizione-occupazionale-laureati_o.pdf>.

16. Francesco Orazi and Marco Socci, *Il popolo di Beppe Grillo* (Ancona: Cattedrale, 2008), 35–8.

17. "I giovani laureati in fuga dagli ordini," *Report of Il Sole 24 ore,* Milano: June 13, 2011, 1–3.

18. "Professionals," *Report of the Termometro politico*: http://forum.termometropolitico.it/discussione-politica/politica-nazionale/119967-ordini-professionali, 2011>.

19. Carboni, *La società cinica,* 31–56.

20. Massimo Bergami, (2009), "Una classe dirigente non di puro rispecchiamento," in *Third Report Generare classe dirigente*, 29–63. Also, see Carlo Carboni, "Elites and the democratic disease," in Andrea Mammone and Giuseppe Veltri, eds., *Italy Today: The Sick Man of Europe* (New York: Routledge, 2010), 23.

21. Even Silvio Berlusconi, for a few hours in July 2011, aired the idea of abolishing professional orders, but the proposal was quashed by a letter signed by 22 senators to the president of the Chamber, also a lawyer (see Ainis, *Privilegium,* 123).

22. While there is no clear evidence that greater competition lowers tariffs and rates or improves quality, there is evidence that it gives impetus to productivity, especially in services. The benefit of liberalization in this sector is estimated at between 1.5 and 3% of Italian GDP.

CHAPTER 42

···

THE COOPERATIVE
MOVEMENT

···

VERA ZAMAGNI

THE Italian cooperative movement has a number of distinctive features. First, it was never organized as a neutral, apolitical, non-religious movement, as in most countries. The deep-rooted propensity towards cooperation that has characterized substantial sections of the Italian population has led not only to a plurality of ideal inspirations of the movement, but also to the formation of separate umbrella organizations.[1]

The early cooperatives that emerged during the second half of the nineteenth century were spin-offs of Friendly Societies. These cooperatives were mainly of a liberal character and were strongly influenced by the ideals of Giuseppe Mazzini, one of the Italian intellectuals who fought for the Risorgimento.[2] A second group of cooperatives materialized with the advent of Italian socialism towards the end of the nineteenth century, while a third group emerged from the Catholics' social commitment, as promoted by Pope Leo XIII in his famous encyclical on the conditions of the working classes, *Rerum Novarum*, published in 1891. The three sources of inspiration of the Italian cooperative movement have often been represented by the colors of the Italian flag: green (the liberal cooperatives), red (the socialist-communist cooperatives), and white (the Catholic cooperatives). Fascism unified the movement in 1926, but it was a temporary achievement; after World War II the plural nature of the Italian cooperative movement reappeared.

This multiplicity of ideals and proposals the movement has been able to offer is at the basis of a second characteristic of the Italian cooperative movement, namely its wide diffusion across Italy. Cooperation is stronger in certain areas than in others (at the top there are two regions: Trentino, the home of white cooperatives, and Emilia-Romagna,[3] the headquarters of the red and green cooperatives), but it can be found across the whole of Italy.[4] The importance in Italy of the cooperative movement was recognized by the 1948 Constitution, which contains an article (45) devoted to cooperation, upon which there was a wide-ranging agreement on the part of all political forces:

The Republic recognizes the social function of cooperation with a mutual and non-profit character. The law promotes and supports its diffusion with suitable means and guarantees and with the appropriate controls that its aims are fulfilled.

At the end of World War II there was a rush to create cooperatives in various fields, expanding the number of those already in existence (probably over 12,000, with 3 million members inherited from the fascist period). This was the result of both a spontaneous effort by the population to produce employment opportunities and meet basic needs and also an intentional strategy on the part of those who had been engaged in the Resistance movement to associate themselves in business activities that expressed their solidarity. The two largest historical umbrella organizations were reconstituted: the Confederazione Cooperativa Italiana (later Confcooperative, which originated in 1919, of Catholic inspiration) was reconstituted on May 5, 1945. The Lega Nazionale delle cooperative e mutue (later Legacoop, which originated in 1886) was reconstituted on September 3, 1945. It included socialists, communists, and also a liberal component, part of which, however, departed in 1952 to form the Alleanza Generale delle Cooperative Italiane (AGCI), which is the third largest Italian umbrella organization[5]. These organizations recreated not only their national apparatuses, but also their local branches that presided over local strategies.

The period 1951–71 was years of "business as usual" for the Italian cooperative movement. It was only after the first oil crisis in the middle of the 1970s that a new phase started, with a strengthening of the cooperative movement and the creation of a new wave of coops. This paralleled the new stance that the trade unions adopted in the same decade (see Chapter 41, this volume). The available histories of all the major consumer coops and of many other large coops show upward spurts in size as a result of numerous mergers and of organizational restructuring.[6] Coops did not share the trend towards fragmentation which was prominent among firms in Italy at the time, but on the contrary, they tended to maintain their average size and the number of large cooperatives increased substantially.

This allowed coops to be better equipped to face the difficulties of the two decades of the 1990s and 2000s, in which, while the Italian economy was growing poorly or not at all, coops enlarged employment and improved their competitiveness, gaining market share. Using employment as our indicator, in 1951 cooperatives employed 2 percent of the private sector employment, a share that had gone down to 1.9 percent in 1971, but increased to 2.8 percent in 1981, 4 percent in 1991, 5.8 percent in 2001, and 7 percent in 2011. A picture of the coops belonging to the three largest umbrella organizations in 2011 is reported in Table 42.1. The additional employment of the remaining coops is estimated at 200,000 people, but data on these are scanty. Figures refer to the direct employment of coops and do not include employment in joint stock companies owned by coops or in companies not incorporated as cooperatives which work for coops (especially the large consumer coops), so that we can say that the economic impact of coops is substantially larger than that which emerges from Table 42.1.

Table 42.1 The Italian Cooperative Movement in 2011

	Number of cooperatives	Turnover (in billions of euro)	Members	Employees
Legacoop[§]	15,500	79	9,000,000*	493,000
Confcooperative	20,000	67	3,100,000	547,000
AGCI	7,832	8	440,000	92,000
Total	43,332	154	12,540,000	1,132,000
% increase over 2006	+5.5	+10.6	+8.4	+13

Notes: *the very large number of members of Legacoop is mostly because a large majority of the coops in retailing belong to this organization §: 2012

Sources: figures come from the three main cooperative umbrella organizations and include social cooperatives.

Italian cooperatives are present in all sectors of the economy, but in some they have a prominent position. In the distributive trade, the two cooperative organizations (Coop, which is made up of consumer cooperatives, and Conad, which is formed by retailers cooperatives) in 2011 reached a share of a third of the organized retailing business. At the same date in agro-industry a third of the Italian gross salable production was processed by cooperatives (but 60 percent in northern Italy), while some of the most important companies in the food industry are cooperative. Of the ten largest Italian general contractors in the building trade in 2011 three are cooperatives, but the consortium of 230 construction cooperatives (CCC, which includes the three largest), is the most important general contractor in Italy, with a turnover in 2010 of 3.5 billion euros. Cooperative banks have a quarter of the market, and include popular banks.[7] The second largest insurance company in Italy is a joint stock company (Unipol) quoted at the stock exchange, but controlled by cooperatives. Social coops delivering welfare services today number more than 12,000, employ 380,000 workers and deliver approximately half of the Italian social services.[8] Cooperatives also have an important presence in facility management, in catering, logistics, transportation, dock services, media, cultural, and professional activities.

The success of cooperativism in Italy is due partly to the support that Italian legislation has granted to the capitalization of coops and partly to the ability to build networks (groups and consortia) and bring about mergers, with substantial help coming from the umbrella organizations.[9] These networks may be of a horizontal (local), vertical (sectorial), or complementary nature, and they have often paved the way to mergers that have created larger cooperative corporations.[10] This has led to the strengthening of production processes, because networks have increased productivity and competitiveness, bringing about the expansion of the cooperative sector. In the next section I will explain the relations of the cooperative movement with Italian politics, which produced the legislation that is favorable to the growth of cooperatives, and I will then illustrate some networks.

COLLATERALISM AND COOPERATIVE
LEGISLATION

To understand why Italian legislation has strengthened the capitalization of cooperatives we have to resort to what in Italy has been labeled "collateralism," namely the mutual support that cooperative umbrella organizations and parties have offered to each other for a very long period of time. It has been much more than an "exchange" of votes for favorable legislation. These relations were rooted in a common global *Weltanschauung*, which encompassed economic interests, but also the general organization of society. Cooperatives shared with the Democrazia Cristiana (DC) inspiration from Catholic social doctrine; Legacoop had militant members of the Partito Comunista Italiano (PCI) and Partito Socialista Italiano (PSI) who shared a belief in the Marxist paradigm, while AGCI members had ideals of solidarity which were politically supported by the Partitio Repubblicano Italiano (PRI) and Partito Socialdemocratico Italiano (PSDI). It can be stated that all post-World War II parties before the Forza Italia of Silvio Berlusconi had their cooperative "branch." [11] We can follow in some details the evolution of the political relations of the two largest umbrella organizations to understand the different approaches, to review the legislation which was issued under the pressure of the cooperative movement, and explain the final overcoming of collateralism.

The connection of Confcooperative with the DC was natural, but by no means without conflict, because the DC has always hosted a plurality of factions. The cooperative Catholic organization was mostly originally formed by farmers' cooperatives, rural banks, and housing cooperatives. The great importance of farmers' cooperatives made it difficult from the very beginning to separate out Confcooperative's role with reference to another powerful Catholic organization of farmers, the Coldiretti, energetically led for many decades by Paolo Bonomi. Coldiretti rallied small farmers, some of whom were also members of farmers' cooperatives, which were not happy to be represented by Confcooperative. At the most, Coldiretti was prepared to allow Confcooperative to play the role of partner in negotiations with the trade unions, but was not willing to externalize the political and entrepreneurial roles of its coops. This division of labor was refused by Confcooperative, not without great internal conflicts.[12] An agreement was signed between the two organizations only in 1963, but it proved to be temporary.[13] In the 1970s, the leftist faction of the DC Forze Nuove led by Carlo Donat Cattin left Confcooperative, and in 1975 formed another umbrella organization (Unione Nazionale delle Cooperative Italiane, or UNCI), which has never had a solid life and was dismantled officially by the government in 2013 as it was functioning poorly.

In view of these facts, we can speak in relation to Confcooperative of an "imperfect collateralism": there was some convergence of purpose between Confcooperative and the DC, but the umbrella organization of the white coops was pushed to act more autonomously as a result of the lack of an "organic" and privileged connection with the DC. It had to have an autonomous presence in Rome, where on October 27, 1950 it inaugurated its headquarters. It joined the ICA (International Cooperative Alliance) in 1948 and opened up direct relations with America. When the EU started, Confcooperative opened up its offices in Brussels, to monitor legislation and undertake lobbying activities directly. Relationships with Legacoop had to be kept separate, but they joined forces when a new law was advocated. In the second half of the 1970s things appeared to improve. In 1977 the DC was persuaded to launch the "First [and only, up to 2015] national congress on cooperation," but when in the 1980s a number of Confcooperative member coops had difficulties, no direct help came from a DC which was already in decline. The 1990s, with the disappearance of the DC, witnessed the final disengagement of Confcooperative from political parties, although most of its members continued to vote for central parties. The most important implication of this fragmentation of the Catholic cooperatives has been that in general Confcooperative has kept its coops smaller, although in some cases (banks, social coops, farmers' cooperatives) federations and/or consortia have constituted tight and well-organized networks.

As for Legacoop,[14] its collateralism with the PCI/PSI was in contrast complete and organic. The leftist galaxy had at the beginning of the post-World War II period, after its defeat in the 1948 elections, the following shape: the communist party was the place where the targets of the opposition to the DC were conceived; the CGIL (the Italian General Confederation of Labor, the communist-socialist trade union) provided the militant force for the fights against capitalism and capitalists, while cooperation was seen as having a transitory role of economic support to the long-term revolutionary strategy. For this reason, in general the red cooperatives were administered by socialist managers, because communists were to preside over the ideological role.[15] It was only in 1962 that for the first time in an official document of the PCI it was recognized that it was unacceptable to confine cooperation to a subordinate role, but it took another 15 years before a complete revision of the position of cooperation inside the PCI could take place. In the XV Congress of the PCI in 1978, cooperation was no longer considered a transitory component of the left, but a stable part of society as a "third sector" of the economy (after the capitalist and the state-owned companies).[16]

Meantime, the international oil crisis had a negative impact on disposable income, so that consumer cooperatives and construction cooperatives had to be restructured to avoid major failures. It was in this context that the PCI finally enlarged and strengthened its cooperatives, something that proved highly successful, so that the great majority of the largest cooperatives today belong to Legacoop. This was instrumental to the uninterrupted flourishing of the red cooperatives after the demise of the PCI. However, the collateralism of Legacoop with the successor parties of the PCI (Partito Democratico di Sinistra [PDS] and Democratici di Sinistra [DS]) remained stronger than the relations between Confcooperative and the successor parties of the DC (Partito Popolare, UDC). It was only in the new millennium that collateralism also disappeared in Legacoop. Perhaps the last episode was the effort made by Unipol to acquire a major bank in 2005 (BNL, Banca Nazionale del Lavoro), which was carried on in a less than transparent way and was finally unsuccessful. The final seal on the demise of collateralism came with the decision reached in 2011 to build the Alleanza Cooperativa Italiana (ACI), in which

Confcooperative, Legacoop, and AGCI converged, with the intention of building up an integrated cooperative movement. This is an irreversible turnaround of a tradition that had lasted a century and a half, and it came in the same year in which the three leading trade unions reached an agreement to unify representation and collective bargaining (see Chapter 41).

In view of what has been explained above, it comes as no surprise that Italy had legislation favorable to the development of cooperatives. Straight after the introduction of Article 45 in the Constitution, the first law appeared (already approved in December 1947) to spell out the principles implied in the Constitution. Called the "Basevi" law from the name of Alberto Basevi, who drafted it, it not only made official the usual cooperative rules (one head one vote, open door, a minimum of nine members, a ban on members who had a private business in the same field, a ban on the distribution of indivisible reserves, even in the event of liquidation), but it introduced compulsory registration into a registry, which allowed cooperatives to be eligible for the subsidies that national or local governments introduced (very limited at the beginning), and granted the supervision of cooperatives to their umbrella organizations, reserving to the Ministry of Labor the supervision of cooperatives which did not join any umbrella organization. This supervision was meant to ascertain every two years how closely the cooperatives had adhered to the rules set by legislation.

Nothing relevant happened for the next two decades, up until the 1971 bill, called the "small reform" (Law 127, 2/17/1971), which recognized members' loans as a crucial element to increase capital available to cooperatives. This had to be agreed upon with the Bank of Italy, because cooperatives performed some of the roles of banks, and it implied a lighter taxation of deposits when made with cooperatives as compared with normal banks. The sector where members' loans became more important was consumers' cooperatives, given the very large number of members and the ease of depositing and withdrawing money on the part of members. As the history of consumer cooperatives (Coop) has shown, the substantial investments made in the 1980s and 1990s, which allowed Coop to become the Italian leader in retail distribution, were largely financed through members' loans that covered more than half of the necessary funds.

Even more important was the bill approved in 1977, following the already mentioned national congress, that allowed undistributed profits set aside in indivisible reserves not to pay the corporate tax, a measure that increased self-finance considerably, because it was easy for the presidents of cooperatives to win the support of members in not distributing profits, with the argument that by putting them to indivisible reserves there was a considerable tax advantage. In March 1983 a new bill was passed (Law 72, labeled Visentini after the minister Bruno Visentini who produced it), granting to cooperatives the permission to fully own or have a majority stake in a capitalist corporation. In this list of laws relevant to cooperatives, one cannot forget Law 381 of 1991 on social cooperatives: this was not meant to strengthen capitalization, but to recognize the different nature of social cooperatives, which had a multi-stakeholder board and serviced the local community rather than members alone (called "external mutuality," a principle recognized by the International Cooperative Alliance in 1995 as the seventh principle of cooperation). Another step towards making additional financial resources available for cooperatives was made by Law 59, approved in 1992, which allowed cooperatives to have members who only supplied capital (*socio sovventore*) and to issue special privileged shares (*azioni a partecipazione cooperativa*). Another important measure introduced by Law 59 was the obligation to devote 3 percent of cooperatives' profits to a fund managed by each of the umbrella organizations; this was intended to strengthen the cooperative movement through the creation of new cooperatives and the restructuring of some of the existing ones.

As mentioned above, Silvio Berlusconi's governments have been the only ones not favorable to cooperatives. As a result of Article 45 being in the constitution and the great support cooperatives have in Italian public opinion, the attack was directed only at lessening the fiscal support granted to them by the state. Berlusconi's finance minister Giulio Tremonti basically moved in two directions with the 2003 legislation: on the one hand it restricted state support only to cooperatives defined as "at prevalent mutualism," in which more than half of the business was done with members; on the other it cut to 30 percent the amount of undistributed profits that could be set aside to indivisible reserves without paying corporate tax. This measure allowed the government to raise revenues (the estimate was around 500 million euros per year), and the cooperative movement had to rely even more than before on the increased efficiency of its business.

NETWORKS

As Italian business activity in general refrained from adopting the big business approach (with a few exceptions), it had to develop networking among firms much more extensively than in other economies, to substitute strong economies of specialization for the missing economies of scale. There is a large literature on the "industrial districts," made up of small firms bunching in a specific geographical area for the production of different brands of the same basic product (jewels, saddles for bicycles, spectacles, ceramic tiles, packaging machinery, brakes, etc.). Italy is internationally competitive in about a thousand niche products produced by small and medium-size firms, which are tied together in networks by subcontracting and collaborative relations. This is known in Italy as "Fourth Capitalism," because it arose chronologically after capitalist corporations, state-owned companies, and industrial districts. Cooperatives tend to practice the ties typical of the fourth capitalism more intensively and formally than other firms. The networking of cooperatives has been studied extensively for Legacoop, but it extends also to the other umbrella organizations.

The period from the 1970s to 2014 can be divided up in four subperiods as far as the Italian economy is concerned: two of growth (1975–90 and 1996–2007) and two of difficulties (1991–5 and 2008 to 2014). In all periods, the profitability of the larger cooperatives continued to grow, which was the main reason why cooperatives have increased their propensity to enlarge once they have decided to effectively compete in the market. We could thus hypothesize that Italy's cooperatives were led out of marginality by two movements: the first between the end of the 1970s and the beginning of the 1980s focused on the general consolidation of individual cooperatives, with mergers and the creation of consortia on a limited geographical scale. Mergers were more easily carried through inside Legacoop because of the central position the PCI still had over the entire left. Many of the difficulties that followed, such as *Mani Pulite* (Clean Hands),[17] which paralyzed the building industry, were of an exogenous nature, and contributed towards reinforcing in the cooperatives the belief that size was important, because the larger cooperatives had an advantage in terms of profitability, organization, market, and lobbying power. The second wave of growth (1996–2007) saw the formation of "cooperative groups," reinforcing the already existing practice of creating complex networks of cooperative and non-cooperative companies.

A good example of this is represented by the consumers' cooperatives, dominated by Legacoop. As mentioned above, there are two Legacoop organizations currently operating within this sector. The first is the Associazione Nazionale Cooperative di Consumo (ANCC), which in 2004 included 160 COOP-brand consumers' cooperatives (of which the top nine account for 90 percent of total turnover) reaching a market share of 18 percent with a single wholesale structure—Coop Italia, created in 1967. Coop Italia has more recently offered its wholesale services to other groups of consumers' cooperatives and retailers' cooperatives which were not members of Legacoop (Sait, Sigma, and Despar), plus some small capitalist chains (e.g. Il Gigante), putting in place a "Centrale Italiana," which has achieved in 2010 a share of the wholesale market, reaching 23 percent. The second Legacoop organization within the retailing sector is the Associazione Nazionale Cooperative Dettaglianti (ANCD), which organizes consortia of cooperatives of retailers (including primarily Consorzio Nazionale Dettaglianti [CONAD] and other smaller brands) with a turnover that accounts for 12 percent of the total turnover of large-scale retailing, and some 3000 sales outlets. In February 2006, CONAD set up the very first cooperative based on European law—Coopernic—jointly with the Belgian chain Coruyt (the third largest in Belgium), the Swiss Coop (the second largest in Switzerland), the French chain E. Leclerc (the leading hypermarket chain in France), and the German Rewe Group (Germany's second largest chain). Coopernic boasted in 2009 a turnover of 96 billion euros and 17,500 sales outlets. Taken as a whole, Legacoop organizes directly more than one-third of Italy's large-scale retailing activity, and this share is growing, albeit slightly, through the crisis years.

A similar trend can be detected in the construction sector, where a national consortium has been set up. The biggest step forward was taken in 1978 with the merger of the powerful consortia of Bologna (1912), Modena (1914), and Ferrara (1945), under the name of CCC (Consorzio Cooperative Costruzioni). Following this step, a project was drawn up to unite all the consortia in the other Italian regions with the CCC (by far the largest), in order to create a national consortium (by the same name) capable of coordinating the Legacoop's strategy within the construction industry. This objective was achieved in 1990. The final step consisted of the incorporation of the Acam (Consorzio Nazionale cooperative approvvigionamenti—National Consortium of Building

Cooperatives Suppliers), that is, the consortium of cooperatives servicing the construction industry.

The services sector has also witnessed the creation of a national consortium, Consorzio Nazionale Servizi (CNS).[18] Set up in 1977, but only really operative from the second half of the 1980s, it brings together more than 200 cooperatives operating in the following sectors: facility management, transport, porterage, custodial and cleaning services, ecology, catering, and tourism-cultural services. The initial governance of this consortium has not been easy, often paralyzed by inner conflicts between the larger and the smaller cooperatives. A stable equilibrium was finally reached in 1998, and this spurred a sustained growth of its turnover, moving at constant 2004 prices from 161 million euros in 1999 to 384 million in 2004. This growth has been partly the result of the comparative advantage a consortium has in producing integrated services (facility management), implying the use of different specializations and the coordination of different cooperatives.

Coordination has proven more complicated in the food and farming sector where, while there has been growth in average company size as a result of mergers, the creation of cooperative groups for specific areas of production has appeared the best solution. The largest group affiliated to Legacoop can be found in the dairy sector (Granlatte-Granarolo),[19] but there are large cooperative groups present in Parmesan production (Granterre), wine (GIV, CAVIRO), fruit and vegetables (Apofruit Italia), large-scale crops, their by-products and services (Progeo), and meat (Unipeg). The other cooperative umbrella organization, Confcooperative, is also very active in this sector, in the form of a number of large cooperative groups such as Conserve Italia.

Another area where a form of overall system governance has been developed is that of the cooperative credit banks, which belong to Confcooperative.[20] This area witnessed an acceleration in concentration and growth during the 1990s, and today the credit unions have consolidated their position. The degree of autonomy of the 400 cooperative banks still in existence is high, but the National Federation has organized a tight network of centralized services. As has already been mentioned, the Confcooperative's degree of concentration is not as great as Legacoop's, resulting in just a few large-scale cooperatives concentrated mainly in the food and farming sector. The Confcooperative has, however, an extremely strong national consortium (Consorzio Gino Mattarelli [CGM]), grouping together 79 local consortia of social cooperatives providing personal services. Legacoop too has a large number of social cooperatives with a strong national association (Legacooperativesociali).

CONCLUSIONS

The relations between cooperatives and the Italian political structure were tight up to the 1990s, although not uniformly so, because the Italian cooperative movement has not

Table 42.2 The Costs and Benefits of Collateralism

Costs	Benefits
Fragmentation and duplication of bureaucratic structures	Political parties' support for cooperatives
Instrumental use of cooperatives by political parties	Intrinsic motivations by members to remain collaborative in their behavior
Involvement in internal faction fighting among single parties	Strong network economies

been a single one and competing parties were different. A cost-benefit analysis listing the costs and benefits of "collateralism" is to be found in Table 42.2.

My opinion is that on the whole benefits exceeded costs, but this was due to a number of external factors. The first is that cooperation is the best way for Italians to overcome their strong individualistic attitude to company management. Firms remain small in Italy primarily because Italians prefer to work for themselves and by themselves. Cooperatives in which members matter and profits are distributed to members or reinvested in the company are seen as second best, whenever a small firm is not suitable. The second factor is that cooperators were encouraged to run firms that could successfully compete in the market, this being done through powerful umbrella organizations that developed services and strategies. Parties helped in restructuring, merging, building networks that were considered necessary for the survival of cooperatives, and to pass laws that helped to strengthen cooperatives' capitalization, but they relied on their umbrella organizations for guidelines. Of course cooperatives financed their supporting party in the elections, but because their profitability was not high, strong financial support never came to Italian political parties from this source. In this, cooperatives were very different from state-owned corporations.

A third factor to explain why collateralism was not anathema to cooperatives is the competition among the various umbrella organizations. In particular, the PCI, which did not have much of a chance to form a national government (but instead was present at the local level), could not allow its cooperatives to fail, and therefore strengthened them from a managerial and business point of view. The most important implication of this was that the red cooperatives did not remain limited to the "working class" and low-quality products, but moved rapidly to cater for the middle classes, thereby preventing a fall in their market share similar to that experienced, for instance, in Great Britain.

All these factors explain the resilience of Italian cooperatives to the 2008 crisis. They have strong managerial capabilities and enjoy a good market position so that they can react positively. There are still, however, three major challenges that cooperatives have to face: they have to a) provide the cooperative system with a cultural background that is capable of bringing past theorization on cooperatives up to date; b) develop ways of administering in a "cooperative" way large cooperatives; and c) open up cooperatives to international cooperation. The building up of ACI, leading to the unification of the Italian cooperatives, gives the coops critical mass so they can strengthen further, but the courage to be innovative does not automatically stem from sheer size. It stems from the commitment of members and managers to the ideals of justice and solidarity which justify the sheer existence of cooperatives, a commitment that cannot be taken for granted.

Notes

1. For a general overview of the development of the Italian cooperative movement in the world context, see Stefano Zamagni and Vera Zamagni, *Cooperative Enterprise: Facing the Challenge of Globalization* (Cheltenham: Edward Elgar, 2010).
2. In Italy the party that adopted this approach was the PRI.
3. See Tito Menzani, *La cooperazione in Emilia-Romagna* (Bologna: Il Mulino, 2006).
4. It must be mentioned, however, that southern Italy is the home of smaller and less solid cooperatives.
5. In 1975 a fourth umbrella organization was formed—UNCI (National Union of Italian Cooperatives)—out of a splinter from Confcooperative; in 2004 a fifth one, Unione Italiana delle Cooperative (UNICOOP), on the activities of which there is very little information, and in 2013 a sixth one, Unione Europea delle Cooperative (UECOOP), formed by Coldiretti; once again this wanted to become autonomous from Confcooperative (see text). These umbrella organizations include few and small coops, and will not be dealt with here. It must also be mentioned that it is possible for an Italian cooperative not to belong to any umbrella organization or to belong to more than one umbrella organization (something that was practiced in the past to pave the way to mergers or to compact networks), but numbers are small.
6. See Vera Zamagni, Patrizia Battilani, and Antonio Casali, *La cooperazione di consumo in Italia* (Bologna: Il Mulino, 2004).
7. Although at the international level Italian popular banks are still included in the cooperative sector, in Italy they are not considered to be part of it any longer, as a result of being exempted since 1948 from the application of cooperative principles, other than one head one vote and a limit to capital ownership by members to 0.5 percent of total capital. In fact, they are placed in a dubious legislative position, because they are neither "true" coops nor "true" capitalist enterprises. The Bank of Italy has been pressing for a legislative reform of popular banks in this awkward state, but only in 2015 did the government decide to demutualize the ten largest popular banks, while leaving the others as they were. Some of them have merged with capitalist banks, but the economic importance of those which still retain their original incorporation is substantial: they have more than one-sixth of all banking activity.
8. This is the number of the social cooperatives in ACI.
9. There are various forms of consortia, but they are all characterized by the fact that the cooperatives belonging to them are administratively and financially independent. In general, they share the services offered to the consortium's members and they enjoy common strategies in advertising and work procurement.

10. A detailed study of Italian cooperative networks can be found in Tito Menzani and V. Zamagni, "Cooperative Networks in the Italian Economy," *Enterprise and Society*, 11, no. 1 (January 2010), 98–127.

11. Only the small PLI did not express support to coops, but its political influence was negligible.

12. See Pietro Cafaro, *Il lavoro e l'ingegno. Confcooperative: premesse, costituzione, rinascita* (Bologna: Il Mulino, 2012).

13. See endnote 5.

14. A full account of this issue can be found in Vera Zamagni and Emanuele Felice, *Oltre il secolo* (Bologna: Il Mulino, 2006).

15. See Renato Zangheri, Giuseppe Galasso, and Valerio Castronovo, *Storia del movimento cooperativo in Italia. La Lega Nazionale delle Cooperative e Mutue, 1886–1986* (Turin: Einaudi, 1987).

16. The expression "Third Sector" today generally defines all the non-capitalist business organizations, but at the time it was not employed in such a way. In a stricter definition, the Third Sector today includes only non-profit organizations, leaving coops in a category of their own.

17. It was a process of denunciation of widespread corruption in public tenders.

18. See Patrizia Battilani and Giuliana Bertagnoni (eds.), *Cooperation Network Service. Innovation in Outsourcing* (Lancaster: Crucible Books, 2010).

19. This group unites both "red" (left-wing) and "white" (Catholic) cooperatives.

20. See Pietro Cafaro, *La solidarietà efficiente. Storia e prospettive del credito cooperativo in Italia (1883–2000)* (Bari: Laterza, 2001).

PART VIII

POLITICS, CULTURE, AND SOCIETY

....

CHAPTER 43

CINEMA AND TELEVISION

....

STEPHEN GUNDLE

BEFORE the 1980s it was not customary to pay much attention to the impact of the mass media on Italian politics for the simple reason that the party system that came into being in the postwar years seemed relatively impervious to innovation. So entrenched were loyalties and so important were party machines and subcultures in mobilizing the electorate that neither cinema nor television was held to have the power to shape outcomes.[1] In the course of the 1980s, all this changed, as the political system and the parties adapted, sometimes with evident difficulty, to a fast-changing society. The expansion of local and private television, the decline of filmgoing as a leisure activity, the fall in conventional political participation, the declining relevance of once powerful ideologies, the emergence of the leader as personality, and an increasing interpenetration of entertainment and politics all forced analysts to rethink some of the categories that had up until then been used to explain Italian politics and political culture.[2] By the time Silvio Berlusconi "entered the field" in 1994, there was a widespread understanding that television had been central in reshaping political communication, mainly by eroding established patterns of social and cultural hierarchy to foreground consumption and entertainment. Berlusconi's success was by no means solely due to his personal control of three television channels, but the medium contributed to his 1994 electoral triumph in a number of ways.[3]

Looking back at the developments of the 1980s and 1990s, it is possible to see the growing importance of television in political communication not so much as heralding the inevitable, belated modernization of a static system, but rather as the product of a specific phase in Italian political history. That phase was marked by the crisis of the party system as a whole, the growing dominance of mass culture, wider secularization, increasing prosperity and individualization, challenges to male hegemony in some areas of society, and increasing receptiveness on the part of both elites and the people to imported (especially American) ideas, techniques, and goods. It was also a period in which the power of corporate interests in the media sector asserted itself first with no and then little regulation, and the long-established proportional electoral system was exchanged for a majoritarian one.

To explore the impact on Italian politics of the two most influential media of the twentieth century, four themes will be considered. First, changes over time in the dynamics of campaigning will be explored. Second, the mediatization of political personnel will be discussed. Third, attention will be given to the treatment of politics in cinema. Finally, some reflections will be advanced on the question of whether the media can be held responsible for narrowing the gap between politics and entertainment.

CINEMA, TELEVISION, AND ELECTIONEERING

In the postwar years, party organization was the key instrument of political communication. It interfaced with the public in a variety of ways: via the press and propaganda, and the work of activists, which included such institutions as graffiti, the spoken newspaper (*giornale parlato*), the wall newspaper (*giornale murale*), the debate with adversaries (*contradittorio*), the residents' meeting and the speaker rally.[4] The Socialist and Communist parties were the first to establish large membership organizations and assert a capillary presence in society. The Italian Communist Party (PCI) organized collateral associations, festivals, sports, and youth activities. The Christian Democrats (DC) were slower to establish an organizational presence, and at first relied heavily on the Church and the support of Catholic lay associations. However, longstanding Catholic interest in the mass media, which included the experience of Vatican radio and documentary cinema, equipped the party to assert control over the radio and the newsreels of *La Settimana Incom*.[5] The state media had been quite even-handed in the immediate postwar years,[6] but in the run up to the parliamentary elections of 1948 and afterwards, impartiality evaporated. Backed by the United States and the Church, the DC used its position of vantage to develop a media strategy that incorporated crude negative propaganda as well as concrete proposals and images of a probable future of prosperity.

As far as cinema is concerned, the party's approach can be summarized in four points. First, it used the tools of state power to censor, suppress, or obstruct the foreign distribution of films deemed to be leftist, including several belonging to the acclaimed Neorealist current. Second, it supported or commissioned a variety of documentaries of a political or religious nature. Third, it provided state support for the building of parish cinemas, which became a key site for the consumption of cinema amounting by the mid-1950s to around one-third of movie theaters in the country.[7] Fourth, it counted on the "indirect efficacy" of Hollywood films in favoring a pro-Western outlook.[8]

The PCI proved to be less able at developing cinematic propaganda. Although the left was very active in the field of cinema, party leader Palmiro Togliatti ruled out any involvement in the production of fiction films.[9] Even though the party was structured in such a way that activism and face-to-face interaction, often mediated by the press, were privileged, it did, however, create a section for the production of propaganda films.[10] The main problems were, first, that the resulting material was often censored or banned, and, second, that the quantity of films was far inferior to the newsreels and official documentaries which were shown every week in cinemas. Where the party proved most influential was in the sphere of art cinema. Although the PCI's relationship with Neorealism was neither as straightforward nor as supportive as might be thought, broad backing was given to films which explored the plight of ordinary people and which rejected the conventions of commercial filmmaking.[11] By the 1950s, cinema was the field of culture in which the party counted its widest influence and deployed the greatest energies, even though its stake in distribution and exhibition was very limited.[12]

Cinema remained a central force in Italian leisure until the 1970s, even though the advent of television in 1954 introduced changes to the media system. By all accounts, television did not immediately alter the way parties campaigned. So strong were political and religious subcultures that they were able to mediate the impact of the medium and condition responses to it. Election broadcasts, which began in 1960, took the form of a press conference in which politicians responded to the questions of a panel of print journalists. This gave them an insider feel in terms of language and address. Despite the institutional view that the role of the mass media was to act as a force for national integration and legitimation, politicians tended to communicate in a way that was geared to reinforcing established support rather than appealing to the undecided.[13] They knew that partisan audiences gathered in public places to jeer or to cheer their favorites. Communist leader Togliatti had used calm tones on the radio in the postwar years, while sometimes striking a more aggressive note in rallies. On television, despite considerable provocation from hostile journalists, he managed to maintain his authority and erudite reputation.[14] The left-wing press amplified his words and used them to counter any doubts at the grass-roots.

For many years the Communists regularly attacked biased news broadcasts on radio and television.[15] However, they never advanced specific proposals for wider access or democratic control. Significant changes came first with the advent of the center left in 1963, which entailed the creation of a second public television channel, and the Constitutional Court's rulings of the early 1970s, which brought about a shift in control over television from the government to parliament, via a committee on which all parties were represented, and the creation of a third channel.[16] These reforms brought some variety and pluralism to current affairs, although the bulk of resources were commandeered by the DC-dominated RAI-1 channel. The changes also heralded a certain "autonomization" of election campaigns. For the first time, Francesca Anania notes, "the media system and the political system began to interact, each seeking to affirm its respective logic and its respective goals."[17]

None of the parties paid much attention to television as a medium of entertainment or consumption, also because advertising had been bounded by strict rules and contained within a daily dedicated container program known as *Carosello*. Thus the extraordinary, sudden development of commercial broadcasting and the formation of three dominant networks, all of which were owned by the mid-1980s by Berlusconi's Fininvest company, heralded dramatic changes. These occurred in a context in which the structures of the parties and the subcultures were significantly weaker than before and less able to absorb novelty.[18] This situation was exacerbated by the economic growth of the 1980s, which brought increases in consumption, an expansion of the tertiary sector, and greater individualism.

By 1983, television was no longer a medium which parties could hope to exploit on their own terms. First the private networks and then RAI developed a series of spaces and programs which greatly increased coverage, while channeling it toward specific audiences or types of encounter which were centered more on issues and which brought the personal qualities of politicians into focus. Parties and candidates moreover invested in electoral advertising spots.[19] The PSI, especially, skillfully used new techniques to gain media attention, constructing an image of modernity, dynamism, efficiency, and vitality, breaking a pattern of debate focused largely on the DC and PCI. But the DC swiftly adapted, presenting spots in the 1983 and 1987 campaigns which recalled the reassuring soft-focus advertisements of the Barilla company.

The collapse of the old party system following the end of the Cold War and the exposure of widespread corruption opened a phase in which television enjoyed unprecedented dominance in national life. It performed agenda-setting functions, provided the main forums in which political debate took shape, set the dominant values, and furnished the personalities who dominated public discourse. Grass-roots organization remained important, but with few exceptions the old institutions of campaigning such as the open-air rally lost much of their capacity to sway opinion. The multiplication of channels, broadcast hours, and opportunities for appearances also created a campaigning context in which the impact of a single show such as *Tribuna politica* was reduced. Indeed, the whole press conference format began to look very rigid and tedious.

It would be wrong to attribute the success of Berlusconi in the March 1994 elections to his position as the owner of television channels. No less important were the threat of a left victory and the weaknesses of the center right in the context of a changed electoral system, his unique ability to connect with the self-employed, and his connections to football and consumption. But he ably deployed television and used his mastery of its language in the course of his campaign. The importance of television to Berlusconi can be gauged by the way he systematically resisted all attempts in the course of a political career lasting 20 years to divest him of control or ownership of his media empire. Indeed, as prime minister he successfully expanded his influence into many corners of RAI, securing for example the banishment of performers and presenters of whom he disapproved.

As long as commercial television possessed a unique capacity to shape society's values and behavior, Berlusconi could harness its dreams. Not even repeated failure to fulfill his election promises damaged fundamentally his capacity to mobilize the center-right vote. But the diversification of broadcasting following the advent of satellite television and the arrival in Italy of Sky, and the creation of the La 7 channel, heralded a reduction in his capacity to control the media environment. The transformation of social communication through new media undermined the centrality of television and created opportunities for political mobilization though the very different channels of the Internet and social media. The success of the Five Star Movement of Beppe Grillo in 2013 offered testimony that it was possible even to ignore the medium in building support. The age of television was not over, but there was no doubt that the age in which national terrestrial broadcasting determined the rhythms, forms, and places of debate, set the agenda, and shaped the public image and popularity of politicians belonged to the past.

The Politician from Sacred Figure to Celebrity

In the postwar years, all leading politicians went out of their way to assume quite modest, conventional profiles. While a handful of minor politicians (notably Giannini of L'Uomo Qualunque and the Monarchist shipping magnate Achille Lauro, who became mayor of Naples) were colorful and histrionic, the leaders of the DC and the PCI, De Gasperi and Togliatti, eschewed personalization. In this respect, they established a basic pattern that would become the norm under the republic. Politicians were men of dignity and vision who revealed little or nothing of their family lives and private tastes. Politicians may occasionally have mixed with celebrities or been photographed with them, but had little in common with them save for being recognizable through the press and newsreels.[20]

The large gap between the worlds of politics and celebrity in the 1950s and 1960s was theorized by the sociologist Francesco Alberoni, who argued that stars fulfilled specific functions in society by virtue of their being a "powerless elite" (a revision of C. Wright Mills's concept of the "power elite").[21] Film stars were more likely to be female, young, and beautiful, as well as less well educated, than politicians. The leading figures of the Christian Democrats (De Gasperi, Fanfani, Pella, Leone, Andreotti, and so on) were by no stretch of the imagination good-looking men and, with the partial exception of Fanfani, they did little or nothing to assert themselves in a dynamic way. The authority that some leading figures commanded and the aura that surrounded them stemmed not from the media but from the social conditions of the postwar years, which, for Angelo Ventrone, "favoured forms of *sacralization* of politics and devotion toward leaders, due to the widespread need to rebuild models of collective identification that allowed for an overcoming of the lacerations caused by the war."[22] It was reinforced by the way the political realm itself was configured as a source of symbols and meanings. Cinema played a part in this. The Vatican-produced film profile of Pius XII, *Pastor angelicus*, in 1942 had enhanced the image of the pope. Togliatti, in the wake of the assassination attempt of July 1948, would become the subject of a subcultural cult, which was captured and cultivated by the film marking his return to political life in September 1948 (*Togliatti è ritornato*). The film was a rare case of a Communist production which was widely shown within left-wing and party circles and used to stimulate fund-raising.

Nevertheless, television heralded some innovation. In the view of Walter Veltroni, "television began to select political personnel according to new parameters; no longer was it solely rectitude, competence and a good biography that counted but the ability to communicate not only in public squares but in the domestic context using the same instrument employed by Henry Salvador and Abbe Lane."[23] Thus a man such as the fiery Communist Giancarlo Pajetta managed, by his inventiveness and sharp tongue, to overcome to some degree the restrictions of the *Tribuna politica* format. He repeated watchwords and used stunts like pointing to an empty chair to highlight the absence of a prominent Christian Democrat accused of corruption.

Television became in this way a sphere in which it was assumed that a shared public opinion could be constructed. It was a space of justice in a way, in which all who held responsibility were expected to be present and to justify themselves. Over time, as the medium came to be a feature of the domestic environment, the political climate became less tense, and social values were reconfigured through the consumer society, politicians were drawn little by little into a new dimension. While it remained the norm for their personal and family lives to be largely concealed, the personality and manner of being of politicians changed. Men such as Aldo Moro and Enrico Berlinguer were not televisual politicians, but they presented human qualities, occasionally smiled, and spoke more directly to spectators in terms they could readily understand. For Veltroni, the tele-visual "magic" of Berlinguer consisted mainly of his face, which he used to hold in his hand, his timid air, and slight Sardinian accent.[24] He also cleverly used the medium to make key announcements, such as his 1981 declaration that the "propulsive stimulus of the October revolution" had run its course. He was aware that these would reverberate widely in the press and public opinion.

The leading politician who was the first to develop a form of showbusiness profile was Andreotti. The author of novels and other books, as well as press columns, and a dispenser of witticisms, he was a cautious machine politician who was not averse to appearing as a guest on non-political shows. Not by chance, he was also the favorite target for the gentle impersonations of Alighiero Noschese, who first started to send up politicians on television in 1969. Three times he was awarded a "Telegatto" statuette by TV listings magazine *Sorrisi e canzoni tv*. His award was for "best politician."

Although he was a product of the old school, the first Socialist President of the Republic, the octogenarian Sandro Pertini, elected in 1978, broke the mold of institutional reserve to become highly visible and vocal. Lacking formal power, but possessed of great energy, he used the popularity he acquired to speak on behalf of the people and castigate the political elite. He was often out of step with his party, but the Socialist leadership of the 1980s also innovated in the field of communication. It was the first to seek to embrace the language and values of entertainment television. Inevitably, this was more a cosmetic shift than a substantial one since the process of political selection within parties had changed little and the negotiational nature of the party system meant that political issues dominated rather than policy issues.

Thanks in part to the alliance of interest he forged with Berlusconi, Craxi exploited the opportunities that were offered by commercial television and the illustrated press for personality politics. He adopted a more casual attitude and dress, brought his wife into the public realm, publicized his travels and holidays, and mixed with heterogeneous elites. With his decisive manner, he struck a different tone to other leaders.

Berlusconi's dramatic formation of Forza Italia in the wake of the collapse of the old party system in 1992–3 heralded the first ever entry into the political realm and then government of a figure from outside the institutional elite. Already famous, and endowed with the image of a dynamic business leader, he mostly discarded conventional political language for a type of personal narration. By telling his own story, he drew people in and offered them a shared experience and a vision. These two aspects were separate in some respects, but they were fused in the glamorous lifestyle which Berlusconi projected. An immensely wealthy man, he publicized his homes and beautiful family as proof of his promise to bring wider prosperity to everyone. Unlike any politician since Mussolini, he projected a physical image of energy and vitality.[25] Unlike Mussolini, though, he adopted not a stern profile but a seductive one encapsulated in his broad smile.[26] He created a type of personalization that was influenced by consumerism and celebrity. In this respect, if not others, he offered a template to a man such as Matteo Renzi to develop a youthful, innovative profile more in tune with contemporary culture than conventional politics. This entailed regular informal appearances on television, the use of private life to build popularity, the projection of a measure of charm, the simplification of language, and the triumph of ballyhoo over substance in political gatherings.

THE REPRESENTATION OF POLITICS IN CINEMA AND TELEVISION

Despite Italian cinema's long record of engagement with social issues dating back to postwar Neorealism, politics did not featured strongly in films. This situation had something to do with censorship but also much to do with the way political forces were organized in society and the type of engagement they encouraged. In the heyday of Italian art cinema, directors made films which were seen as commenting on the state of society without imparting unambiguous political messages. Fellini, who has been described, perhaps surprisingly, as "the most political of Italian directors," offered his own take on culture and politics in films including *La dolce vita* (1960) and *Prova d'orchestra* (1978), but never represented the world of contemporary politics.[27] Visconti, long regarded as the pre-eminent Communist director, was taken to have a political agenda, but so unclear was this on occasions that, after the release of his emigration drama *Rocco e i suoi fratelli* (1960), he was obliged to write an article to clarify that his message was progressive rather than retrograde.[28] In so far as leading filmmakers tackled political questions, they preferred to do so by treating historical themes and episodes, as Visconti did in his Risorgimento dramas *Senso* (1954) and *Il gattopardo* (1963), Fellini in the Fascist-set *Amarcord* (1973), or Bertolucci in *Il conformista* (1970) and *Novecento* (1976).

Rather it was the various branches of the comedy genre which proved most alert to politics as subject matter. In the 1950s, a number of films featured political allusions or scenarios. The popular Neapolitan comic actor Totò often included gags or quips of a political nature and developed a sketch (included in the film *Totò a colori*, 1952) in which he played the part of a complaining citizen who offends a deputy's dignity by first buttonholing him in the compartment in a sleeping car they are obliged to share, and then constantly touching him. Totò's characters were old-fashioned and backward-looking; his attitude toward power was of the client-patron type. Alberto Sordi, the Roman actor who supplanted him as the most popular comic performer, developed a gallery of social types in the course of the 1950s and 1960s who sometimes brushed up against figures of power, for example in *Il vigile* (Luigi Zampa, 1960), in which his zealous traffic cop clashes with the mayor of Rome (played by Vittorio De Sica). Occasionally, he also played political men, most notably in *Il moralista* (Giorgio Bianchi, 1959), in which he is an earnest young Catholic activist—loosely based on several figures including Oscar Luigi Scalfaro and Agostino Greggi—whose moralistic campaigning conceals involvement in a prostitution racket.

Once the political climate changed in the early 1960s, comedy could engage more broadly with politics and even inject some elements of realism. The film *Gli onorevoli* (Sergio Corbucci, 1963) includes mention of some real politicians (the Christian Democrats Mario Scelba and Aldo Moro) and all the main parties, some of whose rallies are shown using actual documentary footage. Set during an election campaign, it also includes some fictional parties, notably the monarchist Partito Nazionale per la Restaurazione, whose unworldly candidate Antonio la Trippa is played by Totò. A variety of political candidates are mocked (Gino Cervi's wealthy publisher turned Liberal senator is sabotaged by a gang of boys including his own son; Franca Valeri's proto-feminist Christian Democrat gets muddled up with some street prostitutes and falls in love with a man paid to get her photographed in a compromising position). The only party to be thoroughly ridiculed is the neo-fascist Movimento sociale italiano, whose candidate, Prof. Mollica (Peppino De Filippo), is lampooned not on the basis of some personal situation but rather in relation to his virility.

The film offers an interesting snapshot of campaigning practices in the early 1960s. Conventional rallies, posters, leaflets, loudspeaker vans, and so on still dominate. But it is evident that the medium of television has introduced change. Cervi's character is keen to harness football to his cause, and he shows a film featuring the game to supporters. De Filippo's character allows himself to be persuaded by a television producer that he should wear make-up to appear on *Tribuna politica*. Transformed by lipstick, false eyelashes, nose pads, and a curly blonde wig, he looks like a grotesque showgirl. Indeed, a gathering of supporters is shown aghast as he appears on the screen decked out in a sequined costume amongst a line of dancing girls. The issue of whether television, with its intimate, domestic focus, actually heralded a form of feminization of politics would not be explored further until comedienne Sabina Guzzanti impersonated Massimo D'Alema and, more famously, Berlusconi in the early 2000s.[29]

For the most part, comedy was limited or mild, especially on television. Politicians were extraordinarily sensitive to any ridicule or satire and those, such as Guzzanti and her brother Corrado, or Beppe Grillo in the early 1990s, who practiced it risked sharp criticism and sometimes exile from the screen. While television programs featuring political satire were always highly controversial, and programs exposing political malfeasance rare, cinema, taking advantage of its greater freedom, gave rise to the heterogeneous genre of the political film. One of the keys to the continuing success of Italian cinema in the age of television lay in its ability to tackle issues and questions that did not get aired on the small screen. Political films were mostly dramas and often dealt with episodes that had resonated with public opinion. Terrorism was a key theme, with the kidnap and murder of Moro in 1978 being the subject of films by Giuseppe Ferrara (*Il caso Moro*, 1986) and Marco Bellocchio (*Buongiorno notte*, 2003).[30] Docudramas such as *Diaz* (Daniele Vicari, 2012) (an exposé of the events behind the police assault on activists at the Genoa G8 in 2001) were genuine efforts to bring issues fully to light, while documentaries such as Sabina Guzzanti's *Viva Zapatero* (2005) and *Draquila* (2011) combined comedy with a form of campaigning investigation.

In general, politicians have not been represented in a positive light in fiction or entertainment. If representations can in some way be taken to be indicative of public esteem, then it would have to be concluded that this is low. While some individuals may have enjoyed high reputations, many have not. This was perhaps most evidently the case in the period between the late 1980s and early 1990s when the old postwar party system was losing credibility and then fell, amid the *Tangentopoli* scandals. A filmmaker with a special appeal for left-inclined younger spectators, Nanni Moretti offered a sympathetic portrayal of the existential crisis of a Communist official in *Palombella rossa* (Nanni Moretti, 1989), before playing a repellent minister in *Il portaborse* (Daniele Luchetti, 1991) and directing *Il caimano* (2006), a critique of the Berlusconi phenomenon. Andreotti was the target of no less devastating a critique in Paolo Sorrentino's full-length satirical biopic *Il divo* (2008). The film provided an inventive fantasy portrayal of the one-time eternal minister who had survived for decades in the snake-pit of DC politics. Andreotti, who had never seemed bothered by impersonations and timid barbs, had even appeared briefly as himself in Sordi's comedy film *Il tassinaro* (Alberto Sordi, 1983). However, the now elderly seven-times prime minister was far less pleased with Sorrentino's film, dubbing it a *mascalzonata* (low blow).[31]

The persistence of certain entrenched political practices despite the changes to the party system, the electoral system, and public indignation at corruption, makes for a certain continuity in the representation of politics. While drama may be linked to specific episodes, comedy can exaggerate tics, types, and traits. Antonio Albanese's corrupt right-wing Calabrian politician Cetto La Qualunque (who debuted on television before starring in the film *Qualunquemente*, 2012) was a minor local Berlusconi in his cynical use of feminine beauty, a grotesque example of the type of arrogant and self-serving bluffer who increasingly figured in the mind of a disillusioned public as the archetypal politician.

Politics and Entertainment

The increasing role of the mass media in social communication in the 1980s and 1990s led to concerns that entertainment was becoming a debasing *lingua franca*. In *Amusing Ourselves to Death*, critic Neil Postman analyzed the phenomenon and argued that political communication had become trivialized since the word, which had been central in the nineteenth century, had given way to the image.[32] As a result, public business had become "a vaudeville act."[33] In one respect, Postman was right. The rise of mass culture created expectations of entertainment, altered attention spans, presented certain human types as trustworthy and worthy of admiration. But two observations undermine his argument. First, early mass politics was less cerebral and wordy than Postman implies. As the first analysts of mass politics, Moisei Ostrogorski and Roberto Michels, showed, popular public speakers were more likely to be hypnotic "spellbinders" who could electrify a crowd than rational communicators.[34] Rallies were accompanied by hullabaloo, music, and commerce. Second, there is only limited evidence that entertainment has shaped the practices of selection or operation of the political elite. The successful politician, in certain contexts, may have a pleasing outer appearance. He may be charming and endowed with an attractive smile. But, beneath this patina, he is still likely to be male, middle-aged, and well educated.

In a context such as the Italian political system, the predominant style of politics was removed from entertainment; it had its own language, codes, lifestyle, and ethos. But this made it compelling in its own way. It mattered because big issues were at stake and this fact gave meaning to its rituals and events. This also carried over into television. With at first just one and then two state channels, the broadcast *Tribuna politica* had the capacity to capture the attention and become an unrivalled event. It offered a rare chance to see prominent politicians and watch them do battle with their interrogators. This specificity of the political, its seriousness and importance, was what gave it its own purchase on popular culture, which included its appeals for film comedy and drama.

However, politics and entertainment nonetheless came into contact. The return of democratic mass politics after 1945 coincided with a steady expansion of cultural industries and increases in cultural consumption. From the earliest postwar period, actors and filmmakers were courted by parties which sought their endorsement and involvement. In particular, the watershed election of 1948 saw a concerted campaign to mobilize actors (even Hollywood stars were troubled) to support the DC or the alliance of the Democratic Popular Front. Later, the left-wing subculture drew stars in via a variety of initiatives including beauty contests, film campaigns, and festivals. They also served as general cheerleaders at election time. Throughout the 1950s, *La Settimana Incom* newsreels featured stars such as Totò, Anna Magnani, and Aldo Fabrizi going to vote or discussing (in very general terms) their voting intentions.

From the 1970s personalities were recruited directly into political roles. In truth, this practice began with writers and intellectuals, as parties reached out to civil society in compiling their election lists. In the 1980s it became more commonplace, as the Radicals, Socialists, and Christian Democrats offered candidatures to prominent and less prominent personalities from the worlds of television, cinema, and popular music. These added luster and interest to the parties and provided them with a connection to popular culture. At a time of waning interest in conventional politics, they provided a cosmetic brushstroke. But it was also perhaps a consequence of the shaping power of entertainment, which was duly grasped and at some level acknowledged. As Veltroni put it, parties once tried to slip their spokesmen in as guests on talk shows and human interest broadcasts, "while in reality it was *Dallas* and *Beautiful* which were changing narrative practises, values, and the order of what was important in the eyes of public opinion."[35]

There were no examples of the sort seen in India, Pakistan, and South America of celebrities bidding to take on a prominent role, although for a period in the early 1990s the enormous television audiences won by popular singer and actor Adriano Celentano for his semi-improvised monologues on contemporary affairs, delivered in prime time on RAI-1, presaged a possible innovation of this nature.[36] For some observers, it was Forza Italia that turned this hypothesis into reality. The relationship in this case between entertainment and politics was original because television was not an exterior medium but a constituent part of the project. Veteran quiz-master Mike Bongiorno, who left RAI for Fininvest in 1979, played the part of John the Baptist in sponsoring and anointing his employer before the eyes of the public. Hailing from the world of showbusiness as well as business proper, Berlusconi provided a new take on the "politician-as-celebrity" phenomenon so deplored by Postman.[37] Although never a professional entertainer, he brought the razzamatazz of advertising and celebrity to politics. The attention paid to appearances and the creation of an upbeat mood were signs of this. The much-criticized practice of *velenismo* (showgirlism) referred primarily to the way Berlusconi offered slots in his election lists to young women of attractive appearance, sometimes drawn from television, but with little political experience.[38] More broadly it related to the commitment to conveying notions of optimism, escapism, beauty, and sex appeal.

Glamour, understood as an enticing image or enhanced reality strictly related to consumption and resting on precisely the above values, combined with wealth, movement, fashion, and fame, had only rarely been drawn directly into politics in Italy.[39] One reason was the different orders of values that obtained in the two spheres. According to Alberoni, stars functioned as a "transgression elite"; they were allowed to exhibit wealth, conduct disorderly personal lives, and break conventions precisely because they were distant from power.[40] Politicians by contrast were expected to conform to prevailing values. The exhibition of wealth was not, for them, permissible because it suggested corruption or at least a gap between their experience of life and that of their electors. Another factor was the legacy of Mussolini. The Duce did not figure in collective memory as a man of glamour but, up until the late 1920s, he harnessed many aspects of celebrity and presented an image via photography and newsreels that was broadly compatible with movie-star glamour.[41]

The high levels of television viewing among categories including housewives, the old, and the less well educated explains in part the ease with which entertainment bled into the political sphere. But, as has been seen in this chapter, politics was drawn into this mediatized world in several ways and was influenced by it. A relative decline in the centrality of cinema and television in the public sphere does not mean that there will be any rapid eradication of this influence. In the era of instant celebrity, the politician on the rise is inevitably subject to pressures and expectations which bring him or her within the realm of celebrity. Beppe Grillo owed his public standing to television, even if his subsequent long banishment from Italian screens led him to build his Five Star Movement through new media. The former stand-up comic draws more from the sphere of entertainment than from conventional politics. In an age in which the centrality of television appears to belong to the recent past, this is perhaps its most enduring, and most dubious, legacy.

Notes

1. As Francesca Anania observes, "the influence of the media system on politics was low at this time." See "Legami pericolosi: la comunicazione politica nell'era della televisione," in M. Ridolfi (ed.), *Propaganda e comunicazione politica: storia e trasformazioni nell'età contemporanea* (Milan: Bruno Mondadori, 2004), 245–262, at 253.

2. Terms such as agenda-setting, media logic, political arena, electoral market, opinion maker, and personalization suggested that the perception of the workings of the public sphere had changed. On these issues, see G. Pasquino, "Mass media, partito di massa e trasformazioni della politica," *Il Mulino* 4 (1983); R. Mannheimer and G. Sani, *Il mercato elettorale* (Bologna: Il Mulino, 1987); S. Gundle, "Italy," in D. Butler and A. Ranney (eds.), *Electioneering* (Oxford: Oxford University Press, 1992), 173–201.

3. P. McCarthy, "Forza Italia: The New Politics and Old Values of a Changing Italy," in S. Gundle and S. Parker (eds.), *The New Italian Republic: From the Fall of the Berlin Wall to Berlusconi* (London: Routledge, 1996), 130–146.

4. A. Ventrone, "Forme e strumenti della propaganda di massa nella nascita e nel consolidamento della Republica (1946–1958)," in Ridolfi, *Propaganda e comunicazione politica*, 211–220.

5. See A. Sainati (ed.), *La Settimana Incom: cinegiornali e informazione negli anni 50* (Turin: Lindau, 2001).

6. A. Amato, "Informazione radiofonica e potere politico prima della televisione," in Ridolfi, *Propaganda e comunicazione politica*, 238–241.

7. On the DC and PCI strategies in relation to the media, in the aftermath of Fascism's development of state control, see D. Forgacs and S. Gundle, *Mass Culture and Italian Society from Fascism to the Cold War* (Bloomington: Indiana University Press, 2007), 197–232, 247–20.

8. Ventrone, "Forme e strumenti," 223.

9. C. Lizzani, *Il mio lungo viaggio nel secolo breve* (Turin: Einaudi, 2007), 109.

10. G. Fantoni, "Red Screens: The Cinematic Production of the Italian Communist Party (1946–1979)," University of Strathclyde PhD thesis, 2013.

11. S. Gundle, "Neorealism and Left-wing Culture," in P. Bondanella (ed.), *The Italian Cinema Book* (London: Palgrave Macmillan, 2013).

12. G.P. Brunetta, *Storia del cinema italiano dal 1945 agli anni Ottanta* (Rome: Editori Riuniti, 1982), especially the chapter entitled "La battaglia delle idee: il fronte della sinistra."

13. Anania, "Legami pericolosi," 253.

14. R. Calasso, "Palmiro il telegenico," *Corriere della Sera*, March 6, 1988. Quoted in A. Grasso, *Storia della televisione italiana* (Milan: Garzanri, 1992), 131–132.

15. G. Crapis, *Il frigorifero del cervello: il PCI e la televisione da "Lascia o raddoppia" alla battaglia contro gli spot* (Rome: Editori Riuniti, 2002).

16. On these innovations, see S. Gundle, "Television in Italy," in J. Coleman and B. Rollet (eds.), *Television in Europe* (Exeter: Intellect Books, 1997), 61–76; and M. Hibberd, *The Media in Italy* (Maidenhead: Open University Press, 2008), 75–89.

17. Anania, "Legami pericolosi," 256. See also Gundle, "Italy," 178–183, 185–198.

18. S. Gundle, *Between Hollywood and Moscow: The Italian Communists and the Challenge of Mass Culture, 1943–91* (Durham, NC: Duke University Press, 2000), 165–193.

19. Gundle, "Italy," 186–192.

20. De Gasperi appeared on the cover of the magazine *Oggi* with actress Linda Christian at the time of her Rome wedding to Hollywood star Tyrone Power. See also M. Marsili, "De Gasperi and Togliatti: Political Leadership and Personality Cults in Postwar Italy," *Modern Italy*, 3:2 (1998), 249–262.

21. F. Alberoni, *L'elite senza potere: ricerca sociologica sul divismo* (Milan: Vita e Pensiero, 1963); C. Wright Mills, *The Power Elite* (New York: Oxford University Press, 1956).

22. Ventrone, 221. See also F. Ceccarelli, "Quando il capo era quasi sacro," *La Repubblica*, December 5, 2013, 31.

23. W. Veltroni, *I programmi che hanno cambiato l'Italia* (Milan: Fetrinelli, 1992), 270. Salvador and Lane were two popular early television entertainers, both of them foreign.

24. Veltroni, *I programmi che hanno cambiato l'Italia*, 271.

25. M. Belpoliti, *Il corpo del capo* (Parma: Guanda, 2009), 84–97.

26. S. Gundle, "Il sorriso di Berlusconi," *Altrochemestre*, 3 (1995), 14–17.

27. Ettore Scola, quoted in A. Minuz, *Viaggio al termine dell'Italia: Fellini politico* (Soveria Mannelli: Rubettino, 2012), 11.

28. See Gundle, *Between Hollywood and Moscow*, 100.

29. C. Watters, "Being Berlusconi: Sabina Guzzanti's Impersonation on Stage and Screen," in D. Popa and V. Tsakona (eds.), *Studies in Political Humour* (Amsterdam: John Benjamins, 2011), 167–189.

30. More widely on terrorism in film, see A. O'Leary, *Tragedia all'italiana: Italian Cinema and Italian Terrorisms, 1970–2010* (Oxford: Peter Lang, 2011).

31. He later withdrew this remark. See Anon. "Andreotti assolve "Il divo": non è una mascalzonata," *Corriere della Sera*, June 9, 2008, 31.

32. N. Postman, *Amusing Ourselves to Death: Public Discourse in the Age of Showbusiness* (London: Methuen, 1985), 45–49.

33. Ibid., 161.

34. See S. Gundle, "Le origini della spettacolarità nella politica di massa," in Ridolfi, *Propaganda e comunicazione politica*, 3–24.

35. Veltroni, *I programmi che hanno cambiato l'Italia*, 271. *Beautiful* is the Italian title of the American soap opera *The Bold and The Beautiful*.

36. See S. Gundle, "Adriano Celentano and the Origins of Rock and Roll in Italy," *Journal of Modern Italian Studies*, 11:3 (2006), 367–386, at 385–386.

37. Postman, *Amusing Ourselves to Death*, 135–137.

38. S. Gundle, "Berlusconi, Sex and the Avoidance of a Media Scandal" in M. Giuliani and E. Jones (eds.), *Italian Politics: Managing Uncertainty* (Oxford: Berghahn, 2010), 59–75.

39. S. Gundle, *Glamour: A History* (Oxford: Oxford University Press, 2008), 5–6.

40. Alberoni, *L'elite senza potere*, 30: "Stars can be a social fantasy because power is barred to them."

41. S. Gundle, "Besaß Mussolini Glamour? Zur fotografischen Inszenierung des Duce," *Zibaldone*, 55 (2013), 39–50.

CHAPTER 44

THE PRESS

PAOLO MANCINI

IF one looks at the history of Italian journalism, and print press in particular, it is not difficult to see two "ancestral roots" in its birth and later development: the literary and the political.[1] In part this definition can be applied to television as well.

The literary roots can be found in the professional figures of those who initiated journalism in Italy. It is evident also in the content and the discourse of the news and in the more general attitude toward journalism, in its forms of recruitment and career advancement. Today's situation seems to maintain most of these characteristics.

As in many other countries, in Italy journalism was initiated as an instrument of educated elites for internal discussion within their own group and circulation of their own products: the first journalists were intellectuals, writers, poets, artists. Most of them became journalists as they were moved by normative and educational goals. It is not by chance that among the first journalists there were a large number of priests. They played an important role in the establishing of Italian journalism, contributing to set and reinforce its main educational function that remained as a feature of Italian journalism for decades.[2] Obviously these figures, intellectuals, writers, priests, brought into journalism their specific discourse, their way of writing, and the topics in which they were interested.

This initial "literary public sphere" was soon transformed into a "political public sphere": newspapers, even those that were born as "literary gazettes," became also, if not mainly, instruments for political and ideological struggle.[3] As we all know, this root of modern journalism is common to many countries in the world, but it seems to be a particular feature of journalism in most of the Mediterranean countries.[4]

Jean Chalaby offers a very vivid image of this: indeed, he has pointed out the differences that exist between the origins of journalism in France and in the Anglo-American world. The title of his article, "Journalism as Anglo-American Invention," is striking: there are clear differences, he points out, between the French model of journalism and the one that developed in Great Britain and the United States that has set the normative foundations of the profession that have become dominant. The former overlaps deeply with politics and literature: those who used to work for the newspaper industry felt their job was some sort of provisional fallback before entering a literary or intellectual career. Their writing was very much affected by this attitude, as was their news selection. Anglo-American journalism was born and developed within a completely different environment: it very soon broke most of the bonds with its literary origin, and rather than assuming an intellectual attitude it was influenced by what have been defined "fact centered discursive practices."[5] Instead of looking at different literary genres, British and American journalists tended toward simple writing, description, accuracy; in essence, Anglo-American journalism became closer to what is recognized today as "news reporting." Moreover, the French transformation into a liberal democracy arrived much later, taking longer than in Great Britain, and the entire process of transformation was more violent. Journalism was deeply involved with this struggle, with single journalists and media outlets both taking part in the battle for political change so that a different tradition of interventionism and partisanship was established. The canons of objective reporting did not find a place, or at least not until very late, in the history of French journalism.

The birth and evolution of the Italian print press was not different and, in many aspects, showed even more extreme aspects than in France. Indeed the two legacies, both literary and political, have remained unchanged for a long period, and a genuinely market- oriented press appeared very late in Italy, even later than in France and in most Western countries. It was Napoleon who started the tradition of a "political" press in Italy and, following this initial development, print press had an important role in Italian Risorgimento: many of the people who "*hanno fatto l'Italia unita*" (made a unified Italy) (Mazzini, Cavour, Cattaneo) were either journalists themselves or courageously used the newspapers to pursue their battle and reach their goals. The habit persisted: the best example of this well-rooted tendency to use newspapers as political tools was Benito Mussolini himself. From the pages of *Il Popolo d'Italia* (The Italian People) he conducted his campaign in favor of the Italian intervention in the First World War, while later his newspaper became the paper of the Fascist Party and therefore an important instrument for its organization.

The fall of Fascism and the resistance against Fascists and Nazis represented another opportunity to reinforce the partisan nature of Italian print press: indeed, the anti-Fascist clandestine press already existed during the period of dictatorship and, in this case too, represented an important instrument for the organization of all groups opposing Fascism. With the fall of Fascism, British and American Allies allowed, as they did in other parts of occupied Europe,[6] the circulation of those papers that were clearly showing anti-Fascist attitudes and positions.[7] Obviously this furthered an already existing attitude toward newspapers' and journalists' political involvement.

Partisanship Today

The more recent history of Italian journalism has moved along this very well-established path. From the old "party press parallelism,"[8] the Italian print press moved to "political parallelism": during the postwar period, but even before that, political parties used to own their own newspapers, as in many other Western countries: *L'Unità* was the newspaper of the Communist Party, *Il Popolo* was the newspaper of Christian Democracy, *L'Avanti* was the property of the Socialist Party, and all the other Italian political parties had their own papers as well. This party press was used to spread party ideas and messages, and was also an organizational tool.

With the secularization process, the commercialization of the entire mass media system that began during the 1980s, and the progressive weakening of the traditional mass parties, the party press progressively lost its main function as an agency of political socialization. The main shift took place in 1992–3 with *Tangentopoli*, with the disappearing of most of the traditional Italian parties and the progressive decrease in economic resources at their disposal. Progressively the party press disappeared, many party newspapers were closed, others were sold to private owners, mostly indirectly linked to the old party owner (this was the case with *L'Unità*). Today the assumed readership is not party members but citizens who share with a particular newspaper general views of society, and general political options and preferences. No longer is there the newspaper of the Communist party, but there exists a leftist newspaper, a rightist newspaper, and so on.

Indeed, political parallelism has replaced party press parallelism: newspapers are not linked to party organizations anymore, but they still maintain a high level of partisanship, being oriented to an educated readership with a well-defined political orientation. The best example of the persistence of the two legacies, literary and political, is offered in the statement with which Eugenio Scalfari, editor and founder of *La Repubblica*, inaugurated the first issue of his newspaper, today the newspaper with the largest circulation in the country: "this newspaper is a bit different from others: it is a journal of information that doesn't pretend to follow an illusory political neutrality, but declares explicitly that it has taken a side in the political battle. It is made by men who belong to the vast arc of the Italian left."[9] Further on he referred explicitly to the "new leftist decision makers." In 1976 Scalfari started a newspaper that made an explicit political choice, a stated leftist option, addressing a presumably educated public. There are many other examples of this.

In the era of political parallelism, the traditional partisanship of Italian newspapers can be seen as three dimensions: content, professionalism, and readership. There is no doubt that everyone is able to understand the leftist orientation of *La Repubblica* (not just because it was clearly stated by its founder, Eugenio Scalfari, but because it emerges clearly from its content, approach, and discourse). The "*dieci domande*" (ten questions) that the newspaper addressed daily for months to Silvio Berlusconi about his sex scandals were a clear indicator of where the newspaper stands. Indeed, these questions were clearly aimed at pointing out the bad behavior of Berlusconi.[10]

Il Giornale is a rightist outlet not just because it is owned by the brother of Silvio Berlusconi but mainly because in all its pages it clearly shows a solid rightist orientation. *Libero* is another rightist newspaper, while *Il Fatto quotidiano* is clearly a leftist newspaper in content and approach. Many other print outlets can be classified on the basis of a leftist/rightist axis.

Very frequently, professionals working within the print press (the situation in television is the same) have a more or less clear political affiliation. Most of the journalists working within a leftist oriented newspaper have a leftist personal orientation, and vice versa for those working for rightist outlets. In most cases there is homogeneity between personal attitudes and the wider ideological and political attitudes of the news outlets. This affects both the selection of news and its treatment. It is rooted in the history of Italian journalism that was described earlier: the overlapping between journalism and politics was born when newspapers were established to support and spread political ideas, to reach specific goals; progressively this attitude became dominant, and has lasted well beyond what happened in most Western democracies.

Many journalists have been and still are political actors as well, and believe they have to play a political role. With these words another important, and in this case controversial, journalist, Giuliano Ferrara, starts one of his books: "I intend journalism as a nasty craft, as a political title … I don't like journalism as a profession … as a fair profession."[11] This is not an isolated statement of the overlapping between political involvement and journalism: a recent study has shown that more than 12 percent of Members of Parliament are either journalists or were formerly journalists; in the United Kingdom this number decreases to 6.5 percent and in Germany to 3.9 percent.[12] This is another confirmation that the journey between mass media and politics is not a rare one, and is much more frequent in Italy than in other Western democracies.

Finally, the Italian print press is addressed to a partisan readership: leftist citizens read leftist newspapers, rightist citizens read rightist newspapers. This widespread behavior affects most general Italian cultural consumption, and in an even more dramatic way it affects television consumption. Concluding their study of the 2008 election campaign, two political scientists, Legnante and Sani, write that "the importance of television is associated with one of the major characteristics of the election in the Second Republic: the alignment between electoral choices and TV consumption."[13]

The high level of partisanship of the Italian print press, and in general of the entire media system, has to be connected to what has been defined as a polarized-pluralist political system. It has featured in Italy in the past years,[14] and still persists today:[15] there is an extreme distance between the positions of the different parties: there are "anti-system parties," that is parties that aim to destroy and radically change the political system and not to win elections; political debate is very harsh; there is disagreement over the so-called rules of the game; political involvement of citizens is high. This was the situation in postwar Italy but it is still in operation today, as, for instance, the experience of Movimento Cinque Stelle shows. In this context, newspapers and other means of communication often overlap with political parties; they cooperate with political parties to support their battle within a polarized political system.

One of the main consequences of what has been said so far is the elite nature of the Italian print press that was and still is addressing an educated public of relatively few readers. Indeed, if compared with other countries, the circulation of Italian newspapers is very low: in the last report of the World Association of Newspaper and News Publishers Italy is last in Europe among the Western European countries as to print press reach, just after Spain.[16] The much-quoted article that the journalist Enzo Forcella wrote in 1959, significantly titled "*Millecinquecento lettori*" (1,500 readers and now published as a book), offers a very vivid image of the low level of circulation of Italian newspapers: "A political journalist in our country can count on fifteen hundred readers: the ministers, and subsecretaries (all of them), members of Parliament (some), party and trade unions leaders, the top clergy and those industrialists who want to show themselves well informed."[17]

It is not by chance that this article by Forcella is quoted in most of the volumes and articles on Italian journalism, as it catches with much precision and simple words one of the featuring characteristics of Italian journalism: its elite nature that mixes partisanship with a main focus and discourse addressed to an educated readership. A real mass market has never developed for the Italian print press: indeed, it has remained an "important" communication tool, but its importance lies in the fact that it circulates within small elites that play a major role in the public decision-making process, and not because it reaches a wide readership.

There is one main consequence of the elite dimension of the Italian print press: the small number of readers is not able to produce sufficient profits for the publishers, neither are they able to attract sufficient resources from the advertising market. Because of their elite nature, Italian newspapers have never represented a profitable business and have never been able to survive solely from their own resources. Consequently the so called "*editoria impura*" (impure publishing industry) has developed: progressively, corporations, businessmen, enterprises with economical interests outside the publishing industry have acquired most Italian newspapers that did not have enough publishing revenue to survive. Capecchi and Livolsi consider that already in 1920 the largest part of Italian newspapers were in the hands of banks, iron and steel industries, textile industries, and insurance companies.[18] This situation has lasted for many decades and there are still very few "pure" owners of the press, that is owners whose revenues depend just on the publishing industry and not on other business areas. To take just a few examples: Fiat (the Italian car factory) owns the third daily in terms of circulation, *La Stampa*; the second largest daily *Il Corriere della sera* is the property of a conglomerate formed by banks and industrialists; *La Repubblica* is the property of a businessman with interests in different fields; the economic activities of the Berlusconi family are spread across the daily *Il Giornale* and numerous weeklies.

The mass media historian, Peppino Ortoleva, has talked of this as "*lobbying all'italiana*" (lobbying Italian style): in Italy lobbying is not regulated by law and is hardly conceived as a "legal" activity, newspapers are used by business, corporations, and the like to intervene and to affect the public decision-making process;[19] Italian newspapers "*are* lobbying." There exists a very obvious case: the daily *Il Giorno* was established in 1956 by the chairman of the powerful state-owned Italian oil company ENI. As one of the journalists involved in the foundation of *Il Giorno*, Piero Ottone, writes: "the main aim of the daily was that debating in the public sphere against the newspapers owned by private industries that were involved in a continuous struggle against the State owned industries."[20] For those years *Il Giorno* represented an important publishing innovation, and many important future journalists were trained within its news organization. Nevertheless, it was clear that the main interest of the daily was applying pressure in favor of state-owned industries, not just disseminating news and making money.

Other instruments to help overcome the low profits of the Italian print industry have been State press subsidies. They have allowed the survival not just of the party press but of most of the Italian dailies, following a policy that has been frequently criticized for its lack of transparency, and for its general approach, which does not make a clear distinction between newspapers that are organs of groups and newspapers that exist just to make a profit. The instrumental use that political parties and even single politicians have made of the opportunities offered by press subsidies has also been frequently criticized. At the end of the 1990s, following a more general tendency in many European countries, press subsidies have experienced substantial cuts.

There is no doubt that the political legacy of the Italian print press is best expressed by the experience of the party press that I discussed earlier. This structural factor has deeply influenced the general level of partisanship, not just in the party press. It has also affected the recruitment of most Italian journalists. Indeed, the party press has contributed to diffuse and reinforce the idea that journalism is a political tool, an opportunity for mobilization but essentially an opportunity to take an active part in the decision-making process. At the same time, the party press has recruited and educated journalists, and, given the Italian way in which the profession is entered, has also been a route that allows young people to embark upon a journalistic career.[21] Therefore it has had a double role within the larger Italian mass media system. On one side, the party press has directly animated the public sphere: the positions of a party being made public through the newspapers has forced other news outlets to take a position regarding the issues that were being raised. A lively partisan debate was the consequence. At the same time, the idea of newspapers as political tools and not as neutral instruments that disseminate news has been reinforced and legitimized.

PRINT PRESS TODAY

The "commercial deluge" of the 1980s,[22] which deeply reshaped the mass media system in a large part of Europe, did not bring to an end the two traditional legacies of Italian journalism. Indeed, after the increase in the circulation of dailies that took place between 1980 and 1990, which followed the dramatic development of the entire mass media system, the print press market fell back to its previously poor state. It reached a peak of seven million copies at the end of the 1980s from the low five million readers that had been the Italian newspapers' circulation for decades, but then, within a few short years, it went back to its traditional level. In the 1980s the entire media system underwent a dramatic development. Above all, this involved radio and television: many new media enterprises were established, and an Italian catchphrase of those years was "Thousands of televisions flourished." The print press too enjoyed this period of dramatic and sudden development. But when the moment ended newspaper circulation soon dropped to its traditional level, still substantially dominated by television, which continued to grow in reach for many years. Print has therefore remained close to its elite model while television conquered and then maintained its position as the "true" mass medium, also reinforcing its role as main agenda-setter for the Italian public sphere. Italian print press is characterized by its minority role compared with television: television is the "true" mass medium addressing a wide audience, while print press remains close to its elite circulation and its restricted readership, which, nevertheless, is composed by "*quelli che contano*" (those who are in power).

The imbalance between print press and television obviously affects the total advertising investment: television is able to attract the largest part of advertising resources while print press gets a very minor part.[23] This imbalance perpetuates the dominance of television.

In spite of what has been said so far, the newspaper industry still plays an important role in influencing the public debate and in establishing a dominant "opinion climate." Those who read newspapers in Italy (and those who contribute to the newspaper either as sources of information or as commentators and editors) are those people, "1500 people," who are in charge of taking public decisions. They have the power to affect the decision-makers or work for and are associated with those agencies, such as the newspaper industry itself, that circulate among these people and play a major role in connecting them.

In other words, the Italian print press has "horizontal functions": it is an instrument that connects elite members who are placed at the same level, or very close levels, within the public decision-making process. They are politicians, journalists, businessmen, intellectuals, columnists, union officials, and so on who through the newspapers discuss each other, negotiate, and try to reach or influence an agreement. The sphere of print becomes a place where different forces try to set up a climate of opinion that supports their positions and ensures a powerful position for the forthcoming negotiations. "Lobbying Italian style" seems to be the right definition for the role of the Italian print press: in spite of its low level of circulation among "common people," it plays an important role among the elite.

The role that the print press plays in Italy is very different from the traditional one that liberal thought entrusts to the press. Indeed, according to this view, which features in most Western democracies, the press is supposed to play a "vertical function," transferring information and knowledge from top down; from those who possess information and decision-making power to those who need to be supplied with information and knowledge. In Italy the press circulates essentially among those who already possess information and power: through the press different organized groups within society try to ensure a better position for themselves when they negotiate with other groups and to determine a climate of opinion that will help them to reach their goals.

While these elites use the newspapers to circulate their messages, at the same time the print press represents for them an instrument that provides insight into the situations they are facing, for interpretation and evaluation, informed comments, behind-the-scenes information. Indeed, Italian newspapers are crowded with this genre of articles; on the contrary, it is not possible to say that they are crowded with "stories," to use this term as understood in the dominant professional ideology. As a well-known, and very controversial, Italian journalist has titled one of his most famous books, the Italian print press is symbolized by "*La scomparsa dei fatti*" (the disappearing of the facts).[24] It does not report on events and on facts but mostly deals with comments, evaluations, interpretations, which are often not separated by simple reporting. These articles are the ones that interest the elite. Decision-makers have to know what Angelo Panebianco, Ernesto Galli della Loggia, and Eugenio Scalfari (some of the main commentators in the most important newspapers) have written that same day before entering any negotiation deals; while other journalists, such as Indro Montanelli and Oriana Fallaci, perfectly embody the figure of an educated journalist addressing an educated readership.

The commercial deluge of the 1980s has not modified this habit: on the contrary it has deepened some of the already existing features. Indeed, there is no doubt that, as already stated, commercialization has also involved the print press. Because of the progressive decrease in State subsidies, it has increasingly become market-driven, while party newspapers have progressively disappeared.

The new commercial logic has not determined the end of the deeply rooted partisanship and elite orientation. Partisanship has mixed with commercialization. Language and discourse have become more extreme in order to reach and to maintain a readership that is mostly segmented on the basis of political, ideological, and cultural affiliations. As there is no possibility of reaching a new consumer within a market already fractured by the existing links of cultural and ideological fidelity and a high level of political polarization, each news outlet only needs to further confirm their traditional readers in their own opinions.

These links are maintained and reinforced through the use of harsh language: the underlining of possible consequences through "negative" campaigns that construct and reinforce the idea of the "enemy," of the "other." There are hundreds of examples of this strategy, which also represents a clear strategy of segmentation. The famous "*dieci domande*" (ten questions) that for months the leftist daily *La Repubblica* asked Italian Prime Minister, Silvio Berlusconi, about his sex scandals, represented a clear and strong political attack, but also a successful market strategy through which *La Repubblica* convinced and reinforced its readership. On the opposite side, *Il Giornale* launched heavy attacks against Gianfranco Fini, who was Berlusconi's opponent in their common party, Il Popolo della Libertà. This is another segmentation strategy this time concerning rightist readers. New and very partisan journalists have emerged: Marco Travaglio, Michele Santoro, Alessandro Sallustri, and many others mix partisanship with a high level of dramatization to address their segmented audiences.

There is no doubt that the arrival of Silvio Berlusconi in the political arena increased the level of partisanship in the Italian news media, polarizing even further their attitudes. Indeed, Berlusconi and his media enterprises have represented a clear division of the political landscape of the country: for and against Berlusconi has been for many years the distinguishing feature not just of the political scene but also of the entire news media system. Journalists are divided in two conflictual, noisy fields: those who are against Berlusconi and those who are in favor.

At the same time Berlusconi and his media empire have acted following a market logic by meeting the already existing partisanship so that both leftist and rightist newspapers are deeply involved in polarizing all those issues that could have some political impact and at the same time represent so-called "customer loyalty"; they use loud words and discourse to attract and strengthen links with their specific readership. I have defined this attitude as "dramatized polarization,"[25] it is common to the entire Italian mass media system and not just to print press, which derives from a well-rooted elite and partisan nature mixed with the exigencies of market competition and segmentation.

Today new media are completely reshaping the existing landscape: newspaper readerships are decreasing, young people go on line to catch their news, journalistic routines are dramatically changing. This is not just the case in Italy; rather it is a very well-observed global situation, within which print press is going to have a completely new role.

What Kind of Professionalism?

What has been said so far has clear consequences on the professional identity of Italian journalists working within both print press and television. In spite of a high level of institutionalization,[26] and the existence of an organization, Ordine dei Giornalisti, recognized by law, professional identity is weak. Formally a shared corpus of professional rules exists,[27] but in everyday activities these rules find very rare application and respect. The decisions and sanctions taken by Ordine dei Giornalisti are rarely applied.[28] Very frequently the figure of journalist overlaps with other professional figures (very often journalism and politics are mixed), and this further undermines professional identity.

This contradiction between formal membership of an organization, recognized by law, on one side, and actual everyday behavior, on other, constitutes a stable and widespread feature of Italian society at large, where a high level of formalism usually struggles with informality. In this sense the existence of a formal, representative organization clashes continuously with everyday behaviors that contradict the principles that this organization is trying to uphold.

In this case too, the contradiction has very well-rooted origins in the history and development of Italian journalism, mainly in the print press. For decades journalists' recruitment has been based on clientelistic relationships rather than on merit and professionalism;[29] it has depended, and, in large part, still depends, on links between the owners of the media outlets and journalism employement seekers. These links may be familial (sons of journalists become journalists themselves), political (recruitment

is based on common political affiliation), or refer to different clientelistic and particularistic links (friendship, etc.). This represents another clear case of the contradiction
between the widespread particularistic habit that features in Italian society at large
and addresses most everyday behaviors, and the formal aspiration toward universalism that finds very rare application in the country and mainly serves as an illusory
legitimizing tool.

This widespread habit has deeply contributed to the undermining of the possibility
that professional standards and rules may be set and shared. Self-regulation is weak,
therefore, and journalism is often regulated by the legislator, as is the case at the time of
writing with the theme of publishing tapping from judicial proceedings, which is raising
a very colorful debate and violent disagreements among journalists, who have not been
able to set a framework of rules regarding this issue that are accepted by all professionals.

Today new media tend to increase the confusion that exists within professional journalism, as those who blog and work within social networks are not professional figures;
often they do not have any specific journalistic education, while their main goal is often
promoting their own ideas and opinions, following and reinforcing already existing attitudes among legacy news media.

Notes

1. Alberto Asor Rosa, "Il giornalista: appunti sulla fisiologia di un mestiere difficile," in *Storia d'Italia* (Turin: Einaudi, 1981), 1229–1257.
2. Giuseppe Ricuperati, "I giornalisti italiani fra poteri e cultura dalle origini all'Unità," in *Storia d'Italia* (Turin: Einaudi, 1981), 1085–1132.
3. Jurgen Habermas, *The Structural Transformations of The Public Sphere* (Cambridge, MA: MIT Press, 1989).
4. Daniel Hallin and Paolo Mancini, *Comparing Media Systems. Three Models of Media and Politics* (Cambridge: Cambridge University Press, 2005).
5. Jan Chalaby, "Journalism as an Anglo-American Invention. A Comparison of the Development of French and Anglo-American Journalism, 1830s–1920s," *European Journal of Communication*, 11, (1996), 303–326.
6. Peter Humphreys, *Media and Media Policy in Germany: The Press and Broadcasting since 1945* (Oxford: Berg, 1994).
7. Alejandro Pizarroso Quintero, *Stampa, Radio e Propaganda. Gli Alleati in Italia 1943–1946* (Milan: Franco Angeli, 1989).
8. Colin Seymour Ure, *The Political Impact of Mass Media.* (London: Constable, 1974).
9. Eugenio Scalfari, "Un giornale non neutrale," *La Repubblica*, January 14, 1976.
10. These are the famous ten questions addressed to Silvio Berlusconi: 1) Mr. President, how and when did you first meet Noemi Letizia's father?, 2) During the course of this friend-ship how many times, and where, have you met?, 3) How would you describe the reasons for your friendship with Benedetto Letizia?, 4) Why did you discuss candidates with Signor Letizia who is not even a member of the PDL?, 5) When did you get to know Noemi Letizia?, 6) How many times and where have you met Noemi Letizia?, 7) Do you take an interest in Noemi and her future or support her family economically in any way?, 8) Is it

true that you promised Noemi you would help her career in show business or in politics?, 9) Veronica Lario said you "frequent under-age girls." Do you meet any others or "bring them up?," 10) Your wife says that you are not well and that "you need help." What is your state of health?

11. Giuliano Ferrara, *Radio Londra* (Milan: Leonardo, 1989).

12. Antonio Ciaglia, "Democrazie in primo piano. Un'analisi comparata del rapporto tra politica e sistema dei media in tre paesi europei" (unpublished PhD dissertation, Istituto Italiano di Science Umane, Florence, 2012).

13. Guido Legnante and Giacomo Sani, "Una breve campagna elettorale," in Itanes [Italian National Elections Studies], *Il ritorno di Berlusconi* (Bologna: Il Mulino, 2008), 29–45.

14. Giovanni Sartori, *Parties and Party System: A Framework for Analysis* (Cambridge: Cambridge University Press, 1976).

15. Daniel Hallin and Paolo Mancini, *Comparing Media System: Three Models of Media and Politics* (Cambridge: Cambridge University Press, 2005).

16. Source: Wan-Ifra, World Press Trends, Report 2012 (Darmstadt: Wan-Ifra, 2012).

17. Enzo Forcella, "Millecinquecento lettori" (Rome: Donzelli, 2004), 3.

18. Vittorio Capecchi and Marino Livolsi, *La stampa quotidiana in Italia* (Milan: Bompiani, 1971).

19. Peppino Ortoleva, "Il capitalismo italiano e i mezzi di comunicazione di massa," in Fabrizio Barca, *Storia del capitalismo italiano* (Rome: Donzelli, 1997), 237–263.

20. Piero Ottone, *Preghiera o bordello* (Milan: Longanesi, 1996).

21. To exercise the profession of journalist in Italy one needs to become part of Ordine dei giornalisti (Order of journalists) and to pass a professional exam. Until a few years ago you could take the exam only if you had been hired for a period of two years by a news organization.

22. Jay Blumler, *Television and the Public Interest* (London, Newbury Park, and New Delhi: Sage, 1992).

23. Last data demonstrate that television gets around 56 percent of the available advertising resources while print press gets just 15.45 percent, the rest being divided among the other means of communication (Source: Federazione Italiana Editori Giornali), *La stampa in Italia 2009–2011* (Rome: Federazione Italiana Edirori Giornali, 2011).

24. Marco Travaglio, *La scomparsa dei fatti* (Milano, Il saggiatore, 2006).

25. Paolo Mancini, "The Italian Public Sphere: A Case of Dramatized Polarization," *Journal of Modern Italian Studies*, 18(3) (2013), 335–343.

26. To become a journalist in Italy, one has to pass before a committee appointed by the Ordine dei Giornalisti.

27. Professional rules are considered within the Ordine dei Giornalisti itself.

28. The case of a journalist working in a daily who was accused of being paid by the Italian secret service and was therefore disbarred by Ordine dei Giornalisti is well known. He was then elected as a Member of Parliament and continued to work as a collaborator for another daily.

29. Giovanni Bechelloni, "The Journalist as Political Client in Italy," in Anthony Smith (ed.), *Newspaper and Democracy* (Cambridge, MA: MIT Press, 1980).

CHAPTER 45

···

THE INTELLECTUALS

···

NADIA URBINATI

EXPLORING the public role of intellectuals allows us to examine the relationship of culture with politics in societies where the opinion of the people is an essential component of political legitimacy and stability. Hence Niccolò Machiavelli wrote that the prince has to "feel" he is affected by the people and the people have to "feel" they affect the prince; and David Hume defined opinion as a "force" that makes the many easily governed by the few and the few unable to escape the control of the many.[1] Although no government can survive long if opinion is truly against it, the ways in which people form their opinions in favor or against a government vary. When governments started to seek the support of their subjects they contributed, unwillingly, to the opening of a door to a politically active public. The eighteenth century was the time in which public opinion acquired the nobility of a liberating authority, and scholars were expected to be the enlightened interpreters of social relations and costumes for the sake of people's well-being, both moral and political. In Jean-Jacques Rousseau's *The Social Contract*, "*l'opinion*" was the soul of the general will, as it could make the people feel the law was their own voice, not a mere means of coercion.[2] Beginning with the Enlightenment, therefore, "the men of culture" felt the civil duty of liberating general interest from both "the *auctoritas* of the prince, independent of the convictions and views of the subjects" and the irrational emotions and factional interests of fickle crowds.[3] The intellectuals positioned themselves between those two forces and claimed the responsibility of convincing both of them on how to lead politics toward goals that they judged reasonable and desirable for all.

Clearly, the role of intellectuals exceeds that of mere experts. Intellectuals have no expertise or technical competence whatsoever although they claim the authority to be the counselors of the sovereign, in particular when the sovereign is a collective subject such as the nation or the people.[4] It goes beyond the remit of this chapter to investigate why, in Europe and Italy in particular, intellectuals have enjoyed such an outstanding moral authority in the age of democratization. It may be reasonable to assume that in the old Continent the process of democratization was grafted into the nation, and nations were, as Benedict Anderson explained, artificial creations by intellectuals and political leaders.[5] Whatever the reasons, the public role of savants intersected with the inclusion of the illiterate in the political nation. This top-down process of nation creation was the result of a laborious work of opinion formation that had to win over stubborn resistance from the old estates and acquire credence among those who were to be included.[6] This is the theoretical and historical context within which I propose we situate the role of intellectuals in Italy.

In what follows I argue that this role gained momentum with the Risorgimento and developed through four types of intellectual engagement: the first was concerned with "making the Italians" and belonged to the liberal phase of national unification; the second was concerned with "transforming" society in order to achieve a fully inclusive state; the third was concerned with "constructing" democratic institutions and the citizenry; and the last, which is closer to our time, was concerned with "saving Italy" from its moral vices. While for the liberal intellectuals of the second half of the nineteenth century the inclusion of the many in the political nation was far in the future and required earlier steps such as literacy and private property, for their socialist and democratic critics, political inclusion was to take place for the sake of a deeper transformation in Italian society. Both views were disrupted by colonialism and World War I, and were then stopped and repressed by Fascism. The democratic renaissance of the Italian state after World War II changed the role of intellectuals, in that the main problem awaiting the republic was that of forming critical minds and making public opinion work as a check on politicians and institutions. However, the deplorable performance of the Italian republic in the late twentieth century made some intellectuals think that public criticism was inadequate in order to redeem Italy since the vices to be cured did not pertain so much to institutions but to the moral fabric of its citizens and politicians. Thus, beginning with its unification, Italy produced four types of intellectual: the liberal, the transformative, the public critic, and the accuser or moralizer. I use these terms broadly, conscious that a short chapter cannot do justice to this important theme, its complexity and articulation, and its protagonists.

MAKING THE ITALIANS

In pre-unified Italy, enlightened scholars engaged in persuading the rulers (through journals, discussion clubs, and pamphlets) to enact reforms that would advance programs of public utility. As it appears in the works of some among the leading authors of the eighteenth century, such as Gaetano Filangieri, Cesare Beccaria and Pietro Verri, the *philosophes* proposed redesigning political institutions and changing legal codes so as to make their states serve better the needs of a society that a market economy was making more dynamic and therefore in need of normative regularity and functional behavior on the part of the public.[7] In the nineteenth century, this progressive work was changed in order to fulfill the specific goal of edifying a constitutional nation-state in a country whose population was highly disparate in all respects. The political inclusion of the many in a state whose territory had been divided into many regions and for centuries ruled by foreign oligarchies was interpreted by the followers of Camillo Benso, Count of Cavour, the leader of the liberals who achieved the unification (1861), as a patient work of formation of mores in which the many had to participate only as passive recipients.[8] Patriots and thinkers who prefigured a process of national unification did not think that a "*volgo che nome non ha*" (a nameless plebs)—as Alessandro Manzoni defined the Italians in his 1822 poem *Adelchi*—was competent enough to share in government. The food of feeling is action, as John Stuart Mill wrote in commenting on the national movements of emancipation on the Continent. Yet the liberals of the peninsula were insensitive to this maxim and, with the exception of Giuseppe Mazzini and republican patriots such as Carlo Pisacane and Carlo Cattaneo, had no doubt that transforming the "*volgo*" into "one people" was a task the people were unable to fulfill by themselves. In a unified Italy, the Italians were expected to achieve citizenship competence through obedience only.[9]

The function of the intellectuals consisted in bringing the meaning of the people to the people, yet not by the people: this was the sense of the famous line by Massimo d'Azeglio (1860) that once Italy was made it would be necessary to make the Italians. "Making the Italians" was a demiurgic task that state institutions had to fulfill with the work of the most competent. To liberals (Catholic moderates such as Niccolò Tommaseo or secularists such as Bertrando Spaventa), the extension of suffrage had to be postponed to a time when the educational work of the institutions was accomplished. To the Destra Storica (the liberal party that led the unification), "making the Italians" meant making law-abiders and loyal subjects to the realm, but also active supporters of the bond of nationality, ready to sacrifice their life if needed. It meant to make all Italians contribute to the general interest by paying taxes, serving in the military (a few years after the unity, the Italian government began colonial conquests in Africa), and obeying with as little resistance as possible and as much patriotic spirit. To achieve these goals, the Italian state established a system of public schools, and Italian society promoted a variety of cultural and artistic activities, from museums and theaters to associations of mutual help held by parishes and socialist cooperatives, thus initiating a permanent initiative for acculturation and socialization. In addition, a bureaucratic class (civil and military) began to be formed and selected. "Making the Italians" meant first of all making the modern state some centuries later than in other European countries.[10]

Early difficulties for the liberal project arrived with the Risorgimento.[11] The first strong blow of criticism and a denunciation of the decline of morality and liberal values—with the complaint of a lack of an "ethical sense of the state"—came from the first generation of patriots and liberals, conservative and progressive alike, for instance Pasquale Villari, Francesco De Sanctis, and Marco Minghetti. The last-named identified the locus of political corruption not in the parliamentary model per se but in the Continental design of the state, with its plan of social policies and a strong administration of society. As he showed through a detailed comparative analysis of patronage in the United States, England, Germany, and France, the Continental paradigm was more conducive to corruption as it involved parties in the administration.[12] Minghetti published his book in

1881, a few years after "*trasformismo*" was inaugurated by a large coalition government that made the parliamentary opposition too weak to be able to check on the state's policy of infrastructure construction (railroads and state buildings such as tribunals, public offices, and schools). That large coalition—the first of several—allowed some decades of stability, yet also the growth of a rapacious political class that a narrow electorate could hardly check and the liberal constitution ("*Statuto*") hardly contain and control. The unhappiness of Italian politicians with alternation in government revealed their lack of trust in their political adversaries; hence the Italian political class preferred strong majorities and consensus.[13] This meant that representative institutions worked poorly and elections did not deter corruption and change in leadership. An outcome of this distorted implementation of representative government was the nurturing of a closed and self-referential political elite, distant from and hated by the people. Minghetti's diagnoses would later on be paraphrased by critics of parliamentarianism from the right and the left, such as Giovanni Papini and Giovanni Prezzolini (and their journal *La Voce*) and Piero Gobetti (and his journal *La rivoluzione liberale*).[14]

The first important work of the liberal intellectuals, moderate and conservative, consisted therefore in denouncing electoral politics because of its compromising nature and its litigious yet accomplice political parties. Their second important work consisted in showing through a careful study of Italian society how unification had betrayed the promises of Risorgimento and, rather than emancipating the Italians, had produced "the social question" and the "Southern Question," names of a complex national malaise: an enormous social inequality both in the agrarian South and the industrial North, popular disaffection with the state, and some pockets of rebellion in the South ("*brigantaggio*").[15] The dismay felt at government based on consent inspired Gaetano Mosca's theory of the ruling class, which was meant to prove that despite the adoption of elections, the "actual power has remained partly in the hands of the wealthiest classes."[16] Mosca's realist political science of elite formation stirred generations of intellectuals, conservatives such as Vilfredo Pareto, who gave the name of "ideology" to "the fiction of 'popular representation,'"[17] social radicals such as the historian Gaetano Salvemini and the founder of the Communist Party Antonio Gramsci, liberals such as Gobetti, and Catholics such as Luigi Sturzo, the founder of the Partito Popolare.[18] Except for Pareto, all of them resolved in their own way to give the game of politics and ideology the nobler goal of building a new social pact, which could bridge the gap between the few and the many and overcome the vices of parliamentarianism.

BETWEEN TRADITION
AND TRANSFORMATION

In the early years of the twentieth century, the project of "making the Italians" seemed to have failed and liberalism with it; this was blamed either because it was unable to create strong executives and put an end to social contestations (even at the cost of violating the liberal guarantees contained in the *Statuto*) or because it chose to represent the exclusive interests of the dominant classes (industrialists and agrarians) against the working and popular classes. In sum, the liberal state seemed to be either too weak or too arrogant, incapable of combining the protection of the legal order with political inclusion. Hence, a few decades after the unification, the role of intellectuals intersected with the problems of corruption, a shaky legality, and the inefficiency of the parliamentary system, which were soon rendered as signs of a divorce between the "legal country" and the "real country." "Making the Italians" ended up meaning obedience without consent.

The narrative of the "two Italys" was destined to become a permanent feature of the work of the public critic, a theme that crossed the entire ideological spectrum and unified several generations of scholars. The doctrine of the ethical state that Giovanni Gentile developed, and became the ideology of the Fascist state, was born out of that narrative, as the myth of a new political order that was needed in order to deliver the Risorgimento's promise of "making the Italians."[19] Fascism was fed by criticism of the liberal state, which from the end of the nineteenth century had become increasingly radical. Fascism reinterpreted in an anti-liberal way the belief that amending that failed experience would be possible by overcoming the dualism between coercion and consensus, even at the cost of repressing liberty: making the Italians obey with enthusiasm by creating a totalizing state.[20]

Yet disaffection with the liberal project also inspired another answer. To understand this we have to reflect on the fact that the Latin root of the term "intellectual" signifies the man of letters but also denotes a group of people separated from all other groups, particularly those who know nothing. The *literati* entail the *illiterate*. This oppositional logic lingered in the traditional vision against which Gramsci theorized the view of the "organic intellectual," a group that was not separated from the many but worked in conjunction with them in order to emancipate the entire society from class and cultural divisions. To the Communist Gramsci, and to some extent the liberal Gobetti, traditional intellectuals were a burden, scholars who viewed themselves as detached depositories of uncontaminated values and ideas, autonomous from all classes, almost indifferent to the social conditions of the many, and eager to defend their impartial status.[21]

In the aftermath of World War I, the "abstract idealism" of superior principles and values was theorized by Julien Benda, who in *La Trahison des Clercs* (1927) accused the "intellectuals" of betraying their vocation by siding with their respective nation or their class, thus becoming political and partisan. Two years before Benda, the philosopher Benedetto Croce had condemned those Italian men of culture who had put their wisdom in the service of ideologies in his seminal "Manifesto degli intellettuali anti-fascisti," written as an answer against Gentile's "*The Manifesto of Fascist Intellectuals*" (1925).[22]

In criticizing the "betrayal of the intellectuals" argument, Gramsci intended to question the self-portrayal of the scholars as guardians of the autonomy of culture from the ruling class or indeed any other social class. He accused traditional intellectuals of hypocrisy, since every government was the expression of some organized interests and in need of an ideology if it wanted to win consensus for its plans and rule with as little resistance as possible from the state's subjects. Mosca inspired Gramsci here, who had early on detected the strategic formation of consent: representative government needed the tribunal of the public in order to both select and control its political class. Extending this line of thought, Gramsci developed the idea of overcoming the "two Italies" through a process he called "passive revolution," a gradual transformation in popular mentality and culture led by the intellectuals. Thus the latter acquired a transformative role, since they would help construct a political program by unifying the many needs scattered throughout society in a hegemonic narrative. [23]

THE TRANSFORMATIVE INTELLECTUAL

Although the Enlightenment was the age in which the public role of intellectuals took shape in a form that is familiar to us today, in Italy this issue dated back to the humanist republics, which were already the scene of tension between the *literati* and holders of political power, and between political stability and the popular element. Both in *The Prince* and his *Discourses*, Machiavelli vindicated the political role of the scholar who devoted his knowledge of human psychology and ancient history to devise noble objectives and models that the prince or the people would have to follow. Moreover, he ended his *Prince* with an "exhortation" to "redeem Italy" from its status of subjection, "more enslaved than the Jews … beaten, robbed, wounded, put to flight."[24] In the tradition of republican humanism, political culture was therefore not a scholastic enterprise, but a reflexive and searching work that sought practical actualization; it was a "useful" and pragmatic culture that claimed responsibility for promoting the good of the city. This vision permeated a transformative view of the intellectual among scholars who shaped their political identity during Fascism (1922–43) as exiles, examples being Carlo Rosselli and the patriots who took part in the clandestine movement "Giustizia e Libertà," or political prisoners, such as many Communists and socialists.[25] The collapse of the Fascist regime and resistance against both Fascists and Nazis forged a new generation of citizens who were animated by the goal of transforming Italian society.[26] There was not unanimity on the interpretation of that transformative role, though, not even among the Communists, as the polemic between the novelist Elio Vittorini (in *Il Politecnico*, the journal he founded) and the general secretary of the Italian Communist Party (PCI), Palmiro Togliatti, showed. That clash pertained yet again to the humanist meaning of the role of the scholar. The PCI's leader accused Vittorini's ideal of keeping culture and politics distinct to be the remnant of an anachronistic view of the intellectual as superior to and detached from the world of social interests, much as Croce had taught. According to the Italian Communists, Vittorini's view had been displaced by Marxism, which had demonstrated that politics and culture were not autonomous domains but the reflection of economic interests.[27]

Starting with the end of the nineteenth century, it is clear that the relationship between culture and politics went through a deep change because of the diffusion of

Marxism among reformist and socialist movements. Yet in the twentieth century, with the mythical impact of the Soviet Revolution on popular opinion and with political parties becoming the home of ideological identification for large masses of followers, the issue of the role of intellectuals became directly associated with the construction of electoral consent. Thus, to the leaders of the Communist Party, there were two issues debated above all others: the criticism of the humanist representation of men of culture as an independent class; and the criticism of a newly born vision of politics as the domain of competent practitioners who regarded political decisions as a matter for social sciences and departments of political sciences rather than ideology and political parties. Culture as the site of uncontaminated values and politics as a profession: the transformative intellectuals meant this to be an answer to both the humanist view and the scientific view.

Yet not unlike the humanist tradition, the transformative role of intellectuals unavoidably retained an aristocratic character. Its paternalistic nature was destined to clash with the democratic evolution of society. In fact, the decline of the transformative role of intellectuals coincided with the actualization of democracy, the appraisal of *doxa* as the character of political opinions. The leading role of the wise few could claim to be "maieutic" when democratic institutions were still on a distant horizon, like a desideratum or a goal to be fought for. It started to decline as soon as democracy became an institutional reality, a political process of decision-making regulated by consented procedures that presided over the formation and change of political majorities. We may say that the political authority of intellectuals followed a process that was inversely proportional with the implementation of electoral democracy. Democratic Italy was the theater of two modes of interpreting the public role of intellectuals: as philosophers who were organic to a party, and as thinkers who were public critics.

Compared with liberal pre-Fascist Italy, when the *literati* claimed a superior status, that relationship was inverted with democracy so that culture, if it wanted to play a public role of some kind, needed to side with a political party, the main protagonist of political life. Willing to be transformative, culture needed to be in the service of a party that could, with the instruments of propaganda, lead citizens toward a new majority rather than a new social order. The electoral system changed the nature of both the party and the intellectuals.

THE PUBLIC CRITIC

The transformative ideal of the intellectual found itself operating within an international order that was hostile to its project and moreover blocked *ex ante* any chance that this goal would win an electoral majority. In a climate of Cold War Manichaeism, the transformative view clashed with liberalism that shaped the construction of representative democracy. An exemplary event in that ideological climate was the politics of dialogue that the political philosopher Norberto Bobbio initiated in 1954 with the

PCI, and in the course of which he proposed a new kind of intellectual who opposed the transformative one. The anti-Erasmian Bobbio challenged the Communists to embrace democracy, and in performing a dialogue with them he wanted to prove, against Cold War Manichaeism, that a critical approach to ideas was naturally oriented toward public dialogue among people who held opposite political projects and yet accepted the risk of changing their mind through a frank discussion.[28] Bobbio proved with the dialogue he entertained with the Communist philosopher Galvano della Volpe and the leader of the PCI, Togliatti, that intellectuals in a democratic society could not be "organic to a class" since their goal was not so much unifying a mass of believers under an ideal of future society but conquering an electoral majority, and thus accepting compromises with other ideas. In a society ruled by opinions, a new and urgent role that intellectuals could play was that of blocking and denouncing power, raising problems, challenging institutions to deliver what they promised, most of all promoting pluralism of political opinions so as to make democracy work.[29]

Bobbio listed four models of intellectuals as they emerged in the twentieth century: traditional philosophers (with the mission of preserving the supreme values of civilization); experts (with the mission of opposing the trivialization of politics in the name of competent decisions); transformative intellectuals (with the mission of engaging in politics by siding with one political party); and public critics, who disseminated doubts and asked questions in a Socratic manner. The last model was consistent with the intellectuals in a democratic society performing the "critical and stimulating function of the *philosophes*, yet not their constructivist project of the good society."[30] Bobbio expressed some concern about the disappearance of critical intellectuals at the expense of either the "*partiticità della cultura*" or technical and political expertise.[31] Indeed, his four models pivoted around a basic dualism: on the one side there was either the myth of pure lovers of truth or the identification of politics with a church-like mission (whether religious or secular, Catholic or Communist); on the other side there were the answers to these myths, which were of two kinds: either stressing the role of the experts who treated politics as problem-solving or stressing the role of public critics. Bobbio did not consider the positivistic model of politics to be in tune with a democratic society; he saw it as a dangerous temptation to substitute the free and public process of deliberation with the myth of an unpolitical administration of society (the Partito dell'Uomo Qualunque founded by Guglielmo Giannini in 1949 represented that myth; in more recent times, Mario Monti's government in 2011–12 tried to convey the same message, while Beppe Grillo's Five Stars Movement also shares in the vision of a politics made of "objective data" against ideologies and political parties).

Even more critical of the identification of culture and politics was Luigi Einaudi, a renowned liberal economist and the first elected president of the Italian republic, who proposed a four-partition scheme. In his *Conoscere per deliberare* (1954), Einaudi drew an interesting map that can help us understand some contemporary mutations of representative democracy affected by both technocracy and populism.[32] According to Einaudi, in a democracy (which in his mind essentially meant procedural electoral democracy) we may detect four types of intellectuals: the theorist, the technician, the politician, and the demagogue (Einaudi himself proposed this order). The *theorists* ("*teorici*") are scholars who theorize the guidelines of interpretation of public issues by combining normative ideas of justice and political analysis. The *technicians or experts* ("*tecnici*") are students who have acquired specific competence in some domains and can be profitably employed in the service of theorists and politicians, yet are not political actors themselves. The *politicians* (citizens involved in politics and elected representatives) play the difficult task of choosing some among the various solutions and proposals that experts devise; and should have the capacity and courage to "drop analyses and solutions that are politically popular" but imprudent, and to endorse even unpopular policies. The politicians are capable of rhetoric but should not follow passively the opinion of the public nor that of the experts. Public intellectuals in modern society are a synthesis of these three typologies.

As for the *demagogues* ("*dottrinari*"), according to Einaudi they are a denial of the theorists because unlike them, who are ready to change their mind in a frank dialogue, do not change their opinions which are not falsifiable assumptions ("*punti di vista*"). The demagogue "knows already what he has to say" because the "viewpoint of his social and political faith" contains already "the right solution." The "*dottrinario*" is like the guardian of dogmas and can flourish in all political camps, including liberalism. Einaudi did not fantasize about a time when democracy would become the home of competent technicians, nor did he think it feasible that deliberation could occur without some general criteria of justice that guided political judgment in selecting problems and making decisions. Einaudi suggested that experts also might risk becoming dogmatic scholars if their specialized knowledge did not content itself with being auxiliary to political deliberation.

The new democratic society, Bobbio and Einaudi agreed, would need a combination of different intellectual functions, some of which were to be performed by competent and expert professionals, and some by the citizens themselves as political leaders, whom the practice of participation would contribute toward forming. Democracy demands several kinds of intellectuals rather than just one. As an open and dissenting society, it also needs public intellectuals who, like the wasps in the comedy by Aristophanes, question, stimulate, and challenge both politicians and public opinion.

THE ACCUSER AND MORALIZER

In its early democratic decades, Italian society was a rich laboratory of political experimentation at both institutional and social level. We should mention some of the reforms that changed Italian society and culture quite radically. The 1970 law instituting regional decentralization gave a more important role to local public life and the cities, while grassroots participation led society toward a rapid process of cultural liberalization that spread beyond state institutions and changed lifestyles and morals: by the 1970s and 1980s, Italian citizens were able to win referenda legalizing divorce and abortion, while the parliament passed a new law on family and marriage that erased patriarchalism. It was as if universal suffrage (adopted in 1945) had produced its effect, since the most radical changes occurred precisely in those social domains in which women and the new generation had suffered subjection because of their political exclusion. In the early stages of democratization, the intellectual discourse reflected the democratic process of liberation. The public critic was the most likely to absorb and understand it, although being criticized from both the radical perspective (leaders of the student movement in the 1960s and 1970s, and radical critics of constitutional democracy such as Antonio Negri) and the realist and moderate one (the critics of the Enlightenment tradition of the *philosophes*, such as the philosopher Augusto del Noce and the historian Ernesto Galli della Loggia). Yet the strength of Bobbio's and Einaudi's position somehow reflected that of Italian politics at a time when governing society essentially meant fulfilling the democratic promises.

This lively process of democratization also had the effect of making civil society a much more active protagonist; its claim for an autonomous voice would shake the way in which politics functioned. Society sought to have a more representative presence in politics, and this changed the nature of political parties. An indication of this was Bettino Craxi's leadership of the Italian Socialist Party (PSI), which changed the style and language of politics and indeed the political culture. The early stage of Craxi's leadership (he was elected Secretary of his party in 1976) brought into political discourse a new interpretation of a just society that was keener to learn from American political philosophy than from Italian Marxism. Journals such as *Politeia* and *Problemi della transizione*, cultural activities promoted by the Fondazione Giangiacomo Feltrinelli of Milan and the Fondazione Lelio e Lisli Basso of Rome, were just few of the many centers of intellectual elaboration in those fertile years in public life. The philosophers Salvatore Veca and Remo Bodei were representatives of this new intellectual course, which tried to combine transformative visions with the role of public critics.[33]

Yet Craxi's leadership changed the relationship within the left and also between the left and the social forces, which were no longer, or not necessarily, unions or labor organizations, but above all the emerging classes of managers and professionals. Stronger connections between politics and business facilitated public behavior that was fed up with rules and legality and more interested in strengthening political influence (the 1984 law that allowed the tycoon Silvio Berlusconi to own some national television stations was an example of this climate of political clientelism). In a few years, "dirty hands in politics" became a central theme in public discourse.[34] The decline of public morality would change citizens' perception of political parties as associations for the promotion of special interests; and while in the short run clientelism seemed able to expand the opportunities of growth for some, in the long run it eroded the sense of the law while engrossing the public debt of the state. Moreover, Craxi's plebiscitarian leadership loosened the controlling function of the party, and this made corruption an easier practice, as the leader of PCI, Enrico Berlinguer, detected in his prophetic speech in parliament in 1981.

Affarismo was the name of the combine between politics and private interests. Its outcome was *manipulite* (cleaning hands) or the prosecution and condemnation of an entire political class (which started in 1992). Among the several collateral consequences of the expansion of justice because of the the expansion of corruption, two of them pertained to the role of the intellectuals: anti-party sentiments among citizens and the transformation of parties into machines for consolidating the power of the elected (*la casta*, in Marco Travaglio's words and the title of a successful book by Gian Antonio Stella); and what Giovanni Sartori called *videocracy*, or the hegemonic role of television in dictating the content and style of politics.[35] The intellectuals became media experts and managers of the image of the new political leader, Silvio Berlusconi, the symbol of these two collateral consequences. The pervasiveness of corruption in the age of Berlusconi's governments also changed the role of intellectuals from public critics in the tradition of the *philosophes* to accusatory scourges of Italians and their moral vices, in the tradition of Savonarola's sermons against Medici's corruption and the despotic rule in humanist Florence (Maurizio Viroli has epitomized Berlusconi's supporters as sellers of their freedom in exchange for favors, sexual, economic, or political). *Saving Italy*, as the title of Paul Ginsborg's book states, has become the mission of the new intellectuals.[36]

The divorce between private morality and public morality—in fact the subjection of public behavior to private interests—has marked the style of public criticism in the *ventennio berlusconiano*. On some occasions, as in the case of Roberto Saviano (the author of the book *Gomorra*, who has been put under a police protection program after he received life threats by *camorra* bosses), the life of the public critic itself has become testimony for the state of illegality and corruption. On other occasions, as with Bill Emmot's articles in *The Economist*, a foreign opinion maker has played the role of an external judge of Berlusconi's politics and has become a very authoritative voice in Italian public opinion. Post-*manipulite*, issues as diverse as illegality, despicable and vulgar behavior by elected officials, bureaucratic incompetence, and state inefficiency have been rendered mainly in one style: that of censorial denunciation and moral condemnation. Rescuing Italy from its vices has become intellectuals' task, with no indication of the means by which this can be attained.

Years ago, the sociologist Alessandro Pizzorno interpreted the paradox unfurled by this moralist style as a sign of the decline of political language and judgment and their replacement with the language and judgment of subjective morality and taste. The centrality of symbols over programs, of the personality of the leader over the collective of party supporters, has translated into the centrality of moral qualities over political qualities in the formulation of political judgment by citizens and public critics alike. Political virtues (prudence, competence, compromise, etc.) have declined and personal virtues (aesthetic, transparency, authenticity, etc.) have become central both in actuality and in the work of critics. However, moral condemnation has not translated into a decline in corruption; if anything, it has made the public seek for more scandals to be viewed and criticized.[37] The practice of transparency, in the name of which the Five Stars Movement acquired such a spectacular gain in the national elections of February 2013, can be interpreted as the late child of a political opinion that has embraced the moral style of denunciation. The paradox of this moralizing approach is that it does not offer politics any feasible strategy for solving its problems, unless the state becomes an illiberal ethical community with the mission of making its subjects virtuous. Finally, denunciation is primed to mobilize a negative kind of power, judgment, which does not foster citizens' political participation, but demoralizes it instead. The growth of electoral abstention in the last two decades is one of the side effects of a citizenship that has lost trust in politics and does not find in the intellectuals arguments that will restore it. One recent book has the telling title of *Intellettuali del piffero: come rompere l'incantesimo dei professionisti dell'impegno*, in which the author claims that democratic citizens need to "kill the father," or emancipate themselves from the paternalism of the *maîtres à penser*.[38] Although after World War II the intellectuals took on themselves the task of reforming, transforming, or scourging democratic citizens, their moral authority gradually faded away. In contemporary Italy, the intellectuals are perceived somehow as preachers who claim an unwarranted superior cognitive and moral authority over their fellow citizens.

Notes

1. Niccolò Machiavelli, *The Prince,* in *Selected Political Writings,* ed. and trans. David Wootton (Indianapolis, IN: Hackett, 1994), chap. 18; David Hume, "On the First Principles of Government," in *Political Essays,* ed. Knud Haakonssen, (Cambridge: Cambridge University Press, 1994), 16.

2. Jean-Jacques Rousseau, *On the Social Contract or Principles of Political Rights,* in *Basic Political Writings,* trans. Donald A. Cress (Indianapolis, IN: Hackett, 1987), bk. 2, ch. 12.

3. Jürgen Habermas, *The Structural Transformation of the Public Sphere: An Inquiry into a Category of Bourgeois Society* (1962), trans. Thomas Burger with Frederick Lawrence (Cambridge, MA: MIT Press, 1991), 90.

4. The bibliography on the subject is immense; see at least John Gross, *The Rise and Fall of the Man of Letters: A Study of the Idiosyncratic and the Humane in Modern Literature* (London: Macmillan, 1969) and the collection edited by Philip Rieff, *On Intellectuals: Theoretical Studies, Case Studies* (New York: Doubleday, 1969).

5. Benedict Anderson, *Imagined Communities: Reflections on the Origin and Spread of Nationalism* (1983), revised ed. (London: Verso, 1991), 5–7.

6. The most comprehensive work on the Italian intellectuals and the one that inspired me in writing this chapter is Alberto Asor Rosa, *La cultura,* in *Storia d'Italia* (Turin: Einaudi, 1975), vol. 4, pt. 2: *D'all Unita àoggi.*

7. Franco Venturi, *Settecento riformatore; da Muratori a Beccaria* (Torino: Einaudi, 1979).

8. See Denis Mack Smith, *Cavour* (London: Weidenfeld and Nicolson, 1985); Alberto Mario Banti, *Il Risorgimento italiano* (Rome and Bari, Laterza, 2004).

9. Franco Della Peruta, *I democratici e la rivoluzione italiana. Dibattiti ideali e contrasti politici all'indomani del 1848* (Milan: Feltrinelli, 1974).

10. Albero Mario Banti and Paul Ginsborg, eds., *Storia d'Italia. Annali,* vol. XXII, *Il Risorgimento* (Turin: Einaudi, 2007).

11. Francesco De Sanctis, "Le due sinistre," (1874) in Francesco De Sanctis, *I partiti e l'educazione della nuova Italia,* ed. Nino Cortese (Turin: Einaudi, 1970), 35–6 (where he used expressions such as "malaise" and "discontent" in order to describe the opinion of the Italians on the performance of the state).

12. Marco Minghetti, *I partiti politici e la ingerenza loro nella giustizia e nell'amministrazione* (Bologna: Zanichelli, 1881).

13. "The state could not make without a constitutional parliamentary opposition" Francesco De Sanctis, *La letteratura italiana nel secolo XIX. Scuola liberale. Scuola democratica. Lezioni*, ed. Francesco Torraca, with an introduction by Benedetto Croce (Naples: Morano, 1920), 372; on the tendency of the Italian parliamentary politics toward large coalitions since the time of Cavour see Massimo L. Salvadori, "Il liberalismo di Cavour," in *Cavour, l'Italia e l'Europa*, ed. by U. Levra (Bologna: Il Mulino, 2011).

14. Eugenio Garin, *Cronache di filosofia italiana (1900–1943). Quindici anni dopo 1945–1960* (Rome and Bari: Laterza, 1975).

15. Leopoldo Franchetti and Sidney Sonnino, *Inchiesta in Sicilia* (first ed. 1877; Firenze: Vallecchi, 1974); Pasquale Villari, *I mali dell'Italia. Scritti su mafia, camorra e brigantaggio*, ed. Eugenio Garin (Florence: Vallecchi, 1995).

16. Gaetano Mosca, *The Ruling Class*, trans. Hannah D. Kahn, ed. Arthur Livingston (New York: McGraw-Hill, 1939), 389.

17. Vilfredo Pareto, *The Mind and Society*, 4 vols., trans. Andrew Bongiorno and Arthur Livingston (New York: Harcourt, 1935), vol. 4, § 2244.

18. Sturzo's Catholic political party (founded in 1919) interrupted de facto the forbidding command to Catholics not to be involved in politics that the Vatican decreed in retaliation against the end of the papal state as an effect of national unification.

19. Giovanni Gentile, *Fascismo e cultura* (Milan: Fratelli Treves, 1928). The issue on whether a "Fascist culture existed" has been the object of an important debate after World War II, which we can simply mention by recalling at least two of its most important representatives: Renzo De Felice, *Intervista sul fascismo* (Bari: Laterza, 1975) and Norberto Bobbio, *Profile of Twentieth-Century Italy*, trans. Lydia G. Cochrane (Princeton, NJ: Princeton University Press, 1995).

20. Gabriele Turi, *Il fascismo e il consenso degli intellettuali* (Bologna: Il Mulino, 1980) and Gabriele Turi, "Giovanni Gentile: Oblivion, Remembrance, and Criticism," *Journal of Modern History*, 70/4 (December 1998), 913–933.

21. Antonio Gramsci, *Odio gli indifferenti* (Milano: Chiare lettere, 2011). As for Piero Gobetti's role in the redefinition of the intellectual as a militant for an emancipatory vision of liberalism, see a collection of his essays: *On Liberal Revolution*, ed. Nadia Urbinati (New Haven, CT: Yale University Press, 2000).

22. Benedetto Croce's Manifesto was published in the May 1, 1925 issue of the journal *La Critica*; concerning his view of the aristocratic function of the "repubblica letteraria" see his *Storia d'Europa nel secolo diciannovesimo* (1932), ed. Giuseppe Galasso (Florence: Adelphi, 1991). On the cultural politics of fascism, and the role of its most intellectual journal *Il Primato*, see Luisa Mangoni, *L'interventismo della cultura: intellettuali e riviste del fascismo* (Roma-Bari: Laterza 1974). After WW2, an important and highly debated issue was that of the conversion of young Fascists to anti-fascism; see Ruggero Zangrandi, *Il lungo viaggio attraverso il fascismo* (Milano: Mursia, 1998); and Luca La Rovere, *L'eredità del fascismo. Gli intellettuali, i giovani e la transizione al postfascismo 1943–1948* (Torino: Bollati Boringhieri, 2008). Equally compelling has been the debate on the strategy of "dissimulation" of anti-fascist ideas adopted by intellectuals during the Fascist regime (or *nicodemismo* as Bobbio defined it); *A Political Life: Norberto Bobbio*, ed. Alberto Papuzzi, trans. Allan Cameron (London: Polity Press, 2002). For an English overview on the *vexata quaestio* of the intellectuals and fascism see Rocco Bubini, *The Other Renaissance: Italian Humanism Between Hegel and Heidegger* (Chicago and London: University of Chicago Press, 2014).

23. See, Eugenio Garin, *Intellettuali italiani del XX secolo* (Rome: Editori Riuniti, 1974).

24. Machiavelli, *The Prince*, 77.

25. Carlo Rosselli, *Liberal Socialism,* trans. William McQuaig, with an introduction by Nadia Urbinati (Princeton, NJ: Princeton University Press, 1994).

26. Claudio Pavone, *A Civil War: A History of the Italian Resistance*, trans. Peter Levy, introduction by Stanislao Pugliese (London: Verso, 2013).

27. The debate is documented in *Il Politecnico*, an anthology ed. M. Forti and S. Pautasso (Milan: Rizzoli, 1975).

28. The "neutral" attitude of the man of culture as epitomized by Erasmus of Rotterdam was rendered by Bobbio with the formula "neither with you nor against you," Norberto Bobbio, "Intellettuali e vita politica in Italia" (1954), in Norberto Bobbio, *Politica e cultura* (1955), new ed. with an introduction by Franco Sbarberi (Turin: Einaudi, 2005), 108.

29. Bobbio, *Politica e cultura*, 97–112; Nadia Urbinati, "Liberalism in the Cold War: Norberto Bobbio and the Dialogue with the PCI," *Journal of Modern Italian Studies* 8 (2003), 578–603.

30. Norberto Bobbio, "Intellettuali e classe politica" (1954), reprinted in Norberto Bobbio, *Il dubbio e la scelta. Intellettuali e potere nella società contemporanea* (Rome: Carrocci, 1993), 35.

31. Ibid., 36.

32. Luigi Einaudi, "Conoscere per deliberare" (1954), in Luigi Einaudi, *Prediche inutili* (Turin: Einaudi, 1962).

33. For an excellent reconstruction of post-World War II Italian political culture see Remo Bodei, *We, the Divided: Ethos, Politics and Culture in Post-war Italy, 1943–2006,* trans. Jeremy Parzen and Aaron Thomas (Toronto: Agincourt Press, 2006).

34. For a history of Craxi's ascendancy and decline see the autobiographical essay by Valdo Spini, *La buona politica. Da Machiavelli alla terza repubblica. Riflessioni di un socialista* (Venice: Marsilio, 2013).

35. Gian Antonio Stella, *La casta* (Milano: Rizzoli, 2008); Giovanni Sartori, *Homo videns* (Rome and Bari: Laterza, 2000).

36. Maurizio Viroli, *The Liberty of the Servants*, trans. Antony Shugaar (Princeton, NJ: Princeton University Press, 2012); Paul Ginsborg, *Salviamo l'Italia* (Turin: Einaudi, 2010).

37. Alessandro Pizzorno, *Il potere dei giudici. Stato democratico e controllo della virtù* (Rome and Bari: Laterza, 1998), 45–63. For a critical analysis of the decline of political culture in the Left see Salvatore Biasco, *Per una Sinistra pensante* (Venice: Marsilio, 2009).

38. Luca Mastrantonio, *Intellettuali del piffero: come rompere l'incantesimo dei professionisti dell'impegno* (Venice: Marsilio, 2013).

CHAPTER 46

....

PUBLIC ETHICS AND POLITICAL CORRUPTION IN ITALY

....

DAVID HINE

SINCE the 1980s it has become increasingly clear that corruption can be endemic in democracies as well as non-democracies. The former are generally better placed to combat corruption, but their advantage is relative not absolute. Democratic rules provide no complete guarantee that office-holders will not exploit office for personal gain, and competitive elections are sometimes unable to prevent dishonest or manipulative individuals winning power or staying there even after being exposed as corrupt. The transparency of public procurement processes, perhaps the major source of corruption in democracies, is certainly not a complete guarantee of probity in the spending of public money. Public ethics has thus become a major governance issue not just in emerging economies, but in some advanced democracies.[1]

Public ethics can be defined positively as civic virtue, or negatively as improper or corrupt behavior. Civic virtue involves sustained voluntary commitment by office-holders to the rules and principles that keep politics clean. These principles include lawfulness, the ethos of public service, transparency, accountability, and moral leadership. Civic virtue requires a sustained effort to ensure that all those holding public office, whether elective or permanent, are properly socialized into these high standards. Unfortunately cashing out positive virtues into observable and measurable behavior is difficult. Most academic discussions therefore focus on the negative: public ethics as measured by the absence of corruption and impropriety.

Here too, however, there are definitional issues. Some commentators prefer a definition rooted in hard law, seeing corrupt political acts as those prohibited by law. Others stress that political conduct in modern societies can be controversial without being strictly illegal.[2] Politicians are capable of evading laws, immunizing themselves against their effects, or adjusting them to suit their own needs and behavior. Even without such adjustments, and even when not strictly illegal, political practices can often seem unacceptable or sub-standard. Examples would be recruitment or contracting practices in the public sector that lack properly-specified rules on conflict of interest, or party funding by powerful interests, or many forms of lightly regulated lobbying activity. It is hard to formulate conflict of interest rules that do not leave many loopholes. Moreover, in modern democracies politicians have the legislative power to vote themselves formidable resources out of which they, and a surrounding, extensive, and well-paid political class can enjoy surprisingly generous lifestyles.

Few democracies have learned lessons about entrenched corruption and legally underpinned impropriety more painfully than Italy. Since the first explosion of widespread corruption cases in the early 1990s Italy has woken up to the deeply rooted nature of its political corruption, and the great, if unquantifiable, cost of corruption in terms of resource allocation and of the legitimacy of public office holders. But the country has struggled to resolve these problems. There have been programs aimed at preventing corruption, and voters have supported a succession of politicians and parties claiming to stand for clean and frugal government. But there have been few satisfactory solutions. There has been progress in some areas in reducing the substantive misallocation of public resources (though at significant cost in complex procedures and delayed spending), but there has been little progress in terms of public confidence in the political and administrative class. It is the psychological dimension of poor ethical standards—the dramatic decline in public trust—which seems to have been the most injurious consequence of Italy's two-decade-long struggle with corruption.

THE EVIDENCE: A REPUTATION
FOR CORRUPTION

We cannot, because of corruption's mostly hidden essence, know how much political corruption exists in Italy. The data from police investigations and court cases are fragmented, particularly those recording definitive convictions, which are often arrived at only many years after the original investigation, making annual data unreliable.[3] Moreover, there are good reasons for thinking that cases which make it to the judicial system are only the tip of the iceberg. What is clear is that the country enjoys the dubious reputation of having, among the long-standing democracies of Western Europe, much the largest and most embedded problem of corruption. The authorities in Italy endorse this reputation. When the Council of Europe's Group of States against Corruption (GRECO) inspected Italy in 2008, as part of its evaluation program, it reported that its interlocutors among Italian officials displayed "a widely shared perception ... that corruption in Italy is a pervasive and systematic phenomenon which affects society as a whole."[4] Numerous parliamentary, judicial, and government reports on the problem from the 1992 *Tangentopoli* scandal onwards had already arrived at the same conclusion.[5]

The most frequently quoted evidence in support of the claim comes from NGOs outside Italy that have assembled databases from survey evidence of perceptions of corruption. This has allowed the construction of comparative cross-national rankings, which, despite the difficulty of absolute quantification, are one of the best ways of assessing whether a country has an abnormally high level of corruption.

The two best-known perceptions rankings are the Transparency International Corruption Perceptions Index (CPI) and the World Bank's World Governance Indicators (WGI).[6] The former is calculated using the combined scores from a number of assessments (rankings, not hard scores) using different methodologies and a changing number of countries. It has existed in various forms since the 1990s. Given the distorting impact of historical experiences (dictatorship, communist hegemony) and of country size, the best comparators for Italy are similar-sized and long-standing European democracies. The data for Italy suggests a dramatic deterioration in standing since 2001, compared to the UK, Germany, France, and (less long-standing as a democracy) even Spain. The rankings of these four have been more stable. In 2001, they ranged from 13th to 23rd place overall and in 2013 (albeit with a different internal ordering) from 13th place to 40th. The Italian ranking fell from 29th place in 2001 to 69th place in 2013. A similar picture emerges from the "control of corruption" index within the WGI. The Italian percentile ranking is significantly below that of comparable west European countries over three data points between 2002 and 2012. By 2012, indeed, Italy was seriously adrift from France, Germany, the UK, and again even Spain. It was already adrift in 2002, but while these other four managed to hold a roughly stable ranking over the decade, Italy's percentile ranking slipped from 72nd to 58th percentile.

The slippage in the *Transparency* CPI ranking in some ways seems even more dramatic. However, the reality is exaggerated by the expansion in the number of countries included. Between 2001 and 2013 this almost doubled, from 91 to 175. It is sometimes ignored that an index based on *relative* positions, but with fairly stable absolute levels of corruption over time for most countries will, as more countries are added, lower the position of a country which, like Italy, was initially not as far from the median ranking as other European countries. Italy was 29th in 2001, when the median ranking was 45th. Importantly, 26 of the 91 countries *not* present in the rankings in 2001, but included by 2011, ranked *above* Italy when they joined. Had these been included earlier, Italy's own ranking would probably have been far lower in 2001. Using a very crude adjustment calculation, Italy really slipped not from 29th to 69th, but more realistically from something like 55th to 69th.

It is doubtful whether this is reassuring. Although Italy might already have ranked low in 2001, its four major West European comparators would still have been roughly where they were, because only about three of the 26 relevant new entrants were higher placed than the four comparators. Italy's decline is not as dramatic as headlines in newspapers sometimes proclaim; its 2001 starting point understates the gap between it and its fellow European countries. But its decline is still marked in absolute terms, as well as relatively. If the rankings are meaningful Italy is certainly an outlier in European terms, particularly given its uninterrupted record of democracy since 1945.

More recent panel-based research by Eurobarometer on the populations of the 28 members of the European Union, conducted in 2009 and repeated in 2011, reveals a similar story. On most counts ("corruption is a major problem," "corruption is present in national institutions," "the country is more corrupt than others in Europe," "corruption is part of the national business culture"), Italians ranked their country as corrupt: generally putting it in the top five to eight most corrupt EU member-states, and always well beyond the European average. None of the post-1945 democracies ranked worse than Italy, and some post-1989 Central and East European members were also rated more highly than Italy. Only Greece, on some issues Spain, and Portugal, of the EU-15 era of member-states ranked worse than Italy.[7]

Hard data on cases of corruption, as opposed to perceptions and comparative rankings of perceptions, are more difficult to assess. Strikingly, as the two main official commentaries published in the last decade observe, the trends in arrests, charges, and convictions usually run in the opposite direction from those of corruption perceptions and panel surveys.[8] After reaching an immediate post-*Tangentopoli* peak in 1996 (1714 definitive convictions for corruption and *concussione* (abuse of office for the purposes of extortion), it dropped away more or less steadily over the following decade, falling to 239 in 2006, 341 in 2007, and 295 in 2008. The absence of effective comparability between crime definitions in different jurisdictions makes it difficult to interpret such figures. There are moreover other forms of corruption (theft of public property, abuse of office) not included in the headline data reported in the main official reports. These reports come from the two successive agencies established to design new anti-corruption strategies. Both interpret the disparity between rising perceptions of corruption and falling conviction rates as evidence not of an improving climate for ethics and propriety, but as a failure of public policy to sustain anti-corruption efforts. This view is indeed widely shared in academic commentary.[9]

Relating the conviction data to direct experiential evidence, moreover, reinforces the picture. Survey evidence indicates a very high level of direct citizen experience of bribery. In the 2009 and 2011 Eurobarometer corruption surveys, 17 percent and 12 percent respectively of those surveyed in Italy reported they had been asked to pay, or offered, a bribe,[10] and in similar *Transparency* surveys in 2010 and 2013 respectively 13 percent and 5 percent of respondents, directly or via a family member, had been asked for bribes in relation to the provision of public services covering health, the police, licenses and permits, and so on.[11] When perhaps one in ten members of the population reports direct experience of administrative corruption, but the number of successful convictions per year is numbered in the low hundreds, there is strong prima facie evidence of an entrenched culture of corruption within which corrupt administrators feel protected and about which citizens feel powerless, knowing that efforts to fight back are likely to be, at best, pointless, and at worst against their own interests. In the 2013 *Transparency* survey, the proportion of respondents willing to become involved in anti-bribery initiatives if faced with corruption was the lowest of all pre-1989 EU member states.[12]

The issue of corruption remains a difficult one for researchers, given how much of it is invisible to the authorities. Research methods are gradually improving, but they sit against a background of inadequate data, changing opportunities for corruption, and no clear agreement on what level of corruption might be called "normal" or "acceptable," as opposed to pathological. One approach developed recently in Italy by the Scuola superiore della pubblica amministrazione is a so-called Excess Perceived Corruption Index (ECPI).[13] This index effectively uses the Human Development Index (HDI) to control for factors which should mitigate against corruption, thereby generating an expected regression line mapping results from corruption perceptions indices against the HDI. The resulting data generates a rank-ordering of corruption control, adjusted for the factors inherent in the HDI (state capacity, education, freedom, etc.). In the project findings, Italy in fact occupied *penultimate* place in the ECPI, a finding that in 2012 occasioned a good deal of press comment about Italy being "worse than Ghana."[14]

EXPLANATIONS OF ITALIAN CORRUPTION

There is thus very clear evidence of Italian exceptionalism. Its causes are more difficult to pin down. Corruption takes many forms. Several different actors are involved: at the partisan level elected politicians, party officials, party advisers and consultants; at the administrative level civil servants, both senior and junior, regulators, public-sector managers, senior police, judicial, and military figures. How these groups interact with one another and with the business and commercial groups that are the sources of money, goods, and services in kind that corruption provides, varies greatly from case to case. Some corruption is large scale and can be said to have a national profile—kickbacks on major public contracts that will go to individual office-holders or to political parties or factions. Some is regionally or locally concentrated: for example, the frequent cases of corruption in health-service procurement, or in the contracting out of services at local government level.[15] Here too, the beneficiaries will be both individuals and parties. Most corruption, particularly that of which ordinary citizens have direct experience, is petty in scale: corrupt exchanges between low-level bureaucrats, such as tax officials or the police, to exempt a citizen from tax, or a fine, or to provide a permit. However, studying what motivates an individual or group to break the law in any *particular* case—expectations of impunity, fear of coercion from criminals, or from internal peer pressure—does not answer the more fundamental underlying question: why a climate exists in which individuals believe, on a much larger scale than in comparable democracies, that engaging in corrupt acts is acceptable, or at least feasible, and can be undertaken at relatively low risk. To answer that question a broader theory is required than one which is merely the sum of accounts of particular cases and practices, however illuminating such cases might be.

Until the 1990s, it could be said that there was no meta-theory of Italian corruption. Indeed, although it was recognized that there was a good deal of corruption, it was surprisingly little discussed among political scientists, compared to problems of political immobilism and ideological polarization. Partly this was because theories of good governance and how to achieve it were only just coming into their own at NGO level, and because there were few measures by which to judge Italy's exposure to corruption in comparative perspective. Rather, explanations of corruption were derivatives of models of the broader Italian political culture. Accounts of Italian political culture tended to focus on key features: the presence of deeply entrenched clientelistic political relationships, especially in the south; ideological fragmentation (the division between a Catholic and a communist subculture, each with its own territorial heartland in different parts of the center-north); and parties that were strong in terms of their control over policymaking, but internally weak through intra-party factional competition.

Clientelism was not quite synonymous with corruption, even though some, like Edward Banfield, saw it as "the moral basis of a backward society."[16] It was subtly different because in the early post-war decades there were only weak legal protections preventing public office-holders from showing arbitrariness and favouritism in public employment and the award of contracts. So clientelism was simply the highly personal way in which mass political relationships worked and a way to build political parties. Such relationships were implicitly corrupt in their discriminatory effect, but their illegality was doubtful, and given the relative lack of autonomy from political control of the police and judiciary in that era, were never likely to generate large-scale corruption cases to test their status.

Ideologically rooted subcultural competition for its part generated two effects adversely impacting on corruption. It focused public debate on very broad ideological choices, not on pragmatic dimensions of policymaking, and secondly it gave the two dominant parties a natural political monopoly in their territorial heartlands. Because one of the two—the Italian Communist Party (PCI)—was stigmatized as ineligible for national government by a majority of the other parties, it also gave the other, the Christian Democrats, the status of permanent governing party. Both effects diminished incentives for those in power to focus on governance quality. When growth was high and taxes and borrowing could fund generous public spending, the governing parties could just about afford to ignore the impact on their electoral support of corrupt and poor-quality governance. Until 1992 the impact was corrosive but not catastrophic. Party leaders on balance preferred the very tangible money they earned from kickbacks to the hypothetical votes they might have earned from doing something about clientele politics and corruption. They also needed these resources for the purposes of intra-party factional competition. So for four decades, Italy's political culture had fewer incentives to address corruption and clientelism than parties in more competitive systems.

After 1992, when growth slowed and the cost of public borrowing soared, *Tangentopoli* forced corruption higher up the political agenda, and the impact of corruption switched from the merely corrosive to the catastrophic. Both main governing parties, the Christian Democrats and the Socialists, were destroyed almost overnight, and party politics became, for the first time, openly competitive and bi-polar. Voters had a choice, and appeared to be ready to focus on governance quality. Yet as we have seen, these changes turned out not to generate the paradigm shift toward clean government that many Italians had hoped for. The judicial authorities for a time were more successful in their pursuit of at least some perpetrators of corruption, but corruption cases continued to erupt, many of a large-scale and serious nature. Regional government, which in the 1990s saw significant expansion of its role, was a new repository for corruption. Political parties became, if anything, even more rapacious in their use of public resources, and the lifestyles of political leaders seemed ever more detached from ordinary voters.

The puzzle that students of Italian corruption have grappled with in the last two decades has therefore been that the broad path-dependent explanation rooted in elements of the political culture just outlined no longer seems an adequate account, even if elements of it still seem significant. In any case, the pattern of corruption that emerged from the 1990s onwards did not any longer entirely square with the model we have described. For example, more instances of corruption appeared to emerge in the economically advanced areas of the country—*Tangentopoli* exposed corruption rooted largely in Lombardy—while a larger number of major scandals seemed to involve banks, businesses, and public-service suppliers at national level, and were increasingly associated with illicit party funding. Moreover, while after 1994 there was a fundamental reworking of the Italian party system, this did not translate into great political successes for parties or movements that made the demand for vigorous action against corruption an unambiguously central element of their political platform. There were anti-party protest movements aplenty. Some, such as the Northern League, quickly turned into quasi-establishment parties and eventually themselves became corrupt. Only Italia dei Valori could claim to make the ethical issue its central plank, and for its troubles it won 4.4 percent in the general election of 2008 and by the election of 2013 had all but disappeared. As we see in the next section, progress toward measures to address corruption was in fact notably slow until after 2011, and in some respects legislation passed by the governments of Silvio Berlusconi in the 2001–6 legislature put new obstacles in the way of anti-corruption drives.

Explanations of Italian corruption from the 1990s onwards have, not surprisingly, shifted in the direction of efforts at greater theoretical and social-scientific precision. The growing interest shown by development economists has clearly influenced this, with a series of articles seeking to model corruption processes in Italy.[17] For the most part these are rational-choice accounts, which focus on the structure of interests and incentives political actors hold, and the institutional incentives or disincentives to corrupt behavior extant in the system.[18] Most accounts seek to formalize and in principle quantify the factors already discussed in this article: the financial rewards; the probabilities of detection; the degree of protection against prosecution or electoral sanction actors can expect; and the degree of monopoly power over jobs, licenses, contracts, and so on that particular officials enjoy. Such models nevertheless seem unrealistic unless they can somehow incorporate a role for values. A clinical risk/reward calculus does not seem a realistic account of how office-holders' behavior is determined.

Taking up this challenge, Donatella Della Porta and Alberto Vannucci, two of the most prolific modern writers on Italian corruption, recognized the value of the economic account but provide a complementary analytical perspective which emphasizes, through close study of the judicial evidence that came to light after 1992, what they call a "hidden order or corruption" in Italy.[19] Ultimately, their insight is an elaboration of a very simple, norm-based explanation within an institutional framework. They see the key issue for an individual in deciding whether to act corruptly as being the extent of his or her insulation from norms and values which emphasize the collective good inherent in ethics and propriety. Values count, therefore, but they count to the extent that the density of complex and stable networks counteracting honesty reduces uncertainty and risk for the potentially corruptible political actors. A society like Italy, they say, having reached a high-corruption equilibrium, can sustain that level of corruption if it evolves and adapts in the face of new challenges. Della Porta and Vannucci see key adaptations in Italy in the rise of brokers and middle-men as, after *Tangentopoli*, party organization became weaker and less directly relevant as a conduit for corruption. They also see it in moves to shore up confidence in the invulnerability of networks of corruption in the face of judicial disruption by changing the law to make prosecution harder; and in the exploitation of new forms of public–private partnership.

The richness of this neo-institutional account is compelling. Its key elements are *expectations* and *densities*. If those with the capacity to act corruptly see corruption as a norm or a necessity, because they are surrounded by dense networks offering a high probability of avoiding detection and punishment, or a strong need to avoid isolation or discrimination at work by participating in corrupt activities themselves, then sustained judicial energy will be insufficient to eradicate corruption. Through this, the account certainly provides insights for policymakers in dealing with corruption, though, like the others, it remains a high-level account which seems resistant to verification or refutation other than through the extensive process-tracing that lies at the heart of the authors' methodology.

Responses to Corruption

If social scientists have struggled to provide a coherent explanation of Italy's high level of corruption, the Italian authorities seem to have done little better when trying to deal with it. One striking feature is the absence of a dedicated and holistic anti-corruption program for over a decade after the events of 1992. The office of the High Commissioner against Corruption was established only in 2003. Its first occupant, Gianfranco Tatozzi, a former appeal court judge, resigned in frustration after two years in office, citing poor resourcing and executive lack of interest in his work—and this lack of interest was from the center-left government not a right-wing one. The office was formally downgraded two years later by the incoming Berlusconi government, suffered various changes of name, and re-emerged under Mario Monti's government in 2012 as the National Anti-corruption Authority. Its main tasks are to stimulate improvements in the performance of central government departments in devising anti-corruption programs. Its staff is modest—around 20 as of 2014—and its role is not formally investigative or prosecutorial.[20]

One of its main goals is to shift the focus in Italian anti-corruption policy from detection and punishment to prevention, for which it recognizes that an enormous cultural change is required in both the political class and public officials. Clearly that does not mean in any sense going soft on the detection and prosecutorial side, but simply recognizing that to rely on more law and more prosecutions will not be enough. The evidence of the 1990s makes that clear. The consequence of *Tangentopoli* was an intense but short-term boost in judicial success rates, peaking in 1996, but thereafter tailing off to a pre-scandal norm. Seen in perspective, that peak was accounted for by the momentum of short-term cooperation with prosecutors by those involved in corruption as their protective networks collapsed. It was also aided by the political vacuum of the time, and by the exceptional cohesion and energy of the Milanese investigative team. Subsequently new and less penetrable networks re-emerged, existing networks raised their defenses, and the political class recovered its nerve. The latter was well aware that while the most egregious acts of administrative corruption could and should be suppressed, a wholesale confrontation with ethics and corruption in Italian public life would raise questions about relationships between parties and business, and the sources of financial support for politics, right across the political spectrum.

Meanwhile the reconstruction of the Italian center-right posed a new ethical issue in the shape of Silvio Berlusconi's evident conflict of interest as both a national political leader and, between 1994 and 2011, four-times prime minister, while owning (but not, in his account, controlling the policy of) formidable business interests, including Italy's main private-sector television network. From the moment he entered politics Berlusconi himself faced sustained judicial investigation in a series of cases not about the central ethical issue of conflict of interest itself, but about a host of other matters concerning his business interests.

The toxic nature of those issues for Italian politics over an exceptionally long period is hard to overemphasize. Italy had a prime minister who was almost constantly embroiled in judicial cases. These cases gradually moved from the lawfulness of particular business practices (tax avoidance schemes, behavior in take-over bids) to much more sensational matters, such as the bribery of members of the Italian Senate, under-age prostitution, abuse of office, and perverting the course of justice. The extensive guarantees inherent in the judicial process ensured that each case was long drawn-out, and several cases expired under the time limits, but eventually in 2013 Berlusconi received a definitive conviction (and suspended jail sentence) for tax evasion.

The political consequences themselves, in the fraught and enduring political stalemate that followed the collapse of his government in November 2011, were formidable, greatly complicating the process of coalition-building under the governments of Mario Monti, Gianni Letti, and Matteo Renzi. But no less significant in the fight against corruption were the long drawn-out judicial processes that preceded Berlusconi's first definitive conviction. To deal with it, the center-right developed a strong narrative that attacked the alleged political bias of the entire judicial system. It was a narrative that divided Italians, but struck a chord at least with those impatient with the undoubted inefficiency of the system, its slow and costly procedures, and the poor quality of much of its work. That this systemic inefficiency had little or nothing to do with the substantive cases against Berlusconi, still less with entrenched corruption in public life more generally, was a secondary issue. The center-right's counter-attack served to weaken the political momentum that might otherwise have continued in support of Italian judicial investigators and anti-corruption agencies after *Tangentopoli*. It fitted too with other electoral narratives played by the center-right in the 1990s and thereafter. The claim of persecution assisted the center-right in its efforts to counter charges that Forza Italia, Berlusconi's own party, benefited from connections with politicians in the south closely connected with organized crime. It also complemented the center-right's case, at times getting close to a collusive embrace of systematic tax evasion by Italian business, that the Italian fiscal system was a conspiracy against freedom and enterprise.

The Berlusconi issue therefore complicated rather than clarified efforts to address systemic corruption. The center-left was in power from 1996 to 2001 and again briefly from 2006 to 2008. Had it developed a less ambivalent attitude toward anti-corruption policy, the issue might have distilled out into a left-right issue. But the center-left itself was periodically embroiled in scandals. It certainly shared some of the concerns about the inefficiency of the judicial system, and it seemed at a loss to know how to deal with the Berlusconi issue. It took until after the 2013 general election for it to take a strong stand against Berlusconi's continued eligibility for public office, and even then only on the back of new legislation that disqualified those found definitively guilty of a criminal offence. But despite decrying Berlusconi's position at the polemical level, the center-left consistently shied away from tackling the conflict-of-interest issue head on. The result was that the center-left never put itself at the head of a determined public demand for a program that made anti-corruption measures a top government priority. This may in any case have been because from the mid-1990s onwards the issue was actually not of high salience to Italian voters. As we have seen, there were parties that expressed generic protest at the state of Italian politics (the radical left, the Northern League, and Italia dei Valori) but it was only after the financial crisis of 2008, and the great economic contraction that followed, that real anger built, and when it did so, it came in a destructive form, fuelling the electoral charge of the highly unsettling Five Star Movement. Corruption seems to have been part of the mix in this anger, particularly in connection with a growing perception that the political class was the one area of the public sector that was not being asked to take financial cuts. Indeed, the debate about the burgeoning cost of politics, subsidies to political parties, and excessive parliamentary salaries became a central ethics issue in the years after 2008.[21] Eventually, necessary cuts began to be imposed, but only long after the damage had been done, because here too, as with Silvio Berlusconi's attacks on the judiciary and on the taxation system, the political class as a whole, in its unwillingness to address its privileged position, had already undermined its legitimacy to set standards and values for the whole of public life.

It is this leadership level, as well as in the dense networks of collusive certainty explained by Della Porta and Vannucci, that Italy's high-corruption equilibrium seems particularly difficult to tackle. There is no obvious model that shows how a democracy moves away from a high-corruption equilibrium. Many advanced democracies offer models of low-corruption equilibria, in which a range of preventative measures including clearly defined ethical principles for public service, appear to be effective. But the causal difference between a society that simply articulates ethical principles—as, in formal terms, Italy does—and one in which public office-holders really internalize those values, and in which the moral costs of impropriety are high and certain, is hard to pin down. The opportunities for corruption will certainly not go away. Business structures and public infrastructure are constantly changing, offering ever-present opportunities for illegality. So a society that does not inoculate itself fully seems highly likely to revert to corruption even after the most formidable of shocks, as 1992 showed.

It is evident then that standards in Italian public life will only improve when there is strong leadership from the top, and when there are effective mechanisms to socialize public office-holders at lower levels. Leaders of the established parties were for long unable to set that tone. They had strong interest in securing contractual kickbacks to sustain parties that were out of touch with ordinary voters, and in using public diffidence or even hostility to public officials to justify the behavior of some key political leaders. Their parties depended on exploiting fiscal resources to fund lifestyles that eventually became grossly offensive to ordinary Italians. All these features of the party system neutralized their moral standing. They also blunted the political class's willingness and ability to throw resources at corruption elsewhere in public life. The result is that since the 1990s a set of values—new codes of conduct, new operating procedures, new so-called "sunshine laws"—has emerged from the still weak and under-resourced institutions charged with the ethical transformation. But they have continued to sit well above the political and administrative machinery they are supposed to penetrate. Voters who care sufficiently about party-political corruption have not yet found a way to signal to parties and their leaders that they want a different, less corrupt, party system. Public-sector managers and administrative leaders have been unable fully to infuse their own workforces with the spirit of new codes of conduct and operational procedures which change the behavior of the recalcitrant but sizable minority that remains willing to engage in corruption. All that said, spotting a turning point in public values and political behavior is impossible until well after a trend has become evident. The consequences of 1992 seemed striking and immediate in their impact on the governing parties but in retrospect were premature and superficial. The events of more recent years (this chapter was written in 2014), while ambiguous, nevertheless contain at least some grounds for hope that an understanding of the costs and dangers of corruption for the Italian economy and society are finally becoming better understood.

Notes

1. The literature on modern public ethics and corruption is formidable, having grown exponentially in the last two decades. See especially S. Rose-Ackerman (ed.) (2006), *International Handbook of the Economics of Corruption*, Cheltenham, Edward Elgar,

especially chapters 1–8, which cover the theoretical underpinnings of a number of the institutional issues covered in this chapter.

2. M. Philp (1997), "Defining Political Corruption," *Political Studies*, 45, 436–462.

3. For analyses of available data see, in summary A. Vannucci (2009), "The Controversial Legacy of 'Mani Puliti': A Critical Analysis of Italian Corruption and Anti-Corruption Policies," *Bulletin of Italian Politics*, 1.2, 236–238; in more detail Greco—Group of States against corruption (2009), *Evaluation Report on Italy*, Strasbourg, July 2, <http://www.coe.int/t/dghl/monitoring/greco/evaluations/round2/reports(round2)_en.asp>, and Ministro per la pubblica amministrazione e la semplificazione (2012), *La corruzione in Italia: per una politica della prevenzione*, Rome.

4. Greco—Group of States against corruption (2009), *Evaluation*, 6.

5. Camera dei Deputati: Comitato di studio (1996), *Rapporto al Presidente della Camera dei deputati*, Rome, 23 October, Comitato di studio per la prevenzione della corruzione; Alto Commissario Anticorruzione, *Il fenomeno della corruzione in Italia (1° mappa dell'Alto Commissario Anticorruzione)*, Rome, December 2007; Ministro per la pubblica amministrazione e la semplificazione, *La corruzione in Italia: per una politica della prevenzione*, Rome, 2012.

6. See respectively: Transparency International (2013) *Global Perceptions Index*, http://cpi.transparency.org/cpi2013/; and World Bank (2013) World Governance Indicators <http://info.worldbank.org/governance/wgi/>.

7. Commission of the European Union, Directorate General for Information: Special Eurobarometer 374, *Corruption*, February 2012.

8. Alto Commissario Anticorruzione, *Il fenomeno della corruzione*, 38–41; Ministro per la pubblica amministrazione e la semplificazione, *La corruzione*, 7–8.

9. See, inter alia, D. Della Porta and A. Vannucci (2007), "Corruption and Anti-Corruption: The Political Defeat of 'Clean Hands' in Italy," *West European Politics*, 30.4, 830–853.

10. Commission of the European Union, Directorate General for Information (2012): Eurobarometer, *Attitudes of Europeans towards Corruption*, 325, wave 72.2, Brussels, November, 2009, and Special Eurobarometer 374 (2012), *Corruption*.

11. Transparency International (2010), *Global Corruption Barometer*, 46 http://www.transparency.org/cpi2010/results, and *Global Corruption Barometer*, 2013, 33 http://cpi.transparency.org/cpi2013/results/.

12. Ibid., 39.

13. Scuola superiore della pubblica amministrazione (2012); <http://integrita.sspa.it/?page_id=6040>. The research builds on intuitions that are set out systematically in J. Svensson (2005) "Eight Questions about Corruption," *Journal of Economic Perspectives*, 19.3, 19–42.

14. *Corriere della Sera*, "Corruzione, gli italiani sfiduciati 'Qui siamo peggio del Ghana'," October 22, 2012.

15. The regional experience of corruption, including the spectacular cases of corruption in several of Italy's largest regions, most notably in 2011/12 in Lombardy and Lazio, is discussed in M. Cerruto (2013), "La delegitimazione della classe politica regionale," *Istituzioni del Federalismo*, 34.2, 477–507. The article also provides a useful and salutary insight into the generous pay that Italy's more than 1,000 full-time elected regional councilors enjoy, along with equally generous discretionary allowances.

16. E. Banfield (1958), *The Moral Basis of Backward Society*, New York: Free Press.

17. See for example A. Del Monte, Erasmo Pagagni (2007), "The Determinants of Corruption in Italy: Regional Panel Data Analysis," *European Journal of Political Economy*, 2, 379–396.

18. R. Klitgaard (1988), *Controlling Corruption*, Berkeley: University of California Press.

19. D. Della Porta and A. Vannacci (2012), *The Hidden Order of Corruption. An Institutional Approach*, Farnham: Ashgate. See also, by the same authors (1999), *Corrupt Exchanges: Actors, Resources and Mechanisms of Political Corruption*, New York: De Gruyter.

20. For an account of its work see ANAC (Autorita Nazionale Anti-Corruzione e per la valutazione e la trasparenza delle amministrazioni pubbliche) (2013), *Rapporto sul primo anno di attuazione della legge N. 190/2012*, Rome.

21. M. Giacone (2008), *Il costo della politica*, Milan: Franco Angel.

CHAPTER 47

···

WOMEN IN POLITICS

···

DONATELLA CAMPUS

ITALIAN women achieved the franchise quite late in comparison with other countries. During the fascist period, the female population had been politically mobilized through a number of organizations for women, but only in 1946, immediately after World War II, were women given the right to vote. In principle, the advent of the suffrage should have promoted the reach of equal participation in politics; however, the process of female political emancipation was only at its beginning. The parties of the new Italian Republic encouraged women's mobilization through the creation of their own female organizations,[1] but they were much less prone to promote their political representation in the institutions of the new-born Republic. Although the two main parties, the Christian Democratic Party (DC) and the Communist Party (PCI), had a large number of female voters and supporters, they never gave proportionate space to women.[2] It should be said that, albeit on the basis of different ideologies, both had a quite traditional view of the role of women in society. It has been observed that the leftist party, the PCI, also regarded female emancipation as "essentially an economic question," and Communists "were reluctant to address issues like inequality within marriage, sexuality and divorce."[3] As a consequence, for a long time, female politicians remained a minority, relegated to secondary roles and excluded from leadership positions. This scenario did not change even with the collapse of the First Republic and the emergence of new parties, as these were no more sensitive to the political mobilization of women and their representation in state institutions.[4]

Starting in the 1970s, a cultural change concerning the issues of reproduction, sexuality, and gender relations took place thanks to the role played by women's movements. Although they consisted of a constellation of groups with no proper unified national organization, "feminists were important in setting the agenda and posing the questions that made reform seem important."[5] During the decade 1970–80 there were many changes in Italian legislation toward equal opportunities and women's rights. Above all, a new Family Law (1975) was introduced to reflect a change from a patriarchal model to another more attentive to the interests of all family members (see Chapter 35, this volume). By defeating a fierce Catholic opposition, divorce had been legalized a few years before (1970). Other turning points were the 1977 Parity Law and the fight about abortion rights, which culminated with its legalization (1978 abortion law) and the referendum of 1981.[6]

Notwithstanding such achievements, the impact of Italian feminism on state institutions was limited. It should be said that the women's movement was characterized by a substantial "anti-institutionalism,"[7] that is to say it did not claim for a gender redistribution of power in formal political institutions, but rather chose to concentrate its efforts on a cultural transformation. As a consequence, despite the above mentioned advancements of the 1970s and 1980s in relation to gender and family relations, the male monopoly over formal politics and state institutions proved to be resistant to any call for equality.[8] In particular, during those years, the problem of the scarcity of women in elected and executive offices was never prioritized.[9]

By the 1990s, among many other developments in the strategies and organization of women's groups (see Chapter 49, this volume), growing attention on the problem of female underrepresentation in government and in the policy process revitalized the debate about how to elect and appoint more women and to further women's concerns through public policies.[10] Although the implementation of equal treatment for women in politics is still ongoing, in recent years some goals have been achieved in terms of women's presence in formal political institutions and of action programs for women. The following sections will deal with specific questions about similarities and differences in the political activism of women and men, about female political representation in legislatures and assemblies, and about women's presence within the ruling elites and amongst the top policymakers.

THE POLITICAL PARTICIPATION
OF ITALIAN WOMEN

Although differences in political activism vary in different activities and contexts, an extended literature has highlighted the existence of recurrent gender disparities when it comes to traditional modes of political participation.[11] In Italy, in a general framework of fundamental disinterest in politics and low participation—as systematically observed by all empirical studies since the seminal book *The Civic Culture* by Almond and Verba[12]—the female population has always been in line with international trends that show women as less politically active.[13] Women participate less than men in most common forms of political activism, such as taking part in street demonstrations or in rallies, volunteering for a political party or a candidate, or donating funds to parties.[14] Predictably enough, differences between the sexes diminish with the increase of education and socioeconomic status. However, what is worth noting is that they are also decreasing in the younger cohorts of citizens,[15] confirming the well-known thesis by Inglehart and Norris that gender difference is likely to diminish over time.[16]

Another fundamental aspect is that Italian women are less interested in politics than men.[17] This attitude may well be connected to a lower female exposure to political information. As a matter of fact, empirical research confirms that women collect less political information than men.[18] However, such gender differences should not be overemphasized, since, as observed above, a lack of interest in politics is a common phenomenon and affects the whole Italian population. Nevertheless, the attitude of women toward politics appears somewhat different under selected qualitative dimensions. Some aspects must be stressed: for instance, according to a report on the relationship between women, politics, and institutions in Italy,[19] a not negligible percentage of respondents (42 percent) is still convinced that men are more competent on political issues. Among them, answers do not differ greatly by gender: a high percentage of women (41 percent) said men are more knowledgeable. This may suggest the existence of a female preference for keeping political orientation a private matter, and perhaps less of a predisposition to involve themselves in public. Female political discussion also usually occurs within families as Italian women in general list relatives, and especially husbands, among the people with whom they most frequently discuss politics.[20]

Notwithstanding the low levels of interest in politics and participation, it is nonetheless true that in Italy for a long time the voting turnout has been very high, and women are no exception. In particular, in the first decades of the Italian Republic, the prevalence of the so-called vote of belonging, based on strong political subcultures, guaranteed mass electoral support to the main political parties.[21] Political identities were shared by whole families and communities. Therefore, even if women participated less than men in political activities, and most of them continued to be excluded from higher political offices, they voted in proportions similar to men.

Owing to the many changes in the political system that occurred in the early 1990s, electoral participation has largely decreased, from over 90 percent in the years before 1979 to 75 percent in the 2013 elections. Women's abstention appears now slightly above that of men (around 3 percent difference in the 1990s and 2000s).[22] A gender gap is particularly evident in the older population, but it is reduced, if not reversed, among younger cohorts.[23] On average, however, the differences in turnout between the two sexes are limited, and cannot be regarded as the indicator of a remarkable change.

On the other hand, voting behavior and ideological orientation patterns have been characterized by a notable evolution which has produced an evident reduction in gender differences. Especially in the first decades of the Italian Republic, women voted more for conservative parties, mainly for the Christian Democratic Party.[24] The primary reason lies in the fact that the influence exerted by the Catholic Church through its network of organizations and local parishes was likely to be stronger on women, who were more regular churchgoers. The Italian female inclination to vote more for right-wing parties—a phenomenon called the "traditional gender gap" —was actually consistent with the trend in several other countries, especially Catholic ones. In particular, De Vaus and McAllister found that in the early 1980s women were still significantly more conservative than men in a group of Western European countries, including Belgium, France, Spain, and Italy.[25]

According to the development theory of gender realignment at the cross-national level,[26] the phase of traditional gender gap has been followed by a decrease of the female support for conservative parties and, then, by a realignment with the parties of the left (the so-called "modern gender gap"). This trend has been visible in many countries and is commonly attributed to an increase in female education and occupational status and a process of secularization. In Italy studies have confirmed the existence of a process of dealignment that started in the 1970s and consisted of a female shift from conservative to left-wing voting. In contrast to other European countries, however, evidence for the appearance of a modern gender gap is more nuanced. According to Giger, Italy has also reached the usual modern gender gap at the end of the 1990s, albeit at a slower pace than other countries.[27] By contrast, after looking at elections between 1968 and 2006, Corbetta and Cavazza offer clear evidence of the disappearance of the traditional gender gap, but do not support the observation of a female realignment with the parties of the left.[28] It is worth noting that female voting preferences, in particular those of older women and housewives, have been considered a substantial determinant of Silvio Berlusconi's success.[29] In general, however, the analysis of the age cohorts has shown that, while a conservative attitude prevails among older women, younger generations are more leftist.[30] This is not only because men and women have become more socially similar, but above all because social differences—in education, employment, religiousness—influence voting choices in Italy much less than in the past. This is especially true for younger people.[31]

WOMEN AND POLITICAL OFFICES: THE END OF UNDERREPRESENTATION?

In 2013 women made up almost one-third of Italian Members of Parliament, a peak in the history of the Italian Republic. In the international rankings,[32] Italy now comes before countries such as France and the UK, and is closer to the percentages of female representatives in Germany and Spain. It is a notable improvement from the previous election of 2008 when women were only 20.3 percent of those elected. Above all, it is a clear difference from the past decades, when Italy stood behind the majority of European countries.

What has happened in the early years of the twenty-first century to boost the proportion of women legislators? A body of literature has highlighted that female representation depends on cultural, socioeconomic, and political factors.[33] While both the culture of gender equality and fair economic conditions are supposed to influence women's access to legislative offices, in this section we will focus especially on the third class of variables. Political variables include, on the one hand, party organization and candidate selection, that is to say how party elites control the access to the nomination of candidates; on the other hand, the electoral law, that is to say the voting formula, the characteristics of the lists, the dimension of districts, the number of seats in Parliament and, last but not least, the adoption of some forms of positive action.

In the 2013 Italian elections some important changes helped to increase female representation. A key role was played by gender quotas. The issue of quotas had been on the political agenda since the first years of the Second Republic, but its opponents were able to stop any attempt to introduce a mandatory quota law (only in 1995 were quotas introduced, but they were soon abolished).[34] Supporters of quotas either on the left or on the right were not influential enough to overcome the fundamental disinterest of the political class toward the issue of the scarce presence of women in the political institutions. Another important factor was the fact that, as mentioned above, Italian feminist groups have traditionally preferred to focus on other areas of political action. It has been observed that political representation was delegated to the men of the allied leftist parties.[35] As a consequence, without the pressure exerted by highly motivated social groups, for a long time the underrepresentation of women legislators has not entered public debate as a true problem for the quality of democracy.[36]

Given the obstacle posed to a quota law, pressure groups within parties pushed toward the adoption of so-called "soft" quotas, which are a form of voluntary positive action employed by parties to guarantee a certain share of women on their lists. Soft quotas are supposed to be weaker instruments than legislative quotas; however, in many countries they have proved to be a good measure for improving the overall context for women.[37] Of course, the effectiveness of soft quotas is strictly dependent on the compliance and collaboration of party leadership.[38] Already in the 2008 election the Partito Democratico (PD) employed party quotas, but at that time the absence of a regulation for the placement of women on closed lists meant a large number of them were allocated in unelectable positions. In 2013 the PD's soft quota interacted virtuously with the introduction of primary elections, which allowed voters to give two preferences, one of each gender. The combination of these two factors substantially improved the proportion of women in competitive positions on the lists. In general, primaries were crucial in enhancing female representation. Both the parties that have elected more women, the PD and the Movimento Cinque Stelle, have involved their party members in the selection of candidates. Such a method has increased the number of women placed in the closed party lists, and consequently the number of women elected to the Italian Parliament.

What should we expect in the future? In 2012 the electoral law for local elections was reformed by including some forms of positive action (Law 215/2012). Therefore, the number of female representatives in local politics has already increased and is supposed to continue increasing over time.[39] At the national level a new electoral law, already nicknamed "Italicum", has been recently approved (Law 6 May 2015, see details in Chapter 11, this volume). The Italicum adopts proportional representation (PR) and includes several forms of positive action. Lists of candidates are semi-open: in each district the first candidate is blocked and selected by parties, while all the other candidates are on an open list and elected on the basis of preferential voting. Among the heads-of- list candidates, neither gender should occupy more than 60 percent of the total number of the heads.

of-list candidates in all districts of each region. This means that, in the worst of cases, a party should have at least a 40 percent of women at the top of their lists in the districts of each region. The other candidates are in an open list that must alternate women and men. Moreover, voters may express up to two preferences, in favor of candidates of different gender (if both are of the same gender only the first preference will be considered valid). Apparently all such measures should enhance female representation. In any case it is worth noting that the new law has overcome the obstacles historically posed to the introduction of a quota law and marks a step forward in the direction of an equal gender representation.

Leadership Positions: A Continuing Marginality

If the number of women in elective offices has been slowly increasing, still relatively few women serve in positions of political leadership. In the higher echelons the influence of women is limited and totally disproportionate. It should be stated that such a state of affairs in politics mirrors the top positions in other spheres—from diplomacy to judiciary, from universities to the bank system.[40] In the world of business, the difficulties in breaking the glass ceiling for top managers have convinced legislators to introduce law quotas in managing boards (Legislation 120/2011). However, the absence of women in political leadership positions is especially striking. No woman has ever acted as President of the Republic or prime minister. No woman has ever been the leader of a large party. The only female politicians who have reached notable public visibility and popularity are Nilde Iotti, a Communist MP who was President of the House of Deputies for many years, and Emma Bonino, a long-time activist of the Radical Party, who served as European Commissioner and was proposed as a candidate for President of the Republic. Bonino also took part in several Italian governments in different roles (among others as Minister of Foreign Affairs in the Letta government). In this regard, it should be said that, at least, the composition of recent governments led by Mario Monti (2011–13), Enrico Letta (2013–14), and Matteo Renzi (2014–present) has marked a reduction of the gap between Italy and other industrial advanced democracies.[41] Before such developments, Italian governments mostly confined women in ministries that deal with the so-called "compassion issues," such as education, health care, environment, and equal opportunity.

The paucity of political women leaders in Italian politics is confirmed by further evidence in local administration: for example, the small number of Presidents of Regions (currently only 2 out of 20). Women mayors are a minority (11.8 percent) and mostly concentrated in small municipalities.[42] In sum, the top elective offices in local administration are still in the hands of men. The most common explanation is that women's political careers are penalized by party elites who tend to perpetuate a male dominance.

This should be regarded as the effect of the natural tendency of any party oligarchy to preserve its power, and therefore to limit access for new forces. However, gender differences in the predisposition toward political leadership and in the motivation for pursuing higher political offices should be taken into consideration. Empirical evidence has shown that women appear less ambitious than men and are less likely to think they are qualified to run for office.[43] In Italy, a body of research on politicians has confirmed the existence of notable gender differences in perceiving obstacles to a political career.[44] First of all, Italian female politicians complain that the political world is still under male dominance, and list a series of *external* obstacles posed by unfriendly party and media environments. However, a second critical factor concerns some *internal* obstacles. If political ambition is defined in terms of office-seeking without any service connotation, then women appear to be less ambitious than men. In comparing personality traits and values of Italian female politicians and voters, Caprara and colleagues found that politicians are more extrovert, energetic, and open than ordinary women, which sounds quite consistent with the choice of pursuing a political career.[45] However, those basic personality traits are not matched by differences in attitudes toward power. Indeed women politicians do not seem to value power more than other Italian women. Rather, they appear more concerned about achievements in terms of policies and collective outcomes. Further research concerning Italian politicians of both sexes confirmed previous findings that men tend to focus on self-enhancement values, including the achievement of power, whereas women give more importance to self-transcending values, including benevolence and universalism.[46]

Clearly such a predisposition for a different concept of politics, far from the traditional masculine ideals of power as strength and dominance over people, has substantial consequences for how women feel about leadership. This may be especially crucial in a country like Italy, where, owing to the historical scarcity of women leaders, political leadership is almost exclusively associated with a male image of power. Without a number of role models from whom to gain inspiration, it is not surprising that women are not at ease with the competiveness associated with leadership, and may see top positions as stressful and demanding. In light of this, a necessary step to reach gender equality in leadership does not require just the removal of external obstacles, but also a further investment in self-reflection and empowerment.

A final point to be stressed is the relationship between the mass media and women politicians. Women in politics complain that obtaining visibility for their ideas through the media is one of the hardest things to cope with.[47] This is not just a subjective perception. In fact, the 2012 electoral law on local elections included access to media among the issues to be ruled according to a principle of equal opportunity. The legislators' sensitivity to this topic highlights the existence of a problem concerning women politicians' lack of visibility or, at least, a concrete difficulty in obtaining fair and unbiased coverage. It should be stressed that such a phenomenon does not just concern Italy. The Global Media Monitoring Project,[48] which documents women's visibility in the world's news media, has found clear evidence of the fact that the media tend to reproduce patterns of gender inequality. In comparison with the world average (only 24 percent of the people heard or read about in print, radio, and TV news are female), however, the Italian female to male ratio is even lower: 18 percent versus 82 percent. If one focuses specifically on news subjects in topics relating politics and government, female subjects are only 14 percent of the total. Among politicians who are news subjects, the percentage of women is 11 percent versus 89 percent of men. In sum, female Italian politicians have good reason to complain about discrimination, especially if one makes a comparison with the larger coverage given to European colleagues.[49]

Above all, the significant Italian peculiarity is the gap between different kinds of visibility given to women in the news: whereas they are rare in the role of key actors or in the function of experts and spokespersons, they are much more visible as "common people" who offer their own opinion or proffer their personal experiences.[50] These findings confirm that there exists a general problem of acknowledging female authoritativeness and centrality in the public sphere. The continuous undervaluation of women in authoritative functions by the media reproduces and also reinforces the exclusion of women from the political leadership. As media coverage exerts considerable effects on women's electability, it is clear that this is an area of policy where legislators may intervene and, above all, journalistic professional codes should be reconsidered.

Notes

1. Perry Willson, *Women in Twentieth-century Italy* (Houndmills: Palgrave Macmillan, 2010), 130.
2. Alisa Del Re, "I paradossi di genere nella rappresentanza," in Franca Bimbi (ed.), *Differenze e diseguaglianze. Prospettive per gli studi di genere in Italia* (Bologna: Il Mulino, 2003), 215–240.
3. Willson, *Women in Twentieth-century Italy*, 131.
4. Del Re, "I paradossi di genere nella rappresentanza."
5. Willson, *Women in Twentieth-century Italy*, 158.
6. For details of the campaign for legalizing abortion, see Willson, *Women in Twentieth-century Italy*; Patrick Hanafin, *Conceiving Life. Reproductive Politics and the Law in Contemporary Italy* (Aldershot: Ashgate, 2007).
7. Anna Di Lellio, "Il femminismo," in Gianfranco Pasquino (ed.), *La Politica Italiana. Dizionario critico 1945–95* (Rome and Bari: Laterza, 1995), 235–245.
8. Donatella Della Porta, "The Women's Movement, the Left and the State: Continuities and Changes in the Italian Case," in Lee Ann Banaszak, Karen Beckwith, Dieter Rucht (eds.), *Women's Movements facing the Reconfigurated State* (Cambridge: Cambridge University Press, 2003), 48–68. Chiara Saraceno, "La protesta delle donne: un successo con molte ombre," in Anna Bosco and Duncan McDonnell (eds.), *Politica in Italia. Edizione 2013* (Bologna: Il Mulino, 2012), 219–236 extends the analysis to the most recent experiences of women's movements, such as "Se non ora quando?", born in 2011 to protest against the "objectivation" and sexualization of the image of women in Italian politics.
9. Marila Guadagnini, "Gendering the Debate on Political Representation in Italy: A Difficult Challenge," in Joni Lovenduski (ed.), *State Feminism and Political Representation* (Cambridge: Cambridge University Press, 2005), 130–152.

10. Del Re, "I paradossi di genere nella rappresentanza"; Della Porta, "The Women's Movement, the Left and the State: Continuities and Changes in the Italian Case."

11. Nancy Burns, Kay Lehman Schlozman, and Sidney Verba, *The Private Roots of Public Action*. (Cambridge, MA: Harvard University Press, 2001); Ronald Inglehart and Pippa Norris, *Rising Tide: Gender Equality and Cultural Change around the World* (Cambridge: Cambridge University Press, 2003).

12. Gabriel Almond and Sidney Verba, *The Civic Culture. Political Attitudes and Democracy in Five Nations* (Princeton, NJ: Princeton University Press, 1963). Luciano Bardi and Gianfranco Pasquino, "Politicizzati e Alienati," in A. Parisi and H. Schadee (eds.), *Sulla soglia del cambiamento. Elettori e partiti alla fine della Prima Repubblica* (Bologna: Il Mulino, 1995), 17–42.

13. Guido Legnante, "La partecipazione politica ed elettorale," in Marco Maraffi (ed.), *Gli italiani e la politica*. (Bologna: Il Mulino, 2007), 235–264.

14. Linda Sabbadini, *Partecipazione politica e astensionismo secondo un approccio di genere*, Istat. Istituto Nazionale di Statistica, 2006, <http://www.istat.it/istat/eventi/2006>; Istat, *La partecipazione politica: differenze di genere e territoriali. Anno 2009*, <http://www.istat. it>.

15. Istat, *La partecipazione politica: differenze di genere e territoriali. Anno 2009*.

16. Inglehart and Norris, *Rising Tide: Gender Equality and Cultural Change around the World*, 126.

17. For an analysis of determinants of interest in politics differentiated by gender see Paolo Segatti, "L'interesse per la politica: diffusione, origine, cambiamento," in Marco Maraffi (ed.), *Gli italiani e la politica*. (Bologna: Il Mulino, 2007), 39–72.

18. Istat, *La partecipazione politica: differenze di genere e territoriali. Anno 2009*, tab.5.

19. Rinaldo Vignati, *Donne, politica e istituzioni* (Compa e Istituto Cattaneo, 2004).

20. Mattei Dogan, "Political Discussion, Views of Political Expertise and Women's Representation in Italy," *European Journal of Women's Studies*, 17(3) (2010), 249–267.

21. Arturo Parisi and Gianfranco Pasquino, "Relazioni partiti-elettori e tipi di voto," in Arturo Parisi and Gianfranco Pasquino (eds.), *Continuità e mutamento elettorale in Italia*, (Bologna: Il Mulino, 1977), 215–249.

22. Sabbadini, *Partecipazione politica e astensionismo secondo un approccio di genere*; Dario Tuorto, "La partecipazione al voto," in Paolo Bellucci and Paolo Segatti (eds.), *Votare in Italia: 1968–2008*. (Bologna: Il Mulino, 2010), 53–82.

23. Tuorto, *La partecipazione al voto*.

24. Mattei Dogan, "Le donne italiane tra cattolicesimo e marxismo," in Alberto Spreafico and Joseph La Palombara (eds.), *Elezioni e comportamento politico in Italia* (Milano: Edizioni di Comunità, 1963), 475-94; David De Vaus and Ian McAllister, "The Changing Politics of Women: Gender and Political Alignment in 11 Nations," *European Journal of Political Research* 17(3) (1989), 241–262; Piergiorgio Corbetta and Nicoletta Cavazza, "From the Parish to the Polling Booth: Evolution and Interpretation of the Political Gender Gap in Italy 1968–2006," *Electoral Studies*, 27 (2008), 271–284; Piergiorgio Corbetta and Luigi Ceccarini, "Le variabili socio-demografiche: generazione, genere, istruzione e famiglia," in Paolo Bellucci and Paolo Segatti (eds.), *Votare in Italia: 1968–2008* (Bologna: Il Mulino, 2010), 83–148.

25. De Vaus and McAllister, "The Changing Politics of Women: Gender and Political Alignment in 11 Nations."

26. Inglehart and Norris, *Rising Tide: Gender Equality and Cultural Change around the World*.

27. Nathalie Giger, "Towards a Modern Gender Gap in Europe? A Comparative Analysis of Voting Behavior in 12 Countries," *The Social Science Journal* 46 (2009), 474–492.

28. Corbetta and Cavazza, "From the Parish to the Polling Booth: Evolution and Interpretation of the Political Gender Gap in Italy 1968–2006."

29. Mario Caciagli, "Come votano le donne," in Mario Caciagli and Piergiorgio Corbetta (eds.), *Le ragioni dell'elettore* (Bologna: Il Mulino, 2002), 113–138.

30. However, the exception of 2008 elections when young males voted for the left more than their female counterparts raises a question if the trend must be considered as irreversible. See Corbetta and Ceccarini, *Le variabili socio-demografiche: generazione, genere, istruzione e famiglia.*

31. Corbetta and Cavazza, "From the Parish to the Polling Booth: Evolution and Interpretation of the Political Gender Gap in Italy 1968–2006."

32. In 2013 women elected in the House of Deputies were 198 (31.4 percent); in the Senate 92 (28.9 percent). As for the single or the lower houses, these are the percentages in other countries: World average 21.2 percent; European average 24.4 percent; France 26.9 percent; Germany 32.9 percent; Spain 36 percent; UK 22.5 percent. All data from <http://www.ipu.org/iss-e/women.htm>, accessed June 10, 2013.

33. For a review and a discussion of the existing literature see Manon Trembley, "Conclusion," in Manon Trembley (ed.), *Women and Legislative Representation* (Houndmills: Palgrave Macmillan, 2012, 2nd ed.), 239–254.

34. Del Re, "I paradossi di genere nella rappresentanza"; Marila Guadagnini, "Gendering the Debate on Political Representation in Italy: a Difficult Challenge."

35. Della Porta, "The Women's Movement, the Left and the State: Continuities and Changes in the Italian Case," 65.

36. Guadagnini, "Gendering the Debate on Political Representation in Italy: a Difficult Challenge."

37. Anne Stevens, *Women, Power and Politics* (Houndmills: Palgrave Macmillan, 2007), 106.

38. Trembley, "Conclusion," 250.

39. A first analysis of data from the 2013 local elections shows that the number of women in municipal councils doubled. <http://cise.luiss.it/cise/2013/06/13/doppia-preferenza-raddoppiano-le-donne-nei-consigli-comunali/> accessed July 1, 2013.

40. For a general discussion, see Saraceno, "La protesta delle donne: un successo con molte ombre."

41. Mario Monti cabinet (November 2011–April 2013), set a record with the appointment of three women in key ministries: Anna Maria Cancellieri as Minister of Internal Affairs; Elsa Fornero as Minister of Labour and Welfare; Paola Severino as Minister of Justice (the first in the history of the Italian Republic); in Enrico Letta's cabinet (April 2013–February 2014) female ministers are 7 out of 21; Matteo Renzi's cabinet (from February 2014) has reached parity, with 50 percent women.

42. ANCI (2013), La rappresentanza di genere nelle amministrazioni comunali italiane, <http://www.anci.it/Contenuti/Allegati/Dossier%20La%20rappresentanza%20di%20genere%20nelle%20amministrazioni%20comunali%20italiane.pdf>.

43. Jennifer Lawless and Richard Fox, *It Takes a Candidate. Why Women do not Run for Office.* (Cambridge: Cambridge University Press, 2005).

44. Donata Francescato, Minou Mebane, Mauro Giacomantonio, and Marco Lauriola, "Glass-Ceiling or Labyrinths? Confronting Two Competing Hypotheses on why Women still have Limited Access to Powerful Positions in Politics," paper presented at

the International Society of Political Psychology Conference, Paris, July 2008; Donata Francescato, Minou Mebane, Mauro Giacomantonio, and Marco Lauriola, "The Construction of Two Short Factor-marker Scales measuring Women Perceived Obstacles (WIPOS) and Women's Coping Efficacy (WIPOCS) in Politics," *TPM* 15 (3) (2008), 113–165; Donata Francescato and Minou Mebane, "Donne politiche," in Patrizia Catellani and Gilda Sensales (eds.), *Psicologia della Politica* (Raffaello Cortina: Milano, 2011), 253–270.

45. Gianvittorio Caprara, Donata Francescato, Minou Mebane, Roberta Sorace, and Michela Vecchione, "Personality Foundations of Ideological Divide: A Comparison of Women Members of Parliament and Women Voters in Italy," *Political Psychology* 31 (2010), 739–762. The article also shows that, with respect to a list of basic values, in the top positions there are benevolence (preservation and enhancement of the welfare of people with whom one is in frequent personal contact) and universalism (understanding, appreciation, tolerance, and protection for the welfare of all people and for nature). It is worth noting, however, the existence of some associations between values and ideological orientations: tradition, power, and security were related to center-right affiliations; universalism was related to center-left affiliations.

46. Minou Mebane, Donata Francescato, and Michele Vecchione, "Do successful women politicians maintain more feminine values and traits compared to their male colleagues?" Paper presented at International Conference of Psychology, Capetown, 2012.

47. Francescato, Mebane, Giacomantonio, and Lauriola "Glass-Ceiling or Labyrinths? Confronting Two Competing Hypotheses on why Women still have Limited Access to Powerful Positions in Politics"; Francescato and Mebane, *Donne politiche*.

48. Global Media Monitoring Project, *Who makes the news?*,2010. http://www.whomakesthenews.org.

49. For instance, in Spain 25 percent; in Germany 20 percent, in Greece 27 percent.

50. As for the functions of news subjects, Italian female percentages are: Experts (12 percent); Spokespersons (17 percent); Subjects (18 percent); Eye witnesses (31 percent); Personal experience (44 percent); Popular Opinion (67 percent). While also the global average for first three functions are quite low (29 percent; 19 percent, 23 percent), there is a notable difference for the second group of functions (29 percent; 36 percent; 44 percent), for which Italy has a score higher than the average.

CHAPTER 48

....

IMMIGRATION

....

GIUSEPPE SCIORTINO

THE dominant icon of international migration to Italy is the overcrowded boat crossing the Mediterranean, ferrying destitute immigrants bound for a life of makeshift camps and odd jobs. To realize how dominant this iconic perception is, it is enough to search for "immigration" and "Italy" in Google Images, then have a quick scan of the results. As for the policies enacted by the Italian state, it is usually taken for granted, in the academic literature and in international public opinion alike, that they are utterly irrational, largely ineffective, and more than occasionally cruel. The attitudes of Italian society toward foreign immigrants are summarized with equal ease as immature, complacent, and frequently racist.

As with most stereotypes, there is a kernel of truth. Boats do indeed cross the Mediterranean in perilous and often fatal journeys. The southern Mediterranean is one of the most dangerous maritime areas for migrants and refugees, where thousands of deaths have been recorded in recent years. Italy has a sizeable irregular foreign population, estimated in 2012 at around half a million. Makeshift camps and vagrant sites exist in several locations, particularly in the south, especially during the labor-intensive phases of agricultural activities. There is a recorded presence of sweatshops, which employ foreign workers in appalling working (and living) conditions.

The country is also known for its frequent changes in immigration legislation. One of the favorite Italian policy tools has traditionally been the regular enactment of amnesties.[1] A large section of the foreign population in Italy has acquired its legal status through one of these, after a spell of irregular work and abode. It is equally true that Italian political discourse shows a widespread tolerance for offensive statements and essentialist rhetorical tropes, particularly in reference to Islam.[2]

To make a general portrait out of these broad brushstrokes, however, would be a mistake. The dominant vision of immigration in Italy may appear self-evident, but it is actually complacent and sometimes orientalist. It is a serious obstacle in developing an adequate analysis of the Italian migratory experience; and it conceals the fact that the Italian case is a variation on broader European trends. The elements highlighted by these stereotypes play well on television, but are far from being the most structurally relevant, as well as being increasingly inaccurate.

Most irregular migrants in Italy, as in any other European country, are not clandestine but have entered legally and subsequently overstayed their visas.[3] During the last decades, illegal border crossing has become difficult, as demonstrated by increasingly risky travel and the steep increase in prices requested by smugglers.[4] The boats so often seen on television are nearly exclusively carrying refugees, whose entry is not a matter of ineffective border controls but of the legal protection guaranteed by the non-refoulement principle of international refugee laws. Many of the immigrants they carry see Italy as a transit point, as they already have relatives (and plans) in other European countries. The volume of arrivals varies substantially from one season to another, contingent upon geopolitical constraints. A large majority of the current incomers are citizens of other EU member states, family members legally reunited, and migrants who enter the country with a regular visa and subsequently overstay.[5] The size of Italy's irregular foreign population, numbering in the hundreds of thousands, does not seem to be extraordinary in the EU context.[6] The recent downturn in the economy has strongly reduced the attractiveness of irregular migration, while the EU Eastern Enlargement, besides regularizing overnight a large number of irregular residents, has also provided a large number of foreign workers with a regular status. Irregular migrants are consequently a small minority of the foreign population living in Italy.[7]

There is room to argue that the received view embedded in the dominant stereotype is unable to account for a phenomenon that is clearly more complex and multilayered. It surely obscures the features of immigration that are bound to be the most fateful in the long term for the Italian economy. Foreign workers play an increasingly crucial role in managing the enduring difficulties of keeping a stagnating economy afloat and adjusting to a conservative-style welfare state with an aging population. Only by taking into account this context does it become possible to understand some important features of Italian immigration policy, such as the recurring use of amnesties and a stable commitment, in spite of recurrent failures, to an active labor immigration policy for low-skilled foreign workers.

DESPITE THE DOWNTURN: ITALY'S ENDURING LABOR IMMIGRATION

There is no doubt that Italy has been experiencing a massive immigration flow. The 4,387,721 foreign citizens registered as regular residents at the beginning of 2013, making up a little less than 7 percent of the population, may not seem particularly impressive in comparison with other Western countries; but their number has more than tripled in less than a decade. Between 2005 and 2010, the immigrant population in Italy has increased, on average, by 400,000 individuals each year, the vast majority of which are new arrivals. Italy has also been one of the countries most affected by the eastern enlargement of the EU. With more than a quarter of the current foreign population made up of EU citizens—entitled from the beginning to a consistent set of legal, social, and (limited) political rights—the whole migratory scenario has changed dramatically in a few years.

The recent economic downturn has severely curtailed the growth rate of the foreign population, but it has not completely frozen labor mobility. In 2009, when Italy recorded one of the worst gross domestic product (GDP) performances in the last 30 years, the foreign population actually increased more than in the previous year. In February 2011, when the website designed to receive applications for the 98,000 work visas allotted by the government for non-EU workers was activated, nearly 400,000 applications were filed in less than two days, half of them within the first 30 minutes. By the end of 2012, 134,576 employers had filed applications for the latest of a long series of amnesty programs for irregularly employed foreign workers. No matter how gloomy the macroeconomic outlook of the country is, Italy remains an attractive migratory destination.[8]

In many ways, immigration to Italy is very similar to the classical European labor migration of the 1960s in northern European countries. It is, in fact, overwhelmingly an inflow of foreign *workers*, bound to fill shortages in low-skilled labor sectors, and later their families (the only concession to the postmodern condition being that the typical first migrant is now often a woman). The foreign population in Italy is characterized by a comparatively high labor market participation rate. Even the participation rate of foreign women, if much lower, is still higher than the EU average. More remarkably, the percentage of foreign residents in gainful employment is markedly higher than that of Italian citizens in the same cohorts.

Another strong similarity with the classical European labor migration of bygone days is reflected in the fact that current migratory flows largely consist of manual laborers. Seventy-six percent of foreign workers in 2009 were employed in low-skilled occupations (compared to 32 percent of natives). A full third of unskilled workers in the Italian economy have a non-Italian citizenship.[9]

The current migratory dynamics are to be understood in the context of the Italian economy's evolving structure. Over the last decade, long before the downturn, Italy's economic performance has been comparatively dismal, with a sharp decrease in the growth of the real GDP caused largely by the lack of growth in labor productivity.[10] A large portion of the Italian economy is concentrated in construction and labor-intensive services. These sectors, largely shielded from globalized competition, are characterized by an extremely large number of small companies and businesses that are unable to realize significant economies of scale or to use the factors of production efficiently. Other than resorting to tax evasion, their survival and profitability is increasingly based on lowering labor costs and increasing the flexibility of working hours and labor contracts. These are the sectors that have been among the main beneficiaries of the labor market reforms carried out since 2000, which have been primarily centered on protecting labor market "insiders"—the baby boomer cohort—while at the same time implementing strong deregulation targeted at increasing flexibility at the margins.[11] Employees in these sectors—being exactly the kind of workers the welfare state was originally designed to protect—have enjoyed a relatively high level of protection from the traditional risks of the industrial working class. But they have paid for such protection with severe constraints on wages matched by comparatively high levels of taxation. Wage moderation notwithstanding, the loss of productivity growth has made Italy one of the Western European countries with the highest cost of labor per product unit. In all sectors, a vicious circle of loss of product competitiveness and labor deskilling has become increasingly evident.

The "bright" side of these dynamics has been the emergence of a strong demand for unskilled, cheap labor. During the last decade, the absolute number of employed individuals has markedly increased, and (before the economic downturn) the number of jobseekers had reached a historical low. The main problem, however, was that a supply of low-skilled, poorly paid, and highly flexible jobs does not match the expectations of young Italians. Even if the education revolution in Italy has been late and is still uneven, its effects are increasingly at odds with an economy that is structurally unable to provide the medium- and high-skilled jobs that new entrants to the labor market seek. This explains why native jobseekers are nearly always young people looking for their first jobs. Coupled with the fact that they usually live with their parents, many of them are able to wait for a "proper" job, even in times of economic downturn. The past two decades have strengthened Italy's dual labor market, where there is a large supply of potential workers for the limited number of middle- and high-skilled jobs, while at the same time a growing demand for low-skilled and unskilled workers faces a tight labor market.

Immigration to Italy has always been tightly intertwined with the growing demand for low-skilled, low-paying jobs. Seen in this context, the (often maligned) Italian habit of enacting frequent amnesty programs for the irregular resident population appears quite effective. These programs have transferred a large number of immigrants from the shadow economy to the formal, low-skilled labor sector, where they were badly needed. Once in the lower strata of Italian occupational structure, however, foreign workers have found it remarkably difficult to move up the ladder, even if only to slightly more qualified jobs. The (comparative) ease with which a foreign worker may find a job in the country is paid for by the lack of chances for subsequent occupational mobility.[12] The economic downturn seems to have strengthened and further accelerated this dynamic. The crisis has hit the middle-skilled and high-skilled strata, where foreign workers are underrepresented, particularly hard. At the same time, it has triggered further pressure towards a compression of labor costs. This has translated, in turn, to an enduring demand for foreign workers. The best example of this dynamic is provided by the construction sector, which according to the latest data employs 17 percent of the foreign workforce (nearly exclusively males). Since 2009, the downturn has caused an intense (and still incomplete) restructuring of the sector. This does not imply, however, the consolidation of firms into larger units that are able to operate in more complex markets, but rather their further fragmentation. There has been both a sharp decrease in the number of skilled and semi-skilled jobs (largely the province of native workers) and a feeble increase in low-skilled jobs, a large number of which have been filled by foreign workers.

Even if the economic downturn has had only a mild impact on the employment rate of immigrants, it has, however, produced consequences that are reflected in the quality of their jobs and their living standards. Foreign workers are much more likely to be employed in unstable jobs, experiencing much more frequent spells of unemployment than natives.[13] They are three times more likely than natives to be underemployed, and their career chances do not improve with immigration seniority. In recent years, the salary gap between natives and immigrants has widened and the percentage of working poor in foreign households has increased. The traditional dualism of the Italian labor market, in short, is becoming not only sharper but also increasingly polarized in "ethnic" terms.

IMMIGRATION AS A PILLAR
OF THE WELFARE STATE

The interplay of immigration flows and labor markets dynamics is contingent upon the structure and strains of the Italian welfare regime. The Italian welfare state is strongly worker-oriented, centered around the male breadwinner model and tailored to provide services primarily through social insurance, which is contingent upon previous work performance. In principle, this model should be neutral in terms of the native/immigrant distinction, as all its benefits are by definition open to all members of salaried occupations. A specific feature of the Italian welfare state, however, makes immigrants de facto net contributors: Italian social expenditure is largely focused on servicing pensions, both for retirees and survivors (Italy spends roughly twice as much as the Organisation for Economic Co-operation and Development (OECD) average on pensions). The main reason foreign workers contribute much more than they receive from pension funds is demographic. Among the resident foreign population, there are eight adults of working age out of any ten foreign residents, with the remaining two usually minors. In principle, this difference should disappear in the long run, with the aging of current immigrant workers; but in reality this will not be the case. In 1996, when it had become clear that the Italian pension system—based on pay-as-you-go defined benefit principles—was no longer sustainable, it was reformed by switching to a defined-contribution system. The transition has been arranged in a way that kept the benefits of the previous system largely intact for those already within it, while the new—and much less generous—system was to be applied to all new entrants. The vast majority of foreign workers, and all Italian youngsters, fall into the latter category. This situation provides further incentive for the Italian state to be very generous with the regularization of employed immigrants.

The weight of pension expenditures on the budget, as well as the pressing need to service Italy's outstanding national debt, implies that many other types of welfare program are non-existent or heavily underfunded, leaving all new social risk configurations (including those typical of large-scale immigration flows) disregarded.[14] In contrast to other European countries, immigrants are very unlikely to become welfare burdens, however hard they try.

At the same time, it is possible to argue that immigration has become one of the main pillars of the Italian welfare regime.[15] The Italian Republic, like other conservative-style welfare states in Europe, entrusts its main welfare tasks to households, supporting them through monetary transfers rather than through the direct provision of services. Italian households consequently operate as general contractors, integrating the services they may self-produce with the small services in kind they can acquire from public bodies and the services they acquire on the market. Like any general contractor, they constantly face a *make-or-buy* choice. The self-production of services, however, has become an increasingly difficult strategy for Italian households in the last decades. Living standards have improved. The number of dual-career households has increased, albeit slowly. Lower rates of fertility have produced smaller households. The aging of the population has increased the number of households where one (or more) members cannot satisfy basic exigencies through internally generated activities, in a context marked by a pervasive cultural resistance to entrust elderly persons to institutions (regardless of their actual or potential quality). These trends create a strong demand for services acquired outside the household. As the supply of state-provided services has been stable or has even shrunk, much of the demand has been directed toward the private market for personal services.

The main problem, however, is that purchasing personal and household services is not easy. The mechanism is part and parcel of what is known in the literature as *Baumol Cost Disease*.[16] Because the productivity of personal services cannot be increased easily through organizational and technical means, and the salaries of service workers may stay in line with what is considered a "decent" wage, the necessary services will be too costly for many households. Wages will outpace productivity, thereby pricing the services out of the market. If, on the contrary, salaries offered in the service sector follow its productivity, the jobs provided by this sector will be highly unappealing and avoided by all those who can do so. In both cases, the lack of an adequate supply of affordable services puts a serious strain on the relationship between the male breadwinner model, embedded in the conservative-style welfare regime, and the realities of an aging population and an increasing female labor participation rate. Immigration may thus be considered a creative adaptation to the challenge of preserving the established welfare regime in a changing social environment.

Since the early 1970s, immigrants have helped to ease the strain, providing market-based personal and household services to Italian households at affordable prices.[17] Once it began, the flow of domestic workers quickly reached a self-perpetuating stage. Workers already active in the local labor market act as triggers for further waves of new arrivals, using their own reputations as guarantees for the reliability of new workers.

The importance of the migratory dimension of the domestic services market is easy to document. It is the only sector of the Italian economy largely dominated by foreign workers: for each native employed in this sector, there are three foreign workers. It is the sector that absorbs 40 percent of all female foreign workers and 20 percent of overall foreign employment. The demands of carework, moreover, are structural rather than cyclical. Half of the jobs for foreign workers since the economic downturn have been in this sector. It has provided the background for original women-only migratory systems, which have sometimes been able to develop into a mass phenomenon in a short space of time.[18]

The demand for domestic services is also among the main preconditions for large-scale irregular migration flows. Live-in carework, the usual entry job in this sector, provides food and housing as part of the salary and, because it takes place within private homes, is effective in shielding the migrant (and the employer) from all kinds of controls. Not by chance, while the presence of irregular immigrants in other sectors has been decreasing over time, the opposite has occurred in the domestic service sector. It currently provides a little less than half of all jobs available to irregular migrants.[19] As will be seen in the next section, the growing importance of foreign domestic work as a pillar of the welfare regime has increasingly shaped the priorities of Italian immigration policy.

THE DISMAL FATE OF THE ITALIAN ACTIVE LABOR MIGRATION POLICY

Italy is one of the very few Western European countries that has always acknowledged the need for low-skilled foreign workers. Such acknowledgment has also implied an effort to implement an active labor immigration policy.[20] Such policies, however, have largely failed in preventing the development of large-scale irregular flows, ending up acting as a tool for their quick regularization "from within." They have also quickly abandoned the promotion of an *immigration choisie*, restricting themselves to the management of the labor demand within the domestic services sector. Both outcomes are partially linked to some peculiarities of the Italian case; but they are also contingent upon the difficulties that *any* active policy would encounter when applied to the labor demand in a low-growth economy.

The basic assumption of Italian labor migration policy is predicated upon the assumption that the encounter between foreign labor supply and demand has to occur before immigration begins. Employers must file a request for a specific worker while he or she is still abroad. The state authorizes such requests if they are compatible with the so-called *carrying capacity* of the country, a notion that may be roughly interpreted as the volume of new entries that is compatible with the available supply of jobs, housing, and social services.[21] The main policy tool is the yearly decree that establishes new work visas and sets the criteria for their allocation.

For approximately two decades, however, planning for the flows of foreign labor has proved elusive. Previously, planning was largely ritual, as the main source of legal foreign labor was provided by periodic amnesties. When, at the end of the 1990s, the new policy was actually implemented, there was a generalized expectation in the country, shared by employers and immigrants alike, that hiring an irregular immigrant and waiting for the next amnesty was the easiest and cheapest option.

Since 1998, the size of the established contingents of immigrants has become noticeable, and has been accompanied by administrative efforts to make the policy work. Its impacts, however, have always largely been disconnected from the intended economic goal, for reasons both internal to the policy process and to the ways in which various social actors have reacted to it.

As an internal process, the main difficulty in utilizing the yearly decree consistently in tandem with a policy of labor market reform has been the prioritization of control measures over integration measures. One of the main reasons that Italy began seriously promoting an active labor immigration policy was the need to "make a deal" with the main sending and transit countries such as Albania, Tunisia, and Morocco. Since 1998, Italy has started to reserve a large proportion of the entry slots for citizens of these countries in exchange for their collaboration in emigration control and readmission of their deported citizens. This exchange has been relatively effective, contributing to diminishing rates of clandestine immigration and higher rates of deportations. But it has also had the consequence of making a large part of the labor contingent irrelevant with regard to skill-based criteria.

A second and important difficulty is related to the neo-corporatist framework, with the involvement of trade associations and trade unions, within which the planning process takes place. The actors involved are representatives of mature, and comparatively large-scale, industrial sectors, which are absorbing only a small percentage of incoming foreign labor. The employers who are actually using the most foreign labor—small farms, small businesses, and households—are not usually members of organized interest bodies and are thus excluded from the game. A third problem is that while amnesties may always be presented as remedial action for previous governments' mistakes, the setting of a yearly contingent makes governments appear as if they actually desire further immigration, thus providing a weapon for all kinds of populist movements.

The most fateful factor, however, is related not to the policy process, but rather to the radical mismatch that has emerged between the *conceptual* design of immigration policy and the actual dynamics of labor markets.

First, Italian labor migration policy presupposes an ordered world of treaties between states, a restricted number of employers that are able to plan their labor demand over the medium term, and the functioning of neocorporatist committees able to police their constituencies and negotiate realistic options. Immigration to Italy is embedded in a strikingly different reality. Although foreign workers have been able to join the industrial working class, it has occurred primarily in small enterprises. Most of the current demand for foreign labor originates in labor-intensive agriculture, in small firms active in the service sector, and in private households. Here, employers are rarely able to plan their labor demand in advance, and very often—this is especially true with households—they act under the pressure of sudden opportunities and constraints. For them, the very idea of hiring someone who is not personally known to them does not even cross their minds. Because formal credentials and certification by public bodies are useless, they look for workers who can be tested directly and employed on the spot, perhaps after having been recommended by someone who is well known to them, usually another trusted worker. Only 4 percent of the foreign workers employed in Italy in 2008 found their job through some kind of formal agency or job center.[22]

Second, an active immigration policy requires a certain degree of control over the labor market. No selective process for admitting newcomers will work if there is widespread tolerance of the irregular employment of those who are already in the country. In Italy, however, this is a Herculean task. Most employers, and large sectors of public opinion, do not regard the hiring of an undocumented migrant as a criminal action. Putting cases of serious abuse, violence, or overexploitation aside, hiring migrants is often considered a gracious, sometimes even a charitable, act. Public opinion strongly supports the deportation of foreign criminals, misfits, and troublemakers, but such measures are nearly always considered too harsh for "honest" irregular workers. Although heavier employer sanctions have been introduced, they have never been systematically implemented, both because of the lack of an adequate administrative infrastructure, and, above all, because of the fear of the political backlash they would trigger in a country where approximately 17 percent of the GDP is undeclared.

The difficulties of enacting an adequate planning program in this context have thus evolved, over the last decade, into an implicit compromise that defines the yearly contingent as a recurring "mini-amnesty," one that is not even particularly disguised. A large number of foreign workers enter every year as tourists, become working tourists, and overstay their visa, waiting for the next round of amnesty. Once their visas are granted, they return to their home country, pick up their visas at the Italian embassy, and return to their workplace as "newly arrived" workers. As a way of managing the irregular population, this compromise has significant advantages, allowing for a trial period that fits the exigencies of employers and (often) workers. It also keeps the spell of irregularity in the biographies of most immigrants reasonably short. But it implies that Italian immigration policy, far from steering the flows, is actually steered *by* them.

Because the yearly decree has become a tool for filtering access to the legal labor market, it has quickly lost any ambition to contribute to labor market reform. Attempts in 2001 to 2006 to provide incentives for high-skilled foreign workers, which resulted in utter failure because of a lack of demand, have been silently abandoned. Since 2007, the yearly decrees have been increasingly targeted at sustaining the Italian welfare regime through the regularization of domestic and careworkers. Satisfying the strong labor demand of Italian households, who by now regard the availability of foreign care labor as a de facto welfare right, is both politically uncontroversial and structurally needed. In 2006, 12 percent of the contingent had been allocated to domestic and careworkers. In 2008, apart from the country-based quotas, the entire contingent was reserved for domestic workers. In 2009, not wanting to appear as if it was promoting further immigration, the government did not issue the yearly decree, but introduced in its budget reform package a new amnesty, restricted only to irregular immigrants employed as housekeepers or careworkers. Since 2010, apart from the country-based quotas, the entire contingent has been reserved for careworkers. Immigration policy developments are increasingly constrained by the externalities of the strained welfare regime.

THE NEW ITALIANS

Italian immigration policy, being focused on flows, has traditionally paid little attention to the long-term processes of immigrant settlement. For a long first phase, the nearly exclusive administrative actor in the management of the foreign population was the home ministry, responsible for the granting and renewal of the *permesso di soggiorno*, the short-term permit that was a formal precondition for entering the labor market, for renting a flat, and gaining access to many social resources. There was a fairly consistent preference for the maintenance of a substantial amount of discretionary action even in the case of migrants who had been in the country for years. At the beginning of the twenty-first century, a majority of the foreign population could still rely only on short-term residence permits, which had to be renewed at short intervals. As a matter of fact, the first elements of a long-term residency status were introduced in Italian legislation only in 1998 (and very restrictively implemented subsequently). The legal stabilization of the foreign population in Italy is less than a decade old. Only in recent times, and mostly thanks to the pressure of the EU directive on long-term residents,[23] has a growing percentage of the foreign population acquired a "denizen" status.

Such lack of policy attention has not prevented, however, a remarkable process of settlement. The initial waves of individual "pioneers" have quickly given way to robust networks of families and kinship networks. The evolution of many migration systems—far from following the fashionable "circular" or "transnational" models celebrated by policy experts—have brought about in many cases a much more traditional model of long-term settlement, with private housing, family reunification, and diminishing involvement in the country of origin. Foreign families have become actors in the urban housing markets, where they rent, and sometimes even buy, their own flats. They have also slowly rooted themselves in the spaces and layers of sociability of urban areas, particularly in working-class neighborhoods. Social and symbolic boundaries have proven somewhat porous. Today, eight Italians out of ten have some kind of personal relationship with at least one person with an immigrant background.[24] One-tenth of the weddings celebrated in the country have at least one partner, much more frequently the bride, with a non-Italian citizenship. Overall, the settlement process has been aptly labeled by Maurizio Ambrosini as one of "subordinate inclusion," where immigrants are able to root their presence—going beyond the initial conditions of deprivation and gaining a modicum of social recognition—without noticeably altering their (low) positions in the pecking order of Italian society.[25] The living and working conditions of immigrants markedly improve during their first years in Italy, but the effects of immigration seniority cease soon afterwards.[26]

The most important consequence of this trend has been the emergence of a large segment of "non-immigrant foreigners," made up of children born in the country to foreign parents or brought to Italy at an early age. On the whole, more than one-fifth of the foreigners living in Italy are minors. Students with foreign nationality in Italian schools have moved from 0.06 percent in 1983–4 to nearly 10 percent in 2014–15. Studies carried out on the children of immigrants seem to agree on the lack of serious cultural and social cleavages within Italian classrooms: children of immigrants and children of natives—helped by the strong inclusionary logic of the Italian school system—intermingle reasonably easily and seem to hold fairly similar values and aspirations.[27] At the same time, there are marked differences in educational outcomes, with children of immigrants being strongly overrepresented among students with delayed schooling, students who fail the yearly exams, or pupils who receive the lowest grades. Children of immigrants are also more likely to drop out of school. They tend to enroll in vocational, rather than academic, career paths.[28] There is consequently a strong risk that the inequalities associated with immigration are going to be reproduced intergenerationally.

Conclusions

Contrary to widespread stereotypes, immigration to Italy is not a tale of destitute, clandestine migrants bound to a life of deviance and marginality. It is largely a story of classical labor migration, oriented towards providing needed workers for the unskilled and low-skilled segments of the Italian economy. What differentiates the current immigration flows to Italy from the pre-1973 experiences of northern European labor-importing countries is the political economy framework within which they take place. Far from answering labor shortages created by high rates of economic growth, foreign workers in Italy are actually "pulled" by the strong demand for flexible and cheap labor originating in the workings of a low-growth, low-productivity, mature economy and also in the growing difficulties of sustaining a conservative-style welfare regime. In this context, the various rounds of immigration policy reforms have been relatively successful in curtailing clandestine migration and in keeping the size of the irregular immigrant population within manageable limits. But they have largely failed both in the goal of planning the flow of new workers and in designing a reasonable path to actual citizenship for the foreign population that is now a stable and pervasive feature of the Italian social landscape.

Notes

1. Marzio Barbagli, Asher Colombo, and Giuseppe Sciortino, eds., *I sommersi e i sanati. Le regolarizzazioni degli immigrati* (Bologna: Il Mulino, 2004).
2. Giuseppe Sciortino, "Islamofobia all'italiana," *POLIS* 16, 1 (April 2002), 103–123.

3. Claudia Finotelli and Giuseppe Sciortino, "Through the Gates of the Fortress: European Visa Policies and the Limits of Immigration Control," *Perspectives on European Politics and Societies*, 14, 1 (February 2013), 80–101.

4. Asher Colombo, *Fuori controllo? Miti e realtà dell'immigrazione in Italia* (Bologna: Il Mulino, 2012).

5. Martina Cvajner and Giuseppe Sciortino, "Dal Mediterraneo al Baltico? Il cambiamento nei sistemi migratori italiani. La fatica di cambiare," in Raimondo Catanzaro e Giuseppe Sciortino, *Rapporto sulla società italiana* (Bologna: Il Mulino, 2009), 23–53.

6. See the estimates at <http://irregular-migration.net>.

7. Gian Carlo Blangiardo, *La presenza straniera in Italia. XVI rapporto sulle migrazioni. F. Ismu* (Milan: Franco Angeli, 2011).

8. Chiara Saraceno, Nicola Sartor, and Giuseppe Sciortino, eds., *Stranieri e diseguali* (Bologna: Il Mulino, 2013).

9. Istat, *L'integrazione nel lavoro degli stranieri e dei naturalizzati italiani* (Rome: Istat, 2009).

10. Emilio Reyneri, "Immigration in Italy: Trends and Perspectives" (2007), Retrieved July 25 2011, <http://www.portalecnel.it/Portale/indlavdocumenti.nsf/0/466486C57FF3FF42C12 5737F0050A9EC/$FILE/Reyneri-%20Immigration%20in%20Italy.pdf>.

11. Paolo Barbieri, "Italy: No Country for Young Men (and Women)," in Hans-Peter Blossfeld, Sandra Buchholz, Dirk Hofäcker, and Kathrin Kolb, eds., *Globalized Labour Markets and Social Inequality in Europe* (London: Macmillan, 2011), 108–145.

12. Emilio Reyneri and Giovanna Fullin, "Low Unemployment and Bad Jobs for New Immigrants in Italy," *International Migration*, 49, 1 (February 2011), 118–147.

13. Chiara Saraceno, Nicola Sartor, and Giuseppe Sciortino, eds., *Stranieri e diseguali* (Bologna: Il Mulino, 2013).

14. Foreigners, moreover, are by definition excluded from what may be considered the largest indirect welfare program in Italy: the provision of sinecures in public administration and state-controlled bodies. As they require Italian citizenship and state-recognized educational credentials, the presence of foreign workers in this sector is minimal or non-existent.

15. Giuseppe Sciortino, "Immigration in a Mediterranean Welfare State: The Italian Experience in a Comparative Perspective," *Journal of Comparative Policy Analysis*, 6, 2 (August 2004), 111–128.

16. William J. Baumol, *The Cost Disease* (New Haven, CT: Yale University Press, 2012) and "The Macroeconomics of Unbalanced Growth," *American Economic Review*, 57, 3 (June 1967), 415–426.

17. Raimondo Catanzaro and Asher Colombo, eds., *Badanti e Co. Il lavoro domestico straniero in Italia* (Bologna: Il Mulino, 2009), and Maurizio Ambrosini, *Irregular Migration and the Invisible Welfare* (London: Palgrave Macmillan, 2013).

18. Martina Cvajner, "The Presentation of Self in Emigration Eastern European Women in Italy," *The ANNALS of the American Academy of Political and Social Science*, 642, 1 (July 2012), 186–199.

19. Gian Carlo Blangiardo and Stefania Rimoldi, "Flussi ridotti e più disoccupazione," *Libertà Civili*, 4, 1 (January–February 2011), 115–127.

20. Giovanna Zincone, "The Making of Policies: Immigration and Immigrants in Italy," *Journal of Ethnic and Migration Studies*, 32, 3 (April 2006), 347–375.

21. Luca Einaudi, *Le politiche dell'immigrazione in Italia dall'unità a oggi* (Bari: Laterza, 2007).

22. Istat, *L'integrazione nel lavoro degli stranieri e dei naturalizzati italiani* (Rome: Istat, 2009).

23. Chiara Saraceno, Nicola Sartor, and Giuseppe Sciortino, eds., *Stranieri e diseguali* (Bologna: Il Mulino, 2013).
24. Istat, *I migranti visti dai cittadini* (Rome: Istat, 2012).
25. Maurizio Ambrosini, Rosangela Lodigiani, and Sara Zandrini, eds., *L'integrazione subalterna: Peruviani, Eritrei e Filippini nel mercato del lavoro milanese* (Milan: Fondazione Cariplo-ISMU, 1995).
26. Chiara Saraceno, Nicola Sartor, and Giuseppe Sciortino, eds., *Stranieri e diseguali* (Bologna: Il Mulino, 2013).
27. Gianpiero Dalla Zuanna, Patrizia Farina, and Salvatore Strozza, *Nuovi italiani: i giovani immigrati cambieranno il nostro paese?* (Bologna: Il Mulino, 2009) and Martina Cvajner, "Migrant Friendships, Migrant Loves – Taking the Sociability of Second Generations Seriously," *Journal of Modern Italian Studies*, 16, 4 (September 2011), 465–477.
28. Davide Azzolini, Philipp Schnell, and John Palmer, "Educational Achievement Gaps Between Immigrant and Native Students in Two New Immigration Countries: Italy and Spain in comparison," *The ANNALS of the American Academy of Political and Social Science*, 643, 1 (September 2012), 46–77.

CHAPTER 49

....

SOCIAL MOVEMENTS

....

DONATELLA DELLA PORTA

ITALY has a history of sustained protest, which peaked in the 1970s with the development of quite radical social movements. The postwar labor movement had been fairly militant and politically repressed; the first offensive wave of strikes in the large northern factories at the beginning of the 1960s was a prelude to the widespread mobilization to develop later in the decade. From the mid-1960s, new types of social movements began to emerge. Prior to 1973, collective action expanded into various sectors of society, in what Sidney Tarrow has described as part of a "cycle of protest."[1] Protest then declined in the mid-1970s, leaving small and radicalized left-libertarian movements in its wake. In the 1980s, we witnessed instead the growth and "institutionalization" of the new social movements. The new millennium opened with a "return to the street," with the global justice movement developing from a dense network of social movement organizations that had undergone a process of apparent specialization of discourses, moderation of tactics, and organizational structuration in the 1990s.[2]

In what follows, using categories well established in social movement studies,[3] I will synthesize research results on the internal characteristics (organizational structure, repertoires of action, and identity framing) of the left-wing movements, locating their developments within a complex structure of political opportunities and constraints.[4]

RADICALIZATION PROCESSES: THE 1960S AND 1970S

In the 1960s and 1970s, attention to social movements mainly focused on processes of radicalization. Violence developed during the cycle of protest that peaked in the late 1960s, with the largest wave of strikes in the history of the Italian Republic. Originating in schools and universities, protest spread to various social groups and geographical levels. In the late 1960s, student protest often took the form of occupation of educational buildings, escalating during police intervention and assaults by neofascists. Initially spontaneous, or at least loosely organized, violence was justified as "defensive." As mass protest declined in the 1970s, however, the New Left groups began to organize. At the margins of the student movement, the first underground group, the Red Brigades (Brigate Rosse, BR), was founded in 1970. In the ensuing years, especially up to 1973, protest spread in factories and cities with various claims on themes such as labor rights, housing conditions, and the price of public transport, all framed mainly within a class discourse. It was also during these years that the women's movement began to spread, with all its innovative capacity.[5]

Throughout the protest cycle, forms of action escalated as students and workers joined in protest campaigns and together clashed with police and neo-Fascists. About one-third (36 percent) of the 4980 protest events Tarrow studied from the period between 1966 and 1973 involved violence.[6] The years leading up to 1971 showed an increase in both total protest events and violent incidents, although the episodes of violence increased less; afterwards, although both declined, the violent component declined less, with the percentage of violent cases being higher than the average for the entire period. At the same time, there was a shift in the type of violence, with semi-military forms substituting for the spontaneous violence of the beginning of the cycle. While violent encounters between competing groups and police peaked in the early 1970s, attacks on persons and things increased as the conflict declined. Also, while violence in the late sixties occurred mainly during mass demonstrations and was justified as "defense" against attacks from outside, in the 1970s violence was organized by smaller groups. It was in these daily confrontations with the radical right and the police that marshal bodies specializing in the use of violence—the *servizi d'ordine*—gained influence within their respective organizations.[7] The presence of terrorist organizations, founded in 1970, contributed to radicalize the debate. Fueled by conflicts with the police and political opponents, this radicalization involved only small groups within much broader peaceful movement milieus.

Between 1974 and 1976, mobilization declined, especially in the factories, where the effects of the economic crisis were immediately felt. Despite some successful campaigns—such as the one in support of the law that legalized abortion, which was challenged by a Catholic-driven referendum—the attempts of the New Left to gain electoral support in 1976 failed, as did the Partito Comunista Italiano (PCI)'s hopes to win a majority of seats. As the unions and the PCI rushed to stigmatize violence, semi-military violence spread, producing harsh debates as well as splits in the left-libertarian movement family. While other movements declined, a wave of youth protest peaked in 1977, and an anti-nuclear campaign against the construction of twenty nuclear plants emerged strongly at the end of the decade.

Many small groups developed from the crisis of the New Left, adapting an "autonomy" ideology, which looked beyond the working class to the more marginal social strata. Quickly radicalizing in increasingly lethal conflicts with neofascists and police, these groups provided the recruitment basis for tiny underground organizations that disappeared after low-level violence, and later for some larger groups such as the Red Brigades, Front Line (Prima Linea, PL), and the Communist Fighting Formations

(Formazioni comuniste combattenti, FCC). These underground organizations frequently emerged from the paramilitary groups within the autonomous collectives.

However, what came to be known as the 1977 Movement was short lived. Protest collapsed especially after the Red Brigades' 1978 kidnapping and assassination of the president of the Christian Democratic Party, Aldo Moro, and the anti-terrorist emergency laws voted in by the so-called "government of national unity" that was elected in the same year with the external support of the Communist Party. This period encompassed the highest number of left-wing terrorist attacks, with 57 attacks against people in 1978 as well as in 1979, and 35 in 1980. Although the number of attacks remained high during the first years of the new decade, most of the underground groups, with the sole exception of the RB, disappeared.

The internal dynamics of radicalization interacted with some characteristics of the structures of political opportunities and constraints, which were characterized by the strong repression of the labor movement and the left in the 1950s as well as the *conventium ad excludendum*, which continued to keep the PCI out of national governments in the following decades. The traditional link between institutional and movement politics on the left was challenged in this period, however, as some institutional openings towards the PCI coincided with the increasingly harsh repression of the movements to its left.[8]

Moderation in the 1980s and the 1990s

When collective action reappeared in the 1980s, after the "lull" in the late 1970s, it had very different characteristics: the impact of socialist ideology waned with the decline of the New Left groups, and many of the organizational and cultural characteristics often described as peculiar to the New Social Movements emerged. An important moment in this phase was the 1981–3 peace movement campaign against the planned NATO deployment of cruise missiles in various European countries, with its emphasis on non-violent forms of action and its broad support. Throughout this decade and the following, the institutionalization of social movements, as well as their interactions with local and national parliaments and governments, were central issues. Environmental associations developed in this period along with women's organizations. These groups tended to organize at the local level, characterized by a pragmatic attitude and often by involvement in the Third Sector, although maintaining their critique of hierarchical, "macho" politics. Citizens' committees flourished in the cities as well as in the countryside, protesting against pollution as well as on security issues. Youth protest (and counterculture) developed in squatted "social centers."[9]

The classical social movements of the 1970s (characterized by universalistic identity, strategies of action founded on protest, and reticular organizational structures) seemed to evolve into four different forms: a) *public interest groups*, characterized by universalistic identity but with a focus on single issues, strategies of intervention based on lobbying and concertation, and bureaucratized organizational structure with paper memberships; b) *voluntary associations*, characterized by universalistic identity, strategies of intervention based on the supply of services, and permanent organizational structures, both participatory and reticular; c) *citizens' committees*, characterized by localistic identity, strategies of action that privileged protest, and participatory organizational structures, flexible and with low levels of coordination; and d) *countercultural communities*, characterized by universalistic identities, strategies of intervention based on cultural (sometimes commercial) activities and (sporadically) protest, and spontaneous and reticular organizational structures.

Several studies have indicated the development of formal, centralized, well-structured organizations lobbying for the public interest in areas where movements developed: environmental politics is a main example.[10] As for the *identity* of these environmental actors, research suggests a weakening of the ideological cleavage between conservationist and ecological approaches that had been seen in the 1970s and 1980s.[11] At the *organizational* level, environmental associations gained widespread public support, which in turn provided rich material and human resources for their organizations. Notwithstanding their spread on national territory, however, environmental associations still relied mainly upon activism and members' contributions. Even formal organizations were often just "networks of networks" of local groups. As for their *action* strategies, our environmental associations seemed to be increasingly involved in both moderate and policymaking-oriented forms of action, including lobbying and the performance of services contracted out to them by local governments.

In addition to forms of lobbying, many social movement organizations of the 1990s moved towards what, with an awkward neologism, was called Ngo-ism. These groups developed in the direction of voluntary associations, oriented to "practice the objective" via the supply of services, either to members or to the public. This path seems to be particularly widespread, for instance, in the women's movement,[12] whose discourse in this period combined parity and diversity, focusing on a new *citizenship* with equal rights for various groups. The discourse on special rights for special groups of citizens was approached with a high degree of *pragmatism*: ideological divisions declined in importance, with an apparent growth in optimistic attitudes. In the new groups, women from different backgrounds cooperated: feminists from the small consciousness-raising groups, together with women with a "double presence" in the left-wing parties and the women's movement.

In the 1990s, along with this pragmatic approach, women's involvement in the Third Sector pushed rank-and-file feminist groups to transform themselves, from the *organizational* point of view, into voluntary associations oriented towards the provision of various services. The cultural and welfare associations that arose from within the women's movement shared some common characteristics. Notwithstanding increasing formalization and professionalization, the emphasis on *participation* was maintained, and with it a reticular structure bridging various *networks* of local groups active in various regions on the same issues, and of women's groups active on different issues in the same towns. As far as *repertoires of action* are concerned, many women's movement organizations focused on pressure politics—with systematic contacts with the media, parties, and local governments. Moreover, thanks to the "brokerage" function of the (Old) Left, women's organizations were available to open negotiations with state institutions, particularly at the local level. In the movement, the idea developed of a *"gendered mediation,"* that is, of relationships with institutions mediated by women occupying positions in local government.

Protest in this period often organized around spontaneous committees of citizens, rooted in the territory. As for their *identity*, the committees were formed on ad hoc themes, often faced in reactive ways (opposition to decisions of the public administration), and asking for limited interventions. In this picture, the citizens' committees were sometimes seen as supporters of NIMBY (Not In My Back Yard) attitudes—materialists moved by conservative behavior and selfish motivations who, potentially, resisted social change. Research on citizens' committees in Italy indicates that they shared an orientation towards defense of the quality of life for one's own territory, combined with calls for larger participation.[13] From the *organizational* point of view, the committees seemed to be weakly structured. They imitated the organizational structure of movements of the past, and this, despite the presence of formal statutes, was non-hierarchical and flexible, with rare moments of coordination for occasional city mobilizations. Regarding forms of *action*, protest remained a fundamental resource, but it assumed a moderate form, was very mediatized, and privileged influence on public decision-makers over the construction of collective identity. The critical attitude towards existing forms of political representation did not prevent the committees from lobbying public powers and, even more important, despite their low level of formalization, taking part in consultation and political mediation. These efforts met with some success in finding allies in the local institutions and in the bureaucracies, even succeeding at times in blocking decisions (for instance, the installation of infrastructures with a high environmental impact) and attracting public investment in their area.

During these years, the residual signals of radical conflict, at least on a symbolic level, remained especially present in juvenile subcultures. In fact, the self-managed squatted social centers formed the bases of mobilization of the most radical wings of protest campaigns—from those seeking peace to those against racism. These centers have been defined as spaces for the development of a political counterculture, strongly critical of all the expressions of the left, old and new, which were accused of attempts at "normalization." Their *organizational* structure was extremely decentralized. Although constituting a diffused phenomenon—over 100 were counted in the early 1990s—the centers were only very loosely coordinated, mainly via magazines and musical centers.[14] The assembly was still a main democratic institution. The theorized organizational model was in fact the net "constituted of knots, independent one from the other, but connected by a web of knowledge."[15] Their main form of *action*—the occupation of sites in disuse, to be transformed into "temporarily autonomous zones"—brought the young people of the centers to clashes with the authorities and the police, who were sent to perform orders of clearance. However, the social centers were not characterized in this period by a violent repertoire. Although clashes with racist groups occasionally escalated, these did not seem to start a spiral of radicalization comparable to those of the 1970s. Relationships multiplied, instead, between social centers and public administration, with social centers sometimes providing functions of service supply or the realization of specific projects, financed with public funds. Different social and cultural activities developed in the autonomous social centers, often finding support and alliance among the local people. In the musical market, social centers nurtured new trends and launched groups destined for fame. Although considered as radical, the social centers were not isolated from other movement organizations, nor often from parties and interest groups.

Alter-Politics in the Global Justice Movements and Anti-Austerity Protests

At the beginning of the 2000s, formal associations, voluntary groups, youth centers, and city committees converged in a global justice movement (GJM), characterized by its heterogeneity.[16] Along with the active involvement of organizations originating in the labor movement and an impressive presence of groups of Catholic background, the movement included activists from the social centers of the 1990s as well as the "new" social movements of the 1970s and 1980s. Notwithstanding its heterogeneity, the Italian GJM featured dense networks, with converging demands for social justice and democracy from below expressed by all of its sectors.

In its emerging phase, the Italian GJM referred to a set of elements common to the movements of the 1980s and 1990s. First, there was an emphasis on differential rights and continuing demands for participation from below, challenging the corruption of representative politics. In addition, these organizations' increasing involvement, not only in the formation but also in the implementation of public policies, brought them into increasing contact with traditional third-sector organizations. Additional changes in the political environment contributed to successful networking: Throughout the 1980s and 1990s there was a weakening of the Old Left, the main institutional ally of the movements, with the main successor party of the PCI, the Democrats of the Left (DS), moving toward an openly reformist position in the social democratic tradition. The relationship between the movements and the institutional left—which was characterized above all in this period by temporary alliances on specific issues (such as peace)—became increasingly conflictual in the mid-1990s, with the return to government of the center-left coalition and its austerity policies. This shift contributed to the development of grassroots trade unions, but also to increasing opposition from within the institutional unions, bringing these sectors of the workers' movement into closer contact with social movement organizations and voluntary associations. Additionally, the government decision to participate in military interventions, including in the former Yugoslavia, strained relationships between the center-left parties and the peace movement.

Networking around issues of (social, political, ecological) global justice was favored by international developments as well. Especially in the early days, the Zapatista insurrection in Mexico provided an important point of reference, particularly for the social centers. Collaboration and mutual influences among groups from diverse cultural and political traditions gradually developed during the organization of a series of counter-summits and international campaigns such as Jubilee 2000 or the anti-war protests.[17] The success of the November 1999 protests against the third conference of the World Trade Organization (WTO) in Seattle accelerated the processes of cross-fertilization and aggregation in Italy. The broad coalition realized on that occasion increasingly led Italian social movement organizations with quite different backgrounds to concentrate, for the sake of common campaigns, more on their commonalities than on their differences. In 2000, various successful coordination efforts brought together social centers, solidarity and voluntary organizations (both secular and Catholic), and a movement sector closer to the traditional left in protests against, among others, NATO (National Atlantic Treaty Organization), the OECD (Organisation for Economic Co-operation and Development), and a fair on biotechnology in Genoa.

These experiences formed the basis for the organization of the protests against the G8 in Genoa in July 2001, launched at the first World Social Forum (WSF) in January 2001. More than 800 groups came together in the Genoa Social Forum (GSF), characterized by a very thin structure and an inclusive approach that relied largely on the resources put at its disposal by the member organizations. The GSF managed to attract organizations that had previously refused to join similar coordination efforts—all the more remarkably since adherence required the signing of a "work agreement" specifying the types of protest initiatives that were accepted and banned under its umbrella.

Compared with its precursors, the "movement of movements" was characterized far more by the presence of weak ties among groups maintaining differentiated organizational models. It was, in fact, the co-presence of different traditions that made more structured models of coordination obsolete: The capacity to coordinate and cooperate while preserving one's own specificity seemed to be a precondition for the effective collaboration of groups with different social, cultural, and political backgrounds in a global mobilization. From the very beginning, the activists of the GJM considered this plurality a positive factor and one of its strengths, as the movement was successful in putting together groups and organizations from different generations and various political and cultural backgrounds, remobilizing old activists and mobilizing new ones.

The movement's "network of networks" structure is in fact evident in the main mobilizations. The various "souls" of the movement aggregated into thematic sectors: the solidarity and voluntary associations, both Catholic and secular, around the Lilliput network in the ecopacifist sector; Attac and the organizations of the more institutional left in the anti-neoliberal sector; and the social centers, in particular the White Overalls and the Network for Global Rights, in the anticapitalist sector. Although located in

different movement sectors, these organizations largely shared the same concerns, facilitating frame-bridging. Condensing the target on neoliberal globalization allowed a logical connection between the various sectoral problems by attributing them to the same
macro-cause. In fact, the movement documents focus especially on democracy from
below and on social justice linked to the principle of solidarity, to environmental justice,
and to peace. The self-definition as "a movement for a globalization from below" emphasized first and foremost the stigmatization of a "top-down" representative democracy.
The movement was critical of both national institutions, thought to be powerless or at
best inadequate to guide globalization, and of supranational ones, because of the specific policies they adopt and their deficits in democratic accountability. These cognitive
connections reinforced the relations between different organizations and sectors: Social
justice was directly linked with the frames of the "old" social movements (unions, left-
wing parties, and radical anticapitalist movements); environmental justice bridged the
frames that emerged with new social movements; the solidarity frame was widespread
among religion-based movements. Having defined causes and effects, and asserting that
"a different world" and "another Europe" were possible, people were called to mobilize
in collective action. The call for struggle, mobilization, meetings, and communication
both inside and outside the movement expressed de facto demands for democracy. In
this context, explicit reference was made in the Genoa call for the right to protest "not to
be subjected to groundless restrictions."

While non-violent, the GJM did experience moments of heavy repression, the brutal
repression at the Genoa G8 in 2001 being a particularly vivid example. State authorities,
in Italy as elsewhere, mainly blamed the movement for these incidents, which they saw
as being caused by the violent action repertoires of some of its sectors and exacerbated
by a generally ambiguous attitude toward the problem of violence. The dominant reaction of Italian institutional politics toward the emerging movement was in fact to present it as primarily a public order problem. In Genoa as well as at numerous other protest
events organized by the GJM, the police did not apply in a coherent way the "negotiated
management" or "de-escalation" strategies developed in the 1970s in the face of increasingly heterogeneous movements with violent fringes.[18]

Among other explanations (e.g. the plurality and horizontality of the movement,
which made dialogue with the police more complicated, and the incomplete democratic
reform of the Italian security forces), a main cause for the violent escalation lay in the
political marginalization of the GJM. Not only did the Italian center-right government
refuse to acknowledge the movement as a partner to be talked with, instead seeing and
presenting it mainly as a problem of public order; but the center-left institutional actors,
during and after Genoa, also expressed mistrust toward the movement. The traditional
tendency of the PCI to disown any autonomous opposition movement to its left, as well
as uneasiness with the GJM critiques of the policies of privatization of public utilities
and deregulation of the labor market that the DS had actively supported, might explain
this closure. To the institutional left—even to those sympathetic to its aims—the movement remained a phenomenon that stimulated politics, "being a marker" for the problems to be addressed. At the same time, the institutional left continued to insist on its

political monopoly, considering the movement incapable of developing answers to the world's problems. The reawakening of interest in more participatory forms of politics was, therefore, viewed by social democratic parties as a danger. Although part of the electoral reservoir of the institutional left, activists also challenged a party model built around elected representatives and relating to the electorate through mass media communication experts and opinion pollsters.[19]

The importance of the collapse of the traditional party system—to be attributed to the fall of the Berlin Wall on the one hand, and to political corruption scandals on the other—has to be particularly stressed. This breakdown "liberated" large sectors of communist- and Catholic-inspired voluntary organizations from their traditional party allegiance. At the same time, with the increasingly moderate course of the DS (the largest successor party of the PCI), the role of the Old Left as an ally, a patron, or a broker for social movements diminished.

Some of the characteristics of the Italian GJM can be traced back to developments within the left-wing social movement families during the 1990s: a diminishing importance of (New) Left ideology; an increasing pragmatism with concentration on concrete projects, accompanied by the development of specific skills and expertise; the willingness to forge alliances with groups of different political and cultural backgrounds, but involved in projects with similar objectives. Also important were phenomena emerging more at the margins of the dominant social movement organizations: the growing importance of grassroots union organizations; the rise of a new generation of activists; a return to direct action.

Part of the global justice movement remobilized in the anti-austerity protests that started in 2008, although these also involved new generations of activists converging with conflicts on various territory against the construction of large infrastructure, such as the high-speed train in Val di Susa or the bridge over the Strait of Messina,[20] as well as the mobilization of precarious workers.[21] Beginning in 2008, indeed, protests developed against the retrenchment of the welfare state, the commodification of citizens' social rights, the growth of unemployment, and the explosion of jobs with low protection (part-time, precarious) in the labor market. Research on contentious politics in 2011 indicated that, if the *acampadas* (protest camps) were indeed less visible than in Spain or Greece, Italy was nevertheless marked by significant conflicts on social issues.

Indeed, political opportunities seemed to be opening up at the domestic level. The center-right government, led by Silvio Berlusconi, was visibly weakening, as its leader became more and more involved in political scandals and increasingly politically isolated. In June, the referenda against the privatization of the water supply, nuclear energy, and so-called "*ad persona* laws" (which protected Berlusconi in its trials)—as well as the defeat of the center-right in local elections—led to expectations of an intensification in protest, involving multiple social and political actors on multiple, bridged, issues. These expectations seem confirmed by research based on systematic searches of a main daily newspaper. Protests in the 2010s indeed largely targeted the government, with a strong focus on social issues: 37 percent of the protest events registered were called for by unions, and 47 percent involved workers mobilized on labor rights, with an additional

22 percent of students protesting against austerity measures.[22] However, social issues were also bridged with concerns about the quality of Italian democracy (in particular on issues of freedom of the press and citizens' equality before the law).[23] Moreover, a multiplicity of actors tended to network in these protests, which at times seemed able to weaken Berlusconi's coalition.

One might have expected this broad oppositional networking—facilitated by the presence of a common (and much stigmatized) enemy—to produce alliances between social movements and other actors such as political parties, thus reducing those tensions with institutional politics that had been identified in the analysis of the Indignados and Occupy movements.[24] Instead, not only did these protests resonate in their social claims with those of the movements, but so did the criticism of liberal democracy that they expressed. Research based on surveys at ten protest events in Italy between 2011 and 2013 indicates in fact that protest on social issues was bridged with extremely low and declining levels of institutional trust, although it included calls for more political intervention to address social inequalities. While the Partito Democratico (PD) converged with Berlusconi's Il Popolo della Libertà (PdL) in supporting the governments led by Mario Monti and then by Enrico Letta, social movement activists expressed increasingly higher levels of dissatisfaction with the institutional center-left, which was in fact losing voters, sympathizers, members, and activists.

Conclusion

In sum, the political weakness of the left-wing parties contributed to the very important role of left-wing social movements in Italy. In part influenced by the cross-national diffusion of ideas by social movements at the transnational level, however, they underwent a specific trajectory, affected by the internal resources of the social movement sector as well as by the external constellation of allies and opponents. In general, social movements on the left showed a particularly strong mobilizing capacity in the cycle of protest that started in the late 1960s, as well as in the peace movement of the early 1980s and the global justice movement at the turn of the millennium. Traditionally, a tendency to ally with the institutional left has been reflected in the framing and organizational structure of the movements. While strong repression as well as physical conflicts with the radical right radicalized social movements in the 1970s, the 1980s and early 1990s tended towards moderation and pragmatic relations with the institutional system, mixing protest with forms of lobbying as well as participation at various levels of policymaking. By the 1990s, and with more strength in the next two decades, the scandals of political corruption as well as the various moves of the main left-wing party towards the center of the political spectrum increasingly strained relations between social movements and party politics, with growing autonomy of social movements but also increasing problems in channeling their demands in the institutional system. While no radicalization of the forms of action ensued this time, social movement activists strongly mistrusted the main institutions of representative democracy, instead attempting to develop forms of democracy based on participation and deliberation.[25]

NOTES

1. Sidney Tarrow, *Democracy and Disorder. Protest and Politics in Italy, 1965–1975* (Oxford and New York: Oxford University Press, 1989).
2. Donatella della Porta, *Movimenti collettivi e sistema politico* (Bari: Laterza, 1996)
3. Donatella della Porta and Mario Diani, *Social Movements: An Introduction* (Oxford: Blackwell, 2006).
4. On political leaders and ideas, see Chapter 45, this volume.
5. Judith Hellman, *Journeys among Women. Feminism in Five Italian Cities* (Cambridge: Polity Press, 1987).
6. Donatella della Porta and Sidney Tarrow, "Unwanted Children. Political Violence and the Cycle of Protest in Italy, 1966–1973," *European Journal of Political Research*, 14, 6 (1986), 615.
7. On terrorist groups, see Chapter 50, this volume
8. Donatella della Porta and Herbert Reiter, *Polizia e protesta. L'ordine pubblico dalla liberazione ai "no global"* (Bologna: Il Mulino, 2004); Donatella della Porta, Abby Peterson, and Herbert Reiter (eds.), *Policing of Transnational Protest* (London: Ashgate, 2008).
9. Donatella della Porta, *Movimenti collettivi e sistema politico* (Bari: Laterza, 1996).
10. Donatella della Porta and Mario Diani (with the collaboration of Massimiliano Andretta), *Movimenti senza protesta? L'ambientalismo in Italia* (Oxford: Blackwell, 2004).
11. Mario Diani, *Isole nell'arcipelago* (Bologna: Il Mulino, 1988), 47.
12. Della Porta, *Movimenti collettivi e sistema politico*; see also Chapters 35 and 47, this volume.
13. Donatella della Porta (ed.), *Comitati di cittadini e democrazia urbana* (Soveria Mannelli: Rubbettino, 2004).
14. AA. VV., *Comunità virtuali. I centri sociali in Italia* (Roma: Manifestolibri, 1994).
15. Ibid., 12.
16. Donatella della Porta, Massimiliano Andretta, Lorenzo Mosca, and Herbert Reiter, *Globalization from Below* (Minneapolis: The University of Minnesota Press, 2006).
17. Donatella della Porta (ed.), *The Global Justice Movement* (New York: Paradigm, 2007).
18. Della Porta and Reiter, *Polizia e protesta*.
19. Della Porta (ed.), *The Global Justice Movement*.
20. Donatella della Porta and Gianni Piazza, *Voices of the Valley, Voices of the Straits: How Protest Creates Communities* (New York: Berghahn Books, 2008).
21. Alice Mattoni, *Media Practices and Protest Politics. How Precarious Workers Mobilize* (Farnham: Ashgate, 2012).
22. Donatella Della Porta, Lorenzo Mosca, and, Louisa Parks, L. (2012) "2001 Subterranean Politics and Visible Protest on Social Justice in Italy," in Mary Kaldor and, Sabine Selchow (eds.), *Subterranean Politics in Europe* (Basingstoke: Palgrave Macmillan, 2015), 60–93.
23. Ibid.
24. See, for example, Donatella della Porta, *Can Democracy be Saved?* (Cambridge: Polity Press, 2013).
25. Ibid; see also *Donatella della Porta, Social Movements in Times of Austerity* (Cambridge: Polity Press, 2015).

CHAPTER 50

TERRORIST MOVEMENTS

ANNA CENTO BULL

THE Italian First Republic went through a prolonged period of political violence from the late 1960s to the mid-1980s that can only in part be classified as "terrorism." Indeed, terrorism is notoriously a controversial concept and has not been universally applied by scholars. Its controversial nature continues to be relevant in Italy today, since this term constitutes a crucial fault line between those who use it in order to condemn the "anti-democratic" and extremist violence of the "years of lead" and those who view the violence of that period primarily as a politically motivated and (to some extent) justifiable "armed struggle" against an "undemocratic" state.

Despite the controversy around the use of the term terrorism, it remains a useful concept that helps to distinguish between the various types of violence practiced in Italy in those years and their perpetrators. Terrorism, in fact, refers to acts of organized violence carried out by small groups operating in semi-clandestine or clandestine fashion, as opposed to mass "spontaneous" violence carried out during protest demonstrations or strikes.[1] Its victims tend to be found among the civilian population, and they are considered merely as "instruments" in the ultimate goal of targeting "the state authority,"[2] or of "sending a message to a target audience in the hope that members of this audience will alter their behavior [. . .] in ways the perpetrators believe desirable."[3] Furthermore, terrorism has a strong element of theatricality and makes use of the media to achieve wide resonance and secure maximum publicity.[4]

These definitions, however limited, clearly set terrorist acts and movements apart from the more widespread and generally unorganized political violence which often characterized mass protest demonstrations in the 1960s and early 1970s, and in so doing they can contribute to a more general interpretation of the origins of terrorism. According to Della Porta and Catanzaro, in fact, it is precisely the transition from mass violence of a mainly "spontaneous" nature to small-group terrorist violence that needs explaining, as opposed to understanding the genesis of terrorism in ways that largely discount the wider sociopolitical context. While this transition concerns primarily the trajectory followed by the radical left movement in the 1970s, a comparable question relates to the emergence of terrorist groups on the right, which were prepared to upgrade their bombing attacks so as to target human victims and cause bloody massacres.

In light of the definitions provided above, one of the questions that needs addressing is: what do we mean by terrorism and terrorist movements in relation to the Italian case? The answer is that we should distinguish between two types of terrorist violence and terrorist groups.[5] The first type of organized violence fits closely with the mainstream definitions of terrorism, as it both targeted innocent victims as "instruments" and relied on a highly symbolic and theatrical dimension. It consisted of bombing attacks, initially aimed at damaging property and later focusing on human targets. The most prominent of these included the one perpetrated in Piazza Fontana, Milan on December 12, 1969, which left 17 people dead and 88 wounded, and a massacre in Brescia on May 28, 1974, which targeted an anti-fascist demonstration and resulted in eight people dead and 103 wounded. There were also various bloody attacks on crowded trains. A later massacre was carried out on August 2, 1980 at Bologna railway station, leaving 85 dead and 200 wounded. The responsibility for these attacks went unclaimed, with the result that investigators into the 1969 Milan bombing followed various possible trails of inquiry, initially attributing the massacre to a small group of anarchists. The latter included Pietro Valpreda and Giuseppe Pinelli, who died while being interrogated in the Milan police headquarters on December 15, 1969. His largely unexplained death later gave rise to a hate campaign against the police commissar responsible for his interrogation, Luigi Calabresi, himself assassinated by a left-wing squad on May 17, 1972. However, subsequent investigations into the Milan attack revealed that the culprits were to be found among extreme-right groups. The trials on the bombing massacres typically lasted several decades and concluded with unsatisfactory verdicts of acquittal for lack of evidence. Despite this, the trials were able to establish that this type of terrorism was carried out by extreme-right neo-fascist groups inspired by radical thinkers.

The second type of terrorism consisted of armed attacks against representatives of the state, such as *carabinieri*, magistrates, prison officers, or indeed people whose work contributed to strengthening the democratic process, including architects, journalists and university professors. This type of violence was exercised primarily by left terrorist groups acting in competition with each other and inspired by revolutionary ideologies. In the course of the 1970s, extreme-right terrorist groups also adopted similar terrorist techniques, targeting magistrates, police and *carabinieri*, and largely imitating their left counterparts, even though they constituted a small minority in comparison to the left groups. Whether or not the right groups adopted guerrilla tactics as an alternative, or rather as complementary, to bombing attacks, remains a moot point among scholars and commentators.

Having established the nature of terrorist violence and the main perpetrators, we need to consider why terrorist groups emerged in Italy and were able to operate over a prolonged period of time. Understanding when and why terrorist movements emerged in Italy also helps us to account for their decline and ultimate defeat. The answers to these questions are not straightforward, even though there is a general consensus among scholars regarding the role played by key factors in promoting the transition from unorganized to organized violence and from attacks on property to attacks on human targets. It is also the case that interpretations of Italian terrorism have over the years been influenced by different theoretical and methodological approaches, which have in turn privileged a structural-sociological interpretation, a psychological one, and, more recently, a mystical-religious one, largely in line with the move away from social structural explanations and with the emergence of the so-called cultural turn in the social sciences.

Italian terrorism, however, cannot be properly understood without taking into account the international as well as the domestic context, and the ways in which the actions and goals of the different terrorist groups intersected and overlapped with the strategies of various political actors, including state actors, in the light of the Cold War. This analysis in turn allows a better understanding of the limits as well as the successes of the Italian state's fight against organized violence and throws light upon the long-standing legacy of terrorism in terms of both (lack of) truth and justice and divided memories.

The next two sections address these issues in relation to each type of terrorist technique and terrorist movement. The analysis then switches to assessing the end of terrorism and its legacy in the country today, and then provides a conclusive assessment.

NATURE, ORIGINS, AND SCOPE OF RIGHT TERRORISM

After the war many neo-fascists joined clandestine organizations until the Movimento Sociale Italiano (MSI) was formed in 1946, providing a political home to all those who were nostalgic about the regime but also by and large accepted the democratic system. However, the MSI witnessed a series of splits from radical groups over the years, leading to the formation of Centro Studi Ordine Nuovo (ON), set up by Pino Rauti in 1956, and Avanguardia Nazionale (AN), set up by Stefano Delle Chiaie in 1959, as well as other minor groups, all of which theorized the use of organized violence. From the late 1960s both ON and AN were seriously implicated in terrorist attacks and many of their members and leaders were subsequently charged with being responsible for bombing massacres. While successive trials lasting several decades have often found it impossible to identify individual culprits, the responsibility of ON was recently acknowledged by the Italian Supreme Court, the Court of Cassation, in a verdict on the Milan 1969 bombing delivered in 2005.

ON and AN merged in 1975 and gradually lost their dominance within the extreme-right extra-parliamentary galaxy. Other groups came to the fore, including Ordine Nero, Costruiamo l'Azione, and Terza Posizione. The latter two theorized the need to overcome left–right divisions and advocated a hybrid form of Nazi-Maoism. A splinter group from Terza Posizione, the Nuclei Armati Rivoluzionari (NAR), set up in 1977, predicated a form of "armed spontaneity," with reference to the almost total absence of a coherent ideology as the inspiration for their actions. These groups were influenced by the "armed struggle" of the leftist revolutionary groups and caused the assassination of a number of people, for which crimes they were later charged and found guilty. However, the two leaders of the NAR, Giuseppe Valerio Fioravanti and Francesca Mambro, together with Luigi Ciavardini, were later also charged and found guilty for the 1980 massacre at Bologna station. As we shall see, there are more lingering doubts over the perpetrators of this massacre than concerning the culprits of previous bombing attacks, despite the fact that in this case the judicial trial ended with a clear guilty verdict for the three members of the NAR.

There are various interpretations as regards the origins of extreme-right terrorism in the shape of bombing attacks. One interpretation, which is at least partially supported by judicial evidence, postulates that neo-fascist groups started to theorize the need for organized violence as a prelude to a *coup d'état* in the mid-1960s, in parallel to the perceived rising threat posed by left-wing movements and parties in the context of the Cold War. This theorizing was part of a wider "Strategy of Tension," devised in collaboration with sectors of the army, the secret services, and Freemasonry, and possibly backed by international forces opposed to the formation of center-left governments in Italy after 1963 and fearful of the social movements of the late 1960s.[6] The neo-fascists thus became one of a number of "co-belligerents" ready to adopt terrorist techniques in order to secure a number of aims. For the neo-fascists, the main aim was the formation of an authoritarian government, while for their co-belligerents it may have consisted more simply in curbing the activities of the left movements and/or sending a clear warning to the Partito Comunista Italiano (PCI). The 1968 students' revolt and the 1969 workers' unrest precipitated the situation, as they were seen as the antechamber of a revolutionary attempt to destabilize and possibly take over the state. Hence the timing of the first bombing massacre and its "false flag" character, designed to put the blame on the anarchist and by extension the entire leftist movement, can both be explained within this interpretative framework. This reading of the bombing campaign generally restricts the "Strategy of Tension" to the period 1969–74, when a *coup d'état* might have seemed feasible, given the authoritarian regimes already established in Southern Europe. However, the fall of these regimes in 1974–75 put an end to such aspirations. The interpretation itself is fairly plausible but it cannot explain all the massacres. The Brescia bombing, for instance, explicitly targeted leftist demonstrators; hence it cannot be labeled "false flag" terrorism. For this reason some have attributed it to a revenge act on the part of the neo-fascists after their allies discarded the Strategy of Tension. The motives for the 1980 Bologna bombing are also still obscure, despite the outcome of successive trials.

Beyond this "rational" interpretation steeped in Cold War politics, we find explanations that take into consideration sociological, ideological, and psychological factors in accounting for the use of bombing attacks against civilians on the part of neo-fascist groups. First, neo-fascists in Italy after the war felt ghettoized and marginalized from both politics and society. They had to witness the triumph of their enemies, with their main adversary, the Communists, being fully legitimized in the new anti-fascist Italian

Republic from which by definition they themselves were excluded.[7] Added to this there appears to have been a generational transmission of psychological attitudes and ideological values from those who had adhered to the Italian Social Republic to their children, who grew up sharing the ideals of their parents and their negative feelings towards democracy.[8] Feelings of resentment and grievance, in turn, coupled with an increasing sense of impotence, especially when faced with the growing popularity of the left, drew a number of them to theorize recourse to violent means. Their main inspiration was Julius Evola, a radical thinker who in the postwar period spurred neo-fascists to adopt a "warrior spirit" and an attitude of total intransigence as the only antidote to military defeat and democratic decadence.[9]

It is easier to explain the genesis of the armed struggle among extreme-right groups in the mid-1970s. As outlined above, it originated in part from the imitation of left terrorism and in part from a gradual escalation of violent tactics used in skirmishes with the police and left groups. The later neo-fascist groups ostensibly rejected links with ON and AN, whom they had come to believe guilty of having connived with sectors of the state. By contrast, the later groups claimed to be fully independent from, and openly targeted representatives of, state institutions. While continuing to adhere to Evola's ideas on the warrior spirit, they appeared to interpret it in a more individualistic and "spontaneous" manner than the previous groups. This is the reason why there are lingering doubts over the culprits for the Bologna bombing, which many believe are to be found in international terrorist groups rather than home-grown neo-fascist ones operating in connivance with sectors of the state. Others, by contrast, argue that the autonomy of these later groups in relation to state bodies has been greatly exaggerated.[10]

NATURE, ORIGINS, AND SCOPE
OF LEFT TERRORISM

The most notorious of these groups, the Red Brigades, were formed officially in 1970 but were pre-dated in embryonic form by other organizations that theorized the need for organized violence. The Red Brigades were the most hierarchical of the terrorist groups on the left, bent on privileging a military/elitist approach to a revolutionary conquest of power. While their early activities focused on targeting industrial factories to gain support among workers, they later opted to deliver a full-scale "attack on the state," especially after the group's founders, Renato Curcio and Alberto Franceschini, were captured by the *carabinieri* in 1974 and were replaced by a more bloodthirsty leadership. Armed attacks against representatives of the Italian state intensified, initially aimed at "kneecapping" the targeted victims, later at killing them. In 1978, the Red Brigades succeeded in striking to the heart of the state when they kidnapped Aldo Moro, the Christian Democratic strategist behind the decision, taken in the early 1960s, to include the Socialist Party in coalition governments and the subsequent decision to collaborate with the Communist Party in the so-called Historic Compromise (1976–9). Indeed Moro was kidnapped on March 16, 1978 while on his way to Parliament where a new government headed by Giulio Andreotti with the external support of the Communists was to be sworn in. On May 9 the Red Brigades dumped his body in a car in Rome, symbolically halfway between the headquarters of Christian Democracy and the Communist Party. Another influential group, Prima Linea, tended to privilege organized violent actions similar to the Red Brigades' while opting to remain close to grassroots social movements, especially the "1977 movement," which renewed in a more violent form the mass protests of the 1960s and early 1970s. Other lesser groups developed in the course of the 1970s, each with its own leaders and specific goals.

An influential interpretation concerning the origins of left terrorism that has largely stood the passing of time is that put forward by Della Porta and other scholars who took part in a research project promoted in the 1980s by the Bologna-based Istituto Cattaneo. As they argued, Italian terrorism must be seen as related to a mass protest cycle that took place between 1966 and 1973. As the protest movement started to wane, so violence escalated, with an increase in the number of competitive actors, greater factionalism, and greater police repression leading to the emergence of semi-clandestine organizations that "eventually adopt[ed] organized terror as their major tool."[11] In short, the emergence of terrorist groups was explained by the "dynamic of the cycle" (as well as by ideology) rather than by "structural causes"[12] (see also Chapter 49, this volume). Furthermore, Della Porta's research shows that both radicalization and de-radicalization must be explained taking into account the micro, miso, and macro levels. At the individual level, attention should be paid to beliefs and attitudes as well as psychological factors. On the miso level, the focus should be on the ways in which groups recruit members and supporters, cement a collective identity and set up efficient organizations, or, conversely, lose support, start to fragment, and become prone to mistakes. At the macro level the focus should be on changing political opportunity-structures.[13]

Other scholars stress the importance of ideology above all other factors. As in the case of right terrorism, left terrorism is seen as having been inspired by radical revolutionary ideas, which various thinkers were at the time elaborating and/or popularizing, including Antonio Negri, Oreste Scalzone, and Giangiacomo Feltrinelli. In this context, some have argued that extreme-left terrorism must be placed within a long-standing cultural and intellectual tradition that in Italy played a major role in transmitting revolutionary ideas across different generations.[14] Revolutionary myths also played a part, especially the myth of a "New Resistance," which inspired young people to emulate the gestures of the partisans.[15] More recently, Orsini placed the emphasis on a mystical-fanatical process of radicalization, dubbed DRIA ("disintegration, reconstruction, integration and alienation"), as the main explanation for the terrorist "mind-set." Despite acknowledging the relevance of the historical-political context, Orsini's interpretation in effect sees radicalization largely as a self-contained and self-standing process.[16]

Finally, as in the case of right terrorism, the issue of "*Cui prodest?*" has been raised over the years by various scholars and commentators, who have argued that the Red Brigades did not act alone, at least after the arrest of Curcio and Franceschini in 1974.[17]

In their view, the new leadership, especially Mario Moretti, significantly changed the nature and strategy of the Red Brigades and had links with secret services from both the Western and Eastern blocks, determined to prevent the "Historic Compromise," seen as destabilizing the international political order. One of the strongest proponents of this interpretation is Giuseppe De Lutiis, who in a recent interview stated explicitly that "Both Western and Eastern powers had a common interest in sabotaging the Historic Compromise." He added: "I would exclude the possibility that the Red Brigades acted autonomously. Of course, 2950 *brigatisti* out of 3000 were certainly acting in good faith but in the case of a small number of high level leaders I would rule it out."[18]

THE DECLINE AND DEFEAT
OF TERRORISM IN ITALY

In the first half of the 1980s terrorism in Italy started to wane, and later it effectively came to an end, despite a few isolated episodes in the 1990s. A dual order of factors contributed to this outcome. First were state responses to terrorism, which can be grouped under the headings of repression and legislative incentives. Second was a process of disengagement within the terrorist movements themselves. In addition, we need to take into account the phenomenon known as backlash, which occurs when the wider public turns decisively against the terrorists. This can be crucially important in facilitating the end of a terrorist phase, since there often exists a support system as well as sympathy towards the terrorists' goals, even if there may also be condemnation of their means.

As far as state responses are concerned, scholars and experts agree that after an initial period of uncertainty and disorientation the Italian state was able to put into place effective intelligence and police operations, coupled with a foresighted legislation that is often hailed as a pioneering example of best practice.[19] The government passed two laws in 1980 and 1982 that initially offered incentives, in the shape of reduced sentences, to individual terrorists who agreed to collaborate with judicial investigators (so-called *pentiti*) and in 1987 formally extended this approach to all those who "dissociated" from violence, whether or not they were prepared to reveal information about fellow comrades. Furthermore, in 1986 the state approved the so-called Gozzini law that introduced more humane prison conditions, while encouraging inmates to establish relations with the outside world. Of great importance was also the establishment, in the early 1980s, of "homogeneous areas" in the prisons, where all those who were neither *pentiti* nor hardliners were housed without fear of retaliation from their ex-comrades.

As regards disengagement within the terrorist movements, at the individual level psychological factors appear to have been especially relevant. Feelings of disillusionment and impending defeat among the terrorists still at large led to infighting and burn-out, thus contributing to their demise. Among imprisoned terrorists, a process of self-reflection led to a growing sense of having wasted one's life and wishing to be given a second chance, which in turn was facilitated by the re-establishment of affective relations and the more humane prison conditions introduced in the 1980s. Furthermore, many chaplains and nuns became interlocutors of the imprisoned terrorists and acted as intermediaries between them and prominent Church figures, above all Cardinal Carlo Maria Martini, who became a key advocate for reconciliation.[20] This explains why, with a dramatic and much publicized gesture, Prima Linea left three bags full of weapons in the Archbishop's palace in Milan on June 21, 1984, thereby signaling the end of the "armed struggle."

As for a backlash against the terrorists among wider society, there is some evidence that this can be traced back to the assassination of Aldo Moro in 1978 and Guido Rossa in 1979. Rossa was a union delegate and Communist Party member from the Genoa Italsider plant who had denounced a fellow worker for acting in connection with the Red Brigades. According to Drake, after Rossa's murder "the Red Brigades became a pariah in the factories" and the first seeds of self-doubt started to penetrate the organization.[21] The view that the murders of Aldo Moro and Guido Rossa precipitated a backlash is supported by a number of former terrorists in their memoirs, even though others deny their relevance, claiming instead that their defeat had been of a purely military character.[22]

The Legacy of Terrorism

Italian terrorism has left a heavy legacy, and there is still a sense that the country has not dealt adequately with its recent violent past. This has been caused by a variety of reasons. First, retributive justice has only been partially successful in delivering clear-cut verdicts. It has been most successful with regards to left terrorism, even though the "incentive" legislation of the 1980s resulted in some very lenient sentences for multiple murderers, to the chagrin of the victims and their relatives. By contrast, the judicial trials on the bombing massacres dragged on for several decades and concluded only recently, typically with unsatisfactory and ambiguous verdicts of "not guilty" for lack of evidence delivered to the (mainly) neo-fascist defendants.[23]

If justice has only been partially obtained, truth has remained elusive. In particular, the role of the Italian state in right terrorism remains a sore and moot issue, as successive trials unearthed very considerable evidence concerning the behavior of the secret services and parts of the armed forces and the political class, in aiding and abetting right terrorists or at least in helping them escape prosecution. Furthermore, there are lingering doubts concerning the behavior of the state towards left terrorism, as it is suspected of having allowed the latter some margins of maneuver in order to keep the Communist Party at bay. While new revelations, mainly of a journalistic nature, have constantly kept this issue in the spotlight, the state has remained silent and the political class has opted not to open state archives to public scrutiny, despite a law approved in 2007 that set a limit of 30 years to state secrecy.

The way in which terrorism came to an end also left a legacy, as it successfully ensured the social reintegration of former terrorists but left the victims and their relatives feeling isolated and abandoned by the state. For many years the victims stayed silent, with just a few exceptions, while the former terrorists published their memoirs and enjoyed a degree of notoriety in the media. In the last decade this situation has been redressed at least in part, with the relatives—especially the children—of the victims also publishing their own memoirs. The two sets of memoirs offer contrasting reconstructions and representations of the past, and there is still a lack of dialogue between their perspectives, despite a few pioneering attempts. The plight of the victims has also been partially redressed with the establishment of an official Day of Memory in 2007. The chosen date was May 9, the day when the body of Aldo Moro was discovered in Rome.

Terrorism has also left a legacy in so far as, while the political class during the Second Republic opted not to embark on a process of truth telling and truth recovery,[24] it has nevertheless made use of the memory of terrorism as a weapon with which to discredit political adversaries. On the right, Berlusconi and his allies repeatedly denied any involvement of neo-fascism or indeed parts of the state in the bombing massacres, and instead promoted a revisionist campaign aimed at attributing all responsibility for terrorism to the left. In 2010 and 2011 the government refused to send representatives to the annual commemoration for the 1980 Bologna massacre, accusing the victims of promoting a left agenda. On the radical left, terrorism is remembered primarily in its right variety, and as having been masterminded by covert forces in order to stop the advance of the Communist Party. Berlusconi himself is portrayed as an important element of continuity with this underhand and corrupt system of power.

Finally, the continuing existence of mutually exclusive narratives and representations of the violent past can provide renewed justification for the use of terrorist means. The assassination of Marco Biagi, a government labor law consultant, in 2002, and the kneecapping of Roberto Adinolfi, head of a nuclear energy company, in 2012 brought widespread condemnation and remained isolated episodes. However, in the face of a further deterioration of the sociopolitical climate prevalent in the country, a possible escalation of violence cannot be ruled out.

Conclusion

The terrorist movements that raged in Italy from the late 1960s to the early 1980s can be (and have been) explained on the basis of a linear interpretation, according to which they were inspired by radical ideologies, gradually escalated their actions following various stages of radicalization, were initially underestimated by the state but were later effectively dealt with thanks to military actions and a pioneering "incentive" legislation. From this perspective, the Italian state is seen as having faced down a very dangerous challenge while successfully defending and preserving its own democratic institutions and the rule of law.

An alternative non-linear interpretation, while accepting that the terrorist movements largely originated of their own accord, views their development and trajectories as being closely interlinked with both domestic and international forces that were external to the movements themselves but had an interest in promoting their activities (in the case of right terrorism) or in allowing them some margin of maneuver (as in the case of left terrorism).

These two interpretations and their numerous variants have survived to this day and given rise to a vast literature of a mainly journalistic nature. The numerous memoirs written by former terrorists and by the victims and their relatives also take a stance in relation to these controversial issues, with most ex-terrorists denying any involvement with external forces and many victims convinced that they and the Italian public have not been told the full truth concerning the political "masterminds" behind left and right terrorism. The political class, in turn, has displayed unity in its decision to honor the victims without embarking in a process of truth-telling, but has also shown continuing deep cleavages and mutual antagonism in its partisan and selective use of the memory of terrorism. In this context, it can be argued that, despite terrorism having been successfully defeated, Italy has not yet been able to work through its difficult recent past and to achieve wider social and political reconciliation.

NOTES

1. Donatella Della Porta and Sidney Tarrow, "Unwanted Children: Political Violence and the Cycle of Protest in Italy, 1966–1973," *European Journal of Political Research*, 14, 5–6 (November 1986), 607–32. See also Raimondo Catanzaro, ed., *La politica della violenza* (Bologna: Il Mulino, 1990), 206.

2. Isabelle Sommier, "'Terrorism' as Total Violence?," *International Social Science Journal*, 54, 174 (December 2002), 473–481 (474).

3. Leonard Weinberg and William Lee Eubank, *The Rise and Fall of Italian* (Boulder, CO: Westview Press, 1987), 2.

4. Bruce Hoffman, *Inside Terrorism* (New York: Columbia University Press, 1999), 185–96; Brian Jenkins, *International Terrorism: A New Kind of Warfare* (Santa Monica, CA: The Rand Corporation, 1974).

5. The analysis does not include the terrorist murders and bombing attacks carried out by the Mafia. On Mafia violence, see Chapter 51, this volume.

6. Franco Ferraresi, *Minacce alla democrazia: la Destra radicale e la strategia della tensione in Italia nel dopoguerra* (Milan: Feltrinelli, 1995); English edition *Threats to Democracy: The Radical Right in Italy after the War* (Princeton, NJ: Princeton University Press, 1996, reprinted as e-book in 2012). See also Anna Cento Bull, *Italian Neofascism. The Strategy of Tension and the Politics of Nonreconciliation* (New York and Oxford: Berghahn, 2007).

7. Francesco Germinario, *L'altra memoria. L'Estrema destra, Salò e la Resistenza* (Turin: Bollati Boringhieri, 1999) and *Estranei alla democrazia: negazionismo e antisemitismo nella destra radicale italiana* (Pisa: Biblioteca Franco Serantini, 2001). See also Marco Tarchi, *Esuli in patria: i fascisti nell'Italia repubblicana* (Parma: Guanda, 1995).

8. See for instance John P.G. Veugelers, "Dissenting Families and Social Movement Abeyance: The Transmission of Neo-fascist Frames in Post-war Italy," *The British Journal of Sociology*, 62, 2 (June 2011), 241–261.

9. On the influence of Evola, see Richard H. Drake, "Julius Evola and the Ideological Origins of the Radical Right in Contemporary Italy," in Peter H. Merkl, ed., *Political Violence and Terror: Motifs and Motivations* (Los Angeles: University of California Press, 1986), 61–89; Franco Ferraresi, "Julius Evola: Tradition, Reaction, and the Radical Right," *European Journal of Sociology*, 28, 1 (May 1987), 107–51; Paul Furlong, *Social and Political Thought of Julius Evola* (Abingdon: Routledge, 2011).

10. Among the former we find Adalberto Baldoni and Sandro Provvisionato, A che punto e' la notte? (Milan: Vallecchi, 2003) and Gianluca Semprini, *La strage di Bologna e il terrorista sconosciuto. Il caso Ciavardini* (Milan: Bietti, 2003); among the latter Franco Ferraresi, *Minacce alla democrazia: la Destra radicale e la strategia della tensione in Italia nel dopoguerra* (Milan: Feltrinelli, 1995) and former neofascist terrorist Vincenzo Vinciguerra. See his *Ergastolo per la liberta. Verso la verita sulla strategia della tensione* (Florence: Arnaud, 1989) and *Camerati addio. Storia di un inganno, in cinquant'anni di egemonia statunitense in Italia* (Trapani: Edizioni di Avanguardia, 2000).

11. Della Porta and Tarrow, "Unwanted Children: Political Violence and the Cycle of Protest in Italy, 1966–1973," 613.

12. Ibid., 611.

13. Donatella della Porta, "Guest Editorial: Processes of Radicalization and De-radicalization," *International Journal of Conflict and Violence*, 6, 1 (2012), 4–10. See also her "Leaving Underground Organizations: A Sociological Analysis of the Italian Case" in Tore Bjørgo and John Horgan, eds., *Leaving Terrorism Behind: Individual and Collective Disengagement* (London and New York: Routledge, 2009), 66–87.

14. See especially the works by Richard Drake, notably his *Apostles and Agitators: Italy's Marxist Revolutionary Tradition* (Cambridge, MA: Harvard University Press, 2003) and *The Revolutionary Mystique and Terrorism in Contemporary Italy* (Bloomington: Indiana University Press, 1989). For a discussion on the different models of Italian intellectuals, see Chapter 45, this volume.

15. Philip Cooke, *The Legacy of the Italian Resistance* (Basingstoke: Palgrave Macmillan, 2011), ch. 5.

16. Alessandro Orsini, *Anatomia delle Brigate Rosse. Le radici ideologiche del terrorismo rivoluzionario* (Soveria Mannelli: Rubbettino, 2009). English edition: *Anatomy of the Red Brigades: The Religious Mind-set of Modern Terrorists* (Ithaca, NY: Cornell University Press, 2011).

17. See especially Roberto Bartali, Giuseppe De Lutiis, Sergio Flamigni, Ilaria Moroni, and Lorenzo Ruggiero, *Sequestro di verità. I buchi neri del delitto Moro* (Milan: Kaos, 2008); Giuseppe De Lutiis, *Il golpe di Via Fani. Protezioni occulte e connivenze internazionali dietro il delitto Moro* (Milan: Sperling & Kupfer, 2007); Sergio Flamigni, *La tela del ragno. Il delitto Moro* (Milan: Kaos, 2005).

18. The interview with Giuseppe De Lutiis took place on October 22, 2012 and is available on YouTube: <http://www.youtube.com/watch?v=MlNj Vc_Fk08>.

19. See especially Martha Crenshaw "How Terrorism Declines," *Terrorism and Political Violence*, 3, 1 (Spring 1991), 69–87; Donatella della Porta, "Institutional Responses to Terrorism: The Italian Case," *Terrorism and Political Violence*, 4, 4 (Autumn 1992), 151–171; Alison Jamieson, *The Heart Attacked: Terrorism and Conflict in the Italian State* (London

and New York: Marion Boyars, 1989); Leonard Weinberg and William Lee Eubank, *The Rise and Fall of Italian Terrorism* (Boulder, CO: Westview Press, 1987).

20. Anna Cento Bull and Philip Cooke, *Ending Terrorism in Italy* (Abingdon: Routledge, 2013).

21. Richard Drake, "Ideology and Terrorism in Italy: Autobiography as a Historical Source," in Leonard Weinberg, ed., *Political Parties and Terrorist Groups* (London: Frank Cass, 1992), 50.

22. Cento Bull and Cooke, *Ending Terrorism in Italy*.

23. Anna Cento Bull, *Italian Neofascism. The Strategy of Tension and the Politics of Nonreconciliation* (New York and Oxford: Berghahn, 2007). Recently, in July 2015, a Milan Court of Appeal found a former prominent neo-fascist and a former intelligence agent guilty for the 1974 Brescia bombing. The verdict was welcomed and hailed as 'historic' by the victims.

24. Anna Cento Bull, "The Italian Transition and National (Non) Reconciliation," *Journal of Modern Italian Studies*, 13, 3 (2008), 405–421.

CHAPTER 51

··

MAFIA, CAMORRA, AND 'NDRANGHETA

··

LETIZIA PAOLI

THE Sicilian Cosa Nostra, the Calabrian 'Ndrangheta, and the Neapolitan camorra—in short, southern Italian mafia organizations—are frequently seen as the epitome of organized crime. This essay argues, however, that southern Italian mafia organizations are an exception in the panorama of organized crime in most developed countries, and Western Europe in particular. Given their size, longevity, organizational and cultural complexity, and multi-functionality, Italy's mafia organizations are fundamentally different from the ephemeral and mostly small-scale enterprises that continually form and disband in the illegal markets of developed countries, including Italy itself, hoping to earn fast money with the production or distribution of prohibited goods and services.

From an analytical point of view, four characteristics distinguish mafia organizations in Italy and a few other "mafia-type organizations" elsewhere, such as the Italian-American Cosa Nostra, the Chinese Triads, the Japanese Yakuza, and the Russian thieves-in-law,[1] from other forms of organized crime:[2]

1) the organizations' longevity;
2) their organizational and cultural complexity;
3) their claim to exercise a political dominion over their areas of settlement—a claim that has over the decades been at least partially recognized by the local population and parts of the official government; and
4) their resulting ability to control legitimate markets.

In this chapter, I argue that Cosa Nostra and the 'Ndrangheta meet all four characteristics, whereas several groups of the camorra meet the latter two.

In the first section of this chapter, I provide an introduction to these three (sets of) criminal organizations, and allude to other crime groups that are sometimes mistakenly presented as mafia. The following four sections are devoted to the analysis of the four distinguishing characteristics of mafia organizations. In the last section, I conclude by briefly summarizing government and societal anti-mafia action from the early 1990s onwards, and considering how mafia groups have reacted to it.

COSA NOSTRA, THE 'NDRANGHETA, AND CAMORRA: AN INTRODUCTION

The Sicilian Cosa Nostra (i.e., "Our Thing") is a confederation of about 150 groups, mostly located in the western part of Sicily, particularly the provinces of Palermo, Trapani, and Agrigento.

The 'Ndrangheta is also a confederation of about 150 groups. They all originate at the southernmost tip of the Italian peninsula, the Calabria region, mostly from the provinces of Reggio Calabria and Vibo Valentia. In the dialect of Greek origin that is still widespread in Calabria, the word "'Ndrangheta" means "society of the men of honor" and still has a decidedly positive connotation. Unlike Cosa Nostra, the 'Ndrangheta also includes groups located outside its home region, particularly in the Northern Italian regions of Lombardy, Piedmont, and Liguria, as well as in several foreign countries, most prominently Germany, Canada, and Australia.

The number of formal members of the 'Ndrangheta is currently estimated by law enforcement officials to be at least 10,000. Five hundred of them, organized in about 25 groups, are active in Lombardy. No exact estimate is known for Cosa Nostra but, according to the same and other sources, their number could be as low as 2,000, down from 3,000 in the mid-1990s. Cosa Nostra has traditionally been much more selective in its recruitment policies than the 'Ndrangheta, has also been more seriously hit by law enforcement action, and has seen its popular legitimacy more seriously challenged than its Calabrian counterpart.[3]

Unlike the first two organizations, the third, the camorra, does not even constitute a confederation but rather consists of a multiplicity of independent criminal groups and gangs that are located in the province of Naples, the capital of the Campania region, and the surrounding areas, particularly the Caserta province north of Naples. Although they are collectively known as camorra, these gangs and groups have different characteristics and modus operandi, and often enter into violent conflict with each other. Some of them are well-established family businesses that, much like Sicilian and Calabrian mafia groups, claim to exercise a political dominion over their neighborhoods or towns and systematically infiltrate local government institutions, often enjoying the protection of high-level national politicians as well. One of them is the "cartel" of mafia-type camorra groups, the Casalesi, active in the Caserta province, which has been very effective in setting up legitimate businesses with proceeds of crime and in gaining control of several local economic sectors. Some of these mafia-type camorra groups have emissaries and operations in Italy's center-north (primarily neighboring Latium but also Piedmont, Emilia Romagna, and Tuscany), several EU member states, above all Spain, as well as South America and the US.[4]

Other camorra groups have less long-lasting formations that develop around a charismatic chief, usually a successful gangster. These groups aim at profit-making primarily through illegal businesses, most frequently illegal drug trafficking, although they may also be able to exercise some control on local legal activities and public life. Finally, there are also loose gangs of juvenile and adult offenders, which—according to police sources—belong to the sphere of common rather than organized crime. The composition of many camorra gangs and the alliances among them can be so unstable that law enforcement agencies often have difficulty in charging and sentencing the members of these groups for the offense of being involved in a mafia-type criminal organization.[5]

A few other criminal coalitions and gangs located in eastern and southern Sicily and in northern Calabria, such as the Stidda in the Agrigento and Caltanissetta provinces and the Sacra Corona Unita in Apulia, are also frequently referred to as mafia in the Italian debate. However, their internal cohesion and political and economic resources are much lower than those of Cosa Nostra or 'Ndrangheta groups. The Sacra Corona Unita, which was founded in the early 1980s, no longer exists as a single viable organization.[6]

The terms "organized crime" and "mafia" are also increasingly used to refer to foreign criminals operating in Italy.[7] With the rare and occasional exception of a few Chinese crime groups,[8] though, foreign criminal groups and actors as well as the non-mafia Italian criminal enterprises make no claim to exercising political authority and do not approximate even closely the longevity and organizational and cultural complexity of southern Italian mafia organizations.[9]

LONGEVITY

As already mentioned, longevity and organizational and cultural complexities constitute the first two defining characteristics of mafia organizations—and both are fully met only by Cosa Nostra and the 'Ndrangheta. Historical research since the 1980s has demonstrated that antecedents of the contemporary Sicilian and Calabrian mafia groups were active from the 1880s, if not before.[10]

The same continuity cannot be ascertained in the case of the camorra. Certainly, in order to strengthen their internal cohesion and legitimacy, many contemporary camorra groups utilize the symbols and rituals of the nineteenth-century camorra. This was an organization that shared several cultural and organizational similarities with its Sicilian and Calabrian counterparts, although it distinguished itself through its concentration in the city of Naples, and its plebeian background. Unlike Cosa Nostra and the 'Ndrangheta, however, the contemporary Campanian crime groups do not directly derive from their nineteenth-century forerunner.[11]

ORGANIZATIONAL AND CULTURAL
COMPLEXITY

Cosa Nostra and 'Ndrangheta's internal structure and cultural apparatus of legitimation have few parallels in the world of crime for their complexity and sophistication. The groups within these organizations are often called families but are clearly distinct from the members' biological families, particularly in Cosa Nostra. In the 'Ndrangheta, male relatives are still regarded as an asset for mafia bosses, who often try to have as many relatives as possible affiliated with the mafia group.[12] However, because of the larger size of 'Ndrangheta groups, these also have a much more complicated internal structure than their Sicilian counterparts, which are often composed of fewer than ten members. In the 'Ndrangheta, some mafia groups are composed of up to 100–200 people. In order to protect the mafia bosses, an internal ranking system has developed, divided into higher and lower sections in each group—and only the older, higher-ranking members have access to the higher section.[13]

In both mafia organizations, the individual groups have their own ruling bodies—the distinguishing trait of an organization, according to Weber.[14] Starting from the 1950s, moreover, super-ordinate bodies of coordination were established—first in Cosa Nostra and, during the 1990s, in the 'Ndrangheta as well. Composed of the most important family chiefs, they are known as "commissions." Although these bodies have often been glamorized, they cannot be compared to the board of directors of a company, as the mafia commissions have historically been rarely in charge of the planning or coordination of profit-making activities. Rather, they were set up primarily to mediate conflicts within the two organizations and regulate the use of violence against mafia members of other units and high-level government officials, so as to avoid unnecessarily attracting law enforcement attention.[15] According to law enforcement sources, the two Cosa Nostra commissions—coordinating the families of the Palermo province and those of the whole region—were disbanded at the turn of the century. It had become too dangerous to bring together the most important representatives of mafia groups in the same place at any one time, and, in any event, most of them were imprisoned.[16] By contrast, the 'Ndrangheta's commission seems to have gained authority in recent times.[17]

The unity of the two confederations does not depend on the coordinating commissions, however. Rather, it is guaranteed by the sharing of common cultural codes and a single organizational formula—a state of affairs that is also highlighted by mafia defectors.[18]

Cosa Nostra and the 'Ndrangheta also have a sophisticated cultural apparatus, consisting of symbols, rituals, and a set of rules comparable to the normative order of a simple society. At its core are two subcultural codes: honor and *omertà*. Traditionally widespread in many pre-modern Mediterranean societies, the code of honor essentially requires a man to defend his person and property, including his women(!), by himself, that is, without resorting to law enforcement authorities. The concept of *omertà* partially overlaps with honor but also emphasizes the duty to keep secret the internal affairs—and in Sicily even the existence—of the mafia organization.[19]

The most powerful ritual of both organizations is the initiation ceremony, through which "status and fraternization contracts" are imposed on new members.[20] They are required to assume a permanent new identity—that is, to become a "man of honor," subordinating their previous allegiances and even life to the mafia membership—to consider the other members as "brothers," and share what anthropologists call a regime of "generalized reciprocity" with them.[21] This regime is premised on altruistic behavior without the expectation of short-term reward.

While the status and fraternization contracts underlying mafia memberships appear and indeed are old-fashioned, they can be very effective in guaranteeing the cohesion of an illegal group and the members' subordination to their bosses. They can also help foster trust and collaboration among the individual members and thus help each of them to achieve their own goals. There is, however, a major constraint under which they operate: namely, mafia status and fraternization contracts can only be effectively imposed upon persons who are already socialized to a certain mafia subculture and are thus willing to internalize the mafia group expectations and values. This first major constraint has limited the pool of suitable candidates for both organizations, which only recruit people of Sicilian or Calabrian descent. Second, since the 1970s, the mafia ideology of "honor and brotherhood" has been increasingly challenged by the mafia members' growing preoccupation with profit-making. This in turn stems from the modernization process that has taken place in southern Italy since the 1960s and made wealth a precondition for being recognized as "a man of honor."[22] Third, in Sicily, the Corleonesi—that is, the mafia bosses from the town of Corleone who gained power over the whole Cosa Nostra during the 1980s and remained dominant until Bernardo Provenzano's arrest in 2006—also contributed to the weakening of mafia ideology by ruthlessly killing dozens of mafia members, violating many of Cosa Nostra's rules, and thus unwittingly ending up increasing the number of defectors.[23]

POLITICAL DOMINION

Cosa Nostra and the 'Ndrangheta, along with several mafia-type camorra groups, share another important characteristic. Unlike most other contemporary organized crime groups, the southern Italian mafia organizations do not content themselves with producing and selling illegal goods and services. Although these activities have acquired a growing importance over the past 30 years, neither the trade in illegal products nor the maximization of profits has been their primary goal in the past or is in the present.[24]

In fact, it is hardly possible to identify a single goal: Cosa Nostra, the 'Ndrangheta and the mafia-type camorra groups are multifunctional organizations and throughout their history have always engaged, sometimes simultaneously, in power- and profit-oriented activities. However, in contrast to the criminal enterprises populating today's illegal markets, the exercise of political domination has always been very important for the ruling bodies of Cosa Nostra, the 'Ndrangheta, and mafia-type camorra groups.[25] These bodies claim, above all, an absolute power over their members. They control every aspect of their members' lives, and they aim to exercise a similar power over the communities where their members reside.

It is important to stress that mafia power had for a long time a higher degree of effectiveness and legitimacy than that of the government. In western Sicily and southern Calabria, mafia groups successfully policed the general population, settling conflicts, recovering stolen goods, and enforcing property rights. Even government institutions, though formally condemning mafia violence and occasionally repressing it, usually came to terms with mafia power; in the territories under its control, the maintenance of public order was de facto entrusted to the mafia leaders.[26]

Even after World War II, mafia bosses particularly in Sicily were considered respectable and suitable partners by many politicians from the dominant Christian Democracy party and were highly appreciated for the voting blocs they could mobilize. Giulio Andreotti, one of the most important Italian politicians in the postwar period,[27] well symbolizes these "evil pacts." In 2004, Andreotti was found guilty by Italy's Supreme Court of abetting Cosa Nostra until 1980, although he could not be convicted owing to the statute of limitations.[28] Especially in Sicily, many "men of honor" were themselves actively involved in political life and held important political positions at the city, regional, and even national levels. One of them, Vito Ciancimino, even became mayor of Palermo in 1968,[29] after being responsible for public works during the administration of another Christian Democrat politician with very close ties to the mafia, Salvo Lima. Thanks to such high-level political patronage, two other "men of honor," the Salvo cousins, gained a private concession to collect taxes in Sicily under very favorable conditions, and became two of the wealthiest people in Sicily.[30]

Even today, although many mafia rules are no longer systematically enforced, mafia groups continue to exercise a certain "sovereignty" through a generalized system of extortion. As a state would do, they tax the main productive activities carried out within their territory. Moreover, whenever *mafiosi* are asked to mediate conflicts, guarantee property rights, and enforce rules compatible with their own legal order, such as those concerning female honor (virginity), they do not hesitate to intervene.[31]

Although ever larger strata of the southern Italian population are increasingly critical of mafia power and ideology, mafia bosses still have few difficulties in finding hidden allies among politicians eager to obtain mafia groups' electoral support. Since the adoption of an ad hoc bill in 1991, over 200 city councils were dismissed, a few two or three times, for being "polluted" or conditioned by mafia groups.[32] Proving the latter's persistent influence, 25 such councils were dismissed in 2012 alone, including for the first time a regional capital, Reggio Calabria.[33] Numerous investigations in the three affected regions have demonstrated that even regional and national politicians continue to accept, and even seek, mafia electoral support in exchange for various favors. The former president of the region of Sicily, Totò Cuffaro, started serving a seven-year prison sentence in 2011 for having abetted Cosa Nostra.[34]

Although mafia groups usually favor colluding with politicians, some of them, particularly those in the Cosa Nostra, have repeatedly directed their military power against government officials or representatives who had become a threat to their interests. Between the late 1970s and the early 1990s in particular, Cosa Nostra assassinated dozens of policemen, prosecutors, judges, and politicians. Cosa Nostra's challenge to state power reached a climax in 1992–93. In 1992, the group murdered the Palermitan judges Giovanni Falcone and Paolo Borsellino in two spectacular bomb explosions. In 1993, in an effort to demonstrate the national power of the mafia, it organized a series of terrorist bombings in Rome, Florence, and Milan.[35] Since then, most mafia groups have realized that such "excellent cadavers," drawing the attention of the public and of law enforcement, are not in their own best interests, and have generally abstained from them. In Calabria, however, 'Ndrangheta groups have intimidated numerous local politicians, prosecutors, and judges since 2005 through minatory letters, phone calls, and property damage.[36]

THE CONTROL OF MARKETS

Thanks to their political and military power, mafia groups have frequently been able to gain control of legal markets in their strongholds. Only in its simplest form does extortion merely entail the (forced) transfer of money, the so-called *pizzo*. Often it involves a payment in kind, the purchase of unnecessary protection services or goods at a higher price, or *mafiosi*'s coerced participation in a company or public contract. From the 1950s onwards, mafia members in Sicily and subsequently in Calabria and Campania, set up building companies to gain subcontracts for the clearance of major public works sites, and progressively raised their ambitions in the following decades. In the 1980s, building companies close to mafia groups were able to secure a large share of the public works contracts in the three regions, by entering into corrupt agreements with government and national building company representatives.

Thanks to better controls, mafia groups' grip on large building projects seems to have declined since then.[37] However, the groups' reach has diversified considerably and covers all kinds of services for the public administration, from garbage collection and disposal to health sector procurements.[38] Through a combination of violence and the abundant financial resources gained through illegal activities, some mafia groups have also been able to establish control over other local market sectors. Starting in the 1970s, for example, mafia groups in specific parts of Sicily and Campania have controlled the local supply of cement. In the 1990s, a series of 'Ndrangheta groups monopolized the meat sector in Reggio Calabria.[39] Mafia groups are also discovering new sectors, such as alternative energy. In 2013 one of the largest Italian wind energy entrepreneurs was identified as a "straw-man" of an important Cosa Nostra boss; all of his companies and properties, allegedly worth over 1.3 billion euros, were seized.[40]

A peculiarity of the camorra groups is the distribution of a wide range of counterfeit products, which are partially manufactured in the Naples and Caserta provinces and partially imported from China. Camorra groups are also proficient in the counterfeiting of currencies, which they then sell to crime groups all over Europe.[41] Because of the groups' numerous criminal activities and international reach, the US Obama administration identified "the Camorra" (falsely understood as a single organization) as one of the four most threatening organized crime groups from the US perspective in 2012.[42]

Mafia control over legal and illegal markets should not be exaggerated, however. Despite their power, mafia groups have not been able to guarantee themselves a monopoly in any sector of the legal or even the illegal economy outside southern Italy. Research done in Belgium and the Netherlands,[43] where the two of the largest European entry points for Colombian cocaine are located, provides no empirical support for the claim frequently heard in Italy that the 'Ndrangheta has "a de facto monopoly on the import of Colombian cocaine into Europe."[44]

Other studies show that when mafia groups move to Northern Italy or abroad they rarely seek to exercise a political dominion but rather merely engage in profit-making legal and illegal activities, even if they seek alliances with local entrepreneurs,[45] a point admitted even by Europol.[46] Outside their strongholds and the 'Ndrangheta's older settlements in Canada and Australia, southern Italian mafia groups have rarely developed ties with politicians or government officials. However, the dismissal of five city councils in Italy's center-north, three of them in 2012, demonstrates that they can do so, and is a worrying sign.

Even the investment of crime proceeds in foreign properties or companies is too often mistaken for control of local market sectors. The mere fact that mafia groups invest proceeds of crime in foreign countries does not automatically suggest that the groups are also able to exert some sort of undue control on a specific economic sector. In the case of Cosa Nostra, its power is not unchallenged even within its strongholds. Given the rigidity of their recruitment policies, in fact, Cosa Nostra groups often find themselves in a minority position with their local competitors and are hence unable to control the local underworld.[47]

Whatever the uncertainties about the extent of mafia groups' wealth and the reach of their economic power, there is no doubt that southern Italian citizens and companies pay a high price for mafia groups' control of the local economy. Campania, Calabria, and Sicily are the poorest regions of the country, have a GDP per capita that is about half of that recorded in the richest regions in the North, and, with the partial exception of Sicily, have been most seriously hit by the current global financial crisis.[48] According to an analysis made by Censis, at least 30 percent of southern Italian companies are negatively affected by mafia-type organized crime, for example because they have to pay higher business costs or face restrictions in business choices concerning suppliers, workers and customers.[49] Southern Italian companies also face indirect costs: according to a Bank of Italy study, companies located in mafia groups' strongholds pay interest rates up to

30 percent higher than those located in non-mafia areas.[50] In another Bank of Italy study, the arrival of mafia-type organized crime in the two southern Italian regions of Basilicata and Apulia, which were considered immune to it until the 1970s, was reported to have resulted in reduced growth of 15 percent in GDP per capita in 30 years, largely owing to lower private investments.[51]

THE COMEBACK OF ANTI-MAFIA?

The murders of judges Giovanni Falcone and Paolo Borsellino in 1992 represented a turning point in the century-long relation between mafia groups and the larger society. In fact, they set in motion an unprecedented reaction by law enforcement agencies and a broad section of the southern Italian population.

The law enforcement reaction profited from both the great improvement in intelligence about Cosa Nostra and investigative methods achieved with the first Palermo maxi trial and a series of new acts passed in 1991 and 1992. In addition to the act allowing the dismissal of city councils, these acts established a new police agency specializing in the fight against mafia-type organized crime, the Direzione Investigativa Antimafia (DIA), and an agency facilitating information exchange between the divisions of the local prosecutors' offices specializing in mafia cases, the Direzione Nazionale Antimafia. They also created a witness protection program and set up a very harsh prison regime for the heads of mafia groups (known as 41bis in Italy).[52]

After 1992–93, law enforcement action against mafia groups became both intensive and very effective, as recognized even by the then-leader of Cosa Nostra, Bernardo Provenzano, in a wiretapped conversation.[53] Almost all Sicilian mafia bosses, some of whom had been on the run for decades, were arrested, along with hundreds of their associates. The DIA issued over 9,436 arrest warrants between 1992 and 2011, and 1,897 of them were related to members of Cosa Nostra or other Sicilian crime groups.[54] Bearing in mind the earlier estimate of 2,000 Cosa Nostra "made" members, the DIA figures suggest that the chances of being arrested have become very high for these members, especially if one recalls that three other police agencies are also involved in anti-mafia action in Italy.

Although the pressure initially focused on Cosa Nostra, it gradually extended to camorra and 'Ndrangheta groups as well. Over the same 20-year period, for example, the DIA issued 2,799 and 2,582 arrest warrants against camorra and 'Ndrangheta members, respectively. Indeed, mafia members were not only arrested but also convicted and given long prison sentences.[55] As of June 2013, for example, 6,758 Italian citizens were imprisoned for the offence of belonging to a mafia-type criminal organization (416bis) and 645 of them were subject, as of December 2009, to the special incarceration regime for mafia members.[56]

The financial drain has also been unprecedented. The DIA alone seized assets worth 11 billion euros from the three sets of mafia groups over the 1992–2011 period and confiscated assets worth 1.8 billion euros.[57] For the first time, moreover, prosecutors not only charged mafia members but also their political protectors. Whereas the most prominent trials against Andreotti and Corrado Carnevale, the former President of a section of Italy's Supreme Court, largely backfired, several other lower-level politicians and government officials accused of favoring mafia groups have been brought to trial, and some of them have been convicted—such as the already-mentioned former President of the Region of Sicily, Cuffaro, and Marcello Dell'Utri, formerly Silvio Berlusconi's right-hand man.[58]

Many of these high-level investigations have been made possible by the contributions of former mafia members turned witnesses (known as *pentiti* in Italy). At its peak in 1996, 1,214 *pentiti* were under the state protection program; after a 35 percent decline in the following years owing to criticisms of *pentiti*'s reliability and judicial contributions and the adoption of restrictive amendments to the witness protection program, the *pentiti*'s number started growing again, reaching 1,093 in 2011.[59] The *pentiti*'s boom in the 1990s and their recent growth suggest that the choice to defect is not only the result of a cost-benefit assessment at the moment of a *mafioso*'s arrest but also reflects the long-term de-legitimation process undergone by mafia groups.[60] Significantly, in recent years, several female relatives of mafia bosses have decided to break with their past and family, and filed for protection.[61]

Cosa Nostra, the 'Ndrangheta and camorra groups have responded in several ways to the intensification of anti-mafia repression. Cosa Nostra gave up the open challenge to state sovereignty pursued in the early 1990s, while all three sets of mafia groups have radically reduced the level of homicidal violence committed by their members. Between the peak year of 1991 and 2011, in fact, mafia murders decreased by 93 and 97 percent in Calabria and Sicily respectively and by 88 percent in Campania, in spite of the anarchy typical of the camorra.[62]

More generally, mafia groups have also tended to focus on entrepreneurial activities that do not to raise much social alarm, such as extortions, usury, manipulation of public tenders, and, as far as possible, drug trafficking. In Sicily, changes were also recorded in the very organization of extortions. According to the DIA, all producers, and not just the large companies as in the past, are now asked to pay a contribution to Cosa Nostra, but contributions are kept low to prevent popular resentment from reaching critical dimensions.[63]

The societal reaction to the 1992 murders was in fact part of a broad long-term process of delegitimation of mafia subculture and values, which started after World War II. This was initially promoted by a small number of primarily Sicilian elites but gained popular support for the first time after the murder of General Carlo Alberto Dalla Chiesa in Palermo in 1982. After a period of retreat in the late 1980s, the anti-mafia movement strongly expanded from the early 1990s onwards, mobilizing large numbers of people in Sicily and, to a lesser extent, also in other southern Italian regions. This process involved new actors such as the Italian, and above all the Sicilian, Employers' Association and the Catholic Church, which had previously remained silent, and led to the establishment of numerous anti-mafia and anti-racket (i.e., against extortion) associations. As a result of this slow but probably inexorable delegitimation process, traditional mafia values of honor and *omertà* no longer find public supporters.

However, other typical Italian values and institutions, such as family and patronage ties, remain broadly accepted and constitute the shared cultural background of *mafiosi* and considerable parts of the Italian society. These values and institutions also form the basis for corrupt agreements between *mafiosi* and politicians and particularistic exchanges between the latter and considerable parts of the southern Italian electorate. Furthermore, in regions affected by chronic unemployment and sharply hit by the post-2008 economic crisis, a career in the mafia or crime looks attractive to many youngsters with poor education and few hopes of finding a job in the legal economy, and who thus provide an inexhaustible reserve army of criminal manpower. Especially in the Naples area, members of the camorra groups—with their lavish mansions and flashy lifestyles—are still role models for many youngsters from marginalized neighborhoods.[64]

Despite the recent law enforcement successes in the fight against mafia groups, therefore, the road ahead is still a long one, and it would be a terrible mistake to claim premature victory.

NOTES

1. See Jay S. Albanese, "The Italian-American Mafia," Vadim Volkov, "The Russian Mafia: Rise and Extinction," Ko-Lin Chin, "Chinese Organized Crime," and Peter Hill, "The Japanese Yakuza," in Letizia Paoli, ed., *Oxford Handbook of Organized Crime* (Oxford: Oxford University Press, 2014), 142–176 and 219–253. See also Letizia Paoli, "The Paradoxes of Organised Crime," *Crime, Law and Social Change*, 37, no. 1 (2002), 51–97.

2. On the dominant forms of organized crime in Western countries, see Martin Bouchard and Carlo Morselli, "Opportunistic Structures of Organized Crime," in Paoli, ed., *Oxford Handbook of Organized Crime*, 288–302, and Europol, *SOCTA 2013: EU Serious and Organised Crime Threat Assessment* ('s-Gravenzande: Deventer, 2013).

3. For the data, see Ministero dell'Interno, Relazione semestrale sull'attività svolta e i risultati conseguiti dalla Direzione Investigativa Antimafia- gennaio—giugno 2012, 2012: 16 and 28–70, <http://www.interno.gov.it/dip_ps/dia/page/relazioni_semestrali.html>; Commissione parlamentare d'inchiesta sul fenomeno della mafia e sulle altre associazioni criminali, anche straniere. Audizione del Procuratore Distrettuale Antimafia di Reggio Calabria, dottor Giuseppe Pignatone, XVI legislature, September 21, 2010, and Europol, Threat Assessment: Italian Organised Crime (File No: EDOC#667574 v8), June 2013. For the differences between Cosa Nostra and the 'Ndrangheta, see Letizia Paoli, *Mafia Brotherhoods: Organized Crime, Italian Style* (New York: Oxford University Press, 2003) and "Mafia and Organised Crime: The Unacknowledged Successes of Law Enforcement," *West European Politics*, 30, no. 4 (2003), 854–880. For the 'Ndrangheta's international expansion, see Commissione parlamentare d'inchiesta sul fenomeno della criminalità organizzata mafiosa o similare. *Relazione annuale sulla 'Ndrangheta*. 2008, Doc. XXIII, n. 3, XV legislature.

4. Europol, Threat Assessment, 12 and 17 and Roberto Saviano, *Gomorrah. A Personal Journey into the Violent International Empire of Naples' Organized Crime System* (New York: Picador, 2008).

5. The offense of mafia-type criminal organization was inserted in Italy's Penal Code in 1982 as Article *416bis*, transforming the meta-juridical concept of mafia into an ad hoc juridical category. Accordingly, a mafia-type criminal organization consists of three or more persons "who belong to it make use of the power of intimidation afforded by the associative bond and the state of subjugation and criminal silence (*omertà*) which derives from such a bond to commit crimes, to acquire directly or indirectly the management or control of economic activities, concessions, authorizations or public contracts and services, either to gain unjust profits or advantages for themselves or for others or to prevent or obstruct the free exercise of the vote and to obtain votes for themselves or others during elections." For analysis of the offence, see G. Turone, *Il delitto di associazione mafiosa* (Milan: Giuffrè, 2012). See also Ministero dell'Interno, Relazione semestrale ... 2012, 130–137.

6. Ministero dell'Interno, Relazione semestrale sull'attività svolta e i risultati conseguiti dalla Direzione Investigativa Antimafia nel primo semestre del 2002. 2002: 57–64, <http://www.interno.gov.it/dip_ps/dia/page/relazioni_semestrali.html>.

7. E.g., Ministero dell'Interno, Relazione semestrale ... 2002, and Monica Massari and Stefano Becucci, eds., *Mafie nostre, mafie loro. Criminalità organizzata italiana e straniera al Centro Nord* (Milan: Comunità, 2001).

8. Osservatorio socio-economico sulla criminalità. La criminalità organizzata cinese in Italia. Caratteristiche e linee evolutive (Rome: CNEL, 2011), <http://www.cnel.it/53?shadow_documenti=18490>.

9. Ministero dell'Interno, Relazione semestrale ... 2012, 239–275. See also Paoli, "The Paradoxes of Organised Crime."

10. E.g., Paolo Pezzino, *Una certa reciprocità di favori. Mafia e modernizzazione violenta nella Sicilia postunitaria* (Milan: Angeli, 1990) and Salvatore Lupo, *History of the Mafia* (New York: Columbia University Press, 2009).

11. Isaia Sales, "Camorra," in Enciclopedia Treccani, ed., *Appendice 2000* (Rome, Treccani, 2001), 468–469, 468. See also John Dickie, *Blood Brotherhoods: A History of Italy's Three Mafias* (New York: Public Affairs, 2014).

12. Pino Arlacchi, *Mafia Business: The Mafia Ethic and the Spirit of Capitalism* (Oxford: Oxford University Press, 1988), 137.

13. Paoli, *Mafia Brotherhoods*, 40–51; Procura della Repubblica presso il Tribunale di Reggio Calabria, Decreto di fermo di indiziato di delitto—artt. 384 e segg. c.p.p.—nei confronti di A. A.M.+156, 2010.

14. Max Weber, *Economy and Society* (Berkeley: University of California Press, 1978), 48.

15. Paoli, *Mafia Brotherhoods*, 51–64.

16. Aaron Pettinari, "Operazione Perseo: 99 arresti. Decapitata la nuova 'cupola,'" *Antimafia duemila*, December 16, 2008, <archivio.antimafiaduemila.com/rassegna-stampa/30-news/11656-operazione-perseo-99-arresti-decapitata-la-nuova-cupola.html>.

17. Procura della Repubblica presso il Tribunale di Reggio Calabria, Decreto di Fermo.

18. Paoli, *Mafia Brotherhoods*, 51–52.

19. Paoli, *Mafia Brotherhoods*, 72–75, 108–112 and 120–140.

20. Weber, *Community and Society*, 672.

21. Marshall D. Sahlins, *Stone Age Economics* (Chicago: Aldine Atherton, 1972), 193–200.

22. Paoli, *Mafia Brotherhoods*, 89–100.

23. Alexander Stille, *Excellent Cadavers: The Mafia and the Death of the First Italian Republic* (London: Jonathan Cape, 1995).
24. Paoli, *Mafia Brotherhoods*, 141–164 and Europol, Threat Assessment, 5–9.
25. Diego Gambetta, *The Sicilian Mafia: The Business of Private Protection.* (Cambridge, MA: Harvard University Press, 1993).
26. Commissione parlamentare d'inchiesta sul fenomeno della mafia e sulle altre associazioni similari, *Relazione sui rapporti tra mafia e politica con note integrative*, doc. XXIII, no. 2, XI Legislature (Rome: Camera dei Deputati, 1993).
27. Giulio Andreotti was a member of parliament from 1948 until 2013, prime minister seven times, and a government minister countless times.
28. Corte Suprema di Cassazione, Sentenza n.49691/2004, 2004.
29. Massimo Ciancimino, and Francesco La Licata, *Don Vito. Le relazione segrete tra Stato e mafia nel racconto di un testimone d'eccezione* (Milan: Feltrinelli, 2010).
30. Umberto Santino, *L'alleanza e il compromesso. Mafia e politica dai tempi di Lima e Andreotti ai giorni nostri* (Soveria Mannelli: Rubbettino, 1997).
31. Paoli, *Mafia Brotherhoods*, 154–172.
32. Vittorio Mete, *Fuori dal comune: lo scioglimento delle amministrazioni locali per infiltrazioni mafiose* (Acireale: Bonanno, 2009).
33. Elisa Ciccarello, "Mafia, governo Monti ha sciolto 25 comuni: 'Con Cancellieri niente mediazioni," *Il fatto quotidiano*, December 7, 2012, <http://www.ilfattoquotidiano.it/2012/12/07/mafia-governo-monti-ha-sciolto-25-comuni-cantone-con-cancellieri-niente-mediazioni/438429/>.
34. Corte Suprema di Cassazione. Sentenza 19 aprile 2011 n. 15583.
35. Stille, *Excellent Cadavers*.
36. Ministero dell'Interno, Relazione semestrale ... 2012, 71–79.
37. Ministero dell'Interno, Relazione semestrale ... 2012, 327–340. See also Antonio La Spina, "The Fight Against the Italian Mafia," in Paoli, ed., *Oxford Handbook of Organized Crime*, 594–612.
38. E.g., Procura della Repubblica presso il Tribunale di Reggio Calabria, Decreto di Fermo.
39. Paoli, *Mafia Brotherhoods*, 153; see also Procura della Repubblica presso il Tribunale di Reggio Calabria, Decreto di Fermo, 2083–2580.
40. Salvo Palazzolo, "Confisca miliardaria al re dell'eolico," *La Repubblica*, April 4, 2013, 20.
41. Ministero dell'Interno, *Relazione semestrale . . . 2012*, 131; Europol, Threat Assessment, 17.
42. US Department of Treasury. Treasury Sanctions Members of the Camorra. August 1, 2012.
43. Kleemans, Edward and Henk van de Bunt, *Georganiseerde criminaliteit in Nederland* (The Hague: Boom, 2007) and Letizia Paoli, Victoria A. Greenfield and Andries Zoutendijk, "The Harm of Cocaine Trafficking. Applying a New Framework for Assessment," *Journal of Drug Issues*, 43, no. 4 (2013), 407–436.
44. Commissione parlamentare, Relazione annuale sulla 'Ndrangheta, 19.
45. Paulo Campana, "Eavesdropping on the Mob: The Functional Diversification of Mafia Activities across Territories," *European Journal of Criminology*, 8, no. 3 (2011), 213–228.
46. Europol, Threat Assessment, 8.
47. Paoli, *Mafia Brotherhoods*, 159–60.
48. SVIMEZ, *Rapporto Svimez 2013 sull'economia del Mezzogiorno* (Bologna: Il Mulino, 2013).
49. Censis, *Il condizionamento delle mafie sull'economia, sulla società e sulle istituzioni del Mezzogiorno* (Roma: Censis, 2009), 42–47.

50. Emilia Bonaccorsi di Patti, *Weak Institutions and Credit Availability: The Impact of Crime on Bank Loans* (Banca d'Italia Occasional Paper No. 52, 2009).

51. Paolo Pinotti, *The Economic Costs of Organized Crime: Evidence from Southern Italy* (Banca d'Italia Working Paper 868, 2012).

52. E.g., La Spina, "The Fight Against the Italian Mafia."

53. Ministero dell'Interno, 2001. Relazione semestrale sull'attività svolta e i risultati conseguiti dalla Direzione Investigativa Antimafia nel secondo semestre del 2000, <http://www.interno.gov.it/dip_ps/dia/page/relazioni_semestrali.html>.

54. Direzione Investigativa Antimafia. Valori dei sequestri e delle confische dal 1992—2011 e dati complessivi ordinanze di custodia cautelare, <http://www.interno.gov.it/dip_ps/dia/page/rilevazioni_statistiche.html>.

55. Direzione Investigativa Antimafia. Valori dei sequestri.

56. Ministero della Giustizia, Anno giudiziario 2010: Relazione del Ministero—Dipartimento dell'amministrazione penitenziaria, 2011; and Ministero della Giustizia, Detenuti presenti per tipologia di reato. Situazione al 30 Giugno 2013, <http://www.giustizia.it/giustizia/it/mg_1_14_1.wp?facetNode_1=0_2&previsiousPage=mg_1_14&contentId=SST935038>.

57. Direzione Investigativa Antimafia. Valori dei sequestri.

58. "Dell'Utri, la Cassazione conferma la condanna a 7 anni," May 14, 2014, *La Repubblica*, <http://www.repubblica.it/politica/2014/05/09/news/dell_utri_sentenza_cassazione-85677592/ntimafia>.

59. Ministero dell'Interno. Relazione al Parlamento sulle speciali misure di protezione, sulla loro efficacia e sulle modalità generali di applicazione—1 luglio—31 dicembre 2011. 2012, <http://www.interno.gov.it/dip_ps/dia/page/relazioni_semestrali.html>.

60. Paoli, *Mafia Brotherhoods*, 94–100.

61. Lirio Abbate, *Fimmine ribelli: Come le donne salveranno il paese dalla 'ndrangheta* (Milan: Rizzoli, 2013).

62. Istat, *Statistische giudiziarie penali* (Rome: Istat, Annual).

63. Ministero dell'Interno, *Relazione semestrale sull'attività svolta e i risultati conseguiti dalla Direzione Investigativa Antimafia nel secondo semestre del 2005* 2006, 20–1, <http://www.interno.gov.it/dip_ps/dia/page/relazioni_semestrali.html>.

64. Europol, Threat Assessment, 12.

PART IX

EXTERNAL RELATIONS

CHAPTER 52

ITALY AND THE ATLANTIC ALLIANCE

MARIO DEL PERO

GEOPOLITICAL imperatives can shape geographical imagination. One needs, however, to seriously stretch the meaning of geography to render Italy "North Atlantic." Highlighting to President Truman the pros and cons of Italy's inclusion in the Atlantic Alliance, Secretary of State Dean Acheson, who personally favored Italy's participation, was very explicit: "Italy is not physically on the Atlantic ocean," he wrote. Admitting it into the Alliance would extend the "commitments of the Parties beyond the North Atlantic areas and into the Mediterranean," raising legitimate questions "as to why Greece and Turkey were not also included."[1]

The president concurred; and so did the most senior members of the Senate Foreign Relations Committee, who initially opposed extending the invitation to Italy. On the left, there was also uneasiness: Italy was a young and frail democracy, had been a fascist enemy during the war, and the arms restrictions clauses of the 1947 Peace Treaty greatly limited its potential contribution to the Alliance. Furthermore, it was not a member of the United Nations, and that undermined one of the arguments of the supporters of the Pact: its full compatibility with the UN charter. "By what stretch of reasoning can Italy be classed as a North Atlantic power?," the *Washington Post* asked rhetorically: "would it not be just as logical to include Greece or Turkey or Egypt or, for that matter, Poland and Russia, which front on the Baltic and Arctic as Italy fronts on the Mediterranean?"[2]

Not Atlantic, not a member of the United Nations, militarily weak, and punished, Italy was also politically unstable and could easily go over to the enemy camp, given the presence of the strongest pro-Soviet Communist Party of the (soon to be) Western world. Everything was therefore against Italy's admission into the Alliance. But despite everything, Italy was in the end accepted among the original signatories of the North Atlantic Pact. Geographical common sense notwithstanding, in 1949 the High Seas reached the Italian shores and Italy thus became nominally "North Atlantic."[3]

Various factors converged in helping Italy's bid. France intensely lobbied for the inclusion of its neighbor, in order to balance Anglo-American preponderance and extend the security guarantee of the Alliance to its Algerian departments. The US Joint Chiefs of Staff repeatedly emphasized the increasing strategic importance of the Mediterranean and of the Italian islands. Italy's Prime Minister Alcide De Gasperi, Foreign Minister Count Carlo Sforza, and ambassador to the United States Alberto Tarchiani all worked hard to promote the case of Italy and win over the many skeptics within the governmental coalition and the dominating party, the Christian Democrats (Democrazia Cristiana, DC), who opposed participation to the new Alliance.[4]

The most important element was Italy's vulnerability, however. Rebuffing Italy could mean pushing it towards a position of neutrality and non-alignment, weakening those pro-US forces that had won the 1948 elections and bet on the alliance with Washington. Furthermore, such a choice would be incongruous with the parallel process that had progressively inserted Italy within a US-led web of economic interdependences and interconnections.

The paradox, and the irony, were quite striking. Italy became "Atlantic" not because of what it had and could offer, but because of what it lacked and needed; because, in other words, it was a problem more than an asset. As frequently during the Cold War, the geopolitical significance of Italy, and the attention the United States dedicated to it, was a function of its problems: what rendered the country important was its fragility more than its strength, what it was more than what it did or tried to do.

These basic contradictions have marked Italy's history in the Atlantic Alliance. This history must therefore be studied by focusing on three different elements:

a) The operational role played by Italy in the Alliance and its organization, NATO.
b) Italy's political and diplomatic activism within the Alliance and the constant, and often frustrated, efforts of the Italian governments to count more, challenging consolidated intra-Alliance hierarchies.
c) The interplay between foreign policy and domestic politics, the Alliance and its structures being present in Italy, and, more importantly, constituting a crucial vehicle of legitimization for domestic political forces.

These three dimensions, and their interplay, shaped the history of Italy's participation in the Atlantic Alliance throughout the various phases of the post-World War II period.

1949–1963

After the signing of the North Atlantic Pact, the main problem for the United States was to effectively co-opt Italy within the Alliance, while exploiting the possibility to station troops and bases on the peninsula. Both the Truman (1945–53) and the Eisenhower (1953–61) administrations pressured the Italians to contribute more to the common defense effort. Particularly during the early 1950s, the US urged Italy, along with other members of the community, to rearm, redirect its industrial production to satisfy

NATO's military needs, and accept the inclusion of the Federal Republic of Germany (FRG) within the Western security area. This last goal induced the United States to finally support the ill-devised plan to create a European Defence Community (EDC), a supranational institution where West German units would be placed under a European military and political authority.

The Italian government often resisted these pressures and American requests to share more of the "Atlantic burden." Just as with the Marshall Plan, Italy was eager to receive US off-shore procurements and the economic stimulus they provided; much less so to use them as requested by Washington. Finally, and to the chagrin and dismay of the United States, the Italian government signed the treaty that in 1952 created the EDC, but then tried to tie its parliamentary ratification to the solution of the dispute with Yugoslavia over the city of Trieste, which was still divided in two zones, administered respectively by the Allied Military Government and the Yugoslav government.

The EDC never saw the light, finally killed by the French National Assembly in August 1954. This was just the first of a long list of transatlantic disputes destined to mark the history of the Atlantic community. In a pattern that was cyclically reproduced in the following decades, the Americans accused the Europeans (and the Italians) of not doing enough and hiding behind America's protection (and high defense spending), while the Europeans (and the Italians) denounced America's arrogance and quasi-imperialism.[5]

Reciprocal frustrations notwithstanding, both sides were getting something in return: military protection and political support for the Italian government; bases, troops and semi-imperial privileges for the United States. In 1954 the two sides signed an agreement regulating the status of US/NATO forces deployed in Italy (the so-called Status of Forces Agreement). The accord defined the rights, and indeed privileges, of American soldiers present in Italy, who fell solely under US criminal jurisdiction. Furthermore, several US and NATO military installations were established, the more important being the air base of Aviano, in the North East, where in 1955 the United States Air Forces in Europe moved its Italian operations, and the base of Bagnoli, near Naples, site of the Allied Forces Southern Europe, the main NATO command in the Mediterranean area.

In exchange, the Italian government hoped to become more influential within the Alliance. Rome justified its request to count more by emphasizing the shifting geopolitical equilibria of the Cold War, the increasing importance of the Middle East, and, consequently, of the Mediterranean. Within NATO, the main goal of the Italian government was to challenge the "first-tier status" of Great Britain, France, and the FRG, which had joined the Alliance in 1955. Political and symbolic considerations played a role in this almost desperate search to enhance Italy's prestige and international recognition.[6] Just as many other countries, Italy harbored ambitions to develop a nuclear arsenal or be part of a nuclear multinational group within NATO. But the Italian government sought also to count more by emphasizing the non-military aspects of the Alliance and the necessity to give substance to Article 2 of the North Atlantic Treaty, which stressed the importance of encouraging economic collaboration among the member states.

Finally, this effort was matched by the attempt to build (or, at least, pretend to build) a "special relationship" of sorts with the senior American ally. The Italian ruling elites did not miss a chance to stress, and overplay, their Atlantic allegiance and commitment, inducing many commentators to frequently caricature Italy as the "Bulgaria of the West." A caricature this reference indeed was. Throughout the entire Cold War, and more intensely in this first phase, there was a huge gap between realities and perceptions, rhetoric and policies, words and deeds. The post-De Gasperi Christian Democratic leaders ambiguously tried to pursue different, and possibly incompatible, goals: to count more within the Alliance; constantly prove their Atlantic and anti-Communist credentials; use US support and endorsement in the domestic and intra-DC quarrels; free-ride in the Cold War, through the promotion of autonomous initiatives; dilute the military character of the organization, to satisfy a domestic public opinion (which included many Catholics) uneasy with the Atlantic community, as well as with the idea of a permanent security alliance with the United States.

Striking a balance among these different objectives was virtually impossible. Contradictions, ambiguities, and inconsistencies inevitably ensued. In the late 1950s and early 1960s they were epitomized by the so-called policy of "Neo-Atlanticism," promoted by the Italian president, Giovanni Gronchi, a leftist Christian Democrat elected in 1955, who in the past had expressed reservations about Italy's participation in the Atlantic Alliance, and by Amintore Fanfani, a less volatile DC member, who was Prime Minister (and also Foreign Minister) in 1958–59 and then again from July 1960 to June 1963.

Wrapped in the rhetoric of the "bridge" that Italy was, allegedly, between two civilizations—East and West, Christianity and Islam—"Neo-Atlanticism" was invoked to justify several over-ambitious initiatives, primarily aimed at fostering good relations with the Arab world that often irritated the senior US ally. Washington doubted Italy's reliability and diplomatic weight, and rarely considered Rome an ally on a par with France, Great Britain, and the FRG.

Meanwhile, the interplay between international (and transatlantic) dynamics and domestic politics operated not just in the attempt of many non-Communist politicians and groups to exploit the relationship with the United States for their own political goals, but also in the decision to use Atlantic structures to anchor Italy to the Western security system more closely. Clandestine, and later very controversial, structures were thus created in order to have them in place had Italy been lost legally (i.e. through electoral results) to the Communist camp or had Western Europe been invaded by the Soviet Union. The most notorious of these "stay-behind" organizations was *Gladio* (from the name of the Roman sword *Gladius*), a paramilitary structure that was part of the clandestine program of NATO.[7] Still to be told, the story of *Gladio* offers a paradigmatic example of the sort of dual allegiance imposed by the Cold War, and its partitions, to Italian political forces, who could be asked to choose between allegiance to the constitution of the Italian Republic or to the international alliance of which Italy was now a member.[8]

EARLY 1960S–LATE 1970S

The elements that had early informed Italy's behavior in (and attitude towards) Atlantic institutions—desire to count more, attempts to free ride, interplay between international relations and domestic politics, the illusion that there could be a special relationship with the United States—were clearly on display even during the second phase of the post-1945 period that covers most of the 1960s and the 1970s.

This period was marked by the long season of détente between the two superpowers. Italy's reaction to bipolar détente was similar, in its fundamental ambiguity, to that of most European members of the Alliance. On the one side détente promised to reduce tensions, and thus the risk of conflict, in Europe. Furthermore, it seemed to offer the possibility to engage economically the USSR and the countries of the Soviet bloc, opening opportunities for profitable investments and exchanges. On the other hand, bipolar détente appeared to further consolidate US/Soviet hegemony in Europe, freezing the geopolitical status quo, and reducing the strategic importance of the continent—and therefore the ability of European nations to influence international relations and processes.

Additional factors shaped the response of Italy, and of its main political forces, to détente. For conservative groups, particularly within the Democrazia Cristiana, détente represented a major threat: the reduction of Cold War tensions risked removing their main, external source of legitimization, namely anti-Communism. On the contrary, the Christian Democratic left saw détente in a different light: as a structural change that could free Italy from the Cold War straightjacket and pave the way for the formation of center-left governmental coalitions that included parties not necessarily pro-Atlantic. Once again, the interplay between international dynamics and domestic politics proved to be deep and inescapable.

This "nexus" shaped two important processes that marked Italian politics in the 1960s and the 1970s: the formation of the first center-left government, which included the formerly pro-Soviet Socialist Party (Partito Socialista Italiano, PSI) in 1963; and the "historical compromise" launched by the Secretary of the Italian Communist Party (Partito Comunista Italiano, PCI), Enrico Berlinguer, that would eventually lead to a DC minority government supported also by Communist members of Parliament in 1976. In both cases, the leaders of the two main Italian leftist parties felt they had to prove their Atlantic allegiance. In January 1962, Pietro Nenni, the PSI leader, published an important article in the journal *Foreign Affairs*. While reiterating the PSI's difference from other Western European socialist parties and its "opposition to military pacts and alliances," Nenni admitted that withdrawing from NATO would "jeopardize the European equilibrium." Fourteen years later, the PCI's secretary Enrico Berlinguer used similar concepts during an interview for the main Italian daily *Il Corriere della Sera*. "I don't wish Italy to leave NATO," Berlinguer declared: "within the Atlantic Pact, Italy can contribute to consolidate the international equilibria and freely build socialism."[9]

The United States reacted differently to these two "openings to the Left," first to the Socialists and then to the Communists, because the times, the Italian interlocutors, and also the US administrations were different. Despite divisions within the State department and among his main advisers, Kennedy finally gave his blessing to the DC-PSI alliance, hoping it could adopt those progressive reforms the Kennedy modernizers believed necessary to fully "Westernize" the country.[10] The Ford, Nixon, and, albeit less rigidly, Carter administrations instead adamantly opposed the historical compromise and the idea that the PCI could enter the governmental coalition as a junior partner of the Christian Democrats. Central, once again, were the potential political and symbolic repercussions within the Atlantic sphere. Henry Kissinger, at the time Secretary of State, put it with his characteristic bluntness:

> "When you imagine what communist Governments will do inside NATO ... it doesn't make any difference whether they [the Italian Communists] are controlled by Moscow or not. It will unravel NATO and the European community into a neutralist instrument. And that is the essence of it. Whether or not these parties are controlled from Moscow—that's a subsidiary issue ... A Western Europe with the participation of communist parties is going to change the basis of NATO ... to bring the communist into power in Western Europe ... would totally reorient the map of postwar Europe."[11]

This period was also marked by two other common and quasi-structural features of Italy's experience within the Atlantic Alliance: Rome's attempts at free-riding and US propensity to meddle and interfere in Italian domestic affairs. Italy's ambition to balance autonomous foreign policy initiatives with public declarations of Atlantic loyalty persisted. The radical challenge of French President Charles De Gaulle, which eventually led France to abandon the NATO military integrated command in 1966, somehow obfuscated Italy's ambiguities and feeble Atlanticism. Washington certainly appreciated the Italian government's support of the United Kingdom's request to join the Common European Market (which was eventually vetoed by France). But the Italian governments did not renounce the country's ambition to find a distinctive role in the international system and the Atlantic community. It therefore continued promoting ambitious, and often unrealistic, foreign policy initiatives. Among them were attempts to mediate in the Vietnam conflict, offering peace plans that both sides, the United States and North Vietnam, ultimately rejected. Amintore Fanfani, at the time Foreign Minister in the government of the leftist DC Aldo Moro, expressed reservations and criticisms towards the US intervention in Indochina, provoking the angry reaction of the Italian ambassador to Washington, Sergio Fenoaltea, who resigned, protesting a behavior he deemed incompatible with Italy's alliance, and special relationship, with Washington.[12]

On the US side, the growing frustration with the perceived lack of progress in Italy, the persistent strength of the Italian Communist Party, and what was often considered to be Italy's half-hearted and opportunistic Atlanticism produced a more rigid attitude and a change of strategy. Already in 1965, Kennedy and Johnson's National Security

Advisor McGeorge Bundy had complained about the propensity of Italian actors to exploit the Cold War and extract aid and concessions from Washington while offering little in return. Bundy urged a drastic reduction of American covert funding for anti-Communist parties: "we have not been getting our full money's worth," he wrote to Johnson.[13]

President Richard Nixon (1969–74) and his National Security Advisor, Henry Kissinger, had even less patience with Rome, and did not share Bundy's faith in liberal/progressive solutions for Italy's problems. They believed Italy had to be anchored more solidly to the Atlantic bloc. To achieve this goal, they were ready to support very conservative anti-Communist groups, to whom they channeled unprecedented levels of covert aid, particularly during Graham Martin's tenure as ambassador in Rome (October 1969—February 1973).[14]

Kissinger, Nixon, and Martin were certainly less sensitive than their predecessors to protecting the frail Italian democracy. What they hoped for, however, was not an authoritarian response: a Greek or Chilean solution of sorts. What they were aiming at was pressuring the DC to the right and inducing it to adopt a more consistent and reliable "Atlantic" approach.

During the 1970s, the entire Southern European flank of the Atlantic Alliance and the Western security system appeared to be at risk, however. Greater Soviet activism in the region seemed to combine with the political and economic difficulties of the local allies of the United States, Italy included, in helping to make the area unstable and more permeable to Communist influence. Because of its economic difficulties, political instability, and often volatile and unpredictable foreign policy, Italy was thus often caricatured as the "soft underbelly" of the Atlantic Alliance: an unreliable partner, always at risk of going to the other camp by legal (i.e. electoral) means. Throughout the 1970s, America's rough pressures and interferences were nevertheless contained by the other European members of the Atlantic Alliance. Within NATO, in the new unofficial forum of the richest and most industrialized states (G6 and then G7) as well as in ad hoc quadripartite summits of French, American, British, and German representatives, the Italian malaise was ultimately managed via multilateral channels, similar to what happened in the complex democratic transitions that took place at the time in Greece, Spain, and Portugal.[15]

The 1980s and the End of the Cold War

The usual ambiguities and contradictions of Italy's Atlanticism characterized even the last decade of the Cold War. The collapse of détente and the renewal of tensions between the two superpowers—the brief but intense "second Cold War" of the early 1980s—seemed to re-cement the Atlantic cohesion that had often been shattered in the previous two decades. This renewed, albeit brief and partial, Atlantic unity led to the decision in 1979 to install medium-range ballistic and ground-based missiles (the so-called "Euromissiles") in the territory of European NATO members in response to the Soviet deployment of the SS-20. NATO's was a dual track decision, since the "Euromissiles" were to be installed only four years later, in 1983, if negotiations with the Soviets to remove the SS-20 failed.

West Germany made its acceptance of the missiles on its territory conditional on the analogous availability of at least one other member of the Alliance. Italy stepped in, despite the opposition of the PCI and large segments of public opinion, and the consequent mobilization of what soon became a broad pacifist movement. Central in this regard was the role played by the Socialist Party and its new, controversial, and energetic leader Bettino Craxi, who adopted an uncompromising anti-Soviet and anti-Communist stance, justified through frequent denunciation of the oppressive nature of the Soviet regime and its constant violation of basic human and political rights. After the 1970s, the discourse and politics of human rights had occupied the center stage of international relations. Human rights thus offered a bridge of sorts—political, ethical, and even discursive—between the European (and Italian) non-Communist left and sectors of the New Right that were governing at the time in the United States and Great Britain. Again, however, considerations of domestic politics played an important role. Just as Nenni had 20 years earlier, Craxi found an important vehicle of political legitimization in stressing his (and his party's) Atlantic allegiance and commitment. In the case of the new Socialist leader, Atlanticism and neo-liberalism converged in conferring the necessary investiture to be a legitimate governmental actor: in August 1983, Craxi became the first Socialist in Italy's history to be appointed Prime Minister.

The decision to join France and the United States in the multinational peacekeeping/ enforcing contingent that was dispatched to Lebanon in 1982 to mediate in the civil war was connected to the desire of the Italian government to prove its Atlantic trustworthiness and enhance its international prestige. But the Lebanese operation ended up revealing, once again, Italy's peculiarity within the Atlantic Alliance as well as the partiality of its Atlanticism. While France, and even more the United States, tended to side with one faction in the conflict and aimed to contain the influence of Islamic groups, the Italian government repeatedly stressed the purely humanitarian concern of the operation and the necessity to remain above the fray. In doing so, Italian political leaders as well as the military on the field resorted to traditional discursive tropes that stressed Italy's role as a bridge between two civilizations and special connection to the Arab world.[16]

Similarly to many of his DC predecessors, Craxi adopted a pro-Arab (and pro-Palestine) stance that often irritated the senior American ally. This approach led to a major diplomatic crisis in 1985, when a group of Palestine terrorists hijacked the Italian cruise ship *Achille Lauro* off the Egyptian coast and killed an American passenger. After a testy exchange with President Reagan, Craxi refused to consign the terrorists to the US: a decision lauded, at the time and retrospectively, across the political board and often presented as a bold and rare example of Italy's ability to stand up to the United States and its pressures.

The crisis of the *Achille Lauro*, and the successive tensions between Italy and the United States over the decision of Reagan to bomb Libya, did not cause the escalation many feared. They were indicative, however, of the persistence in Italy's foreign and Atlantic policy of traits that rendered it a partner not always reliable or credible, in the eyes of the United States and of the most important members of the Alliance.

THE POST-COLD WAR PERIOD

The end of the Cold War led many experts and commentators to predict the inevitable collapse of NATO: a relic of the past, it was often argued, that had lost its *raison d'être* with the collapse of the Soviet Union and the Communist bloc. The Alliance appears indeed to have spent most of the post-Cold War period seeking a rationale for its survival and existence, as testified by the numerous attempts to imagine a new mission and define—in NATO's typical argot—a new "strategic concept."[17]

NATO justified and conceived its enlargement to the East in terms remarkably similar to those used in 1949 with Italy: as a way to facilitate the post-authoritarian transitions in Central-Eastern Europe and consolidate the frail democracies created on the ruins of the former Soviet bloc. But in the post-Cold War scenario, NATO also invented for itself a new, and far less regional, role as peacekeeper and enforcer that led to an expansion of its operations well outside the original Eurocentric perimeter.

Once again, just as in 1949, geopolitical considerations shaped and stretched geographical imagination, rendering the original Central-European core of the Alliance less central, if not marginal. NATO and US installations in the area were decommissioned and closed, including important facilities in Italy, while the number of US troops in Europe was drastically reduced (from the peak of about 400,000 soldiers permanently based in Europe in the early 1950s to the current 80,000).

In this changed, and still mutable and capricious, scenario, the role of Italy within the Alliance and the impact of the Alliance on Italian politics have remained important. The renewed geopolitical centrality of the Middle East, and the greater commitment of the United States in the area, have accentuated the importance of NATO's Southern Flank. This was true during the two Gulf Wars (1991 and 2003). But even the dramatic civil war in the former Yugoslavia, and NATO's intervention first in Bosnia (1995) and then in Kosovo (1999), showed the persistent strategic relevance of Italy and of NATO's installations in the country (particularly the base of Aviano).

Meanwhile, within Italy controversies over the country's role in the Alliance and participation in its missions have continued unabated. Furthermore, 'Atlanticism' remained a sort of litmus test of political legitimacy for Italian political actors. This was clear in the three main post-Cold War international crises that have involved the Atlantic community: the previously mentioned Gulf wars, and the intervention in the former Yugoslavia.

During the first Gulf War, launched in reaction to the Iraqi invasion of Kuwait, the Italian government and political parties responded with typical ambiguity. Italy joined the multinational operation led by the United States, and actively participated in the air raids launched over Iraq. But it did not renounce its ambitions to mediate in the dispute, offer unrealistic peace proposals, and pretend to represent a special interlocutor for the part of the Arab world that had sided with the Iraqi regime.[18]

The intervention NATO undertook in Kosovo in 1999 and the bombing of Serbia also proved very controversial. Large sectors of Italy's public opinion were against it, while leftist minority parties within the governmental coalition led by Massimo D'Alema—the first former Communist Prime Minister in Italy's history—imposed strict (and ultimately disregarded) operational constraints to the participation of the Italian military. Once again, joining the Atlantic bandwagon appeared to offer a political dividend, and a legitimization of sorts, to an ex-Communist like D'Alema, Atlanticism still representing the decisive test for defining the international reliability of Italy's governmental forces. Italy's support of the intervention, and active involvement in military operations, was justified by frequent references to the evolving post-Cold War strategic scenario and the consequent necessity to redefine the role and objectives of the Atlantic Alliance. According to this reading, which made more palatable Italy's continuing involvement in the Alliance to sectors of the domestic left, the Yugoslav wars proved the continuing relevance of NATO as a stability guarantor and peace "enforcer" on the continent. The consequence, somehow paradoxical for the formally very pro-EU left that governed the country in the late 1990s, was to strengthen the bilateral relationship with the United States to the detriment of plans to forge a more autonomous European security policy.[19]

Similar considerations informed the behavior of Silvio Berlusconi, the media tycoon and center-right political leader who was Prime Minister at the time of the second Gulf War in 2003, which led to the final collapse of Saddam Hussein's regime in Iraq. Italy had participated in the NATO operation in Afghanistan (the International Security Assistance Force) since its inception. Despite the opposition of a clear majority of the Italian public to the military intervention in Iraq, Silvio Berlusconi—a controversial figure, suffering himself from a deficit of legitimacy outside Italy—decided to side unequivocally with the US administration of George W. Bush and tried to extract maximum political advantage from this decision. The firm Atlantic and pro-US posture of the Berlusconi government happened during one of the worst crises in the history of NATO, when several commentators predicted the inevitable end of the Atlantic Alliance.[20] The ensuing transatlantic divide revealed, once again, the tension between Italy's full loyalty to the United States within the traditional Atlantic structure and its support of the plans to expand EU capabilities in the security sphere.

Conclusions

The role of Italy in the Atlantic Alliance, and the impact of the Alliance on Italy's foreign policy and domestic politics, have inevitably changed over time, as a consequence of the evolution of the international system and of US and Italian foreign policy priorities and interests. During the different phases of the post-1945 period that I have identified in this essay, there have also been, however, remarkable continuities in the "Atlantic story" of Italy. Three are the main structural elements of this story. The first is Italy's partial, and somehow instrumental, Atlanticism. Like many other allies of the United States, Italy has tried to exploit its role as a junior partner of the United States to extract concessions and gain advantages. This attempt often informed and qualified the behavior of Italy within the Atlantic alliance. The second trait is represented by the "national/international nexus" and the peculiar condition of the Italian republic—where the strongest pro-Soviet Communist Party of the West legally operated—during the Cold War. NATO and its structures were involved in Italy and its politics; more important, Atlanticism came to represent a sort of litmus test for those political forces and individuals who aspired to govern: a way to assess their political maturity and indeed legitimacy. Finally, there was a belief, spread across the political board, that geography, history, and culture conferred on Italy a unique role within the Atlantic Alliance: that of a bridge between the West and the East, Christianity and Islam, that rendered it a unique and credible interlocutor with the Arab world.

Notes

1. *Memorandum by the Secretary of State*, March 2, 1949, *Foreign Relations of the United States* (hereinafter FRUS), 1949, Vol. 4: Western Europe (Washington DC: Government Printing Office, 1975), 142.
2. "Misshapen Pact," *The Washington Post*, March 18, 1949; Holmes Alexander, "Atlantic Pact isn't Sacred. It Should Be Discussed," *The Los Angeles Times*, March 28, 1949.
3. Mario Del Pero, "When the High Seas Reached the Italian Shores. Italy's Inclusion in the Atlantic Communitas," in Marco Mariano (ed.), *Defining the Atlantic Community: Culture, Intellectuals, and Policies in the Mid-Twentieth Century* (London: Routledge, 2010), 161–173.
4. Among the many works on Italy's inclusion in the alliance see Antonio Varsori, "*La scelta occidentale dell'Italia (1948–1949)*", *Storia delle Relazioni Internazionali*, no. 1 and 2 (1985), 95–159 and 303–368; Pietro Pastorelli, *La politica estera italiana del dopoguerra* (Bologna: Il Mulino, 1987); Timothy E. Smith, *The United States, Italy and NATO, 1947–1952* (London: Macmillan Press, 1991); Alessandro Brogi, *L'Italia e l'Egemonia Americana nel Mediterraneo* (Florence: La Nuova Italia, 1996); Guido Formigoni, *La Democrazia Cristiana e l'Alleanza Occidentale* (Bologna: Il Mulino, 1996).
5. Mario Del Pero and Federico Romero (eds.), *Le crisi transatlantiche in prospettiva storica* (Rome: Edizioni di Storia e Letteratura, 2007).
6. Alessandro Brogi, *A Question of Self-Esteem: The United States and the Cold War Choices in France and Italy, 1944–1958* (Westport, CT: Praeger, 2002).
7. Daniele Ganser, *NATO's Secret Armies: Operation Gladio and Terrorism in Western Europe* (London: Frank Cass, 2005).
8. Franco De Felice, "Doppia lealtà e doppio stato", *Studi Storici*, no. 3 (July–September 1989), 493–563
9. Pietro Nenni, "Where the Italian Socialists Stand," *Foreign Affairs*, no. 1 (January 1962), 213–223; Giampaolo Pansa, "Berlinguer conta 'anche' sulla NATO per mantenere l'autonomia da Mosca", *Corriere della Sera*, June 15, 1976.

10. Leopoldo Nuti, *Gli Stati Uniti e l'apertura a sinistra. Importanza e limiti della presenza americana in Italia* (Rome and Bari: Laterza, 1999).

11. *Meeting Secretary of State's Staff,* January 12, 1975 and July 1, 1976, National Archives and Record Administration, College Park, Maryland (NARA), RG59: General Records of the Department of State, Lot File 78D443: Transcripts of Secretary of State Kissinger's Staff Meetings, 1973–1977, Box 6 and Box 10.

12. On the resignation of Fenoaltea see Antonio Varsori, *L'Italia nelle relazioni internazionali dal 1943 al 1992* (Rome and Bari: Laterza, 1998), 164.

13. *Memorandum From the President's Special Assistant for National Security Affairs (Bundy) to President Johnson,* August 4, 1965, in FRUS, Vol. 12: *Western Europe,* Washington, Government Printing Office, 2001, <http://history.state.gov/historicaldocuments/frus1964-68v12/ch3>, last accessed August 20, 2013.

14. Lucrezia Cominelli, *Gli Stati Uniti e la crisi italiana degli anni Settanta* (Milano, Le Monnier, 2014); Roberto Gualtieri, "The Italian Political System and Détente," *Journal of Modern Italian Studies,* no. 4 (December 2004), 428–449.

15. Mario Del Pero, Víctor Gavín, Fernando Guirao, and Antonio Varsori, *Democrazie. L'Europa meridionale e la fine delle dittature* (Rome: Le Monnier, 2010).

16. On the nature and ambiguities of Italy's participation to peacekeeping and peace-enforcing operations see Piero Ignazi, Giampiero Giacomello, and Fabrizio Coticchia, *Italian Military Operations Abroad: Just Don't Call it War* (Basingstoke: Palgrave Macmillan, 2012).

17. For the latest exercise see NATO, *Active Engagement, Modern Defence: Strategic Concept for the Defence and Security of the Members of the North Atlantic Treaty Organization,* November 2010; <www.nato.int/strategic-concept/pdf/Strat_Concept_web_en.pdf>, accessed August 23, 2013.

18. Antonio Varsori, *L'Italia e la fine della Guerra Fredda. La politica estera dei governi Andreotti (1989–1992)* (Bologna: Il Mulino, 2013).

19. Luca Ratti, *Italy and NATO Expansion to the Balkans* (Rome: Carocci, 2004).

20. Geil Lundestad (ed.), *Just Another Crisis? The United States and Europe since 2000* (Oxford and New York: Oxford University Press, 2008).

CHAPTER 53

··

GLI ESAMI NON FINISCONO MAI

Italy and the European Union

··

VINCENT DELLA SALA

EDUARDO De Filippo's 1973 play *L'esami non finiscono mai* (The Exams Never End), has as its central character Guglielmo Speranza, a middle-class civil servant who hopes that he will finally find happiness after successfully passing what he hopes will be his last test in life. His existential search provides an apt metaphor for Italy's relationship with European integration. Italy's central role in the creation and evolution of the European Union, and the latter's impact on domestic policy and politics, have been inexorably tied to deeper questions about domestic politics and Italy's modernization. Each time Italy "passed" one of the European tests—entering into the original six, being ready for the single market, joining the euro—the expected sense of having completed a process of political and economic development remained elusive. The story of Italy's relationship with Europe is of a never-ending quest to be European and to complete Italy's modernization. Inevitably, the relationship has been shaped by and has affected domestic politics.

Italy's relationship with Europe has been largely the domain of historians and, perhaps, it is for this reason that it has been examined primarily chronologically. Italian political science, as elsewhere in Europe, made the European Union and its impact on Italy a focus of attention relatively late. There are four main themes which emerge from both scholarly and political commentary on Europe: Italy at the center of Europe, both as a founding member but also as one of the "Big Four" member states alongside Germany, France, and the United Kingdom; European integration as part of the process of modernization of Italian political, social, and economic life; Europeanization, not only making Italy more "European" but also trying to influence European decisions and politics; and the frayed but enduring consensus that Italy has a rightful place in Europe and that Europe is central to Italy's postwar political and social order. All four threads have woven their way through Italy's history with and in Europe; and all four have come to a head in the recent economic crisis in the EU and Italy.

The aim of this chapter is two-fold. First, it will illustrate how the four narratives mentioned above have woven together a story of Italy as a "good European" always pushing for "more Europe," and for more Europe in Italy. Second, it will look at some of the consequences of the recent economic crisis and how they have led to the growing sense that Italy might be starting to show the strains of having sat one exam too many without the desired result. While support for the European project and ideal remains, the challenges of the single currency have revealed processes of economic and social modernization that have not been fully completed.

ITALY AT THE HEART OF EUROPE OR THE LEAST OF THE GREAT POWERS?

The conventional textbook account of Italy's decision to take part in the nascent European project at the end of World War II was that this was an opportunity for Italy to emerge from the ashes of war and the shadow of 20 years of Fascist rule in order to prove its democratic credentials and become a credible actor on the international stage.[1] The circumstances of the first decades of the Cold War contributed to the sense that Italy was an equal partner in postwar Europe. Germany remained divided and on the front lines of superpower rivalry; moreover, the legacy of the interwar period ensured that it would be more willing to deal with other European partners on an equal footing. France was dealing with the end of its colonial empire as well as political instability in the 1950s, and Britain chose not to join the EEC. By the time it eventually joined in 1973, its period of imperial supremacy was a distant memory along with its industrial base. The other members of the EU were politically important, and even former imperial powers, such as the Netherlands, were small in size and perhaps not as important geopolitically as Italy. It was not a stretch for Italian political leaders to claim that Italy was indeed one of the four great powers of Europe.

It was a claim that was strengthened by the central role played by leading figures, such as Alcide De Gasperi and Altiero Spinelli, in guiding the political process that led to the creation of the European Coal and Steel Community but also in providing it with intellectual and even moral leadership.[2] Italy and its leaders were very much part of a postwar generation of political figures who looked to Europe as the way in which to construct a new social order based on liberal, but also social and Christian, democracy. The European project was not something imposed on Italy as a price to pay to rejoin the family of nations but an integral part of a democratic Europe that Italy helped to construct. This narrative was reinforced over the decades with the prominent roles assumed in the European Commission by figures such as Franco Maria Malfatti, Romano Prodi, Mario Monti, and Emma Bonino.

However much the narrative of Italy as one of the Big Four has affected Italy's role in Europe and been part of the domestic politics of European integration within Italy, it is complementary to another concern—captured by the notion of Italy as the "least of the great powers"—which has also characterized Italy's relationship with Europe. The central theme here is that there is a mis-match between Italy's material power—namely Italy's commitment and role in the Atlantic Alliance, its membership of the G7 and the size of its economy, and the relative durability of its industrial base—and the status or position accorded to it within the EU. Discussions about whether Italy is a pygmy or giant in the EU, or its Cinderella, reflect a much more deep-rooted concern with understanding whether Italy's relative power and influence correspond to its status in the EU.[3] These concerns begin from the premise that while Italy has been central to the European project from the start, it was not axiomatic that its weight in the EU matched its size or historic role. Indeed, conventional accounts often either ignore Italy's role or take it as marginal. It is also noteworthy that some of the more critical positions on Italy's role have been taken by former EU officials, who have looked at Italy within the broader evolution of integration; or have been frustrated by the impact of recent Italian governments on Italy's role.[4] Contemporary historians such as Antonio Varsori have provided much more detailed and nuanced accounts of the complex relationship Italy has had with the EU and other member states. As Varsori points out, the narrative of Italy as a minor player was often constructed by scholars (mostly French- and English-speaking) who had little knowledge of Italian and the rich historiography produced by Italian (but also American) historians that painted a much more central role for Italy in both Europe and the transatlantic alliance.[5] What this literature generally demonstrates is that Italy's ability to shape outcomes in the EU tends to vary according to different issues, domestic political conditions, the alignment of political forces in other member states, and its own ability to mediate across the different constellations of forces in the EU.

Whether Italy is seen as a pygmy or a giant is not so important as the extent to which Europe, and Italy's capacity to shape outcomes, have served to meet the country's strategic interests. Moreover, as Mario Del Pero demonstrates in Chapter 53 of this volume, international legitimation was used for domestic purposes, and this was no more the case than it was with European integration. In this sense, there is a broad consensus that close economic and political cooperation, with deeper forms of integration, has been one of the pillars of Italy's postwar political order and economic foundation. Measured against this yardstick—that Italy needed to be central to a peaceful and prosperous Europe to have these qualities at home—the relationship has been a successful one. Italy has not been at the margins nor has Europe been peripheral to Italy's political and economic development. However, constantly trying to prove that Italy is and deserves to be at the centre of the European project has remained a test that continues to shape political debate. The collapse of the Berlusconi government in 2011 was equally due to the perception that it was responsible for the growing marginalization of Italy in Europe as it was to his mishandling of the economy.

The European Road to Italian Modernization

A related theme to that of Italy's place in Europe is how integration has helped complete a process of modernization which started later than in some of the other member states and had an erratic trajectory until the second half of the last century. There is a longer story here, going back at least to Italian unification as part of a broader historical transformation of the state in Europe. In its postwar incarnation, both political and academic commentators see European integration as the continued modernization of state and society in the continent in which Italy was a willing and central participant.[6] A different interpretation is that Italy has not been able to become truly modern on its own, needing some sort of external pressure or commitment to bring about the societal and institutional changes to keep pace with the modernization processes of its European partners.

In the early phases of the integration process, European integration was seen as the means by which Italy could prove its commitment to the fledgling Atlantic Alliance and, if not atone, at least help forget the country's belligerence in the interwar period.[7] Anticipating a narrative which was to be central to the enlargement to other post-Fascist or authoritarian member states (Portugal, Spain, and Greece) and post-Communist member states, Europe was to be a guarantee of the country's development into a functioning liberal democracy with a market economy. The real "danger" was seen in the presence of the largest Communist Party (the Partito Comunista Italiano, PCI) outside the Soviet world and the perception that Italy had somehow not fully developed "modern" institutions or political culture.[8]

In political debate, clearly anchoring Italy in European institutions was another way in which to delegitimize the PCI and brand it as "anti-system."[9] The EU's clear links with Italy's position within the transatlantic alliance and its emphasis on liberal economic principles could hardly be seen as mobilizing either the PCI's base or its leadership. On the other hand, the PCI leadership made efforts as early as the 1950s to ensure that the European question would not be the source of ideological conflict, and sought to promote a pragmatic approach to Italy's position.[10] While the party wanted to be seen as responsible and a reliable partner for the national unity government in the second half of the 1970s, it still argued for a more democratic Europe that was not in the hands of monopoly capital. But the Communist card worked both ways, as Italian Prime Minister Andreotti was keen not to have Italy's position on the European Monetary System dictated by the PCI, while Communist leader Enrico Berlinguer wanted to strengthen relations with European Social Democratic parties.[11]

By the time the Maastricht treaty was signed and Italy committed itself to entering the single currency, there was a broad consensus across all the major parties of the First Republic, and those that followed in their wake, that both the single market and the single currency were opportunities to bring about change in Italy. The *vincolo esterno* was not seen as an intrusion into Italian sovereignty but as a necessary but not necessarily sufficient condition for a series of policy changes that would help the country "modernize" its institutions and policies. Books with titles such as *Condannata al Successo?* and *Salvati dall'Europa?* captured the sense that meeting the test of being part of a transformed European economy would bring about important political and policy changes which would allow Italy to meet the challenges of a post-Cold War world.[12] The question mark at the end of the titles was significant, in that while Europe may have been a catalyst for change, this required a degree of political agency by Italian political actors to seize the opportunities created, especially by the drive for Economic and Monetary Union.[13] They seemed to be asking whether Italy would pass the latest test.

Much of the narrative of Italy's modernization was tied up with the quest to enter the single currency.[14] It provided an opportunity to find a broad consensus on policy reforms to meet the convergence criteria, but also to provide answers to new and not so new policy challenges such as rigidity in labor markets, female employment rates, education and training, and so on. The single currency also provided arguments for "modernizing" the Italian state. This included not only introducing new structures and principles to public administration, trying to catch the new public management wave sweeping the industrialized world, but also rescaling the state.[15] This came in the form of privatization; for example, dismantling IRI, the state-holdings company established in the 1930s, and generally redrawing boundaries of state intervention in the economy. It also came in the form of an attempt to redraw the boundaries between the central state and regions. While Italy did not become a federal republic, the period since the 1990s has seen a gradual shift of responsibilities to the sub-national level. This "modernization" process was further developed by a rebalancing of competencies and attempts to rationalize spending with the reform of Section V of the second part of the Constitution in 2001. The drive to enter the single currency also enhanced attempts to redress the balance of power between the legislature and the executive as well as centralize power in the latter.

European integration was to be the instrument that would help Italy complete a process that had been anything but smooth or linear.[16] The argument about modernization was applied to almost the entire span of issues related to politics, policy, and polity, from creating a social democratic party in Italy along northern European lines to reforming welfare state institutions and policies. Yet modernization can be a never-ending process and not necessarily an endpoint. Europe, and especially the internal market and the single currency, provided a window of opportunity for wide-ranging changes. In many ways, it was not lost, and in recent decades the nature of the Italian state, its institutions, and politics have been transformed radically; and often this has been, directly or indirectly, attributed to European integration. Arguably, no other member state of the EU-15 can claim to have had a complete change in its political parties and party system, new electoral laws, redrawing of central and sub-national competencies, privatization, welfare state reform; and the list goes on. Yet as we will see in the second part of this chapter, there is still the sense that there are more European exams to sit.

Europeanization

The previous section can also lead us to conclude that there are few of the old EU-15 member states to which the notion of "Europeanization"—understood primarily as the transformation of domestic policies and politics in accordance with European rules—has garnered so much attention. This is primarily because it often raises a number of interesting contrasts, usually in the form of "misfits" between domestic and European policies. The discussion here is not so much about completing a transformation of the state and society, as implied by modernization, but about the extent to which Italy needed to adapt its policies and politics to comply with commitments made at European level.

There is not the time or space here to discuss the various ways in which the concept of Europeanization has been used; suffice to say that it is a process that involves not just adaptation to European rules and commitments by member states but also the ways in which these states try to ensure that their preferences affect European choices.[17] While a great deal of attention has been placed on the extent to which Italy has been a "policy taker," having to adjust and adapt to European rules, there also has been some attention on the extent to which Italy has looked to shape European decisions to promote domestic and national interests.[18] This dynamic relationship, both top-down and bottom-up, has in the background the stated position of nearly every postwar Italian government in favor of making the Union "ever closer." What emerges is a complex relationship in which Italy often finds itself scrambling to meet European standards—the push to reach the convergence criteria for the single currency being the best example—but also plays a key role in determining choices made at European level. As Quaglia and Radaelli argue, the center-right governments of Silvio Berlusconi tried the latter approach, seeking to affect European choices at their source, while center-left governments tended to use Europe as a lever to effect change domestically.[19]

Interestingly, the extent to which Italy has or is being "Europeanized" has not been a source of intense political debate. Even high-profile cases, such as the opposition to Italy's nominee to the European Commission Rocco Buttiglione on grounds that his views on gender roles were not consistent with broader European values, did not generate a great deal of flag-waving or reflection about whether or not Italy wanted to share those values. If anything, what generates discussion is the extent to which Italy has not been able to fully exploit what is on offer from Europe or has failed to comply with European law.[20] One area of Europeanization that has received a great deal of attention is regional policy and structural funds.[21] It provides a good illustration of the ways in which Italy sought to affect European policy while at the same time its own structural weaknesses prevented Italian regions from fully exploiting the resources.[22] Regional development, or the lack of it, has been a central theme since unification, but there was little debate or contestation when this became essentially a European policy with little national discretion. This did not, however, eliminate the impact of domestic politics and institutions, as these became obstacles to Italy's capacity to fully exploit structural funds. A series of reforms have sought to provide greater powers to central institutions as well as enhance the regions' capacity to meet European eligibility criteria.[23]

ELITE AND POPULAR CONSENSUS

With rare exceptions, the dying days of the Berlusconi government being a notable one, there has been a political consensus that not only was Italy one of the central players in Europe but that it should be; and that this centrality was due in no small part to the unconditional commitment Italy had made to creating an ever closer union since the immediate postwar period. As mentioned earlier, even those parties which were ideologically predisposed to refute some of the central pillars of the European project never seriously challenged whether Italy should be part of Europe, or vice versa. Amongst political and economic elites, European integration was used by nearly the entire political spectrum as a way to legitimize their claim to governing the country or for being seen as a legitimate political actor (as was the case of the Italian Communist Party for most of the postwar period). In the literature on Euroskepticism, Italy is at best (or worst) considered as having a "soft" form of Euroskepticism with very few traces of outright opposition to the process and pace of integration. Alongside elite consensus, Eurobarometer and other national and international surveys have consistently reported high levels of public support for the EU and European integration.[24]

Moreover, there has been a significant degree of continuity in support amongst political elites over the last half-century despite the important changes in the nature of political parties and party systems.[25] While knowledge about Europe remains relatively low amongst voters, and European issues have not been salient even in European Parliament elections, parties have nonetheless made efforts to express their support for integration.[26] The result is that, until recently, European integration was a resource and not a constraint for policymakers seeking to generate support for policy measures. The "permissive consensus" which helped push integration forward was very much present in Italy and was part of domestic politics and policymaking, especially in the pre-euro period.

ITALY AND EUROPE AFTER THE CRISIS

The crisis, and what it represents for Italy's economic and political development, has highlighted a number of challenges that Italy faces and raised questions about the relationship between Italy and the European Union. Italy's entry into the single currency was greeted with relief, enthusiasm, and more than a little disbelief. It was able to bring down its public sector deficit from double digits at the time it signed the Maastricht treaty to

2.7 percent of GDP when decision time came in 1998. A combination of lower borrowing costs, some spending cuts, tax increases, and use of innovative financial instruments at a time of relatively strong growth helped achieve what seemed unreachable at the start of the process. But the heady days of celebrating the new Italian "miracle" were a distant memory as Italy and Europe prepared to celebrate the tenth anniversary of the launch of the euro in 2012. In November 2011, Mario Monti's technocratic government replaced that of Silvio Berlusconi, after months of extreme uncertainty in financial markets that led to spiraling borrowing costs and worries about the sustainability of Italian public finances as well as the future of Italian banks.

Italy's problems started long before the instability in financial markets brought an end to the Berlusconi government in November 2011. Italy's period in the single currency has been characterized by low growth, declining productivity, a loss of competitiveness, and market share in world trade. With the public debt overhang from the 1980s, a stagnating economy meant that public finances would always remain under close scrutiny by market operators. Being in the eurozone promised (and delivered) lower borrowing costs while removing devaluation as a policy instrument to regain lost competitiveness. It also brought into relief, and under closer scrutiny of international financial markets and institutions, its policymaking record in responding to new and old challenges. As Giuseppe Bertola argues in Chapter 37, the *vincolo esterno* did not have the desired effect of bringing about major structural changes to macroeconomic governance.

The economic crisis has led much political commentary to consistently place Italy in the "periphery," lumped in with other member states that have run into problems such as Greece but especially Spain. The narrative of the "sick man" of Europe with the potential to sink the euro overtook Italy's traditional place as a pivotal state. There are a number of problems with this story. First, while Italy continued to carry a huge public debt load, it had maintained its commitment with respect to borrowing requirements, especially after being subject to the excessive deficit procedure from 2009 to 2013. There was a broad consensus amongst all the political parties to keep deficit levels below the 3 percent level set by European commitments and to aim (and achieve) a primary surplus. While even some of the "core" members of the Eurozone, such as France and the Netherlands, struggled to meet the 3 percent threshold, Italy remained committed to fiscal discipline regardless of who was in government. European institutions could find much to criticize in Italy's policy mix, but lack of fiscal discipline, which condemned Greece and Portugal to the periphery, was not one of them.

Second, while there was no doubt that the Berlusconi government was isolated in the Eurozone and had lost the confidence of financial markets by the middle of 2011, Italy remained a pivotal member of the EU with a degree of leverage. Indeed, by the end of 2011, Prime Minister Monti was being hailed as the savior of the single currency and, along with help from the European Central Bank, was able to bring down the "spread" (the difference between German and Italian borrowing costs) from historic to much more manageable levels. Even Enrico Letta, the head of a fragile national unity government, was accorded a central place in discussions about how to address various elements of the economic crisis in 2013. The point here is that Italy's centrality to the European economy has remained, and its capacity to affect European choices continues to be shaped by a range of factors that make it difficult to lump it into the "periphery."

What the crisis has meant is that Italy can no longer take for granted that it will continue to play this pivotal role. Paradoxically, while the governance of the European Monetary Union (EMU) has meant that national politics will continue to dictate fiscal policy, the stability of the Eurozone is very much affected by the domestic politics of its 18 members. It is a club that does not choose who gets to sit around the table, but it can try to make life difficult for anyone seen to cause instability for others, as was all too apparent in the last months of the Berlusconi government. On August 5, 2011, the then President of the European Central Bank (ECB), Jean-Claude Trichet, and his appointed successor and Governor of the Bank of Italy at the time, Mario Draghi, penned a letter to Prime Minister Berlusconi. It stated explicitly what the Italian government had to do if it wanted to benefit from the ECB's intervention in secondary debt markets. It set off an exchange of missives between the European institutions and the Italian government in October and November 2011, which had two striking features. First, there was nothing new in the reforms that were being solicited. More than a list of conditions to be met in return for help in financial markets, they were an admonition of the inability of Italian governments of all political stripes in the period since the Maastricht treaty to carry out basic structural changes that should have been part of being in the single currency. Second, it is hard not to read the letters from both sides and not notice an underlying lack of faith in the political will to carry out reforms. The Berlusconi response was full of vague references and promises that were not so different from those presented by Italian governments during the previous 20 years. On the other hand, Commissioner Olli Rehn's punctilious note asking for clarifications contained 39 sets of questions and requests that no government, let alone a fragile one on its last legs, could have responded to with a clear set of answers and commitments. More interestingly, the positions on Italy were transformed practically overnight when Mario Monti formed a government with the backing of a large part of Berlusconi's former parliamentary majority, and with a program which only marginally addressed the issues raised in the Trichet and Rehn letters.

The recent crisis has also highlighted that while the single currency was an opportunity to effect changes to Italian politics, policy, and institutions it was one that was, at best, only partially exploited. The euro did lower borrowing costs, introduced price stability, and anchored monetary policy, but these were largely consequences of European decisions and were not driven internally. European integration continues to shape most, if not all, aspects of Italian life, from universities to food, but major reforms of large parts of the economy and social relations remain unimplemented.[27] Structural reforms to product and labor markets were still lacking or largely ineffective, along with a public administration still considered to be too cumbersome and costly. Modernization and Europeanization, understood here in terms of adapting to European rules, continued to be largely incomplete processes.

Conclusion

What has emerged with the economic crisis, and more generally with Italy's experience with the single currency, is a growing political debate about whether Europe continues to be the route to modernization; and if so, whether it provides a route that Italy still wants to take.[28] The success of populist movements is dealt with in Chapter 18 in this volume, but the growing doubts about where Europe is going and whether Italy wants to take part is more widely diffused than the success of single parties. There remains an elite consensus, albeit frayed, that Italy needs Europe and that Europe needs Italy, but polls no longer place Italians amongst the most enthusiastic supporters of the European project.[29] The challenge for policymakers is that while Italy has many more exams to sit before emerging from the crisis and completing the process of adapting to the crisis, broader public opinion seems to indicate that it is not so sure it wants to stay in school.

Notes

1. Frank Roy Willis, *Italy Chooses Europe* (Oxford: Oxford University Press, 1971).
2. Daniela Preda, *Alcide De Gasperi, federalista europeo* (Bologna: Il Mulino, 2004).
3. Sergio Fabbrini and Simona Piattoni (eds.), *Italy in the European Union: Redefining National Interest in a Compound Polity* (Lanham, MD: Rowman & Littlefield Publishers, 2008).
4. Bini Olivi (1998), *L'Europa difficile: Storia politica dell'integrazione europea 1948–1998* (Bologna: Il Mulino, 1998); Giancarlo Chevallard, *L'Italia Vista Dall'Europa: Testimonianza da Bruxelles* (Soveria Mannelli: Rubbettino Editore, 2008).
5. Antonio Varsori, *La Cenerentola D'Europa? L'Italia e L'Integrazione Europea Dal 1947 a Oggi* (Soveria Mannelli: Rubbettino Editore, 2010), 17.
6. Mario Telò, "Italy's Interaction with the European Project, from the First to the Second Republic: Continuity and Change," *Comparative European Politics*, 11, no. 3 (2013), 296–316.
7. Antonio Varsori, *L'Italia nelle relazioni internazionali dal 1943 al 1992* (Bari, Roma: Laterza, 1998).
8. Gabriel Almond, Gabriel and Sidney Verba, *The Civic Culture: Political Attitudes and Democracy in Five Nations* (Princeton, NJ: Princeton University Press, 1963).
9. Giacomo Benedetto and Lucia Quaglia, "The Comparative Politics of Communist Euroscepticism in France, Italy and Spain," *Party Politics*, 13, no.4, (2007), 478–499.
10. Richard Dunphy, *Contesting Capitalism?: Left Parties and European Integration* (Manchester: Manchester University Press, 2004).
11. Jeffrey Frieden, "Making Commitments: France and Italy in the European Monetary System, 1979–1985," in Barry Eichengreen and Jeffry Frieden (eds.), *The Political Economy of European Monetary Unification* (Boulder, CO: Westview Press, 1994), 25–46.
12. Maurizio Ferrera and Elisabetta Gualmini, *Salvati dall'Europa?* (Bologna: Il Mulino, 1999); Giorgio Freddi, Giuseppe Di Palma, and Sergio Fabbrini (eds.) (2000), *Condannata al successo? L'Italia nell'Europa integrata* (Bologna: Il Mulino, 2000).

13. Michele Salvati, "Moneta unica, rivoluzione copernicana," *Il Mulino*, 46, no. 1 (1997), 5–23.

14. Vincent Della Sala, "From Maastricht to Modernization: EMU and the Italian Social State," in Andrew Martin and George Ross (eds.), *Euros and Europeans: Monetary Integration and the European Model of Society* (Cambridge: Cambridge University Press, 2004).

15. Edoardo Ongaro, *Public Management Reform and Modernization: Trajectories of Administrative Change in Italy, France, Greece, Portugal and Spain* (Cheltenham: Edward Elgar, 2010).

16. Mario Telò, "Italy and the Idea of Europe," in Justine Lacroix and Kalypso Nicolaidis (eds.), *European Stories: Intellectual Debates on Europe in National Contexts* (Oxford: Oxford University Press, 2010).

17. Paolo Graziano and Maarten P. Vink (eds.), *Europeanization: New Research Agendas* (London: Palgrave Macmillan, 2006).

18. Sergio Fabbrini (ed.), *L'europeizzazione dell'Italia: l'impatto dell'Unione Europea sulle istituzioni e le politiche italiane* (Roma: Laterza, 2003); Claudio Radaelli and Fabio Franchino, "Analysing Political Change in Italy," *Journal of European Public Policy*, 11, no. 6 (2004), 941–953.

19. Lucia Quaglia and Claudio Radaelli, "Italian Politics and the European Union: A Tale of Two Research Designs," *West European Politics*, 30, no.4 (2007), 924–943.

20. Tommaso Padoa-Schioppa, "Italy and Europe: A Fruitful Interaction," *Daedalus*, 130, no. 2 (2001), 13–44.

21. Marco Brunazzo, *Le regioni italiane e l'Unione Europea: accessi istituzionali e di politica pubblica* (Roma: Carocci, 2005).

22. Marco Brunazzo, Marco and Simona Piattoni, "Italy and Regional Policy," in Sergio Fabbrini and Simona Piattoni (eds.), *Italy in the European Union. Redefining National Interest in a Compound Polity* (Lanham, MD: Rowman and Littlefield, 2008), 51–65.

23. Paolo Graziano, *Europeizzazione e politiche pubbliche italiane: Coesione e lavoro a confronto* (Bologna: Il Mulino, 2004).

24. Teresa Ammendola, Teresa and Pierangelo Isernia, "L'Europa vista dagli italiani: i primi vent'anni," in Maurizio Cotta, Pierangelo Isernia, and Luca Verzichelli (eds.), *L'Europa in Italia: Elite, opinione pubblica e decisioni* (Bologna: Il Mulino, 2005).

25. Maurizio Cotta, Pierangelo Isernia, and Luca Verzichelli (eds.), *L'Europa in Italia: élite, opinione pubblica e decisioni* (Bologna: Il Mulino, 2005).

26. Nicolò Conti and Vincenzo Memoli, Vincenzo, "Italian Parties and Europe: Problems of Identity, Representation and Scope of Governance in the Euromanifestos (1989–2004)," *Perspectives on European Politics and Society*, 11, no.2 (2010), 167–182.

27. Lucia Quaglia, "The Europeanisation of Macroeconomic Policies and Financial Regulation in Italy," *South European Society and Politics*, 18, no.2 (2013), 159–176.

28. Pier Virgilio Dastoli and Roberto Santaniello, *C'Eravamo Tanti Amati: Italia, Europa e poi?* (Milan: Università Bocconi Editore, 2013).

29. Christophe Roux and Luca Verzichelli, "Italy: Still a Pro-European, but not a Fully Europeanised Elite?," *South European Society and Politics*, 15, no.1 (2010), 11–33.

CHAPTER 54

ITALY AND THE MEDITERRANEAN AFTER WORLD WAR II

ROBERTO ALIBONI

MEDITERRANEAN AUTONOMY AND ATLANTIC ORTHODOXY IN THE COLD WAR (1940S–1970S)

With the end of World War II, the Italian pro-Western political forces divided between those fully accepting the Atlantic Alliance's constraints and those eager to alleviate those constraints with a view to enjoying more freedom in both domestic and foreign affairs, in other words between "orthodox" and "reformists." All of them wished to provide Italy with a degree of national autonomy and a more specific, prestigious role within the Alliance—an aspiration reflected in a very broad trend called "Neo-Atlanticism."[1] However, while the orthodox thought Italy's role was best supported and upgraded by sailing in convoy with its allies, reformists were convinced that Italy had to take an autonomous path.

This contrast, revolving essentially around Italian–American relations, continued throughout the first part of the so called First Republic (1940s–1980s). In the period considered in this section, the driving force among the reformists was the left wing of the Democrazia Cristiana (DC) (see Chapter 21, this volume), which took prominence as soon as the De Gasperi-Sforza duo left. In the DC left-wing's efforts to win more autonomy for Italy within the Atlantic space and in its relations with the United States, the Mediterranean policy played a prominent role.

The DC left wing's interest in the Mediterranean was driven by ideological preferences as well as political goals. Ideologically, they aimed at a non-capitalistic society, based on traditional values, social, and familial cohesion. They continued the system of mixed economy and the state-owned firms, established in the 1930s during Fascism and mostly led by distinguished Catholic managers. In this system, the Ente Nazionale Idrocarburi (ENI) and its leader, Enrico Mattei (see Chapter 27, this volume)—himself from the DC left-wing's ranks—played a decisive role. Moreover, in keeping with the Catholic Church's universalistic values, they were firmly anti-colonialist and broadly attracted by and supportive of Third World countries, in particular in the Mediterranean area, the cradle of their own and the other two monotheistic religions deriving from Abraham (as preached by Giorgio La Pira, mayor of Florence and another important member of the DC left wing).

Politically, the DC left wing sought to set out the domestic and international conditions for decoupling the Socialists (see Chapter 16, this volume) from the Communists (see Chapter 15, this volume), thus making possible a coalition with it. In this respect, a Mediterranean policy attesting to Italy's autonomy from the Atlantic bonds would have facilitated its domestic agenda. At the same time, the anti-colonialist and non-capitalist features of its Mediterranean policy would have been able to attract the Partito Socialista Italiano (PSI).

Led as it was by the DC left wing, what did Italy's Mediterranean policy entail?[2] The contours of a post-World War II Italian policy toward the Mediterranean began to emerge when the UN took its final decision on Italy's colonies in 1951. While Italy had hoped to retain its colonies, all it obtained was a ten-year trust mandate on Somalia. Strongly criticized by parties and public opinion alike, the government, headed by De Gasperi (see Chapter 26, this volume), decided to make virtue of necessity and opted to shift to a broadly anti-colonialist approach. This approach worked. It brought Italy closer to the United States, already its key partner. Furthermore, it made for easier and more fruitful relations with the Mediterranean countries that were then trying to rid themselves of French and British colonial domination.

However, what could have been developed into a tranquil proximity policy of good relations was seen by the DC left wing (and ENI) as an opportunity to advance their domestic and international objectives in a more strategic perspective. Thus, the DC left wing's leaders devised a policy intended to take advantage of Italy's favorable relations with the Mediterranean Arab countries so as to act as a bridge between the region and the West and thus take on a special role in transatlantic relations. Despite the anti-colonialist convergence with the United States, which was tested in the framework of the Suez Canal crisis,[3] it would not have been possible, especially after that crisis, to promote this Italian role without or against the United States. As a result, between 1956 and 1957, the DC left wing, in particular the then President of the Republic Giovanni Gronchi, tried to convince the United States to have "permanent preliminary consultations" with Italy with regard to Mediterranean issues, that is—as written by Sergio Romano—to act as if Italy were the West's "attorney" in the region.

While President Gronchi's "strategy" was flatly rejected by Foster Dulles in the Paris Atlantic Council of December 1956, the DC left-wing policy was cleverly resumed by Amintore Fanfani when, at the beginning of July 1958, he formed his government with the Partito Socialista Democratico Italiano (PSDI) (see Chapter 16, this volume), a first step toward the alliance with the PSI. Fanfani was on the same nationalist and pacifist track as Gronchi, Mattei, and La Pira, but was more articulate and astute politically. He pursued the double-faceted policy promoted by Gronchi (of friendship with both the Arabs and the Americans), but was less naive and more balanced toward the United States. [4] In 1958, he accepted the installation of Jupiter and Thor intermediate-range missiles in Italy, and, when De Gaulle tried to prevent the UK from entering the then European Community at the beginning of the 1960s, Italy sided with the UK and the United States, which had a strategic interest in the UK membership.

While Italy's self-perceived intimacy with the Arab countries continued to dominate Italy's Mediterranean policy under Fanfani, its convergence with the United States as anti-colonialist countries in the Mediterranean soon began to decline. After the Suez crisis, while France headed toward "Gaullisme," the Algerian crisis, and then its "politique arabe," the UK drew closer to the United States, initiating a policy of privileged relations destined to stay. In January 1957, President Eisenhower asked Congress to use force in case of Soviet expansion in the Middle East and, in 1958, the United States sent an expeditionary corps to Lebanon to respond to the ousting of King Feysal in Iraq by a nationalist military coup. After that, the Cold War expanded to the Middle East and the Mediterranean, and the United States, supported by the UK, quickly began to take over the imperial role of the former European colonial powers. Gradually, the United States became the enemy of Arab nationalism. Consequently, Italian Mediterranean policy lost its important nexus with the United States and became a pro-Arab policy hard to sustain in the framework of Italy's Atlantic and American alliances. In fact, by the mid-1960s, the DC left wing's Mediterranean policy had substantially run out of steam. Furthermore, the PSI, in coalition with the DC since 1963 (see Chapter 16, this volume), had proved to be far more interested in East–West detente and disarmament than in the Mediterranean.

In 1967, the Arab–Israeli war moved the Socialists to tilt from their traditional pro-Israel stance toward the Arabs via the Palestinian nationalist cause. Furthermore, in 1968 the evolution of the Vietnam War brought the anti-Americanism naturally embedded in the DC left wing's ideology to the fore. While nothing changed at the governmental level, Catholic anti-Americanism merged with the anti-Americanism dominant among the Socialists and Communists to become a movement with strong support and empathy for the Third World, going beyond Italy's previous focus on the Mediterranean. This anti-American movement in support of the Third World contributed to preparing for the attempt to enlarge the centre-left coalition to include the Communists, the so called *Compromesso Storico* (see Chapter 22, this volume), which dominated Italian domestic politics until its failure at the end of the 1970s.

The 1970s were for Italy years of domestic terrorism and deep economic crisis in which its foreign policy suffered a considerable decline. In this period, civil society nurtured a movement supporting the Third World and Palestinian nationalism, but this movement could not be translated into any governmental foreign policy. Aldo Moro spoke frequently about the Mediterranean and was instrumental in inserting a section on the Mediterranean into the Helsinki Final Act. Nevertheless, Italy's Mediterranean policy actually withdrew from center stage.

Toward the End of the Cold War: Risks from and Initiatives toward the Mediterranean (1980s)

In the 1980s, the last decade of the Cold War, Italy's foreign policy was affected by two significant developments that had an impact on its Mediterranean policy. First, a debate on security, initiated in the 1970s as a consequence of a number of strategic and geopolitical shifts in the southern approaches to Italy and Europe (the "south" in the Italian literature), came to bear upon the Mediterranean as well.

Second, there was a substantial shift in the domestic political arena, setting out the conditions for a new and active foreign policy cycle, in which both foreign, military, and Mediterranean policies acquired momentum. This shift emerged with Partito Repubblicano Italiano (PRI) Giovanni Spadolini's two governments in 1981–82, followed by two unusually stable governments headed by PSI Bettino Craxi from August 1983 to April 1987. These governments and the *Pentapartito* (see Chapter 23, this volume) coalition they represented (DC, PSI, PSDI, PRI, and the Partito Liberale Italiano (PLI)) essentially put an end to the issue of the Partito Comunista Italiano (PCI)'s participation in government (see Chapter 22, this volume), which had dominated the Italian political debate in the 1970s, in the same way that the Opening to the Left (see Chapter 21, this volume) had in the 1950s–1960s. In this new context, the secular-led governments of the 1980s were able, like De Gasperi's earlier centrist coalitions, to conduct a foreign policy that was not strictly functional to domestic politics. The dialectic between autonomy and Atlanticist orthodoxy remained, but it was far less politically significant than before and, despite well-known incidents, such as in Sigonella, allowed for a period of positive inter-Atlantic and Italy–US relations.

The "Risk from the South" Debate

Until the beginning of the 1970s, the instability in the Mediterranean deriving from the process of decolonization and the rise of Arab nationalism had in no way been perceived as a threat to Europe's security. However, in 1973, the oil shock following the Yom Kippur war generated an initial perception of the Mediterranean as a security concern, thereby opening the "risk from the south" debate. In subsequent years, this perception was confirmed and magnified by incidents of Palestinian terrorism in Italy and Europe, the Lebanese civil war and the spilling over of radical Islamism from the Middle East to Europe, the rearmament race in practically all countries south of the Mediterranean, the revolution in Iran (followed by the Iran–Iraq war), and Sadat's assassination.

Italy's academic and military quarters took note of these developments,[5] engendering an array of pioneering analyses of the conceptual distinction between threats (from the East–West context) and risks (from the "south"), the multidimensional and multidirectional nature of the emerging risks, and the tendency toward a diffusion of power in addition, if not as an alternative to the existing bipolar concentration (concepts that were all to constitute the backbone of the 1991 NATO doctrine after the end of the Cold War).[6] The debate's core concept was that Italy was facing risks that were independent from the East–West confrontation and that required a national political and military response.

The risk from the south debate arose in conservative academic and military quarters and was essentially rooted in nationalist feelings: the need for Italy to find a way to emancipate itself from the legacy of the World War II defeat and to be able to act within the alliance as a peer nation. At the end of the day, the debate was once again on Italian autonomy within the Alliance, though this time it proceeded from substantive issues (risks from the south) rather than the complex DC left wing's ideological and political agenda. While the DC left wing had used Italy's supposedly special relations with the Arabs to explain the need for autonomy in the Mediterranean, now it was the emerging risks from the south. As soon as the debate expanded, the nationalist drift brought about by the debate on the risks from the south was opposed by other experts and military, who—recreating the opposition between Atlantic "orthodox" and "reformists"— maintained that the risk from the south added to the usual Atlantic security picture without replacing it.[7]

Unlike the disputes between Atlanticists and nationalists in the previous period, the risk from the south debate did not generate problems in relations with the allies and the United States. The latter could only welcome Italy's efforts at military modernization, as long as these efforts remained compatible with the Alliance's purposes.

While plans for military modernization to deal with the risks from the south failed to be completely accomplished, though, and were then interrupted by the economic and political crisis that hit Italy in the early 1990s, the 1980s debate and efforts helped Italy develop its capabilities for participating in post-Cold War international peace support operations, thus attenuating, if not overcoming, its marginality complex. Inadvertently, it also helped Italy envision a more adequate strategic space than the Mediterranean, by enlarging its experience to the whole Middle East. These two trends contributed to shaping its post-Cold War policy.

Socialist Initiative in the Mediterranean

The debate just illustrated and the activities it promoted were an important dimension of the wider re-emerging tendency toward activism and responsibility in Italian foreign policy in the 1980s, especially with regard to the Mediterranean. This was also attested to by political initiatives such as the 1980 Italian decision to guarantee Malta's neutrality—that is, to avoid the mercantile use of the island's geopolitical location by its leadership (Laborite Dom Mintoff) to the advantage of non-Western powers. While Italy failed to rein in Mintoff's leanings, this policy, further to Italy's participation in multinational military missions, proved that Rome was prepared to take on substantive responsibility in the area within the Alliance's framework.

In parallel with these various developments, the PSI, led by Craxi (see Chapter 29, this volume) promoted a bold policy of Mediterranean political cooperation aimed at asserting Italy's role as part of a kind of regional Euro-Mediterranean expression of solidarity. In a sense, Craxi was influenced by the analyses predicating Italy's and Europe's security on the risks coming from the south. He was convinced that the Palestinian conflict played a central role in generating these risks, and that its resolution would thus remove the primary source of those risks and ensure peaceful and secure relations across the Mediterranean.[8] In his vision, the issue regarded the whole EU and, for this reason, he thought that a solid European effort was needed to achieve a solution. In his view, southern Europe, mostly led at that time by Socialist governments, had to play a mediating role to make northern-central EU members coalesce in a shared Euro-Mediterranean agenda of security and cooperation.

Relations among southern European Socialist parties, along with their relations with the parties and governments in the south-eastern Mediterranean countries, were very active during the 1980s. However, the Socialists did not manage to translate these activities into EU policies, nor to organize any form of structured or regular cooperation among southern European countries themselves or between them and Arab Mediterranean countries. Only between 1989 and 1991, at the end of the policy period under consideration, with the Cold War already over, did some initiatives come from southern Europe's governments and the Italian Socialist Foreign Minister Gianni De Michelis: support for the Union of the Arab Maghreb, the setting up of the "Five plus Five" Western Mediterranean grouping of countries, and the proposal to convene a Conference on Security and Cooperation in the Mediterranean (in the same vein as what Aldo Moro had proposed in the 1970s). None of them succeeded, as the United States, (via the intervention to liberate Kuwait and the subsequent organization of the Middle East Peace Conference in Madrid), took the lead in 1991 and overrode all European initiatives in the region. As we shall see, only in 1995 did the Europeans again take the initiative by launching the Euro-Mediterranean Partnership, EMP, in a completely new political context.

While the Euro-Mediterranean side of the Socialist policy was proving weak, Foreign Minister Giulio Andreotti developed an active bilateral diplomacy with the Arab states. At the same time, Craxi and the PSI promoted intense relations, in particular, with the Organization for the Liberation of Palestine. More often than not, this made the more orthodox Atlanticist component of the *Pentapartito* nervous, causing disputes apparently similar to those from the 1950s to the 1970s. As a consequence of the Sigonella incident in 1986,[9] the PRI withdrew from the government, even though the United States moved more cautiously (within ten days of the end of the incident, President Reagan had sent Craxi a personal letter underscoring the solid bond between the two countries). In fact, in those years a broad Euro–American understanding had emerged on Arafat as the only convenient interlocutor, although the US was generally less trusting of him and his organization than the Europeans. In the end, most American agencies and the Department of State agreed with the Italian interpretation of the incident as an anti-Arafat move coming from the Palestinian opposition.

All in all, Craxi's government proved an asset for the Alliance by drawing a line with respect to the extreme left in Italy, stabilizing the country, participating in a number of multinational missions, and allowing for the installation of the SS2os (not only in Italy, like Fanfani with the Jupiter-Thor missiles, but in Europe). It did not take the United States long to see that this time Italy's autonomy in the Mediterranean, despite some divergence, was fully compatible with the Alliance's bonds, and that there was no reason to risk a shift toward the left by the PSI in Italy's domestic political balance as a reaction to US pressures.[10] This is why the subsequent incident in April 1986—the American bombing of Tripoli and Benghazi, culminating in the launching of two Libyan missiles against a US monitoring installation on Italy's Lampedusa islet—caused a lot of ado but no political disruption in Italy–US relations.

Changes in the Second Republic (1990s–2000s)

The end of the Cold War caused a systemic crisis in Italy's domestic politics, which led to the dissolution of, first, the PCI and then the DC and all the other parties. The crisis ushered in a bipolar system of sorts (see Chapter 25, this volume): on the right, it gave way to a conservative/populist coalition of previously nonexistent parties; on the left, to the formation of a reformist Democratic Party alongside a set of minor parties, all striving to adapt their traditional legacies to new realities.

In the deeply changed post-Cold War international environment, dominated by the United States, the Democratic Party, while emerging as a loyal supporter of the Atlantic Alliance, believed that US supremacy needed to be balanced by making multilateralism more effective, and strengthening, above all, the EU. In particular, in the Mediterranean the left thought it had to pursue its historical objectives of peace and security by contributing to developing a multilateral, primarily Euro-Mediterranean policy.

The right-wing coalition, led by Silvio Berlusconi, brought in a less idealistic and cooperative vision. The new international context was seen as an opportunity to pursue Italy's national interests, keeping a distance from the EU and staying close to the United States and its supremacy. The right-wing coalition did not show any interest in the Mediterranean as a regional project of democratic transformation and was convinced that US policies in the area served Italy's interests well. Strengthened cooperation with

President George W. Bush in the 2000s, when Berlusconi steadily held power, led Italy's military and political engagement as far away as Afghanistan and Iraq. In this framework, with regard to the Mediterranean, the center-right coalition focused on developing bilateral relations with a set of preferential partners, acting essentially in a broad national (and conservative) perspective.

The two coalitions governed in two quite different periods, that is, before and after 9/11. While under Clinton's presidency an agenda of democratic transformation through international cooperation made sense, after 9/11 the old system of Euro–American alliances was substantially modified with security, securitization, and national/nationalist perspectives prevailing everywhere.

The Center-Left Governments: International Cooperation in the 1990s

The center-left was in power throughout the 1990s with the exception of the first Berlusconi government's nine months from May 1994 to January 1995. Then it governed again from May 2006 to May 2008, with Prodi's second government.

Led by liberal-reformist leaders, such as Giuliano Amato, Carlo Azeglio Ciampi, Romano Prodi, Massimo D'Alema, and Lamberto Dini, the center-left governments were convinced that it would be better for Italy to pursue its interests by playing an active role within the alliances and multilateral organizations in general, rather than nationally.

In this context, Italy's Mediterranean policy increasingly identified itself with committed participation in ongoing international efforts, with a view to building a new EU and European role in the Mediterranean area. In 1993–4, Ciampi and Beniamino Andreatta, the Foreign Minister, supported the setting up of the Mediterranean Forum for Dialogue and Cooperation and prepared the stage for Italy's participation in the launching of the Euro-Mediterranean Partnership (then established at the November 1995 Barcelona Conference during the short, first Berlusconi government). Similarly, at the beginning of the 1990s, Italy, alongside Spain, took initiatives to make NATO commit itself to the Mediterranean. This contributed to the setting up of the NATO Mediterranean Dialogue in 1994.

In 2000, while the Euro-Mediterranean policy remained the center-left coalition's flag-policy, international and EU failures in solving the Israeli–Palestinian conflict made the Arabs believe that political cooperation with the Europeans within the EMP was fruitless, and substantially put an end to Arab interest in it. In subsequent years, the broad decline in EU political cohesion deepened the EU Mediterranean policy's decay. Curtailed by the Arabs' lack of interest and the Europeans' lack of political initiative, by the mid-2000s, the EU Mediterranean policy de facto represented a sheer developmental rather than a political agenda.

Nevertheless, in 2006–08, when Prodi returned to Palazzo Chigi, on two important occasions the left went back to its Euro-Mediterranean flag-policy. First, to help keep peace in south Lebanon at the end of the 2006 Israeli–Hizbollah conflict, the Italian government took initiatives to strengthen the United Nations Interim Force in Lebanon (UNIFIL), successfully involving the EU with a view to turning its own initiative into an EU one.[11] Second, it skillfully contributed to the process which in 2008 led to the establishment of the Union for the Mediterranean (UFM), replacing the Euro-Mediterranean Partnership.[12] However, in a profoundly changed Mediterranean context, while the UFM marked the end of the EU Euro-Med policy rather than its revitalization, the UNIFIL operation—in itself a success—was unable to help change the trend toward weakening of the EU's foreign and security policy. In conclusion, at the beginning of the 2010s, Mediterranean policy had become an empty container. Italy's center-left was left with Mediterranean rhetoric rather than any policy.

The Center-Right Coalition: Nationalism and Bilateralism in the 2000s

In the 2000s the center-right governed from 2001 until 2011, with the exception—as said—of the second Prodi government in 2006-08. While the left maintained—and after 9/11, like many other Europeans, deepened—its critical attitude toward US policy in the Mediterranean and the Middle East (the inclusion of all political Islamist actors in the category of terrorist, the promotion of an unarticulated Western notion of democracy, the alliance with undemocratic Arab regimes as bastions against Islamism, the approach to the Israeli–Palestinian conflict), Italy's right-wing governments fully espoused this policy. In the Mediterranean, Berlusconi's government strengthened bilateral political relations with Egypt, Tunisia, Libya, and Jordan, while improving business relations with all countries in the area, including Syria. In a historical shift, it initiated a policy of staunch political support for Israel.

While Italian diplomacy contributed to the EU Euro-Mediterranean routine, the government had no national policy toward the Mediterranean as a region. In tune with the United States, Italy addressed Mediterranean and Middle Eastern issues in what was for Rome an unusual global perspective.

However, the Mediterranean remained important for its proximity. Besides strengthening bilateral political and business relations, in the 2000s Italy dealt with two important issues related to the Mediterranean area: its complex relations with Libya and increasing immigration (in which its relations with Libya played—and still play—a special role).

The combination of Libya's importance for Italy's energy security (as a result of ENI's investments) and Gaddafi's insistence on considering Italy's colonial legacy unsettled created, after the Libyan revolution of 1969, a durable and complex national issue with which all Italian governments had to deal, independently of their different approaches to the whole area: no Italian leader failed to enter Gaddafi's famous tents in the desert or the Bab el-Aziza compound.[13]

In the 1970s, Italian governments succeeded in developing a privileged relation with Libya, although this relation was always haunted and spoiled by Gaddafi's demands for compensation related to colonial domination. In the 1980s, Italy had also difficulties in balancing its relations with Libya with US pressure on the country. During the long period of Lockerbie sanctions, relations almost had to be frozen. However, the day after the sanctions were lifted on April 6, 1999, Lamberto Dini, then Foreign Minister, was the first to visit Tripoli. In a few months, he was followed by Massimo D'Alema, in his capacity as Italy's premier.

Though the center-left had opened the way, it was Berlusconi who put an end to the historical dispute on the colonial legacy that had vexed the emergence of a nevertheless privileged Italian–Libyan relationship. Berlusconi was facilitated in his task by the complete end to American–Libyan tension when, in 2003, Gaddafi unexpectedly renounced possession of weapons of mass destruction. However, it was undoubtedly the realism of his Mediterranean approach, his business sense, and his interest in Gaddafi as a bastion against Islamism that brought about the breakthrough. On August 30, 2008, the two countries signed an important Treaty of Friendship, Partnership and Cooperation in Bengazhi. In Sirte, on March 2, 2009, Berlusconi presented formal apologies for Italy's colonial past. In June 2009, Gaddafi visited Rome for the first time (among eccentric gestures and harsh criticism from the Italian media and political figures). In 2009, the contentious Italian–Libyan relations seemed happily settled.

The other center right Mediterranean concern was immigration. In the 2000s, the governments led by the right-wing parties passed restrictive and conservative legislation to contain legal and strictly counter illegal immigration. In the Mediterranean, this policy proved relatively successful with respect to flows of economically driven migrants coming from North Africa (sometimes West Africa, for example Senegal). The government fostered externalization policies by concluding readmission agreements and increasing immigration quotas and financial aid to cooperating sending countries. In contrast, the same legislation proved unfit to manage refugees and other clandestine immigrants from south-Saharan Africa or other countries farther afield, who cross North Africa and then the sea. Gaddafi's Libya, a non-sending country, employed immigration to manipulate its complex relations with Italy, providing and withdrawing cooperation and becoming, at the end of the day, the most important sailing point for migrants wanting to reach Italy; hence the importance of the agreements signed by Berlusconi with Gaddafi.[14]

In sum, Italy's policy on migration appears to be a most problematic aspect of its Mediterranean policy. As Libya is a migration conduit to Italy, after the fall of Gaddafi, who actually contained immigration, this country and immigration are bound to remain two relevant stumbling blocks for future Italian foreign policy toward the area.

EPILOGUE

In the 2000s, the changes in American foreign policy triggered by 9/11 were more important in modifying and weakening Euro-American alliances than those that occurred in the previous decades. The outcome has been a kind of renationalization of European allies' foreign policies. The foreign policy of Italy's right-wing political parties—independently of their ideological preferences—has followed this trend. In previous decades, the search for a Mediterranean role was functional to providing Italy with a degree of autonomy in the context of its alliances (whether in a nationalist or leftist perspective). But with the erosion of these alliances during the late 1990s, in the 2000s there was no longer any reason to seek that autonomy: in the emerging global world, Italy was willy-nilly reacquiring its full national autonomy.

Nevertheless, without the support of its old alliances, Italy was emerging in the new context as a weak country, unprepared to sustain an autonomous national foreign policy. The center-right government—consciously or not—got around this difficulty by setting Italy's foreign policy fully in the shadow of US policy. That allowed Berlusconi to carry out his policy of promoting national interests and bilateral relations in the Mediterranean quietly and successfully. Yet when, in 2011, the uprisings in Tunisia, Egypt, and Libya convinced President Obama to abandon the old Arab allies and leave the door open to the ascent of Islamist parties, Berlusconi was badly taken aback and the poor sustainability of his nationalist foreign policy was laid bare. He hesitated for a long time before agreeing to the intervention against Gaddafi, yet in the end, he had to go along with the major Western countries as he had neither the means nor a way to oppose their policy, as the Russian Federation did later in Syria.

In this new scenario, with the center-left government led by Matteo Renzi—who replaced Enrico Letta as prime minister in 2014—Italy as a national power appears as isolated and impotent in the Mediterranean as the previous center-right governments led by Silvio Berlusconi and Mario Monti. The key variable is the presence of a strong allied framework: if the latter does not work or is weakened, Italy can hardly manage any significant Mediterranean policy.

NOTES

1. Paolo Cacace, *Venti anni di politica estera italiana (1943–1963)* (Rome: Bonacci, 1986), ch. 42.
2. Roberto Gaja, *L'Italia nel mondo bipolare. Per una storia della politica estera italiana (1943–1991)* (Bologna: Il Mulino, 1995); Sergio Romano, *Guida alla politica estera italiana. Dal crollo del fascismo al crollo del comunismo* (Milan: Rizzoli, 1993); Antonio Varsori, *L'Italia nelle relazioni internazionali dal 1943 al 1992* (Bari: Laterza, 1998).
3. Federica Onelli, "L'Italia e la crisi di Suez del luglio 1956: potenzialità e limiti del neoatlantismo," in Matteo Pizzigallo (ed.), *Cooperazione e relazioni internazionali. Studi e ricerche sulla politica estera italiana del secondo dopoguerra* (Milan: Franco Angeli, 2008), 67–104.

4. Leopoldo Nuti, "Italian Foreign Policy in the Cold War: A Constant Search for Status," in Maurizio Carbone (ed.), *Italy in the Post-Cold War Order. Adaptation, Bipartisanship, Visibility* (Lanham, MD, Boulder, CO, New York, Toronto, Plymouth: Lexington Books, Rowman & Littlefield Publishers, 2011), 25–45.

5. See Virgilio Ilari, "La percezione del 'rischio minaccia da Sud' in Italia," in Carlo Maria Santoro (ed.), *Rischio da Sud. Geopolitica delle crisi nel bacino mediterraneo* (Milan: Franco Angeli, 1996), 53–101.

6. Carlo Maria Santoro, *Rischio da Sud. Geopolitica delle crisi nel bacino mediterraneo,* op. cit.; Alessandro Colombo, "La percezione italiana dei 'rischi da sud' tra l'ultima fase della Guerra Fredda e il mondo post-bipolare," in Massimo De Leonardis (ed.), *Il Mediterraneo nella politica estera italiana del secondo dopoguerra* (Bologna: Il Mulino, 2003), 107–134.

7. Maurizio Cremasco, "Le possibili situazioni di crisi e gli eventuali scenari di confronto. Quale strumento militare per farvi fronte?," in Maurizio Cremasco (ed.), *Lo Strumento militare italiano. Problemi e prospettive* (Milan: Franco Angeli for Istituto Affari Internazionali, 1986), 53–71.

8. Antonio Badini, "Introduzione," in Stefania Craxi (ed.), *Bettino Craxi. Pace nel Mediterraneo* (Venice: Marsilio for Fondazione Craxi, 2006), 11–16.

9. Alessandro Silj (ed.), *L'alleato scomodo* (Milan: Corbaccio, 1998).

10. Joseph La Palombara, "The Achille Lauro Affair: A Note on Italy and the United States," *Yale Review*, 75, 4 (October, 1986), 542–563.

11. Anna Caffarena, "La guerra israelo-libanese e il rilancio di un multilateralismo efficace," in Jean-Louis Briquet and Alfio Mastropaolo (eds.), *Politica in Italia. I fatti dell'anno e le interpretazioni. Edizione 2007* (Bologna: Il Mulino, 2007), 189–207.

12. Roberto Aliboni and Fouad Ammor, *Under the Shadow of "Barcelona": From the EMP to the Union for the Mediterranean*, EuroMeSCo Paper, 77, February 2009, <www.euromesco. net/index.php?option=com_content&view=article&id=1142%3Apaper-77-under-the-s hadow-of-barcelona-from-the-emp-to-the-union-for-the-mediterranean&catid=102% 3Aprevious-papers&Itemid=102&lang=en>.

13. Arturo Varvelli, "Italia e Libia. Storia di un rapporto privilegiato," in Karim Merzan and Arturo Varvelli (eds.), *Libia. Fine o rinascita di una nazione?* (Roma: Donzelli, 2012), 109–135.

14. Emanuela Paoletti, *The Migration of Power and North South Inequalities. The Case of Italy and Libya* (New York and Basingstoke: Palgrave Macmillan, 2011).

INDEX

Page references to Figures or Tables will be in *italics*, while references to Endnotes will be followed by the letter 'n' and note number.